The Modern Language Association of America

Reviews of Research

Victorian Prose: A Guide to Research. Edited by David J. DeLaura. 1973.

Anglo-Irish Literature: A Review of Research. Edited by Richard J. Finneran. 1976.

Victorian Fiction: A Second Guide to Research. Edited by George H. Ford. 1978.

Victorian Periodicals: A Guide to Research. Edited by J. Don Vann and Rosemary T. VanArsdel. 1978.

Victorian Fiction: A Guide to Research. Reprint of 1964 edition. Edited by Lionel Stevenson. 1980.

Recent Research on Anglo-Irish Writers: A Supplement to Anglo-Irish Literature: A Review of Research. Edited by Richard J. Finneran. 1983.

The Transcendentalists: A Review of Research and Criticism. Edited by Joel Myerson. 1984.

The English Romantic Poets: A Review of Research and Criticism. Fourth edition. Edited by Frank Jordan. 1985.

THE

ENGLISH

ROMANTIC

A Review of Research

FOURTH EDITION

Edited by

Frank Jordan

POETS

and Criticism

John Clubbe   Stuart Curran

Mary Lynn Johnson   Frank Jordan

Karl Kroeber   Max F. Schulz

                     Jack Stillinger

The Modern Language Association of America
New York   1985

Library of Congress Cataloging in Publication Data
Main entry under title:

The English romantic poets.

  (Reviews of research)
  Includes bibliographies and index.
   1. English poetry—19th century—History and
criticism.   2. Romanticism—England.   3. English
poetry—19th century—History and criticism—Bibliography.
I. Clubbe, John.   II. Curran, Stuart.
III. Johnson, Mary Lynn, 1937–   .   IV. Series.
PR590.E5   1985   016.821'7'09   85-7216
ISBN 0-87352-262-1
ISBN 0-87352-263-X (pbk.)

PR
590
E5
1985

First printing, 1985.
Second printing, 1986.

Published by The Modern Language Association of America
10 Astor Place, New York, New York 10003

Contents

Preface

The fourth edition of *English Romantic Poets: A Review of Research and Criticism*, unlike the second and third editions, is not a revision but a new work. Because the scholarly and critical writing on the Romantic poets has, since the third edition, been exceedingly plentiful and exceptionally probing and because the writing on literary theory, to which the Romantics seem indispensable, has been uncommonly provocative, all concerned in this enterprise agreed that the authors had to start afresh if they were to do justice to this rich harvest. Accordingly, the seven chapters have been entirely rewritten. The fourth edition is, however, intended to be complete. Although our purpose has been to give maximum consideration to recent writing, we have treated all works in historical context so that readers might keep proportion, seeing contemporary scholarship and criticism in perspective.

The most striking change in the fourth edition is the inclusion of Blake. Whereas in 1972 (or in 1969, when the third edition was projected) it was not possible to steal Blake from the companion volume on the minor Romantic poets and the essayists, it was not only possible but eminently desirable in 1980, when the present volume was planned, to rectify the unfortunate association of Blake with minor poetry. Nearly as conspicuous, I trust, is the uniting of Coleridge the poet and Coleridge the philosopher in a single chapter written by a single author. In mending this multiple split we rectify another unfortunate state of affairs.

The first chapter to be finished arrived in early 1982; the last one, in mid-1983. Consequently, there is some discrepancy in coverage. But when reading copy all the authors endeavored to include as many of the important items from subsequent years as they were able to know about and gain access to before rounding off their tasks. These last are more likely to be books than articles, given the tardiness of the annual bibliographies.

Increasingly, present-day scholar-critics are reluctant to hide or minimize the differences that distinguish the six poets. The movement and its label now secure, thanks to the successful efforts of those who earlier fought so valiantly to rescue the good name of Romanticism from the slurs of its detractors, today's authorities feel free to let the subject have its head. In keeping with this trend, the authors of the seven chapters have been free to organize their materials in the ways they deemed most appropriate. For this reason each chapter is provided with its own table of contents.

Even though each chapter represents finally the knowledge and judgment of one scholar, the project has been a cooperative venture. The contributors have read each other's chapters, much to their mutual benefit and greatly to the assistance of the editor. Moreover, other Romantics scholars have read chapters or parts of chapters in which they were expert; still others have alerted us to forthcoming publications or provided us with copies of their books and articles, sometimes before they were generally available. University presses, too, have on occasion assisted us by supplying copies of books that for one reason or another were inaccessible. Specific acknowledgments are made in the chapters as appropriate.

It remains to note that the names of previous authors have been dropped from the title page, since they bear no responsibility for the fourth edition, and to express the gratitude of the new authors and of Romantics scholars generally for their past labors on behalf of the study of Romantic poetry. Some of them are now with us only in spirit; others continue to add to our knowledge, augment our understanding, and quicken our appreciation of the subject with their books and articles. We their successors hope that this latest review will serve the present generation of Romantics scholars as well as its predecessors seem to have served earlier generations.

F. J.
October 1984

Abbreviations in References

ABELL	Annual Bibliography of English Language and Literature
AI	American Imago
AJES	The Aligarh Journal of English Studies
AL	American Literature
AN&Q	American Notes and Queries
AntigR	Antigonish Review
ArielE	Ariel: A Review of International English Literature
ASch	The American Scholar
AUMLA	Journal of the Australasian Universities Language and Literature Association
BB	Bulletin of Bibliography
BBr	Books at Brown
BC	The Book Collector
BIQ	Blake: An Illustrated Quarterly
BIS	Browning Institute Studies
BJA	British Journal of Aesthetics
BJRL	Bulletin of The John Rylands University Library of Manchester
BLR	Bodleian Library Record
BMMLA	The Bulletin of the Midwest Modern Language Association
BNL	Blake Newsletter
BNYPL	Bulletin of the New York Public Library
BRH	Bulletin of Research in the Humanities (formerly BNYPL)
BRMMLA	Rocky Mountain Review of Language and Literature
BS	Blake Studies
BST	Brontë Society Transactions
BSUF	Ball State University Forum
BuR	Bucknell Review
ByronJ	The Byron Journal
CBEL	Cambridge Bibliography of English Literature
CE	College English
CEA	CEA Critic: An Official Journal of the College English Association
CentR	The Centennial Review
CGP	Carleton Germanic Papers
ChLB	Charles Lamb Bulletin
CIEFLB	CIEFL Bulletin
CIS	Cahiers Internationaux de Symbolisme
CL	Comparative Literature

CLAJ	Comparative Language Association Journal
CLQ	Colby Library Quarterly
CLS	Comparative Literature Studies
CML	Classical and Modern Literature: A Quarterly
CollG	Colloquia Germanica
CP	Concerning Poetry
CQ	The Cambridge Quarterly
CR	The Critical Review
CREL	Cahiers Roumains d'Etudes Littéraires: Revue Trimestrielle de Critique, d'Esthétique et d'Histoire Littéraires
CRCL	Canadian Review of Comparative Literature
CritI	Critical Inquiry
CritQ	Critical Quarterly
DHLR	D. H. Lawrence Review
DNB	Dictionary of National Biography
DR	Dalhousie Review
DUJ	Durham University Journal
EA	Etudes Anglaises
E&S	Essays and Studies
EC	Etudes Celtiques
ECS	Eighteenth-Century Studies
Edda	Edda: Nordisk Tidsskrift for Litteraturforskning
EDH	Essays by Divers Hands
EIC	Essays in Criticism
EJ	The English Journal
ELH	(formerly Journal of English Literary History)
ELN	English Language Notes
ELT	English Literature in Transition
ELWIU	Essays in Literature
EM	English Miscellany
ERP3	English Romantic Poets, third edition
ES	English Studies
ESA	English Studies in Africa
ESC	English Studies in Canada
ESQ	ESQ: Journal of the American Renaissance (formerly Emerson Society Quarterly)
Expl	Explicator
ForumH	Forum (Houston, Tex.)
FR	French Review
GaR	The Georgia Review
GQ	German Quarterly
GRM	Germanisch-Romanische Monatsschrift
HAB	The Humanities Association Review
HES	Harvard English Studies
HLB	Harvard Library Bulletin

HLQ	Huntington Library Quarterly
HR	Hispanic Review
HTR	Harvard Theological Review
IJP	International Journal of Psychoanalysis
JAAC	Journal of Aesthetics and Art Criticism
JAmS	Journal of American Studies
JArabL	Journal of Arabic Literature
JBalS	Journal of Baltic Studies
JEGP	Journal of English and Germanic Philology
JES	Journal of European Studies
JGE	Journal of General Education
JHI	Journal of the History of Ideas
JJQ	James Joyce Quarterly
JML	Journal of Modern Literature
JMRS	Journal of Medieval and Renaissance Studies
JNT	Journal of Narrative Technique
JTS	Journal of Theological Studies
JWCI	Journal of the Warburg and Courtauld Institutes
KR	Kenyon Review
KSJ	Keats-Shelley Journal
KSMB	Keats-Shelley Memorial Bulletin
L&P	Literature and Psychology
LC	The Library Chronicle
LCUT	Library Chronicle of the University of Texas
L&H	Literature and History
MFS	Modern Fiction Studies
MLN	Modern Language Notes
MLQ	Modern Language Quarterly
MLR	Modern Language Review
MLS	Modern Language Studies
MP	Modern Philology
MQ	Midwest Quarterly
MSE	Massachusetts Studies in English
N&Q	Notes and Queries
NCF	Nineteenth-Century Fiction
NCTR	Nineteenth-Century Theatre Research
NDQ	North Dakota Quarterly
Neophil	Neophilologus
NEQ	New England Quarterly
NLH	New Literary History
NM	Neuphilologische Mitteilungen
NYRB	New York Review of Books
OJES	Osmania Journal of English Studies

OL	Orbis Litterarum
ORev	Occasional Review
P&L	Philosophy and Literature
PAPS	Papers of the American Philosophical Society
PBSA	Papers of the Bibliographical Society of America
PLL	Papers on Language and Literature
PLT	PLT: A Journal for Descriptive Poetics and Theory
PMLA	Publications of the Modern Language Association of America
PoeS	Poe Studies
PQ	Philological Quarterly
PR	Partisan Review
PRR	The Journal of Pre-Raphaelite Studies (formerly Pre-Raphaelite Review)
PSt	Prose Studies
PTRSC	Proceedings and Transactions of the Royal Society of Canada
QQ	Queen's Quarterly
QR	Quarterly Review
REL	Review of English Literature
RES	Review of English Studies
RHL	Revue d'Histoire Littéraire de la France
RLC	Revue de Littérature Comparée
RLM	La Revue des Lettres Modernes
RLMC	Rivista di Letterature Moderne e Comparate
RLV	Revue des Langues Vivantes
RMS	Renaissance and Modern Studies
RP&P	Romanticism Past and Present
RS	Research Studies (Pullman, Wash.)
RSH	Revue des Sciences Humaines
RUS	Rice University Studies
SA	Studi Americani
SAB	South Atlantic Bulletin
S&W	South and West
SAP	Studia Anglica Posnaniensia
SAQ	South Atlantic Quarterly
SB	Studies in Bibliography
SBHC	Studies in Browning and His Circle
SC	Stendhal-Club: Nouvelle Série. Revue Trimestrielle
SCB	South Central Bulletin
ScLJ	Scottish Literary Journal
SCR	South Carolina Review
SECC	Studies in Eighteenth-Century Culture
SEER	Slavic and East European Review
SEL	Studies in English Literature
ShawR	Shaw Review
SHR	Southern Humanities Review
SIR	Studies in Romanticism

SLitI	Studies in the Literary Imagination
SN	Studia Neophilologica
SoR	Southern Review (Baton Rouge, La.)
SoRA	Southern Review (Adelaide, Australia)
SP	Studies in Philology
SQ	Shakespeare Quarterly
SR	Sewanee Review
SSF	Studies in Short Fiction
SSL	Studies in Scottish Literature
SUSFL	Studi Urbinati di Storia, Filosofia e Letteratura
TDR	The Drama Review
TLS	[London] Times Literary Supplement
TSE	Tulane Studies in English
TSL	Tennessee Studies in English
TSLL	Texas Studies in Language and Literature
TxSE	Texas Studies in English
UKCR	University of Kansas City Review
UTQ	University of Toronto Quarterly
UTSE	Studies in English (University of Texas)
VIJ	Victorians Institute Journal
VN	Victorian Newsletter
VP	Victorian Poetry
VPN	Victorian Periodicals Newsletter
VQR	Virginia Quarterly Review
WascanaR	Wascana Review
WC	The Wordsworth Circle
WVUPP	West Virginia University Philological Papers
WWR	Walt Whitman Review
XUS	Xavier Review
YCGL	Yearbook of Comparative and General Literature
YES	Yearbook of English Studies
YFS	Yale French Studies
YR	The Yale Review
YULG	Yale University Library Gazette
YWES	Year's Work in English Studies
ZAA	Zeitschrift für Anglistik und Amerikanistik

THE ROMANTIC MOVEMENT IN ENGLAND

Frank Jordan

Contents

This chapter is organized to highlight the scholarship and criticism on Romanticism in England published since the third edition of *English Romantic Poets: A Review of Research and Criticism* (1972). Accordingly, many earlier essays and books, especially those now of limited use to Romantics scholars, are reviewed succinctly or simply listed or sometimes omitted altogether. Occasionally, I have referred readers to the third edition (hereafter cited as *ERP3*) for titles and commentary that it was not possible to accommodate in the present essay. This is particularly the case for studies of the literature of the later eighteenth century (the so-called pre-Romantic period), to which Ernest Bernbaum gave such generous space in the first two editions (1950, 1956). So energetic and, I would argue, so exciting, not to mention complex, is the study of the Romantic period itself since World War II that it is difficult to justify attending to writing that does not bear directly on the subject—at least not in the finite form of a chapter. As it is, I have had to omit both articles and books—I trust the less worthy ones—in order to give shape to and shed light on material that would otherwise resemble the realm of Chaos and Old Night. As a rule of thumb, I have restricted my review to items purporting to deal with the cultural phenomenon we call Romanticism or with the historical movement in England we designate the Romantic period. This means, in particular, that items primarily concerned with one or two of the poets or their poems are reserved for consideration by my colleagues in the succeeding chapters. When departing from this rule, I have attempted to justify my procedure except in cases where my reasons are self-evident. Finally, I should say a word about the topical arrangement of the material. Other arrangements were considered but abandoned as unworkable, at least for me. Readers will discover, I hope, that the separate categories resulting from such a scheme are more apparent than real, for I have taken care, without employing a tedious system of cross-references, to underscore the recurring preoccupations, issues, controversies, motifs, methods, and perspectives that, like repeated images in poems, point to the very real and quite remarkable patterns to be discerned in Romantics studies. Whatever else one may think or say about Romantics scholars, they cannot be accused of ignoring each other. Indeed, perhaps their most impressive feature is the celerity and sincerity with which they respond to the scholarly and critical outpourings of their peers. Whether or not this feature makes for progress in understanding the Romantic poets and their movement is, of course, one of the issues that currently concerns and occasionally divides us. This chapter, if it enables readers to come to some conclusion on that score, will have achieved an objective beyond its aim.

Bibliographies

George Watson's edition of *The New Cambridge Bibliography of English Literature,* volume 3 (1969), which combines volume 3 of the 1940 edition with the relevant section of the 1957 supplement and extends the whole through 1967, may still be the greatest single source of books and articles concerning the Romantic movement. But given the ever-proliferating scholarship in the field and, more important, the ever-changing perspectives therefrom, Watson's volume is, with each passing year, less and less adequate for scholars' needs. Surveys from the same era such as Richard Harter Fogle's "The Romantic Movement," in *Contemporary Literary Scholarship: A Critical Review* (ed. Lewis Leary, 1957), and René Wellek's "Romanticism Re-examined," in *Concepts of Criticism* (ed. Stephen G. Nichols, 1963), and also in *Romanticism Reconsidered* (ed. Northrop Frye, 1963), are likewise now of limited use, though interesting for the concepts of Romanticism implicit in the assessments these veteran scholars make. Fogle's *Romantic Poets and Prose Writers,* a compilation for the Goldentree Bibliographies series (1967), needs updating if it is to continue to serve the undergraduate and beginning graduate students for whom it was designed. Donald H. Reiman's *English Romantic Poetry, 1800–1835: A Guide to Information Sources* (1979) is the only reasonably current bibliographical guide in book or essay form to be recommended. It is, however, first-rate, thanks to the author's thorough knowledge of the subject and his incisive annotations. Reiman's guide is necessarily selective, particularly with regard to articles, but the important books are there, and major articles not caught up in books are included. Two other volumes in the same series are also useful to Romantics scholars: Harris W. Wilson and Diane Long Hoeveler, *English Prose and Criticism in the Nineteenth Century: A Guide to Information Sources* (1979), and L. W. Conolly and J. P. Wearing, *English Drama and Theatre, 1800–1900: A Guide to Information Sources* (1978).

Serious students of the period must rely primarily, now as before, on the annual bibliographies. The oldest of these, dating back to 1919, is *The Year's Work in English Studies,* a publication of the English Association of London. It is more concerned with reviewing important new items—articles as well as books—than with providing a full listing of new titles. *The Annual Bibliography of English Language and Literature,* sponsored since 1920 by the Modern Humanities Research Association, offers a much more extensive listing and notices reviews. Both annuals typically run several years behind. The most complete and most efficiently produced of the annual bibliographies, initiated in 1922 by the Modern Language Association of America, is the *MLA International Bibliography of Books and Articles on the Modern Languages and Literatures.* An international project since 1957 and subsequently many times enlarged, it is, in a word, indispensable for scholars in any literary or related field. The Romantic period and the Romantic writers are covered in volume 1. By some good fortune, Romantics scholars have, besides these three annuals, two additional bibliographical resources of their own. *The Romantic Movement: A Selective and Critical Bibliography,* for many years now under the general editorship of David V. Erdman, is a movable feast (in *ELH,* 1937–49; in *PQ,* 1950–64; in *ELN,* 1965–78; published as a separate volume by Garland Press, 1979–) but nonetheless a feast for all its migrations, though with the move to Garland rich man's fare. It provides full reviews of major studies and brief notices of consequential ones; it describes or summarizes important articles; and it indicates reviews, sometimes with a hint as to their tone. For the convenience of researchers, the first thirty-five years (1936–70) were collected and indexed by A. C. Elkins, Jr., and L. J. Forstner in

1973. The introduction by David Erdman provides an interesting history of the project and indirectly offers some perspective on the development of literary scholarship in the last fifty years. The second specialized annual is the Current Bibliography of Keats, Shelley, Byron, Hunt, and their circles, published since 1952 in the *Keats-Shelley Journal.* It combines the best features of the others—thorough listing, annotation, indication of reviews—with some special features of its own to make it the most useful of the lot for scholars whose authors come within its province. The preliminary sections, "Current Bibliography" and "Books and Articles Relating to English Romanticism," can be consulted profitably by all Romantics scholars. In 1964, the first twelve years (1 July 1950–30 June 1962) were collected by David Bonnell Green and Edwin Graves Wilson; in 1974 Robert A. Hartley collected the next thirteen years (1 July 1962–31 Dec. 1974).

Finally, one should note the journals that regularly devote issues or parts of issues to annual reviews. Best known of these is "Recent Studies in Nineteenth-Century English Literature," which has appeared in the Autumn number of *Studies in English Literature* since 1961, with a different reviewer each year. The books reviewed (no articles), partly Romantic, partly Victorian, are those received by the editor. Since 1973, the *Wordsworth Circle* has given over its entire Summer number to reviews of current books, many but not all of them concerned with the Wordsworth circle, which group the editors interpret liberally. The highly independent judgments of C. C. Barfoot have been a feature of the Dutch journal *English Studies* since 1970. Barfoot reviews only a handful of books under the heading "Current Literature [year]: Criticism . . . Biography," but his piquant remarks are a reader's, if not an author's, delight. Review articles have become too numerous to list, much less discuss, here. Several of the best are cited later in this chapter at points where their arguments are pertinent.

Histories and Guides, Backgrounds and Introductions, General Studies

The last decade has produced few new histories or guides. The trend in Romantics scholarship is increasingly toward theoretical work, with strong emphasis on critical method, resulting in what is variously described by those who practice and advocate it as "philosophical criticism" or "interpretation." Though not without interest, the earlier histories and guides reviewed in previous editions of this volume—C. H. Herford's *The Age of Wordsworth* (1897; 3rd rev. ed. 1899); George Saintsbury's *A History of Nineteenth-Century Literature (1780–1895)* (1896); Legouis and Cazamian's *History of English Literature* (1924; latest rev. ed. 1971); Ernest Bernbaum's *Guide through the Romantic Movement* (1930; 2nd ed. 1949); Samuel Chew's *The Nineteenth Century and After (1789–1939)*, in *A Literary History of England,* edited by A. C. Baugh (1948; 2nd ed. by Richard Altick, 1967)—are, unfortunately perhaps, not much consulted these days by students of the period. And even the more contemporary histories—David Daiches' *A Critical History of English Literature* (1960) and the two volumes in *The Oxford His-*

tory of English Literature, volume 9 by W. L. Renwick, which treats the years 1789–1815 (1963), and volume 10 by Ian Jack, which treats the years 1815–1832 (1963)—are seldom cited in recent scholarship, though the Daiches volume is useful enough and the Jack volume, critically provocative at times even for advanced students, is more than serviceable. The Renwick volume cannot, however, be recommended, because it is outdated in its perspective and unsympathetic to its subject. Boris Ford's Pelican guide on the Romantics (1957) was reissued as volume 5 of *The New Pelican Guide to English Literature: From Blake to Byron* (1982).

Jean Raimond's *Visages du romantisme anglais* (1977) emphasizes detail and complexity. The six poets share the stage with Scott, Southey, Clare, and the gothic novel. The most distinctive feature of Raimond's study, however, is the dividing of Romanticism, following De Quincey, into two types: the objective and the subjective. This last, the romanticism of interiority, characterizes most of the major poets, who work from within. J. R. de J. Jackson's *Poetry of the Romantic Period* (1980), volume 4 of the Routledge History of English Poetry, is not a conventional work. A "history of poems rather than of poets," it juxtaposes the poems of the six major poets (plus Burns and Cowper) to those of poets we now label minor or worse, in the belief that "such interplay between great writers and the illustrious obscure is the stuff of which the best Romantic poems are made." Jackson's organization is by literary contexts familiar to readers and writers of the period rather than by modern literary contexts (e.g., genres) or by chronology. Curious in procedure and format, Jackson's history is also curious for the absence of a thesis or an idea of history. A. D. Harvey's *English Poetry in a Changing Society, 1780–1825* (1980) shares Jackson's goal of establishing the actual literary context in which the great Romantic poets wrote and were read. This context, he insists, is not the work of only a few: "The basic fact about any culture, which tends to be neglected by students of literature, is that the contributors to a cultural environment are to be numbered in scores and hundreds, not in ones and twos. The purpose of the following study is to bring the scores and hundreds back into the picture." Though Harvey does not exclude sociopolitical explanations for Romanticism, he concentrates on literary ones, in part because he thinks the French Revolution explanation for poetic change overrated. By this account of English Romanticism, Byron, Scott, and Campbell, with considerable help from the likes of Bloomfield and Moore, were responsible for the dethronement of the Augustans; they were the writers who made it possible for the less representative geniuses—Blake, Wordsworth and Coleridge, Shelley and Keats—to flourish. What Jackson has done with poems John Purkis has done with pictures and poems in *The World of the English Romantic Poets* (1982). By demonstrating pictorially the greater images that recur in Romantic poetry, he seeks to illuminate the poetry, sometimes simply by juxtaposing images from different contexts, sometimes by explicating the symbolism of image sequences. Starting and ending with the greatest of the images—that of Prometheus—the author creates a familiar social history of English Romanticism, one amply supported by the poetry and powerfully reinforced by the pictures.

To the general background studies designed especially for today's student by Leonard M. Trawick—*Backgrounds of Romanticism: English Philosophical Prose of the Eighteenth Century* (1967)—and by Karl Kroeber—*Backgrounds to British Romantic Literature* (1968)—we can add Brian Hepworth's *The Rise of Romanticism: Essential Texts* (1978). Trawick's volume includes eight excerpts from the writings of such intellectuals as Hartley, Duff, and Godwin. Kroeber's volume, which is not restricted to philosophical backgrounds, includes pieces by thirteen prominent social, intellectual, and art historians of the twentieth century. Both collections provide informative introductions and responsible reading lists. Hepworth's "texts" are taken from some twenty-seven writers, ranging from Thomas Burnet to Wordsworth. The selection, as the introductory "history of ideas" in poetry and philosophy points out, is intended to show the continuity—more convincing than the contrast, in Hepworth's eyes—between the eighteenth century and Romanticism. The so-called pre-Romantic world Hepworth prefers to call Romantic.

If the writing of histories, guides, and backgrounds has abated, the collecting of essays intended to introduce students to scholarly issues or to critical trends in the study of Romanticism—an enterprise greatly stimulated by the enthusiasms of the 1960s—proceeds apace. Two of the earlier such collections have even gone into second editions, as if to monitor the changing fads and fortunes of the subject. Chief of these is M. H. Abrams' *English Romantic Poets: Modern Essays in Criticism* (1960; 2nd ed. 1975). Abrams justifies the second edition (which drops eight essays and adds thirteen) by claiming that the debate about the Romantic achievement, the focus of the first edition, is now resolved in favor of the Romantics, whose would-be detractors among modern writers are now seen to be themselves latter-day Romantics. The second edition is thus free to represent what Abrams refers to as "drastic shifts in sensibility and poetic standards during the generation or so just past"—that is, the upheavals that characterized Romantics literary scholarship in the 1960s and early 1970s. The second collection to undergo revision is Robert F. Gleckner and Gerald E. Enscoe's *Romanticism: Points of View* (1962; 2nd ed. 1970). About half the revised volume, which is solely Gleckner's work, is new; but the essays retained from the first edition have been reedited, the introduction expanded, and each chapter supplied with a bibliographical note. Shiv Kumar's *British Romantic Poets: Recent Revaluations* (1966), a collection similar to these others, is now of interest primarily to students of the history of Romantic criticism. So, too, the collections of essays conceived as companions to the second edition of this volume and to its counterpart on the minor Romantic writers—*The Major English Romantic Poets: A Symposium in Reappraisal* (ed. C. D. Thorpe, Carlos Baker, and Bennett Weaver, 1957) and *Some British Romantics: A Collection of Essays* (ed. James V. Logan, John E. Jordan, and Northrop Frye, 1966). Scholars interested in the very considerable contributions of Abrams, Frye, Lionel Trilling, and René Wellek to Romantics studies will not want to miss the most distinguished collective effort of reappraisal of the 1960s: *Romanticism Reconsidered,* four papers selected from those read at the English Institute in 1962 and edited by Frye (1963). Other items in this category from this era are Anthony Thorlby's *The Romantic Movement* (1966), a more serious version of the Gleckner and Enscoe volume, and John B. Halsted's *Romanticism: Problems of Definition, Explanation, and Evaluation* (1965), an assortment of essays taken from the more or less standard studies. Howard E. Hugo's slightly earlier *The Romantic Reader* (1957) is a fat anthology of excerpts from Romantic poetry and prose ordered so as to picture the age of Romanticism in all its variety of subject and mood. By contrast, an item from the late 1960s—Harold Orel and George Worth's *The Nineteenth Century Writer and His Audience: Selected Problems in Theory, Form, and Content* (1969), six essays by members of the English faculty at the University of Kansas—addresses a single subject. Two of the six essays deal with Romantic poets.

Contributions in this genre from the 1970s and beyond not conceived as festschriften (see below) are *Romanticism: Vistas, Instances, Continuities* (ed. David Thorburn and Geoffrey Hartman, 1973); *Studies in Relevance: Romantic and Victorian Writers in 1972* (ed. Thomas M. Harwell, 1973); *European Romanticism* (ed. I. Sőtér and I. Neupokoyeva, 1977); *Romantic and Modern: Revaluations of Literary Tradition* (ed. George Bornstein, 1977); and *The Romantics* (ed. Stephen Prickett, 1981). Nine of the eleven essays in the Thorburn and Hartman volume were delivered as lectures at Yale in 1970–71. Written from a revisionist impulse, the essays seek to develop a broadened concept of Romanticism in ways hinted at by the language of the title. The Harwell compilation, an item in the University of Salzburg's Romantic Reassessment series, includes six essays on the Romantics, five of them specific to a single poet. The Sőtér and Neupokoyeva volume is comparative literature on the grand scale. Its distinctive perspective is the socialist ideology of its contributors, who also seek to broaden the concept of Romanticism by expanding it to comprehend the critical and historical perspectives of Eastern Europe. The Bornstein volume, like the "Continuities" section of the Thorburn and Hartman book, stresses the affinities of Romantic and twentieth-century writers, with particular attention to irony as a common ground. The Prickett volume, five essays (two of them, plus introduction, by Prickett himself) by faculty at the University of Sussex, forms part of the Methuen series entitled "The Context of English Literature." Thus, it possesses a singleness of purpose and unity of design neither desired nor achieved in the other collections. (These collections and the festschriften discussed just below will be identified subsequently in this chapter by the last names of their editors, as, for example, "in Thorburn and Hartman" or "in Hilles and Bloom.")

Festschriften worthy of being carried over from the previous edition are *The Age of Johnson* (ed. Frederick W. Hilles, 1949) and *From Sensibility to Romanticism* (ed. Frederick W. Hilles and Harold Bloom, 1965). Though the former, a tribute to Chauncey B. Tinker, contains only two essays on the Romantics, the latter, a tribute to Frederick A. Pottle, is a rich compilation. More recent items are *The Morality of Art: Essays Presented to G. W. Knight by His Colleagues and Friends* (ed. D. W. Jefferson, 1969); *Le Romantisme anglo-américain: Mélanges offerts à Louis Bonnerot* (ed. Roger Asselineau et al., 1971); *Romantic and Victorian: Studies in Memory of William H. Marshall* (ed. W. Paul Elledge and Richard L. Hoffman, 1971); *Nineteenth-Century Literary Perspectives: Essays in Honor of Lionel Stevenson* (ed. Clyde de L. Ryals, 1976); and *Literature of the Romantic Period*

1750–1850 (ed. R. T. Davies and B. G. Beatty, 1976). This last volume, beyond its intent to honor Kenneth Muir by members of his sometime department at Liverpool University, hopes to promote an "enquiry into the problem of the homogeneity of Romantic literature." A late item in this category is *Romantic Texts, Romantic Times: Homage to David V. Erdman,* a special issue of *Studies in Romanticism* (Fall 1982), which opens with an interview of Erdman and his wife, Virginia, by Morris Eaves, editor of the issue. A group of unrelated essays follows; it is, in turn, followed by groups of essays on Blake (ed. Eaves) and Coleridge (ed. Carl Woodring) and reviews of recent Romantics texts (ed. and introd. Donald H. Reiman). Of related interest is this journal's celebration (Winter 1982) of its majority by inviting a number of important scholars to reminisce about "How It Was" in the days before the advent of *SIR.* Together the two issues testify to the gusto with which this fine journal has, from its beginning, served the cause of interpreting Romanticism. *An Infinite Complexity: Essays in Romanticism* (ed. J. K. Watson, 1983), the latest of the festschriften, celebrates neither a scholar nor a journal but rather the 150th anniversary of the University of Durham.

   The trend in Romantics scholarship mentioned at the beginning of this section has made particularly problematic the old category of "general studies"—those overviews of a literary period that fall somewhere between histories and specialized treatises because they attempt to be comprehensive by considering all the Romantic writers, more or less equally, in the light of a particular perspective or thesis or because they attempt to consider Romanticism in all or most of its aspects or topics. One can understand why collections of essays such as those reviewed just above have proliferated. Increasingly, there is the recognition that no single book can be adequate to Romanticism in its complete manifestation—and, on the part of wiser scholars, that no single concept or theory of Romanticism can or should be encased in amber, where it is allowed to harden into dogma. John W. Ehrstine, for example, in "A Calling of the Wits Together: A Recent Romantic Theory" (*ESQ,* 1972), argues that books that leave open the door to other theories serve Romantics studies best. The very language currently used to speak of the subject—for example, "vistas, instances, continuities" or "affinities" or "perspectives"—reflects this recognition. Hence, few recent books on English Romanticism, no matter how central their topic or how fully they explore it, presume to deal with all the poets or all the critical and philosophical problems that the poets raise. And thus the items to be discussed here are not as many as one might expect.
   Ernest Bernbaum, in the first two editions of this volume, cited Oliver Elton's *Survey of English Literature, 1780–1830* (1912) as still valuable for revealing the impact of Romanticism on the traditional literary forms. And so it is. Graham Hough's *The Romantic Poets* (1953) is a relatively modest effort to discuss Romantic poetry according to the lights of modern scholarship and criticism. Hough has no particular thesis to advance or critical method to champion. Not so M. H. Abrams' *The Mirror and the Lamp: Romantic Theory and the Critical Tradition* (1953; rpt. 1958). One of the most distinguished of all works of American literary scholarship, it became an instant classic, boosting the morale of

Romantics scholars in a period when such a tonic was badly needed. Classifying Romantic poetry and poetics as expressive (symbolized by the lamp) and hence sharply distinguished from mimetic art and aesthetics (the mirror), Abrams created an image of Romanticism as a radical break with the dominant tradition of Western art from its beginnings through the eighteenth century, a point of view that has had tremendous currency in the last thirty years. Encyclopedic in scope and in format, *The Mirror and the Lamp* is perhaps the work to which most Romantics scholars return most often, using it as they would a reference work. Edward E. Bostetter's *The Romantic Ventriloquists: Wordsworth, Coleridge, Keats, Shelley, Byron* (1963; rpt. 1975) derives its title from a favorite Romantic analogy for the poetic imagination, "the ventriloquistic image of the aeolian harp." Taking issue with Earl Wasserman's claim that the Romantics created a new cosmic syntax (see *The Subtler Language* below), Bostetter argues that the Romantics inherited this syntax from the eighteenth century and that it ultimately failed them because it was inadequate for their needs. Scholars can take and have taken issue with this book, but it continues to stimulate those who pick it up. Harold Bloom's *The Visionary Company: A Reading of English Romantic Poetry* (1961; rev. ed. 1971) is much further from Hough, Abrams, and Bostetter than publication dates might suggest. His "reading" is, of course, not only unlike theirs or that of traditional literary scholars but also unlike that of anyone else, though his approach to Romanticism is now widely disseminated among younger scholars, who reflect it in their own writing. This approach will be taken up at length later in this chapter. Suffice it to say here that if Bloom, in *The Visionary Company*, privileges Blake and the apocalyptic strain in Romanticism, he also makes room for Byron and even gives a chapter to Beddoes, Clare, Darley, and other writers usually ignored. With this study the mythic approach to Romantic literature can be said to have "arrived" and is brilliantly exploited. The only earlier study resembling Bloom's in the slightest is D. G. James's *The Romantic Comedy* (1948). Though James's objective is to trace the development of the Romantic spirit as it changed and matured over a period of thirty-odd years, he finds certain constants, among the most prominent being the interest of the Romantic poets in mythology and their need to employ it. James saw the Romantic movement as a quest for an adequate literary form; Bloom sees it as a quest, albeit an internalized quest, for "the real man, the imagination." The first scholar to devote a book to the subject was Hoxie N. Fairchild, *The Romantic Quest* (1931), for whom the objectives of the quest were to be found in naturalism, medievalism, and transcendentalism. A devil's advocate of Romanticism, Fairchild persisted in judging the quest and its consequences negatively. Magnus Irvine, *The Unceasing Quest* (1940), dwelt on the Romantics' quest for perfection; David Perkins, on *The Quest for Permanence: The Symbolism of Wordsworth, Shelley, and Keats* (1959; rpt. 1965). This last quest study is probably the most rewarding.

Anyone nostalgic for the 1960s radical version of Romanticism—that is, Blake is the figure central to English Romanticism, which is indissolubly tied to avatars of the revolutionary movement from 1780 to 1830; the dream of Romanticism "n'est pas derrière nous; il est la jeunesse du Monde"—will relish Paul

Rozenberg's *Le Romantisme anglais: Le défi des vulnerables* (1973), which witnesses to Abrams' perception of "drastic shifts in sensibility and poetic standards" in that decade. Since criticism emanates from the university and since the university is synonymous with the "establishment"—hence, with resistance to revolution—Rozenberg forgoes the assistance of other scholars; except for Harold Bloom, counterculture figures are the author's sole mentors. The only other books to be discussed here are the companion studies of David Morse, *Perspectives on Romanticism: A Transformational Analysis* (1981) and *Romanticism: A Structural Analysis* (1982). Together they suggest how quickly mainstream Romantics scholarship has left the more extreme and simplistic platforms of the 1960s behind, as well as how philosophically sophisticated Romantics criticism has become in just a few short years. The first volume is "transformational" analysis in the sense that "everything is produced by transformation out of something else"; emerging from something else, Romanticism "is always on the point of becoming something else." The second volume is "structural analysis" in the sense that Romanticism is represented "as a series of characteristic intellectual structures rather than as a climate of opinion, an ambience or sea through which the individual authors as fishes move." Morse's purpose in using such terms is to signal his distance from the New Criticism, the roots of which, he acknowledges, are to be found in Romanticism. Still, he is unsparing in his censure: "A cardinal axiom of Romanticism was that of uniqueness, singleness and particularity of everything in the universe, and such an assumption has pervaded modern literary criticism with consequences so catastrophic that they verge on deliberate mystification and anti-intellectualism." The first volume, after correcting the misreadings by Foucault and Derrida of eighteenth-century discourse in order to describe accurately the nature of Romantic discourse (the language of which is "plural and perspectival"), examines the continuity between Protestantism and Romanticism, the impact of Smollett's fiction on Romantic narrative, and the preoccupation of Romantic writers with the infinite (and the problems this preoccupation produced, e.g., the derogation of painting and the exaltation of music). A final chapter focuses on what Morse chooses to call the "conflict between the monoscopic and the polyscopic," that is, between the traditional orientation of Western culture to truth and perspective and the new orientation of Western culture fostered by Romanticism to relativity and perspectives—to "contradiction and manysidedness." Ultimately, Morse proceeds "from a position in the late twentieth century that Romanticism is grasped not as a thing in itself but as a part of a system of differences in Western culture." The second volume examines three fields of Romantic discourse—the gothic, the historical drama and historical novel, the artist figure in the folktale and in English Romantic poetry—in which the Romantic writer, through particular figures and motifs, addresses political, social, and professional issues. Despite Romanticism's cult of the individual, Morse insists, "there are no individual ways of looking at the world; collective ways are the only ways we have." Not all that follows in this chapter is polyscopic or perspectival in the strict sense of Morse's studies, but much of the more recent writing on Romanticism is. Collective ways of looking at the world of Romantic poetry are on the increase.

Natural Supernaturalism and Romantic Irony

M. H. Abrams' *Natural Supernaturalism: Tradition and Revolution in Romantic Literature* (1971) may be said to inaugurate the decade under special review in this volume. Eagerly anticipated as the second major work on Romanticism by the author of *The Mirror and the Lamp* (1953), it is consistent with the earlier work in viewing Romanticism as a transformation of Western culture wrought by poets and philosophers, especially in England and Germany in "collateral developments," in response to "the spirit of the age" or revolution in society and politics. As his title suggests, the Romantics were concerned with the old as well as the new, intent on preserving as well as destroying. In the face of progressive and accelerating secularization, they set out, in Abrams' words, "to reconstitute the grounds of hope and to announce the certainty, or at least the possibility, of a rebirth in which a renewed mankind will inhabit a renovated earth where he will find himself thoroughly at home." This they accomplished by secularizing Biblical myths, most especially the myth of providential design. Abrams' Romantics are in themselves reconcilers of opposites, being not either poets or philosophers—not one or the other—but both at once. Hence Wordsworth—and especially the Wordsworth of Coleridge's grand design—is, for Abrams, the "great and exemplary poet of the age, and his Prospectus [to *The Recluse*] stands as the manifesto of a central Romantic enterprise against which we can conveniently measure the consonance and divergences in the writings of his contemporaries." And from the Prospectus, it is Wordsworth's marriage metaphor, the wedding of mind and nature, that Abrams chooses to focus the argument of *Natural Supernaturalism* —"a prominent period-metaphor which served a number of major writers, English and German, as the central figure in a similar complex of ideas concerning the history and destiny of man and the role of the visionary poet as both herald and inaugurator of a new and supremely better world." With special but selective attention to Keats and Carlyle in England and to Schiller, Hegel, and Hölderlin in Germany, Abrams pursues the development of the new mythology of natural supernaturalism—the revolution in consciousness—to the present day by examining the psychoautobiographies of numerous writers in the Romantic and post-Romantic tradition, with special emphasis on the plot of the "circuitous journey" common to their lives and works. Continually comparative, *Natural Supernaturalism* is important reading for students of Continental Romanticism and of twentieth-century American poetry as well.

It was several years before the impact of *Natural Supernaturalism* became clear. From the vantage point of the sequel decade, it would appear that Abrams' imposing study was rather more a culmination of his and others' study of Romanticism than it was a departure from the theories and trends of Romantics scholarship in the decades since World War II. As such, it will remain invaluable for years to come. Like *The Mirror and the Lamp* and several of Abrams' "classic" essays, *Natural Supernaturalism* is a landmark of Romantics scholarship to be consulted again and again for its eloquent statements about the Romantic enterprise and for its perceptive accounts of individual authors and works. But it is not, to judge from subsequent studies, either the last word on Romanticism or the whole story of that subject. As it turned out, "Romantic irony" rather than "natural supernaturalism" became the watchword of the 1970s. To oversimplify a bit, Abrams himself provided the impetus for the more skeptical appraisals his book received when he remarked in the Preface that he omitted Byron "altogether; not because I think him a lesser poet than the others but because in his greatest work he speaks with an ironic counter-voice and deliberately opens a satirical perspective on the vatic stance of his Romantic contemporaries." For years, Romantics studies had been omitting Byron—and omitting Blake, who, though he figures in *Natural Supernaturalism,* can hardly serve as major support for Abrams' argument, given his celebrated visceral reaction to Wordsworth's Prospectus. When one takes into account the traditional critical methods of Abrams and remembers that even his approach to Wordsworth is, by some renderings, conservative, then one has a general idea of why *Natural Supernaturalism* was greeted by both enthusiastic admiration and respectful reservation.

Seven years after *Natural Supernaturalism* appeared, Cornell University honored Abrams with a symposium, the papers for which were published in *High Romantic Argument: Essays for M. H. Abrams* (ed. Lawrence Lipking, 1981). The first part of the volume recognizes Abrams' special contribution to Wordsworth studies, with essays by Geoffrey Hartman and Jonathan Wordsworth; the second part reviews and assesses Abrams' scholarly achievements as a whole, with essays by Wayne Booth, Thomas McFarland, Lawrence Lipking, and Jonathan Culler, to which Abrams offers a witty but dead serious response, reaffirming his stand in the critical disputes of the day: "depite immersion in the deconstructive element of our time, I remain an unreconstructed humanist."

Anne K. Mellor's *English Romantic Irony* (1980) is perhaps the most direct reply to Abrams. Like him, she views Romanticism as a reaction by poets and philosophers to social and political upheaval, but she reads that reaction differently. Like him, too, she uses German writers to shed light on the English Romantics, but she chooses a different set. The reaction Mellor detects is philosophical skepticism, which manifests itself as Romantic irony: "Romantic irony is both a philosophical conception of the universe and an artistic program." Perceiving the world as chaotic and incomprehensible rather than as divinely ordered and therefore knowable, Romantic ironists find their values in change and process; hence they are not pessimists or nihilists either. If they must continually deconstruct their own texts just as they must continually deconstruct the myths that project ascertainable truths and deify their creators, so too they must continually construct new texts, for Mellor insists on the significance of both terms: "the authentic romantic ironist is as filled with enthusiasm as with skepticism. He is as much a romantic as an ironist." His art, consequently, "simultaneously creates and de-creates itself." In doing so, Mellor is at pains to distinguish her brand of deconstruction from that of modern deconstructionists. The principal theorist of Romantic irony is Friedrich Schlegel, whose concept provides her with a paradigmatic model for discussing individual works. Mellor's book is not, therefore, so much an attack on *Natural Supernaturalism* as a supplement to it, filling in the acknowledged omissions. (Indeed, Abrams outlines a book much like Mellor's in the essay "Rationality and Imagination in Cultural History: A Reply to Wayne Booth" [*Critl,* 1976] and boasts that he could almost imagine writing it.) If Abrams privileges the Romantic work that is confident, idealistic, and closed or resolved, Mellor gives priority to the work that is open-ended, inconclusive or indeterminate, unsuccessful in reconciling opposites—the work that affirms the creative process but not necessarily the product. Purely in terms of proportion, it would seem that Abrams included more than he omitted. Mellor's approach allows her to give Byron his due, but the other English writers with whom she is preoccupied, Keats and Carlyle, are equally important to Abrams.

The second half of *English Romantic Irony* is devoted to the "perimeters" of the mode, as defined by the guilt of Coleridge and the fear of Carroll: when philosophical skepticism eventuates in guilt or fear, then Romantic irony is not possible. Mellor's mode would appear to be more an exclusively nineteenth-century phenomenon than Abrams' "natural supernaturalism." But by her own account, Mellor's investigation is a more modest enterprise—and not the less informative for that. If one must choose between natural supernaturalism and Romantic irony, Mellor makes the latter seem an attractive prospect, particularly when it is compared with more recent ironic modes.

A second book appearing in the same year (1980), Tilottama Rajan's *Dark Interpreter: The Discourse of Romanticism,* is also a counterversion or countervision of Romanticism as expounded by Abrams, Frye, and others. What Abrams proposes as the revolutionary element of Romanticism—"a natural supernaturalism based on the imagination"—Rajan labels its most conservative element, for by her account the Romantic rhetoric of affirmation is compensatory: its effect is to deny the vision that the universe is discontinuous and chaotic in poems that "deconstruct their own affirmative postulates." More so than Mellor, Rajan is a student and practitioner of deconstructionist criticism and, as such, is obligated to use the language implicit in her method of inquiry, but it should be said at once that she clearly and carefully enunciates her principles and procedures. Moreover, there is method to her method, for she finds certain Romantic theorists to be forerunners of modern deconstruction theorists; her method, to some degree, is their method and not an alien or ahistoric form of discourse. Rajan qualifies her disagreements with Abrams and his school. It is not that they have failed to recognize the darker elements of Romantic works; it is just that they have not given them enough credit: "The darker elements in Romantic works are not a part of their organic unity, but rather threaten to collapse this unity." Similarly, Rajan qualifies her agreement with Paul de Man, Jacques Derrida, and other modern discourse theorists. She does not propose that the deconstructed Romantic text replaces the surface text: "it is also necessary to recognize that the text cannot simply be replaced by a subtext, and that the official content of a work does not cease to exist because it is undermined from within. It is because the doubts buried in subtexts are not necessarily 'truer' than the affirmations urged in texts that Romanticism is less decisive in its commitment to self-irony than de Man sometimes supposes." Put succinctly, Rajan's position is that "the current debate between organicist and deconstructionist critics over the nature of Romanticism was originally waged by the Romantics themselves and was not resolved in favor of either side." Where Abrams relies on Hegel and Mellor on Schlegel for the critical perspective to deal with Romantic poems, Rajan goes to Schiller, Schopenhauer, and Nietzsche, resulting in a more complex, if more flexible, paradigm, in line with her desire not to oversimplify the dialectical relationship of text and subtext, of transcendentalism and skepticism—of illusion and its deconstruction in Romantic literature. The most striking difference between Rajan's book and Mellor's is that, where, for the latter, Byron would seem to be the starting point and principal example of Romantic irony, he is negligible to the point and purpose of the former. Shelley, Coleridge, and especially Keats receive the bulk of Rajan's attention. More so than Mellor even, she is reluctant to extend her idea of Romanticism beyond the Romantic period as traditionally defined. The qualifications Rajan accumulates as she proceeds may give one pause, but her work is the more ingratiating for them.

Along the way of her analysis, Rajan reminds us that, in Edward E. Bostetter's *The Romantic Ventriloquists* and D. G. James's *The Romantic Comedy* (see above), the view of the Romantics being put forth by the present-day ironists critics was in part anticipated. Bostetter she labels a "proto-deconstructionist." A latter-day champion of "Bostetter's Critical Method: The Romantic Truth-Tellers" (*Paunch,* 1974) is Arthur Efron, who extends Bostetter's thesis to Blake.

Still a third study that by implication questions the Abrams or positive tradition of Romanticism is David Simpson's *Irony and Authority in Romantic Poetry* (1979), which originated in the belief that there is a place for a concept of Romantic irony in English Romantic literature, a concept that is "coinstantaneous with, rather than caused by, developments in the German tradition." Simpson's view of Romanticism, like Mellor's and Rajan's, is relatively negative because it describes Romantic poetry as "organized to make us confront the question of authority, especially as it pertains to the contract between author and reader." Romantic irony, therefore, is the reader's questioning of the Romantic writer's "meaning of what he says both as we receive it into our own codes and canons of significance and as it relates to the context of the rest of his utterances, their moods and voices." But it is also the Romantic artist's studied avoidance of determinate meanings ("indeterminacy" is Simpson's key term), the "refusal of closure," and a good deal more. Although Simpson's book has in common with Rajan's the new vocabulary of the newer criticism (and he mixes and spreads it liberally), it is perhaps closest to hers in its desire to demonstrate that the Romantics anticipate recent critical theory or, in the special terms of Simpson's book, that current arguments about the authority of the text and, in particular, about the hermeneutic circle (E. D. Hirsch is an especially prominent figure in Simpson's own critical circle) are themselves Romantic in origin. Simpson is closest perhaps to Mellor in stressing the doubleness of Romantic works as they both assert authority and seek reception and, simultaneously, sabotage that authority and require interpretation, thus making of reading as well as of writing a process of "deconstruction and reconstruction, where meaning must be perpetually established and re-established." He also invites comparison with Thomas McFarland, whose treatment of organicism in *Romanticism and the Forms of Ruin* (1980) is discussed later in this chapter.

Simpson's book has nowhere near the methodological precision of the other two and hence perhaps nothing resembling their clarity, but there are some benefits to his looser method, among them his attention to neglected Romantic works such as Wordsworth's poems "On the Naming of Places" and his explanation of why, with the advent of Romanticism, the child replaces the traveler as the dominant metaphor of literature.

For Peter Conrad in *Shandyism: The Character of Romantic Irony* (1978), the fourth book of the decade to treat this special subject, it is not necessary to go to Germany for paradigms or to deconstruction aesthetics for methods. Rather, Romantic irony for him is a characteristically English phenomenon, first manifested fully in *Tristram Shandy*, a work that, by combining without inverting or subverting the Shakespearean or dramatic categories of tragedy and comedy, anticipates both the ethics and aesthetics of Romanticism: irony is that point in the process where comedy and tragedy meet. Like Simpson's, Conrad's notion of Romantic irony is a little slippery, involving various sorts of transformations, including that of the reader's role in literature. Moreover, Conrad is not by any stretch of the imagination a conventional scholar. As is his wont, he mixes literary criticism with art history, literary theory with musicology, and ranges freely among the national literatures and artistic cultures of Western Europe. One may wish for more systematic analysis or—especially where painting is concerned— more plates to examine as one tries to appreciate Conrad's interpretations. But anyone who can suggest that we might view the Shandys as "a group of alternately blithe or dizzy or gravely sensitive Wordsworthians before their time" will never be accused of boring his readers.

Books do not, of course, tell the whole story. Several articles of note also examine Romantic irony. Ernst Behler, in "Techniques of Irony in Light of the Romantic Theory" (*RUS*, 1971), attempts to point up the distinction between classical and Romantic irony and to explain the shift from one to the other at the end of the eighteenth century. Of special interest, given Conrad's theme, is Behler's suggestion that Romantic irony flourished in practice during the eighteenth century, culminating in (rather than beginning with) *Tristram Shandy*. Romantic irony is, then, the belated giving of a name to something already existing in literature. (Behler cites the wise fool in Shakespeare, Don Quixote, etc.) Of special interest, too, is Behler's association of the double with Romantic irony. Byron is, of course, the English Romantic most useful to Behler in illustrating the techniques of this mode. Raymond Immerwahr's "Romantic Irony and Romantic Arabesque prior to Romanticism" (*GQ*, 1969) is of interest to English Romanticism chiefly for two reasons: (1) it demonstrates that the germ of irony is contained in the very word "romantic," and (2) it claims that *Tristram Shandy* is the most important channel for transmitting arabesque stylistic techniques (arabesque being a version of Romantic irony) to the Romantic movement. Squarely centered on the English Romantics, at least the second generation of them, Stuart M. Sperry's "Toward a Definition of Romantic Irony in English Literature" (in Bornstein) agrees with the essays of Mellor, Rajan, and Simpson in viewing Romantic irony as a state of mind, an awareness of indeterminacy, that arises, in part, unconsciously. Both Keats and Shelley, according to Sperry, struggle for insight that is "never secure from the pervasive ironies of human experience." Byron's irony differs, especially from Keats's, in being fully conscious and deliberate: *Don Juan* is the nineteenth century's best illustration of this mode. From the perspective of Romantic irony—from this alternative account of English Romanticism, therefore—Byron is not a Romantic writer to be accommodated by Morse Peckham's negative Romanticism or Bloom's Promethean quest; rather he becomes the exemplary poet of the age, against which the others are to be measured. In the Victorian period, Romantic irony went underground, in Sperry's reading, eventually to emerge in the modern novel.

Both Mellor and Rajan acknowledge the precept and example of Cyrus Hamlin, the author of two essays on Romantic irony, for their own critical thinking. The later essay, "Platonic Dialogue and Romantic Irony: Prolegomenon to a Theory of Literary Narrative" (*CRCL*, 1976), takes issue with part of Behler's essay, in particular with his distinction between classical and Romantic irony and his history of Romantic irony (both derived from Schlegel). For Hamlin, Plato's dialogues are self-reflexive narratives and thus are models of Romantic irony, self-reflexive discourse being the constitutive element of the mode. Thus, Platonic dialogues and the European novel, in which Hamlin sees Romantic irony emerging, can be said to provide a hermeneutics of literature, a basis for a theory of literary narrative (not confined to the novel). Hamlin's earlier essay, "The Temporality of Selfhood: Metaphor and Romantic Poetry" (*NLH*, 1974), is concerned with pointing up the gap between the theory of metaphor in Romanticism—that of symbolic form, in which opposites are fused or unified—and the practice—that of metaphoric form, in which the tension or discontinuity between opposites is not resolved, resulting in a dialectical structure that can be called ironic. To adopt Hamlin's position is to argue for a revision of the literary history that links modern theories of metaphor with Romantic theories of the imagination, something that Mellor resists in "On Romantic Irony, Symbolism and Allegory" (*Criticism*, 1979). As in her book, she would reconcile, using Romantic irony as she conceives it, allegory or metaphor and symbol: "the romantic-ironic work sustains two modes of figural discourse without privileging one over the other."

The scholar chiefly identified with undermining the privileged status of the symbol in the literary history and criticism of the Romantics is, of course, the late Paul de Man. Representative of his argument is the essay "The Rhetoric of Temporality," in *Interpretation: Theory and Practice* (ed. Charles Singleton, 1969). In asserting the superiority of symbol over allegory, critics (among them Abrams, Wimsatt, and Wasserman) have perpetuated the deliberate "self-mystification" of the poets themselves, who employed symbol to hide from the painful knowledge that the self cannot identify with the nonself, the subject with the object ("an act of ontological bad faith"), and that it is illusory to think otherwise. Symbol is the rhetorical mode of this illusory identity; allegory is the mode of difference and distance from nature, the perception of which is the authentic Romantic experience, whether it be German, French, or English. The tension between symbol and allegory, not the substitution of symbol for allegory, is, thus, the true figural rhetoric of Romantic poetry. Whether allegory and irony go hand in hand, as theorists are prone to suggest, is, however, problematic. De Man uses "A Slumber Did My Spirit Seal" to show that they need not. They are, however, linked "in their common discovery of a truly temporal predicament. They are also linked in their common de-mystification of an organic world postulated in a symbolical mode of analogical correspondences or in a mimetic mode of representation in which fiction and reality coincide. It is especially against the latter mystification that irony is directed." Two essays in *Blindness and Insight: Essays in the Rhetoric of Contemporary Criticism* (1971)—"Literary History and Literary Modernity" and "Lyric and Modernity"—also argue for a revision of literary history necessitated by the allegorization of poetry, "the distinctive characteristic of modernity in the lyric." The metaphors of blindness and insight function for de Man much as those of mirror and lamp do for Abrams: they are a convenient shorthand for his thesis. His posthumous *The Rhetoric of Romanticism* (1984) collects eight essays dating from 1956 and adds two new ones. Not the "historical reflection on Romanticism" deflected by "local difficulties of interpretation" that constitute *Allegories of Reading* (1979), the collection represents "the main bulk" of what de Man has written on Romanticism.

Gunnar Berefelt, "On Symbol and Allegory" (*JAAC,* 1969), is more interested in chastising the Romantic writers who made the distinction than in correcting modern theorists who wish to negate or subvert it in some way. His complaint is that the Romantics treated symbol and allegory as antithetical because they failed to distinguish different levels of symbolic functioning. Allegory is one level of symbolism, what Berefelt calls "composed symbol." These articles debating allegory and symbol are not merely peripheral to the larger debate of natural supernaturalism versus Romantic irony. The scholars who would privilege allegory over symbolism or even equate it with symbolism undermine the High Romantic argument that has prevailed in Romantics scholarship for several decades and the Coleridge-derived tradition of Romantic aesthetics on which it is founded. Not just the books and essays of Abrams are called into question, but also those of René Wellek, W. K. Wimsatt, Albert Gérard, and on and on. Symptomatic of the trend is Gay Clifford's book *The Transformation of Allegory* (1974), which, though it attends little to the Romantics except to note their hostility to allegory, constitutes a defense of allegory as a mode of discourse whose moment may have returned—a good thing, in Clifford's view.

In this section I have of necessity restricted the discussion to those works that concern English Romantic writers. It cannot but be obvious, however, that German literature and German literary scholars are often the starting point for any concept of Romantic irony. For those who read German and wish to delve deeper, there are specialized studies of the subject by Helmut Prang, *Die Romantische Ironie* (1972); Ernst Behler, *Klassische Ironie. Romantische Ironie. Tragische Ironie: Ursprung dieser Begriffe* (1972); Ingrid Strohschneider-Kohrs, *Die Romantische Ironie im Theorie und Gestaltung* (1960). And there is an oft-cited English-language Columbia dissertation by Morton Gurewitch entitled *European Romantic Irony* (1957). D. C. Muecke includes Romantic irony within *The Compass of Irony* (1969).

Before leaving *Natural Supernaturalism* and its controversies, I should at least note that Abrams' neglect of Romantic irony, with the consequent effort of those offended by this omission to make compensations, is not the sole reservation voiced about the book, as anyone addicted to reviews is well aware. One review essay in particular, Jerome J. McGann's "Romanticism and the Embarrassments of Critical Tradition" (*MP,* 1973), faulted Abrams for not being nearly historical enough. By summoning Romantic writers ignored by Abrams he demonstrates the limitations and distortions that result when the Romantic tradition is defined as a Judeo-Christian tradition and, especially, when Christian is restricted to Protestant. McGann's complaints also apply, of course, to Harold Bloom's interpretation of Romanticism, leading McGann to suggest alternatives for Romantics scholarship and criticism predicated either on the expansive model of Northrop Frye or on a "flexible set of interacting limits" whereby the investigation of Romanticism can be narrowed so as to avoid oversimplification, distortion, and, especially, sheer loss of valuable Romantic works and writers. McGann's recommendation is illustrated, as one might expect, by his own work on Byron and Swinburne and, most recently, by his *Romantic Ideology: A Critical Investigation* (1983), of which the thesis is that "the scholarship and criticism of Romanticism and its works are dominated by a Romantic Ideology, by an uncritical absorption in Romanticism's own self-representations." Taking Heine for his mentor, McGann pursues a historical method of criticism because it enables him to underscore the difference of the past and its artistic culture from the present and its artistic culture. Only by clarifying and promoting this difference, he asserts, can we hope to improve social conditions ·or advance learning. McGann is not the only voice to insist on the historical difference of Romantic from post-Romantic culture; Karl Kroeber has for some time been sounding much the same theme. But McGann's volume is the most single-minded effort "to free present criticism from the crippling illusion that such a past establishes the limits, conceptual and perceptual, of our present and our future." As such, it presents quite possibly an even stronger challenge to the Abrams tradition of Romantics criticism than do the several books and essays of the Romantic ironist critics because it is a more radical alternative to that tradition than theirs.

Akin to McGann's work is Patrick Parrinder's *Authors and Authority: A Study of English Literary Criticism and Its Relation to Culture 1750–1900* (1977), a revisionist account of literary criticism that examines the English critical tradition of crediting literature with the force of an ideology, a notion that emerged in the Romantic period. Accordingly, Parrinder devotes one chapter to Wordsworth, whose "prefaces had pioneered the claim that to accept the authority of a new volume of poems was to accept a particular social ideology," and another to the rest of the Romantic critics, all of whom follow Wordsworth in attributing to literature a power worthy of competing with sociopolitical power. Parrinder shows just how potent this Romantic culture of art has been right down to our time. The failure of traditional histories of criticism to recognize this connection between author and authority and its origin in Romanticism can be traced, Parrinder suggests, to the institutionalizing of criticism in the universities and the subsequent monopoly on notions of criticism they have exercised. This Romantic notion is not, in his view, the only possibility, nor should it be.

Earlier Controversies

The present-day, largely good-natured, and even conciliatory controversies come as no surprise to those scholars who have personally observed the course of Romanticism since World War II and even before. It has long been embattled from both within and without. The familiar story of the latter—the attacks by first the New Humanists and second the New Critics—is told at length in *ERP3* (59–65). It will suffice here to touch on the central features. Offended by what they perceived to be ethically irresponsible and philosophically unsound literature, Paul Elmer More in *Shelburne Essays* (1910, 1913) and Irving Babbitt in *Rousseau and Romanticism* (1919) attacked specific Romantic poets and general Romantic thought—Babbitt in language calculated to draw sharp fire. C. H. Herford, Hugh I'A. Fausset, Lawrence Hyde, and especially Ernest Bernbaum, among others, counterattacked. Most of the combatants and their weapons were spent by the late 1930s. Those who took up the cause later—for example, J. W. Beach and E. M. W. Tillyard—tended to have personal connections with the issue: Beach had been Babbitt's student at Harvard; Tillyard had known some of the British humanists.

The New Critics, successors to the New Humanists in the war against Romanticism, did more damage than their predecessors. Many of them exceptionally talented poets, they attacked Romanticism on two fronts, as philosophy and as art, to the end of expounding and applying a theory of literature that would interpret and defend their own philosophies and poems. T. E. Hulme, *Speculations: Essays on Humanism and the Philosophy of Art,* ed. Herbert Read (1924), commenced the hostilities with some colorful language: "Romanticism then, and this is the best definition I can give it, is spilt religion." T. S. Eliot's Harvard lectures of 1932–33, published as *The Use of Poetry and the Use of Criticism: Studies in the Relation of Criticism to Poetry in England* (1933), delivered an equally devastating blow. Meantime, I. A. Richards had supplied the New Critics with the psychological and aesthetic principles with which to wage the battle. Eliot's reputation drew scores of poets and scholars of modern poetry to the ranks, among them William Empson, Laura Riding, and Robert Graves in England and Edmund Wilson, John Crowe Ransom, Cleanth Brooks, and Allen Tate in America—all names more familiar now than the names of those who came to the defense of the Romantics, many of them distinguished scholars—for example, D. G. James, Eric R. Bentley, E. E. Stoll, R. S. Crane, Richard Harter Fogle, and Douglas Bush. As late as 1949, David Daiches could write in *TLS* (29 July): "The school that maintains that the essence of poetry is paradox, and that Keats must be proved paradoxical before he can be shown to be a great poet, is the ascendant critical school in the United States today."

Two essays by Fogle—"Romantic Bards and Metaphysical Reviewers" (*ELH*, 1945) and "A Recent Attack upon Romanticism" (*CE*, 1948)—proved to have the winning strategy. Shrewdly, he revealed that, for all their claims to affinity with the metaphysical and neoclassical poets—with the anti-Romantic tradition—the New Critics and the modern poets they championed were at bottom Romantics themselves, rebelling against their own heritage in order to make a place for themselves. In the 1950s, Murray Krieger, Richard Foster, and Frank Kermode elaborated this strategy in a series of complementary books and essays (see *ERP3* 64–65). Meantime, scholars began to assess the damage. The more charitable among them gave the New Critics their due and professed to think that, on the whole, they had done Romanticism good service: "Damn braces. Bless relaxes."

The story of fighting within the ranks of Romanticism is nearly as familiar and should not properly be labeled fighting at all. I refer to the contest among scholars to respond to A. O. Lovejoy's conclusion, reached in a series of essays spanning twenty-five years (1916–41), that so many are the varieties of Romanticism that the term is useless: it should be used in the plural or not at all. A review of definitions proffered in the years before and during Lovejoy's work (see *ERP3* 49–51) would tend to confirm his conclusion. Moreover, such was the respect for Lovejoy that for a time no one ventured to refute him. But refutation did eventually come, first from the philosopher Bernard Phillips, in "Logical Positivism and the Function of Reason" (*Philosophy*, 1948), and then from the literary scholar René Wellek, in "The Concept of 'Romanticism' in Literary History" (*CL*, 1949; rpt. *Concepts of Criticism*, 1963), an essay that asserted the general coherence and integration of the Romantic movement by arguing that the Romantics held in common a view of nature as organic, a view of the imagination as creative and thus the source of art, and a view of the method of art as symbolic and mythic.

Like Lovejoy before him, Wellek reiterated and supplemented his argument in subsequent essays and books. Among the essays, two may be especially noted: "Romanticism Re-examined" (cited above) and "German and English Romanticism: A Confrontation" (*SIR*, 1964; rpt. *Confrontations*, 1965). The former expressed Wellek's belief that the scholarship of the 1950s pointed to the same conclusions he had arrived at in 1949 and that the argument for the validity of the term Romanticism had in fact been won: "they all see the implication of imagination, symbol, myth, and organic nature, and see it as part of the great endeavor to overcome the split between subject and object, the self and the world, the conscious and the unconscious. This is the central creed of the great Romantic poets in England, Germany, and France. It is a closely coherent body of thought and feeling." At the same time, the essay surveyed the important scholarly writing on the subject, both in this country and abroad, between 1949 and 1963. The second article confirmed Wellek's claim that he was not insensitive to the very real differences within the national literatures of the Romantic movement by demonstrating the peculiar character of German Romanticism when compared to English Romanticism. The concept of a coherent movement was most expansively elaborated, of course, in Wellek's *History of Modern Criticism 1750–1950*, volume 2, *The Romantic Age* (1955; rpt. 1966), which in its scope is without peer among modern Romantics studies. To be sure, Wellek did not convince everyone that Romanticism is a valid literary term—least of all Lovejoy, who in the preface to *The Reason, the Understanding, and Time* (1961) reiterated his objection to the word Romanticism and even to the question of what Romanticism is. But the definition he championed is now widely accepted.

Not far behind Wellek in taking up the challenge of Lovejoy was Morse Peckham, without doubt the liveliest polemicist on the field. For Peckham, the answer to Lovejoy was to be found in the later pages of Lovejoy's own *The Great Chain of Being*, wherein is implied the very definition of Romanticism that the author had earlier proclaimed impossible. Seeing himself as a reconciler of Lovejoy and Wellek, Peckham claimed, in "Toward a Theory of Romanticism" (*PMLA*, 1951), that the three ideas by which the former argued for the inconsistency of Romantic thought and art (organicism, dynamism, diversitarianism) and the three by which the latter argued for its consistency (organicism, imagination, symbolism) could all be derived from a root metaphor, the organic metaphor of the structure of the universe, or "dynamic organicism." The values of Romanticism so defined are change, imperfection, growth, diversity, the creative imagination, and the unconscious. In order to comprehend Byron in his definition, however, Peckham was forced to speak of a negative Romanticism and a positive Romanticism, by analogy with Carlyle's Everlasting No and Everlasting Yea, and in doing so provided skeptical readers or those merely offended by his tone and procedure with the opportunity to scoff. In the following year, Peckham wrote of "The Triumph of Romanticism" (*Magazine of Art*, 1952), referring to modern art in general as the triumph of nineteenth-century Romanticism. By the 1960s, however, Peckham had become less confident about the theory he had so vigorously proposed. In a sequel to the original article, "Toward a Theory of Romanticism: II. Reconsiderations" (*SIR*, 1961), he retracted the definition that he had formerly assigned to Romanticism and bestowed it instead upon the Enlightenment in its last and highest phase. (These essays and the ones discussed below are gathered in *The Triumph of Romanticism: Collected Essays*, 1970.) *Beyond the Tragic Vision* (1962), the culmination of Peckham's original efforts, continued this line of thinking and thus preferred "Enlightenment" to "Romanticism." An ambitious attempt to explain the unparalleled change in the mind and thought of people in the West that occurred in the eighteenth century—the change that has made so imperative an adequate definition of Romanticism in the first place—the book surveys very generally the old ways by which human beings oriented themselves to the world before the modern period and then shows, by ranging widely among the major artists of the nineteenth century, the new way that emerged from the disintegration of the old—the way of the self that projects value on the world and so creates its own orientations. For his title Peckham drew on Nietzsche's vision of a joy that is deeper than woe, a vision that indicates the true source of being for the truly modern person, the imaginative mind. Still later essays—"Romanticism: The Present State of Theory" (*Pennsylvania Council of Teachers of English Bulletin* 12, 1965) and "The Dilemma of a Century: The Four Stages of Romanticism," in *Romanticism: The Culture of the Nineteenth Century*, ed. Peckham (1965)—did not represent significant shifts in position. The latter might be described as a condensed version of *Beyond the Tragic Vision*, with some few refinements; the former, while it offered a brief account of Peckham's theory as it evolved from 1951 to 1965, was primarily a quest for allied opinions. In the process of the quest, Peckham made it abundantly clear that he was not one of those whose opinions converged with Wellek's or anyone else's. The character of Peckham's writing was not calculated to win wholesale acclaim. Response ranged from open contempt to keen excitement. But the controversies he deliberately provoked in what he called "interim reports" (see "On Romanticism: An Introduction," *SIR*, 1970) must themselves be accounted contributions toward a theory of Romanticism. Many another scholar's wits were sharpened by them.

Yet a third scholar whose writing over a period of years contributed significantly to the effort to validate Romanticism is Northrop Frye, in the minds of many people the chief apostle of archetypal or myth criticism of our time. Frye's brilliant study of Blake, *Fearful Symmetry* (1947; 3rd ed. 1969), though restricted to that poet, is not unrelated to his more general studies of Romanticism, for Blake is crucial to Frye's interpretation of the Romantic movement. Nor is his *Anatomy of Criticism* (1957), the widely influential apology of myth criticism, beside the point. But most relevant here are two of Frye's essays, "The Drunken Boat: The Revolutionary Element in Romanticism," in *Romanticism Reconsidered* (rpt. *The Stubborn Structure: Essays on Criticism and Society,* 1970), and "The Imaginative and the Imaginary," in *Fables of Identity* (1963), and his volume *A Study of English Romanticism* (1968; rpt. 1983). It cannot be said that these and related essays in *Fables of Identity* duplicated themselves, but it is possible to see running through them Frye's belief that Romanticism denotes the beginning of the first major change in the encyclopedic myth derived largely from the Bible that dominated the literature and philosophy of Western Europe for centuries prior to 1800—a change that replaced the old myth, which attributed the projection of reality to God and nature, with a new one, which recovered the projection of reality to human beings themselves, in particular to their creative imaginations. With special attention to the imagery of poetry, Frye demonstrated the change from an exterior reality to an interior one on the four levels of being in which people in the West have been traditionally framed—heaven, Eden, nature, hell. The new images, which convey the new myth, are symptomatic of the general transformation of literary genres by which Frye also defined Romanticism. That he saw Romanticism as having its center of gravity in the creative arts makes more tenable his theory that, though we may have had a post-Romantic movement in the twentieth century, we have not yet, to judge from the imagery of modern poetry, created a new myth or even some new patterns of myth, nor have we reverted to the old one. The problems with Frye's approach to literature were conveniently raised in Irene H. Chayes's "Little Girls Lost: Problems of a Romantic Archetype" (*BNYPL,* 1963), which, while discussing the Persephone archetype in Blake's Lyca, Wordsworth's Lucy Gray, and Keats's Madeline, posed the larger question of what her method could contribute to the understanding of a literary period such as the Romantic. Chayes's article is fair-minded, recognizing both gains and losses.

Romantic Consciousness and Romantic Self

In his preface to a volume of essays entitled *Romanticism and Consciousness* (1970), Harold Bloom suggested that the advanced criticism of Romanticism had increasingly identified Romantic self-consciousness as the most central problem in defining our own relation to the Romantic poets. The impetus for this trend was the writing of certain European scholars variously labeled "the Swiss School," "the Geneva School," or "critics of consciousness." Laurent LeSage provided an introduction to their work and some extracts from it in *The French New Criticism* (1967). Of the many critics he discussed, Georges Poulet was the most familiar to scholars this side of the Atlantic, in large part because he alone had written about the English Romantic poets, first in the article "Timelessness and Romanticism" (*JHI*, 1954) and then in the book *The Metamorphoses of the Circle* (1966). Like his fellows, Poulet was concerned with describing the consciousness of the poet in its conflict with the phenomenal world as this consciousness can be discerned in his or her poetry, but from the beginning Poulet focused on the poet's consciousness of time and space. Thus, the article contends, with particular reference to Coleridge, that the Romantics brought eternity into time, thereby converting God's timelessness to that of human beings. Similarly, the book, based on the premise that the circle is the most constant form whereby people have represented their consciousness of time and space, contends, again with special attention to Coleridge, that the Romantics through consciousness of the self (the center or point of the circle) returned to the nonself (the periphery of the circle). Romanticism becomes the "taking possession by consciousness of the fundamentally subjective character of the mind," or the retreat of the mind to its centermost point, from which it returns reinvigorated and in quest of a circle, that is, of self-realization. In the fourth volume of his *Etudes sur le temps humain —Mesure de l'instant* (1968), Poulet returned to the Romantic experience of the eternal moment in human and terrestrial time, anticipating Richard Jackson's account of the Romantics' experience of time, in "The Romantic Metaphysics of Time" (*SIR*, 1980), which posits that time is the creation of imagination, a synthesis formed when consciousness perceives the gap between eternity and temporality. Short or long, the Romantic poem, "a form of indefinitely expanded moment," gives expression to this metaphysics. J. Hillis Miller, in "The Literary Criticism of Georges Poulet" (*MLN*, 1963), described Poulet's work in largely favorable terms; but Geoffrey Hartman, in "Beyond Formalism" (*MLN*, 1966; rpt. *Beyond Formalism*, 1970), questioned Poulet's approach, particularly as it postulates a Romantic or period consciousness. Poulet's results, he found, were not greatly different from those of a historian of ideas like Lovejoy.

Not that Hartman was hostile to phenomenological criticism. He was identified with it himself, especially in his two books on Wordsworth, but also in his essays, for example, "Romanticism and 'Anti-Self-Consciousness'" (*CentR*, 1962; rpt. *Beyond Formalism*, 1970, and *Romanticism and Consciousness*, 1970), which treats consciousness as the remedy to self-consciousness. Richard Haven's book on Coleridge, *Patterns of Consciousness* (1969), was a fair sample of the trend. But Bloom's own essay, reprinted from the *Yale Review* (1969), "The Internalization of Quest Romance," remains the best introduction to it. Here Romanticism is seen as a revival and internalization of the quest romance, whose movement is from nature to freedom of the imagination—from Promethean man to "the real man, the imagination." The goal is expanded and intensified consciousness; the obstacle to the goal, self-consciousness or solipsism. The hero of internalized romance is, of course, the poet who quests for "mature powers" by turning away from outer nature to inner self. The "monuments" of this antinature movement are the great poems of Romanticism, but especially *The Prelude* and *Jerusalem,* for Bloom the finest long poems of the nineteenth century. (A fuller discussion of Bloom follows shortly.) Reviewing the history of the effort to define Romanticism in the twentieth century as a prelude to discussing the most recent efforts, Peter L. Thorslev, Jr., in "Romanticism and the Literary Consciousness" (*JHI,* 1975), confirmed Bloom's analysis: Romantics studies of the 1960s and early 1970s are chiefly concerned with consciousness, with phenomenology. Most of his examples are discussed elsewhere in this chapter, for "consciousness" has become in Romantics studies a buzzword nearly as pervasive as "imagination." Two items he cites, Edward Engelberg's *The Unknown Distance: From Consciousness to Conscience, from Goethe to Camus* (1972) and James Twitchell's "Romanticism and Cosmic Consciousness" (*CentR,* 1975), are appropriately mentioned here. Engelberg's book includes chapters on Byron and Wordsworth; Coleridge is its guiding spirit. His argument—and strong conviction—is that we must restore to their original unity conscience and consciousness, overcoming the fascination of the nineteenth century, especially, with their dialectical potential. Twitchell writes in the venerable tradition of protesting that Romanticism cannot be defined and then proceeding to define it. The consciousness that the Romantics strove for was the supra or cosmic consciousness, the highest possible level of consciousness, because at this level they were released from their senses, from nature. (Only Wordsworth, Twitchell claims, was ambiguous about this.) Such consciousness—a near mystical state or secular epiphany—is the solution to the Romantic problem—to selfhood—because it represents the loss of self-consciousness, of ego. Any summary of Twitchell's article will make it sound more brash than in fact it is.

The word "self," like the word "consciousness," may be used to organize a variety of books and articles appearing in the 1960s and 1970s. The first to sound the theme is Wylie Sypher's *Loss of Self in Modern Literature and Art* (1962), a book provocative in its effort to characterize the shifts in the concept of self from the Romantic period to the present and encouraging in its prophecy of a new humanism that Sypher labels "post-existential," but some Romantics scholars may have difficulty in crediting Sypher's premise that the Romantic self is represented by the Byronic man. George Boas's "The Romantic Self: An Historical Sketch" (*SIR,* 1964) seems more sober and, though far shorter, is more comprehensive. The theme of Romantic individualism is also the subject of two other articles that do not entirely agree: Peter L. Thorslev, Jr.'s "The Romantic Mind Is Its Own Place" (*CL,* 1963), a useful essay on the familiar topic of Romantic satanism, which concept Thorslev explains well but does not question, and Frederick Garber's "Self, Society, Value, and the Romantic Hero" (*CL,* 1967), a stimulating article that challenges the traditional view of the Romantic mind as autonomous, the Romantic hero as morally and spiritually isolated from society. Similar in point to his earlier article is Thorslev's later "Incest as Romantic Symbol" (*CLS,* 1965), which concludes that incest is the "symbol of the Romantic psyche's love affair with self and of its tragic isolation in an increasingly alien world." By far the most important contribution of the 1960s to the subject—and a seminal interpretation of Romanticism—is Earl Wasserman's "The English Romantics: The Grounds of Knowledge" (*SIR,* 1964). Wasserman asserts that the fundamental problem of Romanticism for the Romantics themselves was to define the relation between self and nature, subject and object. His essay not only demonstrates the centrality of this epistemological problem to the Romantics and thus to any effort by scholars to define their movement but also testifies to the radical diversity of the Romantics as witnessed by their solutions to the problem and thus cautions us against seeking to reconcile all opposites in our anxiety to establish definitions.

The first study of the 1970s was Fred Kaplan's *Miracles of Rare Device: The Poet's Sense of Self in Nineteenth-Century Poetry* (1972), which looks closely at the structure and imagery of some major poems (four of them Romantic) to support the author's premise "that a major key to Romantic poetry is an understanding of how the artist reveals in his poetry his concern with himself as an artist and with his art." The Romantic poem is self-consciously an "act of the mind"; as such it initiates a tradition of poetry characterized by the tendency of poets to doubt their own creativity. Romantic poems offer examples of both success and failure in overcoming this doubt. John Holloway's *The Proud Knowledge: Poetry, Insight and the Self, 1620–1920* (1977) is a more ambitious undertaking. The Romantics, like some of their predecessors and many of their successors, are involved in a quest of the aspiring mind for the proud knowledge of the self, the truth of which is the realization that the human mind is capable of conceiving and pursuing the quest for the self within the self and discovering that the pursuit is self-validating. New poems arise to express this new quest. Some of them, however, attend to the radical alternative—to the dark side of this motive, which is the rejection of the quest. The Romantics and Victorians especially face and struggle to overcome the dark side. Wordsworth is singled out as the poet who sees the integrity of those who choose not to make the pursuit. Robert Langbaum is a third scholar who interprets modern literature in terms of self and identity. The first part of *The Mysteries of Identity: A Theme of Modern Literature* (1977) is entitled "The Romantic Self"; its single chapter is "Wordsworth: The Self as Process." Subsequent parts of the book trace the decline and eventual reconstitution of the Romantic self in Victorian and early twentieth-century literature. The terms "self" and "identity" have by now a trendy ring, as Langbaum admits, but readers of *The Poetry of Experience* (1957) know his talent for turning the superficial into the substantive. Langbaum's interpretation of Romanticism as the modern literary tradition has been more influential than one might suspect, given his mild style and modest procedure of letting literature speak for itself. Meena Alexander, in

The Poetic Self: Towards a Phenomenology of Romanticism (1979), posits Romanticism as establishing the norm for all explorations of the self, falling as it does between Hume's skepticism about the unified self and the fragmented images of the self espoused by modernism. For Alexander, Romanticism is defined by its perspectival view of truth: subjectivity is the ultimate source of human value. She explores not only the positive consequences of this phenomenology but also the tragic ones: for some Romantics the subjective structures they achieved undermined the interpretive acts that created them. The normative Romanticism emphasizes the reciprocal relationship of subject and object, self and other as in the Coleridgean model of self-construction. Alexander's particular concern is to demonstrate that "the structures of human memory bear within them the imprint of the spatial existence of the lived body through which alone they have been generated." Accordingly, in her analyses of poems—she begins with Coleridge's conversation poems—she seeks "to highlight the task of the lived body in establishing the poetic self." This task is accomplished through the creation of a poetic space in which the speaking voice of the poetic self quests for values. The poetic type of this phenomenological structure is "Tintern Abbey." Alexander devotes an entire chapter to *The Prelude,* however, before moving on to Arnold, Whitman, Baudelaire, and an epilogue on Sartre, Proust, Beckett, and Robbe-Grillet. The latest book—Frederick Garber's *The Autonomy of the Self from Richardson to Huysmans* (1982)—may very well be the best. In an earlier essay—"Nature and the Romantic Mind" (*CL,* 1977)—Garber proposed that Romanticism shows a variety of engagement of the self with the world, ranging from the use of nature to illustrate affairs of mind to a convergence in which consciousness blends with the universe or with another being. In the book he develops what he calls the dialectic of aloofness and association, charting the variety of aspects of self-making by "artisans of consciousness" with its ups and downs, its experiences of continuity and discontinuity. "The practitioners of Romantic consciousness offered no single solution to the question of what they deemed best within themselves. . . . They agreed only on the importance of the fact of consciousness itself. After that there was only divergence." Garber's work is comparative literature at its most exciting. As background to these books, there is John O. Lyons' *The Invention of Self: The Hinge of Consciousness in the Eighteenth Century* (1978), which approaches the Romantics at many points but always stops short of encountering them directly. Lyons' work relies heavily on prose, which is the subject of *Interspace and the Inward Sphere: Essays on Romantic and Victorian Self* (ed. Norman A. Anderson and Margene E. Weiss, 1978). Two essays on the prose of Coleridge and De Quincey and six on Victorian writers are intended to illuminate the continuity between Romantic and Victorian prose in its search for the self by constructing that self. A second background study that actually reaches the foreground in a concluding chapter on "Self as Creative Genius: William Blake" is Stephen D. Cox's *"The Stranger within Thee": Concepts of the Self in Late-Eighteenth-Century Literature* (1980).

Romanticism and Criticism

Explicit in the foregoing pages has been the theme of Romanticism and criticism, with an emphasis on what Walter Reed has referred to as "the peculiar coordination of the two terms, the conjunction of the discourse traditionally termed 'philosophy' and the discourse traditionally termed 'poetry' that has pertained since the cultural revolution of the later eighteenth century in Europe now known as Romanticism" (*TSLL,* 1981; the essay is an introduction to papers presented at a 1978 colloquium at the University of Texas). Actually, the version of this chapter in *ERP3* implied such a conjunction in Romantics studies, namely, by the special attention given to the work of Harold Bloom, Geoffrey Hartman, Morse Peckham, Northrop Frye, and René Wellek. Here I wish to bring the story of these scouting scholar-critics up to date—here, in this manner, because their work in the last decade has taken them well beyond English Romanticism (though not necessarily away from it). Moreover, we are beginning to see the fruits of their early endeavors in the books and articles of their students. Some scholars are through-and-through disciples of one or the other of these modern gurus; others simply quote them by way of asserting their credentials to perform in the increasingly challenging and bellicose arena of literary criticism.

Harold Bloom is decidedly the most spectacular flower in this bountiful bouquet of critics. Better known than many a novelist or poet of comparable achievement, Bloom has become the nearest thing we have to a household word in literary criticism, especially in this country. And with good reason, for since his early books on Blake and Shelley and his *The Visionary Company* (1961; rev. 1971 with a brief prologue "on the historical backgrounds of English Romantic poetry and an epilogue relating my study to some current phenomena"), he has in a compulsive series of works, both discursive prose and fiction, constructed a theory of poetry, replete with an idiosyncratic vocabulary, that explains most major poets in the English tradition from Blake to Stevens as well as several contemporary poets, among them A. R. Ammons and John Ashbery, by reference to a tradition of "strong poets" in the line of Milton whose achievement is wrought out of an "anxiety of influence," a weakness that, paradoxically, they manage to convert to strength by swerving from said influence—that is, by deliberately misreading the precursor poet's works, they make space in which their own creative imagination can flourish and triumph. (Bloom himself acknowledges Walter Jackson Bate as his own precursor, particularly the Bate of *The Burden of the Past and the English Poet,* discussed later in this chapter.) Bloom has prevailed (where he has prevailed), in part because of the sheer fascination such exuberance of prolix creativity inspires in scholars of less energy and less boldness, in part because of the stimulation a genuinely new (or nearly new) theory of poetry provokes even when it is rejected wholesale or accepted only in pieces. Scholars of either persuasion can point, for every flash of brilliant insight, to misreadings of texts far in excess of what is acceptable in scholarly discourse. Some would go further to suggest that Bloom's sin against criticism has been to substitute the critic for the poet, extending the concept of misreading to intolerable limits. Several years ago Jerome J. McGann suggested that "the intellectual history of Romantic scholarship is even now moving beyond Bloom's formulations..." ("Romanticism and the Embarrassments of Critical Tradition" [*MP,* 1973]). He may have been right, but, if so, not all Romantics scholars perceived the change of wind so quickly as he—especially, perhaps, Bloom himself.

Bloom's books, listed parenthetically at the end of this paragraph in order of their appearance, are, finally, the record of Bloom's own evolving understanding of Romanticism and of his quest for the form of criticism required to elicit that understanding; thus, they are characterized not only by the excitement of epiphanic insights and passionate endorsements but also by subtle refinements and large-scale revisions, though so spectacularly subjective in manner that changes in matter are sometimes obscured. Perhaps we can expect that in its late phases Bloom's Romanticism, like Blake's myth, will simplify its system, if not cast it off altogether—"Husk & Covering into Vaccuum evaporating revealing the lineaments of Man." Meantime, belated graduate students requiring shortcuts to Bloom's thought might consult the several articles that tend to herald new books or recapitulate old ones: "To Reason with a Later Reason: Romanticism and the Rational" (*Midway,* 1970) compares the "High Romantics" (the six Romantic poets), in whom the power of mind is "awesome," with later Romantics (Yeats and Stevens), in whom it is "intermittent," as they demonstrate that our rationalizations or rationalisms must be overthrown if we are fully to explore our humanity. "The polemic of Romantic poetry, which is to say of most vital modern poetry, is directed against inadequate accounts of reason, not against reason itself." It is thus easy to see why, for Bloom as for Abrams, Wordsworth is the "exemplary Modern Poet, the Poet proper," as he says in a second essay "Clinamen or Poetic Misprision" (*NLH,* 1972), which anticipates *The Anxiety of Influence: A Theory of Poetry* (1973), though in the essay Bloom proposes "not a new poetics, but a wholly different practical criticism," one that attempts to read a poem as the poet's misreading of the precursor poet because this is the way poets themselves read poetry. Such a proposal, if adopted and implemented, would provide us a true history of modern poetry because it would be based on "the accurate reading of these revisionary swerves." Still insisting on "The Necessity of Misreading" (*GaR,* 1975), Bloom is by now preoccupied with how canons are formed, how tradition is made. He is also preoccupied with the readers of poems, wishing to disabuse them of their desires for poetry and their illusions about it. Readers are being invited to become misreaders—which is to say, to become interpreters, not simply critics. Once aware of themselves as "belated," they are in a position to preserve their own diminished creativity—a position they share with the modern or Romantic poets, with Bloom himself, and, as Bloom's aesthetic theory evolves into a cultural theory, with Americans both in general and in particular. Reading becomes the equal of writing, if not the more equal of the two. Probably it is this aspect of his revisionist theory that has most alienated traditional critics. The upshot of Bloom's antithetical criticism is that, if it saves the reader of poetry, it may leave that person with nothing to read—nothing, that is, but interpretations of poems. Or so Bloom's spoilers have it (for example, Gerald Graff in *Literature against Itself,* 1979). Bloom and his Yale associates would argue just the opposite: as Geoffrey Hartman puts it in the title essay of *The Fate of Reading and Other Essays* (1975), "One wonders how long it will be before the tale itself disappears because we do not—are unable to—read it any more." (*Shelley's Mythmaking,* 1959; *The Visionary Company: A Reading of English Romantic Poetry,* 1961; rev. 1971; *Blake's Apocalypse: A Study in Poetic Argument,* 1963; *From Sensibility to Romanticism,* ed. with F. Hilles, 1965; *Yeats,* 1970; *Romanticism and Consciousness,* ed. 1970; *The Ringers in the Tower: Studies in Romantic Tradition,* 1971; *The Anxiety of Influence: A Theory of Poetry,* 1973; *A Map of Misreading,* 1975; *Kabbalah and Criticism,* 1975; *Poetry and Repression: Revisionism from Blake to Stevens,* 1976; *Figures of Capable Imagination,* 1976; *Wallace Stevens: The Poems of Our Climate,* 1977; *The Flight to Lucifer: A Gnostic Fantasy,* 1979; *Deconstruction and Criticism,* 1979; *Agon: Towards a Theory of Revisionism,* 1982; *The Breaking of the Vessels,* 1982. I have not listed the several editions of poetry and prose for which Bloom is responsible, although to undergraduate and beginning graduate students he is probably best known for his "Commentary" on *The Poetry and Prose of William Blake,* ed. David V. Erdman, 1965; rev. 1982.)

Geoffrey Hartman, often associated with Bloom because of their geographical proximity and because of kindred critical presuppositions—for example, their mutual belief that criticism, like poetry, is a creative act—is in many ways his opposite. Increasingly, Hartman has become one of America's chief exponents of criticism, urging Anglo-American literary scholar-critics to abandon their provincial, narrow notion of criticism and to take as models their European counterparts, of whom Hartman has been an eloquent interpreter and transmitter. In this respect, he has assumed the image of a latter-day Matthew Arnold, at once insisting on the importance of criticism to culture and on the need for a vastly better criticism, sometimes called "philosophical criticism." Hartman has no shockingly original theory of poetry to champion, but his own criticism, in being richly informed by linguistics, psychology, philosophy, and anthropology as well as by the literary traditions of Germany and France, is a model of the criticism he advocates. Hartman is a comparatist in the fullest sense of the word. It is our good fortune that the Romantic writers, especially, of course, Wordsworth, have received such a large share of his attention.

Like Bloom, Hartman has interspersed his books, listed parenthetically at the end of this paragraph in order of appearance, with essays that reflect his principal critical concerns and positions. A short essay first published in the *Wordsworth Circle* ("Theories on the Theory of Romanticism," 1971; rpt. *The Fate of Reading,* 1975) surveys the needs of Romantics studies at that point and suggests a varied program of research and criticism for Romantics scholars. His multi- and interdisciplinary perspective on problems is the thread linking these suggestions. At this time the need to study criticism is simply one among many demonstrable needs. By 1976, Hartman's interests for himself and for Romanticism have come to center on criticism. The essay "Crossing Over: Literary Commentary on Literature" (*CL,* 1976) is something of a manifesto for a new criticism: "Literary criticism is now crossing over into literature. For in the period that may be said to begin with Arnold—a period characterized by increasing fears that the critical would jeopardize the creative spirit, and self-consciousness the energies of art—literary criticism is acknowledged at the price of being denied literary status and assigned a clearly subordinate, service function. There is no mystery in the fact, only irony, that literary commentary today is creating texts—a literature of its own." True to his professed belief in the value and utility of literary history, Hartman reminds us, however, that, even within the period now coming to a close, criticism as literature (the essay as distinct from the article) is to be found in the aesthetic criticism of, for example, Wilde. True to his belief in the value and utility of comparative literature and comparative studies, he cites Derrida's *Glas* as an example of contemporary criticism as literature. An essay of the same year, "Literary Criticism and Its Discontents" (*CritI*, 1976), attempts to put what is happening in criticism into perspective, illustrating what is one of Hartman's great gifts, the capacity to set aside the polemical mode at which he excels for the genuinely helpful descriptive assessment of the function of present-day criticism. Throughout the essay Hartman compares the "post-New Critical critics" with the New Critics in language that is respectful to both. To be sure, Hartman's explanation of the former becomes at times a defense—for example, he argues for the necessity of a demanding style, for the natural and desirable elitism of criticism, and for the desirability of plurality in criticism (something Abrams and Wayne Booth have argued about in print)—but in the main he attempts to quell the fears and reduce the anxieties of those threatened by the newer critics, for whom theory, he claims, is a text but not a privileged text. His most telling point perhaps is his assertion that revisionist criticism "has already rescued the Romantic poets from modernist snobbishness." And though it is not the case that the rescue is solely the work of revisionist critics or at least of critics of Hartman's and Bloom's ilk, still, when one recalls the fate of the Romantic poets at the hands of the New Criticism, then it is hard to gainsay Hartman's statement. Besides, he is appropriately modest about the principles of revisionist criticism: "In the present ferment...I see mainly the *creative* force of the *critical* spirit, as it questions such honorific terms as 'creative' or 'primary' or visionary; or feels trapped by a neoclassical concept of unity; or shows how all vision is revision—the strong if negative extension of canonized texts." Having begun on the melancholy note that Renaissance humanism is fast coming to an end in our society, he finishes with the encouraging idea that revisionist criticism might be seen as a rearguard humanism, revisionist critics attempting to strike a balance between solipsism and materialism. Critical of humanist cant, revisionist critics are not, in Hartman's eyes, dehumanists. The essay anticipates Hartman's books *Criticism in the Wilderness: The Study of Literature Today* (1980) and *Saving the Text* (1981), the latter recalling by its title Hartman's disavowal of the label "deconstructionist" in the essay introductory to *Deconstruction and Criticism* (1979). (On this point see also his "The Use and Abuse of Structural Analysis: Riffaterre's Interpretation of Wordsworth's 'Yew Trees'" [*NLH*, 1975], an essay written in response to a structuralist analysis of Wordsworth's "Yew Trees" by Michael Riffaterre [*NLH*, 1973].) The third and last essay I will cite here is "A Short History of Practical Criticism" (*NLH*, 1979; rpt. *Criticism in the Wilderness*, 1980), where Hartman, speaking as a pedagogue, exposes the shortcomings and failures of practical criticism, the touted method of the New Critics, in the university classroom. If the humanities are lost, it will be the fault of practical criticism, long since estranged from the humanities, not that of revisionist criticism, which, along with composition theory, has outflanked practical criticism. The former two have both come of age, matured to become adult or philosophical criticism, Hartman argues; practical criticism never grew up. For Hartman as for Bloom, then, criticism can arrest the decline of the humanities if anything can; it can address the "belatedness" of our spiritual-psychological-intellectual condition; it can save us from losing the ability to read altogether. Along with Bloom, he has, in Richard Poirier's words, provided Anglo-American scholars, most especially Romantics scholars, with "a kind of star trek in the theory of poetics." (*The Unmediated Vision: An Interpretation of Wordsworth, Hopkins, Rilke, and Valéry,* 1954; *André Malraux,* 1960; *Wordsworth's Poetry, 1787–1814,* 1964; rpt. with Retrospect, 1971; *Hopkins: A Selection of Critical Essays,* ed., 1966; *Beyond Formalism: Literary Essays 1958–1970,* 1970; *Romanticism: Vistas, Instances, Continuities,* ed. with D. Thorburn, 1973; *The Fate of Reading and Other Essays,* 1975; *Akiba's Children,* 1978; *Deconstruction and Criticism,* 1979; *Criticism in the Wilderness: The Study of Literature Today,* 1980; *Saving the Text: Literature/Derrida/Philosophy,* 1981. In addition, Hartman has edited Wordsworth's poetry and prose as well as selected essays from the English Institute.)

More so than Bloom or Hartman, Frye has left Romanticism per se behind to pursue a project announced many years ago, a study of the Bible as the chief source of those stories or myths that European artists have consistently used to create or re-create the imaginative universe we know as Christian civilization, an endeavor not dissimilar to Abrams' in *Natural Supernaturalism.* The first volume of this project, entitled *The Great Code: The Bible and Literature,* appeared in 1981; a second volume is soon to follow. Frye's title is taken from Blake, and readers familiar with Frye's career will find its direction appropriate, if not inevitable. They will also find his literary theory of archetypes and myths largely unchanged and his critical practice of adducing patterns of recurrence and change in myth from poetic images—here he revels in typology—unimpaired and possibly unsurpassed. By way of preparing for *The Great Code,* Frye dispensed with the other and lesser source of stories that European artists have invariably drawn upon, the folktales, or, in their literary form, romances—the secular contrary to the biblical myths—in a volume fittingly entitled *The Secular Scripture: A Study of the Structure of Romance* (1976). If Blake can be seen as a distant inspiration for *The Great Code,* Scott is the deepest Romantic root of the earlier volume, which grew, Frye tells us, out of an abandoned essay on the Waverley novels. As such, *The Secular Scripture* is mostly concerned with prose fiction, especially with the revolutionary power of popular romance to revitalize the weary realism that replaces by displacement romance formulas in sophisticated literature. Harold Bloom's review for the *New York Times Book Review* (18 Apr. 1976) offers a quick grasp of the differences between the master and his most celebrated pupil as well as an eloquent tribute to the man who is possibly Romanticism's most venerable theoretician.

Morse Peckham's latter-day contributions to the study of Romanticism have been overshadowed both by the iconoclastic character of his own earlier work and by the even more unsettling character of the work of new theorists on the scene. But important Romantics scholars, for example, Michael Cooke, have testified to the continued impact of Peckham on their thinking. His essays of the late 1960s and early 1970s have been collected in *Romanticism and Behavior* (1976), a companion volume to *The Triumph of Romanticism* (1970). The title of the second book is a plain but accurate clue to Peckham's more recent speculations. Having decided that he could not understand Romanticism without theories of language, art, cultural history, and epistemology, Peckham in the course of his investigations determined that these theories in turn could not be understood without a theory of behavior. Negative Romanticism and Positive Romanticism become, in the terms of behavior theory, responses to the cultural trauma that precipitated Romanticism, namely, the collapse of explanation itself. For Peckham it is only Negative Romanticism that recognizes the response as such; hence it is the subtler, historically progressive Romanticism. If Peckham thereby separates himself from the Abrams school—that of apocalyptic, redemptive, explanatory Romanticism—and as a consequence appears to align himself with the antiredemptive, antiexplanatory Romanticism of the Romantic irony school, he nevertheless attributes the "astonishing culturally innovative dynamism of high explanatory culture and its exemplification for the past 180 years" to the "fundamental incoherence of these two modes of response to cultural trauma." Now, however, Peckham prophesies a turn in Romantics scholarship: "As [the redemptive notion of art is destroyed], I think we will see in the scholarship of Romanticism a turning away from the still fashionable limitation of Romanticism to its relatively superficial apocalyptic or redemptive mode, and a turning toward its more penetrating tradition, the anti-explanatory, the antiredemptive, the refusal to accept any consolation for the irresolvable tension of human existence." (Thomas McFarland's *Romanticism and the Forms of Ruin* is testimony to the accuracy of this prophecy.) Peckham's 1965 book, *Man's Rage for Chaos,* recapitulated and considerably modified in the 1978 essay "Perceptual and Semiotic Discontinuity in Art" (*Poetics*), expands this theory of Romanticism to art, which Peckham sees—and thinks avant-garde artists see—as an adaptional device for escaping cultural controls that are always inadequate. It is a human defense. Artists have come to accept perceptual and semiotic instability as the only means of transcending the limits of cultural control. (A useful analysis of Peckham's functional theory of literature is John Reichert's, in *Making Sense of Literature,* 1977. Larry W. Gasser and Jack Gifford's proposal to make materialism the third foot of a tripod, in "Classicism, Romanticism, Materialism, All Three" [*Rendezvous,* 1975], finds inspiration in Peckham. And Lawrence Wynn's "The Shaping Spirit: Nineteenth-Century Quests for Order" [*Interpretations,* 1976] situates his survey of these quests in the argument between Austin Warren [*Rage for Order*] and Peckham.)

René Wellek's energies in recent years have been devoted to completing his monumental *History of Modern Criticism,* of which the volume covering the Romantics appeared in 1955, and to defending the critical positions he has established in a series of brilliantly learned essays conveniently collected in *Concepts of Criticism* (1963), *Confrontations* (1965), *Discriminations: Further Concepts of Criticism* (1970), and *The Attack on Literature and Other Essays* (1982). A late example, characteristic of Wellek's incisive judgments and formidable learning, is the essay "The New Criticism: Pro and Contra" (*Critl,* 1978; rpt. *The Attack on Literature and Other Essays,* 1982), wherein New Criticism is defended against the unwarranted charges of formalism, aestheticism, scientism, and close reading. He does not, characteristically, mince words on the role of criticism vis-à-vis poetry: "criticism is always subordinated to creation." Though Wellek faults the New Critics for being Anglocentric, he makes no effort to conceal his "conviction that the New Criticism has stated or reaffirmed many basic truths to which future ages will have to return. . . ." Also worth serious attention is Wellek's "The Fall of Literary History," in *Geschichte-Ereignis und Erzählung* (ed. Reinhart Koselleck and Wolf-Dieter Stempel, 1973; rpt. *The Attack on Literature and Other Essays,* 1982), wherein he explains the decline of literary history and the proposals to reform it in such a way as to leave no doubt that he is still our comparatist par excellence. Ultimately, he proceeds to explain why the so-called new literary history "promises only a return to the old one. . . ." Wellek, long since convinced that history cannot be divorced from criticism and that criticism is so many acts of judgment predicated on prior commitment to certain value schemes, has come lately to believe that there is no evolution in the history of critical argument and possibly in the history of poetry: "There is no progress, no development, no history of art except a history of writers, institutions and techniques. This is, at least for me, the end of an illusion, the fall of literary history." An extraordinary statement from the author of *The History of Modern Criticism*!

Most of the complaints against the post–New Criticism or philosophical criticism are aired and documented by John Clubbe in "The 'Folklore' of English Romanticism" (*Mosaic,* 1981). By Clubbe's account, criticism (he begins with Arnold) has never done Romanticism justice: "we have had little progress in the art of criticism, although fads come and go." Where criticism of Romanticism has almost consistently failed us, he believes, is in assisting us to understand the Romantics within the "humanistic perspective they themselves desired." Arnold, Eliot, Brooks, Bloom, Peckham—Clubbe's representative critics—have all failed on this score. When Clubbe moves to current criticism, he finds a humanistic perspective on the Romantics, if anything, still more remote. His particular prescription for criticism, if it is ever to make any progress in the illumination of Romantic poetry, is for it to return in language to "basic English" and in matter to "the poetry itself." Clubbe's is not a call for the return of the New Criticism. Like some of the critics he rebukes, he faults Anglo-American academic criticism for its weak or nonexistent literary history and its insularity from the literature and literary history of Europe. (In this regard, see Clubbe's review essay "Romanticism Today," *Mosaic,* 1974.) His collaboration with the late Ernest J. Lovell, Jr., *English*

Romanticism: The Grounds of Belief (1983), gives voice in a major way to these concerns: "We wish to embody a perspective that takes its stand not in a chosen methodology but in a regard for human life in all its bewildering complexity. Such a perspective may become a strength if readers find fewer traditional biases in this avowedly revisionist study than in comparable books." In a series of inter-related essays, one on each poet, plus two synthesizing chapters, Clubbe and Lovell demonstrate that, for all their differences (some of them simply functions of the two generations involved), the Romantics are unified by kindred enthusiasms, similar preoccupations, and shared assumptions about life and art. Polemics aside, this book is an excellent introduction to Romanticism for serious students of any age. Clubbe is not, of course, alone in wishing to divert Romantics criticism from its present theoretical preoccupations, as many reviews of critical studies published in the 1970s attest, among them M. H. Abrams' energetic reply to Wayne Booth's critique of *Natural Supernaturalism* (*CritI,* 1976). As yet, however, such wishing has not been gratified; signs of radical change in the state and character of Romantics criticism are relatively few, and even those few not very clear. The latest teaching text on the market—John L. Mahoney's *The English Romantics: Major Poetry and Critical Theory* (1978)—is symptomatic of just how extensive the preoccupation with theory is.

A cautionary voice, if not a complaint, about some of the new directions in criticism is raised by Harold E. Toliver, in a searching book entitled *The Past That Poets Make* (1981). Wordsworth, Shelley, and Keats figure prominently in Toliver's defense of literary history, even if they and Romantic theorists such as Coleridge and Hazlitt anticipated the antihistorical tendencies of modern criticism, thus contributing to the "precarious existence" of literary history in our time. "The fact remains," Toliver contends, "that unlike stars in a constellation, which appear to the eye to be ever present and almost uniform, literary texts differ from one another in ways that can only be explained on historical grounds." Toliver's book is not an attack on Romantics criticism in general or on specific Romantics critics. Richard Hoffpauir's two essays " 'Kubla Khan' and the Critics: Romantic Madness as Poetic Theme and Critical Response" (*ESC,* 1976) and "The Failure of Romantic Mythology" (*Compass,* 1979) are, however, precisely that. In the spirit of Leavis, Hoffpauir debunks, in the first article, the Coleridge poem, Romantics criticism, and, to some extent, Romanticism itself. In the spirit of Winters, he attributes the critical debilities of Abrams, in the second essay, to Romantic poetry or to what he calls the "Fallacy of mythic form," which prevents Abrams from recognizing that the better Romantic poets are Southey, Landor, and Byron. The only comparable attack in recent years is by Philip Hobsbaum, first in "The Romantic Dichotomy" (*BJA,* 1976) and then in *Tradition and Experiment in English Poetry* (1979). After quoting Arnold's indictment of the Romantics for their insufficient knowledge, Hobsbaum, in the book, remarks: "We can add to his diagnosis. Not only did the Romantics not know enough, but they were hardly ever in control even of that which they thought they knew." Such hostile writing is reminiscent of the 1920s and 1930s, when the battle between the humanist New Critics and the academics raged. Fortunately for Romanticism, the weapons used by these latter-day assailants are obsolete.

If Toliver makes a brief for literary history, Lawrence Lipking makes one for literary lives in *The Life of the Poet: Beginning and Ending Poetic Careers* (1981), albeit it is literary lives with a difference. Lipking contends that "every major Western poet after Homer . . . has left some work that records the principle of his own poetic development." Until we recognize that "the life of the poet is often the life of the poem"—until we see poets as they come to see themselves and wish us to see them—we do not read them well. Lipking begins and ends with Keats, who serves as paradigm par excellence for his theory. Blake's *Marriage of Heaven and Hell* also figures prominently in an early section of the book. Romantics scholars particularly may not find Lipking's new ways of reading poems so very new.

Romantic Imagination, Romantic Will, and Romantic Sublime

The previous version of this chapter gave considerable space to the subject of the imagination or Romantic imagination as increasingly the primary concern and chief focus of Romantics studies. Still valuable are the studies by C. M. Bowra (*The Romantic Imagination,* 1950), Ernest Tuveson (*The Imagination as a Means of Grace: Locke and the Aesthetics of Romanticism,* 1960), H. W. Piper (*The Active Universe: Pantheism and the Concept of Imagination in the English Romantic Poets,* 1962), and Alethea Hayter (*Opium and the Romantic Imagination,* 1968)—all of which, except Bowra's book, look at the subject from the special point of view implied in their titles. The articles cited there (see *ERP3* 47–48) by Northrop Frye, A. S. P Woodhouse, N. P. Stallknecht, and others are also still worthy of mention, though the ones specifically preoccupied with the distinction between imagination and fancy need to be read in the light of more recent research, especially that of Thomas McFarland (see the Coleridge chapter). Several phenomena of the sixties, seventies, and early eighties have affected our notion of the Romantic imagination rather significantly: the admission of Blake into the Romantic pantheon, the great strides in Byron criticism, the reinterpretation of Romanticism by the post–New Critics discussed elsewhere in this chapter and book, and the appearance of James Engell's *The Creative Imagination: Enlightenment to Romanticism* (1981). Blake's appearance in the present volume and John Clubbe's review of Byron scholarship in chapter 5 bear witness to the first and second of these phenomena. It remains for me, here, to deal with Engell's book, which is impressive for the courage of its aim as well as for the clarity of its achievement. Engell's study is straight history of ideas. Moreover, it is tricked out with no idiosyncratic theory of history or literature or esoteric vocabulary. Readers familiar with Wellek's Coleridge chapter in his *History of Modern Criticism* will recognize Engell's derivational approach to Romantic theory; but his study is revisionist in its thesis that the creative imagination is the creation of the eighteenth century, with some refinements by Coleridge. The Romantic poets had the idea—or cluster of ideas—at hand ready for application. Herein, according to

Engell, is the secret of their amazing productivity: as artists, they played the crowning role in the effort to overcome dualism, the motive for the eighteenth-century writers who initiated the effort. In one sense, Engell's view suggests a return to the old pre–Romanticism, but he is not concerned with the rivalry of literary periods. And if by describing the later eighteenth century as the "Enlightenment creating Romanticism, primarily by developing the idea of the imagination" he restores significance to that period, he does not do so at the expense of the Romantics' achievement. Engell's procedure is to trace the history of the idea as it gradually replaces that of the great chain of being and thus separates the modern worldview from the Renaissance outlook, becoming finally a zeitgeist. Most chapters focus on one or two individuals who promoted or otherwise contributed to this evolution, for example, Hobbes and Locke or, later, Goethe and Keats. This last pairing indicates another important feature of the book. Since the idea of creative imagination developed in both Germany and England in somewhat parallel chronology, Engell employs the comparative method to elucidate his subject. Not theoretically exciting, Engell's book is nonetheless a satisfying work because it is so very lucid, solid, comprehensive, and informative; by the time he has traced the chameleon image to an early eighteenth-century treatise by Zachary Mayne or demonstrated the early use of "plastic" to modify "imagination," one is willing to concede the argument and then some.

Other studies of the creative imagination inevitably pale by comparison, but Romantics scholars can learn from some of them, even so. Jean Starobinski's title "Remarques sur l'histoire du concept d'imagination" (*CIS,* 1966) suggests kinship with Engell's book, but the author invokes history to make a plea for the relativity of the concept: imagination is relative to the milieu, the times, the traditions in which it occurs. It follows that the critical task is to observe the imaginative power as it operates in the human context, when and wherever it comes into view. *The Evidence of the Imagination: Studies of Interactions between Life and Art in English Romantic Literature* (1978), a collection of essays by Romantics scholars, edited by Donald H. Reiman, Michael C. Jaye, and Betty T. Bennett, makes much the same point. The sixteen essays on the six major Romantic poets, plus Mary Shelley, Peacock, and Claire Clairmont's niece Pauline, are intended to demonstrate the primacy of the text—the evidence of imagination—in literary scholarship and criticism: the work of art must be fully understood in its biographical and historical context before it can be used to document any critical theory of imagination. A reference in the preface to "ignorant critics" hints at polemics; invocation of the humanist argument for literature, especially for literature taught in the classroom from the human (biographical-historical) perspective of the scholars included here, reveals the colors under which this volume skirmishes. The editors' claims for the quality of the essays are entirely justified. A slight article by Gerald Enscoe, "Some Thoughts on the Liberated Imagination" (*MLS,* 1972), also faults the professors of liberated imagination for failing to cultivate it either in themselves or in their students. According to Roland A. Duerksen, in "The Critical Mode in British Romanticism" (*RP&P,* 1983), academics would serve Romanticism and particularly the creative imagination better if they were to group the six poets by perceptual difference rather than by chronological convenience. He proposes the label "traditional Romantics" for those poets who extended but did not break with neoclassical rationalism—Wordsworth, Coleridge, Byron—and the label "critical Romantics" for those who did—Blake, Shelley, Keats. It is the latter, Duerksen fervently believes, who "raised the questions or joined the issues that have confronted the world of artistic endeavor since their time." This realignment Duerksen also finds useful in differentiating among modern revolutionists: Herbert Marcuse resembles the traditional Romantics; James Agee, the critical Romantics.

Helen Regueiro's *The Limits of Imagination: Wordsworth, Yeats, and Stevens* (1976), as her three authors would suggest, does not buck the fashionable critical trends. As she defines it, the imagination struggles "to triumph over self-consciousness and even reality," to transcend "the dialectic in which the two are engaged," and to redeem "the poetic self from its imprisonment in temporality." Such struggle, paradoxically, intensifies rather than resolves the dialectic, leading to solipsism or poetic silence. The limits of imagination are, thus, those beyond which the imagination cannot be affirmed without self-destruction. Although Regueiro makes an effort to distinguish her work from that of the critics she quotes, she is not altogether successful.

Another scholar who examines the dangers of solipsism is A. D. Nutall in *A Common Sky: Philosophy and the Literary Imagination* (1978). It is the empiricists who, according to Nuttall, laid the ground for solipsistic fear in their hostility to experience; they removed us from the reality of the external world, commencing a regression in philosophy that continues today (via Berkeley, Hume, the English Romantics, Eliot). "Thus the boy Wordsworth grasping at the wall may serve as an emblem of modern literature." Mary Warnock's *Imagination* (1976) is also a philosopher's work with a philosopher's purpose: "to bring Wordsworth and Coleridge into a framework of professionally philosophical thinking, about the very subject matter with which they were concerned as poets." In particular, she tries to show that the concept of imagination is the only means of connecting ordinary perception and extraordinary perception, that is, of symbolizing. The concept of imagination that emerges is, Warnock admits, Romantic because the Romantic "version is true, and fits the facts." Moreover, she puts a high value on this imagination, quoting *The Prelude* and Mill, and concludes by urging that so vital a human "power in the mind" be taken into account in theories of education. Edith Cobb's *The Ecology of Imagination in Childhood* (1977) is sociological in approach, but, like Warnock, Cobb affirms the Romantics' argument for fostering and preserving the imagination so active and healthy in the child. Cobb's inspiration is Keats and Wordsworth. Andrew Brink, "On the Psychological Sources of Creative Imagination" (*QQ*, 1974), narrows the focus to art, seeking to demonstrate that psychoanalysis can help to explain the uses of art by artists—and expose artists' motivations—and thus can function in the interest of the humanities.

Two studies shift us from the academy to the political arena. Thomas R. Edwards, *Imagination and Power: Study of Poetry on Public Themes* (1971), includes a chapter "The Revolutionary Imagination," with subsections on Blake, Shelley, Wordsworth, and the idealization of art. For all eras, Edwards is most interested in the problematic relationship of poetry or imagination to politics. Accordingly, with the Romantics, he focuses on the difficulties they "faced in integrating imagination and political enthusiasm," the paramount one being their tendency to effect such union by changing their concern for "immediate social and political reality" into "some symbolic paradigm that the mind can possess more easily than the intractable stuff of the public world itself." Eleanor Wilner, *Gathering the Winds: Visionary Imagination and Radical Transformations of Self and Society* (1975), is especially interested in the visionary imagination in its apocalyptic-millennial form as a response to extremity and crisis in the human condition. The nineteeth century is the center of her book; she uses Blake, Beddoes, and Yeats to demonstrate, respectively, the instance of positive response (apocalyptic imagination) to crisis, the instance of negative response, and the instance of contrived response or accommodation. Wilner is attractively modest in her claims and properly respectful of the "rebellious imagination." Not to be left out is *The Economics of the Imagination* (1980) by Kurt Heinzelman. Although this is a work of literary criticism, the texts criticized are economic tracts and poems. Heinzelman wishes to write about political economy and its effect on literature but also about metaphor, the meeting ground of economist and poet. He calls the effort "an intersystemic analysis of the language and logic which poetic and economic 'systems' share." A chapter on Blake explores his struggle to transform the economic imagination to the aesthetic imagination. A chapter on Wordsworth presents the stamp collector as seeking to "retrieve economic discourse from its mismanaged and facile rhetorical forms and thus to construct a cogent poetics of labor value." This poetics Heinzelman broadens to Romantic poetics: "In Wordsworth's economy the *reader,* the nominal 'consumer,' must also be a *productive* laborer. Indeed, Wordsworth's labor theory affirms that *only* in the exchanges of poetry is 'productive consumption' not an oxymoron—an unreal word—but a powerful transformation and overbalancing of that getting and spending which lay waste our powers." And we are back to familiar territory. But it's been quite a trip!

Denis Donoghue's Ker Memorial lecture *Imagination* (1974; expanded as chapter 2 in *The Sovereign Ghost: Studies in Imagination,* 1977) is an engaging comparison of the imagination "in its standard Romantic version," with its post-Romantic accounts and with its structuralist renderings. Donoghue's lack of partisanship—"structuralism emphasizes destiny, Romanticism freedom. The tension is at worst tolerable, at best fruitful"—is refreshing.

The titles make it convenient to group such couplings as Margaret R. Higgonet's "Bachelard and the Romantic Imagination" (*CL,* 1981), Lilian Furst's "Kafka and the Romantic Imagination" (*Mosaic,* 1970), and Alan Frost's "Captain James Cook and the Early Romantic Imagination" (in *Captain James Cook: Image and Impact,* ed. Walter Veit, 1972). The first two are informative articles; the last is mainly entertaining.

Finally, for the Macmillan Casebook series, John Spencer Hill has gathered extracts from the poets and modern critical studies in *The Romantic Imagination* (1977). The poets do not include Blake and Byron; the critical studies were all written before 1970.

If studies of the Romantic imagination are plentiful, verging on abundant, studies of the Romantic will, the agent of or complement to imagination, are at a dearth. Michael G. Cooke is to be congratulated for considering so important but strangely neglected a topic in *The Romantic Will* (1976). In theory he locates his study in the current preoccupation with Romanticism and consciousness, which, for Cooke, is a dynamic of perception and morality or metaphysics—it is "engaged." This metaphysics of engagement is consummately expressed, for the Romantics, in the concept of will. Thus, not to recognize the role of the will in the development of imagination—to concentrate exclusively on perception—is to miss the drama of Romantic poetry and so emerge with only a partial appreciation of it. In accord with this belief, Cooke examines, with the help of philosophical underpinnings erected in the first chapter, the relation of "will and the art of being" in a representative range of poems, beginning with "The Ancient Mariner." Readers of Cooke's study may become so engrossed in his subtle readings (even occasionally to the point of quarreling with them) that they lose sight of the raison d'être for the readings—the more so because Cooke rarely lets his thesis stand in the way of provocative digressions. But his final chapter confirms both the theme of the book and its vital importance to the Romantics and to their interpreters.

Cooke's later book, *Acts of Inclusion: Studies Bearing on an Elementary Theory of Romanticism* (1979), lies in theory somewhere between the unitary or organic theories of Romanticism and the fragmentary or ironic theories. By "inclusion" Cooke means "universality," and his book attempts to study "a new and explicit interest in the paradoxes of inclusion, that is, in universality." Cooke grants the Romantics' dialecticism, their need to achieve radical reconciliation, and in fact their inclusion of opposites in their work, but he is more concerned to recognize "that they proposed acts of inclusion as their ground or goal." Along with Garber and others who defend the virtues of Romantic irony, Cooke asserts that Romantic irony, in its effect, does less "to undermine faith and romance than to increase awareness of actuality and, thus, to suggest a richer, more complex, more challenging ground for a faith that would better withstand its challenges." By an "elementary theory" of Romanticism Cooke means, then, that Romanticism "entails an impulse and a demand for a principle of comprehension. It takes the form, characteristically, of an act of inclusion." In this work Cooke organizes his argument according to "generic and thematic and formal issues," the better to cover the territory. Sections not to be missed are the chapter "The Feminine as the Crux of Value" and the postscript "Prose in the Romantic Period." Cooke, of Romantics scholars, has one of the keenest minds for detecting subtle connections between contemporary and Romantic social phenomena (Cooke's belief that the Romantic period recovers a place of substantial power for women in poetry emerged in a mini-essay of 1971: see "The Editor's Lookout," *SIR*, the Summer issue); he also manages, better than most, to make use of complex and conflicting critical theories without becoming ensnared by them. Moving from Byron to the Byron-inspired subject of the Romantic will to a compelling theory of Romanticism well grounded in the full range of Romantic poetry is no mean achievement.

Two essays of the last decade are devoted to Cooke's topics. Ben F. Ward's "The Romantic Recovery" (*SHR*, 1978) argues for the validity of "Romantic" as a viable philosophical category; Romantic art is one of inclusion (among other things). Ward's overly emphatic article is not nearly so careful as Cooke's longer work. John R. Reed's "Inherited Characteristics: Romantic to Victorian Will" (*SIR*, 1978) examines the relationship of the Romantics and Victorians from the concept of the will and concludes that the Romantics engaged the argument of free will versus necessity and transmitted it to the Victorians. Where the former were expansive in their view of the will, however, the latter were contractive, not unwilling to expand but anxious to consolidate at the same time. In Philip Drew's broader perspective, *The Meaning of Freedom* (1982), the Romantics occupy a prominent place, for the author believes that a history of ideas—in this case, the idea of free will—should be interdisciplinary. Moreover, Drew argues with some passion that poets and novelists have carried an equal voice with philosophers and other intellectuals in debating the issue of free will. The Romantic period, he finds, strikingly replicates the period 1590–1620: "We have there...the same sudden surge of belief in the freedom and power of the individual, followed in each case very rapidly by doubts, mistrust of the new liberty and disillusion." The newest and most comprehensive contribution to the subject is Peter L. Thorslev, Jr.'s *Romantic Contraries: Freedom versus Destiny* (1984), an impressively learned account of these two concepts in the history of philosophy, with particular attention to their value, when correctly defined, for elucidating and distinguishing among the Romantic alternatives—the organic universe, the gothic universe, and the open universe—to the mechanized universe of the Enlightenment. The present confusion in Shelley criticism about the distinction between "necessity" and "destiny" points to the timeliness of Thorslev's enterprise. His careful study is the more persuasive for his recognition (and the flexibility therefrom) that poets "are not professional philosophers—although in the Romantic age the two disciplines were more closely allied than ever before or since—and we do not expect of them a lifelong intellectual consistency, nor even an orderly and rational evolution of ideas and attitudes." Even so, Thorslev argues, the Romantics were more serious about their philosophical suppositions than some of their present-day interpreters allow. Hence the obligation, he insists, to read them accurately.

One version of the Romantic imagination—the "egotistical sublime"—has received special attention in the last ten years or so, most notably by the late Thomas Weiskel. With all the critical paraphernalia of the Yale critics, the structuralists, and the semioticians, Weiskel, *The Romantic Sublime: Studies in the Structure and Psychology of Transcendence* (1976), sets out to do for the Romantic sublime what Samuel Monk, *The Sublime: A Study of Critical Theories in XVIII-Century England, 1674–1800* (1935; rpt. with new preface 1960), did for the eighteenth-century sublime. Because of Monk's work the absence of "a point of view for the larger drama of Romantic transcendence" is all the more conspicuous, Weiskel feels. The "structure and psychology" of his title are, respectively, linguistic (or semiotic) and Freudian, specifically, the Freudian concept of sublimation, whereby the Romantics—Wordsworth especially—experienced and coped with the anxiety of modernism. And it is from this "point of view," he believes, that the sublime still speaks to us—not as ideology but as inspirational psychology for illuminating, if not resolving, problems of identity. Weiskel's is an engaged book and has been called "brilliant"; whether it is engaging depends on the reader's tolerance for hard words and hard thoughts struggling to find each other. Many a reader of the humanist persuasion has wished for less matter and more art. Weiskel's book fits almost perfectly, however, the prescription for criticism written by Hartman, who, with Bloom, was one of the author's acknowledged mentors. An article by Jan Cohn and Thomas H. Miles, "The Sublime: In Alchemy, Aesthetics and Psychoanalysis" (*MP*, 1977), charts the history of the word "sublime" from alchemy through aesthetics to psychoanalysis or from "sublime" to "sublimation." The separation of the sublime from the beautiful in aesthetics was crucial in preparing for the third stage of development. Marshall Brown's "The Pre-Romantic Discovery of Consciousness" (*SIR*, 1978) also links the sublime in the Romantic period with the problem of identity. The Romantic style, he believes, was engendered by the perceived need to deconstruct the eighteenth-century style or the "urbane sublime" in order to give expression to a single value—self-consciousness or personal identity. Both the history of ideas and the history of poetry, he argues, should therefore be subsumed under a general history of consciousness. For W. P. Albrecht, too, in *The Sublime Pleasures of Tragedy: A Study of Critical Theory from Dennis to Keats* (1975), the sublime has become, by the Romantic period, a psychological state, though one less vexed than that spelled out in Weiskel's theories. The critical theory Albrecht elucidates reveals a merging of the sublime and tragedy to the point where tragedy gives pleasure because of the sublime's capacity to unite knowledge and emotion, making "all disagreeables evaporate." The latest psychological study of the sublime, inspired by Wallace Stevens' poem "The American Sublime," is James B. Twitchell's *Romantic Horizons: Aspects of the Sublime in English Poetry and Painting, 1770–1850* (1983). Twitchell's focus is by intent narrow—the visual sublime or "how the romantic artist's eyes lift from the palpable designs of natural landscape to the gathering activity at the horizon"; his objective is to discover whether poets and painters, when engaged in this motion, envisioned the same thing. In pairing Romantic poets and painters (his couplings are not the usual ones) Twitchell joins the avant-garde of Romantics criticism (see below, under "Romantic Literature and the Other Arts"); in defining the sublime as that which mediates between the conscious and the mystical, bringing its practitioner to the threshold of new consciousness but not farther, he builds on his own earlier work (see above, under "Romantic Consciousness and Romantic Self"). Theresa M. Kelley's "Wordsworth, Kant, and the Romantic Sublime" (*PQ*, 1984) is also concerned with accuracy of definition. A critical difference in the "role accorded reason and fear" in Kant and Wordsworth is, she argues, overlooked. Consequently, neo-Kantian readings of Wordsworth's sublime distort both the poet and, through him, the Romantic sublime itself.

the spirit of Wordsworth, Weiskel complains that the categorizing of the eighteenth-century sublime, like the categorizing of the mind, diminishes the subject. An instance of this practice, the "religious sublime," provides the title for a book by David B. Morris: *The Religious Sublime: Christian Poetry and Critical Tradition in 18th-Century England* (1972). An extension of Monk's pioneering work, Morris' book takes up, near the end, the "radical transformation of the religious sublime" by Wordsworth, Coleridge, and Blake. Keats's phrase for Wordsworth's imagination—the "egotistical sublime"—is, for Morris, a key to the how and what of the transformation of the religious sublime by the Romantics. The religious ideas of the old sublime passed through the individual imaginations of the poets, emerging with new clothes.

Romantic Religion, Romantic Myth, and Romantic Occult

In *ERP3* (37), I referred students interested in Romantic religion to the books and articles of Vilhelm Gronbeck, Murray Roston, John Herman Randall, James Benziger, Hoxie N. Fairchild, and A. S. P. Woodhouse—all of which can still be consulted profitably. The newer studies to be discussed here are not necessarily superior. Henry Chadwick, "Romanticism and Religion," in *The Future of the Modern Humanities*, ed. J. C. Laidlaw (1969), attempts to say just what effect Romanticism had on religion: it meant the transfer of interest from ontology to psychology, from the object of faith to the subjective act of believing—in short, it produced a shift to the subjective that still characterizes religion. Besides, it brought art and religion together by providing a common language for aesthetic and religious experience, it stimulated study of the psychology of religion, and it promoted the comparative study of religion. Chadwick sees gains and losses for religion. F. X. Shea, S. J., "Religion and the Romantic Movement" (*SIR*, 1970), writes in much the same vein. Romanticism, by relocating reality in experience, destroyed the "other world" but left intact the human need for transcendence. We should change our images for Romantic religion from male to female, he suggests, to reflect a domesticated religion. A revived religion was the gain; a dead faith was the loss. A third essay to suggest that the modern world is the Romantic world and that modern religion (and also the study of religious history) is born with Romanticism is Sydney E. Ahlstrom's "The Romantic Religious Revolution and the Dilemmas of Religious History" (*Church History*, 1977). To various degrees, these writers define Romanticism as a spiritual or religious phenomenon in part or in toto. Bernard M. G. Reardon, "Religion and the Romantic Movement" (*Theology*, 1973), goes so far as to call Romanticism a religion bearing all the attributes of Romantic poetry, but as such it causes Romanticism to seem remote to us; it is Romantic humanism, not Romantic religion, that we still feel close to. For Christopher Clausen, "Poetry as Revelation: A Nineteenth-Century Mirage" (*GaR*, 1979; rpt. *The Place of Poetry*, 1981), the notion that poetry might become the salvation of religion was misguided; poetry was not able to save itself, much less religion, and experienced a decline in the nineteenth century. Pointing in somewhat the same direction is Derek Colville's *Victorian Poetry and the Romantic Religion* (1970), which formulates a visionary and confident Romantic poetry as a critical norm against which to measure a compromised, problem-ridden Victorian poetry.

The Reardon essay mentioned above takes up the inspiration Romanticism provided for the revival of Catholicism. Michael H. Bright, "English Literary Romanticism and the Oxford Movement" (*JHI*, 1979), looks at the consequences for literature and religion of shared characteristics; he finds that poet and priest are both exalted, poetry and theology are both transmitted through symbolism, and imagination and religious faith both achieve the same end, spiritual truth. By far the most important new study, however, is Stephen Prickett's *Romanticism and Religion: The Tradition of Coleridge and Wordsworth in the Victorian Church* (1976). Perhaps his most significant point is the inextricable relationship between literary criticism and theology in nineteenth-century England, a relationship he demonstrates by showing how the tradition of Wordsworth's and Coleridge's Romanticism—their emphasis on the ambiguous nature of human experience and on a language that expresses this ambiguity (i.e., the symbol), a language associated with ideas of creativity and development—was fostered and interpreted by Victorian men of letters so as to inform and form the theology of the Victorian church. A single instance of this process is explored by Sheridan Gilley, in "John Keble and the Victorian Churching of Romanticism" (in Watson). Nor does the story stop with the nineteenth century. R. J. Reilly brings Romantic religion into the twentieth century with his *Romantic Religion: A Study of Barfield, Lewis, Williams, and Tolkien* (1971).

In quite another vein is Walter H. Evert's "Coadjutors of Oppression: A Romantic and Modern Theory of Evil" (in Bornstein). Analyzing Romantic works, with special attention to "Christabel" and "The Cenci," and twentieth-century works, especially *One Flew over the Cuckoo's Nest, A Clockwork Orange,* and *Terminal Man,* Evert hypothesizes that, in the modern mind, "the nature of absolute evil is the insidious and inevitable corruption of good *into* evil, a corruption that is successful precisely in proportion to the real purity of the good." On the general subject of Romantic morality we now have a full-scale study, Mark Roberts' *The Tradition of Romantic Morality* (1973). For Roberts, the morality of the present age is Romantic morality, which he defines as belief in the "energy of the soul." This energy, the sole source of true values and the principal guide to conduct, the Romantics and their heirs "divinise," with the unfortunate result that the forms of action such energy takes become inconsequential. Roberts' analysis of Romantic morality is ultimately negative: "Romantic morality . . . does not attempt to solve moral problems so much as to avoid them." Blake and Wordsworth are the High Romantics Roberts deals with. R. G. Woodman, "Satan in the 'Vale of Soul-Making': A Survey from Blake to Ginsberg" (*HAB*, 1974), finds that the Romantics' heretical theory of soul making—the necessity of enlisting in the devil's party—was short-lived because the moral intensity of their vision dissipated rapidly. In recent times only literary hacks have professed to follow in their footsteps, sign enough that modern-day Romanticism is an "exhausted impulse which is unable to contain within itself the vision it has inherited."

Murray Roston's *Prophet and Poet: The Bible and the Growth of Romanticism* (1965) is now supplemented by E. S. Shaffer's *"Kubla Khan" and* The Fall of Jerusalem: *The Mythological School in Biblical Criticism and Secular Literature, 1770–1880* (1975). If the discovery of the Bible as literature played a formative part in Romantic poetry, so did the higher criticism of the Bible that developed in Germany. In fact, Shaffer would argue, we cannot understand literary Romanticism, especially Coleridge, if we do not attend to the reception and practice of the higher criticism in England. The author makes test cases of "Kubla Khan," a poem often described as pure poetry, and Hölderlin's odes. Shaffer's book not only proposes the higher criticism as an intermediary between philosophy and literary criticism and, hence, as a new method of literary criticism but also demonstrates the great benefits of the comparative method. From still another perspective we see how radical a break with the past the Romantics made. The very latest book on the religious derivation of Romanticism, Richard E. Brantley's *Locke, Wesley, and the Method of English Romanticism* (1984), argues the other way. "Wesley's mediation of Locke's thought," Brantley finds, "is an immediate context of English Romantic poetry: Blake, Wordsworth, Coleridge, Shelley, and Keats . . . resemble each other in their formulations of experience, which echo Wesley's." Besides its provocative thesis and cogent demonstration, Brantley's richly learned book is distinctive for its critical-theoretical awareness, implicit throughout and explicit in the postscript, which reminds us only too well of how far literary scholarship has advanced since Frederick C. Gill essayed the same subject, in *The Romantic Movement and Methodism: A Study of English Romanticism and the Evangelical Revival* (1937; rpt. 1954).

One of the biblical myths that underwent profound change in this period was the myth of the fall. In *Some Versions of the Fall: The Myth of the Fall of Man in English Literature* (1973), Eric Smith has a chapter entitled "Romantic Attitudes." Wordsworth and Coleridge, more than the other poets, were interested in the fall for the potential of motiveless evil it depicted and hence as an answer to Godwin's position that all evil was susceptible to rational explanation. Too, they were interested in the fall as a myth of the state of the specially gifted poet.

Religion and myth are, of course, subtly intertwined, especially in the Romantic period. In both we tell ourselves stories of our origins, among other things, and "origins" is a recurrent word in Romantics studies of the recent past. In the interpretations of Romanticism by the post–New Critics especially, the Romantic poets are presented as preoccupied with their origins, specifically, their poetic and spiritual origins in their precursors, usually Milton. Leslie Brisman's *Romantic Origins* (1978) makes explicit this running theme in much of our latest criticism and theory by underscoring the intensity and variety of the Romantics' myths of origins. For Brisman two of the great motivating powers behind the Romantic movement are, in fact, "the desire to know correctly a state which no longer exists, and the desire to express one's awareness of the fictionality of such a state." His study ranges over all the major Romantics and throws in Darley for good measure but originates in Rousseau and culminates in Wordsworth. Brisman is one of the newer critics whose style seems calculated to make us sympathize with Douglas Jerrold, who, when taking up *Sordello* after a severe illness in which he had been irrational, thought he had lost his mind. With application, however, the book yields its meaning even if the reader, like the Romantic poets, is made to feel "that he is cut off from the real line and the reality about him." In a more conventional sense of both myth and origins Marilyn Gaull deals with the Romantics and creative myths in her article on Wordsworth and Darwin (see below).

Brisman distinguishes between the Romantics' concern for originality and their preoccupation with myths of origins. The Romantics may not have been particularly eager to claim originality, but some of their interpreters are highly sensitive to charges that they were copiers. Thomas McFarland, in "The Originality Paradox" (*NLH,* 1974), elaborates a paradoxical theory of originality ever present in any literate culture. Romanticism may have heightened the paradox but hardly invented it. Plagiarism, in McFarland's analysis, becomes "a practice that participates in and is witness to the paradox that surrounds the entire conception of originality." Norman Fruman, "Originality, Plagiarism, Forgery, and Romanticism" (*Centrum,* 1976), objects to grouping plagiarists of the period and then explaining away their plagiarisms through an accommodating theory of Romanticism. The paradox he emphasizes is the harsh attitude of the Romantic age to unacknowledged borrowings. Modern notions of authorial rights and literary property date from that time.

One way of appreciating the new ways of thinking and writing about myths and mythology in the Romantic period is to mention the one older book given over to the topic: Douglas Bush's *Mythology and the Romantic Tradition in English Poetry* (1937; rpt. 1969), which, for all its age, is still impressive scholarship. E. B. Hungerford's *Shores of Darkness* (1941), Albert J. Kuhn's "English Deism and the Development of Mythological Syncretism" (*PMLA,* 1956), and Alex Zwerdling's "The Mythographers and the Romantic Revival of Greek Myth" (*PMLA,* 1964)—specialized studies that take us into the intellectual ferment of the later eighteenth century, when syncretists and other speculative mythologists were reestablishing myth by advancing claims for its service to religion—must now take second place to Stuart Curran's thorough investigation of the subject, in *Shelley's Annus Mirabilis* (1974), especially the chapter "The Key to All Mythologies." A still more recent account—and a good overview—is provided by Paul J. Korshin's learned *Typologies in England, 1650–1820* (1982). Chapter 6 specifically treats "Typology and Myth"; the Romantic poets figure prominently in the later chapters "Typology and Prophecy" and "The Typology of Everyday Life." Bush's later *Pagan Myth and Christian Tradition in English Poetry* (1968) rehearses each major Romantic poet's use of Greek myth (Blake's excepted) but contends that this use is always classical and secular. In 1975, Burton Feldman and Robert D. Richardson, Jr., published a large work entitled *The Rise of Modern Mythology, 1680–1860,* which mixes essays and relevant documents, creating an anthology of sorts. The Romantic period is divided into three sections, each with its own essay: one on German Romanticism, another on English, and a third on American. At present the same authors are editing for Garland Publishing, under the title of *Myth and Romanticism*, "A Collection of the Major Mythographic Sources Used by the English Romantic Poets" (their subtitle). When completed it will comprise twenty-five titles. The inadequacies of both Bush and Feldman-Richardson are exposed in Theresa M. Kelley's "Proteus, Nature, and Romantic Mythography" (*WC*, 1980), which shows how Wordsworth invokes the ancient symbolic function of Proteus and Triton not to celebrate but to subvert nature. "In this strategy we find a truer portrait of Romantic adaptations of classical mythology than that once offered by Douglas Bush and recently supported by Richardson and Feldman."

Several Romantics scholars of late have sidetracked Romanticism and religion and circumvented Romanticism and myth for Romanticism and the occult. The Spring 1977 issue of the *Wordsworth Circle*, guest edited by Anya Taylor, is devoted to the subject. Taylor's introductory essay specifies the several ways in which the occult is relevant to the study of Romanticism and thereby sets the stage for the essays, involving most of the major poets, that follow. At the same time she provides a bibliographical essay of the topic, pointing out, for example, that occult themes have entered mainstream Romantics studies through the work of both M. H. Abrams (the third chapter of *Natural Supernaturalism*) and Harold Bloom (his use of the Lurianic kabbala to elucidate the anxiety of influence in English poetry). Taylor's book, *Magic and English Romanticism* (1979), argues that the Romantics' interest in the occult is compatible with their humanism; they search for "some unprovable powers" because they "desire to affirm the existence of spirit, of imagination, and of freedom in the face of exclusively physical hypotheses." Among other things, Taylor's book throws light on the complex relationship of Wordsworth and Coleridge. Its chief merit, aside from information, is the restraint with which she handles a subject uncongenial to many scholarly minds. Somewhat related in purpose and material is Wallace Jackson's *The Probable and the Marvelous: Blake, Wordsworth, and the Eighteenth-Century Critical Tradition* (1978), which argues that in the mid-eighteenth century a renaissance occurred in poetry inspired by discontent with the inadequacies of the prevailing Augustan tradition. Proposing to recover the central English tradition, this renaissance prefigured the still greater renaissance we now call Romanticism. Jackson's title refers to the parameters within which the early rebel poets worked. "More than any other theme, the permissible limits of the marvelous consistent with the delineation of probable human action and response shaped the revaluations of mid-century. . . . It is this theme, also, and the revitalized employment of it, that directed the mythopoeic lyrics of those late revolutionary poets we know as the first Romantics." By "first Romantics" Jackson means Blake and Wordsworth. And by "marvelous" he refers to something approximating the sublime, especially the religious sublime, rather than the magical in the sense of the occult. More adventurous is James B. Twitchell's *The Living Dead: A Study of the Vampire in Romantic Literature* (1981). Like Frankenstein's monster, Twitchell claims, "the vampire is one of the major mythic figures bequeathed to us by the English Romantics";

he may even be "the most enduring and prolific mythic figure we have." Reason enough to study him (or her)! Twitchell begins by tracing the progress of the vampire out of folklore and into serious art; he concludes with the adaptation of the myth to explain the creative process of art. Twitchell claims that the book was fun to write; it is fun to read as well.

Romanticism and Science

Stephen Prickett remarks in his study of Romanticism and religion that "the full impact of Romanticism on the physical sciences has yet to be studied." Maybe so; there has been no Marjorie Nicolson or Basil Willey to do for Romantic poetry and science, physical or biological, what we have for the relationship of literature and science in the seventeenth and eighteenth centuries. But, of late, scholars have given us some valuable articles in which, if we cannot discern a consensus, we can at least detect the issues at stake. Edward Proffitt, in "Science and Romanticism" (*GaR,* 1980), contends that "even in its extreme manifestations, romanticism is not simply divorced from science. And in its less extreme manifestations . . . it is in fact an ally to a very substantial degree." The alliance is in procedure, not in the scientific model of reality, which is mechanistic. Proffitt contends further that, in the long run, the Romantics were the better scientists: the mechanistic model of science has been proved by physicists to be the subjective model. He takes up modern ecology, physics, generative linguistics, several brands of psychology, structuralism, and phenomenology—all of which, by Proffitt's account, support his contention. William Stephenson, "Romanticism and Modern Science" (in Harwell), finds that contemporary science is based on the Romantic worldview of an organically expanding universe. He chooses for illustration the anti-Newtonian view of modern physics that mass and energy are two manifestations of the same phenomenon, that space and time are a relativistic continuum. Both Romanticism and contemporary science are open systems, both admittedly subjective. Leo Marx, in "Reflections on the Neo-Romantic Critique of Science" (*Daedalus,* 1978), thinks that Romanticism anticipated most of the themes in current criticism of science, particularly its claims to legitimacy as a mode of cognition and as a social institution. The same spectrum to be discerned in the Romantic period—Wordsworth, Coleridge, and Carlyle in the middle; Shelley and Blake at the two extremes—he sees in our time, with Theodore Roszak corresponding to Blake. According to Wylie Sypher, *Literature and Technology: The Alien Vision* (1968), the first Romantics were receptive to science, associating their poetry of experience with the empirical mode of science, but the later Romantics (the realists and aesthetes), in his view, resorted to method rather than experience to validate their emotions, resulting in the "technical alienation of art." For Walter J. Ong, S.J., *Rhetoric, Romance, and Technology: Studies in the Interaction of Expression and Culture* (1971), "Romanticism and technology . . . are mirror images of each other, both being products of man's dominance over nature and of the noetic abundance which had been created by chirographic and typographic techniques of storing and retrieving knowledge and which had made this dominance over nature possible." Concentrating on Wordsworth's attitude toward poetic diction, he concludes that "romantic poetic was the poetic of the technological age." Keith Connelly, in "Modernism, Science and Romanticism" (*Four Decades of Poetry, 1890–1930*, 1976), pursues an idea similar to Sypher's. Modernism and modernist criticism allied themselves with forces opposed to Romanticism, remaking the artist to fit the image of the critic, of the scientist. If Marx deplores the institutionalizing of science, Connelly equally deplores the institutionalizing of poetry and criticism, calling for a revival of Romanticism. A recent article connecting "The Rise of Modern Science and the Genesis of Romanticism," by Hans Eichner (*PMLA*, 1982), argues forcefully against any significant impact of Romanticism on the history of science. In fact, Eichner labels Romanticism a "desperate rearguard action against the spirit and the implications of modern science." Through this action Romanticism liberated the arts themselves from "the constraints of a pseudoscientific [classicist] aesthetics" but failed to alter the course of science. Robert O. Preyer, "The Romantic Tide Reaches Trinity: Notes on the Transmission and Diffusion of New Approaches to Traditional Studies at Cambridge, 1820–1840," in *Victorian Science and Victorian Values: Literary Perspectives* (ed. James Paradis and Thomas Postlewait, 1981), suggests otherwise. Particularly at Trinity College, the organic philosophy of Wordsworth and Coleridge did much to stem the tide of utilitarianism in scientific studies as in the liberal arts curriculum. Leading practitioners of the new science at Cambridge—for example, William Whelwell, Adam Sedgwick, George Peacock—exerted considerable influence on students who were to dominate British science for the rest of the century.

Several essays take up specific points of comparison between Romantic poetry and physical science. D. M. Knight's "Chemistry, Physiology and Materialism in the Romantic Period" (*DUJ*, 1972) is primarily a gloss on a passage from *Aids to Reflection,* where Coleridge extols the advances of chemistry and physiology in terms indicating that these sciences, once associated with materialism, were separated from it in the Romantic period. An earlier article, "The Physical Sciences and the Romantic Movement" (*History of Science,* 1970), cautiously explores the question of the Romantics' impact on physics and chemistry and vice versa. Knight comes to no fast conclusions but does succeed in exemplifying for other scientists that literary history and the study of language or metaphor are helpful in generating the history of science. Cecil Y. Lang, in "Romantic Chemistry" (*Courier* [Syracuse Univ. Lib.] 1973), argues that chemistry, via Goethe's *Elective Affinities,* transformed the vocabulary of romantic love in English poetry. He credits Shelley's poetry with introducing the new vocabulary but fails to consider Hazlitt's critical essays as a possibility. Charles A. Culotta, "German Biophysics, Objective Knowledge, and Romanticism," in *Historical Studies in the Physical Sciences,* ed. Russell McCormmach (1973), points out that German Romanticism is the cultural context from which biophysics sprang, its rise not in opposition to, but somewhat in tandem with, Romanticism. Again, the bond is with the experimental sciences. Stephen C. Brush, *The Temperature of History: Phases of Science and Culture in the Nineteenth Century* (1978), in a chapter entitled "Romanticism and

Realism," suggests that only in physics were conditions favorable for Romanticism, for "a leap of the imagination; physics was ready for a unitary theory of natural forces." Literary scholars may take some comfort from Brush's chapter; his grasp of literary Romanticism is about as unsophisticated as many a literary scholar's grasp of physical science.

Two articles explore the implications of the theory that Julian Jayne explores in *The Origin of Consciousness in the Breakdown of the Bicameral Mind* (1977) for reading Romantic poetry and Romantic literary history. Edward Proffitt, "Romanticism, Bicamerality, and the Evolution of the Brain" (*WC,* 1978), suggests that Jayne's theory might explain why poetry of the last two hundred years—Romantic poetry—is a diminished thing. Judith Weissman, "Vision, Madness, and Morality: Poetry and the Theory of the Bicameral Mind" (*GaR,* 1979), uses Jayne's theory to depict a struggle in the nineteenth century between consciousness and the bicameral mind. The Romantics in particular elevated "a whole complex of emotions and experiences previously undervalued in literature, many of which can be related to the qualities of the pre-conscious, bicameral mind as Jayne describes it."

Biological science, as well as physical science, continues to receive attention. Older scholars know the pioneering studies of Joseph Warren Beach, *The Concept of Nature in Nineteenth-Century English Poetry* (1936), and Alfred North Whitehead, *Science and the Modern World* (1925), discussed along with several related essays in *ERP3* (27 – 28). To these earlier names and titles they will want to add that of Patricia M. Ball, whose *The Science of Aspects: The Changing Role of Fact in the Work of Coleridge, Ruskin and Hopkins* (1971) narrows the subject of the Romantics and nature to three writers' observations of fact or the natural world and the consequent differences to be detected in their recordings of these observations. Like her earlier *The Central Self* (1968), this volume takes us deeper into the ins and outs of the Romantic imagination, especially as received and transmuted by Victorian writers. Ria Omasreiter, *Naturwissenschaft und Literaturkritik im England des 18. Jahrhunderts* (1971), includes a chapter on imagination that finishes with Coleridge. The link between science and poetry, established in the eighteenth century, is the imagination. Thomas McFarland's learned chapter "Coleridge's Doctrine of Polarity and Its European Contexts," in *Romanticism and the Forms of Ruin* (1981; see below under "Romantic Forms and Modes" for a full discussion), investigates the background of one of the most complex and pervasive ideas shared by science and poetry in the Romantic period. He ranges far beyond Coleridge, much to the enlightenment of all Romantics scholars. H. A. M. Snelders' "Romanticism and Naturphilosophie and the Inorganic Natural Sciences, 1797 – 1840" (*SIR,* 1970) is not, unfortunately, concerned with England. Desmond King-Hele has examined "The Influence of Erasmus Darwin on Wordsworth, Coleridge, Keats, and Shelley" (in Asselineau et al.). For his influence on Blake, see Nelson Hilton's review essay "The Spectre of Darwin" (*BIQ,* 1981). Marilyn Gaull, in "From Wordsworth to Darwin: 'On to the Fields of Praise'" (*WC,* 1979), takes the reverse tack, examining the influence of poets on science, specifically, of Wordsworth and his *Excursion* on Darwin's creation myth in *The Origin of Species.*

Sir Peter B. Medawar, drawing especially on the Romantics, tried to argue in "Science and Literature" (*Encounter,* 1969) that the two are inimical because they invariably compete rather than cooperate. But Morse Peckham argues for similar behavior in scientists and poets. His essay "Romanticism, Science and Gossip" (*Shenandoah,* 1972) finds several grounds of sympathy between the two, but he is chiefly interested in the way both react when pushed to the wall while justifying their activities: they fall back on knowledge for its own sake, a sophisticated form of gossip, in that it discourages inquiry, testing, and so forth. At such times, both reveal their estrangement from the world.

Romanticism, Politics, and Society

The second part of Abrams' title for *Natural Supernaturalism*—"Tradition and Revolution in Romantic Literature"—points to an enduring, if not universally held, interpretation of Romanticism, namely, that it is fundamentally revolutionary literature spawned by social revolution. Abrams' earlier "English Romanticism: The Spirit of the Age," in *Romanticism Reconsidered,* ed. Northrop Frye (1963), remains perhaps the best statement of this view—after Hazlitt's, that is. An even more conspicuous pairing of Romanticism and revolution occurs in Howard Mumford Jones's *Revolution and Romanticism* (1974), a wide-ranging, richly detailed book on the complex relationships in art and thought between the New World and the Old—his third book on this subject, which now extends from 1492 to 1915. Not perhaps to be recommended to the specialist Romantics scholar, if most reviewers are to be believed, the book may serve the general reader quite well. Carl Woodring's *Politics in English Romantic Poetry* (1970) is, by contrast, the ideal work for scholars, for when it comes to sheer scholarship, Woodring is unsurpassed. A wealth of highly detailed information is herein adroitly organized and deftly analyzed to demonstrate the intricate interconnections of personal experience, political event, and poetic act for the Romantics. Without going to extremes, Woodring seeks to show that politics was more of a generative force for Romantic poetry than is sometimes recognized. Woodring's book and those books by David Erdman and others on the politics of specific Romantic poets have superseded the older studies of Crane Brinton and earlier scholars discussed in *ERP3* (37–38). If the depth and the breadth of the subject are now well defined, however, the length is still disputed. Some insist that the Romantic revolution is a thing of the past; some, that it is still with us and even reinvigorated. In either view, there is cause apparently for grieving or for rejoicing. Taking Burke as his master, Peter J. Stanlis, in "The Modern Social Consciousness" (*ORev,* 1974), sees the "Romantic politics of revolution" as a disaster for civilization. George Yost, "The Romantic Movement of Today, and Earlier" (*ForumH,* 1972), sees "remarkable resemblances between the English Romantic scene and the present scene in America" and thinks they are our best hope for understanding present-day American society. Howard O. Brogan, "The English Romantics: Revolution, Reaction, and the 'Generation Gap' " (*JGE,* 1974), concentrates on a specific relevance, the generation gap between first- and second-generation idealists in times of fundamental and rapid change; like Yost, he thinks the Romantics can shed helpful light on the problem. Peter L. Thorslev, Jr., "Romantic Writers and the Now Generation" (*WC*, 1971), thinks Romanticism is or can be especially valuable to the youth of today if their teachers can show them "that the moral and social as well as the esthetic dilemmas they face were no less real and painful for the great Romantic poets, and that sometimes, at least, the Romantics found solutions." Occasionally, writers who affirm the value of Romanticism for society fault critics for converting the poets' efforts to repudiate orthodoxies into orthodoxies. D. A. Beale, "The Trumpet of a Prophecy: Revolution and Politics in English Romantic Poetry" (*Theoria*, 1977), is such a writer. For Beale "it may be that Romanticism was that moment in Western Cultural history when poetry and politics fused in a total imaginative sense of the nature of Man: that Freedom was the essential condition of Man's humanity." Charles Rosen and Henri Zerner, in reviewing Hugh Honour's *Romanticism* (see below, under "Romantic Literature and the Other Arts"), chastise the author for giving to aesthetic forms and images a fundamental and inalterable meaning when the Romantics themselves were always giving new meanings to old forms (*NYRB*, 22 Nov. 1979), a theme that they have expanded on in *Romanticism and Realism: The Mythology of Nineteenth-Century Art* (1984), discussed later in this chapter.

Not to be omitted in this context is the work of Jacques Barzun, whose *Romanticism and the Modern Ego* (1943; rev. as *Classic, Romantic and Modern,* 1961) interprets the Romantic movement as fundamentally a social and political phenomenon, its art and philosophy as responses to the political desire for personal freedom within collective action. Because he saw the cultural history of the nineteenth and twentieth centuries as Romantic in nature, Barzun took seriously the connections he believed to exist between Romanticism and such modern political phenomena as Fascism and Nazism, just as he took seriously the connections he saw between Romanticism and such later aesthetic movements as realism, naturalism, symbolism, and cubism. His aim was to show that Romanticism, despite the efforts to kill it or to assert its demise in the 1920s and 1930s, was anything but dead and gone. The revised book simply provides an epilogue to the earlier one, bringing Barzun's story up-to-date. As in *The Energies of Art* (1956) and "Romanticism Today" (*Encounter,* 1961), he argues that Romanticism by the Romantic act of abolition or annihilation, which has been the aesthetic of art since World War II, is at long last coming to an end. Romanticism was a great symphony, its last three movements represented by realism, naturalism, and symbolism; modernism is the coda that proclaims the end of the music, which is to say, the death of art. Other veteran interpreters of Romanticism from a social perspective are R. W. Harris (*Romanticism and the Social Order, 1780 – 1830,* 1969) and Allan Rodway (*The Romantic Conflict,* 1963). These writers differ in their approaches as well as in their assessments of Romanticism's original achievements, lasting consequences, and staying power, but both succeed in representing Romanticism as something far broader than an isolated aesthetic phenomenon. So does Frank A. Lea, in *Voices in the Wilderness: From Poetry to Prophecy in Britain* (1975), a sequel to his *Ethics of Reason* (1975). The author begins with three chapters on Blake, Wordsworth, and Carlyle, writers who in a period of revolution were devoted, like their German contemporaries, to exposing and countering the abuse of reason by materialist philosophers and propagandists. The Romantics "aspired to a social revolution that would make the world safe for Shakespeare . . . . " This revolution would, in other words, reintegrate heart and head, relocate the universal in the particular, and reunite words and things. In Lea's view, the only revolution they achieved was a literary one, but they were not without some social impact. Lea's comparative analyses of the three writers are exceptionally shrewd. Renée Winegarten, in *Writers and Revolution: The Fatal Lure of Action* (1974), attributes the "varied archetypes of literary revolutionism" to the English Romantics, who saw in social revolution the salvation of human beings traditionally looked for in religion and, lured by the active nature of revolution, appropriated it via analogy for poetry. In doing so, she argues, they confused the quite different claims of art and revolution, which are not friends but rivals. Moreover, so persuasive were the Romantics that artists ever since have assumed the truth of the analogy, to the debasement, Winegarten believes, of both art and revolution. This is a provocative critique of Romantic culture. So is the collection of essays, *1789: Reading Writing Revolution. Proceedings of the Essex Conference on the Sociology of Literature,* July 1981 (ed. Francis Barker et al., 1982). Graham Pechey's "1789 and After: Mutations of 'Romantic' Discourse" tries to bring together in a complementary way the oversights of two isolated but influential kinds of Romantic discourse: the one preoccupied with the nexus of text and history, which is mostly the work of English and Marxist critics, and the one preoccupied with the specificity of Romantic poetry as a signifying practice, which is largely American in origin and deconstructionist in method. Catherine Belsey's "The Romantic Construction of the Unconscious" argues that psychoanalysis has a discursive, textual history of its own, dating from the late eighteenth and early nineteenth century. The texts are certain gothic novels and several of Wordsworth's poems, including *The Prelude.* Belsey's account of these texts leads her to conclude that psychoanalysis is radical discourse. Antony Easthope's "Novelty and Continuity in English Romanticism: A 'Lucy Poem' " asserts that Romanticism is not a break with tradition so much as a recuperation and sustaining of the tradition of bourgeois poetry. By continuing to provide for the subject as transcendental ego, albeit in a novel way—Romanticism developed a vehicle for eliding the distance between subject and object analogous to the child's experience of unity in the primary state of narcissism—English Romanticism claims its inheritance. Other essays in this collection dwell on single poets, for example, Blake.

Beale's article (cited above) carefully distinguishes between Romantics and radicals. N. Stephen Bauer, in a pair of articles—"Romantic Poets and Radical Journalists" (*NM,* 1978) and "Romantic Poetry and the Unstamped Political Press, 1830–1836" (*SIR,* 1975), looks at the use of the poets by radicals in the periods of 1817–24 and 1830–36. Whether the poets were invoked as allies or enemies of radical causes, whether they were quoted to illustrate current woes or future perfections were very much matters of journalistic convenience. Bauer does, however, point out a shift of Romantic poetry from the center of the radical movement to the periphery in the later period, when poets were no longer considered political personalities. These essays are very much in Woodring's vein.

Marilyn Butler's *Romantics, Rebels and Reactionaries: English Literature and Its Background, 1760–1830* (1981) proceeds in opposite fashion from Jones's big book. She cites the need for cultural and chronological discriminations within Romanticism if we are to understand the relationship between art and society. Moreover, she sides with those scholars who find the so-called Romantic revolution an eighteenth-century or Enlightenment phenomenon to which the Romantics responded. One sign of this view is the label "neoclassicist" that she uses for the younger Romantics. The author of books on Austen, Edgeworth, and Peacock, Butler involves Romantic novelists and essayists in her revision of English social history, resulting in a scope broader than Woodring's and narrower than Jones's. Not all will agree with her categories or with who fits them, but she has contributed a stimulating book to an almost hopelessly complicated area of inquiry.

War is both background and foreground to Romantic politics. Betty T. Bennett has reminded us vividly of this by collecting *British War Poetry in the Age of Romanticism: 1793–1815* (1976). One section of her introduction discusses "War Poetry and Romanticism"; she concludes it by asserting that "Wordsworth and Coleridge, Shelley and Byron celebrated the individuality of the common man, but it was the popular war poetry that, for the first time in British literary history, put the common man center-stage." The trauma of revolution when theory comes up against practice is interestingly presented in Paul Hamill's "Other People's Faces: The English Romantics and the Paradox of Fraternity" (*SIR,* 1978), which suggests that, before they could realize the ideal of fraternity, the Romantics discovered they had first to recognize the problem of fraternity—namely, the dark side of human nature in its communal as well as its individual manifestation. In "Ideas of Human Perfection" (*Theoria,* 1975), David G. Gillham includes Blake and Wordsworth among the literary figures who contributed ideas. The medieval past was a source of both negative and positive notions of human nature, its strengths and its shortcomings. Alice Chandler's *A Dream of Order: The Medieval Ideal in Nineteenth-Century English Literature* (1970) is the first substantial new treatment of the subject in its positive form. The Romantics are minority figures in her broad canvas, but Scott and the three Lake Poets are important to her investigation. Mark Girouard's *The Return to Camelot: Chivalry and the English Gentleman* (1981) is the second. It presents the code of medieval chivalry as exerting a continuous though weakening influence on British ideals of behavior until the late eighteenth century, when it "acquired a new intensity and new characteristics." Of the Romantics, only Scott is central to Girouard's well-told story, but this is an engrossing book, which in its final chapter, "The Great War," touches on the subject of an equally engrossing book, Paul Fussell's *The Great War and Modern Memory* (1975). Just as that conflict discredited the ideal of the chivalrous gentleman, so it cast a shadow on the literature and art that depicted war as the testing ground of chivalry, some but by no means all of it (witness Byron's attack on such notions in *Don Juan*) Romantic art. Garold N. Davis' "Medievalism in the Romantic: Some Early Contributions" (*BRMMLA,* 1974) is of little value.

The industrialization to which the medieval "dream of order" was a response continues to receive scholarly attention though not perhaps of the quality of E. P. Thompson's classic work *The Making of the English Working Class* (1963; rpt. 1968). Raymond Williams' *Culture and Society: 1780–1950* (1959; rpt. 1966) attends particularly to the way in which the Romantics responded to the Industrial Revolution, noting that, as time went on, they became more accepting of social changes and more cooperative with nonartists in working to ameliorate the negative effects. The Romantics figure prominently, too, in Williams' *The Country and the City* (1973), helping to chronicle and to further a division or sense of division greatly aggravated by the Industrial Revolution. Williams' brilliant, sensitive exposition of socialist ideology is in marked contrast to the socialist propaganda of John D. Clay in "English Romantics and the Working Class" (*Literature and Ideology,* 1973), where the Romantics are presented as expounding their theories to confuse people rather than to enlighten them about political issues. (But see S. V. Pradhan's "Romantic Poetics: A Critique of Marxist Critiques" [*CIEFLB,* 1977] for the shortcomings of Williams' Marxist analysis of the Romantics.) The latest major Marxist reading of the Romantics is the joint effort of David Aers, Jonathan Cook, and David Punter, *Romanticism and Ideology: Studies in English Writing 1765–1830* (1981). (Punter's *Blake, Hegel and Dialectic,* 1982, for all its focus on Blake, has implications for the other Romantic poets.) The authors of this volume seek to cure modern scholars of the habit of taking the Romantics at their own word, especially when it comes to their word about opposing the contemporary sociopolitical order in England. E. P. Thompson and other present-day Marxists to the contrary, the Romantics, they believe, were not important critics of capitalism but, rather, political naifs at best. A salutary piece of work, it should be read, however, in company with Michael Fischer's "Marxism and English Romanticism: The Persistence of the Romantic Movement" (*RP&P,* 1982), which sets forth the Marxist critique of Romanticism (the Romantics complied with their age and thus betrayed their own good intentions) and the Marxist response (Marxists overcame the limits they perceived in Romanticism, rescuing it from its own self-deception) before proceeding to argue that, on the contrary, Marxists did not and have not transcended the limits of Romanticism, a persistent phenomenon.

Alasdair Clayre has produced a most attractive volume, *Nature and Industrialization: An Anthology* (1977), with a section on nature and Romantic literature that includes eleven extracts from the poets and gives "Frost at Midnight" and "Tintern Abbey" in full. Francis D. Klingender, in *Art and the Industrial Revolution* (ed. Arthur Elton, 1947; rev. and exp. 1968), illuminates the interpenetration of art and technology, especially in a chapter entitled "The Age of Despair," which includes, for example, a section on "Satanic mills." And Ivanka Kovačević has edited *Fact into Fiction: English Literature and the Industrial Scene, 1750–1850* (1975). "Fiction" in the title means, however, just that: prose fiction. Finally, I might mention here George Steiner's "In Bluebeard's Castle: Some Notes towards the Re-Definition of Culture. 1: The Great Ennui" (*Listener,* 18 Mar. 1971; the first chapter of his book by the same title, 1971) for its proposal that the revolutionary energies not consumed when the revolutionary hopes of the 1790s and early 1800s collapsed were diverted to industry, which diversion obscured a corrosive ennui that was the reaction to these dashed hopes and that survived to account for some of the more debilitating and enigmatic aspects of twentieth-century culture.

In "Mme de Staël and the Woman of Genius" (*ASch,* 1975), Ellen Moers suggests that, in *Corinne et Italie,* the French author did for women what Byron did for men: "dramatized the romantic ego in all its extravagance, pain, and glory." But, then, women of genius were a type apart. To judge from the materials, what the Romantic revolution accomplished for ordinary women is highly debatable. Cooke, in *Acts of Inclusion* (see above), argues that the Romantic period produced "a sense of the natural but untapped power of the feminine which, because it had so little social or political expression, was doing less than it should for the masculine and for the human" and relates this to the "revolutionary impulse in romanticism." Cooke, it must be emphasized, is speaking of a pursuit of the feminine in the nineteenth century before "the depersonalization of the industrial revolution and the collectivization of imperial advances rendered men, as well as women, subjects and instruments of amorphous institutions," that is, of a time when a Wordsworth had the imagination and courage to represent the ideal in human growth as "feeling intellect." Helen E. Haworth, " 'A Milk-White Lamb That Bleats'? Some Stereotypes of Women in Romantic Literature" (*HAB,* 1973), using different evidence, comes to different conclusions: the Romantics, for the most part, stereotyped women in several roles, all domestic. In a second article, "Romantic Female Writers and the Critics" (*TSLL,* 1976), she argues that women writers were condescended to in a variety of ways by readers and critics. Along the same lines Lynne Agress, *The Feminine Irony: Women on Women in Early Nineteenth-Century English Literature* (1978), proposes that women writers and intellectuals themselves perpetuated society's biases against women (herein the irony of her title) and that, consequently, to know the nineteenth-century woman only through the women who wrote about her is to know her inaccurately. Agress seldom draws on the resources of Romantic poetry even when they are glaringly relevant; besides, her discussions of Dorothy Wordsworth and Austen are inadequate. A strongly psychological thesis is advanced by J. M. Hawthorn in "The Strange Deaths of Sally, Ann, Lucy and Others" (*Trivium,* 1971). The idea is that the Romantic poets used death or death fantasy as a mechanism for gaining control of their own characters or of those they associated with sexual love, that is, women. "Porphyria's Lover" is contrasted with the Lucy poems as a crude use of death fantasy to control the beloved. A less exotic account of women in the poetry of the Romantics is that of Irene Tayler and Gina Luria, whose essay "Gender and Genre: Women in British Romantic Literature" forms a chapter in Marlene Springer's volume *What Manner of Women: Essays on English and American Life and Literature* (1977). If in Romantic poetry women were largely restricted to the role of muse, appearing only as projections of the male poets' own creative egocentricity, in the novel they were allowed both self-exploration and self-determination, making that genre woman's "analogue to the poetry of the male Romantic poets" and, in doing so, initiating a new genre in prose fiction, the Victorian novel. This is a valuable essay.

Both Cooke and Haworth cite Mary Wollstonecraft—Cooke in association with Wordsworth and the promise Romanticism held out to tap the power of the feminine, Haworth in association with the Romantics who perpetuated the female stereotype of domesticity. No one even dimly aware of trends in scholarship can have failed to notice the industry that has grown up around Wollstonecraft in the last several decades. Claire Tomlin (*The Life and Death of Mary Wollstonecraft*, 1974), Edna Nixon (*Mary Wollstonecraft*, 1972), and Ralph Wardle (*Mary Wollstonecraft: A Critical Biography*, 1951)—to name three—have written biographies. Wardle and Carol Poston have edited her letters (1979). And Oxford and other presses have given us new editions of her works. Equally important is the scholarly attention paid to Wollstonecraft's talented daughter, Mary Shelley, by talented Romantics scholars. We now have multiple editions of her masterpiece, *Frankenstein,* with critical commentary by Harold Bloom (1965), M. K. Joseph (1969), and James Rieger (1974). Her stories and tales have been meticulously edited by Charles E. Robinson (1976). And Betty T. Bennett is scrupulously editing her letters, with volumes one and two of a projected three already published. Critical studies keep pace with editorial efforts. For specific titles, see the Shelley chapter. Whatever the final judgment on the part played by the Romantic poets in the liberation of women, such activity on behalf of women writers by Romantics scholars is praiseworthy.

Butler's study (see above) attends to rebels and reactionaries, moving the poets in and out of the categories as particular circumstances and documents dictate. John P. Farrell, in *Revolution as Tragedy: The Dilemma of the Moderate from Scott to Arnold* (1980), has had the happy idea of attending to the moderate—the writer attracted to revolution but also repulsed by it, resulting in a struggle between consciousness and conscience—and in so doing has written the best book on Romantic politics since Woodring's. Farrell's moderates—who include Scott and Byron as well as Carlyle and Arnold—bear some resemblance to the Romantics depicted by Romantic ironist critics: sharing in the developing "historical consciousness" of the period, as they must, they both witness and bear witness to a shift in the concept of the tragic, which is now seen to reside not in the flawed individual but in the flawed world. Like Shakespeare's characters, the moderates seem to exist in what Farrell calls a "dialectical dance," a motion that separates them from both an active past and an anticipated future. The four writers' resourcefulness in illuminating the moderate's dilemma in revolution by resorting to the Shakespearean model, in Farrell's view, elevates the moderate to a position of status, for in the moderate resides the most acute development of the historical consciousness—the keenest perception of revolution, namely, that it is tragic because nothing disappears: "Revolution is simply the ironic form in which history comments on its own continuity." Farrell's study makes it easier to dismiss William Walling's complaint ("Hegel,—hélas!" in *PR,* 1975) that Romantics scholars have failed to produce a method for demonstrating the causal relationship between politics—specifically, the French Revolution—and Romantic literature.

Romantic Philosophy and Romantic Psychology

The theory of Romanticism that stresses organic unity as the visionary ideal of the Romantic poets and organic form as the symbolic expression in art of this vision is at the core of the current debate between the natural supernaturalists and the Romantic ironists discussed above. But others have also questioned the unity theory, especially L. J. Swingle, in a series of articles that, in retrospect, can be seen to lead to a major challenge. "On Reading Romantic Poetry" (*PMLA,* 1971) cautions us against two errors of reading Romantic poetry, that of manipulating it to make it express the doctrine we expect to find there (the "creative" error) and that of condemning it for not providing what we expect (the "condemnatory" error). Rather, Swingle suggests, we should follow a model of reading that allows the poetry to disrupt our equilibrium and to communicate a sense of the experiential data behind the "constructs men impose upon the cosmos." Romantic poetry creates a drama in which the reader is to participate dramatically; open-ended, it asks for open minds. A second article, "Romantic Unity and English Romantic Poetry" (*JEGP,* 1975), deplores the growing fashion of Romantic unity, inspired by Abrams' book, because it obscures the distinctions between the poets' metaphysics and their poems, which are about oppositions, not unities. The tension between what the Romantics envision—harmony—and what they experience—discord—is for some of the poets reconciled ("tension as unity") but not for others who deny such a paradox. Unity is thus not characteristic of the Romantics' experience and, if we read carefully, not what we find when we compare Romantic poets. Still a third article, "The Romantic Emergence: Multiplication of Alternatives and the Problem of Systematic Entrapment" (*MLQ,* 1978), states most clearly Swingle's position. The problematic rather than the attributional approach to defining Romanticism is likely to be most rewarding. In line with recent thinking, he argues that the Romantics' problem was not a skimpy inheritance of systems from the eighteenth century but rather the reverse, an overabundant inheritance. They were faced with a proliferation of systems leading to a "multiplication of seemingly viable but conflicting alternatives." This perspective causes Swingle to claim that "The heartland of English Romantic territory . . . is to be found within the space that opens out between the claims of competing systems." The Romantic mind is in that middle space; "what renders the potentially Romantic mind actively Romantic is the persistence of indeterminism." A kindred spirit is Morris Eaves, who, in "Romantic Expressive Theory and Blake's Idea of the Audience" (*PMLA,* 1980; rev. for *William Blake's Theory of Art,* 1982), also finds a larger role for the reader or audience of Romantic poetry than Abrams' expressive theory seems to allow. The familiar view that in Romantic poetry the artist displaces the audience is not, he claims, the whole story, only part of it, only one phase of the artist-audience relationship. In another phase, Romantic poetry generates an audience and, by extension, an idea of social order, one based on the highly personal, even loving, relationship of poet and reader, to which imagination is the key. Like Swingle, Eaves reminds us of distinctions obscured by the reductive blandishments of theories that promise to comprehend all cases.

Meanwhile G. N. Giordano Orsini, in *Organic Unity in Ancient and Later Poetics: The Philosophical Foundations of Literary Criticism* (1975), reminds us of the obligation to know the derivation of the theory we so freely apply in Romantics criticism. And in *Organic Form: The Life of an Idea* (1972), G. S. Rousseau has edited four essays by himself, G. N. Giordano Orsini, Philip C. Ritterbush, and William K. Wimsatt that explore the implications—philosophical, scientific, and poetic—of the "idea." A useful bibliography of works on organic form completes the volume. Still of interest are two essays focused on the eighteenth century: James Benziger, "Organic Unity: Leibniz to Coleridge" (*PMLA*, 1951), and R. Cohen, "Association of Ideas and Poetic Unity" (*PQ*, 1957). Donald Wesling, "The Inevitable Ear: Freedom and Necessity in Lyric Form: Wordsworth and After" (*ELH*, 1969), provides a picture of literary history in which periods of organic poetry ("form as proceeding") are contrasted with periods lacking such poetry, for example, the period of imagism. Wesling's organic or "continuous poem" is used to classify modern American and English poets. For organic theory in the other arts, there is Philip C. Ritterbush's *The Art of Organic Form* (1968).

Orsini, introducing his subject (see above), insists that scholars master the philosophical underpinnings of criticism. The history of Romantics criticism shows that, in fact, scholars have for years been busy relating the aesthetic ideas and critical precepts of the Romantic poets and prose writers to the philosophical traditions from which they emerged. One of the two essays on the Romantics in *English Literature and British Philosophy: A Collection of Essays*, ed. S. P. Rosenbaum (1971), is M. H. Abrams' "Mechanical and Organic Psychologies of Literary Invention" (the other, by Northrop Frye, is on Blake). If this sort of scholarship seems less popular today, it may well be because so many Romantics scholars are now interdisciplinary in method, mixing philosophy with psychology, linguistics, history, and practical criticism to the end of "interpretation." Even so, there are recent contributions (not yet discussed in this chapter) to the history of ideas. We still have, for example, interest in Romantic Platonism. David Newsome, *Two Classes of Men: Platonism and English Romantic Thought* (1974), starting from Coleridge's famous remark in the *Table Talk* for 2 July 1830—"Every man is born an Aristotelian, or a Platonist . . . . They are the two classes of men, beside which it is next to impossible to conceive a third"—studies the role of Platonism, actual and supposed, in the philosophical speculations of the Romantic poets and some of their disciples. (Many years before, L. I. Bredvold examined "The Tendency toward Platonism in Neo-Classical Esthetics" [*ELH*, 1934], and later Kathleen Raine explored "Thomas Taylor, Plato and the English Romantic Movement" [*BJA*, 1968; *SR*, 1968].) Wendell V. Harris, *The Omnipresent Debate: Empiricism and Transcendentalism in Nineteenth-Century English Prose* (1981), writes about the same division that interests Newsome but thinks his own terms are preferable to Coleridge's. Coleridge is the only one of the poets (by virtue of his prose) to figure in Harris' treatise. Neither Harris nor Newsome is immediately concerned with critical theory. But John O. Hayden, *Polestar of the Ancients: The Aristotelian Tradition in Classical and English Literary Criticism* (1979), offers an alternative to Abrams' postulates in *The Mirror and the Lamp,* rejecting Abrams' four divisions (mimetic, pragmatic, expressive, objective) of criticism in favor of three divisions—evaluation, literary theory, and creative theory. Focusing on the second, which he divides into Aristotelian, Neoclassical Rationalist, and Romantic, Hayden then proceeds to locate Wordsworth and Coleridge—indeed, all the so-called High Romantics—in the Aristotelian category. Romantic literary theory is that of pure poesis, of art for art's sake. With something more than scholarly enthusiasm, Ernest Lee Tuveson, *The Avatars of Thrice Great Hermes: An Approach to Romanticism* (1982), urges that, if we distinguish between hermeticism and Neoplatonism, we understand Romanticism better, for "in its truest guise" hermeticism is democratic. Romanticism, he believes, not only benefited from hermetist ideas but also did much to spread them widely.

Both Wallace Jackson and Martin Kallich have also followed Orsini's injunction and given us studies linking philosophy with critical theory. Jackson, in *Immediacy: The Development of a Critical Concept from Addison to Coleridge* (1973), traces the development of "immediacy" or "aesthetic affectivity" as a criterion for aesthetic judgment and as an explanation for aesthetic creativity. As such it is one of the stones from which the Romantic concept of imagination was carved. Kallich, in *The Association of Ideas and Critical Theory in Eighteenth-Century England* (1971), provides the history of a psychological method in English criticism, setting the stage for the first generation Romantics and, Kallich suggests, for much critical thinking since. See also R. Cohen, "Association of Ideas and Poetic Unity" (cited above).

It is, of course, philosophy as aesthetics that literary scholars are most prone to study. Robert C. Holub, in "The Rise of Aesthetics in the Eighteenth Century" (*CLS,* 1978), sees the rise of aesthetics as coincident with the movement to distinguish aesthetics from philosophy—a visible but incoherent process in which other branches of philosophy (metaphysics and theology) decline as aesthetics emerges. General studies of Romantic aesthetics written before 1970 include Annie E. Powell's (Mrs. A. E. Dodds's) *The Romantic Theory of Poetry: An Examination in the Light of Croce's Aesthetic* (1926), M. H. Abrams' *The Mirror and the Lamp: Romantic Theory and the Critical Tradition* (1953), Raymond Immerwahr's "The First Romantic Aesthetics" (*MLQ,* 1960), P. W. K. Stone's *The Art of Poetry, 1750–1820* (1967), Herbert Mainusch's *Romantik Ästhetik: Untersuchungen zur englischen Kunstlehre des späten 18. und frühen 19. Jahrhunderts* (1969), and M. A. Goldberg's *The Poetics of Romanticism: Toward a Reading of John Keats* (1969). Obviously, these writers differ in scope, approach, and point of view. Stone, for example, is inclined to see more originality in Romantic poetics than Goldberg is. And Immerwahr traces the aesthetics of Romantic poetry to the medieval popular romance by way of landscape gardening. Abrams' book, discussed earlier, clearly dominates the field.

One of the more intriguing subjects of aesthetics is beauty, with or without its frequent companion "the sublime" and occasional companion "the picturesque." Jerome Stolnitz, in " 'Beauty': Some Stages in the History of an Idea" (*JHI,* 1961), traced the decline of beauty in modern aesthetics to the eighteenth century, where it first began to lose ground because of its intimate connection with the concept of genres. Stolnitz's other article of the same year, "On the Origins of 'Aesthetic Disinterestedness'" (*JAAC,* 1961), prompted supplementary notes in the same journal on "critical disinterestedness" (by Marcia Allentuck) and "religious disinterestedness" (by Rémy G. Saisselin) and finally a second article, by Jerome Schiller, proposing "An Alternative to 'Aesthetic Disinterestedness'" (*JAAC,* 1964). A more recent article by Stolnitz, "'The Aesthetic Attitude' in the Rise of Modern Aesthetics" (*JAAC,* 1978), reiterated his argument that the rise of disinterestedness and the decline of beauty—that is, modern aesthetics—is an eighteenth- and early nineteenth-century development. Wladyslaw Tatarkiewicz, "The Great Theory of Beauty and Its Decline" (*JAAC,* 1972), also credited the Romantics with helping to bring on beauty's decline. Albert Hofstadter, meantime, offered a rather different idea of beauty and modern aesthetics in "The Aesthetic Impulse" (*JAAC,* 1973), which characterizes the aesthetic impulse as one toward beauty followed by the impulse to move away from beauty (i.e., the antiaesthetic); both impulses are stages of more basic human impulses such as that for freedom. Romanticism is one example of the antiaesthetic stage because Romantic art shows that human freedom is not finally expressible through art. And we are still living in this stage. Kathleen Raine's "An Essay on the Beautiful" (*SoR,* 1979) attributes the Romantics' notion of beauty to Thomas Taylor in particular.

Besides the items discussed immediately above and in the section on the Romantic sublime, there is W. J. Hipple, Jr.'s *The Beautiful, the Sublime, and the Picturesque in Eighteenth-Century British Poetic Theory* (1957), an attempt to differentiate these three aesthetic categories. Perhaps the best essay on "the picturesque moment" in art is Martin Price's piece by that name in Hilles and Bloom's *From Sensibility to Romanticism.*

The three s's—sincerity, sentimentalism, and sensibility—also continue to surface. To Henri Peyre's *Literature and Sincerity* (1963); Patricia M. Ball's "Sincerity: The Rise and Fall of a Critical Term" (*MLR,* 1964); and Herbert Read's *The True Voice of Feeling: Studies in English Romantic Poetry* (1953) and "The Romantic Revolution," in *The Tenth Muse: Essays in Criticism* (1957), we must add Leon Guilhamet's *The Sincere Ideal: Studies on Sincerity in Eighteenth-Century English Literature* (1974), a modest historical account of the development of sincerity as a literary standard, referring to the ideal both of a perfectly guileless human behavior and of an uncorrupted social state. Guilhamet praises David Perkins' *Wordsworth and the Poetry of Sincerity* (1964) for establishing the merits of his subject. His final chapter demonstrates how "the giants of sincerity," Blake and Wordsworth, are related in their concern for sincerity to the earlier figures Guilhamet has treated at length. And, of course, there is Lionel Trilling's searching volume *Sincerity and Authenticity* (1972), which begins with an account of the origin and rise of sincerity, "a salient, perhaps a definitive characteristic of Western culture for some four hundred years," and proceeds to tell of its fall in the twentieth century, to be replaced by authenticity. Donald Davie, "On Sincerity: From Wordsworth to Ginsberg" (*Encounter,* 1968), argues that the so-called new "confessional" poetry of Robert Lowell and others is not new at all; rather, "Confessional poetry has come back with a vengeance; for many years now it is the poetry that has been written by the most serious and talented poets, alike in America and Britain." About such poetry the most appropriate question to ask is, "Is the poet sincere?" Considered "an impertinent and illegitimate question" by the New Critics, it "can never again be out of order."

Sentimentalism—as Guilhamet indicates, very closely related to sincerity—is for Richard O. Allen, in "If You Have Tears: Sentimentalism as Soft Romanticism" (*Genre*, 1975), a serious alternative in life and in the literature about life to other, harder forms of Romanticism. Many novels, past and present, actually intermix the two. A better account of the term is in R. F. Brissenden's *Virtue and Distress* (1974), in the chapter entitled " 'Sentimentalism': An Attempt at Definition."

More important is sensibility, the term that has been used as a label for the later eighteenth century; see, for example, Northrop Frye's "Towards Defining an Age of Sensibility" (*ELH*, 1956; rpt. *Fables of Identity: Studies in Poetic Mythology*, 1963). But Roland Mortier refuses "sensibility" or other such labels for the end of the eighteenth century in his " 'Sensibility,' 'Neoclassicism,' or 'Preromanticism'?" (*Eighteenth-Century Studies Presented to Arthur M. Wilson*, ed. Peter Gay, 1972), on the grounds that neoclassicism and sensibility or pre-Romanticism exist happily together, enriching each other; his illustrations are from ruins and tombs. G. S. Rousseau's "Nerves, Spirits, and Fibres: Towards Defining the Origins of Sensibility," in *Studies in the Eighteenth Century*, volume 3, edited by R. F. Brissenden and J. C. Eade (1976), traces the origins of sensibility to the later seventeenth century, following a suggestion of R. S. Crane in "Suggestions toward a Genealogy of 'The Man of Feeling' " (*ELH*, 1943; rpt. *The Idea of the Humanities*, 1967). Surprisingly, Rousseau's exercise in defining sensibility turns out to support Harold Bloom's definition of Romanticism, which, as Rousseau reminds us, commences in *The Visionary Company* with "The Heritage of Sensibility." Bloom, with Frederick W. Hilles, edited a collection of essays charting the movement *From Sensibility to Romanticism* (1965). Since many titles on sensibility do not make the connection, readers are hereby referred to Rousseau's excellent notes and to pages 8–10 of *ERP3* for additional items.

Robert Currie's *Genius: An Ideology in Literature* (1974) takes up another aspect of aesthetics important to Romanticism. His theory of genius as the alienated individual who will save others from their alienation—whether it be alienation from the self or from society—is not complimentary to the Romantic genius or hero, the concept of which "derives its dynamic from the inescapable deficiency of the many who fall short of the ideal." The Romantic genius' transcendental realm tends, thus, to be highly selective, if not elitist. Currie's book should be read in connection with Paul Kaufman's "Heralds of Original Genius" (*Essays in Memory of Barrett Wendell*, 1926), Hans Thüme's *Beiträge zur Geschichte des Geniebergriffs in England* (1927), and Ruth O. Rose's "Poetic Hero-Worship in the Late Eighteenth Century" (*PMLA*, 1933). The only contribution that falls between is Geoffrey Hartman's "Romantic Poetry and the Genius Loci" (*The Disciplines of Criticism: Essays in Literary Theory, Interpretation, and History*, ed. Peter Demetz et al., 1968; rpt. *Beyond Formalism*, 1970), which characterizes the later eighteenth-century poets as attempting to marry the visionary

and prophetic temperament (the ancient genius loci) with the rational temperament (the English poetic genius).

Finally, there is the encompassing aesthetic of taste. By consulting W. J. Bate's
From Classic to Romantic: Premises of Taste in Eighteenth-Century England
(1946; rpt. 1961) and Stanley Edgar Hyman's *Poetry and Criticism: Four Revolutions in Literary Taste* (1961), one can learn the basic history of "taste" as an aesthetic premise and critical tool. (For the titles of several essays before Bate, see
ERP3 21.) Bate's volume is, in fact, still one of the best chronicles of changing
aesthetics and their effect on art in the eighteenth century. Unlike some of the
authors mentioned above, Bate is not jealous of the reputation of the eighteenth-
century writers or of the Romantics, as his two magisterial and sympathetic biographies of Johnson and Keats attest. In this he, along with Earl Wasserman in *The
Subtler Language: Critical Readings of Neoclassic and Romantic Poems* (1959),
has done much to repudiate the protectionist strategies of other scholars,
promoting a scholarship that stresses continuity, evolution, and compromise
rather than discontinuity, abrupt change, and originality. His later *The Burden of
the Past and the English Poet* (1970) unites the Augustans, the Romantics, and all
poets since the Renaissance in a common dilemma that puts their differences,
major and minor, into perspective. Bate's scholarship of applied humanism coupled with intellectual rigor and formidable erudition is difficult to improve on.
The taste for pleasure in art has interested another well-known humanist scholar,
the late Lionel Trilling, whose essay "The Fate of Pleasure" (*Partisan Review,* 1963,
and *Romanticism Reconsidered,* 1963; rpt. *Beyond Culture,* 1968) attributes to
Wordsworth and Keats this bold innovation in the aesthetics of art and then proceeds to trace the cultural ramifications of their audacity.

It was, of course, Coleridge who in the Romantic period decried the dearth
of philosophy in Britain and evolved, as a partial remedy for the shortcomings of
educational institutions, his concept of the clerisy. Newsome, above, gives attention to the Platonic elements in the concept. Ben Knights devotes a short book to
the subject, *The Idea of the Clerisy in the Nineteenth Century* (1978). Coleridge's
and Wordsworth's interest in the Bell or "mutual instruction" system of education is the subject of Philip E. Hager's "The English Romantics and Education"
(*AntigR,* 1976). Both poets initially approved Bell's system, which Bell himself introduced in Kendal, but Wordsworth eventually suspected that it discouraged development of the imagination. The great educational value of Romantic poetry is
the subject of Helmut Viebrock's "A Defence of (the Teaching of English Romantic) Poetry" (*Archiv für das Studium der Neueren Sprachen und Literaturen,*
1975). Coleridge's mentor Boyer would not likely agree with Viebrock's somewhat murky notion of pedagogy. For information in highly readable form about
the schools and schoolmasters of Wordsworth, Coleridge, Byron, Shelley, Keats,
and Southey, see Morris Marples' *Romantics at School* (1967). The complete
range of schools available to middle- and upper-class boys at the time is represented by the six poets.

A great deal of what has gone before in this chapter testifies directly or indirectly to the pervasive role of psychology and psychological theory in modern lit-

erary criticism. Once scholars were likely to complain bitterly about this; now most of them expect it. Senior scholars—Frye, Bloom, Hartman, Langbaum—and junior—Ragussis, Onorato, George—alike shape their methods, in part or in total, according to the concepts of Freud, Jung, or some lesser-known predecessor or successor. In this respect especially, Romantics scholarship has become unapologetically interdisciplinary. There remain to be mentioned here, consequently, only a few items not already treated elsewhere. Alan Weissman, in "The English Romantics and Modern Psychology" (*Centerpoint,* 1975), emphasizes the fertile ground of Romanticism for the combined application of psychology and literary criticism by pointing to anticipations of Freudian and Jungian theory in the English Romantics and faults the twentieth century for ignoring their fine insights into psychology. Jason Y. Hall, in "Gall's Phrenology: A Romantic Psychology" (*SIR,* 1977), calls our attention to a Romantic psychology—Romantic because it relied on such concepts as organicism, striving, and uniqueness—much in advance of Freud's or Jung's, one embraced by some of the later Romantics in France and America and some of the Victorian novelists. Gerald B. Kauvar, in "The Psychological Structure of English Romantic Poetry" (*Psychoanalytic Review,* 1977), identifies the central modality of English Romantic poetry as a symbolic debate between the legitimate claims of the daily world and the equally legitimate and real claims of the imagination. He then restates this modality in a series of psychoanalytic terms. Arguing that the debate is not progressive, he identifies Romanticism's most successful poems as those that focus on the attempt (usually a failure) to develop beyond the nurtured state, to resolve Oedipal conflicts. A still more recent item is Simon Stuart's combined application of psychology and literary criticism in *New Phoenix Wings: Reparation and Literature* (1979). Here the psychology is Melanie Klein's theory of reparation as the origin of creativity; the literature to which it is applied includes poems of Blake and Wordsworth, the central literary figures in his study. Klein also figures prominently in Barbara A. Schapiro's *The Romantic Mother: Narcissistic Patterns in Romantic Poetry* (1983), though Heinz Kohut and Otto Kernberg provide the theoretical framework for this analysis of the relationship of the Romantic poets (Shelley, Keats, Coleridge, Wordsworth) to the woman, the image of which, Schapiro argues, is central to their poetry. As the title implies, she focuses chiefly on the poets' root relationship with the woman (that with the mother), which affects not only poetic imagery but poetic style and theme as well. Ambivalence in this relationship, when internalized, results in a split ego, which in turn results in the condition of pathological narcissism peculiarly strong in the English Romantics. But Schapiro distinguishes "differences in the levels of narcissistic regression as well as in the strength and intactness of the ego involved." Wordsworth emerges as the poet most successful in overcoming narcissism, allowing women their wholeness and humanity. All four poets, however, in grappling with a condition that is also ours, have much to teach us. Schapiro's analysis is undertaken in the belief that it can shed light on the structure of Romantic poems, sometimes revealing coherence where none was thought to exist. Finally, Ross Woodman, in "Shaman, Poet, and Failed Initiate: Reflections on Romantic and Jungian Psychology" (*SIR,* 1980), provides a searching critique of Romanticism through Jung's own critique of Romanticism, which Woodman considers one of the best. In Jung's analysis and Woodman's assessment, the Romantics' failure is symbolized by the Ancient Mariner, who, though he does make the return journey (not all Romantics do), denies the knowledge he has gained. The importance of Romanticism's failure is that it "demonstrates the discrepancy existing at present between the demands of our global village . . . and the level of consciousness at which we continue to function."

Romanticism and Language

Romantic poetry has benefited in the last few years from the current interest in linguistic theory and its implications for literary criticism. The premier scholar in the field, however, remains Josephine Miles, whose work, as Michael Ragussis attests, few critics have advanced. Many of her earlier essays are collected in *The Vocabulary of Poetry* (1946) and *The Primary Language of Poetry in the 1740's and 1840's* (1950). Changes in the diction of poetry with which Miles is concerned in these volumes become important evidence for changes in the mode of poetry with which she is concerned in "The Romantic Mode of Poetry" (*ELH,* 1953), subsequently one of four chapters on the Romantics in *Eras & Modes in English Poetry* (1957; rev. ed. 1965). In general, the book argues for the validity of the period concept of English literature; in particular, the chapters on the Romantics demonstrate the advent of a new or Romantic mode of poetry, the lyrical narrative of dramatic confrontation, or the new ballad. This new structure, which serves a new substance—a new attitude—justifies, in Miles's opinion, our grouping of the five major poets (but not Blake) as Romantics. Her latest volume, *Poetry and Change: Donne, Milton, Wordsworth, and the Equilibrium of the Present* (1974), catches up more recent essays but, like its predecessors, bears witness to Miles's double interest in language and art—the cooperation of language and art in poetry—and her belief that literature provides an especially "fine frame for the study of change." Though changes in the language of poetry support period concepts, they are not revolutionary. From the point of view of diction, consequently, Romanticism is not a revolutionary phenomenon. Miles's admirers will appreciate her later article "Values in Language; Or, Where Have *Goodness, Truth* and *Beauty* Gone?" (*CritI,* 1976) for its generous and encouraging answer to the question the title poses. (For a contrary view of Miles's work, see Robert Gleckner's review of *Poetry and Change, BNL,* 1976). If any one word can be said to differentiate Romantic from Augustan poetry it is probably "joy." That this should be so is the topic of John Lucas' "The Poet in His Joy: How and Why a Word Changes Its Meaning During the Eighteenth Century," the third chapter in his *Romantic to Modern Literature: Essays and Ideas of Culture 1750–1900* (1982). Clifford Siskin's "Revision Romanticized: A Study in Literary Change" (*RP&P,* 1983) seeks "to historicize our understanding of the Romantic use of revision" in the service of change. In particular, Siskin points to several literary changes characterizing the shift from the Augustan Age to the Romantic period in which revision plays a central role: "the rise of developmental thinking, the forging of sympathetic author-reader relationships, and the formation of interpretive procedures." The changes, in turn, account for connections between Romantic discourse and our own.

Other books on the language of poetry mentioned in *ERP3* still worthy of attention are Donald Davie's *Purity of Diction in English Verse* (1952), Bernard Groom's *The Diction of Poetry from Spenser to Bridges* (1956), and R. A. Foakes's *The Romantic Assertion: A Study in the Language of Nineteenth-Century Poetry* (1958). Of these, Foakes's book, which distinguishes the poetry of the nineteenth century from that of the twentieth as poetry of assertion, not of conflict—as poetry committed to "images of impression," not to metaphor—is probably the most rewarding. Davie's book, as a 1966 postscript makes clear, is ultimately a manifesto for "the movement" poetry of the 1950s. Newer books are Arthur Sherbo's *English Poetic Diction from Chaucer to Wordsworth* (1976), Irving Massey's *The Uncreating Word: Romanticism and the Object* (1970), Michael Ragussis' *The Subterfuge of Art: Language and the Romantic Tradition* (1978), and Jerzy Peterkiewicz' *The Other Side of Silence: The Poet at the Limits of Language* (1970). Sherbo is interested in restoring the good name of poetic diction, which even Wordsworth helps him to do. Massey is interested in reversing the movement toward "unnamability," to which Romanticism—the intersection of the objective and subjective view of the world—contributed by fostering a distrust of language. Eventually, reality demands a name; the ethics of silence is, in Massey's view, not only undesirable but also unnecessary. Ragussis, following Lawrence, who followed Freud, is interested in the literary tradition—Romantic and post-Romantic—of art as a cure for regression. The language of art can function within the text to create a dialogue between heart and mind that effects cures no less impressive than those wrought by the dialogue of analyst and analysand. Wordsworth is the "omega" of the tradition. Peterkiewicz is not so disturbed about silence as Massey, for poets today are at the frontier of silence, which must be crossed if they are to enter the real present. Peterkiewicz' poets, among whom the Romantics figure prominently, desire to die with poetry, to go beyond words—the sublime of poetry. He envisions the poet creating without language and, thus, communicating directly, in "some unrecordable form moulded from silence." Robert Gleckner sees the "silence" of the Romantics, in "Romanticism and the Self-annihilation of Language" (*Criticism,* 1976), as at once the depth of their despair at the fragile, mortal nature of human discourse and the height of their joy in total communication and communion. The latter, the "self-annihilation" of the title, is the Romantic concept of language, the loss of which in our culture Gleckner laments. Frank D. McConnell, on the other hand, in "Romanticism, Language, Waste: A Reflection on Poetics and Disaster" (*BuR,* 1972), rues the stranglehold Romanticism has on us; structuralism and linguistics have merely confirmed us in seeing resemblances between our imaginative lives and those of the Romantics: we both are preoccupied with language as structure; we both are radically skeptical of certitude in any form; we both produce waste in reading and writing alike.

Ragussis concludes with an epilogue on the echo, which he sees as the word's criticism or the spirit of irony present in the mind's reflection of itself. John Hollander's *The Figure of Echo: A Mode of Allusion in Milton and After* (1981) is concerned with echo in one poet's mind of another poet, but his echo also possesses revisionary power, generating new figuration. The Romantics are indispensable to Hollander's point. James K. Chandler, "Romantic Allusiveness" (*CritI,* 1982), is also concerned with echo, but specifically with the poets' rhetorical use of allusion, a neglected aspect of Romantic rhetoric. Examining the intention at work in Romantic lyrics, he finds that allusion appears as the "intentional representation of unconscious influence"—that is, as a rhetorical slip of the tongue, followed by the discovery of allusion. Romantic poems can thus be viewed as dramas "about . . . poetic influence"; the crowning example is Wordsworth's echo of *Paradise Lost* early in Book 1 of *The Prelude,* which consequently becomes a reflection on its own composition. Oxymoron, like allusive echo, is not peculiar to Romantic poetry; but Jean Perrin, in "Imaginaire et rhétorique: l'oxymoron dans la poésie romantique anglaise" (*Recherches et travaux, l'imaginaire,* 1977), thinks it a key to the Romantic imagination.

Romantic Images and Themes

The scholars who pay tribute to M. H. Abrams in *High Romantic Argument* concentrate on his "use of changes in radical constitutive metaphors as one key to important shifts in the intellectual and cultural history of the West." And with good reason: through *The Mirror and the Lamp, Natural Supernaturalism* (marriage metaphor), and "The Correspondent Breeze: A Romantic Metaphor" (*KR,* 1957; rev. for *English Romantic Poets: Modern Essays in Criticism,* 1960; 2nd ed. 1975), he is memorably identified with this approach to Romanticism, one now widely adopted by his fellow Romantics scholars. One who follows Abrams in viewing Romanticism as a great cultural shift is Patricio V. Monis, who in "The Romantic Literary Symbol" (*Unitas,* 1975) argues that the literary symbol used today is a new mode of perception developed by the Romantics to deal with the ontological reaction to the "stark mechanistic universe of the age of science." Monis eventually moves on from English Romanticism to the French symbolists and, in doing so, recalls Frank Kermode's *Romantic Image* (1957), the notable study of the continuity of Romantic and twentieth-century poetry as demonstrated through images of isolation and suffering as the sources of joy, pain, and fear from which art is born. Yeats's dancer is the image on which Kermode's thesis ultimately focuses. Similarly, David Perkins' study of Romantic symbolism in *The Quest for Permanence: The Symbolism of Wordsworth, Shelley, and Keats* (1959; rpt. 1965) discovers the key to Romantic poetry in its symbols, especially those that achieve a sense of permanence for art and artist in a world "Where youth grows pale, and spectre-thin, and dies." More recently, Suzanne Nalbantian has contributed *The Symbol of the Soul from Hölderlin to Yeats: A Study of Meton-*

ymy (1977). Nalbantian, careful not to overgeneralize, finds no uniform pattern among the Romantics but rather three uses of the soul symbol: to convey the ascendant nature of human beings and their transcendent moments, to communicate, conversely, their depths of being and descendent propensities, and to represent their horizontal position as souls in jeopardy. This last forecasts the direction and image the soul takes as it departs from characteristic Romantic conceptions and uses of it. Wordsworth and Hölderlin particularly associate the soul with prisons, the subject of a book (*La prison romantique: Essai sur l'imaginaire,* 1975) and an essay ("The Happy Prison: A Recurring Romantic Metaphor," in Thorburn and Hartman) by Victor Brombert, who is little concerned with English writers other than Byron but whose ideas—especially that of the double movement within the prison theme—are often suggestive for English Romantics more generally.

Terry J. Castle's "Lab'ring Bards: Birth *Topoi* and English Poetics 1660–1820" (*JEGP,* 1979) takes us from permanence to change, from soul to body. Castle examines the shifts in the significance of metaphors for poetic activity drawn from bodily functions between 1660 and 1820, looking especially at the metaphor of the poet as one who conceives, gives birth to, and nurtures a child. She concludes, validating Abrams' theory of metaphor, that the Romantics reverse the Augustans, who disliked the analogy because of its natural, organic implications, converting their predecessors' distaste to pleasure. Thomas R. Frosch's "The New Body of English Romanticism" (*Soundings,* 1971) also derives from Abrams in surveying a development in the Romantic poets that Frosch labels a "secularization of the resurrection" and in examining the ways in which this development informs the workings of visionary imagery, specifically the imagery of the body, which the Romantics perceive as both diseased and renovated. Both individually and communally, this body is one in which all the senses participate in conversation, the ear equally with the eye, resulting in a dialectic of continuous resurrection—a marriage of the Romantic commitment to image (to the eye) and of the Romantic recognition that images are impossible. Frosch's impressive article anticipates his important book on Blake. Here perhaps I should mention again Paul J. Korshin's "The Development of Abstracted Typology in England, 1650–1820," in *Literary Uses of Typology from the Late Middle Ages to the Present* (ed. Earl Miner, 1976; reworked for *Typologies in England, 1650–1820,* 1982), which enumerates the kinds and causes of typology in the Romantic period, concluding with the generalization that the "aspect of the figural system which appealed to most English Romantic poets is natural typology, or typology abstracted from theological concerns to natural phenomena and normal aspects of human behavior." The breeze of Abrams' essay applies here. So, too, the natural phenomena singled out for attention by other scholars. Robert M. Maniquis, in "The Puzzling *Mimosa*: Sensitivity and Plant Symbols in Romanticism" (*SIR,* 1969), demonstrates that the Romantics used the mimosa to imply not only a state of feeling but also a state of being. It is one of the crossing points of science and poetry. August Wilhelm Hoffmeister, in *Die Blume in der Dichtung der englischen Romantik* (1970), analyzes meticulously the flower imagery of Romantic poetry, with a backward look at *The Seasons* and *The Botanic Garden* before plunging into *Songs of*

Innocence and of Experience. And one flower, the rose, is the subject of a chapter in Barbara Seward's *The Symbolic Rose* (1960). H. B. de Groot, "The Ouroboros and the Romantic Poets: A Renaissance Emblem in Blake, Coleridge, and Shelley" (*ES,* 1969), examines the use of the circling snake figure by Romantic poets; the significance of the emblem, he finds, varies from poet to poet. In a rather obvious article, "Romanticism's Singing Bird" (*SEL,* 1974), Frank Doggett shows the bird as typically associated with the poet or with the muse of the poet; it also recaptures from the Middle Ages its association with the human soul, for which see Beryl Rowland's beautifully conceived and produced *Birds with Human Souls: A Guide to Bird Symbolism* (1978). She begins with the albatross.

Grander natural phenomena are also subjects of inquiry. One should begin by citing Arden Reed's *Romantic Weather: The Climates of Coleridge and Baudelaire* (1983), for by Reed's account Romantic literature is full of weather, albeit a different weather from that found in neoclassical literature. The Enlightenment repressed the weather; Romanticism, "itself . . . a kind of weather or atmospheric disturbance [variously described as] storms, frontal systems, isobars, low pressure zones," tended to lift the repression. Reed's claim that "to take a reading of the weather requires taking literary criticism out of doors" is no mere boast. The book is much more than a study of metaphor, but it is W. H. Auden, in *The Enchafèd Flood or The Romantic Iconography of the Sea* (1951; published the preceding year with a different subtitle), who attempts to understand Romanticism by isolating the image of the sea. He takes as his text Wordsworth's dream of the fleeing Bedouin in *The Prelude,* but before he is done, *Moby-Dick* has become as important to his thesis as Wordsworth's poem. Lena Beatrice Morton's *The Influence of the Sea upon English Poetry from the Anglo-Saxon Period to the Victorian Period* (1976) would appear, from its format, to be a published dissertation and, from its bibliography, one written many years ago. She finds Romantic sea poetry markedly different from that of earlier periods, but this difference—the Romantics spiritualize the sea—would not seem to alter the way we read this poetry. Some years ago, Marjorie Hope Nicolson, in *Mountain Gloom and Mountain Glory: The Development of the Aesthetics of the Infinite* (1959), attended to that other grand natural phenomenon so crucial to Romantic poets, tall or short, for acquiring perspective and surveying prospects. Now Fred V. Randel, in "The Mountaintops of English Romanticism" (*TSLL,* 1981), has taken up the subject—or rather one aspect of it: that type of Romantic poem "which ponders what it means to be on top of a land mass that juts up above its surroundings." Randel develops a chapter of literary history that affirms the dialectical character of Romantic poetry; the poems he explores debate the views attained from their mountaintop experiences.

Harmony is on occasion the mood of the mountaintop, even if, for the Romantics, the harmony of the spheres has given way to the harmony of organic nature. Sue E. Coffman, in *Music of Finer Tone: Musical Imagery of the Major Romantic Poets* (1979), is curious to know why the Romantics found music to be such an appropriate metaphor and why they sometimes praised music itself, given their notable lack of interest in musical performance. She discovers the answers in the capacity of music to suggest organic unity and harmony. The Romantics, she claims, actually contributed to the philosophy of music by supplementing the music of the concert hall with the music of nature. John Hollander's lecture *Images of Voice: Music and Sound in Romantic Poetry* (1970) goes further in suggesting that English poetry, in walking out on music and into nature, substituted the music of sound for the sound of music. Erland Anderson's *Harmonious Madness: A Study of Musical Metaphors in the Poetry of Coleridge, Shelley and Keats* (1975) discusses the poets' knowledge of music and their use of this knowledge. Musical metaphors, he claims, are crucial in Coleridge, Shelley, and Keats but not in Blake, Wordsworth, and Byron. Anderson's clumsy prose belabors the obvious and gives the reader little credit for any knowledge of music.

Robley Evans' "The House and the Well in English Romantic Poetry," in *Symposium on Romanticism: An Interdisciplinary Meeting* [Connecticut Coll.], edited by Pierre Deguise and Rita Terras (1977), attempts, with special attention to Wordsworth and D. G. Rossetti, to chart Romantic careers by images of movement (water) and stasis (house). Although a suggestive article, its generalizations about Romantics and Victorians are not fully warranted by the evidence. With Evans' article we have a bridge from natural phenomena to human phenomena, among them, human love. Frederick L. Beaty, in *Light from Heaven: Love in British Romantic Literature* (1972), has provided us with the only comprehensive book on this obviously important subject, imaged by several Romantic poets as "light from heaven." Beginning with the proposition that the Romantics refused to acknowledge the incompatibility of love and reason, Beaty proceeds to argue that love is a pervasive concept associated with nearly all of the Romantics' favorite speculations; in particular, it tends to become for them the social and spiritual counterpart of the imagination and the individual. Romantic "kinds" of love from comic to philanthropic are the subjects of Beaty's five chapters. One type—"marital"—is also the subject of Susan M. Levin's "The Great Spousal Verse: The Marriage Metaphor in English Romantic Poetry" (*SCR,* 1975), which finds motives for the "magnificent marriages" in Romantic art in the inability of Romantic artists "to establish successful marriages in real life...." Gerald Enscoe's *Eros and the Romantics: Sexual Love as a Theme in Coleridge, Shelley and Keats* (1967) attends to the theme of sexual love as it illustrates the shift in cosmic and moral orientation in Romanticism—especially, where sexual love is concerned, a shift away from the orthodox Christian ethos and toward the modern psychological ethos. As Enscoe sees it, this shift is not completed by the Romantics. Drawing on Peckham's "dynamic organicism," he presents the three poets as initiating the change from love as an inherently evil force leading the individual to damnation to love as a potentially good force leading the individual to psychic regeneration. That the Romantics, their publishers, and their readers were far more "Victorian" about verbal accounts of sexual love than common opinion has it is the subject of Helen E. Haworth's " 'The Victorian Romantics'—Indecency, Indelicacy, Pornography and Obscenity in Romantic Poetry" (*PLL,* 1974). Jean H. Hagstrum, in "Eros and Psyche: Some Versions of Romantic Love and Delicacy" (*CritI,* 1977), wishes to point up the imaginative affinity of the pre-Romantics and Romantics for this myth. He chooses to concentrate on one interpretation, that which stresses the delicacy of narcissistic solitude and involution, leading to unisex figures: "the achievement of delicacy we have discussed anticipates an influential modern idea, that to feminize life may in fact be to civilize it."

Louise Vinge's *The Narcissus Theme in Western European Literature up to the Early Nineteenth Century* (1967) mentions the English Romantics only in the last few pages. The most indelicate of mythical figures, Pan, is fully explored in the Romantic period by Patricia Merivale, in *Pan the Goat-God: His Myth in Modern Times* (1969). For the most part she hears but does not see Pan in Romantic poetry, where he loses the allegorical vividness he displays in earlier literature. By universalizing Pan, the Romantics make him invisible. Prometheus, on the other hand, is both universalized and highly visible, according to Christian Kreutz, in *Das Prometheussymbol in der Dichtung der englischen Romantik* (1963). Kreutz argues that Prometheus symbolizes both the political and the spiritual crisis of the age and the creative and human potential that responds to crisis: "Schließlich ist Prometheus das Symbol des Menschen." Raymond Trousson's *Le Thème de Prométhée dans la littérature européenne* (1964; 2nd ed. 1976) gives full treatment to the English Romantics, including Mary Shelley. Walter A. Strauss's *Descent and Return: The Orphic Theme in Modern Literature* (1971) argues that the Orpheus myth is the antithesis of the Prometheus myth and, further, that all modern literature falls "within the area delimited by these two points of reference, rebellion [Prometheus] and refusal [Orpheus]." The English Romantic poets can be split between the two myths, and their names appear in Strauss's book, but he focuses on Continental writers because "the theme of Orpheus does not figure prominently or decisively in modern English literature." (Léon Cellier, *L'Épopée humanitaire et les grands mythes romantiques* [1954; rev. 1971], would agree with Strauss on the importance of the Orpheus myth for Continental literature from Romanticism to our own time. See his appendix "Le Romantisme et le mythe d'Orphée.") Articles on other classical figures are Lyna L. Montgomery's "The Phoenix: Its Use as a Literary Device in English from the Seventeenth to the Twentieth Century" (*DHLR*, 1972), which turns up little use in the nineteenth century, and Jerome J. McGann's "The Beauty of the Medusa: A Study in Romantic Literary Iconology" (*SIR*, 1972), which shows that Medusan beauty, Praz to the contrary, was not a negative beauty to Shelley, Pater, Swinburne, or Morris.

Two additional image studies both attest to the dramatic shift in ontology and epistemology in the later eighteenth century. Jacques Bousquet, *Les Thèmes du rêve dans la littérature romantique* (1964), proceeding from a linguistic method, argues that Romantic dreams function to compensate for the monotony of daily life; the same images, sky and hell, of medieval dreams are emptied of their religious and moral content. Romantic dreams to 1850 present a succession of paradises—in the sky, in nature, in platonic love—and a succession of hells—in the underground, in the city, and in the nightmare. Bishop C. Hunt, Jr., in "Travel Metaphors and the Problem of Knowledge" (*MLS*, 1976), detects a new pattern of travel metaphor commencing in the eighteenth-century novel and continuing in Romantic poetry. Where once traveling—a metaphor for learning—was circular, implying that the world can be known, it is now linear, implying the endless extension of knowledge, hence an unknowable world. The linear journeys of Romantic travelers do not square, students will be quick to notice, with the circular journeys of Romantic poets recounted in *Natural Supernaturalism*. For Bernard Blackstone, Georg Roppen, and Richard Sommer, Romantic poetry is by and large travel literature precisely because it is a poetry of movement and the Romantic poets are "mental travellers." Blackstone's *The Lost Travellers: A Romantic Theme with Variations* (1962) works this theme through the six major poets, but Blake is his point of departure. Roppen and Sommer, in *Strangers and Pilgrims: An Essay on the Metaphor of Journey* (1964), trace their metaphor from antiquity to Wordsworth before looking at the English Romantics, for whom the journey has become "The Individual Quest." Blackstone's study is interesting and informative if not especially revealing; the volume by Roppen and Sommer is too clumsy to be of much value. Colette Le Yaouanc's *L'Orient dans la poésie anglaise de l'époque romantique (1798–1824)* (1975) has neither drawback. The book both explains why the Orient appeared in major poetry of the Romantic period and defends Romantic Oriental poetry as a type. With Le Yaouanc's study we move a long way from the traditional view of orientalism as escapism.

Hunt's theory may help to suggest why David Simpson asserts, in *Irony and Authority in Romantic Poetry* (discussed earlier), that the child has replaced the traveler as the dominant metaphor of the Romantic period. Extending the point, Christopher Clausen, in "Tintern Abbey to Little Gidding: The Past Recaptured" (*SR*, 1976; rpt. *The Place of Poetry*, 1981), thinks most important Victorian and twentieth-century poetry is a search for Wordsworth's childhood, that is, a poetry of lost faith associated with a lost childhood—in short, "Tinternabulism." Some of his evidence—poems dominated by churches—is a little shaky; and his poetic tradition, blatantly exclusive. U. C. Knoepflmacher's "Mutations of the Wordsworthian Child of Nature," in *Nature and the Victorian Imagination,* ed. Knoepflmacher and G. B. Tennyson (1977), qualifies the influence of the Wordsworthian and Romantic child on the Victorians, whose attitude is characteristically ambivalent, thanks to a mix of nostalgia and criticism with which they receive this legacy. Jean H. Hagstrum's " 'Such, Such Were the Joys': The Boyhood of the Man of Feeling," in *Changing Taste in Eighteenth Century Art and Literature* by Robert E. Moore and Jean H. Hagstrum (1972), locates the father of Wordsworth's and Coleridge's Romantic child in the pre-Romantic child of the eighteenth century. So does Peter Coveney's *Poor Monkey: The Child in Literature* (1957; rev. as *The Image of Childhood: The Individual and Society: A Study of the Theme in English Literature,* 1967). With the revolution in sensibility in the latter part of the eighteenth century, the "literary tide was full set towards the shores of Feeling, and bore with it the fragile craft of the Romantic child.... With Blake we have the first coordinated utterance of the Romantic Imaginative and spiritually sensitive child." From Blake, Coveney moves on to Wordsworth and Coleridge, evolving, as he proceeds, the thesis that, for the modern writer, the child became a "symbol of the greatest significance for the subjective investigation of the Self," an inquiry that "became the *raison,* and in some cases, the strength of his art." In some instances, notably with Wordsworth, the growth and development resulting from this self-study was outward and progressive; in others, inward and regressive. "The history of the child in nineteenth-century literature does in fact display both the weakness and the strength of all romantic art. . . ." The other chief study of the Romantic child in recent years is Robert Pattison's in *The Child Figure in English Literature* (1978). But Pattison's study is deliberately limited to the conjunction of the child figure in literature with two ideas fundamental to Western culture: the concept of the Fall of man and the concept of original sin. From this perspective the child takes on a new coloring in the Romantic period because it is attached to new sentiments, namely, that the child is evidence neither that human beings by nature must fall nor that by nature they attest to original sin. The cult of feeling founded by Rousseau and propagated by Wordsworth explains how the child is transformed from an object of intellection to one of sentiment. Reinhard Kuhn's method (intertextual), purpose (to achieve a better understanding of real children by proposing a phenomenological description of their fictional counterparts), and scope (Western literature), in *Corruption in Paradise: The Child in Western Literature* (1982), result in only passing reference to the English Romantics, with the exception of Wordsworth, who is central to his penultimate chapter on the resonance of children's voices in modern poetry. If not particularly noteworthy for Romantics studies, Kuhn's book represents a considerable advance on previous investigations of its subject. Rousseau is, of course, also responsible for another Romantic hero, the noble savage, who is the subject of Peter L. Thorslev, Jr.'s "The Wild Man's Revenge," in *The Wild Man Within: An Image in Western Thought from the Renaissance to Romanticism,* ed. Edward Dudley and Maximillian E. Novak (1972). Thorslev identifies several versions of the noble savage or wild man in order to show that he is a projection of writers' psychological needs and cultural attitudes. The wild man's revenge comes about when civilized man is forced to "recognize that the only source of evil, as well as the only sanction of value, is within himself."

Recent studies of the Romantic hero actually have little to do with English Romantic poetry. Walter L. Reed's *Meditations on the Hero in Nineteenth-Century Fiction* (1974) is preoccupied with the novel of several nations. Lilian R. Furst's "The Romantic Hero, or Is He an Anti-Hero?" (*SLitI,* 1976; rpt. *Contours of Romanticism,* 1979) suggests that the Romantic period produced a hybrid type halfway between hero and anti-hero; this hybrid Romantic hero lacks the self-irony that would complete the transformation of hero to anti-hero. Furst draws only on Byron from the English Romantics. Raney Stanford, "The Romantic Hero and That Fatal Selfhood" (*CentR,* 1968), is, like Reed, mostly interested in heroes of fiction. Principally, though, he is eager to see both the Romantic hero and the term "anti-hero" disappear, persuaded that their lingering makes it difficult to appreciate the true heroes of modern fiction, who do exist and are worthy of the name. John Ower's "The Aesthetic Hero: His Innocence, Fall, and Redemption," in *Literature and History,* ed. Harry R. Garvin (1977), which expands on Auden's notion of the aesthetic hero in *The Enchafèd Flood* (see above), is more charitable. Ower traces the aesthetic hero's origins to the spiritual vacuum created by the disintegration of the old world order that commenced in the Renaissance. The Romantics, for whom the aesthetic hero is a paradigm of the spiritual history of Western man in a time of crisis, were preoccupied especially with the second and third stages of this hero's career, his ineluctable fall and problematic redemption. If Byron's Manfred images the fallen hero whose fall is not redeemed because the conflict between traditional and existential value systems is unresolved, his Prometheus and, more so, Shelley's Prometheus shadow forth the hero whose fall is resolved in redemption, mirroring the fall and regeneration of Western culture. This resolution derives from the assimilation of Prometheus to Christ. For Ower, the reconciliation of old metaphysics and new values is not so much a retreat as it is an alternative to existentialism, in the twentieth century as well as in the nineteenth. To James D. Wilson, *The Romantic Heroic Ideal* (1982), the Romantic hero is also an alternative to existentialism and, hence, is more traditional than modern. Earlier studies have erred, he believes, in restricting the hero to a single type, usually the satanic rebel, and in denying his moral identity. Although Wilson argues for variety in the Romantic hero, he subscribes to the idea of a unified Romantic movement: wherever and however the Romantic hero appears, he is defined by the moral ideal of self to which he aspires and by the intensity with which he strives, rarely with success, to attain it.

Two distinct social types—the Jew and the dandy—are studied in Harold Fisch's *The Dual Image: The Figure of the Jew in English and American Literature* (1971) and in Jerome J. McGann's "The Dandy" (*Midway,* 1969). By Fisch's assessment the Romantic poets were mainly compassionate and tolerant in representing Jews. McGann sees the dandy as a specifically Romantic icon (unlike, say, Satan). As such, the dandy represents the attempt to come to terms with individuality; finally, dandyism is an iconography of imagination (if not of nature).

Romantic Forms and Modes

The quintessentially Romantic form, the fragment, which was the subject of Ilse Gugler's *Das Problem der fragmentarischen Dichtung in der englischen Romantik* (1944) and of D. F. Rauber's "The Fragment as Romantic Form" (*MLQ,* 1969), still teases the minds of scholars. Rauber contended that the fragment is the perfect formal solution to the Romantic poet's problem of reflecting the infinite and indeterminate world. In doing so, he anticipated the Romantic ironists—David Simpson, for example—for whom the fragment is also a solution to the problem of the relationship of poem to reader, for whom, in turn, the fragment functions as heuristic stimulus to creative response. Writing about "Kubla Khan" as fragment in *The Other Side of Language,* Jerzy Peterkiewicz remarks: "The Romantics wanted to see their visions in the way they saw ruins, broken up and abandoned. Then they imagined the whole, and tried to leap into the dark. . . ." Thus, he strikes a chord that Thomas McFarland, in *Romanticism and the Forms of Ruin: Wordsworth, Coleridge, and Modalities of Fragmentation* (1980), expands into a Mahlerian symphony. From incompleteness, fragmentation, and ruin—the "diasparactive trio"—he builds an image of life, manifest in the biographies of Wordsworth and Coleridge and definitive "in a certain perspective" of Romanticism. The experience of fragmentation, the sense of part, is the complement to the longing and striving for unity and wholeness: diasparative form is the polar opposite of organic form. As for fragments as vehicles of writing, McFarland cites not just the usual poems but also *Don Juan* and *The Excursion* as well as prose pieces. The most vital work of Coleridge and Novalis is to be found in their fragments. Before he has done, McFarland has subsumed Wellek's famous definition of Romanticism into his own, with dazzling results. McFarland's book is, for many reasons, one of the most important contributions to the theory of Romanticism—an essential corollary to the studies of Wellek, Abrams, and other advocates of the organicism theory. Though not concerned particularly with fragments or ruins as literary structures, Laurence Goldstein's *Ruins and Empire: The Evolution of a Theme in Augustan and Romantic Literature* (1977) has affinities with McFarland's book. Goldstein pursues his theme in America as well as in England, but it is Wordsworth's career he most desires to illuminate by studying "a literary tradition that values the ruin sentiment, the vicarious experience of dying and rising, as a necessary ordeal in the regaining of self-mastery, and through self-mastery, joy." From McFarland to Goldstein is a rather sharp descent. But Alethea Hayter's explanation of the Romantic fragment in *Opium and the Romantic Imagination* (1968) is hardly more stimulating: opium may stimulate the imagination, but it destroys the will to follow through to completion with the great plans born under its inspiration.

Three older essays on form and structure in Romantic poetry are still of great value for getting one's bearings in this demanding but fascinating region of exploration: W. K. Wimsatt's "The Structure of Romantic Nature Imagery," in *The Verbal Icon: Studies in the Meaning of Poetry* (1954); Elizabeth Nitchie's "Form in Romantic Poetry," in Thorpe et al., *The Major English Romantic Poets* (1957); and M. H. Abrams' "Structure and Style in the Greater Romantic Lyric," in Hilles and Bloom, *From Sensibility to Romanticism* (1965). All three essays are concerned with characteristic Romantic poems as they resemble or differ structurally from their predecessors and successors; all three have much to say about Coleridge, organic form, and the poem as symbolic structure; and all three make convincing cases for the impressive artistry of the poems they study. (For a major challenge to this reading of the Romantic lyric, see the writing of Paul de Man, discussed earlier.) So, too, does Albert S. Gérard's *English Romantic Poetry: Ethos, Structure, and Symbol in Coleridge, Wordsworth, Shelley, and Keats* (1968), which, building on earlier studies, is particularly successful in showing how the Romantic experience of organic unity is given organic form through imagery, structure, and symbol. More recent essays on the Romantic lyric include Uwe Böker, "Lyrik der englischen Romantik," in *Epochen der englishchen Lyrik*, ed. Karl Heinz Göller (1970), who suggests that the Romantics wrote lyrics as alternatives to novels; James Bunn, "Circle and Sequence in the Conjectural Lyric" (*NLH*, 1972), who proposes that the nineteenth-century lyric be regarded as a conjecture rather than as a finished thing because, like conjecture, it is both a circling back and a moving forward; John Holloway, "The Epiphany-Poem in the Romantic Period" (in Asselineau et al.), who sees this type as a distinct, basic poetic mode defined and established by the examples he locates in Clare, Blake, Wordsworth, Keats, and Shelley; Robert Langbaum, "The Epiphanic Mode in Wordsworth and Modern

Literature" (*NLH,* 1983), who wants to show the significance of Wordsworth's innovation for modern poetry and prose fiction, especially the short story ("the epiphanic mode is to a large extent the Romantic and modern mode—a dominant modern convention"); and Klaus Egbert Faas, "Die deskriptive Dichtung als Wegbereiter der romantischen Naturlyrik in England" (*GRM,* 1972), who locates the origins of the Romantic nature lyric in "Windsor Forest." Arunodoy Bhattacharyya has written a book entitled *The Sonnet and the Major English Romantic Poets* (1976), the first such general study. Designed for Indian students, Bhattacharyya's book is critically unsophisticated, as he admits, but enthusiastic about the historical significance and artistic merit of Romantic sonnets.

First, Robert Daniel, "Odes to Dejection" (*KR,* 1953), and then Irene H. Chayes, "Rhetoric as Drama: An Approach to the Romantic Ode" (*PMLA,* 1964), and Kurt Schlüter, *Die englische Ode: Studien zu ihrer Entwicklung unter dem Einfluss der antiken Hymne* (1964), directed our attention to the special qualities of the Romantic ode. With all the bravura of the post–New Criticism, Paul Fry, in *The Poet's Calling in the English Ode* (1980), distinguishes the ode—Romantic and otherwise—from the hymn, to which it is rather a satanic answer. For Fry the ode is always ironic (or dialectic) because of its doubtful relation to vocabulary; "more steadily than any other mode" it raises questions "about the aesthetic shibboleth of the unified whole"—an extreme statement somewhat characteristic of this book. Cyrus Hamlin also writes about the Romantic ode as establishing a rhythm of opposing attitudes—a dialogue—never fully integrated and resolved, in "The Hermeneutics of Form: Reading the Romantic Ode" (*Boundary 2,* 1979), though Hamlin's interest is in developing and testing for criticism a hermeneutics of form (from Hegel) applicable to the entire tradition of European literature. "Dejection: An Ode" is the prototype of the Romantic ode as dialogue. John Jump offers a few pages on the Romantic ode in his monograph *The Ode* in the Critical Idiom series (1974). Whatever the differences in these studies, it would appear that we have some consensus now on the distinction of the Romantic ode; for the hymn as it may have influenced the ode, see Samuel F. Pickering, Jr.'s "Mrs. Barbauld's *Hymns in Prose:* 'An Air-Blown Particle' of Romanticism" (*SHR,* 1975). Jonathan Culler, in "Apostrophe" (*Diacritics,* 1977), detects two forces in poetry, apostrophic and narrative. The lyric (Culler discusses Romantic odes incidentally) is characteristically the triumph of the apostrophic. From the apostrophic, therefore, we turn to the second force or narrative.

Ballads in the Romantic period are the subject of Albert B. Friedman's *The Ballad Revival: Studies in the Influence of Popular on Sophisticated Poetry* (1961) and of Karl Kroeber's *Romantic Narrative Art* (1960). Kroeber's book is not, of course, limited to the art of the ballad, and it is particularly valuable for charting a course through a large and—in the instance of minor poets especially—little-known territory. Hermann Fischer's *Die Romantische Verserzählung in England* (1964) is the sole study devoted exclusively to the verse tale. Exhaustively thorough, it examines all the tales by major and minor Romantics in an effort to evolve a historical classification. George Malcolm Laws, Jr., in *The British Ballad: A Study in Poetic Imitation* (1972), is concerned to show the role of the broadside and the folk ballad in the literary ballads that consciously imitate them. Without such knowledge, we cannot understand, judge, and appreciate the literary ballad, which assumes importance for the first time in the Romantic period. Lionel Stevenson, "The Mystique of Romantic Narrative Poetry" (in Elledge and Hoffman), eliminates from "the category of essentially Romantic art" those narrative poems, Romantic and Victorian, whose method is not calculated to induce spontaneous imaginative participation by the reader in the narrating or creating of the story. Seeking a quarrel with the antihistorical bias of much modern criticism, Walter L. Reed, in "A Defense of History: The Language of Transformation in Romantic Narrative," in *Literature and History*, ed. Harry R. Garvin (1977), attempts to describe the formal structure of history and story in Romantic narrative. If we are to understand Romantic narrative, he claims, we need to recover the experience of history as story or at least the hope of such experience. Romanticism as history asks us to look not just at origins and endings but also at the historical passage between the two. Reed focuses on the two basic forms in which, at deep level, this passage is narrated: evolution and revolution. By means of these complementary forms, the Romantic mind is enabled not only to dominate a world of change but also to participate in it. Among the Romantic minds Reed examines in this stimulating essay are those of Mary Shelley, Wordsworth, Keats, Shelley, Austen, and Emily Brontë. He concludes by suggesting that, if Romanticism is the recovery of "a certain power of telling stories, a partial magic of discourse that takes possession of discourse in its alien, written form," it is neither the positive nor the negative extreme that modern criticism makes it out to be—all the more reason, he implies, to hang on to it.

Romantic poetry as epic poetry can hardly be the innocent topic these days that it once might have seemed to be. First Northrop Frye and then Harold Bloom appropriated the Romantic long poem for romance, albeit perhaps romance with a difference or "internalized romance." The 1960s produced two important studies of the epic in the Romantic period: D. M. Foerster's *The Fortunes of Epic Poetry: A Study in English and American Criticism, 1750–1950* (1962), which incorporates three articles published previously, and Brian Wilkie's *Romantic Poets and Epic Tradition* (1965). Though Foerster and Wilkie make the same apology for their work (the absence of any study of the epic after 1800 except for Tillyard's *The Epic Strain in the English Novel*, 1958), Foerster is preoccupied with the fate of epic as genre in the nineteenth and twentieth centuries; Wilkie, with some Romantic poems that evidence a strong epic intention. The titles of the two books are thus accurate (if, in the case of Wilkie, modest) designations. The 1970s have proliferated essays and books on the subject. A. D. Harvey, "The English Epic in the Romantic Period" (*PQ*, 1976), examines the thirty epics actually published in or just before the nineteenth century, a rash of them in the 1790s and early 1800s, and groups them by theme (national, biblical, chivalric, explorative, and oriental). Harvey's epics (not *The Prelude* or *Don Juan*) reflect more the major social interests (war, America, etc.) of British readers of the time than their philosophical or aesthetic-literary concerns. Both Edward Proffitt and Stuart Curran are concerned with poems that do not fit Harvey's definition. In "The Epic Lyric: The Long Poem in the Twentieth Century" (*RS*, 1978), Proffitt claims that the epic lyric or lyric long poem, the mode toward which many twentieth-century poets strive, originates with *The Prelude,* the archetypal long poem of the last two hundred years, thereby confirming the proposition that Anglo-American poetry of the last two centuries is of a piece. In "The Mental Pinnacle: *Paradise Regained* and the Romantic Four-Book Epic," in *Calm of Mind: Tercentenary Essays on* Paradise Regained *and* Samson Agonistes *in Honor of John S. Diekhoff* (ed. J. A. Wittreich, 1971), Curran advances a strong claim for the epic as the major genre of the Romantic period and for that period as the "heyday of the English epic," in "terms of both numbers and insight into the potential of the genre." Moreover, it is *Paradise Regained* rather than *Paradise Lost* that is the model for the Romantic epic or four-book epic (e.g., *Jerusalem, Endymion, Prometheus Unbound*). The "eminence of *Paradise Lost* as model"—an eminence much augmented by the poetics of Harold Bloom especially—"has obscured the equal if not greater significance of *Paradise Regained.*" Curran's article is the only one of the group likely to stimulate a revision of literary history. Thomas A. Vogler's *Preludes to Vision: The Epic Venture in Blake, Wordsworth, Keats, and Hart Crane* (1971) reflects in its title some of the same caution Wilkie exhibited throughout his book. Vogler sets out to distinguish the epic urge from the formal conventions of epic in order to explain how the epic has, in fact, survived well into the twentieth century. It is the outer form of epic that has changed so as to obscure the survival of epic; the inner form of epic has endured, making it possible to find the epic in works of our time, though the problems whereby that inner form is realized have changed: poets can no longer find to hand a common ideology of authority and value, traditionally the core of epic poetry. The problems and the solutions to them in such "preludes to vision" as *Milton, The Prelude, The Fall of Hyperion,* and *The Bridge* are the heart of Vogler's thoughtful book.

The pastoral, which John Stevenson studied in "Arcadia Re-settled: Pastoral Poetry and Romantic Theory" (*SEL,* 1967), is also Herbert Lindenberger's subject in "The Idyllic Moment: On Pastoral and Romanticism" (*CE,* 1972), which extrapolates from Shakespeare's pastoral moment a definition of pastoral in the modern world—a kind of island in time that gains its intensity from the tension it creates with the historical world—that transcends literary periods. Such islands are to be found in Rousseau, Shelley, Byron, and Wordsworth among the Romantics. If Laurence Lerner, *The Uses of Nostalgia: Studies in Pastoral Poetry* (1972), can find little pastoral in Romanticism (Wordsworth is the great "unpastoral poet" in English poetry), Harold E. Toliver, *Pastoral Forms and Attitudes* (1971), is more discerning, devoting three chapters to the Romantics' efforts to reconcile social and transcendental themes, which have a natural inclination to separate, as reflected in the conflict between industrial and Romantic views of nature. Their struggle determined the character of pastoral from the Romantic period to the present day.

Unlike other forms, the epitaph remains the subject of a single essay, Ernest Bernhardt-Kabisch's "The Epitaph and the Romantic Poets: A Survey" (*HLQ,* 1967). And Robert Langbaum's influential *The Poetry of Experience: The Dramatic Mon-*

ologue in Modern Literary Tradition (1957), for better reasons, is still the standard treatment of the dramatic monologue. The Victorians loom larger in Langbaum's work than the Romantics do, as one would expect, but they, along with their successors the twentieth-century symbolists, are shown to be in the Romantic tradition of poetry, which is the poetry of experience. The distinctive form that this poetry takes is the dramatic monologue of Tennyson and Browning, but Langbaum traces the roots of the form to the dramatic lyrics of the Romantics and detects its branches in the symbolist poems of Eliot and Pound. Ralph W. Rader, in "The Dramatic Monolog and Related Lyric Forms" (*CritI,* 1976), seeks to correct both Langbaum and Elder Olson by claiming the dramatic monologue for lyric poetry and by subtly distinguishing the grades of dramatic versus expressive quality we find in poems all considered at some point dramatic monologues.

Stuart Tave, in *The Amiable Humorist: A Study in the Comic Theory and Criticism of the Eighteenth and Early Nineteenth Centuries* (1960), charted the change from unamiable to amiable humor that differentiates the Augustans from the Romantics. Subsequently, Allan Rodway, in *English Comedy: Its Role and Nature from Chaucer to the Present Day* (1975), has looked at Romantic comedy in the larger context of English comedy. Between Augustan comedy and Regency comedy he finds no major comic writer other than Burns. But with Austen, Peacock, Byron, and Shelley we have four comic writers whose work conforms to Rodway's idea of comedy—that it functions as a mode of psychological warfare. These four Romantics mock the opposition of neoclassicism and Romanticism, producing a Romantic satire—Romantic because it starts from feelings rather than, like Augustan satire, from conventions or ideas. Mark Storey's *Poetry and Humour from Cowper to Clough* (1979) is not so selective: all the major Romantic poets "are directly concerned with the implications of humor and what happens if it is allowed into poetry." They come to see that humor is one solution to the problem of accommodating the self in poetry—a particularly acute problem for the Romantics, whose poems tend to be about themselves; it can work as both a controlling and a liberating device. This "line of humour" culminates for Storey in Clough. Marilyn Gaull, in "Romantic Humor: The Horse of Knowledge and the Learned Pig" (*Mosaic,* 1976), argues that, to locate humor in the Romantic period, we must go to popular culture, especially to the theater with its afterpieces of farce, burlesque, or pantomime. Her further point is that popular humor became allied with street humor or humor of survival (oral culture), the characteristics of which appear in the written culture as parody. Parody, for the age that succeeded the Augustan, was the appropriate sequel to satire. Edward Duffy, in "The Cunning Spontaneities of Romanticism" (*WC,* 1972), is also concerned with parody as the means whereby the Romantics, using traditional forms of literary expression imposed on them, cunningly achieved spontaneity. We have not been alert to this cunning, he claims, because we have been too quick to take the French Revolution as metaphor for the Romantic movement, a metaphor Duffy finds distracting. Abundant in parody, Romantic literature is also rich in the grotesque, according to Christian W. Thomsen, *Das Groteske und die englische Literatur* (1977), who defines the grotesque as a mode that, replacing tragedy and comedy, gives to the ugly and the evil the same rights as obtain for the beautiful and the sublime; thus, it is hospitable to mingled reactions to art and life. A. J. M. Smith's "Non-sense Poetry and Romanticism," in *Essays in Honor of Russel B. Nye* (ed. Joseph Waldmeir, 1978), postpones Romantic humor and parody to the Victorian period. The nonsense poets, by his account, take Romantic poetry, which is halfhearted nonsense, and, extending it to its logical end, achieve exuberant nonsense poetry. Extension is often achieved through parody, but it is appreciative parody.

In turning to technical aspects of Romantic poetry, I would cite first John Hollander's "Romantic Verse Form and the Metrical Contract" (*Romanticism and Consciousness,* 1970; rpt. *Vision and Resonance: Two Senses of Poetic Form,* 1975). Hollander is concerned with the elements of "convention which link a metrical style or type to a whole poetic genre and, hence, a poet's choice of meter to a larger intention." He demonstrates just how aware the Romantics were of such metrical contracts even when choosing to dismiss or subvert them. Hollander's essay is obligatory reading. Janet Ruth Heller, in "Enjambment as a Metrical Force in Romantic Conversation Poems" (*Poetics,* 1977), uses the conversation poems of Coleridge and Wordsworth to illustrate how run-on lines alter the rhythmic con-tours of verse. And James Bailey, *Toward a Statistical Analysis of English Verse: The Iambic Tetrameter of Ten Poets* (1975), using the Russian linguistic-statistical method, shows changes in some features of iambic tetrameter (no changes in other features) when we compare Russian and English metrics; Wordsworth and Blake are two of the ten poets whose iambic tetrameter is analyzed. Another tech-nical approach to the Romantics is Donald Ross, Jr.'s "Stylistics and the Testing of Literary Hypotheses" (*Poetics,* 1978). Ross hopes to build an empirical theory of literature, using the EYEBALL computer program, by which literary theories—for example, Wordsworth's in the 1815 Preface—can be tested. I might close this sec-tion by alluding to Barbara Herrnstein Smith's *Poetic Closure* (1968), which uses Romantic poems as examples of the different sorts of closure she identifies; no one kind of closure, it would seem, is characteristic of Romantic poetry.

The situation of Romantic drama changed dramatically during the 1960s and 1970s. No longer is there a paucity of scholarship on this topic. To Allardyce Nic-oll's *A History of Early Nineteenth Century Drama* (1930; rev. 1955), Newman Ivey White's "The English Romantic Writers as Dramatists" (*SR,* 1922), and Bertrand Evans' *Gothic Drama from Walpole to Shelley* (1947) have been added Richard M. Fletcher's *English Romantic Drama, 1795–1843: A Critical History* (1966) and John W. Ehrstine's "The Drama and Romantic Theory: The Cloudy Symbols of High Romance" (*RS,* 1966). Fletcher sets out to demolish the logical fallacies that plague the criticism and judgment of Romantic drama, suggesting at one point that the "Romantic playwright was fortunate to precede the modern critic." He also defines Romantic drama as poetic drama, of which *The Borderers* is the first instance and *Remorse* the first performed example. The promise of poetic drama was initially thwarted by the double phenomena of neo-Elizabethanism and the Byronic hero; Victorian commercialism ultimately sealed its fate. Ehrstine suggests that Romantic drama failed, at least in the form of the play, because its theory—that drama is mental, interior, imaginative—was incompatible with the conventions of traditional drama. One should note here as well the chapter in Patricia M. Ball's *The Central Self: A Study in Romantic and Victorian Imagination* (1968) on Romantic plays, which she claims are "central efforts of the Romantic imagination, not peripheral mistakes."

Joseph W. Donohue's *Dramatic Character in the English Romantic Age* (1970) reiterates Ehrstine's view of Romantic dramatic theory but, in addition, shows how it developed from Jacobean drama and how it reflected the contemporary cultural milieu. "The Revival of Elizabethan Drama and the Crisis of Romantic Drama" is also N. W. Bawcutt's subject (in Davies and Beatty). By championing the Elizabethans disparaged by the eighteenth century and using them as a standard to judge contemporary drama, the Romantics rewrote literary history, he claims, in such a way as to make their own plays evidence for a continuing decline. Terry Otten's *The Deserted Stage: The Search for Dramatic Form in Nineteenth-Century England* (1972) interprets the plays of Byron, Shelley, Tennyson, and Browning as experiments in dramatic form, some of them limited successes in the effort to find objective form for subjective matter. Otten's dismissal of most nineteenth-century plays raised the dander of Michael R. Booth, who offers "A Defence of Nineteenth-Century English Drama" (*Educational Theatre Journal,* 1974); the problem with literary scholars, he complains, is that they habitually see drama as text instead of as theater. Booth is the principal worker in this once-neglected vineyard. He has edited five volumes of *English Plays of the Nineteenth Century* (1969–76), providing us with representative dramas, comedies, farces, pantomimes, extravaganzas, and burlesques from throughout the century. Students of Romanticism can now judge the nineteenth-century theater for themselves. He has also written the bibliographical essay "Nineteenth-Century Drama" for *English Drama: Select Bibliographical Guides* (ed. Stanley Wells, 1975) and served as one of the editors for volume 6 (covering 1750–1880) of *The Revels History of Drama in England* (1975). L. W. Conolly and J. P. Wearing have supplied us with *English Drama and Theatre, 1800–1900: A Guide to Information Sources* (1978), in which all the Romantic poets except Blake are included.

Books by Pratyush Ranjan Purkayastha (*The Romantics' Third Voice: A Study of the Dramatic Works of the English Romantic Poets*) and Om Prakash Mathur (*The Closet Drama of the Romantic Revival*) appeared in the same year (1978). Both propose to redress the neglect of their subject but are otherwise little alike. Purkayastha insists on examining the plays as drama rather than as literature and admonishes us not to try to put them into a single mold. Though he repeats a number of the critical platitudes Fletcher derides, he is commendably pragmatic. The time was out of joint, he concludes, for the dramatic abilities of the Romantic poets to prosper. Mathur, in lumping Romantic plays together as closet drama, goes against the critical principles of both Fletcher and Purkayastha, but is, even so, less contentious than the former and critically more sophisticated than the latter. Mathur's argument is that "[t]he English drama of the Romantic Revival . . . presents the rare phenomenon of the almost complete divorce of the literary element from the theatrical." This divorce, characteristic of the theater itself in the Romantic age, is definitive of closet drama at its purest. Erika Gottlieb's *Lost An-*

gels of a Ruined Paradise: Themes of Cosmic Strife in Romantic Tragedy (1981) looks at *The Borderers, Remorse, Otho the Great, Manfred,* and *The Cenci* for their common thematic and generic traits. The result is the best explanation yet for the Romantics' failure to write great drama or tragedy. Central to all five plays, Gottlieb finds, are a saintly heroine's loss of innocence and a child's crime against a father or father figure. All five, thus, reenact the basic myth of the loss of innocence and subsequent loss of Paradise. Moreover, she argues, the plays do not achieve tragic catharsis, because with the collapse of the new system created by the Enlightenment—that is, with the failure of the French Revolution to establish the political and human ideals spawned by the philosophes—the Romantics lost faith in human beings, who are in some mysterious way irreparably flawed. Gottlieb's study may, in the way of myth criticism, be overschematized, but no one before her has managed to give such a coherent account of English Romantic drama. By comparison with these books, J. C. Trewin's "The Romantic Poets in the Theatre" (*KSMB,* 1969) is negligible. It perpetuates, as does Allardyce Nicoll's *English Drama: A Modern Viewpoint* (1968), the outmoded judgment the other books seek to challenge and lay to rest. Joseph W. Donohue's "Burletta and the Early Nineteenth-Century English Theatre" (*NCTR,* 1973), by contrast, is precisely the sort of research requisite to bringing about a revision of literary history. So, too, is his *Theatre in the Age of Kean* (1975), which offers a refreshing perspective on the history of the Romantic theater, while at the same time commending the subject to other researchers by calling attention to the "abundance and complexity of the records" extant. Theater in the age of Kean is not important because it "paved the way" for the late nineteenth-century theater, he claims. "On the contrary, it commands our interest on its own account." Marilyn Gaull, "Romantic Theatre" (*WC,* 1984), would seem to agree. It is the popular theater, especially pantomime and melodrama, she argues, that is genuinely Romantic. Like Romantic poetry and prose, it assimilated public and private forms, adapting them to new purposes. Byron and George Coleman the Younger figure in *Essays on Nineteenth Century British Theatre . . .* (ed. Kenneth Richards and Peter Thomson, 1970); and Byron, alone of the English Romantics, appears in E. Saprykina's "Some Distinctive Features of the Romantic Theory of Drama" (in Sótér and Neupokoyeva), an essay that argues the informative role of Italian Romantic drama and dramatic theory in European Romanticism. Michael Goldman's "The Ghost of Joy: Reflections on Romanticism and the Forms of Modern Drama" (in Bornstein) is not about Romantic drama but rather about the serious error modern drama made in adapting the Romantic feeling of being cut off from the joy of life to dramatic representation.

The leap from play to film is easily made these days. In "The Visionary Cinema of Romantic Poetry" (*William Blake: Essays for S. Foster Damon,* ed. Alvin Rosenfeld, 1969; rpt. *The Ringers in the Tower,* 1971), Harold Bloom compares what he calls the cinema of Romantic poetry to film, with the plaudits going to the poetry, whose cinema, because it is visionary and not visual, takes us far deeper imaginatively than film does. Frank D. McConnell has since given us *The Spoken Seen: Film and the Romantic Imagination* (1975). His thesis is that film, the ascendant art form of the twentieth century, perpetuates and extends the aesthetic concerns and issues of literary Romanticism and, possibly, realizes the Romantic ideal of art as total representation. With film, we, like Adam, awake and find the dream true. McConnell's engaging study, interesting to literature and film students alike, gives new life, as he claims, to the cliché that we still live in a Romantic era.

Whether or not this chapter should attend to the novel in the Romantic period is a moot point. The German idea that the novel is the characteristic expression of Romanticism has never traveled well, but as more and more Anglo-American critics rely on German literary theory for interpretive tools, the idea appears more and more frequently, if incidentally, in Romantics studies, especially those that explore Romantic irony. Symptomatic too, perhaps, is the repeated effort of Romantics scholars to appropriate *Tristram Shandy* for Romanticism. And it may be worth remembering that some Romantic poets themselves were aware of the close proximity of the poem and the novel, a point developed by John Speirs in *Poetry toward Novel* (1971). L. J. Swingle's "The Poets, the Novelists, and the English Romantic Situation" (*WC,* 1979) outlines the current dispute about whether to extend the concept of English Romanticism to include novelists of the period, reckoning the gains and losses before proceeding to develop an approach to Romantic literature that suggests that "the principal novelists of the Romantic period belong within the Romantic company"—an approach that, instead of diminishing one or the other group in order to effect a vague kinship, illuminates both poets and novelists as they respond in similar ways to a common perception of the world as characterized by intellectual indeterminacy. Scholars attracted to this notion of the Romantics' view of things but offended by the language in which it is often expressed nowadays will want to take note. Swingle's graceful, meticulous reading and comparing of Romantic texts is worth worlds of brilliant aperçus and dizzying theory. The novelists Swingle examines are Austen and Scott, especially the former. Some of the other essays in the same issue of the *Wordsworth Circle* (Spring 1979; ed. Swingle and Gene W. Ruoff), which is devoted to British Romantic fiction, depart from the major novelists to consider Hogg, Charlotte Brontë, and Lady Caroline Lamb. Introducing the general topic are three brief papers (revised) given at the 1978 MLA meeting of the English Romantics division by Kroeber, McGann, and Langbaum. They provide the background for Swingle's opening remarks about the present dispute. (Romantic fiction was also the topic for the division's 1971 MLA meeting, where five papers published in the Autumn 1971 issue of the *Wordsworth Circle,* ed. Frank Jordan, under the general rubric of "Imagination and Reality in Romantic Fiction" were discussed.) Perhaps because Austen and Scott dominated their initial effort, Swingle and Ruoff put together a second issue of the *Wordsworth Circle* (Autumn 1979), "Regionalism in British Romantic Fiction." Their introduction points to some interesting distinctions between the Romantic poets and Scott, who retain the mystery of the unfamiliar or remote region, and the regional novelists, who, sensing that knowledge is power, eliminate such mystery. (The role of the *Wordsworth Circle* in expanding the subject matter of Romantics studies and thereby strengthening our grasp of Romanticism is to be warmly commended.) A third group of novelists in the Romantic period—Robert Bage, Elizabeth Inchbald, Thomas Holcroft, and William Godwin—are the subject of Gary Kelly's *The English Jacobin Novel, 1780–1805* (1976), which argues that in the 1790s the younger Jacobins became Romantics, appreciating the power of imagination and feeling. The later novels of Holcroft and Godwin reflect this metamorphosis by transforming the Jacobin novel into the Romantic novel.

The one book of the 1970s that focuses squarely on the problem, Robert Kiely's *The Romantic Novel in England* (1972), for all its merits as a series of readings of chosen texts, is disappointing in its failure to say something of significance about its titular subject. No thesis or definition emerges from Kiely's analysis, unless it is the implication that, as his choices would suggest, the Romantic novel is the gothic novel or usually so. Rather similar in not pushing a thesis is Hubert Teyssandier's *Les Formes de la création romanesque à l'époque de Walter Scott et de Jane Austen, 1814–1820* (1977), but the six years he isolates define a rich and coherent field of research, according to the author, one in which several distinct types of fiction coexist and thrive. For each type there are both mediocre and superior examples. The difference is the Romantic imagination, which can transform and even enrich the systems of literary conventions with which all the novelists work. Michael Munday explains the difference otherwise in "The Novel and Its Critics in the Early Nineteenth Century" (*SP*, 1982). His investigations reveal something of a symbiotic relationship between novels and reviews in the first decades of the Romantic century: better novels produced better reviews, which in turn stimulated still better novels. By the 1820s, consequently, the status of the novel was greatly improved.

The presence of Charlotte Brontë in the first Swingle-Ruoff collection and of Emily Brontë in Kiely's book points to the strong tendency of scholars to find the Romantic novel, like Romantic painting, outside the Romantic period proper. Several recent books illustrate this tendency. Charles Schug, *The Romantic Genesis of the Modern Novel* (1980), is convinced that Romantic aesthetics informed the modern novel, but some fifty years after the Romantic period. To prove it, he spends a chapter on Romantic poetry and another on Romantic form before taking up Henry James. (Daniel Mark Fogel is of like mind in his *Henry James and the Structure of the Romantic Imagination* [1982].) Ioan Williams, *The Realist Novel in England: A Study in Development* (1975), reads the English novels of the Romantic period as conservative and hence unreceptive to Romantic ideas but, as such, preparing the ground for the realist novel that flourished afterward. Donald D. Stone, in *The Romantic Impulse in Victorian Fiction* (1980), though carefully discriminating what aspects of Romanticism informed which Victorian novelists and in which Romantic writers or works those aspects are seen, also finds the impact of Romanticism on the novel to be a Victorian phenomenon. A specific instance is explored in Michael E. Hassett's "Compromised Romanticism in *Jude the Obscure*" (*NCF*, 1971). With "English Romanticism as a Source of Character and Motif in Joyce's *Portrait*" (*SAB*, 1977), Jack Weaver moves well beyond the Victorian period, and with *River of Dissolution: D. H. Lawrence and English Romanticism* (1969), so does Colin Clarke, who thinks that recognizing Lawrence's debt to the English Romantic poets can solve some of the critical cruxes in a novel like *Women in Love.* Demonstrating the "not inconsiderable part" played by the Romantics—especially Byron, Shelley, and Blake—in Joyce's imaginative life is the aim of Timothy Webb's " 'Planetary Music': James Joyce and the Romantic Example," in *James Joyce and Modern Literature* (ed. W. J. McCormack and Alistair Stead, 1982). With "Doris Lessing and Romanticism" (*CE,* 1977), Michael L. Magie confirms the impact of Romanticism on a major novelist of our era. Erich Kahler, *The Inward Turn of Narrative,* trans. Richard and Clara Winston (1973), goes in the opposite direction: "With *Tristram Shandy* we have reached the threshold of Romanticism." And Ernest Bernbaum, "What Kinds of Modern Prose Fiction Would the Romantics Admire?" in his *Guide through the Romantic Movement* (2nd ed. 1949), looks to novels not yet written to "interpret life as [Romantic] Imagination truly discloses it." As yet, it seems, we are more inclined to seek and find the Romantic novel outside the precincts of the Romantic period, the gothic novel notwithstanding.

The tendency to identify the gothic novel as the type of Romantic novel, sometimes more by default than by cogent reasoning, is itself warmly debated these days. F. R. Hart's "Limits of the Gothic: The Scottish Example," in *Studies in the Eighteenth Century,* ed. Harold E. Pagliaro (1973), calls attention to the dispute and at the same time makes suggestions for lines of inquiry that might help to resolve it. Hart refers specifically to the debates in the pages of *PMLA* between Robert D. Hume and Robert L. Platzner, following Hume's "Gothic versus Romantic: A Revaluation of the Gothic Novel" (*PMLA,* 1969). He thinks that before such an issue can be resolved we need to cultivate a fuller cultural and historical understanding of the gothic tendency in literature, for example, to look at Scottish practitioners such as Smollett, Scott, and Hogg and to determine the historical dimensions of the gothic. Scholars, Hart charges, are too eager to indulge in "generic essentializing" before they know enough about the historical diversity and cultural variation of a genre. At this time in Romantics scholarship, determinations that gothic is or is not Romantic are decidedly premature. A second important article on the subject, in the same volume, is Frederick Garber's "Meaning and Mode in Gothic Fiction." Like Platzner, Garber thinks the gothic is a meeting of modes and thus a peculiarly rich form of literature, especially since the modes are allowed to retain their discreteness. Such a view of the gothic consorts nicely with Swingle's ideas of Romanticism and thus prepares the way for bringing the two into harmony.

Whether the gothic novel is the Romantic novel or a subtype of the Romantic novel or neither of the above, it is the subject of much research and criticism these days—a trend well under way in the 1960s (see *ERP3* 16–18, for discussion of books and articles before the 1970s). Two scholars in particular, Sir Devendra P. Varma and G. Richard Thompson, have been especially industrious in making the gothics themselves available to modern readers. So far, Arno Press has published three volumes comprehending thirty titles under Varma's editorship, as well as the revised dissertation of William Emmet Coleman, *On the Discrimination of Gothicisms* (1980), which concludes with a chapter on Romantic gothicism. Thompson has edited fifteen *Romantic Gothic Tales, 1790–1840* (1979), with fifty-odd informative pages covering "Gothic Fiction of the Romantic Age:

Context and Mode" and a useful bibliography. A few years earlier, Thompson collected critical essays in *The Gothic Imagination: Essays in Dark Romanticism* (1974). His general view is that "The Gothic is the dark counterforce to optimistic Romanticism." Elizabeth MacAndrew's *The Gothic Tradition in Fiction* (1979) makes no use of Romantic poetry. Coral Ann Howells, in *Love, Mystery, and Misery: Feeling in Gothic Fiction* (1978), by contrast, draws repeatedly on the poets to establish her position that the gothic novel, which falls within the genre of the Romantic novel, had most to contribute to English fiction in the area of feeling or the whole nonrational side of experience. Interest in the gothic novel declined eventually because the Romantic poets and Scott did what the gothic novelists were doing and did it better. The gothic novel going about the same business as Romantic poetry is also important to A. M. Rustowski, "Convention and the Generic Instability of the English Gothic Novel" (*SAP*, 1976), who quarrels with Montague Summers because he failed to see the "basic instability of the gothic novel as type," the consequence of its dynamic form, by which it reveals its close if anticipatory relationship with Romantic literature. Both the novelists and the poets, in experiencing the same ontological crisis, underwent the same stages of development, from "terror gothic" to "horror gothic." David Punter, *The Literature of Terror: A History of Gothic Fictions from 1765 to the Present Day* (1980), goes so far as to argue, in a chapter entitled "Gothic and Romanticism," that the Romantic poets articulated images of terror—specifically, images of the wanderer, the vampire, and the seeker after forbidden knowledge—that exercised "a potent influence over later literary history." Robert L. Stevens, "The Exorcism of England's Gothic Demon" (*MQ*, 1973), takes a contrary position in suggesting that the gothic never caught on in England or America because the Anglo-Saxon writers show genius for function and normalcy. The genius for opposite traits, especially nihilism, is Continental, showing up among the English Romantics only in Blake. Hence it is easy for England to exorcise its gothic demon—unfortunately, in Stevens' eyes, since nihilism can be useful. A book such as Judith Wilt's *Ghosts of the Gothic: Austen, Eliot, and Lawrence* (1980) suggests that Stevens may be looking for the gothic in the wrong places, for Wilt argues that these three mainstream novelists embrace the gothic in their fictions. As Masao Miyoshi indicated in *The Divided Self: A Perspective on the Literature of the Victorians* (1969), the modern literary sensibility, divided against itself, is tied to the gothic novel. Linda Bayer-Berenbaum's *The Gothic Imagination: Expansion in Gothic Literature and Art* (1982) is interdisciplinary, comparing literature with painting and architecture in order to find the common denominator of gothic, which turns out to be the promise it offers of expanded consciousness and intensified reality—reasons for its appeal today as yesterday.

Additional criticism can be located by consulting Frederick S. Frank's "The Gothic Novel: A Checklist of Modern Criticism" (*BB*, 1973). Plot summaries of some two hundred English gothic novels can be located in Ann B. Tracy's *The Gothic Novel: 1790–1830* (1981), which includes an index to motifs.

Romantic nonfictional prose has also come a long way in the past two decades, but as yet most studies focus on individual writers or works. Thus Marie H.

Law's *The English Familiar Essay in the Early Nineteenth Century* (1934) is still a standard text. And M. R. Watson's studies—"The *Spectator* Tradition and the Development of the Familiar Essay" (*ELH,* 1946) and *Magazine Serials and the Essay Tradition, 1746–1820* (1956)—are still important. One significant addition is Laurence Stapleton's *The Elected Circle: Studies in the Art of Prose* (1973), which attends with critical acumen to both Hazlitt and De Quincey. A second is John R. Nabholtz' "Romantic Prose and Classical Rhetoric" (*WC,* 1980), which proposes the tradition of classical rhetoric that derives from Aristotle, the principles of which were part of the Romantics' education, as the best way to understand their argumentative prose, a far greater quantity of writing than their familiar essays or impassioned pieces. Nabholtz demonstrates this proposition with Coleridge. Readers interested in Romantic diaries as they compare with diaries of other periods should consult Robert A. Fothergill's *Private Chronicles: A Study of English Diaries* (1974). And those who wish to explore Romantic autobiography might start with William C. Spengemann's *The Form of Autobiography* (1980), in which "philosophical autobiography," the successor to "historical biography," is illustrated exclusively by Romantics (Rousseau, Wordsworth, and De Quincey). All the signs point to autobiography as the coming subject of Romantics studies. Indeed, it has already arrived in some quarters, for example, Wordsworth studies. As Michael Cooke remarks in "Modern Black Autobiography" (in Thorburn and Hartman), "it is no mere coincidence that autobiography first cuts its own stream in the literary landscape toward the end of the eighteenth century, or as a sign of the Romantic movement." Jerome Hamilton Buckley would appear to agree. In *The Turning Key: Autobiography and the Subjective Impulse since 1800* (1984), a major study of the function rather than the form of nonfictional autobiography, he cites *The Prelude* as "the archetypal subjective poem in the language." For Buckley, the proper function of autobiography is to achieve a balance between self and society or "an ennobling interchange" of inner and outer, by charting a course from individual psychological discovery to a general psychology. No wonder that "Wordsworth's poem remains exemplary in its demonstration that the edge of meaning lies never far beyond the prose of ordinary experience." When it comes to autobiography, the question of genre is, for Paul Jay, vexed. Hence he prefers to concentrate, in *Being in the Text: Self Representation from Wordsworth to Roland Barthes* (1984), on the uses to which authors have put self-reflexive literary forms and, even more so, on "the impact of changing ideas about the psychological 'self' and the literary subject" on these forms. *The Prelude,* he suggests, "provides a unique insight into the paradoxes of literary self-representation in a period when the self was coming to be thought of less as the creation of a deity and more as the construction of humankind's own mental powers." As such, it has been instructive to autobiographical writers well into the modern period. More titles may be located in Harris W. Wilson and Diane Long Hoeveler, *English Prose and Criticism in the Nineteenth Century: A Guide to Information Sources* (1979).

The contemporary reception of Romantic poetry is now to be known for the reading. William S. Ward indicated his interest in the subject as far back as 1945 in an essay for *PMLA:* "Some Aspects of the Conservative Attitude toward Poetry:

1798–1820." In 1972 he provided a list of over 15,000 reviews in the two-volume *Literary Reviews in British Periodicals 1798–1820: A Bibliography.* In 1977, he covered the years from 1821 to 1826; and in 1979, from 1789 to 1798. (In the interim he provided an *Index and Finding List of Serials Published in the British Isles, 1798–1832* [1953] and *British Periodicals & Newspapers, 1789–1832: A Bibliography of Secondary Sources* [1972]. Two years later he gave us a *Supplementary List* to the *Index* [*BNYPL,* 1974].)

Taking advantage of new technology available to publishers, Donald H. Reiman has compiled in nine volumes nearly all the known reviews of five Romantic poets' first editions (not, of course, Blake's poems) appearing between 1793 and 1824, as well as selected reviews of a later date, in *The Romantics Reviewed, 1793–1830: Contemporary Reviews of British Romantic Writers* (1972). Many reviews of their contemporaries are also collected. Beside the monumental labors of Ward and Reiman, those of others appear negligible, but small selections have their purpose, for example, John O. Hayden's *Romantic Bards and British Reviewers: A Selected Edition of the Contemporary Reviews of the Works of William Wordsworth, Samuel Taylor Coleridge, Byron, Keats and Shelley* (1971). Hayden's informative introduction is backed up by his earlier study of *The Romantic Reviewers 1802–1824* (1969). Preceding Hayden with selections were John Wain, with *Contemporary Reviews of Romantic Poetry* (1953); H. S. Davies, with *The Poets and Their Critics,* volume 2, *Blake to Browning* (1962); and Patricia Hodgart and Theodore Redpath, *Romantic Perspectives . . .* (1964). The first uses extracts from the three leading critical quarterlies to assess the reception of five Romantic poets plus Tennyson. The third, presenting perspectives from all sorts of contemporary prose, not just reviews, is limited to the early Romantics. But Redpath came out with a sequel volume, *The Young Romantics & Critical Opinion, 1807–24 . . .* in 1973.

Besides the reviews themselves, we have studies like Hayden's of the reviewers and studies of the journals, for example: John Clive's *Scotch Reviewers: The Edinburgh Review, 1802–1815* (1957) and his "The *Edinburgh Review:* The Life and Death of a Periodical" in *Essays in the History of Publishing in Celebration of the 250th Anniversary of the House of Longman, 1724–1974,* ed. Asa Briggs (1974); and J. H. Alexander's *Two Studies in Romantic Reviewing: Edinburgh Reviewers and the English Tradition* and *The Reviewing of Walter Scott's Poetry: 1805–1817* (1976). As far back as 1940, J. J. Welker, "The Position of the Quarterlies on Some Classical Dogmas" (*SP,* 1940), demonstrated that the reviewing journals were not as hostile to Romanticism as had been supposed. The work of Hayden, Clive, and others based on more information has confirmed his thesis. We now know that neither Keats nor any other Romantic poet was killed by the reviewers, who, on the whole, did rather well by the new poets. Thanks to Donald Thomas, *A Long Time Burning: The History of Literary Censorship in England* (1969), we now know a great deal also about how the Romantics figure in the long struggle of British writers to be free of censorship. The latest research tool in this area is *British Literary Magazines: The Romantic Age, 1789–1836* (ed. Alvin Sullivan, 1983), with an introduction by John O. Hayden. It provides profiles compiled by forty-two scholars of eighty-four journals, adequate testimony to Sullivan's claim that "the Romantic movement was embraced by more journals, reviews, and miscellanies than any other."

Romantic Literature and the Other Arts

The interdisciplinary imperative more and more Romantics scholars invoke these days has implications for the study of literature and the other arts as well as for the study of literature and psychology or economics. Their research is greatly facilitated by the annual *Bibliography on the Relations of Literature and the Other Arts*. Published under the same title from 1952 to 1967 by the AMS Press, since 1968 it has been sponsored by the MLA Division on Literature and Other Arts and produced at Dartmouth College, where Steven Scher chairs the collecting committee. And *Blake: An Illustrated Quarterly* is a regular source of information and discussion on literature and the other arts, especially, of course, literature and the visual arts. Several scholars—Jacques Barzun, Morse Peckham, Wylie Sypher, for example—characteristically consider painting and music in their theoretical studies of modern art. H. G. Schenk's *The Mind of the European Romantics: An Essay in Cultural History* (1966) is still, however, the one study that attempts a full cultural history of European Romanticism without privileging one or another discipline or art form. All the major Romantic poets except Blake appear in his "Dramatis Personae," which includes, among the English characters, Carlyle, Pugin, Scott, Southey, and Turner as well. Eric Newton's *The Romantic Rebellion* (1962) is heavily oriented toward the visual arts. Efforts to pin down a Romantic style in the arts include Frederick B. Artz, *From the Renaissance to Romanticism: Trends in Style in Art, Literature, and Music, 1300–1800* (1962), and Ulrich Weisstein, "Romanticism: Transcendentalist Games or 'Wechselseitige Erhellung der Künste'" (*CollG*, 1968). Artz's idea that neoclassicism and Romanticism are parallel movements may strike literary scholars as peculiar, though art and music historians are quite familiar with it. Weisstein's failure to find a distinctively Romantic style, unless style be defined as weltanschauung, is disappointing, if not surprising. Edmund Blunden's "Romantic Poetry and the Fine Arts" (*Proceedings of the British Academy*, 1942) remains a pleasantly readable sketch of the subject.

In a class by itself but concerned equally with poetry, painting, and music is Donald Sutherland's *On, Romanticism* (1971). (Sutherland does not think there is Romantic architecture or sculpture.) An essay on style, conducted with great wit and written in the antithesis of academic prose, it distinguishes Romantic style from classic and baroque: "I mean . . . by the romantic an immoderate sympathy with Becoming, Time, Change, and Many." Having established a critical vocabulary for Romantic art (mostly familiar terms such as imagination, potentiality, indetermination), Sutherland proceeds to discuss Romantic forms, taking Shelley, *Don Giovanni*, Tasso, Pompeian painting, and Vergil as exemplars. Obviously, Sutherland's three styles have little to do with conventional definitions. And yet he does associate artistic style with historical period. The baroque style, for example, is that of our own time. Sutherland's title and every word of his madcap book express his wish that it were otherwise.

For various reasons—the legacy of "ut pictura poesis" in the Romantic period, the explosion of interest in Blake in the second half of our century, the revival of interest in Romantic painting since World War II as witnessed by major exhibitions of large (Turner) and small (Allston) talents alike, together with publications of catalogues raisonnés, artists' notebooks and memoirs, biographical and critical studies—it is the connections between Romantic poetry and Romantic painting that dominate comparative study of the arts. Besides Chauncey B. Tinker's *Painter and Poet: Studies in the Literary Relations of English Poetry* (1938), we now have Mario Praz's *Mnemosyne: The Parallel between Literature and the Visual Arts* (1970), J. R. Watson's *Picturesque Landscape and English Romantic Poetry* (1970), Raymond Lister's *British Romantic Art* (1973), *Images of Romanticism: Verbal and Visual Affinities,* edited by Karl Kroeber and William Walling (1978), Hugh Honour's *Romanticism* (1979), and William Vaughan's *Romanticism* (1977; published in the United States as *Romantic Art* in 1978). Praz begins by elaborating theoretical problems of "ut pictura poesis" in order to clear the way for "a common link between the various arts." His tactic is to find that link, not in themes or ideas, but in modes and expressions that reflect deep structural affinity. In the nineteenth century this structural affinity can be termed telescopic (or dualistic), microscopic (or monistic), and photoscopic. The distinction between telescopic and microscopic Praz illustrates with the "plan" that, according to Coleridge, governed the writing of *Lyrical Ballads;* photoscopic refers to the new alliance between painting and photography in the later nineteenth century that replaced the earlier, strong bond of mutual inspiration between painting and literature. In formulating his tactic Praz gives considerable credit to the ideas of Rudulf Zeitler, *Die Kunst des neunzehnten Jahrhunderts* (1966). J. R. Watson starts with the tradition of the picturesque; he explores the ways in which it directed the Romantic movement and, conversely, the ways in which the Romantics modifed it by adding feeling to seeing, imagination to fancy, and so forth. (Pioneering work in the picturesque is Christopher Hussey's *The Picturesque: Studies in a Point of View,* 1927. For other studies of the picturesque, see above, under "Romantic Philosophy and Romantic Psychology.") Watson's "Turner and the Romantic Poets," in *Encounters: Essays on Literature and the Visual Arts,* edited by John Dixon Hunt (1971), proposes that "however varied our discrimination of romanticisms may be, in England they are all united in the work of Turner." On the related subject of landscape, one might continue with Adele M. Holcomb, "More Matter with Less Art: Romantic Attitudes toward Landscape Painting" (*Art Journal,* 1977). The writers were influential in cultivating an awareness of the local sources of British landscape painting. And even today they can be an invaluable interpretive key to this same painting. John Barrell, in *The Dark Side of the Landscape: The Rural Poor in English Painting 1730–1840* (1980), draws on the poetry of Wordsworth to help explain the imagery of Constable's paintings, much as in *The Idea of Landscape and the Sense of Place,*

1730–1840: An Approach to the Poetry of John Clare (1972) he uses Wordsworth to assist him in describing Clare's sense of place (which is as remote from Wordsworth's, he believes, as it is from Thomson's or Young's). The standard work on landscape and its impact on poetry and other arts for many years, Elizabeth Manwaring's *Italian Landscape in Eighteenth-Century England* (1926), has been greatly augmented, if not superseded, by Barrell's work and still more so perhaps by the proliferating studies of Ronald Paulson, in particular his *Literary Landscape: Turner and Constable* (1981) and *Representations of Revolutions (1789–1820)* (1983). The earlier book explores "what purpose the literary (or its converse, the reaction against the literary) served" for Turner and Constable. Paulson begins by invoking Wordsworth. The later book is, in the author's mind, closely related to the earlier because he views "landscape painting as *the* artistic equivalent of the political upheaval" we label revolution. It is also related by what is most distinctive about Paulson's interpretations—the Freudian methodology that habitually refers aesthetic categories to psychological ones (for example, the progression from sublime to beautiful or the regression from picturesque to grotesque becomes Oedipal or oral-anal in psychological translation). This approach, in turn, is what holds together a somewhat disparate collection of essays. All the artists invoked saw the "phenomenon of revolution . . . as a personal psychomachia. . . ." Still a third scholar whose present interests are in comparing literature and landscape painting is James A. W. Heffernan, author of *The Re-creation of Landscape: A Study of Wordsworth, Coleridge, Constable, and Turner* (1984). All four artists, he argues, were ambitious to recreate landscape in their respective arts in such a way as to bridge the gap between the spatial and the temporal arts. The book incorporates two recent articles by Heffernan, "Space and Time in Literature and the Visual Arts" (*Yearbook of Comparative Criticism,* 1984) and "Wordsworth, Coleridge, and Turner: The Geometry of the Infinite" (*BuR,* 1984), and one earlier essay, "Reflections on Reflections in English Romantic Poetry and Painting" (*BuR,* 1978). This last proposes the fascinating thesis that, for the Romantic artists, reflections in water are superior to the objects reflected because they embody an ideal world or a contrast to reality.

Raymond Lister examines "The Spirit of Romanticism" in its manifold appearances before taking up the "main categories in which British Romantic painting was expressed"—portraiture, both psychological and visionary; historical and topical painting; book illustration; and landscape. Because he thinks literary Romanticism preceded Romanticism in visual art, which "remained under the influence of literature," he constantly draws on poetry to illustrate this "spirit." Blake, as one might expect from Lister's earlier work, dominates the book, especially his aesthetic doctrine of the minute particular. The Kroeber-Walling volume is a collection of essays, most by literary scholars, that attempts to represent the state of the art in the comparative study of literature and (mostly) painting. The emphasis is on affinities, not influences, and on the concrete particulars of time, place, and circumstance rather than on generalizations and isms. The author of several essays and a book that compare specific poems and paintings, Kroeber is the acknowledged leader among Romantics scholars in such comparative work in the last decade, as much for his pursuit of profitable methods by which to compare the arts as for his actual performance, which is always provocative and frequently exhilarating. Implicit in Kroeber's work is the theory of Romanticism that characterizes this volume and especially his own essay "Romantic Historicism: The Temporal Sublime": "The primary thrust of Romantic art was toward neither apocalypse nor transcendence but toward the representation of reality as historical process." As such, it is an important alternative to theories currently enjoying wide favor, one with serious implications in that it does not allow for the return of undifferentiated Romanticism in our or any day. Kroeber's theory, with its embracing of the Romantic experience as open-ended and transitional, resembles that of the Romantic ironists, but his analogies are more likely to come from archaeology, ecology, or chemistry than from psychology or philosophy. Several of the other essays—James A. W. Heffernan's "The English Romantic Perception of Color" (very different from the Augustan), R. F. Storch's "Abstract Idealism in English Romantic Poetry and Painting," Martin Meisel's "The Material Sublime: John Martin, Byron, Turner, and the Theater"—are appropriately mentioned here as dealing with more than one or two Romantic figures. As the titles suggest and Kroeber stresses, both the art of Turner and the aesthetic of the sublime are somehow central to grasping the relationship of the arts in the Romantic movement. A fine piece on Turner by another literary scholar with comparative proclivities is Max Schulz's "Turner's Fabled Atlantis: Venice, Carthage, and London as Paradisal Cityscape" (*SIR,* 1980).

Hugh Honour, unlike Kroeber and his confreres (but like most art critics), shies away from definitions or paradigms of Romantic style. But his *Romanticism* establishes a rich context for the visual arts, in part by resorting frequently to the poets for points of comparison. A review of Honour's book forms part of the first chapter in Charles Rosen and Henri Zerner's *Romanticism and Realism: The Mythology of Nineteenth-Century Art* (1984), a series of interconnected essays (originally appearing in the *New York Review of Books*) concerned with underscoring the often neglected polarity between avant-garde and official art in accounts of nineteenth-century art, as well as with emphasizing the folly of that art history which perpetuates the distinction between high and low art when, in fact, the "progressive abolition" of the distinction is a hallmark of Romanticism. William Vaughan's *Romanticism* (1977) resembles Honour's book rather than Rosen and Zerner's. Said to be introductory, Vaughan's book is actually quite a thorough survey, copiously illustrated. Whatever Romanticism may be, it has, in Vaughan's eyes, a positive meaning for the art of the early nineteenth century. By contrast, Johannes Dobai's *Die Kunstliteratur des Klassizismus und der Romantik in England,* volume 3 (1977), covering the period from 1790 to 1840, is an enormous, erudite tome, which only scholars with strong powers of endurance are likely to use. A single chapter surveys the literature on art by some fifteen writers from Wordsworth (and his sister) to Jane Porter. Hazlitt receives a separate chapter, Coleridge is treated in a chapter on aesthetic theory, and Blake is grouped with painters and sculptors. In a decidedly more popular vein is Peter Quennell's *Romantic England: Writing and Poetry, 1717–1851* (1970). Sir Kenneth Clark's *The Romantic Rebellion* (1969), the text of a widely viewed television series, is also intended for the general reader. Painters organize the book. Two folio volumes,

Marcel Brion's *Romantic Art* (1960) and Michel Le Bris's *Romantics and Romanticism* (1981), have little beyond their size in common. Brion, who subscribes to the Paterian view that Romanticism is a constant of the human mind and thus a recurrent phenomenon in human history, concentrates on the period 1750 to 1850 only so as not to risk "losing sight of the target itself." That target includes architecture and sculpture. Otherwise, his is a conventional book. Le Bris charts a highly personal course through Romanticism, taking as his inspiration Novalis' words: "We dream of traveling through the world. But isn't the world within us? We little know the depths of our own mind. The mysterious road goes inward." A committed Romantic, he admits to designs on his readers; specifically, he seeks to free them from their complicity with totalitarianism in order that they may take up the song of Romanticism, the burden of their own creativity.

Of considerable, if tangential, interest is Bryan Jay Wolf's *Romantic Re-Vision: Culture and Consciousness in Nineteenth-Century American Painting and Literature* (1982), a book that employs contemporary literary theory in the service of revising "our understanding of the nature of American Romantic painting" and of redefining "the enterprise of criticism necessary to recapture that visual heritage." Coleridge is no little help to Wolf in revealing "the radical modernism undergirding American culture of the nineteenth century." Scholars of British Romanticism should find particularly rewarding the chapter on Washington Allston, which includes a trenchant analysis of *Biographia Literaria.*

Articles of special interest to literary scholars are Roy Park's "'Ut Pictura Poesis': The Nineteenth-Century Aftermath" (*JAAC,* 1969), on the ambivalence of Coleridge and Hazlitt toward this concept; Claire Pace's "Claude the Enchanted: Interpretations of Claude in England in the Earlier Nineteenth-Century" (*Burlington Magazine,* 1969), especially by Keats, Hazlitt, and Haydon; Frederick W. Hilles' "Reynolds among the Romantics," in *Literary Theory and Structure: Essays in Honor of William K. Wimsatt,* ed. Frank Brady et al. (1973); and R. W. Liscombe's "The Commencement of Real Art" (*Apollo,* 1976), on the divergence of the critics' prophecies and the actual influence of the Elgin Marbles on Romantic art.

There are, of course, any number of books on Romantic painting itself. Of late one of the most prolific authors in this field is Robert Rosenblum. His *Transformations in Late Eighteenth-Century Art* (1967) was followed by *Modern Painting and the Northern Romantic Tradition, Friedrich to Rothko* (1975); that tradition includes Blake, Palmer, and Turner. Sandwiched between is an article—"The Dawn of British Romantic Painting, 1760–1780," in *The Varied Pattern: Studies in the 18th Century,* ed. Peter Hughes and David Williams (1971)—that locates almost every innovation in painting later called Romantic in the twenty years 1760 to 1780. Rosenblum's art history is theoretically ambitious. Another valuable piece is Frederick J. Cummings' "The Problem of Artistic Style as It Relates to the Beginnings of Romanticism," in *Irrationalism in the Eighteenth Century* (ed. Harold E. Pagliaro, 1972). This essay recommends looking at late eighteenth-century art as "the battle of styles," that is, as a choice of three visual alternatives—atelier (medieval), academy or modal (Renaissance), research and "the critical evaluation of experience." Painters who chose this last style, which includes experience of the past, of human emotions, of literature, and of the observed world, were the first Romantic painters or indeed the first modern artists. Lorenz Eitner, author of one of the essays in the Kroeber-Walling collection, has a very useful volume, *Neoclassicism and Romanticism, 1750–1850: Sources and Documents* (1970). Chapter 4, "Twilight of Humanism," treats the Romantics. William Gaunt's elegant *The Great Century of British Paintings: Hogarth to Turner* (1971) puts more emphasis on the eighteenth century.

The principal study of the relationship between sculpture and poetry in the Romantic period remains Stephen Larrabee's *English Bards and Grecian Marbles: The Relationship between Sculpture and Poetry, Especially in the Romantic Period* (1943), which chronicles the movement in poetry away from mere description of statues toward interpretation of their inner meaning—as in Wordsworth's lines on the statue of Newton. Nancy M. Goslee, "From Marble to Living Form: Sculpture as Art and Analogue from the Renaissance to Blake" (*JEGP*, 1978), begins and ends with Blake, who in *Milton* reshapes sculpture's history. With Los as sculptor, sculpture is transformed from marble to living form. Nicholas Penny's *Church Monuments in Romantic England* (1977) examines the most prevalent sculptures of the day and occasionally invokes the Romantic poets as evidence of a similar sensibility in literature. The churches that housed Penny's monuments and their secular counterparts are the subjects of several works now fairly old, for example, Ronald Bradbury's *The Romantic Theories of Architecture of the Nineteenth Century, in Germany, England and France* (1934), which views the Romantic movement as literary in inception. As the new poetic sensibility spread to other fields, architecture came within its sphere of influence. Bradbury's focus, for the section on England, is the Gothic Revival, as is Agnes Addison's, in *Romanticism and the Gothic Revival* (1938; rpt. 1967). Romantic architecture, by Addison's account, is not a new style but a revival of old styles, especially the Greek and the medieval. In this backward motion, it resembles the first of the three modern architectural styles, Renaissance style, which also turned to ruins (those of Rome) for its idiom. Restricting herself to the Gothic Revival, Addison associates it specifically with Romantic nationalism but does not think that, in England, the Gothic Revival was dependent on the literature of the Romantic movement, Walter Scott notwithstanding. Kenneth Clark's *The Gothic Revival, an Essay in the History of Taste* (1928) anticipated both Bradbury and Addison. J. Mordaunt Crook, *The Greek Revival: Neo-Classical Attitudes in British Architecture, 1760–1870* (1972), has furnished us with the other half of the story. And Sacheverell Sitwell, *British Architects and Craftsmen: A Survey of Taste, Design, and Style during Three Centuries, 1600 to 1830* (1945), provides the wide-angled view. For the lasting influence of Romantic architectural theory, we have Richard P. Adams, "Architecture and the Romantic Theory: Coleridge to Wright" (*Architects' Quarterly*, 1957).

Raymond Immerwahr, "The First Romantic Aesthetics" (*MLQ*, 1960), has traced the genesis of Romantic aesthetics to the art of landscape gardening. To be added to those studies cited elsewhere in this chapter and book are Edward

Malins' *English Landscaping and Literature* (1966) and Kenneth Woodbridge's *Landscape and Antiquity: Aspects of English Culture at Stourhead 1718–1838* (1970), which focuses on the most glorious instance of this art form in Britain. B. Sprague Allen's two-volume *Tides in English Taste (1619–1800): A Background for the Study of Literature* (1937) also attends to landscape gardening as it describes new movements in the arts that precede and sometimes anticipate the Romantic period. But the best way with which to conclude this section is to mention John Dixon Hunt's *The Figure in the Landscape: Poetry, Painting, and Gardening during the Eighteenth Century* (1976), a study that attends to the sibling relations of not two but three arts and insists that eighteenth-century poems (early, middle, and late) incorporating new and changing attitudes toward landscape gardening were "crucial" to the Romantics.

The warnings sounded by René Wellek, W. K. Wimsatt, and others about the confusions literary critics perpetrate when comparing the arts may have deterred literary scholars from investigating the relationships between poetry and music especially. Similarly, one encounters relatively few music theorists or historians who seem comfortable in comparative study. Certainly such scholar-interpreters of Romantic music and literature as Charles Rosen are rare. But the field is not vacant. M. H. Abrams reminded us in *The Mirror and the Lamp* that the Romantics themselves pointed to music rather than painting as the sister art to poetry. And Herbert M. Schueller, in "Literature and Music as Sister Arts: An Aspect of Aesthetic Theory in Eighteenth-Century Britain" (*PQ,* 1947) and "Correspondences between Music and the Sister Arts, according to Eighteenth-Century Aesthetic Theory" (*JAAC,* 1953), has pursued "ut musica poesis" into the eighteenth century, where Romantic aesthetics have their origin. His "The Use and Decorum of Music as Described in British Literature, 1700–1780" (*JHI,* 1952) is also of interest for the Romantic period.

Invariably, authors of books on Romantic music fall back on definitions of Romanticism formulated by Romantic writers or by their literary scholars and critics. Even more than the visual-arts historians, they profess to be hopelessly perplexed by the complexity of the movement and tend to cite Lovejoy as ally and comforter in their dilemma. At the same time they are prompt to endorse a change from "ut pictura poesis" to "ut musica poesis" as symptomatic of Romanticism and eager to adopt the glowing tributes paid to music by Romantic writers, usually at the expense of all the other arts, including poetry. Alfred Einstein's *Music in the Romantic Era* (1947), though it is not often comparative, bears some similarity to current theories of Romantic poetry in its view of Romantic music as characterized by contrasts unified by the two principles of sheer sound—the common obsession of all Romantic composers—and lateness—the common burden fostered by the knowledge of music's long history. Fredrich Blume, *Classic and Romantic Music* (trans. 1970), stresses the simultaneous development of Romantic music and literature as further developments of classicism. He tends to take the Romantic writers and composers (his examples are predominantly German) at their word, making for enthusiastic prose. Like so many music historians (and art historians, too), he gets caught in the classic-romantic trap. Barry S. Brook, in

"Sturm und Drang and the Romantic Period in Music" (*SIR*, 1970), sees early Romantic literature and Romantic music as parallel precisely because both reveal the classical-romantic duality. Kenneth B. Klaus, in *The Romantic Period in Music* (1970), views Romanticism in music as an attack on the classical system of tonality and a corresponding search for something new, which materializes eventually as atonality. Romantic art generally is, for Klaus, so many paradoxes—paradoxes recognized but not resolved. Rey M. Longyear, in *Nineteenth-Century Romanticism in Music* (1969; 2nd ed. 1973), explores at length the topic "Romanticism and Music," resorting frequently to comparisons of literature and music. Longyear thinks Romantic writers had a greater influence on Romantic composers than the other way round. Of particular interest to literary scholars should be his article "Beethoven and Romantic Irony" (*Musical Quarterly,* 1970). He relies on the same theories of Romantic irony that Mellor, Rajan, and Simpson do. Peter le Huray and James Day propose that, in order to understand the word "romantic" when applied to music, music historians need to examine the "testimony" of the Romantics themselves. Accordingly, they have collected and edited the pertinent materials, in *Music and Aesthetics in the Eighteenth and Early Nineteenth Centuries* (1981), thereby enabling students to experience firsthand the aesthetic issues that, in debate, produced the notion of Romantic music. A projected second volume is to contain "evidence of the ways in which aesthetic attitudes were given practical expression."

If one has time for only one work on Romanticism and music, it should be Jacques Barzun's splendid two-volume *Berlioz and the Romantic Century* (1950; 3rd rev. ed. 1969) and, in particular, the essay entitled "The Century of Romanticism." A model of cultural and intellectual history, Barzun's study is fully informed by a scholar's knowledge of Romantic literature and its criticism; moreover, Barzun, in other books, has himself helped to elucidate and validate the concept of Romanticism, particularly in its continuum and later aesthetic manifestations. More recent is Conrad L. Donakowski's *A Muse for the Masses: Ritual and Music in an Age of Democratic Revolution, 1770–1870* (1977), a cultural history bordering on anthropology, refreshing in its attention to the less spectacular mass movements of the time. Like other scholars, Donakowski is preoccupied with the aesthetic change from "ut pictura poesis" to "ut musica poesis," which he sums up as "Make life not geometry but music." Music becomes, with the Romantic age, the chief means of popular "participation in politics, art, religion, and life generally." The composer becomes first among artists, the main hope of realizing the Romantic goal of reintegrating "the western psyche and culture under leadership of artistic insight." The heart of Donakowski's book is the section on these two themes: artist as hero, music as communication. The English Romantics are not prominent in this richly multidisciplinary work, but they are cited occasionally. Even so, the literary scholar can learn much about the musical expression of motifs pervasive in Romantic poetry—for example, the quest for childhood innocence (in hymns), the return to nature (in a restored plain chant), the search for organic wholeness (in a reclaimed Renaissance polyphony). Donakowski's conclusion makes it clear that he has not been writing of a dead culture: "Each autumn of romanticism has...become a second spring"—

understandably so, for "that cluster of geniuses who began as humanists . . . formed our modern ego and its consciousness." Donakowski's book is not to be missed. Nor is James Anderson Winn's *Unsuspected Eloquence: A History of the Relations between Poetry and Music* (1981), which, if not the last word, is the latest on the interest of poets and composers in one another's art during the Romantic period in England, as well as during earlier and later periods. Winn cites as one of the causes of Romanticism "those changes in poetry brought about by attempts to make it aspire, in Pater's famous phrase, 'to the condition of music.'" But he also argues that "the condition was a myth, an inaccurate notion of music as an immediate language of the passions without syntactic or formal restraints." Some of Winn's best pages analyze the results of this misunderstanding of music—first, on Romantic poetry (not, by any means, all bad results), and, then, on music, which eventually succumbed to the literary myth of itself. Finally, George Graham's "Toward a Definition of Romanticism in Music" (*QQ*, 1965) explores traditional definitions with the goal of showing their weaknesses.

Two books on Romantic opera appeared a year apart. Lectures given at Cornell in 1937–38 by Edward J. Dent were edited by Winton Dean and published as *The Rise of Romantic Opera* (1977). Dent's context includes literature. Characteristically brash is Peter Conrad's *Romantic Opera and Literary Form* (1978), a slim volume that argues that virtually every literary form is more significant to opera than the drama is, the novel being the closest analogue. Jean-Pierre Barricelli, in "Romantic Writers and Music: The Case of Mazzini" (*SIR*, 1975), is also concerned in part with opera as a form with the potential to realize Mazzini's program for a new music that would reconcile German or harmonic music with Italian or melodic music and, in doing so, unify human society. But Mazzini was highly critical of current opera, finding hope for his dream only in Beethoven. No Romantic writer inspired more composers of opera than Scott. According to Jerome Mitchell, *The Walter Scott Operas: An Analysis of Operas Based on the Works of Sir Walter Scott* (1977), only Shakespeare is the source of more libretti. His book strikes, therefore, at the heart of the subject, which by Mitchell's account can lead literary scholars a merry chase. It was not, of course, just composers of opera who were interested in setting Romantic literature to music. Scott, Byron, and others were fairly besieged at times by songwriters. Bryan N. S. Gooch and David Thatcher, in *Musical Settings of British Romantic Literature* (1982), have cataloged all known musical settings, published and manuscript, of Romantic literature. The variety of musical form given Romantic poetry by composers would seem to reflect the variety of poetic form from which they had to choose.

Two books that are of great value for Romantics studies, though they are restricted to the eighteenth century, are Lawrence Lipking's *The Ordering of the Arts in Eighteenth-Century England* (1970) and James S. Malek's *The Arts Compared: An Aspect of Eighteenth-Century British Aesthetics* (1974). Lipking treats the effort in the second half of the century of such writers as Walpole, Reynolds, T. Warton, and Johnson to order the arts of painting, music, and poetry by establishing their histories and by guiding the tastes of their audiences. Malek treats the effort to find bases from which to compare the arts so as to make clear their similarities and differences. Following in the wake of these efforts, the Romantic poets were inevitably better informed both about the nature of each art and about the relationship of one art to another than their predecessors were, even if they were, consequently, also more anxious about the role and the future of their preferred art form.

English Romanticism Abroad

Given the title of this volume, it is inappropriate to attend to Romanticism outside England except where English Romanticism is involved, as in general studies of the movement that invoke the English Romantics or in comparative studies that feature them. Already, examples of both have been cited in this chapter. Some of English Romanticism's most prominent scholars—for example, Wellek, Peckham, Frye, Hartman, Kroeber—are comparatists, their writing typically comparative. And, as I have stated before, newer scholars in the field, especially those of strong theoretical bent, are giving a comparative coloring to trendsetting books and articles. Moreover, one of our principal journals, *Studies in Romanticism,* is devoted to promoting the comparative and interdisciplinary study of Romanticism. A separate section at this point in the chapter serves, then, only to catch up important items not mentioned heretofore and to recall titles from the third edition still of consequence.

Certainly one of the most memorable of the earlier studies is Mario Praz's *The Romantic Agony* (1931; trans. 1933), which gave enduring fame to some of the more sensational features—the erotic, satanic, pathological—of Romantic literature wherever it flourished. Two comparative symposia of the early 1940s—"Romanticism: A Symposium" (*PMLA,* 1940) and "Symposium of Romanticism" (*JHI,* 1941)—are of historical interest; they complement but do not duplicate each other. Largely of historical interest now, too, is Paul Van Tieghem's *L'Ere romantique: Le romantisme dans la littérature européenne* (1948), a work impressive in its accumulation of materials but disappointing in its use of them. H. G. Schenk was really the first scholar to succeed in presenting a readable account of European Romanticism. His *The Mind of the European Romantics: An Essay in Cultural History* (1966) offers a familiar concept of the Romantic mind—contradictory, dissonant, conflicted—but it enables Schenk to integrate literature, philosophy, religion, painting, and music into a full cultural history of European Romanticism. Between Van Tieghem and Schenk, both René Wellek and Henry H. H. Remak investigated the common features of European Romanticism or, more accurately, the relative consensus on what those features may be. Wellek's 1963 bibliographical essay "Romanticism Reconsidered" (cited earlier) seeks to show a growing area of agreement among American and European scholars about Romanticism, especially in the period from 1949 to 1963. Remak, in two essays—"West European Romanticism: Definition and Scope," in *Comparative Literature: Method and Perspective* (ed. N. P. Stallknecht and Horst Frenz, 1961), and "A Key to West European Romanticism?" (*CollG,* 1968)—tends toward lists and charts in the manner of Van Tieghem but interprets his data to discover a common denominator in the Romantics' attempt "to heal a break in the universe." Remak seems aware of his proximity to Wellek, who in demonstrating a growing area of agreement is at the same time suggesting that his own notion of Romanticism is being widely accepted.

The comparatist scholar most completely preoccupied with illuminating European Romanticism in the last decade or so is Lilian Furst. An early article—"Romanticism in Historical Perspective" (*CLS*, 1968; rpt. *Comparative Literature: Matter and Method*, ed. A. Owen Aldridge, 1969)—rehearses the history of Romanticism in England, Germany, and France in order to demonstrate the lack of a unified movement across national boundaries. As such, it heralds a book with nearly the same title—*Romanticism in Perspective*—published the following year (rpt. 1972). Furst's perspective stresses the differences rather than the likenesses between national Romantic movements· but sees "creative renewal" inherent in each of them. The volume on Romanticism for Methuen's Critical Idiom series (1969; 2nd ed. 1976) is written from the same point of view. In *The Contours of European Romanticism* (1979), a collection of earlier but revised essays, she develops further her view that Romanticism is "multeity in unity." Along with many of her contemporaries, she finds the pursuit of "contours" (or "configurations" or "affinities") more rewarding because less problematic than the pursuit of definitions. Contours—whether seen from archetypal, historical, or aesthetic perspective—can and do overlap; definitions tend to set apart. Furst's most recent contribution, *European Romanticism: Self-Definition* (1980), allows readers to compare central Romantic texts (or excerpts therefrom).

'Romantic' and Its Cognates: The European History of a Word (1972), a collection of essays tracing the history of the word "romantic" in Western Europe and Russia, edited by Hans Eichner, supersedes all previous accounts (see *ERP3* 50). The essays are written by specialists in the languages and literatures for which each is responsible. Raymond Immerwahr has written the chapter on the word in England and elsewhere before 1790; George Whalley, on the word in England during the Romantic period. Curiously, Whalley is reluctant to use critically or descriptively the term "romantic" that is his subject (see, in this regard, his earlier essay "Literary Romanticism" [*QQ*, 1965] and that of Irving Massey, "The Romantic Movement: Phrase or Fact?" [*DR*, 1964]). Moreover, his essay is as much criticism as history. Generally, however, the authors keep to the historical method. Henry H. H. Remak brings up the rear with a chapter "Trends of Recent Research on West European Romanticism," the emphasis being on post-1960 scholarship; he claims a consensus among scholars on the definition of Romanticism as propounded especially by Wellek. The result is an enormously informative volume and a credit to comparative literature. *Die Europäische Romantik*, by Ernst Behler and eight other scholars (1972), follows a similar plan, though the emphasis here is more literary than linguistic. In the introduction Behler himself writes on the idea of European Romanticism in critical thought. The eight essays that follow take up the subject country by country, including Poland. Helmut Viebrock contributes the essay on the English Romantics.

The earlier of two recent books on German-English literary relations in the Romantic period is Rosemary Ashton's *The German Idea: Four English Writers and the Reception of German Thought 1800–1860* (1980). The four writers are Coleridge, Carlyle, G. H. Lewes, and George Eliot. Ashton's study, thanks to its sharp focus, tells a coherent story, one that links up on occasion with Shaffer's book on biblical criticism. The later book, Amala Hanke's *Spatiotemporal Consciousness in English and German Romanticism: A Comparative Study of Novalis, Blake, Wordsworth, and Eichendorff* (1981), though also preoccupied with only four writers, is more ambitious. The author proposes to demonstrate, through a metacritical examination of the four writers, nothing less than "a common denominator of the thought of the age, both in England and Germany." That denominator is the Romantic spatiotemporal consciousness, the paradigm for which emerges from the apparently diverse but actually similar responses of the four Romantics to the experience of time and space. For this paradigm, dialectic in mode and circular in form, Hanke is admittedly indebted to Abrams' *Natural Supernaturalism,* but she argues that, because of "the German late Romantic return to organized religion," Abrams' secular, psychological model of Romantic consciousness as it seeks redemption of mind and nature through the confrontation with time and space needs to be modified to include orthodox Christian belief regarding sin, fall, and salvation. The narrow focus of Ashton's book and the metacritical bent of Hanke's mean that, for the larger story, scholars must still consult earlier studies by A. C. Bradley, *English Poetry and German Philosophy in the Age of Wordsworth* (1909; rpt. *A Miscellany,* 1929); F. W. Stokoe, *German Influence in the English Romantic Period, 1788–1818* (1920); V. Stockley, *German Literature as Known in England, 1750–1830* (1929); and Eudo C. Mason, *Deutsche und englische Romantik* (1959). Horst Oppel's comparative essay "Englische und deutsche Romantik" (*Die neueren Sprachen,* 1956; incorporated into his *The Sacred River* [1959] and reprinted with slight changes in *Versdichtung der englischen Romantik: Interpretationen,* ed. Teut A. Riese and Dieter Riesner, 1968) is now surrounded by essays on the German influence on English literature and on the literature of the English Romantics in Germany, making up three chapters in volume 2 of his *Englisch-deutsche Literaturbeziehungen* (1971). Additional contributions in essay form are René Wellek's "German and English Romanticism: A Confrontation" (*SIR,* 1964; rpt. *Confrontations,* 1965) and, indirectly, Geoffrey Hartman's "Romanticism and 'Antiself-Consciousness' " (*CentR,* 1962; rpt. *Romanticism and Consciousness,* ed. Harold Bloom, 1970). Future students of the subject should benefit enormously from the ten volumes containing over 1,500 reviews of German literature in British periodicals, compiled and edited by John Boening under the title *The Reception of Classical German Literature in England, 1760–1860: A Documentary History from Contemporary Periodicals* (1977).

Highly specialized books such as Wellek's *Immanuel Kant in England, 1793–1838* (1931), E. D. Hirsch's *Wordsworth and Schelling: A Typological Study of Romanticism* (1960), and Werner W. Beyer's *The Enchanted Forest* (1963) are not likely to be superseded altogether, though in the case of Wellek's book modifications—some by Wellek himself—are now indicated.

Students requiring a survey of French influence on English literature in the period must still depend on Marcel Moraud's *Le Romantisme français en Angleterre de 1814 à 1848*...(1933). Our knowledge of English-French relations in the Romantic period has been greatly advanced, however, by Margery Sabin's *English Romanticism and the French Tradition* (1976). Her comparisons are made to the end of affirming the strong national and hence separate literary traditions of England and France. "My first and last impression has been that French and English writers in this period have done the same things well." Sabin's long and illuminating comparison of Rousseau and Wordsworth invokes Hazlitt but also points to a comparative essay by her mentor, Paul de Man, "Structure intentionelle de l'image romantique" (*Revue Internationale de Philosophie*, 1960; trans. for Bloom's *Romanticism and Consciousness*). Jacques Voisine's *J.-J. Rousseau en Angleterre à l'époque romantique: Les Ecrits autobiographiques et la légende* (1956) is now joined by Edward Duffy's *Rousseau in England: The Context for Shelley's Critique of the Enlightenment* (1979), which makes a case for *The Triumph of Life* as the most ambitious effort in English Romantic poetry to mythologize Rousseau. Like Sabin, Margaret Gilman, in "Revival and Revolution in English and French Romantic Poetry" (*YFS*, 1950), points to differences deriving from national traditions but for a somewhat different purpose: she wishes to account for the supposed inferiority of French Romantic poetry to English. If the recent comparative studies suggest less rather than more literary influence—find the contrasts more striking than the similarities—there is still the occasional piece that goes in the other direction. One such is John C. E. Greene's "Maurice de Guérin, Barbey d'Aurevilly et les romantiques anglais: Étude sur le poème en prose" (*CRCL*, 1978), which finds English roots for the French poem in prose.

Beyond any doubt, the most provocative comparative work on English and French Romanticism since Sabin's study is Arden Reed's *Romantic Weather: The Climates of Coleridge and Baudelaire* (1983). A long opening section reviews the history of the idea of weather, to the end of revealing the several ways in which that idea "can help us to calibrate the transition from Classic to Romantic." Meteorological figures, Reed observes in reference to Abrams' brief for the plant as the seminal image for Romantic poems, "are at least as pervasive as botanical ones in the literature of the period." When turning to the texts of Coleridge and Baudelaire, Reed employs the strategies of deconstruction as "the most adequate way to apprehend the activity of the weather, to track the vapors that are the flux and reflux of the imagination in the poetry of Baudelaire and Coleridge." Comparatists may well find Reed's interchapter "Abysmal Influence," where he links Coleridge and Baudelaire through a story De Quincey told concerning Piranesi's engravings of Rome, his most intriguing. The engraver's abyss-labyrinth-prison becomes, in Reed's skillful hands, a figure for influence. "While it traps the artist, the prison also liberates by unleashing astonishing energies."

From France comes the first major study of Anglo-Irish literature in the Romantic period, Patrick Rafroidi's *L'Irlande et le romantisme: La littérature irlandaise-anglaise de 1789 à 1850 et sa place dans le mouvement occidental* (1972; trans. Lucille Watson and Margaret Stanley Vaughan, as *Irish Literature in England: The Romantic Period (1789–1850)*, 1981). Concerned to show the impact of the Romantic poets—especially Wordsworth, Shelley, Byron—on Irish poets, Rafroidi also wishes to show the reverse, that is, the impact, at times, of Irish writers on English poets. The importance of Rafroidi's subject is that from such Romantic crosscurrents Irish literature derived the makings of greatness. In Esteban Pujals' *El romanticismo inglés: Orígenes, repercusión y relaciones con la literatura española* (1969), we also have now a full study of British Romanticism's impact on Spanish literature, beginning with the pre-Romantic period in both countries. Pujals' subject casts certain minor figures, for example, Blanco White and Robert Southey, in leading roles and mixes American writers freely with British. Especially useful is the author's discussion of translations.

From the eastern side of Europe come two volumes devoted to European Romanticism, in which British Romantics figure as appropriate: I. Sőtér's *The Dilemma of Literary Science* (1973; trans. Éva Róna, 1979) and *European Romanticism,* edited by Sőtér and I. Neupokoyeva (1974; trans. Éva Róna, 1977). In the former, Sőtér seeks generally to extend this comparative study of Romanticism by including Central and Eastern European literature, notably Hungarian, and particularly to take issue with Van Tieghem's concept of pre-Romanticism. In the latter, Sőtér and Neupokoyeva have collected essays—all comparative and some interdisciplinary—by other scholars that treat, from the socialist perspective, broad topics such as "The Romantic Attitude to Nature" or "Romantic Literature and Music." Inevitably, some of the essays are better than others, but all are in various degrees informative by virtue of their range and point of view. The attention to Byron's plays, for example, in E. Saprykina's "Some Distinctive Features of the Romantic Theory of Drama" goes far beyond that given them by most Anglo-American scholars. Another scholar to expand the geographical (and chronological) borders of Romanticism is Hubert F. Babinksi. *The Mazeppa Legend in European Romanticism* (1974) traces the sources of the popular legend to Eastern Europe in the seventeenth century. Babinski's engrossing book is precisely the sort of study that vindicates the practice of comparative literature. His concentration on the Mazeppa story enables him eventually to compare Eastern European Romanticism with that of the West and ultimately enables him to characterize the Romantic imagination in its fullest manifestation as "mystical." That a common quality of Romanticism, Eastern and Western, is a sharp awareness of the inadequacy of existing modes of communication is the thesis of Monica Partridge's "Romanticism and the Concept of Communication in a Slavonic and a Non-Slavonic Literature" (*RMS,* 1973). Urging scholars of Russian literature to pay less attention to Byron and Scott and more attention to *Lyrical Ballads,* Partridge engages in an extended comparison of Wordsworth and Coleridge with Pushkin, by way of setting the example. Ultimately, though, she suggests why Russian and English Romanticism, for all they had in common, developed so very differently. Going still farther east, James Whipple Miller looks at "English Romanticism and Chinese Nature Poetry" (*CL,* 1972), not so much to point up similarities but to underscore differences, the most important of which center in the Chinese poet, who does not subscribe to the concept of creative imagination and hence does not acknowledge the special status it confers on the poet. Geographically farther from Britain than China, Australia is, of course, in every other respect infinitely closer. It should come as no surprise, therefore, that Australian poetry, according to Noel Macainish, in "Symbol, Pageant, Sequence—A New Kind of Australian Poem" (*Westerly*, 1977), long under the influence of English Romanticism—especially Romantic ideas of symbolism and poetic language—continues, albeit in new ways, to reflect the Romantic heritage.

Any number of studies treat the relationships of England and Italy in the Romantic period. Chief among them are Margaret C. W. Wicks, *The Italian Exiles in London: 1816–1848* (1937); C. P. Brand, *Italy and the English Romantics: The Italianate Fashion in Early Nineteenth-Century England* (1957); Herbert Barrows, "Convention and Novelty in the Romantic Generation's Experience in Italy" (*BNYPL*, 1963); and Kenneth Churchill, *Italy and English Literature, 1764–1930* (1980). For the Romantics' knowledge and use of Dante, Boccaccio, and Tasso, there are the studies of W. P. Friederich, "Dante and English Romanticism," in *Dante's Fame Abroad, 1350–1850* (1950); Oswald Doughty, "Dante and the English Romantic Poets" (*EM*, 1951); H. G. Wright, *Boccaccio in England from Chaucer to Tennyson* (1957); and C. P. Brand, *Torquato Tasso: A Study of the Poet and of His Contribution to English Literature* (1964). The most distinguished contribution to date, however, is Karl Kroeber's *The Artifice of Reality: Poetic Style in Wordsworth, Foscolo, Keats, and Leopardi* (1964). Kroeber's book, which is concerned with the advent of a new style in poetry that he calls Mediterranean, provides first-rate evidence for an international Romanticism while at the same time observing its fundamental diversity.

One of the essays in the Sőtér and Neupokoyeva collection examines the "Romantic Writers and the Classical Literary Heritage," with special attention to the profoundly personal, lyrical feeling of the Romantics for the great artists of the past, with whom they seem to sense a "co-presence" and "co-participation." Greco-Anglo literary relationships can be approached through Harry Levin's *The Broken Column: A Study in Romantic Hellenism* (1931), which maintains that the true spirit of ancient Greece was given a too sentimental interpretation in English Romantic literature; through Terence Spencer's *Fair Greece, Sad Relic* (1954), the definitive study to date of philhellenism in English literature; through Eugene N. Borza's "Sentimental Philhellenism and the Image of Greece," in *Classics and the Classical Tradition: Essays Presented to Robert E. Dengler*... (1973), which argues that sentimental philhellenism derives from Shelley rather than from Byron and chastises classics scholars for following the lead of Shelley rather than that of Byron, who escaped (as most scholars have not) the sentimental view of Greece; through John Buxton's *The Grecian Taste: Literature in the Age of Neo-Classicism, 1740–1820* (1978); and through Timothy Webb's *English Romantic Hellenism, 1700–1824* (1982), a selection of readings on the subject. Spencer's study is relevant largely because of Byron; Buxton's has chapters on Shelley and Blake (as well as on Landor and Peacock).

For all the attention to Anglo-American literary relations in recent times, full-scale comparative studies of English and American Romanticism are relatively rare. We have nothing comparable in scope, for example, to Stephen Spender's *Love-Hate Relations* (1974). Still, there are several essays of note, chief among them Tony Tanner's provocative "Notes for a Comparison between American and European Romanticism" (*JAmS*, 1968). Originally a talk, Tanner's piece inclines to distinctions rather than resemblances. Wystan Curnow, in "Romanticism and Modern American Criticism" (*SIR*, 1973), argues that American Romantic literature has much to gain from the new ideas of Romanticism implicit in the approaches to British Romanticism of critics like Peckham, Wasserman, and Langbaum—that is, from a "Romantic criticism"; only such criticism can do justice to American Romantic literature. Single American writers continue, of course, to be studied in the light of British Romanticism. Richard Harter Fogle's "Nathaniel Hawthorne and the Great English Romantic Poets" (*KSJ*, 1972–73) shows, in a well-tempered essay, that the relationship of Hawthorne and the British Romantics has been underrated. Michael G. Yetman, in "Emily Dickinson and the English Romantic Tradition" (*TSLL*, 1973), taking his departure from Bloom's essay "The Internalization of Quest Romance," wishes to put to rest the view of Dickinson as a latter-day metaphysical; rather, he argues, her tradition is the English Romantic tradition critically received. Nearly ten years later Joanne Feit Diehl has published a book-length study of the same subject: *Dickinson and the Romantic Imagination* (1981). Also indebted to Bloom, Diehl puts even greater stress on Dickinson's reinterpretation of the Romantic tradition but, in doing so, underscores that Romanticism is indeed her tradition. V. P. Chari, in "Walt Whitman and the Language of the Romantics" (*EA*, 1977), suggests that Whitman early and late—and despite efforts to break free—reflected the critical assumptions and values of Romanticism and that, in fact, his later poetry reveals a deepening of Romantic lyricism stemming from Wordsworth. Raymond Benoit's *Single Nature's Double Name: The Collectedness of the Conflicting in British and American Romanticism* (1973) takes us far beyond the Romantic movement either in Britain or in America by extending the Romantic movement in America to the present day. After establishing the primacy of Coleridge to Romantic philosophy and poetics, Benoit treats the Americanizing of Romanticism in the nineteenth century and, eventually, in the twentieth century by Snyder, Stafford, Wilbur, and Nemerov. By comparison—or even by itself—John Press's "English Romanticism and American Poetry" (in Asselineau et al.) is a superficial essay on the subject of how American poetry (or the best American poetry) reacted to English Romanticism. Jay Parini, *Theodore Roethke: An American Romantic* (1979), deals with Roethke's debts to the English Romantics, particularly Blake and Wordsworth, but his emphasis is on the American manifestation of Romanticism. One of Roethke's mentors is the subject of Carl Rapp's *William Carlos Williams and the Romantic Ideology* (1984). Charles Altieri's *Enlarging the Temple: New Directions in American Poetry during the 1960s* (1979) uses Coleridge and Wordsworth as the sources of, respectively, modernist poetics rejected by poets of the 1960s and postmodernist poetics adopted in its place. Lest we forget, Clarice Short's *The English Romantics and America: Dream and Reality* (1974), a lecture given at the University of Utah, reminds us that the English Romantic poets were intensely interested in America. Wordsworth and Coleridge used William Bartram to represent the Romantic view of nature in America: green. Byron used Daniel Boone to represent the Romantic view of the natural individual in America: free, thus good. And Coleridge, Byron, and Shelley used George Washington to represent the Romantic view of the social individual in America: free to acquire and wield power without becoming its victim.

English Romanticism often goes abroad, of course, through translation, the subject of R. Kvič's "Translating English Romantic Poetry," in *The Nature of Translation: Essays on the Theory and Practice of Literary Translation* (1970). After advancing a theory of translation—the four steps or phases of translation and the three checks for faithfulness of translation—Kvič turns to instances. Many of them are woefully inadequate, but it is possible to demonstrate successful translations of Keats in Serbo-Croatian and of Shelley in both Czech and Polish.

Romanticism Past, Present, and Future

The relation of the Romantics to the literary past is best approached through Walter Jackson Bate's fine essay *The Burden of the Past and the English Poet* (1970). In feeling the past to be burdensome—restricting and inhibiting—the Romantics were, he shows, true offspring of the eighteenth-century writers, the first to experience the problem and to reckon with it. In responding to the burden with honesty and courage, as their immediate predecessors had shown them how to do, in openly admiring the Renaissance masters and deliberately striking out to emulate them, the Romantics discovered the freedom to become great artists in their own right and thereby transformed burden into blessing. A short but provocative essay by Harold Bloom, "First and Last Romantics" (*SIR*, 1970), affirms Bate's ideas. (See above under "Romanticism and Criticism" for Bloom's full-blown theory of the Romantics' relation to their predecessors.) For the most part, books and articles on this subject belong in the chapters subsequent to this, but it is appropriate to mention here some items of a general character.

Milton's special importance to the Romantics has never been in doubt—witness R. D. Havens' *The Influence of Milton on English Poetry* (1922), but because Milton is the principal cause of anxiety for the Romantics in the antithetical readings of Harold Bloom (see especially *The Anxiety of Influence*) and others, in recent years studies of this relationship have greatly proliferated, even to the point of stimulating the creation of a journal (entitled originally *Milton and the Romantics*, more recently called *Romanticism Past and Present*). Besides the work of the senior Yale critics, in which Milton figures repeatedly, there is Leslie Brisman's *Milton's Poetry of Choice and Its Romantic Heirs* (1973). Armed with the theory of burden (Bate) and of poetic revision (Bloom), Brisman sets up a scheme of choice between willed and unwilled (self-conscious or natural) poetry, borrowed from William Empson. Milton, who himself chose to be the subjective poet, is the model of the conscious will for the Romantics, most especially Wordsworth. The poetry of both is thus the poetry of choice, a "romantic achievement" for Milton as for his legatees. Proportionately, only a small part of the book is devoted to the "Romantic heirs." Joseph Anthony Wittreich, Jr., in "Cartographies: Reading and Misreading Milton and the Romantics" (*Milton and the Romantics*, 1976), sifts the strengths and weaknesses of Bloom's interpretations. In a series of books and articles, however, he has made this subject very much his own bailiwick. "Milton, Man and Thinker: Apotheosis in Romantic Criticism" (*BuR,* 1968) corrects the received view that Romantic criticism of Milton is narrow in interest (i.e., limited to his great artistry) or radical in perception (i.e., magnifying and distorting Satan). Better than Augustan or Victorian criticism, Romantic criticism holds Milton the man, the poet, and the thinker in balance. By way of supporting this point, Wittreich edited a fat volume entitled *The Romantics on Milton: Formal Essays and Critical Asides* in 1970, followed in 1972 by a note, "Milton's Romantic Audience" (*AN&Q*)—not as extensive as we might suppose. In 1975 appeared *Milton and the Line of Vision,* a collection of essays designed to show that, in his own line, which is the line of vision (not of wit), Milton's influence on English poetry has been salutary or inspirational and not, as Eliot for a time believed, debilitating. The essays also seek, by examining both Milton's relationships with some of his predecessors and the relationships of some of his successors with him, to clarify the Miltonic tradition in English poetry, which Wittreich here and elsewhere designates the tradition of prophecy, "whose holding spool is the Bible—its prophecies and especially the Book of Revelation." Most recently, Wittreich has expanded the theses and insights of his earlier writings to form a full-length study, *Visionary Poetics: Milton's Tradition and His Legacy* (1979). A work of historical criticism, Wittreich's book exemplifies how much yet remains to historical criticism. Specifically, for Milton, it must "show more clearly the extent to which ... 'Miltonic Romanticism' is one of the main sources of post-Miltonic poetry." And this is Wittreich's goal. Only the first part of Wittreich's title—"tradition"—is realized in this volume; a sequel, now under way, will treat the "legacy." A further sign of Romantic interest in Milton may be found in Jerome A. Kramer's " 'Virtue, Religion, and Patriotism': Some Biographies of Milton in the Romantic Era" (*Milton and the Romantics,* 1977).

No other predecessor of the Romantics has received comparable attention, not even Shakespeare, whose connections with the eighteenth century, by contrast, have been extensively studied (see *ERP3* 19). R. W. Babcock's *The Genesis of Shakespeare Idolatry, 1766–1799: A Study of English Criticism of the Late Eighteenth Century* (1931), which investigates the key theme, is supplemented by Earl Wasserman's "Shakespeare and the English Romantic Movement" in *The Persistence of Shakespeare Idolatry,* ed. Herbert M. Schueller (1964). Wasserman speculates on whether Shakespeare's plays, in the Romantic period, passed beyond idolatry, their status in the eighteenth century, to become the sources of archetypes. He concludes that, though a tendency in this direction can be observed, the Romantics were on the whole too close to Elizabethan England to engage widely in such use of Shakespeare. Even so, Samuel Schoenbaum's chapter on the Romantics in *Shakespeare's Lives* (1970) indicates that the Romantic critics—Lamb, Hazlitt, Coleridge—"effected a transformation in the way that Shakespeare was read and understood." The Romantics did not, however, write biographies of the Bard, preferring to concentrate on his works. John Crawford's *Romantic Criticism of Shakespearian Drama* (1978) is, in fact, restricted to criticism of four plays—*Hamlet, Antony and Cleopatra, King Henry V,* and *The Merchant of Venice.* The author is motivated by the belief that the Romantic school of Shakespeare criticism has been and still is the most influential and by the personal conviction that characterization, which the Romantics stressed, is the "heart of any dramatic creation." For the larger picture—the Romantics on the whole of Shakespeare—we still depend on Augustus Ralli's *A History of Shakespeare Criticism,* volume 1 (1932).

The important subject of Dryden's and Pope's influence on the Romantics is investigated by Upali Amarasinghe in *Dryden and Pope in the Early Nineteenth Century* (1962). Stanley Archer's "A Dryden Critic of the Romantic Period" (*SCB,* 1973)—one Thomas Green of Ipswich—adds a mite to the evidence of continued esteem for the neoclassical poets during the Romantic period. The principal item for this period, however, is Harold Orel's *English Romantic Poets and the Enlightenment: Nine Essays on a Literary Relationship,* in *Studies on Voltaire and the Eighteenth Century* (vol. 103, ed. Theodore Besterman, 1973). Orel provides an essay each on Burns, Blake, Coleridge, Wordsworth, Scott, Byron, and Keats and two on Shelley. No new definitions of the Enlightenment or of the Romantic movement emerge from these essays, which focus on aspects of the relationship, not on the nature of it; and Orel proffers no unifying concept or thesis. One comes away from the book, however, more persuaded of the continuity of the two periods than of the discontinuity. A series of essays by E. H. King on James Beattie, if they overstate the Scottish poet's influence on Romanticism, nevertheless fill a vacuum in the account of the Romantic poets' literary roots. "James Beattie's Literary Essays (1776, 1783) and the Evolution of Romanticism" (*SSL,* 1974) argues that we have not paid enough attention to the origins of Romantic criticism, which is not so original as Romantics scholars like to think. "James Beattie's *The Minstrel* and the Romantic Poets" (*Aberdeen Univ. Rev.,* 1976) argues that, after Gray's elegy, Beattie's poem was the most popular and influential poem of its time, its hero, Edwin, the prototype of the young Romantic poet we see in *The Prelude, Alastor,* and *Childe Harold's Pilgrimage.* "James Beattie and the Growth of Romantic Melancholy" (*ScLJ,* 1978) repeats to some extent the earlier essays before going on to argue that Beattie's Romanticism because it is Scottish is real, as evidenced in his distinctive, fresh melancholy. King's writing is a believer's cause: the recovery of Beattie from neglect. Burns, the subject of one of Orel's chapters, is the subject also of Raymond Bentman's "The Romantic Poets and Critics on Robert Burns" (*TSLL,* 1964). The Romantics looked on Burns as a spiritual kinsman and both felt and acknowledged his influence—a point of view not common in twentieth-century criticism.

Two essays by L. J. Swingle take us into the Romantic period itself. In "Late Crabbe in Relation to the Augustans and Romantics: The Temporal Labyrinth of His *Tales in Verse*" (*ELH,* 1975), he distinguishes Crabbe from the Augustans but not to make of him a Romantic: "Crabbe stands on the modern side not only of the Augustans but also of the Romantics. He nudges us a step down the literary road toward the uneasy eden of *A Child's Garden of Verses,* where the world is so full of a multitude of things." In "Stalking the Essential John Clare: Clare in Relation to His Romantic Contemporaries" (*SIR*, 1975), Swingle asks us to judge Clare by his own axioms, not by those of his contemporaries. The result is a poet who contrasts sharply with Wordsworth (he does not project his own mind on nature), Keats (he is not afraid to look "too far into the sea"), and Tennyson (he does not anguish over a "nature red in tooth and claw"). Swingle is one of the few scholars to take seriously the much proclaimed obligation to investigate the whole Romantic period and not just that part constituted by the six poets. These essays strike one like gusts of clean, fresh air. May they stir corresponding breezes, if not gales, in other scholars.

Just as scholars no longer care to seal off the Romantics from their predecessors or, to use a more fashionable term, precursors, so scholars no longer care to isolate the Romantics from their successors, Victorian and twentieth-century poets, to whom they are related in much of the writing about "traditions," "continuities," "affinities," and so on, by the term "High Romantics." As Kerry McSweeney has put it, in "Romantic Continuities and Mutations: Browning to Stevens" (*HAB*, 1979): "Perhaps the major critical orientation of the past twenty years in English studies has been the recognition of the essential continuity and the essentially Romantic basis of British and American poetry from the beginning of the nineteenth century to the present." In a sympathetic essay, "Three Blind Men and the Elephant: The Problem of Nineteenth-Century English" (*NLH*, 1982), William C. Spengemann urges that we abandon the categories Romantic, Victorian, and American literature (three blind men), retaining the single category of nineteenth-century English literature (elephant), the period from the American Revolution to World War I. Thus we will be able to see the period as it actually is, one object characterized by a debate between two ideas of reality (objective-external form versus subjective-formless energy)—not a new debate but one conducted with a new urgency. Any number of articles and books seek to continue the story of Romanticism beyond the Romantic period proper. Max F. Schulz's "The Perseverance of Romanticism: From Organicism to Artifact" (*Clio*, 1974), beginning with the title, is a case in point. The article traces a shift in the relationship of art and nature—symbiotic, in Schulz's view—reflected in metaphor. As the idea of nature changed to reflect the views of Darwin and others, the metaphor for art changed accordingly; for the Romantic metaphor of art, the organism, artists substituted the modern metaphor of artifact, resulting in the diminishing of art. Carl Woodring has also traced the post-Romantic relations of nature and art, which he sees as polarities, in "Nature and Art in the Nineteenth Century" (*PMLA*, 1977). As a result of photography, Darwin, and aestheticism, we moderns are descended from both Rousseau and Wilde; we have not been forced either to reconcile the two or to choose between them. A related item is George Stavros' "Oscar Wilde on the Romantics" (*ELT*, 1977), which argues for Wilde's return to the Romantic naturalism he had abandoned when, in his last years, he quoted approvingly from *The Excursion, The Borderers,* and the sonnets. (For similar essays and books—for example, Leon Gottfried's *Matthew Arnold and the Romantics,* 1963, the latest of several books on this topic, or Timothy Peltason's "Tennyson, Nature, and Romantic Nature Poetry," *PQ*, 1984—readers should consult the *MLA Bibliography* on Victorian poetry.) In *The Rural Tradition: Rural Perspectives in Poetry from Wordsworth to the Present* (1980), W. J. Keith traces the tradition of Wordsworthian nature poetry to R. S. Thomas and beyond: "For all the rural poets since his time the example of Wordsworth is supreme." Keith's attention to Wordsworth's experiments with point of view and perspective, in this beautifully written book, shows why this should be true. In *Supreme Fictions* (1978), Brian John traces the tradition of Romantic vitalism from Blake to Lawrence through Carlyle and Yeats. He finds that tradition still alive in the "Children of Albion," those present-day poet-disciples of Blake.

Wendell V. Harris, in "Where Late the Sweet Birds Sang: Looking Back at the Victorians Looking Back at the Romantics Looking Back . . ." (*VP,* 1978), asks what is Victorian about Victorian poetry. It is, he finds, what it did with Romanticism: it subsumed it and then retrenched in order to minimize risks. Along the same lines, Kenneth Allott, in "Victorian Poetry and the Legacy of Romanticism" (in Davies and Beatty), views early and mid-Victorian poetry as Romantic poetry trying to serve two masters, the poets' imaginations and their age. "This results in a worried art." It also results, thinks Allott, in the absence of masterpieces in Victorian poetry. Patricia M. Ball, in *The Heart's Events: The Victorian Poetry of Relationship* (1976), finds the Romantics' legacy to Victorian poetry—at least when it comes to love poetry—inadequate. The Romantics tended to take their emotional journeys alone; the Victorians, with others. In doing so, they discovered a new theme, that of relationship ("let us be true to one another"), and were compelled to develop a technique for expressing it. Some of Wordsworth's and Byron's lyrics may, however, have provided them with hints of how to go about it. Derek Colville's *Victorian Poetry and the Romantic Religion* (1970) is an effort at reformulation and, through it, restoration. The core of Romantic poetry, he believes, is the expression of vision; the periphery is a "world-outlook . . . of staggering sureness and faith." As such, Romantic poetry is not a chaotic phenomenon; as such, too, Romantic poetry can provide "a critical norm against which to examine major Victorian poetry which deals with problems of world-outlook." Colville's objective with this "Romantic approach" is to convince moderns concerned with "questions of outlook and belief" that Victorian poetry, especially that of Arnold, Tennyson, and Browning but also the writing of Ruskin and Wilde, has more to offer than they may suspect. More sophisticated is the study of Barbara Fass, *"La Belle Dame sans Merci" and the Aesthetics of Romanticism* (1974), which takes Keats and his poem as touchstones for the theme of the dichotomy of art and life in later English and Continental literature. Whether la belle dame is femme fatale or good fairy—whether the muse of art is demon or agent of divine inspiration—is a widespread aesthetic problem for writers in the Romantic tradition. Walter D. Reinsdorf, in "Poiesis, Mind, and Reality: Romanticism to Imagism" (*Journal of Altered States of Consciousness,* 1978–79), argues that Romanticism was the critical point in the shift from viewing poems as objective forms signifying prior realities to seeing them as parts of a creative process—from viewing the poets as metaphor makers to seeing them as perception shapers, with the final emphasis on neither poems nor poets but readers.

Romanticism in twentieth-century poetry is a vexed subject. Scholars go round and round on such questions as whether it is in fact present and in what form, whether it is on the wane or on the increase and what are the signs, whether it is undesirable or desirable and in what sense, and so forth. An important effort in earlier criticism was the exposing of anti-Romantic poets and critics for their blindness, willful or otherwise, to the sources of their own art and theory in Romanticism. A late contribution to this endeavor is Ronald Primeau's "On the Discrimination of Hulme: Toward a Theory of the 'Anti-romantic' Romanticism of Modern Poetry" (*JML*, 1974). By Primeau's account, Hulme is an "important figure for the development of modern poetry not in spite of, but *because* he reflects so clearly its romantic stance." Primeau locates Hulme's Romanticism—and thus modern poetry's—in his epistemology: reality is a matter of mental perception or construction. Wolfgang Riedel, in *Die Arbeit der Dichter: Vergleichende Studien zur dichterischen Subjecktivität in der englischen Romantik und Moderne* (1979), also argues that modern or at least early modern poetry is created on the same epistemological grounds as Romantic poetry. (The English summary for non-German readers might as well be in German.) Two of the moderns frequently associated with their Romantic forebears are, of course, Hardy and Yeats. See, for example, Michael Alexander's "Hardy among the Poets," in *Thomas Hardy after Fifty Years* (ed. Lance St. John Butler, 1977), which compares Hardy and Wordsworth, and George Bornstein's "Yeats and the Greater Romantic Lyric" (in Bornstein), which argues that Yeats "crossed visionary autonomy of Blake and Shelley with poetic structures from Wordsworth, Coleridge, and Keats" to produce eight poems in this special form of lyric. Bornstein's *Transformation of Romanticism in Yeats, Eliot, and Stevens* (1976) extends this essay to the book-length proposition that modern poetry is written in the tradition of Romantic poetry. (For interesting suggestions of how scholars can improve both influence study and literary history, see Bornstein's "Victorians and Volumes, Foreigners and First Drafts: Four Gaps in Postromantic Influence Study" [*RP&P*, 1981].) Donald H. Reiman, in "Wordsworth, Shelley, and the Romantic Inheritance" (*RP&P*, 1981), carefully delineates the "temperamental affinities between individual Romantic poets and particular modernist poets, all of whom inherit collectively the ontological and epistemological problems and perspectives that faced the Romantics." Noteworthy is his argument that Wordsworth and Shelley, who between them divided the "empire of Romantic tradition," were the representative Romantics to both the Victorian and the modernist poets. Characterizing this split as "pastoral" versus "Gothic," he groups Auden and Stevens under the former, Eliot and Yeats under the latter. Reiman's account of poetic influence is tendered in opposition to Harold Bloom's. Christopher Clausen is another scholar who is more impressed with the continuity in poetry since the end of the eighteenth century than with the discontinuity. He finds this continuity, in *The Place of Poetry: Two Centuries of an Art in Crisis* (1981), in the poets' efforts to "find or make a place for [their] art in a world that has seemed ever more hostile or indifferent." Clausen sees the effort as usually unsuccessful, resulting in the decline of poetry. He gives the Romantics considerable credit, however, for granting poetry a lease on life: "Romanticism brought about a sustained revival of serious poetry that appealed to a broad audience, thereby mitigating to an impressive degree not only the alienation of the artist that was itself to become a theme of Romantic art, but also the dehumanizing effects of nineteenth-century industrial and scientific progress." Clausen ends with an account of the present place of poetry, also the topic of a book by Robert Pinsky, *The Situation of Poetry: Contemporary Poetry and Its Traditions* (1977). The traditions Pinsky identifies are modernist and, before that, Romantic. Along with Bornstein, Reiman, and Clausen, he discerns a continuity between modernist-contemporary and Romantic poetry. In particular, the Romantics passed on to their successors their conflicts "between conscious and unconscious forces within the mind" and, with them, "responses to and assumptions about these conflicts." This "Romantic persistence" looms large in the poems written since 1957 that are Pinsky's main interest. The latest treatment of the subject is Carlos Baker's *The Echoing Green: Romanticism, Modernism, and the Phenomena of Transference in Poetry* (1984). In part 1 Baker assesses the five "ancestral voices" of Wordsworth, Coleridge, Byron, Shelley, and Keats; in part 2 he examines their "modern echoes" (and those of Blake) in the poetry of Yeats, Frost, Stevens, Eliot, and Auden. Critically current but not theoretically modish, Baker's study is attractively restrained in the claims it makes for the convergence of Romanticism and modernism. The examples of influence he cites are many, but they do not add up to massive infiltration. Rather, the transfers are selective and idiosyncratic. Because of the individual tastes and temperaments of the moderns, it could not be otherwise. Between the covers of this book Baker has gathered more information on his subject than anyone before him; he has communicated it more expertly than anyone after him is likely to do. One last book to equate modern and Romantic poetry is Octavio Paz's *Children of the Mire: Modern Poetry from Romanticism to the Avant-garde* (trans. Rachel Phillips, 1974). Paz argues that modern poetry is born in English and German Romanticism and that it is unified by its attempt "to found a tradition on the only principle immune to criticism because it is the condition and consequence of criticism: change, history." Since Romanticism the poetic imagination has been building monuments on ground undermined by criticism. And it goes on doing so, fully aware that it is undermined. The central chapter, on the High Romantics, provides the title of the book. The essays in *Romanticism, Modernism, Postmodernism* (ed. Harry R. Garvin, 1980) explore not only the complex relationships of the three literary "periods" but also the problematic utility of the critical terms themselves.

Less sanguine about modern poetry is Edwin Webb, who in "Poetry and the Culture of Feeling" (*New Universities Quarterly,* 1978) suggests that it risks "atrophy and the impoverished response" because it fails to recognize, as the Romantic poetry did not, the importance of feeling to poetic composition; it tends not so much to make the poem as to manufacture it. Somewhat in the same vein is Rosemary Stephens' "The Spirit of Romantic Poetry: Heritage of the Modern Poet" (*S&W,* 1971), which seeks to encourage those writing today in the spirit of the Romantics by prophesying that they will one day be recognized. Such uncritical enthusiasm for Romantic poetry is rare these days. For earlier and more substantial instances of the appreciative genre—for example, the celebrated books of G. Wilson Knight and, later, the writings of Paul Goodman—readers are referred to *ERP3* (66–67). Stephens and other starry-eyed nostalgics would do well to read Karl Kroeber's witty and provocative essay "The Relevance and Irrelevance of Romanticism" (*SIR*, 1970). Kroeber's reservations about the return of Romanticism are still pertinent, though perhaps less urgently so than a decade ago. This time round we might give the last word to Raymond Immerwahr, who in "Romanticism: Past and Present" (*CGP*, 1974) urges us to examine the constructive and destructive potentials of twentieth-century Romanticism in order to work more effectively for the preservation of society. After considering the process by which Romanticism arose, the psychological and emotional needs it has served, and the contributions it has made to the crisis of our civilization, he concludes that Romanticism past and present—first and last—is better qualified to criticize social and cultural ills than to propose cures. The turn to Romanticism in the third quarter of the twentieth century, like the original turn to Romanticism, is a reaction to the boredom and banality of the sociocultural environment. Hence the cure—and the future—cannot be more Romanticism but a "pre-romanticism" or a "para-romanticism": Carlyle to the contrary, the cure is not in the disease. The success of Immerwahr's prescriptions is difficult to predict. His very language for a new culture, retaining as it does the term "romanticism," suggests just how problematic it is to leave Romantic culture, dissipated and dispirited as it may be, behind. More, the inclusive acts of Romantics studies these days would seem to be taking us deeper into the subject, bringing us more in harmony with the sources of that culture rather than leading us beyond it. Dennis Taylor, who in "Natural Supernaturalism's New Clothes: A Recurrent Problem in Romantic Studies" (*WC*, 1974) asks and answers several fundamental questions about Romanticism, puts the case best. He concludes that there "seems to be no way in which one can become a post-Romantic or anti-Romantic poet." For "there is no way to be a true Romantic poet; there is no way to be any other kind of poet. There is no way to rebel against Romanticism; there is no way to accept it." Whatever the dilemma, whatever the prognosis for escaping it, Romantics scholars continue to offer us perspectives on Romanticism that simultaneously devour and proliferate the phenomenon, destroy and preserve texts, bewilder and enlighten readers. Gradually, students of the period are learning to live with or at least cope with the anxieties of poetic influence (not to mention the traumas of critical influence), the binary oppositions of poetic vision, the deconstructive or indeterminate or ironic character of poetic texts—and with the new language devised or old language revived (no worse than Coleridge's, surely) to express these new perspectives, perhaps because we have been shown, sometimes convincingly, that the new methods of inquiry and the abysses of interpretation they seem to open were anticipated by the Romantics themselves. At times it seems that the harder we try to leave the High Romantics behind, the more certain we are to find ourselves at their feet again. This is not to say, however, that the feud between the theorists and the humanists, as it is commonly phrased, is spent. Whether or not peace is possible or even likely in the near or distant future is not a prophecy I care to make. Perhaps such a peace is not even desirable: "Though a quarrel in the streets is a thing to be hated, the energies displayed in it are fine; the commonest Man shows a grace in his quarrel." If, on the one hand, the quarrels in Romantics scholarship and criticism can be likened to street fights and, more important, if the sequel part of Keats's perception follows for scholar-critics, then the price we pay for harmony may be too high by far. If, on the other hand, Keats's speculation does not apply, then we might fall back on Blake's prescription for progression and hope that the contraries that characterize our disputes are genuine. Just who are the angels and who the devils it would not become me to say.

WILLIAM BLAKE

Mary Lynn Johnson

Contents

General Remarks

The inclusion of a section on Blake in this fourth edition of a standard reference work on the "major English Romantic poets" would not occasion comment were it not for one awkward fact: there was no such section in any of the three previous editions. Writing the introductory chapter on Romanticism for the first edition (1950), Ernest Bernbaum must have felt uneasy, for just the year before, in the preface to a new edition of his own *Guide through the Romantic Movement,* he had proudly called attention to his prescience in placing Blake "not among the pre-Romantics, but in the forefront of the Romantics" as early as 1930. Of necessity, bibliographical teams of the Modern Language Association operate more conservatively, but in partial remediation for the oversight of 1950, Carolyn Washburn Houtchens and Lawrence Huston Houtchens slipped Blake in with the minor poets in their companion volume, *The English Romantic Poets and Essayists: A Review of Research and Criticism* (1957; rev. 1966). When the third edition of the review of major poets was planned, Blake was omitted only because the review in Houtchens and Houtchens was still current. But the misplacement of Blake has long annoyed users of both reference works, including the editor of the present volume.

As newer interpretations of Romanticism gained acceptance—a topic discussed by Frank Jordan in his introductory chapter to this volume—and especially after the appearance of Northrop Frye's *Fearful Symmetry* in 1947, Blake was discovered not at the fringes of the Romantic movement but at its center. With Wordsworth, he came to exemplify the midcentury ideal of the Romantic poet as a mythmaker who struggles to repair the rift between subject and object, consciousness and the unconscious. At present in the United States, where many of our most influential critical theorists have been interested in Romanticism, perception of Blake is again shifting: he is now viewed less as a mythmaker than as one who penetrates the structures of language and myth only to subvert them. What effect contemporary efforts to "desecrate the canon" will have on the reputation of Blake as a latecomer to Parnassus is unforeseeable, but he will not again be thought of apart from the Romantics, however their movement is conceived in the future.

Historically, Blake studies developed in isolation from scholarship on early nineteenth-century poetry not only because Romanticism itself was conceived so as to exclude Blake but also because Blake's work cuts across boundaries between academic disciplines and historical periods. An engraver by trade, Blake published his literary works in "Illuminated Printing," a medium of his own invention. Usually he brought together words and pictures within a single page design, which he then etched, printed, and watercolored. Each copy of each individually produced handmade book came into existence as a unique work of art, recreated rather than replicated with each new issue—for even when Blake printed several copies at once, he seems to have assembled, colored, and stitched together the pages as needed to fill orders, one book at a time. Blake's laborious method of publication and narrow system of distribution necessarily limited the size of his contemporary audience. His customers and friends thought of him primarily as a graphic artist; his books of poetry, because they were privately published, were ignored by reviewers. Moreover, the genre in which he realized his mature ideas—illuminated epic-length poems amazing in their mythical shape, prophetic voice, and quasi-biblical style—resists anthologizing. Such passages from Blake's later books as were quoted up through the 1950s were usually displayed to confirm the truism that such stuff is at best unreadable, at worst indicative of incipient madness. Reproductions of his colored etchings were inadequate in both quality and quantity. Thus Blake was perceived almost exclusively as the author of his most familiar and accessible book, in its verbal form only. The naive mode of *Songs of Innocence and of Experience* (1789–94), coupled with the accident of the author's mid-eighteenth-century birthdate, made it convenient for literary historians to classify him with Robert Burns as the most gifted of what used to be called the pre-Romantics. This partial view, once academically institutionalized, tended to be self-perpetuating. Few textbooks on the Romantic period published before 1960 attempt to recognize the importance of either the designs or the later poetry.

No single critical view of Blake dominates the 1980s as S. Foster Damon's did after 1924 and as Northrop Frye's did for decades after 1947. The most significant contributions to Blake studies of the last fifteen years have been in basic scholarship—new editions, bibliographies, facsimiles, and catalogs. Only a critical biography is lacking. Recent criticism has not yet absorbed these advances in scholarship, but certain trends are discernible. Critics of the eighties have finally liberated themselves from the preoccupation of working out fine points of the "myth" or "system" derived from the formulations of Frye, though Blake's special uses of iconographic conventions, biblical typology, and literary archetypes continue to command attention. The importance of his intense social concern, revealed by David V. Erdman and others, is everywhere acknowledged. The relevance of his pictorial work to an understanding of his poetry—a major focus of the criticism of the sixties and seventies—is now rarely questioned. Recent Freudian, Marxist, feminist, and semiotic studies show little concern for Blake's mysticism, Neoplatonism, or use of esoteric sources, except, on occasion, as justification for finely drawn extrapolations. Instead, they focus on affinities between his philosophical, theological, psychological, and political insights and those of our own century. Just on the horizon are sophisticated investigations of his theories of language, meaning, and aesthetic structure, along with specialized considerations of individual works. Further thoughts on the state of Blake studies appear at the conclusion of this chapter.

Because this essay is a review and guide rather than a historical survey, it directs readers to the most useful or interesting works on Blake at present and keeps silent about most superseded publications, although it points out a few prominent milestones along the way. The volume of Blake studies has increased exponentially in bursts during the twenties, the forties and fifties, and especially since 1960; obviously, the only way to avoid overwhelming the reader with mere lists of titles—which are conveniently available in the enumerative bibliographies and checklists reviewed under "Aids to Research"—is to leave out a great deal.

To economize on primary references, I suppress many subtitles and normalize minor anomalies in punctuation, and I rely on phrases like "previously mentioned" as shorthand for "check the index." Frequently mentioned collections of essays on Blake are described at the beginning of the "General Studies" section, with abbreviations explained in note 3; references to Blake journals are explained in note 1.

I omit most brief notes, most foreign language publications, most dates of photoreprints, most books that refer to Blake only as part of a larger theoretical or historical study, most general books on Romanticism, and almost all dissertations and privately printed books. The large section called "Studies of Individual Works" is the most selective, for reasons that anyone who checks the swelling columns on Blake in recent MLA bibliographies will understand. It is confined—particularly with respect to *Songs*—to essential informative notes and the most valuable, interesting, or controversial commentaries on the most widely studied poems and designs. Throughout this chapter, however, in order to define issues and encourage further research, I occasionally cite weak or erroneous works if they serve to call attention to promising and undeveloped areas of inquiry or if they have established themselves in positions of influence.

Aids to Research

The scholar hoping to investigate Blake's unique works of art requires guidance well beyond the range of ordinary bibliographies. At every point, the line between Blake's poetry and designs is difficult or impossible to draw. The illuminated books, the only works Blake himself chose to publish, have come to be considered more authoritative than his few unillustrated publications in letterpress. Blake produced eighteen of these illuminated books; among them, it happens that those that have most interested critics also pose special problems for editors and bibliographers. *The Book of Thel* (1789), *Songs of Innocence and of Experience* (1789–94), *Visions of the Daughters of Albion* (1793), *The Marriage of Heaven and Hell* (?1793), *America* (1793), *Europe* (1794), *Milton* (?1808), and *Jerusalem* (?1818) all exist in multiple versions, most of which have been touched up by the hand of the artist after printing. Dating is difficult. A title page sometimes bears an etched date a year or more earlier than the watermarks visible in the earliest copy Blake printed; for example, both *Milton* and *Jerusalem* are dated 1804 on their title pages but were first printed no earlier than 1808 and 1818, respectively. Variant copies were sometimes issued over wide intervals: the latest version or "edition" of *Songs*, for example, appeared more than thirty years after the earliest. Copies of *Songs* and several other books vary even in the selection and arrangement of their constituent plates. As editors and critics become ever more cognizant of minute verbal and pictorial differences among copies, they need more accurate facsimiles and more finely detailed bibliographical descriptions.

Not only are practically all the pages of Blake's central canon "illuminated" in some way, but there are also strong visual elements in many of his other books of poetry and a textual side to most of his drawings and paintings. Unillustrated manuscript poems are limited to the ballads of the Pickering Manuscript (?1808), "The Everlasting Gospel" (?1818), and the satirical and miscellaneous verses in the Notebook. Of published works, Blake's three productions in ordinary commercial type are also unillustrated: *Poetical Sketches* (1783), run off in a small printing never offered for sale; *The French Revolution* (1791), cancelled in press; and *Descriptive Catalogue* (1809), sold as a polemical guide to his exhibition of paintings and drawings. But both text and design are important in *Tiriel* (?1789), the Notebook or Rossetti Manuscript (?1787–?1818), and *Vala* or (retitled) *The Four Zoas* (?1796–?1807). Blake's pictorial responses to the Bible and to Milton, Young, Gray, Bunyan, Dante, Chaucer, and Spenser also function as literary criticism and reward attention by students of literature. Even the commercial book illustrations Blake engraved after his own or other artists' designs sometimes deserve consideration as works of art—for example, his woodcuts for a school text of Vergil (1821). An especially hard-to-classify publication is Blake's engraving of the classical statue of the *Laocoön* group (?1818–20), which he reinterpreted as Jehovah, Satan, and Adam struggling within the coils of good and evil, on a plate covered with engraved aphorisms on art and its relationship to money, empire, and religion. With all these complexities to keep in mind, the Blake scholar requires a wide shelf of highly specialized works of reference.

REFERENCE WORKS

The indispensable aids to research can be named briefly and without hesitation. Almost all have appeared within the last two decades. The largest and best-stocked warehouse of information is the colossal *Blake Books,* by G. E. Bentley, Jr. (1977), which fully describes everything written by Blake and lists almost everything (excluding only reviews) published about him. For recent works and for a sampling of reviews, the critical section of *Blake Books* should be supplemented, cautiously, by Joseph Natoli's brash and breezy annotated checklist, *Twentieth-Century Blake Criticism: Northrop Frye to the Present* (1982), along with checklists in the specialized periodicals described below. Also essential to research on Blake are the complete catalogue raisonné by Martin Butlin, *The Paintings and Drawings of William Blake* (1981), and David V. Erdman's convenient set of black-and-white reproductions of the central canon, *The Illuminated Blake* (1974), which contains a stimulating though often speculative plate-by-plate commentary. Erdman (with others) also prepared a computerized *Concordance* (1967) in the Cornell series, keyed to a corrected version of the then-standard Keynes text (discussed below). S. Foster Damon's *Blake Dictionary* (1965) contains concise though occasionally idiosyncratic interpretive identifications of characters and symbols, and the 1979 reprinting includes a useful index by

Morris Eaves. G. E. Bentley, Jr.'s *Blake Records* (1969), discussed under "Biographical Resources," compiles all known documents about Blake, including statements about him by his contemporaries. Other bibliographical information of first importance appears in books discussed under "Editions, Facsimiles, and Reproductions," particularly in the notes to the standard texts prepared by Bentley, by Erdman, and by Sir Geoffrey Keynes, as well as Keynes's notes to the Blake Trust series of facsimiles, Erdman's notes to the facsimile of the Notebook, and Bentley's notes to the facsimile of *Vala*. To understand the status of any text from Blake's illuminated books, the critic should carefully study at least the appropriate Blake Trust facsimile and compare facsimiles of differing copies.

Bibliographies. With the publication in 1977 of Bentley's *Blake Books*, scholarly drudgery has been simplified if not sweetened. Within Bentley's twelve hundred pages of nearly four thousand items resides an entire library of bibliographies, as his subtitle indicates: "Annotated Catalogues of . . . Writings in Illuminated Printing, in Conventional Typography, and in Manuscript, and Reprints Thereof, Reproductions of his Designs, Books with his Engravings, Catalogues, Books He Owned, and Scholarly and Critical Works about Him." Bentley's sections of descriptive bibliography must be measured against the previous work of Geoffrey Keynes, who devised the basic descriptive codes still in use. Keynes's *A Bibliography of William Blake* (1921; rpt. 1969) was the first full-scale descriptive bibliography of all of Blake's writings, whether illuminated, commercially printed, or in manuscript. In his section on the illuminated books, following the lead of John Sampson in his edition of Blake's *Poetical Works* (1905), Keynes brought order to the welter of variants among numerous handmade versions of the same work by labeling each separate copy of each illuminated book with a letter of the alphabet reflecting its relative position in the total run of copies (A for the earliest through D, for example, in a four-copy series). This masterwork became outdated only as additional copies came to light. In *William Blake's Illuminated Books: A Census* (1952; rpt. 1969), Keynes and Edwin Wolf II corrected Keynes's 1921 section on the illuminated works—though significant inaccuracies remained, of the sort detailed in Thomas E. Connolly's "A Blakean Maze" (*BS* 3: 1 [1970]), on the British Museum's three copies of *Songs*.[1] The Keynes-Wolf *Census* also reorganized items in a new alphabetically labeled series to accommodate newly discovered copies and reflect a better understanding of their chronological ordering. These Keynes-Wolf alphabetical tags have become so firmly established, so necessary for transactions among scholars, art auction houses, librarians, and collectors, that Bentley wisely did not again adjust them to fit more recent chronologies.

The Keynes-Wolf *Census* also established a standard page ordering for each illuminated book to simplify comparisons between inconsistently foliated copies. Since Blake arranged no two copies of *The Book of Urizen* identically, for example, there can be no "authorial order" for this poem: one takes one's bearings from the Keynes-Wolf reference number for each plate and the identifying letter for each copy. When Keynes assigned numbers for the plates, however, he was not as farsighted or as consistent as with his alphabetical tags for copies: therefore,

Bentley has replaced the Keynes-Wolf combination of Arabic and small Roman numerals with an all-Arabic system, which he employs also in his own edition of *William Blake's Writings* (1977). With *Milton*, unfortunately, he held to Keynes's choice of Copy A as the standard, thus reducing the additional pages in copies C and D to nonnumerical status. But most of Bentley's renumberings make excellent sense. The inevitable transition from Keynes-Wolf to Bentley numbers, though as awkward as the transition from English to metric weights and measures, will be beneficial in the long run; meanwhile, scholars must use clumsy dual citations.

Bentley vastly amplifies the Keynes-Wolf quantitative data on illuminated books, but he makes no attempt to preserve, clarify, and correct their useful qualitative remarks on the character of individual copies. His occasional comments on pen work, printing quality, and palette appear only as examples in summary passages. Factual details provided in the Keynes-Wolf copy-by-copy notes, such as "18 plates on 10 leaves," are relegated in *Blake Books* to fine-print tables, thus of course facilitating comparisons but inconveniencing the viewer of any single copy. The exhaustive descriptions of the works in "Illuminated Printing" would have been much easier to use if Bentley had separated these published books from Blake's ephemeral and minor writings, such as inscriptions on drawings, and if he had kept the primary materials apart from reprints and modern editions. These latter might well have been combined, under a broader heading, with the items listed under "Collections and Selections."

Besides modernizing Keynes's work, Bentley corrects and brings up to date his own. The sections on reproductions of drawings and paintings, book engravings, catalogs and bibliographies, books owned by Blake, and biography and criticism (with its addendum) extend *A Blake Bibliography: Annotated Lists of Works, Studies, and Blakeana* (1964) by Bentley and Martin K. Nurmi. That Bentley, working alone, could have compiled and annotated lists of such magnitude is astounding. Ironically, though, for almost all practical purposes, the very comprehensiveness of the section on criticism is a mixed blessing—for, as Bentley himself notes, "Dozens, scores, even hundreds of these articles and books . . . are hardly worth the trouble to look up," and "a great many" are merely distressing. Numerous titles not only in familiar European languages but also in Japanese, Chinese, Bulgarian, and various Scandinavian and Slavic languages (usually translated but unannotated) attest to the poet's worldwide reputation and the bibliographer's devotion, but few add to the store of knowledge about Blake. Bentley's terse annotation of hundreds of entries, "particularly when the titles are obscure," with "normally descriptive rather than evaluative" comments, often falls short of its intended purpose. The understandable exasperation of an oversaturated reviewer flares out in sarcastic one-line brush-offs, particularly when Bentley tries to engineer the self-condemnation of some critics by turning their own words against them in atypical phrases made to appear ridiculous without context. As a corrective, Natoli's paragraph-length annotations, despite occasional lapses, are worth consulting: the selectivity of *Twentieth-Century Blake Criticism* and its quotations from reviews make it, for many purposes, more use-

ful than *Blake Books,* even though it is poorly organized, with too many
overlapping categories.

In the vast domain of *Blake Books,* the recovery of awkwardly pigeonholed
works is made difficult by Bentley's decision to drop the cross-referencing system
used in Bentley-Nurmi. The extensive index does not quite take care of every situation. Some random examples: a person interested in Blake's illustrations of
the Bible would naturally consult the "Bible" category under "Reproductions"
but would thereby overlook Keynes's *William Blake's Illustrations to the Bible*
(1957), which is listed among the chronologically arranged museum, sale, and exhibition catalogs. Only by working through the fifty-three "Bible" entries in the
index, as of course a conscientious scholar would do, could one uncover this important compilation of reproductions. The point is not that the book is
misclassified; it *is* a catalog, but it is also a collection of reproductions on a single
theme. Cross-references would also help locate Irene Tayler's *Blake's Illustrations
to the Poems of Gray* (1971), which rightly appears under "Criticism," though it is
also a catalog. Darrell Figgis, despite his 117 pages of commentary, is demoted to
"editor" of *The Paintings of William Blake* (1927), which appears under "Reproductions," not "Criticism." And anyone interested in the history of Blake's appearance in exhibitions, by running through the chronologically arranged "Catalogues" section, would come up with two official catalogs for the International
Exhibition of 1862 but would miss a three-page comment by Tom Taylor in his
Handbook of Pictures in the International Exhibition of 1862, listed under "Criticism." Since there is no index listing for "exhibitions," a seeker would have to
chance upon this entry, as I did. (The index performs one commendable service
unavailable in many other standard reference works: it cross-lists writers who
have published under more than one name. This service is of obvious benefit to
female scholars in particular.) As for the general organization, *Blake Books* is not,
as they say about certain computer programs, "user-friendly." One misses
Keynes's 1921 subdivisions: the separation between exhibition and sale catalogs,
for example, and the classification of engraved works according to whether they
were designed, engraved, or both designed and engraved by Blake. And yet the
inconvenience must be put in perspective. *Blake Books* is absolutely the first
book, after a good edition, that a serious scholar should acquire. With it should
be kept Bentley's "Supplement" and Robert N. Essick's review, which also contains supplementary entries; both appear in *Blake: An Illustrated Quarterly* (no.
43, 11: 3 [1977 – 78]).

Bentley's introductory survey in *Blake Books,* "Blake's Reputation and
Interpreters"—like his more condensed introduction to *Blake: The Critical Heritage* (1975)—judiciously evaluates major scholarship through 1974. In either the
longer or the shorter version, Bentley's is by far the best recent and general
guide to criticism on Blake. Bentley's titles for subsections make up a neat
outline of Blake's critical reception from the year of his death through the early
1970s: " 'A Genius with a Screw Loose': 1757 – 1863," "The Achievement of Public
Stature: 1863 – 1893," "A Bibliography, a Text, and Source Studies: 1921 – 1946," "A
Man for Our Time: 1947 – 1974." These epochs memorialize major publications:

Alexander Gilchrist's *Life of William Blake, 'Pictor Ignotus'* (1863), E. J. Ellis and W. B. Yeats's *The Works of William Blake* (1893), Geoffrey Keynes's *A Bibliography of William Blake* (1921), and Northrop Frye's *Fearful Symmetry* (1947). For work published before the middle sixties, the more detailed survey by Frye, supplemented by Nurmi, in the Houtchenses' volume (1966) should be consulted. Condensed general guides appear in Erdman's contributions to A. E. Dyson's *English Poetry: Select Bibliographical Guides* (1971) and in *Blake's Poetry and Designs,* edited by Mary Lynn Johnson and John E. Grant (1979). Hugh J. Luke, Jr.'s "William Blake: *Pictor Notus*" (*PLL,* 1966) and especially his "A Decade of William Blake" (*Prairie Schooner,* 1973 – 74) survey useful criticism and offer wise counsel on acquisitions. Roger Easson, "On Building a Blake Library" in *Sparks of Fire* (an anthology described below), describes interesting personal choices that include novels about Blake and "A Note on Some Other Books of Interest for the Student of the Transformative Consciousness: A View from the 1980s." Donald C. Mell, Jr.'s annotated bibliography in *English Poetry, 1660 – 1800: A Guide to Information Sources* (1982) is recent, brief, and reliable.

Annual annotated checklists of Blake scholarship, once published in journals, are now put out in typographic photo-offset, in costly hardcover editions, often behind schedule: the bibliography of the Romantic movement, edited by Erdman (*ELH,* 1937 – 49; *PQ,* 1950 – 64; *ELN,* 1965 – 80), is now published by Garland Press; that of the eighteenth century, with a Blake section edited by Paul J. Korshin (*PQ,* 1968 – 74), by the American Society for Eighteenth-Century Studies. Earlier issues have been republished in conveniently indexed multivolume sets: *The Romantic Movement Bibliography: 1936 – 1970,* edited by A. C. Elkins, Jr., and L. J. Forstner (1973), and *The Eighteenth Century: A Current Bibliography: 1928 – 1969,* edited by Curt A. Zimansky (1970). These extremely valuable bibliographies, particularly the one on the Romantics, exhibit understandable failings: annotations by divers hands are uneven in reliability; items published late in the year are listed but usually go unannotated in succeeding years and so slip into obscurity (though occasionally items are reviewed two years running). Blake's place in the annual reviews of scholarship published in *Studies in English Literature* over the past two decades appears to be determined by the taste and stomach of individual reviewers: he has been tossed like a hot potato—or firecracker—between eighteenth-century and nineteenth-century specialists, sometimes falling to the latter (1961 – 62, 1964, 1966, 1970), sometimes to both (1965, 1967, 1969), and sometimes to neither (1963, 1971). Since 1972 the nineteenth-century reviewer has accepted full responsibility. To sample British reactions and double-check for publications in other languages, the American scholar should also consult *The Year's Work in English Studies* (1921–   ), as well as the *Annual Bibliography of English Language and Literature* (1921–   ) of the Modern Humanities Research Association. Nonannotated checklists appear annually in the *MLA International Bibliography* (1970–   )—continued from the annual bibliographical number in *PMLA* (1922 – 69)—and in *Blake: An Illustrated Quarterly,* formerly *Blake Newsletter* (1967–   ). The timely *Humanities Index* (1974–   ), a sequel to *Social Sciences and Humanities Index,* helps run down essays published as parts of books. For notice of articles almost as soon as they appear, the bimonthly *New Contents: English and American Literature* (1979–   ) and the weekly *Current Contents: Art and Humanities* (1979–   ) are useful. Articles on Blake's pictorial works are listed in *Art Index* (1929–   ), which provides a separate listing of works reproduced. Especially helpful in tracing foreign language publications and major exhibition catalogs are the annotated art bibliographies: *Artbibliographies Modern* (1972–   ), formerly *LOMA* (*Literature on Modern Art*) (1969–71); *Répertoire d'Art et d'Archéologie* (1910–   ; published quarterly in improved format since 1973); and a semiannual computer-assisted abstracting and indexing service now published by the J. Paul Getty Trust, *RILA: Répertoire International de la Littérature de l'Art* (1975–   ).

Aside from the present essay and Bentley's index, the only convenient guides to criticism of individual works are the now-dated and typographically scrambled listings in R. H. Fogle's Goldentree bibliography, *Romantic Poets and Prose Writers* (1967) and the annotated checklists in Natoli's *Twentieth-Century Blake Criticism* (1982). Natoli's coverage is spotty, sometimes compromised by perfunctory or cheap-shot annotations and sensationalized accounts of the wranglings and snipings of Blakeans, but his judgments are refreshingly independent, and there is no doubt that the book is a valuable timesaver. For helpful annotations of about one hundred and fifty well-chosen items, see the Blake section in Mell's *English Poetry, 1660–1800*.

Catalogs.   After *Blake Books,* the next essential but costly reference book a dedicated scholar will want to save up for is Martin Butlin's long-needed two-volume catalogue raisonné, *The Paintings and Drawings of William Blake* (1981), wherein Blake's entire oeuvre in the nonreplicative visual arts is not only cataloged but also richly illustrated. The volume of plates, including 251 in color, excludes only designs in major series that have been reproduced elsewhere, etchings and engravings, and of course lost and inaccessible works. This splendid catalog, the subject of a special issue of *Blake: An Illustrated Quarterly* (no. 61, 16: 1 [1982]), is already initiating a new era in Blake studies for literary critics and art historians alike. Butlin, an art historian himself, evenhandedly shows respect for both disciplines, frequently citing Blake's writings and the comments of literary critics. Now at last scholars can compare pictures executed in different media, during different periods, and—at least in imagination—reunite works dispersed in collections around the globe. Essick's extensive review essay in the special Butlin issue of the *Quarterly* gives a fuller sense of the depth, breadth, reliability, and importance of this masterful catalog than can be suggested here.

There is no similarly comprehensive, fully illustrated catalog of all Blake's work in the print media. Neither David Bindman's *The Complete Graphic Works of William Blake* (1978) nor the books it supersedes—Lawrence Binyon's *The Engraved Designs of William Blake* (1926; rpt. 1967) and Keynes's *William Blake's Engravings* (1950; rpt. 1972)—are concerned with Blake's engravings after other artists, which sometimes depart from their sources in interesting ways.

A. G. B. Russell's *The Engravings of William Blake* (1912; rpt. 1968), though complete in its day, is only partially illustrated. The rather sketchy entries in Bindman's fully illustrated *Graphic Works* sometimes require supplementation from Russell, Binyon, and Keynes. Robert N. Essick's *The Separate Plates of William Blake* (1983) is a meticulously annotated, comprehensively illustrated catalog of single prints that builds upon and supersedes Keynes's *Engravings by William Blake: The Separate Plates* (1956). Its color and black-and-white reproductions are superb. Still incomplete is a projected fully illustrated catalog of Blake's commercial engravings: Robert N. Essick and Roger Easson's *William Blake: Book Illustrator* (1, 1972; 2, 1979; 3, in preparation); in volumes published so far, fine details of prints are hard to make out. Scholars would find convenient a one-volume illustrated checklist of engravings, excluding illuminated books, based on material covered in Essick's *Separate Plates,* Essick and Easson's *Book Illustrator,* Bindman's *Graphic Works,* and the "Engravings" section of Bentley's *Blake Books*—that is, a present-day Russell. Remaining gaps in the reference shelf would have to be filled by separate catalogs and the editions discussed in the next section.

Of the two journals dealing exclusively with Blake and related topics—the semiannual *Blake Studies,* founded in 1968 by Kay and Roger Easson, and *Blake: An Illustrated Quarterly* (formerly *Blake Newsletter,* 1967–77), edited by Morton D. Paley and Morris Eaves—only the latter is bibliographically oriented. Besides an annual checklist, now compiled by Thomas L. Minnick and Detlef W. Dörrbecker, the *Quarterly* has published Robert N. Essick's "Finding List of Reproductions of Blake's Art" (nos. 17-18, 5: 2 [1971]); Everett Frost's checklist of slides, posters, and postcards (no. 33, 9: 1 [1975]); Peter Roberts' checklist of musical settings (no. 28, 7: 4 [1974]); checklists of works on Blake in various non-English languages; annual summaries of art sales (usually by Essick); and handlists of major collections, including those of the Department of Prints and Drawings of the British Museum (by P. Morgan and G. E. Bentley, Jr., no. 20, 5: 4 [1972]), the Rosenwald Collection of the Library of Congress (by Ruth Fine Lehrer, no. 35, 9: 3 [1975–76]), and, in a single issue (no. 44, 11: 4 [1978]), the Essick collection (by Janice Lyle), the Metropolitan Museum of Art, the Boston Museum of Fine Arts, the Fogg Art Museum, and the Victoria and Albert Museum (by Paley).

In addition to the handlists published in the *Quarterly,* the scholar should check the separately published inventories of important Blake collections. The Blake section of *The Lessing J. Rosenwald Collection* (in the Library of Congress), with a preface by Frederick R. Goff (1977), includes that portion of Rosenwald's Blake collection which is now in the Library of Congress; the rest, in the National Gallery of Art, has not been fully cataloged. David Bindman's *William Blake: Catalogue of the Collection in the Fitzwilliam Museum, Cambridge* (1970) includes a supplementary listing of Sir Geoffrey Keynes's collection, willed to this museum; Keynes describes his collection in more detail in his own *Biblioteca Bibliographica* (1964). C. H. Collins Baker's *Catalogue of William Blake's Drawings and Paintings in the Huntington Library,* revised by R. R. Wark (1969), excludes the illuminated books covered in Essick's handlist in *BIQ,* mentioned above. Most of the information in Martin Butlin's fully illustrated *William Blake: A Complete Catalogue of Works in the Tate Gallery* (1971), reappears in his *Paintings and Drawings*. Butlin's "The Blake Collection of Mrs. William T. Tonner" (*Bulletin, Philadelphia Museum of Art,* 1972) briefly annotates works that have since, for the most part, become the property of that museum. G. E. Bentley, Jr.'s *The Blake Collection of Mrs. Landon K. Thorne* (1971) catalogs works that have since, with some exceptions, entered the Pierpont Morgan Library. Helen D. Willard's *William Blake, Water-color Drawings, Museum of Fine Arts, Boston* (1957) is slenderly annotated; the Blake section of W. G. Constable's *Catalogue of Paintings and Drawings in Water Color, Museum of Fine Arts, Boston* (1949) contains more detailed notes. Blake's Dante designs in the National Gallery of Victoria, Melbourne, are reproduced without annotation in a pamphlet introduced by Ursula Hoff (1961). Six Blakes in the Pollok House, Glasgow, are described by Alasdair Auld in a pamphlet (c. 1970). Still without published catalogs of their Blakes are the Houghton Library of Harvard, that portion of the Rosenwald Collection in the National Gallery of Art, that portion of the Pierpont Morgan Library's holdings outside the Thorne Collection, the Paul Mellon Collection (in process of being donated to the Yale Center for British Art), and the collections in the Glasgow University Library, the Whitworth Gallery (Manchester), the Ashmolean (Oxford), the Cincinnati Art Museum, the New York Public Library, and the Rosenbach Foundation (Philadelphia). A well-indexed one-volume compendium of handlists of Blake collections, arranged regionally, would facilitate the planning of research trips and the ordering of photographs. For Blake's written work only, this desideratum is fulfilled by the helpful "Table of Collections" in Bentley's *William Blake's Writings,* discussed under "Editions."

Sale catalogs are not reviewed here because most information in them is available in Bentley's *Blake Books.* The most important exhibition catalogs are the following: Edwin Wolf II and Elizabeth Mongan's *William Blake, 1757 – 1827,* for the Philadelphia exhibition of 1930; Martin Butlin's *William Blake,* for the Tate Gallery exhibition of 1978; David Bindman's catalogs for two important exhibitions: *William Blake: Kunst um 1800,* at the Kunsthalle, Hamburg (1975), and *William Blake: His Art and Times,* at the Yale Center for British Art and the University of Toronto (1982). Several of Bindman's interpretative points have appeared in other forms in his catalog of the Fitzwilliam Museum and in his *Blake as an Artist,* discussed under "Criticism." Also valuable are Charles Ryskamp's *William Blake Engraver,* for the 1969 Princeton exhibition; A. S. Roe's notes for a 1965 exhibition at Cornell; Robert R. Wark's notes for 1965 – 66 exhibitions at the Huntington, *William Blake and His Circle;* Frederick Cummings' *Romantic Art in Britain* for the 1968 Detroit show; the team-annotated *William Blake and the Art of His Time,* edited by Corlette Walker for the Santa Barbara exhibition of 1976; Harvey Stahl's *William Blake: The Apocalyptic Vision,* introduced by Bruce Daryl Barone, for a 1974 exhibition at Manhattanville College. Finally, Kerrison Preston's *The Blake Collection of W. Graham Robertson* (1951) contains interesting impressionistic comments by Robertson, whose collection, dispersed at his death, has enriched museums on both sides of the Atlantic.

BIBLIOGRAPHICAL ESSAYS

Bibliographical research on Blake has been dominated by his trio of great editors. The dating of his script, based on his idiosyncratic formation of the letter *g*, has been debated by David V. Erdman, the discoverer of this phenomenon, and G. E. Bentley, Jr., in *Blake Newsletter* (no. 9, 3: 1 and no. 10, 3: 2 [1969]). Bentley has also written on bibliographical problems in *The Four Zoas* (*MLN*, 1956; *TSE*, 1958), *America* (*SIR*, 1966), and the Pickering Manuscript (*SB*, 1966) and on textual problems in general (*Editing Eighteenth-Century Texts*, ed. D. I. B. Smith, 1968). Erdman has attacked Bentley's edition of *Vala*, discussed problems of editing this work, and proposed new arrangements (*Library*, 1964). He has also written on "The Everlasting Gospel" (in *From Sensibility to Romanticism*, ed. Frederick W. Hilles and Harold Bloom [1965]) and on textual questions generally (in *William Blake: Essays for S. Foster Damon*, ed. Alvin H. Rosenfeld, 1869). His "The Suppressed and Altered Passages in Blake's *Jerusalem*" (*SB*, 1964, followed up in 1965) demonstrates his uncanny ability to reconstruct lost lines, though one crucial reconstruction, on Blake's notion of "Writing," turned out to be unfounded, as acknowledged in another "temporary report" (*BIQ* no. 65, 17: 1 [1983]). Several of Sir Geoffrey Keynes's bibliographical essays were reprinted in his *Blake Studies* (rev. 1971); he has also explained the development of his editions of Blake in *English Studies Today* (ed. G. I. Duthie, 1964) and has provided detailed bibliographical information (*BC*, 1981) about the recently rediscovered copy BB of *Songs*. (Designations like "copy BB" refer to the Keynes-Wolf system described above; see also n. 2.) This copy, with plates from other books, receives attention in Robert N. Essick, "New Information on Blake's Illuminated Books" (*BIQ* no. 57, 15: 1 [1981]). Detlef Dörrbecker describes copy Y of *Innocence* in "Innocence Lost and Found: An Untraced Copy Traced" (*BIQ* no. 59, 15: 3 [1981–82]).

In "William Blake as a Private Publisher" (*BNYPL*, 1957), Bentley accounts for the failure of the 1802 and the 1805 sales of Hayley's *Ballads*. In "For Friendship's Sake: Some Additions to Blake's Sheet for 'Designs to a Series of Ballads' (1802)" (*SB*, 1976), Karen G. Mulhallen continues an earlier study of Blake's use of surplus paper from the *Ballads* project, namely, Bentley's "The Date of Blake's Pickering Manuscript; or, the Way of a Poet with Paper" (*SB*, 1966). Michael Phillips' "Blake's Corrections in *Poetical Sketches*" (*BNL* no. 14, 4: 2 [1970]) describes the eight copies Blake annotated; his "William Blake and the 'Unincreasable Club': The Printing of *Poetical Sketches*" (*BNYPL*, 1976) shows good reasons for identifying John Nichols as the printer of Blake's first volume; and his "The Reputation of Blake's *Poetical Sketches*" (*RES*, 1975) investigates early promotional efforts. Francis Wood Metcalf corrects the bibliographical notes in Bentley's edition of *Tiriel* in "Toward a More Accurate Description of the *Tiriel* Manuscript" (*BNL* no. 13, 4: 1 [1970]). Christopher Heppner, "Blake and *The Seaman's Recorder*" (*BIQ* no. 45, 12: 1 [1978]), corrects Bentley's misattribution in *Blake Books*. Robert N. Essick and Morton D. Paley, "The Printings of Blake's Designs for Blair's *Grave*" (*BC*, 1975), offer a foretaste of their book on this project, *Robert Blair's The Grave, Illustrated by William Blake: A Study with Facsimile* (1982), discussed under "Pictorial Works." Charles Ryskamp [with Thomas V. Lange], "A Blake Discovery" (*TLS,* 14 Jan. 1977), announces variants of Blake's engravings in an extra-illustrated volume acquired by the Pierpont Morgan Library. William F. Halloran, "William Blake's *The French Revolution:* A Note on the Text and a Possible Emendation" (*BNYPL,* 1968), argues for a rearrangement of several lines; his proposal has influenced editions by Stevenson, Erdman, and Bentley, discussed below. In adjoining articles (*BIQ* no. 64, 16: 4 [1983]), Thomas V. Lange and Joseph Viscomi expose as forgeries plates 4 and 9 of *America* copy B (Pierpoint Morgan Library). Michael J. Tolley describes *America* copy N and *Europe* copy I in "The Auckland Blakes" (*Biblionews and Australian Notes & Queries*, 1967). A. W. J. Lincoln, "Blake's 'Europe': An Early Version?" (*N&Q,* 1978), analyzes a proof copy, and Edward Larrissy attempts to reconstruct a draft text underlying both *America* and *Europe* (*N&Q,* 1983). Some textual snarls in *Vala,* or *The Four Zoas,* are partially untangled by Andrew Lincoln, David V. Erdman, John Kilgore, and Mark Lefebvre in a special issue of *Blake: An Illustrated Quarterly* (no. 46, 12: 3 [1978]). In a posthumous contribution Geoffrey Keynes published some recently discovered lines by Blake, "The Phoenix to Mrs. Butts" (*TLS,* 14 Sept. 1984), sparking an interpretation by John Adlard (*TLS,* 21 Sept. 1984).

Editions, Facsimiles, and Reproductions

For the same reason that Blake's visual and verbal productions cannot be discussed separately, the categories of edition, facsimile, catalog, bibliographical study, and commentary often overlap—for example, in G. E. Bentley, Jr.'s generously illustrated edition of Blake's *Writings,* David V. Erdman's *The Illuminated Blake* (mentioned above), Erdman's and Donald K. Moore's edition of Blake's Notebook, Irene Tayler's book on Blake's designs for Gray's poems, and the Clarendon edition of Blake's *Night Thoughts* designs, as well as many of the Blake Trust facsimiles with Sir Geoffrey Keynes's scholarly apparatus. I have tried to discuss in logical places, with frequent cross-references, these and other works that serve several purposes.

TEXTS

Principles of textual scholarship like those developed for Shakespeare studies by W. W. Greg and amplified by Fredson Bowers cannot be made to apply to Blake's etched and engraved texts, which were usually individually modified: each copy of each book that left Blake's hands was, in effect, a new edition, even if the copperplates from which the book was printed were not technically in an altered "state." Copies of the same work made in the same year usually differ in hand-altered details. Blake freely varied the printed punctuation—and sometimes even the words— with pen or brush, and he often added, subtracted, or rearranged pages. Lines were occasionally printed in an early copy, masked or erased in a later copy, and restored in a still later copy. No fair copies in manuscript exist for any illuminated book; the master plates etched by Blake were sold for scrap metal in the nineteenth century. Thus no Ur-texts or final revisions can be established. Variants cannot be arranged in the neat tree diagrams that Jack Stillinger uses to present solutions to textual problems in Keats.

Duplication of Blake's unconventional punctuation is impossible with mechanical typography: ornamental flourishes have a status halfway between punctuation and decoration; other marks are used idiosyncratically and are unstable among different copies of the same work. To illustrate with a hypothetical but by no means atypical example, an editor might have to decide whether to accept a period (because it appears in eight out of ten copies of the work at hand), a comma (because it is used in the earliest copy), a colon (because there seems to be an extra dot in the latest copy, though it is elongated enough to be interpreted with equal validity as an exclamation point), or a semicolon (because a collation of all printed copies suggests that this may have been the mark, improperly inked, that was originally etched on the copperplate). Or is the best course simply to suppress the mark altogether because it confusingly breaks into a grammatical unit? Only in our century have Blake's zealous and patient editors confronted such questions; no definitive answers are possible. No editor, however conscientious, will ever be capable of producing an immaculate text. No two editors, however highly principled, will ever agree.

Editorial principles appropriate to Blake's unique texts have evolved slowly, in the process raising critical understanding, which in turn has advanced criticism to the point that ever more faithful texts are needed. For almost a hundred years after Blake's death there was no complete scholarly edition of his work. Notoriously intrusive repunctuation and rewording characterized nineteenth-century editions, as may be seen in Dante Gabriel Rossetti's selection of lyrics in Gilchrist's 1863 biography, William Michael Rossetti's 1874 Aldine edition, and the 1893 *Collected Works* edited by Edwin J. Ellis and W. B. Yeats. The stories behind these editions are recounted in Deborah Dorfman's *Blake in the Nineteenth Century* (1969) and in articles reviewed with "Influence" studies. John Sampson, in his "New and Verbatim Text" of the *Poetical Works* (1905), set the direction for this century by scrupulously preserving Blake's exact wording and orthography, whether etched, handwritten, or in letterpress, and by supplying variant readings from collations of several copies of each illuminated book. Sampson's edition of the lyric poetry was supplemented by the equally scholarly *Prophetic Writings*, edited by D. J. Sloss and J. P. R. Wallis (1925), which contains interpretative notes and an "Index of Symbols" that prefigure Damon's 1965 *Dictionary*. Geoffrey Keynes's three-volume Nonesuch edition (1925) was the first complete edition; from it were derived his one-volume *Poetry and Prose* (1927; rev. 1939) and later his *Complete Writings* (1957; corr. 1974), the basis for Erdman's *Concordance*, mentioned above.

But the Sampson, Sloss-Wallis, and Keynes editions all cautiously attempted to normalize Blake's punctuation. As new scholarship developed around the Keynes edition, with its successive improvements, the need arose for a more transparent text. David V. Erdman's nonrepunctuated *Poetry and Prose*, with a commentary by Harold Bloom (1965; rev. 1982 as *The Complete Poetry and Prose of William Blake*) has tended, especially in America, to supplant Keynes as the standard text. Because the 1965 Erdman edition omitted some minor correspondence, most of the designs, and full bibliographical descriptions of original documents (and because Bloom's commentary did not cover all works), still another scholarly complete edition was justifiable: G. E. Bentley, Jr.'s two-volume *William Blake's Writings,* copiously illustrated and heavily annotated, appeared in the Oxford English Texts series in 1978. Far less freely than Keynes, Bentley alters Blake's punctuation, signaling typographically that some kind of change has occurred. Bentley reproduces three quarters of the designs in black and white and describes all designs, whether reproduced or not. His editorial apparatus is much fuller than Erdman's or Keynes's, especially in descriptive bibliography. His interpretative notes are intended as objective descriptions and identifications only. Meanwhile, Erdman's edition has been revised; the 1982 complete edition, with improved readings, has been designated an approved text by the Modern Language Association.

In principle and in practice, Erdman and Bentley differ sharply, although each is a painstaking editor. A major difference between the two editions is that Erdman provides reconstructions of numerous deleted lines that Bentley does not accept. Thus, depending on one's independent ability to confirm or reject Erdman's readings, one may praise Erdman's sharp eyes and deeply learned intuitions or be grateful for Bentley's uncompromising conservatism. The editors differ, too, in their methods of establishing textual authority for the illuminated books. For both, the text rests on the hypothetical final state of the original copperplate (now lost). Erdman seeks to reconstruct this plate by inductions derived from collations of several printed versions of each work; Bentley seeks the same goal by adhering to a single printed copy as copy text. Neither Bentley nor Erdman accepts a highly finished, heavily retouched late copy as being in principle more authoritative than the original plate, though both occasionally incorporate readings from retouched copies. Erdman and Bentley also render Blake's whimsical and expressive punctuation differently. When Erdman must choose between a comma and a period, he accepts the larger mark on the grounds that it could not have appeared in print unless it had been actually etched on the plate, while the smaller mark could have been an improperly inked comma. In attempting to preserve Blake's punctuation while refusing to accept any one copy text as decisive evidence of what was etched on the original plate, Erdman arrives at eclectic readings. For example, Blake's printed copies contain far more colons than exclamation points, but the appearance even in one copy of an exclamation point is enough to convince Erdman that this mark must have been the one actually etched (the colons being merely underinked), and so Erdman's edition includes more exclamation points than can be found in Blake's own publications. Bentley, on the other hand, relies on a single, often atypical copy text—a posthumous, uncolored one, usually—on the theory that it is most similar to the final state of the plate, though sometimes for the sake of convenience he chooses some other copy, almost always a lightly colored one. But which is really closer to what Blake wanted his reader to see—a plain copy closely resembling his etched plate or a highly finished copy on which the letters and punctuation have been carefully redelineated by the hand of the author, designer, and printer? And how useful are Bentley's signaled changes in Blake's punctuation, since they reveal only that a change has been made but conceal the original mark that has been altered or removed? E. B. Murray's thorough review of Bentley's edition (*BIQ* no. 55, 14: 2 [1980–81]) contrasts sample passages from Bentley and Erdman, discusses the importance of Blake's hand-finished details, and clearly explains why it is virtually impossible to establish consistent editorial principles, especially for recording and emending Blake's punctuation. The "Santa Cruz Blake Study Group" presents a long review of the 1982 Erdman edition that deplores the mediation of all modern printed texts, points out a few erroneous or questionable transcriptions by Erdman, objects to Bloom's commentary, and reflects on editorial procedures in general (*BIQ* no. 69, 18: 1 [1984]).

Erdman's revised 1982 edition, the *Complete Poetry and Prose,* is still compact and inexpensive enough to be used in the classroom. At the same time, its fidelity to its own principles ensures its continued use as a primary working text for scholars. But Bentley's text, with its fuller apparatus, including detailed bibliographical descriptions, must also be consulted, and its readings checked against Erdman's. Unfortunately, since the two editions number plates and even lines differently, comparisons are inconvenient, and dual citations are necessary. For reference to Blake's letters, Bentley's fully annotated edition and Keynes's *The Letters of William Blake* (3rd ed. 1980) are usually preferable to Erdman's edition because they identify Blake's correspondents, locate and describe the documents, and identify topical and literary allusions. A few factual shortcomings in Keynes's generously illustrated edition of the letters, repunctuated for the general reader, are pointed out in Bentley's review in *BIQ* (no. 59, 15: 3 [1981–82]). A bonus in Bentley's edition is a detailed note on the workings of the British postal system, which provides a framework for interpreting dates and times postmarked in different districts.

There is no complete set of interpretative notes for all Blake's works. The fullest and most satisfactory, by W. H. Stevenson in Longman's Annotated English Poets series (1971) and by Alicia Ostriker in the Penguin series (1977), cover all the poetry but no prose except for *The Marriage of Heaven and Hell.* Selected editions by F. W. Bateson (1957), Hazard Adams (1970), and Mary Lynn Johnson and John E. Grant (1979) provide concise but comprehensive introductions and notes. Selections for use in both secondary schools and colleges are very well annotated in two British series, Macdonald and Evans' Annotated Student Texts, by R. B. Kennedy (1970), and Wheaton Studies in English, by A. S. Crehan (1976). Bloom's commentary in Erdman's *Complete Poetry and Prose,* though it omits consideration of *Songs* and many shorter works, is frequently rewarding on the prophecies, but it provides little factual information and identifies only "the most crucial of Blake's literary allusions and historical references." Johnson reviews many of these annotated texts in a survey and checklist of classroom editions (*BNL* no. 37, 10: 1 [1976]). (A four-volume bilingual edition translated by Pierre Leyris, *Oeuvres de William Blake* [1974–83], contains well-reproduced illustrations; the first, second, and fourth volumes are introduced by Leyris, the third by Jacques Blondel. Editions in an impressive variety of languages may be found in *Blake Books.*)

Perhaps now is the time to consider whether a team-edited *Blake Variorum,* one worthy of standing on the same shelf with *Blake Books* and the Blake *Concordance,* would be both feasible and desirable.

FACSIMILES OF ILLUMINATED BOOKS

In addition to sound texts, the Blake scholar requires faithful facsimiles, preferably with full but unobtrusive critical and bibliographical notes. To some degree, an accurate facsimile of one of Blake's originals delivers the text directly, without the necessity of scholarly intervention: each reader becomes in effect an editor as well. But without specialized information on variants it is difficult to progress beyond a naive impression of a single copy of a work that exists in multiple versions. Ideally, then, the editor of a scholarly facsimile should provide a transcript of the text, with or without modern punctuation, a description of the designs, and suggestions for interpreting both, considering other copies of the same poem, other works by Blake, bibliographical evidence, and leading critical appraisals. In practice, probably because reproduction of an illuminated book entails such formidable problems, most editors of facsimiles simply arrange for reproduction and provide a few introductory remarks.

Beginning in the 1880s, in editions of fewer than one hundred copies, William Muir produced with uneven success handmade color facsimiles of most of the illuminated books, and Ellis and Yeats embellished their edition with crudely redrawn monochrome lithographs. The best moderately priced and widely distributed facsimiles are the color collotypes published by Dent in the 1920s and 1930s and the six- and eight-color offset reproductions published by Oxford University Press in the 1970s; both include some critical commentary. Most of the illuminated books have also been reproduced in color microfilm by the E. P. Group of Companies of Wakefield, Yorkshire (formerly Micromethods, then E. P. Microform). These filmstrips, photographed from six wonderful originals in the Fitzwilliam Museum, seven originals in the British Museum, and the Blake Trust facsimile of *Jerusalem* (described below), are also available as slide sets. E. P. has also filmed the Bunyan series (Frick Museum) and a colored copy of the *Night Thoughts* engravings (Soane Museum). Colors by E. P. are usually reliable when fresh, but—as with all slides—they are subject to decay unless kept in dehumidified cold storage.

A true facsimile, full scale and in color, is of course expensive to produce. For accuracy almost to the point of forgery, so that slight dissatisfactions arise only after minute comparisons with the originals, no reproductions come close to the complete series of magnificent hand-stenciled facsimiles brought out by the Blake Trust at the instigation and under the editorship of Geoffrey Keynes; these were executed under the supervision of Arnold Fawcus by the craftworkers of the Trianon Press, Jura, France. Keynes's "The William Blake Trust," in *William Blake: Essays for S. Foster Damon,* edited by Alvin H. Rosenfeld (1969), reviews the history of this project. These very expensive books, most of which appeared in numbered editions of four to six hundred, may be found in research libraries. The remaining stock of Bernard Quaritch, the original distributor, is now sold by Maggs Brothers of London; earlier issues occasionally turn up in rare-book dealers' catalogs, such as those of Ben Abraham Books of Thornhill, Ontario, which specializes in Blake. Keynes's interpretive notes on the designs have varied in depth over the three decades in which the series was published. His brief bibliographical statements, though they sometimes contain new information, are usually so closely focused on a single copy that Bentley's *Blake Books* should be the primary point of reference. Individual titles in the series are discussed below. With the death of Fawcus in 1979 and of Sir Geoffrey in 1982, this series has virtually come to an end, having fulfilled its primary mission of duplicating at least one copy of each illuminated book. Work on a Blake Trust facsimile of Blake's designs for the Book of Job is being completed by a team of editors.

G. E. Bentley, Jr., had long planned a five-volume *Microfiche Edition of William Blake's Colored Works in Illuminated Printing* with the University of Chicago Press. The microfiche edition would have offered every library access to every page of every book Blake colored, thus fulfilling a long-cherished communal dream of scholars. But foundation support for photography could not be secured, and the project was canceled in 1984. John E. Grant and others at the University of Iowa have produced an interactive videodisc for local use from Grant's own slide collection, and they project a comprehensive archive of Blake's images for general distribution. The distancing effect of reproduction by microfiche or videodisc of course prevents readers from experiencing differences in size, format, paper texture, depths of imprinting, and the subtler tones of inks and washes, but this loss would be more than offset by the opportunity, at one sitting, to view widely scattered works, some in remote private collections. And a virtually indestructible microfiche or videodisc record would help ensure that Blake's works produced on acidic "wove" paper will be known in some form to future generations. Yet because Blake was a book designer who created pages that can be lovingly turned by hand, his readers will continue to want, in addition to nonbook forms of reproduction, beautiful facsimiles on paper that recreate his works of art in their original format.

The scholar needs a practical reference work on the illuminated texts as well. The halftone reproductions in Erdman's portable and cheap *The Illuminated Blake* (1974) are useful reminders of the originals in color. Erdman's full though sometimes quirky commentary on the designs, ranging over everything from major symbols to gnat-sized arabesques, should routinely be consulted. But Erdman does not attempt to provide detailed bibliographical information or transcriptions of the texts, nor does he consistently note how many copies are believed to exist and which of these have previously been published in facsimile. In many cases, photographs from various sources form a composite copy rather than a reproduction of any single copy. *America, Europe,* and *Jerusalem* have been sharply reduced; the text plates of *For the Sexes: The Gates of Paradise* have been enlarged. But the convenience of having all the plates together and the insights in the commentary far outshine minor imperfections noted by G. E.

Bentley, Jr. (*UTQ,* 1975). The works in illuminated printing are also reproduced in black and white in Bindman's *Graphic Works* and Bentley's *Blake's Writings.*

Aside from the Blake Trust series, the most heavily annotated facsimile editions aimed at a scholarly audience have been produced in the United States. The American Blake Foundation sponsored two short-lived series of two titles each: G. E. Bentley, Jr.'s editions of *America* (1974) and *Europe* (1978), and Kay and Roger Easson's editions of *The Book of Urizen* (1978) and *Milton* (1978). Also, the New York Public Library and Brown University copublished Nancy Bogen's edition of *The Book of Thel* (1971). Despite the good intentions and expertise of the editors, each of these American editions is marred by notable errors of fact or interpretation. Nevertheless, the student of Blake's illuminated books should seek out these and other facsimiles, attempting to compare as many variant copies as possible in facsimile, while recognizing that some facsimiles will be useful primarily for their physical fidelity to the original, others for their notes or critical commentary, and still others for their textual scholarship. Even those that distort Blake's hues at least give some inkling of an otherwise inaccessible copy. In conscience, our generation should accept gracefully the mediation of facsimiles; the rare originals, on brittle, acidic paper, must be consulted sparingly if they are to be preserved beyond our own time.

Because study of facsimiles is essential to critics, because *Blake Books* does not guide readers to available facsimiles (they are intermingled, in chronological order, with other editions), and because the convenient records of facsimiles in the Keynes-Wolf *Census* are now out of date, a guide to facsimiles is in order. I survey all Blake facsimiles except those that are both inaccurate and scarce. I list illuminated books first—in a modified chronological order similar to the arrangements in Erdman's and Bentley's editions—followed by illustrated manuscripts, unillustrated manuscripts, and finally Blake's major pictorial series. (Several books listed here as facsimiles or reproductions could also be discussed as catalogs, editions, or critical works.) For each of the illuminated books, so that the status of a given facsimile is clearer, I provide approximate dates of the earliest and latest copies believed to have been finished and issued by Blake himself, the total number of copies believed to have been published by Blake, the alphabetical copy designations of those copies that have been reproduced, and the 1984 location of their originals. Throughout, it should be assumed that the Blake Trust facsimile is to be preferred above all others.[2]

Both *All Religions Are One* (one copy) and *There Is No Natural Religion* (13 copies) were probably etched around 1788 and printed about 1794 to 1815; they were left in loose, uncollated sheets. These closely related works, apparently Blake's first efforts in illuminated printing, have similar and largely speculative printing histories. The Blake Trust facsimile of *All Religions Are One* (1970), reproduced by color photography rather than by stenciled watercolors, is based on copy A (Huntington), the only virtually complete copy, supplemented by a title page from the Keynes collection. Some color discrepancies are noted in a review by Kay Parkhurst Easson (*BS* 5: 1 [1972]). Since no complete copies of *There Is No Natural Religion* exist, the Blake Trust facsimile (1971) reproduces pages in copies C, G, F, and L. Keynes's important bibliographical notes reconsider the page ordering and the relationship of this work to its companion tractate.

For *The Book of Thel* (title page 1789; printed 1789–1815, in 16–18 copies), the Blake Trust facsimile (1965) reproduces copy O (Rosenwald Collection, Library of Congress); E. P. reproduces both copy G (Fitzwilliam) and copy D (British Museum). The composite copy in *The Illuminated Blake* includes three plates from copy N (Cincinnati). Mary Lynn Johnson and John E. Grant reproduce the title page of copy N in color in *Blake's Poetry and Designs* (1979).

Nancy Bogen's *The Book of Thel: A Facsimile and a Critical Text* (1971) reproduces copy M (Berg Collection, New York Public Library). Because this edition is exemplary in format and methodology, though not in execution, it calls for detailed consideration. To establish her text, Bogen collates seventeen copies: the sixteen finished copies Blake is known to have produced plus the uncolored proofs in the Pierpont Morgan Library. Her table of variants and her notes on coloring are often unreliable, probably because she had to rely on slides in some cases. In punctuating her transcription, Bogen selects the largest mark of punctuation, according to Erdman's principle that smaller variants result from insufficient inking. Her unprecedented thoroughness in collating copies led to a significant discovery: the second "gentle" on plate 1, line 13, was printed as "gently" (without retouching) in copies K and R, indicating that these are in a "first state," earlier than the rest of the copies. Bogen also posits a "third state" for copies I and J, in which two lines on plate 6 are missing, because she thinks they were gouged from the plate itself rather than—as the thinned and roughened paper indicates—erased after printing. According to the "third state" hypothesis, copies I and J would have to be the latest of all copies; stylistically, however, they appear to be earlier than the elaborately finished copies N and O. In her introduction Bogen reviews previous scholarship and advances "A New Interpretation," which has not found wide acceptance. Most of her explanatory notes on the text are helpful; those on the designs contain some eccentric identifications of plant and animal forms. On balance, this book is useful as a record, in fairly accurate color, of copy M and as an example of features that a scholarly facsimile edition ought to have.

For *Songs of Innocence* (title page 1789; issued 1789–?1818, in about 25 versions), the Blake Trust facsimile (1954) used copy B (Rosenwald Collection, Library of Congress), which is also nicely reproduced photographically in color—without an editor—in an inexpensive paperback by Dover (1971). *Druckgraphik von William Blake aus der Sammlung Neuerburg,* an exhibition brochure from the Wallraf-Richartz Museum of Cologne (1982), includes two color reproductions from copy Y ("Laughing Song," enlarged, and "The Blossom") and two in black and white.

Songs of Innocence and of Experience (title page 1794; issued 1794–?1826, in about 28 versions) is best known in copy Z (Rosenwald Collection, Library of Congress), the original of the Blake Trust facsimile (1955). The hand-painted Blake Trust facsimile was then reproduced photographically in color by Orion Press (1967) and reissued by Oxford University Press (1970), with some blurring of details. Keynes's interpretative notes for the 1967 and 1970 editions ingest bits of Wicksteed, Erdman, Damon, and Hirsch with insufficient grains of salt. An anonymously edited color reproduction of the *Experience* portion of copy Z, apparently made from the Blake Trust facsimile, was published by Dover (1984). For a photographic color reproduction of copy T (British Museum), itself a composite of parts of a copy in Blake's later style with pages from earlier copies, see Werner Hofmann's *William Blake: Lieder der Unschuld und Erfahrung* (1975). In separate volumes of *Innocence* in 1926 and *Experience* in 1927, Ernest Benn published the whole of copy A in a color facsimile, with some rearrangements and substitutions. E. P. reproduces both British Museum copy B and Fitzwilliam copy AA. The Huntington Library has published, in color enlargements, a selection of sixteen pages from the two copies of *Songs* in its collection (E and N), with a brief introduction by James Thorpe (1976).

Monochrome prints from sixteen electrotype plates made directly from Blake's originals (with the exception of the title page for *Experience,* which seems to be made from a crude imitation) appeared in Gilchrist's *Life,* discussed under "Biographical Resources." Now both the original copperplates and the Gilchrist electrotypes have been lost or destroyed, but several duplicate sets of electrotypes exist; Keynes has published prints from these plates in the two editions of his *Blake Studies*—half in the first, half in the second. In 1983 the Manchester Etching Workshop announced a very limited edition of sixteen prints made from a set of duplicate electrotypes (except that a new and more accurate etching has been made to replace the botched title page for *Experience*). This workshop used handmade ink and paper, a rolling press similar to Blake's, and colors mixed according to eighteenth-century recipes. The printmaker was Paul Ritchie, and the commentator was Joseph Viscomi. The prints have been colored by hand, without the aid of stencils, on the model of Copy B (British Museum). A splendid plan for a color facsimile of Copy W (King's College, Cambridge)— announced with gorgeous gold-touched sample pages (*Book Collector,* 1980)— was abandoned (according to Sir Geoffrey Keynes in correspondence, 1981).

Bindman, *Graphic Works,* reproduces the whole of *Songs of Innocence and of Experience,* copy B (British Museum), in black and white. Wicksteed's *Blake's Innocence and Experience,* discussed under "Criticism," reproduces (mostly in halftone) the whole of an eclectic *Songs,* intermingling plates from all three copies in the British Museum (A, B, and T) and from copy AA in the Fitzwilliam. Photographs of *Songs* in *The Illuminated Blake* are taken from copy I (Widener, Harvard) and from the electrotypes made for Gilchrist's biography. As Mary Ellen Reisner points out in *BIQ* (no. 40, 10: 4 [1977]), the Folcroft facsimile of the uncolored posthumous copy *b* at Harvard has been deceptively retouched.

There are three color facsimiles of *Visions of the Daughters of Albion* (title page 1793; printed 1792–?1815, in 17 copies). The Blake Trust facsimile (1959) is based on copy C (Glasgow University), E. P. on the more richly colored copy P (Fitzwilliam), and the Dent facsimile (1932) on copy A (British Museum). The latter includes a commentary by John Middleton Murry.

Of *The Marriage of Heaven and Hell* (issued ?1793–1827, in about 11 copies), faithful color facsimiles of three distinctively beautiful copies have been made: the Blake Trust facsimile of copy D, Rosenwald Collection, Library of Congress (1960); the Dent facsimile of copy I, one of two in the Fitzwilliam Museum, Cambridge (1927); and the remarkably inexpensive Oxford University Press facsimile of copy H, the other Fitzwilliam copy (1975). Copy I is also reproduced by E. P. and—via the Dent facsimile—by Clark Emery in a clear black-and-white paperback edition (1962), with a long introduction aimed at beginning students. Halftone reproductions of twenty-four (of twenty-seven) plates of Copy C (Pierpont Morgan Library) accompany June Singer's Jungian study, *The Unholy Bible* (1970; rpt. 1973). Bindman, *Graphic Works*, reproduces copy B (Bodleian, Oxford).

Commentaries accompanying facsimiles of this work are particularly astute. Max Plowman analyzes the structure of the *Marriage* and describes nine copies for the Dent edition. Geoffrey Keynes, building upon an essay by Erdman and others in the Paley and Phillips festschrift for Keynes (discussed under "Criticism"), provides penetrating observations on all aspects of the designs for the Oxford facsimile. John Beer, however, questions its color quality and some of Keynes's points of interpretation (*BIQ* no. 41, 11: 1 [1977]).

For *America* (title page 1793; issued ?1793–1821 in 12–14 copies), the Blake Trust reproduces copy M, from the Paul Mellon Collection (1963), also the basis of an anonymously edited color reproduction by Dover (1984). E. P. reproduces copy O, one of two in the Fitzwilliam Museum. But most copies of *America*, printed usually in blue or green ink on white or cream paper, were designed by Blake as uncolored books. One of these, copy E (Rosenwald Collection, Library of Congress), has twice been made into a facsimile: first as an unbound set of line reproductions and halftones, without commentary (and mislabeled as copy C), put out by *Blake Newsletter* (1975), and then as a complete scholarly edition (in the clothbound version) published by the American Blake Foundation, *Materials for the Study of William Blake*, volume 1 (1974), edited by G. E. Bentley, Jr., with an annotated checklist of secondary material in English by Roger R. Easson. *The Illuminated Blake* conflates and reduces by one third pages from copies N (Auckland, New Zealand) and K (Yale). The whole of copy K, greatly reduced, accompanies Erdman's article on *America* in *Blake's Visionary Forms Dramatic*, cited under "Criticism." In "America, Everyone?" (*BNL* no. 36, 9: 4 [1976]), Erdman compares the demerits of his, the *Newsletter*'s, and Bentley's facsimiles, harshly objecting to Bentley's editorial work. Bindman, *Graphic Works*, reproduces copy F, British Museum.

Europe (title page 1794; issued 1794–?1821, in 9–11 copies) is reproduced as a Blake Trust facsimile (1969) based on pages from copies B (University of Glasgow) and G (Thorne Collection, Pierpont Morgan Library): this composite facsimile was apparently the basis of an anonymously edited color reproduction by Dover (1984). E. P. reproduces copy K (Fitzwilliam). For uncolored reproductions, *The Illuminated Blake* uses copy I (Auckland, New Zealand), reduced by one third, and the American Blake Foundation uses copy H (Harvard) in *Materials for the Study of William Blake*, volume 2 (1978). The latter was published as a portfolio of loose sheets, with editorial commentary by Bentley and an annotated checklist by Robert N. Essick (who also reviewed the Blake Trust *Europe* in *Kenyon Review,* 1970). Bindman, *Graphic Works,* reproduces the whole of copy B.

Two copies of *The Song of Los* (title page 1795; issued in five copies) have been reproduced in full. Copy B (Rosenwald Collection, Library of Congress) is the one selected by the Blake Trust (1975); E. P. uses copy A (British Museum). *The Illuminated Blake* uses portions of copies A, E, and D (reduced).

The Book of Urizen (title page 1794; issued 1794–?1818 in 7 copies) appears as a Blake Trust facsimile (1958) of copy G (Rosenwald Collection, Library of Congress). The Dent facsimile (1929) follows copy A (British Museum) and concludes with a discussion by Dorothy Plowman of such matters as the derivation of Urizen's name from the Greek word for "to limit." An inexpensive, excessively reddish photographic color facsimile of copy G by Easson and Easson (1978) is marred by some editorial inaccuracies and interpretative eccentricities; see Stuart Curran's severe review (*BIQ* no. 55, 44: 3 [1980–81]). E. P. uses copy D (British Museum); *The Illuminated Blake* reproduces copy B (Thorne Collection, Pierpont Morgan Library). The introductory essay in Clark Emery's blurry halftone reproduction of the Blake Trust facsimile (1966) dwells on parallels between *Urizen* and Gnostic thought.

The Book of Ahania (title page 1795) was issued in only one copy. The Blake Trust facsimile (1973) restores the original frontispiece from a loose sheet in the British Museum to reconstitute this unique copy, the bulk of which is in the Rosenwald Collection of the Library of Congress. E. P. has not reproduced *Ahania.*

The Book of Los (title page 1795) was also issued in only one copy. The technical difficulties of imitating the layers of opaque pigments used in *Ahania, The Book of Los,* and *The Song of Los* stymied the wizards of the Trianon Press until fairly recently. The unique copy of *The Book of Los* in the British Museum was issued as a Blake Trust facsimile in 1975 and was also filmed by E. P.

For *Milton* (title page 1804; issued ?1808–?1818 in 4 copies), there are color reproductions of copy D (Rosenwald Collection, Library of Congress) by the Blake Trust (1967), copy A (British Museum) by E. P., and copy B (Huntington) by Easson and Easson of the American Blake Foundation for Shambala Press (1978). Some shortcomings of the latter are pointed out by Joseph A. Wittreich, Jr. (on the text) and Morton D. Paley (on the plates) in *BIQ,* no. 49, 13: 1 [1979]). Thus the only copy that has not been fully reproduced is copy C (New York Public Library), but two color plates from this copy appear in Johnson and Grant's *Blake's Poetry and Designs,* and many plates in monochrome appear in Bentley's *Blake's Writings.*

Jerusalem (title page 1804; produced ?1818–?1826, in 5 complete copies—4 of which are uncolored—and one partial copy, colored) was the first project of the Blake Trust. There are now Blake Trust color facsimiles of both the sumptuous and brilliant copy E in the Paul Mellon Collection (1951) and the more subdued copy B (private collection), which consists of the first chapter only (1974). To represent the four uncolored copies, the Blake Trust also reproduced copy C in heliogravure from a private collection (1952); a companion volume of commentary by Joseph Wicksteed soon followed (1953). Minna Doskow's *William Blake's Jerusalem* (1982) contains a complete reproduction of copy C, filmed from the Blake Trust facsimile. *The Illuminated Blake* reproduces copy D (Harvard), and Bindman's *Graphic Works* reproduces copy A (British Museum). Only copy F (Pierpont Morgan Library) remains unreproduced. E. P.—though it credits the British Museum for the colored copy of *Jerusalem* from which its slides and microfilm were made—actually reproduces Paul Mellon's copy E, the only complete colored copy, probably from the British Museum's copy of the Blake Trust facsimile.

Blake's final works in illuminated printing—the aphoristic *Laocoön* engraving (c. 1820; 2 copies), the single sheet containing *On Homer's Poetry* and *On Virgil* (c. 1821; 6 copies), and the illuminated playlet *The Ghost of Abel* (title page 1822; 4 copies)—are all uncolored. Copy A of the first work, copy B of the second, and copy B of the third, with related drawings, were published in one volume, *Blake's Last Testament,* by the Blake Trust (1976). Keynes's notes point out for the first time Blake's departures from his model, the cast of the *Laocoön* group in the Royal Academy. (Because Blake's title for this work begins—in Hebrew lettering—with the first syllable of God's ineffable name, it is usually referred to by its more widely recognized classical title; Blake's own title, transliterated, would be *Yah and His Two Sons.*) Keynes's facsimile edition inspired a special meeting at the MLA convention, prepared for by Irene Tayler's "Blake's Laocoön" and an announcement by David Bindman of an early state of the engraving, both in *BNL* (no. 39, 10: 3 [1976]). *The Illuminated Blake* reproduces copy D of *On Homer's Poetry* and copy D of *The Ghost of Abel.* Bindman's *Graphic Works* reproduces copy B of the *Laocoön,* copy A of *On Homer's Poetry,* and copy A of *The Ghost of Abel.*

Other books of designs fit somewhat uneasily into the category of illuminated books. In its first edition, *The Gates of Paradise,* under the prefixed title *For Children* (1793; 5 copies), was not a literary work at all but a book of emblems, captioned designs. In its second edition, however, under the supratitle *For the Sexes* (?1818; 12 copies), Blake added an introductory poem, further inscriptions under seven of the sixteen engravings, and two concluding poems. Neither edition was colored. Along with sample variants from other states of the engravings, Keynes published facsimiles of the two editions, with a thorough bibliographical analysis and a new census of copies, in a three-volume set put out by Trianon Press (1968). In this edition, the original of *For Children* is copy D (Rosenwald Collection, Library of Congress) and that of *For the Sexes* is copy F (Huntington). *The Illuminated Blake* reproduces copy E of *For Children* and copy G of *For the Sexes* (both from the Mellon collection), and Bindman, *Graphic Works,* reproduces copy A of both series (Rosenwald Collection, Library of Congress).

The British Museum's copies of Blake's collections of opaquely color-printed plates from various illuminated books, known as *The Small Book of Designs* (1794–96) and *The Large Book of Designs* (?1794), have been filmed in color by the E. P. Group of Companies. A second copy of the *Small Book,* now dispersed, contains gnomic inscriptions in Blake's handwriting. Sample pages, including inscriptions, are reproduced in the Keynes-Wolf *Census* (from *Urizen* 1), in *Graphic Works* (from *Urizen* 1 and 13), and in Butlin's *Paintings and Drawings* (from

Urizen 22). Butlin (see "Reference Works") describes and reproduces the pictorial area of both series.

OTHER FACSIMILES

The illustrated manuscripts known as *Tiriel* (?1789), the Notebook (?1787–?1818), and *Vala* or *The Four Zoas* (?1796–?1807) have all been published in black and white in scholarly facsimile editions. In *Tiriel: Facsimile and Transcript of the Manuscript* (1967), G. E. Bentley, Jr., reunites with the poem eight of the twelve full-page illustrations originally meant to accompany it, comments helpfully on their interrelationship and on bibliographical and interpretive matters, and transcribes the text, signaling editorial punctuation. Erdman's unrepunctuated text in *Poetry and Prose* differs in several readings, some of which Bentley later accepted in his edition of the *Writings*. Certain medial periods in Erdman's text appear in the facsimile, however, to be unintentional specks—smaller or much closer to parts of letters than are the dots used elsewhere in the manuscript for punctuation. Color reproductions of some of the designs and information about them can be found in Butlin's *Paintings and Drawings*. Francis Wood Metcalf's 1970 article in *Blake Newsletter,* mentioned under "Bibliographical Essays," corrects some of Bentley's descriptions.

 The Notebook of William Blake: A Photographic and Typographic Facsimile, edited by David V. Erdman, with the assistance of Donald K. Moore (1973; corr. rpt. 1977), uses infrared photography to make faint or erased lines in this precious manuscript-sketchbook visible; for ordinary scholarly purposes, the facsimile is more useful than the original in the British Museum. Moore's ingenious typographical imitation of Blake's text, upside down, sideways, and in swirls, allows for easy comparison between transcript and photocopy in any position. Thus the Erdman-Moore facsimile supersedes the one edited by Keynes (1935) and the bibliographical study based on it by Bunsho Jugaku (1953). The introduction announces Erdman's discovery—from inconsistent patterns of stains—that the pages are no longer in their original order; Erdman also detected from erased or canceled numberings that Blake had planned several different sequences of emblems before he created *The Gates of Paradise.*

 Settling on a correct transcription and a satisfactory editorial arrangement of the *Vala* manuscript is undoubtedly the most troubled area of Blake scholarship, even within the mind of a single editor and certainly between rival editors. Close to the forefront of the long and distinguished line of books on Blake published by Oxford University Press is Bentley's staggering full-scale replica of the atlas-size manuscript *William Blake's Vala* (1963). Complete with massive editorial support services, it appears on first acquaintance to be the definitive edition. But the protean manuscript is so difficult to decipher and arrange, especially in Night VII, that so far Bentley and Erdman have not been able to agree on transcriptions, fix the status of words that Keynes's edition records as deleted, or synchronize their correlations among archaeological layers of revisions on different pages—nor has one convinced the other that he has correctly deduced the evolution of the poem either from internal evidence or from the physical evidence of the manuscript and its supplementary scraps. The conflicting editions are too complex and the evidence too technical to review briefly—or perhaps at all—but the user of Bentley's *Vala* facsimile should at least be aware of Erdman's review (*Library,* 1964) and should compare Erdman's and Bentley's newer transcriptions in their recent editions with the photographic facsimile, with Stevenson's edition, and with the essays on the text by Erdman, Andrew Lincoln, John Kilgore, and Mark Lefebvre in *BIQ* (no. 46, 12: 2 [1978]). This special issue on *Vala* announced an Italian translation, with commentary on the designs, to accompany a facsimile edited by Cettina Magno. An English-Italian version of this project by Magno and Erdman, with reduced infrared photographs to clarify details, is ready for publication. In 1983 Swallow Press brought out a nonscholarly transcription by Landon Dowdey, assisted by Patricia Hopkins Rice, which sets the repunctuated text in prose paragraphs "integrated" with photolithographic reproductions of more than 120 engravings and drawings selected from throughout Blake's work. With infrared photographs as illustrations, John E. Grant has corrected some of Bentley's notes on the drawings (in *Blake's Sublime Allegory,* cited under "Criticism"). H. M. Margoliouth's *Vala: Blake's Numbered Text* attempted to excavate the earliest complete stratum of text and to provide a bibliographical and critical analysis, but it is not certain that all parts of Margoliouth's numbered text represent any one discernible stage of completion of the poem. Interpretation of internal evidence is equally controversial. Both Bentley and Margoliouth perhaps exaggerate the indications in Blake's patterns of revision that he underwent an abrupt conversion from radical secularism to Christianity, yet Erdman's resistance to their whole line of argument sometimes seems harder than the evidence itself.

Photographic facsimiles of unillustrated manuscript works include *The Pickering Manuscript* (Pierpont Morgan Library), introduced by Charles Ryskamp (1972); *Letters from William Blake to Thomas Butts,* made up of beautiful collotype reproductions on odd-sized sheets, edited by Keynes (1926); and a hard-to-read "photoreprint" of Blake's annotated copy of Lavater's *Aphorisms on Man,* learnedly introduced by R. J. Shroyer (1980). A facsimile edition of Blake's annotated copy of Bishop Watson's *Apology for the Bible* was edited by G. Ingli James (1984). A sample page of text and sketches from *The Island in the Moon* is reproduced (reduced) in Bentley's *Writings*; three other pages appear in Wicksteed's *Blake's Innocence and Experience*; Goran Malmqvist's 1979 Swedish edition and translation of the *Island* includes a complete facsimile, and R. J. Shroyer also plans a facsimile edition. Of interest only as a sample of Blake's clerkly handwriting during his residence in Felpham is the facsimile (without an editor) of Blake's secretarial transcript of Hayley's translation of an Italian poem, misleadingly entitled *Genesis: Verses from a Manuscript of William Blake* (1952). This document should not be confused with Blake's own "Genesis Manuscript," reproduced in Butlin's *Paintings and Drawings.* Finally, the original edition of *Poetical Sketches* (1785), in letterpress, was reproduced in facsimile without editorial comment in 1926. For a recent census of copies, see Geoffrey Keynes's essay *"Poetical*

Sketches," in his *Blake Studies* (1971) and Michael Phillips' "Blake's Corrections in *Poetical Sketches" (BNL* no. 14, 4: 2 [1970]); for reproductions of Blake's hand corrections in copy F, see D. F. McKenzie (*Turnbull Library Record,* 1968).

REPRODUCTIONS OF PICTORIAL WORKS

Because much of Blake's imaginative criticism exists in pictorial form, literary scholars also require access to his major illustrations of other writers and his serial works on single themes. Butlin's *Paintings and Drawings,* mentioned under "Aids to Research," reproduces many of these and discusses items in series as aesthetic entities. Butlin's catalog should be the primary point of reference for all the works it describes, since his notes are more recent and accurate than those in most separate catalogs. Specialized critical studies centering on Blake's illustrations may be found in the "Criticism" section under "Pictorial Works." Additional reproductions of pictures from various series may be located through two previously noted aids to research in *Blake Newsletter:* Essick's "Finding List" (1971) and Frost's checklist of slides (1975). With the advent of Butlin's *Paintings and Drawings,* these listings are no longer the essential research tools they once were, but they still help to locate such things as color reproductions of pictures that Butlin publishes only in black and white. Convenient sources of slides, in addition to E. P. Group of Companies, include Sandak, Inc., the American distributor for Tate Gallery items; Budek Films and Slides; the Miniature Gallery; and the Boston Museum of Fine Arts. The British Museum always has a number of Blake slides at its sale counter. Many of the major Blake repositories mentioned under "Catalogs" occasionally sell Blake items, and most will make slides on special order.

Blake's first undertaking in interpretative illustration was also/by far his largest. In 1795 he began a series of 537 watercolor designs to surround the printed text of Young's *Night Thoughts.* Forty-three of these atlas-scale designs were published in 1797 as engravings to illustrate the first four "Nights" of Young's poem. Most of the original watercolors remained unpublished until the long-awaited appearance in 1980 of *William Blake's Designs for Edward Young's Night Thoughts,* edited by John E. Grant, Edward J. Rose, and Michael J. Tolley, with David V. Erdman as coordinating editor. A companion volume of commentary has been in preparation for many years. This Clarendon edition reproduces all 537 designs and the engravings in black and white, in reduced size, along with related drawings and 80 color plates, two of which contain small reproductions of eight colored engravings. A long introduction reviews the publication history and states of engravings, provides a new census of colored engraved copies (divided according to "White Death" and "Green Death" color schemes), interprets the frontispieces for the two volumes of watercolors, and concludes with a checklist of scholarship. (The whole series of designs is described but not reproduced in Butlin's *Paintings and Drawings.*) Detlef W. Dörrbecker (*BIQ* no. 62, 16: 2 [1982]) bemoans the quality of the Clarendon reproductions, especially those in color, and the misplaced emphases of the introduction; Thomas V. Lange's "A Rediscovered Colored Copy of Young's *Night Thoughts" (BIQ* no. 59, 15: 3 [1981–82]) points out some shortsightedness in the Clarendon editors' numbering system for colored copies of the engraved edition; Grant's response reviews key aspects of the project (*BIQ* 18: 3 [1984–85]). Color microfilms of the complete set of watercolors and of a colored engraved copy ("White Death" type) are sold by E. P. Group of Companies. In *Illustrations to Young's Night Thoughts Done in Water-Colour by William Blake* (1927), Geoffrey Keynes edited a selection of thirty of the designs; these are beautifully reproduced almost full size in expensive collotype, with five in color that is much clearer, brighter, and more delicate than anything in the Clarendon edition. Keynes reprints his introductory essay for this edition in his *Blake Studies* (1949; rev. 1971). In 1975, Robert Essick and Jenijoy La Belle edited a photographic facsimile of the 1797 engraved edition (reduced about 35%). In addition to supplying the bibliographical details and an annotated checklist of scholarship, they call attention to such features as the upward, downward, and circular movements in the designs, which "whirl" about Young's text and expand it "both spatially and iconographically."

In the same format and on the same "elephant" paper as the *Night Thoughts* designs (but with a smaller text area leaving more room for pictures), Blake in 1797–98 created for Nancy Flaxman an illustrated volume of Gray's poems (the date was established by Mary K. Woodworth [*N&Q*, 1970]). All 116 designs appear in color, full size, in the Blake Trust facsimile edited by Keynes (1972); a selection of color plates based on this facsimile (the remainder in black and white) was published about the same time, with the same title: *William Blake's Water-Colour Designs for the Poems of Thomas Gray.* In *Blake's Illustrations to the Poems of Gray* (1971), which combines "catalogue with commentary," Irene Tayler shows that Blake breathed new life into Gray's fanciful figures by illustrating them literally and going on "to make connections and arouse feelings only dimly present" in Gray's poems. Where Blake's designs veer from Gray's conscious intentions so as to form a principled critique, Tayler's commentary is of course most rewarding, as in her essay, "Metamorphoses of a Favorite Cat," in *Blake's Visionary Forms Dramatic* (published a year earlier, but substantially identical to a section of her book). Keynes's and Tayler's catalogs supplant H. J. C. Grierson's *William Blake's Designs for Gray's Poems* (1922).

Blake's comprehensive pictorial commentary on the Bible appears in two series, both executed for Thomas Butts: one is in tempera (1799); the other in watercolor (c. 1800–05); each is presented separately in Butlin's *Paintings and Drawings.* The two series, along with other miscellaneous biblical illustrations, are intermingled in biblical order in Keynes's *William Blake's Illustrations of the Bible* (1957), now useful primarily for its seven magnificent large-scale color reproductions. Blake's decorations for Hayley's library (1800) were reproduced and described by Thomas Wright in *The Heads of the Poets by William Blake* (1925) and, in greater detail and with a reconstructed plan of the placement of the portraits in the library, by William Wells and Elizabeth Johnston in *William Blake's 'Heads of the Poets'* (1969). The designs by which Blake the artist was best known during his lifetime, illustrations for Robert Blair's *The Grave* (1806), appear in Robert N. Essick and Morton D. Paley's *Robert Blair's The Grave, Illustrated by William Blake: A Study with Facsimile* (1982), discussed below. This detailed exposition supplants *Blake's Grave: A Prophetic Book,* with a commentary by S. Foster Damon (1963), and the photographic reprint, without commentary, published by Double Elephant (1969, 1973).

The poet for, upon, and with whom Blake released most of his illustrative and interpretative powers was John Milton. Butlin's section on the Milton illustrations (1801–25) in *Paintings and Drawings* is the most convenient, comprehensive, and reliable single source of descriptions and reproductions (though uneven in color fidelity). A color slide set of Blake's designs for *L'Allegro* and *Il Penseroso* is sold by the Pierpont Morgan Library; the series is reproduced in color with Blake's inscriptions in Adrian Van Sinderen's *Blake: The Mystic Genius* (1949). Pamela Dunbar's *William Blake's Illustrations to the Poetry of Milton* (1980) was the first full-scale study of all the Milton designs. Nearly a hundred halftone plates show all versions of Blake's Milton designs and related sketches, but some are cropped, reversed, misidentified, or of poor quality. Dunbar claims to examine the designs in relation to their texts, their "symbolic detail, Blake's attitudes toward Milton, and the artist's . . . 'system,'" and she attempts "to assess the artistic merits of the Milton plates and, where relevant, to suggest pictorial sources for them." Dunbar's insights are less original than her footnotes indicate, and her bibliography lists no item published after 1975. Stephen C. Behrendt's handsomely produced critical study *The Moment of Explosion: Blake and the Illustration of Milton* (1983) includes twenty-four generously proportioned but somewhat discolored color plates of the two sets of *Paradise Lost* illustrations. Blake's relationship to Milton—a complex subject that also, of course, requires consideration of *The Marriage of Heaven and Hell* and *Milton: A Poem,* as well as detailed interpretations of the illustrations—is further discussed under "Criticism."

In the 1820s, during the last seven years of his life, Blake surpassed himself in the novelty and variety of his illustrations. In 1820, he for the first time designed woodcuts (and executed several). Transcending their occasion, a school text of Vergil, they became the inspiration of Samuel Palmer and the other young artists who brightened Blake's old age. The best facsimile of these woodcuts is not a facsimile at all but a set of modern pulls from the original blocks, much more carefully printed than the originals: Iain Bain, David Chambers, and Andrew Wilton's *The Wood Engravings of William Blake for Thornton's Virgil* (1977). Blake's pedestrian copper engravings for this textbook have not, to my knowledge, been reproduced. Blake's watercolor illustrations for Bunyan's *Pilgrim's Progress* (1824–27) were reproduced in color for the Limited Editions Club, edited by G. B. Harrison and introduced by Geoffrey Keynes (1941); this reproduction is available on microfilm from the E. P. company. In *Blake Newsletter* (no. 23, 6: 3 [1972–73]), G. E. Bentley, Jr., discusses the inscriptions on the Bunyan designs, and James T. Wills comments on and reproduces an additional drawing for the series—the only one not in the Frick Collection. This extra design had been identified by Martin Butlin in *BNL* (no. 19, 5: 3 [1971–72]). E. P. has the Frick Museum's Bunyan designs on color microfilm. A book on the series by Gerda Norvig is said to be in the works.

In 1821, Blake completed tracings begun by John Linnell from Blake's 1805–10 Job watercolor series for Butts. Linnell then commissioned a set of engravings, *Illustrations of the Book of Job* (1825); this is the one work by Blake that is universally respected by art historians. Nearing completion is a Blake Trust facsimile of the whole Job project: the Butts and Linnell watercolors, a smaller set of wash drawings preliminary to the engravings (the "New Zealand" set, now believed to be a copy), the engravings themselves, many related pencil drawings, and complete and partial sets of colored engravings, with editorial comments by Bindman, Essick, and Lindberg. Lawrence Binyon and Geoffrey Keynes edited for the Pierpont Morgan Library a facsimile of the watercolor sets (in full color), the engravings, and some related sketches in *The Illustrations of the Book of Job* (1935). The New Zealand (now Mellon) set was also reproduced in color with comments by Philip Hofer (1937). Reproductions of the engravings in S. Foster Damon's *Blake's Job* (1966; rpt., reduced size, 1969; full size, 1982) are accompanied by a plate-by-plate commentary that owes some points to Joseph Wicksteed's influential *Blake's Vision of the Book of Job* (1910; rev. 1924). An inexpensive paperback facsimile for general readers, *The Book of Job Illustrated by William Blake* (1976), contains the complete biblical text, acceptable reproductions, and an undocumented digest of previous criticism by Michael Marqusee. Commentaries by Andrew Wright and Kathleen Raine are mentioned under "Criticism." Bo Lindberg's *William Blake's Illustrations to the Book of Job* (1973) is both a catalog and a meticulous scholarly study of every aspect of this project, with particular attention to Blake's media and techniques and his iconography.

The crowning task of Blake's life was to illustrate Dante's *Divine Comedy* (1824 – 27), another of his commissions from Linnell. There being no Blake Trust facsimile of the watercolors, one can be grateful indeed for Milton Klonsky's *Blake's Dante* (1980), which—including the dust jacket—reproduces in acceptable color 48 of the 102 designs and in black and white the remainder of the designs and the seven engravings, all in substantial (though reduced) format. Klonsky's design-by-design commentary, with a few new wrinkles, reinforces the standard commentary, Albert S. Roe's *Blake's Illustrations to the Divine Comedy* (1953). Roe's chapter on Blake's symbolism, mentioned under "Criticism," concisely outlines the structure of Blake's thought and art. Though Roe was unable to examine the large body of Dante designs in Melbourne, he provides a learned and illuminating exposition of the series from an art-historical perspective, hampered occasionally by his tendency to identify figures and motifs rather too closely with characters and symbols in Blake's poetry. Roe's monochrome reproductions, reduced, were made from the portfolio of larger black-and-white reproductions of the watercolors published by the Arts Council of Great Britain (1922; reissued by Da Capo Press, with the addition of reproductions of the engravings, in 1968). The Blake Trust published a portfolio of the seven engravings in 1978. An exhibition catalog edited by Corrado Gizzi, *Blake e Dante* (1983), contains 23 color plates, 132 black and white reproductions, and several appreciative essays. A lavish Milanese magazine, *FMR* (1984), published by Franco Maria Ricci, contains ten exceptionally large and clear color reproductions and a commentary on Dante by Jorge Luis Borges.

Blake illustrated Chaucer and Spenser not in sets of designs but in panoramic cavalcades of characters. The best commentary on the tempera *Sir Jeffery*

Chaucer and the Nine and Twenty Pilgrims on Their Journey to Canterbury (?1808) is Blake's own in the *Descriptive Catalogue* for his 1809 exhibition; others are discussed under "Criticism." The best reproduction is by the Athena poster company of London; the lighter colors in the smaller and more expensive reproduction by the New York Graphic Society are less faithful. Blake discussed his engraving of this subject (1810) in "A Public Address to the Chalcographic Society," which remained in rough draft in scattered passages in his Notebook. A fine reproduction of the engraving is sold by the Huntington Library and Art Gallery. The quarrel with Cromek over both the Chaucer engraving and the designs for Blair's *Grave* is the subject of several biographical articles by Bentley and by Dennis Read, described below. The tempera known as *The Characters in Spenser's "Faerie Queene"* (?1825) is well reproduced in color, in large format, with a detailed description by John E. Grant and Robert E. Brown in "Blake's Vision of Spenser's *Faerie Queene*: A Report and an Anatomy" (*BNL* no. 31, 8: 3 [1974–75]). Extra reproductions were made by the journal to be sold separately.

Of general interest is the large reproduction, without commentary, of *Epitome of Hervey's Meditations on the Tomb,* published as a special insert by *Blake Studies.* W. J. T. Mitchell reproduces and comments briefly on Blake's major depictions of a favorite theme in "Blake's Vision of the Last Judgment," a leaflet issued by *Blake Newsletter.* Examples of preliminary drawings for several of Blake's serial illustrations, as well as two of his "Enoch" drawings, appear in Geoffrey Keynes's *Drawings of William Blake: 92 Pencil Studies* (1970), a condensation of Keynes's compilations of 1927 and 1956. *The Blake-Varley Sketchbook of 1819,* edited by Martin Butlin (1969), is not directly related to Blake's poetry or pictorial criticism; it is, however, the best showcase of Blake's "Visionary Heads."

Biographical Resources

A modern critical and scholarly biography of Blake has not yet been published. For the present, the fullest and most accurate source of information on his life is *Blake Records* (1969), compiled and annotated by G. E. Bentley, Jr. This large and generously illustrated book contains the raw material for all future biographies. Despite Blake's emphatic denial that truth can be found in "Public RECORDS," Bentley manages to arrange such things as commercial receipts, tax accounts, early reviews, and memoirs of Blake's acquaintances and their descendants so that they form a coherent and engrossing documentary history. An added convenience is that Bentley's reliable texts of early published accounts of Blake make citation of the scattered original sources unnecessary for most purposes. These include Benjamin Heath Malkin, *A Father's Memoirs of His Child* (1806); John Thomas Smith, *Nollekens and His Times* (1828); and Allen Cunningham, *The Lives of the Most Eminent British Painters, Sculptors, and Architects,* volume 2 (1830), which is partly based on Smith. All three, with others, are reprinted in photographic facsimile by Joseph Anthony Wittreich, Jr., *Nineteenth-Century Accounts of William Blake* (1970), which supersedes reprints by Arthur Symons in *William Blake* (1907). *Blake Records* also includes scholarly texts of memoirs not published in Blake's lifetime: Henry Crabb Robinson's diary and reminiscences and Frederick Tatham's narrative. As a sidelight, Mark Reed, in "Blake, Wordsworth, Lamb, Etc.: Further Information from Henry Crabb Robinson" (*BNL* no. 12, 3: 4 [1970]), reports on an 1848 letter from Robinson, and in the same *Newsletter* issue Paul F. Betz's "Wordsworth's First Acquaintance with Blake's Poetry" argues that Wordsworth copied poems from Malkin's preface in 1807. Moving brief character sketches in *Blake Records* include those by Blake's disciples Linnell, Palmer, Calvert, and Richmond; see also Bentley's "William Blake, Samuel Palmer, and George Richardson" (*BS* 2: 2 [1970]). The biographical section of Bentley's *William Blake: The Critical Heritage* (1975) arranges excerpted material from *Blake Records* under topical headings. The section on Blake's "Forgotten Years," a chronological arrangement of 1831–62 comments, may be regarded as an extension of *Blake Records.* A visual supplement to *Blake Records* may be found in Keynes's *The Portraiture of William and Catherine Blake,* a Trianon Press facsimile (1977), and a visionary summation of Blake's life appears in Bo Lindberg's series of paintings (reproduced in monochrome in *Sparks of Fire,* 1983).

The first full-scale study of Blake's life and works, Alexander Gilchrist's *Life of William Blake: Pictor Ignotus* (1863; rev. 1880), will remain a primary source because Gilchrist recorded interviews and correspondence with Blake's surviving friends without documenting his sources or preserving original letters; so far as could be verified by Bentley, however, Gilchrist's reports are accurate. After his death in 1861, his widow, Anne, organized a team of Blake enthusiasts to help her complete the work: D. G. Rossetti wrote the final chapter and edited some of the poems; W. M. Rossetti compiled annotated catalogs of the drawings and paintings for the second volume; William Haines cataloged the engravings; A. C. Swinburne did research on the prophetic writings; and for the 1880 edition Frederick J. Shields described many of the designs for Young's *Night Thoughts.* Between the two editions of Gilchrist, A. C. Swinburne's *William Blake* (1869)—discussed under "Criticism"—brought out new biographical information and speculation derived from Blake's acquaintance Seymour Kirkup. Gilchrist's *Life,* inspirational in style and outlook, plays down Blake's radical ideas on politics, psychology, and religion in order to idealize him as an otherworldly artist-hero aided by his faithful helpmate. Gilchrist succeeded beyond all expectations in rescuing Blake's name from oblivion; his book generated exhibitions, new editions, and critical studies for the rest of the century. His lack of documentation was partially remedied in 1943 (rev. 1945) by Ruthven Todd in an Everyman edition. At his death Todd left a much more fully annotated edition of Gilchrist, for which G. E. Bentley, Jr., now seeks a publisher (*BIQ* no. 62, 16: 2 [1982]).

During our century the major competitor or supplement to Gilchrist's *Life* has been Mona Wilson's generously illustrated *Life of William Blake* (1927; rev. 1948, ed. by Keynes, 1971). Proceeding from a healthy skepticism toward Gilchrist, Wilson uncovered fresh, verifiable sources such as the Farington Diary and made use of Symons' criticisms of Gilchrist. Unlike Gilchrist, Wilson made no apology for her subject, and she was more vehement than Gilchrist in defending Blake's sanity, since she regarded the charge of madness as an excuse to avoid grappling with the prophetic books. She also pointed out sources and interrelationships among Blake's works that have never been properly assimilated into later criticism. Although she did not wholeheartedly endorse the mystical bias of S. Foster Damon's pioneering study of Blake's symbolism (1924, discussed under "Criticism"), she attempted to apply the Damon model of stages in the Mystic Way not only to Blake's prophetic poetry but also to the phases of his life. Both Gilchrist and Wilson include far more flat paraphrase of Blake's longer works than would now be thought desirable.

Michael Davis' brief popularization (without footnotes) of material from Gilchrist, Wilson, and Bentley, *William Blake: A New Kind of Man* (1977), publishes numerous photographs of supplementary interest from out-of-the-way collections. Thomas Wright's *The Life of William Blake* (1929; rpt. 1969), though factually unreliable, is worth seeking out for its photographs of places associated with Blake, now much altered in appearance. Herbert Jenkins (Herbert Ives) was, with Wright, a pillar of the Blake Society, which flourished in England early in this century. His articles identifying the probable location of Blake's unmarked grave in Bunhill Fields and examining the documentary history of Blake's trial were reprinted, with others, in his *William Blake* (1905). In a section of *William Blake's Jerusalem* (1953), Joseph Wicksteed conveys a strong impression of Blake's birthplace, a structure which has since been razed. Blake's homes are located and photographed in Paul Miner, "Blake's London Residences" (*BNYPL,* 1958); photographs and maps appear also in Bentley's *Blake Records.* John Adlard, in "Los Enters London" (*ES,* 1973), identifies a mundane locale. Stanley Gardner is writing a book on Blake's London. H. M. Margoliouth's unpretentious *William Blake* (1951) is based on assiduous detective work on Blake's early years. Jack Lindsay's readable *William Blake: His Life and Work* (1978) describes the man and the poet with facility but provides little new critical insight or factual detail. His footnotes, compressed to the point of unintelligibility, do not acknowledge in detail the extent of his indebtedness to Gilchrist and to Bentley's *Blake Records.* Raymond Lister's *William Blake: An Introduction to the Man and His Work* (1968) is a pleasant popular account.

An illuminating close-up of Blake from the other side of the glass is provided in *Blake's Hayley* (1951) by Morchard Bishop (Oliver Stoner). This wonderfully entertaining book about Hayley's dealings with Cowper, Romney, and others refers extensively to articles by Kenneth Povey, a Sussex County historian in the late twenties. Bentley's "Blake, Hayley, and Lady Hesketh" (*RES,* 1956) adds more details. Morton D. Paley, "Cowper as Blake's Spectre" (*ECS,* 1968), traces through Hayley and other mutual acquaintances Blake's idea of Cowper, whom Blake never met in the flesh. To round out information on Blake's trial for sedition, one should consult Keynes's essay in his *Blake Studies* (1971) and Bentley's "A Footnote to Blake's Treason Trial" (*N&Q,* 1955) and "Blake's Trial Documents" (*BIQ* no. 53, 14: 1 [1980]). Bentley has hit other highs and lows of Blake's dealings with his patrons in "Thomas Butts: White Collar Maecenas" (*PMLA,* 1956), "William Blake and 'Johnny of Norfolk'" (*SP,* 1956), "A. S. Mathew, Patron of Blake and Flaxman" (*N&Q,* 1958), "Blake's Engravings and His Friendship with Flaxman"

(*SB,* 1959), "The Promotion of Blake's *Grave* Designs" (*UTQ,* 1962), "Blake and Cromek: The Wheat and the Tares" (*MP,* 1974). More about the Cromek episode appears in Dennis Read's "Blake and the Chalcographic Society" (*PQ,* 1981), and more on earlier patronage in H. M. Margoliouth's "Blake's Mr. Mathew" (*N&Q,* 1951). Bentley's "The 1821 Edwards Catalogue" (*BIQ* no. 68, 17: 4 [1984]) sheds light on the publisher of Blake's *Night Thoughts* designs. Leslie Parris, "William Blake's Mr. Thomas" (*TLS,* 5 Dec. 1968), identifies another of Blake's patrons, and Robert N. Essick, "William Blake and Sir Thomas Lawrence" (*N&Q,* 1978), reports on still another. Erdman's "Blake's Nest of Villains" (*KSJ,* 1953) reviews the Hunt brothers' misperception of the artist. His "Blake's Early Swedenborgianism: A Twentieth-Century Legend" (*CL,* 1953) shows that Blake's heritage was basically Anglican, possibly with Baptist influence. And Nancy Bogen, "The Problem of William Blake's Early Religion" (*Personalist,* 1968), reconsiders the question without reaching secure conclusions. Raymond H. Deck, Jr., "New Light on C. A. Tulk, Blake's Nineteenth-Century Patron" (*SIR,* 1977), suggests a source of the Swedenborgian legend. The long-standing speculation that Blake was acquainted with the Neoplatonic philosopher Thomas Taylor was confirmed by James King in "The Meredith Family, Thomas Taylor, and William Blake" (*SIR,* 1972). Marcia Allentuck, "Blake, Flaxman, and Thomas: A New Document" (*HLB,* 1972), helps fix the date of Blake's first *Comus* designs. Blake's scanty knowledge of Hebrew is exposed by Arnold Cheskin, "The Echoing Greenhorn: Blake as Hebraist" (*BIQ* no. 47, 12: 3 [1978–79]). Sheila Spector dismisses some of Cheskin's charges by citing differences between Jewish and Christian traditions of construing Hebrew words (*BRH,* forthcoming).

All the biographical essays in Keynes's *Blake Studies* are informative, especially those on Blake's relations with Linnell and Stedman. Keynes's "Blake's Library" has been supplemented by Bentley in "Additions to Blake's Library" (*BNYPL,* 1960), revised for *Blake Books.* Both Bentley and Keynes also clear up confusions with contemporaries sharing Blake's name: the former in "A Collection of Prosaic William Blakes" (*N&Q,* 1965), the latter in "Engravers Called Blake," in *Blake Studies.* Harold Bruce, "William Blake and Gilchrist's 'Remarkable Coterie of Advanced Thinkers'" (*MP,* 1926), attacks the nineteenth-century legend that Blake regularly dined in Joseph Johnson's circle of radicals. More on Johnson and his circle may be found in Leslie F. Chard's "Joseph Johnson: Father of the Book Trade" (*BNYPL,* 1975) and his "Bookseller to Publisher; Joseph Johnson and the English Book Trade, 1760 to 1810" (*Library,* 1977), F. B. Curtis' "Blake and the Booksellers" (*BS,* 6: 2 [1975]), and Gerald P. Tyson's *Joseph Johnson: A Liberal Publisher* (1979). David V. Erdman documents Godwin's lack of interest in Blake in *N&Q* (1953 and 1954). Richard J. Shroyer's "The 1788 Publication Date of Lavater's *Aphorisms*" (*BIQ* no. 41, 11: 1 [1977]), E. B. Murray's "A Suggested Redating of a Blake Letter to Thomas Butts" (*BIQ* no. 51, 13: 3 [1979–80]), Morton D. Paley's "The Truchsessian Gallery Revisited" (*SIR,* 1977), and Mary K. Woodworth's "Blake's Illustrations for Gray's Poems" (*N&Q,* 1970) clear up some other matters. Unpublished materials in the Flaxman, Linnell, and Cumberland papers will aid future biographers; see, for example, G. E. Bentley, Jr., *A Bibliogra-*

phy of George Cumberland (1975). A full-scale critical biography is reported to be in preparation by Aileen Ward.

Criticism

The phenomenon derided in some quarters as the "Blake industry" simply reflects the industriousness and genius of Blake himself, who wrote, designed, etched, and colored so many works deserving of close study that an ever-growing community of industrious scholars has not yet encompassed, let alone exhausted, the range of his achievement. To be sure, Blake attracts his share of cranks, incompetents, and authors of unnecessary articles. But conscientious and dedicated scholars must not be deterred from assessing.the bibliographical intricacies of Blake's texts, the voluminousness and variety of his publications, the depth and richness of his ideas and symbols, and the brilliance of his technical effects. As long ago as 1928, Joseph Wicksteed observed to Max Plowman that "Blakists, whether they agree or disagree, combine together to produce a kind of ferment of creative effort and diligent labour, and, as Blake himself would most fervently claim, our 'enemies' are often amongst our best spiritual friends."

Regrettably, however, Blake's ideal of spiritual friendship is clouded in exchanges between art historians and literary critics, Britons and Americans, eighteenth-century specialists and Romanticists, not to mention disputes among (and between) Christians, Neoplatonists, humanists, atheists, Marxists, idealists, formalists, feminists, deconstructionists, and all the rest. Some American literary specialists in Romanticism may be guilty, in private, of belittling what they see as the insouciant gentlemanly amateurism of the British literary critic, the conservative aesthetics of the neoclassicist, or the narrowly academic taste and methodology of the art historian, any of which may contribute to the devaluation or exclusion of some of Blake's best and most interesting work. Conversely, from British, neoclassicist, or art-historical points of view, much Blake criticism from America seems repellently ingrown, jargon-ridden, critically undiscriminating, and ill-informed about the artist's techniques, materials, training, and cultural milieu. Transatlantic interdisciplinary journals and festschriften, along with the moderating influence of Canadian and Australian critics, help bridge these gulfs; the "ferment" Wicksteed approved may yet bring forth the intellectual bread and wine of the "New Age" Blake foresaw.

It is pleasant, meanwhile, to speculate that this ferment contributes to the awesome scholarly longevity of our senior Blakeans. Geoffrey Keynes, the master of them all, published his first study of Blake, begun many years earlier, in 1921 and his last in 1981, a year before his death at ninety-five. S. Foster Damon's publications on Blake, 1924 to 1969, stop just short of his death in 1971. Jack Lindsay's Blake books were published in 1927 and 1978. Milton O. Percival, whose seminal study of Blake was published in 1938, remained active into his nineties. Such comparative juveniles as Northrop Frye, who first came to notice with *Fearful Symmetry* in 1947, and David V. Erdman and G. E. Bentley, Jr., who began publishing major articles in the fifties, continue to set the pace for all others. Blakists are not factory drudges; they are industrious because there is so much yet to do, and time is short even for the energetic blessed with length of life.

GENERAL STUDIES

Expanding interest in Blake has led to the founding of two learned journals and the development of a large international scholarly community, with branching subspecialties. During the 1970s it was not uncommon for the Modern Language Association to sponsor two or three Blake seminars during the same annual meeting. Blake has been the subject of an unusually large number of festschriften and other collections of essays. Since miscellanies are by nature difficult to characterize and evaluate, notable items in each of the following landmark collections will be discussed under appropriate headings later in this section.

The Divine Vision: Studies in the Poetry and Art of William Blake by Scholars from Three Continents, edited by Vivian de Sola Pinto (1957), was a bicentennial tribute announcing a new wave of interest in Blake. *William Blake: Essays for S. Foster Damon,* a broad-based anthology edited by Alvin H. Rosenfeld (1969), represents most approaches and schools of thought. *Blake's Visionary Forms Dramatic,* edited by David V. Erdman and John E. Grant (1970), emphasizes the interrelationship of poetry and design. *Blake's Sublime Allegory,* edited by Stuart Curran and Joseph Anthony Wittreich, Jr. (1973), is a narrow-gauge examination of *The Four Zoas, Milton,* and *Jerusalem,* often in technical language. *Blake in His Time,* edited by Robert N. Essick and Donald Pearce (1978), focuses on the visual arts. Two collections that speak more directly to larger audiences are *William Blake: Essays in Honour of Sir Geoffrey Keynes,* edited by Morton D. Paley and Michael Phillips (1973), and *Interpreting Blake,* edited by Michael Phillips (1978). *William Blake and the Moderns,* edited by Robert J. Bertholf and Annette S. Levitt (1982), considers Blake's affinities with twentieth-century poets, novelists, and thinkers. Blake enthusiasts outside academe are well represented in *Sparks of Fire: Blake in a New Age,* edited by James Bogan and Fred Goss (1982), an ebullient montage of essays (some previously published), meditations, poems, drawings, graffiti, musical settings (a recording enclosed), a horoscope—and a few critical and bibliographical pieces. At least two more collections of new essays are in prospect: *Unnam'd Forms: Blake and Textuality,* edited by Thomas A. Vogler and Nelson Hilton (1985), and *Blake and the Argument of Method,* edited by Donald Ault, Mark Bracher, and Dan Miller. Both feature contemporary critical approaches by younger scholars.[3]

The most important collection made up largely of previously published work is Sir Geoffrey Keynes's *Blake Studies* (1949; rev. 1971). Robert N. Essick's carefully selected, well-indexed *The Visionary Hand* (1973) brings together major statements on Blake's art, several of which had become difficult of access. The following collections, as is usual in compilations intended primarily for students, consist mostly of old chestnuts sprinkled with a few lemons, but they are certainly convenient: *Discussions of William Blake,* edited by John E. Grant (1961);

Blake: A Collection of Critical Essays, edited by Northrop Frye (1966); *Twentieth Century Interpretations of Songs of Innocence and of Experience,* edited by Morton D. Paley (1969); *William Blake, Songs of Innocence and of Experience: A Casebook,* edited by Margaret Bottrall (1969); and the "Criticism" section of *Blake's Poetry and Designs,* edited by Mary Lynn Johnson and John E. Grant (1979). The snippets in Judith O'Neill's *Critics on Blake* (1970) are too chopped up to be useful: only three essays are unabridged, and each of these is readily available in one or more of the competing collections.[4]

The more useful of the two American journals on Blake is *Blake Newsletter* (1967–   ), retitled in 1977 *Blake: An Illustrated Quarterly,* edited by Morton D. Paley and Morris Eaves, because, in addition to critical and scholarly articles and reviews, it publishes checklists, notes, and news of meetings, exhibitions, and the like. The semiannual *Blake Studies* (1968–   ), edited by Kay P. Easson and Roger R. Easson, has published important critical interpretations and reviews but has been erratic in publication dates, printing, and quality of articles; as its most recent issue appeared in 1980, it is effectively defunct. Two journals that emphasize Blake have brought out special issues: *Colby Library Quarterly* 12 (1977) and *Bulletin of the New York Public Library* 61 (1957), 64 (1960), and—under its new title of *Bulletin of Research in the Humanities*—84 (1981). The editors of both journals—Erdman of *BRH* and John H. Sutherland of *CLQ*—welcome submissions on Blake. Special Blake issues have also appeared in *Huntington Library Quarterly* 21 (1957) and *Studies in Romanticism* 13: 3 (1974) and 16: 2 (1977). I have not seen the following foreign Blake journals or special numbers: *Messages* 1 (1939), in French, and *Blake* [and] *Whitman* (1931–32), *Eigo Seinen: The Rising Generation* 67 (1927) and 103 (1957), and *Mizue* [watercolor painting] 882 (1978), in Japanese. The contents of the first three foreign journals are retrievable through Bentley's *Blake Books,* reviewed under "Reference Works"; see also Kazumitsu Watarai's bibliography under "Reputation, Influence, and Affinities."

Literature and Philosophy.   *Introductions.* The best current introductory books on Blake are mutually supplementary. Martin K. Nurmi's philosophically oriented *William Blake,* though solid and very clearly written, is hampered by its disregard of the designs and its remoteness from some of the texts. Milton Klonsky's psychedelically energized *William Blake: The Seer and His Visions* (1977), which is fully illustrated, should be read with a book like Nurmi's as ballast. Morton D. Paley's beautifully illustrated *William Blake* (1978) wavers occasionally from its intended introductory level and says much less about the poetry than about the designs. For the shorter poems, John Holloway's *Blake: The Lyric Poetry* (1968) is a clear, well-informed, and generally reliable introduction, as is his Open University course guide (1984), which contains helpful historical supplements, both visual and verbal. Geoffrey Keynes's selection of color reproductions from the Blake Trust facsimiles in *A Study of the Illuminated Books of William Blake: Poet, Printer, Prophet* (1965), along with Martin Butlin's *William Blake* (1966), in the Tate Gallery Little Books series, as well as his 1978 exhibition catalog, are good introductions to Blake's art; see also those mentioned under "Art and Theory." Of essay-length introductions to the poetry and the ideas, the

best are Northrop Frye's often-reprinted articles "Blake's Treatment of the Archetype," *English Institute Essays, 1950* (1951), "Blake after Two Centuries" (*UTQ*,
1957), and "The Keys to the Gates" (1966), along with Jean H. Hagstrum's "Blake's
Blake," in *Essays in History and Literature* (ed. Heinz Bluhm, 1963) and Harold
Bloom's "William Blake," in his *The Visionary Company* (1961; rev. 1971). Clear
and well-balanced enough for a general reader, though not intended as an introduction, is Martin Price's concise and perceptive section on Blake in *To the Palace of Wisdom* (1964; rpt. 1970). Pierre Berger's scholarly 1907 study, translated
by D. H. Conner as *William Blake: Poet and Mystic* (1914), has become obsolete;
Phillipe Soupault's *William Blake* (1928; trans. J. Lewis May, 1928) retains some
value as art appreciation.

French readers have a solid brief introduction in Francis Léaud's *William
Blake* (1968). Jacques Blondel's *William Blake, émerveillement et profanation*
(1968) provides clear reproductions from *Songs* (some in color) but overemphasizes Gnostic tradition and the polarities suggested by his title, particularly
in discussing the longer poems. The misguidance proffered in Pierre Boutang's
longer study, *William Blake* (1970), has been exposed by Simone Pignard (*BNL*
no. 22, 6: 2 [1972]). An exchange between Pierre Leyris and Boutang is translated
by Lee Johnson (*BNL* no. 15, 4: 3 [1971]). See also Henri Lemaitre's "William Blake,
vision et poésie" in *Le Romantisme anglo-américain* (ed. Roger Asselineau et al.,
1971) and his "William Blake, un poétique visionnaire de la figure," *Cahiers du
Romantisme anglais* (1975). For Italians, Claudia Corti's *Il Primo Blake, testo e
sistema* (1980) purports to be an introduction; Nemi D'Agonisto's "William Blake"
(*EM*, 1957) is a bicentenary tribute. Bo Lindberg's "William Blake" (*Finsk
Tidskrift*, 1971) is an introduction in Finnish. Other foreign language introductory
works are traceable in *Blake Books*.

A. C. Swinburne's *William Blake* (1869; ed. Hugh J. Luke, 1970) was the first
extended effort to bring the prophetic books to the attention of the general
reader. Swinburne's monograph throbs with the energy of a youthful advocate of
sexual liberation. His gift for quoting the most exciting and readable passages
from the longer prophecies anticipates that of Harold Bloom in *Blake's Apocalypse* (1963), and his appreciative analyses of Blake's designs are still worth reading. As Frye cautions in his review in the Houtchenses' volume, however,
Swinburne's conception of a "sadist or diabolist" Blake influenced Shaw and
Gide and is reflected in Mario Praz's *The Romantic Agony* (1933) and in D. G.
James's *The Romantic Comedy* (1948). Swinburne's study, ignored in its time, was
a ripple in the wake of the 1863 Gilchrist *Life*. In the next Blake boom—sparked
by Keynes's 1921 *Bibliography*, ushering in the Age of Damon—the leaders were
Max Plowman, Joseph Wicksteed (discussed below), and John Middleton Murry.
In *Introduction to the Study of Blake* (1927; rpt. 1967) and in shorter essays,
Plowman originated the now-axiomatic ideas that the illuminated books constitute Blake's central canon and that texts and designs should be seen as an artistic
unity. Murry's *William Blake* (1933; rpt. 1964), without recourse to the designs,
emphasized Blake's revolutionary theology and clarified his themes of self-
annihilation and the struggle with the Spectre. After 1947, in the early years of
the Age of Frye, two new introductions appeared. Bernard Blackstone's indepen-

dent-minded *English Blake* (1949) surveys Blake's "life and teachings," with emphasis on teachings, in relation to British tradition, both rationalist and antirationalist. H. M. Margoliouth's readable *William Blake* (1951), now factually out of date, is somewhat distorted by his theory that Blake underwent a sudden Christian conversion. In addition, William Gaunt's *Arrows of Desire* (1956) lightly sketches the background of Blake's "Romantic World," mostly in the realm of art.

Because of an intractable hostility to Blake's later works, D. G. Gillham's *William Blake* (1973) and Stanley Gardner's *Blake* (1968) cannot be recommended except for Gardner's excellent topo-political chapter, "Blake's Westminster." Stewart Crehan's *Blake in Context* (1984) is good on social and political background. Victor Paananen's superficial and derivative *William Blake* (1977) in the Twayne series was roundly condemned by all reviewers. Kathleen Raine's *Blake* (1971) in the Praeger World of Art series and Ruthven Todd's *William Blake the Artist* (1971) work fairly well as picture collections. But Raine's book is marred by the Neoplatonic bias of the commentary and by deficiencies in color fidelity, and the small format of Todd's book allows little room for text or pictures. William Vaughan's *William Blake* (1977) is an attractive album of color reproductions. Carolyn Keay's *William Blake: Selected Engravings* (1975) must be shunned absolutely because, with few exceptions, its reproductions are based on crude redrawings. F. R. Leavis' "Justifying One's Valuation of Blake," an hourlong speech printed in the festschrift for Keynes, is actually an anti-introduction, a belated response to T. S. Eliot's once-influential "William Blake" (1920; rpt. *Selected Essays, 1917–1950,* 1964, and in *Blake's Poetry and Designs*). The most reliable arm's-length introduction for those who find in Blake "so much that repels" is D. W. Harding's brief essay in *The Pelican Guide to English Literature* (1957; rpt. *Experience into Words,* 1963).

Comprehensive Views. The proverbial industriousness of Blakists does much to explain why the two greatest works of general criticism were both long in gestation: S. Foster Damon's *William Blake: His Philosophy and Symbols* (1924) was rewritten repeatedly over a ten-year period, and Northrop Frye's *Fearful Symmetry* (1947; 3rd ed. 1969) took ten years and five complete rewritings, "of which the third and fourth were half as long again as the present book" (1962 Preface). David V. Erdman's more specialized historical study, *Blake: Prophet against Empire* (1954; 3rd ed. 1977), painstakingly prepared over a long period, has been diligently corrected and reconsidered in later editions. The fortitude of the bibliographers is equally reminiscent of Blake's hero Los. Geoffrey Keynes's *Bibliography* (1921) was begun in 1908, substantially completed before World War I, and then rewritten either two or three times (Bentley's and Keynes's accounts vary) at the instigation of the great editor John Sampson, who as consultant to both Oxford and Cambridge University presses twice rejected the reworked manuscript; this monumental work was finally published by the Grolier Club of New York. G. E. Bentley, Jr., began his decade of worldwide travel and research for *Blake Books* (1977) while the Bentley-Nurmi *Blake Bibliography* (1964) was still in press. If less patient recent authors had emulated the dogged and heroic persistence of these seminal writers on Blake, fewer works of clarification and rectification would now be needed.

Those interested in glimpsing the personalities behind some of these books will enjoy reading Keynes's *'Religio Bibliographici'* (1952), which includes the story of his 1908–21 labors on the *Bibliography;* Keynes's *The Gates of Memory* (1981), which recounts the history of his adventures as a World War I surgeon, bibliophile, friend of Rupert Brooke, and member of the Bloomsbury circle of his brother John Maynard Keynes; J. T. C. Oates's sketch of Keynes (*BC,* 1964); Bentley's portrait of Keynes as *Fons et Origo* in the 1973 Keynes festschrift; Max Plowman's letters, *Bridge into the Future* (ed. D[orothy] L. P[lowman], 1944); Damon's "How I Discovered Blake" (*BNL* no. 3, 1: 3 [1967]); selections from Damon's journal edited by Catherine Brown (*Books at Brown* [1981]); Frye's "Reflections in a Mirror" in *Northrop Frye in Modern Criticism* (ed. Murray Krieger, 1966) and his "The Road of Excess" (1963; rpt. *The Stubborn Structure,* 1970); and Morris Eaves's interview with David Erdman (*SIR,* 1982).

In Blake studies, almost every interpretative avenue paved during this century radiates from Damon's *Philosophy and Symbols.* His thesis that a master configuration of interrelated symbols underlies everything Blake wrote was the foundation from which Frye worked. His extended analyses of *The Four Zoas, Milton,* and *Jerusalem,* with the fourfold schema laid out in the chapter "Cosmography" and in diagrams throughout, have entered into all subsequent views of Blake. Since Damon, scholars who avoid the later works have been on the defensive. Damon's plate-by-plate commentary on the designs, though without reproductions, anticipates Erdman's *The Illuminated Blake,* mentioned above. His arcane research opened areas entered by Milton O. Percival, Kathleen Raine, Désireé Hirst, and Morton D. Paley, all discussed below. His chapter on metrics, "The Chariot of Genius," reads like an abstract of Alicia Ostriker's fuller study, *Vision and Verse in William Blake* (1965). Upon his line-by-line model are constructed Bloom's commentary in the Erdman edition and Stevenson's annotated Longman edition, and upon his general comments rest Keynes's introductions to the Blake Trust facsimiles. Implicit in his chapter "Illustrations to Others" are whole books about Blake's designs: Roe's and Klonsky's on Dante, Tayler's on Gray, Essick and Paley's on Blair's *Grave,* Grant, Rose, Tolley, and Erdman's on Young's *Night Thoughts,* and Essick and Easson's on commercial book illustrations–all discussed elsewhere. Even such small points as echoes of Watts's hymns, children's books, and nursery rhymes in *Songs of Innocence* are continually being rediscovered by scholars who neglect to look first in Damon.

Damon's great limitation, despite his caveat that "Blake had a horror of fixed symbols" and "did not wish his works to be translated with the aid of an easy key," lies in the rigidity of his allegorizations. For Damon in 1924 (less so in his 1965 *Dictionary*), Blake was a mystic first, a poet second, and a painter third; steps in the "Mystic Way" determine the shape of his whole canon as well as of individual poems like "The Mental Traveller." This position was promptly attacked by Helen White in *The Mysticism of William Blake* (1927). Inevitably, in application, either Blake's poem or Damon's scheme breaks down. Tiriel's offspring, for example, are allegorized first as warring religious sects (their father being aged Religion and his dying wife Inspiration); then abruptly the daughters become the senses and the sons the liberal arts. For Damon, *The Marriage of Heaven and Hell*—probably because it is so resistant to systematic allegorization—is a mere "scrapbook." In discussing *Marriage* and *Visions of the Daughters of Albion,* however, Damon makes clear that his mystical Blake is no ascetic; like A. C. Swinburne in *William Blake* (1869) and Wicksteed in *Innocence and Experience* (1928), Damon emphasizes Blake's advocacy of the "improvement of sensual enjoyment" and sexual delight. He also observes variations in the illuminated books (for example, in 19 copies of *Songs*) and recognizes that "each copy of each book" is an artistic whole, with its own "chord of color" and interrelationship of pages.

The main difference between the synoptic approaches of Damon and Frye may be dramatized in one sentence: Damon wrote that "Blake's method of concealing his ideas is known as Symbolism"; for this sentence to make sense to Frye, it would have to be turned inside out: Frye would say that symbolism, as is especially clear in Blake's work, is the way poets reveal rather than conceal their ideas. Frye considers Blake a visionary rather than a mystic and emphasizes his clarity, his utter detestation of Mystery, the Great Whore of Babylon. Blake's coherent symbolic structure is to Frye the fullest expression of a system that underlies all literature, at least in the Western tradition, and is dimly shadowed forth in dreams and primitive myth; this system corresponds to the structure of the human imagination. Blake's symbolism, as Frye puts it in his 1962 preface, is "a distinctive but normal adaptation of the language of poetry." All Blake's art, then, is both "an attempt to achieve absolute clarity of vision and a beginner's guide to the understanding of an archetypal vision of which it forms part." To learn to read Blake aright is to learn to read all literature with greater pleasure and fuller understanding.

Fearful Symmetry, obedient to the proportions of Blake's engraved canon, concentrates on the longer, later, and more baffling "prophetic books." These are difficult, Frye has stated elsewhere, because it was not possible to make them any simpler. Blake could not use familiar metaphors for his radical epistemology, theology, and social analysis—the subjects of Frye's three opening chapters—because personifications of classical and biblical myth had grown ineffectual through overuse. The thorny surface of Blake's major works, precisely because it is incomprehensible by conventional aesthetic standards, draws the reader to a mythic, archetypal, or anagogical level of meaning. At this point in Frye's argument it is reasonable to object that if an elaborate critical apparatus for understanding Blake is merely something that "has to be got up like so much Gothic" (Frye quotes Douglas Bush's objections in his 1969 preface), it cannot be worth acquiring. Frye answers that Blake teaches the "grammar" of an "imaginative iconography" that informs all poetry. According to Frye, the depths we reach, with difficulty, in Dante, Spenser, and Blake make us suspect how much we are missing beneath the "smooth, readable surface" of Homer, Shakespeare, and Chaucer. The main reason *Fearful Symmetry* was so hard for Frye to write was that, without realizing it at the time, he was simultaneously evolving what was to become *Anatomy of Criticism* (1957), his own Blake-influenced theory of criticism.

Frye's theoretical interests account for some of the blind spots in *Fearful Symmetry*. At times Frye's pronouncements are based on inspired extrapolations from Blake rather than on what Blake actually wrote: that is, Frye's symmetry is more symmetrical than Blake's. This is perhaps easiest to see in his large table of Zoas, Emanations, and their associations in which "a number" of entries "have been added merely to complete the pattern, and a number are mere guesses"; the same might be said about Damon's similar table, with which Frye's conflicts at several points. Frye objects to interpretations of Blakean or intellectual allegory in corporeal terms that call for a "continuous translation of poetic images into a series of moral and philosophical concepts," such as the equation of Los with Time or Prophecy, or of Urizen with Reason (as in Damon); yet Frye considers Blake "so conscious of the shape of his central myth that his characters become almost diagrammatic," no more than "intellectual ideographs." Frye's grand scheme allows for little or no development, experimentation, or inconsistency as Blake worked with themes and characters over the course of a career that spanned five decades, nor does it accommodate Blake's designs.

Frye supports some interpretations of particular poems only by reference to his own monomyth, not to specific texts in Blake that stubbornly refuse to cooperate. In *Urizen,* for example, Blake mentions "Eternals" but not Albion or Eternal Man, the all-important personage who first appears in *The Four Zoas*; and in both *Urizen* and *Ahania* the character Fuzon, son of Urizen, is entirely distinct from Orc, son of Los, a different kind of rebel. But since Fryean unity and symmetry require a smoothing out of anomalies, Frye assumes that Albion, though unnamed, is one of the Eternals in *Urizen,* and that Fuzon is only a by-form of the archetypal rebel Orc.

The most influential critics of the past thirty years have seen Blake's work almost exclusively through Frye's wide-angle X-ray lens in *Fearful Symmetry* and the magisterial general essays already mentioned. Such terms as the "consolidation of error" and the "Orc cycle" have so lodged in the common critical vocabulary that their origin in Frye is recalled only with effort, in such reminders as David V. Erdman's corrective "Note on the Orc Cycle" (in *BVFD*). Frye commented in his 1962 preface that in a sixth rewriting he might have been "more concerned with the reader's superficial difficulties with the texts and the designs, less concerned with recreating Blake's thought and attitude in my own words"; in his 1969 preface he remarked that he would now prefer a "fully documented commentary" to his "extended critical essay in the Swinburne tradition" on "Blake as an illustration of the poetic process." But only Frye could have written the *Fearful Symmetry* we have; thanks to Frye, it does not now take a Frye to write new versions of the "more conventional book" he sometimes wishes *Fearful Symmetry* had been. As Bentley remarks in *Blake Books, Fearful Symmetry* is "probably the most comprehensive, learned, illuminating, and profound book on Blake of this or any other era." It is also the wittiest and most exhilarating. Young scholars should either buy the book in hardback or be prepared to wear out several paperback copies of the study that forms the continental divide of Blake criticism.

Either before or immediately after gaining the Olympian summit of Frye's *Fearful Symmetry* and well before surveying the political scene in David V. Erdman's monumental *Blake: Prophet against Empire*, reviewed below, the explorer of Blake's poems should establish a firm footing in detailed analyses of individual poems, the most provocative of which appear in Harold Bloom's early works: *The Visionary Company* (1961; rev. 1971), *Blake's Apocalypse* (1963; rev. 1970), and the commentary in the Erdman edition (1965; virtually unchanged in the 1982 edition). Bloom excels in conveying distinctive tonal and textural qualities—the ingenious verbal intricacies of the shorter poems, the nervous energy of the Lambeth books, and the sweep, turbulence, and splendor of the longer prophecies. He has the most sensitive ear of any Blake critic: it is possible to discover through his quotations a breathtaking passage overlooked in the setting of Blake's own rhetoric. (Except in the revised edition of *The Visionary Company*, however, he does not deign to provide the amenity of line references.) Other critics may be less uneven, less capable of unintentional misreadings, less wearily ironic about the Bard's role in *Songs of Innocence and of Experience*, less swayed by bibliographical interpretations of the Bard's Song in *Milton*, more helpful with Blake's transformations of his sources, or more interested in his designs, but none offers better companionship for the development of one's own skill in reading Blake closely.

But on the harsh Freudian (or Darwinian) "psychic battleground" of Bloom's tetralogy in "antithetical criticism"—*The Anxiety of Influence* (1973), *A Map of Misreading* (1975), *Kabbalah and Criticism* (1975), and *Poetry and Repression* (1976)—critics who merely clarify and explicate are "weak." To become a strong poet or an imaginative critic, the Bloomian ephebe—who is apparently always imagined as male—must struggle to clear space for himself by "misreading" his literary father: this is supposedly the way Blake and the other Romantics, anxious over their "belatedness," misread Milton and created the Romantic crisis poem. Bloom's more recent books, which seem to appear semiannually, have gone still further in this direction and are outside the scope of this review. Just as Frye's Blake led his critic from *Fearful Symmetry* to *Anatomy of Criticism*, so Bloom's Blake is proclaimed in *The Anxiety of Influence* to be "the most profound and original theorist of revisionism to appear since the Enlightenment and an inevitable aid in the development of a new theory of Poetic Influence." Bloom develops his theory of influence not by exposition, usually, but by perverse aphorisms, in the manner of Blake's Proverbs of Hell, or by psychodramatic anecdotes, as in the Memorable Fancies. A few of Bloom's theories—which are purposely phrased so as to frustrate efforts at practical application—have been put to use by Leslie Brisman, to name one. But Bloom's insistence on misinterpreting poems in relation to tangential precursor texts (setting "London" and "The Tyger" against passages in Ezekiel and Job, for example) results in distortions of the sort exposed in Michael Ferber's "London and Its Politics" (*ELH*, 1981), cited below.

After the taut, energetic work published by Bloom in the early sixties, John Beer's twin volumes, *Blake's Humanism* (1968) and *Blake's Visionary Universe*

(1969), seem slack and diffuse, oblivious to Bloom's interpretative advances. Neither the relationship between Beer's two books nor the meaning of their titles is clear: *Humanism* deals mostly with earlier works but includes *Milton,* while *Universe* deals mostly with later works but includes *Poetical Sketches.* In both books, long stretches of paraphrase blur original insights, and Blake's characters seem mechanically to ascend and descend a stepladder from single to fourfold vision. Rewards come through specific suggestions, such as the development of Damon's parallel between the lion of Spenser's Una and that of Blake's Lyca (in *Humanism*) and through deft summations of existing knowledge—for example, on the relationship between industrial mills and the mills of the mind and on the difference for Blake between the architecture of Stonehenge and the Gothic cathedrals. The numerous visual sources Beer proposes are frequently suggestive. Reviewers in England rightly praised his jargon-free diction and his independence of critical cliques. He has clearly identified some persistent ambivalences in the poet's thought: is Blake a theist or a Christ-centered atheist? a mystic or a social realist? does he approve of or disdain the flesh and the natural world? does imaginative vision have any authority outside the human mind? Beer's answers are partly that the catchall term "humanism" reconciles many polarities and partly that Blake held different beliefs at different times (favoring sexual liberation in *Visions of the Daughters of Albion,* for example, and transcendence of sexual desire in *Jerusalem*).

More recently, and with much sharper focus, Leopold Damrosch, Jr., has analyzed similar contradictions that he finds both inherent in Blake's thought and irreconcilable in Western culture. These Damrosch considers to be the source of Blake's power as a poet—but also the reason that Blake constantly revised his myth without ever being able to make it internally consistent. In *Symbol and Truth in Blake's Myth* (1980), Damrosch investigates four interrelated areas: epistemology, reflected in poetic tension between sense perception and vision; psychology, reflected in tension between the isolated self and the self integrated into a universal humanity; ontology, reflected in tension between immanent and transcendent divinity; and aesthetics, reflected in tension between the idea of art as salvation and the notion that it involves the imposition of spurious form. For Damrosch, Blake's poems "fail to achieve coherence at just the points where his ideas refuse to be reconciled." The epistemological and ontological (or theological) areas are for most readers, I think, more deeply problematic than the other two. Contradictory statements about nature, the senses, and God can indeed be found throughout Blake's work, even in letters and marginalia. But much of what Damrosch calls contradiction might more accurately be called evidence of Blake's imaginative ability to hold opposites in solution—in order to contrast fallen and regenerated perspectives or to tease and educate through paradox or to open thought through wordplay, metaphor, and dialectical struggle. A Coleridgean perspective on "symbol" and a less commonsensical idea of "truth" would obviate the tension implied in the title. Because Damrosch challenges Blake's ideas while respecting his power as a thinker, however, his book has compelled orthodox Blakeans to reexamine their premises.

Contexts, Sources, and Approaches. The best-established specialized approach to Blake at present is the historical-political one. The outstanding book in this area is David V. Erdman's influential *Blake: Prophet against Empire* (1954; 3rd ed. 1977). Erdman encapsulates his method in "Blake: The Historical Approach," *English Institute Essays, 1950* (1951), often cited as a model for historical criticism. Erdman discovers direct allusions to contemporary events even in seemingly private and obscure images or in biblical and literary figures. Abundant circumstantial detail, references to the popular press, and reproductions of political cartoons clarify the social and political issues of Blake's place and time. Erdman makes vivid the robust Englishman who jostled in the streets and combated through visionary art the moral blindness of his reactionary, war-waging country. Despite all disclaimers, though, Erdman's penetration to the "historical level" has given many readers the impression that this is to be taken as the only or most important of Blake's concerns. For example, the flat announcement that Enitharmon's quarrel with Los in Night II of *The Four Zoas* "predicts, in short, the coup of Brumaire" has the unintended effect of diminishing the strong psychological, epistemological, and theological implications of this episode. Historically, though, Erdman's overstatements were necessary as correctives to the "mystical" view of Blake, and he tempers them in the ample footnotes of his revised editions.

Erdman's this-worldly Blake had previously been detected independently by Mark Schorer in *William Blake: The Politics of Vision* (1945; paperback abridgment, 1959) and by J[acob] Bronowski, *William Blake: A Man without a Mask* (1944; reintroduced in 1965 [rpt. 1969] as *William Blake and the Age of Revolution*). Schorer's historical readings, padded with excessive quotations, are less successful than his chapters on the development and decay of Blake's mythic structure in relation to his worldview. His clear, concise statements on myth are frequently quoted by specialists in other areas. According to Schorer, by attempting to incorporate too much into his system, Blake destroyed its aesthetics and produced a misshapen image of his anarchistic politics; nevertheless, "whatever deplorable results the system may have had in Blake's forms, it is still unexhausted as an imaginative complex, and will remain so." In his 1965 introduction, Bronowski modestly describes his own work as an outline later filled in by Erdman and confirmed by Schorer. Bronowski is particularly interested in Blake's position as a practitioner of a declining handicraft during the dawning of the Machine Age. His humane learning and vigorous prose style also distinguish his briefer popularizations, such as his centennial tribute, "A Prophet for Our Age" (*Nation,* 1957). Corroborating material on the status of the artisan may be found in E. P. Thompson's landmark study *The Making of the English Working Class* (1963; corr. rpt. 1968). Morris Eaves's prizewinning essay "Blake and the Artistic Machine: An Essay on Decorum and Technology" (*PMLA,* 1977), discusses the iconographic significance of Blake's method of production. Related topics enter into Marxist and feminist commentaries discussed below. A clear overview of Blake's position on revolution, in both its pre-Bastille and modern senses, informs Aileen Ward's "The Forging of Orc: Blake and the Idea of Revolution" (*TriQuarterly,* 1972). Crehan's introduction *Blake in Context,* mentioned earlier, is a fresh look at Blake's social environment from the left.

Other global views of Blake urge influences of a Neoplatonic, Gnostic, kabbalistic, Swedenborgian, or Boehmian origin. One of the first—and still among the best—of the arguments that Blake's "logical and coherent system" is the "culmination of a long tradition" of heterodoxy stemming from Orphic, Pythagorean, Hermetic, alchemical, and other sources is Milton O. Percival's under-documented *William Blake's Circle of Destiny* (1938; rpt. 1964). Without claiming to provide the one and only key, Percival subordinates his sources and analogues to his outline of Blake's pattern of thought. His topic-by-topic organization is easy to follow and anticipates many of Frye's insights in a more straightforward, if less rich, formulation. Recent major advocates of the esoteric approach are, in order of productivity and influence, Kathleen Raine, George Mills Harper, and Désireé Hirst, each of whom has been viewed by most American critics as a distorter of Blake's thought. In the late fifties and early sixties, Raine and Harper, working independently, named as primary source Thomas Taylor "the Platonist," a Neoplatonic translator and evangelist whose works they have since collaborated in editing. Their speculation that Blake knew Taylor personally has since been borne out in James King's discovery, cited under "Biographical Resources," that Blake actually took geometry lessons from him. But the Raine-Harper case for a deepseated attraction to Neoplatonism remains shaky: the essentially dualistic "Perennial Philosophy" conflicts with Blake's reiterated aphorism that "every thing that lives is holy," his urging of "the improvement of sensual enjoyment," his "devilish" suggestion that "man has no Body distinct from his Soul," his sense of the joy emanating from "every particle of dust," his hatred of Mystery, his hero's smashing of the occult secrets of the Smaragdine Tablets in *Jerusalem,* and his general hostility to all things Greek, particularly in his later years.

The methods and emphases of the esoteric critics vary considerably. Harper is reasonably cautious about applying his theories to the interpretation of whole poems. In *The Neoplatonism of William Blake* (1961), he provides a useful history of Platonic thought in England, an account of the influence and circle of Thomas Taylor, and an explication of Blake's major symbols through parallels with Taylor, while admitting that Blake may have arrived at his own version of Platonic idealism entirely on his own. Blake's frequent references to preexistence and, in later years, to "Eternal Forms" shadowed forth in the "Vegetable world," as well as his condemnation of some aspects of nature, accord with Neoplatonic thought, and Harper is careful to point out that such favorite Blakean notions as "Multitudes" in eternity are *not* in these sources.

To Raine, however, in *Blake and Tradition* (1968; excerpted in *Blake and Antiquity,* 1977) and numerous related articles and shorter books, Blake can be understood only in the light of "traditional metaphysics" preserved in remnants of "the ancient Mysteries," for he draws on "the royal language of poetry and the other arts," the "cosmic analogy" of a universal "language of symbolic discourse," now all but lost. Raine's good intentions of indicating "the degree of certainty or doubt" about Blake's knowledge of specific sources are not always carried out, and her inattention to what she calls "those mechanical matters to which the modern academic world attaches such inordinate importance," such as documentation and dating, is damaging. When dates cannot be satisfactorily aligned, she all

too frequently falls back on the suggestion that the work that supposedly influenced Blake was available before publication in manuscript or through conversation. The bulk of Raine's book consists of long quotations linked to Blake by brief
comments; at times, however, the source passages really do resonate against
Blake's poetry: discussions of *Tiriel,* "The Chimney Sweeper" of *Innocence,* and
Urizen, to name only a few, are very well conducted. On Swedenborgian thought
generally, Raine is consistently helpful. The book would have been much stronger
if weaker links had been struck out. Raine's lavish illustrations are fascinating in
themselves and often are clearly related to Blake's work—for example, the striking similarity between Blake's diagram of "Milton's track" and the one of Christ's
path in Law's translation of Boehme, which Blake is known from external evidence to have admired. For some of her most fervently espoused hypotheses,
such as the idea that Blake's Arlington Court Picture (1821) illustrates Porphyry's
commentary on the Cave of Nymphs in the *Odyssey,* her score is about fifty-fifty:
details of the nymph's buckets, spinning, and weaving fit well; details of the dominant male figure not at all. (Furthermore, as Rodney M. Baine has shown [*PQ,*
1972], Blake's knowledge of this symbolism, used also in *Thel,* could have come as
easily from the notes in Pope's translation of Homer as from Thomas Taylor.) Jean
H. Hagstrum, "Kathleen Raine's Blake" (*MP,* 1970), discusses Raine's views further.

Hirst's *Hidden Riches* (1964) surveys traditional symbolism from the Renaissance to Blake, as well as the lives and times of the symbolists. Hirst claims that,
in approaching Blake "without a knowledge of the tradition upon which he drew,
the reader is in . . . the position of an intelligent Mongolian Buddhist attempting
to fathom *Paradise Lost* without any knowledge of the Bible, any acquaintance
with European letters, or any understanding of the Christian vision." Her
discussion of the kabbala, Paracelsus, Boehme, and William Law (Boehme's translator) is intriguing, but most of this material, which dips into family histories of
various members of theosophical groups over a three-hundred-year period, has
no bearing on Blake. Denis Saurat's earlier study, *Blake and Modern Thought*
(1929), traces the movement of kabbalistic, Gnostic, Druidic, Hindu, and Celtic
lore through eighteenth-century European circles of illuminati. Sergio Givone,
William Blake: Arte e religione (1978), goes over much of the same ground as
Saurat. In the 1969 festschrift for Damon appear three articles of related interest:
Asloob Ahmad Ansiri, "Blake and the Kabbalah," on Jewish mystical teachings;
Piloo Nanavutty, "*Materia Prima* in a Page of Blake's *Vala,*" on alchemical learn-
ing; and G. M. Harper, "The Divine Tetrad in Blake's *Jerusalem,*" on numerology.
Ansiri had been anticipated by Bernard Fehr, "William Blake und die Kabbala"
(*Englische Studien,* 1920), and Fehr's student Waldemar Bagdasarianz, *William
Blake: Versuch einer Entwicklungs-geschichte des Mystikers* (1935). But the most
thorough and informative essay on Blake's knowledge of kabbala is Sheila
Spector's carefully documented and impartial survey "Kabbalistic Sources—
Blake's and His Critics'" (*BIQ* no. 67, 17: 3 [1983–84]), which reviews sources avail-
able to Blake and corrects decades of critics' mistaken assumptions. The work of
Frye and others suggests, nevertheless, that the Bible and a trained literary sensibility throw a more searching light into the prophecies than esoteric learning has
done so far; Hirst's analogy of the Mongolian Buddhist simply does not hold.

Boehme, Paracelsus, Swedenborg, and the Cambridge Platonists also loom large in Morton D. Paley's *Energy and the Imagination: A Study of the Development of Blake's Thought* (1970). But unlike the extremists of the esoteric school, Paley does not claim to have found a key. He cites these theosophists, along with such contemporary new-consciousness seers as Norman O. Brown, as part of a "background" set up to outline Blake's uniqueness. According to Paley, although Blake's meanings "may in part be construed from the internal logic of the poem," they also depend "at least in part on meanings established elsewhere," such as in Boehme; yet "we must beware of assigning sources too narrowly, or of mechanically transferring a meaning from one context to an entirely different one." Paley argues persuasively that Blake, in shifting the heroic role from Orc to Los, moved from a doctrine of liberation through release of energy to one of regeneration through creative labor. At times, however, long quotations displaying vaguely analogous ideas and images merely lie inert, in contrast to the highly suggestive passages from Bryant and Mallet that actively support his discussion of *The Marriage of Heaven and Hell*. In " 'A New Heaven is Begun': William Blake and Swedenborgianism" (*BIQ* no. 50, 13: 2 [1979]), Paley analyses Blake's "complex and shifting attitude" toward that faith and explains controversies within London's New Jerusalem Church, some of which had been touched on earlier by John Howard (*PLL*, 1968; *BS* 3: 1 [1970]). Stuart Curran, "Blake and the Gnostic Hyle" (*BS* 4: 2 [1972]), explores Blake's avenues of access to Gnostic tradition, as does Piloo Nanavutty, "Blake and Gnostic Legends" (*AJES*, 1976). Andrew J. Welburn, "Blake's Cosmos: Sources and Transformations" (*JEGP*, 1981), does what most commentators on the Blake-Boehme relationship fail to do: he emphasizes Blake's originality, as does Eugene J. Harding in his article on *Urizen* (see "Criticism"). Mary V. Jackson, "Blake and Zoroastrianism" (*BIQ* no. 42, 11: 2 [1977]), suggests some parallels. Leonard Trawick's "Blake's Empirical Occult" (*WC*, 1977), one of three essays on Blake in a special issue on the occult, levelheadedly surveys this field, earlier explored by John Senior, *The Way Down and Out* (1959).

An earlier context study also deals learnedly with theosophic material and brings out Blake's sometimes subversive transformations of his sources: Peter Fisher's posthumously published *The Valley of Vision: Blake as Prophet and Revolutionary* (1961), which is dulled somewhat by his "dry Aristotelian style," as Frye charitably describes it in his introduction. Fisher's excellent (and often reprinted) "Blake and the Druids" (*JEGP*, 1959), largely absorbed into his book, may be supplemented by A. L. Owen's *The Famous Druids* (1962) and confirmed by Lois Ziegelman's "Blake, the Druids, and the Regeneration of Generation" (*University of Hartford Studies in Literature*, 1983). Fisher's position in "Blake's Attacks on the Classical Tradition" (*PQ*, 1961) is implicitly challenged in articles by Andrew Wilton, David Bindman, and Paley, mentioned under "Art and Theory," and in Irene Chayes's "The Presence of Cupid and Psyche" (in *BVFD*) and her "Plato's *Statesman* Myth in Shelley and Blake" (*CL*, 1961). Albert J. Kuhn, "Blake on the Nature and Origins of Pagan Gods and Myth" (*MLN*, 1957), relates Blake's theory of the relation of sacred and profane antiquity to the mythographies of Swedenborg, Bryant, and John Hutchinson. Edward B. Hungerford's *Shores of Darkness* (1941) and Ruthven Todd's chapter on Blake and the "eighteenth-

century mythologists" in *Tracks in the Snow* (1946) are also relevant in this connection. Paley, "William Blake, the Prince of Hebrews, and the Woman Clothed
with the Sun," in the festschrift for Keynes, makes a strong case for the influence
on Blake—in a negative way—of Richard Brothers and Joanna Southcott. John
Beer, "Influence and Interdependence in Blake," in *Interpreting Blake,* meditates
on levels of influence and their evidential criteria, using sometimes rather tenuous examples of each.

Most literary historians, partly because of the bias of their training, remain
unconvinced that Blake drew his essential nourishment from sources farther
afield than the Bible and the master poets of the English tradition, especially
Milton. Yet no comprehensive study of Blake's use of biblical sources has yet been
published. Fortunately, Paul Miner's densely packed article in the Damon
festschrift, "Visions in the Darksom Air: Aspects of Blake's Biblical Symbolism,"
goes a long way toward showing how the Bible ignited Blake's imagination. Michael J. Tolley's notes on "The Everlasting Gospel" (*N&Q,* 1962 and 1968) and his
identification of biblical references for W. H. Stevenson's annotated Longman edition (1971), along with many of his other articles, make one impatient for the
publication of a fuller study growing out of his 1974 London University dissertation. H. M. Margoliouth collects biblical and literary references on human sacrifice in "Notes on Blake" (*RES,* 1948). Sheila Spector examines evidence that Blake
had access to Hebraic language and thought through channels open in his time
(*BRH,* forthcoming).

Leslie Tannenbaum's study of Blake's response to both exegetical and pictorial modes of scriptural interpretation, *Biblical Tradition in Blake's Early Prophecies: The Great Code of Art* (1982), might well be reviewed under more than one
heading. The first four chapters compile information on the Bible as Blake and
his contemporaries saw it; the separate chapters on each of the "Lambeth Books"
offer significant insight into that important category of Blake's writings and will
be referred to again under "Studies of Individual Works." The four introductory
chapters show that Blake's art and thought derive not only from his direct
engagement with the Bible itself but also from the interpretative traditions surrounding it "that were being actively tested and revised in his own time." Blake's
notion of prophetic form seems to follow principles enunciated by well-known
biblical commentators whom the poet might easily have read; his designs and
metaphors accord with the aesthetics of biblical figuration even more closely
than with the *ut pictura poesis* tradition; his recreation of the Bible through
"sublime allegory" draws on his profound understanding of biblical typology.
Tannenbaum's extensive bibliography and informative footnotes are in themselves worth the price of the book. He handles even the drier aspects of his subject with grace and élan.

The presence of Milton in Blake's imagination, from early childhood on, was
so strong that "influence" seems inadequate as a metaphor. In *Angel of Apocalypse: Blake's Idea of Milton* (1975), Joseph Anthony Wittreich, Jr., places in appropriate contexts three instances of Milton's impact on Blake. First, he examines
Blake's pictorial representations of Milton in relation to portraits of Milton en-

graved by others. Second, he explores traditional and innovative elements in Blake's own illustrations of Milton's poems—*Paradise Regained,* in particular—in relation to prevailing eighteenth-century misinterpretations of Milton's themes. Third, with particular attention to *The Marriage of Heaven and Hell* and with reference to commentaries on biblical prophecy of the seventeenth and eighteenth centuries, he argues that Blake and Milton belonged to a "tradition" of revolution in both politics and aesthetics, which they expressed and promoted by merging epic with biblical prophecy to create a new poetic form. An epilogue advances a cooperative theory of poetic influence, in opposition to the anxiously competitive one of Harold Bloom. Wittreich's Blake looks to Milton as John the Divine looked to Daniel—as a fellow prophet whose work is in part understood but in part also requires reinterpretation or correction. Wittreich holds that Blake did not find Milton's theology obsolete; on the contrary, he understood it as boldly innovative, revolutionary. Blake's task then was to liberate the true Milton from the misconstruals of conservative interpreters and illustrators who had encumbered his radical ideas with the errors of orthodoxy. (Hayley, surprisingly, comes off as a protoradical who showed Blake the way to understand Milton; F. E. Pierce, in "The Genesis and General Meaning of Blake's *Milton*" [*MP,* 1927], had earlier pointed out a few suggestive sentences in Hayley's *Life of Milton.*) According to Wittreich, Blake is a "peerless" critic of Milton whose idea of the poet "resembles the current idea of him" and indeed reaches beyond it.

Preliminary or supplementary versions of some ideas in *Angel of Apocalypse* may be found in several of Wittreich's shorter statements: "The 'Satanism' of Blake and Shelley Reconsidered" (*SP,* 1968), the introduction to his extremely useful compilation *The Romantics on Milton* (1970), "'Opening the Seals': Blake's Epics and the Milton Tradition," in *Blake's Sublime Allegory,* "'Sublime Allegory': Blake's Epic Manifesto and the Milton Tradition" (*BS,* 1972), "Domes of Mental Pleasure: Blake's Epics and Hayley's Epic Theory" (*SP,* 1971), "Blake's Milton: 'To Immortals, . . . A Mighty Angel'" (*MiltonS,* 1978). On Blake's visual images of Milton, Karen Mulhallen offers some refinements of Wittreich's ideas in "William Blake's Milton Portraiture and Eighteenth Century Iconography" (*CLQ,* 1978), and Bentley throws out a sidelight in speculating that Blake reworked a Cipriani etching for a commercial edition (*UTQ,* 1981). Some sketchy point-for-point correspondences between Milton's major works and Blake's are suggested by S. Foster Damon, "Blake and Milton," in *The Divine Vision,* and links between their lives, personalities, and philosophies by Denis Saurat, *Blake and Milton* (1935). Studies by Leslie Brisman, Jackie DiSalvo, Pamela Dunbar, Stephen C. Behrendt, and others are cited in connection with *Milton* or the illustrations to Milton's poems, and as always Frye's *Fearful Symmetry* should not be overlooked.

In comparison with Milton, other literary influences pale. Robert F. Gleckner's projected book on Blake and Spenser may well establish that literary connection as next in importance. Spenser's influence, obvious in Blake's *Faerie Queene* painting, is also mentioned throughout David Wagenknecht's *Blake's Night* (1973) and in the source studies of John Beer. Fleeting echoes of other poets may be pursued in notes and sections of books listed in Bentley and Natoli. Most of Blake's profound relationships with major literary figures were developed through his illustrations of their writings and are mentioned under "Pictorial Works." Studies of his reworkings of Renaissance emblem books and Protestant hymns are mentioned under "Art and Theory" and in connection with *Songs of Innocence and of Experience*. B. H. Fairchild's slim monograph *Such Holy Song: Music as Idea, Form, and Image in the Poetry of William Blake* (1980), which incorporates a 1975 *Blake Studies* article, contains some useful observations about the music in the air in Blake's time and the patterning of vowels in *The Four Zoas*, but its elaborate musical analogies are highly conjectural. John Adlard's *The Sports of Cruelty: Fairies, Folksongs, Charms, and Other Country Matters in the Work of William Blake* (1972) samples the delights of subliterary traditions that "English Blake" may have absorbed.

Blake's latter-day transmogrification in critical opinion from "pre-Romantic" to Romantic does not cut him off from his eighteenth-century roots, as Frye has shown in "Towards Defining an Age of Sensibility" (*ELH*, 1956; rpt. *Eighteenth-Century English Literature: Modern Essays in Criticism*, ed. James L. Clifford, 1959), and in Frye's *Fables of Identity* (1963). See also Mona Wilson, "The Twilight of the Augustans" (1927; rpt. *Essays and Studies*, 1935). Several writers on Blake's visual art, discussed below, examine stylistic links with his contemporaries. His literary and philosophical affinities and antipathies are concisely presented by Frye in "The Case against Locke," the opening chapter of *Fearful Symmetry*. Jean H. Hagstrum, in "William Blake Rejects the Enlightenment," *Studies on Voltaire and the Eighteenth Century* (1963; rpt. *Blake*, ed. Frye), outlines the reasons for Blake's attacks on neoclassical psychology and aesthetics, antirevolutionary epistemology, and deistic religion, all of which "had in fact invaded the deepest recesses of his being." In *The Creative Imagination: Enlightenment to Romanticism* (1981), James Engell discusses Blake's idea of imagination at some length because it clarifies and exemplifies the thought of Blake's contemporaries, and it allows the historian of ideas to review an almost incredible number of currents and tributaries, with Blake at the confluence. (In the section on nature, however, Engell makes Blake's views too compatible with Wordsworth's; this may explain his anachronistic statement that Blake deeply admired the Simplon Pass section of *The Prelude*.) Martin K. Nurmi's "Negative Sources in Blake," in the 1969 collection of essays for Damon, deals with the poet's creative reactions to Newton's limits, Descartes's vortices, and Thomas Burnet's cosmology. Harry White's "Blake and the Mills of Induction" (*BNL* no. 40, 10: 4 [1971]) deals with Blake's objections to empiricism, inductive reasoning, and the scientific method generally. Joanne Witke traces Blake's responses to Berkeley and Hume in "Blake's Tree of Knowledge Grows Out of the Enlightenment" (*Enlightenment Essays*, 1972). Stephen D. Cox, in *"The Stranger Within Thee": Concepts of the Self in Late-Eighteenth-Century Literature* (1980), argues sketchily that Blake adapted empiricist principles to combat Lockean empiricism—for example, the principle of selective perception. (See also the opening chapter of Leonard Deen's *Conversing in Paradise* [1983], David Punter's chapters on the universal individual and on selfhood in his *Blake, Hegel, and Dialectic* [1983], Christopher Heppner's article on Thel's identity under "Studies of Individual Works" and, in contrast, William Dennis Horn's "William Blake and the Problematic of the Self," in *William Blake and the Moderns,* for Freudian, Bloomian, and Gnostic comparisons, and Pagliaro's article on self-annihilation, mentioned elsewhere.) Punter's ambitious study of Blake's relationship to nineteenth-century philosophy, *Blake, Hegel, and Dialectic,* just mentioned, attributes Blake's and Hegel's parallel revival of dialectical thinking to the social, epistemological, and cultural upheavals of their era; a debate on Blake's dialectic, with respect to Marx, Derrida, and modern interpretations of Hegel, has begun with Nelson Hilton's review (*BIQ* no. 68, 17: 4 [1984]) and Punter's response (*BIQ* no. 69, 18: 1 [1984]). Some of the same contexts for Blakean dialectic are considered more plainly in Hazard Adams' *Philosophy of the Literary Symbolic* (1983). Leonard M. Trawick, "William Blake's German Connection" (*CLQ,* 1977), responsibly investigates some ideas and images possibly transmitted to Blake through Lavater and Fuseli. Daniel Stempel's "Blake, Foucault, and the Classical Episteme" (*PMLA,* 1981)—a tour de force in the avoidance of concrete nouns—remotely applies to Blake's use of language Foucault's idea that the Enlightenment "episteme," or total interrelationship of patterns of thought, may be detected in "Classical" discourse based on naming.

Donald Ault's style in *Blake's Visionary Physics* (1974; rpt. 1975) also lacks the common touch, but the Blake-Newton current arcs across the gap nonetheless. Noting the need for a full-scale treatment of this subject, Marjorie Hope Nicolson, in "Epilogue: The Poetic Damnation of Newton," in her *Newton Demands the Muse* (1946), had questioned "whether Blake could have hated Newton so heartily had he not responded to him more than he was willing to admit." According to Ault, Blake creates new contexts for such terms as "void," "vortex," "center," and "circumference" in order to expose as Newtonian metaphor what has been presented as the objective structure of reality. In the organization and development of his book, Ault attempts to approximate some of Blake's poetic and perceptual shock effects. Thus, one of the few sections detachable from his whole design is the clear geometrical analysis of Blake's 1795 color print *Newton.* Mathematically inept readers will be unable to follow the details of Ault's exposition, even with the help of his diagrams, but everyone can catch the excitement of his claim that Blake understood and objected to Newton on grounds more defensible than literary critics have ever dared imagine. Ault's sequel, "Incommensurability and Interconnection in Blake's Anti-Newtonian Text" (*SIR,* 1977), augurs a large study, in press, on radical narrative in *The Four Zoas.* Ault suggests that Blake uses irreconcilable narrative systems to block the reader's formation of a false integration through massive suppression of conflicting data, as in Newtonian cosmology.

Stuart Peterfreund, "Blake and Newton: Argument as Art, Argument as Science" (*Studies in Eighteenth-Century Culture,* 1981), attempts to examine the Blake-Newton relationship more closely but trips up on small inaccuracies; he explores related questions in "Blake on Space, Time, and the Role of the Artist" (*STTH: Science/Technology and the Humanities,* 1979). Laraine Fergensen, "Blake's 'Eternal Now': A Prophetic Vision of Post-Newtonian Physics" (*STTH:*

Science/Technology and the Humanities, 1980), with help from Edwin Abbott's classic mathematics satire *Flatland,* reflects on Blake's Einsteinian vision of space-time: "We (and Blake), trying to see into the four-dimensional nature of the universe, are in a position similar to that of the Square . . . who is made aware of the third dimension by a Sphere." Blunt, Gage, and Essick discuss the Newtonian imagery of Blake's color print *Newton* and the frontispiece for *Europe* in works considered under "Art and Theory." F. B. Curtis, "Blake and the 'Moment of Time': An Eighteenth Century Controversy in Mathematics" (*PQ,* 1972), relates Eno's "Moment" in *The Four Zoas,* Night I, to a dispute about the material existence of the "Moments" in Newton's theory of fluxions. Ronald L. Grimes discusses "eschatological time" in his contribution to *Blake's Sublime Allegory,* included in his book *The Divine Imagination* (1972). Mollyanne Marks, "Time as Hero in Blake's Major Prophecies" (*Studies in Eighteenth-Century Culture,* ed. Ronald C. Rosbottom, 1976), thinks that temporal dislocations force the conception of time back "where Blake thinks it properly must be, in the perceiving consciousness." This subject also comes up in Brisman's *Milton's Poetry of Choice and Its Romantic Heirs,* discussed elsewhere, and in several articles on *Milton.* Most articles and sections of books on Blake's conceptions of time and space—and there are many—simply elaborate on Frye's explanation in *Fearful Symmetry* of the Eternal Now, as opposed to "clock-time" and "yardstick space." Nelson Hilton, "The Spectre of Darwin" (*BIQ* no. 57, 15: 2 [1981]), reviews evidence of Blake's interest in scientific information disseminated through Erasmus Darwin's works; see also David Worrall's "William Blake and Erasmus Darwin's *Botanic Garden*" (*BNYPL,* 1975), especially for his discussions of *Thel* and *Visions of the Daughters of Albion,* and the articles by Carmen Kreiter and David Charles Leonard mentioned in connection with *The Book of Urizen.* Bernard Blackstone, *The Consecrated Urn* (1959), had earlier pointed out the Blake-Darwin connection. Mark Greenberg, in "Blake's 'Science' " (*Studies in Eighteenth-Century Culture,* 1983), reviews the shifting meanings Blake associated with this term. Bryce J. Christensen, in "The Apple in the Vortex" (*P&L,* 1982), reconsiders Blake's relation to Newton and Descartes.

Blake's theological position has been located near the edges of orthodoxy, atheism, and points between. Solid chapters in J. G. Davies' *The Theology of William Blake* (1948) expose the corrupt eighteenth-century Anglican establishment and advance speculations later verified in Erdman's "Blake's Early Swedenborgianism: A Twentieth-Century Legend" (*CL,* 1953). As a Christian communicant addressing fellow worshipers of "our Lord," however, Davies dilutes both Blake's heterodoxies and centrist Christian doctrines. By the end of the book he has Blake accepting an only slightly truncated version of the Apostle's Creed: the reprobate Christ is explained away as no more than an "overliteralistic misinterpretation of the Evangelists' records." At the other pole, in what Blake might call the Voice of the Devil, Thomas J. J. Altizer, *The New Apocalypse: The Radical Christian Vision of William Blake* (1967), boldly anatomizes the most involuted theological formulations in Blake and at the same time proclaims him the prophet of something called "Christian atheism," which in fact is Altizer's own Death-of-God movement, famous in the 1960s (see his *The Gospel of Christian Atheism,* 1966).

The distance between Altizer and Davies may be measured by their comments on the Atonement: to Davies, Blake's interpretation of the Crucifixion as a "perpetual example of self-sacrifice" preserves the essentially orthodox idea of reconciliation while rejecting only the "penal or juridical theory"; to Altizer, the transcendent God emptied himself once and for all into the historical Jesus, and in Jesus' death God himself perished and Satan was self-annihilated. At this point Altizer abandons Blake for Hegel (thereby earning the disapproval of Thomas Merton, "Blake and the New Theology" [*SR*, 1968; rpt., with his "Nature and Art in William Blake," in *The Literary Essays of Thomas Merton*, 1982]) to proclaim that the profane reality of creation moves through a dialectical process toward apocalyptic reunification in the "Great Humanity Divine," a final coincidence of opposites. According to Eileen Sanzo, "Blake, Teilhard, and the Idea of the Future of Man," in *William Blake and the Moderns*, this dialectical movement is evolutionary, utopian, and millenarian rather than apocalyptic. William Walling, "The Death of God: William Blake's Version" (*DR*, 1968), discusses Blake's anticipations of Nietzsche and others. On the whole, Altizer comes considerably closer than Davies to the paradox of the Blakean Christ, but he overshoots the precise point at which radical and traditional elements intersect.

Whether and in what sense Blake's outlook should be considered Christian in the later prophecies depends on the way Jesus' redemptive action or power is interpreted. Kathleen Raine, in "Blake's Christianity," a 1976 lecture included in her *Blake and the New Age* (1979), describes Blake's Jesus as the Universal Self that we experience through self-annihilation, with the aid of the arts. Jean H. Hagstrum traces the steps leading up to Blake's reacceptance of Christian principles of nonviolence and forgiveness in "The Wrath of the Lamb: A Study of Blake's Conversions," in *From Sensibility to Romanticism* (ed. Frederick W. Hilles and Harold Bloom, 1965). Ronald L. Grimes's *The Divine Imagination: William Blake's Major Prophetic Visions* (1972), a study in the "phenomenology of religion," takes on the aesthetic and theological problems posed by the intrusion into prophetic narrative of the redemptive action of Blake's Jesus, criticizes Altizer's theory of *kenosis,* and claims that Blake's prophecies are "at once literature and literary criticism, . . . religion and religious criticism (theology)." A. L. Morton's pamphlet-length *The Everlasting Gospel* (1958) views Blake against the antinomian tradition of the Ranters and other seventeenth-century sects and suggests that he shared with them the idea of Joachim of Flora that the Everlasting Gospel is a third testament that opens a new age of spiritual freedom under the Holy Ghost. H. Summerfield precisely registers the degrees of difference Blake demarcates within the Godhead in "Blake and the Names Divine" (*BIQ* no. 57, 15: 1 [1981]). R. D. Stock's *The Holy and the Daemonic from Sir Thomas Browne to William Blake* (1982) touches on Blake only in the eighth and final chapter, "Religious Love and Fear in Late Eighteenth Century Poetry: Smart, Wesley, Cowper, Blake." Harold Pagliaro, "Blake's 'Self-Annihilation': Aspects of Its Function in the *Songs,* with a Glance at Its History" (*English,* 1981), discusses the religious traditions underlying this concept.

Kathryn R. Kremen glances over Blakean Christianity in a long, choppy section of *The Imagination of the Resurrection: The Poetic Continuity of a Religious*

Motif in Donne, Blake, and Yeats (1972), which consists mostly of scattered assertions, paraphrases and restatements of well-accepted critical views. In articles on
Milton and *Jerusalem,* discussed below, Mary Lynn Johnson and William E. Phipps
also seek a better understanding of Blake's Christology. Charles J. Sugnet, "The
Role of Christ in Blake's *The Four Zoas*" (*Essays in Literature,* 1976), though
shaky on details of Blake's revisions, usefully emphasizes the importance of
Christ's redemptive role and its influence on Blake's modifications of the Zoas,
particularly of Los. Uncompromisingly orthodox ideas of redemption are reas-
serted by Lawrence Mathews in " 'The Value of the Saviours Blood': The Idea of
Atonement in Blake's *Milton*" (*WascanaR,* 1980) and "Jesus as Saviour in Blake's
Jerusalem" (*ESC,* 1980). These articles legitimately attack the adamantly nontheist
positions of other critics, but Mathews succeeds no more than Davies in driving
the black sheep safely within the fold. Leslie-Ann Hales, in "The Figure of Jesus
Christ in William Blake's *Jerusalem*" (*Heythrop Journal,* 1983), argues with spirit
and sophistication that Blake's Jesus is transcendent as well as immanent, an
extrahuman redeemer as well as a personification of the human imagination;
hence Blake is authentically Christian, though unorthodox. François Piquet considers the incarnation in "Le Tragique et la différance" (*EA,* 1983). Hagstrum's
"Christ's Body," in the 1973 festschrift for Keynes, probes the "disconcerting originality" of the Blakean Christ's physical presence, with particular reference to his
Michelangelesque appearance. At the "glowing core" of Blake's vision, according
to Hagstrum, "the Poet stands before Christ open-armed and receptive but as a
distinct and separate identity"; this conception of the body of Christ preserved
his mystical thought from vagueness and insubstantiality.

This vivid sense of physicality, minus the Christian dimension, informs
Thomas Frosch's phenomenological study *The Awakening of Albion: The Renovation of the Body in the Poetry of William Blake* (1974). Frosch holds

> that renewal for Blake is not a transcendence but a reorganization of the
> given, that his critique of ordinary perception centers on an attack on
> perspectivism, that Blake conceives of the imagination as a perceptual,
> rather than purely mental, capacity, and that, ultimately, his proposal is
> for a metamorphosis of the senses through their engagement in the
> process of work.

Frosch criticizes Frye's rather cerebral distinction between sense and imagination—or perception and interpretation—because it obscures Blake's point that
expansion of sense perception liberates the imagination. He finds Robert F.
Gleckner's important article "Blake and the Senses" (*SIR,* 1965) correct in its response to Frye but too diagrammatic, cryptic, and inconclusive. Frosch clarifies
Blake's ideas on sense perception and sexuality in relation to the myth of fall and
regeneration, but he fails to establish that in Blake the risen body is no more than
a temporal reorganization of corruptible flesh. When he comes to the Pauline imagery of resurrection in "To Tirzah," as he does much too fleetingly for a book on
this subject, he despiritualizes it by fiat, in reverse allegory: the Mortal Part *is*
"the body as it is perceived naturalistically"; putting off mortality *means* "putting

off the consciousness of the body as a natural object." He evades Blake's paired rhetorical questions in the final preface to *Jerusalem:* "What is Mortality but the things relating to the Body, which Dies?" "What is Immortality but the things relating to the Spirit, which Lives Eternally!" He translates the apocalyptic scenes of universal resurrection in *The Four Zoas* and *Jerusalem* into corporeal terms without clarifying them: the senses are replaced by "faculties, which, as separate entities, themselves drop out to be replaced by a fourfold organ of imagination, the body of Albion," but that entity in turn is more accurately described "as a risen activity than as a risen body." It would seem that Blake's later ideas on regeneration cannot be discussed in absolute terms of either flesh or soul; perhaps St. Paul's (and Hagstrum's) concept of the "spiritual body" is after all what Blake wanted to get at when he engraved this phrase on the design for "To Tirzah"—or perhaps the subject is best left as one of the irreconcilable contradictions that Damrosch faces up to in his book, discussed above.

Blake's ideas on sexuality have been equally controversial. His marriage to the submissive Catherine was idealized by his early biographers, but his approval of the "Lineaments of Gratified Desire" was seen by Swinburne and later by the critics of the twenties as straightforward advocacy of Free Love. The apparent contradiction between his life and his principles has frequently been read backwards (usually irresponsibly) into the tangled sexual relationships of his heroes and heroines. Paul Miner's "William Blake's 'Divine Analogy' " (*Criticism,* 1962) traces the biblical and mythic background of Blake's idea that "the act of sex in its imaginative form" becomes "a propitiatory offering, a sacrifice of the selfhood"; for the female, the intact hymen is analogous to the mysteriously veiled holy of holies. Parallel symbolism based on male anatomy is developed in E.J. Rose's "Circumcision Symbolism in Blake's *Jerusalem*" (*SIR,* 1968). David G. Riede, in "The Symbolism of the Loins in Blake's *Jerusalem*" (*SEL,* 1981), discusses the anatomical precision and biblical allusiveness of a whole complex of genital and sexual images. Diane Christian, "Inversion and the Erotic: The Case of William Blake," in *The Reversible World: Symbolic Inversion in Art and Society* (ed. Barbara A. Babcock, 1978), deals not with Freudian inversion but with Blake's overturning of prohibitions against the fulfillment of desire. In *Light from Heaven* (1971), F.L. Beaty reviews statements on love and sexual freedom by the Romantics generally. A clear and deeply informed psychobiographical essay, John Sutherland's "Blake: A Crisis of Love and Jealousy" (*PMLA,* 1972) follows Blake's shifts in emphasis from the celebration of sexual love to pessimism about the torments of jealousy to a more comprehensive myth that includes both possibilities in the opposition between the seductress Vala and the bride Jerusalem. The sexual themes of pivotal poems in the Pickering Manuscript are also discussed thoroughly in Hazard Adams' book on Blake's shorter poems, taken up below. Two articles in *Blake's Sublime Allegory* bear on this subject: Hagstrum's "Babylon Revisited, or the Story of Luvah and Vala" contrasts fallen, unfallen, and regenerated forms of sexual expression in Blake's later epics, and Grant's "Visions in *Vala:* A Consideration of Some Pictures in the Manuscript" scrutinizes partially erased pencil sketches of figures copulating in various nonstandard ways. (Feminist perspectives on Blake's representation of woman will be taken up shortly.)

After reviewing the Jungian efforts of W. P. Witcutt's *Blake: A Psychological Study* (1946) and June K. Singer's *The Unholy Bible* (1970) in *Blake Books,* Bentley remarked with good reason that there had been "mercifully few" psychological interpretations of Blake. There is still no Jungian study that can be recommended unreservedly. In *Blake and the Assimilation of Chaos* (1978), Christine Gallant argues that "*only* through attention to the changing pattern of Jungian archetypes" in Blake's revisions of *The Four Zoas* do we see his myth changing "from a closed, static system to a dynamic, ongoing process." But her attempt to compare Jung's unconscious with "chaos" in Blake fails because she makes "chaos" mean too many different things over the course of Blake's development: in *Urizen* alone, she tries to gather eternal flux, nonexistence, and Urizenic order into this amoebic term. She is more successful when she compares Jung's mandala to Blake's images of order, such as Golgonooza, and when she analyzes *Milton* as portraying a process of individuation. Oddly, she does not note Jung's own brief comments on Blake's art in "Psychology and Literature" (1930; trans. 1933; rev. 1950; trans. R. F. C. Hull in *The Spirit in Man, Art, and Literature,* 1971) and his use of Blake's designs as illustrations for *Psychology and Alchemy* and in his last work, "Approaching the Unconscious," in *Man and His Symbols* (1964). Eileen Sanzo, "Blake and the Great Mother Archetype" (*Nassau Review,* 1978), attributes Blake's negative images of women not to misogyny but to the innate duality of the powerful archetype of the mother. G. W. Digby's *Symbol and Image in William Blake* (1957) and Kathleen Raine's *The Human Face of God* (1982), both reviewed below, are also of special interest to Jungians.

Freudian studies of Blake, prophesied in W. H. Auden's "Psychoanalysis and Art Today" (1935; rpt. in *The English Auden,* ed. Edward Mendelson, 1977), have been slow in developing. Marion Milner's 1958 essay on the Job designs is discussed under "Pictorial Works." The Oedipal intensity of conflicts between Los and Orc and between Urizen and Fuzon must have been remarked in hundreds of college classrooms, but perhaps because Frye had absorbed these into his "Orc Cycle" the point was long neglected in print except for passing remarks by, for example, Bloom in *Blake's Apocalypse.* Daniel J. Majdiak and Brian Wilkie opened the subject in "Blake and Freud: Poetry and Depth Psychology" (*Journal of Aesthetic Education,* 1972). Diana Hume George, in an article revised for inclusion in her highly original book *Blake and Freud* (1980), became the first to observe that Blake, unlike Freud, presents the Oedipal conflict from the point of view of the father. Damrosch, in *Symbol and Truth in Blake's Myth,* comments on the absence of a Blakean concept of the unconscious (as something unknowable) and of a historical self, and he apparently perceives Blake's denial of the "reality principle" as a shortcoming. John Sutherland in "Blake and Urizen," in *BVFD,* attributes to Blake's own "psychic history" in relation to father figures his "deeply ambivalent feelings about that aspect of human mental activity which he allegorized as Urizen." In the opinion of the literary critic Randel Helms in "Blake at Felpham: A Study in the Psychology of Vision" (*Literature and Psychology,* 1971), Blake suffered temporarily from a condition bordering on "schizophrenic paranoia." Margaret Storch, in "The 'Spectrous Fiend' Cast Out: Blake's Crisis at

Felpham" (*MLQ,* 1983), interprets the lines on the old man, the thistle, and Los as Blake's release of rage against his father and his assimilation of the father's power into the son at a new level of creative maturity. Brenda Webster's *Blake's Prophetic Psychology* (1983) is a thumpingly obvious, rattlingly old-fashioned Freudian study: as in her similar book on Yeats, Webster picks through the poetry for evidence of the man's unconscious problems with sibling rivalry, desire for the breast, anxiety about incestuous thoughts, and the like. Her lack of subtlety is perhaps not a handicap in her examination of the scatological imagery of *The Island in the Moon* and *The Book of Urizen*. Occasionally, however, she gives the poet credit for having brilliant psychological insights that he used in art with a conscious understanding of their significance. And her view from outside the tradition of Blake scholarship can be refreshing, as in her reexamination of Blake's feelings about women. Elaine M. Kauvar, in "Blake's Interpretation of Dreams" (*AI,* 1984), draws close parallels with Freud. In *New Phoenix Wings* (1979), Simon Stuart attempts to approach Blake's idea of the creative imagination by way of Melanie Klein's psychoanalytic theories. Like Gallant and Webster, however, he fails to discriminate consistently among interpretative assumptions. His parallels between Blake's and Klein's symbolic constructs are illuminating: lapses occur when he uses Klein's fables to analyze Blake's own infant psyche rather than his mature art.

Diana Hume George's enterprise is of another order. According to the dust jacket of *Blake and Freud,* her book is a reading of "Blake as a psychoanalytic critic and of Freud as a poet" in "a new kind of psychoanalytic literary criticism." An opening chapter of juxtaposed texts creates the illusion that Blake wrote marginalia on Freud. (Morris Dickstein, coincidentally, manipulates a similar conceit—derived from Borges and Bloom—for his appreciative general essay "The Price of Experience: Blake's Reading of Freud," in *The Literary Freud,* ed. Joseph Smith, 1980.) George's Blake not only anticipates all that is most original in Freud but also acts as his own revisionist. George usually manages to keep the Freudian vocabulary from clashing with Blake's own language and sensibility, and she represents the poet as artistically in control of what he dredges up from the unconscious. In "A Little Girl Lost," for example, Ona's response to her father's "loving look" is

> terror, because what she faces in his eye is the dread of incest. Their terror becomes mutual because their repressed fear and desire are also mutual.... [Ona] is also responding to yet another forbidden impulse, her aggressive and hostile feelings toward the father for presenting prohibitions in the first place, which produced the fear her lover overcame.

George's respect for both Freud and Blake as thinkers is apparent except when she uses Blake as a club against Freud, miscast as a failed prophet. A footnote confessing dissatisfaction with her draft commentaries on *The Four Zoas,* George's key text for "reading Blake as a psychoanalytic critic," raises hopes of a follow-up book before long.

Whether Blake's conscious purposes in creating metaphors of the female were undermined by unconscious conflicts has only recently become a matter of controversy, to which George devotes a whole chapter, revised from a previously published article. Mainline critics (notably Frye) deny antifeminist bias in Blake's concept of the "Female Will," the natural power that suffocates one's humanity and is enacted in the social sphere by women in their roles as domineering mothers and coy mistresses. The usual explanation for this degradation of the feminine principle is that Blake was merely using traditional gender personifications for spirit (male) and matter or nature (female), and anyhow he had championed woman's cause in *Visions of the Daughters of Albion* (possibly under the influence of Mary Wollstonecraft herself), and besides, full humanity is represented not in the male but in the unfallen, archetypal androgyne (an image reviewed in Diane Long Hoveler's "Blake's Erotic Apocalypse: The Androgynous Ideal in *Jerusalem*" [*Essays in Literature,* 1979]). The incongruity between Blake's advocacy of liberation for both sexes and his use of feminine metaphors for the most deeply fallen fragments of humanity was first confronted by Irene Tayler (*BMMLA,* 1973; rpt. *Blake's Poetry and Designs,* 1979). The issue was analyzed independently by Susan Fox in "The Female as Metaphor in William Blake's Poetry" (*CritI,* 1977), with the telling observation that "no woman in any Blake poem has both the will and the power to initiate her own salvation, not even the strongest and most independent of his women, Oothoon." Blake's view of woman, with special reference to Ololon's annihilation at the end of *Milton,* was inconclusively debated by Arthur Efron and Margaret Wooster in several numbers of *Paunch*: "Bostetter's Critical Method: The Romantic Truthtellers" (no. 36 [1974]), "On Blake's 'Streams of Gore': An Exchange" (no. 40–41), and "Another Round" (no. 42–43 [1975]).

Since about 1970, Blake's male-female symbolism has been an increasingly popular topic for dissertations and articles, ranging from Karleen Middleton Murphy's general reflections in " 'All the Lovely Sex': Blake and the Woman Question" and "The Emanation: Creativity and Creation" (both in *Sparks of Fire,* 1982), to Margaret Storch's harsh psychoanalytic attack in "Blake and Women: Nature's Cruel Holiness" (*AI,* 1981), to Catherine Smith's well-considered broader critique in "The Invention of Sex in Myth and Literature" (in *The Binding of Proteus,* 1980), to David Punter's psychohistorical analysis, with Fielding as a foil, in "Blake, Trauma, and the Female" (*NLH,* 1984). A recent special issue of *Blake: An Illustrated Quarterly* (no. 63, 16: 3 [1982–83]) considers some interrelated questions, with mixed success: Nelson Hilton, "Some Sexual Connotations," reveals more about Hilton's own psychoverbal proclivities than about Blake's; Anne K. Mellor, "Blake's Portrayal of Women," shows from Blake's poetry that the female element remains subordinate even in the apocalyptic reunion of male and female, but her arguments for his androcentrism on the basis of visual sources are less persuasive; Michael Ackland, "The Embattled Sexes: Blake's Debt to Wollstonecraft in *The Four Zoas,*" establishes the pervasiveness of Wollstonecraft's influence and shows that Blake liberated her sexual radicalism from the rationalistic and moralistic conservatism of her philosophical outlook. The best-balanced essay on this complex subject, Alicia Ostriker's "Desire Gratified and Ungratified: William Blake and Sexuality," acknowledges that in Blake a "richly developed anti-patriarchal and proto-feminist sensibility" coexists uneasily with a "homocentric gynophobia." Ostriker has the generosity to forgive "a large poet's large inconsistencies" as well as a great prophet's inability fully to transcend his own time.

In her own consideration of the question, Diana Hume George defends Blake's apparent antifeminism in the same way that she defends Freud's—as an accurate representation of the status quo, in which women do indeed collaborate in their own dehumanization: present reality must first be recognized if it is to be changed. She acknowledges, however, that in adapting conventional symbols Blake "eventually restricted his capacity to portray the feminine" because of un-avoidable "problems of symbol formation that express themselves in the [gendered] limitations of language." One rock turned over repeatedly by feminist critics exposes the sexism inherent in the language and metaphors of nonfeminist critics even when they are trying to be right-minded. It is an encouraging sign of change that in "Blake's Idea of Brotherhood" (*PMLA,* 1978), Michael Ferber considers the problem of women's place in Blake's metaphors of fraternal companionship and membership in one body, as well as the problem of what Blake meant by "self-annihilation" as a form of atonement or martyrdom. Tom Dargan attempts to refine Ferber's position in "Forum" (*PMLA,* 1979); the questions are also addressed in Damrosch's book, mentioned previously. These matters are independently considered from a Marxist perspective by David Aers, "Blake: Sex, Society, and Ideology" (in *Romanticism and Ideology,* ed. David Aers, Jonathan Cook, and David Punter, 1981).

There is as yet no comprehensive Marxist critique of Blake, though one was attempted in G. R. Sabri-Tabrizi's *The "Heaven" and "Hell" of William Blake* (1973), an arbitrary allegorization, vitiated by factual and interpretative error, of Blake's response to Swedenborg. John Middleton Murry, *William Blake,* had earlier been sympathetic to a Marxist-Christian ideology. D. Aers, "William Blake and the Dialectics of Sex" (*ELH,* 1977), attempts a Marcusean interpretation of the revolutionary and counterrevolutionary feminine consciousness expressed by Oothoon and Enitharmon. Jackie DiSalvo argues—reductively but provocatively—that Blake criticizes Blake's unconscious representations of the emerging bourgeois state and the patriarchal Puritan family in "William Blake on the Holy Alliance—Satanic Freedom and Godly Repression in Liberal Society" (*WC,* 1972) and "Blake Encountering Milton: Politics and the Family in *Paradise Lost* and *The Four Zoas*" (in *Milton and the Line of Vision,* ed. Wittreich, 1975). In her more fully developed feminist-Marxist analysis, *War of Titans: Blake, Milton, and the Politics of Religion* (1983), DiSalvo shows brilliantly that Blake deconstructs classical and biblical myths, and interpretations thereof, to reveal the "history of social, sexual, cultural, and psychological evolution" that they had covered up. Considering Los and Enitharmon as metalworker and textile maker, Fred Whitehead attempts comparisons with "the iconography of working-class socialist art" as represented by Soviet posters in "William Blake and the Radical Tradition," in

Weapons of Criticism: Marxism and the Literary Tradition (ed. Norman Rudich, 1976). Kurt Heinzelman's essay on Blake and the "Economics of the Imagination" (*MLQ*, 1978; incorporated into his 1980 book with this title) attends to Blake's economic metaphors and his allusions to British monetary problems in order to suggest that Blake was "reimagining" political economics by viewing labor as the fundamental determinant of value. According to Graham Pechey's "The London Motif in Some Eighteenth-Century Contexts: A Semiotic Study" (*L&H,* 1976), Blake's "London" releases the city motif from its "ideological anchorage" in Whig mercantile capitalism; in a "free play of literary signifiers," through "ironic reiteration and allusion," it provides "both a powerful polemical riposte to a century of consensus and a new view of the city"; compare David Punter's "Blake's Capital Cities" in *London in Literature* (ed. Neil Taylor and Simon Edwards, 1979). See also Crehan's *Blake in Context,* already mentioned.

Although David Punter exaggerates whatever identification Blake made between humanity and its expression in social organization, his thoroughly documented, closely reasoned articles reveal important aspects of Blake's thought from a Marxist (or more specifically Marcusean) perspective. In "Blake: Creative and Uncreative Labour" (*SIR,* 1977), he interprets the different kinds of work performed by Los or directed by Urizen as Blake's representations of actual systems of production, not as metaphors for conflicting epistemologies. In "Blake, Marxism, and Dialectic" (*L&H,* 1977), he justifies the apparent incompatibility between the clarity of Blake's social vision and the opacity and elitism of Blake's choice of style and medium on the grounds that more straightforward communication would be delusive, as both language and commonsense perception are "tainted with domination." Insofar as Blake's characters define themselves by their work, Punter maintains that Blake looks toward the "dialectical assertion of the inseparability of human activity and human consciousness" and anticipates Marx's concept of the alienation of the worker from his labor. But Blake's is not a class-based analysis of exploitation: Urizen, as capitalist, is afflicted by his own repressions in the same way as his underlings are. And Blake's idea of the reformation of consciousness, like Hegel's but unlike Marx's, retains much of the idealist and apocalyptic heritage of his period of history. In "Blake: Social Relations of Poetic Form" (*L&H,* 1982), Punter attempts to show that Blake rejected established genres and chose popular and Gothic forms for political reasons. His aforementioned *Blake, Hegel, and Dialectic* (1982), heavily philosophical in orientation, remains at a considerable distance from Blake's poetry, except for chapters on the *Marriage* and *The Four Zoas.* A new essay, "The Sign of Blake," is forthcoming in *Criticism.* "Blake: 'Active Evil' and 'Passive Good,' " in *Romanticism and Ideology* (ed. Aers, Cook, and Punter, 1981), glances at Blake's philosophy of work. Peter Middleton, on poetics, and Edward Larrissy, on structure, tie Blake's art to his politics in *1789: Reading, Writing, Revolution* (ed. Francis Barker, 1982). Publications on working-class ideologies by A. L. Morton, D. V. Erdman, E. P. Thompson, and Morris Eaves have been noted earlier. On general sources, contexts, and approaches, additional suggestions are considered in the section on Blake's art.

Themes, Symbols, Styles. Other general studies of Blake's poetry take up such traditional literary concerns as language, metrics, imagery, myth, and genre. The opening paragraph of Erdman's preface to the computer-assisted Blake *Concordance* (1967; listed with "Reference Works") suggests the limitations of any quantitative analysis of Blake's lexicon:

> We may have expected to find MAN, LOVE, ETERNAL, and EARTH among Blake's most used words, but not DEATH so near the top or NIGHT so far ahead of DAY. And among those used only once we may be struck to see how many were memorably effective in their single impacts. . . .

In a 1950 English Institute paper incorporated into her *Eras and Modes in English Poetry* (rev. ed. 1965), Josephine Miles tabulated, sans computer, the most frequently used content words in a "thousand lines from the beginnings of almost all his major works, a hundred lines from each" (but according to her post-concordance afterthoughts in "Blake's Frame of Language" in the 1973 festschrift for Keynes, the sample had been drawn from "the first two hundred lines" of major poems). This sampling indicated to Miles that the staples of Blake's heavily adjectival vocabulary are by and large those of his age, though Blake used more repetition than his contemporaries did and also relied on such special words as *eternal, red, starry, terrible, furnace,* and *wheel.* After correcting Erdman's frequency lists by setting aside prose occurrences and combining singular and plural forms, Miles found essential agreement between her semiscientific data base and the complete *Concordance* word counts of 20,000 lines. These frequencies suggest to her that Blake looks out and up "from death and from night and from son and man, and from earth, these being Blake's major nouns"; his more ethereal terms appear much less often.

Robert F. Gleckner, apparently working from his own word count or from general impressions, suggests in "Blake's Verbal Technique," in the 1969 festschrift for Damon, that Blake's adjectives reflect changes in perspective as his canon developed. In *Innocence,* nouns and adjectives display "a kind of indissoluble grammatical and dictional unity"; in *Experience,* this unity is disrupted, the adjectives becoming deliberately inappropriate to the nouns they limit. In the later poetry, Blake's coherent language mocks the incoherence it represents through such manipulations as wordplay, ambiguity, "adjectival nouns or nounlike adjectives," and verbal irony; but see Gleckner's thoughtful review of Miles (*BNL* no. 36, 9: 4 [1976]). In "Blake's Diction—An Amendatory Note" (*BS* 7: 2 [1975]), J. Walter Nelson denies that Blake's verbal inventiveness derives primarily from his imaginative manipulation of a common word stock and credits him with numerous coinages. Roger Murray, "Blake and the Ideal of Simplicity" (*SIR,* 1974), on the basis of eighteenth-century rhetorical theory, finds that Blake achieved the effect of simplicity by combining "few and recessive" slow-moving verbs with a clustering of gerunds and participles that "agitate the interstices between verbs." A related point, overlooked by Murray, is made in the central portion of Edward J. Rose's "Visionary Forms Dramatic: Grammatical and Icono-graphical Movement in Blake's Verse and Designs" (*Criticism,* 1966), on Blake's "synchronization of parts of speech with his symbolism." With copious footnotes to his own dissertation, Ronald Clayton Taylor, "Semantic Structures and the Tem-poral Modes of Blake's Prophetic Verse" (*Language and Style,* 1979), dissects "as-pect" (as opposed to tense), particularly in Blake's verbals. Without referring to Erdman's *Concordance* or to the work of Miles or Gleckner, D. Ross, in "An EYE-BALL View of Blake's *Songs of Innocence and of Experience,*" in *Computers in the Humanities* (ed. J. L. Mitchell, 1974), describes a program for stylistic analysis that he and Robert Rasche developed. Since the program detected few stylistic differences between *Innocence* and *Experience,* it is unlikely that the preliminary statistics on Blake will, as Ross hopes, provide a standard for analyses of other poets.

Contemporary fascination with language as a self-reflexive system is begin-ning to influence Blake studies. Gleckner pursues Blake's diction beyond words in "Most Holy Forms of Thought: Some Observations on Blake and Language" (*ELH,* 1974). Referring often to Fredric Jameson's *The Prison-House of Language* (1972), Gleckner examines the poet's use of fallen language, babble, or "mere si-militudes of the Word" to create a "transcendent or translucent syntax" that has the capacity to reconstruct Eternity by embodying (and annihilating) error and organizing vision. Gleckner claims that "everything [Blake] says about anything" is "translatable into a comment upon language, words, the poet's task, reality." Peggy Meyer Sherry's Derrida-inspired piece, "The 'Predicament' of the Auto-graph: 'William Blake' " (*Glyph,* 1978), deals with "the problematics of the line as a source of difference and figuration"; the design woven into Blake's signature "is both a reflexive link and a disruption of its text" that points to the inseparability of drawing, writing, and the epistemology of reading. V. A. De Luca, questioning commonly accepted etymologies in his "Proper Names in the Structural Design of Blake's Myth-making" (*BS* 8:1 [1978]), discusses Blake's coinages as self-referential "verbal icons" that tend to generate new names by repatterning their own phonetic material, thus forming clusters that hold together both phonetic-ally and mythically. Francis Wood Metcalf, "Reason and 'Urizen': The Pronuncia-tion of Blakean Names" (*BNL* no. 21, 6: 1 [1973]), looks for metrical clues to pro-nunciation. In "Pictures of Speech: On Blake's Poetic" (*SIR,* 1982), Aaron Fogle carries to ludicrous extremes his search for "pictures-in-letters"; the three letters of "Orc"—to take his strongest example—are seen as a circle followed by two in-complete circles, a broken chain.

Similar wordgames form the core of Nelson Hilton's handsomely illustrated *Literal Imagination: Blake's Vision of Words* (1983): puns, anagrams, homonyms, orthographic variants, graphic patterns, semantic changes, hypothetical etymolo-gies—all indicate to Hilton that Blake places pressure on certain nodal words "to the point where they break their husks and reveal . . . 'all.' " In this dazzling display of "polysemous" and "multidimensional" words, it is frequently unclear whether the fracturing and anagrammatizing of line after line of Blake is sup-posed to reveal something Blake did—intentionally or unintentionally—or merely to entertain anyone who shares the author's jeu d'esprit. But at his best Hilton makes genuine discoveries at the molecular level of poetic language, grinding stony structures to dust so that he can identify the organelles of Blake's "syntagms." Parts of the book have been published separately as "Blake in the Chains of Being" (*The Eighteenth Century: Theory and Interpretation,* 1980) and "Spears, Spheres, and Spiritual Tears: Blake's Poetry as 'The Tyger'" (*PQ,* 1980). Blake's use of language is considered also by Leopold Damrosch and by Hazard Adams, discussed elsewhere, and by Peter Middleton in a two-part paper "The Revolutionary Poetics of William Blake" in *1789* (ed. Francis Barker, 1982) and in *Oxford Literary Review* (1983), emphasizing the ideological implications of his unstable syntactic units and his use of texts that call attention to their textuality.

Analysis of Blake's metrics has not yet caught up with advances in linguistic science and postmodern poetics. Building on Damon and on George Saintsbury's *History of English Prosody* (1910; rpt. 1961), Alicia Ostriker, in *Vision and Verse in William Blake* (1965), taxes conventional scansion systems to accommodate Blake's rhythmic effects. As one would expect, counting beats works better for the earlier poems than the later ones. Although Ostriker recognizes the metrical originality of the free-verse "Argument" and biblically rhythmic "Song of Liberty" in *The Marriage of Heaven and Hell,* she holds steadfastly to an accentual base: Blake was scarcely on "speaking terms with his meter" by the time he reached plate 98 of *Jerusalem,* on which variations in the usual "eight-stress" line "seem to be nine and ten feet long." In contrast, John Hollander's "Blake and the Metrical Contract," in *From Sensibility to Romanticism* (ed. Hilles and Bloom, 1965), takes Blake's "subversion of English meter" as something of a virtue, an anticipation of Whitman and Hopkins. After surveying the relationship between meter and the ethos of different genres, Hollander suggests that Blake was trying "to evolve a whole metrical system to serve as an alternative to the normal one." William Kumbier, in "Blake's Epic Meter" (*SIR,* 1978), uses musical notation to register quantity as well as stress, in accordance with the tendency of Blake's "rhythmic units and phrases to define themselves over a sequence of lines, rather than in any [one] line." Edith Sitwell's introduction to *The Pleasures of Poetry* (1931) contains an interesting analysis of Blake's sound patterns. Kathleen Raine's "A Note on Blake's 'Unfettered Verse,'" in the festschrift for Damon, gives examples of Blake's sensitivity to the rhythms of spoken English "tensed against" his lines of six, seven, and eight stresses. Harold Fisch, *Jerusalem and Albion* (1964), briefly relates Blake's versification to that of Hebrew poetry. Theodore Roethke, "Some Remarks on Rhythm," in *On the Poet and His Craft* (ed. Ralph J. Mills, Jr., 1965) also briefly analyzes metrical variations in "The Poison Tree" (noted by Jenijoy La Belle, *BS,* 9 [1980]). In the first section of "On the Verbal Art of William Blake and Other Poet-Painters" (*Linguistic Inquiry,* 1970), the master grammarian Roman Jakobson subjects "Infant Sorrow" to intense linguistic and structural analysis and discovers a stunning "relational geometricity." A nonmetrical linguistic follow-up to Jakobson's piece, moving across sentence boundaries, appears in E. L. Epstein, "Blake's 'Infant Sorrow'—An Essay in Discourse Analysis," *Current Trends in Stylistics* (ed. Braj B. Kachiv and Herbert F. W. Stahlke, 1972), but it is of interest primarily to linguists. Perhaps a future study of Blake's metrics, building on Ostriker, will adopt more sophisticated notational systems capable of representing early and late rhythms with equal fidelity.

Most studies of Blake's symbols and metaphors are concerned with specific patterns of imagery. Two general articles on metaphor award Blake poor marks, but for diametrically opposite reasons. According to Matthew Corrigan, "Metaphor in William Blake: A Negative View" (*JAAC,* 1969), "Blake's metaphors represent transferences of a rigid and even stark sort; he is not in his use of metaphor a particularly subtle poet, and we are disappointed if we read his poetry attempting to find nuance of detail or of word," for Blake is "a philosophical *naif,* a poet insensitive to words, uninteresting in syntax," whose metaphors carry only an intellectual charge. W. H. Stevenson, in "On the Nature of Blake's Symbolism" (*TSLL,* 1973), declares, on the contrary, that Blake's symbols, instead of pointing to anything in the world of ideas, merely express the poet's own compulsive fears and desires: the consistency of his images arises from his psychology, not from his artistry or philosophy. Stevenson grudgingly concedes that certain recurrent figures—Urizen, for example—are not "simply thrown up by the emotional vision that engendered a certain poem, as the Poison Tree is"; they do require "a certain amount of planning." This strange attitude occasionally makes itself felt in the otherwise sensitive annotations in his edition, described earlier.

In implicit opposition to both Corrigan and Stevenson and in alignment with Gleckner's "Most Holy Forms of Thought," mentioned earlier, Hazard Adams, "Blake and the Philosophy of Literary Symbolism" (*NLH,* 1973; extended in "Blake, *Jerusalem,* and Symbolic Form," *BS* 7: 2 [1975]), observes that the poet anticipates "twentieth-century ideas of 'symbolic form' and constitutive poetic language." In Blake, creation of language is equivalent to the creation of consciousness, especially in *Jerusalem,* where a mythic language that unites subject and object competes with antimythic language that points outward to things. Art, continually re-creating language, is continually devoured by the antimetaphoric languages it generates, and they in turn must be continually reshaped into their opposite. Adams is primarily interested in the implications of these ideas for critical theory, as developed in his comprehensive *Philosophy of the Literary Symbolic* (1983).

The best brief introduction to Blake's "system" is probably still Albert S. Roe's chapter "Blake's Symbolism"—in his *Blake's Illustrations to the Divine Comedy* (1953; rpt. *The Visionary Hand* and elsewhere); it distills the wisdom of Damon, Percival, and Schorer though unaccountably omitting reference to Frye. Karl Kiralis' influential introductory essay "Intellectual Symbolism in Blake's Later Prophetic Writings" (*Criticism,* 1959; corr. and abr. rpt. *Discussions,* ed. Grant) sorts Blake's major symbols into "personal, geographical, British-mythical, and Biblical" categories, pointing out that, when possible, Blake defines his symbols within his poems or provides ample contextual clues. Frye's essays mentioned under "Literature and Philosophy: Introductions" in this section are helpful at many levels of study. Recent criticism has tended to reject the idea that Blake's symbols have stable meanings; the impossibility of fixing a symbol within a single cognitive frame is emphasized in Donald Ault's analysis of "incommensurability" (see above). Margaret Storch, "The Very Image of Our Conceptions: Blake's Allegory and the Role of the Creative Poet" (*BRH,* 1980), argues that Blake's epic works are publicly "allegorical," not privately "symbolic"; his "allegory establishes a permanent set of concrete signs for mental processes and makes possible the transfer of ideas between the spiritual realm and social reality." The reader's share in assigning meaning is emphasized in Jerome McGann's "The Aim of Blake's Prophecies and the Uses of Blake Criticism," Stuart Curran's "The Structures of *Jerusalem,*" and Roger Easson's "William Blake and His Reader in *Jerusalem,*" all in *Blake's Sublime Allegory.*

The essential content of most articles on specific literary symbols is clear from their titles—except for those in the subtle and far-ranging work of Edward J. Rose, the most prolific writer on Blake's symbolism. He extrapolates freely from Blake's particulars, among which he forges often-obscure associative links. His concise opening paragraphs and launching points in quoted passages are therefore likely to be firmer than his full expositions are. For example, in "The Shape of Blake's Vision" (*BuR,* 1977), Rose moves from imagery of the eye as orb (contracting) and as vortex (expanding), to its expressions in tear and eye-beam, to associated images of circle, womb (or "mind-womb"), phallus, stars, "eye-I," "voice-eye," and finally to permutations of abstracted letter shapes of "LOS," used as page designs. Rose's "The Gate of Los: Vision and Symbol in Blake" (*TSLL,* 1978) deals with imaginative perception in a timeless moment. " 'Mental Forms Creating': 'Fourfold Vision', and the Poet as Prophet in Blake's Designs and Verse" (*JAAC,* 1964) develops the paradox that a fourfold vision of essential oneness characterizes the unfallen perspective within our fallen world and is expressed in Blake's recurring designs and page layouts. "Blake's Metaphorical States" (*BS* 4: 1 [1971]) takes "state" or "class" to be both metaphor and "metaphorical process." " 'Forms Eternal Exist For-ever': The Covenant of the Harvest in Blake's Prophetic Poems," in *Blake's Sublime Allegory,* is about symbolic uses of the seasonal cycle. The titles of two related articles, "Blake's Human Insect: Symbol, Theory, and Design" (*TSLL,* 1968) and "Blake's Human Root: Symbol, Myth, and Design" (*SEL,* 1980), are reasonably self-explanatory. "The Symbolism of the Opened Center and Poetic Theory in Blake's *Jerusalem*" (*SEL,* 1965; excerpted in *Blake's Poetry and Designs*) illuminates not only *Jerusalem* but all Blake's poetry by showing how eternity enters into finitude through the creative moment in time, the visionary atom in space, and the annihilated center of one's selfhood. "Blake's Fourfold Art" (*PQ,* 1970) takes up Blake's quadraplex symbolism of the human body—as skeletal abstract (Ulro), scarlet robe or circulatory network (Generation), cosmic giant (Beulah), or work of art (Eden). Other articles by Rose—on *Milton, Jerusalem,* Blake's mythic character types, his theories of art and design, and other topics—are noted in appropriate places.

In studies of particular themes, images, and symbols, the visual and verbal strands cannot really be separated. Dennis M. Welch's "Center, Circumference, and Vegetation Symbolism in the Writings of William Blake" (*SP,* 1978) reworks familiar ground except in his treatment of the ambiguous vortex symbol, which is the subject also of Mark Greenberg's "Blake's Vortex" (*CLQ,* 1978); see also W. H. Stevenson's "Circle, Centre, and Circumference in Blake" (*Ibadan Studies in*

English, 1970) and W. J. T. Mitchell's stimulating comments in *Blake's Composite Art,* mentioned later, and in his "Metamorphoses of the Vortex: Hogarth, Turner, and Blake" (*Articulate Images,* ed. Richard Wendorf, 1983). Blake's vegetation symbols intertwine with the symbol traced in Paul Miner's "The Polyp as a Symbol in the Poetry of Blake" (*TSLL,* 1960): both the rooted vine and the polyp depict the encroachments of the natural upon the human. Denis Donoghue gives a lively account of Blake's imaginative dominance of brute nature in *Thieves of Fire* (1974). Other aspects of Blake's ambivalence toward nature—or outright rejection of it—are considered by Barbara Lefcowitz in "Blake and the Natural World" (*PMLA,* 1974), Elaine M. Kauvar in "Landscape of the Mind: Blake's Garden Symbolism" (*BS* 9 [1980]), and Nelson Hilton in "Blake and the Mountains of the Mind" (*BIQ* no. 56, 14: 4 [1981]). Rodney M. Baine projects a book-length study of plant and animal symbolism. Eileen Sanzo, "Blake and the Symbolism of the New Iron Age," in *The Evidence of the Imagination* (ed. Donald H. Reiman et al., 1978), argues that Blake saw the positive side of the Industrial Revolution. According to V. A. De Luca, "The Lost Traveller's Dream: Blake and the Seductions of Continuity" (*ArielE,* 1980), Blake was drawn to the wanderer as an expression of a state "neither here nor there"; but with Los, who travels on a plottable journey, he came to accept and transcend discontinuities. Morton D. Paley unravels "The Figure of the Garment in *The Four Zoas, Milton,* and *Jerusalem*" in *Blake's Sublime Allegory.* As for urban imagery, Kenneth R. Johnston's "Blake's Cities: Romantic Forms of Urban Renewal" (in *BVFD*) elucidates the historical and mythic significances of London, Jerusalem, and Golgonooza; see also Edward J. Ahearn's "Confrontation with the City" (*HSL,* 1982). (Articles on the city by Graham Pechey, David Punter, E. P. Thompson, and Michael Ferber are described under Marxist criticism or under explications of "London.") W. T. Jewkes's title is self-explanatory: "Blake's Creation Myths as Archetypes of Art," in *Directions in Literary Criticism* (ed. S. Weintraub and P. Young, 1973). Paul A. Cantor's exciting study of the creation myth in *Urizen* is cited below.

The transactions between time and eternity expressed through Blake's variations on a traditional symbol have been studied by H. B. De Groot, "The Ouroborus and the Romantic Poets: A Renaissance Emblem in Blake, Coleridge, and Shelley" (*ES,* 1969), and—less fully—by Daniel Hughes, "Blake and Shelley: Beyond the Uroboros," in the Damon festschrift; this volume also contains Albert S. Roe's "The Thunder of Egypt," on the association of Egypt with materialism. Sheila Spector's "Death in Blake's Major Prophecies" is forthcoming in *Studia Mystica.* Until recently, critics were content with Damon's identification of stars with Urizenic materialism. Now complications in Blake's celestial imagery have been introduced in Nicholas O. Warner's "Blake's Moon-Ark Symbolism" (*BIQ* no. 54, 14: 2 [1980]) and in "Blake and the Night Sky" (*BRH,* 1981), the title of a special section on Blake's use of various constellations that includes David Worrall's "The Immortal Tent," David V. Erdman's "Art against Armies," and Paul Miner's "Visionary Astronomy." To point out Blake's adaptation of an image from Stedman's *Narrative,* three overlapping notes unfortunately do the work of one: James Bogan, "Vampire Bats and Blake's Spectre" (*BNL* no. 37, 10: 1 [1976]); Geoffrey Keynes, "Blake's Spectre" (*BC,* 1979); Alice Mills, "The Spectral Bat in Blake's Illustrations to *Jerusalem*" (*BS* 9 [1980]). The relationship between Blake's "Ghost of a Flea" and Hooke's drawing of a microscopic enlargement of a flea's head was noted by Charles Singer (*Endeavor,* 1955) and developed further by Keynes (*BNYPL,* 1960; rpt. in his *Blake Studies,* 1971).

For twenty-five years Henri Petter's *Enitharmon: Stellung und Aufgabe eines Symbols in dichterischen Gesamtwerk William Blakes* (Swiss Studies in English, 1957) has stood out as the fullest investigation of a single figure or character in Blake. As a "Janusfigur" between time and eternity who partakes of the natures of both Jerusalem and Vala, working usually but not always against regeneration, Enitharmon is "typisch weiblich und typisch menschlich." Petter acknowledges Blake's antifeminist tendencies but does not see them as a defect in his vision. Leonard W. Deen's *Conversing in Paradise: Poetic Genius and Identity-as-Community in Blake's Los* (1983) deals with the sweeping themes indicated in the title, not with Blake's characterization of Los. The following articles consider the Spectre as a quasi character: C. William Spinks, "Blake's Spectre," in *Studies in Relevance* (ed. Thomas Harwell, 1973); Edward J. Rose, "Blake and the Double: The Spectre as *Doppelgänger*" (*CLQ,* 1977); Mary Lynn Johnson and Brian Wilkie, "The Spectrous Embrace in *The Four Zoas,* VIIa" (*BIQ* no. 46, 12: 2 [1978]). Rose considers Los and his attributes from angles too various and complex to discuss briefly: "Los: Pilgrim of Eternity" (in *Blake's Sublime Allegory*) is about time as Paul Tillich's "Kairos"; "The Spirit of the Bounding Line: Blake's Los" (*Criticism,* 1971) is on imaginative delineation; and "The Gate of Los: Vision and Symbol in Blake" (*TSLL,* 1978) is on the temporal and spatial penetration, through vision, of infinitesimal particulars. Rodney M. Baine's "Blake's Sons of Los" (*PQ,* 1984) elucidates British and biblical allusions. Despite the strained title and vocabulary of George Quasha's "Orc as a Fiery Paradigm of Poetic Torsion" (in *BVFD*) Orc emerges as a principle of renewal and creative power, capable of breaking through the dull round of Frye's "Orc cycle." Rose, in "Good-bye to Orc and All That" (*BS* 4: 2 [1972]), sees Orc as "a symbol of thwarted creativity," a dramatization of "frustrated desire or misdirected energy," which, in art, generates the literature of protest. Orc's political and psychological dimensions have also been considered in articles by Aileen Ward and Randel Helms, cited in other connections. The psychological themes developed in John Sutherland, "Blake and Urizen" (in *BFVD*) and Jean H. Hagstrum, "Babylon Revisited, or the Story of Luvah and Vala" (in *Blake's Sublime Allegory*), have already been mentioned. Several studies of Blake's personages, individually or collectively, remain in the form of unpublished dissertations.

Generic classification of Blake's works has strained critical ingenuity. With his customary imaginative vigor, Harold Bloom has come up with two highly suggestive ways to look at the longer works: one is described in "The Visionary Cinema of Romantic Poetry" (1968; rpt. *Ringers in the Tower,* 1971, and the festschrift for Damon), the other in "The Internalization of Quest-Romance" (*YR,* 1969; rpt. *Romanticism and Consciousness,* ed. Bloom, 1970, and elsewhere). For the first essay, Bloom's examples of "auditory and visual counterpoint," a surrealistic, cinematic phantasmagoria, are drawn from *The Four Zoas.* For the second essay, all three major long poems exemplify the internalized quest-romance, the "Roman-

tic Movement from nature to the imagination's freedom," in which the social self
is destroyed through its struggle "to widen consciousness as well as to intensify
it," while "shadowed by a spirit that tends to narrow consciousness to an acute
preoccupation with self."

One of the two best-established terms for the genre of the longer poems is
"prophecy," favored by Frye and set in historical context by Wittreich (for example, in "Painted Prophecies: The Tradition of Blake's Illuminated Books," in *Blake
in His Time* [1978]). The other is "epic," the subject of Thomas Vogler's *Preludes
to Vision: The Epic Venture in Blake, Wordsworth, Keats, and Hart Crane* (1971)
and of Brian Wilkie's "Epic Irony in *Milton,*" in *BVFD.* In " 'The Illustrious Dead':
Milton's Legacy and Romantic Prophecy" (*Milton and the Romantics,* 1980),
Wittreich also suggests that the word "song" in a number of Blake's titles carries
prophetic overtones. Wittreich's essays in the definition and history of the epic
prophecy or prophetic epic include " 'Sublime Allegory': Blake's Epic Manifesto
and the Milton Tradition" (*BS* 4: 2 [1972]); "Domes of Mental Pleasure: Blake's
Epics and Hayley's Epic Theory" (*SP,* 1971); "Opening the Seals: Blake's Epics and
the Milton Tradition," in *Blake's Sublime Allegory* (1972); and the epilogue to his
Angel of Apocalypse: Blake's Idea of Milton (1975), a book that incorporates several earlier articles. Judith Wardle, "Satan, not Having the Science of Wrath, but
only of Pity" (*SIR,* 1974), questions Wittreich's nomination of Hayley as a source
of Blake's theory of genres.

David Wagenknecht, in *Blake's Night: William Blake and the Idea of Pastoral*
(1973), eschews any consideration of "pastoral in the vulgar sense." Part 1, on the
earlier poems, summons remote analogies from Renaissance art, Spenser, and
Richard Cody's theory of pastoral as solutions to contrived problems in *Poetical
Sketches* and *Songs.* At times a search for novelty and a confusion about country
matters unseemly in a pastoralist produce odd speculations—for example, that
the two ewes on the second plate of "Spring" are somehow "parents" of the lamb
and that the lioness in the tailpiece of "The Little Girl Lost" may be a male tiger.
On Blake's adaptation of Spenser's Una and the Lion, however, previously pointed
out by Damon and Beer, Wagenknecht writes persuasively, and his discussions of
Thel and of *The Four Zoas* raise important issues, discussed below. Part 2, which
refers only sporadically and distantly to the ostensible thesis and emphasizes
Milton rather than Spenser, contains an analysis of Night VII of *The Four Zoas,*
based on a reconsideration of the textual relationship between both of the "seventh" Nights (detailed in his appendix C). Wagenknecht's "idea" of pastoral,
stated twice in the book, is that "the ordinary world of extensive, fallen vision includes the imaginative wherewithal for that world's intensive, visionary transformation"; though at times productive of local insights, this thesis takes in too
much territory and gets too far away from the ordinary meaning of pastoral in literary criticism.

In *Fearful Symmetry,* Frye suggested that satire may have been Blake's "real
medium": certainly this bent is evident in *An Island in the Moon, Songs of Experience, The Marriage of Heaven and Hell, The Book of Urizen,* the Notebook
squibs, and "The Everlasting Gospel." Robert F. Gleckner, in "Blake and Satire"
(*WC,* 1977), compares Blake's tone and spirit in the *Island* to passages in Samuel

Butler, Henry Carey, and Sterne, and he calls for a fuller study of Blake's "satirical background." Irene Tayler, in "Blake Meets Byron on April Fool's" (*ELN*, 1978), comments on his playfulness. Comparing Blake with the Augustans in excellent discussions of the *Marriage* and *Urizen*, Martin Price, in *To the Palace of Wisdom* (1965), points to Blake's shifting of the satirical norm "from moral judgment to a standard of energy." Essays by England, Kirk, Tannenbaum, Mitchell, and Erdman cited under "Studies of Individual Works" indicate the range of Blake's satiric styles. David Simpson, *Irony and Authority in Romantic Poetry* (1979), and Steven E. Alford, *Irony and the Logic of the Romantic Imagination* (1984), share with Bloom, Leader, and Wagenknecht a concern with Blake's maneuvers as an ironist.

First and finally, of course, Blake is one of the very greatest lyricists in English. Unlikely as it may seem, John Holloway's modest booklet in a series for "the advanced Sixth Former and the university student," *Blake: The Lyric Poetry* (1968), which I have classified with the introductory studies, is the most comprehensive treatment of Blake's achievement in this mode. After relating *Poetical Sketches, Songs,* and the Pickering Manuscript to hymns and other verse popular in the eighteenth century, Holloway places Blake with Shakespeare and Wordsworth as a writer of the kind of lyric that adheres to familiar forms. Though "lyricism such as Blake's is not a technical success," its strength lies in its buoyant vitality and its scathing social protest. In "Burns, Blake, and the Recovery of Lyric" (*SIR*, 1982), Leopold Damrosch, Jr., characterizes the two poets as lyricists of "impersonal subjectivity," using a phrase of Susanne Langer's. Blake's use of the ballad form is briefly discussed in Hazard Adams' *William Blake: A Reading of the Shorter Poems* (1963), reviewed under "Studies of Individual Works," and in Alicia Ostriker's *Vision and Verse in William Blake,* mentioned above.

Reputation, Influence, and Affinities. Blake's abject obscurity during and long after his lifetime—his being, as Gilchrist's subtitle puts it, a *pictor ignotus*—is, paradoxically, one of the most famous aspects of his legend. The other is his supposed madness. When in middle age he annotated Reynolds' *Discourses* during the first decade of the nineteenth century—the period of his greatest epics and his biblical designs—he accurately said of himself, "I am hid." In 1824 Charles Lamb speculated that "Robert" Blake had fled "Whither, I know not, to Hades, or a Mad House"—this when Blake had yet to illustrate *Pilgrim's Progress, The Divine Comedy,* and probably *Paradise Regained*; to engrave his *Job* designs; and to finish some of the most splendid copies of his illuminated books.

A full, clear, and accurate impression of Blake's contemporary reputation and after-fame may be derived from the convenient compilation of excerpts from published and unpublished sources in G. E. Bentley, Jr., *William Blake: The Critical Heritage* (1975); most appear also in Bentley's *Blake Records* (1969). Several of the published sources are reproduced in facsimile in Wittreich's *Nineteenth-Century Accounts of William Blake* (1970). As Bentley has shown, contemporary reviews of Blake's poetry were confined to comments on the lyrics from *Poetical Sketches* and *Songs of Innocence and of Experience,* which Malkin had included in the introduction to his 1806 memoirs of his son (mentioned under "Biographical Resources"). These lyrics, condemned by the *Literary Journal* (1806), *British Critic* (1806), *Monthly Review* (1806), and *Monthly Magazine* (1807), were tolerated by the *Annual Review* (1807). Blake's best-known designs, the inventions for Blair's *Grave* (1808), were pilloried by Robert Hunt in the *Examiner* (1808) and by the *Antijacobin Review* (1808) and were praised moderately by the *Monthly Magazine* (1808), warmly by the *Repository of Arts* (1810), and equivocally and belatedly by the *Quarterly Review* (1826). A few commercial engravings received brief, usually unfavorable notice. Of all the reviews, the one Blake took most to heart was Robert Hunt's attack on the 1809 Exhibition and its *Descriptive Catalogue* in the *Examiner* (1809)—which characterized Blake as an "unfortunate lunatic" and described the flesh tones in one of his masterpieces as "exactly like hung beef "—only a year after Hunt's ridicule of the *Grave* designs. Unknown to Blake at the time, however, Henry Crabb Robinson was attempting—to little effect—to launch Blake's German reputation with "William Blake, Künstler, Dichter, und Religiöser Schwärmer" (*Vaterländisches Museum,* 1811). Surprisingly, even before Robinson's account was published, Jean Paul Friedrich Richter had privately recorded his admiration of the *Night Thoughts* designs; this fact was discovered by Werner Hofmann and was publicized in English by Detlef W. Dörrbecker (*BIQ* no. 42, 11: 3 [1977]). Robinson supplemented Malkin's information with his own strong impression of the 1809 Exhibition and the *Night Thoughts* and *Grave* designs. If Robinson's appreciative though somewhat patronizing article had appeared in a British magazine, it might have helped alleviate Blake's darkest years of poverty and isolation.

Unpublished judgments on Blake by his contemporaries were not always significantly different from what was said in reviews. Praise by the Wordsworth circle was lukewarm, but his "madness" was at least considered "interesting." Coleridge's generally high ratings of the *Songs* are mentioned under "Studies of Individual Works." Lamb admired "The Tyger" and "The Chimney Sweeper" (of *Innocence*) and was impressed by the 1809 exhibition. Although the mythic structures of Blake and Shelley are strikingly similar, as Damon, Bloom, and others have emphasized, there is no evidence of contact between them or their work; Melanie Bandy's *Mind-Forg'd Manacles: The Problem of Evil in Shelley and Blake* (1981) is, therefore, a study of analogues.[5] Blake's fellow artists gave him mixed notices. Romney once compared Blake's inventiveness with Michelangelo's; Flaxman, the Fuseli circle, and even some of the rank-and-file Academicians admired his invention but not his execution. That he was at least known to exist after even Fuseli and Johnson had ceased to employ him is reflected in Janet Warner's "A Contemporary Reference to Blake" (*BNL* no. 36, 9: 4 [1976]). Within Swedenborgian groups, selections from the *Songs* circulated throughout the "forgotten years," as Raymond H. Deck, Jr., has discovered: "Unnoticed Printings of Blake's Poems, 1825– 1852" (*BNL* no. 40, 10: 4 [1977]). Martin Butlin's " 'The Very William Blake of Living Landscape Painters' " (*BNL* no. 27, 10: 1 [1976]) announces an 1845 reference in the *Illustrated London News* that reveals that Blake's name meant something to the general reader even in the pre-Gilchrist era. In 1863,

Gilchrist's *Life* ended the period of obscurity and began to dissipate the specter of insanity.

Bentley's admirable introduction to *William Blake: The Critical Heritage,* abridged from "Blake's Reputation and Interpreters" in *Blake Books,* gives an aerial view of the development of Blake's reputation from his time to ours. Deborah Dorfman's *Blake in the Nineteenth Century* (1969), heavily though confusingly documented, goes into the interesting complications of the making of Gilchrist's biography and the cavalier editorial work of D. G. Rossetti. Suzanne Hoover's contributions to *Blake Newsletter* (1971–72) and the festschrift for Keynes take the story further and fill in significant details. Louis W. Crompton's 1954 dissertation, "Blake's Nineteenth Century Critics," remains a valuable supplement to Dorfman. John Sampson's "Blake Parodies: 1895–1913," in his *In Lighter Moments* (1934), could entertainingly be brought up to date and expanded to include cartoonists' adaptations of Blake's designs.

The anglocentric focus of Bentley's introductory essay and of Hoover's and Dorfman's surveys may be broadened through Uwe Böker's "Die Anfänge der europäischen Blake-Rezeption" (*Arcadia,* 1981), which reveals the depth of Blake's influence on the decadent and symbolist movements on the Continent, particularly among such literati and advanced tastemakers as Gide, Rudolf Kassner, Stefan Zweig, Betocchi, Ungaretti, and Montale; Yeats was the primary transmitter. For more detail, Anna Balakian's "The Literary Fortune of William Blake in France" (*MLN,* 1956) may be supplemented by an unpublished 1978 dissertation, Joanne Barbara Wieland-Burston's "Blake in France: The Poet and the Painter as Seen by French Critics in the Nineteenth and Twentieth Centuries." See also Simone Pignard's "Blake in French: An Interview with Pierre Leyris" (*BNL* no. 36, 9: 4 [1976]), a translation of Françoise Wagener's interview with Blake's translator in *Le Monde* (12 July 1974), which mentions essays on Blake by Julien Green, George Bataille, and Marcel Brion. Other reports on Blake's public and academic reputation outside the English-speaking world have appeared in the *Newsletter* and *Quarterly:* for example, G. E. Bentley, Jr.'s "Blake among the Slavs: A Checklist" and Detlef W. Dörrbecker's "Blake Goes German: A Critical Review of Exhibitions in Hamburg and Frankfurt, 1975" (with a list of popular articles inspired by the exhibitions), both in *BIQ* no. 41, 11: 1 (1977); N. G. D. Malmqvist's "Blake in China" (*BIQ* no. 49, 13: 1 [1979]); Gu Jing-yu's "Unlisted Articles on Blake Published in China" (*BIQ* no. 68, 17: 4 [1984]); Kazumitsu Watari's "A Bibliography of William Blake in Japan, 1969–1977" (*BIQ* no. 47, 12: 3 [1979]). So Woong Ko's 1977 dissertation, "A Study of Japanese Criticism of William Blake's Poetry," may serve as a companion to Watari's bibliography.

Blake's immediate disciples were all artists, notably the adoring young band headed by Samuel Palmer, mentioned under "Biographical Resources." Their line of influence—from the Ancients to the Pre-Raphaelite Brotherhood to art nouveau and beyond—is traced under "Art and Theory." On the literary side, Blake was virtually without influence until the making of the Gilchrist *Life,* when he attracted D. G. Rossetti as editor and A. C. Swinburne as critic. As both poet and painter, Rossetti promoted Blake's reputation within the orbit of the P.R.B., but resemblances between his work and Blake's, whether verbal or visual, are not

striking: see Kerrison Preston's superficial *Blake and Rossetti* (1944) and Gregory
Walter's very general "Blake and Rossetti" (*English Record,* 1978), which sticks to
literature and uses Rossetti as a foil to set off Blake's superiorities. R. W. Peattie, in
"William Michael Rossetti's Aldine Edition of Blake" (*BIQ* no. 45, 12: 1 [1978]),
supplements Dorfman's account by drawing on WMR's unpublished papers.
Swinburne's 1868 monograph *William Blake,* a spin-off from his work on the
Gilchrist project, has already been mentioned as the first serious and enthusiastic
effort to bring Blake's poetry and designs, including the longer prophecies, to
the attention of a wider public. But nothing of Blake rubbed off on Swinburne's
own work except what Swinburne read into *The Marriage of Heaven and Hell*
(see Julian Baird, "Swinburne, Sade, and Blake: The Pleasure-Pain Paradox" [*VP,*
1971]).

Swinburne helped plant the seed of Blake's reputation and influence in
America by corresponding with Whitman (see *Walt Whitman Newsletter,* 1958).
Thanks to Whitman's interest in Blake and to the widow Anne Gilchrist's matri-
monial interest in Whitman, together with her need to support herself while
wooing him, many original Blakes passed from her collection to American pur-
chasers and thence to our museums (according to Evan H. Turner's foreword to
Butlin's "The Blake Collection of Mrs. William T. Tonner," *Bulletin: Philadelphia
Museum of Art,* 1972). American connoisseurs appreciated Blake's work much
earlier than did the English; the Boston Museum of Fine Arts amassed one of the
earliest collections, and the Lessing J. Rosenwald Collection of the Library of Congress contains the world's richest concentration of the illuminated books. Thanks
to the generosity of American donors, however, Blake's Notebook, the *Night
Thoughts* designs, and some other treasures now reside in the British Museum.
(See also Raymond Earl Blois's 1941 dissertation, "The American Reputation and
Influence of William Blake.")

On the Whitman-Blake literary relationship, the most substantial articles are
also the most recent: Donald Pease's "Blake, Whitman, and Modernism: A Poetics
of Pure Possibility" (*PMLA,* 1981), the same author's "Blake, Whitman, Crane: The
Hand of Fire," in *William Blake and the Moderns,* and Martin Bidney's "Structures of Perception in Blake and Whitman: Creative Contraries, Cosmic Body,
Fourfold Vision" (*ESQ,* 1982). Pease examines the shifting relationships between
epic and prophecy and the flow of inspiration from *Milton* to *Leaves of Grass* to
The Bridge. With a broad brush, Bidney outlines some affinities between Blake's
and Whitman's ideas but handles the question of influence quite loosely. On
Crane, Blake, and epic prophecy, Thomas Vogler's *Preludes to Vision,* previously
cited, is also highly relevant.

With Edwin John Ellis, Yeats edited *The Works of William Blake, Poetic, Symbolic, and Critical* (1893), in three volumes, with 296 lithographs and a "Memoir
and Interpretation," and in the same year, working alone, the one-volume Muses
Library edition. Yeats and Ellis were the first of their generation to read *Vala,*
which then lay in unsorted sheets in the hands of John Linnell's elderly descendants. The editing experience was of supreme importance to Yeats as a poet, as
suggested in Raymond Lister's quotations from Yeats's letters and private notes in
"W. B. Yeats as Editor of William Blake" (*BS* 1: 2 [1969]), but from the point of

view of Blake's readers, it was a disaster. The text, biography, criticism, and reproductions are all unreliable if not outright fabrications—for example, the notorious claim that Blake the Londoner was in fact a Dublin-born Irishman named
O'Neill. Yeats's effect on Blake's reputation was to turn Blake from poverty-
stricken eccentric to occultist and archmystic. Ian Fletcher, in "The Ellis-Yeats-
Blake Manuscript Cluster" (*BC,* 1972), examines some of Ellis' papers, and James
McCord, in "John Butler Yeats, 'The Brotherhood,' and William Blake" (*BRH,*
1983), documents an 1869 circle of Blake's admirers that included Ellis and Yeats's
father.

In his own work, Yeats refers to Blake constantly, most fully in "William
Blake and the Imagination" (1897) and "William Blake and His Illustrations to the
Divine Comedy" (1896), both published in his *Ideas of Good and Evil* (1903) and
reprinted in his *Essays and Introductions* (1961). Yeats also comments interestingly on the *Night Thoughts* designs in "The Message of the Folk-lorist" (1893;
rpt. *Uncollected Prose,* ed. John P. Frayne, 1970—not in *Blake Books*). Yeats's
Behmenist Blake is a "too literal realist of the imagination," a "symbolist who had
to invent his symbols." Hazard Adams, in *Blake and Yeats: The Contrary Vision*
(1955; with corr. pref. 1968) and afresh in "The Seven Eyes of Yeats," in *William
Blake and the Moderns,* has made the fullest and most discriminating investigation of the Yeats-Blake relationship. Only the first chapter of *Blake and Yeats* is
directly concerned with influence, for Adams is mainly interested in comparing
the poets' aesthetic theories and patterns of symbolism and with outlining Yeats's
perception of Blake. According to Adams' recent essay, Yeats picked up the following basic concepts from Blake: "Contraries and Negations"; center and circumference; a negative, moralistic idea of the religious; the importance of forgiveness of
sin; the idea that all belief is an image of truth; the centering of imagination upon
"Minute Particulars"; and the permanence of imaginative forms. To this list might
be added the vortex, as discussed in *Blake and Yeats.* Adams makes clear that
Yeats's devotion to Blake had "little effect on his poetic style" except for scattered
verbal echoes; in Yeats's prose "Blake's influence was mixed and filtered through
John Butler Yeats's Pre-Raphaelitism and occultist thought."

Northrop Frye, in "Yeats and the Language of Symbolism" (*UTQ,* 1947), contrasts Yeats with Blake, as does W. H. Stevenson in "Yeats and Blake: The Use of
Symbols" in *W. B. Yeats* (ed. D. E. S. Maxwell and S. B. Bushrui, 1965), while
Kathleen Raine's "Yeats's Debt to William Blake" (*Texas Quarterly,* 1965) places
them both in the Neoplatonic tradition; see also D. S. Lenoski, "The Symbolism of
the Early Yeats: Occult and Religious Backgrounds" (*SLitI,* 1981). Harold Bloom's
sometimes bewilderingly speculative and impressionistic comments on Blake
and Yeats appear first in "Yeats and the Romantics," in *Modern Poetry* (ed. John
Hollander, 1968): "Yeats began as a mock or decadent Romantic, and matured into
a true one, a genuine inheritor of the fulfilled renown of Blake and of Shelley,
the apocalyptic myth-makers among the Romantics," but Yeats's misconceptions
of "Blake-as-mystic" and "Blake-as-arcane-speculator" still distort criticism. In his
deflationary book *Yeats* (1970), particularly in the chapter on *A Vision,* Bloom sets
Blake up as a point of light and sanity from which Yeats whirled downward into
"mumbo-jumbo" to become an apostle of "natural religiosity" rather than of the

Romantic imagination. Raymond Lister's slim volume, *Beulah to Byzantium: A Study of Parallels in the Works of W. B. Yeats, William Blake, Samuel Palmer, and Edward Calvert* (1965), touches on some further signs of possible influence.

In contrast to Yeats, James Joyce published nothing directly on Blake; all that survives is a portion from the middle of a holograph manuscript of a speech, in Italian, that Joyce delivered in 1912 at the University of Trieste (in *James Joyce: The Critical Writings,* ed. [and trans.?] Ellsworth Mason and Richard Ellman, 1959). If this speech had been made in English to readers brought up on the Ellis-Yeats edition, its thesis would have been startling: "It seems to me that Blake is not a mystic." Joyce felt that Blake's ability to unite mystical feeling with a sense of formal precision and keenness of intellect reflected the influence of both Michelangelo and Swedenborg. Joyce's Blakean sources are considered by Northrop Frye, "Quest and Cycle in *Finnegans Wake"* (*James Joyce Review,* 1957); Karl Kiralis, "Joyce and Blake: A Basic Source for *Finnegans Wake"* (*MFS,* 1958–59); Robert F. Gleckner, "Joyce and Blake: Notes toward Defining a Literary Relationship," and Morton D. Paley, "Blake in Nighttown," both in *A James Joyce Miscellany,* 3rd series (ed. M. Magalaner, 1962); also in Clive Hart, *Structure and Motif in "Finnegans Wake"* (1962); John Clarke, "Joyce and Blakean Vision" (*Criticism,* 1963); and Gleckner's very circumstantial and persuasive "Joyce's Blake: Paths of Influence," in *Blake and the Moderns.* Gleckner, among other things, presents evidence that Joyce used Yeats's Muses Library edition rather than the Ellis-Yeats edition of the same year, contra Anita Gandolfo, "Whose Blake Did Joyce Know and What Difference Does It Make" (*JJQ,* 1978). Karl Kroeber's "Delivering *Jerusalem"* in *Blake's Sublime Allegory* briefly contrasts Joyce's ornate wordplay with Blake's unadorned, aggressive repetitions. See also Patrick J. Keane's "Time's Ruins and the Mansions of Eternity" (*BRH,* 1983).

D. H. Lawrence, G. B. Shaw, Dylan Thomas, and Theodore Roethke all acknowledged the influence of Blake. Constantine M. Stavrou, "William Blake and D. H. Lawrence" (*UKCR,* 1956), broadly compares the two writers' ideas of space, time, eternity, and spontaneity. Vivian de Sola Pinto, "William Blake and D. H. Lawrence," in the festschrift for Damon, reviews the history of Lawrence's interest in Blake, points out parallels between their lives and times, and discusses affinities between their ideas of the importance of "sensuous understanding" and the damage done by overdevelopment of abstract thought and mechanized labor. Myra Glazer, in "Why the Sons of God Want the Daughters of Men: On William Blake and D. H. Lawrence," in *William Blake and the Moderns* (revised from an essay simultaneously published in *Hebrew University Studies in Language and Literature,* 1982), discusses the primal state of fourfold unity and the fall into sexual division and repressiveness. See also Glazer's "For the Sexes: Blake's Hermaphrodite in *Lady Chatterley's Lover"* (*BuR,* 1978) and W. D. McGinnis, "Lawrence's 'Odour of Chrysanthemums' and Blake" (*RS,* 1976). Shaw himself endorsed Irving Fiske's Shavian Tract, *Bernard Shaw's Debt to William Blake* (1951; rpt. *G. B. Shaw: A Collection of Critical Essays,* ed. R. J. Kaufmann, 1966); see also D. J. Leary's "Shaw's Blakean Vision: A Dialectic Approach to *Heartbreak House"* (*Modern Drama,* 1972) and Valli Rao's "Vivie Warren in the Blakean World of Experience" (*ShawR,* 1979) and her " 'Back to Methuselah': A Blakean Interpretation" (*Shaw Annual,* 1981). On Thomas and Blake, see Joseph Anthony Wittreich, Jr., "Dylan Thomas' Conception of Poetry: A Debt to Blake" (*ELN,* 1969), and Harry Williams, "Dylan Thomas's Poetry of Redemption: Its Blakean Beginnings" (*BuR,* 1972); Thomas himself in *Adelphi* (1935) praises Blake's vocabulary but not his wisdom. On Roethke and Blake, see Jenijoy La Belle's "William Blake, Theodore Roethke, and Mother Goose: The Unholy Trinity" (*BS* 9 [1980]), about Roethke's response to the *Songs,* and her *The Echoing Wood of Theodore Roethke* (1976), on the child's passage from innocence to experience; and Jay Parini, "Blake and Roethke," in *William Blake and the Moderns,* a not entirely reliable treatment of Blakean resonances in Roethke's *The Lost Son.*

Many—but not quite all—the allusions to Blake in Joyce Cary's *The Horse's Mouth* (1944) have been identified by Andrew Wright in his edition of the novel (1957) and in his *Joyce Cary: A Preface to His Novels* (1958). Hazard Adams, in "Blake and Gulley Jimson: English Symbolists" (*Critique,* 1959), parallels the lives and theories of the artist-heroes; his *Joyce Cary's Trilogies* (1984) refers frequently to Blake. Annette S. Levitt, in "The Miltonic Progression of Gulley Jimson" (*Mosaic,* 1977), sets up Blake's *Milton* as a model for Gulley's development, and in " 'The Mental Traveller' in *The Horse's Mouth,*" in *William Blake and the Moderns,* she makes good use of Cary's unpublished charts and notes to follow his reading of Blake's poem. Further observations on Cary's Blake appear in Ann P. Messenger's "A Painter's Prose: Similes in Joyce Cary's *The Horse's Mouth*" (*RE: Arts and Letters,* 1970) and Hugh Miller's "Blake and Gulley Jimson in Joyce Cary's *The Horse's Mouth*" (*AntigR,* 1978). According to James A. W. Heffernan, "Politics and Freedom: Refractions of Blake in Joyce Cary and Allen Ginsberg," in *Romantic and Modern* (ed. George Bronstein, 1977), Blake represents artistic independence to Cary and political liberty to Ginsberg.

The extraordinary communion between Blake and Ginsberg includes eerie experiences of direct auditory revelation, which Ginsberg vividly describes to Thomas Clark in *Writers at Work: The Paris Review Interviews* (3rd ser., ed. George Plimpton, 1967); see also Alison Colbert, "A Talk with Allen Ginsberg" (*PR,* 1971); Jan Kramer, *Allen Ginsberg in America* (1968); and Paul Portugés, *The Visionary Poetics of Allen Ginsberg* (1978). Inspired by Blake's own voice, heard spiritually, Ginsberg tuned the *Songs* for voice, pump organ, kazoo, and other instruments; see the reprint of Ginsberg's notes in "To Young or Old Listeners: Setting Blake's *Songs* to Music, and a Commentary on the *Songs*" (*BNL* no. 15, 4: 3 [1971]), which is immediately preceded by Morris Eaves's review; Ginsberg's notes are also reprinted in *Sparks of Fire* (1982).[6] Alicia Ostriker, "Blake, Ginsberg, Madness, and the Prophet as Shaman," in *William Blake and the Moderns,* is concerned with Ginsberg's interpretation of the prophetic role.

A list of all the poets, novelists, and culture critics who have come under Blake's spell would be tedious to compile; a few names will suggest the range of his influence and appeal. At least three distinguished poets besides Yeats and Eliot have written appreciative introductory essays: W. H. Auden, "A Mental Prince" (*Observer,* 17 Nov. 1957); Howard Nemerov, "Two Ways of Imagination" (1964; rpt. *Reflections on Poetry and Poetics,* 1972); and Kenneth Rexroth, "The Works of Blake" (1968; rpt. *The Elastic Retort,* 1973). Howard T. Young, *The Line in the Margin: Juan Ramón Jiménez and His Readings in Blake, Shelley, and Yeats* (1980), documents Jiménez' receptivity to the verbal and visual influence of Blake. Kerker Quinn, "Blake and the New Age" (*Virginia Quarterly Review,* 1937), skims over Blake's influence on several modern poets; Charles G. Hill, "André Gide and Blake's *Marriage of Heaven and Hell*" (*CLS,* 1966), discusses creativity and Satanism; Robert Bly, "Looking for Dragon Smoke" (*Stand,* 1967), calls for more of Blake's spirit in American poetry; Jerome J. McGann, "Blake and a Tradition" (*Poetry,* 1970), names Blake the father of the "wildman" school; Robert J. Bertholf, "Robert Duncan: Blake's Contemporary Voice," in *William Blake and the Moderns,* sees Duncan as Blake's heir; A. S. Crehan includes a 1971 *London Magazine* interview of Ted Hughes by Egbart Faas, referring to Blake, in his edition of Blake's *Selected Poetry and Letters* (1976). To my knowledge, Blake's influence on Sylvia Plath and on Gary Snyder has not been studied in detail. Michael Horowitz' *The Children of Albion* (1970), an anthology of "underground" British poetry supposedly in the line of Blake, caused a stir in *TLS* (10 Nov. and 29 Dec. 1972) and *Books* (1972). The most recent investigation of Blake's influence on Doris Lessing is Susan Levin's "A Fourfold Vision" in *William Blake and the Moderns.* Maurice Sendak has often stated that he goes to Blake for inspiration; see Jennifer R. Waller, "Maurice Sendak and the Blakean Vision of Childhood" (*Children's Literature,* 1977). The possibility that George MacDonald's admiration for Blake colored his Victorian fantasies for children has not been explored. Blake deeply influenced American hippie culture in the 1960s both directly and through Ginsberg and others, including R. D. Laing, *The Divided Self* (1965), Norman O. Brown, *Life against Death* (1959) and *Love's Body* (1966), Theodore Roszak, *The Making of a Counterculture* (1969) and *Where the Wasteland Ends* (1972), and Colin Wilson, *Religion and the Rebel* (1957). In two of Wilson's novels, *Ritual in the Dark* and *The Glass Cage,* the heroes are Blake enthusiasts; the latter book is reviewed by Stuart Curran (*BS* 2: 2 [1970]).

The modern poet most temperamentally and philosophically resistant to Blake's influence nevertheless paid grudging tribute, in his role as critic, to Blake's "peculiar" and "terrifying" honesty. T. S. Eliot's 1920 essay "William Blake," mentioned earlier, represents Blake as a writer who, forced to make do without a "framework of accepted and traditional ideas," cobbled together a system that reflects a certain "meanness of culture." Eliot's Blake lacked proper respect for scientific objectivity; he was a poet of "genius" but not a "classic." Ernest J. Lovell, Jr., "The Heretic in the Sacred Wood," in *Romantic and Victorian* (ed. W. Paul Elledge and Richard L. Hoffman, 1969), revealingly tracks Eliot's vacillations, inconsistencies, self-protective maneuvers, and hidden sources of attraction to Blake through several of his essays and informal remarks. Leroy Searle, "Blake, Eliot, and Williams: The Continuity of Imaginative Labor," in *William Blake and the Moderns,* argues that William Carlos Williams—who knew little of Blake—is much closer in spirit than Eliot cared to be.

Discussions of the influence of Blake on twentieth-century critical theory have inevitably centered on the system of Northrop Frye. In "Blake and the

Postmodern," in the festschrift for Damon, Hazard Adams defends Blake-influenced criticism, with Frye as prime exemplar, against the attacks of W. K. Wimsatt's "Horses of Wrath: Recent Critical Lessons," in his *Hateful Contraries* (1965), and Murray Krieger's *A Window to Criticism* (1964). See also Michael Fischer's "The Legacy of English Romanticism: Northrop Frye and William Blake" (*BIQ* no. 44, 11: 4 [1978]) and his "The Imagination as a Sanction of Value: Northrop Frye and the Uses of Literature" (*CentR,* 1977). Adams develops further insights into Blake's theory of "constitutive" metaphorical language and symbolic form in "Blake, *Jerusalem,* and Symbolic Form" (*BS* 7: 2 [1975]): Blake "has had a germinal influence on the theories of numerous modern writers and [has] made the most complete utterance of a philosophy of literary symbolism in his time"; he provides "a transition from purely neoclassical English views of language to those developing in the later nineteenth and earlier twentieth centuries." Blake plays a central role in Adams' *Philosophy of the Literary Symbolic,* previously mentioned.

Peter L. Thorslev, Jr., "Some Dangers of Dialectic Thinking with Illustrations from Blake and His Critics," in *Romantic and Victorian,* deplores what he sees as disturbing critical tendencies, which he calls the "Either-Or Syndrome," the "absolutizing of abstractions," and the "Both-And Syndrome." Michael Fischer's "Blake's Quarrel with Indeterminacy" (*New Orleans Review,* 1984) reveals fundamental incompatibilities between Blake's ideas of meaning and those of contemporary critics who, for a variety of reasons, hold that meaning is undecidable. Further theoretical studies might deal with Bloom's emergent system or bring Adams' work on Blake's philosophy of language and form in line with the contemporary Franco-American outlook. Young Blake scholars already seem adept in writing of Blake in language appropriate to the era of Derrida, as indicated in essays to be published in the volumes edited by Vogler and Hilton and by Ault, Bracher, and Miller (mentioned under "General Studies"); for a look ahead, see my conclusion, "Trends and Prospects."

Art and Theory.   No literary critic reads much of Blake without wanting to know more about his art. Important distinctions among Blake's roles as "inventor" or designer, engraver, printmaker, and painter are often blurred in the minds of scholars unread in art history and inexperienced in studio art. The best general introduction is Martin Butlin's "The Art of William Blake," in his catalog for the 1978 Tate exhibition; his bibliography points to further milestones in criticism. Introductory books by Paley and Todd, mentioned earlier, feature Blake's art. But precious few art historians have cared to write at length on Blake, for reasons that Robert N. Essick summarizes in "Meditations on a Fiery Pegasus," a "Preludium" to *Blake in His Time* (1978), and in his introduction to the standard essays collected in *The Visionary Hand* (1973). The cliché most damaging to Blake's reputation as an artist—in his time and ours—is the charge that he had original ideas but was unable to execute them. His draftsmanship, sense of proportion, knowledge of anatomy and perspective, and even his skill as an engraver have been so widely disparaged that generations of art students have turned their attention elsewhere. If literary critics have ventured too far into unfamiliar terrain, they have done so because criticism abhors a vacuum.

A pioneering investigator of Blake's visual sources was C. H. Collins Baker, "The Source of Blake's Pictorial Expression" (*HLQ*, 1941; rpt. *The Visionary Hand*). Anthony Blunt's series of introductory lectures, *The Art of William Blake* (1959), was the first book-length application to Blake's work of the "ordinary methods of art history." Although Blunt takes as "fact" that Blake "had little natural facility as a painter" and that a number of his works are "clumsy," he admires his formal and technical originality. On Blake's sources and his affinities with his contemporaries, Blunt speaks with authority, particularly in his stimulating specialized articles in the *Journal of the Warburg and Courtauld Institutes:* "Blake's *Glad Day*" (1938), "Blake's 'Ancient of Days': The Symbolism of the Compasses" (1938), "Blake's *Brazen Serpent*" (1943), and "Blake's Pictorial Imagination" (1943). Kerrison Preston, in "A Note on Blake's Sources" (*Apollo,* 1965), collected additional parallels as an amateur without attempting art-historical analysis.

David Bindman's *Blake as an Artist* (1977) is a chronological survey of Blake's development from the point of view of a professional art historian. Bindman respects Blake's genius and has taken the trouble to read and understand the later poetry and to acquaint himself with its body of exegesis. His footnotes are packed with information of the kind that most literary critics do not know how to get at; his 182 plates, though occasionally poorly reproduced or mislabeled, are an education in themselves. But since a really detailed life-and-works study of Blake's art cannot be done in 250 pages, commentary thins out to make mere coverage possible. Bindman begins with Blake's apprenticeship and ends with his death; there is no attempt at an introductory or concluding overview. Such lively sections as the one on the structure, themes, and techniques of the biblical tempera series, however, arouse expectations of more detailed studies to follow. On specific sets of designs, art historians have already written standard works: Roe's book on the Dante designs and Lindberg's on the Job series, classified under "Catalogs."

Several other art critics have made brief but interesting remarks on Blake. Roger Fry, in "Three Pictures in Tempera by William Blake" (1904; rpt. *Vision and Design,* 1920, 1956), dissents from the common judgment that Blake was a divinely inspired amateur to claim that his finished paintings show him in secure command of his technique, though his "majestic and profound ideas" had to be clothed in "the worn-out rags of an effete classical tradition." Fry's exchange with S. P. Kerr, Douglas Jerrold, Greville MacDonald, and A. G. B. Russell in "Blake and British Art" (*Nation,* 1913–14) contains fascinating revelations about British ideas of art. Nikolaus Pevsner's "Blake and the Flaming Line," a chapter in his *The Englishness of English Art* (1956; rpt. 1964), refers directly to Blake's art in only a few paragraphs—on the medieval weightlessness of Blake's figures and the abstract geometry of his compositions—but these paragraphs are essential reading precisely because they are embedded in this excellent compact analysis of English art. Robert Rosenblum's seminal study, *Transformations in Late Eighteenth Century Art* (1967), remarks on the primitivistic regression of Blake's style from illusionistic traditions: the "fluent, wraithlike contours" of Blake's figures "no longer need exist in the rational spatial ambiance" of Renaissance perspective. Rosenblum provides a footnote on the few accounts of Blake's art he considers to be of interest to art historians, among them Ulrich Christoffel's *Malerei und Poesie: Die Symbolisische Kunst des 19. Jahrhunderts* (1948) and his own well-known dissertation, "The International Style of 1800: A Study in Linear Abstraction" (1956; rpt. 1976).

To counterbalance the stereotype of Blake as a wholly isolated visionary, most source studies by art historians use the term "borrowings" and emphasize memory above inspiration. In contrast, literary critics—who are largely self-educated in iconographical studies—so delight in Blake's originality that they assume (as we shall see) that his derived images were as imaginatively purposeful as his literary allusions and take seriously his boast that every "Blur or Mark" has discernible significance. And indeed in Blake's greatest work his powerful dislocations of borrowed forms call for interpretative approaches other than, or supplemental to, those ordinarily employed in art history. Kenneth Clark's Blake chapter in *The Romantic Rebellion* (1973), the text of his television series, popularizes the view that Blake was an inspired naif who didn't always know what to do with his visionary images, many of which were actually irrelevant recollections of traditional motifs. This notion Clark probably derived, by oversimplification, from Joseph Burke's "The Eidetic and the Borrowed Image: An Interpretation of Blake's Theory and Practice of Art," in *In Honour of Daryl Lindsay* (1964; rpt. *The Visionary Hand*). Burke, an art historian indebted to the source studies of Collins Baker and Blunt, to which he makes some additions, proposes a connection between Blake's "visions" and the perceptual phenomena designated "eidetic" by the psychologist E. D. Jaensch—remembered images that are involuntarily reimprinted on the retina. Motifs from other artists fused into sharply delineated forms that came to Blake as visions, or eidetic images; these he executed in firm outline, in accordance with his aesthetic theory favoring the linear style. Burke also points out parallels between Blake's assessment of this style and that of the art historian Heinrich Wölfflin. Although Burke clearly has no intention of impugning Blake's powers of invention, the involuntary nature of the eidetic process takes something away from the active imagination.

Compared with all other aspects of his art, Blake's day-to-day toil as an engraver seems most foreign to students of literature. In Robert N. Essick's handsomely produced, generously illustrated scholarly treatise *William Blake, Printmaker* (1980), as to a lesser degree in Raymond Lister's *Infernal Methods: A Study of William Blake's Art Techniques* (1975), one acquires some sense of the recalcitrance of Blake's media and materials. Essick reconstructs the procedures Blake learned from his master, Basire, and perhaps from early technical handbooks, the formation of his taste from study of prints by and after the old masters, and the development of his insight into the economics, aesthetics, and social conditions of his trade. (This latter area is the focus of Eaves's 1977 *PMLA* article, already mentioned.) Throughout, Essick demystifies engravers' tools and procedures to explain Blake's technical experiments, and he demonstrates that Blake's techniques are intimately related to his style, subject matter, metaphoric structure, and aesthetic theory. Essick's study assimilates and virtually supersedes every-

thing listed in his extensive bibliography, although Bo Ossian Lindberg questions
some points in a review (*BIQ* no. 59, 15: 3 [1981–82]). For an informative survey
of Blake's period from the connoisseur's standpoint, with considerable attention
to printmaking processes, see Stephen Calloway's "The English Romantic Tradition," in his *English Prints for the Collector* (1980).

Exactly how Blake etched the plates for his illuminated books was first studied experimentally by William Hayter, Joan Miró, and Ruthven Todd, as reported
by Todd in "The Techniques of William Blake's Illuminated Printing" (1948; rev.
ed., *The Visionary Hand*). Evidence that dikes and terraces controlled the level of
the etching acid was discovered by John Wright through experimentation based
on scrutiny of the electrotypes made for Gilchrist's *Life*. From his own experimentation, Essick confirms some of the findings that Wright published in two
long-winded articles: "Toward Recovering Blake's Relief-Etching Process" (*BNL*
no. 26, 7: 2 [1973]) and "Blake's Relief-Etching Methods" (*BNL* no. 36, 9: 4 [1976]).
But Essick shows that, to facilitate commercial printing, the Gilchrist electrotypes
were much more deeply etched than Blake's original plates could have been;
thus Todd and Wright were misled. Essick, with G. E. Bentley, Jr., "William Blake's
Techniques of Engraving and Printing" (*SB*, 1981), accepts the testimony of Blake's
friends—and some textual indications—that Blake was skilled enough in mirror
writing to pen his texts in reverse directly on the plates in an acid-resistant liq-
uid. Keynes and most other authorities—Lindberg in particular—think he wrote
normally on paper and transferred by counterproof; this point will continue to
be debated, as will the question of the depth of biting. In *Printmaking*, Essick
does not push his much-discussed earlier theory that Blake symbolically associated entrapment with the "linear net" of crosshatching—a standard method of
representing shade and modeling in engraving: see "Blake and the Traditions of
Reproductive Engraving" (*BS* 5: 1 [1972]; rpt. *The Visionary Hand*). Anne Maheux,
"An Analysis of the Watercolor Technique and Materials of William Blake" (*BIQ*
no. 68, 17: 4 [1984]), provides a thorough technical report on procedures and pigments Blake used on works now in the Fogg Art Museum; in the same issue of
the *Quarterly* Joan K. Stemmler reports on Blake's source of information from
Cennino. For further specifics, see Essick's *The Separate Plates of William Blake*
(1983), mentioned above.

There seems to be no more precise or convenient term for Blake's synergis-
tic verbal-visual art form than "illuminated book." Northrop Frye's "Poetry and
Design in William Blake" (*JACC*, 1951) opened the way for Jean H. Hagstrum's
William Blake, Poet and Painter: An Introduction to the Illuminated Verse
(1964), which in turn led to W. J. T. Mitchell's *Blake's Composite Art: A Study of the
Illuminated Poetry* (1978). In adjoining articles (in *BVFD*) Hagstrum buttresses
his position that Blake worked within the eighteenth-century "sister arts" tradition against Mitchell's argument that Blake's work is a drastically original departure from it. See also Edward J. Rose, "*Ut Pictura Poesis* and the Problem of Pictorial Statement in Blake," in *Woman in the Eighteenth Century and Other Essays*
(ed. Paul Fritz and Richard Morton, 1976). Despite their differences, all these
critics—along with Erdman in *The Illuminated Blake*, Keynes in his introduc-

tions to the Blake Trust facsimiles, and such essayists on particular plates as John E. Grant and Morris Eaves—share premises they have helped to make axiomatic: Blake's poetry and designs are inseparably interrelated, though the designs do not directly depict what the texts describe, nor do the words serve as captions for the pictures. To express their interrelationship, Frye adduces musical analogies like Wagnerian opera, counterpoint, and syncopation. Blake's specific innovations in page layout and book design are considered by Kay Parkhurst Easson, "Blake and the Art of the Book," in *Blake in His Time*; A. W. Sewter, "William Blake and the Art of the Book" (*Manchester Review*, 1959–60); and G. Ingli James, "Blake's Mixed Media: A Mixed Blessing" (*E&S*, 1977).

In his 1964 book, Hagstrum briskly announced an end to the era of reading Blake's words in isolation from their designs. After placing Blake's page designs in the context of medieval illuminated Bibles, Books of Hours, Renaissance emblem books, mannerist paintings, master engravings, and eighteenth-century commercial book illustrations, Hagstrum considers examples of illustration (discrete designs set in compartments within the texts they depict), decoration (text with border), and illumination (in which the relationship of page layout and textual content is most intimate and complex)—or combinations of the three. Though he considers *Milton* and *Jerusalem* "failures as composite art," he admits that the "gaucheries and irrelevancies" of *Jerusalem* are "somehow overcome" by the cumulative effect of the whole. Hagstrum's strongly stated value judgments occasionally break in on his exposition, but his analysis of the illuminated books in relation to pictorial tradition prepares the reader to agree that Blake "molded the sister arts, as they have never been before or since, into a single body and breathed into it the breath of life."

Though Mitchell borrows from Hagstrum his title phrase, *Composite Art*, he discerns no merging of the two "sisters" into one body. On the contrary, he emphasizes "dialectics," "interplay," "orchestration," "cinematic transformation or conversion," and even "rivalry" between the two media. According to Mitchell, the "unity" of Blake's art "depends upon the vigorous independence of its component parts"; the result is "a marriage of equals." Mitchell seeks the principles behind Blake's reshaping of the traditions surveyed by Hagstrum; he asks why, for example, Blake places "a Michelangelesque nude in a Romanesque or Gothic space." Mitchell claims that Blake used recurrent linear motifs not as features of a consistent iconography but as keys made to unlock particular sensory processes. The viewer's senses and the illuminated page are doors of perception that communicate through variations on certain basic forms associated also with verbal image clusters: the circle (eye), spiral (ear), arabesque (tongue), and arch (nose) are "multisensory elements of existential (not visual) space." Blake's designs in *Jerusalem* are "vortices which draw the reader inward, into a dialectic of ironies, ambiguities, paradoxes, and concentric unfoldings"; his style becomes the "objective correlative of his epistemology." This last point is developed more fully in "Style as Epistemology: Blake and the Movement toward Abstraction in Romantic Art" (*SIR*, 1977).

Concerning himself with theory of Romantic form and the interplay between distinct systems of symbolism, Mitchell examines problematic works representative of three different styles, themes, and periods: *Thel, Urizen,* and *Jerusalem.* He writes on the texts first, then the designs, which he tries to see as "pictures in a world of pictures." As Hagstrum would be the first to admit, Mitchell's premises, his interpretative acuity, and his opportunity to absorb recent scholarship have taken him much further into *Jerusalem* than Hagstrum would have thought possible or desirable fourteen years earlier. According to Mitchell, Blake's art forms are "critiques of their own mediums" and imply "the ability of man to create his vision." His poetry and designs converge on the central icon of the human body within an abstract space so as to suggest that "the shape and significance of spatial reality is not objective or given, but derives its form and meaning from the human consciousness that inhabits it."

The image of the body is central also to Anne Kostelanetz Mellor's *Blake's Human Form Divine* (1974), another book on Blake's art by a literary critic. Mellor contends that "form," considered both intellectually and stylistically, was a problem for Blake: he came to value firm outline in art at a time when philosophically he viewed form itself—particularly enclosure within the body—as evil. So Blake's theory and practice of art went through well-defined stages: from the "severely closed" forms of *Songs of Innocence* (1789) to the "more open forms of some of the *Marriage of Heaven and Hell* designs" that express the liberation of energy (1793) to a pivotal period in which a style based on linear depiction of heroic nudes conflicted with his thematic concern with closed intellectual and social systems and the fall of infinite mind into corporeal existence (1794–95). After going rapidly through these intellectual and aesthetic reversals, he then resolved his stylistic and philosophical conflicts through the closed yet infinite figure of Jesus, the "human form divine" (1805–27). But somewhere between the shifting meanings Mellor attaches to closed or "tectonic" form and Blake's diversity of styles within each period, the neat formulation breaks down. Throughout his career Blake consistently worked for the release of "the bounded" (a term of 1788) by means of the clarification of vision, which in life and art requires "the bounding line" (a term of 1809): this is a paradox, not a conflict. Blake's sadness or indignation over the self-limitations of the fallen senses is not the same as "hatred" of the body; see Rose's quadruple perspective on Blake's body symbolism in his poetry, "Blake's Fourfold Art," mentioned above. On the relationship between iconography, style, and philosophy, Mellor's book inevitably suffers in comparison with Mitchell's later and more sophisticated study. But Mellor is very good at spotting suggestive details—for example the comparison of the misericords at Chichester cathedral with the gargoyles of the *Vala* designs and the neglected biblical context of the motto to *Jerusalem.* It is surprising that Mitchell footnotes Mellor only twice.

When literary critics write on art, for better or worse, they feel most at home in studying iconography and the relationship of design to meaning. Eban Bass, *"Songs of Innocence and of Experience:* The Thrust of Design," in *BVFD,* though not cited by Mellor or Mitchell, anticipates them both in attending to abstract patterns in Blake's compositions. In her influential essay "Blake's Use of Gesture," also in *BVFD,* Janet A. Warner presents a valuable primer of Blake's gestural iconography and a brief catalog of other motifs; see also her "Blake's Figures of Despair: Man in His Spectre's Power," in the festschrift for Keynes (1973). Icono-graphic studies assume, of course, some basis of consistency in coding. According to Mitchell, Blake's abstract shapes in themselves are "not put to the use of a consistent iconography"; Bass, in contrast, tries too schematically to show that, at least in *Songs,* the abstract forms do convey specific meanings. Warner has it both ways: repeated human gestures and other recurrent images have "consistent symbolic meanings," but these may be in fallen or unfallen states, "apocalyptic or demonic," "benevolent or malevolent," according to context. Since Mitchell and Warner are analyzing Blake's designs at different levels of abstraction, however, their views are not necessarily incompatible. Warner attends to Blake's mastery of the conventions of a body language that is certainly clearly intelligible also to choreographers (see n. 6 above). Blake's deeply ambiguous visual images—of the sort noted in Mitchell's books and articles, Norvig and Glazer-Schotz's analysis of *Songs,* Murray's discussion of *Visions,* and Dilworth's speculations on *Milton*—pose theoretical questions that will probably attract increasing critical attention. Stephen Leo Carr, in "Visionary Syntax: Non-tyrannical Coherence in Blake's Visual Art" (*Eighteenth Century: Theory and Interpretation,* 1981), sees Blake as opposing eighteenth-century book illustrators' methods of organizing parts into a whole: "Blake's designs enact a freeplay of particulars within a larger, coherent form" that is determined by its own bounding lines; thus Blake's style encourages multiple construals and is rich in visual puns and metaphors. Nicholas O. Warner, in " 'The Eye Altering Alters All': Blake and Esthetic Perception" (*CLQ,* 1983), compares Blake's theories and practice to E. H. Gombrich's concept of "the beholder's share" and Wolfgang Iser's theory of readers' response. Studies of unambiguous motifs and designs include M. Volpi Orlandini's "La figura ammantata" (*Qui Arte Contemporanea,* 1974), on the solitary cloaked figure; Detlef Dörrbecker's "That Man be Separate from Man" (*Jahrbuch der Hamburger Kunstsammlungen,* 1977), on the development of one despairing figure from pencil sketch to finished engraving; and Minna Doskow's "The Shape of Limitation: A Visual Pattern in the Illuminated Works of William Blake" (*CLQ,* 1981), on the double arch. Misidentifications and methodological errors in Clyde R. Taylor's "Iconographical Themes in William Blake" (*BS* 1: 2 [1969]) were immediately pounced upon by John E. Grant and Martin Butlin in the next issue. See also Nicholas Warner's "The Iconic Mode of William Blake" (*Rocky Mountain Review* [1982]) and Janet Warner's 1984 book, mentioned below.

A curator and a historian of ideas may be expected to differ on the subject of Blake's originality in using sources within the range surveyed by Blunt and critically assessed by Hagstrum. For example, Andrew Wilton's large collection of loose parallels in "Blake and the Antique" (*British Museum Yearbook,* 1976), announces itself as "merely an extended footnote" to Blunt. Wilton is not cited in Morton D. Paley's more sharply focused essay " 'Wonderful Originals'—Blake and Ancient Sculpture," in *Blake in His Time;* the two present similar reading lists of works on the antique that Blake might have known. But while Wilton assumes that Blake recalled his sources only unconsciously, Paley thinks that in recasting them he "clearly intends the source to be recognized" as part of the new meaning. In "Blake and the Language of Art: From Copy to Vision" (*CLQ,* 1977), Janet

Warner points out several of Blake's visual quotations of standard works that she also thinks were intended to be recognized by his viewer as part of a common language of archetypal gestures and stances. Warner's *Blake and the Language of Art* (1984), further develops this line of thought. According to Bindman, "Blake's Theory and Practice of Imitation," also in *Blake in His Time,* the conflict in Blake between his well-schooled admiration of Greek art and his later theory that it was not inspired nourished "one of the more bizarre artistic theories in the history of art": the British idea—by no means original with Blake—that Greek artists copied divinely inspired Hebrew originals. Nancy M. Goslee's sweeping essay "From Marble to Living Form: Sculpture as Art and Analogue from the Renaissance to Blake" (*JEGP,* 1978) collects comments on sculpture generally, made by Blake and many others. Paley's "The Fourth Face of Man: Blake and Architecture" (in *Articulate Images,* ed. Richard Wendorf, 1983) demonstrates the importance of architectural motifs; his "How to Read Blake's Pictures" in *The Continuing City* (1983) is a superb guide.

Emblem books, picture books of mottoes paired with allegorical figures, may be thought of as textbooks in "the language of art." Hagstrum locates the illuminated books within the emblem tradition, and Piloo Nanavutty, "Blake and Emblem Literature" (*JWCI,* 1952), relates particular plates to Blake's designs. Mary Lynn Johnson, "Emblem and Symbol in Blake" (*HLQ,* 1974), follows the interplay between traditional iconography and Blake's fusions and innovations, as illustrated in *Gates of Paradise* and the flower plate of *Songs.* (Other emblem studies are included with criticism of *Gates of Paradise.*) Judith Wardle has written several learned articles on the subject: "The Influence of Wynne's *Emblems* on Blake" (*BNL* no. 34, 9: 2 [1975]), " 'For Hatching Ripe': Blake and the Educational Uses of Emblem and Illustrated Literature" (*BRH,* 1978), "Blake and Iconography: Analogues of Urizen and Vala" (*CLQ,* 1978), and "William Blake's Iconography of Joy: Angels, Birds, Butterflies and Related Motifs from *Poetical Sketches* to the Pickering Manuscript" (*BS* 9 [1980]). Aquilino Sanchez Perez' *Blake's Graphic Work and the Emblem Tradition* (1982), which I have not seen, is favorably reviewed by Joseph S. Salemi (*BIQ* no. 69, 18: 1 [1984]).

David Bindman, "Blake's 'Gothicised Imagination' and the History of England," in the festschrift for Keynes, explains that in Blake's day advanced artists associated the Gothic style not with piety but with simplicity and purity, which had been corrupted by tyrannical power. Blake's program for a cycle on English history, which includes subjects from "British Antiquity" and extends to the apocalyptic future, does not reflect a taste for the Gothic at this early period of his career. Two overlapping and inconclusive essays in *Blake in His Time* also deal with Gothic form. Roger R. Easson's "Blake and the Gothic" assembles sketchy evidence as to what the term meant in the eighteenth century, a task also performed by Edward J. Rose in his more solid and scholarly "The 'Gothicized Imagination' of 'Michelangelo Blake.' " Rose attempts to demonstrate that Michelangelo's influence modulated Blake's interpretation of Gothic style, but neither Easson nor Rose has come fully to grips with what "Gothic" meant to Blake. Rose has also analyzed Blake's positive and negative responses to two great painters who affected him deeply: "Blake and Dürer" (*CLQ,* 1980) and

" 'A Most Outrageous Demon': Blake's Case against Rubens" (*BuR*, 1969; rpt. *The Visionary Hand*). In "Blake and Tibaldi" (*BRH*, 1978), Irene H. Chayes enumerates some resemblances without the support of external evidence.

In two fine articles, "Blake and the Iconography of Cain," also in *Blake in His Time*, and "Transformations of Michelangelo in William Blake's *The Book of Urizen*" (*CLQ*, 1980), Leslie Tannenbaum ponders the significance of Blake's borrowings. Blake's reinterpretation of Cain "selects and extends [aspects of earlier] pictorial traditions in order to comment upon the more orthodox use of those traditions by his contemporaries." His reworking of Michelangelo's images liberates them from Reynolds' systemizations. Jenijoy La Belle speculates on Blake's own systemizations of Michelangelo: on Aby Warburg's *"pathos formulae"* in "Blake's Visions and Re-Visions of Michelangelo" in *Blake in His Time* and (less effectively) on correspondences in organization of sequential designs in "Michelangelo's Sistine Frescoes and Blake's 1795 Color-Printed Drawings: A Study in Structural Relationships" (*BIQ* no. 54, 14: 2 [1980]). Irene Chayes, in "Blake's Ways with Art Sources: Michelangelo's *The Last Judgment*" (*CLQ*, 1984), focuses on Michelangelesque figures and themes in plates 5 and 6 of *America* to make numerous valuable general observations, though without reference to progress made by Tannenbaum and La Belle. Blake's debt to Michelangelo had been traced earlier by Giorgio Melchiori in *Art and Ideas* (1961) and in *Michelangelo nel Settecento Inglese* (1950) and briefly analyzed by Mellor in *Blake's Human Form Divine*. There is no detailed and comprehensive study of Blake's relationship to Raphael: the comments of Blunt, along with briefer statements by Beer in *Blake's Visionary Universe* and Erdman's "Front Matter" (*BNYPL*, 1976), make a start.

At the outset of "Blake and British Art: The Gifts of Grace and Terror," in *Images of Romanticism: Verbal and Visual Affinities* (ed. Karl Kroeber and William Walling, 1978), Jean H. Hagstrum makes the startling claim that his subject is "largely an uncharted terrain." In substantial sections his nearly simultaneous article "Blake and Romney: Gifts of Grace and Terror," in *Blake in His Time*, duplicates his exploration of this area, which earlier had been entered several times by Bindman and others. Hagstrum arranges the artists closest to Blake according to Burkean beautiful-sublime contraries with specific application to relationships between Blake's *Thel* and Romney's black-chalk Psyche drawings. Alexander Gourlay and John E. Grant, "The Melancholy Shepherdess in Prospect of Love and Death in Reynolds and Blake" (*BRH*, 1982), find unexpected parallels between *Thel* and a Reynolds portrait, and Gourlay provides a source for Reynolds (*BRH*, 1983). Blake's debts to Gillray are recorded by David V. Erdman (*Art Quarterly*, 1949), and Nancy Bogen (*AN&Q*, 1967). Victor Chan, in "Blake, Goya, Flaxman, Romney, and Fuseli: Transcriptions and Transformations of a Dantesque Image" (*Arts Magazine*, 1981), traces a complex of derivations from Flaxman's *Caiaphas and the Hypocrites*. Standard works on Flaxman contribute little on his relationship with Blake beyond minor corrections of Gilchrist. William Pressly, *The Life and Art of Barry* (1981), touches on the Blake-Barry connection. Gert Schiff's apparatus in his catalogue raisonné *Johann Heinrich Füssli 1741–1825* (1973) contains the soundest and freshest evaluation of the Blake-Fuseli relationship. D. H. Weinglass amplifies some points in a review (*Art Bulletin*, 1980), and Peter

Tomory detects a minor borrowing (*Burlington Magazine,* 1975). Blake also affects British art through his young disciples: see Laurence Binyon's "The Engravings of William Blake and Edward Calvert" (*Print Collector's Quarterly,* 1917; rpt. *The Visionary Hand*) and the reproductions in his *The Followers of William Blake: Edward Calvert, Samuel Palmer, George Richmond, and Their Circle* (1925; rpt. 1968), and separate books on Calvert by Raymond Lister (1962) and on Palmer by Geoffrey Grigson (1947), with added information in Lister's " 'The Ancients' and 'the Classics' " (*SIR,* 1975). Grigson's "Painters of the Abyss" (*Architectural Review,* 1950) considers Blake with Mortimer, Barry, and Fuseli. In connection with an exhibition of works by Blake's followers at the Huntington Art Gallery, a special number (*HLQ,* 1983) contains papers by Gerald E. Bentley, Jr., Robert N. Essick, Shelley M. Bennet, and Morton D. Paley. Rediscovered in the mid-nineteenth century by the Rossettis, Blake's influence extends through them to Beardsley and others, as shown in Robert Schmutzler's "Blake and Art Nouveau" (*Architectural Review,* 1955), an essay absorbed into his 1963 book (abr. 1977, trans. 1978). Blake's best-known British follower in recent times is Paul Nash. Clearly, the time is opportune to consolidate our knowledge of Blake's relationship to British art. The exhibition organized by David Bindman for the Yale Center for British Art and the University of Toronto in 1982–83 should stimulate further study.

Recently Blake has been viewed in the company of some of his northern European contemporaries. Robert Rosenblum, *Modern Painting and the Northern Romantic Tradition* (1975), bypasses French art to trace a line of Romanticism through Friedrich, Blake, Runge, and Palmer on into nineteenth- and twentieth-century movements in which elements of Romanticism are revived; Mitchell sharply raps Rosenblum's "beguiling oversimplifications" (*BIQ* no. 43, 11: 3 [1977–78]). In "German Romantic Painting in International Perspective" (*Yale University Art Gallery Bulletin,* 1972), Rosenblum compares Carstens and Runge to Blake and Friedrich to other British artists. G. Syamken, "Die 'Tageszeiten' von Phillip Otto Runge und 'The Book of Job' von William Blake" (*Jahrbuch der Hamburger Kunstsammlungen,* 1975), suggests that Blake could have known of Runge through Crabb Robinson, the collector Karl Aders, or the publisher Friedrich Perthes. David Bindman's essay "Blake and Runge," in *Runge: Fragen und Antworten* (1979), is the freshest treatment of this relationship, touched on earlier by Hans Tietze, "Blake und Runge" (*Der Kreis,* 1927), and Jorg Traeger, *Phillip Otto Runge* (1975). Edith Hoffman, "Some Sources of Munch's Symbolism" (*Apollo,* 1965) traces Munch's marginal use of small floating figures through Klinger to Blake. Briganti, *I pittori dell' immaginario* (1977), surveys the rise of visionary and psychological expression in the art of Blake's period, primarily in England and Germany. In the nature of visual critical responses rather than "influenced" works are several design series: Bo Lindberg's on Blake's visionary life, mentioned under "Biographical Resources," J. Salzman's photomontage *The Steps of Urizen: Visions of a Journey* (1975), and Leonard Baskin's *Blake and the Youthful Ancients* (1956) and his *The Auguries of Innocence by William Blake* (1959).

Blake the aesthetician is most familiar as debunker of other people's theories in such rude quips as "To Generalize is to be an Idiot." The highlight of *Tyger,* Adrian Mitchell's tasteless musical comedy at the National Theatre in 1971, was the staging of Blake's antiestablishment annotations to Reynolds as cockney wisecracks over a pint at the local, hurled at the impervious televised image of Sir Joshua. Scholars, by contrast, have politely attempted to reconcile the nonmember and the president of the Royal Academy by arguing, for example, that Blake's paranoia and prejudice blinded him to Reynolds' unexceptionable statements (or made him declare that someone else wrote the good parts) or that Reynolds changed his position over the years of delivering the lectures, as the middle ground of taste shifted, or that Blake and Reynolds merely used different terminology for the same ideas. These and other palliative explanations may be gleaned from some of the half-dozen expositors of Blake's view of Reynolds. The most helpful discussions are Bindman's in *Blake as an Artist,* Hazard Adams' in "Revisiting Reynolds' *Discourses* and Blake's Annotations," in *Blake in His Time,* and Robert R. Wark's in his edition of *Discourses on Art by Sir Joshua Reynolds* (1959; rev. 1975).

Blake's aesthetic principles in the verbal and visual arts should not be separated. They are surveyed from a Continental standpoint by Johannes Dobai, "William Blake als Kunst-theoretiker," in *Kunst und Kunsttheorie des XVIII. Jahrhunderts* (ed. Gerhard Charles Rump, 1979). V. A. De Luca, in "Blake and the Two Sublimes" (*Studies in Eighteenth-Century Culture,* 1982), learnedly distinguishes the Burkean sublime (which lies behind Reynolds) from the biblical sublime (as interpreted by Lowth) and finds both blended in Blake's prophetic style. François Piquet, in "Blake peintre du sublime et critique de la transcendance," *Nature et Surnature,* from the Centre du Romantisme Anglais (1977–78), also contrasts Blake's and Burke's ideas of the sublime with respect to Blake's visual art. David B. Morris, in *The Religious Sublime* (1972), analyzes the rhetoric and imagery of "The Tyger" on the basis of eighteenth-century theories of the sublime. Thomas Weiskel's *The Romantic Sublime* (1976), discussed in connection with *The Four Zoas,* is a major contribution to a theory of the Blakean sublime. Hazard Adams' earlier study "The Blakean Aesthetic" (*JAAC,* 1954; rpt. *The Visionary Hand*) is concerned primarily with Blake's principles in relation to literary art, viewed against the epistemological terminology of his time.

Morris Eaves's *William Blake's Theory of Art* (1982) has the effrontery to take everything Blake said about art seriously, as if it all fits together, makes sense, and is exemplified in Blake's practice. And by the time Eaves gets through expanding and interconnecting Blake's metaphors in marginalia, letters, prefaces, advertisements, catalogs, and notebook essays, the whole framework of ideas somehow clicks together at the center to form an expressive theory of art mounted on a sturdy tripod of artist-work-audience interconnections. As in the early work of M. H. Abrams and Morse Peckham, Eaves splits cultural history cleanly into mimetic-mechanistic-neoclassical versus expressive-organic-Romantic schools and periods. Eaves, concerned with Blake's aesthetics in relation primarily to the visual arts, holds that Blake "reestablishes Enlightenment principles on

romantic grounds" by redefining traditional aesthetic terms and reorganizing relationships among artist, art, and audience. Eaves seeks to "establish Blake's own
standards in their own terms by extending the conceptual plot initiated by the
metaphor of line." Instead of using Blake's elevation of "line" above color as
Bindman and others have done, as evidence of a basic adherence to neoclassical
academic principles, Eaves holds that Blake romanticized his linearism by
associating line with imagination and vision rather than with intellect and fidelity
to natural forms. For Blake, the outline is active, not static; drawing an outline expresses the artist's genuine identity and delineates the vision within his
imagination—not in nature. And so with other terms both within and without the
Blakean aesthetic: what Eaves has to say about "expression," "originality," "decorum," and "conception and execution" clarifies and interrelates Blake's principles. The final section, which appeared first as "Romantic Expressive Theory and
Blake's Idea of the Audience" (*PMLA,* 1980), runs in a supple Fryelike movement
through "phases" of artist-to-audience relationships and their sociological implications. Eaves wastes some time shadowboxing with artist-reviewer Tom Phillips:
he perversely misunderstands the plain English of Butlin and some other art historians; he (wrongly, I think) interprets some of Blake's more outrageous claims
as satirical or parodic. But *Blake's Theory of Art* is a clever and spirited book that,
because it celebrates rather than apologizes for Romantic expressive theory, will
comfort and enlighten anyone interested in the Romantics generally.

There is still room for study of Blake's conceptions of—and possible derivations from—the work of early Italian painters and sculptors: Giotto, for example, mentioned in both *An Island in the Moon* and the Notebook, and Fra Angel-
ico, mentioned in Palmer's letter to Gilchrist. It would be useful to have an
illustrated compilation of Blake's probable sources of information on all the
painters, engravers, connoisseurs, and art historians whose names he mentions,
from Pliny on Apelles to the magazine and newspaper reviews of his contemporaries. The illustrations in such a monograph should be detailed enough to demonstrate the qualities he admired in engravings of Dürer, Goltzius, Sadeler, and
Edelinck and those he detested in Woollett and Strange (through their hacks
Browne and Aliamet), Hall, and Bartolozzi.

STUDIES OF INDIVIDUAL
WORKS

Illuminated Books. *Songs of Innocence and of Experience.* Isolated explications of individual poems in *Songs of Innocence and of Experience* now serve little purpose except as school exercises. Commentaries contribute to scholarship
to the degree that they consider multiple contexts and perspectives: the relationship of each poem to its accompanying design, its "contrary" poem in the companion volume, its depiction of the "state" of either Innocence or Experience, its
dramatic situation, its positioning by Blake in his various arrangements of *Songs,*
its style of finishing that makes up the distinctive character of the specific copy in
which it appears, its relationship to other works by Blake, its sources and ana-

logues in other literature and art, and its political, social, psychological, theological, philosophical, and (perhaps) biographical implications. As might be expected,
critics prefer to work on oblique or ironic relations between the poem and one
or more of its contexts—for example, the contrasts between its subject matter, on
the one hand, and its speaker, design, or contrary poem, on the other.

The first full-length commentary on *Songs,* Joseph Wicksteed's *Blake's Innocence and Experience* (1928), emphasized the interconnectedness of the poems
and their inseparability from their designs—all clearly reproduced, along with
Notebook drafts and sketches. Despite Wicksteed's impressionistic critical technique, exclamatory and flowery style, and pietizing of the more radical ideas in
the *Experience* cycle, his book remains influential (for good or ill) because of his
theory that left-right distinctions in the designs represent material and spiritual
directions (suggested first in his book on the *Job* designs), his sexual interpretation of "The Blossom" and other poems, his insistence on the higher authority of
the illuminated books over works in manuscript or conventional printing, and his
enthusiasm over Blake's "modernity" in thought and poetics.

Wicksteed's readings remained practically unchallenged for more than thirty
years. Then Robert F. Gleckner, *The Piper and the Bard: A Study of William Blake*
(1959), taking as much care to avoid the designs as Wicksteed had taken to discuss
them, provided fresh texts to support explications relating individual poems to
the general plan of the whole—and to "The Structure of Blake's Poetic," as the
opening chapter is called. In the interval between Wicksteed's and Gleckner's
books had appeared, of course, Frye's *Fearful Symmetry.* As Wicksteed had absorbed Damon's "Mystic Way" into his idea that the interweaving of joy and sorrow is the theme of *Songs,* so Gleckner accommodated his interest in the perspectives of the Piper and the Bard to Frye's archetypal view. Neither Wicksteed
nor Gleckner finds any of the authorial arrangements of *Songs* useful as an
organizing principle. Gleckner connects poems through symbolic associative
clusters and arranges them to show the soul's progression from Innocence
through Experience to a "higher innocence," a much-repeated term that many
readers think of as having originated in Blake rather than in Gleckner. Gleckner
collects ancillary evidence from close readings (and new texts) of other poems of
the same period—*Tiriel, Thel, Visions,* and the *Marriage*—and from general references to the later prophecies. Lacunae are frankly confessed: at the time he wrote
The Piper and the Bard, Gleckner did not understand some poems and naturally
emphasized those that supported his thesis. His occasional efforts to show that
certain poems fail ("The Ecchoing Green," for example) usually indicate only that
they fail to conform to the critic's scheme. Gleckner's enduring contributions to
the study of *Songs* have proved to be his observation of recurring themes and
image patterns (day and night, lost and found) and his emphasis (in theory if not
always in practice) on the importance of the angle of narration, as outlined in his
often reprinted essay "Point of View and Context in Blake's Songs" (*BNYPL,* 1957).

On Gleckner's heels in the early sixties followed several books wholly or
partly on the *Songs:* Harold Bloom, *The Visionary Company* and *Blake's Apocalypse,* previously mentioned; Hazard Adams, *William Blake: A Reading of the
Shorter Poems* (1963); E. D. Hirsch, *Innocence and Experience: An Introduction*

to Blake (1964). Like Gleckner and Bloom, Adams derives from Frye the principle that Blake's shorter pieces must be seen in relation to the whole of his achievement; unlike them, he shows some interest in Blake's visual arts as well, primarily as decorations. His *Reading of the Shorter Poems* brings both New-Critical and archetypal methods to bear on the lyrics, with particular attention to their verbal texture, related images in Blake's other works, and the symbolic conventions of literature generally. Through diagrams, he explores the fallen and unfallen states of the major archetypes of tree, human body, and city and applies his generalizations in sensitive, well-disciplined readings of *Songs,* made still more useful by his large annotated bibliography of previous criticism. His analyses of the longer and more complex lyrics of the Pickering Manuscript are particularly rewarding.

Frye's observation in *Fearful Symmetry* that Innocence and Experience satirize each other has had the unfortunate effect—for which Frye is not responsible—of encouraging ironic readings of everything that rings out loud and clear in the *Songs,* at least everything that is optimistic and celebratory. The state of Innocence and the character of the Bard in *Experience* have received the brunt of the ironic onslaught. The tradition of faulting the Bard, dating from a debate between René Wellek and F. R. Leavis (*Scrutiny,* 1936), continues in Bateson's 1957 annotations to the poems. Bloom and many of his successors seem to regard the pessimistic outlook of Earth in "Earth's Answer" as if it were a fuller and more genuine comprehension of the human situation than the vision of the Bard in "Introduction" to *Experience* and "The Voice of the Ancient Bard." That is, the point of view of Earth is used to correct and criticize that of the Bard rather than the other way around. Further, those ironies that expose the limitations of Innocence are allowed to overbalance equally strong ironies at the expense of Experience, except in *Experience* poems like "Nurse's Song," where the speaker's neuroses, frustrations, and hypocrisies are egregious.

Recently even the delicate designs of Innocence have been interpreted ironically. Although Bloom, like Gleckner, ignores Blake's designs, Zachary Leader in *Reading Blake's 'Songs'* (1981) follows Wicksteed in scrutinizing them along with the poems. But Leader is an even heavier ironist than Bloom, and his critical procedure is even more impressionistic than Wicksteed's. He so peeps and botanizes on the vines, blossoms, tendrils, and swirls of the *Innocence* designs that no sense of joy and unity is left intact. Leader's book has the theoretical virtue, however, of urging respect for the character and integrity of each individual copy of *Songs* produced by the artist himself. And when the ironic perspective suits the poem, the perceptions of Bloom and often of Leader sharpen one's critical awareness. Bloom's readings of "The Chimney Sweeper" and "Holy Thursday" of *Innocence,* the "Nurse's Song" of both states, and "Ah! Sunflower" in *Experience* are particularly fine, as are Leader's reading of "The Ecchoing Green" and his primary interpretation of the design for the second plate of "A Cradle Song."

In *Innocence and Experience* (1964) E. D. Hirsch examines *Songs,* in its multiple arrangements, according to his theory that Blake's work should be separated into distinct periods on the basis of changes in philosophy and outlook (see also his "The Two Blakes" [*RES,* 1961]). As in F. W. Bateson's introduction to *Se-*

lected Poems of William Blake (1957; rpt. *Casebook,* ed. Bottrall), Hirsch opposes the practice of reading short lyrics as microcosms of Blake's thought and symbolism and questions whether the separate poems in *Songs,* in view of Blake's rearrangements, are even members of a whole. Many of Hirsch's readings of the *Innocence* poems, taken one by one, respond to the pervading spirit of that work. His evidence is sufficient to indicate at least some change in Blake's religious thinking during this period. Hirsch cannot demonstrate, however, that Blake went through a totally naturalistic period in which he repudiated the whole concept of Innocence. His analyses of separate poems sometimes suffer from entanglement in a system more rigid and arbitrary than anything he objects to in Wicksteed and Gleckner; even bibliographical evidence is bent to the shape of a hypothetical spiritual autobiography reminiscent of Dowden's interpretations of Shakespeare's comedies and tragedies as utterances from "On the Heights" and "In the Depths."

Gleckner's emphasis on the filtering effects of multiple lenses (those of the individual speaker, the Piper or the Bard, and of Blake the author, for example) has been exaggerated in efforts by subsequent critics to detect a dramatic situation even in songs that lack an identified speaker: for example, D. G. Gillham, *Blake's Contrary States* (1966), and Brian Wilkie, "Blake's *Innocence and Experience*: An Approach" (*BS* 6: 2 [1975]). By placing the bland maxims of *Songs* in the context of eighteenth-century moral reasoning, Heather Glen, "Blake's Criticism of Moral Thinking in *Songs of Innocence and of Experience*," in *Interpreting Blake* (ed. Phillips, 1978), skillfully draws out the disturbing tonalities through which Blake exposed their inadequacies. So far, so good; but her reading of "London" as a reflection of the speaker's distorted psychological processes does violence to Blake's unequivocal denunciation of social evil. In *Vision and Disenchantment: Blake's Songs and Wordsworth's Lyrical Ballads* (1983) Glen sensitively reads *Songs* against eighteenth-century children's verse and makes illuminating comparisons with Wordsworth's poems. Robert F. Gleckner and Mark Greenberg are preparing a volume of new pedagogical essays on *Songs* for the MLA Approaches to Teaching series.

Excellent brief comments on particular poems in relation to *Songs* as a whole appear in C. M. Bowra, "Songs of Innocence and of Experience," in his *The Romantic Imagination* (1949; rpt. *Casebook*); Martin Price, *To the Palace of Wisdom* (1965); and John Holloway, *Blake: The Lyric Poetry* (1968). A. E. Dyson and J. Lovelock, in "The Road of Excess: Blake's *Songs of Innocence and of Experience*," in *Masterful Images* (1976), offer sensitive readings of "The Shepherd" and "The Sick Rose." Stimulating remarks on individual poems, especially in *Experience*, redeem Stanley Gardner's *Infinity on the Anvil* (1954; rpt. 1965), which rejects the later poetry outright. Of the collections of reprinted commentaries on *Songs* mentioned earlier, Paley's *Twentieth Century Interpretations* is the best balanced; it also contains a good though very brief annotated reading list. Two crisply written appreciations of the *Songs* in the no-nonsense British style, both of which originally appeared in *Politics and Letters* (1947), were reprinted in Bottrall's *Casebook*: S. F. Bolt's "The Songs of Innocence," and Wolf Mankowitz' "The Songs of Experience." Both read individual songs in relation to each whole collection, and both—in the year *Fearful Symmetry* was published—feel that the prophetic books claim too much attention. Bolt deplores the "substitution of exegesis for criticism" in Blake studies because it has caused *Songs of Innocence* to be neglected. In Bottrall's generous selection of criticism by Blake's contemporaries appears an interesting unsigned laudatory piece in *London University Magazine* (1832), probably by C. A. Tulk. Coleridge's intriguing annotations on Blake in a letter to Tulk (rpt. *Discussions* and *Poetry and Designs*) are clarified by B. R. McElderry (*MLQ,* 1948; rpt. *Discussions*) and analyzed by Michael Ferber (*MP,* 1978).

Major bodies of commentary on *Songs* have also appeared in separate articles. In addition to *The Piper and the Bard,* Gleckner has written some of the best brief explications we have, for example on "Holy Thursday" and "The Human Abstract," both discussed below. Even his overly speculative essays like "The Strange Odyssey of Blake's 'The Voice of the Ancient Bard' " (*RP&P,* 1982) are valuable in calling attention to interpretative cruxes. John E. Grant, another substantial essayist on the individual plates of *Songs,* has specialized in intensive (sometimes overdetailed) analyses of copy-to-copy variations in the *Experience* designs, with reference to the accompanying text, other designs by Blake, designs by other artists, and the pitfalls of interpretation into which previous critics have fallen: "The Art and Argument of 'The Tyger' " (*TSLL,* 1960; rev. and rpt. in *Discussions*); "Interpreting Blake's 'The Fly' " (*BNYPL,* 1963; rpt. *Blake,* ed. Frye); "Two Flowers in the Garden of Experience," in Rosenfeld's festschrift for Damon (1969); "The Fate of Blake's Sun-Flower: A Forecast and Some Conclusions" (*BS* 5: 2 [1973]). The assumptions underlying the pileup of information in Grant's articles are that pictorial details are as important a part of Blake's meaning as verbal details and that the full significance of these details is intelligible only within contexts provided by Blake. Grant seeks to identify the angle of vision in each poem as it relates to that of Blake the author.

The relationship of *Songs* to emblem books has been discussed by Hagstrum and by Nanavutty, Johnson, and Wardle, in articles mentioned under "Art and Theory." Comparisons with children's books and hymns for children have come up in books by Damon, Mona Wilson, Holloway, Leader, Essick, and Glen, as well as the following: Vivian de Sola Pinto, "William Blake, Isaac Watts, and Mrs. Barbauld," in his anthology of essays *The Divine Vision;* Martha Winburn England, "Blake and the Hymns of Charles Wesley" (*BNYPL,* 1966), a serial article reprinted in her and John Sparrow's *Hymns Unbidden* (1966); Nick Shrimpton, "Hell's Hymnbook: Blake's *Songs of Innocence and of Experience* and their Models," in *Literature of the Romantic Period, 1750–1800* (ed. R. T. Davies and B. G. Beatty, 1976); Porter Williams, Jr., "The Influence of Mrs. Barbauld's *Hymns in Prose for Children* upon Blake's *Songs,*" in *A Fair Day in the Affections* (ed. Jack M. Durant and M. Thomas Hester, 1980); and J. R. de J. Jackson, *Poetry of the Romantic Period* (1980).

Robert Mikkelsen's "William Blake's Revisions of the *Songs of Innocence and of Experience*" (*CP,* 1969)—overlooked in *Blake Books*—relates revisions to changes in meaning in "Nurse's Song" and "Holy Thursday" of *Innocence* and "The Fly," "The Tyger," and "A Poison Tree." Michael Phillips, "William Blake's

Songs of Innocence and *Songs of Experience* from Manuscript Draft to Illuminated Plate" (*BC,* 1979), with meticulous attention to shades of ink and with the advantage of analysis of the Notebook in the Erdman-Moore edition, traces the text-and-design evolution of "London" and of several poems in *Innocence.* Gerda Norvig and Myra Glazer-Schotz, "Blake's Book of Changes: On Viewing Three Copies of the *Songs of Innocence and of Experience*" (*BS* 9 [1980]), point out some of Blake's subtle variations in application of finishing touches.

Anyone seeking to understand Blake's Innocence apart from Experience—both as a collection of poems and as a state of mind—should pore over the pages of Price, Bloom, and Hagstrum and make use of the insights of Bowra and Bolt and the best passages on individual poems in Hirsch. Beyond that, Donald Dike's "The Difficult Innocence: Blake's Songs and Pastoral" (*ELH,* 1961) lays bare the "precarious vulnerability" of Innocence and the tough honesty of Blake's pastoralism. John Wiltshire contrasts Blake and Wordsworth in "Blake's Simplicity" (*CQ,* 1971). Wallace Jackson, "William Blake in 1789: Unorganized Innocence" (*MLQ,* 1972), included in his book *The Probable and the Marvelous* (1978), seems bent on undoing all developments since Damon: *Innocence* "has no seriatum unity, no accretively established context of symbols, no dialectical relationship among its parts."

The pathos of the Innocent's resistance to oncoming experience has drawn critics to "The Little Black Boy" and "The Chimney Sweeper," where the clash of perspectives, intensified by embedded quotations of secondary characters, is felt most sharply. Mark Van Doren, in *Introduction to Poetry* (1951; rpt. *Discussions*), close-reads "The Little Black Boy" without reference to the design or to *Songs* as a whole. Van Doren is alert to the inner contradictions of this utterance but sees them all as expressive of the boy's pure and invincible faith. For A. E. Dyson (*CQ,* 1959) the boy transcends the bitterness of Experience through acceptance of love. Myra Glazer, "Blake's Little Black Boys: On the Dynamics of Blake's Composite Art" (*CLQ,* 1980), fruitfully compares pictorial treatments of the story in *Songs of Innocence* alone (copy B) and in an *Innocence and Experience* version (copy Z), but her analysis of the text itself is overingenious. Both Howard H. Hinkel, "From Pivotal Idea to Poetic Ideal: Blake's Theory of Contraries and 'The Little Black Boy'" (*PLL,* 1975), and C. N. Manlove, "Engineered Innocence: Blake's 'The Little Black Boy' and 'The Fly'" (*EIC,* 1977), see the boy as deluded. Gleckner's "Blake's Little Black Boy and the Bible" (*CLQ,* 1982) places the imagery of sun and light in the context of the first Epistle of John. Cecil Anthony Abrahams' interesting comments on the poem appear in his article on *The Song of Los.*

Others have elucidated historical or rhetorical details in individual poems. Martin K. Nurmi's "Fact and Symbol in 'The Chimney Sweeper' of Blake's *Songs of Innocence*" (*BNYPL,* 1964; rpt. *Blake,* ed. Frye) is one of the most eye-opening things ever written on *Songs,* an account of the horrors of an eighteenth-century sweep's existence that underlie the ironies of Blake's "innocent" perspective. The list of required readings on this poem need not extend further than Nurmi, but Porter Williams, Jr., in "'Duty' in Blake's 'The Chimney Sweeper' of *Songs of Innocence*" (*ELN,* 1974), and James Harrison (*Expl,* 1978) also reinforce the irony of discrepant perspectives. Robert Gleckner's "Irony in Blake's 'Holy Thursday'" (*MLN,* 1956) does for this poem in *Innocence* something of what Nurmi did for the "Sweeper" by laying out the historical context of the orphans' procession, making the obtuseness of the self-satisfied observer crystal clear. Thomas E. Connolly's "The Real 'Holy Thursday' of William Blake" (*BS* 6: 2 [1976]) shows that the day of the annual charity school service was neither Ascension Thursday nor Maundy Thursday but a variable springtime date. L. W. Cowie's "Holy Thursday" (*History Today,* 1977) illustrates the history of the ceremony over the course of a century. David V. Simpson's "Blake's Pastoral: A Genesis for 'The Ecchoing Green'" (*BIQ* no. 51, 13: 3 [1979]), though shapeless and overlong, usefully explores the iconography of the village oak. Rodney M. Baine and Mary R. Baine, "Blake's Blossom" (*CLQ,* 1978), argue that the speaker is a mother holding her child. Michelle Leiss Stepto, "Mothers and Fathers in Blake's *Songs of Innocence*" (*YR,* 1978), looks for the root of the Female Will in the gentle mothers of Innocence and the darkening of vision in images of the heavenly father. Jim S. Borck defends the expressive pointing in "Blake's 'The Lamb': The Punctuation of Innocence" (*TSL,* 1974). Rita Munson, "Blake's 'Night'" (*Unisa English Studies,* 1984), argues that "Night," frequently placed last in *Innocence,* is the most comprehensive vision of the innocent condition in that it looks toward Experience yet should not be read cynically. Thomas E. Connolly and George R. Levine, "Pictorial and Poetic Design in Two Songs of Innocence" (*PMLA,* 1967), discuss the haloed figure in "The Little Boy Found" as mother rather than Christ, thus inciting John E. Grant to occupy early issues of *Blake Newsletter* with a running debate (nos. 2, 3, 6, 7 [1967–68]).

In Blake's "final" arrangement of *Songs,* "The Little Girl Lost" and "The Little Girl Found" joined "A Little Girl Lost" in the *Experience* volume. The central issue in the lost-and-found poems about Lyca is whether the little girl's journey from her parents' home to the lions' desert takes her from life to death, innocence to experience, sexual unawareness to the threshold of sexual knowledge, or—as Kathleen Raine and other Neoplatonic critics hold—from preexistence to material incarnation. Blake's decision to transfer these two poems from *Innocence* to *Experience* also raises the question of how Lyca's situation is related to Ona's sexual trauma in "A Little Girl Lost." The best considerations of these matters are the least dogmatic. Irene H. Chayes's "Little Girls Lost: Problems of a Romantic Archetype" (*BNYPL,* 1963; rpt. *Blake,* ed. Frye) suggestively associates Lyca with Wordsworth's Lucy Gray and Keats's Madeline as variations on the Kore or Persephone figure, with the Lucy of Wordsworth's Goslar lyrics and Coleridge's Christabel further in the background. In "Blake and Tradition: 'The Little Girl Lost' and 'The Little Girl Found'" (*BNL* no. 13, 4: 1 [1970]), Chayes rescues the poems from Raine's otherworldly interpretation while recognizing the imagery in Thomas Taylor as one of many possible sources and analogues of Blake's symbolism. Michael Ackland takes up the transitional status of these poems in "Blake's Problematical Touchstones to Experience: 'Introduction,' 'Earth's Answer,' and the Lyca Poems" (*SIR,* 1980). Norma A. Greco, in "Blake's 'The Little Girl Lost': An Initiation into Womanhood" (*CLQ,* 1983), interprets Lyca's experience—with the aid of Mircea Eliade and Erich Neumann—as a death to her limited self and a rebirth into sexual maturity. Stuart Peterfreund's "The Name of Blake's Lyca Re-Examined" (*AN&Q*, 1975) and John Adlard's "The Age and Virginity of Lyca" (*BNL* no. 23, 6: 3 [1972 – 73]) struggle with cruxes.

The thorns, scratches, and soot awaiting explicators of the *Experience* poems have deterred no one. "The Tyger," of course, is the *Hamlet* of Blake criticism. Winston Weathers' *William Blake: The Tyger* (1969) gathers—in addition to excerpts from books—the following essays. Jesse Biers, "A Study of Blake's 'The Tyger' " (*Bucknell University Studies*, 1949), sees the tiger as both "that outward, powerful, tormenting evil that frustrates man" and the perverse inward self; to the mystic, these are not irreconcilable with ultimate good. Martin K. Nurmi, "Blake's Revisions of *The Tyger*" (*PMLA*, 1956), finds in the drafts ample evidence that Blake was working toward a complex affirmation of the tiger's divinity, etched in the final version. Philip Hobsbaum, "A Rhetorical Question Answered: Blake's Tyger and Its Critics" (*Neophil*, 1964), thinks the poet does not know who made the Tyger because there may be no answer; he echoes Frye's advice in "Blake after Two Centuries" to "leave it a question" and chides critics for attempting to do otherwise. Footnoting an excellent summary of previous criticism, Morton D. Paley, "Tyger of Wrath" (*PMLA*, 1966; rpt. Paley, *Twentieth Century Interpretations*, and absorbed into his *Energy and the Imagination*), notes the vocabulary of the religious sublime and faint parallels in Boehme and others and concludes that Los is the creator. Rodney M. Baine, "Blake's 'Tyger': The Nature of the Beast" (*PQ*, 1967), also explores images of Boehme and Swedenborg, along with physiognomical treatises, to show that the tiger is overwhelmingly associated with ferocious cruelty. In an essay written especially for the Weathers volume, Kay Parkhurst Long, "William Blake and the Smiling Tyger," using a reader-response approach, suggests that the poem parodies the Urizenic compulsion to find answers; through nonsense, it evokes "a kind of absurd laughter" that frees us to see many tigers, the inexhaustible possibilities within an imaginatively perceived universe.

A condensed version of Hazard Adams' "Reading Blake's Lyrics: 'The Tyger' " (*TSLL*, 1960; rpt. *Discussions*) appears in his 1963 book. Adams argues that the visionary power creates the tiger; to the opaque fallen eye, the beast is horrendous, but to the visionary "the tiger symbolizes the primal spiritual energy which may bring form out of chaos" and unite human beings with a rejected part of themselves. John E. Grant's "The Art and Argument of 'The Tyger,' " already mentioned, contrasts the fearful Tyger of the poem, who appears within history, with the bedraggled Tyger of the design, who is viewed from a more optimistic or prophetic perspective than the speaker alone has achieved. Kathleen Raine's "Who Made the Tyger?" (*Encounter*, 1954) reasons that God made the Lamb, but that Elohim, a lower demiurge, made the fallen world, including the Tyger. Paul Miner's " 'The Tyger': Genesis and Evolution in the Poetry of William Blake" (*Criticism*, 1962) traces connections with Blake's other references to tigers. In a pair of articles, Coleman O. Parsons usefully lays out the pictorial and cultural contexts of the poem and picture: "Tygers before Blake" (*SEL*, 1968) and "Blake's 'Tyger' and Eighteenth Century Animal Pictures" (*Art Quarterly*, 1968). Mary R. Baine and Rodney M. Baine perform a similar service in "Blake's Other Tygers, and 'The

Tyger'" (*SEL,* 1975). Warren Stevenson, "'The Tyger' as Artefact" (*BS* 2: 2 [1969]), classifies previous critics—to his own satisfaction—as "moralists," "synoptists," "rhetoricians," and "revisionists" and goes on to develop his own prosodic analysis; this discussion reappears in his *Divine Analogy: A Study of the Creation Myth in Blake and Coleridge* (1972). Robert O. Bowen identifies allusions to Daedalus, Icarus, and Prometheus in *The Explicator* (1949). In his introduction to the Viking Portable edition of Blake (1946), Alfred Kazin acutely analyses the rhetoric and rhythm of the poem, as do M. L. Rosenthal and A. J. M. Smith in *Exploring Poetry* (2nd ed. 1973). G. H. Pechey and E. H. Paterson discuss the poem in *Theoria* (1966 and 1967). Of possible value to linguists is E. L. Epstein's all-but-unreadable "The Self-Reflexive Artefact: The Function of Mimesis in an Approach to a Theory of Value for Literature," in *Structure and Style in Literature: Essays in the New Stylistics* (ed. Roger Fowler, 1975): his analysis of "The Tyger" is intended as the showpiece of the essay. In two versions of the same article—"Blake's Revolutionary Tiger" in *Articulate Images* (ed. Richard Wendorf, 1983) and "Blake's Lamb-Tiger," a chapter of *Representations of Revolution (1789–1820)* (1983)— Ronald Paulson attempts to read the poem as the response of a timid observer to the moral paradoxes generated by the French Revolution. Other worthwhile articles and notes on this poem are listed in Bentley's and Natoli's bibliographies. The search for critical novelties—and for answers to the overwhelming question—may conveniently be concluded with a glance at David Morice's not-to-be-missed comic strip in *Sparks of Fire* (rpt. *Poetry Comics,* 1982), which at last reveals the true nature of the Tyger's Frankensteinian creator. Gluttons for punishment may prefer Stanley Fish's parodic interpretation of the poem as an allegory of digestion in *Is There a Text in This Class?* (1980), a spoof provoked in part by Epstein's article.

"London" holds a fascination for explicators second only to "The Tyger." Sometime in the 1970s, perhaps with a push from Gillham's aforementioned *Blake's Contrary States,* there occurred a marked shift in the poem's perceived center of gravity—from the city to the speaker. The strongest forces influencing this shift are Bloom's "Blake and Revisionism" in his *Poetry and Repression* (1976) and Heather Glen's "The Poet in Society: Blake and Wordsworth on London" (*L&H,* 1976), along with her previously noted article in *Interpreting Blake.* For both Bloom and Glen, the speaker partakes of the corruption he seeks to expose. Bloom selects Ezekiel 9 as his precursor text, a passage also cited by Glen: here the prophet sets marks on the foreheads of selected inhabitants of Jerusalem. Bloom considers Blake's speaker deficient in "prophetic direction and prophetic purpose" as he wanders about setting marks upon Londoners. Glen recognizes that the external evil is real enough, but since the poet is "implicated and defined by his society," his repetitiveness is "relentless, restrictive," "thin and obsessive," and "imaginatively bankrupt" (but in her *Vision and Disenchantment,* previously mentioned, she sees the speaker as having a viewpoint close to Blake's own). Of several responses to Glen in *Literature and History,* the fullest is Gavin Edwards' linguistic analysis in "Mind-Forg'd Manacles: A Contribution to the Discussion of Blake's 'London'" (*L&H,* 1979). Graham Pechey's valuable though obscure essay "The London Motif in Some Eighteenth-Century Contexts: A Semiotic Study" has been mentioned in connection with Marxist-semiotic criticism. David Punter, "Blake and the Shapes of London" (*Criticism,* 1981), makes the point that the novelty of Blake's city poem lies in its identification, behind surface phenomena, of a "sinister and intricately connected system"; once it has been recognized as such, it can be changed. But E. P. Thompson's important essay "London," in *Interpreting Blake,* goes furthest toward restoring to the poem its searing "moral realism." Thompson follows the development of the political and apocalyptic overtones of Blake's language through stages of revision, politely rejecting Glen's denigration of the speaker in the adjacent essay.

The linguist Archibald A. Hill, in "Imagery and Meaning: A Passage from Milton, and from Blake" (*TSLL,* 1969; rev. in *Constituent and Pattern in Poetry,* 1976), works out semantic principles bearing on the metaphorical structure of this poem and on interpretive problems generally. D. H. Rawlinson, in "An Early Draft of Blake's 'London,' " in *The Practice of Criticism* (1968), demonstrates Blake's skill and inspiration in revising. V. Doyno's "Blake's Revision of 'London' " (*EIC,* 1972) points out, among other things, the acrostic of "HEAR" in the third stanza, and F. W. Bateson adds a postscript on the shift of power to the people in the last two stanzas, as the diseased harlot becomes "the avenging angel of capitalist *hubris.*" Karl Kiralis, in " 'London' in the Light of *Jerusalem*" (*BS* 1: 1 [1968]), urges recognition of the city's human form as developed in the epic. According to Max Duperray, "A la source de la ville fantastique: 'London' de William Blake" (*EA,* 1975), Blake's vision of the city prefigures well-known recent treatments of the modern city as a hellish phantasmagoria perceived by a night wanderer. John B. Radner's "The Youthful Harlot's Curse: The Prostitute as Symbol of the City in Eighteenth-Century English Literature" (*Eighteenth-Century Life,* 1976) contrasts the harlot of "London" with prostitutes described by Steele, Boswell, Johnson, Goldsmith, Fielding, and Wordsworth. Grant C. Roti and Donald L. Kent, in "The Last Stanza of Blake's 'London' " (*BIQ* no. 41, 11: 1 [1977]), adduce medical evidence in support of the accepted association of the "curse" with venereal disease, opposing Bloom's bizarre notion that it is menstruation. Jonathan Culler, *The Pursuit of Signs: Semiotics, Literature, Deconstruction* (1981), uses disagreements on "London" and particularly on "appalls" to demonstrate that interpreters, even though they reach different conclusions, rely on identifiable interpretative conventions to give shape to their experience of the poem. Finally, for a well-balanced, richly comprehensive study of "London" and the critical system surrounding it, including a sound appraisal of all major points in previous criticism, see Michael Ferber's " 'London' and Its Politics" (*ELH,* 1981).

From Damon to Hirsch to the present, there is next to no agreement on the meaning of "The Fly" or on the degree of sympathy the reader should have with the speaker. Grant, "Interpreting Blake's 'The Fly,' " already mentioned, reads the text against the picture and finds the speaker callous, a poor reasoner, "in error," though "Blake does not despise him for it." Hagstrum, "The Fly," in the Damon festschrift, using many of the same parallel readings as Grant, considers the speaker to be Everyboy, thoughtless but not guilty. An exchange between Michael J. Tolley and Hagstrum (*BS* 2: 1 [1969]) refines Grant's and Hagstrum's positions. Warren Stevenson, "Artful Irony in Blake's 'The Fly' " (*TSLL,* 1968), reiterates

Grant's point that the discrepancy between text and design is purposeful, as is the ironic incongruity between tone and subject matter. Gleckner, "Blake, Gray, and the Illustrations" (*Criticism,* 1977), making up for his confession in *The Piper and the Bard* that he did not understand the poem, starts from Damon's idea that Blake "reversed" Gray's idea of the fly; the speaker, who is imaginatively wrong, is "in a sense both Gray's speaker and Gray himself." Thomas E. Connolly, "Point of View in Interpreting 'The Fly'" (*ELN,* 1984), argues unpersuasively that (despite the if-then connection between stanzas 4 and 5) the Bard is the speaker of the fourth stanza.

The enigmatic self-containment of "The Sick Rose," its insulation from any point of external reference, has intrigued all commentators. Reuben A. Brower, "The Beautiful Gate of Enjoyment," in his *The Fields of Light* (1951), uses the poem to demonstrate his technique of reading from smaller to larger configurations of meaning. As phrased by John Neubauer, "The Sick Rose as an Aesthetic Idea: Kant, Blake, and the Symbol in Literature," in *Studies in Eighteenth-Century Culture: Irrationalism in the Eighteenth Century* (ed. Harold E. Pagliaro, 1972), "the poem is a single image with no commentary, no generalization, no hint at allegorical intention," and it is tantalizing precisely for this reason. After demonstrating the shortcomings of psychosexual, moral, social, and archetypal readings, Neubauer suggests that the poem illuminates Kant's concept of the "aesthetic idea," which is something that occasions much thought, yet conveys no definite thought adequate to its implications. For an undergraduate audience, T. R. Henn discusses the poem's "obscurity" in *The Apple and the Spectroscope* (1951). Michael Riffaterre, in "The Self-Sufficient Text" (*Diacritics,* 1973), attempts to analyze the poem on the basis of internal evidence alone, to "determine to what extent the literary text is self-sufficient." He wishes to avoid not only the referential fallacy but also "reference to the corpus of topoi, themes, and motives." His "reading" is quite successful, but he brings in numerous instances of traditional rose and worm imagery to establish the stereotype of their inherent polarity, so that in the end the poem is understood in relation to other poems after all. On the basis of discrepancies between text and design, J. F. Berwick, "*The Sick Rose:* A Second Opinion" (*Theoria,* 1976), considers the speaker—a sexually troubled female—to be the one who is sick, while in the design the rose, luxuriant in foliage, bends down toward the worm and in human form stretches out her welcoming arms.

On other songs, Grant's previously mentioned articles on the flower poems—which review earlier criticism—should be considered, along with Bloom's interpretation of the Sunflower's aspiration as a state of eternal frustration, G. M. Harper's incidental remarks on the Clytie myth in "The Source of Blake's 'Ah! Sun-Flower'" (*MLR,* 1953), and Hilton Landry's emphasis on erotic desire in "The Symbolism of Blake's Sunflower" (*BNYPL,* 1962); Johnson's article on emblem literature is also pertinent. Thomas N. Berninghausen's "The Marriage of Contraries in 'To Tirzah'" (*CLQ,* 1984) is the most thorough consideration to date of one of Blake's most difficult and demanding poems. On point of view in "The Clod & the Pebble," Hagstrum, in *Restoration and Eighteenth-Century Literature* (ed. Carroll Camden, 1963), argues that the reader's sympathies should lie with the Pebble because it has a healthy natural desire to please itself through aggressive physical love. Max F. Schulz (*PLL,* 1966) objects that neither Clod nor Pebble can stand as an absolute: the Clod is too meek and passive, the Pebble too insensitive; it is up to the Bard, who sees beyond their limitations, to place them in fruitfully ironic opposition.

Jakobson's illuminating linguistic analysis of "Infant Sorrow" was mentioned earlier; the fascinating process of the poem's composition is studied in Donald K. Moore's "Blake's Notebook Versions of *Infant Sorrow*" (*BNYPL,* 1972). John Bender and Anne Mellor, in "Liberating the Sister Arts: The Revolution of 'Infant Sorrow'" (*ELH,* 1983), argue that the poem and design rebel against the sister arts tradition in that with this combination Blake "presents the theoretical possibility of the nondependency and nonunification of the verbal and visual codes." Philip Gallagher, "The Word Made Flesh: Blake's 'A Poison Tree' and The Book of Genesis" (*SIR,* 1977), treats the poem as a countermyth correcting the biblical account of the Fall and the doctrine of original sin. The ever-skeptical F. W. Bateson uses the same poem as a proof-text in "Myth—A Dispensable Critical Term" (in *The Binding of Proteus,* 1980). Robert F. Gleckner's "William Blake and the Human Abstract" (*PMLA,* 1961) remains the best explication of the relationship between "The Human Abstract" and "The Divine Image." D. H. Rawlinson's "Relevance and Irrelevance in Response: Another Blake Poem," in his *The Practice of Criticism,* offers a lesson in responsible interpretation of "The Human Abstract." John Adlard, "The Garden of Love" (*BNL* no. 16, 4: 4 [1971]), shows that binding with briars was a traditional way to protect new graves, as illustrated at the bottom of Blake's plate. Rodney M. Baine, "Blake's 'The Little Vagabond'" (*Expl,* 1968), suggests that since Dame Lurch would have been recognized as a schoolmistress, Blake's indictment applies to the school as well as to the church. Stephen D. Cox, "Adventures of 'A Little Boy Lost': Blake and the Process of Interpretation" (*Criticism,* 1981), asks why this poem in *Experience* has been passed over by critics or made to mean nearly the opposite of what it seems to say. Expert readers have acquired great power over the text by assimilating it to Blake's larger systems of meaning and ignoring or neutralizing its troublesome side, namely, the boy's forthright argument for egotism in love. Cox proposes guidelines for interpreters: never neglect the meaning most accessible to nonspecialists; always consider evidence both for and against the proposed reading; don't sweep aside disturbing or anomalous aspects of the poem; keep the text open.

The best introduction to all the *Songs* is Frye's often reprinted essay "Blake's Introduction to *Experience*" (*HLQ,* 1957), which explicates "Introduction" and "Earth's Answer" together as a crystallization of Blake's whole system of symbolic thought. But Frye's respectful view of the Bard has recently been challenged. Those of us who take it for granted that the speaker of the "Introduction" is, to say the least, a reliable witness of Experience—prophetic, visionary, and imaginative—now find ourselves on the defensive. It is no longer possible to assume with Frye, as Schulz had done in his explication of "The Clod & the Pebble," that the Bard prefigures Blake's later hero Los—not Los as he is in *Urizen,* of course, but as he becomes in *The Four Zoas, Milton,* and *Jerusalem.* In books and articles already mentioned, Bateson, Bloom, Leader, Gleckner, and others have represented the Bard—in "Introduction," "The Voice of the Ancient Bard," and certain visionary passages in *Songs*—as authoritarian, error-prone, hypocritical, or worse. David V. Simpson's critique of "The Voice of the Ancient Bard," in *Irony and Authority in Romantic Poetry* (1979), shares their suspicions. The argument that the speaker of "London" is tainted by the world of experience, as advanced by Heather Glen and others, also reinforces the attack on the Bard's credibility.

Anyone aspiring to write a new full-scale study of *Songs* should, of course, assimilate the best that has gone before and strike the right balance between attention to the whole and to its parts. A new commentator should understand verbal and visual details in relation to the collection as a whole, the interplay between Innocence and Experience, and the meanings emphasized by Blake's rearrangements and retouchings, always keeping in mind the wider context of Blake's work and his place in relevant intellectual, literary, and pictorial traditions. Above all, the analytic voice should not drown out the glad pipings and notes of woe sounded by Blake's singers. The paragon who can manage all this without crushing the poetry, withering the designs, or discouraging new readers may not yet have appeared among us.

The Shorter Prophecies and Visionary Narratives. Two books have concentrated on the prophetic poems Blake wrote before he moved to Felpham in 1800. The first of these may now be considered entirely superseded; the second will keep its place as a standard work of criticism for years to come. Emily S. Hamblen's *On the Minor Prophecies of William Blake* (1930)—according to Damon's introduction—was "made deliberately independent of any other research." Not surprisingly, it consists largely of paraphrase. In contrast, Leslie Tannenbaum's erudite *Biblical Tradition in Blake's Early Prophecies: The Great Code of Art* (1982) brings centuries of exegetical and illustrative traditions to bear on Blake's "Lambeth books." Tannenbaum's book, which has already been discussed under "Contexts, Sources, and Approaches," is filled with insights into *The Marriage of Heaven and Hell, America, Europe, The Song of Los, Urizen, Ahania,* and *The Book of Los.* John Howard's uneven book *Infernal Poetics* (1984) attempts to show what constitutes Blake's "Bible of Hell."

Nancy Bogen's "Selected References" in her facsimile edition of *The Book of Thel* (1971) provides a convenient starting point for research on the earliest and most delicate of the illuminated narratives. Of the separate essays on Bogen's list, two stand out because they address the moral issue of self-sacrifice, first raised in H. M. Margoliouth's *William Blake.* In so doing, they depart from the firmly established Ellis-Yeats tradition—espoused by Frye and Damon—that Thel is an unborn soul who chooses not to enter the "death" of corporeal existence or, as in Bloom's version, to descend from Beulah to Generation. The first of these exceptional articles, Robert F. Gleckner's "Blake's *Thel* and the Bible" (*BNYPL,* 1960), though rich in new perceptions of the work, mercilessly attacks Thel's coldness, self-protectiveness, and timidity. Michael J. Tolley's milder characterization of Thel as a "selfish innocent" in *"The Book of Thel* and *Night Thoughts"* (*BNYPL*, 1965) hardly requires the dubious support of Young's poem. Together, however, Gleckner and Tolley shifted critical attention from the metaphysical to the moral sphere, where it now rests.

According to Mary Lynn Johnson's "Beulah, 'Mne Seraphim,' and Blake's *Thel,"* (*JEGP*, 1970), Thel's dialogues with natural objects intensify, by stages, her sense of existential and ontological crisis; her final shriek is at last a naked, authentic response to the anxieties voiced from the grave by her "buried self." In *Blake's Composite Art,* already discussed, W. J. T. Mitchell points to the irreconcilable difference between the reassuring answers Thel obtains by questioning others about death and the shock she receives when she herself explores her grave. He notes too the "absence of any finite moral norm"; Blake has "stripped away all the superior vantage points from which we might pass judgment" on the heroine. The designs convey "the rich sense of paradox and ambiguity latent in the apparent clarity of the poem," which is complete without pictures. In Wagenknecht's *Blake's Night,* mentioned earlier, almost buried under all the observations proclaimed by the author to be "interesting," lie several interpretative nuggets: "Blake's underlying concern . . . is with the relation between perception, or vision, and one's existential condition. . . . Thel, in her self-communion in the form of imaginary conversations, creates the images . . . against which in the end she rebels." Unlike many male critics who chide Thel for rejecting the destiny imposed on her by her anatomy, Wagenknecht observes sympathetically that her "dilemma is especially sharp because she is a woman"—conditioned not to act but to be acted upon.

In Bogen's own "New Interpretation," Thel hears in the complaining voice from her own grave her future adult role as "protester," a role she rejects in her present state of immaturity. Anne Kostelanetz Mellor, "Blake's Designs for *The Book of Thel:* An Affirmation of Innocence" (*PQ,* 1971), justifies Thel's flight as that of an innocent who wisely rejects the evils of experience to remain in Har, where she will eventually find fulfillment in love and motherhood. Roland A. Duerksen, "The Life-in-Death Theme of 'The Book of Thel' " (*BS* 2: 2 [1970]), tries to endorse Gleckner's sexual interpretation without relinquishing the earlier doctrine of preexistence. Christopher Heppner, " 'A Desire of Being': Identity in *The Book of Thel"* (*CLQ,* 1977), views Thel's crisis in the light of concepts of personal identity in Locke, Hume, Leibniz, and Swedenborg. According to Donald R. Pearce, "Natural Religion and the Plight of Thel" (*BS* 8: 1 [1978]), Thel retreats from experience because she has been nurtured on false naturalistic doctrines. Dennis Read, "Blake's 'Tender Stranger': *Thel* and Hervey's *Meditations"* (*CLQ,* 1982), detects verbal parallels that suggest to him that Blake's poem is an "anti-Graveyard School argument." Marjorie Levinson, " 'The Book of Thel' by William Blake: A Critical Reading" (*ELH,* 1980), allegorizes Thel as "the idea of Desire working out its motivation" and proclaims that not Thel but the "act of speech" is the protagonist of the piece. A supposed "foregrounding of the speech-act" in *Thel* has apparently encouraged this peculiarly contorted interpretation.

Miltonic parallels, noted generally by Damon and Schorer, are developed in detail by Rodger L. Tarr, " 'The Eagle' versus 'The Mole': The Wisdom of Virginity in *Comus* and *The Book of Thel*" (*BS* 3: 2 [1971]), and by Annette S. Levitt, "Comus, Cloud, and Thel's 'Unacted Desires' " (*CLQ,* 1978). Michael Ferber, in "Blake's *Thel* and the Bride of Christ" (*BS* 9 [1980]), establishes a coherent basis for biblical references collected by Gleckner and others by relating them to the imagery of the Song of Songs, but he breaks off without showing exactly what this contributes to our sense of Thel's "spiritual failure."

Many theories about *Thel* stem from a long-established derivation of the heroine's name from the Greek word for "wish" or "will" or "desire." Now everything must be reconsidered in the light of E. B. Murray's "Thel, *Thelypthora,* and the Daughters of Albion" (*SIR,* 1981), a rediscovery of a once-notorious tract on polygamy (or against seduction) published in 1780–81 by Martin Madan, a Methodist clergyman. Madan's coinage *Thelypthora* translates as "the ruin of woman." According to this tract, sexual union itself constitutes a marriage in the eyes of God: the seducer of a virgin, even if already married, is obligated to accept responsibility for his conquest by making her an additional wife. Although Madan's theories seem remote from Thel's conversations with animated natural objects, Murray argues that in 1789 the word "Thel" could have had no other connotations than those evoked by Madan's title. Tolley had previously suggested in a footnote the derivation from "woman," though he did not note the currency of the word through Madan or point out that the root word is spelled with an eta rather than an epsilon. (Emily S. Hamblen had extracted the name from a different root, meaning "soft persuasive charm.")

By comparison with *Thel,* critical response to *Visions of the Daughters of Albion* has been meager, though the heroine, Oothoon, is universally regarded as one of Blake's most compelling and sympathetic figures. Jane E. Peterson, "The *Visions of the Daughters of Albion*: A Problem in Perception" (*PQ,* 1973), presents in an early footnote a fairly complete but awkwardly organized working bibliography, sorted under four nonparallel headings: Neoplatonic, historical or biographical, "free love," and the movement from innocence to experience. Peterson's promising idea that the poem dramatizes Blake's theory of perception freezes into a stern assessment of each character's precise degree of deviation from correct perception; in the end Oothoon herself, along with her impercipient lovers, is blamed for seeing only with her outward eye. If Peterson had considered John Middleton Murry's commentary in his 1933 Dent facsimile edition, mentioned earlier, she might have found guidance: "the devastating criticism of current sexual morality of which Oothoon is the vehicle" is "simply part of a larger vision: it is implicit in the realization that body is a portion of soul discerned by the five senses." A year later, in his *William Blake,* Murry published a fuller interpretation, "The Awakened Woman," using Lawrentian sexual doctrine as a foil and identifying the theme as "the passing of a woman's soul from innocence through experience to a new innocence." Roland A. Duerksen's "The Life of Love: Blake's Oothoon" (*CLQ,* 1977) registers general approval of the heroine and her principles.

That historical criticism need be neither dry nor reductive is made manifest in David V. Erdman's often-reprinted "Blake's Vision of Slavery" (*JWCI*, 1952; incorporated into his *Prophet against Empire*). Erdman passionately delineates Blake's antislavery position by pointing out correspondences between *Visions* and John G. Stedman's *Narrative* of the horrors of the slave system in Guiana, for which Blake made unforgettable engravings. Henry H. Wasser's "Notes on the *Visions of the Daughters of Albion* by William Blake" (*MLQ*, 1945), weakened by biographical inaccuracies, suggests the possible influence of Mary Wollstonecraft as writer and personal acquaintance. Vernon E. Lattin, "Blake's Thel and Oothoon: Sexual Awakening in the Eighteenth Century" (*Literary Criterion* [India], 1981), argues that Blake presents "opposite types of eighteenth-century females" in *Thel* and *Visions* by contrasting Thel's "passive ambivalence" with Oothoon's awareness of "woman's sexual awakening as the way of vision and freedom."

D. G. Gillham's neglected article "Blake: *Visions of the Daughters of Albion*" (*WascanaR*, 1968), which became the best chapter in his *William Blake*, advances the theory that Bromion and Theotormon are complementary types, virtually two halves of one being, who contrast with Oothoon's complex but integrated sense of self. Through their speeches Blake caricatures leading philosophies of the Enlightenment. Bromion is a sensationalist, Theotormon a rationalist: "The one denies real identity to the knower while the other denies substantial reality to what is known." Mark Bracher, in "The Metaphysical Grounds of Oppression in Blake's *Visions of the Daughters of Albion*" (*CLQ*, 1984), proceeds further along these lines without reference to Peterson or Gillham: Oothoon's authentic being is denied by both the empiricist-hedonist Bromion and the idealist-theocentrist Theotormon. E. B. Murray, "A Pictorial Guide to Twofold Vision: Copy 'O' of *Visions of the Daughters of Albion*," in *Sparks of Fire*, considers Bromion an aspect of Theotormon and even finds a suggestion of his profile hidden in Theotormon's bouffant hair on plate seven of the highly finished British Museum copy of the work. (Weird optical effects of this kind, some in the manner of M.C. Escher, are not uncharacteristic of Blake, as noted also in the study of the three British Museum copies of *Songs* by Norvig and Glazer-Schotz, cited earlier, and in Dilworth's essay on "Milton's track," mentioned later. Clear instances of this peculiarity have never been brought together for study, and the question of accident versus intentionality has never been properly addressed—but see essays by Carr and N. Warner reviewed under "General Studies: Art and Theory.")

Howard H. Hinkel, "From Energy and Desire to Eternity: Blake's *Visions of the Daughters of Albion*" (*PLL*, 1979), takes this poem to mark a transition in Blake's understanding of apocalyptic change—from external revolution as in *Marriage* and *America* (both also probably first printed in 1793) to transformation of consciousness in a moment of vision, as in the later epics. Yves Denis, "William Blake: 'Visions des Filles D'Albion' " (*Temps Moderne*, 1970), places the work in the sexual-political milieu of the late 1960s. In *Acts of Inclusion* (1979), Michael G. Cooke discusses the theme of forgiveness as contributing to the Romantic understanding of "consequences": Oothoon's forgiveness of Theotor-

mon "extends and authenticates her *forgiveness of herself.*" Mark Anderson, in
"Oothoon, Failed Prophet" (*RP&P,* 1984), argues that the heroine's continuing desire for Theotormon's approval stifles her visionary powers and focuses the reader's attention on her tragedy rather than her prophetic message. According to
John G. Moss, who, like Peterson, does not cite Gillham, the poem is "meticulously arranged as a forensic oration," an eight-part Ciceronian argument. Verbal
and visual structural units should be further considered by someone able to pick
up where W. H. Stevenson left off in his annotated Longman edition (1971). Susan
Fox's feminist essay and Michael Ackland's essay on Wollstonecraft, both cited
earlier, as well as interpretations by Bloom and others mentioned in the "General
Studies" section, should not be overlooked. Good as they are in their separate
ways, though, the various studies of important aspects of this poem seem never
to converge upon a firm critical center; Oothoon wails on just at the margin of
our comprehension.

Max Plowman's discovery of the verbal-visual "chapters" of *The Marriage of
Heaven and Hell* (in his 1927 Dent facsimile) is compatible with Martin K.
Nurmi's often-excerpted study *Blake's Marriage of Heaven and Hell* (1957), in
which the organization of the alternating themes of the work is compared with
"the A B A' of the ternary form in music." According to Nurmi, the first section
introduces the idea of progression through contraries, the second deals with expanded sense perception, and the third returns with modulations to the theme
of contraries; each major section is in turn made up of secondary contrasting
units, usually an expository segment followed by a "Memorable Fancy." Nurmi's
historical and critical survey of fundamental Blakean concepts in the *Marriage*
remains central. So too does Harold Bloom's highly compressed "Dialectic in *The
Marriage of Heaven and Hell*" (*PMLA,* 1958; rpt. in his *Ringers in the Tower,*
1971, and in *English Romantic Poets: Modern Essays in Criticism,* ed. M. H.
Abrams, 1960, first ed. only). Bloom discusses the work in more detail in his
Blake's Apocalypse. Martin Price presents an excellent brief analysis in *To the
Palace of Wisdom,* already mentioned

What Plowman did for the structure of the *Marriage* and Nurmi did for its
major themes, Bloom has done for its genre. In *Blake's Apocalypse,* he places it in
the subcategory of satire that Frye designated "Menippean" in *Anatomy of Criticism* (1957)—a boisterous medley of prose and verse, an "anatomy." Refining this
point, Leslie Tannenbaum, in "Blake's News from Hell: *The Marriage of Heaven
and Hell* and the Lucianic Tradition" (*ELH,* 1975), argues that Blake fuses
Christian-prophetic and classical-satirical elements to create "prophetic satire"
for the purpose of "subverting all previous epics and prophecies" in preparation
for his later works in the revolutionary genre of "epic-prophecy." According to
Lawrence Lipking, "Blake's Initiation: *The Marriage of Heaven and Hell,*" in
Woman in the Eighteenth Century and Other Essays (ed. Fritz and Morton, 1976;
rpt. in his *The Life of the Poet,* 1981), the work belongs to a distinct but nameless
literary kind with "a long and honorable history"; this genre he christens "The Initiation," a type familiar in "various portraits of artists as young men." Mary V.
Jackson's "Prolific and Devourer: From Nonmythic to Mythic Statement in *The
Marriage of Heaven and Hell* and *A Song of Liberty*" (*JEGP,* 1971) has Blake work-

ing out variations on the system of contraries through a repertoire of styles until in the concluding song he arrives at mythic condensation, which he uses in his subsequent writings.

Bloom's primary explications of the shorter narrative units of the *Marriage* have remained standard points of reference. Taking up the episodes in which Blake and the Angel show each other their "eternal lot," Morris Eaves, in "A Reading of Blake's *Marriage of Heaven and Hell,* Plates 17–20" (*BS* 4: 2 [1972]), traces imagery of Blake's etching process. David V. Erdman, in "The Cave in the Chambers," a postscript to his bibliographical essay in the 1969 festschrift for Damon, allegorizes hell's printing house as Blake's workshop. Robert F. Gleckner points out parallels with *The Faerie Queene,* book 2, in "Edmund Spenser and Blake's Printing House in Hell" (*SAQ,* 1982). Hazard Adams, in "Blake, *Jerusalem,* and Symbolic Form" (*BS* 7: 2 [1975]), reads the expository section on the ancient poets as a parable of the collapse of metaphorical language. Previously noted studies by Morton D. Paley and John Howard suggest shades of meaning that only the Swedenborgian community would have perceived.

In a probing semiological study, *"The Marriage of Heaven and Hell:* A Text and Its Conjecture" (*Oxford Literary Review,* 1979), Graham Pechey argues that Blake adopts the rude and irreverent tone of such plebeian genres as the chapbook and the radical political pamphlet to dislocate and profane the high philosophical themes of polite culture. Pechey breaks through Plowman's and Nurmi's structural analyses to uncover chiasmus: "Themes and motives of the first half [seven of fourteen sections] return in the second," in reverse order and in a different modality. The brilliance and vigor of Pechey's ideas shine through the miasma of his up-to-date terminology; no one should write on the *Marriage* without working through this article.

In the introduction to his facsimile edition, mentioned earlier, Clark Emery had partially anticipated Pechey's intricate pattern of reversals. In addition to the pamphlet and the chapbook that Pechey mentions as models, others have been proposed: the children's primer in Gary J. Taylor, "The Structure of the *Marriage*: A Revolutionary Primer" (*SIR,* 1974); the Bible in Edward Terry Jones, "Another Look at the Structure of *The Marriage of Heaven and Hell* " (*BNL* no. 40, 10: 4 [1977]), and in Randel Helms, "Blake's Use of the Bible in 'A Song of Liberty' " (*ELN,* 1979). Helms also clarifies a puzzling episode in "Why Ezekiel Ate Dung" (*ELN,* 1978). Michael E. Holstein's fine article "Crooked Roads without Improvement: Blake's 'Proverbs of Hell' " (*Genre,* 1975) shows that Blake reinvigorates the aphoristic form by grafting the depleted shoot of philosophic tradition to the sturdy stock of folk wisdom. Mark Roberts, "Blake and the Damnation of Reason" in his *The Tradition of Romantic Morality* (1973), uses the Proverbs to expound Blake's doctrine of energy. Hatusko Niimi, "The Proverbial Language of Blake's *Marriage of Heaven and Hell* " (*SEL* [Japan], English no. [1982]), contrasts the Proverbs with the aphoristic expressions of Trusler, Fuseli, and Reynolds.

Pechey excuses himself from discussing the designs by declaring them "very much a subordinate element in the whole." A sounder justification would have been to acknowledge that David V. Erdman and his associates Tom Dargan and Marlene Deverell-Van Meter, "Reading the Illuminations of Blake's *Marriage of*

Heaven and Hell," in the 1973 festschrift for Keynes, with their magnifying-glass scrutiny even of interlinear capriccios, have left very little for anyone else to discover. Keynes managed to make a few refinements in his notes for the Oxford University Press facsimile edition, already mentioned. Both Keynes and the Erdman team provide clear, precisely labeled enlargements of the minuscule designs.

The "Lambeth books" or shorter prophecies lend themselves particularly well to historical interpretation. In addition to identifying topical references and allusions to Joel Barlow's *Vision of Columbus* in *Prophet against Empire,* David V. Erdman has written the best single essay on a shorter prophecy—*"America:* New Expanses" *(BVFD;* rpt. *Blake's Poetry and Designs)*—in which he "reads" both text and pictures "as an acting version of a mural Apocalypse." Erdman shows that the book begins in silence, with the tableaux of frontispiece and title page, and builds to the sound of thunders and war clarions in the text. His introductory remarks on the seventh plate of *Jerusalem* and the notes on the Mundane Shell and the Orc Cycle are also valuable.

David E. James, "Angels out of the Sun: Art, Religion, and Politics in Blake's *America"* *(SIR,* 1979), considers the embarrassing disparity between Blake's revolutionary aims and his difficult style and expensive means of publication, which ironically restricted his audience to initiates and connoisseurs. James contends that Blake, rejecting the division between mental and physical labor, enacted the conjunction of spiritual and material reality prophesied in the poetry. Ronald Schliefer, "Simile, Metaphor, and Vision: Blake's Narration of Prophecy in *America"* *(SEL,* 1979), claims that Blake articulates "the transformation of simile to metaphor"; the poem enacts its prophecy and marks the entrance of Orc into history. As background for these and other interpretive comments, Bentley's important bibliographical essay, already noted, should be kept in mind. W. H. Stevenson, "The Shaping of Blake's *America"* *(MLR,* 1960), infers from a collation of copies that the poem underwent "piecemeal" development in response to current events.

Vincent A. De Luca, "Ariston's Immortal Palace: Icon and Allegory in Blake's Prophecies" *(Criticism,* 1970), takes the abrupt intrusion of a mythic dimension, the self-contained account of Ariston's Atlantis, as an example of an "iconic" passage. Such passages interrupt the narrative sequence by introducing transcendent, highly charged, but tantalizingly self-enclosed images that alter tone and syntax to produce a sudden insight. According to Deborah Dorfman, " 'King of Beauty' and 'Golden World' in Blake's *America:* The Reader and the Archetype" *(ELH,* 1979), the "text generates conflicts that resist resolution" yet demand interpretation. Possible negative overtones in the passage were first picked up by Dennis M. Welch, "America and Atlantis: Blake's Ambivalent Millennialism" *(BNL* no. 22, 6: 2 [1971]).

Commentaries on other poems in the "continent" sequence can be quickly listed. Michael J. Tolley's *"Europe:* 'To those ychain'd in sleep,' " in *BVFD,* the only substantial essay on that work, examines text and designs with particular reference to Blake's political reworking of Milton's *On the Morning of Christ's Nativity.*

Leslie Tannenbaum's stimulating chapter on *Europe* in his *Biblical Tradition* errs, I think, only in representing the Shadowy Female in the Preludia of *America* and *Europe* as two separate figures. Bibliographical notes by Lincoln and Larrissey have already been mentioned. Carol P. Kowle, "Plate iii and the Meaning of *Europe*" (*BS* 8: 1 [1978]), examines links between the first page of text (present in only two copies) and the rest of the poem but fails to fulfill the very large implication of her title. *The Song of Los* was quite neglected until David V. Erdman's "The Symmetries of the *Song of Los*" (*SIR*, 1977). According to Erdman, the two subdivisions of this work, "Africa" and "Asia," are "prophecy foreshortened to song" and are built to enclose the longer poems, as cues in the text indicate. James McCord's "Historical Dissonance and William Blake's *The Song of Los*" (*CLQ*, 1984) is a straightforward explication confirming the received interpretation. Cecil Anthony Abrahams, *William Blake's Fourfold Man* (1978), draws on both historical scholarship and the work of present-day African poets in his intensive analysis of the "Africa" section, extending his notice to "The Little Black Boy," *Visions of the Daughters of Albion,* and other passages on slavery and racial stereotyping. Of the other prophecies of the Lambeth period, only *The Book of Urizen* has accumulated a long bibliography. The solitary essay on its sequel, Morton D. Paley's "Method and Meaning in Blake's *The Book of Ahania*" (*BNYPL*, 1966), incorporated into his *Energy and Imagination,* centers on Fuzon as Blake's critique of blind rebellion, a nonapocalyptic release of energy. The third work in this trilogy, *The Book of Los,* has attracted no attention outside the standard works of Damon, Frye, and Bloom, except for Sibyl C. Jacobson's sketchy presentation of parallels in "The Creation and Fall in *The Book of Urizen* and *The Book of Los:* A Study of Corresponding Images" (*CP,* 1974). Patricia Cramer's interesting psychological study "The Role of Ahania's Lament in Blake's *Book of Ahania*" (*JEGP,* 1984) complements both Paley's essay and Gallant's Jungian study.

The involuted intrinsic and extrinsic puzzles of *The Book of Urizen* (entitled in early printings *The First Book of Urizen*) are difficult to explain, let alone straighten out. To begin with, the fact that this work has full-page illustrations but no fixed page order would seem to preclude large-scale structural analysis or the detection of verbal-visual correlations. Quite to the contrary, however, three major articles on structure were published almost simultaneously: W. J. T. Mitchell, "Poetic and Pictorial Imagination in Blake's *Book of Urizen*" (*ECS,* 1969; rev. as part of *Blake's Composite Art,* 1978); Karl Kroeber, "Graphic-Poetic Structuring in Blake's *Book of Urizen*" (*BS* 3: 1 [1970]); and Robert E. Simmons, "*Urizen:* The Symmetry of Fear," in *BVFD* (1970); these were soon followed by Morris Eaves, "The Title-Page of *The Book of Urizen*" in the Keynes festschrift (1972), and Mollyanne Marks, "Structure and Irony in Blake's 'The Book of Urizen'" (*SEL,* 1975).

It is convenient to begin with Kroeber because his essay is "*not* an interpretation" but rather "a definition of formal principles of interaction between verse and pictures." He points out that Blake's poetry is "locked into" the pictorial and graphic unit of the engraved plates; the sequence of plates could be varied (very freely indeed in the case of the full-page designs in *Urizen*), but the aesthetic integrity of single plates could not be violated. He provides a handy table of sequential variations among the seven copies (maddeningly, the Keynes-Wolf "ideal order," which he also lists, does not match any of these). The chart does not quite show that the text-bearing plates remain in reasonably stable positions, as the article itself makes clear; the contrast between the first and last plates, for example, is essential to the meaning of the work and was never varied. Kroeber anticipates the better-known theories of Mitchell and Eaves by emphasizing that "Blake's pictures depict not what we perceive but how we perceive." His emphasis on "the equal independence of the two modes," with the graphic system acting as a "counterthrust" to the verbal, is strongly reiterated in Mitchell's work.

Unfortunately, Kroeber's chart of variations—essential to any study of the work—was unavailable to Simmons, whose intricate system of parallels and contrasts among all twenty-eight plates is based on the "ideal" Keynes-Wolf ordering, which corresponds only some of the time to any one of Blake's own arrangements. Where the bilateral symmetries happen to fit an actual copy, however, they fit quite well; and as Hagstrum notes (in one of the many miscellaneous comments by essayists and editors that oddly crowd the footnotes of *Blake's Visionary Forms Dramatic*), the kind of symmetrical structure Simmons detects resembles the chiasmus of Hebrew poetry, a pattern mentioned also in Pechey's article on *The Marriage of Heaven and Hell*. Simmons correctly notes Blake's frequent expression of parallels through "opposites as well as similars": mortality may be signified by both births and deaths, causality by both causes and effects, division by both unions and separations. By means of linguistic ambiguities and the compounding of meaning through the designs, Blake causes the finite, symmetrical, fixed universe of Urizen to imply (and arouse a longing for) the infinite, sensual, and changing sphere of the Eternals. Mitchell's essay, reworked for *Blake's Composite Art* without consideration of Kroeber's article, independently bears down on the "atemporal, antisequential" quality of the designs as a "deliberate formal device, a way of augmenting the antinarrative elements disclosed by the text." The eighteen stable plates provide a framework within which the ten movable plates are varied. The designs on the stable plates, though nonillustrative, parallel the movement of the narrative. The "epic wit" of *Urizen* overturns the Miltonic pantheon and subjects the "potential egotism and megalomania of the bardic role" to ironic criticism.

Mitchell's perception that Blake recognized something of himself in Urizen as well as Los was developed in another way by John Sutherland in "Blake and Urizen" (*BVFD*), cited among the psychological studies of Blake. Mitchell's conception of "epic wit" is further developed in Leslie Tannenbaum's "Blake's Art of Crypsis: *The Book of Urizen* and Genesis" (*BS* 5: 2 [1972]), revised for his *Biblical Tradition in Blake's Early Prophecies* (1982). Tannenbaum presents the work as a sustained satiric interpretation of Genesis that is "deeply indebted to the literary and exegetical traditions" surrounding that book, particularly Gnostic tradition (as discussed also in Clark Emery's introduction to his facsimile edition). The agents of creation and fall, Urizen and Los, reflect the two distinct conceptions of the Creator in Genesis—as Elohim and Jahweh (or Jehovah) in separate strands of the intertwined narrative. Paul A. Cantor's *Creature and Creator: Myth-Making and English Romanticism* (1984) contains an excellent chapter on Urizen, "The Demonic Creator." Mitchell and Tannenbaum each advance a parodic interpretation of the title page: in Mitchell the Creator is a two-fisted writer-illustrator: in Tannenbaum the Judge is a blind inscriber in the books of Life and Death. These ideas are compatible with Eaves's more detailed "reading" of the title page in his brief contribution to the Keynes festschrift.

Tannenbaum's study appeared too late to influence Mollyanne Marks's article "Structure and Irony," but the two present complementary theses. Marks feels that Blake's "sustained use of irony explains his apparent and otherwise inexplicable redundance" as well as his use of similar images for both creation and fall. In writing and designing, Blake "imitates the ordering process he mocks," yet his irony saves him from "becoming what he beholds." The "subject, structure, and images of the poem insist that the poet's mind mirrors the reality he challenges and that a fallen consciousness is fallen indeed." The problem of self-consciousness and the self-doubt of the imagination becomes central to the later poems, *Jerusalem* in particular, and it has been increasingly the focus of critical interest in Blake's work as a whole. According to Marc Rosenberg, "Style and Meaning in *The Book of Urizen*" (*Style*, 1970), Blake's style reflects his "imaginative ontology." Partly through syntactic dislocations, the metaphors or similes introduced as aspects or attributes of something else abruptly take on an existence of their own at the "literal" level. The comparison of Urizen's shadow to such things as a spiderweb, a female in embryo, and something "twisted like to the human brain" that metamorphoses into the "Net of Religion," all work to dissolve the barrier between literal and physical planes of reality, "short-circuiting our linguistic and perceptual habits."

Carmen S. Kreiter, in "Evolution and William Blake" (*SIR*, 1964), attributes to Blake's probable acquaintance with the surgeon John Hunter and his collection of preserved fetuses the amazingly accurate and up-to-date anatomical, physiological, and embryological imagery in *Urizen*, even to the point of anticipating the principle that "ontogeny recapitulates phylogeny." David Charles Leonard, "Erasmus Darwin and William Blake" (*Eighteenth-Century Life*, 1978), considers Darwin a more likely source of Blake's knowledge of embryology (see also David Worrall's article, cited above). The commentary section in Easson and Easson's 1978 facsimile edition focuses on human embryology (without documentation) and also attempts to work out an elaborate analogy with methods of book production. Eugene J. Harding, "Jacob Boehme and Blake's 'The Book of Urizen'" (*Unisa English Studies*, 1970), shows how Blake transformed one of his likely sources. More passive assimilation is suggested in most other studies of Blake and Boehme, but P. H. Butter, "Blake's *Book of Urizen* and Boehme's *Mysterium Magnum*," in *Le Romantisme anglo-américain* (ed. Roger Asselineau et al., 1971), finds differences rather than similarities. Harald A. Kittel's "*The Book of Urizen* and *An Essay Concerning Human Understanding*," in *Interpreting Blake*, claims only that "portions" of the work "may be read as" satire against Lockean epistemology; Urizen's fall "gains in significance" if so read, but the poem is "neither a systematic nor an explicit critique of the *Essay.*" In the end, for *Urizen* as for all of Blake's difficult works, Dorothy Plowman's deceptively simple advice in her 1929 facsimile should be fastened to the heart with hoops of steel:

> There are books that will explain to you the meaning of every word Blake wrote, but when you have read them all through you will not know as much about *The Book of Urizen,* as if you had spent half an hour poring over one of Blake's own pages.

When Plowman herself, as mother of a newborn, first opened the poem, she understood only one phrase, the "globe of life blood trembling"; to her credit, she had the courage to start from there.

The Longer Prophecies. Some awkwardness and distortion will obviously result from my reserving consideration of *Vala,* or *The Four Zoas,* for a later section, for it has strong ties with the finished illuminated poems *Milton* and *Jerusalem*: this linkage was recognized by Stuart Curran and Joseph Wittreich when they gathered the essays for *Blake's Sublime Allegory* (1973). In all three long poems, the discontinuities, dislocations, and shocks to the reader's system of expectations have recently been interpreted as enactments of central themes: that is, blocked avenues to spiritual regeneration are opened through the artist's relentless assaults on the reader's epistemological and perceptual centers of resistance. In all three poems, a search for linear narrative continuity has come to be considered futile; the true structure is revealed in what Frye calls "a single simultaneous pattern of apprehension" in "The Road of Excess" (1963; rpt. *The Stubborn Structure,* 1970). A thread running through much of the commentary on *Milton* and *Jerusalem* and implicit in essays on *The Four Zoas* (see those by McNeil and Ault, for example) comes to the surface in Hazard Adams' "Blake and the Muse" (*BR,* 1967): these are "poems, in a sense, about their own composition." In spite of these affinities, consideration of *The Four Zoas* must be postponed; Blake's achievement is more clearly recognized if his published illuminated works are set apart as a "canon" distinct from those he never etched, printed, or offered for sale. *The Four Zoas* was a work perpetually in progress; *Milton* and *Jerusalem,* though no two finished copies of either work are exactly alike, did achieve canonical status.

The organization of this review—merely the most workable of the compromises considered—has the further drawback of separating scholarship on *Milton* from that on two related topics: Miltonic influences on Blake's poetry and Blake's pictorial criticism of Milton's work. *Angel of Apocalypse: Blake's Idea of Milton* (1975), by Joseph Anthony Wittreich, Jr., unites these areas of concern. Along with other general studies of Blake's relationship to Milton, *Angel of Apocalypse* is considered above, under "Contexts, Sources, and Approaches"; along with other books and articles on the Milton illustrations, Pamela Dunbar's and Stephen Behrendt's books are mentioned below, under "Pictorial Works."

Milton appears slightly more hospitable to new readers than does *Jerusalem.* For one thing, it is only about half as long. Familiar names can be spotted within the morass of Blakean neologisms: the title page refers to John Milton and quotes a famous line from *Paradise Lost;* one scene appears to take place in the front garden of "Blake's Cottage at Felpham," according to the caption under a realistic-looking picture; plates labeled "William" and "Robert" depict Blake himself and his own brother. Surely, the naive reader thinks, I can manage this one. But once the threshold is cleared, recognizable props are knocked down from all sides—and by then it is too late to back out. Many weary and exciting months or years later the initiate emerges from an experience like nothing else in literature, cherishing some flickering insights that need to be kept alive, strengthened, and made available to others. Thus it happens that *Milton* has been read, reread, taught, and written about more often than either *The Four Zoas* or *Jerusalem.*

During the middle to late seventies, three books and one special number of *Blake Studies* were devoted to *Milton.* A fourth book, Mark Bracher's *Being Form'd: Thinking through Blake's Milton* (1984), has just been announced. The most rewarding of the full-length studies is Susan Fox's admirably plainspoken and orderly *Poetic Form in Blake's* Milton (1976), a patient and detailed account of structural correspondences between book 1, on Milton, and book 2, on Ololon. Fox's common sense, unpretentiousness, and determination to keep a steady eye on the poem in its fullest form, copy D, inspire confidence. Her complex system of correlations—perhaps easier to grasp as a whole in its more condensed earlier appearance, "The Structure of a Moment: Parallelism in the Two Books of Blake's *Milton*" (*BS* 2: 1 [1969]) — sets forth the "overriding structural principle" that governs the otherwise "delirious chaos" of multiple perspectives and simultaneity of events in the narrative. Wittreich, for his own purposes in *Angel of the Apocalypse,* independently outlines the basic system of parallels with admirable clarity and succinctness:

> Book I is concerned with the making of the poet, Book II with the making of the poem. . . . The Songs of Beulah in Book II find their structural analogue in the Song of the Bard in Book I. In each instance, the songs provide the immediate philosophical context for the book they preface: the Song of the Bard evolves a theory of psychological types, and the Songs of Beulah enunciate Blake's philosophy of contraries and his conception of states and individuals. In each book, the songs are followed by a descent [of Milton in I and of Ololon in II]. . . . Book I ends with a vision of the time-world, Book II with a vision of eternity of which the time-world is an image.

In Fox's view, such parallelism is actually "the theme of the poem realized concretely as its narrative." Her examples of echoes, cyclical patterns, paired verse paragraphs, and the like go far toward establishing her claim that the poem is precisely ordered down to the last detail. Pictorial parallels are relegated to an appendix. By concentrating so narrowly on internal architecture, however, Fox impoverishes the effect of some of the richest passages of biblical and Miltonic al-

lusion in all of Blake's poetry. At some points the verbal parallels seem forced for
the sake of mechanical symmetry. But expert discussions of the general plan of
the work and of such ideas and images as Eternity, the Vortex, and the garment
more than make up for minor shortcomings.

John Howard, *Blake's Milton: A Study in the Selfhood* (1976), begins by
noting that in Blake's time the "psychological language necessary to express the
conflict between [impulses of self-imprisonment and self-liberation] had not yet
been created"; therefore, Blake invented "sublime allegory," using a symbolic
structure that would accommodate his vision of the interplay of cosmic, historical, artistic, and personal forces within the human psyche. Howard ignores all
visual features; he is primarily interested in Blake's psychological insights and
their applications. About half the book consists of "background" to Blake's key
ideas, with emphasis on his concept of the paralyzing, inhibiting system of inner
restraints that he called the "Selfhood" and the metaphor of the journey within.
Although the subjects are familiar, Howard freshens them with pithy quotations
or paraphrases—for example, Priestley on materialism, Swedenborg on the relationship between the material and the physical, Abraham Tucker on the vehicular
body. Some of his best points, however, are buried in discursive footnotes that
should have been incorporated within the text, such as his two-page discussion of
the Bard's Song and his tantalizing speculation that Urizen's name is derived
from *orizon* or *ourizen,* the horizon line in "Renaissance studies of the art of perspective" (unidentified).

If it is fair to say that Fox reduces *Milton* to its formal structure and that
Howard reduces it to elementary principles of psychology, then David E. James,
Written Within and Without: A Study of Blake's Milton (1978), too frequently reduces it to a restatement of its own dicta, so that one develops a claustrophobic
sense of being trapped inside the poem. James breaks the work into five main
sections: the Bard's Song, Milton's response, and Milton's exploration of his
shadow in book 1 and Ololon's journey and the final apocalypse in book 2. Narrative dislocations and the fragmenting of time and space (compared at one point
to cubist techniques in painting) challenge the audience's reading habits in order
"to modify quite specifically and radically our whole perceptive process." James
usefully disentwines the main narrative threads to allow separate consideration
of Milton's heroic actions, which consist largely of "statements of insight, of perceptions in which he either recognizes past errors or affirms new truths." The
poem reenacts the inspired moment in which Blake rejected political solutions in
favor of artistic ones; simultaneously, it re-creates the process of its own creation
and awakens the creative powers of the reader. James makes only "incidental reference" to the pictures; all three books on Blake, indeed, are concerned almost
exclusively with verbal structure. Debate on *Milton* should probably also take
note of four long reviews: Fox's review of James (*BIQ* no. 49, 13: 1 [1979]), Leslie
Brisman's review of Fox and Morris Eaves's review of Howard (both in *SIR,* 1977),
and Mary Lynn Johnson's review of Fox and Wittreich (*Milton and the Romantics,*
1976).

The gem of the special *Milton* number of *Blake Studies,* edited by Karl
Kroeber for the 1973 MLA convention, is W. J. T. Mitchell's "Style and Iconography

in the Illustrations of Blake's *Milton*" (*BS* 6: 1 [1973]), a companion to his essay of the same year on the text, "Blake's Radical Comedy: Dramatic Structure as Meaning in *Milton*," in *Blake's Sublime Allegory*. As in his later book, *Blake's Composite Art*, Mitchell prefers to consider text and design separately. In "Blake's Radical Comedy," he traces the sequential unfolding of Blake's "vision of a providential resolution to history" in three waves: the Bard's Song, which calls Milton; Milton's descent, which calls Ololon; and Ololon's descent, which calls "a multitude of responses." Each of these waves "plays a variation on the basic comic pattern of disintegration and restoration of order." The descents—actually a single movement—of Milton and Ololon reunite poet and audience; Milton's action shows how to die and struggle, Ololon's how to live and hope. Poetry, like everything else that is created, is not an end in itself but a means of liberation; Blake created "a system that would self-destruct." In "Style and Iconography," Mitchell asks why the proportion of pictorial to textual space is smaller in *Milton* than in the other illuminated books and why the style seems uneven. On iconography, he asks why almost every full-page design is "grounded" on a horizon line and why the work has so few sexually or stylistically "well-developed" female figures. Mitchell speculates that Blake deemphasized pictures as a reaction to Hayley's interest in commercial success, that he included some plates cut in a primitive style to illustrate his ideas on varying perceptions, that he laid out a firm horizon to call attention to the theme of descent, and that the female nudes are immature to suggest the theme of unfulfilled potentiality. The fully virile male nudes, on the other hand, are depicted in poses that, to Mitchell, suggest homoerotic contact, a visual variation on the verbal theme of the brotherhood of poets and prophets. Together, Mitchell's articles on text and design suggest that, in seeking appropriate pictorial and verbal forms for his theme of "Eternal Annihilation," Blake deliberately built in unsettling peculiarities; we enter the book "not to rest in contemplation of its formal beauties, but to be propelled . . . into our own imaginations."

Also in the special issue of *Blake Studies*, Mary Lynn Johnson's "'Separating What Has Been Mixed': A Suggestion for a Perspective on *Milton*" briefly considers Blake's Christology in relation to a pattern based on the conversion of sets of twos into threes, the release of true Contraries from their covering by the illusory Negation; Milton's actively imaginative contemplation of a work of art contrasts with that of the uninspired audience of the Eternals of Albion. Thomas W. Herzig, "Book I of Blake's *Milton*: Natural Religion as an Optical Fallacy," suggests that the depiction of nature in the first book complements the treatment of natural religion in the second; false religion is based on a limited perception of the natural world and its supposed laws, but by the end of book 1 both Milton and the reader have undergone a process of perceptual reeducation. Jeffrey Mitchell, "Progression from the *Marriage* into the Bard's Song of *Milton*," shows the development of Blake's ideas on the contraries. In the *Marriage*, the prolific and the devouring must remain enemies; in *Milton*, Rintrah and Palamabron maintain a harmonious tension in opposition to the true enemy, Satan, "the principle of the fear of being." David V. Erdman, "The Steps (of Dance and Stone) That Order Blake's *Milton*," visualizes the designs as "stills . . . from numerous perspectives" of a "two-part dance opera, with all the world as its stage" and Felpham as stage center. He notes the startling frequency with which designs emphasizing the human foot appear, as in the half-title designs for both books; the full-plate tableau of Rintrah, Palamabron, and Satan; the plate on which Milton's foot divides the word "Self-hood" as he rises to overthrow Urizen"; and, of course, the full-plate designs of "William" and "Robert" receiving the star.

Notice of another major publication should be repeated in this connection: the 1978 color facsimile of copy B of *Milton,* with Kay Parkhurst Easson and Roger R. Easson as editors and commentators. The color photography, though a bit harsh, makes this beautiful book available for study and enjoyment in a popular format. But people who pick up this edition unwarily will have a strange first encounter with the poem. The novelty of the long commentary is its attempt to relate Blake's theory of perception and his diagram of "Milton's track" to nineteenth-century notions of the anatomy and physiology of the eye. The theory might well have been put forward in a thoroughly documented article, or it might usefully have been introduced as a tentative suggestion; the trouble here is that it is merely asserted, without any indication of its novelty, as a baseline for new readers. The bibliography, since it contains no articles at all, is practically useless. For example, the cornerstones of Blake's poetic universe are laid out in Northrop Frye's "Notes for a Commentary on *Milton*" (in Pinto's *The Divine Vision,* 1957), an essay that should be at the top of any reading list not only on *Milton* but also on *Jerusalem* and *The Four Zoas.*

Authors of all three full-length studies of *Milton* owe much to Edward J. Rose, "Blake's *Milton*: The Poet as Poem" (*BS* 1: 1 [1968]), who insists that any "linear analysis" is doomed to failure; the work of art is "complete yet never finished because it is the shape of vision expanding." As in Milton's "Apology for Smectymnus," the poet "ought himself to be a true poem." Andrew M. Cooper, "Blake's Escape from Mythology: Self-Mastery in *Milton*" (*SIR,* 1980), strains Rose's and Mitchell's theories past the breaking point: "*Milton* the poem self-annihilates just like Milton the character," and the poet "recovers the self-expressive vigor he lost through the entropy of creation." According to Harold Fisch's "Blake's Miltonic Moment," in the festschrift for Damon, the new characterization of Los as "the spirit of biblical poetry" marks the beginning of a new phase of Blake's work, with Milton as the agent of the transformation. For Blake, true epic is lyrical, conceived in "an ecstatic moment of vision"; dialogue becomes "a thrilling and continuing monologue" since all the characters blend and fuse and all divisions are abolished. Albert Cook's "Blake's *Milton*" (*Costerus,* 1972) contains some interesting observations on Blake's septenary as being somehow akin to Milton's handling of accents and caesuras, especially over the long haul of the verse paragraph. Thomas Dilworth, "The Hands of *Milton*: Blake's Multistable Image of Self-Annihilation" (*Mosaic,* 1983), hampered by the upside-down printing of a diagram, views hand-shaped flames in "Milton's track" against a tradition of unsettling perceptual effects in art. Florence Sandler, "The Iconoclastic Enterprise: Blake's Critique of 'Milton's Religion'" (*BS* 5: 1 [1972]), deals resourcefully with Blake's use of the apocalyptic structure of successive unveilings to present his sympathetic reinterpretation of Milton, whom he loves "only just this side idolatry." At issue are doctrines of atonement and marriage, which Sandler places in patristic and Miltonic contexts.

Stuart Curran, "The Mental Pinnacle: *Paradise Regained* and the Romantic Four-Book Epic," in *Calm of Mind*, edited by Joseph Anthony Wittreich, Jr. (1971), mentions *Milton* as one of the Romantic poems in the line of Milton's brief epic, with its themes of self-purification and the return to paradise. Brian Wilkie, "Epic Irony in *Milton*" (*BVFD*), suggests that Blake and Milton are like all other epic poets in locating their works "in the line of an epic ancestry" while at the same time criticizing the values of earlier epics. Through Blake in *Milton*, Milton vicariously retracts additional errors that he had previously been unable to detect. Blake uses epic machinery in both traditional and subversive ways, overturning other epic traditions in essence but not in form: for example, he rejects the antifeminist bias of previous epics while endorsing it on a symbolic level in his conception of the Female Will, and he repudiates war but preserves the metaphor of warfare. Wittreich takes quite a different view of Blake's relationship to Milton and to epic tradition. He claims in "Opening the Seals: Blake's Epics and the Milton Tradition," in *Blake's Sublime Allegory,* that "Blake's deepest roots are planted in the epic tradition that by Spenser and Milton was tied to the tradition of prophecy"; they had already created "a new kind of epic poetry" with Revelation as a structural model. Wittreich's " 'Sublime Allegory': Blake's Epic Manifesto and the Milton Tradition" (*BS* 4: 2 [1972]) reviews eighteenth-century misconceptions of Milton's legacy to support his claim that "Blake, rather than shifting the direction in which Spenser and Milton moved the epic poem, follows the course set by them to its logical conclusion," though obviously Blake goes much further in arresting narrative movement. Both Milton and Blake "fracture the traditional relationship between the epic poet and his audience," which is transformed "from a theatre of readers to a house of interpreters." "Blake's Milton: 'To Immortals, . . . A Mighty Angel' " (*MiltonS,* 1978), crystallizing insights scattered throughout *Angel of Apocalypse* and Wittreich's earlier articles, elucidates *Milton* as "both a criticism and a celebration" of Milton's work. As the only poem "in which one poet elevates another to the rank of epic hero," Blake's *Milton* mythologizes Milton's own breakthrough, within his lifetime, from previous errors into the radical theology of *Paradise Regained.* For Wittreich, Milton has no need to undergo a purgation or to repudiate anything in his final vision; Blake's task is rather to liberate Milton's work from false traditions promulgated in eighteenth-century misinterpretations. In the "Epilogue" to *Angel of Apocalypse,* Wittreich states that Blake criticizes Milton "as a man, an intellect, and an artist," and he faults Frederick E. Pierce, "The Genesis and General Meaning of *Milton*" (*MP,* 1927), for maintaining "that only Milton's commentators *and not Milton* are the objects of Blake's criticism." But the weight of all Wittreich's books and articles is surely on the same side as Pierce; both critics suggest that the self-corrected Milton of *Paradise Regained* requires no correction from Blake.

Blake's conception of time and space, examined in general articles that have already been considered, seems especially problematic in *Milton.* Peter Alan Taylor, "Providence and the Moment in Blake's *Milton*" (*BS* 4: 1 [1971]), finds providence operating both in history and in the timeless moment of inspiration; the two converge when the symbols of the lark and the wild thyme are viewed from multiple perspectives. (Sources for the wild thyme, beyond *Midsummer Night's Dream,* have been proposed by John Adlard, "Blake and the Wild Thyme" [*Folklore,* 1976], and Elaine Kauvar, "Los's Messenger to Eden: Blake's Wild Thyme" [*BNL* no. 39, 10: 3 (1976–77)].) Yvonne M. Carothers, "Space and Time in *Milton*: The 'Bard's Song,'" in *Blake in His Time,* fruitfully compares Blake's and Kant's (later) ideas on space and time as intuitive organizing principles within the mind; she then contrasts Blake's position with Lessing's assignment of time to poetry and space to painting. But this groundwork is put to little use in her attempt to demonstrate from the Bard's Song that space-time coordinates "not only function as organizational principles but also comprise Blake's entire art." The Bard, repeatedly breaking in with direct admonitions to the audience, belies her claim that he "vanishes behind the 'Song' throughout its narration." Leslie Brisman's section "Blake and the Eternals' Time" in *Milton's Poetry of Choice and Its Romantic Heirs* (1973) follows Blake's re-viewing of biblical history as recounted in *Paradise Regained* to make room for his own prophecy. He "rewrites the history of Milton's choice by himself arresting the moment of choice," opening old stories to new endings (thus canceling the historical time between texts) and repeatedly returning to moments of creation and fall (thus abolishing ordinary narrative temporality). Albert J. Rivero, "Typology, History, and Blake's *Milton*" (*JEGP,* 1982), finds the model of biblical typology helpful in reconciling instantaneous action with the sequentiality of such events as the Bard's Song and Milton's descent. From the perspective of Eternity, events occur within a single moment, but they must be sequentially unfolded to be perceptible to the corporeal understanding, as in the typological approach to the Bible. Rivero's essay coincides in subject with Leslie Tannenbaum's fourth chapter, "Sublime Allegory: Blake's Use of Typology," in *Biblical Tradition in Blake's Early Prophecies* (1982), but whereas Rivero claims that typological exegesis had been discredited by Blake's time, Tannenbaum indicates that it was very much alive.

Certain sections of the poem invite more detailed analysis. Its most famous lines, known as the "Jerusalem" hymn and made popular in Sir Hubert Parry's 1916 musical setting, appear only in copies A and B. Nancy M. Goslee, " 'In Englands green & pleasant Land': The Building of Vision in Blake's Stanzas from *Milton*" (*SIR,* 1974), reads the "Jerusalem" anthem as a metaphoric microcosm of both *Milton* and *Jerusalem.* On tone and meaning, see also G. W. Arms et al. in *Explicator* 1943 and John Wain and W. W. Robson, " 'Intention' and Blake's *Jerusalem*" (*EIC,* 1952). Sophia B. Blaydes and Philip Bordinat analyze the use of the hymn in two movies, *The Loneliness of the Long Distance Runner* and *Chariots of Fire* (*Literature/Film Quarterly,* 1983).

Few would disagree that the Bard's Song is the most confusing part of the poem, particularly in its C and D versions, which contain additional plates. Eve Teitelbaum, "Form as Meaning in Blake's *Milton*" (*BS* 2: 1 [1969]), in considering the relation of the Song to the process of Milton's self-redemption, correctly observes that (at the time she wrote) interpretation of the Song had been almost entirely confined to the biographical level, as Rose also had noted. She proposes an aesthetic allegory based on Blake's concepts of the Beautiful Man (Palamabron), Strong Man (Rintrah), and Ugly Man (Satan). James Rieger, " 'The Hem of Their Garments': The Bard's Song in *Milton*," in *Blake's Sublime Allegory*, also repudiates historical and biographical interpretations and reads the conflict among Los's sons as a warfare within the imagination, "an affective rather than a facultative psychomachia." The audience is deliberately misled; because the Edenic and natural levels are discontinuous, the prophet must boggle finite understanding in order to rouse the imagination. The strongest section of John H. Sutherland's "Blake's *Milton*: The Bard's Song" (*CLQ*, 1977) challenges Erdman's identification of Rintrah with Pitt, though without reference to Teitelbaum and Rieger.

At last we come to the end of the poem, to quite different ways of asking questions about text and design. Through rhetorical questions, Peter Butter, "*Milton*: The Final Plates," in *Interpreting Blake*, resurrects "poetic quality" and intelligibility as critical issues. Butter finds Blake's concept of Satan as both a character and a state particularly troublesome, a "muddle"; he seems to have missed the crucial point that Milton refuses to annihilate Satan as a character or outward being because he has discovered the state of Satan within himself. Butter is of course right to demand that a poet mean something; such demands from British critics probably help keep American critics honest. The classes of Prolific and Devouring ought not to be reconciled if there is to be "Progression" in criticism. Butter leaves open the possibility that Blake's apparent obscurities or confusions will become "clear or meaningfully ambiguous" on further consideration, but his general tone renders this outcome unlikely. A different kind of interim report—a progress report as well—is recorded by John E. Grant, "The Female Awakening at the End of Blake's *Milton*: A Picture Story, with Questions," in *Milton Reconsidered* (ed. John Karl Franson, 1976). Grant poses thoughtful theoretical questions about various kinds of poetic-pictorial alignments before investigating some ambiguous or "conditional" depictions of female figures near the end of the poem. His "provisional considered answers" to his own questions set up a pictorial sequence with the regeneration of the female principle as the controlling theme.

Feminine regeneration is also an issue in Irene Tayler's "Say First! What Mov'd Blake? Blake's *Comus* Designs and *Milton*," in *Blake's Sublime Allegory*. Considering Ololon's and Leutha's major speeches, Wayne Glausser, "*Milton* and the Pangs of Repentance" (*BIQ* no. 52, 13: 4 [1980]), distinguishes four levels of repentance corresponding to four kinds of faultfinding: in Ulro, you are guilty; in Generation, I am guilty; in Beulah, no one is guilty; in Eden, we are mutually guilty and must forgive one another. Ololon's final speech reveals that she has found the way to Edenic repentance; she recognizes conflict as a part of her essence, a Blakean version of original sin, and at this point her feminine portion enters Ulro, a void that becomes a womb. Donald H. Reiman and Christina Shuttleworth Kraus, "The Derivation and Meaning of 'Ololon' " (*BIQ* no. 62, 16: 2 [1982]), convincingly trace the name not to "ululation," as Frye had suggested, but—following Peter Fisher—to a Greek word meaning an ecstatic cry of women to the gods.

Two current books on *Jerusalem* take complementary approaches. Minna Doskow's *Structure and Meaning in William Blake's Jerusalem* (1982), considerately providing a "General Outline for the General Reader," argues that the poem is a "kaleidoscopic whole" in which basic motifs, rearranged with each chapter, reveal different perspectives on the single theme of Albion's sleep and reawakening. Morton D. Paley's *The Continuing City: William Blake's Jerusalem* (1983), the best overall commentary by far, sets the poetry and designs against their various traditions, considers the history of millenarianism in relation to Blake's idea of Jerusalem, analyzes the poem's two central myths (Albion, Jerusalem, and Vala; Los, Enitharmon, and the Spectre), and takes up the question of form, using Joseph Mede's conception of "synchronism" in Revelation as an aid. Doskow's workmanlike plate-by-plate guide, which assumes that Blake produced a coherent work with a "fit" though nonspecialized audience in mind, maximizes order and relationship, while minimizing or ignoring obscurities and inconsistencies; for a critique of her "strategies," see De Luca's review (*BIQ* no. 69, 18: 1 [1984]). Doskow includes a complete facsimile of the illuminated poem (copy C); Paley provides a wealth of illustrations of instructive sources and analogues.

The only other full-scale study, now almost thirty years old, is Joseph Wicksteed's *William Blake's Jerusalem* (1953), which was published by the Blake Trust in the same format as its 1952 monochrome facsimile of copy C, as companion volumes for the Trust's resplendent color facsimile of copy E. A general introduction to Blake's thought and to the poem itself leads into a plate-by-plate commentary on text and designs. Wicksteed's disregard of *Fearful Symmetry*, along with his diffuse enthusiasms and stab-in-the-dark approach to Blake's symbolism, imparts an antique flavor belied by his shrewd observations on Blake's London and its environs and his sharp eye for pictorial details. His overworked and overly rigid system of left-right symbolism can open mind-altering vistas, such as his observation that Blake's arrangement of the words "Sheep" and "Goats" on the third plate places the reader in the position of the soul facing judgment before the page itself. In 1964, William R. Hughes published a "Simplified Version" of *Jerusalem*, with a commentary very much in the Wicksteed tradition that may be initially helpful to some new readers.

One number of *Blake Studies* is devoted to *Jerusalem* (7: 1 [1974]). E. B. Murray, "*Jerusalem* Reversed," takes the principle of reversal—reflected in reversals of names, roles, situations, meanings, narrative and dramatic patterns—as a key to meaning. Mollyanne Marks, "Self-Sacrifice: Theme and Image in *Jerusalem*," follows the opposition between selfhood and the attainment of a higher level of consciousness, mainly through Los and the character Blake. Irene H. Chayes, "The Marginal Designs on *Jerusalem* 12," attends to meanings revealed by details of clothing, gestures, attributes, with reference to similar figures and objects elsewhere in Blake; this, she feels, is "the kind of analysis that could profitably be made of most of the minor designs in *Jerusalem*." The three approaches in this number of *Blake Studies*—through symbolic structure, theme, and iconography—typify much recent work on the poem.

By far the most pressing concern of critics of *Jerusalem* has been with the problem of form or structure. Things have moved a long way since W. H. Stevenson's petulant objection—in "Blake's *Jerusalem*" (*EIC,* 1959)—to the poem's "artificially invertebrate structure," whatever that means. Stevenson considered the four prefaces a "suspiciously symmetrical" overlay on a work consisting almost entirely of digressions and padding. (It is hard to understand why someone with this view of a mature epic would choose to edit and annotate Blake's complete poetical works—and harder still to understand how he was able to make so good a job of it. But an intense love-hate relationship with Blake seems endemic to one strain of British criticism—witness T. S. Eliot, F. R. Leavis, F. W. Bateson.) Stevenson's sense that the poem lacks a coherent structure is not shared by others. During the first two thirds of this century, critics searched for a simple key in the four-chapter layout. Damon took the first chapter as a fall into Beulah, the second as a fall into Generation, the third as presenting both the triumph of error and the main Christian events, and the fourth as a description, by stages, of the awakening. According to Frye, the four chapters depict fall, struggle, redemption, and apocalypse, with imaginative vision brought in simultaneously "with the body of error which it clarifies." Karl Kiralis, "The Theme and Structure of Blake's *Jerusalem*" (in *The Divine Vision*), defines the structure as "one of interfolded growth" and the theme as the maturing of humankind into harmony and wholeness. After the general introduction of chapter 1, Kiralis considers chapters 2–4, addressed to Jews, Deists, and Christians, to be related to the "Three Regions" of "Childhood, Manhood & Old Age," named near the end of the poem. Edward J. Rose, "The Structure of Blake's *Jerusalem*" (*BuR,* 1963), points out correspondences in reverse between chapters 2 and 4 and then suggests that each chapter is ruled by a Zoa, in the following order: Tharmas, Luvah, Urizen, Los; chapter 1, not 4 as claimed by Kiralis, deals with old age. The conceptual modes of the four chapters are psychological, sociological, rational, and visionary. The subject and structure are really one, linked through man's regenerating perceptual power. V. A. De Luca, "The Changing Order of Plates in *Jerusalem,* Chapter II" (*BIQ* no. 64, 16: 4 [1983]), reconstructs an early arrangement and suggests that Blake's changes after publication reflect reconsiderations of his visual design, not thematic or verbal modifications.

Insistence on the oneness of subject and structure also undergirds recent arguments, though critics of the 1970s have made a virtue of necessity by claiming that *Jerusalem* is *supposed* to be confusing because its subject is itself, its own making. According to Hazard Adams, "Blake, *Jerusalem,* and Symbolic Form" (*BS* 7: 2 [1975]), *Jerusalem* "self-consciously embodies the principles of poetic construction as its content or subject"; it is "about itself or is itself *being made.*" It possesses neither beginning nor ending; instead, we come in upon it, remain in its present time, and end with its imagining of Jerusalem as an ongoing state of potentiality. Roger R. Easson, "William Blake and His Reader in *Jerusalem,*" in *Blake's Sublime Allegory,* also argues that *Jerusalem* is "a poem about itself, about the relation between the author and his reader"; it "may be read as" being "about the experience of reading *Jerusalem.*" Easson finds "two warring and diverse structures"—one being a sublime allegory of Albion's fall and redemption, the other "the great obscuring veil of narrative" that becomes for the "reasoning" reader a source of frustration. The right kind of reader will strip away the "superficial four-chapter structure" to discover a perfect fourfold entity telling the double story of Albion and Los in sixteen scenes, "two cycles of eight scenes each." One reviewer has gone so far as to call Easson's article a hoax; I think it is a sincere house of cards built on a solid foundation—the perception that Blake's outrageous demands on his reader are purposeful and in the long run conducive to the reader's reeducation. In another essay in *Blake's Sublime Allegory,* Stuart Curran lets slip the incautious remark that "no sophisticated reader confesses himself lost in its midst, unable to comprehend the plate he is reading." It may be true that readers who wish to appear unflappable refrain from admitting anything—but the difficulties assuredly remain, and no candid reader need blush to acknowledge them. Probably Curran meant only to combat know-nothing Stevensonesque attacks on the poem as something totally incomprehensible and formless. Curran descries no fewer than seven structures: "A primary structure of four divisions," "a two-part structure [contrasting] Ulro and Eden; a three-part structure whose pivots are climactic representations of the fallen state; a threefold and a fourfold division within each chapter stressing the dialectical mode of the poem; a sixfold division emphasizing the continuity of major events; a second three-part structure [surrounding] Albion's world with Los's perspective; and a sevenfold structure of epic prophecy." Can even a sophisticated reader help feeling confused?

According to Henry Lesnick, "Narrative Structure and the Antithetical Vision of *Jerusalem*" (in *BVFD*), "specific plates which introduce and conclude each of the four chapters help to define the material included in each chapter." The turning point comes with the appearance of the Covering Cherub at plate 89, about halfway through the fourth chapter; the first three chapters depict successive stages of the fall, and the last half of the fourth chapter depicts restoration. In "The Function of Perspective in Blake's *Jerusalem*" (*BNYPL,* 1969), Lesnick refines Wicksteed's suggestion that the page itself has an "inside" and "outside"; for example, the doorway through which Los steps in the frontispiece is the same as "Death's Door" in *The Gates of Paradise,* seen from the perspective of Eternity.

For structural models, critics have turned most naturally to the Bible. According to Harold Bloom, "Blake's *Jerusalem*: The Bard of Sensibility and the Form of Prophecy" (*ECS,* 1970; rev. *Ringers in the Tower,* 1971), the flamelike form of the poem freely follows that of Ezekiel, with the Merkabah or divine chariot as central image. Both works emphasize individual responsibility and self-purgation. But the form of *Jerusalem* is "twisted askew by too abrupt a swerve or *clinamen*" from Ezekiel; this means that, according to Bloom's theory of influence, Blake self-protectively held back from identifying himself too closely with his precursor. Randel Helms, "Ezekiel and Blake's *Jerusalem*" (*SIR,* 1974), patiently considers "difference-in-similarity" in structure, prophet-audience relationship, key images (wheels, fourfold city-temple), and verbal echoes. David Sten Herrstrom, "Blake's Transformations of Ezekiel's Cherubim Vision in *Jerusalem*" (*BIQ* no. 58, 15: 2 [1981]), pursues Ezekiel motifs throughout Blake's work, without the help of Grant's "The Visionary Perspective of Ezekiel" (*BS* 4: 2 [1972]). Joanne Witke, "*Jerusalem*—A Synoptic Poem" (*CL,* 1970), sets up the four Gospels as structural model, with attention to what Blake may have known of exegetical attempts to "harmonize" the four; most of her support comes from Matthew and chapter 1 of *Jerusalem.* James Ferguson, "Prefaces to *Jerusalem*," in *Interpreting Blake,* takes a closer look at the four addressees as organizing devices. James L. Bogan, "Apocalypse Now: William Blake and the Conversion of the Jews" (*ELN,* 1981), contrasts Blake's conciliatory approach in the preface to chapter 2 with the insulting tone of contemporary pamphlets supposedly aimed at Jewish audiences.

Discussions of structure modulate, of course, into discussions of theme. Jane McClelland, "Dramatic Movement as a Structuring Device in Blake's *Jerusalem*" (*CLQ,* 1977), organizes the poem around Los's actions of forgiveness and creative labor (complementing Marks's essay). According to Michael G. Cooke, *The Romantic Will* (1976), in a movement of "alternation-as-confrontation" Los gains control over his Spectre or destructive will; the affirmation in *Jerusalem* of "the poet's will to act as an independent construct" entails "a certain defect and isolation for any work," for the more a work is about itself, the less it can be about anything else. Cooke's idea that self-reflexivity in *Jerusalem* exemplifies a profound danger in Romanticism contrasts with Hazard Adams' more sanguine view. William E. Phipps, "Blake on Joseph's Dilemma" (*Theology Today,* 1971), supplies a brief history of the ancient heresy of Jesus' illegitimate birth, which is endorsed by Blake in the beautiful scene between Mary and Joseph on plate 61; Phipps then defends Blake's use of this material as the vehicle of a fundamental Christian truth. Rodney M. Baine's "Blake's Sons of Los" (*PQ,* 1984) explains complex biblical allusions.

On particular symbols and images, see E. J. Rose's major articles—"Blake's Hand: Symbol and Design in *Jerusalem*" (*TSLL,* 1964), "The Symbolism of the Opened Center and Poetic Theory in *Jerusalem*" (*SEL,* 1965), "Wheels within Wheels in Blake's *Jerusalem*" (*SIR,* 1972), and "Circumcision Symbolism in Blake's *Jerusalem*" (*SIR,* 1968)—as well as David G. Riede, "The Symbolism of the Loins in Blake's *Jerusalem*" (*SEL,* 1981). On other symbols, see Cary Nelson, "*Jerusalem*: A Fourfold Vision of the Human Body," in his *The Incarnate Word* (1972), mostly on womb imagery; G. M. Harper, "The Odyssey of the Soul in Blake's *Jerusalem*" (*BS* 5: 2 [1974]); James Bogan, "Blake's City of Golgonooza in *Jerusalem*: Metaphor and Mandala" (*CLQ,* 1981); David M. Wyatt, "The Woman Jerusalem: *Pictura* versus *Poesis*" (*BS* 7: 2 [1975]). David Worrall's "Blake's *Jerusalem* and the Visionary History of Britain" (*SIR,* 1977) documents the underpinning of Blake's myth in records of legendary antiquities, some of which are rather remote. A pioneering essay on the relationship of visual details to lines of text, Claudette Kemper's survey of minutiae in "The Interlinear Drawings in Blake's *Jerusalem*" (*BNYPL,* 1960) overstates its case against right-left currents of movement but presents good examples of "visual tensions" in the work. David E. Latané, Jr., focuses on the frontispiece in "The Door into Jerusalem" (*RP&P,* 1983).

Closing in on particular plates, Michael J. Tolley explains biblical references in plate 12 (*BIQ* no. 13, 4: 1 [1970]); Chayes's discussion of visual sources for this plate has already been noted. Deirdre Toomey and Morton D. Paley propose sources for plate 25 (the disemboweling of Albion), in *BNL* (no. 19, 5: 3 [1971–72]): he in Poussin and she in a School of Fontainebleu engraving. Toomey also compares variant copies of this plate (*BNL* no. 22, 6: 2 [1972]), whereupon Essick cautions against calling a variant a "state" unless the plate itself has been altered (*BNL* no. 27, 7: 3 [1973]). W. D. Paden and Gerhard H. W. Zuther observe changes Blake made in the embracing couple on plate 28 (*N&Q*, 1965). Judith Ott gives possible sources for plate 76, the bird-man (*BNL* no. 38, 10: 2 [1976]), and for plate 14 (*BIQ* no. 68, 17: 4 [1984]). Ben F. Nelms (*BS* 5: 2 [1973]) analyzes plates 96–100. Other significant contributions have already been noted: Mitchell's chapter on *Jerusalem* in *Blake's Composite Art,* Carr's "William Blake's Print-Making Process in *Jerusalem*" (*ELH,* 1980), Erdman's bibliographical articles "The Suppressed and Altered Passages in Blake's *Jerusalem*" (*SB,* 1964) and "Blake's *Jerusalem:* Plate 3 Fully Restored" (*SB,* 1965). Erdman notes a new reading of a key phrase on plate 3 in his 1982 textual notes on the *Complete Poetry* (for an enlarged photograph of this plate, see the cover of *BIQ* no. 69, 18: 1 [1984]).

Other Illuminated Writings. The Gates of Paradise, in both its first edition as *For Children* and its revised form as *For the Sexes,* is in style and format an emblem book and is viewed within that tradition by Nanavutty, Johnson, and Wardle in articles previously cited. Wardle's " 'For Hatching ripe': Blake and the Educational Uses of Emblem and Illustrated Literature" (*BRH,* 1978) also contains an informative appendix, "Blake's Knowledge of Emblem Literature." Hagstrum and Mitchell discuss this tradition, and Chauncey Brewster Tinker, *Painter and Poet* (1938), has pointed out some possible sources. Yet Joseph S. Salemi, "Emblematic Tradition in Blake's *The Gates of Paradise*" (*BIQ* no. 59, 15: 3 [1981]), writes with no awareness of Nanavutty, Johnson, or Wardle or of the essay by Parisi cited below: this carelessness renders his reproductions of traditional emblems the most useful part of his essay.

George Wingfield Digby, *Symbol and Image in William Blake* (1957), relates both *Gates of Paradise* and the mysterious work known as the Arlington Court Picture to Blake's whole structure of symbolism, as seen through Jungian analytical psychology and mystical tradition. Much of what he says will seem arbitrary to beginning students, but his general interpretation of the *Gates* is suggestive, and his style is perfectly clear and unpretentious. Gail Kmetz, "A Reading of Blake's *The Gates of Paradise*" (*BS* 3: 2 [1971]), restricts herself to strictly Blakean terms; her essentially hopeful interpretation is closer to Digby than perhaps her sparse footnotes indicate. In two condensed paragraphs in his 1966 essay "The Keys to the Gates" (cited under "General Studies: Introductions"), Frye reads the sequence as a closed natural cycle. Frank M. Parisi, "Emblems of Melancholy: *For Children: The Gates of Paradise,*" in *Interpreting Blake,* focuses on the 1793 form of the work, before the introductory and concluding verses and longer captions were added. His footnotes tend to obscure the relative importance of some previous critics (i.e., Digby becomes a "see also"); others are not mentioned at all (e.g., Erdman's commentary in *The Illuminated Blake,* which reproduces both the 1793 and the 1818 editions; Wardle's 1975 essay, which includes comments on plate 7, the one page that Parisi inexplicably leaves out; and Mellor's chapter in *The Human Form Divine,* which, like Beer's *Blake's Humanism,* anticipates

Parisi's pessimistic interpretation). Parisi's plate-by-plate commentary on Blake's traditional symbolic framework is particularly fine on the frontispiece, plate 12 (Ugolino), and plate 13 (prophetic deathbed scene). To press his thesis, however, he minimizes "hope" in plate 13 and the optimistic hints of the last three plates, evident in the eager haste of the traveler.

Mature consideration of *The Ghost of Abel* properly begins with Leslie Tannenbaum's penetrating essay "Lord Byron in the Wilderness: Biblical Tradition in Byron's *Cain* and Blake's *The Ghost of Abel*" (*MP*, 1975), which looks for the exact point at which Blake and Byron part company. According to Tannenbaum, Blake approved Byron's rejection of retributive justice, but he saw that Byron lacked a vision of atonement, of liberation from his own "self-defeating skepticism." Tannenbaum relates Blake's illuminated closet drama to the medieval mystery form and his doctrine of self-sacrificial atonement to exegetical traditions. Without awareness of Tannenbaum, Martin Bidney looks into the same area; in "*Cain* and *The Ghost of Abel*: Contexts for Understanding Blake's Response to Byron" (*BS* 8: 2 [1979]), he first translates *Cain* into Blakean terms and then shows how Blake's "dramatic epiphany" points the way beyond Byron's conclusion in vengeance and despair. Thomas A. Reisner's double-barreled essay, "Cain: Two Romantic Interpretations" (*Culture*, 1970), is also pertinent. On the *Laocoön* plate, in addition to Tayler's already cited article (*BNL* no. 39, 10: 3 [1976–77]), see David E. James's "Blake's *Laocoön*: A Degree Zero of Literary Production" (*PMLA*, 1983); provocative though muddled, it is the fullest treatment so far.

Other Writings. The poems of Blake's adolescence, published in ordinary typeface by his friends as *Poetical Sketches,* were first studied in bibliographical and critical detail by Margaret Ruth Lowery, *Windows of the Morning* (1940). Lowery marshals page after page of parallel quotations to exhibit Blake's affiliations with scores of other poets from Shakespeare to Collins. John W. Ehrstine, *William Blake's Poetical Sketches* (1967), contributes no outstanding new insights. Michael Phillips, "Blake's Early Poetry," in the festschrift for Keynes, besides footnoting a convenient "select bibliography," attempts to trace Blake's developing sense of his own vocation. In the same volume, Tolley begins "Blake's Songs of Spring" with a Christian interpretation of "To Spring." In "Blake and the Progress of Poetry" in the festschrift for Damon (rpt. in his *Beyond Formalism*), Geoffrey H. Hartman argues that the poems on the seasons are actually about poetry and its westward movement. Irene H. Chayes, "Blake and the Seasons of the Poet" (*SIR*, 1972), imagines the speaker rotating through four "states" of mind as the seasons revolve around him. L. C. Knights, "Early Blake" (*SR*, 1971), analyzes a group of eight contiguous poems with first-person speakers that deal with experience, sexual love in particular. James McGowan, "The Integrity of the *Poetical Sketches*" (*BS* 8: 2 [1979]), takes a close look at the order of the poems, the movement from calm lyricism to transitional uncertainty to terror or frustration in the fragmentary final pieces. Bibliographical essays by Phillips, Keynes, and McKenzie also contain observations of critical importance. But the anchor commentary on *Poetical Sketches* will probably be Gleckner's *Blake's Prelude* (1982), which examines the poems in the context of Shakespeare, Spenser, Milton, and the late eighteenth century without anachronistically drawing on the later work for "interpretative assistance." Incorporating Gleckner's "Antithetical Structure in Blake's *Poetical Sketches*" (*SIR,* 1981) and his earlier "Blake's Seasons" (*SEL,* 1965), *Blake's Prelude* is ingenious, provocative, perhaps a trifle thesis-ridden, and—like all Gleckner's work—it will be highly influential.

For many years scholars have worked on dates and real-life identifications of characters in *An Island in the Moon*: Jane M. Oppenheimer, "A Note on William Blake and John Hunter" (*Journal of the Hist. of Med. and Applied Science,* 1946); Nancy Bogen, "William Blake's 'Island in the Moon' Revisited" (*Satire Newsletter,* 1968); Rodney M. Baine and Mary R. Baine, "Blake's Inflammable Gass" (*BNL* no. 38, 10: 2 [1976]); R. J. Shroyer, "Mr. Jacko 'Knows What Riding Is' in 1785: Dating Blake's *Island in the Moon*" (*BIQ* no. 48, 12: 4 [1979]). Shroyer's argumentation and documentation suggest that his edition of the *Island* (advertised 1984) will be excellent; see also Malmqvist's Swedish edition, mentioned earlier. Martha W. England, "The Satiric Blake: Apprenticeship in the Haymarket" (1969; abr. in *BVFD*), on Samuel Foote's theatrical entertainments, and Eugene Kirk, "Blake's Menippean *Island*" (*PQ,* 1980), propose differing satiric traditions for the work. Kirk makes the stronger case, though at many points the two need not be mutually exclusive. According to William Royce Campbell, "The Aesthetic Integrity of Blake's *Island in the Moon*" (*BS* 3: 2 [1971]), the work is organized as a Hogarthian "Progress," showing Quid's developing disaffections. Everett C. Frost identifies a quotation from John Taylor the Water Poet (*N&Q,* 1979).

On *Tiriel* there are few items of importance beyond Bentley's facsimile and Metcalf's correction, mentioned earlier, and accounts in the standard works by Frye, Bloom, and Gleckner (the latter having first appeared in *PQ,* 1951). Both Nancy Bogen and Mary S. Hall, in adjoining articles in *BNYPL* (1970), suggest that Blake derived some names and images from Bryant's *New System,* an analytic mythography that he helped illustrate. William F. Halloran, "Blake's *Tiriel*: Snakes, Curses, and a Blessing" (*SAQ,* 1971), classifies the work with *Thel* and *Visions of the Daughters of Albion* as an early prophetic poem on despair and the possibility of recovery. Essick, "The Altering Eye: Blake's Vision in the *Tiriel* Designs," in the festschrift for Keynes, looks for ways in which the illustrations embody "in rudimentary form" Blake's later themes and motifs. Bindman's Fitzwilliam catalog and his *Blake as an Artist,* previously mentioned, suggest a close visual parallel for the second design in a painting by Barry. Hans Ostrom's "Blake's *Tiriel* and the Dramatization of Collapsed Language" (*PLL,* 1983) focuses on linguistic implications. The fullest study, Stephen C. Behrendt's " 'The Worst Disease': Blake's *Tiriel*" (*CLQ,* 1979), disputes occult sources in Raine and Mellor's theory that Har and Heva's geriatric state of well-preserved innocence is a good thing. Behrendt interprets both text and designs as condemning "an entire Reason-oriented cultural system" in which all the characters are in error. See also David Fuller's "The Translation of Vision" (*DUJ,* 1982).

On *The French Revolution,* David G. Halliburton's article "The *Figura* and Yesterday's News" (*SIR,* 1965) defines Blake's genre and metaphorical base: the poem is a "figural prophecy" that fails because its characters and events are too closely tied to factual events. William F. Halloran, "*The French Revolution*: Revelation's New Form" (*BVFD*), sees a symmetrically organized prophecy on the model of Revelation that expands the reader's perception until revolution is seen as revelation. Halloran's bibliographical article, already named, is also a major contribution. Joel Morkan, "Blake's Ancient Forests of Europe" (*BIQ* no. 24, 6: 4 [1973]), explains the feudal "forest rights" of French peasants.

On the Notebook, the apparatus in Erdman and Moore's edition is of primary importance. See also Moore's article "Infant Sorrow," noted above, and Erdman's "Terrible Blake in His Pride," in *From Sensibility to Romanticism*. Tolley traces Blake's biblical sources for "The Everlasting Gospel" in *N&Q* (1962 and 1968); Jean Hall, "Blake's *Everlasting Gospel*" (*BS* 4: 1 [1971]), grapples uncertainly with Blake's radical theology, and Randel Helms, "The Genesis of *The Everlasting Gospel*" (*BS* 9 [1980]), relates the probable sequence of revisions and the biblical allusions to the development of Blake's Christology. In the Houtchenses' review volume, Frye remarked that "the days of looking into one's heart to write about Blake are over," but his optimism was premature: G. Wilson Knight's self-validating psycho-Nietzschean reading, "The Chapel of Gold," in *Interpreting Blake,* totally lacks a sense of audience. Walter Pache and Ursula Salacki, "Blake and Ovid" (*BS* 4: 1 [1971]), point out that a desecration of altars by a snake in Ovid is somewhat similar to the situation at hand. Gleckner, "Blake's 'I Saw a Chapel all of Gold' " (*CLQ,* 1979), footnotes a reliably selected and tersely annotated bibliography and cites key passages in Milton and Spenser to support his reading of the poem as a correction of the errors of orthodoxy. Nicholas Warner (*Expl,* 1983) calls attention to the Anglican ritual of the bishop's rapping with a serpent-headed crozier to consecrate a new church. G. J. Finch " 'Never Pain to Tell Thy Love': Blake's 'Problem Poem" (*BS* 4: 1 [1971]), unpersuasively argues that the poem "runs counter to intention" because of Blake's own mixed feelings about self-giving love.

For the beautiful, disturbing poems of the Pickering Manuscript, Adams' commentary in *William Blake: A Reading of the Shorter Poems* holds up as the best overall treatment, accompanied by Bloom's economical readings in *Blake's Apocalypse.* On the most overpowering poem in the collection, "The Mental Traveller," already the subject of several dissertations, some older theories have been gathered in *Literary Symbolism* (ed. Maurice Beebe, 1960): W. M. Rossetti's identification of the speaker as an "explorer of mental phaenomena" who observes "the career of any great Idea or intellectual movement," Damon's "five stages" in the "life of mystic," Mona Wilson's adumbration of Frye's "Orc cycle," and Joyce Cary's interpretation of the history of art in *The Horse's Mouth.* John H. Sutherland, "Blake's 'Mental Traveller' " (*ELH,* 1955; rpt. *Discussions,* ed. Grant, and *Critics on Blake,* ed. O'Neill), identifies Blake himself as the speaker who views archetypes in eternity through a perceptual vortex: the male babe is Orclike and the female babe, who remains free, is the creative imagination or its product. Paley, "The Female Babe and 'The Mental Traveller' " (*SIR,* 1962; rev. in his *Energy and the Imagination*), sees the narrator as a "pseudo-naive" satirist of our human entrapment within the "bound circle which is both the subject and the structure of the poem"; the female babe is a manifestation of the Female Will. Nurmi, "Joy, Love, and Innocence in Blake's 'The Mental Traveller' " (*SIR,* 1963), diagrams the action—the fallen world—in concentric circles that have several points of potential opening whenever humanity is ready to bring on the Apocalypse. The female babe, "fierce love born of such joy as Experience provides," escapes the trap. Gerald E. Enscoe, "The Content of Vision: Blake's 'Mental Traveller'" (*PLL,* 1968), also sees the female babe as a way out; in his psychosexual reading, the mental traveler himself and the birth episodes also offer hope. Irene Chayes's 1962 article on Plato's *Statesman* myth as a source identifies the basic pattern as a spiral; Arthur Adamson, "Structure and Meaning in Blake's 'The Mental Traveller'" (*Mosaic,* 1974), thinks Spengler's model of historical cycles is analogous; James Twitchell, "'The Mental Traveller,' Infinity, and the 'Arlington Court Picture'" (*Criticism,* 1975), reprinted in his *Romantic Horizons* (1983), thinks the poem is modeled on the mathematical symbol of infinity; Izak Bower and Paul McNally, "'The Mental Traveller': Man's Eternal Journey" (*BIQ* no. 12: 3 [1978–79]), plot "the theological cycle of Man's fall from and return to Eden." As things stand, the crucial questions are whether the female is good or evil and whether the circle opens at any point.

There are two major commentaries on the final Pickering poem: John E. Grant's "Apocalypse in Blake's 'Auguries of Innocence'" (*TSLL,* 1964)—not in *Blake Books*—and Janet Warner's "Blake's 'Auguries of Innocence'" (*CLQ,* 1976). Grant focuses on the beginning and ending in relation to Blake's "epistemology and his conception of prophecy and eschatology," with emphasis on the story of Jonah. He draws out the ambiguities and connotations of the title and the first four lines (a formula for achieving apocalypse), which are fulfilled in the contrasting views of God in the last eight lines; a modification of his "editorial arrangement" is adopted in the Erdman text. Warner, following Blake's own arrangement, finds coherent "lexical sets" on such themes as cosmology, time, nature, humanity, prophecy, religion, emotion, commerce, clothing, wounding, and doubt and belief, which she thinks are arranged according to a kind of musical structure. Reisner and Reisner explain a contemporary allusion (*Expl,* 1977), and John Adlard brings up some convincing analogues in folk art in *The Sports of Cruelty* (1972).

Standard interpretations of *The Four Zoas* in preexisting critical and textual studies are consolidated and amplified by Brian Wilkie and Mary Lynn Johnson, *Blake's "Four Zoas": The Design of a Dream* (1978), which reaches out to first-time readers. Their old-fashioned concern with thematic coherence, organizational and metaphorical patterns, and psychological states has earned the praise of some reviewers and the disdain of others. They append a list of varying accounts of the Fall and a selected bibliography. Wilkie and Johnson unquestioningly use the 1965 Erdman textual arrangement, despite W. H. Stevenson's queries about the beginning of Night II and the status of Night VIIb (*BNL* no. 3–4, 1: 3–4 [1967]), and Paley's and Wagenknecht's reconsideration of both Nights VII in *Energy and the Imagination* and *Blake's Night,* previously mentioned. A special issue of *Blake: An Illustrated Quarterly* (no. 46, 12: 2 [1978]) includes editorial reassessments by Andrew Lincoln, Erdman, John Kilgore, and Mark Lefebvre, which led to changes Erdman incorporated into his 1982 edition. This special issue also includes critical and historical articles by Nelson Hilton on "The Sweet Science of Atmospheres" (backgrounds in Swedenborg and in the science of Blake's time),

Terence Allan Hoagwood on "The Philosophick Cabbala" (parallels in Henry More's Neoplatonic redaction of Genesis), and Johnson and Wilkie on the "Spectrous Embrace" (the acceptance of doubt and negativism in Romantic art).

Stout critics have faced up to the wildest and most forbidding aspects of the poem. Helen T. McNeil, "The Formal Art of *The Four Zoas*" (in *BVFD*), describes it as an "epic of situations" that operates "without a context, even a Blakean one"; the reader, lost in a chaotic limbo and subjected to abrupt shifts in perspective without the orientation of cause-effect sequences or mimetic links with the known world, is shocked into identifying with the fallen Albion and partaking in his redemption. Thomas Weiskel, "Darkning Man: Blake's Critique of Transcendence" in his *The Romantic Sublime* (1976)—overlooked by Wilkie and Johnson—takes Blake's "analytic critique of sublimation" as supplementary to Kant's theory of the sublime, and he concentrates on aesthetic, religious, and psychological aspects of the sublime in the Urizen-Ahania scene in Night III. Leslie Brisman, "Re: Generation in Blake" in his *Romantic Origins* (1978), searches behind five major explanations of how Albion fell ill, as various characters reinterpret "history" to place themselves at its beginning. The conflicting accounts challenge the very idea of a definitive "beginning" and lead to Los's acceptance of a "consciousness of fictionality"; Brisman's Blake anticipates Derrida without falling into nihilism. James C. Evans, "The Apocalypse as Contrary Vision: Prolegomena to an Analogical Reading of *The Four Zoas*" (*TSLL*, 1972), calls for an abandonment of allegorical readings and a recognition that the poem "is not linearly but symmetrically organized."

Two adjoining articles appear in *PQ* (1977). Martin Bidney's "Urizen and the Comedy of Automatism in Blake's *The Four Zoas*" draws on Bergson's theory of the comic, a juxtaposition of automatism with vitality, as a way of understanding "Urizen's fall from the sublime to the ridiculous, from creative flexibility to stasis and repetition." Victoria Myers, "The Dialogues as Interpretive Focus in Blake's *The Four Zoas*," analyzes nine narrations of the Fall for evidence of both differences that reveal nuances of character and similarities that hint at the primal unfallen state. Bentley, "The Failure of Blake's *Four Zoas*" (*TSLL*, 1958), thinks the poem was destroyed by revision. George Mills Harper, "Apocalyptic Vision and Pastoral Dream in Blake's *Four Zoas*" (*SAQ*, 1965), discovers a cyclical view of history—a return to pastoral Eden rather than a breakthrough to the City of God. Wagenknecht pursues "the idea of pastoral" in earlier and later versions of the poem in two chapters of *Blake's Night*. Andrew Lincoln's "Blake's Lower Paradise: The Pastoral Passage in *The Four Zoas*, Night the Ninth" (*BRH*, 1981) explores the ambiguities of the dreamworld that Vala shares with Tharmas and Enion: the dream is perhaps a warning that unless this state is transcended the Fall will recur. Sugnet and Hagstrum discuss Christ's role, in essays already mentioned. A. Grace Wegner identifies a biblical allusion (*Expl*, 1969). Grant's detailed analysis of the drawings for Night III (in *BVFD*) has already been noted. Myra Glazer-Schotz, "On the Frontispiece of *The Four Zoas*" (*BNL* no. 40, 10: 4 [1977]), points out the ambiguous rising-reclining posture of the dreaming figure. Judith Lee, in "Ways of Their Own: The Emanations of Blake's *Vala, or The Four Zoas*" (*ELH*, 1983), views the female figures as characters with novelistic motivations. Jackie

DiSalvo's *War of Titans: Blake's Critique of Milton and the Politics of Religion* (1983)—a book too rich and subtle to yield extracts on short acquaintance—develops Wittreich's reading of Milton scholarship and feminist and Marxian insights to produce a provocative study of Blake's analyses of destructive power relationships embedded in English institutions, particularly the church and the home. Donald Ault's book on the poem is in press. Natoli lists six dissertations, some of which will doubtless become seedbeds for further publications.

Pictorial Works. For each picture or set of illustrations discussed in this section, the most comprehensive list of critiques is to be found in Butlin's *The Paintings and Drawings of William Blake,* a primary resource mentioned under "Aids to Research." Butlin also provides the most convenient—and often the most accurate—reproductions; but see "Reproductions of Pictorial Works" for specialized critical catalogs, many of which also contain commentary. Edward Hodnett's *Image and Text* (1982) includes a chapter on Blake as illustrator, for non-specialized consumption. Bentley's "The Great Illustrated-Book Publishers of the 1790s and William Blake," in *Editing Illustrated Texts* (1980), sets up Blake's historical context.

Before Blake began any of the designs that Butlin rightly calls "The Great Book Illustrations," he made an extraordinary set of twelve large color prints on biblical, Shakespearean, Miltonic, and historical themes. Literary critics have not hesitated to attempt interpretations of these haunting images, eight of which may be viewed in the Tate Gallery, London. In the festschrift for Damon, an art historian and a literary critic contribute adjoining essays on these designs: Martin Butlin, "The Evolution of Blake's Large Color Prints of 1795," and Anne T. Kostelanetz (later Mellor), "Blake's 1795 Color Prints: An Interpretation." Although most American literary critics do not accept Butlin's British and art-historical designation of 1795 as a cutoff date after which "Blake's primary and most successful means of expression ceased to be poetry and its illustration and became purely visual," they are well advised to take Butlin's careful sifting of technical and stylistic features of the designs as an absolutely necessary context for any iconographic study. It was Butlin, too, who discovered that Blake's true title for one famous print was not *Elijah,* as had long been thought, but *God Judging Adam* (*Burlington Magazine,* 1965; rpt. *The Visionary Hand*). Theories of an association between Blake's 1795 interest in color printing and the pessimistic outlook of the Lambeth Books and most of the color prints have been shaken by Butlin's recent bombshell, the discovery that one of these prints, the Butts copy of *Newton* (Tate Gallery), was made on 1804 paper ("A Newly Discovered Watermark and a Visionary's Way with His Dates" [*BIQ* no. 58, 15: 2, 1981]). Bindman, in an afterword on the 1982 Yale-Toronto exhibition (*BIQ* no. 64, 16: 4 [1983]), suggests that differences between two versions of *Newton* "make it unlikely that they were printed from the same surface"—another shock to received opinion, especially in connection with Butlin's discovery of the 1804 watermark. The *Newton* print has been much studied, primarily in relation to the compasses and left-handed symbolism also used in the "Ancient of Days" or frontispiece to

Europe, by Blunt (*JWCI,* 1938) and by Essick (*BS* 3: 2 [1971]); see also Nurmi's "Blake's 'Ancient of Days' and Motte's Frontispiece to Newton's *Principia*" in *The Divine Image.* John Gage (*JWCI,* 1971) emphasizes rainbow-prism imagery. Bo Lindberg's "William Blakes Nebuchadnezzar och Mänskodjuret" (*Taide Historiallisia Tutkimuksia Konsthistoriske Studien,* 1974) is a source study that focuses on the "moral code" of *Nebuchadnezzar.* H. Summerfield's sketchy speculations in "Blake's *Pity:* An Interpretation" (*CLQ,* 1981) are less persuasive than Christopher Heppner's fresh, well-thought-out suggestions in "Reading Blake's Designs: *Pity* and *Hecate*" (*BRH,* 1981).

On Blake's two great sets of illustrations to the Bible, relevant sections of the following books are helpful: Ronald Paulson's brief section "Blake's Bible" in *Book and Painting* (1982), which considers Milton and Michelangelo crucial to Blake's "deconstruction of the Bible" throughout his work; Bindman's discussion of the temperas and large canvases in *Blake as an Artist;* Blunt's grouping of the watercolors in "Blake's Bible," *The Art of William Blake;* Paley's shrewd observations in *William Blake.* See also the following essays: Nanavutty's "She Shall Be Called Woman" in *The Divine Vision;* Grant's "The Visionary Perspective of Ezekiel" (*BS* 4: 2 [1972]), Wicksteed's *The River of Life* (1949); Johnson's "Blake's Judgment on the Book of Judges," on the Samson and Jephthah pictures, in *Reconciliations* (ed. Mary Lynn Johnson and Seraphia D. Leyda, 1983); Essick's review of Butlin (*BIQ* no. 61, 16: 1 [1982]); Christopher Heppner's "The Woman Taken in Adultery: An Essay on Blake's 'Style of Designing' " (*BIQ* no. 66, 17: 2 [1983]); Terence Allan Hoagwood's " 'God Blessing the Seventh Day': Blake's Visions of God and His Biblical Watercolors" (*Studia Mystica,* 1984). A book-length study of the watercolor series, perhaps along lines projected by Johnson or by Kathyrn Gabriella (Kremen), cannot be far in the future.

A commentary on Blake's illustrations for Young's *Night Thoughts* by the Clarendon editors—Grant, Rose, Tolley, and Erdman—is progressing at a glacial pace. Anticipation of this long-promised collaborative commentary has tended to forestall other investigations. Grant's "Envisioning the First *Night Thoughts*" (in *BFVD),* a sort of preview of the full commentary, organizes the designs for Night I into thematic and imaginative units, factually describes them (with some lapses into interpretation), and expatiates on the cross-connections within and among the units. Grant identifies some preliminary and related sketches supplementary to those published in the Clarendon edition (*BIQ* no. 61, 16: 1 [1982]) and reviews problems of interpretation and execution (*BIQ,* 18: 3 [1984–85]). Paley's "Blake's *Night Thoughts:* An Exploration of the Fallen World," in the festschrift for Damon, clearly sets up the framework of the project and touches on its major motifs, but these are occasionally pressed too hard for resemblances to characters and ideas in the prophetic books. H. M. Margoliouth, "Blake's Drawings for Young's *Night Thoughts,*" in *The Divine Vision,* makes some interesting observations about some of the watercolors and their differences from the engraved versions, with particular attention to the figure of Christ. Thomas H. Helmstadter looks into other angles in "Blake's *Night Thoughts:* Interpretations of Edward Young" (*TSLL,* 1970; rpt. *The Visionary Hand*), "Blake and Religion: Iconographical Themes in the *Night Thoughts* (*SIR,* 1971), and "Blake and the Age of Reason: Spectres in the *Night Thoughts*" (*BS* 5: 1 [1972]). Wardle's study of emblem sources, mentioned earlier, is also pertinent.

On the Gray designs, Tayler provides very full and original commentary in her critical catalog *Blake's Illustrations to the Poems of Gray,* along with her overlapping or supplementary articles. Two brief conference speeches on the subject were published in *Fearful Joy* (ed. James Downey and Ben Jones, 1974): Tayler's "Two Eighteenth-Century Illustrators of Gray," on Bentley and Blake, and Ben Jones's "Blake on Gray: Outlines of Recognition." Richard Johnson follows up in "Blake as Audience: The Designs to Gray's 'Ode on the Death of a Favourite Cat,' " in *Reconciliations* (ed. Johnson and Leyda, 1983). Frank A. Vaughn, "Blake's Illustrations to Gray's 'The Bard' " (*CLQ,* 1981), sees the title figure as undergoing an educational redirection of his prophetic energy. Gleckner's article on the Gray designs, mainly about "The Fly," has already been mentioned.

Blake made at least one set of illustrations for most of Milton's major poems. A chapter in Marcia R. Pointon, *Milton and English Art* (1970), surveys the whole subject, and a chapter in Wittreich, *Angel of Apocalypse,* considers Blake's illustrations, particularly those for *Paradise Regained,* in relation to Milton's texts and the illustrative and critical traditions surrounding them. But Pamela Dunbar, *William Blake's Illustrations to the Poetry of Milton* (1980), enjoys the distinction of providing the first detailed exposition of all the subjects from Milton. A book so important should have been better, not only in quality of reproductions but, more importantly, in depth of citations and brightness of commentary. For example, the appearance of Wittreich in Dunbar's bibliography (but not in her footnotes or index) gives no hint of his leading role in this area of Blake studies, and Stephen C. Behrendt's numerous articles are totally ignored. Although Dunbar's book is useful in calling attention to the designs for Milton as a coherent body of pictorial criticism, Behrendt's full-scale study *The Moment of Explosion: Blake and the Illustration of Milton* (1983) will appeal to a more knowledgeable audience than Dunbar's because it engages in productive dialogue with Butlin and with critics across the full range of Blake studies. A third book on the Milton designs has been announced as forthcoming by its author, Bette Charlene Werner.

In reviewing studies of separate sets of Blake's illustrations of Milton, I follow Butlin's chronology, with the caveat that Dunbar, Behrendt, and others occasionally disagree. Since several of the following critiques are concerned with differences between two sets of illustrations for the same poem (one made for Blake's patron Butts, the other for a Mr. Thomas), I mention locations as well as patrons to make identifications easier.

The *Comus* illustrations (an 8-design series in 2 sets: ?1801, for Thomas, now in the Huntington; ?1815, for Butts, now in the Boston Museum of Fine Arts) have been brilliantly illuminated by Irene Tayler. But her perceptive judgments, expressed most fully in *Blake's Sublime Allegory,* are based entirely on the Huntington series. The main line of her psychosexual interpretation, including supporting details on the symbolism of the haemony flower, is taken over wholesale by Dunbar without acknowledgment. Angus Fletcher, *The Transcendental Masque* (1971), reproduces both sets of *Comus* designs in color, though dismally, to support very brief comments. Behrendt's articles, since revised for *The Moment of Explosion,* include "The Mental Contest: Blake's *Comus* Designs" (*BS* 8: 1 [1978]), which argues, on the basis of both sets, that Blake corrects Milton's excessive veneration of chastity not by deviating from the poem but by representing it very literally. Behrendt further discusses Blake's interpretive mode in "The Polished Artifact: Some Observations on Imitative Criticism" (*Genre,* 1977). J. Karl Franson, "The Serpent-Driving Females in Blake's *Comus* 4" (*BIQ* no. 47, 12: 3 [1978–79]), identifies the uppermost figure as Cotytto.

On the *Paradise Lost* designs (12-design series in 2 sets: ?1807, for Thomas, in the Huntington; 1808, for Butts, most now in Boston), Morse Peckham, "Blake, Milton, and Edward Burney" (*Princeton Univ. Lib. Chron.,* 1950), suggests that Blake was indebted to a previous illustrator, and C. H. Collins Baker, "Some Illustrators of Milton's *Paradise Lost* (1660–1850)" (*Library,* 1948), lays out a whole illustrative tradition, to which details are added by Pointon and Wittreich. Merritt Y. Hughes, "Some Illustrators of Milton: The Expulsion from Paradise" (*JEGP,* 1961; rpt. in *Milton: Modern Essays in Criticism,* ed. Arthur E. Barker, 1965), points out that Blake was the first to follow Milton's ambiguously hopeful text rather than the Masaccio-Raphael iconography of despair. The originality of Blake's final design is also noted in Kester Svendson, "John Martin and the Expulsion Scene in *Paradise Lost*" (*SEL,* 1961). David Bindman's "Hogarth's 'Satan, Sin and Death' and Its Influence" (*Burlington Magazine,* 1970) and Robert R. Wark's "Blake's 'Satan, Sin and Death'" in his *Ten British Pictures* (1971) explicate Blake's second illustration.

On the *Nativity Ode* (6-design series in 2 sets: 1809, for Thomas, now in the Whitworth; ?1815, for Butts, now in the Huntington), there is a dispute about dating. The undated Huntington set (which Butlin dates c. 1815) appears to him certainly stylistically later than the dated Whitworth set on the basis of details not clear to the untrained eye, especially when reproductions are used. The finely detailed penwork of the Whitworth set (1809) leads Dunbar to think it must be the later version; she therefore dates the mistier-looking Huntington set a year earlier (c. 1808). On the basis of reproductions only and a reference to the ode in a letter to Butts, Stephen C. Behrendt, in "Blake's Illustrations to Milton's *Nativity Ode*" (*PQ,* 1976), dates the Huntington set even earlier (c. 1803) and reorders the series to bring out Blake's response to the poem's apocalyptic conclusion and Christocentric theology. Behrendt's ordering goes against the arrangements of both Keynes's 1923 set of reproductions and Baker's *Catalogue of William Blake's Drawings and Paintings in the Huntington Library* (rev. R. R. Wark, 1969), and in *The Moment of Explosion* he repudiates the idea. In *Paintings and Drawings,* Butlin summarizes the stylistic evidence for the 1815 date and points out that Behrendt's fifth design is inscribed "No. 3" on the back of the mount. Alexander N. Hutchinson (*Brit. Columbia Lib. Quarterly,* 1972–73) comments on the Whitworth set only.

For illustrations of *L'Allegro* and *Il Penseroso* (12 designs, 6 for each poem, in one set made for Butts, Morgan Library), the interpretations are too diffusely at variance to be characterized briefly. Besides books by Wittreich, Mellor, and

Dunbar, see articles by Rose (a "thematic reading" in *Hartford Stud. in Lit.,* 1970) and by Grant (chatty identifications, accompanied by Judith Rhodes's interesting diagram-cum-explanation of "thematic relationships" in *BIQ* no. 16, 4: 4 [1971]; rpt. *The Visionary Hand*). Grant also discusses negative imagery in the Mirth design as watercolor and engraving (*BIQ* no. 19, 5: 3 [1971–72]) and adds a short note on *L'Allegro* 6 (in *BVFD*). Behrendt comments on poetic maturity in *Il Penseroso* in *Milton Studies* (1973); Kiralis discusses sexual phobias, found even in the final design, in *Milton Reconsidered* (ed. Franson, 1976). J. M. Q. Davies works out the negative implications of the final *Il Penseroso* design in *AUMLA* (1980).

On *Paradise Regained* (12 designs in one set, ?1816–20, Fitzwilliam), the basic articles are Wittreich's "William Blake: Illustrator-Interpreter of *Paradise Regained*" in *Calm of Mind* (ed. Wittreich, 1971), refined in *Angel of Apocalypse;* Franson's "Christ on the Pinnacle" (*Milton Quarterly,* 1970); Gleckner's "Blake's Illustration of the Third Temptation in *Paradise Regained*" (*BIQ* no. 42, 11: 2 [1977])—all of which bring out Blake's approval of Milton's theme of Christ's self-mastery and the manifestation of the divine nature within. J. M. Q. Davies, " 'Embracings are Comminglings': Passion and Apocalypse in Blake's *Paradise Regained* Designs" (*DUJ,* 1981), attempts to show that Blake was more critical of the doctrine of obedience than Wittreich thinks and that he also criticized Milton's sexual attitudes. Bindman's 1970 Fitzwilliam catalog describes and reproduces an alternative design, "Christ in the Wilderness," and James T. Wills, " 'For I Discern thee Other Than thou seem'st' " (*BS* 8: 2 [1979]), identifies another.

Essick and Paley's excellent study and facsimile *Robert Blair's* The Grave *Illustrated by William Blake* (1982) might have been made even more useful by. the inclusion of a brief bibliography of modern criticism. The authors review the history of graveyard poetry and of the Cromek-Schiavonetti scheme, building on the Cromek research of Bentley, mentioned earlier. Dennis Read has carried this work further. Through some oversight, Essick and Paley omit notice of Thomas Helmstadter's " 'Bright Visions of Eternity': Blake's Designs for Blair's *Grave*" (*BS* 8: 1 [1978]), which—among other original points—finds texts to fit even the three unnumbered plates and brings out "ironic tension" between author and illustrator in Blake's emphasis on resurrection.

On the snarling complexities of the Job project, the clearest guidance comes from Bo Lindberg's critical catalog *William Blake's Illustrations to the Book of Job* (1973). The influential pioneering interpretations of Wicksteed's *Blake's Vision of the Book of Job* (1910; rev. 1924) and Damon's *Blake's Job* (1966), both of which show that God is a reflection of Job's state of mind, now seem too rigidly programmatic—in that Wicksteed overemphasized left-right symbolism and Damon insisted too much on the pattern of the Seven Eyes of God. Andrew Wright's *Blake's Job: A Commentary* (1972), largely a recapitulation of well-established critical ideas, touches on new points from time to time; a brief appendix summarizes previous studies. Wright acknowledges but does not really absorb Frye's magisterial essay "Blake's Reading of the Book of Job" in the festschrift for Damon, which treats the designs as a pictorial commentary on the Bible as a whole, with Job as microcosm. Ben Nelms, "Text and Design in *Illustra-*

tions of the Book of Job" (in *BVFD*), interprets Elihu's crucial speech as a positive development. Nelms also makes use of a little-known Freudian interpretation by Marion Milner (Joanna Field), "Psycho-Analysis and Art (in *Psychoanalysis and Contemporary Thought*, ed. John Sutherland, 1958). Jenijoy La Belle, "Words Graven with an Iron Pen: The Marginal Texts in Blake's *Job"* (in *The Visionary Hand*), examines typological and imagistic relationships among biblical texts in the border designs. Diane Filby Gillespie (*CLQ*, 1983) takes the circle as key to the designs, particularly 20, with "pictures within pictures, circles within circles, wheels within wheels." Kathleen Raine's *The Human Face of God: William Blake and the Book of Job* (1982), forthrightly proclaiming itself to be "not primarily a work of scholarship," neither builds on nor corrects Raine's recent predecessors but examines the designs as a vehicle for conveying "universal metaphysical knowledge." Oddly, Raine has some kind words for the accusers and finds Eliphaz' hair-raising apparition to be the "first opening" of Job's understanding. Her concluding chapter usefully compares in detail (for the first time in print, to my knowledge) Blake's and Jung's interpretations of the Book of Job.

Although Blake's panoramic designs for Chaucer (1808) and Spenser (?1825) were executed years apart, for different patrons, each clearly illuminates the other. So far, however, their interrelationship has hardly been considered; the lion's share of attention has gone to the Chaucer picture and its engraving. On the Spenser picture, except for comments in Frye's *Fearful Symmetry* and Damon's *Dictionary*, the Grant-Brown exposition cited earlier (*BNL* no. 31, 8: 3 [1974–75]) stands virtually alone.

Karl Kiralis, "William Blake as an Intellectual and Spiritual Guide to Chaucer's *Canterbury Pilgrims"* (*BS* 1: 1 [1969]), points out patterns of relationship implied by the symmetrical arrangement of figures and details of their clothing and mounts. Kiralis also shows that Blake's quotations correspond to none of the three available editions of Chaucer and surmises that he used Tyrwhitt, possibly supplemented by Speght. In an appendix he reports on five states of the engraving and mentions two colored copies of the first state. Warren Stevenson, "Interpreting Blake's *Canterbury Pilgrimage"* (*CLQ*, 1977), in pursuit of Blake's "sense of ironic ambivalence," reiterates many of Kiralis' points, such as his reasons (following Damon) for identifying the Wife with the Whore of Babylon and the Prioress with Tirzah. Orphia Jane Allen, "Blake's Archetypal Criticism: The *Canterbury Pilgrims"* (*Genre*, 1978), makes some good incidental observations but insists on a procrustean taxonomy. Alice Miskimin, "The Illustrated Eighteenth-Century Chaucer" (*MP*, 1979), compares Blake's design with engravings in the 1721 Urry edition, with the Bell's English Poets edition of 1782–83, and with Stothard's large rival picture—but see corrections by G. E. Bentley, Jr. (*MP*, 1981). Claire Pace, "Blake and Chaucer" (*Art History*, 1980), places Blake's picture within the whole history of British illustrations of Chaucer, bringing in Barry, Mortimer, Rigaud, Hamilton, and Westall, in addition to the engravers noted by Miskimin; she also gives a physical description of the painting itself, which Kiralis and Stevenson knew only in the inaccurate reproduction published by the New York Graphic Society. Betsy Bowden, "The Artistic and Interpretive Context of Blake's 'Canterbury Pilgrims' " (*BIQ* no. 52, 13: 4 [1980]), coincidentally mentions many of the same illustrators; she even goes back to the Ellesmere Manuscript, which in Blake's time was in London. Miskimin, Pace, and Bowden all emphasize the importance of Urry's edition, which contained an engraved processional scene, probably by Vertue. M. E. Reisner, "Effigies of Power: Pitt and Fox as Canterbury Pilgrims" (*ECS,* 1979), argues that the Pardoner and Summoner are based on political cartoons of the leading ministers of state. Finally, Ruthven Todd, "A Tentative Note on the Economics of the *Canterbury Pilgrims*" (*BIQ* no. 41, 11: 1 [1977]), speculates on costs, and Essick and Michael C. Young, "The Posthumous Pilgrimage of the 'Canterbury' Print" (*BIQ* no. 58, 15: 2 [1981]), reveal shady dealings in restrikes.

Considerably less has been written about other major works. Albert S. Roe's thorough study *Blake's Illustrations to the Divine Comedy* (1953) and Milton Klonsky's added observations and color reproductions in *Blake's Dante* (1980) stand as the only major essays in interpretation of these 102 designs. On the *Last Judgment* pictures, besides Blake's own commentary and the *Quarterly's* special leaflet edited by Mitchell, previously cited, see Roe's "A Drawing of the Last Judgment" (*HLQ,* 1957) and Damon's *Dictionary.* Keynes, "The Arlington Court Picture" (1954; rev. in his *Blake Studies* [1971]), describes the picture and recounts its exciting discovery in 1947. It was first called "The Circle of the Life of Man" by Keynes and others, but Keynes came to accept Raine's title "The Sea of Time and Space," on the basis of the Neoplatonic interpretation she published in *JWCI* (1957) and reiterated in her *Blake and Tradition,* mentioned earlier. Digby, *Symbol and Image,* interpreted the picture psychologically as a moment of choice between the light and dark aspects of life; regeneration comes through acceptance of unconscious forces. According to Simmons and Warner (*SIR,* 1971; rpt. *The Visionary Hand*), it represents a "moment of truth," recognition of the fallen condition; the veiled female figure is a demonic Vala. Grant (*BNL* no. 12, 3: 4 [1970] and no. 13, 4: 1 [1970]), with afterthoughts in *SIR* (1971; rpt. *The Visionary Hand*), interprets the lady as a redemptive Jerusalem figure. Both Simmons-Warner and Grant relate various motifs in the design to similar ones elsewhere in Blake and in art traditions generally. Blake's Shakespeare illustrations (set of 6 in the British Museum, made for Thomas) are discussed by W. Moelwyn Merchant, briefly in *Shakespeare and the Artist* (1959), more fully in *Apollo* (1964; rpt. *The Visionary Hand*). Rodney Baine and Mary Baine analyze a preliminary drawing in "Blake's Sketch for *Hamlet*" (*BNL* no. 36, 9: 4 [1976]); Rodney Baine also identified sketches for *Robinson Crusoe* in *BNL* (no. 22, 6: 2 [1972]). A fascinating series of designs for a pseudoepigraphic book was discussed in Allan R. Brown's "Blake's Drawings for *The Book of Enoch*" (*Burlington Magazine,* 1940; rpt. *The Visionary Hand*). Peter Alan Taylor, "Blake's Text for the *Enoch* Drawings" (*BNL* no. 28 7: 4 [1974]), corrects Brown by reading the 1821 translation that Blake actually used. Bentley, "A Jewel in an Ethiop's Ear," in *Blake in His Time,* learnedly compares the drawings not only with the text but also with illustrations by Westall and Flaxman. Essick, in "Blake's 'Enoch' Lithograph" (*BIQ* no. 56, 14: 4 [1981]), explains technical details of the unique print. The Genesis Manuscript (Huntington) has hardly been touched; Butlin's notes in *Paintings and Drawings* suggest exciting possibilities beyond the beginning made by Piloo Nanavutty's "A Title Page in Blake's Illustrated Genesis Manuscript" (*JWCI,* 1947).

Some articles on Blake's miscellaneous drawings and graphic works, even his hackwork, bring up surprisingly interesting information. Keynes's "Blake's Engravings for Gay's *Fables*" (*BC,* 1972) reveals that Blake was sometimes free to improve the designs he engraved professionally. Todd, "Two Blake Prints and Two Fuseli Drawings" (*BNL* no. 14, 5: 2 [1972]), shows that Fuseli allowed Blake considerable latitude as an engraver of his designs. Essick, "The Figure in the Carpet: Blake's Engravings in Salzmann's *Elements of Morality*" (*BNL* no. 45, 12: 1 [1978]), suggests ways to detect Blake's hand in unsigned plates. Bernard Smith, "European Vision and the South Pacific" (*JWCI,* 1950; rpt. in his book of the same title, 1960), shows how Blake modified Hunter's original sketch of an aborigine family. Dennis M. Welch, "Blake's Response to Wollstonecraft's *Original Stories*" (*BNL* no. 49, 13: 1 [1979]), shows how images from a commercial project spilled over into Blake's own work. Dennis M. Read, "A New Blake Engraving: Gilchrist and the Cromek Connection" (*BIQ* no. 54, 14: 2 [1980]), reveals the existence of a proof copy of Blake's original engraving (destroyed by Cromek) for the frontispiece to Malkin's *A Father's Memoirs of His Child.* G. Ingli James, "Blake's Woodcuts Illuminated" (*Apollo,* 1974), reproduces prints from a colored copy of the Vergil woodcuts. Thomas V. Lange, "Blake in American Almanacs" (*BIQ* no. 54, 14: 2 [1980]), announces early piratings of Blake's Stedman plates. Tolley's "Some Blake Puzzles—Old and New" (*BS* 3 [1971]) and John E. Grant's "Addenda" in the same issue discuss some recently discovered sketches, and Philip B. Grant (*BNL* no. 39, 10: 3 [1976–77]) suggests a source for one of them. Essick, "Blake and the Traditions of Reproductive Engraving" (*BS* 5: 1 [1972]), theorizes that Blake equated cross-hatching with mechanical reproduction and with nets and traps. Erdman, "The Dating of William Blake's Engravings" (*PQ,* 1952), and Butlin, "Cataloguing William Blake," in *Blake in His Time,* discuss solutions to problems in dating.

TRENDS AND PROSPECTS

The old order passes; the rough beast slouches. In the humanities, several writers of surveys have recently adopted the term "paradigm shift"—though it is no longer fashionable in the history of science—to describe their own moment of the flux. If a major shift is occurring in Blake studies, as it seems to be, it does not pivot on any one new work of criticism, and no new paradigm is in evidence. Through minute fissures in the polished monolith of *Fearful Symmetry,* we begin to glimpse a Blake more fearful than symmetrical. For the near future the way into Blake's depths, as A. C. Bradley once proclaimed of Wordsworth, appears to lead "through his strangeness and paradoxes, and not around them"—or above some of them, as in Frye's grand construct. A decade ago, for example, the question of Blake's misogyny, like the more general problem of the conflicting details in his myth, was in effect invisible because it had not been treated as an issue by Frye. But the question did not go away; along with other loose ends, it began to work itself away from the seamless whole, to demand attention. The pressure of

critical modernity has also worked its changes. Those who are au courant do not
deal in matters of wholeness, coherence, harmony, or powerful intrinsic meaning. A vocabulary of "seer," "prophet," "vision," and "apocalypse" fairly shouts the
pre-1970 orientation of its framework of ideas. The Blake whom the trendsetters
are now writing about is no poet of "firm perswasion" but a tangled complex of
uncertainties, doubts, mysteries; a generator of subliminal ironies, antitheses, ir-
resolutions, indeterminacies, absences; an inscriber of "texts." For several of the
speakers at a 1982 conference entitled "Blake and Criticism" in Santa Cruz, it
seems that Urizen the compulsive writer has actually replaced Los the artificer
and lover as a guiding genius.

The history of transitions in Blake criticism from the beginning up through
the early 1970s is best told, as I have already said more than once, in Bentley's
"Blake's Reputation and Interpreters" in *Blake Books.* Recently Morris Eaves, "Inside the Blake Industry: Past, Present, and Future" (*SIR,* 1982), in an issue honoring Erdman, has given the rest of the world a delicious opportunity to Eaves-
drop on ten prominent members of the "Blake Establishment" as they conduct an
in-house assessment of their undertaking: Erdman, Essick, Adams, Joseph
Viscomi, Mitchell, Nelson Hilton, Paley, Kroeber, Gleckner, and Grant. No art historian, British or Commonwealth subject, neoclassicist—or feminist scholar of
any gender or discipline—sits on the board of directors of this "little, home-
made, bumptious, and entirely unintimidating world of high Blake scholarship."
These scholars are, of course, conversant with the whole range of schools and movements in Blake studies, even those they do not themselves follow, and the clan is
representative enough to air the main agenda of Blakists within the whole of
academia. For example, most members of Blake's larger critical audience would
agree with Eaves's group that some or all of the following are desirable: a critical
biography that is sensitive to Blake's political, social, intellectual, literary, and artistic surroundings; a more intimate and productive interchange between art historians and literary critics; a rapprochement of critical theory, literary history,
and practical criticism that will produce more sophisticated ways of dealing with
the prophecies; a complete set of high-fidelity color reproductions, perhaps disseminated in microfiche or videodisc; a better understanding of Blake's interpretation of the Bible. There is also some feeling, expressed by Essick, that Butlin's
catalog will lure new generations of art historians into Blake studies, leaving literary critics free to resume their proper function of verbal analysis. Like the regen-
erate Zoas, specialists will return to their appointed stations as in times of old.

Some of the more recent in a long line of thoughtful reviews and essays of
the past ten or fifteen years put the present upheaval in perspective; others are
worth reading for their signposts at earlier crossroads: John E. Grant, "Who Shall
Bind the Infinite and Arrange It in Libraries?" (*PQ,* 1982); V. A. De Luca, "How We
Are Reading Blake" (*UTQ,* 1980–81); Spencer Hall, "Some Recent Directions in
Blake Studies" (*SHR,* 1976); Henri Lemaitre, "État présent des études blakiennes"
(*EA,* 1975); Hugh J. Luke, Jr., "A Decade of William Blake" (*Prairie Schooner,*
1972–74), and his "William Blake: *Pictor Notus*" (*PLL,* 1966); Leonard Trawick,
"The Present State of Blake Studies" (*Studies in Burke and His Time,* 1971); Max
Schulz, review essay in *ECS* (1971); G. E. Bentley, Jr., "Blake Scholars and Critics,"

in two parts (*UTQ,* 1970). See also an unsigned review, "Some Anglo-American Divergencies in the Appraisal of William Blake" (*TLS,* 25 Dec. 1969), and Michael Ackland's narrow review "Blake's System and the Critics" (*AUMLA,* 1980). Outspoken deplorers of most recent trends include such luminaries as the author of the first art-historical study and the coeditor of the *Census* of illuminated books—see Anthony Blunt's "Blakomania" (*YR,* 1972) and "Blake and the Scholars" (*NYRB,* 28 Oct. 1965) and Edwin Wolf II's review of Paley's *William Blake* (*Fine Print,* 1979).

In the middle eighties, formalist and archetypal critics continue bracing themselves for a long-predicted tidal wave of phenomenological, structuralist, semiotic, and deconstructive interpretations of Blake that will reshape the critical landscape. Edward Larrissy, in "Horses of Instruction" (*Art History,* 1983), predicts "a major engagement between Marxian critics . . . and anti-historicist theoreticians" on the embattled plain of Blake studies. Michael Fischer's aforementioned "Blake's Quarrel with Indeterminacy" and Steven Shaviro's " 'Striving with Systems': Blake and the Politics of Difference" (*Boundary 2,* 1982) differ on Blake's compatibility with the tenets and approaches of contemporary critical schools. Several members of Eaves's symposium suggest that the engagement between Blake and deconstruction will be all to the good. The newer criticisms appear to be mellowing and enlisting clearer expositors; meanwhile, critics of older persuasions are learning to formulate harder theoretical questions about what has been left out or left unresolved in Blake's thought and art. It is even possible that Blake, as Mitchell speculates, will "provide a new leavening for critical theory" because he "anticipates so many of the strategies of deconstruction and offers such powerful antidotes to its skeptical and nihilistic tendencies." Will Blake be discovered to have been there always, already? In the next decade's reenactment of the old struggle between Los and his Spectre—with some critics reading the stars, others the void between the stars—we may make progress when the Spectre and Los agree to strike alternate blows on the same anvil.[7]

Notes

[1]Because *Blake: An Illustrated Quarterly* (1967– ; named *Blake Newsletter* until 1977) contains so many items of importance, my citations include the volume and number, the year, and one extra number: from its origin as a mimeographed sheet until volume 18 in 1984, this journal has maintained continuous serial numbers for all issues, without regard to the newer volume and quarterly numbers. My citations give this special issue number before the conventional volume number, thus: *BIQ* no. 61, 16: 1 (1982). These special issue numbers, called "whole" numbers, have perhaps retained informal currency among Blakists because of the awkwardness of identifying issues by date: the Winter issue, the third number in each volume, always spans the old and new years. For most purposes, however, conventional citations are sufficient. Although the MLA *International Bibliography* abbreviates this journal as *Blake,* I have used *BNL* or *BIQ* or, where the context is clear, the *Quarterly,* to avoid confusion with books called *Blake.* The other Blake journal, *Blake Studies* (1968–), should not be confused with Keynes's collection of essays by the same title (1949; rev. ed. 1971). I cite both volume and number for *Blake Studies* because it got so far behind schedule that it dropped dates altogether; the date I use for undated issues is the legal copyright date. No issues

have been published since volume 9, combining numbers 1 and 2, appeared in 1980.

[2]I mention the black-and-white photographs in Erdman's *The Illuminated Blake* (1974) and David Bindman's *The Complete Graphic Works of William Blake* (1978) only when the copies they reproduce are otherwise unavailable. As stated under "Aids to Research," it was Keynes, following John Sampson, who devised the present system of referring to different copies of the same work by letters of the alphabet—"copy A" for the earliest to as many letters as are necessary for the latest. I follow Bentley, *Blake Books* (1977), in extending the system to works not covered by Keynes, while preserving reference letters used in the Keynes-Wolf *Census* (1953). I comment on the pictorial and editorial quality of the facsimiles only to note exceptions. Thus it goes without saying that the hand-stenciled Blake Trust facsimiles are beautifully executed in color (unless otherwise noted); that Keynes's editorial notes for the Blake Trust, though brief and often without comparisons among copies, are reliable; that Erdman's interpretative notes are essential points of reference; and that E. P. microfilms and slides are in color. When I feel that more should be said about a facsimile, I cite a review, often a severe one. For information on reproductions of individual plates, see Essick's already mentioned "Finding List" (*BNL* nos. 17–18, 5: 1–2 [1971]), which I have not attempted to bring up to date. Bentley's *William Blake's Writings* (1978) contains virtually complete facsimiles of all the illuminated books, some in copies not otherwise reproduced, which I neglected to list.

[3]In subsequent references to three of the books mentioned in this paragraph, I use informal abbreviations familiar to most Blake scholars: Rosenfeld's *William Blake: Essays for S. Foster Damon* becomes "the festschrift for Damon"; Paley and Phillips' *William Blake: Essays in Honour of Sir Geoffrey Keynes* becomes "the festschrift for Keynes"; Erdman and Grant's *Blake's Visionary Forms Dramatic* becomes *BVFD*.

[4]When I refer to journal articles that have been included in these collections, I note republication except for those articles best described as "often reprinted"; I ignore reprints of sections of books. The collection edited by Grant is abbreviated *Discussions,* that by Frye as *Blake,* that by Bottrall as *Casebook,* that by Johnson and Grant as *Poetry and Designs.* I note reprints in other kinds of collections, such as casebooks on Romanticism or the collected essays of a single author, only sporadically, as they have come to my attention. If an article first appeared in a periodical other than a learned journal and was later gathered by the author into a volume of essays, I give the date only of the periodical publication, followed by the full citation of the author's volume of essays.

[5]Since the value of general comparisons lies mainly in the eye of the beholder, I merely list some proposed relationships that interested persons may wish to pursue in the standard bibliographies: parallels or contrasts with Dante, by Richard G. Green (*CL,* 1974); with Carlyle, by Albert J. Lavalley (in *Carlyle and the Idea of the Modern* [1968]); with Hawthorne, by Glenn M. Pederson (*NCF,* 1958); with Rimbaud, by Enid R. Peschel (*FR,* 1973); with Kierkegaard, by J. R. Scrimbeour (*Scand. Stud.,* 1975); with Unamuno, by Mario J. Valdes (*UTQ,* 1971); with Eudora Welty, by John B. Vickery (*MLN,* 1961) and by Wayne D. McGinnis (*Notes on Mississippi Writers* [1979]); with Plato, by Harry Lesser (*Philosophy,* 1981); with Mann, by Walter Pasche (*Arcadia,* 1975); with Wallace Stegner, by J. Ellis (*SSF,* 1980); with Pound, by W. St. Flory (*Paideuma,* 1977); with Novalis, by Joachim J. Scholz (*Blake and Novalis,* 1978). See also John Beer's "Blake, Wordsworth, and Coleridge: Some Cross-Currents and Parallels, 1789–1805" (in the festschrift for Keynes) and, for an excellent survey and a checklist of Blake-Wordsworth comparisons, James R. Bennett's "The Comparative Criticism of Blake and Wordsworth" (*WC,* 1983).

[6]Settings by C. Hubert Parry, Benjamin Britten, Ralph Vaughan Williams, Virgil Thomson, Ellen Raskin, and others are reviewed by Peter Roberts (*BNL* no. 28, 7: 4 [1974]) and cataloged in Bryan N. S. Gooch and David S. Thatcher's *Musical Settings of British Romantic Literature* (1982). Eloise Hay, in "Songs of William Blake and Music of Blake's Time" (*Soundings,* 1976), and Martin K. Nurmi (*BNL* no. 40, 10: 4 [1977]) review an interesting concert at the 1976 Santa Barbara conference on Blake. B. H. Fairchild's *Such Holy Song,* already mentioned, considers sources and analogues in folk and classical music. Anthony J. Harding reviews Mike Westbrook's jazz settings commissioned for Adrian Mitchell's musical comedy *Tyger* (*BIQ* no. 58, 15: 2 [1981]); Arthur Farwell's settings are published for the first time by his son Brice (*BIQ* no. 42, 11: 2 [1977]). The making of Vaughn Williams' *Job: A Masque for Dancing* is detailed by Mary Clark, *The Sadler's Wells Ballet* (1955; rpt. *BIQ* no. 45, 12: 1 [1978]); see also Keynes's account of contributions by Gwendolyn Raverat and Ninette de Valois in his *Blake Studies.* Everett C. Frost reviews the British television production of *Job* (*BNL* no. 46, 12: 2 [1978]); Frank M. Parisi analyzes Neil Tennant's and Heidi Parisi's modern-dance choreography for "The Mental Traveller" (*BNL* no. 36, 9: 4 [1976]). Contributions by Tom Nichols and Evan Tonsing to *Sparks of Fire* (1982) indicate further musical experimentation. The effect of Blake on such groups as the Fugs and the Doors in the late 1960s and on Emerson, Lake, and Palmer in the 1970s is beyond my capacity to consider. In 1983, Elliott Hayes's one-man play, *Blake,* opened in Stratford, Ontario, starring Douglas Campbell, with songs by Loreena McKennit. Everett Frost produced *An Island in the Moon* for Pacifica radio in 1979. William Bolcom's full-scale Blake chorale premiered at the Stuttgart Opera in 1984. Notices of cinematic, theatrical, videocast, and musical productions appear from time to time in *Blake: An Illustrated Quarterly* (though they are not indexed, unfortunately). Bentley's *Blake Books* lists "chance findings" in a dozen media, including postage stamps (but not T-shirts), in the introduction.

[7]My work on this review was made easier by a summer grant from the National Endowment for the Humanities (1981), special help from the Coe College library, and by the graciousness of the following presses in supplying review copies, often of very expensive books: Cornell University Press, Oxford University Press, Princeton University Press, Yale University Press, Kent State University Press, and the Harmony Books division of Crown Publishers. Criticism published after my drafting was complete in 1982 is reviewed unevenly, as it happened to come to my attention. I am grateful for access to prepublication copies of books from Princeton University Press, Garland Press, the University of California Press, and the University of Georgia Press. G. E. Bentley, Jr., Morris Eaves, Robert F. Gleckner, John E. Grant, Nelson Hilton, and Morton D. Paley shared news of forthcoming books; Peter Schock helped with library work; Carolyn B. Brown and Alexander S. Gourlay helped with proofreading.

WILLIAM WORDSWORTH

Karl Kroeber

Contents

Introduction

Since the last edition of this volume there have been four developments of outstanding importance for Wordsworthian scholarship. First, the accelerating increase in the quantity of writing about the poet has continued; Wordsworthian criticism is accumulating so rapidly that there is danger that we may lose track of our most useful lines of inquiry. I try not to contribute to this suicide-through-plenitude by reporting selectively, not comprehensively. I try to make my selectivity useful by defining clearly my point of view through frank expressions of opinion as I write in February 1982 (inserting brief notices of subsequently published work).

The second major development has been the success of the *Wordsworth Circle,* which since 1970 has been publishing essays, reviews, bibliographies, and accounts of research in progress, with occasional concentration on special topics, such as the Autumn issue of volume 9 (1978), primarily devoted to more than thirty discussions of teaching Wordsworth. The journal has become the focal point for criticism dealing with Wordsworth, being a primary source for surveys of brief notes and dissertations (both omitted from this report). In looking over the dissertations completed after 1969, for example, I found more than ninety that seemed worthy of attention by specialists. Unsurprisingly, *WC* has been the center of several controversies, but increasingly it has served to extend the effective range of activity of those concerned with Wordsworth's art and social milieu.

The third principal event in our field has been the appearance in strength of the Cornell edition. The volumes so far published are noted individually below, but it may be said here that the series as a whole has become the intellectual center of most recent investigations into Wordsworth's poetry. The series has encouraged careful and textually accurate scholarship, and its salutary influence will be felt for many decades.

Finally, less tangible but most important, is the rise to critical popularity of William Blake. Blake has not displaced Wordsworth as the central figure of Romanticism in England, but the spreading acceptance of Blake's significance has compelled modifications in judgments of Wordsworth and definitions of his place in literary history. Harold Bloom's "The Internalization of Quest-Romance" in a collection of essays he edited in 1970, *Romanticism and Consciousness,* illustrates how Blake's popularity has affected Wordsworthian studies. For Bloom the paradigmatic Romantic quest poem is *Jerusalem,* so it is unremarkable that he discovers Wordsworth's poetry to be distinguished by "the evanescence of any subject but subjectivity" and in no way seeking reconciliation of humankind and nature, its "healing function" being "performed only when the poetry shows the power of the mind over outward sense": so much for Wordsworth's "fitting & fitted," to which Blake objected violently.

The tendency to associate Wordsworth with Blakean antinaturalism, moreover, may be seen as carrying forward a modernist critical view described by Lionel Trilling in his essay "The Fate of Pleasure" in *Romanticism Reconsidered* (ed.

Northrop Frye, 1963). Trilling points out that one of the boldest and most upsetting affirmations in Wordsworth's Preface to *Lyrical Ballads* is that "the grand elementary principle of pleasure" is the foundation for "the naked and native dignity of man." The statement has been largely ignored by modern critics, Trilling suggests, because they feel a "complex antagonism" toward such pleasure, being themselves "in favor of the gratification which may be found in unpleasure." Trilling cites Dostoevsky's Underground Man and Nietzsche as representative of the modernist position antithetical to Wordsworthian pleasure. Their "inside life," Trilling says, is the "characteristically modern conception of the spiritual life," and he notes "how far" from the modernist "imagination is the idea of 'peace' as the crown of spiritual struggle," with the "idea of 'bliss' even further removed." For a modern critic, "that highly developed person who must perforce live the bourgeois life in an affluent society, an aesthetic ethos based on the devaluation of pleasure" must be attractive, particularly since for such a "modern literary personality political life is likely to exist only as it makes occasion for the disgust and rage which are essential to the state of modern spirituality." Although I find Trilling's diagnosis confirmed by much criticism of the sixties and early seventies, an exception is B. R. Breyer, "Wordsworth's Pleasure: An Approach to His Poetic Theory" (*SHR*, 1972); the modernist sensibility he described is now being transformed, and an increasingly profitable interaction between Wordsworthian and Blakean criticism may be rather confidently predicted.

More recent Wordsworthian studies, however, have somewhat depressed me by their prevailingly mournful tone, a tone adumbrated by Thomas McFarland in "Poetry and the Poet: The Structure of Poetic Content" in *Literary Theory and Structure* (ed. Frank Brody, 1973). McFarland thinks all lyrics are "evening lyrics," says that "the ultimate poetic theme is the elegiac theme," and concludes that "great poems are monuments to our lost selves." While one doesn't expect a modern "literary personality" to have sympathy for Wordsworth's faith that the processes of life are intrinsically pleasurable, the contemporary Wordsworthians' gravity discourages, because, when not specious, its superficiality tends to conceal the poet's intense emotionality and tragic vision. The appearance of a merrier tone in Wordsworthian studies might signal a welcome turn from current analysand solemnity toward more authentic intellectual seriousness.

Orders from the front office as well as the logic of my selectivity account for my emphasis on works published since the third edition of this work or therein slighted. Such emphasis Carlyle ridiculed as producing histories in his day giving a sentence to Alfred the Great and pages to George IV. But I assume this scholarly series to be an ongoing one, so that we who in the great perspective of cultural history are insignificant may without guilt enjoy a day in the sun.

Bibliographies

Basic bibliographies of Wordsworthian criticism are the "series" initiated by James V. Logan with his annotated *Wordsworthian Criticism: A Guide and Bibliography* (1947; rpt. 1961), selective for 1850–99, comprehensive for 1900–44. Elton F.

Henley and David H. Stam carried forward this work with *Wordsworthian Criticism 1945–1964* (1965), with Stam publishing another addition, *Wordsworthian Criticism 1964–1973* (1974). This line will be continued by a bibliography selective through 1973 and exhaustive for the subsequent decade, edited and annotated by Mark Jones and Karl Kroeber (1985). N. S. Bauer's *William Wordsworth, a Reference Guide to British Criticism 1793–1899* (1978) is splendidly annotated and cross-referenced. Russell Noyes in a review (*WC*, 1980) lists five minor omissions, principally parodies, and some useful biographical citations not incorporated by Bauer will be found in Walter Swayze, "Early Wordsworthian Biography" (*BYNPL*, 1960), which contains a list of relevant books and articles published up to 1851. A number of nineteenth-century American articles not listed elsewhere among standard bibliographies are found in W. F. Poole, "Bibliography of Review and Magazine Articles in Criticism of Wordsworth" (*Transactions of the Wordsworth Society*, 1884), although Mark L. Reed, who called my attention to this work, notes the inconvenience of the citations by volume number only, without year of publication.

CBEL's listing of Wordsworthian criticism through 1967 is adequate, but since 1970 the *Wordsworth Circle* has provided annual surveys of scholarship along with an issue devoted to reviews of recent books, which—in company with the Wordsworth section of the Romantic Bibliography appearing from 1965 to 1980 in *ELN*, and now available (at huge cost) through Garland, and with the Fall issue of *SEL* with its annual survey of nineteenth-century studies—meet the first needs of those searching recent critical literature. One should not forget, however, the Wordsworth sections in the thorough MLA annual bibliography as well as that of the Modern Humanities Research Association, and *The Year's Work in English Studies* contains sensible commentaries on important contributions of the preceding year, though the *WC* report tends to be more nearly complete. An excellent source for a beginner is *English Romantic Poetry 1800–1835: A Guide to Information Sources* (ed. Donald H. Reiman, 1979), intelligently selective both in general sections and in the pages on Wordsworth and succinctly and reliably annotated.

For reviews from the poet's own day, one may consult part A of *The Romantics Reviewed: Contemporary Reviews of British Romantic Writers* (1972) compiled by Donald H. Reiman, which does not include newspaper notices, and the four volumes of *Literary Reviews in British Periodicals* compiled by William S. Ward: *1789–1797* (1979), *1798–1820* (2 vols. 1972), and *1821–1826* (1977). There is a handy list of several significant reviews in an appendix to John O. Hayden's *The Romantic Reviewers 1802–1824* (1968), and the same author reprints a useful collection of reviews in *Romantic Bards and British Reviewers* (1971). Jack C. Barnes provides "A Bibliography of Wordsworth in American Periodicals through 1825" (*PBSA*, 1958). Herbert Lindenberger's evaluation of "The Reception of *The Prelude*" (*BNYPL*, 1960) has been considerably modified by Carl Dawson in *Victorian Noon* (1979).

Several works mentioned subsequently contain bibliographies for text identification and text analysis, but special notice should be taken of R. S. Woof's "Wordsworth's Poetry and Stuart's Newspapers: 1797–1803" (*SB*, 1962), which lists appearances of Wordsworth's poems in the *Courier* and *Morning Post* and straightens out some of the confusion created by Coleridge's practice of submitting Wordsworth's poems. This matter was first systematically addressed by Jane Worthington Smyser in "Coleridge's Use of Wordsworth's Juvenilia" (*PMLA*, 1950). Among pieces dealing with specific examples of this collaborative confusion are Carol Landon's "Wordsworth, Coleridge and the *Morning Post*: An Early Version of the Seven Sisters" (*RES*, 1960), Stephen M. Parrish's "The Wordsworth-Coleridge Controversy" (*PMLA*, 1958), developing from de Selincourt's discovery that part of "The Three Graves" was composed by Wordsworth; and Parrish and David V. Erdman, "Who Wrote the Mad Monk? A Debate" (*BNYPL*, 1960), with Parrish's latest remarks on these matters found in his *Art of the Lyrical Ballads* (1973) discussed below. Thomas McFarland in *Romanticism and the Forms of Ruin* (1981) devotes several pages to the importance of the "symbiosis" analyzed in the foregoing essays.

Stephen Bauer lists thirty-six poems of Wordsworth's that appeared in anthologies and annuals betweeen 1798 and 1836 in "Wordsworth and the Early Anthologies" (*Library*, 1972). Chester L. Shaver and Alice C. Shaver in *Wordsworth's Library: A Catalogue* (1979) construct a valuable list from the sale catalog of Wordsworth's books in 1859, an 1824 recording of his books and those stored for Coleridge, and a listing of books lent from Rydal Mount from 1824 through 1858, plus a list of "books belonging to Wordsworth in addition to" those found in the documents just mentioned. For collections in libraries in this country, see first George H. Healey's *The Cornell Wordsworth Collection: A Catalogue of Books and Manuscripts Presented to the University by Mr. Victor Emanuel* (1957), with information on more than three thousand items at Ithaca, and Russell Noyes, *The Indiana Wordsworth Collection, a Catalogue* (1978). For other library holdings, see P. M. Zall and E. W. Zall, "Wordsworth in the Huntington Library: A Preliminary Checklist" (*WC*, 1970); Cornelius Howard Patton, *The Amherst Wordsworth Collection: A Descriptive Bibliography* (1936); *The Arthur Beatty Collection, University of Wisconsin Memorial Library* (1960); James A. Butler, "Wordsworth in Philadelphia Area Libraries" (*WC*, 1973), especially for Wordsworthiana at Swarthmore; and William Hale White's *Description of the Wordsworth and Coleridge Manuscripts in the Possession of Mr. T. Norton Longman* (1897) for several important manuscripts now in the Yale Library. Thomas J. Wise's two bibliographies of books now in the British Museum, *A Bibliography of the Writings in Prose and Verse of William Wordsworth* (1916) and *Two Lake Poets: A Catalogue of Printed Books, Manuscripts, and Autograph Letters by William Wordsworth and Samuel Taylor Coleridge* (1927; rpt. 1965) are generally reliable, though with at least one forgery, "To the Queen, 1846," noted by J. E. Walls (*PQ*, 1942). There is no bibliography for the Dove Cottage Library, the principal repository for Wordsworthian manuscripts, although an incomplete and not always reliable listing of the manuscripts, organized according to the earlier numbering system, is found in Reynold Siemens, *The Wordsworth Collection* (1971), and Mark Reed provides an accurate listing of renumbered manuscripts there in his *Chronology...Middle Years* (1975), discussed in the next section. John Clubbe describes "the W. Hugh Peal Collection at the University of Kentucky" (*WC*, 1984), which includes some unpublished letters.

Biographical Matters

The standard biography is *William Wordsworth: A Biography,* 2 volumes
(1957–65), by Mary Moorman, an intelligent, sympathetic study, factually accurate
and judicious in its presentation of evidence and in its estimates of the poet's
strengths and weaknesses. Moorman's aim is biography, not criticism, and she
uses the poetry to illuminate the life. Her assessments of key relations in
Wordsworth's career, to his sister, Coleridge, Annette Vallon, his wife and children, are consistently sensible. Never exciting, Moorman's work is reliable;
though containing little new information, by its careful organizing of known facts
it has reduced the significance of earlier biographical studies. George Wilbur
Meyer, *Wordsworth's Formative Years* (1943), built his presentation on the premise
that *The Prelude* was not a reliable guide to the facts of the poet's life, being filled
with both misrepresentations and self-deceptions, an approach subtilized by subsequent, more psychologically sophisticated critics who find the poet's
"falsifications" revealing profound psychic truths. Meyer's work attracted more
attention than it intrinsically merited when it first appeared because it contro-
verted a mode established by Emile Legouis, whose still-rewarding *La Jeunesse de
Wordsworth, 1770–1798* (1896; trans. J. W. Matthew, 1897; 3rd ed. 1932) presents
the biography as a commentary on *The Prelude*; Legouis, in fact, is the first major
commentator to make *The Prelude* central to an understanding of Wordsworth.
George McLean Harper, *William Wordsworth: His Life, Works, Influence,* 2
volumes (1916; rev. and abr. 1929), a worthy if finally unimaginative book, owed
something to Legouis. But Harper was the first to describe Wordsworth's relationship with Annette Vallon (with further information in *Wordsworth's French
Daughter,* 1921), inspiring Legouis to dig out more material on this—for Wordsworthians of the 1920s—exciting topic in *William Wordsworth and Annette
Vallon* (1922).

The discovery that Wordsworth had had an illegitimate daughter by a
Frenchwoman was made much of in the decade following Harper's books—Sir
Herbert Read's *Wordsworth* (1930) exemplifies the tendency to stress speculatively
the poet's anguish over the relation. But, shocking as this psychological probing
into a hushed-up affair would have been to the poet's nephew, Christopher
Wordsworth, Bishop of Lincoln, who published the official *Memoirs of William
Wordsworth* in 1851 (so much a model of Victorian discretion that even some
Victorians complained), more upsetting suggestions were soon to come. A key
publication was F. W. Bateson's *Wordsworth: A Reinterpretation* (1954; a second
edition, with a new preface somewhat softening the assertiveness of the original,
appeared in 1956). Bateson, advancing the view that some of Wordsworth's best
poetry was produced by inner conflicts, went so far as to suggest that a significant
source of these was the poet's extraordinarily intense feelings toward his sister,
Dorothy. The suggestion, understandably, was not endorsed enthusiastically by
those closest to the Dove Cottage Library. Particularly offensive were some crude
simplifications of Bateson's argument, including Kenneth Clark's in *Civilisation,*

which provoked Mary Moorman's uncharacteristically harsh attack on Bateson in a lecture to the Royal Society of Literature in 1970, available in *Essays by Diverse Hands... Transactions of the Royal Society of Literature* (1972). This essay, in turn, provoked a lively newspaper debate, to be discussed shortly.

For a time, however, attention to Wordsworth's sister was superseded by interest in his mother, or, as Derrideans might have it, her absence. W. W. Douglas in *Wordsworth: The Construction of a Personality* (1967), for instance, employs techniques of modern psychology, particularly as expounded by Melanie Klein and Erik Erikson, to define the poet's "crisis" as efforts to control aggressive and destructive impulses deriving from the loss of his mother. A more extended and purely Freudian interpretation similar to Douglas' is Richard J. Onorato's thoughtful *The Character of the Poet: Wordsworth in* The Prelude (1971), an intelligent, perceptive, clearly written psychoanalytic speculation with insights of value to any Wordsworthian. Barbara A. Schapiro, *The Romantic Mother: Narcissistic Patterns in Romantic Poetry* (1983), using ideas of Heinz Kohut and Otto Kernberg, sharply but unpersuasively attacks Onorato, arguing that Wordsworth's poetry strives "not to recapture the lost mother but to fortify the self in relation to her" and that through his poetry one may observe a progressive integration of the poet's personality through his confronting of his ambivalences about his parents and the hostility and guilt provoked by his experiences in nature. Simon Stuart, *New Phoenix Wings: Reparation in Literature* (1979), provides a Kleinian reading parallel to Schapiro's.

Analysts have paid relatively little attention to Wordsworth's reactions to his father and his father's death, and that this may be a mistake is suggested by Mazzeno's essay cited below, for example, and is asserted by William Gordon in "Autobiography and Identity: Wordsworth's *The Borderers*" (*TSE*, 1972), and by Ronald Paulson in *Representations of Revolution* (1983). Wordsworth evokes unusually clear illustrations of the powers and limitations of psychoanalytic approaches to literary biography. Purporting to illuminate the writing by explaining the psyche, psychoanalytic biographers interpret the writings to construct a hypothetical diagram of their writer's psychic development or retardation. The resulting portrait is, to my taste, usually too schematic to be useful for understanding the subtle and intricate traits of imagination in major literary accomplishments. But the process of fabricating a schema of interior pressures and resistances in a sensitive and conscientious study such as Onorato's does encourage attention both to certain verbal nuances that are easily overlooked and to larger patterns of recurrence defining persistent tensions in the artist's mind.

Deliberately doing something quite different (whose scholarly value is undebatable), Mark L. Reed has produced two books that have changed and will continue to change all Wordsworthian studies: *Wordsworth: The Chronology of the Early Years, 1770–1799* (1967) and *The Chronology of the Middle Years, 1800–1815* (1975). Reed "limits" himself to recording every verifiable, objective event involving Wordsworth or his immediate circle for almost every day of the poet's life, accompanying this record with a detailed and exact chronology of Wordsworth's composition of his poetry or specifications of the bases for the best judgments on this composing progress. There is no speculation about

Wordsworth's personality, his ideas, or his critical principles, but there is an unbelievably extensive record of facts on which evaluations can be based. "Some error and omission must occur in compilation on such a scale," Reed himself says with characteristic scrupulosity, but the thoroughness of his research is matched by his accuracy and his skill at clear organization, exemplified by his indexes, cross-references, and summarizing appendixes. So far as I know, there exist no comparable works for other writers, and all genuine scholarship of Wordsworth for the foreseeable future will be indebted to Reed's labors.

Speculation and opinionated evaluation, properly, will never stop. To me, the most interesting recent speculations concern Wordsworth's relationship to his sister Dorothy, perhaps because in *"Home at Grasmere:* Ecological Holiness" (*PMLA,* 1974) I observed that Wordsworth treats openly "incestuous" feelings rather than only betraying repressed impulses. I was carrying forward F. R. Leavis' comment, in *Revaluation, Tradition and Development in English Poetry* (1936), on the absence "of morbid repression" in Wordsworth's poetry. Although recent studies on Shelley, Byron, and even Jane Austen point toward an openness about the "incestuous" as a widespread feature of Romanticism and though the sensationalism of the topic diminishes as scholars grow out of Victorian moralizing, our age prefers to dwell on secrets, unconscious motives, concealed impulses. We cast the critic in the role of detective uncovering crimes and hidden motives. So Richard E. Matlak, "Wordsworth's Lucy Poems in Psychobiographical Context" (*PMLA,* 1978), sees Lucy as expressive of the poet's ambivalent fantasies about Dorothy, fantasies reinforced by his anguish at his separation from Coleridge, anguish intensified by the latter's emotional attachment to Thomas Poole; Matlack develops his argument in "The Men in Wordsworth's Life" (*WC,* 1978). As important is Donald H. Reiman's polemic for recognizing that the poet's "psychic wounds," including "hidden fears of incestuous passion...and, quite possibly, resentment toward his wife for his own feelings of sexual and creative inadequacy," are a source of his greatest poetry: "The Poetry of Familiarity: Wordsworth, Dorothy, and Mary Hutchinson," *The Evidence of the Imagination,* ed. Donald H. Reiman, Michael C. Jaye, Betty Bennett (1978). Presenting the basic biographical evidence forcibly, Reiman points out, for example, how much of Wordsworth's best poetry was composed during the seven years before his marriage when he lived with Dorothy. Reiman makes good use of Onorato's analyses and justly summarizes the issues heatedly debated in letters to the *Times Literary Supplement,* principally under the heading "Brothers and Sisters," initiated by Alethea Hayter's commendation of Moorman's Royal Society Lecture (see above): 9 August, 23 August, 13 September, 4 October, 1 November, 8 November, 15 November, 22 November, 27 December 1974. This issue will surely be a major focus of Wordsworth studies during the next decade, particularly as scholars bring more sophisticated, less polemical psychological and textual analyses to bear on such documentary evidence as, for example, the newly discovered love letters from Wordsworth to his wife.

Although these thrilling private problems have tended to overshadow other biographical enterprises, several critics have made excellent use of new editions of the poetry and Moorman's and Reed's work to explore social, political, and intellectual aspects of Wordsworth's life, as is indicated in the sections on criticism below. How much of value is yet to be done, however, is suggested by E. P. Thompson's "Disenchantment or Default: A Lay Sermon" in *Power and Consciousness* (ed. Conor Cruise O'Brien and William Dean Vanech [1969]), which treats two "spots" in Wordsworth's and Coleridge's most intimate interactions, Thelwall's visit in July-August 1797 and the decision to go to Germany in March 1798. Thompson's essay conveniently brings together two foci of biographical studies: the relations with Coleridge and Wordsworth's political views. For the latter, one should consult Carl R. Woodring's indispensable *Politics in English Romantic Poetry* (1970). F. M. Todd's *Politics and the Poet* (1957) is less scholarly and less acute about political nuances. The poet's not invariably admirable activities in support of the Lonsdale interest in the 1818 Westmoreland election are treated in J. E. Wells's "Wordsworth and De Quincey in Westmoreland Politics, 1818" (*PMLA*, 1940), extended by W.W. Douglas in "Wordsworth in Politics: The Westmoreland Election of 1818" (*MLN*, 1948), both essays still of use, as is Wells's "Wordsworth and the Railway in 1844–45" (*MLQ*, 1945) though one should not overlook Joanne Dann, "Some Notes on the Relationship between the Wordsworth and the Lowther Families" (*WC*, 1980). Valuable, too, are the Marxist analyses of Michael Friedman in his book discussed below and the same author's "Wordsworth's Grasmere: A Rentier's Vision" (*Polit: A Journal of Literature and Politics*, 1977). Less rewarding is Roger Sales, *English Literature in History 1780–1830: Pastoral and Politics* (1983), who finds origins of the poet's later sympathy for local gentry in poems like "Michael." A good beginning place for relations with Coleridge is William Heath's *Wordsworth and Coleridge: A Study of Their Literary Relations in 1801–1802* (1972), although Coleridgeans have found Heath unfair to their man. Heath shows these months to have been critical in the lives of both poets and decisive in the development of their relationship. H. M. Margoliouth, *Wordsworth and Coleridge, 1795–1834* (1953), is wider in scope but less penetrating and persuasive in judgments of the tensions between the men. Oddly, there are still unresolved doubts about their first meeting—see Robert Woof, "Wordsworth and Coleridge: Some Early Matters," *Bicentenary Wordsworth Studies* (ed. Jonathan Wordsworth, 1970)—and even the planning, cooperation in composing, and the publication of *Lyrical Ballads* are still disputed. Max F. Schulz, in "Coleridge, Wordsworth, and the 1800 Preface to *Lyrical Ballads*" (*SEL*, 1959), argues that the Preface was written by Wordsworth without significant aid from Coleridge, who had been supposed to write it but failed to do so, and thus it became a source for later disagreements. A. M. Buchan, in "The Influence of Wordsworth on Coleridge, 1795–1800" (*UTQ*, 1963), proposes that on balance Wordsworth exercised an inhibiting effect on Coleridge's imagination and selfconfidence during the period from which came *Lyrical Ballads*. Mark L. Reed, "Wordsworth, Coleridge, and the 'Plan' of the *Lyrical Ballads*" (*UTQ*, 1965), argues cogently that the contents of the famous volume were more a product of expediency than of deliberate planning. Earlier, in "The Wordsworth-Coleridge Controversy" (*PMLA*, 1958), Stephen M. Parrish had suggested that the disagreements and cross-purposes originated in even earlier attempts at collaboration on "The Three Graves," "Cain," and "The Ancient Mariner." Doubtless relations between these two gifted but difficult men, their intimacies and estrangements, will continue to attract attention, with more emphasis, I would guess, on the benefits to each.

The drowning of Wordsworth's brother John profoundly affected the poet, and some have seen this tragedy as the beginning of the most drastic changes in his art and philosophy. The event has been treated usefully by E. L. McAdam, Jr., "Wordsworth's Shipwreck" (*PMLA*, 1962), and R. C. Townsend, "John Wordsworth and His Brother's Poetic Development" (*PMLA*, 1966). Frank Prentice Rand, *Wordsworth's Mariner Brother* (1966), is a full biography; more succinct and as valuable is Carl H. Ketcham's introduction to his. edition of the *Letters of John Wordsworth* (1969). Mary Moorman in "Wordsworth and His Children" in *Bicentenary Wordsworth Studies* (1970) surveys the poet's relations with his five children, the deaths of two of whom deeply troubled the poet. This introduces the murky subject of Wordsworth's "later years." Though a decline in the quality of his poetry is denied by no influential critic, a more serious and helpful interest in Wordsworth's later poetry seems to be developing, as is indicated in some items in the criticism discussed subsequently. Here, though, one may single out for special mention among the most sympathetic but not adulatory studies of this phase of the career, first, John Jones, *The Egotistical Sublime* (1954), then Edith C. Batho, *The Later Wordsworth* (1933), and Bernard Groom, *The Unity of Wordsworth's Poetry* (1966).

Among biographical studies with a special focus one may notice: Ben Ross Schneider's *Wordsworth's Cambridge Education* (1957), illuminating both on college life and the intellectual milieu at the end of the eighteenth century, superior to my mind to Z. S. Fink, *The Early Wordsworthian Milieu* (1958), basically an edition of a schoolboy notebook used by Christopher and William; David V. Erdman, "Coleridge, Wordsworth, and the Wedgwood Fund" (*BNYPL*, 1956), arguing that Wordsworth's reaction to a plan for educational reform shaped his ideas on the development of the mind; W. W. Douglas, "Wordsworth as Business Man" (*PMLA*, 1948), which may be compared with V. G. Kiernan, "Wordsworth and the People," in *Marxists on Literature: An Anthology* (ed. David Craig, 1953). C. N. Coe, *Wordsworth and the Literature of Travel* (1935; rpt. 1979), has some utility as an introduction to one of Wordsworth's favorite areas of reading, though inferior to a study of another area of his interest, *Wordsworth's Reading of Roman Prose* (1946) by Jane Worthington Smyser. Smyser's emphasis on Wordsworth's stoicism has provoked disagreement, but her work calls attention to an undeniably important quality of the poet's personality and thought. Frances Blanshard's *Portraits of Wordsworth* (1959) provides reproductions of more than sixty portraits, indicating the poet's eminence in his later years. Mark Reed shrewdly suggests that anyone who has ever found mischievous qualities in Wordsworth's poetry—or has not—might with profit reflect on the image of his twenty-eight-year-old face in Blanshard's first reproduction, that of Shuter's portrait made in 1798.

Two older, amusing, yet revealing works about Wordsworth's life in the Lake Country are T. W. Thompson, *Wordsworth's Hawkshead* (ed. Robert Woof, 1970), filled with every sort of minutia about the conditions of life when the poet was a schoolboy, and Hardwick Drummond Rawnsley's *Reminiscences of Wordsworth among the Peasantry of Westmoreland,* reprinted in 1968 with an introduction by Geoffrey Tillotson from the original, which appeared in *Lake Country Sketches* in 1903, allowing us to see the poet, family, and friends from the not always complimentary view of humble and rustic life. David McCracken in *Wordsworth and the Lake District* (1984) identifies many places referred to in the poems, discusses the relations of poems to actualities intelligently, and provides useful maps and itineraries. As for Wordsworth's landscapes, Americans unable to manage trans-Atlantic fares should not forget Beatrix Potter's admirable scenic renderings, the best, perhaps, in *Mrs. Tiggy-Winkle.* Many of the numberless volumes on Lake District topography and scenery use Wordsworth as a center. Donald E. Hayden, *Wordsworth's Walking Tour of 1790* (1983), records a tour by Hayden and his wife in 1980 following as precisely as possible the trip taken by the poet and his friend Jones 190 years earlier. Hayden's text is concise and helpful, the maps clear and usable, the photographs splendid—the book is as delightful as it is valuable.

There are several popular biographies, the most recent of which is that of Hunter Davies, an unpretentious, sympathetic, well-written survey of the life that gives due weight to the late as well as the early years. Russell Noyes's Twayne *Wordsworth* (1971) is sane and reliable, and Carl R. Woodring's brief *Wordsworth* (1965), though a critical rather than a biographical work, has an outstanding opening chapter, "The Formative Years," and throughout supports literary commentary with a lucid rendering of factual background. Worth remembering also are two highly colored but useful portraits by men who knew Wordsworth: Thomas De Quincey's not always factually true essays on the Lake Poets in *Tait's Magazine,* originally collected in 1882 by David Masson in his edition of De Quincey, as "Literary and Lake Reminiscences," and William Hazlitt's essential "My First Acquaintance with Poets" that first appeared in the *Liberal* in 1823.

Editions

POETRY

By February 1984, nine volumes of the Cornell Wordsworth editions had been published: *The Salisbury Plain Poems of William Wordsworth,* edited by Stephen Gill (1975); *The Prelude 1798–1799,* edited by Stephen Parrish (1977); *Home at Grasmere: Part First, Book First of The Recluse,* edited by Beth Darlington (1977); *The Ruined Cottage and The Pedlar,* edited by James A. Butler (1979); *Benjamin the Waggoner,* edited by Paul Betz (1981); *The Borderers,* edited by Robert Osborn (1982); *Poems, in Two Volumes, and Other Poems, 1800–1807,* edited by Jared Curtis (1983); *Descriptive Sketches,* edited by Eric Birdsall assisted by Paul M. Zall (1984); and *An Evening Walk,* edited by James Averill (1984). Each volume includes photographic reproductions of the manuscripts and simplified "reading texts" along with full transcriptions and complete apparatus criticus. Aiming to recover Wordsworth's earliest versions of longer poems, this series inverts the principles employed in construction of the standard edition of the poems, *The Poetical Works of William Wordsworth, Edited from the Manuscripts, with Tex-*

tual and Critical Notes, five volumes (1941–49; rev. ed. 1952–59) by Ernest de Selincourt and Helen Darbishire. Their basic text is the six-volume edition of 1849–50, the last to have been supervised by the poet, and their copious, lucid notes and appendixes provide material by which one can reconstruct the poet's various revisions. Mark Reed calls attention, in this respect, to the notes in the last of William Knight's much maligned editions (8 vols., 1896), particularly those dealing with Wordsworth's literary sources, notes not repeated by later editors.

The de Selincourt apparatus criticus is by no means flawless, and working back to the original form of poems can be laborious, being not infrequently hampered by the topical (rather than chronological) ordering of the poems, which is, of course, Wordsworth's own. Necessarily, therefore, the Cornell editions repeat much already available in the de Selincourt-Darbishire complete works, but the different format and more comprehensive textual reports bring one closer to a full and accurate charting of what Wordsworth wrote when and of how he changed and reordered his verses. The early claim of the series' general editor that Wordsworth's original versions were the best, in fact, grossly distorts the complexity of Wordsworth's art as a reviser. The Cornell volumes prove that Wordsworth's revisions are more important over a much longer span of time than most scholars had suspected. One does well, of course, to heed the caution of a famous Cornell professor in his commentary on another great Romantic poet, Pushkin, that "an artist should ruthlessly destroy his manuscripts after publication, lest they mislead academic mediocrities into thinking that it is possible to unravel the mysteries of genius by studying cancelled readings." The warning applies to critics rather than to editors, who try to make usefully available the information provided by the large number of manuscripts that Wordsworth chose to preserve. Stephen Gill, "Wordsworth's Poems: The Question of Text" (*RES,* 1983), judiciously discusses dilemmas posed to both editors and readers by Wordsworth's revisions and the recent "editorial creation" of poems. The center of editorial interest, of course, has been *The Prelude,* published posthumously in 1850 (on its reception, see Lindenberger and Dawson, above) and never titled by the poet himself. In 1926, de Selincourt published *The Prelude, or Growth of a Poet's Mind, Edited from the Manuscripts with Introduction, Textual and Critical Notes* (a second, revised edition utilizing new manuscript evidence was brought out by Helen Darbishire in 1959). This volume prints on the right-hand page the text published in 1850 and on the left-hand page the previously unknown "1805" version that Wordsworth read to Coleridge, his poem's addressee. De Selincourt's volume was a principal shaping force in Wordsworthian studies through the 1960s, above all in confirming our century's view, not the Victorians', that *The Prelude* is Wordsworth's most significant poem.

Two works in 1964 triggered reconsiderations of *The Prelude*'s textual history: J. R. MacGillivray, "The Three Forms of *The Prelude* 1798–1805," in *Essays in English Literature... Presented to A. S. P. Woodhouse,* edited by Millar Maclure and F. W. Watt, and John Alban Finch's doctoral dissertation at Cornell, "Wordsworth, Coleridge, and 'The Recluse' 1798–1804." These studies made plausible what MacGillivray called a "proto-Prelude," an idea developed by Jonathan Wordsworth in "The Growth of a Poet's Mind" (*Cornell Library Journal,* 1970) and presented by him and Stephen Gill in "The Two-Part *Prelude* of 1798–99" (*JEGP*, 1973), describing the version used in the third edition of the *Norton Anthology of English Literature* (short *Prelude*s are a godsend to publishers). It is this "two-part" *Prelude* Parrish edited in the Cornell Wordsworth volume mentioned above. A Norton Critical Edition edited by Jonathan Wordsworth, M. H. Abrams, and Stephen Gill, *Wordsworth's Prelude 1799, 1805, 1850* (1979), prints along with the two-part version the 1805 and 1850 texts on facing pages, with the former given modern punctuation (more than Wordsworth used) and the latter edited against manuscripts and corrected texts that distinguish it from de Selincourt's text. In 1977, Jonathan Wordsworth published in *JEGP* "The Five-Book *Prelude* of Early Spring 1804," defining a stage between earlier forms of the poem and the "completed" 1805 version. Robin Jarvis, "The Five-Book *Prelude*: A Reconsideration" (*JEGP*, 1981), points out weaknesses in J. Wordsworth's reconstruction. Cornell plans to publish a thirteen-book *Prelude* edited by Mark Reed and a fourteen-book *Prelude* edited by W. J. B. Owen, and these will, for a time, complete the history of a poem few of the poet's contemporaries knew existed. Helpful for keeping up with the proliferation of *Prelude*s are essays by Michael C. Jaye, "Wordsworth at Work: Ms. RV, Book II of *The Prelude*" (*PBSA*, 1974), and "*The Prelude, The Excursion,* and *The Recluse:* An Unpublished *Prelude* Variant" (*PQ*, 1975); David Ellis, "Origins of *The Prelude*" (*PQ*, 1978); and, above all, Mark Reed's appendix 5 in his *Wordsworth: The Chronology of the Middle Years 1800–1815* (1975). Reed presents the complicated evidence with unfailing clarity and never loses sight of the need to keep in mind *all* testimony to the poet's attitudes toward various drafts. Reed points out, for example, the absence of any hard evidence that Wordsworth regarded any form of *The Prelude* as finished before 1805.

Textual studies of *The Prelude,* along with Jonathan Wordsworth's influential *The Music of Humanity: A Critical Study of Wordsworth's "Ruined Cottage"* (1969), have encouraged interest in the origins of *The Excursion* and the never completed *Recluse.* The volume edited by James Butler in the Cornell series (which subsumes Butler's earlier valuable contributions) develops lines suggested by Jonathan Wordsworth's book and John Alban Finch's "*The Ruined Cottage* Restored: Three Stages of Composition" (originally published in 1967), available in *Bicentenary Wordsworth Studies in Memory of John Alban Finch,* edited by Jonathan Wordsworth (1970). For a debate on the significance of "Pedlar" passages in Ms. D (printed in *The Music of Humanity*), see Jonathan Wordsworth's review of Butler's volume and Butler's reply in *WC,* 1979. On this topic, too, Mark Reed provides a useful summary in *Middle Years,* and at least one earlier study, Thomas M. Raysor's "Wordsworth's Early Drafts of *The Ruined Cottage* in 1797–1798" (*JEGP*, 1956), is worth attention. For *The Recluse*'s one completed book, Beth Darlington's edition of *Home at Grasmere* is essential, especially in confirming the relatively late date of composition of much of this work, a point discussed succinctly by Reed in *Middle Years* and first proposed by John Alban Finch in "On the Dating of 'Home at Grasmere': A New Approach" in *Bicentenary Wordsworth Studies* (1970).

Wordsworth's lyricism has not yet totally been lost sight of in the scramble to identify long poems within long poems, but R. L. Brett and A. R. Jones, who edited

Lyrical Ballads in 1963 (rev. ed. 1965; reissued in 1980), still provide the best edition with useful notes on shifts in ordering of the poems. Paul F. Betz, "The Hands Involved in Yale's Sheets from the Second Volume of *Lyrical Ballads* (1800) Corrected for the Edition of 1802" (*YULG*, 1971), supplements the report on these matters by Frederick Pottle in the same publication in 1966, and James A. Butler in "Wordsworth, Cottle and the *Lyrical Ballads*" (*JEGP*, 1976) prints and comments usefully on five letters bearing importantly on the printing of the collection. "Michael," the final poem in the editions of 1800–05, has been the subject of vigorous discussion since Stephen Parrish's "Michael and the Pastoral Ballad" in *Bicentenary Wordsworth Studies* (1970) centered attention on a "balladic" text. Robert S. Woof (1970) and Jonathan Wordsworth (1971) debated the importance of the poem's mode of origination in articles in *Ariel*, in which publication in 1972 Mark Reed evaluated the controversy in an essay that remains the best "On the Development of Wordsworth's 'Michael,' " observing that "present evidence does not confirm extensive work on a rhymed poem corresponding to *Michael* as more than a possibility in logic." A discussion of other criticism of this poem appears below, but it is appropriate here to mention one other item, Randel Helms's "On the Genesis of Wordsworth's 'Michael' " (*ELN*, 1977), since it takes off from the foregoing controversy.

Eric R. Birdsall discusses "Wordsworth's Revisions to *Descriptive Sketches*: The Wellesley Copy" (*WC*, 1974), and another important Wellesley document is described in Jared Curtis, "The Wellesley Copy of Wordsworth's *Poetical Works, 1832*," (*HLB*, 1980), which shows the poet's relentless use of the four-volume 1832 edition for revisions ranging from rough draft through printer's copy. The Lucy poems continue to attract speculators, and two short notes of 1979 are worth their attention: Brian G. Caraher, "Lucy in Retrospect: A Late Wordsworth Manuscript of 'She dwelt among th' untrodden ways' " (*WC*), and Jared Curtis, "A Note on the Lost Manuscripts of William Wordsworth's 'Louisa' and 'I travell'd among unknown Men' " (*YULG*). More important is Michael C. Jaye's thorough analysis, "William Wordsworth's Alfoxden Notebook: 1798," in *The Evidence of the Imagination* (ed. Donald H. Reiman et al., 1978). The year 1802 is an interesting if difficult one for Wordsworth critics, particularly those who seek to sort out his relations with Coleridge. Jared R. Curtis, *Wordsworth's Experiments with Tradition, the Lyric Poems of 1802* (1971), may be the best place to begin on this topic, for the book contains complete texts of thirty lyrics with full, valuable commentaries, the next book to be consulted then being William Heath's *Wordsworth and Coleridge: A Study of Their Literary Relations in 1801–02*, noted above. Jared Curtis' edition in the Cornell series of Wordsworth's *Poems, in Two Volumes, and Other Poems, 1800–1807*, supersedes Helen Darbishire's edition of *Poems in Two Volumes 1807* (2nd ed. 1952) in all textual matters, but Darbishire's second appendix analyzing metrical forms of the poems remains of value. Alice Comparetti's edition of *The White Doe of Rylstone* (1940) and Abbie F. Potts's edition of *Ecclesiastical Sonnets* (1922) remain the best available for these works.

A handy classroom text is that in the Riverside series, *Selected Poetry and Prefaces of William Wordsworth* (1965), carefully edited and annotated by Jack Stillinger, which includes the complete 1850 *Prelude*. Also relatively inexpensive is the Oxford paper edition of the 1805 *Prelude* in de Selincourt's edition corrected by Stephen Gill (1970). There is also the J. C. Maxwell edition of *The Prelude* (Penguin, 1971; rpt. Yale, 1979), and the Norton triple *Prelude* already mentioned. The Oxford Standard Authors *Poetical Works*, edited by Thomas Hutchinson in 1904 and revised by de Selincourt in 1936, until recently has been the most easily available "complete" one-volume edition, but it lacks margins for scribbling notes, and the print is for small eyes only. Handsomer is the Houghton Mifflin Cambridge edition by A. J. George (1904), which presents the poems in chronological order, though, since George's text is the 1849–50 edition, one reads a "1798" poem in a form it did not attain until many years later (this edition was reissued in 1982 with an introduction by Paul D. Sheats). The same difficulty applies to John O. Hayden's chronologically ordered *William Wordsworth: The Poems*, two volumes (Penguin, 1977; rpt. Yale, 1981), which is too fat but clearly printed, including a number of works not in George and with handy indication of each poem's place (or places) in Wordsworth's arrangement by categories. The selection of poems appearing in chronological order in *William Wordsworth*, edited by Stephen Gill in the Oxford Authors series (1984), uses for its texts the earliest complete state of each poem, which avoids the problem noticed in Hayden's edition but will provoke controversies about what is the "earliest complete state." The old Hutchinson edition just mentioned, incidentally, was the basis for the *Concordance to the Poems of William Wordsworth* by Lane Cooper (1911), compiled too early to have included the 1805 *Prelude*. Cooper's essay "The Making and the Use of a Verbal Concordance" (*SR*, 1919) remains of interest, particularly in its anticipation of some of Josephine Miles's work.

PROSE WORKS

The Prose Works of William Wordsworth, three volumes (ed. W. J. B. Owen and Jane Worthington Smyser, 1974), is one of the splendid gifts to Wordsworth scholars of the past decade. A truly scholarly edition, it supersedes the editions of A. B. Grosart (1876) and William Knight (1896). Owen and Smyser give us two previously unpublished manuscripts related to *A Guide through the District of the Lakes*, nearly a dozen early scraps of prose, five letters published by the poet during the election campaign of 1818, and a reprint of the autobiographical memoranda from Christopher Wordsworth's *Memoirs*. Wordsworth's own notes and comments on his poems, including those dictated to Isabella Fenwick, and observations in private letters (which made up most of Grosart's third volume) are omitted by Owen and Smyser on the grounds of their availability elsewhere. Thoroughness of textual and annotative referencing distinguishes this edition. Texts are printed with every fifth line numbered, so without disfiguring pages the editors can supply copious information where it is most useful. Works are arranged chronologically rather than topically; for printed works Wordsworth's own latest edition is the basic text, for those not published until after his death the final manuscript version. Variant readings from early drafts are preserved.

For the Preface to the *Lyrical Ballads,* the 1800 and 1850 versions appear on facing pages, with published variants from 1802 (and later) noted separately.

For selections, two volumes with nearly the same coverage are Paul M. Zall, *Literary Criticism of William Wordsworth* (1966), and W. J. B. Owen, *Wordsworth's Literary Criticism* (1974). M. L. Peacock's compilation *The Critical Opinions of William Wordsworth* (1950; rpt. 1969) is a useful catalog of the poet's observations on a variety of literary topics, for the most part arranged alphabetically and heavily cross-referenced, its main sections treating literary principles and subjects, other authors and their works, and Wordsworth's own verse and prose; there is an excellent index. Owen's and Smyser's editing of the *Guide through the District of the Lakes,* in *The Prose Works,* with an excellent introduction and a reproduction of an 1835 map, supersedes earlier editions, such as de Selincourt's of 1906. Peter Bicknell, *The Illustrated Guide to the Lakes* (1984), provides contemporary engravings and paintings, modern color photographs, and a good, brief introduction. Gordon K. Thomas has tried to "furnish a reliable photographic reproduction to the original text of 1809" of *William Wordsworth's Convention of Cintra* (1983).

LETTERS

The Letters of William and Dorothy Wordsworth, edited by de Selincourt in six volumes (1935–39), are being thoroughly reedited with new material included in each volume and annotations improved and extended. The present general editor, Alan G. Hill, who has published *The Letters of William Wordsworth: A New Selection* (1984), containing 162 complete letters, eight never before published, reports on progress and plans as follows: volumes of the second edition so far published are *Early Years, 1787–1805,* edited by Chester L. Shaver (1967); *Middle Years, Part I, 1806–1811,* edited by Mary Moorman (1969); *Middle Years, Part 2, 1812–1820,* edited by Moorman and Hill (1970); *Later Years, Part 1, 1821–1828,* edited by Hill (1978); *Later Years, Part 2, 1829–1834,* edited by Hill (1979); *Later Years, Part 3, 1835–1839,* edited by Hill (1982), and the final volume, *Part 4, 1840–1850,* scheduled for publication shortly. This last volume will include an appendix of items not contained in the earlier volumes and will bring to nearly four hundred the number of previously unpublished letters. A supplementary third volume for the *Middle Years* (1806–20), moreover, is currently being edited by Hill and will include the recently discovered love letters of William and Mary as well as many letters of Dorothy not in the earlier volumes. Meanwhile, already available are *The Love Letters of William and Mary Wordsworth,* edited by Beth Darlington (1981), and, for truly wealthy Wordsworthians, a facsimile edition, *My Dearest Love: Letters of William and Mary Wordsworth, 1810* (1981), published by the Trustees of Dove Cottage on handmade paper in six-color reproductions allowing, to quote a reviewer, "wonderful subtlety to the ink blots and smudges produced by haste and time." Those with a more vulgar interest in these letters exchanged when William and Mary had been married eight years and were rearing five children will be rewarded by evidence of the poet's continuing passionate love for his wife. The warmth, even sensuality, of Wordsworth's affection should come as no surprise to careful students of the poet's life though few biographers have recognized how long these energies remained active. The testimony of these letters should chill the suggestions that Wordsworth had little affection for his wife but probably will, by reemphasizing his passionate nature, revive interest in his relations with Annette and ultimately provide ammunition for those who find significance in the strength of his feelings for his sister.

The new complete edition of the letters, unlike de Selincourt's, includes letters to Henry Crabb Robinson, before available only in Edith J. Morley's edition of the *Correspondence of Henry Crabb Robinson with the Wordsworth Circle* (1927), as well as letters published by L. N. Broughton in *Some Letters of the Wordsworth Family* (1942) and previously unpublished letters from the poet to William, earl of Lonsdale, as well as to the earl's son, Viscount Lowther, plus letters published in L. N. Broughton's *Wordsworth and Reed: The Poet's Correspondence with His American Editor, 1836–1850* (1933). John E. Jordan edited the correspondence of De Quincey with the Wordsworths, providing much useful biographical information, in *De Quincey to Wordsworth: A Biography of a Relationship* (1962), and of course the correspondence of Coleridge and Lamb contains much of interest to Wordsworthians.

The Journals of Dorothy Wordsworth, edited by Ernest de Selincourt, two volumes (1941; rpt. 1959), are as indispensable as Helen Darbishire's edition of *Journals: The Alfoxden Journal of 1798* and the *Grasmere Journals 1800–1803* (1958), revised by Mary Moorman (1971), and since reprinted several times. A preview of "The Later Journals" will be found in Carl H. Ketcham's "Dorothy Wordsworth's Journals 1824–1835" (*WC,* 1978). As for other members of the family, *The Letters of Sara Hutchinson from 1800 to 1835* were edited by Kathleen Coburn (1954), *Letters of Mary Wordsworth, 1800–1855* by Mary E. Burton (1958), and *Letters of John Wordsworth* by Carl H. Ketcham (1969).

Some Historical Patterns in Criticism

The amount of Wordsworthian criticism has in recent years so increased while attention to minute particulars has so intensified that it is no longer easy to identify critical categories, let alone trends within categories. So at the risk of repeating too much later, I begin with a pair of essays defining some major historical lines of Wordsworthian study. Jonathan Arac, "Bounding Lines: *The Prelude* and Critical Revision" (*Boundary 2,* 1979), observes that *The Prelude* was a double failure, for it did not enable Wordsworth to write *The Recluse,* nor was he able through the preparatory poem to locate the origin of imaginative power. He therefore ends the 1805 version arbitrarily, simply declaring that the origin has been found, and then works for the rest of his life to "finish" the poem. Arac is challenging M. H. Abrams' view in *Natural Supernaturalism* (1971) that *The Prelude* is triumphantly "circular" in form, "centered in love," a Romantic version of the Christian-

Neoplatonic circuitous progress of the soul back to its original home. Abrams'
interpretation of the poem as attaining harmonious resolution places him in the
tradition of Matthew Arnold, who uses the same figure of the journey in praising
Wordsworth as the poet of consoling joy. Arnold, however, emphasizes the journey rather than its successful conclusion, never insisting, as Abrams does, on the
spatialized vision of the poem as "spiral form." Arac identifies the principal
countertradition of criticism, as had Abrams in his introduction to *Wordsworth,* a
collection of critical essays he edited in 1972, in work by Geoffrey H. Hartman
stemming from A. C. Bradley's "darkly philosophical, brooding poet, hostile to
'sense' and verging on apocalypse." Arac, contrasting himself to the Hegelian
premises he perceives as common to both Hartman and Abrams, however,
prefers a "Kierkegaardian" reading, for him illustrated by Lindenberger's *On
Wordsworth's* Prelude (1963), deriving from Walter Pater, who "presents the vitality
and mobility of writing in *The Prelude*" without, like Abrams, claiming a completed reachievement of the pattern of traditional paradise, fall, redemption or,
like Hartman, emphasizing "a debilitatingly self-conflicting struggle." For Pater-
Lindenberger-Arac readers, the poet's revisions show that he recognized that his
life as a poet depended on disturbance, "shock," and "surprise" and that his "authority" derived not from the stability of truth but from "the lability of moments
in which the world slipped away." Arac finds "human liberation in letting go . . .
such a project as *The Recluse,* and deferring the end, keeping the self suspended
in receptivity like the Boy of Winander."

Arac's reading may be regarded as "postmodern" in its resistance to modernist reductions of temporal actualities to spatialized patterns and in its sympathetic
attention to the occasions of rhetorical complexity. A different kind of theoretical
base for an analogously "antimodernist" approach appears in Charles Altieri's
"Wordsworth's 'Preface' as Literary Theory" (*Criticism,* 1976). Altieri perceives
Wordsworthian criticism through the sixties and early seventies as dominated by
either empirical or idealist approaches, with both positing radical opposition between nature and consciousness. But Wordsworth, in Altieri's view, conceived of a
poetry "not dependent on the opposition between nature and consciousness," a
conception illuminated by Wittgenstein's philosophical grammar, since for both
poet and philosopher, contexts of action rather than formal systems of language
are most important, leading toward the possibility of poetry's disclosing "shared
meanings men live by." Because Wordsworth believes good poetry confers power
on its readers to become aware of what they share with others, he insists that the
utility of poetry is its ability to impart pleasure. The essence of that pleasure is a
harmonizing of mind and nature that can symbolize moral goodness, since the
harmonizing involves an emotionalized awareness of "human agreement," an
awakening of capacities, as the Preface puts it, for a "relationship and love" that
will bind the individual to a community.

Poetry for Wordsworth, then, "neither imitates nor restructures reality but
tries to disclose . . . what we might ordinarily not recognize," above all, what we
as human beings have in common. Hence he champions a poetic language "of
repeated experience and regular feeling." The poet enables us to perceive in
ordinary lives moral forms worth preserving. What preserves is memory, which

Wordsworth believes retains "what is fitted to the nature of the mind." We all share the basic experience of growing up, because we all face the same necessities, so poets by submitting their private, subjective experience to the mind's inherent tendency to preserve what is best for it, discover the felicitous relevance of their experiences to experiences of others. In this fashion, Altieri, who claims as *his* chief ancestor John Stuart Mill, finds Wordsworth's best poetry and most valuable poetic theorizing antithetical to a "radical dichotomy between nature and mind." That split Altieri perceives as the peculiar fault of "modernist" readings of Wordsworth, such as de Man's, which make his poetry "allegorical" and play down the poet's attention to the common rhythms of ordinary experience.

If Altieri and Arac point toward coming lines of development in Wordsworthian studies, their starting point indubitably is the work of Geoffrey H. Hartman, particularly *Wordsworth's Poetry 1787–1814* (1964), which has virtually obliterated memory of his book of exactly a decade earlier, *The Unmediated Vision.* Since its publication *Wordsworth's Poetry* has been the center of the best Wordsworthian criticism, most debates of importance originating in agreement or disagreement with the book. In it, to oversimplify, Hartman minimizes Wordsworthian pleasure to place in the foreground the poet's anguished awareness of a division between processes of his mind and those of the natural world. Hartman's book articulates this view through many detailed and subtly original readings of major poems that intelligent readers will find rewarding and stimulating, whatever their agreement or disagreement with Hartman's thesis, as is shown, for example, by Jeffrey Plank, "Literary Criticism as an Autobiographical Form" (*WC,* 1982), who sees Hartman as incapable of dealing with radical literary changes. This one may expand on by using the "Retrospect" with which Hartman begins the second edition of his book (1971). He has described, he says, "Wordsworth's 'consciousness of consciousness,'" stressing the poet's obsession with place, where he relived in his poetry "the religious struggle between Helenic (fixed and definite) and Hebraic (indefinite, anti-anthropomorphic) representations of the divine." The poet's development is "a matter of converting apocalypse into akedah, or binding to nature, as a preparatory humanizing of an otherworldly power of imagination." The imagination is "otherworldly" because it "tended to seek a separate reality" and the "everyday world was often so inadequate that the imagination preferred withdrawal or ecstasy." Then, as the poet "grows aware of what is within and separates imagination more clearly from nature," he retrospectively recognizes that nature "played an essential though self-transcending role in the growth of the mind."

Even this condensation of a "barest" self-summary may suggest why during a period when few students of literature have manifested significant social, political, or religious commitments, Hartman's reading of Wordsworth has been attractive. Nor is it an accident that, as Hartman's later work shows, his readings are essentially Freudian, in the sense not so much of deducing the poet's psychological state from the evidence of the verse as of interpreting the verse according to the logic and metaphysics (such as they are) of Freudianism. Hartman, in other words, subordinates specific religious, political, or social features of a poetic occasion, broadly its historical dimension, so as to place in the foreground timeless psychological configurations. This approach, as criticism of the seventies illustrates, lends itself to detailed textual analyses, particularly speculation about revisions.

But if Hartman's Wordsworth is a congenial image for recent academics, the image maker is not so readily placed. His intellectual curiosity is based on knowledge of literature and literary theory in several languages. He relishes literary debate and has consistently defended the rights of pure intellectuality. He has always practiced something like what has recently been called the "hermeneutics of indeterminacy," ensuring that the emphasis of his work keeps shifting, so that to regard Hartman's contribution to Wordsworthian criticism solely in terms of his influential book would be misleading. His *Beyond Formalism* (1970), for example, contains essays from the sixties frequently cited, "Romanticism and Anti-Selfconsciousness" and "Romantic Poetry and the Genius Loci," though some critics think "Wordsworth, Inscriptions, and Romantic Nature Poetry" one of Hartman's most influential works. Among more recent essays, one should notice "The Use and Abuse of Structural Analysis" (*NLH,* 1975), answering Michael Riffaterre on "Yew Trees"; "A Touching Compulsion: Wordsworth and the Problem of Literary Representation" (*GaR,* 1977); "Blessing the Torrent: On Wordsworth's Later Style" (*PMLA,* 1978); "Words, Wish, Worth: Wordsworth" in *Deconstruction and Criticism,* edited by Harold Bloom et al. (1979); "Diction and Defense in Wordsworth," *Psychiatry and the Humanities,* volume 4, edited by J. H. Smith (1980); and "The Unknown Language: Wordsworth before Heidegger" in *Languages of Knowledge and of Inquiry* (ed. Michael Riffaterre, 1985). Although ranging widely, these pieces illustrate Hartman's interest in intertextuality, problems of defining "subject" in literature, the special quality of Wordsworthian allusiveness, and Wordsworth's later style.

Some delineation of major trends in criticism is necessary because it takes only the simplest arithmetical test to prove that since 1968 more has been published on Wordsworth than appeared in print between 1798 and that date. Given this quantitative acceleration, one does well to remember that some of the most valuable critiques are among the earliest. Coleridge's comments in the *Biographia Literaria* are usually remembered, but frequently forgotten are some more penetrating observations in his letters, essays, and conversations. His poem "To William Wordsworth" is not only the earliest (by more than a century) but also one of the most sympathetic responses to the 1805 *Prelude,* of which Coleridge was, of course, the addressee. (For different responses to the first *published* version of the poem in 1850, see Lindenberger and Dawson cited above; there is a selection of reactions, including Macaulay's charge that the poem is "Jacobinical, indeed Socialist," included in *The Prelude, 1799, 1805, 1850,* ed. J. Wordsworth et al.) A year after Coleridge's poem was composed, Byron wrote an amicable review of the 1807 *Poems in Two Volumes,* though this did nothing to restrain his later attacks in both verse and prose, beginning with *English Bards and Scotch Reviewers,* and reaching a humorous climax in the suppressed preface to *Don Juan.* The significance of the ambivalences toward Wordsworth's poetry found everywhere in Keats's and Shelley's work has yet to be fully evaluated. Hazlitt's essays, especially "On Mr. Wordsworth's *Excursion*" (1817), "On the Living Poets" (1818), and "On Genius and Common Sense" (1821), with

"Wordsworth" in *The Spirit of the Age* (1825), are vivid and vigorous and have had considerable influence. There are good insights in De Quincey's "On Wordsworth's Poetry." Besides the shrewd, if often casual and not invariably complimentary, remarks of Lamb in his letters, his review of *The Excursion* (shortened and distorted by Gifford) for the *Quarterly Review* in its sympathetic perceptiveness counterbalances Jeffrey's infamous, if not entirely unjust, review in the *Edinburgh Review*: John I. Ades, "Friendly Persuasion: Lamb as Critic of Wordsworth" (*WC,* 1977), is a good recent evaluation of Lamb's insights and of his effect on Wordsworth.

Among the Victorian critics, Matthew Arnold remains historically preeminent, not merely for his Preface to his selection from the poems published 1879 but also for his "Memorial Verses" published in June 1850. Arnold's prefatory essay celebrated Wordsworth as a poet ("his poetry is the reality, his philosophy is the illusion") in reply to Leslie Stephen's article in 1876 in the *Cornhill Magazine,* "Wordsworth's Ethics" (reprinted in *Hours in a Library,* 1879). Much less important, except for its early date, is the laudatory "Essay on the Poetical Works of Mr. Wordsworth" by Sir Henry Taylor (*Quarterly Review,* 1834); but quite significant are the essays of Walter Bagehot, beginning with an article on Hartley Coleridge in 1852, followed by "The First Edinburgh Reviewers" (1855), and climaxing in the rather snobby yet acute "Wordsworth, Tennyson, and Browning, on the Pure, Ornate, and Grotesque in English Poetry" in 1864. These, and even the remarks of G. H. Lewes in the "Principles of Success in Literature" (*Fortnightly Review,* 1865), may now seem more valuable than Stephen's comments, as almost surely will the remarks at various places in *Modern Painters* by John Ruskin and J. C. Shairp's essay in his *Studies in Poetry and Philosophy* (1868), which has been described as the first Hegelian study of Wordsworth and which contrasts the English poet with Rousseau. Altieri's article has suggested that John Stuart Mill's judgments of Wordsworth, both in the 1833 essays "What Is Poetry" and "The Two Kinds of Poetry" and in his *Autobiography* (1873), though well-known, will repay careful reexamination: I should like to see, for example, a thoughtful refutation of Mill's presupposition that much of the strength of Wordsworth's poetry depends on its appeal to a reader's memory of experiences similar to those of the poet. Arac's article implies increasing recognition of Walter Pater's perceptiveness in his essay on Wordsworth, first published in 1874, before both Stephen's and Arnold's, but best known through its reprinting in *Appreciations* (1889). Swinburne in "Wordsworth and Byron" (1884) praises Wordsworth for "harmony and imagination" and for his "tender sublime" and is generally anti-Arnoldian.

From the earliest part of our own century, A. C. Bradley's two lectures of 1903 (*Oxford Lectures on Poetry,* 1909) and his "English Poetry and German Philosophy in the Age of Wordsworth" of 1909 obviously retain much more than antiquarian interest and are written with exemplary verve. Less well-known but by no means obsolete is Alfred North Whitehead's discussion of Wordsworth in "The Romantic Reaction" in *Science and the Modern World* (1925). Contrarily, subsequent developments in criticism give importance to two contrasting works published just over half a century ago: Irving Babbitt's "The Primitivism of

Wordsworth" in 1931, reprinted in *On Being Creative* (1932), summing up and marking the point of precipitate decline in the influence of "New Humanist" antipathy to Wordsworth, and William Empson's *Seven Types of Ambiguity* (1930), setting the pattern of antipathy toward Wordsworth characteristic of much New Criticism with a few pages devoted to demonstrating how the poet in "Tintern Abbey" through misuse of the fourth type of ambiguity muddles the poem. Empson's critique is a delight to read today, for he faults exactly those features that enchant present-day critics, and in this respect Empson's work may seem more germane now than does T. S. Eliot's once influential "Wordsworth and Coleridge" in *The Use of Poetry and the Use of Criticism* (1933)—but this is to underestimate Eliot, as I indicate toward the end of this chapter. Those interested in the relation of transformations of critical opinions to changes in culture during the past couple of generations should notice Aldous Huxley's "Wordsworth in the Tropics," which appeared in *Do What You Will* (1929; first in *YR,* 1924). Travel in equatorial regions, Huxley claims, would have taught the poet that nature is "alien" and, therefore, that one should cultivate schizophrenia, taking Jekyll and Hyde as a model. But rereading this argument with knowledge of Huxley's later progress into mind-expanding drugs in air-conditioned Southern Californian mansions under the tutelage of a guru, one may feel that Huxley has ironically validated Wordsworth's diagnosis of how modern society fosters spiritual sickness.

At this point I ought to survey American academic criticism of this century's first four decades, which, however, I mostly skip, referring those curious about detail to earlier editions of this volume, Logan's bibliography cited above, and Ernest Bernbaum's *Guide through the Romantic Movement* (1930; rev. and enl. 1949), the very datedness of which is spectacularly illuminating. The first major American academic contribution to elucidating intellectual sources of Wordsworth's poetic development was Arthur Beatty's *William Wordsworth: His Doctrine and Art in Their Historical Relations* (1922; rev. 1927), which defended Wordsworth as a philosophical poet by asserting his use of David Hartley's associationalist psychology. The subsequent evolution of academic Wordsworthian studies to a remarkable degree follows developments in psychology, not surprisingly for a poet who claimed the mind as "my haunt, and the main region of my song." In England, Basil Willey in some respects subtilized and broadened the range of "background studies" developed by Beatty in the fine final chapter to *The Seventeenth Century Background* (1934), "On Wordsworth and the Locke Tradition," followed by " 'Nature' in Wordsworth," the conclusion of *The Eighteenth Century Background* (1940). It is nearly fair to regard as reactions to Beatty's argument Melvin M. Rader's *Presiding Ideas in Wordsworth's Poetry* (1931), Joseph Warren Beach's treatment of Wordsworth in *The Concept of Nature in Nineteenth-Century English Poetry* (1936), followed by "Reason and Nature in Wordsworth" (*JHI,* 1940), and Newton P. Stallknecht's *Strange Seas of Thought: Studies in William Wordsworth's Philosophy of Man and Nature* (1945). All three authors bring to the fore idealist rather than empiricist, transcendental rather than associative, sources for Wordsworth's ideas and psychology. Rader draws attention to Plato, Spinoza, Kant; Beach, to the Cambridge Platonists; and

Stallknecht, in the most important of these works, adds to the regular philosophical traditions the more mystical Jacob Boehme. Stallknecht's suggestion that Wordsworth could not bear the freedom his beliefs dictated he should welcome anticipates the darker views of later critics such as Hartman, whose first book on Wordsworth, *The Unmediated Vision* (1954), gave impetus to the important book by David Ferry, *The Limits of Mortality: An Essay on Wordsworth's Major Poems* (1959).

Before turning to these more recent critics, however, I think it necessary to make two points, the first well phrased by Larry J. Swingle in a forthcoming book: "all these studies have made significant contributions in illuminating the philosophical contexts within which Wordsworth wrote his poetry; but . . . they tend to undervalue the distinction between poetic materials and what the poet makes of those materials." One might note that Daniel Stempel, "Wordsworth and the Phenomenology of Textual Constitution" (*P&L,* 1981), believes that Beatty, by misreading Hartley, led many scholars onto the wrong track as to Wordsworth's use of his intellectual heritage, specifically that "Wordsworth's refusal to name the 'something far more deeply interfused' " in "Tintern Abbey" in fact "mirrors his vigorous avoidance of the conventional labels of eighteenth-century piety and his resolve to go beyond them toward a presence sensed as immanent in transcendental consciousness." Second, one ought to recognize that critics have not always attended to how the very idea of nature has been changed by scientists, even as the biologists and physicists working these changes have seldom kept up with changing views of "nature poets." Amusingly behind the times is Charles Hartshorne, "In Defense of Wordsworth's View of Nature" (*P&L,* 1980), who believes nobody ever reads *The Prelude* and that the Simplon Pass episode has been insufficiently analyzed. But Hartshorne's ignorance of the onward march of literary criticism is no more impressive than some critics' ignorance of elementary biology. Hartshorne's listing of five salient features of Wordsworth's view of nature and his explanation of why they constitute a position "to which disciplined inquiry now imposes fewer obstacles than it did 180 years ago" ought not to be ignored. He observes that "the science of Newton and Aristotle" is, indeed, "incompatible with Wordsworthianism," in good part because "Aristotle had not an inkling of the cellular and molecular structure of matter, and Newton's atoms had little in common with the particles, atoms, and molecules of present-day physics." Critics who have discussed Wordsworth and nature on the basis of conceptions that are Newtonian at best and pre-Aristotelian at worst have left open a wide field for fruitful investigation by younger scholars willing to link humanism with modern disciplines concerned with the physical constitution of the natural world.

Wordsworthian criticism beginning in the early sixties tended increasingly to emphasize mind rather than nature. Ferry observes that Wordworth's "love of nature" is conflicted, and his picture of a contradictory division in the poet between "mystical" and "sacramental" impulses to a degree parallels Hartman's later "apocalypse" and "akedah" distinction. Ferry makes good use of the chapters by Basil Willey cited above and D. G. James's *Scepticism and Poetry* (1937), as well as of G. Wilson Knight's "The Wordsworthian Profundity" in *The Starlit*

Dome (1941) and Walter Jackson Bate's *From Classic to Romantic* (1946), but goes farther than anyone before him to argue that "the ideas and feelings in Wordsworth's most important poems are lovingly hostile to the humane world" because the poet hated the mortal limitations by which the natural world circumscribes us. Ferry supports his argument with careful attention "to the special sorts of demands which the poems make on us," demands that he felt had too often been ignored and that anticipate to a significant degree the self-contestations that are the focus of poststructuralist critiques. Ferry sees "vision" as central to Wordsworthian self-contestation, for a "sacramental" view finds that "ordinary nature both aids and obstructs vision"; further complicating matters, Wordsworth was simultaneously a mystic and therefore drawn toward devaluing his own sacramentalist impulses, however complicated. In Ferry's view nature obstructs mystical "direct contact with the Eternal Presences," and for the mystic "Nature must therefore be destroyed," though to the sacramental view nature is precious because it symbolizes the eternal. It is a major virtue of Ferry's book that he emphasizes the temporal, representing the primary struggle in Wordsworth as the contradictory awareness of time and eternity. Most subsequent critics have tended surreptitiously to slide away from the temporal dimensions of the Wordsworth "problem." Had Christopher Salvesen, for example, confronted Ferry on this issue, instead of ignoring him, Salvesen's *The Landscape of Memory: A Study of Wordsworth's Poetry* (1965) would have been a more useful book.

David Perkins' *The Quest for Permanence* (1959) begins with three chapters defining Wordsworth's response to new, essentially modern conditions of life characterized by "instability . . . uncertainty . . . constant change" both in the activities going on around him and in his own mind. The response Perkins sees as a "yearning for a different reality, more stable," a search for "resolutions of the anxieties created by the need for permanence." I think Perkins is mistaken; I believe that Wordsworth, like other Romantics, seeks a permanence not outside flux but within the dynamic process of the vital activity itself, and that is why a definition of the quest within has properly occupied later critics. But Perkins may be right. Crucial to his view, moreover, is the insight that the poet felt continuously a "sense of the gulf between human nature, with all its greedy demands, its turbulent assertions . . . and the rest of nature." This insight, which puts Perkins on the same track with Hartman and Ferry, underlies *Wordsworth and the Poetry of Sincerity* (1964), in which, however, Perkins turns away, as it were, from the Ferry-Hartman direction to concentrate on placing Wordsworth within the developing cultural demand that poetry be written with personal sincerity, whatever the poet's metaphysical or aesthetic commitments. This leads Perkins to concentrate on an aspect of Wordsworth that has been little attended to by critics during the past decade and a half but that, sooner or later, is bound to come to the fore again—namely that Wordsworth's style

declares that some things matter more than art. It premises that "anxiety for Humanity" Keats generously praised in Wordsworth. A great poem,

Wordsworth thinks, does its work...as an example in living, an engagement of the whole being of the poet—his imagination, but also his conscience and intellect....It is this concern for the needs of life beyond the needs of art that purer, more rarefied artists find so hard to forgive.

Despite Perkins and other good critics, including John Danby and Carl Woodring, what might be called the psychoreligious aspect of Wordsworth's career, with its fundamentally ahistorical orientation, dominated Wordsworthian criticism into the seventies. Even M. H. Abrams' monumental *Natural Supernaturalism: Tradition and Revolution in Romantic Literature* (1971), treating "the secularization of inherited theological ideas and ways of thinking," is structured throughout by Abrams' understanding of Wordsworth's spiritual psychology as central to the Romantic movement, that movement conceived of as a diversified yet coherent totality, which, to a large degree, has been determinative of modern culture. "On Man, on Nature, and on Human Life" is what Abrams uses to conclude his book, and he regards the prospectus to *The Recluse* as epitomizing the central Romantic faith in the human power to create a paradisal condition on earth, a faith necessarily reshaped but not abandoned after the failure of apocalyptic hopes aroused by the French Revolution.

I have been surprised however, by how little specific influence Abrams' massive work seems to have exerted during the last decade despite the laudatory reviews it received by publication and even though some of Abrams' earlier essays that underlie key portions of *Natural Supernaturalism*—for example, "The Correspondent Breeze: A Romantic Metaphor" (*KR*, 1957), "English Romanticism: The Spirit of the Age" in *Romanticism Reconsidered* (ed. Northrop Frye, 1963), or the later "Structure and Style in the Greater Romantic Lyric" in *From Sensibility to Romanticism: Essays Presented to Frederick A. Pottle* (ed. Frederick W. Hilles and Harold Bloom, 1965)—have frequently been cited as fundamental. It seems to me, however, that no study of *The Prelude* would be complete if it did not take into account (whether in agreement or disagreement) Abrams' elaborate discussion of the poem. Abrams' insistence on a basically positive and optimistic tendency in Wordsworth lacks appeal to critics searching out anxieties and unresolved crises. But I suspect that *Natural Supernaturalism* should be seen as summing up, even culminating, an academic movement that might be described clumsily as liberal-humanist, that is, the final secularization of theological modes of thinking whose origin Abrams' book describes.

According to Abrams, a version of *Natural Supernaturalism* was completed in 1963, so the book really antedates the later sixties, challenge to the tradition in which Abrams writes. The published book, in fact, includes some polemics against developments of the later sixties, emphasizing the volume's quality as an apologia. None of this should suggest that Abrams has ceased to be a force in academic criticism—his continuing vitality is amply evidenced in *High Romantic Argument: Essays for M. H. Abrams* (ed. Lawrence Lipking, 1981), which includes contributions on Wordsworth by Geoffrey Hartman and Jonathan Wordsworth and on Abrams by Lipking, Wayne Booth, Thomas McFarland, and Jonathan Culler, with a cogently spirited reply by Abrams himself, showing no diminution in his genial combativeness.

Geoffrey Hartman was right to find a forerunner not only in A. C. Bradley but also in Willard Sperry, *Wordsworth's Anti-Climax* (1935), for Sperry was the first carefully to analyze Wordsworth's "self-consciousness" in a fashion fore-telling Ferry and Hartman by picking up Charles Lamb's comment on "The Old Cumberland Beggar." Lamb said that in the poem "the mind knowingly passes a fiction upon herself first substituting her own feelings for the Beggar, and, in the same breath detecting the fallacy, will not part with her wish." Sperry, though not engaging in close critical readings, lays a groundwork for Hartman's concept of Wordsworthian "surmise"; but Sperry, a theologian, not only uses a most unpoststructuralist rhetoric but even questions the validity of "making the imagi-nation itself rather than the objects upon which it is employed" the subject of poetry. But there are possibilities in Sperry not found in Hoxie N. Fairchild's *Religious Trends in English Poetry* (1939—68), whose analysis of Wordsworth in the third volume reflects the author's sectarian bias, though the second volume pro-vides a fair historical survey of the religious temper of Wordsworth's time, on which one may also consult D. LeMahieu, *The Mind of William Paley: A Philoso-pher and His Age* (1976), for an understanding of the most influential orthodox theologian of Wordsworth's age even though he seldom is even mentioned by re-cent discussants of Wordsworth's "transcendental" impulses.

Along the line leading toward Hartman's work one might also notice William Empson's *The Structure of Complex Words* (1951) and, more important, John Jones's *The Egotistical Sublime* (1954). Jones attacks the "lazy assumption that the Romantic poets were all striving to express unity," and by demonstrating how Wordsworth's best poetry is devised to express the more exciting paradox of "solitude-in-relationship," he begins to delineate tensions explored more in-tensely by Ferry and Hartman. Jones's epilogue in particular calls attention to the kind of epistemological subtleties in Wordsworth's poetry that have interested subsequent commentators, though he is more concerned with the continuity of the poet's entire career. Perhaps the best way of indicating changes in critical em-phasis I have been outlining is through a contrast of *Wordsworth: Centenary Studies Presented at Cornell and Princeton Universities,* edited by Gilbert T. Dunklin (1951), commemorating the poet's death, and *Bicentenary Wordsworth Studies in Memory of John Alban Finch,* edited by Jonathan Wordsworth (1970). Two thirds of the contributions to the latter excellent volume make use of care-fully detailed analyses of manuscript sources with scrupulous concern for accu-racy in the exposition of minutiae. Here we see Wordsworthian criticism making its shift from discussion of poems to discussion of texts. The earlier, briefer volume contains only seven essays, all "liberally humanistic," though none avoiding attention to minute particulars where appropriate, especially Earl L. Griggs in his comprehensive "Wordsworth through Coleridge's Eyes" and Frederick A. Pottle's succinctly lucid "The Eye and the Object in the Poetry of Wordsworth." At least as impressive, however, are essays by John Crowe Ransom and Lionel Trilling. Ransom's "William Wordsworth: Notes toward an Understanding of Poetry," despite its titular dependence on Eliot, includes one of the best technical analyses of Wordsworth's poetic devices, along with a brilliant summation of how Wordsworth's "religion of nature" appears in his poetry as a concretion, "massive yet individualized, and its presence . . . likely to enter unexpectedly and dramatically into the consciousness of a boy who is about the business of a boy." In these moments, "the spirit of the natural universe focuses all its terrific power in the given concretion . . . for the purpose of aggressively seeking him out and making itself known to him and giving him its joy." Because of such occasions, Ransom finds Freud of little help in reading Wordsworth, since Freud's "instructive mythology" is of little relevance to a poet who believes we win "individual happiness not by challenging the opposing natural element but by embracing it." For if we "obtain the sense of community with the infinite concretion of the environing world, we may cease to feel like small aliens, even though busy, cunning, and predatory ones." Trilling's essay, "Wordsworth and the Iron Time," being better known, needs less quotation. Trilling argues that Wordsworth's special gift to modern culture is precisely what makes him antithetical to many modern critics, his belief "that life does not have to be justified and feeling affirmed by what is violent, or by that which is proud: the meanest flower is enough."

The Cornell series of texts, preceded by Mary Moorman's completion of her biography and the appearance of Mark Reed's infinitely detailed chronologies, along with uncertainties aroused by the growing influence of new modes of criticism, perhaps made it inevitable that the later seventies should not produce large-scale books of Wordsworthian criticism. Most of the best work of the past few years, at any rate, has been relatively narrow. Even books that seem to claim wide scope often turn out to limit their areas of concentration and, rather than explore adventurously, tend to refine earlier exegeses. So Jeffrey Baker's *Time and Mind in Wordsworth's Poetry* (1980) is unusual in ignoring a good deal of contemporary scholarship and in hesitating to advance on earlier analyses of "unique aspects of Wordsworth's time sense" (though the book contains some good readings, notably of the Arab dream in *The Prelude* and book 1 of *The Excursion*), and Charles Sherry's *Wordsworth's Poetry of the Imagination* (1980), dealing almost exclusively with the Intimations Ode, "Tintern Abbey," and *The Prelude,* centers itself rigorously on the idea of anamnesis, a form of memory that Sherry thinks best defined in Platonic dialogues and that enables a "man to perceive certain permanent, even eternal truths once he remembers to remember them, and through their recollection raise them once again to conscious significance." This view and the small range of poetry he treats probably commit Sherry to the unspectacular conclusion that for Wordsworth it is self-consciousness itself that is recompense for the inevitable growing away from a divine origin.

Two books by an older scholar, John Beer, *Wordsworth and the Human Heart* (1978) and *Wordsworth in Time* (1979), while ranging through many details of the poet's life, work, and the influences on him, define the poet's relations with Coleridge, his balancing of "energy and stasis," and what Beer aptly

terms his "human mysticism." The results are good specific readings and insights
into psychological, intellectual, or literary indebtednesses, but they offer no decisive redefinition of the poet's accomplishment. Beer's books are like those just
mentioned in not articulating Wordsworth's value for a particular moment of critical history. John A. Hodgson, in *Wordsworth's Philosophical Poetry* (1980), like
Beer, ranges widely, aiming to provide a full "history of Wordsworth's metaphysical beliefs." That history Hodgson sees as comprising four phases, first
(1797–98) optimistic belief in "one life," followed by a reaction against the loss
of human "individuality, awareness, and intelligence" (1798–1804), leading
Wordsworth to "memorializing poems" supplying "some enduring, if not immortal, record of individual life." This reaction, in turn, leads to a reconceiving of
godhead as more transcendent than originally envisioned, a reconception climaxing in the Intimations Ode and *The Prelude* (1804–05). But more and more
after 1805 Wordsworth "modifies his metaphysical assumptions," arriving finally
at "something very like the God of Christianity." Such summary perhaps unfairly
emphasizes Hodgson's tracing of a route already thoroughly examined, notably
by Alan Grob in *The Philosophic Mind: A Study of Wordsworth's Poetry and
Thought 1797–1805* (1973). But even many of the particularized readings of
Hodgson add less than one would hope to Paul Sheats's *The Making of
Wordsworth's Poetry, 1785–1798,* another important book published in the same
year as Grob's. Even what Hodgson calls his "counter plot . . . the correlative history of Wordsworth's emblematizing vision" has to a degree been anticipated by
James A. W. Heffernan's *Wordsworth's Theory of Poetry* (1969), although
Hodgson's concern is with the poet as religious man, not as critic. That a commentator so knowledgeable as Hodgson should thus seem so uninnovative suggests that the time was not propitious for comprehensively original work, though
such a time may be near. The slightly oppressive nature of the late seventies' climate is revealed negatively in three books oriented toward explaining the theoretical bases of Romantic literature, each of which one would expect to have
much to say of Wordsworth: David Simpson, *Irony and Authority in Romantic
Poetry* (1979), Anne K. Mellor, *English Romantic Irony* (1980), and Tilottama
Rajan, *Dark Interpreter: The Discourse of Romanticism* (1980). The three books,
in fact, almost entirely ignore Wordsworth, although Simpson's subsequent
Wordsworth and the Figurings of the Real (1982) uses our poet to define in a
stimulating fashion an underlying Romantic epistemology of dynamic interactivity
and an "ethic of the polymorphous."

Lest this outline of broad patterns too grossly simplify the complex world of
Wordsworthian scholarship, however, I mention, before turning to specific
poems as foci of criticism, several books of diverse character as reminders of the
variety of modern academicism. Frances Ferguson's *Wordsworth: Language as
Counter-Spirit* (1977) argues that Wordsworth was deeply concerned with language's relation to consciousness, particularly as language could be used to challenge the reader's and the poet's ability to articulate profound fears and aspirations. Ferguson explores Wordsworth's belief that the affections are fundamental
in psychic life, being the ground of consciousness and perception. Because of this
conviction, the impact of loss of affectional objects was for him traumatic, and his

most imaginative poetry is epitaphic in the sense of endeavoring to recover the irrecoverable.

The radically different approach of Hermann J. Wüscher is revealed by the title of his book, *Liberty, Equality, and Fraternity in Wordsworth, 1791–1800* (1980), which deals with material analyzed more profoundly by Michael H. Friedman in *The Making of a Tory Humanist: William Wordsworth and the Idea of Community* (1979). Friedman, using a combined Freudian-Marxist approach, portrays the poet as having a divided sense of himself—one "princely," grandiose; the other contracted, stinted—and as having sought to resolve this division through the articulating of an ideal human community. He thought the French Revolution offered a community that would provide both stability and scope for his princely self. Yet his own psyche, because of his internalization of paternal authority, from the first resisted and finally led him to abandon that idea for the less effective but more affective ideal of "traditional" community of the Lake Country. But the social and economic forces generated by the Industrial Revolution were destroying that society just as Wordsworth was formulating from it his ideal, and the poet was led to mythicize social relations, so that what had begun in him as acute awareness of real conditions of rural and impoverished life became increasingly a facile, false humanism. Friedman uses Freud and Marx in unusual and impressive ways, and he is the first to employ effectively C. M. L. Bouch and G. P. Jones's *A Short Economic and Social History of the Lake Counties, 1500–1830,* though it has been available since 1961.

David B. Pirie's *William Wordsworth: The Poetry of Grandeur and of Tenderness* (1982), like Simpson's more penetrating *Figurings of the Real* (1982), may illustrate a growing resistance to earlier impositions of reductive philosophic or psychological patterns on the complexity of Wordsworth's poetry, increasingly seen as emerging out of antithetical "convictions which will not surrender to each other." Pirie, who distressingly minimizes the likeness of his observations and ideas to other critics' work and indulges in some tonal infelicities, argues that interpretations based on abstract theories deface the essential self-contradictions and persistently infiltrating ambiguities on which depends the delicate balance between sympathy and skepticism that is Wordsworth's remarkable and enduring attainment. The most recent work of J. R. Watson, *Wordsworth's Vital Soul: The Sacred and Profane in Wordsworth's Poetry* (1982), is disappointing in its development of a good insight that the poet's "early religious apprehension" produced "fundamental, even primitive ideas of the sacred" decisive to the originality of his art. More historical in its treatment of religion's influence in *English Romanticism: The Grounds of Belief* (1983) by John Clubbe and Ernest J. Lovell, Jr. They stress Wordsworth's Anglican background and upbringing and his sympathies with Blake's and Coleridge's beliefs, all three agreeing that imaginative perception is profoundly ethical.

Defying usual critical categories in *Wordsworth's Metaphysical Verse: Geometry, Nature, and Form* (1982) by Lee M. Johnson, who illuminates poems by metrical analyses and their "geometrical extension," which means, primarily, Wordsworth's use of geometrical proportions, especially the golden section (A:B:: B: A+B), for symbolic effect. Johnson, whose fine book on the sonnet I note toward the end of this chapter, argues persuasively that in "Tintern Abbey," the Immortality Ode, *The Prelude,* and *The Excursion* passages emphasizing the transcendental are fully appreciated only when we see how the poem can make "what is most concrete ... most symbolic" through deployment of his knowledge of geometry for defining forms that cannot be measured or defined numerically. A final chapter explores with lucid perceptiveness Wordsworth's "commitment to metrical composition." This is the most original recent book of Wordsworthian criticism—almost, indeed, eccentric. It does not explore deeply enough possible psychic forces expressed through "geometrical" orderings, but it opens up a new mode of investigation.

Another book difficult to classify is *Romantic Contraries: Freedom versus Design* (1984) by Peter L. Thorslev, Jr., whose discussion of Wordsworth appears in chapter 4, "The Organic Universe," centered on the poet's "retreat"—in the religious as much as the military sense—from the strains of intense conscious thought. Thorslev, though indebted to Abrams (notably in an emphasis on parallels between Hegel and Wordsworth), opens a new direction when he squarely confronts what most of us evade, the question of what constitutes the consolation for Margaret's death in "The Ruined Cottage." He finds the answer in Wordsworth's creation of a context of an "organic sublime." Books such as those of Thorslev, Johnson, and Simpson are extraordinarily varied in their methods and purposes. If one adds to them Kenneth Johnston's *Wordsworth and* The Recluse (1984), discussed in the next section, and Don H. Bialostosky's exploration into the dynamics of Wordsworthian narratives by means of a fascinating Bakhtinian "poetics of speech" in *Making Tales: The Poetics of Wordsworth's Narrative Experiments* (1984), noted among works on *Lyrical Ballads* below, it would appear that Wordsworthian studies in the early 1980s are undergoing an unusual diversification as well as expansion. Its principal cause I should guess to be an enriching of "theoretical" approaches by an intensified historical scholarship.

Longer Poems (excluding *The Prelude*)

The Cornell series alone assures continuing attention to Wordsworth's early poetry, and *The Borderers* in particular has steadily attracted commentators eager to define the foundation of the poet's achievement in his "great decade." The remarkable new Cornell edition (1982) of Wordsworth's only play by Robert Osborn will doubtless stimulate even more careful and textually informed analyses. Although *An Evening Walk* and *Descriptive Sketches* are not so important, the new Cornell editions will direct more attention to them, and both have been treated with respect since Hartman's commentaries in his 1964 book. Jonathan Ramsey, for example, in "Seeing and Perceiving in Wordsworth's *An Evening Walk*" (*MLQ,* 1975), stresses the poem's foreshadowing of crucial later issues, and he follows the same line in "The Prelusive Sounds of *Descriptive Sketches*" (*Criticism,* 1978). J. F. Turner is more concerned with intrinsic qualities in "'Various

Journey, Sad and Slow': Wordsworth's *Descriptive Sketches* (1791–2) and the Lure of Pastoral" (*DUJ*, 1976), while Steven E. Sharp usefully defends the poet against "The Unmerited Contempt of Reviewers: Wordsworth's Response to Contemporary Reviews of *Descriptive Sketches*" (*WC*, 1977). Paul D. Sheats's *The Making of Wordsworth's Poetry, 1785–1798* (1973), however, remains one of the best sources for analyses of the early works, especially the juvenilia. Sheats is convincing in showing how early Wordsworth's major attitudes toward art and life developed and how thoroughly he consciously confronted issues posed by the French Revolution. Sheats, incidentally, is one of the few recent critics to bring forward again the importance to the poet of his involvement with Annette.

The Borderers continues to seem the crucial work for evaluating the evolution of the poet's metaphysical and political views and so remains a center for controversy. A recent contribution by David V. Erdman, "Wordsworth as Heartsworth; or, Was Regicide the Prophetic Grounds of Those 'Moral Questions'?" in *The Evidence of the Imagination* (ed. D. H. Reiman et al., 1978), points to possible parallels between the play and events in France, with a bonus of freewheeling speculations of a historical kind. Speculations of another kind animate William A. Gordon's "Autobiography and Identity: Wordsworth's *The Borderers*" (*TSE*, 1972), which represents the play's extreme psychic violence as expressing the poet's rejection of his father. More down-to-earth is Marijane Osborn's "Wordsworth's 'Borderers' and the Landscape of Penrith" (*Transactions of the Cumberland and Westmoreland Antiquarian and Archaeological Society*, 1976), which sees the literal topography as a kind of bedrock for the poet's dramatization of his social and political ideas and, presumably, his psychic problems: an appealing approach. Contrasting interests are exhibited in James W. Pipkin's "*The Borderers* and Wordsworth's Emblems of Solitude" (*SoRA*, 1976) and in W. J. B. Owen's "*The Borderers* and the Aesthetics of Drama" (*WC*, 1975), which sees Wordsworth's Shakespearean material both enriching the significance of his arguments and providing valuable new ways of looking at Shakespeare's works. "Gothic Survival in Literary Drama" is the last chapter in *Gothic Drama from Walpole to Shelley* (1947) by Bertrand Evans, not an important work but a useful reminder of a literary form contemporary critics persistently ignore.

The most consistent focus of controversy over Wordsworth's unperformed play takes its origin in Hazlitt's discussion in *The Spirit of the Age* of Godwinian influence. In recent years the conception of the play as revealing the process of Wordsworth's changing his social and political ideas has become subordinated to analysis of how the work dramatizes the poet's psychic struggles. Early biographers Legouis and Harper, along with de Selincourt, read *The Borderers* as a rejection of Godwin—a position kept alive as late as 1966 by Enid Welsford in *Salisbury Plain: A Study in the Development of Wordsworth's Mind and Art*. H. W. Garrod, in *Wordsworth* (1923—but with some passages still well worth attention), argued to the contrary that the drama implies acceptance of Godwinian solutions. Later scholars have tended to redefine this disagreement not by minimizing Wordsworth's engagement with radical thinking or commitment to appropriate social action in the 1790s but, instead, by emphasizing the complexity of these issues in the poet's day—some sense for which may be gleaned from

Kenneth MacLean's *Agrarian Age: A Background for Wordsworth* (1950) and E. P. Thompson's *The Making of the English Working Class* (1963). The most judiciously concise analysis of how these forces appear in *The Borderers* is Carl Woodring's in *Politics in English Romantic Poetry* (1970). Woodring points out that the play examines "the effects of social disruption rather than its cause" and does not attack reform but gives "half-conscious evidence that narrrowness in argument for reform and progress would have to be abandoned." A fine analysis of the play, stressing biographical implications for the poet in the character Marmaduke's retreat from action, is Roger Sharrock's *"The Borderers:* Wordsworth on the Moral Frontier" (*DUJ,* 1964). R. F. Storch, "Wordsworth's *The Borderers:* The Poet as Anthropologist" (*ELH,* 1969), emphasizes the motif of sexual jealousy as a focus for the conflict between society and the individual. Storch's essay may be regarded as qualifying by limiting the reading of G. Wilson Knight in *The Starlit Dome* (1941), since Knight stresses Wordsworth's passionate ambivalence toward action, suggesting that although the play cannot resolve the issues it raises and to this degree is a failure, it also reveals Wordsworth working toward a new conception of emotional and intellectual energies. Knight, in fact, very nearly anticipates Hartman's interpretation in *Wordsworth's Poetry,* which represents Oswald as forcing Marmaduke into "a new and isolating consciousness," the moral significance of which remains obscure because of Marmaduke's evasive tactic of going into exile. Robert Osborn, however, argues persuasively that Wordsworth is centrally concerned with "the dangers of entering upon, and attempting to perpetuate, the world of dreams which the inversion of relationship between 'inner' and 'outer' entails" in "Meaningful Obscurity: The Antecedents and Character of Rivers" (*Bicentenary Wordsworth Studies*). This valuable article, whose notes admirably survey the entire history of criticism of the drama, is the base for Osborn's recent edition.

No one doubts that in the mid-1790s Wordsworth moved away from the superficially pro-French position revealed in *Descriptive Sketches* to struggle with what Woodring characterizes as "a revulsion against unimaginative rationalism . . . the moral and psychological ground held in common by Paley and Malthus . . . Condorcet, Volney, Priestley, Godwin and Bentham." Everyone is coming to agree, then, that political issues in the early poems carry one to the heart of Wordsworth's evolving philosophic-aesthetic originality. For that reason "Guilt and Sorrow," a poem subject to many transformations over many years, deserves more attention than it has yet received, despite the excellent edition of Stephen Gill, preceded by "'Adventures on Salisbury Plain' and Wordsworth's Poetry of Protest 1795–97" (*SIR,* 1972), and before that by his "Wordsworth's Breeches Pocket: Attitudes to the Didactic Poet" (*EIC,* 1969), which focuses on the 1793 "Salisbury Plain" as poetry of social protest. Although Arthur Beatty pointed to connections between Wordsworth's poem and Joseph Fawcett's poem *The Art of War* (1795) in "Joseph Fawcett: The Art of War" (*Univ. of Wisconsin Studies in Language and Literature,* 1918) more than sixty years ago and M. Ray Adams wrote "Joseph Fawcett and Wordsworth's Solitary" (*PMLA,* 1933) half a century ago, the poems have been little studied, perhaps because, as Gill observes, they do not richly reward purely psychological analysis. A notable exception is provided by Paul D. Sheats in *The Making of Wordsworth's Poetry* (1973), which includes comment on the poems' relation to *The Borderers*, while Francis Celoria, "Chatterton, Wordsworth and Stonehenge" (*N&Q*, 1976), points to the "Battle of Hastings" as a source. But as Sheats and Gill agree, "Salisbury Plain" remains a splendid research topic for any scholar with interest in late eighteenth-century history and in Wordsworth's poems antedating his great decade, for Enid Welsford's *Salisbury Plain: A Study in the Development of Wordsworth's Mind and Art* (1966) fails to confront effectively the most difficult issues posed by the poem. Some of these issues are close to the center of Jonathan Wordsworth's *The Music of Humanity: A Critical Study of Wordsworth's "Ruined Cottage," Incorporating Texts from a Manuscript of 1799 – 1800* (1969). The book, however, is best known for its disentangling of *The Ruined Cottage* and *The Pedlar* from their fusion in the later comprehensiveness of *The Excursion,* a disentangling significantly developed by James A. Butler (see his introduction to his edition of *The Ruined Cottage* and *The Pedlar* cited above). *The Music of Humanity* argues that an essential feature of the poet's achievement is founded in his early commitment to sympathetic love and that this underlying humanitarianism in his art was weakened by his developing aesthetic concept of imagination. In *William Wordsworth: The Borders of Vision* (1982) this view is refined into a consideration of Wordsworth's sense of the human being as a creature of "borderland," rooted in the world of actuality but aspiring beyond the normal range of experience. Jonathan Wordsworth's approach takes off from a line of criticism perhaps best exemplified earlier in John Danby's eloquent *The Simple Wordsworth* (1960), which seeks to demonstrate that Wordsworthian "simplicity is an invitation to a new intimacy, a new discipline, and a new complexity." John Jones, lacking Danby's interest in and ear for the poet's simple lyrics, in *The Egotistical Sublime: A History of Wordsworth's Imagination* (1954) traces a gradual loss of relational power. This power, closely allied to "simplicity" and "humanitarianism" in his early verse, enables the poet at his best simultaneously to represent self as solitary and separate and yet as existing fully only in reciprocal relations with the outer world, thus evoking in his reader a sense of mundane reality unifiedly single and self-sustaining. That this focus on Wordsworth's affectional commitment to common humanity remains important to many readers is illustrated by Frederick Beaty's chapter on Wordsworth and Burns in *Light from Heaven: Love in British Romantic Literature* (1971), centering on Wordsworth's portrayals of deserted women.

Despite the persuasiveness of champions of the early Wordsworth and the value of the Cornell series in restoring early versions, one must recognize that "early" and "late" Wordsworth are not, finally, entirely separable. It is, indeed, the richness and the extended time span of the dialectic between original composition and multiple revisions that give Wordsworth's poetry much of its unique fascination for scholars. Wordsworth, moreover, not only revised and rerevised but also frequently delayed publication, as well as rearranging the order in which he presented his poems—the intricacies of which are discussed below. Because the Wordsworthian critic must consider simultaneously the histories of composition, revision, and editorial arrangement for publication, it is worth recollecting that if we have now more *Preludes* than we can easily accommodate, the early Victorians had none; and the second generation of Romantic poets, along with Scottish critics, had no access to *The Ruined Cottage* or *The Pedlar,* now thrust willy-nilly on modern freshman-anthology buyers. The Romantics had to make do with *The Excursion,* since they lacked even as much of the uncompleted *Recluse* as we possess.

If early Wordsworth, then, is a possession of later times and no one has yet definitively dismissed Jeffrey's dismissal of *The Excursion,* there are at least signs of a movement in the direction of a Keatsian ambivalence toward Wordsworth's longest poem published in his lifetime. Sympathy for the aim of the later style seems to be evidenced in Kenneth Johnston's *Wordsworth and* The Recluse (1984) and in forthcoming studies by Peter Manning, and I suspect that in the next decade much more will be discovered to be interesting in work that received the shortest possible shrift in previous editions of this volume: if nothing else, some of our distinguished critics are themselves aging.

Judson Stanley Lyon, *The Excursion: A Study* (1950), solid but uninspiring, for a good many years dominated the empty landscape of *Excursion* criticism and remains of some value, but the commentaries of E. E. Bostetter in *The Romantic Ventriloquists* (1963) and Geoffrey Hartman in *Wordsworth's Poetry 1787–1814,* although fundamentally negative, will be found by most contemporary readers more interesting and illuminating; serious scholars continue to find useful Don H. Hensley's dissertation "Wordsworth and a New Mythology: A Stylistic Analysis of the Excursion" (Univ. of Wisconsin, 1964). Enid Welsford in *Salisbury Plain* (1966) analyzes structure and symbolism to defend Wordsworth's "emblematic" presentation of nature, and Bernard Groom argues vigorously for a recognition of the significant continuity between "early" and "late" Wordsworth in *The Unity of Wordsworth's Poetry* (1966). Perhaps the most intriguing discussion of the poem in the 1960s appears in H. W. Piper's *The Active Universe* (1962), which frequently is referred to as if it were concerned solely with Wordsworth's early poetry. Piper, it is true, seeks to identify the source of what he regards as Wordsworth's "pantheistic imagination" in the ideas of late eighteenth-century radical thinkers such as Priestley and Erasmus Darwin. But Piper goes on to argue that though Wordsworth and Coleridge shared the stimulation of this radical thinking, they evolved from it two distinct concepts of imagination, set forth in the *Biographia Literaria* and *The Excursion;* the latter Piper associates with Wittgenstein's "seeing as," and he goes on to trace the influence of *The Excursion* on the younger Romantics. Frances Ferguson, in a chapter on *The Excursion* in *Wordsworth: Language as Counter-Spirit* (1977), is less interested in the poem's influence though she does not ignore that issue. She calls attention to Wordsworth's mocking of popular notions of sublimity, even a near challenging of his own "egotistical sublimity," discusses the complexity of the characters' relations (stemming in part from the poet's refusal to grant any one ultimate authority), and insists on the poem's focus on language and reading, illustrated by the maltreatment of *Candide* and the epitaphs of the dalesmen. Carl Woodring in *Wordsworth* (1965) presents the only accurate available summary of the poem, and elegantly defines the work's strengths and weaknesses while elucidating the intricacies of its compositional history in seventeen short pages.

Not surprisingly, most comment in the 1970s has clustered around the first book, within which features of *The Pedlar* and *The Ruined Cottage* are discerned by scrupulous editors. In "'Finer Distance': The Narrative Art of Wordsworth's 'The Wanderer'" (*ELH,* 1972), Reeve Parker judiciously argues that insistence on the superiority of the abridged 1799–1800 version is one-sided, missing the poet's ultimate skill in rendering the "achievement of equanimity" in the face of "recollected misery." Parker usefully compares the treatment of the Wanderer-Narrator relation to that of the Ancient Mariner and the Wedding Guest. An even more vigorous defense of book 1 of *The Excursion* is Philip Cohen's "Narrative and Persuasion in *The Ruined Cottage*" (*JNT,* 1978), while Peter Manning, in "Wordsworth, Margaret, and the Pedlar" (*SIR,* 1976), demonstrates that a "review of the complicated history of Book I" shows "how profoundly intertwined are the stories of Margaret and the Pedlar" and "the underlying coherence of the longer text with which he [the poet] began and to which he returned." Manning credits admiration for the poet's compassionate observation with leading Jonathan Wordsworth in *The Music of Humanity* (1969) to insist on the integrity of *The Ruined Cottage.* Evan Radcliffe, "'In Dreams Begins Responsibility': Wordsworth's Ruined Cottage Story" (*SIR,* 1984), sees the story as justifying the poet's withdrawal from society into the country. The tale of Margaret has, in fact, been admired by many, including Helen Darbishire and F. R. Leavis, first in *Revaluation* (1936), subsequently in "Wordsworth: The Creative Conditions," *Twentieth-Century Literature in Retrospect* (ed. Reuben A. Brower, 1971). *The Ruined Cottage,* however, has been printed as a distinct poem in the *Oxford Anthology of English Literature* and the *Norton Anthology of English Literature,* both of which roundly declare it superior to other versions.

Russell Noyes answers the question, "Why Read *The Excursion?*" (*WC,* 1973), by recommending the poem's eloquence, vivid natural descriptions, and courageous social criticism; while Paul H. Fry, in "The Absent Dead: Wordsworth, Byron, and the Epitaph" (*SIR,* 1978), treats *The Excursion* as one of several "antisublime" epitaphic poems, and William Galperin, "'Imperfect While Unshared': The Role of the Implied Reader in Wordsworth's *Excursion*" (*Criticism,* 1980), studies the poem, with interesting results, from the perspective of reception theory. Thomas McFarland, "Wordsworth on Man, on Nature, and on Human Life" (*SIR,* 1982), develops a probing analysis of the first line of the "Prospectus" to *The Recluse* that accompanied the first edition of *The Excursion* and serves as the starting point for M. H. Abrams' *Natural Supernaturalism.* A valuable contribution is the collection of eight essays by Annabel Patterson (Vergilian qualities and structure), Geoffrey Durrant (death), David Q. Smith (strength of silence and solitude), Stuart Peterfreund (relation to Milton), Barbara T. Gates (free will and determinism), Jim Springer Borck (language used to face sorrow and death), and Peter F. McInerney (indeterminacy of the Wanderer's consolation) in *WC,* 1978—of which perhaps *primum inter pares* is Kenneth R. Johnston's "Wordsworth's Reckless Recluse: The Solitary." Johnston is the steadiest critic of

the later poetry, his work now fortunately concentrated in *Wordsworth and* The
Recluse (1984), including but extending earlier essays, such as "Wordsworth and
The Recluse: The University of Imagination" (*PMLA,* 1982), which, as Johnston says,
gives an "overview" of the argument embedded in his book, probably most valuable in its detailed yet clear analyses of the sequential development of *Recluse*
texts. For Johnston there are three principal phases: the first starts from the origin of the *Recluse* project in 1797, continuing through the completion of the two-
book *Prelude* in 1799; the second begins with the first work on "Home at
Grasmere," 1800–01, ending with its conclusion in 1806; the final segment commences with "The Tuft of Primroses" and concludes with the completion of *The
Excursion.* Johnston's approach enables him to comment on all Wordsworth's
longer poems, and I am arbitrary to single out for special praise his discussion of
"Home at Grasmere" and the difficult "Tuft of Primroses" fragment, which is also
expertly analyzed by James A. Butler, "Wordsworth's *Tuft of Primroses:* 'An Unrelenting Doom' " (*SIR,* 1975). Butler argues that the poet's central symbol of the
vale having failed him, he attempts—unsuccessfully—to use the primroses as a
substitute emblem of hope and serenity. Johnston's treatment of "Home at
Grasmere," along with Muriel J. Mellown's "The Development of Imagery in
'Home at Grasmere' " (*WC,* 1974), may be regarded as correcting the emphasis on
ecological vision in my essay on the poem mentioned previously, though I remain unrepentant. Mellown and I wrote before the appearance of Darlington's
valuable edition (cited above), although Jonathan Wordsworth, "On Man, on Nature, and on Human Life" (*RES,* 1980), now argues against Darlington's compelling evidence of the poem's late completion. Kurt Heinzelman, in a chapter of
The Economics of the Imagination (1980), uses "Home at Grasmere" along with
"Michael" and "Resolution and Independence" to argue that the poet instructs
"the reader in the true meaning of social production" and that Wordsworth's poetics involves an "exchange of labor modelled upon an economic contract." More
convincing is Michael Friedman, "Wordsworth's Grasmere: A Rentier's Vision"
(*Polit,* 1977), which explores the applicability of Raymond Williams' terms to
Wordsworth's idealizations. Bruce Clarke, "Wordsworth's Departed Swans: Sublimation and Sublimity in *Home at Grasmere*" (*SIR,* 1980), through an investigation
of the poem's "elaborate vagueness," shows Wordsworth attempting to codify "a
poetic sensibility that is counter-sublime," while Timothy R. Austin, "Stylistic Evolution in Wordsworth's Poetry: Evidence from Emendations" (*Language and
Style,* 1979), finds "deterioration" or "self-plagiaristic borrowings" through intense examination of selected passages. Laurence Goldstein, in his book *Ruins
and Empire* (1977), devotes much space to the later Wordsworth, in particular
comparing works of the "Grasmere" period to eighteenth-century predecessors
and prototypes, a focus probably explaining his disregard of *The White Doe of
Rylstone,* which might seem appropriate to his topic. This poem still awaits full
critical analysis, though it has attracted some good commentary. Peter Burra, in
his brief but vivid *Wordsworth* (1936), praises the poem highly, making use of
Coleridge's letter of May 1808 on the first completed version. John Jones in *The
Egotistical Sublime* is negative, but his discussion leads into his interesting suggestions on the "baptised imagination." Martin Price's "Imagination in *The White*

Doe of Rylstone" (*PQ,* 1954) is a forerunner of James A. W. Heffernan's vigorous apologia for the emblematic imagination he finds splendidly displayed in the poem in his *Wordsworth's Theory of Poetry* (1969). Barbara T. Gates, in "Wordsworth's Symbolic White Doe: 'The Power of History in the Mind' " (*Criticism,* 1975), sees the doe as symbolizing the revelatory power of the past.

The Prelude

Most major critical books on Wordsworth include at least a chapter devoted to *The Prelude,* often with special attention to the Simplon Pass episode, but the first full-length study to make use of both the 1805 and the 1850 texts provided by de Selincourt was Melvin Rader's *Presiding Ideas in Wordsworth's Poetry* (1931), somewhat updated in *Wordsworth: A Philosophical Approach* (1967), perhaps superior to Stallknecht's *Strange Seas of Thought* (1945) in defining the influence of transcendental thinkers on Wordsworth and just in assessing the impact of associational psychology. After Rader, the next major study is that of Raymond Dexter Havens, *The Mind of a Poet* (1941), lengthy, detailed, arrogantly dogmatic in the academic style of forty years ago but still of value, particularly in drawing attention to crucial passages by thorough discussions and annotations. Mary Burton's *The One Wordsworth* (1942) contains the first, and so far last, extended comparison of the 1805 and 1850 *Prelude*s strongly to favor the later version. In 1954 appeared *Wordsworth's* Prelude: *A Study of Its Literary Form* by Abbie Findlay Potts, which remains the most complete general treatment of the poem's sources but not of the poem's form. In the next decade Herbert Lindenberger provided one of the most useful books given over entirely to the poem, *On Wordsworth's* Prelude (1963). This work, along with the extended chapter of sensitive criticism in David Ferry's *The Limits of Mortality* (1959) and Hartman's discussion in *Wordsworth's Poetry 1787 – 1814* (1964), constitutes the best starting place for anyone taking up seriously criticism of Wordsworth's primary poem. Lindenberger does not give a reading, nor does he press a single thesis. Instead, he gives us "Thirteen Ways of Looking at *The Prelude,*" dealing first with aspects of language, then taking up problems of structure, analyzing the poet's difficulty in shaping a long poem at a time when poetry was beginning to be identified solely with the lyrical mode, and finally turning to problems of time and the poem's "social dimension," including its fortunes in subsequent literary history.

The thrust of Hartman's analysis is defined by the clear if overly simple rejection of it presented by E. A. Horsman in "The Design of Wordsworth's *Prelude*" in *Wordsworth's Mind and Art* (ed. A. W. Thomson, 1969). Horsman argues that *The Prelude* shows "the diversity of relations that are possible between the mind of man and the rest of the universe" and that the poem's energizing core is discovering that "what is to be prized in our being" is to be found by escaping the mind's "false secondary power," which "places a barrier of its own making between the mind and the rest of the world. For Horsman, the Simplon Pass episode is therefore misunderstood by Hartman, who does not recognize that it dramatizes the contrast "between the sterile activity of the mind haunted by itself

and the creative activity of the mind in contact with the external world."
Horsman goes on to argue that the vision from Snowdon in the final book demonstrates that there is "an analogy, in life outside the mind, for the domination
which the mind exerts over 'outward sense,'" and that "the whole scheme of
things seems to thwart the tyranny of the senses." So on Snowdon we encounter
the "kind of experience Wordsworth most values," in which "the mind deals with
and transforms 'the objects of the universe.'" A more sophisticated and complex
response to Hartman will be found in M. H. Abrams' "*The Prelude* as a Portrait of
the Artist" in *Bicentenary Wordsworth Studies* (1970), a redaction of his usefully
elaborate treatment of *The Prelude* in *Natural Supernaturalism*. Mark L. Reed's
"The Speaker of *The Prelude*" in the *Bicentenary* volume centers on the end of
book 6 and the beginning of book 7 to point out that the poem both "describes
the growth of Imagination and demonstrates" it to be a "present mode of
vision . . . not only . . . as it organizes . . . past experience . . . but also . . . as it expresses the nature" of the poet's "present being" at the time of writing. An analogous emphasis will be found in Sybil S. Eakin, "The Spot of Time in Early Versions of *The Prelude*" (*SIR*, 1973), tracing the evolution of the spots of time from
the two-book version to the more extended version to remind us that in judging
the poet's final presentation of those spots we must remember how Wordsworth
"drew inspiration from what he had already written" as well as from nature and
that as powerful an influence on him as the events described "was the suggestive
force of the poetry he wrote from these memories." Pursuing the same general
line, the more Heideggerian Charles Sherry, in "Wordsworth's Metaphors for
Eternity: Appearance and Representation" (*SIR*, 1978), demonstrates how "the act
of recollection recovers the significance of what was revealed in the visitation of
the imagination, and the poet forms from what is left after the passage of the imagination the sign which points . . . backward to what has happened, and forward to
what may come again, and beyond that into eternity."

Frank D. McConnell, *The Confessional Imagination: A Reading of
Wordsworth's* Prelude (1974), provides some good critiques of specific passages.
His thesis, that in addressing the poem to Coleridge Wordsworth exploits the traditional mode of Christian confessional writing, is surprisingly feebly supported,
but some light is thrown on the poem's peculiar narrative form—a matter treated
differently by Thomas A. Vogler, *Preludes to Vision: The Epic Venture in Blake,
Wordsworth, Keats, and Hart Crane* (1971), who sees the form determined by a
search for a heroic subject. Richard E. Brantley, *Wordsworth's "Natural Methodism"* (1975), argues, on occasion persuasively, for the importance of the influence
on Wordsworth of the Evangelical tradition, though conviction is weakened by
some awkwardness in the expression of aesthetic judgments and in the presentation of social history. Leslie F. Chard, *Dissenting Republican* (1972), somewhat
overemphasizes the effect on Wordsworth of dissenting traditions. Still one of
the best commentators on Wordsworth's religious thinking is Stopford A. Brooke,
Theology in the English Poets: Cowper, Coleridge, Wordsworth and Burns (1874),
but Ross Woodman, "Child and Patriot: Shifting Perspectives in *The Prelude*" (*WC*,
1980), argues with considerable effectiveness that we need to understand that
"because nature is grace" Wordsworth can imagine "his own mental growth from

the divinity of childhood and youth to the humanity of adult life." Woodman is one of the few to take full account of the important analysis of the relations between religion and imagination in Wordsworth provided by Gene W. Ruoff's "Religious Implications of Wordsworth's Imagination" (*SIR,* 1973), discussed below in the section "The Critic Wordsworth."

Closer to the more popular concerns of our times is Frederick Garber, *The Autonomy of the Self from Richardson to Huysman* (1982)—who contrasts Wordsworth's attitude to nature to those of Rousseau, Blake, Hölderlin, Emerson—and Morris Golden, *The Self Observed: Swift, Johnson, Wordsworth* (1972). Golden sees Swift preeminently a moralist, Johnson a psychologist, and Wordsworth a poet, claiming that the poet reintegrates the Renaissance-originated division between "literary" and "authorial" selves, assuring us finally that "human union" makes up "for disillusion and individual death." For a darker and stylistically less felicitous view of autobiography but one characteristic of recent preoccupations, one may consult Paul de Man, "Autobiography as Defacement" (*MLN,* 1979), centering on the "Essays on Epitaphs." William C. Spengemann, *The Forms of Autobiography* (1980), sees *The Prelude* as a precursor to the full fictionalizing of the mode in the nineteenth century, while Philip Davis, *Memory and Writing: From Wordsworth to Lawrence* (1984), analyzes Wordsworth's use of the repetition not only to give his verse coherence but also to affirm his identity as a poet.

James H. McGavran, Jr., "The '*Creative* Soul' of *The Prelude* and the 'Sad Incompetence of Human Speech' " (*SIR,* 1977), drawing support from Brantley and McConnell, finds the ultimate truths to which *The Prelude* points beyond human articulation in poetry as the Word of God, so that the poem's language necessarily succeeds and fails simultaneously as a medium of expression. W. J. B. Owen, "The Perfect Image of a Mighty Mind," and John Beer, "Wordsworth and the Face of Things," contiguous essays in *WC* (1979), argue for recognizing in the Snowdon scene an exhibition of how the literary imagination works on nature, Beer stressing how the ambiguous "face of nature" serves to dramatize both the poet's successful transcendence and acceptance of the limits of the human condition. Charles I. Patterson, Jr., "Prophecy and the Prophetic Poet in *The Prelude*" (*SHR,* 1977), by contrast, surveys the "accrual" of prophecy in the poem as "nature becomes less and less the source of Truth but . . . the agent by means of which the mind discovers truth within itself." With Patterson one may compare Geoffrey Hartman's essay in *High Romantic Argument,* edited by Lawrence Lipking (1981), "The Poetics of Prophecy" (indebted to a chapter, "The Visionary Character," in Elinor Shaffer's *"Kubla Khan" and* The Fall of Jerusalem, 1975, on how the Bible came to be regarded as constituted of the diverse kinds of poetic imagination), and R. A. Foakes's "The Power of Prospect: Wordsworth's Visionary Poetry" in *The Author in His Work* edited by Louis Martz and Aubrey Williams (1978), which defines the essence of Wordsworth's linking of "sight" and "vision" to "infusion." John T. Ogden, "The Structure of Imaginative Experience in Wordsworth's *Prelude*" (*WC,* 1975), sees the poem as built on repeated four-stage sequences of imaginative experience and subsequent analogous stages of poetic composition. Two other articles treating issues of compositional unity ought to be read together for their complementarity: Kenneth R. Johnston, "On First Looking into Wordsworth's *Prelude:* Seeing the Whole in the Parts" (*WC*, 1978), and Paul D. Sheats, "Wordsworth's 'Retrogrades' and the Shaping of *The Prelude*" (*JEGP*, 1972).

Ian Reid, "A Naked Guide-Post's Double Head: The Wordsworthian Sense of Direction" (*ELH*, 1976), examines figurative nakedness as imaging a recurrent focus of Wordsworth's poetry, which expresses "a Janus-like awareness of both loss and restoration . . . weakness and renewed strength . . . that the path forward leads him . . . to confront his past . . . through the primal experiences of being lost and exposed." Mary Jacobus, in "Wordsworth and the Language of the Dream" (*ELH*, 1979), presents wide-ranging speculations on links between "vital experiences" and "bookishness," all radiating out from the possibility that "the dream of the Arab Quixote . . . uncovers the fiction . . . on which Wordsworth's poetry" finally depends. More mundanely, W. J. B. Owen analyzes "Literary Echoes in *The Prelude*" (*WC*, 1972), and Stuart Peterfreund considers "*The Prelude:* Wordsworth's Metamorphic Epic" (*Genre*, 1981). Mary Lynn Woolley briefly and modestly demonstrates "Wordsworth's Symbolic Vale as It Functions in *The Prelude*" (*SIR*, 1968), while Robert Young's "The Eye and Progress of His Song: A Lacanian Reading of *The Prelude*" (*Oxford Literary Review*, 1979) is indubitably Lacanian but dubious as a reading of poetry. Max Byrd's *London Transformed* (1978) has some useful comments on urban problems, though R. F. Storch's earlier "Wordsworth and the City: 'Social Reason's Inner Sense' " (*WC*, 1970) should not be overlooked, while William B. Thesing, *The London Muse: Victorian Poetic Responses to the City* (1982), devotes a few pages to Wordsworth's ambivalence in his "pastoral cityscapes." James K. Chandler in "Wordsworth and Burke" (*ELH*, 1980) seeks to controvert M. H. Abrams' view that Wordsworth's "apocalyptic" poetics grew out of revolutionary politics by demonstrating how Burke's *Reflections,* ignored in *Natural Supernaturalism*, became the ironic occasion of the English Jacobin movement's intellectual flowering. An earlier essay on Wordsworth's earlier political "sources" is Z. S. Fink, "Wordsworth and the English Republican Tradition" (*JEGP*, 1948); Ronald Paulson gives most of an important chapter to *The Prelude* in *Representations of Revolution (1789 – 1820)* (1983), and here again one ought to consult Carl Woodring's *Politics in English Romantic Poetry.*

It may be useful at this point to arrange citations sequentially according to the part of Wordsworth's poem on which they focus. David Ellis discusses "Autobiography and Reminiscence in the First Two Books of *The Prelude*" (*CritQ*, 1980), while Mary R. Wedd, in "Wordsworth's Stolen Boat" (*WC*, 1980), explores the possibilities for the actual locale of the famous incident, and J. Robert Barth, S.J., provides a useful commentary, " 'The Props of My Affections': A Note on *The Prelude* II, 276 – 81" (*WC*, 1979). Muriel J. Mellown, "Images of Fancy and Imagination: A Reading of *The Prelude,* Book III" (*DUJ*, 1979), argues that the poet deliberately combines imaginative and fanciful imagery to manifest a temporary weakening of his visionary power, while Michael Black, "On Reading: Some Lines of Wordsworth" (*CritQ*, 1977), deals with the lines on Newton (bk. 3, 58 – 63). John R. Nabholtz, "The Journeys Homeward: Drama and Rhetoric in Book IV of *The Prelude*" (*SIR*, 1971), calls attention to the "Janus-like" theme and structure of this book. C. F. Stone III, "Narrative Variation in Wordsworth's Versions of 'The Discharged Soldier' " (*JNT*, 1974), analyzes the three principal versions of the episode; a more general treatment of the topic will be found in the "reintroduction" concluding Leslie Brisman's *Romantic Origins* (1978), while Don H. Bialostosky's *Making Tales* (1984) includes perhaps the most impressive analysis to date of the Discharged Soldier episode.

J. Robert Barth, S.J., has a succinct discussion, "The Poet, Death, and Immortality: The Unity of the *Prelude*, Book V" (*WC*, 1979), and Michael C. Jaye, "The Artifice of Disjunction: Book 5, *The Prelude*" (*PLL*, 1978), gives a thoughtful analysis of central complexities based on the intricate processes of fabricating the book under "pressure of the expansion of *The Prelude* beyond five books," including inconsistencies in Wordsworth's attitudes toward the proper relation of books to nature. Michael Ragussis, "Language and Metamorphosis in Wordsworth's Arab Dream" (*MLQ*, 1975), argues for an Ovidian source for this famous episode at the beginning of book 5. One may note also as useful David Wiener, "Wordsworth, Books, and the Growth of a Poet's Mind" (*JEGP*, 1975), as well as Joel Morkan's "Structure and Meaning in *The Prelude*, Book V" (*PMLA*, 1972). Cynthia Chase, in "The Accidents of Disfiguration: Limits to Literal and Rhetorical Reading in Book V of *The Prelude*" (*SIR*, 1979), draws attention to accidents in this book to develop a de Manian analysis of Wordsworth's "literalism," which "displays how our general dilemma as interpretive readers of poetry is compounded by our unfailing predicament as critical writers about it." In the same issue of *SIR*, Timothy Bahti, in his aptly titled "Figures of Interpretation, the Interpretation of Figures: A Reading of Wordsworth's 'Dream of the Arab,' " provides a dense exegesis in support of an argument that the relation between "imagination and nature in Wordsworth is always necessarily mediated by rhetorical, textual constructs and situations, and that the 'dialectical' 'binding' of mind and nature . . . reflects a great deal more negativity" than is ordinarily admitted. J. Hillis Miller, "The Stone and the Shell," in *Mouvements premiers: études critiques offertes à Georges Poulet* (1972), anticipates Bahti's thesis which is related also to the equally complex argument of Thomas Weiskel, *The Romantic Sublime: Studies in the Structure and Psychology of Transcendence* (1976). This book contains extensive commentary on Wordsworth, particularly about his anxieties of deprivation, detailing his "astonishing repertoire of defenses," with a lengthy analysis of the Simplon passage as a spot of time. A valuable because sympathetically informed critique of Weiskel's influential volume is Jerome C. Christensen's "The Sublime and the Romance of the Other" (*Diacritics*, 1978).

Having interrupted my sequential progress through *The Prelude*, I interject here the observation that for the past decade book 5 has taken precedence over the Simplon Pass episode as the favored point for critical study, brilliantly carried forward by Peter J. Manning, "Reading Wordsworth's Revisions: Othello and the Drowned Man" (*SIR*, 1983), and Susan J. Wolfson, "The Illusion of Mastery: Wordsworth's Revisions of 'The Drowned Man of Esthwaite,' 1799, 1805, 1850" (*PMLA*, 1984), both of which admirably exemplify the contemporary willingness to explore the ramifying significances of Wordsworth's revisions, an approach I reaffirm in my forthcoming *British Romantic Art*. But the Arab Quixote has been intensely interpreted for a long time, though Havens and Ferry slighted the passage. W. H. Auden used it as his primary text in his reading of the Romantics through the image of the sea in *The Enchafèd Flood; or, The Romantic Iconography of the Sea* (1950). David Perkins, *Wordsworth and the Poetry of Sincerity* (1964), finds "symbolic commonplaces": the "Arab is the poet; the shell is the poem; the dreamer is the audience; and the sea is the reality from which the poem comes and to which it leads." Hartman in *Wordsworth's Poetry* (1964) proposes "that the dream is sent by Imagination to lead the poet to recognize its power, and what the dreamer desires and fears is a direct encounter with Imagination." Richard Onorato reads "the impending apocalypse" as "revelation of a death . . . in the past" (the poet's mother) and of "a desired life beyond it" (*The Character of the Poet,* 1971). Melvyn New thinks "Wordsworth's Shell of Poetry" (*PQ,* 1974) is of a tortoise, from which the first lyre was made—according to Greek mythology. Long ago Jane Worthington Smyser, "Wordsworth's Dream of Poetry and Science: *The Prelude,* V" (*PMLA,* 1956), discussed the fact that the dream belongs to Descartes, while recently Theresa M. Kelley, in "Spirit and Geometric Form: The Stone and the Shell in Wordsworth's Arab Dream" (*SEL,* 1982), effectively uses earlier scholarship to redefine the episode's significance.

I return to sequential progress through *The Prelude.* For the lines on the Grande Chartreuse just preceding the Simplon Pass episode in *The Prelude*'s final version, the largest single addition, see Joseph F. Kishel's valuable "Wordsworth and the Grande Chartreuse" (*WC,* 1981), which analyzes not only the passage's place in *The Prelude* but also its relation to *Descriptive Sketches* and "The Tuft of Primroses." Robert A. Brinkley, in "The Incident in the Simplon Pass: A Note on Wordsworth's Revisions" (*WC,* 1981), argues that the radicalness of the revisions raises fundamental questions about "the process of self-composition and the temporal relations which that process entails." The operative word here is "self-composition," for it points up how the proliferation of *Prelude*s has strengthened what Jonathan Arac calls "textualization of literary history." Freudian "genetic" studies of textual change are increasingly popular, and more of this critical introjection can be expected in the years ahead. Yet two of the most valuable recent essays on the cruxes of book 6 are not so methodologically modish. Isobel Armstrong, "Wordsworth's Complexity: Repetition and Doubled Syntax in The Prelude Book VI" (*Oxford Literary Review,* 1981), shows that "two readings of the same words, two syntaxes" are at work throughout the 1805 *Prelude.* She traces sensitively the intricate mutual pressures of a syntax proposing the world as a construct of the mind and the no less insistent one proposing an autonomous world of both subject and object. Though centered on the descent of the Alps, Armstrong's analysis of the dialogue of reflexive and reciprocal syntaxes locates this "displaced climax" of the sixth book in a context of detailed exegeses of passages from books 5, 10, and 11. Armstrong's powerful essay finds the 1850 version more "Victorian" in clarifying the ambiguities and contradictions that give the 1805 version its peculiar power of assured uncertainty.

Ernest Bernhardt-Kabisch, "Wordsworth and the Simplon Revisited" (*WC,* 1979), is in another fashion representative of a developing tendency in Wordsworthian scholarship. Bernhardt-Kabisch considers not only evidence of various manuscripts but also Dorothy's reminiscence of Wordsworth's revisiting the pass (a return he seems to have regarded rather casually) and earlier commentaries, including the important article by Max Wildi, "Wordsworth and the Simplon Pass" (*ES*, 1959), which has long served as the definitive topographical commentary but which Bernhardt-Kabisch shows (in part through his on-foot investigation of the actual sites) to need modification. His on-the-spot and textual analyses suggest the conclusion "that the setting depicted in the poem was not just a fortuitous factual stage or matrix for a visionary experience, whether apocalyptic or sacramental, but was itself dictated by an anterior visionary urge, the deeply personal need to derive gain from loss, order from chaos." It is the combining of interest in psychological evolution with concern for the historical circumstances in which that evolution occurs—rather than defining it according to an abstract psychological system—that seems to me to have appeal for a growing number of younger scholars.

Books 7 to 11, especially as they treat of the French Revolution, are of course one focal point for the discussions mentioned above in relation to *The Borderers*. Recent directions of these debates may be indicated by a cluster of essays beginning with George Watson's "The Revolutionary Youth of Wordsworth and Coleridge" (*CritQ*, 1976), which presents the older poet's political involvements as more intense and durable, so that Wordsworth was able to look back on his revolutionary sympathies more accurately and penetratingly than Coleridge was. This view is challenged by John Beer, "The 'Revolutionary Youth' of Wordsworth and Coleridge: Another View" (*CritQ*, 1977), who sees a fundamental consistency in the political opinions of both poets in their youth and later. David Ellis, "Wordsworth's Revolutionary Youth: How We Read *The Prelude*" (*CritQ*, 1977), however, claims that the important point is that we read the autobiographical poem as a literary, not a factual, document. This would be too simple a reading for Barbara T. Gates, who has written "*The Prelude* and the Development of Wordsworth's Historical Imagination" (*EA*, 1977), an article related to her "Wordsworth and the Course of History" (*Research Studies of Washington State Univ.*, 1976). Two essays less directly concerned with *The Prelude* but dealing with the issues just mentioned are James K. Chandler's essay noted above and, more original, J. P. Ward, "Wordsworth and the Sociological Idea" (*CritQ*, 1974), who compares and contrasts Wordsworth with August Comte to delineate changes in social sensibility between the revolutions of 1789 and 1830.

John T. Ogden, "The Power of Distance in Wordsworth's *Prelude*" (*PMLA*, 1973), claims that books 7 and 8 prove that distance is necessary to Wordsworth's love for humanity. Donald H. Reiman in a valuable essay treats "The Beauty of Buttermere as Fact and Romantic Symbol" (*Criticism*, 1984), relating the passage in book 7 to its factual basis and to Coleridge's and De Quincey's different treatments of the facts and again suggesting that the structure of *The Prelude* may follow the form of an Italian sonnet. W. J. B. Owen investigates "Two Wordsworthian Ambivalences" (*WC*, 1980) to show how the poet in book 8 uses the sublime to reconcile mixed feelings about the pastoral and the urban. Lore Metzger, "Coleridge in Sicily: A Pastoral Interlude in *The Prelude*" (*Genre*, 1978), analyzes the conclusion of book 11 as representative of Wordsworth's deployment of pastoral topoi.

The most sensational recent treatment of the final books is Gayatri Chakravorty Spivak's "Sex and History in *The Prelude* (1805): Books Nine to Thirteen" (*TSLL*, 1981), which claims that Wordsworth had to exorcise his illegitimate paternity and to reestablish himself sexually in order to declare his imagination restored and that he coped with his experience of the French Revolution by transforming it into an iconic text he could write and read. He thus suggested that poetry was the best cure for oppression and that his life taught humankind this useful lesson. Fully to understand "iconic text" one must consult the author's earlier "Allégorie et histoire de la poésie: Hypothèse de travail" (*Poétique*, 1971). Spivak provides a new way of reading Vaudracour and Julia, but her use of Freud and Marx is considerably less sophisticated than Michael Friedman's, his work being ignored by her. William H. Galperin, " 'Turns and Counterturns': The Crisis of Sincerity of the Final Book of *The Prelude*" (*MLQ*, 1979), less flamboyantly describes how the poem's last books are "less a history of Wordsworth's restoration than a tale of two Wordsworths—a smiling public Wordsworth, determined to bring the poem to its 'appointed' close, and a brooding, private Wordsworth who must accommodate this closural impulse even as he resists it." Galperin's careful reading is persuasive that Wordsworth is afraid of the inadequacy of his imagination, not of its potency. Jeffrey Robinson, "*The Prelude*, Book XIV, and the Problem of Concluding" (*Criticism*, 1974), also calls attention to the poet's aesthetic as well as psychological uncertainties as to the validity of his conclusion. Daniel Stempel, "Revelation on Mount Snowdon: Wordsworth, Coleridge, and the Fichtean Imagination" (*JAAC*, 1971), deals with possible sources for the poet's theory of imagination, while in *Romantic Landscape Vision* (1975), I place the Snowdon scene in the context of the historical development of landscape representation beginning with the great painters of the seventeenth century and Denham's *Coopers Hill*. Richard Schell, "Wordsworth's Revisions of the Ascent of Snowdon" (*PQ*, 1975), sees the later version emphasizing mind whereas the earlier version emphasizes nature; treating the same topic is Alan Liu, " 'Shapeless Eagerness': The Genre of Revolution in Books Nine and Ten of *The Prelude*" (*MLQ*, 1982). Here one may note Joseph F. Kishel, "The 'Analogy Passage' from Wordsworth's Five-Book *Prelude*" (*SIR*, 1979), who analyzes, as does Schell, some hundred lines from manuscript W intended to follow the Snowdon ascent. Richard Gravil's "Wordsworth's Ontology of Love in *The Prelude*" (*CritQ*, 1974) centers on the poem's final book.

Finally, it is worth recalling that the Norton Critical Edition of *The Prelude: 1799, 1805, 1850* provides at a reasonable price an excellent set of texts and drafts, many useful (and some useless) notes, and critical commentaries, though its heavy bias against the 1850 version has been comdemned. Inevitably such a volume tends to concentrate attention on problems of intratextuality at the expense of consideration of the poem's relation to circumstances outside the poet's psyche. But if this volume makes one anticipate a decade of fine-grinding psychological criticism, it at least promises the mills will rest on a solid base.

The Intimations Ode

Ode: Intimations of Immortality has, of course, been intensely studied, but so far as a gross summary may be fair, the history of this criticism may be conveniently encapsulated by two essays, Lionel Trilling's "The Immortality Ode," which first appeared in the *English Institute Annual* in 1941, reprinted in Trilling's *The Liberal Imagination* (1950), and Helen Vendler's critique in "Lionel Trilling and the *Immortality Ode*" (*Salmagundi*, 1978). Trilling's work, centered on a refutation of a reading popular in the twenties and thirties that the ode was a "conscious farewell to art," extends to an interpretation of the poem as representing growing up rather than growing old, and leads, ultimately, to a questioning of the existence of a "particular poetic faculty which may be isolated and defined." The ode in this view embodies a characteristically Romantic uncertainty about human powers and potentialities, dramatized by the unresolved contradiction between the drive toward an imprisoning worldliness in stanzas 5 through 8 and transcendent compensations for loss depicted by stanzas 9 through 11. The conflict remains *successfully* unresolved for Trilling because he perceives the poem as originating in personal experience but expressing more than private conditions of life, conditions affecting people other than poets. Vendler, seemingly in keeping with recent critical preferences, insists that Wordsworth is concerned with the poet's gift, the capacity to make natural things into metaphors of human life. She sees Wordsworth making use of a traditional elegy pattern, in that misgivings and questionings "of sense and outward things" become the "fountain-light," that "foundation on which we construct our later trust in that inward affectional and intellectual reality 'by which we live.' " Pointing to Trilling's failure to recognize the profundity of the satiric harshness of stanza 7 and the theological depth of the answering stanza 8, Vendler demonstrates how the conclusion is a successful human affirmation of "thought arising from feeling," the "acquisition of the power of metaphor" by which the purely sensual and intense feelings of the child are humanly enriched, so that the poet "is no longer a stranger" in the world, longing hopelessly for the " 'imperial palace' whence he came . . . but naturalized in the world, as all its parts become colored by the feeling eye." Thus for Vendler the ode is "self-therapeutic in a fashion exactly in accord with Arnold's sense for Wordsworth's poetry as healing." More important, perhaps, Vendler's analysis reveals the inevitable weakness of criticizing Wordsworth, as Trilling does, in terms of a "modernist sensibility," which seeks the "authority of . . . systematic thought and must fall back on a schema drawn from Freudian doctrine." For us today, Vendler claims, the ode means, most of all, "by its ability to invent, mediating between language of childhood sense and its mirror-language of adult inwardness, a language of disorientation, which conveys the difficulty inherent in the relation of consciousness to sense experience, that difficulty which the great poetry of the Ode so triumphantly overcomes."

It is interesting that as yet Vendler's piece seems to have had little impact. In an important collection of seven essays in the *Wordsworth Circle* (12: 1 [1981]), her essay is considered only by Jeffrey C. Robinson, "The Immortality Ode: Lionel

Trilling and Helen Vendler," who develops at length the contrast between her reading and Trilling's that I've rapidly sketched and who finds her guilty of oversimplifying both the poem and the earlier critic. I disagree. But I regard as healthy Robinson's resistance to oversimplifying, a resistance shared by most of the authors of the *WC* essays. They tend toward careful historical reconstruction of the circumstances (both personal and social) out of which the poem took shape and toward judicious, rather than polemical, analyses of intricate textual cruxes and of the variety of literary influences operating on the poem. Most impressive, perhaps, is Gene Ruoff's " 'Fields of Sheep': The Obscurities of the Ode, I–IV," which begins with a survey of the first extended critical exchange on any of Wordsworth's poems, the score of responses and counterresponses to A. L. Mayhew's query in *N&Q* (1889), "What is the meaning of the line, 'The winds come to me from the fields of sleep'?" eliciting the "sheep" solution. Ruoff observes that all the basic strategies of subsequent "strong" readings of difficult lines such as this appear in the early debate, yet the line remains today not satisfactorily explained. He points out, furthermore, that this line, like most of stanzas I–IV, was never significantly revised, suggesting that "lines which are allowed to stand unchanged over years of compositional activity are inherently privileged, and to locate the source of their privilege is to explain their obscurity." The source of Ruoff's focal line he locates in the complex intertextual development of the ode in relation to poems by both Wordsworth and Coleridge. The principle here illustrated is an important one; in Ruoff's words, "poems exist in time, marked subtly but permanently by vestigial traces of processes of composition which brought them into existence."

In the forty years following Trilling's essay one may notice a variety of studies, first Cleanth Brooks's "Wordsworth and the Paradox of the Imagination" in *The Well-Wrought Urn* (1947), a classic of the New Criticism focused on the poem's imagery and arguing that the loss of childhood vision involves preservation of primal sympathy and, therefore, that the sustenance of a sympathetic imagination is extended. E. D. Hirsch, Jr., has a useful chapter in *Wordsworth and Schelling* (1960), "Both-And Logic in the Immortality Ode." An article in some respects carrying forward this line of understanding is Kenneth R. Johnston's "Recollecting Forgetting: Forcing Paradox to the Limit in the 'Intimations Ode' " (*WC*, 1971). T. M. Raysor in "The Themes of Immortality and Natural Piety in Wordsworth's Immortality Ode" (*PMLA*, 1954), urging a more transcendental reading against Trilling's "naturalism," called forth an immediate counterargument for dualism in the poem by Robert L. Schneider, "The Failure of Solitude: Wordsworth's Immortality Ode" (*JEGP*, 1955). This line of debate reached one climax a decade later with Alan Grob's "Wordsworth's *Immortality Ode* and the Search for Identity" (*ELH*, 1965), which finds Wordsworth's growing dualism resolved in recognition of different levels of being and the poem as a whole registering a conversion from doubt to faith. Florence Marsh, however, in "Wordsworth's *Ode:* Obstinate Questionings" (*SIR*, 1966), argues that the poet, by treating personal mystical loss as if it were a common one, ends by rendering in incompatible fashion the immanence he associates with the child and the transcendence enunciated in the final stanzas. Although I find no one who has specifically challenged Marsh's assertions on the immanence-transcendence conflict, Stuart M. Sperry, Jr., "From 'Tintern Abbey' to the 'Intimations Ode': Wordsworth and the Function of Memory" (*WC,* 1970), has made a strong case for a more accurate discrimination of the variety of functions memory plays for Wordsworth, especially between what Sperry calls the reconstitutive and the premonitory memory, while C. E. Pulos, "The Unity of Wordsworth's Immortality Ode" (*SIR,* 1974), insists that the poem's light symbolism in fact embodies two distinct concepts of truth. Harold Bloom in *A Map of Misreading* (1975) reads the ode as deeply in the shadow of Milton, a position elaborated by Paul McNally in "Milton and the Immortality Ode" (*WC,* 1980), he in turn being supported by Edward Proffitt in *WC* (1980): "Samson and the Intimations Ode: Further Evidence of Milton's Influence." Lucy Newlyn, "The Little Actor and His Mock Apparel" (*WC,* 1983), interestingly explores affinities between stanzas 7 and 8 and "To H. C. Six Years Old."

Another way to consider the history of commentary on the Intimations Ode is to examine it as a focal poem for the two principal strains of Wordsworthian criticism that M. H. Abrams in his introduction to *Wordsworth: A Collection of Critical Essays* (1972) calls the "simple" and the "problematic." The simple Wordsworth is the one described by Arnold, his vision carried forward in the middle years of our century by Helen Darbishire, *The Poet Wordsworth* (1950), John Danby, *The Simple Wordsworth* (1960), and Jonathan Wordsworth, *The Music of Humanity* (1969), among others, and finding its primary critical source in the Preface to *Lyrical Ballads,* which stresses "elementary feelings," "great and simple affections," "universal passions of men," "beautiful and permanent forms of nature" and in which the poet appears in a "naked and simple style . . . a man speaking to men." The problematic Wordsworth, dominant since Ferry and Hartman, originates in A. C. Bradley, who, working from the "Essay, Supplementary to the Preface" in the *Poems* of 1815, stresses not merely sublimity but what is "peculiar" and "strange" in the poetry, something "mystic" or "visionary," a "denial" of the sensible world, as Bradley says, "contradicting or abolishing the fixed limits of our habitual view . . . everything . . . is natural, but everything is apocalyptic." The Intimations Ode's chronological position between the Preface and the "Essay, Supplementary" and its spatial "placing" in Wordsworth's arrangements of his poems in later editions so that it was outside all other categories may be seen as representing its role in the transformation of one Wordsworth (or one image of Wordsworth) into the other.

Such a view is encouraged if one remarks the ode's pivotal position in the Wordsworth chapter of Harold Bloom's *The Visionary Company* (1961) in contrast to Bloom's later comments in *A Map of Misreading,* or even the analysis of "Tintern Abbey" mentioned below. Bloom's criticism of Wordsworth has been against the grain of deconstructive methods, the development of his emotionally charged, expressive commentaries opposing the more "playful" structural-linguistic approaches. In *The Visionary Company* Bloom is surprisingly

Arnoldian. He locates the ode's power in its tapping of primary sympathies involving reciprocity of mind and nature. Although Bloom claims the uniqueness of the ode in the English tradition derives from its dependence on the "prophetic portions of the Hebrew Bible," his own response to the poem is firmly kept in terms of the "humanistic groundings" (as he calls them) of Trilling's commentary. Yet the effectiveness of this early criticism of Wordsworth seems to me to derive from Bloom's genuine religious sensibility that allows him to penetrate further into Wordsworth's emotional implications than have most recent critics, whose talk of "apocalypse," "transcendence," and "sublimity" is unanimated by discernible sympathy with the poet's strong spiritual feelings. Bloom's empathy is particularly impressive because he does not share Wordsworth's "pagan" sensual responsiveness to natural phenomena, above all transformative ones like wind, mist, sleet. But Bloom is acute in registering the emotional potency of Wordsworth's effort to express a sense for the presence of dignity and value in the "simplest" encounters with the natural world.

As Bloom has grown older and increasingly dedicated to systematizing, he has moved away from the strength of his original sympathetic responsiveness to Wordsworth, losing in particular sensitivity to what Vendler calls the "antiphonal" language of the older poet confronting his earlier experiences. Yet Bloom's fundamental Arnoldianism is revealed in his continuing preoccupation with Wordsworth's poetic decline. For Bloom, the fading of powers of interactive reciprocity inevitably means loss of Wordsworth's special genius whereas Bradleyans exhibit a desire to justify the later poetry, if only because in it the gulf between consciousness and nature becomes more explicit. Bloom's early criticism dramatizes those features of Wordsworth's poetry subsequent critics have tended to slight, while the weakness of his later critiques illuminates the strengths in their "problematic" mode of criticism. For both kinds of critics the crux of the Wordsworth "problem" may be located in the poet's conception of memory. If Hartman, for instance, increasingly treats Wordsworth as though the poet were committed to an early Freudian concept of repression, his psyche immobilized into rigid structures determined by traumatic childhood events, so Bloom has moved away from emotional sympathy with the poet's sense for youthful insights into infinity and belief in recollection as a basis for renovation into a mechanistic system of explanation, increasingly abstract in its articulation and removed from the experiential immediacies of specific poems. Bloom's relatively trivial influence on the mainstream of Wordsworthian criticism, then, is due both to his "Arnoldian" bias and to an inability to develop his original intuitive responses into a significant alternative to the Bradleyans' valid insistence that peculiarly Wordsworthian paradoxes and contradictions not be evaded.

Such consideration of critical trends raises the question, at least for someone in my position, of whether the proliferation of criticism serves a worthwhile purpose. Does Paul H. Fry's elaborate reading of the Intimations Ode in *The Poet's Calling in the English Ode* (1980), for example, add to our understanding only through inventing a class "Odes of Presentation"? One can, it is true, detect changes over time in the dominating views of critics. In earlier years, for instance, Wordsworth's long explanation to Isabella Fenwick and his letter to

Catherine Clarkson of December 1814 seem to have been taken more seriously (and perhaps more literally) than in the sixties and early seventies, and earlier critics were more overtly concerned about the ode's "message," its moral or religious validity, with what it said as either false or true, good or bad, the critic judging from a fairly well-defined ethical position. Few among the current generation of critics define their position ethically, and most today are readier than their predecessors to accept a poem as effective even though it does not articulate a definitive philosophic, ethical, or theological judgment. The obvious danger in the later practice is a tendency to sink the peculiarities of Wordsworthian artistry in grandiose generalization about the nature of all poetry. Yet, as I've noted, there now seems a growing trend toward concentrating on the specificity of Wordsworth's circumstances, social as well as psychological, when he composed and revised the ode and, through this concentration, to perceive in the poem definitions of particular problems confronting *a* poet at crucial moments in his life. Vendler's essay, to my mind, suggests how, haltingly and irregularly, humanistic criticism does advance by absorbing previous analyses into more flexibly powerful imaginative acts. This "progress" is dependent less on "bold" new readings and methods than on the simple, patient sifting out from ambitious claims their grains of lasting value. Thus, Paul Magnuson's "The Genesis of Wordsworth's 'Ode'" in the *Wordsworth Circle* collection (1981) proves that there is much of value to be learned from ever more careful analyses of as many of the poem's contexts as possible, and Peter J. Manning's "Wordsworth's 'Intimations Ode' and Its Epigraphs" (*JEGP*, 1983) pursues the significance of the 1807 epigraph from Vergil's fourth eclogue because most "strong" readers have ignored the fact that "My Heart Leaps Up" did not become the epigraph until 1815. Manning sees Wordsworth reversing the Vergilian model by turning inward, that is, by making small appeal to adult masculinity and staying more rigorously within the limits of time rather than evoking eternity. Manning also links the conclusion of the ode to the Arab-Quixote dream in *The Prelude* so as to read the ode as exploiting "the resonance of Christian faith without committing itself to belief in 1807." Later changes, including the replacement of the Vergilian epigraph by "My Heart Leaps Up," then, may be seen as efforts to close off exactly the tensions that give the ode its power. It is praise, not derogation, of Manning and Magnuson that their work is profoundly dependent on what earlier critics have done; like Ruoff, they do not have to invent categories or methodologies in order to criticize, because they are fully engaged both with the poem as a complex historical event and with the history of how that event has been perceived, by the poet as well as by others. Out of such work, it seems to me, is emerging the possibility of more impressive evaluations of the ode's philosophical and ethical implications than were produced thirty to fifty years ago. Even if I am wrong in finding "progress" in our criticism, recent work at least makes apparent the extraordinary degree to which the Intimations Ode has engaged the imaginative energies of critics normally hostile to the slightest hint of didacticism and suspicious of even the appearance of affirmative celebration in poetry.

Lyrical Ballads and *Peter Bell*

Three books provide the basic background for *Lyrical Ballads*. John E. Jordan, in *Why the* Lyrical Ballads? *The Background, Writing, and Character of Words-worth's* Lyrical Ballads (1976), introduces many of the principal critical and histor-ical questions posed by the famous little volume, and Stephen Parrish's *The Art of the* Lyrical Ballads (1973), a recasting of earlier essays, is especially good on de-tailed comparisons between Wordsworth's poems and works by other poets, as well as on Wordsworth's rhetorical and dramatic methods. Those interested in the history of criticism should note that much of Parrish's book appeared in essay form more than a decade earlier and that his arguments for recognizing the dra-matic techniques in the lyrics were an important contribution to Wordsworthian studies of the late 1950s, exemplified by Robert Langbaum's *The Poetry of Experi-ence: The Dramatic Monologue in Modern Literary Tradition* (1957). Langbaum identifies the Romantics, notably Wordsworth, as originating but not fully devel-oping the dramatizing methods of modernist lyricism. Parrish, however, has con-sistently stressed the relation of Wordsworth's rhetoric to his immediate histor-ical circumstances.

The third fundamental book is Mary Jacobus, *Tradition and Experiment in Wordsworth's Lyrical Ballads (1798)* (1976), in which, through careful examina-tions of poems and their sources, Jacobus elucidates how Wordsworth made use of both popular literature and his formal literary heritage. Jacobus, influenced by Jonathan Wordsworth's *The Music of Humanity* (1969), sees 1797–98 as crucial years in the poet's development and therefore does not restrict her attention solely to poems in the *Lyrical Ballads* volume; she presents, for example, an im-pressive case for reading the 1798 *Peter Bell* as a counter to Coleridgean supernat-uralism. This kind of contextual richness and Jacobus' lucidity of analysis are fur-ther illustrated by her essay "Southey's Debt to *Lyrical Ballads* (1798)" (*RES,* 1971), which delineates how the future laureate, despite his critical review of the famous volume, made use of its contents.

The works I've mentioned are all written in the context of a debate about the novelty of the *Lyrical Ballads* initiated by Robert Mayo in "The Contempora-neity of the *Lyrical Ballads*" (*PMLA,* 1954), which claimed that the poems were not so radical a departure from the style and themes of popular poetry of the 1790s as had often been assumed and were indeed "an intense fulfillment of an already stale convention." Charles Ryskamp, "Wordsworth's *Lyrical Ballads* in Their Time" in *From Sensibility to Romanticism* (ed. Frederick Hilles and Harold Bloom, 1965); R. F. Storch, "Wordsworth's Experimental Ballads: The Radical Uses of Intelligence and Comedy" (*SEL,* 1971), centered on "Simon Lee," "The Idiot Boy," and *Peter Bell;* and John E. Jordan, "The Novelty of the *Lyrical Ballads*," *Wordsworth Bicentenary Studies* (1970), all assert to the contrary the originality of the poems, although Parrish's book probably best shows how Wordsworth made original use of conventional materials. Richard Gravil, "*Lyrical Ballads* (1798): Wordsworth as Ironist" (*CritQ,* 1982), regards the poems as subtly parodying contemporary fashions in verse. With Jacobus' work one sees a tendency for the conventional-revolutionary debate to slide toward considerations of what John Danby in *The Simple Wordsworth* (1960) called the poems' "perennial contemporaneity," a quality determined not abstractly but through a firmer fixing of all Wordsworth's early poetry into the complex socioliterary context out of which it emerges; Danby's special contribution was to define the artfulness by which Wordsworth attained the simplicity of his best lyrics. This tendency informs most of the best recent studies, including James H. Averill's *Wordsworth and the Poetry of Human Suffering* (1980), which demonstrates how and why the creating of an adequate literary response to suffering became increasingly difficult for the poet, an approach carried foward by Margaret Garner in "The Anapestic *Lyrical Ballads*: New Sympathies" (*WC*, 1982). Likewise, Paul D. Sheats in *The Making of Wordsworth's Poetry, 1785–1798* (1973) through close readings of individual poems traces Wordsworth's relation to the main line of classical-Renaissance humanism. But Sheats shows that Wordsworth transforms philosophical commonplaces through original use of "passionate" personal experience. As I've already suggested, Sheats's book can profitably be read in conjunction with Alan Grob's nearly contemporaneous *The Philosophic Mind: A Study of Wordsworth's Poetry and Thought, 1799–1805* (1973), defining Wordsworth's change from a poet of philosophic naturalism, or of empiricism, to one whose work is based more on an epistemology of transcendence. In this view, some of the poet's most interesting work is that of his transition from one position to its virtual opposite, "Resolution and Independence" and the Intimations Ode among the poems of 1802 becoming particularly important. For these, Jared R. Curtis, *Wordsworth's Experiments with Tradition: The Lyric Poems of 1802* (1971), should be consulted.

Turning back to works centered on the earlier *Lyrical Ballads*, one may note Stephen Prickett's *Wordsworth and Coleridge: The Lyrical Ballads* (1975), which argues for the volume as a unified totality but not so persuasively as Ruth Cohen, "The 1800 Ordering of *Lyrical Ballads*: Its Moral Purpose" (*Caliban*, 1976), or James Averill, "The Shape of the *Lyrical Ballads*" (*PQ*, 1981), or David McCracken, "Wordsworth's Doctrine of 'Things as They Seem,'" (*WC*, 1982), a fine presentation of the view that the grouping of the 1800 *Lyrical Ballads* illustrates the point in the "Essay, Supplementary to the Preface" (a work perhaps adequately appreciated only by Larry Swingle and, more recently, by Don H. Bialostosky) that poetry treats things as they appear. Marilyn Katz describes "Early Dissent between Wordsworth and Coleridge: The Preface Deletion of October, 1800" (*WC*, 1978), but far more valuable is Susan J. Wolfson, "The Speaker as Questioner in *Lyrical Ballads*" (*JEGP*, 1978), culminating in a fine analysis of "Tintern Abbey" but containing many intelligent descriptions of the "voice of assertive denial." Several "strong" critics would benefit from Wolfson's golden ear for the significance of tonal nuances. Even more original and intellectually stimulating is Don H. Bialostosky, *Making Tales: The Poetics of Wordsworth's Narrative Experiments* (1984), which fruitfully applies Bakhtinian ideas to several of the most important lyrical ballads as well as to an exploration of Wordsworth's Preface.

"Tintern Abbey," of course, continues to be the principal focus of studies of the 1798 *Lyrical Ballads,* as in the splendid concluding chapter of *The Making of Wordsworth's Poetry 1785 – 1798* by Paul Sheats. Equally valuable is Isobel Armstrong, " 'Tintern Abbey': From Augustan to Romantic" in *Augustan Worlds,* edited by J. C. Hilson et al. (1978). Although her footnotes are peppered with errors, Armstrong presents an exceptional reading of the poem's first hundred lines, including detailed analyses of Wordsworth's use of comparatives, prepositions, and participles. She treats the lyric as a turning "back on itself" to "construct out of its past forms ... new possibilities," thus to become a "self-transforming poem" revelatory of the central mode of Romantic lyricism. She demonstrates how Wordsworth transforms the topographical tradition in which he writes by using repetition to enable his mind to interpret itself to itself. This reading owes something to that of C. C. Clarke in his undervalued *Romantic Paradox* (1962), as well as to Christopher Ricks's "Wordsworth: 'A Pure Organic Pleasure from the Lines' " (*EIC,* 1971). Worth notice also are Carl Woodring, "The New Sublimity in 'Tintern Abbey' " in *The Evidence of the Imagination,* edited by D. H. Reiman et al. (1978), and Kenneth R. Johnston, whose very important "The Politics of 'Tintern Abbey' " (*WC,* 1983) shows Wordsworth's dependence on Gilpin, clarifies his relation to the *Philanthropist,* and sets the probable date of his revisit as 14 July 1798, a redating of significance. Two other brief pieces in the *Wordsworth Circle* on the placing and timing of the poem are Geoffrey Little, " 'Tintern Abbey' and Llyswen Farm" (1977), which points out that the farm was rented by John Thelwall in 1798 and that Wordsworth may have used some of its landscape in his poem, and J. R. Watson, "A Note on the Date in the Title of 'Tintern Abbey' " (1979). J. B. McNulty uses both Little and Watson in "Self-Awareness in the Making of 'Tintern Abbey' " (*WC,* 1981) to argue for treating the poem as an ode. There is an important discussion by Albert O. Wlecke in *Wordsworth and the Sublime* (1973), in which the poem is used to examine Wordsworth's "sublime self-consciousness." For Wlecke, the poet's "open-ended sense of self experience in the act of apperception with the phenomena of nature revealed by the act of perception" is "a way of making intelligible the visionary world and of mediating its terrors." Speaking of terrors, Harold Bloom's chapter "Wordsworth and the Scene of Instruction" in *Poetry and Repression* (1976), so far as it is not self-referential, centers on "Tintern Abbey," a poem perhaps not perfectly suited to this critic's *Castle of Otranto* style. Bloom says that the Hermit in line 21 is John Milton. David V. Erdman in a brief note (*WC,* 1977) reproduces a few interesting passages and an aquatint from a guide composed by three painters, Ibbetson, Laporte, and Hassell, in 1793, which should intrigue seekers of the picturesque in and around the abbey.

"Anecdote for Fathers" has recently evoked one quite valuable essay, Laurence W. Mazzeno's "Of Fathers, Children, and Poets: Wordsworth's 'Anecdote for Fathers' " (*Psychocultural Review: Interpretations in the Psychology of Art, Literature and Society,* 1977). By analyzing revisions of the text of this poem occurring over nearly fifty years, Mazzeno demonstrates how the poet both improved the lyric and transformed the narrator from a hostile to a sympathetic father figure. The changes, Mazzeno suggests, reflect an important transformation in the poet's attitude toward representatives of paternity. Jonathan Ramsey, in "Wordsworth and the Childhood of Language" (*Criticism,* 1976), uses a psycholinguistic approach on "Anecdote for Fathers" and "The Idiot Boy" to show how Wordsworth redeems "language from the bondage to the 'noisy world.'" The same author's "Wordsworth's Silent Poet" (*MLQ,* 1976) is similar in method.

Meanwhile back at "The Thorn," debate continues. Recent contributions include Thomas L. Ashton, "The Thorn: Wordsworth's Insensitive Plant" (*HLQ,* 1972), in which the universe is seen as insensitive; Michael Kirkham, "Innocence and Experience in Wordsworth's 'The Thorn'" (*ArielE,* 1974); W. J. B. Owen, "'The Thorn' and the Poet's Intention" (*WC,* 1977), which associates the poem with spots of time; Donald G. Priestman, "Superstition and Imagination: Complementary Faculties of Wordsworth's Narrator in 'The Thorn'" (*JNT,* 1975), which finds the narrator less simpleminded than do critics who favor the "superstitious"; Gordon K. Thomas, "Coleridge Stuck on 'The Thorn'" (*WC,* 1978) and later "'The Thorn' in the Flesh of English Romanticism" (*WC,* 1983); Geoffrey Jackson, "Moral Dimensions of 'The Thorn'" (*WC,* 1979); and Jerome Christensen, "Wordsworth's Misery, Coleridge's Woe: Reading 'The Thorn'" (*PLL,* 1980). These critiques, as well as James H. Averill's, which links his two good chapters on the 1798 and 1800 *Ballads* in *Wordsworth and the Poetry of Human Suffering* (1980), inevitably lead to analyses of Wordsworth's narrative methods, such as Andrew L. Griffin's "Wordsworth and the Problem of Imaginative Story: The Case of 'Simon Lee'" (*PMLA,* 1977). Griffin's remarks on Wordsworth's reader, however, need to be qualified by consideration of Bialostosky's work and Morris Eaves's discussion of Romantic readers in "Romantic Expressive Theory and Blake's Idea of the Audience" (*PMLA,* 1980), and Roger Murray's *Wordsworth's Style: Figures and Themes in the Lyrical Ballads of 1800* (1967) remains one of the most helpful analyses of Wordsworth's rhetoric of this period. Albert E. Wilhelm discusses in more conventional terms the unreliability of the narrator in "The Dramatized Narrator in Wordsworth's *The Idiot Boy*" (*JNT,* 1975), while Don H. Bialostosky, in "Narrative Point of View in 'The Last of the Flock' and 'Old Man Travelling'" (*WC,* 1980), argues persuasively for the skillful effectiveness with which Wordsworth maneuvers readers so as to include them "in the community of pleasure and pain" into which the poet's encounters have brought him.

"Michael," the final poem in the 1800 *Lyrical Ballads,* continues to be held in high esteem, but for increasingly diverse reasons. For example, James Kissane, "'Michael,' 'Christabel,' and the *Lyrical Ballads* of 1800" (*WC,* 1978), sees Wordsworth's poem as a deliberate alternative to "Christabel," the sheepfold standing for Coleridge's unfinished poem, whereas David Sampson, "Wordsworth and the Poor: The Poetry of Survival" (*SIR,* 1984), reads the poem in relation to "The Old Cumberland Beggar." Sheldon Halpern, "*Michael:* Wordsworth's Pastoral of Common Man" (*Notre Dame English Journal,* 1972), draws attention to negative aspects of the protagonist, though Lore Metzger in "Wordsworth's Pastoral Covenant" (*MLQ,* 1976) takes a more positive view of the shepherd. Sydney Lea, "Wordsworth and his 'Michael': The Pastor Passes" (*ELH,* 1978), thinks

Wordsworth hoped to transmit to his successors a legacy of pastoral values, and A. J. Sambrook treats "Michael" in "An Essay on Eighteenth-Century Pastoral, Pope to Wordsworth" (*Trivium,* 1971), and later in *English Pastoral Poetry* (1983), seeing Wordsworth as completing the eighteenth-century "naturalization of pastoral." Robert C. Gordon's "Wordsworth and the Domestic Roots of Power" (*BRH,* 1978) makes a contrast of the poem's moral logic with that of the Cintra tract. Pegeen Brennan in " 'Michael' and the 'Preface' " (*WC,* 1980) argues by writing in blank verse "that 'Michael' is the poem which vindicates / His theory of poetic diction best." A remarkable piece of work. Peter J. Manning in " 'Michael,' Luke, and Wordsworth" (*Criticism,* 1977) treats the poem as a complex self-presentation of the poet, identifying the core dilemma of the poem as best "illuminated by the imbricated Biblical allusions surrounding Luke" wherein "we can descry a boy's—or man's—doubt that he can stand alone without the support of his parents." In direct contrast to Manning's psychoanalytical-archetypal reading, my "Constable: Millais:: Wordsworth: Tennyson," in *Articulate Images* (ed. Richard Wendorf, 1983), uses stylistic comparisons between painting and poetry to argue that "Michael" is characteristically Romantic in shaping a historical perspective from which the reader responds to the work as deliberately controverting its apparent models, such as Abraham and Isaac, Wordsworth's aim being to render not archetypal but ectypal reality, to preserve and celebrate the historical uniqueness of human events.

This seems a good point to say something of the work of scholars whose diverse interests and angles of vision may have a strong effect on the development of Wordsworthian studies in the next few years. Peter J. Manning, whom I've just mentioned, for example, follows Hartman as a dedicated Freudian, but his psychoaesthetics of textual history are connected to an interest in the evolution of genres, as is shown in four rewarding essays, "Wordsworth, Margaret, and the Pedlar" (*SIR,* 1976), " 'My Former Thoughts Returned': Wordsworth's *Resolution and Independence*" (*WC,* 1978), "Wordsworth and Gray's Sonnet on the Death of West" (*SEL,* 1982), and "Wordsworth's *Intimations* Ode and Its Epigraphs" (*JEGP,* 1983). Larry J. Swingle, more philosophically oriented, has in a scattered group of articles sought to place Wordsworth in a conception of Romanticism stressing the rhetorical and experimental nature of Romantic art rather than emphasizing articulation of personal truths or the proclamation of a definitive understanding of the nature of things. "On Reading Romantic Poetry" (*PMLA,* 1971) presents Romantic poems as attempts "to grasp the experiential data that underlie the doctrinal constructs men impose upon the cosmos," and in "Romantic Unity and English Romantic Poetry" (*JEGP,* 1975), "Wordsworth's Contrarieties: A Prelude to Wordsworthian Complexity" (*ELH,* 1977), "The Romantic Emergence" (*MLQ,* 1978), and "Wordsworth's 'Picture of the Mind' " in *Images of Romanticism: Verbal and Visual Affinities* (ed. Kroeber and Walling, 1978), Swingle points up manipulative designs in the poetry intended to provoke the reader into considering how specific psychological situations tend to call forth particular dogmas of art, morality, or social idealism. Finally, Michael Cooke, like Swingle striving to understand individual Romantic poets through analyses of what such diverse artists share, has reassessed conventional attitudes toward the Romantic, with important implications for Wordsworthian studies, in two remarkably ingenious books, *The Romantic Will* (1976) and *Acts of Inclusion* (1979), that defy summary by their subtle relating of minute particulars in specific poems to perceptions of over-arching tendencies of Romanticism.

A good place to begin study of the difficult but important *Peter Bell* is with John E. Jordan's "The Hewing of *Peter Bell*" (*SEL,* 1967), describing the poem's complicated development, and Jordan's "Wordsworth's Most Wonderful as well as Admirable Poem" (*WC,* 1979), which adds twenty years of experience to his com-ments in "Wordsworth's Humor" (*PMLA,* 1958), as well as increased attention to how the poem was received. At least two earlier commentaries are worth going back to, those of Lascelles Abercrombie in *The Art of Wordsworth* (1952) and of Melvin R. Watson in "The Redemption of Peter Bell" (*SEL,* 1964), which empha-sizes comparisons with *The Ancient Mariner,* although this approach to my mind is better developed in Mary Jacobus' *Tradition and Experiment,* discussed a few paragraphs back, while Jacobus' "*Peter Bell* the First" (*EIC,* 1974) delineates how Wordsworth "did much to camouflage elements that had been central to the originality and power" of the earliest version. A different kind of Coleridge com-parison is provided by Leah Sinanoglou Marcus in her illuminating "Vaughan, Wordsworth, Coleridge and the *Encomium Asini*" (*ELH,* 1975). Also useful on sources and traditions is Geoffrey Durrant, "Wordsworth's *Peter Bell,* a Pons Asinorum for Critics" (*WascanaR,* 1966). Charles I. Patterson, Jr., "The Daemonic in *Peter Bell*" (*WC,* 1977), should be considered along with Lawrence Kramer, "That Other Will: The Daemonic in Coleridge and Wordsworth" (*PQ,* 1979). Brian Cosgrove, "Wordsworth's Moonlight-Poetry and the Sense of the 'Uncanny'" (*ArielE,* 1982), treats Peter along with the Idiot Boy and the Discharged Soldier. Gordon K. Thomas in "Rueful Woes, Joyous Hap: The Associate Labor of 'The Id-iot Boy' and 'Christabel'" (*WC,* 1983) sees the poems' complementarity as most significant in their treatment of language perversion, which Thomas regards as central to the original plan of *Lyrical Ballads.* Jack Benoit Gohn in "Who Wrote *Benjamin the Waggoner?* An Inquiry" (*WC,* 1977) determines that it was not John Hamilton Reynolds who wrote the parody *The Waggoner: A Ryghte Merrie and Conceitede Tale in Verse, a Fragment* but John Gibson Lockhart. Whoever the au-thor, this parody, written after the announcement but before the publication of Wordsworth's poem, exactly as happened with Reynolds' *Peter Bell,* parodies not Wordsworth's *Waggoner* but *Peter Bell*—as Reynolds' *Peter Bell* parodies not the poem whose title it uses but "The Idiot Boy." Shelley's valuable *Peter Bell the Third,* which among its other accomplishments does spoof the poem it names—see Jack Benoit Gohn's "Did Shelley Know Wordsworth's *Peter Bell?*" (*KSJ,* 1979)—is discussed in the Shelley section of this volume. David Damrosch, in "Peter Bell Revised" (*WC,* 1980), provides an amusing modern parody and sur-vey of earlier parodies and includes one of the simple arithmetical measures of the "alarming" increase in Wordsworthian studies. Damrosch should complain!

Other Works

Since virtually everyone who has written on Wordsworth has commented on the so-called Lucy poems (my favorite suggestion is Samuel Butler's that the poet got Lucy in trouble and did her in), I'll not attempt a comprehensive listing. A history of the criticism of the poems will, indeed, provide a microcosmic history of Wordsworth's fate amongst critics—I use the future tense because a dissertation on this topic by Mark Jones is nearing completion at Columbia. But even a glance at critiques of recent years reveals the unsurprising predominance of psychological, usually Freudian, readings. Notable is J. Hillis Miller, "On Edge: The Crossways of Contemporary Criticism" (*Bull. of AAAS,* 1979), analyzing "A Slumber Did My Spirit Seal." Richard E. Matlak is more conventionally scholarly in his "Wordsworth's Lucy Poems in Psychobiographical Context" (*PMLA,* 1978). Less persuasive are Norman N. Holland, "Literary Interpretation and Three Phases of Psychoanalysis" (*CritI,* 1976), also focused on "A Slumber," and John Price, "Wordsworth's *Lucy*" (*AI,* 1974). Frances Ferguson in *Wordsworth: Language as Counter-Spirit* (1977) argues that the "sequence" articulates a recognition of Lucy's "absence rather than a re-possessing" and, like much earlier commentary, finds the poems useful for defining, explicitly or implicitly, principles of criticism. To move backward chronologically (for a reason given in the next paragraph), Roger L. Slahey, "At Zero: A Reading of Wordsworth's 'She Dwelt Among the Untrodden Ways' " (*SEL,* 1972), stresses the poetic experience of reflection; Spencer Hall, "Wordsworth's 'Lucy' Poems: Context and Meaning" (*SIR,* 1971), treats the lyrics as expressing an essentially tragic vision; J. M. Hawthorn (*Trivium,* 1971) delineates a special elegiac tradition for Wordsworth's heroine in "The Strange Deaths of Sally, Ann, Lucy and Others"; Geoffrey H. Durrant, in *Wordsworth and the Great System* (1970), perceives the poems' imagery as revealing an underlying conception of how individual identity links to the total cosmos, and Paul de Man's "The Rhetoric of Temporality" in *Interpretation,* edited by Charles Singleton (1969), uses "A Slumber" to define the "Romantic predicament." E. D. Hirsch, Jr., in *Validity in Interpretation* (1967), uses readings of "A Slumber Did My Spirit Seal" by Cleanth Brooks in *Literary Opinion in America,* edited by M. D. Zabel (1951), and F. W. Bateson, *English Poetry: A Critical Introduction* (1950), as a climactic illustration of the problem posed by plausible but irreconcilable interpretations. Abbie Findlay Potts in *The Elegiac Mode* (1967) draws parallels between Wordsworth's poems and those of elegists of antiquity. Geoffrey Hartman in *Wordsworth's Poetry 1787–1814* (1964) explores the relation of the poet's self-consciousness to his subject's incomplete self-consciousness, a reading interestingly foreshadowed by David Ferry in *The Limits of Mortality* (1959), who finds the poet, unlike Lucy, within "the limits of mortality" and therefore only capable of a symbolic relation to the eternity with which Lucy is identified. Warren Stevenson, "Cosmic Irony in Wordsworth's 'A Slumber Did My Spirit Seal' " (*WC,* 1976), develops this view, and Hartman in "A Touching Compulsion: Wordsworth and the Problem of Literary Representation" (*GaR,* 1977) returns to the issue with a careful "psychoaesthetic" analysis suggesting that Wordsworth's poetry may be regarded as "a form of reality-testing."

How scholarship is made use of these days is suggested by the fact that most of the critics I've cited entirely ignore the evidence marshaled by Hugh Sykes Davies in "Another New Poem by Wordsworth" (*EIC,* 1965) that the "Lucy group" or "sequence" is a fabrication of the Victorian Francis Palgrave, abetted by Matthew Arnold and Aubrey de Vere. "A Slumber Did My Spirit Seal" does not, of course, mention Lucy, Wordsworth never spoke of a "Lucy group," and his diverse ways of publishing the lyrics suggest he never conceived of them as forming a unit.

"The Two April Mornings" and "The Fountain" are often referred to as "Matthew poems" and are so studied by Richard E. Matlak on the model of his treatment of the "Lucy" poems in "The Men in Wordsworth's Life" (*WC,* 1978). Larry J. Swingle's essay on "The Two April Mornings" in *Images of Romanticism,* edited by Karl Kroeber and William Walling (1978), is more attentive to psychological aesthetics, as is E. D. Hirsch's careful reading in *Wordsworth and Schelling.* Anne Kostelanetz Mellor stresses the dramatic features of both poems in "Wordsworth's 'Conversations': A Reading of 'The Two April Mornings' and 'The Fountain'" (*ELH,* 1966), while John Danby, in *The Simple Wordsworth,* and Anthony Conran, in an essay in *Wordsworth's Mind and Art,* edited by A. W. Thomson (1969), treat the Matthew and Lucy poems as a group of "Goslar Lyrics," the title of Conran's essay.

"The Solitary Reaper" has been much admired and long has served as a kind of touchstone for Wordsworth's lyric purposes. Both Geoffrey Hartman, *Wordsworth's Poetry 1787–1814,* and Frederick Garber, *Wordsworth and the Poetry of Encounter* (1971), begin their books with lengthy analyses that serve as the foundation for their central theses. Although Garber ultimately compares Wordsworth with poets as diverse as Hölderlin and Wallace Stevens, his principal endeavor is to define the significance of poetry arising from moments of experience when the poet is startled, rebuked, baffled by encounters with an object, scene, event, or person. It is obvious why for him "The Solitary Reaper" and "Resolution and Independence" are paradigmatic, but his approach has value for much of Wordsworth's poetry. Geoffrey J. Finch, "Wordsworth's Solitary Song: The Substance of 'True Art' in 'The Solitary Reaper'" (*ArielE,* 1975), makes an elaborate argument for seeing the lyric primarily as a dramatization of aesthetic experience. A more ingenious and characteristically postmodern reading is that of Helen Regueiro in *The Limits of Imagination: Wordsworth, Yeats, and Stevens* (1976), a third of which is devoted to demonstrating Wordsworth to be a modernist manqué.

Criticism of "Resolution and Independence" as a distinctively Wordsworthian poem may have reached a peak of intensity in the 1960s but certainly began with the poet's vigorous letter to Sara Hutchinson in June 1802—and pride in his accomplishment is reiterated less defensively in an important passage in the 1815 Preface. The biographical foundation for the poem (for which Dorothy's journal entry of 3 October 1800 is central although Wordsworth to Isabella Fenwick emphasized another occasion) was systematically surveyed by George W. Meyer in *"Resolution and Independence"* (*TSE,* 1950), but William Heath's careful commentary in his *Wordsworth and Coleridge* (1970) is better informed and more penetrating in its psychological judgments. Heath sees *The Prelude* as "Resolution and Independence" writ large, in that both represent "a means to the discovery of the imagination," and he makes the point that though the action in the lyric "takes a few moments," because of "the mood of the poet's mind those moments comprehend a life-time." Heath demonstrates that the poem transforms the conventional subject of the "spring-elegy" popular at the end of the eighteenth century and shows that the poets whose destinies Wordsworth reflects on probably include, besides Burns and Chatterton, Bruce, Graeme, Fergusson, and Coleridge.

Among earlier studies worth noting—and in one way or another underlying Heath's commentary—are W. W. Robson in *Interpretations* (ed. John Wain, 1955); Florence G. Marsh, "*Resolution and Independence* Stanza XVIII" (*MLQ*, 1955); Anthony E. M. Conran, "The Dialectical Experience: A Study of Wordsworth's *Resolution and Independence*" (*PMLA*, 1960—especially useful on the influence of Chaucer and Chatterton); Albert Gérard, "*Resolution and Independence*: Wordsworth's Coming of Age" (*ESA*, 1960) and later "A Leading from Above," in *English Romantic Poetry* (1968); Alan Grob, "Process and Permanence in *Resolution and Independence*" (*ELH*, 1961); Stanley Edgar Hyman, "A Poem of Resolution" (*CentR*, 1961); E. E. Bostetter in his *The Romantic Ventriloquists* (1963); A. W. Thomson, "Resolution and Independence," in *Wordsworth's Mind and Art*, which he edited in 1969; and David Eggenschwiler, "Wordsworth's *Discordia Discors*" (*SIR*, 1969). In 1971 Jared R. Curtis, in *Wordsworth's Experiments with Tradition*, devoted a good chapter to the poem, with particular attention to the later version's relation to "The Leech-Gatherer" and including a thorough survey of earlier commentaries.

Among subsequent commentaries of worth are Gorman Beauchamp, "Wordsworth's Archetypal Resolution" (*CP*, 1974); Peter J. Manning, " 'My former thoughts returned': Wordsworth's '*Resolution and Independence*' " (*WC*, 1978); and Irene Tayler, "By Peculiar Grace: Wordsworth in 1802," in *The Evidence of the Imagination*, edited by Donald H. Reiman et al. (1978), which in the mode of Heath discusses the relations of troubles in the poet's personal life to the poems composed in 1802. More recently Robert Essick, "Wordsworth and Leech-Lore" (*WC*, 1981), links the story of the old man to the poet's concern about his own physical and psychic health, and Samuel E. Schulman, "The Spenserian Enchantments of Wordsworth's 'Resolution and Independence' " (*MP*, 1981), traces both the direct influence of the Elizabethan and the impact of James Thomson's modifications of Spenser's manner and aims.

If there seems to have been a slight falling off of interest in "Resolution and Independence" in the past decade, it is paralleled by the criticism of "Elegiac Stanzas," usually known as "Peele Castle," of which my analysis in *Romantic Landscape Vision* (1975) and that of Z. A. Usmani, "Solitude and Wordsworth's Peele Castle Poem" (*AJES*, 1977), appear to be the latest treating the poem as marking a decisive turning point in the poet's career. "Peele Castle," to be sure, never attracted critics in the manner that "Resolution and Independence" did. J. D.

O'Hara, "Ambiguity and Assertion in Wordsworth's 'Elegiac Stanzas'" (*PQ,* 1968), starts from Beaumont's painting, a feature of no interest to Geoffrey Hartman in his valuable pages on the lyric in *Wordsworth's Poetry 1787–1814,* and E. D. Hirsch, Jr., analyzes the poem as expressive of a radical religious-metaphysical change in Wordsworth's views, in *Wordsworth and Schelling* (1960). "Peele Castle" may not be as important a poem as some of us have thought, although it would seem essential to anyone dealing with Wordsworthian sublimity, and I wonder if the time is not ripe for some further reconsideration, as well as a reinvigoration of attention to "Resolution and Independence." Coleridge in the twenty-second chapter of the *Biographia* identified this poem as "especially characteristic" of Wordsworth's art, observing that "there is scarce a defect or excellence in his writings of which it would not present a specimen," but for recent critics whose methods derive in one way or another from structuralist principles, the peculiar and distinctive have not been of overriding interest. A unique exhibition of a specialized craftsmanship seems to many critics now less important than a "text's" illumination of underlying principles of poetry or its illustration of the value of a critical methodology. But almost any shift in the spectrum of our critical approaches seems likely to revive debate over these intensely, almost quintessentially Wordsworthian poems.

The most recent essay on "The Barberry-Tree" is Jared R. Curtis, "Charles A. Elton and Wordsworth's 'New Poem': A Study in Taste" (*WC,* 1980). This poem, which came to light only in 1964, is discussed by Curtis in *Wordsworth's Experiments with Tradition* (1971), its appearance and authenticity having been studied earlier by Jonathan Wordsworth (*CE,* 1966) and Mark L. Reed (*CE,* 1966). Thomas R. Frosch, "Wordsworth's 'Beggars' and a Brief Instance of 'Writer's Block'" (*SIR,* 1982), discusses Wordsworth's difficulties in shaping this poem and the probable psychological causes. David McCracken, "Wordsworth on Human Wishes and Poetic Borrowing" (*MP,* 1982), provides a reading of "The Wishing Gate" that includes a perceptive analysis of Wordsworth's views on literary theft and borrowing, including Coleridge's practices.

David R. Sanderson studies "Wordsworth's World, 1809: A Stylistic Study of the Cintra Pamphlet" (*WC,* 1970) but does not take us too deeply into the work. Gordon K. Thomas, *Wordsworth's Dirge and Promise: Napoleon, Wellington, and the Convention of Cintra* (1971), unfortunately does not really carry us much beyond A. V. Dicey, *The Statesmanship of Wordsworth* (1917), which includes discussion of "Poems Dedicated to National Independence and Liberty." J. E. Wells, "The Story of Wordsworth's 'Cintra'" (*SP,* 1921), was the first to untangle the complexities of the tract's composition and publication. The facsimile edition by Gordon Thomas is noted in the "Editions" section above. Richard D. McGhee, "'Conversant with Infinity': Form and Meaning in Wordsworth's 'Laodamia'" (*SP,* 1971), centers on the poem's classic-romantic tensions.

Among recent essays devoted to the important poem "Nutting" are James W. Pipkin, "Wordsworth's 'Nutting' and Rites of Initiation" (*Interpretations,* 1978), which reads the poem in the light of the ideas of Mircea Eliade, and Douglass H.

Thomson, "Wordsworth's Lucy of 'Nutting' " (*SIR,* 1979), which examines the draft of the poem found in de Selincourt's edition of the poems.

F. H. Langman, "Two Wordsworth Poems" (*SoRA,* 1978), praises Wordsworth's skill at handling supernaturalism in "Poor Susan" and "To Joanna." David Simpson in an interesting essay, "Criticism, Politics, and Style in Wordsworth's Poetry" (*CritI,* 1984), analyzes "Alice Fell" and "Gipsies" in order to explore how "literary statements are inevitably socially referential and allusive."

The two sonnets that have been most analyzed are "The World Is Too Much with Us" and "Westminster Bridge." A swirl of debate in the *Wordsworth Circle* has recently surrounded the former, initiated by the article of Arnold B. Fox and Martin Kallich, "Wordsworth's Sentimental Naturalism" (1977), answered in 1980 by Edward Profitt in " 'This Pleasant Lea' "; meanwhile, David Ketterer in 1979 had written interestingly on " 'Glimpses' in Wordsworth's 'The World . . . ,' " to which Theresa M. Kelley responded in 1980 with "Proteus, Nature, and Romantic Mythography," denying that there is any of the "natural religion" Ketterer finds in Wordsworth; Kelley extended her work in an important essay, "Proteus and Romantic Allegory" (*ELH* 1982), in which she proves against de Man that Romantic poetry can be simultaneously symbolic and allegorical. Charles Molesworth discusses "Wordsworth's 'Westminster Bridge' Sonnet: The Republican Structure of Time and Perception" (*Clio,* 1977), Harvey P. Sucksmith presents "Ultimate Affirmation: A Critical Analysis of Wordsworth's Sonnet, 'Composed upon Westminster Bridge,' and the Image of the City in *The Prelude"* (*YES,* 1976), Patrick Holland explores "The Two Contrasts of Wordsworth's 'Westminster Bridge' Sonnet" (*WC,* 1977), and J. Hillis Miller has a valuable essay on this sonnet entitled "The Still Heart: Poetic Form in Wordsworth" (*NLH,* 1971).

Geoffrey Hartman concentrates on formal matters in his commentary on a late sonnet, "Blessing the Torrent: On Wordsworth's Later Style" (*PMLA,* 1978), while Paul de Man, seeming to disregard his own theories of Romantic literature, gives a fine reading of "Composed by the Side of Grasmere Lake," in *In Defense of Reading,* edited by Reuben A. Brower and Richard Poirier (1962), emphasizing "the delicate balance between direct and imagined vision" in Wordsworth's poem as contrasting with the artificiality of Yeats's "Coole Park and Ballylee, 1931." Thomas R. Edwards comments cogently on a few of the political sonnets in *Imagination and Power: A Study of Poetry on Public Themes* (1971), and Barbara T. Gates deals with the *Ecclesiastical Sonnets* in "Wordsworth's Mirror of Morality: Distortions of Church History" (*WC,* 1981). Alan G. Hill in "On the Date and Significance of Wordsworth's Sonnet 'On the Extinction of the Venetian Republic' " (*RES,* 1979) argues for the poem's composition in 1807, not 1802. Peter J. Manning, "Wordsworth and Gray's Sonnet on the Death of West" (*SEL,* 1982), uses the work attacked in the Preface to *Lyrical Ballads* to explain Wordsworth's ability to attain a "cosmic vantage" in lyrics such as the Lucy poems. The best and most complete work on Wordsworth's sonnets is *Wordsworth and the Sonnet* (1973) by Lee M. Johnson, noted again in the final section of this chapter.

Ronald Schliefer, in "Wordsworth's Yarrow and the Poetics of Repetition" (*MLQ,* 1977), describes how various Yarrow poems employ repetition and allusion to link present to past. Other studies of "gatherings" worthy of attention are Jeffrey C. Robinson, "The Structure of Wordsworth's Memorials of a Tour . . . 1803" (*PLL*, 1977), and Jill Rubenstein, "Wordsworth and 'Localized Romance': The Scottish Poems of 1831" (*SEL*, 1976).

"Yew-Trees" has been intensively studied in the past decade. Gene W. Ruoff, "Wordsworth's 'Yew-Trees' and Romantic Perception" (*MLQ*, 1973), uses phenomenology as articulated by Merleau-Ponty to elucidate the work's elemental wholeness. Michael Riffaterre, "Interpretation and Descriptive Poetry: A Reading of Wordsworth's 'Yew-Trees'" (*NLH*, 1973), seeks to explore the "referential fallacy" by demonstrating that this example of purely "descriptive poetry" exploits grammatical-semantic codes to persuade us that "extreme anxiety, inescapable fear, rooted in an involved consciousness of our very humanness, may be lulled by means as material and elemental as the fear is metaphysical—the monotonous murmur of water." Though paying tribute to the brilliance of Riffaterre's commentary, Geoffrey Hartman draws on his own earlier work, including portions of *The Unmediated Vision* (1954), in "The Use and Abuse of Structural Analysis: Riffaterre's Interpretation of Wordsworth's 'Yew-Trees'" (*NLH*, 1975) to argue that Riffaterre "overlooks the problem of voice or of the poet as intermediary," a flaw inherent in the impersonality of his structural method. A different challenge is posed to Riffaterre by Frederick Bowers in "Reference and Deixis in Wordsworth's 'Yew-Trees'" (*ESC*, 1979), who claims Riffaterre ignores the difference between semantic and deictic features of language. I have no doubt that Riffaterre's fine essay will be drawing fire for years to come, though a brilliant "geometrical" reading by Lee M. Johnson in *Wordsworth's Metaphysical Verse* (1982) introduces a new kind of structural analysis, also controversial.

Relations with Visual Arts and Sublimity

There has been considerable attention given to Wordsworth's relations to the visual arts since Martha H. Shackford in 1945 provided a list (now recognized to be incomplete) of the poet's references to paintings and painters in *Wordsworth's Interest in Painters and Pictures*, but Alexander King's *Wordsworth and the Artist's Vision* (1966) was the first comprehensive study of this topic from a modernist perspective—King suggests an analogy between Wordsworth and Henry Moore, for example. Morse Peckham, however, in *Beyond the Tragic Vision* (1962), provocatively investigates impulses expressed by both poets and painters, focusing principally on Goethe, Wordsworth, Friedrich, and Constable. In a chapter in *The Triumph of Romanticism* (1970), Peckham specifically compares Wordsworth and Constable, as had Lord Kenneth Clark briefly yet eloquently in *Landscape into Art* (1949).

The comparison with Constable is treated most extensively in my *Romantic Landscape Vision: Constable and Wordsworth* (1975), which works inductively from contrastive juxtapositions of specific poems and paintings to definition of underlying similarities. My subsequent work extends the same method to other artists and later periods, as is indicated in my "Constable: Millais:: Wordsworth: Tennyson" in *Articulate Images,* edited by Richard Wendorf (1983), and a chapter on Wordsworth and Turner in my forthcoming *British Romantic Art.* There is an excellent essay by R. F. Storch, "Wordsworth and Constable" (*SIR,* 1966), and the same critic extends his comparison to a contrast with Turner and Shelley, with suggestions as to the psychological basis of differences, in "Abstract Idealism in English Romantic Poetry and Painting" in *Images of Romanticism: Verbal and Visual Affinities,* edited by Karl Kroeber and William Walling (1978). This volume also contains valuable essays by Larry J. Swingle, "Wordsworth's 'Picture of the Mind,' " and James A. W. Heffernan, "The English Romantic Perception of Color," which should be read in conjunction with his "Reflections on Reflections in English Romantic Poetry and Painting" (*BuR,* 1978) and an essay in the same journal, "Wordsworth, Coleridge, and Turner: The Geometry of the Infinite" (1983). J. R. Watson evaluates the personal relations of Wordsworth and Constable, their main connection being through Sir George Beaumont, in "Wordsworth and Constable" (*RES,* 1962), later extended in his *Picturesque Landscape and English Romantic Poetry* (1970). In "Constable, Wordsworth, and Beaumont: A New Constable Letter in Evidence" (*Art Bulletin,* 1982), Mark L. Reed not only provides the transcript of a letter from the painter to the poet but also judiciously analyzes the probable acquaintance each had with the other's work. James B. Twitchell in *Romantic Horizons: Aspects of the Sublime in English Poetry and Painting 1770–1850* (1983) compares "Yew-Trees" with paintings by Wright of Derby.

The more diffuse topic of Wordsworth's relation to aesthetic theories of the later eighteenth century, and particularly those concerned with landscape, has attracted considerable scholarship, a little of it useful. E. A. Shearer and J. I. Lindsay study "Wordsworth and Coleridge Marginalia in a Copy of Richard Payne Knight's *Analytical Inquiry into the Principles of Taste*" (*HLQ,* 1937), this joint examination by the two poets probably marking Wordsworth's first serious confrontation with Kant's ideas about the sublime; Russell Noyes, *Wordsworth and the Art of Landscape* (1968), surveys the field sensibly and accurately for the general reader and includes full references to earlier studies; John Barrell, in *The Idea of Landscape and the Sense of Place, 1730–1840* (1972), is splendidly opinionated and thought-provoking, being especially good in contrasting Clare with Wordsworth. Wordsworth's relation to the picturesque tradition is the specific subject of John R. Nabholtz, "Wordsworth's *Guide to the Lakes* and the Picturesque Tradition" (*MP,* 1964), while Stephen J. Spector, in "Wordsworth's Mirror Imagery and the Picturesque Tradition" (*ELH,* 1977), centers on *The Prelude* and *Home at Grasmere.* These, like more general studies of the picturesque, seem to me likely to be enriched in the near future as we come to a better understanding of the function of interest in the picturesque, often, ironically, obscured by its chief theorists. It served, in fact, as an escape from the polarizations of sublime and beautiful as articulated by Burke, Kant, and other philosopher-aestheticians and was closely linked to patriotic, nationalistic aspirations.

There has been a recent revival of interest in sublimity, stimulated in the case of Wordsworth by the publication of the poet's fragmentary essay "The Sublime and the Beautiful" in the *Prose Works,* edited by Owen and Smyser (vol. 2), commented on by W. J. B. Owen in two essays, "The Sublime and the Beautiful in *The Prelude*" (*WC,* 1973) and "Wordsworth's Aesthetics of Landscape" (*WC,* 1976), as well as by Stuart Peterfreund, "Wordsworth and the Sublime Duration" (*Publications of the Arkansas Philological Assn.,* 1977). Earlier, James A. W. Heffernan had focused on this important topic in "Wordsworth on the Sublime: The Quest for Interfusion" (*SEL,* 1967). Samuel Monk's *The Sublime: A Study of Critical Theories in Eighteenth-Century England* (1935) has been much relied on by literary scholars and is still quite useful, but it ought to be supplemented by more recent professional philosophic work—I recommended, for instance, Mary Warnock's *Imagination* (1976), a lucid and sensible presentation of the relevance of Kant's thinking to these matters, and James Engell's *The Creative Imagination: Enlightenment to Romanticism* (1981), which provides an encyclopedic survey of the history of "imagination." On the interesting history of the word "sublime" one may consult Jan Cohn and Thomas H. Miles, "The Sublime: In Alchemy, Aesthetics, and Psychoanalysis" (*MP,* 1977). Several of the more ambitious analyses of the past few years suffer from inadequate attention to the evidence from the visual arts. Most, for example, have failed to notice how the metaphor of perspective underlying many discussions of sublimity derives from specific developments in art history, as is pointed out by Claudio Guillén in *Literature as System* (1971). A thorough survey, with full attention to the work of earlier scholars, is available in W. P. Albrecht's *The Sublime Pleasures of Tragedy* (1975), with a kind of addendum, "Tragedy and Wordsworth's Sublime" (*WC,* 1977), on the poet's fragmentary essay. To my mind, Albrecht ties Romantic sublimity too closely to its eighteenth-century sources (Carl Woodring suggests that "The New Sublimity in 'Tintern Abbey'" [*The Evidence of the Imagination*, ed. Reiman et al., 1978], is un-Burkean and different in a new fashion from the picturesque and beautiful), but Albrecht's book, despite its concentration on tragedy, is more useful for Wordsworthians than David B. Morris, *The Religious Sublime* (1972).

The most important study of the sublime focused on Wordsworth is that of Albert O. Wlecke, *Wordsworth on the Sublime* (1973). Wlecke finds the "structure of Wordsworth's experience" that the poet refers to as "sublime" a mode of self-consciousness that does not necessarily displace other kinds of awareness, for the "visionary dimension" that sublime self-consciousness discloses does not involve "annihilation of the phenomenal world." On the contrary, Wordsworth, observing that in "nature everything is distinct yet nothing defined into absolute independent singleness," recognizes "the immanence of apperception in perception," which allows "a sense of self that is 'far diffus'd' through time as well as space." The structure of consciousness thus achieved "lacks any principle of limitation," so that an individual form is no longer "seen as a 'punctual Presence' existing at a defined point in space that excludes all other points in space," and a particular moment is no longer isolated but is seen as part of a temporal continuity, contributing to "Being unimpaired."

Wlecke's analysis concentrates on what M. H. Abrams in "English Romanticism: The Spirit of the Age" in *Romanticism Reconsidered,* edited by Northrop Frye (1963), termed "a central paradox . . . of Wordsworth's major period: the oxymoron of the humble-grand," the paradox on which Hazlitt first commented when he observed that Wordsworth, "distinguished by a proud humility, . . . elevates the mean" and strives "to aggrandise the trivial." But whereas Abrams regards Wordsworth's source as "obvious" (the New Testament) and describes the oxymoron as merely another example of secularization of traditional religious attitudes, Wlecke perceives Wordsworth's view as intriguingly original and explores its relations to the poet's view of the processes of memory and of poetic creation. Both processes Wlecke defines as *spreading*; "affective memory" blends "an infinite regression by consciousness into its past subjectivity" with an "intensifying act of self-consciousness in which the soul comes to a progressively incremental sense of its own powers," so to write poetry involving memory is to cultivate "life where hope and memory are as one."

The most discussed recent work on the general topic of Romantic sublimity is that by Thomas Weiskel, *The Romantic Sublime: Studies in the Structure and Psychology of Transcendence* (1976). Weiskel, piling Lacan atop Freud, centers on the Simplon Pass episode in *The Prelude* to define in Wordsworth what Weiskel calls the "vacancy of immanence," arguing that memory becomes in fact "the vacancy, the absolute insufficiency of the *now* . . . objectified as the distance between identities which can be signified." One foundation for this view is so intensely Freudian that Weiskel even claims Wordsworth could not have remembered his childhood, and, despite some modishly elaborate verbiage, Weiskel to a considerable degree simply follows Richard Onorato's delineation of anxieties deriving from the poet's loss of his mother. Weiskel, moreover, does not build on specific evidence marshaled by Wlecke, so that whatever the impressiveness of his Hegelian abstractions, their practical value is likely to be minimal for careful students of the complexities of Wordsworth's practice. Weiskel's intellectual and stylistic contortions, indeed, suggest that the critical fondness for sublime misreadings may be about to yield to factually better informed modes of judging Wordsworth's aesthetic. Such modes may spiral back toward some of the earlier responses to Wordsworthian intricacies; in this instance, one thinks of possible reconsideration of Marjorie Hope Nicolson's comments on Wordsworth's "aesthetics of infinity" in *Mountain Gloom and Mountain Glory* (1959). Symptomatic of such improved scholarship is Theresa M. Kelley's fine essay "Wordsworth and the Rhinefall" (*SIR,* 1984), which goes beyond both Wlecke and Weiskel in carefully analyzing Wordsworth's later reconsiderations of sublimity and "the complex revisionary impulse of his aesthetics."

Predecessors, Contemporaries, Successors

Milton for a long time has most interested students of Wordsworth's predecessors, and Joseph A. Wittreich, in his compendium *The Romantics on Milton* (1970), gives forty-six pages to brief quotations from letters, diaries, prefaces, and poems illustrating Wordsworth's indebtedness. Wittreich makes use of valuable essays by Jared R. Curtis, "William Wordsworth and the Poetry of the Sixteenth and Seventeenth Centuries" (*CLAJ,* 1966), and Bishop C. Hunt, Jr., "Wordsworth's Marginalia on *Paradise Lost*" (*BNYPL,* 1969). The first full book on the subject was H. J. C. Grierson's *Milton and Wordsworth: Poets and Prophets* (1937), but contemporary readers will probably find more stimulating Leslie Brisman's *Milton's Poetry of Choice and Its Romantic Heirs* (1973), which gives a chapter and a good part of its foreword to Wordsworth. Though stylistically diffuse and inclined to credit too much to Milton alone, Brisman makes some good points, notably on "poetic situations." Ross Woodman, "Milton's Satan in Wordsworth's 'Vale of Soul-making'" (*SIR,* 1984), emphasizes the importance to *The Prelude* of *Paradise Regained.*

Milton, however, forms only the tip of this iceberg of scholarship—the past decade alone has produced nearly sixty essays on Wordsworth's more than trivial literary debts and affinities. So rather than take vast space for this topic, I refer the reader back to the bibliographical sources: on these matters, the *Wordsworth Circle*'s annual survey of scholarship is especially helpful. I'll mention here a rather arbitrary selection of items that illustrate various categories of this research so far as it treats particular authors and works, slighting more general studies, such as the chapter by T. J. Diffey, "The Roots of Imagination," in *The Romantics,* edited by Stephen Prickett (1981), which discusses development of the concept and how Wordsworth among others made use of it; Barbara T. Gates's "Wordsworth's Use of Oral History" (*Folklore,* 1974); and Rayner Unwin's *The Rural Muse: Studies in the Peasant Poetry of England* (1954), which distinguishes Wordsworth from "unlearned" predecessors.

Wallace Jackson, "Wordsworth and His Predecessors: Private Sensations and Public Tones" (*Criticism,* 1975), focuses effectively on Gray and Collins, and James E. Swearingen considers "Wordsworth on Gray" (*SEL,* 1974), while Nathaniel Teich treats some issues raised by these studies in "Evaluating Wordsworth's Revolution: Romantic Reviewers and Changing Taste" (*PLL,* 1975). Myrddin Jones, in "Wordsworth and Cowper: The Eye Made Quiet" (*EIC,* 1971), discerns a decisive imaginative advance in the later poet, while Everard H. King studies "Beattie's *The Minstrel* and Wordsworth's *The Excursion:* What the Critics Overlook" (*BRH,* 1980). Raymond Bentman, "Robert Burns's Declining Fame" (*SIR,* 1972), suggests how Burns served Wordsworth as a bridge to certain aspects of Augustan poetry, and John Beer makes some astute remarks on Wordsworth's relations to Burns in *Wordsworth and the Human Heart* (1978). Following Abbie Potts's lead, Vincent Newey, "Wordsworth, Bunyan and the Puritan Mind" (*ELH,* 1974), links the 1805 *Prelude* to *Grace Abounding,* while Bishop C. Hunt, Jr., presents a substantial body of evidence in "Wordsworth and Charlotte Smith" (*WC,* 1970). For Wordsworth and Blake my work has been done for me by James R. Bennett in his superlatively annotated "The Comparative Criticism of Blake and Wordsworth: A Bibliography" (*WC,* 1983). Heather Glen in *Vision and Disenchantment: Blake's Songs and Wordsworth's* Lyrical Ballads (1983), through perceptive analyses of the genres these various poems subvert, provides illuminating comparisons and contrasts.

Despite their impressive tracing down of sources, Douglas Bush, *Mythology and the Romantic Tradition in English Poetry* (1937), and Burton Feldman and Robert D. Richardson, *The Rise of Modern Mythology 1680–1860* (1972), fail to take sufficient account of how Wordsworth used mythology, some understanding of which is shown in Albert J. Kuhn, "English Deism and the Development of Romantic Syncretism" (*PMLA*, 1956), though this topic calls out for new work, not crippled by dependence on the intellectual trivialities of Eliade. It is surprising also that we have as yet no truly extensive work on Wordsworth's use of classical poetry and no impressive studies of his translations from Michelangelo or even of his reworkings of Chaucer. With Rousseau the situation is interestingly different. *Rousseau in England* by Edward Duffy (1979) centers on Shelley, but its remarks on Wordsworth are useful. Margery Sabin's *English Romanticism and the French Tradition* (1976) is largely concerned with Wordsworth, beginning with a detailed contrast between *The Confessions* and *The Prelude*. Sabin sees Rousseau as claiming freedom from artificial and conventional forms yet confined by them, whereas Wordsworth by a deliberate literariness attains originality, particularly in his use of language. The poet celebrates imagination; to Rousseau imagination is to be distrusted, for it leads away from truth. The Frenchman can lay claim to something like total recall because he regards his past as fixed, determinate, while for Wordsworth memories change in time and therefore can be a source of renewal, though for Rousseau they are only a refuge. For Rousseau "le sentiment de l'existence" defines his self-sufficiency in the face of a hostile world, but for Wordsworth the "sentiment of being" points to his feeling of belonging to a larger reality beyond self. Sabin comments intelligently on parallels and differences between Wordsworth, Hugo, Baudelaire, Hopkins, and Yeats, always with an eye to the distinctions between cultural and aesthetic traditions in Britain and France that individual works manifest, modify, or even create. Since so much Wordsworthian criticism has either asserted or assumed an essential identity between Rousseau and Wordsworth, I return to Sabin's book at the conclusion of this chapter.

Theodore E. D. Braun argues—a bit ineffectively—for similarity between Wordsworth's prefaces and Diderot's *Paradoxe sur le comédien* in "Diderot, Wordsworth, and the Creative Process" (*CLS*, 1974), but Braun's topic deserves more careful attention than it has yet received. Geoffrey Hartman's good essay "Wordsworth and Goethe in Literary History" (*NLH*, 1975) focuses on "The Danish Boy" and "Der Erlkönig," and one should not overlook Rudolf Dirk Schier's "The Experience of the Noumenal in Goethe and Wordsworth" (*CI*, 1973), utilizing the Simplon Pass lines and the opening monologue of *Faust II*.

Richard Gravil, "Wordsworth's Second Selves?" (*WC*, 1983), finds our poet "haunting" Geoffrey Hill, W. S. Graham, R. S. Thomas, and Ted Hughes, while W. J. Keith in *The Poetry of Nature* (1980) finds Wordsworth's influence on later "nature poets" such as Clare, Barnes, Hardy, Frost, and Edward Thomas both subtler and more pervasive than is usually recognized. This lack of recognition might explain the relatively unexciting quality of most traditional studies (and there are a great number) of the relation of Wordsworth's poetry to subsequent writers.

Wordsworth's originality creates a special problem; it is not the unquestioned greatness of his achievement that made him difficult for successors. It was more his having opened up new ranges of subject matter, particularly in the realm of subjective psychology, that compelled every lyric poet into "Wordsworth's" path. After Wordsworth, all lyric poets *had* to be "original"—as he had been. He was the first explicitly to insist that a great and original author "must himself create the taste by which he is to be relished." What a bequest to subsequent poets!

Those in our profession today who feel themselves at the critical cutting edge, that is, our leading dust creators, find intimations of Wordsworth everywhere, not because any modern poets could even by the dullest be mistaken for Wordsworth, but because his poetry can be made to seem proleptic (aah!) of issues crucial to all twentieth-century poets. At the same time, the author of "We Are Seven" seems not threatening to the superior insight and importance of modernist writers and, by extension, their critics. I accept the broad, general truth of the proposition that Romanticism inaugurates the modern era of history, but I believe the obsession with a proleptic Wordsworth unfortunate. It requires ignoring profound differences between the end of the eighteenth and the end of the twentieth centuries. The intensifying urgency with which Wordsworth is presented as if he were a contemporary testifies as powerfully as increased use of word processors to the continuing erosion of our era's historical sense. So I am not as enthusiastic as some about Wordsworth's increased popularity in academia during the past two decades—although I admit the bias induced by having to read the results of that popularity. The indubitable rise in his prestige in English departments, moreover, appears to me accompanied by a diminution in esteem for genuinely contemporary poetry, as well as a kind of defensive reaction to the surge in Blake's esteem.

Having thus proved I have no business writing this report, I'll get on with it, suggesting that the problem of predecessors and successors is further complicated by the fact that influences do not always flow in purely literary channels, as is illustrated handily by a pair of essays in the 1979 *Wordsworth Circle.* There Sue Weaver Westbrook shows there is still vitality in the line of research opened by Arthur Beatty three score years ago by examining the impact of both Hartley and Erasmus Darwin in "A Note on Hartley's Theory of 'The Sensation of Chilliness' in Wordsworth's 'Goody Blake and Harry Gill' "; and Marilyn Gaull, in a long, detailed survey entitled "From Wordsworth to Darwin: 'On to the Fields of Praise,' " urges that the poet's Romantic concern for geology helps make his poetry a link between earlier theoreticians and Charles Darwin, whose work influenced more than one writer. On Wordsworth and science, the essay by James H. Averill entitled "Wordsworth and 'Natural Science': The Poetry of 1798" (*JEGP,* 1978) is to be recommended, especially for attention to the poet's debt to *Zoönomia,* a matter touched on also by Desmond King-Hele's *Erasmus Darwin* (1963).

Turning now to Wordsworth's principal "contemporaries," minus Coleridge, treated however inadequately in "Biographical Matters" (above) and in "The Critic Wordsworth" (below), and Blake, because of Bennett's fine bibliography just mentioned, I recommend as the best place to begin "Scott and Wordsworth; Or,

Reading Scott Well," Frank Jordan's essay (*WC,* 1973), though also worth consulting are Kathryn Sutherland's comparison in *Scott and His Influence,* ed. J. H. Alexander (1983) and Donald G. Priestman, "Wordsworth on the Poetry of Walter Scott" (*DR,* 1975 – 76). On Southey, see the essay by Mary Jacobus cited previously and also "A Fresh Comparison of 'The Idiot Boy' and 'The Idiot' " by Elizabeth Duthie (*N&Q,* 1978), which dramatizes vividly Wordsworth's unconventionality. Influence on the younger Romantic poets is appropriately covered in other sections of this volume, but it is worth observing that there is room for more work on this topic even though major studies of Shelley and Keats often consider Wordsworth—Keats's letters to Reynolds of 3 February 1818 and 3 May 1818 frequently being cited—and the specific indebtedness of a poem such as "'Alastor" has been thoroughly analyzed. But the work of Thora Balslev, *Keats and Wordsworth: A Comparative Study* (1962), and J. C. Echeruo, "Shelley on Wordsworth" (*ESA,* 1966), needs to be superseded. One kind of model is provided by Michael G. Cooke, "Byron and Wordsworth: The Complementary of a Rock and the Sea" (*WC,* 1980), which goes beyond his brief but suggestive remarks on *Don Juan* and *The Prelude* in his *Acts of Inclusion* (1979). Byron, because of his political and aesthetic hostility and the so-called conservative character of his verse, is, indeed, too seldom studied in conjunction with Wordsworth, despite connections finer than those of contrast between *Childe Harold* and *The Prelude.* Specially interesting because of the rarity of such studies (except for Cooke's) is Peter J. Manning's "Tales and Politics: *The Corsair, Lara,* and *The White Doe of Rylstone"* (*Byron: Poetry and Politics: 7th Intl. Symposium, Salzburg, 1980,* ed. E. A. Stürzl and J. Hogg, 1981), which, without overlooking the poems' affinities, contrasts them in terms of their relations to the politics of their times and authors. While it is natural that most comparative studies of the two generations of Romantic poets center on images, themes, or forms, there remains much useful analysis to be pursued, one line of which is suggested by Jack Stillinger's final chapter in *The Hoodwinking of Madeline and Other Essays on Keats's Poems* (1971) or, in a more specialized fashion, by Peter J. Manning's "Keats's and Wordsworth's Nightingales" (*ELN,* 1980) and Mario L. D'Avanzo's " 'Ode on a Grecian Urn' and *The Excursion"* (*KSJ,* 1974) or even Ants Oras' "Notes on Introspection and Self-Analysis, Their Function and Imaginal Representation in Shelley" (*NM,* 1972), which contrasts the younger poet with Wordsworth.

Another kind of model worth consideration appears in Cyrus Hamlin's comparison of "reconstructions of experience" in "The Poetics of Self-Consciousness in European Romanticism: Hölderlin's *Hyperion* and Wordsworth's *Prelude"* (*Genre,* 1973), even though we here cross the boundary between "influence" and "parallelism" or "analogues." Yet the affinity of these domains might be more carefully explored with good results, as is suggested by Hartman's discussion of Goethe and Wordsworth already mentioned and, of course, his *Unmediated Vision,* which takes up Rilke, Hopkins, and Valéry, and perhaps even by my *Artifice of Reality* (1964), which pairs poems by Wordsworth and Keats with poems by Foscolo and Leopardi. A different but certainly rewarding approach is that of

Monica Partridge, "Romanticism and the Concept of Communication in a Slavonic and a Non-Slavonic Literature" (*RMS*, 1973), which concentrates on Wordsworth and Pushkin among the first generation of English and Russian Romantics.

Another area in which more work is needed is that of Wordsworth's "minor" contemporaries George Crabbe and John Clare. Works about these two usually take some account of Wordsworth, but we need more attention to parallels and differences by Wordsworthian specialists. Larry J. Swingle's "Late Crabbe in Relation to Augustans and Romantics: The Temporal Labyrinth of his *Tales in Verse, 1812*" (*ELH*, 1975) and "Stalking the Essential John Clare: Clare in Relation to His Romantic Contemporaries" (*SIR*, 1975) are to date the best brief treatments of these topics, though Barrell's book noted above should be consulted for Clare and Wordsworth. Specialized work on a subject almost entirely ignored nowadays is Elizabeth Brewster's "George Crabbe and William Wordsworth" (*UTQ*, 1973), which claims that Crabbe had a strong influence on the metrical practice of the younger poet.

Why the field of Wordsworth and the Victorians is so vast is suggested by the opening of John R. Reed's "Inherited Characteristics: Romantic to Victorian Will" (*SIR*, 1978), which calls Wordsworth and Coleridge "the earliest major Victorian writers." Jonathan Wordsworth discusses a woman often treated as a belated Romantic in "Wordsworth and the Poetry of Emily Brontë" (*BST*, 1972), though the book by Margaret Homans *Women Writers and Poetic Identity* (1980) goes deeper. Janice Carlisle, "A Prelude to *Villette:* Charlotte Brontë's Reading, 1850–52" (*BRH*, 1979), claims a major effect of Wordsworth's poem on Emily's sister. Study of Wordsworth's influence on George Eliot, to cite one more novelist, is now a substantial industry. Recent work includes Henry Auster, "George Eliot and the Modern Temper," in *The Worlds of Victorian Fiction,* edited by Jerome H. Buckley (1975); Robert H. Dunham, "*Silas Marner* and the Wordsworthian Child" (*SEL*, 1976); and Peter Simpson, "Crisis and Recovery: Wordsworth, George Eliot, and *Silas Marner*" (*UTQ*, 1978). Karen B. Mann undertakes the broader topic "George Eliot and Wordsworth: The Power of Sound and the Power of the Mind" (*SEL*, 1980); Jay Clayton describes "Visionary Power and Narrative Form: Wordsworth and *Adam Bede*" (*ELH*, 1979); Deborah Heller Roazen, in "*Middlemarch* and the Wordsworthian Imagination" (*ES*, 1977), finds substantial affinities; and Margaret Homans concentrates on *The Mill on the Floss* in "Eliot, Wordsworth, and the Scenes of the Sisters' Instruction" (*CritI*, 1981). Among earlier works well worth attention are Lillian Haddakin's chapter on *Silas Marner* in Barbara Hardy's *Critical Essays on George Eliot* (1970), along with Q. D. Leavis' introduction to the Penguin edition of *Silas Marner* (1967) and Thomas Pinney's excellent "The Authority of the Past in George Eliot's Novels" (*NCF*, 1966).

Amidst the many commentaries on Arnold's relations to his predecessor, Michael Timko's "Wordsworth's 'Ode' and Arnold's 'Dover Beach': Celestial Light and Confused Alarms" (*Cithara*, 1973) is useful on the specifics of difference between the two poems, but one should begin with the foundations provided by David DeLaura in "The 'Wordsworth' of Pater and Arnold" (*SEL*, 1966) and Leon

Gottfried's *Matthew Arnold and the Romantics* (1963). Donald Rackin, " 'God's Grandeur': Hopkins' Sermon to Wordsworth" (*WC*, 1980), is an impressively thoughtful comparison and includes a survey of earlier Wordsworth-Hopkins studies, with special attention to Geoffrey Hartman's *Unmediated Vision.*

The enormous field of Wordsworth's role in Victorian thought, religion, and critical attitudes is best explored through volumes similar to this one, such as *Victorian Prose,* edited by David DeLaura. The field is not going to be treated adequately here. Robert Langbaum, *The Poetry of Experience* (1957), is still valuable on development of the dramatic monologue. A lively introduction to the aesthetic relations of Romanticism to Victorian, with a good deal on Wordsworth's role, is to be found in Patricia M. Ball, *The Central Self* (1968), and Elizabeth K. Helsinger, "Ruskin on Wordsworth: The Victorian Critic in Romantic Country" (*SIR*, 1978), gives guidance on that important topic. Mary G. Mason, "Wordsworth and Pater's First Imaginary Portrait" (*HLB*, 1971), sees "The Child in the House" as indebted to the poet's ideas on the growth of consciousness, and Sharon Bassett explores "Wordsworth, Pater and the 'Anima Mundi' " (*Criticism,* 1975). Two articles on John Stuart Mill having interest for Wordsworthians if for few others—Karl Britton, "J. S. Mill: A Debating Speech on Wordsworth" (*Cambridge Review,* 1958), and Anna J. Mill, "John Stuart Mill's Visit to Wordsworth, 1831" (*MLR,* 1949)—illustrate the characteristically detailed scholarship in this field of research. Stephen Prickett's thoughtful and careful *Romanticism and Religion: The Tradition of Coleridge and Wordsworth in the Victorian Church* (1976) is a generally valuable work with many useful references, arguing that Wordsworth's pervasive influence sprang from the fact that his poetry was interpreted as showing transcendence not antithetical to naturalism.

James L. Hill's "The Frame for the Mind: Landscape in 'Lines . . . Tintern Abbey,' 'Dover Beach,' and 'Sunday Morning' " (*CentR,* 1974) carries us not only into the modern period but also into American literature. Although there has been good work done in the latter area, this remains one of the promising fields for future research, as is suggested by Jonathan Wordsworth's discussion of affinities in "The Mind as Lord and Master: Wordsworth and Wallace Stevens" (*WC,* 1983). Herbert N. Schneidau's "Pound and Wordsworth on Poetry and Prose" in the good volume *Romantic and Modern: Revaluations of Literary Tradition,* edited by George Bornstein (1977), suggests one kind of rewarding topic. Neill R. Joy, "Two Possible Analogues for 'The Ponds' in *Walden*: Jonathan Carver and Wordsworth" (*ESQ,* 1978), links the American to the *Guide to the Lakes.* Thomas F. Heffernan describes Melville's annotations in his copy of Wordsworth in "Melville and Wordsworth" (*AL,* 1977), while Michael Hinden describes "Poe's Debt to Wordsworth: A Reading of 'Stanzas' " (*SIR,* 1969). Erna E. Kelly, in "Whitman and Wordsworth: Childhood Experiences and the Future Poet" (*WWR,* 1977), stresses similarities between *The Prelude* and "Out of the Cradle Endlessly Rocking." Sydney Lea is less respectful in "From Sublime to Rigamarole: Relations of Frost to Wordsworth" (*SIR,* 1980) and makes use of Frost's shrewd and amusing comments on Wordsworth in the *Cornell Library Journal* (1970); Lea's work bears comparison with David L. Miller's fine "Dominion of the Eye in Frost," *Frost: Centennial Essays,* volume 2 (1974 – 78). Reuben A. Brower, *The Poetry of Robert Frost* (1963), has many simple but apt comparisons between the two poets.

John W. Stevenson, "Seeing Is Believing: Wordsworth's Modern Vision" (*VQR,* 1977), identifies Wordsworth as the source of affirmative features in such moderns as Yeats, Eliot, Stevens, and Roethke; Lawrence Kramer describes "Ocean and Vision: Imaginative Dilemma in Wordsworth, Whitman, and Stevens" (*JEGP,* 1980), while David Simpson, "Pound's Wordsworth; or, Growth of a Poet's Mind" (*ELH,* 1978), draws parallels between the *Cantos* and Wordsworth's longer poems. More ambitious, Robert Rehder, *Wordsworth and the Beginnings of Modern Poetry* (1981), ranges widely, even diffusely, but makes some acute remarks on tradition. George Bornstein, *Transformations of Romanticism in Yeats, Eliot, and Stevens* (1976), works intelligently from the base of Abrams' comments on the "Greater Romantic Lyric," and Frank Kermode's *Romantic Image* (1957) is generally useful but without much for Wordsworthians, who may appreciate more Charles Altieri, "From Symbolist Thought to Immanence: The Ground of Postmodern American Poetics" (*Boundary 2,* 1973). For more specific consideration of our man in the general advance (if that's what it is) of Western culture, there is Brian Wilkie, "Wordsworth and the Tradition of the Avant Garde" (*JEGP,* 1973), crediting Wordsworth with leading the way for artists pursuing novelty for its own sake, and Marion Montgomery, *The Reflective Journey toward Order* (1973), presenting him as a major figure in the emergence of modernism. Jonathan Arac, "Romanticism, the Self, and the City: *The Secret Agent* in Literary History" (*Boundary 2,* 1980), uses Wordsworth to show Conrad's participation in "a major strand of literary history from the period of the French Revolution to the Great War" by pointing out that "Wordsworth's language is more duplicitous" than modernist critics have acknowledged and that Wordsworth and Conrad share the "art of being off center." Nice ending points for this too selective section are essays by Laurence Goldstein, "Wordsworth and Snyder: The Primitivist and His Problem of Self-Definition" (*CentR,* 1977), and Colin Butler, "Margaret Drabble: *The Millstone* and Wordsworth" (*ES,* 1978), Drabble being the author of a vivacious rather than weighty biography of our hero.

The Critic Wordsworth

Thanks to its superficiality, D. D. Devlin's *Wordsworth and the Poetry of Epitaphs* (1981) is an easy introduction to the difficulties of Wordsworth as a critic, particularly since the book is not disfigured by unseemly references to previous scholarship. Although Devlin sails past all the subtleties in Wordsworth's critical pronouncements from the "Advertisement" to the 1798 *Lyrical Ballads* to the 1815 "Essay, Supplementary to the Preface" and the "Letter to a Friend of Burns"

(1816), he does note most of the major statements and does refer to several of the more important letters. To my mind, these would include those to Coleridge (Feb. 1799), Charles James Fox (Jan. 1801), John Taylor (Apr. 1801), John Wilson (June 1802), Sara Hutchinson (June 1802), Sir George Beaumont (May 1805 and Jan. 1808), Lady Beaumont (May 1807), Francis Wrangham (June 1808), Lord Lonsdale (Feb. 1819), W. S. Landor (Jan. 1824), James Montgomery (Jan. 1824), and William R. Hamilton (Sept. 1827 and Dec. 1829). Markham L. Peacock's *The Critical Opinions of William Wordsworth* (1950) is helpful for pursuing letter citations and for his selection of the notes dictated to Isabella Fenwick, an invaluable source for Wordsworth's later opinions.

Devlin states clearly, if too simply, the difficulty of Wordsworth's situation as it has been defined by the best commentators, whom Devlin doesn't trouble to mention: "at the meeting point of . . . Renaissance and Romantic views of poetry and their different implications for the kind of audience the poet will have or will wish to have." At this critical cusp, the epitaph, which can "comprehensively and triumphantly reconcile" the voice of the responsible public speaker and the privacy of the modern poet, becomes pivotal. The three *Essays on Epitaphs* (of which only one was published during Wordsworth's lifetime), therefore, are central to Devlin, though he recognizes that Wordsworth's later poetry is less epitaphic than his earlier.

This seeming discrepancy between critical articulation and success in poetic accomplishment has been discussed more usefully in one of the important works Devlin ignores, James A. W. Heffernan's *Wordsworth's Theory of Poetry: The Transforming Imagination* (1969). Heffernan feels that Wordsworth's theories developed in both subtlety and significance after 1800, as he moved from an idea of poetry as "transcription" to poetry as "transformation" and increasingly emphasized "imagination" rather than "feeling." One may note here that a critic like Jonathan Wordsworth, in *The Music of Humanity,* describes much the same movement but sees it as signaling a *loss* of poetic power. Heffernan, however, tends to rate the later poetry more highly than most do; for example, "the *White Doe of Rylstone,* written in what is most often regarded as the period of Wordsworth's decline, represents rather a terminus ad quem in the gradually heightened exercise of his imaginative power," which for Heffernan is to be associated with emblematizing. By concentrating on principles of fusion, interchange, and "freshness of apprehension—a freshness which is the essence of imaginative apprehension," Heffernan builds a case for seeing a coherent evolution in both Wordsworth's verse and his criticism, and, unlike Devlin, he tries to take fully into account the work of earlier commentators.

An interesting development of Heffernan's position will be found in Gene Ruoff's "Religious Implications of Wordsworth's Imagination" (*SIR,* 1973), which argues that for Wordsworth imagination functions "within the world of phenomenal reality rather than serving as a means of transcending it." This view ought not to be ignored, because the premises of many modern critics do, in fact, uncritically assume a relation between "imagination" and "religion" considerably less complex in Wordsworth than the evidence justifies, a point made in different fashions by Wellek (see immediately below) and earlier by R. D. Havens, *The Mind of a Poet* (1941), who flatly asserts that for Wordsworth imagination "was not an instrument for the discovery of truth." A difficult work, at least for those whose German is wobbly, but important to the question at issue here is Hubert Wurmbach's *Das Mystiche Element in der Dichtung und Theorie von William Wordsworth* (1975), which defines Wordsworth not as a mystic but as part of a tradition of the "mystical doctrine of mediation," which enables him to move his theoretical work beyond the mere opposition of expressive and imitative poetry. A different view is presented by Katharine M. Wilson, however, in her brief discussion of Wordsworth in "Imagination and Mysticism" (*Theoria to Theory: An International Journal of Science, Philosophy and Contemplative Religion,* 1976).

A perfect complement to Heffernan's book appeared in the same year, 1969: W. J. B. Owen's *Wordsworth as Critic.* Owen is concerned primarily with sequential exegesis, slogging, line by line, through each main document in the Wordsworth critical canon, and he pays little heed to earlier commentators — Abrams is mentioned thrice and Wellek not at all. So far as Owen uses any critical framework, it is from M. H. Abrams' *The Mirror and the Lamp: Romantic Theory and the Critical Tradition* (1953), in which Wordsworth plays an important if not dominating role. Abrams' claim for the transformation of mimetic theories of poetry into expressive theories is applied very judiciously to Wordsworth, who is seen by Abrams as committed to essentially an "expressive" point of view that gives primacy to the feeling of the artist rather than to the artist's attempt to reflect reality, yet whose strong leanings to earlier, more mimetic rhetorical attitudes is admirably displayed. Abrams is especially persuasive in urging Wordsworth's reliance on earlier ideas of the common nature of humanity. Yet to my mind, René Wellek's chapter on Wordsworth in volume 2 of his *A History of Modern Criticism: 1750–1950* (1955; rpt. 1966) is superior, because Wellek more thoroughly, even frustratingly, defines the paradoxes and inconsistencies of Wordsworth's criticism as giving it unique strength and interest. While Wellek does not deny a certain evolution of Wordsworth's critical ideas, he finds those ideas "ambiguous or transitional" and insists, furthermore, that we recognize a "distinction between statements in prose and statements in verse." Wellek points out that in the earlier criticism "Wordsworth sounds like a naturalist defending the imitation of folk ballads and rustic speech" but that he actually "assimilates Spenser, Milton, Chaucer, and Shakespeare to his concept of 'nature' without making them over into primitives," in this as in other ways distinguishing himself from some of the superficially similar German theorists and practitioners at the end of the eighteenth century. In the early pronouncements, Wellek sees Wordsworth conceiving of poetry "as primarily a manipulation of human feelings for a purpose: for man's mental and moral health and happiness," not "as the conveyance of moral propositions or truth," and as the poet grew older he became "more simply didactic and instructive." But even this formulation is too simple, because "Wordsworth disconcertingly vacillates among three epistemological principles," concludes Wellek, identifying these as, first, making imagination purely subjective, "an imposition of the human mind on the real world"; second, making the imagination "an illumination beyond the control of the conscious mind and even beyond the individual soul"; and third, and most often, an "in-between position which favors the idea of collaboration" between mind and world.

Among students of Wordsworth's criticism earlier than Abrams and Wellek, one may mention Roger Sharrock, "Wordsworth's Revolt against Literature" (*EIC,* 1953); Newton Stallknecht, *Strange Seas of Thought* (1945); and, way back, Marjorie L. (Barstow) Greenbie, *Wordsworth's Theory of Poetic Diction* (1917), whose concerns carry us toward the specific issues treated in the final section of this chapter. Before turning to those, however, I'll take a moment for a special matter, Coleridge and/against Wordsworth. T. S. Eliot, in his chapter "Wordsworth and Coleridge" in *The Use of Poetry and the Use of Criticism* (1933), regards the older man as the more powerful and influential *critical* mind, best understood in terms of the intensity of Wordsworth's social and political commitments. "You may say that this public spirit is irrelevant to Wordsworth's greatest poems; never-theless I believe that you will understand a great poem like 'Resolution and In-dependence' better if you understand the purposes and social passions which animated its author; and unless you understand these you will misread Words-worth's literary criticism entirely." These passions, for Eliot, are the root of Wordsworth's "profound spiritual revival" in "the mind of an age of conscious change," essential alike to his criticism and to a poetry that is "the expression of a totality of unified interest." Eliot's manner of response to both poetry and criti-cism is hardly in keeping with recent fashions, and he seems equally out-of-date in minimizing the differences and disagreements between Wordsworth and Cole-ridge while portraying their critical endeavors as essentially similar and unified. To my mind, this view is fundamentally correct, in part because of the "symbio-sis" described by Thomas McFarland in *Romanticism and the Forms of Ruin* (1981) and in part because of the different analysis of Stephen Prickett in *Coleridge and Wordsworth: The Poetry of Growth* (1970). Prickett carefully distin-guishes the work and thinking of the two men, but he perceives the distinctions as grounded in basic similarities in religiously oriented ideas of imagination and a parallel understanding of perception as growth, with equivalent development of the ambiguities deriving from each writer's giving importance to "projection" as well as to "receptivity." It is possible to affirm, in fact, that explorations of dif-ferences between the poets' critical pronouncements and practical principles are the base for the work of both McFarland and Prickett, the latter being particu-larly helpful in depicting distinctions between the two poets' equally powerful resistance to mechanistic and deterministic systems.

The opposite position, however, is tenable, though Jean-Pierre Mileur's *Vi-sion and Revision: Coleridge's Art of Immanence* (1982) is not successful on this point, primarily because of his failure (characteristic of Coleridgeans) to recog-nize the complexity of Wordsworth's views, though Mileur's picture of Coleridge dispersing his selfhood as a kind of protest against the Wordsworthian "identity" is not without interest. Because of his focus on Coleridge, however, Mileur fails to take into account the fashion in which the younger man's misinterpretations of Wordsworth's criticism have tended to obscure the originals and their true difference from Coleridge's ideas—the topic of Don H. Bialostosky's extremely valuable "Coleridge's Interpretation of Wordsworth's Preface to *Lyrical Ballads*" (*PMLA*, 1978). Because Bialostosky believes there are crucial differences, he makes a cogent plea for breaking free from the debilitating misconception that the Preface is merely Wordsworth's inept effort to express Coleridgean ideas, that, in George Saintsbury's words, Coleridge was "one of the finest critics in the world" while his friend had "by no means all, or even very many, of the qualifications of a critic" (*A History of Criticism*, 1900–04), or, more recently, in George Watson's words, that "Wordsworth was badly out of his depth as a critic" (*The Literary Critics*, 1962). These views, despite T. S. Eliot, have been so prevalent that there has been surprisingly little useful study of Wordsworth and Coleridge as interdependent critics. The recognition that Wordsworth's Preface is not what Coleridge claimed—"half a child of my own brain"—could be, as Bialostosky says, "momentous for Anglo-American criticism." One should notice here the persistent argument of John O. Hayden for recognition of the importance of the Aristotelian position, in "Coleridge, the Reviewers, and Wordsworth" (*SP*, 1971), *Polestar of the Ancients* (1979), and "Wordsworth and Coleridge: Shattered Mirrors, Shining Lamps?" (*WC*, 1981).

Among the earlier studies that insist on differences between the poets as critics, one should certainly look up Stephen Parrish's "The Wordsworth-Coleridge Controversy" (*PMLA*, 1958) on the matter of point of view and his "Wordsworth and Coleridge on Meter" (*JEGP*, 1960), as well as M. H. Abrams' thoughtful discussions in *The Mirror and the Lamp* (1953) or, for a more concentrated presentation, his "Wordsworth and Coleridge on Diction and Figures" (*English Institute Essays*, 1952). For clear and forceful instances of the Coleridgean bias, one may consult with profit T. M. Raysor, "Coleridge's Criticism of Wordsworth" (*PMLA*, 1939), and C. D. Thorpe, "The Imagination: Coleridge versus Wordsworth" (*PQ*, 1939), but James Engell's introduction to the second volume of the *Biographia Literaria* in the *Collected Coleridge* presents this bias more judiciously. The Coleridge section of this volume cities several works primarily devoted to Coleridge but with valuable remarks on his relations with Wordsworth.

Language, Poetic Forms, the Imagining of Nature

Just when I was starting to recover from the trauma of recognizing this project to be one in which I could only lose friends and create enemies, the horrid realization dawned that there is *no* valid fashion in which to categorize the material I am supposed to be organizing. The problem is not that many items don't readily fit a limited set of categories, for example, A. H. Gomme's "Some Wordsworthian Transparencies" (*MLR*, 1973), which deals with how the poet projects feelings on "imaginary or partly imaginary figures," or Arden Reed's "Abysmal Influence: Baudelaire, Coleridge, De Quincey, Piranesi, Wordsworth" (*Glyph*, 1978), which treats influence as involuntary repetition and distinguishes Wordsworth from the other poets (using the Solitary from *The Excursion* to exemplify) because he gives visionary articulation from the point of view of death, not life. No, the problem is exactly the opposite: both good essays and good books actually fit most, sometimes even all, one's categories. Herein lies the explanation for the failure of the abstract in our discipline; a good piece of humanistic research inevitably penetrates logical classificatory boundaries. So a survey such as this must define its perspective, which determines the source of its system of categorizing and the ground of assignment of items. My comments have defined my system of critical values more precisely than could any abstract statement of them, and I write at the end of February 1982. At this date, it appears that studies of Wordsworthian imagery and tropes, language and syntax, forms and genres are coalescing and interpenetrating. The coalescence manifests important if confusing trends in Wordsworthian criticism since the appearance of the first edition of this volume, trends that in this final section I try to illuminate and evaluate.

Brian Morris, in "Mr. Wordsworth's Ear" (*WC*, 1979), and Jenny Guest, in "Wordsworth and the Music of Humanity" (*CR*, 1978), consider the musical qualities of the verse, the first centering on the poet's sensitivity to natural sound, the second on cadences of speech. John Hollander, "Wordsworth and the Music of Sound" in *New Perspectives on Coleridge and Wordsworth,* edited by Geoffrey Hartman (1972), remains the best starting place for analysis of sound and musicality, the history of which, however, is surprisingly lengthy. The first study I know is that of W. A. Heard, "A Few Thoughts upon Wordsworth's Treatment of Sound" in *Transactions of the Wordsworth Society* (1884). J. C. Smith, *A Study of Wordsworth* (1944), provides a pedestrian but accurate listing of the evidence for the poet's alertness to sound and music—and has the best comment I've encountered on another of Wordsworth's senses: "for olfactory purposes that haughty nose of his was a barren promontory." John Hollander also includes Wordsworth in *The Figure of Echo* (1981), which surveys how Milton's poetry echoes in, and is echoed by, later poetry. But of more value to Wordsworthians is William C. Stephenson, "The Mirror and the Lute: Wordsworth's Fine Art of Poetic Auscultation" (*YES*, 1976), a careful analysis of the poet's use of mirroring and echoing. Stephenson notes that Wordsworth's reverberative technique involves "not naive recovery of something that has been lost but reopening of circuits from the perspective of the original experience." Both Paul Sheats, *The Making of Wordsworth's Poetry* (1973), and Don H. Bialostosky, *Making Tales* (1984), present valuable discussions of metrics, as does Lee M. Johnson in *Wordsworth's Metaphysical Verse* (1982).

Although all criticism of poetry is about language, there are some critics, like Hans Aarsleff, "Wordsworth, Language, and Romanticism" (*EIC*, 1980), developed in Aarsleff's book *From Locke to Saussure* (1982), who address the "problem of language of a poet's epoch," as does Gene Ruoff in "Wordsworth on Language: Toward a Radical Poetics for English Romanticism" (*WC*, 1972), while others concentrate on a specific feature of the artist's linguistic arsenal, as for example Christopher Ricks, "The Twentieth-Century Wordsworth" in *Twentieth-Century Literature in Retrospect,* edited by Reuben A. Brower (1971), who studies Wordsworth's prepositions, or Frances O. Austin, who in "Time, Experience and Syntax in Wordsworth's Poetry" (*NM,* 1969) emphasizes the poet's fondness for the *of*-adjunct, seeing the linguistic separating of a quality of an object from the object so obtained as embodying Wordsworth's hovering between "objective" and "subjective" perception. Closer to Ricks than Aarsleff is C. C. Barfoot, "Key Perspective, the Tonality of Tense in Some Poems of Wordsworth" (*ES,* 1973), dealing mainly with "Peele Castle," "The Solitary Reaper," and "Resolution and Independence" to show the relations of tenses and emotional changes. Robert Holkeboer and Nadean Bishop discuss "Wordsworth on Words" (*WC,* 1975), as does Geoffrey Hartman in a more metaphysically liberated fashion in "Words, Wish, Worth: Wordsworth" in *Deconstruction and Criticism,* edited by Harold Bloom et al. (1979), and in "Diction and Defense in Wordsworth" in *The Literary Freud: Mechanisms of Defense and the Poetic Will,* edited by Joseph H. Smith (1980). Here one might look at an exchange in *Essays in Criticism* begun by Gerald Solomon, "Wordsworth and 'The Art of Lying,' " (1977), which uses a Freudian approach to argue that Wordsworth sought to recapture aspects of his childhood by deliberate confusions in his language. Jane Sturrock replied ("Heaven Lies") in the journal the following year (which includes a feeble rejoinder by Solomon) and pointed out factual errors and improbabilities in Solomon's readings. Julian and Zelda Boyd in "The Perfect of Experience" (*SIR,* 1977) point to Wordsworth's liking for present-perfect verb forms to bring the past into the present. Geoffrey Durrant, "Wordsworth and the Poetry of Objects" (*Mosaic,* 1971), proposes that the poet's "simple language" not merely resists the falsity of poetic diction but also expresses faith in the integrity of his experiences in the phenomenal world. Stephen K. Land, however, in "The Silent Poet: An Aspect of Wordsworth's Semantic Theory" (*UTQ,* 1973), explains the paradox that the poet creates "situations which necessarily transcend language precisely because they are fitting subjects for poetry." Will Christie in "Wordsworth and the Language of Nature" (*WC,* 1983) sees two "natural" languages in the poet's art and his criticism, one transparent, one symbolic. Despite the virtues of these later studies, still one of the best analyses of Wordsworth's rhetoric is Roger N. Murray's *Wordsworth's Style: Figures and Themes in the Lyrical Ballads of 1800* (1967), a book brief, original, and pedagogically useful, though Keith Hinchliffe in "Wordsworth and the Kinds of Metaphor" (*SIR,* 1984) has shown how detailed analyses of "joining—and connecting—words" can reveal Wordsworth's search, especially in *The Prelude,* "for terms in which he can speak simultaneously of mental and physical, rather than driving between them the wedge of analogy."

Michael McKie, in "Shelley, Wordsworth and the Language of Dissent" (*EIC,* 1978), argues against an essay by Richard Cronin in the same journal the previous year, "Shelley's Language of Dissent." Cronin claims that the attempt to transform the relation of ordinary language and poetic diction of the Romantics involved them in a self-contradictory struggle against the very nature of language. An earlier treatment of related issues appears in G. S. Fraser's "Common Speech and Poetic Diction in Wordsworth," in *Tribute to Wordsworth,* edited by Muriel Spark and Derek Stanford (1950). Jim Springer Borck, in "Wordsworth's *The Prelude* and the Failure of Language" (*SEL,* 1973), sees the poet as dissatisfied with language used by adults for dealing with childhood experiences. A Marxist treatment of similar matters is John Clay's "English Romantics and the Working Class" (*Literature and Ideology,* 1973); but A. E. Dyson's "Symbiosis in Wordsworth" (*Critical Survey,* 1973) is more original in suggesting how the poet attains complex effects with simple words, and Richard Payne's " 'The Style and Spirit of the Elder Poets': *The Ancient Mariner* and English Literary Tradition" (*MP,* 1978) addresses thoughtfully Wordsworth's response to archaisms in Coleridge's poem—though the ideas in both of these last two essays may be enriched by consideration of R. D. Havens' essay "Simplicity, a Changing Concept" (*JHI,* 1953). For readers of German, Jurgen Schlaeger, *Imitatio und Realisation: Funktionen Poetischer Sprache von Pope bis Wordsworth* (1974), focuses on the later poet, showing how his verse reflects his new conception of the poem as event, and includes a careful reading of "Tintern Abbey" with discussions of the use of the first person in longer poems.

Just as in commentaries on language one perceives an increasing tendency to insist on the interdependence of language and form, so one recognizes in recent critiques of form a willingness to grapple with complexities arising from the poet's consciousness of the inseparability of linguistic and generic structurings. It seems to be usual now to regard the very dubieties, even confusions, of the poet's experiments with form and ordering as essential to full comprehension of his achievement. Jeffrey Robinson, for example, in his analysis "The Structure of Wordsworth's Memorials of a Tour in Scotland, 1803" (*PLL,* 1977) demonstrates the importance of the poet's additions, deletions, and reorderings, and J. Hillis Miller, in "The Still Heart: Poetic Form in Wordsworth" (*NLH,* 1971), sees the Westminster Bridge sonnet as exemplifying the poet's success at making the problem of form a crucial thematic element in his best work. *Wordsworth and the Sonnet* by Lee M. Johnson (1973), the principal book on the subject, is of interest both for its analyses of specific poems and for suggestions about Wordsworth's final arrangement of his sequences. Johnson sees the sonnets as bearing a "synecdochic" relation to the other poems, but because he works from the final form of the poems his fine work calls out for a follow-up treating more adequately the evolution of Wordsworth's career as a sonneteer and of the sequences. G. M. Harvey, "The Design of Wordsworth's Sonnets" (*ArielE,* 1975), does not provide these, for he concentrates instead on a pattern of interaction he detects in the best examples between a "sympathetic" and an "ironic" voice. Seraphia D. Leyda in "Wordsworth's *Sonnets upon the Punishment of Death*" (*WC,* 1983) defends the poet's argument against superficial misreadings.

In *Romantic Narrative Art* (1960), I addressed Wordsworth's contributions to the development of literary balladry and what I called the "personal epic." Albert B. Friedman's treatment in *The Ballad Revival: Studies in the Influence of Popular on Sophisticated Poetry* (1961) went beyond my modest beginning—though anyone who wants to understand fully popular ballads ought to consult Bertrand H. Bronson, *The Ballad as Song* (1969). As for epic, Brian Wilkie left me far behind with his chapter on Wordsworth in *Romantic Poets and Epic Tradition* (1965). Two years later (1967) appeared Abbie Findlay Potts's posthumously published *The Elegiac Mode: Poetic Form in Wordsworth and Other Elegists,* dealing in particular with the Lucy poems, *Peter Bell,* and *The Prelude* and *The Excursion.* With a more modern orientation Paul H. Fry, in *The Poet's Calling in the English Ode* (1980), gives Wordsworth ample attention. Fry, unlike some moderns, generously acknowledges his debts to his predecessors, notably Kurt Schlüter, *Die Englische Ode* (1964); Carol Maddison, *Apollo and the Nine* (1960); and even George N. Shuster, *The English Ode from Milton to Keats* (1940). Irene H. Chayes, "Rhetoric as Drama: An Approach to the Romantic Ode" (*PMLA,* 1964), only touches on Wordsworth peripherally but is valuable to anyone concerned with his manipulations of this form.

Harold E. Toliver's *Pastoral Forms and Attitudes* (1971), a comprehensive survey of the entire tradition, has three chapters important to Wordsworth's verse and supersedes the historicism of L. N. Broughton's *The Theocritean Element in the Works of William Wordsworth* (1920) and the suggestions of Renato Poggioli in "The Pastoral of the Self" (*Daedalus,* 1959). It is not so far from the pastoral to the epitaphic, as more than one critic has noticed, one route indicated by Geoffrey Hartman's ground-breaking "Wordsworth, Inscriptions, and Romantic Nature Poetry" in *From Sensibility to Romanticism,* edited by Frederick W. Hilles and Harold Bloom (1965). Ernest Bernhardt-Kabisch has two useful essays on the epitaphic, "Wordsworth: The Monumental Poet" (*PQ,* 1965) and "The Epitaph and the Romantic Poets: A Survey" (*HLQ,* 1967), while Paul H. Fry extends the subject in "The Absent Dead: Wordsworth, Byron, and the Epitaph" (*SIR,* 1978). Other works already mentioned that treat this topic include, of course, Devlin's book, W. J. B. Owen's chapter "Essays upon Epitaphs" in his *Wordsworth as Critic* (1969), and Frances Ferguson's *Wordsworth: Language as Counter-Spirit* (1977), the title of which comes from the third of those essays.

Many works already cited, such as those treating "Michael" as pastoral, have much to say about form, as does M. H. Abrams in a more inclusive fashion, not only in his fine "Structure and Style in the Greater Romantic Lyric," in *From Sensibility to Romanticism,* but also illuminatingly, if peripherally, in his comprehensive "English Romanticism: The Spirit of the Age," in *Romanticism Reconsidered,* edited by Northrop Frye (1963). Frye himself, of course, talks a great deal about form, but it is perhaps significant that he says little about Wordsworth in his *A Study of English Romanticism* (1968). Wordsworth's fashion of categorizing is certainly different from Frye's. A book-length consideration of the ramifications of its peculiarities is James Scoggins' *Imagination and Fancy: Complementary Modes in the Poetry of Wordsworth* (1967), perhaps most valuable in suggesting how the categories, especially "Fancy" and "Imagination," are complementary, though Frances Ferguson in *Language as Counter-Spirit* treats the relations more mechanically. The most important essay on this topic is Gene W. Ruoff's "Critical

Implications of Wordsworth's 1815 Categorization, with some Animadversions on Binaristic Commentary" (*WC,* 1978). Ruoff argues forcibly through display of the evidence of Wordsworth's shiftings that the categories express the poet's "awareness of diversity" rather than "his desire for unity," his "proclivity for using form against itself," and his pleasure in seeing works in one class as complementary to those of all other classes. Simplified structural analyses, therefore, seriously distort Wordsworth's accomplishment. Ruoff's dissertation, "Wordsworth's Categorization and Arrangement of His Shorter Poems" (Univ. of Wisconsin, 1970), remains the most complete systematic study of this subject and serves as the basis for the elaborate analyses of Donald Ross, Jr., in "Poems 'Bound Each to Each' in the 1815 Edition of Wordsworth" (*WC,* 1981). Ross in essence confirms Ruoff's judgments, though he is a bit more rigid in his evaluations, but the essay provides some useful tabular evidence. Ross also makes use of Judith B. Herman's sensible and unpretentious "The Poet as Editor: Wordsworth's Edition of 1815" (*WC,* 1978), in which she suggests that one of Wordsworth's motives was to "represent" poems previously misunderstood so as to gain them acceptance. Allan Briesmaster, "Wordsworth as a Teacher of 'Thought' " (*WC,* 1980), provides a careful meditation on several aspects of Wordsworthian form, taking off from Ruoff's suggestions. James A. W. Heffernan's plaintive "Mutilated Autobiography: Wordsworth's *Poems* of 1815" (*WC,* 1979) may appear to be a complaint about the Dartmouth library but in fact is an argument for the issuing of a facsimile of the 1815 edition with a suggestion that its schematic form was an alternative to the dynamically continuous autobiography Wordsworth couldn't bring himself to publish.

The recent interest in the ordering of forms is strikingly different from the interest in description and analysis of imagery that dominated the forties and fifties. There was then a good deal of searching out of patterns of imagery throughout the corpus, though the popularity of New Critical methods assured that there were plenty of studies of specific poems, for example, Kenneth MacLean, "The Water Symbol in *The Prelude* (1805 – 6)" (*UTQ,* 1948), and Cleanth Brooks on the Intimations Ode, already mentioned. M. H. Abrams' "The Correspondent Breeze: A Romantic Metaphor" (*KR,* 1957), James R. Baird's "Wordsworth's 'Inscrutable Workmanship' and the Emblems of Reality" (*PMLA,* 1953), Carl Robinson Sonn's "An Approach to Wordsworth's Earlier Imagery" (*ELH,* 1960), and C. J. Smith's "The Contrarieties: Wordsworth's Dualistic Imagery" (*PMLA,* 1954) give the flavor of that epoch's taste: though each essay uses specific texts and concentrates on particular patterns of imagery, each makes general statements about the poet's characteristic usages and style. R. A. Foakes, *The Romantic Assertion* (1958), and Bernard Blackstone, *The Lost Travellers* (1962), more mechanically find dominant symbols of journeying derived from repeated images. C. C. Clarke, *Romantic Paradox* (1962), begins to point toward later attitudes by dwelling on Wordsworth's use of the words "image" and "form" as well as on figures and syntax. A major realization of the earlier mode is Florence Marsh, *Wordsworth's Imagery* (1952), which, besides discussing Wordsworth's theory of imagery, presents a compendium of recurrent images in the poetry. Marsh's work is analogous to the vocabulary and syntactical studies of Josephine Miles, first in *Wordsworth and the Vocabulary of Emotion* (1942), subsequently in a chapter in *Eras and Modes in English*

Poetry (1957). Miles's work was slightly anticipated by F. B. Snyder's "Wordsworth's Favorite Words" (*JEGP,* 1923), which cites forty-eight such words from the Cooper concordance. William Empson inverts, as it were, Miles's system by concentrating on a single word, "Sense in *The Prelude*," in *The Structure of Complex Words* (1951), whereas Ellen Leyburn more conventionally traces "Recurrent Words in *The Prelude*" (*ELH,* 1949). That works of this type do not now appear frequently is interesting because of our ever more intensely focused attention on details of Wordsworth's syntactic structures, figurative language, and dominant metaphors.

The basic thrust of the stylistically oriented essays of the forties and fifties seems to me in part revealed by Frederick A. Pottle's essay "The Eye and the Object in the Poetry of Wordsworth," in the *Centenary Studies* edited by Dunklin (1951). Pottle, through an analysis of "I Wandered Lonely as a Cloud," defines what we would now call the parameters of Wordsworth's images and tropes by exploring two contradictory statements from the *Lyrical Ballads* Preface: "poetry takes its origin from emotion recollected in tranquillity" and "I have at all times endeavored to look steadily at my subject." To Pottle the second sentence means that so far as the poet's "subject is drawn from nature . . . there is implied a lifelong habit of close, detailed, and accurate observation of the objects composing the external universe." There is a temporal dimension to Wordsworthian accuracy, which is the opposite of mathematical, mechanical, analytic accuracy. Pottle accepts Whitehead's description of the precision sought by Wordsworth, who "dwells on that mysterious presence of surrounding things, which imposes itself on any separate element that we set up as an individual for its own sake." Wordsworth "always grasps the whole of nature as involved in the tonality of the particular instance." Pottle then points out that the "subject" Wordsworth speaks of "is not an object of external nature" but a mental image "seen by not the physical but the inward eye." The mental image that is the poet's subject "accompanies or is the source of emotion recollected in tranquillity; it recurs in memory not once but many times; and on each occasion he looks at it steadily to see what it *means*."

Pottle, therefore, denies that Wordsworth's poetry is "descriptive" in the usual sense. The poet's special accuracy and special subjects lead him to connect "deeply imaginative effects with a sense of infinity"—not nothingness, not absence. For Pottle, Wordsworth's imagination begins "when the edges of things begin to waver and fade out . . . where things are lost in each other, and limits vanish," and through imagination, as one moves from things to persons, oneself and others, "the impression of [personal] joy deepens into social joy."

William Wimsatt, in "The Structure of Romantic Nature Imagery," in his *The Verbal Icon* (1954), illustrates a complementary feature of style studies of the forties and fifties when he cites Wordsworth as one of the Romantic poets reacting against mechanistic (what we today recognize as structuralist) tendencies in the Enlightenment, developing a new kind of "wit," differing from that of the earlier poets such as the metaphysicals in its focus on implications, in making "less use of the central overt statement of similitude." In Romantic metaphor "both tenor and vehicle . . . are wrought in a parallel process out of the same matter"—the tenor "is likely to be subjective . . . not an object distinct from the vehicle." This is why the feat common to Romantic poets is "to read meanings into the landscape," meaning, however, "summoned out of the very surface of nature itself." Surface, not depth. Wimsatt insists that for the Romantics nature is "not transcending but immanent and breathing through all things," and, as Wordsworth supremely illustrates, Romantic poems dramatize "the spiritual through the use of the faint, the shifting, the least tangible and most mysterious part of nature." The Intimations Ode is representatively Romantic in its "blurring of literal and figurative" and "a strange yet artistic warping . . . of vehicle by tenor." This "sleight of words, and imposition of image upon image" is "the *modifying* power of imagination."

Wimsatt and Pottle (and one could cite Carlos Baker's introduction to the Rinehart edition of a selection of Wordsworth's poetry in 1948, with its attention to "superimposition") do not treat Wordsworth as a simple celebrant of the natural world. They are as interested as Hartman in the poet's consciousness, but for them consciousness is inseparable from relationships with other people, the natural world, and the poet's earlier self. I see the reorientation in Wordsworthian studies during the sixties, therefore, as founded not on a new appreciation for the poet's complexities but, rather, on a fundamental simplification: an assumption that alienation, not relation, is essential to Wordsworth, as to all human existences. So Hartman, to cite a central figure, argues for the poet's principal struggle as an effort to overcome alienation. The presupposition of an absolute and unpassable gulf between unself-conscious world and self-conscious mind, between human language and phenomenal actualities, that Altieri has identified as central to recent criticism inverts the assumptions from which Wimsatt and Pottle work, as is made plain in Paul de Man's "The Rhetoric of Temporality," in *Interpretation: Theory and Practice,* edited by Charles Singleton (1969), which in its latter half defines through analysis of "A Slumber Did My Spirit Seal" what de Man calls, significantly, the "predicament" of the Romantics. The "irony" de Man finds in this lyric supports his contention in the earlier portion of his essay that the Romantic poet does not engage in a true dialectic between mind and nature but instead represents nature allegorically, as something unknown, alien, on which the mind imposes its own structure. The essay only develops de Man's earlier "Structure intentionelle de l'image romantique" (*Revue Internationale de Philosophie,* 1960), translated and reprinted with trivial changes in *Romanticism and Consciousness,* edited by Harold Bloom (1970), and later in *Wordsworth: A Collection of Critical Essays,* edited by M. H. Abrams (1972). The climax of de Man's argument is founded on a juxtaposition en bloc of a passage from *La Nouvelle Héloïse,* two passages from *The Prelude* of 1850, and the opening lines of Hölderlin's "Heimkunft." The diverse contexts from which these excerpts have been untimely ripped are ignored, and the apparent indifference to rudimentary standards of scholarship is reinforced when de Man explains his 1850 *Prelude* passage by citing, without indicating that he has switched texts, intervening lines from the 1805 version. But de Man is not indifferent. By asserting the essential identity of three works in three languages spanning nearly a century, one in prose, the others in radically different forms of poetry, he dramatically affirms the preeminence of the critic's idea of an underlying structure. The specific works are of interest only insofar as they enable the critic to fabricate, to "misread."

Like Freudians who apply a ready-made template, de Man does not work inductively, as Wimsatt and Pottle do. Their essays are arranged to persuade us that the numerous and diversified illustrations they have gathered will illuminate implicit principles of ordering in the works they study. Pottle and Wimsatt have the same general style of quotation—many brief citations from a wide range of sources, with frequent use of contrastive quotations to elucidate subtle similarities. Paul de Man uses few large blocks of quotation. The contrast of his method to Wimsatt's is peculiarly impressive because both treat of metaphor. Simply asserting that "after Pope" the structure of poetic language "becomes increasingly metaphorical," de Man shows no interest in specifying the varieties of metaphor that are Wimsatt's interest. The specifics of discrimination are not to be found in de Man, because to him what matters is the gross structure of separation between signifier and signified, human fabrications of language and natural objects. He invariably discusses the separation in terms of "objects" and "words," since he ignores the possibility of a Whiteheadian view. Words and images, "entities engendered by consciousness," originate, he says, by employing "a negation of permanence, the discontinuity of death in which an entity relinquishes its specificity," whereas for "natural entities, like the flower, the process is entirely different" because "all particular flowers can at all times establish an immediate identity with an original Flower, of which they are as many particular emanations." So "natural objects" originate as "a natural emanation of a transcendental principle, as an epiphany . . . the rediscovery of a permanent presence." But "words do *not* originate like flowers . . . the word . . . designates a desire for an epiphany but necessarily fails to be an epiphany." For de Man what characterizes nineteenth-century poetry (essentially identical with Rousseau's eighteenth-century prose) is the reexperiencing and representing of the "adventure" of the "failure" of poetry to draw "closer and closer to the status of the object." The failure is inevitable because no relationship can "exist in actuality" between "matter and consciousness." So for de Man any sense of success in the Simplon Pass episode illustrates that by "imagination" Wordsworth means only the "possibility for consciousness to exist entirely by and for itself, independent of all relationships to the outside world."

An interesting study of some sources of "this curious theory of the uncommensurability of language and reality" in Sartre and Nietzsche (particularly useful on the difference between the latter's "eagerly conserving at the cost of all other values, the sense of being alive" and Wordsworth's power of finding reassurance in the objective realm) is A. D. Nuttall's *A Common Sky: Philosophy and the Literary Imagination* (1974), with several cogent analyses of Wordsworth's views. Development of the de Maniacal approach, extended and intensified by Derridean influences, moreover, seems already to be producing strong countermovements. We are not going to see, however, any simple return to the approach of the fifties, as Vendler's critique of Trilling indicates. There may be some revival of a Whiteheadian understanding of nature, simply because the biological sciences have moved in that direction—although when one observes how so distinguished a thinker as Paul de Man thinks flowers originate, one suspects that it may be some time before even rudiments of contemporary thinking in the life sciences flow into our discipline. But whether criticism draws on internal or external sources, to stay vital it must be self-transforming: it is arguable, for example, that de Man's resistance to the New Criticism, as illustrated in *Blindness and Insight*, accounts for some of his work's first popularity. Whatever the situation in literary art, the anxiety of influence is crippling in critical tradition, as one sees, for example, in Leslie Brisman's *Romantic Origins* (1978). Despite his energy in stylistic subtleties of presentation, reviewers find little in his focal interpretations of the Snowdon vision and the discharged soldier episode in *The Prelude* that adds to the substance of previous critiques. This puzzling failure, arousing the feeling that the criticism ought to be more illuminating than it is, seems a result of the author's reluctance radically to rethink the presuppositions of his mentors. For an instance of the opposite kind, one might cite James H. Averill, who has read Hartman with profit and learned from a conventional critic like Paul Sheats, yet in *Wordsworth and the Poetry of Human Suffering* (1980) strives to consider the poet's work in terms of a new understanding of literary sentimentalism.

The most intriguing harbinger of current rerevisionism now stirring in Wordsworthian studies to my mind is Margery Sabin's unpretentious and little-noticed *English Romanticism and the French Tradition* (1976) previously discussed. The implications of her discriminating between Wordsworth and Rousseau cannot indefinitely be disregarded. Sabin, who acknowledges Paul de Man as her original inspiration, recognizes that the tendency to conflate Rousseau and Wordsworth has flourished since Irving Babbitt early in this century. Freudian critics may become grumpy when shown Wordsworth displaying, in Sabin's words, "the extraordinary, almost miraculous freedom of the mind to re-create itself anew" and treating "the original shape and import of past experience" as not inviolate. Nor will all critics desire to be reminded of Wordsworth's commitment to a "tradition of poets and prophets who allow the human self to become worthy of reverence only because of the individual's bond to other forms of being." Yet the textual evidence is on Sabin's side, which is perhaps why she can afford a modesty of style pleasantly unusual among recent critics emphasizing strength, her style originating, she says, in her "discomfort with the widespread application of identical critical terms to writings... fundamentally different" and her consequent reluctance "to impose other, perhaps equally inadequate or over-restrictive labels."

Sabin's book, finally, points to Wordsworth's essential Englishness. Continental and American critics, for understandable reasons, have not emphasized this point, yet in the perspective of any genuinely comparative study Wordsworth must be recognized as profoundly English. This is not merely a biographical truism; rather, it illustrates a cultural fact of late eighteenth-century Europe. It manifests nationalism, that "creative faculty working in individuals and entire societies alike," theoretically defined by Herder and others, part of what Sir Isaiah

Berlin has identified as "the counter-enlightenment." Sir Isaiah's recent collection of essays (from which I have just quoted) articulating the complexities of this intellectual-aesthetic movement so vital to Romanticism is entitled *Against the Current* (1980), but if I have read the trend of Wordsworthian studies correctly the flow is toward absorption of new methodologies into an increasingly detailed and precise historical criticism.

Note

Warm thanks are due to Mark Jones for his proofreading and checking of citations. The report has benefited from careful readings by Jonathan Arac, Mark Reed, and Carl Woodring. These scholars can lay no claim, however, to credit for any errors of omission or commission, these being solely the product of my genius.

SAMUEL TAYLOR COLERIDGE

Max F. Schulz

Contents

Introduction

Scholarly and critical fashions wax and wane. Many of the issues that exercised generations of twenty to fifty years ago no longer raise an eyebrow. I have accordingly, in deference to current estimates of Coleridge and to immediate concerns (not least being space), summarized older critical positions but left unmentioned many works relevant to these issues and perhaps intrinsically deserving of inclusion but now seldom cited. Someone wishing information about these dated matters may consult the third edition of *ERP.* Together the chapters of the third and fourth editions cover comprehensively the reception of Coleridge over the past 150 years. So that readers may refer to both editions with a minimum of searching, especially when the issues overlap, I have tried to keep the same sequence in the sections on biography and criticism of poetry. Students of Coleridge otherwise should find the present review adequate for most purposes.

Bibliographies

There is need for a new descriptive bibliography of Coleridge's writings. Until that eventuality, Thomas J. Wise's *Bibliography* (1913) and supplement *Coleridge-iana* (1919) will have to do. Although free of forgeries it is not proof against careless ascription. Instances are detailed by George Whalley in "The Publication of Coleridge's 'Prometheus' Essay" (*N&Q,* 1969) and in "Coleridge's Sheet of Sonnets, 1796" (*TLS,* 23 Nov. 1956). Wise's collection of Coleridge first editions, manuscripts, and autograph letters described in *Two Lake Poets* (1927; rpt. 1965) and in his *Catalogue of the Ashley Library* (1922; rpt. 1971) is now in the British Museum. As for the latter, Fran Carlock Stephens reveals in "Cottle, Wise, and *MS. Ashley 408* (*PBSA,* 1974) that Wise's skill in bibliographical sophistication did not protect him from being taken in by the negligence of Cottle's indiscriminate combining of materials, leading Wise to mistake proofs for *Poems* (1796) as proofs for *Poems* (1797). And Mary Lynn Johnson, in reviewing the printing history and giving a working census of annotated copies of *Sibylline Leaves,* in "How Rare Is a 'Unique Annotated Copy' of Coleridge's *Sibylline Leaves?*" (*BNYPL,* 1975), notes in passing additional inaccuracies of Wise. Not strictly bibliographical yet helpful in their enumerative overview are Whalley's "Coleridge's Poetical Canon: Selection and Arrangement" (*REL,* 1966), which surveys the collections from *Poems* (1796) through the 1828, 1829 and 1834 editions, to Sara Coleridge's attempt at a chronological arrangement in 1852 and to the great editions of James Dykes Campbell (1893) and of Ernest Hartley Coleridge (1912), who rely respectively on the 1829 and 1834 editions, and Whalley's "On Reading Coleridge," in *S. T. Coleridge* (ed. R. L. Brett, 1971), which distinguishes between Coleridge's canonical and subcanonical (posthumously published) works and surveys "what books may be profitably read in what order" to get an idea of Coleridge's "work in detail and as a whole." Whalley has also compiled the analyzed list of successive authorized editions of Coleridge in volume 3 of *CBEL* (1969).

The major deposit of Coleridge materials, including the Ottery Collection, is in the British Museum. See the *General Catalogue of Printed Books,* volume 65 (1980), and *Catalogue of Additions to the Manuscripts.* Second in importance is "The Coleridge Collection in Victoria University Library, Toronto," analyzed by H. O. Dendurent (*WC,* 1974). The story of how these two collections after over one hundred years of caretaking by the Coleridge family came into public custody is recited by Kathleen Coburn, *In Pursuit of Coleridge* (1977). In personal terms she tells a fascinating (and for female scholars inspiring) narrative of her search, discovery, and delivery of the Coleridge papers into the sanctums of the British Museum and Bodleian and Victoria College libraries and of her dedication to the lifelong task of editing them.

Coleridgeiana elsewhere is described by diverse hands: at the Royal Malta Library and Palace Archives, Valletta, by Donald Sultana, in *Coleridge in Malta and Italy* (1969); at the Yale University Library, by William Hale White, in *Description of the Wordsworth and Coleridge Manuscripts in the Possession of Mr. T. Norton Longman* (1897), and by Cornelius H. Patton and Frederick A. Pottle (*YULG,* 1934, 1966); at the Huntington Library, by Roberta F. Brinkley (*HLQ,* 1945) and by Paul M. Zall (*WC,* 1971); at the University of Texas, by Fran Stephens (*Library Chronicle of the University of Texas,* 1970, and *The Hartley Coleridge Letters,* 1978); at Cornell University, by George Harris Healey, in *The Cornell Wordsworth Collection* (1957), which contains a section "Coleridge and His Family"; and at the University of Alberta, by Reynold Siemens, in *The Wordsworth Collection: Dove Cottage Papers Facsimiles* (1971), which lists several holographs and transcripts of Coleridge's poems. John Louis Haney's bibliography of 1903 has some continuing value, principally for its lists of portraits, poetical tributes, and parodies and imitations of Coleridge. And Chester L. Shaver and Alice C. Shaver include as part of *Wordsworth's Library: A Catalogue* (1977) the record of about three hundred books owned by Coleridge but in Wordsworth's care from roughly 1809 to 1829.

Annual reviews of Coleridge scholarship and criticism appear in the annual bibliography of the MLA (1922–) and in the sometimes annotated bibliography for the Romantic movement in *ELH* (1937–49), *PQ* (1950–64), *ELN* (1965–79), and since 1980 independently printed by Garland Publishing Company. The two checklists do not always duplicate each other, so both should be consulted. The latter has been collected in *The Romantic Movement Bibliography 1936–70* (7 vols., ed. A. C. Elkins, Jr., and L. J. Forstner, 1973). David V. Erdman's warning to "retrospective users" of this compilation is to the point. They should be aware of its "varying kinds of overlapping and omission in different years, as well as shifts of emphasis over the decades." There is also an annual survey, which includes doctoral dissertations and sparse summary of contents, in *WC* by diverse hands (Marilyn Gaull, 1971; Walter B. Crawford and Edward S. Lauterbach, 1972; Jane Matsinger, 1973–78; David M. Brown, 1979; Joseph S. Burman, 1980). With the Summer 1981 issue only books have been reviewed, by diverse hands.

Coleridgeans are blessed at the moment with several teams of selfless searchers after secondary sources. Richard Haven, Josephine Haven, and Maurianne Adams have compiled in *Samuel Taylor Coleridge: An Annotated Bib-*

liography of Criticism and Scholarship, Volume 1: 1793–1899 (1976) "all published references to Coleridge through 1834,... all books, articles, notes, and reviews exclusively or primarily devoted to him since that date, and all substantial or significant discussions of him in published material primarily concerned with other subjects." The years 1900 to the present in two, possibly three, volumes are being compiled by Walter Crawford, Ann Crawford, and Edward S. Lauterbach. So far, only volume 2, covering 1900 to 1939 (1983) has appeared. It contains, as well, a supplement of close to seven hundred items from 1795 to 1899. The Crawfords and Lauterbach, with Coleridgean zest for the grand project, aim to produce a bibliography so comprehensive and informative that "the most thorough Coleridge scholar can rely on it for all his 'literature search' for the period it covers." They have broadened their principles of selection, from the usual articles, books, reviews, and dissertations concerned explicitly with Coleridge, to encompass editions and anthologies with editorial contributions to Coleridge material and letters, journals, memoirs, autobiographies, and notebooks with unusual or fresh views of Coleridge. They also review items from more than twenty languages, along with translations of Coleridge's works, and extend the listings of Coleridgeiana to the visual and aural: illustrations, cartoons, film, television, radio, theater, videotapes, and sound-slide sets, musical scores and recordings, recorded readings and lectures, parodies and imitations, continuations and completions by other writers of Coleridge's unfinished poems, and a wide variety of other verbal and nonverbal artifacts. The next volume will contain in addition to the main bibliography for the years 1940– the section housing special lists of extraverbal materials. Computer compiled, the work is phenomenally free of errors. Coleridgean in scope and concern for method, this bibliography towers above previous such endeavors, a Xanadu among tract houses.

Until the Crawfords and Lauterbach finish their ambitious undertaking, one will have to make do for the latter part of the twentieth century with superannuated compilations and with checklists that are either highly selective or perfunctorily redactive of the annual bibliographies. The best, but now woefully dated, of the selected bibliographies is Virginia Kennedy and Mary Barton's (1935). Intended as a supplement, Jefferson D. Caskey and Melinda M. Stapper's *Samuel Taylor Coleridge: A Selective Bibliography of Criticism, 1935–1977* (1978) should be used with care, since it multiplies errors and misprints, nonchalantly cites reprints as if they were newly minted, and treats categories such as biography as heterogeneous catchalls for not easily assigned items. More specialized but more reliable is Mary Lee Taylor Milton's *The Poetry of Samuel Taylor Coleridge: An Annotated Bibliography of Criticism, 1935–1970* (1981), also conceived as a continuation of Kennedy-Barton. Entries are abstracted fully and accurately and avoid value judgments. Omitted from this compilation are dissertations, reviews, non-English-language works, most biographies, books on Coleridge that do not offer specific comments on his poetry, and works that do not deal with Coleridge but contain apposite facts and commentary—for example, Mark Reed's note on the dating of "Kubla Khan" in *Wordsworth: The Chronology of the Early Years 1770–1799* (1967). Donald H. Reiman, *English Romantic Poetry, 1800–1835: A*

Guide to Information Sources (1979), provides an intelligent selection, with evaluative annotations, of bibliography, editions (including collected, selected, general, special topic, and individual titles), biographical studies, criticism (subdivided into general, periods, particular works, and themes), and collections of miscellaneous essays. Philip C. Rule's "Coleridge's Reputation as a Religious Thinker: 1816–1972" (*HTR*, 1974), although properly speaking not a bibliography, offers a measured and judicious survey of articles and books on Coleridge as theologian and religious thinker, organized into four periods: 1816–59, 1860–1918, 1919–55, 1956–72. Additional checklists include Richard Harter Fogle's *Romantic Poets and Prose Writers* (1967) with 212 items; John Beer's "Coleridge, 1772–1834" in *English Poetry: Select Bibliographical Guides* (ed. A. E. Dyson, 1971) with 133 items plus an introductory discussion of the scholarship; and Whalley's essay in *S. T. Coleridge* (ed. R. L. Brett, 1971) with 143 items. "The Nineteenth Century: Romantic Period" in the *Year's Work in English Studies*, while limited in its coverage, includes European items that often do not get into the American bibliographies. For those desirous of tracking allusions to Coleridge, Crawford and Lauterbach have made a start with "Coleridge in Narrative and Drama" (*WC*, 1972, 1973), a short-title list of works, principally twentieth-century but some nineteenth, in which something apropos of Coleridge has been identified. Other bibliographies, mostly dated and of suspect value, are described in "Bibliography," *ERP3*.

On the contemporary response to Coleridge's published poems and nonbelletristic writings William S. Ward lists *Literary Reviews in British Periodicals . . . with a Supplementary List of General (Non-Review) Articles on Literary Subjects*, in four volumes: 1798–1820 (2 vols., 1972), 1821–26 (1977), and 1789–97 (1979). Because of the desultory issuing of these volumes, starting in the middle years and subsequently extending the peripheries, one needs to consult more than one volume to find all the reviews listed for some Coleridge publications. Ward's survey in *Some British Romantics* (ed. James V. Logan, John E. Jordan, and Northrop Frye, 1966) of "periodical literature"—reviews, magazines, and weekly journals—and of indexes and books on the subject is a useful place to start for a sense of "the worlds of fine thinking that 'lie buried in that vast abyss.'" Of limited use is William S. Ward's *British Periodicals and Newspapers, 1789–1832: A Bibliography of Secondary Sources* (1972), which lists books and articles written about the newspapers and periodicals of the period (there are seven pages on Coleridge), and Andrew Boyle's *An Index to the Annuals*, volume 1, *The Authors, 1820–1850* (1967), which lists poems, epigrams, songs, and lines of verse appearing in such annuals as *Friendship's Offering* and *Keepsake*.

Three publications have collected contemporary reviews and general estimates of Coleridge's works from 1794 to 1834: J. R. de J. Jackson's *Coleridge: The Critical Heritage* (1970); Donald Reiman's photofacsimile printing of *The Romantics Reviewed: Contemporary Reviews of British Romantic Writers*, part A, "The Lake Poets" (2 vols. 1972), which also gives brief introductions to the periodicals and headnotes to the reviews; and John O. Hayden's *Romantic Bards and British Reviews: A Selected Edition of Contemporary Reviews of the Works of Wordsworth,*

Coleridge, Byron, Keats, and Shelley (1971). All are selective, with Jackson offering the best coverage, especially for the early years through 1797, for which presumably Reiman was unable to find copies that could be efficiently reproduced for facsimile publication, and after 1824, which is Reiman's cutoff date. Jackson contains twenty-five reviews not in Reiman, while Reiman has twenty-three not in Jackson. Thus, both must be consulted in any attempt at inclusiveness for the years 1794–1834. Hayden's collection, restricted in coverage to "the best criticism of the best-known works," numbers less than a third of Jackson's and Reiman's. Supplementing Jackson's, Reiman's, Hayden's, and Haven's (see below) gatherings are Oliver Warner's printing of a favorable review of *Lyrical Ballads* in *Naval Chronicle* ("Coleridge's 'Naval Poetry' and Southey's 'Life of Nelson,'" *N&Q*, 1970), James Ogden and Peter A. Cook's identification of "two early critiques" of "The Ancient Mariner" and of "Love" (*VPN*, 1975), Theodore L. Fenner's "'The Traveller' Reports on Coleridge's 1811 Lectures" (*N&Q*, 1974), and Oskar Wellens' "Henry Crabb Robinson: Reviewer of Wordsworth, Coleridge ["Christabel"], and Byron in the *Critical Review*: Some New Attributions" (*BRH*, 1981). In "Gillman's Discovery of the 'Lost' *Times* Review of *Christabel*: An Aid to Reflection on Community among Scholars" (*WC*, 1975), Mary Lynn Johnson plaintively calls attention to the need for accurate information storage. David V. Erdman replies with an explanation of the unsystematic printing procedures in newspaper offices during the Regency period.

Several works review the reviewers. Derek Roper in *Reviewing before the "Edinburgh" 1788–1802* (1977) essays a fascinating picture of the small circle of writers who fed copy into the omnivorous maws of the eighteenth-century reviews and buttresses Hayden's observation that on the whole the reception of Coleridge's early poems was friendly and helpful and the critical treatment of *Lyrical Ballads* scarcely a hindrance to its success. Hayden in *The Romantic Reviewers 1802–1824* (1969) evaluates the response to Coleridge in the periodicals from 1811 (a review of the *Friend*) to 1818 (of the *Friend* again). In "The Ancient Mariner in the Nineteenth Century" (*SIR*, 1972), Haven analyzes early unpublished responses to and later criticisms of Coleridge's poem, while Adams examines more broadly the "Diverse and Deviant Standards of Poetry Criticism in Victorian Journalism: The Case for Coleridge" (*VPN*, 1977).

Collections of original essays and gatherings of important published articles on Coleridge, in order of appearance, include all-Coleridge or primarily Coleridge issues of *REL* (1966), *WC* (1972), and *SIR* (1972, 1982); *S. T. Coleridge,* edited by R. L. Brett (1971); *New Perspectives on Coleridge and Wordsworth,* edited by Geoffrey H. Hartman (1972); *Coleridge's Variety: Bicentenary Studies,* edited by J. Beer (1974); *Reading Coleridge: Approaches and Applications,* edited by W. B. Crawford (1979); and *New Approaches to Coleridge: Biographical and Critical Essays,* edited by Donald Sultana (1981). Behind most of the essays in *Evolution of Consciousness: Studies in Polarity: Essays in Honor of Owen Barfield,* edited by Shirley Sugerman (1976), stand the informing texts of Barfield, and behind them the informing minds of Coleridge and Rudolf Steiner. Previously published articles on Coleridge are also in *English Romantic Poets: Modern Essays in Criticism*, edited by M. H. Abrams (1975); *Coleridge: A Collection of Critical Es-*

says, edited by K. Coburn (1967); and R. H. Fogle, *The Permanent Pleasure: Essays on Classics of Romanticism* (1974). Casebooks with good selections of historically and critically important essays include Royal A. Gettmann's *"The Rime of the Ancient Mariner": A Handbook* (1966); James D. Boulger's *Twentieth-Century Interpretations of "The Rime of the Ancient Mariner": A Collection of Critical Essays* (1969); and Alun R. Jones and William H. Tydeman's *Wordsworth:* Lyrical Ballads: *A Casebook* (1972).

Editions

Publication of a pioneer editing of all Coleridge's writings—poems, prose, marginalia, lectures, letters, and notebooks—approaches flood tide. The end of the eighties should see most of it completed. After a century and a half of editorial partisanship, timidity, opportunism, and severely defined intentions, Coleridge will enter the twenty-first century with a sublimely conceived and meticulously executed text on which evaluations of him will be based for the next century or more. The chief architect and generalissimo of much of this intimidating task is Kathleen Coburn, ably seconded as associate editor by Bart Winer.

Sponsored by the Bollingen Foundation, the *Collected Coleridge* is a critical edition comprising sixteen titles in an ever-expanding number of volumes, now estimated at twenty-six or twenty-seven. It is arranged according to form of communication, unlike such earlier specialized editions as Thomas M. Raysor's *Coleridge's Shakespearean Criticism* (1930; rpt. 1960), which restricted itself to topic or subject. The works and their editors are *Lectures 1795: On Politics and Religion* (1 vol., 1971), edited by Lewis Patton and Peter Mann; *The Watchman* (1 vol., 1970), edited by L. Patton; *Essays on His Times* (3 vols., 1978), edited by David V. Erdman; *The Friend* (2 vols., 1969), edited by Barbara E. Rooke; *Lectures 1808–1819: On Literature* (2 vols., due 1985), edited by Reginald A. Foakes; *Lay Sermons* (1 vol., 1972), edited by R. J. White; *Biographia Literaria* (2 vols., 1983), edited by James Engell and Walter Jackson Bate; *Lectures 1818–1819: On the History of Philosophy,* edited by Owen Barfield; *Aids to Reflection,* edited by John Beer; *On the Constitution of the Church and State* (1 vol., 1976), edited by John Colmer; *Shorter Works and Fragments,* edited by J. R. de J. Jackson and H. J. Jackson; *Marginalia* (2 vols. to date, Abbt to Hutton, 1980–84, of a projected 5 vols.), edited by George Whalley; *Logic* (1 vol., 1981), edited by J. R. de J. Jackson; *Table Talk,* edited by Carl R. Woodring; *Opus Maximum,* edited by Thomas McFarland; *Poetical Works,* edited by J. C. C. Mays. Each volume carries a chronological table of Coleridge's life and of other historical and literary events at least up to composition and publication of the contents of the volume and often through 1834, frontispiece reproduction of a Coleridge portrait, facsimiles of manuscript and printed pages, statement of editorial policy, editor's introduction, and an index that attempts the impossible—an exhaustive analysis of the contents.

In *CC* 1 Patton and Mann print Coleridge's political lectures and pamphlets of 1795: *A Moral and Political Lecture, Conciones ad Populum,* "Lecture on the

Slave Trade," manuscript version of "Lecture on the Two Bills" and its revised and expanded version published as *The Plot Discovered,* the pamphlet *An Answer to "A Letter to Edward Long Fox, M.D.,"* and his six *Lectures on Revealed Religion.* Appendixes include fragments of theological lectures, which contain an interesting early account of the imagination, a sermon on the text 1 Peter 2.21, the *Star* report of the Bristol Guildhall meetings of 17 and 20 November 1795, the Bristol Petition against the Two Bills, Thomas Beddoes' *A Word in Defence of the Bill of Rights against Gagging Bills,* and *A Letter to Edward Long Fox, M.D.* The introduction is in two parts. The first, jointly authored, gives a chronological account of the political lectures and the events and political associations that aroused Coleridge's "squeaking baby-trumpet of sedition" and reconciles as best the authors can the documented lectures with reports of lectures announced and of lectures delivered. The second part, by Mann, examines the degree to which Coleridge the political reformer is Coleridge the defender of religion and reviews the extent to which Coleridge was reacting against Godwinism. Mann's account defines a youthful radical resisting the extreme philosophy of the revolution but sharing its moral and social concerns and exonerates the "later intellectual progress" of Coleridge as not "an apostasising rejection of his ideas of 1795, but as a more profound exploration and development of them."

In *CC* 2 Patton prints the ten issues of the *Watchman,* from 1 March to 13 May 1796, with a table of contents analyzing each issue. In footnotes he gives the original source of each item, manuscript fragments, textual variants, Coleridge's annotations on two copies of the periodical, and the political and literary background to the various essays, reviews, and news items. In a succinct introduction, Patton sketches the shifting political climate of Whiggish opinion that forms the inception and demise of the *Watchman,* identifies contributors, and analyzes the complex question of Coleridge's journalistic skills and evolving intentions.

Erdman's magisterial collection of Coleridge's *Essays on His Times (CC* 3) in the *Morning Post* (vol. 1) and the *Courier* (vol. 2), with "Conjectural and/or Collaborative Attributions" (vol. 3), adds twenty-nine contributions to Sara Coleridge's sixty-five (*EOT,* 1850) in the *Morning Post,* seventy-four more in the *Courier,* and another seventy-five conjectural and collaborative pieces. As if this unexpected harvest were not enough, Erdman also includes twenty-five letters and drafts of essays that can be construed as part of Coleridge's intended journalistic output. Three additional appendixes contain contemporary attacks on Coleridge in the *Anti-Jacobin,* by Cobbett in the *Political Register,* and by Hazlitt in the *Morning Chronicle*; a list of verse contributions by Coleridge and Wordsworth, with the texts of new conjectural attributions; and puffs and advertisements of Coleridge and his works. Extensive headnotes and footnotes establish the political and personal context of each leader and set forth the internal and external evidence for new attributions. In an introductory essay, "Principles of Attribution," Erdman distills the experience of over twenty years of testing the evidences of attribution (for articles and books on this subject, see "Editions," *ERP3*), concisely characterizes Coleridge's metaphors, and gives a brief analysis of the prose styles of the editorial family at the *Morning Post* and *Courier* during Coleridge's association with them. His introduction is an elegant survey of the journalistic ebb and flow of Coleridge's crying "the State of the political Atmosphere" in the *Morning Post* and *Courier* from 1798 to 1818 certainly, and to 1823 conjecturally, and a bemused albeit subtle analysis of Coleridge's, the editor Daniel Stuart's, and the *Morning Post*'s antiministerial and antiwar oscillations from 1798 to the fall and winter of 1802 – 03. There is room for disagreement with Erdman's sometimes unhedged and unequivocal conjectures and conclusions; and Donald Sultana, "Coleridge's Political Papers in Malta" (*New Approaches to Coleridge,* ed. Sultana, 1981), corrects what he considers Erdman's errors in fact, attribution, interpretation, and emphasis, particularly as regards the July and December 1804 versions of "Observations on Egypt."

In *CC* 4 Rooke prints both the three-volume 1818 *rifacimento* of the *Friend* and the original 1809 – 10 periodical. In footnotes she gives Coleridge's revisions of the 1809 – 10 text for the 1812 publication, as well as his emendations, cuts, and marginal comments noted in copies of the work, plus manuscript deletions and additions. In appendixes Rooke analyzes the colophons of the 1809 – 10 and 1812 versions; describes known annotated copies of the 1809 – 10, 1812, and 1818 versions; collates in parallel columns the folios of the manuscript and the pages of the 1809 – 10, 1812, and 1818 *Friend* and the 1837 (Henry Nelson Coleridge) and *Collected Coleridge* reprints. The introduction gives a full history of the *Friend* from inception to the posthumous edition of 1837 of Henry Nelson Coleridge, detailing "the mundane problems of paper, stamps, and subscribers" that Coleridge struggled with, summarizing the revisions Coleridge made for the 1812 and 1818 publications, and analyzing Coleridge's organization (his "method") of the 1818 *rifacimento.*

Foakes presents Coleridge's *Lectures 1808 – 1819: On Literature* (*CC* 5) for the first time in chronological order, with a headnote to each set of lectures, and to each lecture where there is sufficient evidence to warrant one. For the controversial 1811 – 12 lectures Foakes prints a text necessarily based on Collier's 1811 transcriptions of his shorthand notes (now lost except for several lectures); he includes Collier's 1856 *Seven Lectures on Shakespeare and Milton* (which has almost no authority now, thanks to Foakes's research) and transcriptions of Collier's two surviving shorthand texts. On the circumstances of Collier's sources for his 1856 edition—his diary for the six weeks 11 October – 27 November 1811, his shorthand notes of the lectures, his longhand transcriptions—and their relative reliability, Foakes has reluctantly come to the conclusion that "the best text available of Coleridge's lectures of 1811 – 12" remains at two removes from Coleridge's spoken words and the ideal of an accurate account probably unattainable: see "The Text of Coleridge's 1811 – 12 Shakespeare Lectures" (*Shakespeare Survey,* 1970), *Coleridge on Shakespeare: The Text of the Lectures of 1811 – 12* (1971), and "What Did Coleridge Say? John Payne Collier and the Reports of the 1811 – 12 Lectures," in *Reading Coleridge* (ed. W. B. Crawford, 1979). John F. Andrews underlines the moral of all this in his review essay "The *Ipsissima Verba* in My Diary" (*Shakespeare Studies,* 1975), pointing out the errors and omissions in Foakes's 1971 edition of the 1811 – 12 lectures. Previous presentations of Coleridge's literary criticism—*Literary Remains* (1836), Raysor's *Coleridge's Shakespearean Criticism* (1930; rpt. 1960) and *Miscellaneous Criticism* (1936)—have obscured

Coleridge's development as a critic. Foakes's chronological order illustrates and documents Coleridge's progression from opening lectures seeking to establish general principles, as in the first four lectures of 1808 and of 1811–12, to the late lectures, which he announced as a course of "practical criticism" and which he delivered directly from texts marked with notes that he took into the lecture room. Foakes, in his introduction, reviews Coleridge's attempt to reappraise the nature of critical activity and to establish new principles of criticism. On the vexed question of Coleridge's use of Schlegel's lectures, Foakes notes the absence of any signs of Schlegel's influence before December 1811, with enough evidence in the 1808 and earlier part of the 1811–12 series to confirm Coleridge's general claim that he had reached independently the basic positions set forth in a more structured and coherent framework by Schlegel. Foakes commendably cautions against ascribing precedence and originality to either Coleridge or Schlegel and reminds us that we are inordinately reliant on secondhand reports of what Coleridge said and that Coleridge seems to have acknowledged his debts publicly by displaying the books and commenting on them in the lecture room.

In *CC* 6 the two *Lay Sermons (The Statesman's Manual,* 1816, and *A Lay Sermon,* 1817) are edited by White from their original printings. In editorial and textual footnotes he cites in detail Coleridge's sources, elucidates allusions, and reproduces Coleridge's afterthoughts, corrections, and revisions found in annotated copies of the *Lay Sermons,* as well as changes made in editions of Henry Nelson Coleridge (1839) and Derwent Coleridge (1852). A charming introduction captures the bemusement of contemporaries at Coleridge's sermonizing and the puzzlement of readers at the *Lay Sermons'* mix of religion and political economy.

As "one of the supreme works in the history of literary criticism" by "the most philosophically oriented and informed critic in the English-speaking world," the two-volume text of the 1817 publication of the *Biographia Literaria (CC* 7) is handled with loving care by Engell (responsible for vol. 1) and Bate (responsible for vol. 2). Mindful of the plagiarism issue, they note sources in detail and verbatim. They cite and quote from editions of the German philosophers Coleridge used and, for the convenience of readers, also include parallel references made to standard modern editions. The extensive documentation of sources bears out McFarland's thesis (in *Coleridge and the Pantheist Tradition,* 1969) that Coleridge's mode of composition was to assemble an intricate mosaic of his own and others' statements. Appendix A contains a chart of the exact percentage of matter in the contested chapters taken without acknowledgment from German sources.

The introduction confronts the major questions relating to *Biographia Literaria* that have provoked critics and scholars since its publication: the history and chronology of its composition and publication, its unity, its sources and deployment of them, its fancy-imagination distinctions, and its criticism of Wordsworth. In part 1, Bate narrates fully the stages in growth of the work: the circumstances of its origin and composition, Coleridge's revised intentions, and the distressing farce of its printing and publication. He perceives the original impetus behind the writing of *Biographia Literaria* to be Coleridge's continuing reaction to Wordsworth's poetry and ideas, with a biographical-critical preface and collected poems initially designed as an answer parallel in form to Wordsworth's 1800 preface and poems. The appearance of Wordsworth's 1815 *Poems* with its new preface pronouncing on fancy and imagination reinforced Coleridge's view of his work as a rival twin to Wordsworth's. Accepting Daniel M. Fogel's carefully reasoned "Compositional History of the *Biographia Literaria*" (*SB*, 1977), which corrects E. L. Griggs's (*CL*, 3 – 4) and George Watson's (introduction to Everyman edition, 1956; rpt. 1975) reconstructions of its genesis, Bate has chapters 1 – 4, 14 – 21, and part of 22 completed by the end of July 1815. About then Coleridge began to expand the "philosophical Part," which grew in the next six weeks into chapters 5 through 13. The work underwent a metamorphosis, outgrowing the "prototype" of Wordsworth's preface and poems in the process. Bate suggests tentatively and delicately that Coleridge's truncated discussion of the imagination in chapter 13 may have been caused by the pressure of a printing deadline rather than by insecurity with *Naturphilosophie* and its sources.

In parts 2 and 3, Engell writes a controlled history of the philosophical traditions in both Germany and England that Coleridge was bent on synthesizing, particularly the evolution and reversal of meanings of fancy and imagination in the eighteenth century. Coleridge's "unacknowledged appropriations" from Schelling, Maass, Jacobi, Kant, and Fichte are identified—exactly what and how much and the extent of Coleridge's condensation of them to fit his own unique purposes. Coleridge emerges from this scrutiny "as a barometer" of almost every central issue involving the language of poetry raised from the 1750s to the early 1800s. Nor is he perceived to be, vis-à-vis the developing philosophy in Germany, any more "beholden" to predecessors than are those on whom he is drawing for precedence. In its assimilation of the best of Coleridge criticism and scholarship of the past decade, the introduction distills a new appreciation of Coleridge's contributions to the centuries-old problems of perception, art, and language—and reduces to a historical curiosity J. Shawcross' justifiably influential introduction to his 1907 edition of *Biographia Literaria.*

Colmer follows the second edition (1830), which was revised by Coleridge, for the text of *Church and State* (*CC* 10). In appendixes he reprints Henry Nelson Coleridge's preface to the 1839 edition and the Catholic Emancipation Act of 1829, collects the fragments of Coleridge's manuscript drafts of *Church and State* and fragments of his on the Catholic question and on the origin of the priesthood written about 1821, and lists annotated copies of *Church and State.* Colmer's introduction traces historically the changing attitude toward the relationship of church and state in England, their growing de facto separation by the end of the sixteenth century, and de jure attempts in the eighteenth century to formulate a political alliance between the two estates. During Coleridge's lifetime the acute issue was Catholic emancipation, which he accepted in principle but preferred as a gradual process. He feared emancipation would lead to Ireland's separation from union, ending in the creation of an imperium in imperio. Hence, his chief concern is with ensuring security against foreign alliances. Coleridge's usual grasp of the issues at hand and his characteristic bent on working out the fundamental principles on which to ground national security rather than yield to political expediency is matched by Colmer's conscientious exposition.

One of the glories of the *Collected Coleridge,* and a contribution of incalculable importance to our knowledge of Coleridge's thought, is the multivolumed *Marginalia* (*CC* 12) compiled with selfless devotion and diligence by the late George Whalley and culminating a professional lifetime of pursuing Coleridge's reading, beginning with the oft-cited list of Coleridge's Bristol Library borrowings (*Library,* 1944) and most recently recapitulated in the partly autobiographical account "On Editing Coleridge's Marginalia," in *Editing Texts of the Romantic Period* (ed. John D. Baird, 1972) and in the account of the special status of Coleridge's marginalia in Lamb's books (*ChLB,* 1975). The phrase "book-oriented" assumes definitive lexical meaning when Coleridge is its frame of reference. According to Whalley (who was surely the most knowledgeable on Coleridge's reading habits) Coleridge began copious annotating of books about 1803, with the practice slowly increasing in volume and extent to 1807 – 08, then bursting forth after the interregnum of the *Friend* years again in 1811, and swelling into a flood that ran at full tide until his death twenty-three years later. Manifest in this unflagging marginal activity is Coleridge's perceptive reading—his grasp of flaws in logic, his anticipation of where an argument will lead, and his independent pursuit of an idea—which should help downgrade the issue of plagiarism, softening its hue and cry to calmer tones. The textual apparatus of the *Marginalia* is a triumph over intrinsic difficulties, not least the diplomacy necessary to recapture the quotidian context of Coleridge's mind when writing the annotations, while avoiding the traps of interpretation and explanation. Coleridge's annotations and the relevant textus are tastefully presented for ease of reading in two colors. There are also headnotes on authors, as well as on individual books. Care has been taken to record every bit of marginalia, however trivial it might appear. The edition will eventually contain some 8,000 notes recovered from about 450 titles (nearly 700 volumes) written by some 325 authors. Much can only be dated tentatively or not at all, since Coleridge seldom dated his marginal notes, entered notes at successive readings of the same book, and did not hesitate to annotate second and third copies or different editions of the same book. Except for the *Annual Anthology* and *Omniana,* which are treated as special cases, Coleridge's annotations on proofs or copies of his own works are not included in the *Marginalia* but are cited in the pertinent volumes of the *Collected Coleridge.* Copies still are discovered after publication of the relevant *CC* volume, making necessary such supplementary items as William P. Albrecht's "An Annotated Copy of *The Watchman*" (*WC,* 1978) and Mann's "Annotations by Coleridge in a Copy of *The Friend* (1818)" (*SB,* 1973).

In a gracefully written introduction Whalley provides a history of when and how the books came to be annotated, as best that story can now be reconstructed, with names of those most generous in their lending of books to Coleridge; a history of Coleridge's purchases, ownership, and life with books; an estimate of the contents of the marginalia, the range of their references as a faithful index to the play of Coleridge's mind; and an exposition of Coleridge's and others' assessments (especially Lamb's) of the rich harvest in these books. In annex A Whalley details the history of Sara, Henry Nelson, and Derwent Coleridge's (the first generation's) harvesting of the marginalia and, since 1853, of subsequent editors' (especially H. Nidecker, J. Aynard, T. M. Raysor, and R. F. Brinkley) publishing of small collections of it. In annex B he tells the valuable, if melancholy, story of the posthumous dispersal of Coleridge's books, the loss of Lamb's "ragged regiment" of folios and quartos, and the breakup of the Henry Green collection—ending in the triumphant rescue of many of these books by the British Museum and Victoria College, Toronto, collections.

Except for Alice Snyder's detailed account of the manuscript and excerpt of twenty-odd pages from it (*Coleridge on Logic and Learning*, 1929), the *CC* 13 transcription of *Logic* represents the first full printing of Coleridge's modest exposition of "the Elements of Discourse, or the Criteria of true and false Reasoning deduced from an Analysis of the Reasoning Faculty." Written in 1822–23 as an introduction to Kantian logic for the practical purpose of training the minds of young professional men in methods of thinking, the *Logic* is not meant to be a contribution to the development of philosophy. Besides a description of the manuscript and reconstruction of the work's provenance, its amanuenses and transcribers, its chronology of composition, and its sources, chiefly the *Critique of Pure Reason,* Jackson prints in six appendixes manuscript fragments of a preliminary sort, most in Coleridge's hand, related to the *Logic.* Terse and concentrated, Jackson's introduction adds to our knowledge of Coleridge's daily routine in the 1820s at Highgate, his pedagogical view of himself as contributing to the formation of young minds through the agency of his writings and of his celebrated monologues. Such was the intent of the weekly philosophical classes that he proposed in 1822–23 for "a select number of gentlemen," and that were linked to his writing of the *Logic.* Jackson also shows how the *Logic,* for all its intent of popularizing Kant, reflects the unified movement of Coleridge's mind to grasp the intellectual issues of his time and to integrate them into the intensely partisan theological framework of his thought. Among "the concealed aims" of *Logic* are Coleridge's desire to refute the logically antimoral and anti-Christian concepts of necessity, to dismiss "Hume's system of . . . non-causation" by means of the Kantian redefinition of space and time, and to mediate the contemporary controversy over whether language originates in verbs or nouns. Thus the *Logic* becomes, according to Jackson, "much more than a derivative introduction to Kant." Despite such discriminations, Raimonda Modiano (*WC,* 1982) finds reason to chastise Jackson for "not . . . thoroughly document[ing]" allusions to Schelling and for not differentiating at all times between what is "vintage Kant" and what "vintage Coleridge."

Of the volumes in the *Collected Coleridge* still to be published, original publications and older editions (where they exist) will have to do for a few more years. The *Philosophical Lectures* are available in a skillfully edited but skimpily indexed volume by Coburn in 1949, *Aids to Reflection* in the H. N. Coleridge edition of 1840 (rpt. 1971) and in the W. G. T. Shedd edition of 1853, and *Table Talk* in H. N. Coleridge's editions of 1835 and 1836. In the *Collected Coleridge* edition of the latter, by Woodring, the copy text will be based on the manuscript notebooks of Henry Nelson Coleridge. A second volume will reprint Henry Nelson's second edition of 1836. The new materials are mostly personal, concerning the Coleridge family and prominent members of his circle of friends. Equally of interest are the corrections in dating of the items of conversation as a result of Woodring's success in reconstructing HNC's manuscripts, which are basically diaries with various other materials, frequently transcriptions from Coleridge's letters, notebooks, and marginalia.

Some sense of "The Psychic Economy and Cultural Meaning of Coleridge's *Magnum Opus*" (so the ideal entity is termed) as a conservative "last-ditch stand, at the innermost ramparts of Christianity," against the intellectual currents of scientific empiricism and utilitarian pragmatism can be gathered from McFarland's discussion of it in chapter 6 of *Romanticism and the Forms of Ruin* (1981). Paramount for McFarland is the bias of the *Opus Maximum* (the term commonly used for the manuscript fragments) as a work in reaction to the Enlightenment and in defense of "theological ideals of permanence."

As for Coleridge's *Shorter Works and Fragments,* until the Jacksons complete their edition, the materials remain Coleridgean in their fragmentary and dispersed hints at the readiness of his mind to take up any subject, however distant from his usual literary-philosophical concerns. As earnest of that distant day E. E. Bostetter, editor of the *Shorter Works and Fragments* until his untimely death, summarizes "Coleridge's Manuscript Essay on the Passions" (*JHI,* 1970); Anthony John Harding prints "Coleridge's College Declamation, 1792" (*WC,* 1977) in Latin, with an English translation, and sketches in the background history to its composition; and H. J. Jackson describes the contents of the manuscript "Essay on Scrofula," in "Coleridge on the King's Evil" (*SIR,* 1977), to show that *Theory of Life* began as a digression from the Scrofula essay and prints (in *CL,* 1981) from a manuscript fragment (the first page is missing) "The Historie & Gests of Maxilian," Coleridge's elaboration of an E. T. A. Hoffmann short story. On the controversial questions raised in part by the posthumous circumstances of the contested authorship of *Theory of Life* as a joint effort of Coleridge and James Gillman, J. H. Haeger's near-definitive article "Coleridge's 'Bye Blow': The Composition and Date of *Theory of Life*" (*MP,* 1976) appears to offer all the answers on authorship, dating, sources, reasons for its being written, as well as a judicious reexamination of the previous scholarship. And S. W. Reid, "The Composition and Revision of Coleridge's Essay on Aeschylus' *Prometheus*" (*SB,* 1971), backs up with bibliographical evidence Whalley's announcement (*N&Q,* 1969) of finding two manuscript fragments (in the Duke University Library and in the Berg Collection of the New York Public Library) of the essay on Aeschylus that Coleridge delivered in 1825 to the Royal Society of Literature. Reid also traces its history from initial composition in May 1821 for Hartley Coleridge's use through subsequent transcription and revision to printing in 1834.

Poetical Works (1893), edited by James Dykes Campbell, and *Complete Poetical Works* (2 vols., 1912), edited by Ernest Hartley Coleridge, specimens of the best of late nineteenth-century editorial practice, will be superseded by J. C. C. Mays's projected three-volume variorum edition in *Collected Coleridge*. Volume 1 is tentatively planned to include reading texts of all the significant poems, and at the back textual evolutions, historical notes, originals of translations, identification of allusions, and early versions. Volume 2 will then contain all Coleridge's poems in chronological sequence, including a hundred or more previously uncollected or unpublished, and new versions of nearly every other poem formerly known. Mays aims at recording every variant reading from holograph manuscripts, transcripts, printed versions, and corrected printed versions. Instances of the new material awaiting us in Mays's edition of the poems are given by J. Stevens-Cox and G. Stevens-Cox, "On the Discovery of Two Poems by Samuel Taylor Coleridge in [The Sherborne, Dorset] *Weekly Entertainer," Samuel Taylor Coleridge and Mary Lamb: Two Recent Discoveries* (1971); by Burton R. Pollin, "John Thelwall's Marginalia in a Copy of Coleridge's *Biographia Literaria*" (*BNYPL*, 1970), which includes the first seven lines and closing couplet of Coleridge's sonnet "To John Thelwall"; and by James D. Wilson, "A Note on Coleridge and *The Quarterly Review*" (*WC*, 1975), which reprints marginalia in a presentation copy of *Remorse* (1813). Volume 3 contains the plays, including new texts, annotations of old texts, and drafts of hitherto unpublished short plays. The Schiller translations are on facing pages with the German manuscript version Coleridge used for the *Death of Wallenstein* and a reconstructed version of the lost manuscript of the *Piccolomini*.

Of the other two long-term editions in progress—the letters and the notebooks—the late Earl Leslie Griggs's *Collected Letters* (6 vols., 1956–71) has been completed now for more than a decade. One of its shortcomings is that the critical apparatus, in comparison to the *Collected Coleridge*, is spartan. Another is that there is no comprehensive index. Published at intervals in sets of two volumes at a time, the edition has three separate indexes (in vols. 2, 4, and 6), one for each two-volume set. Volume 6 concludes with two appendixes. The first consists of short essays describing the death and burial, the postmortem examination, the grave, and the will of Coleridge with a full transcription of the latter. The second appendix gives the text of additional letters (1795–1831) not in the chronological series and some letters in volumes 1–6 now reprinted from manuscript. Despite Griggs's fifty-year endeavor to track down Coleridge's letters, they continue to surface, the most recent described and printed by Mann (*RES*, 1974), by Woodring (*Columbia Library Columns*, 1975), and by C. D. W. Sheppard (*N&Q*, 1978).

Three volumes (1957, 1961, 1973) of Coburn's towering edition of Coleridge's *Notebooks* (volume 1, 1794–1804; 2, 1805–07; 3, 1808–19; with a fourth in press and a fifth in the works coedited with Merton A. Christensen) bring ever closer the day when upwards of seventy of Coleridge's "Pocketbooks, the Confidantes who have *not* betrayed me," will be available for all to read. Each volume is bound in two parts, one text and the other notes. Each double volume contains chronological and notebook tables of dates for the entries that appear in it and a mammoth triple index of persons, titles, and place names. One will have to wait until the final volume in the collection for a subject index. The companion volumes of textual notes give analytical descriptions of each notebook. There are also informative appendixes (to vol. 1) on Coleridge's knowledge of German and on his marginal notes on Thomas Taylor's *Proclus* and (to vol. 2) on Coleridge's knowledge of Italian, on his official duties in Malta, on his construction of a cryptogram, on the account in the Maltese political journal *Il Cartaginese* of the sinking of Captain John Wordsworth's ship *The Earl of Abergavenny,* on the contents of Wordsworth MS. M, which accompanied Coleridge to Malta, and on Coleridge's reorganization of Nicholson's observations on weather. Volume 3 spans the time period of Coleridge's lectures, as well as the years when he was writing *Biographia Literaria.* These notebooks contain extensive evidence of his reading in German philosophy and criticism, providing a perspective on the issue of plagiarism in the *Biographia.* Some of the editorial wisdom Coburn has garnered from her marathon bout with Coleridge's "flycatchers" is shared at length in "Editing the Coleridge Notebooks," *Editing Texts of the Romantic Period* (ed. J. D. Baird, 1972).

In a pioneering scholarly effort of such complexity and monumentality as the *Collected Notebooks,* errors and omitted or overlooked facts are bound to surface; yet there have been to date surprisingly few corrections or elaborations of data. Angus Easson, "Coleridge in the Apple-Orchard" (*N&Q,* 1979), explains the second brainteaser of *CN* 1 as a genuine mathematical problem. H. W. Piper, in "Coleridge's Note on Unitarianism, Orthodoxy, and Atheism" (*N&Q,* 1978), and Hartmut Brietkreuz, in "Coleridge's German Vocabulary" (*N&Q,* 1973), argue for corrections in dating and annotating of 1797–98 entries. Mary Lynn Johnson, "Coleridge's Prose and a Blake Plate in Stedman's *Narrative*" (*WC,* 1982), amends the gloss regarding the influence on Coleridge's imagination of Stedman's descriptions of tortured black slaves. Sultana, in "Coleridge's Autographs" (*TLS,* 15 Feb. 1963) and in *Coleridge in Malta and Italy* (1969), challenges Coburn's disposition of some documents, notebook entries, and events associated with Coleridge's Maltese and Italian years. The latter has elicited a lively exchange (see *ES,* 1973 and 1974).

Because of their invaluable commentaries and aperçus specialized gatherings of Coleridge's writings that will probably not be made obsolescent by the *Collected Coleridge* include E. H. Coleridge's facsimile edition of one of the manuscripts of *Christabel* (1907), although its account of "Christabel" manuscripts should be supplemented with Jo Ann Citron's "Two Unrecorded Manuscripts of *Christabel*" (*WC,* 1982); Alice D. Snyder's editing from the *Encyclopaedia Metropolitana* of the *Treatise on Method* (1934), which Coleridge subsequently expanded for the 1818 *Friend;* Coburn's collection of Coleridge's prose pensées in *Inquiring Spirit* (1951; rpt. 1979); R. F. Brinkley's omnium-gatherum *Coleridge on the Seventeenth Century* (1955), whose contents are divided half on "The Old Divines" and half on literary authors, excluding Shakespeare; and Joseph Anthony Wittreich's *The Romantics on Milton* (1970), which attempts a definitive culling of Coleridge's comments on Milton. Finally, a taste for eccentricity spiced with antiquarian perceptions and leavened by critical intelligence will find *Coleridge's Verse: A Selection* (1973), with introduction by William Empson and textual commentary and notes by David Pirie, a fascinating reaffirmation of the nineteenth-century view (officially embalmed in E. K. Chambers' biography) that

"Coleridge wrote only a very few good poems." Empson and Pirie print next to nothing written after "Hymn before Sunrise," not even "To William Wordsworth," and favor early and first versions, which means the "Verse Letter to Sara" instead of "Dejection: An Ode" and, in the case of "The Ancient Mariner," an eclectic text based on the 1800 poem but introducing words, phrases, and lines that restore its initial "impulse and conception" before Coleridge mangled it with successive and "harmful changes where he had fallen out of sympathy with its basic ideas."

Coleridge is the scholar's and critic's delight, because like them he is book-ish. There is a compatibility of intellectual habits—when human frailties of personality are not allowed to intrude—that endears him to much of the academy. It will take at least a generation of scholars to sift through the new riches offered by these editions to arrive at a just evaluation of Coleridge's stature as poet, critic, philosopher, psychologist, theologian, and man of letters and ideas and of his contribution to nineteenth- and twentieth-century British and American thought. A start has been made in this ongoing assessment—a secondary gleaning of the first editorial harvest—as manifested by the following sections of this survey.

Biographies

Imperative in Coleridge studies is a full-dress biography commensurate with the amplitude of the man's intellect and the complexity of his personality. The task is daunting. Few are up to its polymath demands. Among current Coleridge schol-ars, Bate, Coburn, Erdman, and McFarland are perhaps intellectually and sympa-thetically equipped to cut through the clouds of prejudice and misapprehension, to mention only one problem that plagues the Coleridge "biography," to get at the essence of the man and the legacy of his accomplishments. With the note-books, letters, and complete writings of Coleridge soon available in their entirety, we have the materials for a definitive biography, as regards the facts of his life and works and perhaps even the paradoxes of his inner life, that unfathomable human element at the core of his emotional and intellectual contradictions which prompted his contemporaries, and one hundred years of commentators since, to register symptoms in the belief they were locating first causes.

Nineteenth-century attempts to give us the sight and sound of the man need not detain us overlong here (for a detailed survey, see "Biographies," *ERP3*). Al-ready a legend in his lifetime, he inspired many contemporary recollections by the likes of Lamb, Hazlitt, De Quincey, Carlyle, and Keats, as well as by less literarily endowed diarists, journal keepers, and letter writers. Adulation and re-spect is expressed also by the first generation of Victorians—Julius Hare, F. J. A. Hort, F. D. Maurice—and the second generation of Coleridges—Sara, Henry Nel-son, and Derwent—the "Germano-Coleridgeans" John Stuart Mill called them, at-testing to their philosophical-religious allegiances. As Mill's faintly derogatory term indicates, their honoring of Coleridge is not so much biographical in form as ideological in sentiment. The same can be said for that of Mill and Newman, who espoused different philosophical and religious systems of belief. The late

Victorian acknowledgment of the Coleridgean legend, deprecatory and condescending in its assessment of the sage of Highgate, appears in a work like H. D.
Traill's *Coleridge* (1884).

The modern appreciation begins with James Dykes Campbell's biographical
introduction to his edition of the *Poetical Works* (1893), published as a separate
volume the next year (rpt. 1971), and attested to most recently by Whalley as still
"[the] best biography of Coleridge" (*S. T. Coleridge,* ed. R. L. Brett, 1971). For the
first half of this century, the most reliable biography factually was E. K. Chambers'
Samuel Taylor Coleridge (1938). Its moral hostility toward Coleridge, however,
limited its value.

Superseding both these narratives as the standard and most comprehensive
one-volume biography is *Samuel Taylor Coleridge* (1968) by Walter Jackson Bate.
Well paced and proportioned, this biography touches on all the controversial aspects of Coleridge's life, both literary and personal, with fresh perspective: the
poet-metaphysician dichotomy, the plagiarism, the unsystematized philosophy, the
fragmentary theory of imagination, the opium addiction, the psychic dependency,
the unfinished "Kubla Khan" and "Christabel," and the medical history of the
man. For the first time we get a serious treatment of the second half of
Coleridge's life, the years when he functioned as critic, philosopher, and religious
thinker. Bate sees Coleridge as both blessed and cursed with a comprehensive
mind. The most gifted psychological intelligence of his time, "one of the half-
dozen greatest critical interpreters in the history of literature," and an innovative
and farsighted religious thinker, he was forever getting trapped by the largeness
of his vision, by his sympathetic openness to ideas, his eagerness to include
rather than exclude. Both the glory and the failure of Coleridge's intellectual pilgrimage, accordingly, lie in his persistent effort to accomplish all things at once.
Coleridge's was a lifelong search (or at least from roughly 1802 to his death) for
the means philosophically by which the mystery of creation could be answered to
the satisfaction of the claims of (1) traditional Christian theology, (2) modern
epistemology and logic, and (3) "dynamic philosophy," with its inclusion of the
discoveries of science and philosophy.

The most recent biography, Oswald Doughty's *Perturbed Spirit: The Life and
Personality of Samuel Taylor Coleridge* (1981), challenges the "official" domi-
nan e of the Bate biography; yet serious shortcomings with it leave the Bate pres-
entε tion of Coleridge indisputably still the best and most reliable reference. This
is too bad, since Doughty gives the fullest detailed story yet of Coleridge's messy
odyssey through life, including a sympathetic appraisal of Mrs. Coleridge, a recognition of the fun in Coleridge along with his inclination toward an irregular Bohemian existence, and an early-warning sensitivity to the friction developed in
the day-to-day rubbing of the Coleridge-Wordsworth fellowship. The glory of the
book is the third section, covering the years 1816–34, which narrates skillfully
and generously the routine of Coleridge's last years as a member of the Gillman
household, his early crises of incompatibility with the Gillmans, his social triumphs, his parental griefs, his reputation as a talker, and his relationship with
scores of distinguished people. *Perturbed Spirit* has the virtues of a factual biog-

raphy. Street addresses are pinned down, acquaintances identified, dates determined with the care that characterizes Mary Moorman's biography of Wordsworth and Leslie Marchand's of Byron. Unfortunately, Doughty died before completing the biography. Published posthumously, it lacks notes, bibliography, and acknowledgments; hence, there is no way to determine the source of Doughty's information. What makes this need particularly important is that Doughty's perception of Coleridge takes its cue from the bias of E. K. Chambers. Furthermore, Doughty's grasp of Coleridge and of the period owes a large intellectual allegiance to the turn-of-the-century scholars H. D. Traill, Oliver Elton, and George Sampson, whose culturally bound opinions Doughty deferentially invokes. The Coleridge who emerges from these pages is not an attractive person. Doughty seems bent on catching the hint of falsehood in every explanation Coleridge exuberantly concocts and the trace of spite in every jeu d'esprit he irrepressibly is party to. Little sense of the delicacy of Coleridge's feelings is conveyed or of the power of his shaping intellect and imagination. The emphasis is on his habitual backbiting, on his sponging, on his grandiloquent dreams of books never written, and on his sensual overindulgence in food, drink, and narcotics. The explanation given psychologically for Coleridge's hyperemotional state is "anxiety hysteria," although Doughty does not go in for psychoanalysis of Coleridge beyond handy reference to this term. Worse, Doughty misunderstands Coleridge's hopes for Davy and the science of his day, downplays Coleridge's journalistic efforts and his literary relationships, ignores his metaphysical and theological interests, and misrepresents the *Biographia Literaria*. There is no literary analysis and only slight reference to the poetry even when it has biographical relevance. Doughty takes little advantage of recent scholarship and at times distorts narrative chronology, pushing the uninformed reader to pejorative interpretations of Coleridge's intent and act. Significantly, the unsympathetic tone changes to an appreciative one in part 3, the Highgate years, where Doughty delineates a Coleridge principally as he was seen and heard by his contemporaries. Given the insoluble mix of cynic and believer, opportunist and ideologist, manipulator and idealist in Coleridge's psychological makeup, a biographer needs a strong appreciation of his virtues, if not bent of good will, to avoid falling into a supercilious tone regarding the folly and the "round of inconsistencies" (so Hazlitt called them) in his personal dealings with the world. A responsible biography of Coleridge must dwell on the gifts of his mental and imaginative capacities if it is to escape registering contempt for his specious incapacity to cope with the daily demands of life. Doughty has not risen to the challenge as has Bate.

For all their virtues the rigid economy of Bate's one-volume biographical narrative and the self-imposed literary and philosophical restrictions of Doughty's point up the need of a larger scale for the definitive biography of Coleridge, to allow for interpretative criticism of the details of his personal life and of his mental and literary development and to set his life against the background of intellectual history. If Wordsworth, like many others, could call Coleridge "the most wonderful man I have ever known," the definitive biography, if it is ever written, should show something of the reason for such a judgment from one of the most cautious of men. Although it requires correcting and updating in details, Lawrence Hanson's excellent account *The Life of S. T. Coleridge: The Early Years* (1938), which goes up to 1800, takes such a broad view of biography. It interprets, for instance, the early relationship of Wordsworth and Coleridge, discusses the attitude of both toward the French Revolution, gives something of the historical and intellectual background of their opinions, criticizes their poetry, and in general follows the traditions of literary biography, as Campbell, Chambers, and Doughty do not. Unfortunately, Hanson did not continue his account of Coleridge's life in subsequent volumes. Although Paul Deschamps offers the most detailed study of Coleridge's early intellectual development, in *La Formation de la pensée de Coleridge 1772–1804* (1964), he likewise breaks off the narrative halfway through Coleridge's life of mental striving.

The majority of the older single-volume attempts to solve the Coleridge enigma (reviewed in *ERP3*) need to be approached cautiously. As for biographical studies of the last decade, most plead a special thesis or pursue a narrow facet of Coleridge's life, much as past biographies, and therefore share the same shortcomings and limitations.

John Cornwell in *Coleridge: Poet and Revolutionary* (1973) reads Coleridge's youthful radicalism as part of the political, millennial, social, and intellectual ferment of the time; but the gesture toward a fresh examination of the climate of the 1790s is little more than that. Somewhat gratuitously, Cornwell also engages in low-keyed psychologizing of Coleridge's sexual dreams, fears of women and sex, and need for friendships with reliable individuals. Told as a tale of poetic promise lost, the biography raises the tenuous saw that Coleridge the poet was diverted from his rightful metier by the fog of Coleridge the would-be philosopher.

Alethea Hayter has followed up her book *Opium and the Romantic Imagination* (1968) with *A Voyage in Vain: Coleridge's Journey to Malta in 1804* (1973), which pinpoints this episode as having forced Coleridge to face his altered self and to recognize that the once joyous poet had been transformed by guilty dependence on opium into a hopeless aging creature, the generous sympathies of his youth narrowing and petrifying in the gravestone of his heart. The book's virtues are a fast-paced narrative of events not confined to the annus mirabilis period in Coleridge's life and a cinematic device of switching from Coleridge on the *Speedwell* to "the friends and folks back home" that evokes them as living rather than historical personages. Vitiating these virtues are two countereffects: the fictionalized recreation of feelings, conversations, and thoughts, extrapolated in part from Coleridge's notebooks, pushes our willing suspension of disbelief to its limit; and the maritime information, not uninteresting in itself, remains unassimilated into the Coleridgean odyssey and hence irrelevant filler for an already thin thesis. Sultana's *Samuel Taylor Coleridge in Malta and Italy* (1969) is still the best factual coverage of Coleridge's Mediterranean hegira, especially the daily routine of his life on Malta, although the exposition is not consistently lucid or always fair and sympathetic; and Coburn's "Poet into Public Servant" (*PTRSC*, 1960) is the most sensitive exposition of the Coleridgean movement of mind from outer contemplation of things to inner concern with states of feeling and of how this imaginative process underlay his functioning as a civil servant.

Molly Lefebure has weighed in with two books. *Cumberland Heritage* (1970) is a high-spirited tribute from one fell walker to the first and one of the best "fell-pounders," praising Coleridge's mountain instincts, skill, and daring in venturing alone where even Wordsworth went only with a guide. She relives Coleridge's remarkable first-time solitary moonlight expedition over Helvellyn on a walk from Keswick to Grasmere in September 1800 to read part 2 of "Christabel" to the Wordsworths, his reckless solitary ascent of Scafell in August 1802 (for more on that foolhardy exploration, see her "Broad Stand—or Scafell Chimney? A Re-Examination of Samuel Taylor Coleridge's Descent from Scafell," *ChLB*, 1976; rpt. *Cumberland Discovery*, 1977), and his pioneering "grand horse-shoe tour" of Eel Crags to Causey Pike, "today rated one of the classics." The book is also a lively catalog of local lore about the dalesmen among whom Coleridge lived for ten years and Wordsworth all but ten years. Less winning is Lefebure's *Samuel Taylor Coleridge: A Bondage of Opium* (1974), which follows Coleridge's opium-dependent life and career until 1816, when he went to live with the Gillmans, who changed his melodramatic "junky" existence overnight into dull middle-class meritocracy and old age. Lefebure's account of Coleridge's struggle with morphine reliance is moving. She dates his addictive tendency as early as 1795–96 (independently supported by Fred Milne's analysis of " 'Pantisocracy': A Reflection of Coleridge's Opium Use?" (*ELN*, 1972) and his addictive dependence by 1800–01, when he began taking the celebrated "black drop of Kendal" (a stronger opium preparation than laudanum), and has him fully reliant on drugs by 1803. The book had best be read with Griggs's (Introduction, *Collected Letters*, vol. 3; and *HLQ*, 1954) and Bate's more restrained summaries of Coleridge's addiction. Lefebure's sensationalist version of the narcotic psychosis suffered by Coleridge's experimentation—he is presented as a member of a drug-oriented group of the 1790s—and her incautious effort to see Coleridge's laudanum-soaked life through the eyes of his similarly inclined, and not so inclined, friends produces one unexpected bonanza (Coleridge's courtship, marriage, and separation seen sympathetically from his wife's viewpoint) and one surprise (surely one of the harshest indictments of the Wordsworths to be made in years). In " 'Toujours Gai': Mrs. Samuel Taylor Coleridge, 'a Most Extraordinary Character,' Reviewed in the Light of Her Letters" (*ChLB*, 1980), Lefebure continues to resuscitate the personality of Coleridge's much-maligned wife. Lefebure blames their domestic discord on Coleridge's addiction and attributes Mrs. Coleridge's bad image to his morphine lies. Mrs. Coleridge emerges as a woman of acute and constant sense of humor and of strength and fortitude.

Exhibiting the virtues of an old-fashioned homiletics, Basil Willey's *Samuel Taylor Coleridge* (1972) is an "intellectual and spiritual biography" that assumes religion was the "raison d'être" to Coleridge. Accordingly, Willey follows the development of Coleridge's thought, from Unitarianism to full Christian orthodoxy, in his life's task of uniting head and heart, logos theology and historical Christianity, metaphysics and religion. Separate chapters examine Coleridge's major prose works from the *Friend* to *Church and State* (least satisfactory of Willey's expositions), as exempla of Coleridge's teachings that accord with current advanced theology. By that yardstick, *Aids to Reflection*—"his best prose work"—remains a meaningful book today.

The preference of critics and scholars in the recent past has been to explore the drama of Coleridge's mental universe rather than search out new facts about his life. To those biographical items already cited (see also "Biographies," *ERP3*) should be added the following: J. D. Gutteridge, "Coleridge and Descartes's *Meditations*" (*N&Q*, 1973), on evidence that Coleridge was reading Descartes as early as 1795; John Unsworth, "Coleridge and the Manchester Academy" (*ChLB*, 1980), on the likeliest date, early November–early December 1793, when Coleridge might have slipped up from Cambridge to Manchester to see about a vacant classics position; Berta Lawrence, "Coleridge's First Chapel" (*ChLB*, 1974), on the Trim Street Chapel, Bath, where early in 1796, in blue coat and white waistcoat, Coleridge conducted a Unitarian first service, speaking on the Corn Laws, and in a second service on the Hair Powder Tax, to a disappointed congregation; Derek Roper, "Coleridge, Dyer, and *The Mysteries of Udolpho*" (*N&Q*, 1972), on the improbability of Coleridge's having written a review of *Udolpho;* Peter Mann, "Coleridge, Joseph Gerrald, and the Slave Trade" (*WC*, 1977), on a facet of the complicated intellectual climate of the 1790s, with its competing and conflicting pro- and antislavery and reform sentiments, not all public information, with which Coleridge had to contend as he tried to steer an informed and influential course through the events of the day; and Alethea Hayter, "Coleridge, Maturin's *Bertram,* and Drury Lane" (*New Approaches to Coleridge,* ed. Sultana, 1981), on the tangled relationship of *Zapolya* and *Bertram* and Coleridge's critique of the latter.

On relationships with his contemporaries, Beer (ch. 10, *Coleridge's Poetic Intelligence,* 1977) imagines Coleridge as recollected by his friends, highlighting his intellectual ebullience and the "great deal of fun" in him. H. J. Jackson, "Coleridge's Collaborator: Joseph Henry Green" (*SIR*, 1982), reviews "Coleridge's working relationship with Green" from their first meeting to Coleridge's death and Green's struggles as literary executor to supervise publication of Coleridge's manuscript remains. M. A. Hassan further interprets Coleridge's puzzling intentions for his "Letter to Peter Morris, M.D." (*N&Q*, 1972), which Lockhart published purportedly without permission in the September 1820 issue of *Blackwood's Magazine.* This is a matter that Griggs grapples with in headnotes to letters of November 1819 and December 1820 in *Collected Letters* 4 and that Erdman treats of in *WC* (1975). Other assessments of Coleridge's entanglements with review editors are below under "Political Economy and Social Theory" in the section "Prose Writings."

Worth mentioning for the slight views they afford of Coleridge are Woodring's "Sara *Fille*: Fairy Child" (*Reading Coleridge,* ed. Crawford, 1979), which surveys Sara *fille*'s life of devotion to the mind and writings of her father; Whalley's "Thomas Gray: A Quiet Hellenist" (*Fearful Joy,* ed. James Downey and Ben Jones, 1974), which suggests some striking compatibilities of mind between Gray and Coleridge; F. Doherty's "Some First-Hand Impressions of Coleridge in the Correspondence of Thomasin Dennis and Davies Giddy" (*Neophil,* 1979), mainly of Coleridge's affectation, vanity, and endless taste for speaking in similes on visits to the Wedgwood home, Cote House, Surrey, 1798 – 99; John R. Welsh's "An Anglo-American Friendship: Allston and Coleridge" (*JAmS*, 1971); Samuel Schoenbaum's "Dyce's Recollections of Wordsworth, Mrs. Siddons, and Other Notable Persons" (*TLS*, 22 Jan. 1971), which quotes four selections on Coleridge, the two most interesting depicting Coleridge's directions to the actors at Drury Lane on "how certain passages" of *Remorse* "were to be delivered" and (an anecdote by Southey) Coleridge's "metaphysical and long-winded" approach to simple and unambiguous ideas; and the essays in *New Approaches to Coleridge*, edited by Sultana (1981), linking Coleridge in fresh ways with Hazlitt, Scott, Lockhart, Frere, and Tieck.

Two persons—Lamb and Wordsworth—continue to overshadow all others in the intimacy and permanence of their impact on Coleridge. Following up Whalley's "Coleridge's Debt to Charles Lamb" (*E&S*, 1958), Lamb criticism seems determined to measure his intellectual and emotional distance from Coleridge. The reciprocity of two independent but complementary temperaments, one superior of intellect, the other of heart, is set forth by Willey in "Charles Lamb and S. T. Coleridge" (*ChLB*, 1973), by Beer in "Coleridge and Lamb: The Central Themes" (*ChLB*, 1976), and by Jane Aaron in "Charles Lamb, the Apostate: 1796 – 1798" (*ChLB*, 1978). Winifred F. Courtney, *Young Charles Lamb 1775 – 1802* (1982), offers an evenhanded treatment of the Coleridge-Lamb relationship in its early years.

Still unsettled to everyone's satisfaction is the question of the psychological and literary debt Coleridge and Wordsworth owed each other. Then there are the attendant questions of their respective conceptions of the imagination and their conflicts over the dramatic portrayal of characters, over diction and the relation of words to things, and over the relation of the supernatural to the natural. Arguing for the detrimental effect of Wordsworth's self-centered habits of mind on the insecure Coleridge are Griggs (*Wordsworth: Centenary Studies*, ed. G. T. Dunklin, 1951) and A. M. Buchan (*UTQ*, 1963). Less complimentary to Coleridge is William Heath's *Wordsworth and Coleridge: A Study of Their Literary Relations in 1801 – 1802* (1970), which concocts an envious, self-pitying, distastefully personal Coleridge whose excesses serve as a "horrid warning" to Wordsworth. But this book is based on too many flimsy surmises, even resurrecting F. W. Bateson's unsavory suspicions, to lend confidence in its key supposition that the twelve months from November 1801 to October 1802 were crucial for the divergent directions the two men subsequently took. The corpus delicti are the autobiographical verses each wrote that year: "Letter to Sara" and the poem quarried from it, "Dejection: An Ode" (analyzed for their shabby failure to translate domestic unhappiness into poetry), and "Resolution and Independence" (praised for its representation of a reborn Wordsworth who finds in its creation an "authenticity of self" and sense of equilibrium). In the most thorough analysis to date of "The Symbiosis of Coleridge and Wordsworth" (*SIR*, 1972; rpt. as ch. 1 in *Romanticism and the Forms of Ruin*, 1981), McFarland finds in the mutually fructifying exchange involving Coleridge's psychic reliance on Wordsworth and Wordsworth's corresponding intellectual dependence on Coleridge that

Coleridge loses most and Wordsworth gains most. McFarland reviews all their attempts at joint authorship, their collaborations, and their intertwining of thoughts and responses in sequences of poems addressed in part to each other. His conclusion is that the gravitational pull of their minds working against contrary polarizing tendencies created each other as great poets but also extinguished their potential for continued poetic greatness. Coleridge arrested Wordsworth's natural development by deflecting him into the role of philosophical poet, and their estrangement assured Wordsworth's "shipwreck . . . as a poet." Thus were they damned if they did and doomed if they didn't. In essential agreement is Stephen M. Parrish, who raised two decades ago (see *PMLA,* 1958, 1959; *JEGP,* 1960) the question of their "profound disagreement" over the propriety of dramatic poetry, the uses of the supernatural, and the purpose of meter. In *The Art of the* Lyrical Ballads (1973) he has expanded his earlier observations into a full reexamination of the mutual stimulations and inevitable discords that punctuated their poetic partnership. He concludes that, for all the fruitful cross-breeding, in the long run dyspathy governed the famous collaboration to the mutual damage of each one's development as a poet. Generally anti-Coleridgean, Parrish finds especially deplorable Coleridge's critical impatience with the dramatic element in the *Lyrical Ballads.* A case for the conventionality of *Lyrical Ballads* was made by Robert Mayo thirty years ago (*PMLA,* 1954). In another look at their indebtedness to German and English ballads, Parrish argues for their experimental dramatic and narrative technique and for Wordsworth's superior dramatic skills—both unfortunately (in Parrish's eyes) denigrated by Coleridge.

An opposite tack, accentuating what H. M. Margoliouth in *Wordsworth and Coleridge, 1795 –1834* (1953) terms an ennobling interchange between the two poets, is not without its defenders. Stephen Prickett in *Coleridge and Wordsworth: The Poetry of Growth* (1970) contends that the partnership, despite disagreements, adds up to a model of creativity definable as "a single" instance of Romanticism. Hence, their interdependence during their creative years is finally more important for us than are any incompatibilities that may have marred their collaboration. This is also the working assumption of Beer. As a qualification of Bloom's hypothesis (*New Perspectives on Coleridge and Wordsworth,* ed. Hartman, 1972) that Coleridge suffered poetic disablement because of anxiety over Milton's influence, Beer, "Coleridge and Wordsworth: Influence and Confluence" (*New Approaches to Coleridge,* ed. Sultana, 1981), lays out the argument for there being periods of his life—for example, during his close association with Wordsworth from 1797 to 1800—when Coleridge was relatively free of anxiety. In other books and articles Beer has pursued a thorough, sympathetic, and sensitive examination of Wordsworth's unfolding genius within the framework of Coleridge's speculative development of an esoteric world picture that rejects Newtonian mechanics for a complex set of correspondences between the fountainous forces in nature and in animated beings (see below, "General Evaluations" under "Historical and Literary Criticism of the Poetry"): *Wordsworth and the Human Heart* (1978) analyzes Wordsworth's poems in terms of Coleridge's speculations about the heart's cosmic significance, its links with animated nature, and its role in human relationships; and *Wordsworth in Time* (1979) similarly treats of these developing attitudes in terms of human consciousness as part of the time process. Coleridge's esoteric speculations as shaped by Beer come perilously close to providing the Rosetta stone for every thought and word of the two poets during the years of their intimacy, although Beer reiterates that he is not presenting a complete view of Wordsworth, or of the Wordsworth-Coleridge friendship, and that his formulation of Coleridge's thought is conjectural. In "Coleridge, the Wordsworths, and the State of Trance" (*WC,* 1977) and in "Coleridge and Wordsworth: The Vital and the Organic" (*Reading Coleridge,* ed. Crawford, 1979), Beer also finds Wordsworth drawing with fruitful results on Coleridge's abiding effort to link the theories of science and "facts of mind" as mutually confirmatory. R. L. Brett in "Coleridge and Wordsworth" (*S. T. Coleridge,* ed. Brett, 1971) reviews necessarily in more truncated fashion their personal and professionally supportive history from Coleridge's first reading of Wordsworth's poems in 1793 to his writing of *Biographia Literaria.* And Berta Lawrence, *Coleridge and Wordsworth in Somerset* (1970), describes the villages, towns, countryside, and people the two poets would have known and seen daily during their years in Somerset, with family histories of Thomas Poole, John Chester, and other locals of Nether Stowey; while A. S. Byatt, *Wordsworth and Coleridge in Their Time* (1970), places them in the larger context of the social, literary, political, cultural, and educational life of the nation.

Mark L. Reed's "Wordsworth, Coleridge, and the 'Plan' of the *Lyrical Ballads*" (*UTQ,* 1965) is now supplemented by John E. Jordan's dress rehearsal of the events leading to that book's publication. In *Why the* Lyrical Ballads? *The Background, Writing, and Character of Wordsworth's 1798* Lyrical Ballads (1976), Jordan analyzes the critical and environmental climate of taste and opinion into which the poems appeared, their novelty and reception, and the meaning of "lyrical" in the title. Jordan approaches the making of *Lyrical Ballads* as a Wordsworthian so does not concentrate overly on Coleridge's role in these transactions. Contrariwise, Prickett's *Wordsworth and Coleridge: The* Lyrical Ballads (1975) stresses the simultaneous collaboration and conflict characterizing the peculiar tension of the "whole enterprise of the *Lyrical Ballads*" and leading to the evolution of Coleridge's role as coauthor in 1798 to assistant in 1800.

Speculation over Coleridge and Wordsworth's poetic association as regards specific poems continues to be debated. R. S. Woof, "Wordsworth and Coleridge: Some Early Matters" (*Bicentenary Wordsworth Studies in Memory of John Alban Finch,* ed. Jonathan Wordsworth, 1970), raises questions anew about the circumstances of their meeting and of their early poetical association and, in "Mr. Woof's Reply to Mr. [Jonathan] Wordsworth" ("A Note on the Ballad Version of 'Michael,'" *ArielE,* 1971), insists that "A Character" and "Michael" have "no necessary manuscript connection" and that it is wrong to see Coleridge as the model for "A Character" (Reed and Parrish present postmortems of the controversy in *ArielE,* 1972); while James H. Averill, "Another Early Coleridge Reference to *An Evening Walk*" (*ELN,* 1976), decides that their mutual interest in evening poems brought the two poets initially together. James Kissane and Marilyn Katz discuss " 'Michael,' 'Christabel,' and the *Lyrical Ballads* of 1800" (*WC,* 1978) and possible

"Early Dissent between Wordsworth and Coleridge" (*WC*, 1978) over Coleridge's dilatoriness in completing "Christabel" and the decision to delete it from the 1800 *Lyrical Ballads*. Beer, "Blake, Coleridge, and Wordsworth: Some Cross-Currents and Parallels, 1789–1805" (*William Blake: Essays in Honour of Sir Geoffrey Keynes*, ed. Morton D. Paley and Michael Phillips, 1973), examines their millenarian hopes in the 1790s and their contrary ordering of the vegetable and animal worlds; and Anya Taylor (*Magic and English Romanticism*, 1979) reviews the respective attitudes of Coleridge (also in *WC*, 1972) and Wordsworth on the theory and use of magical words.

The principal biographical controversy since the publication of Norman Fruman's *Coleridge, the Damaged Archangel* (1971) has been fought on the battle field of Coleridge's plagiarisms and related plaints of his derivative and unsystematic thought. One can name here only some of the leading combatants of a seemingly never-ending war that has been going on for 150 years. A full and detailed history and evaluation up to the publication of Fruman's book of the charges brought against Coleridge and the defenses offered in exculpation of plagiarisms in his poetry and his prose works is given by McFarland in "The Problem of Coleridge's Plagiarism" (ch. 1 of *Coleridge and the Pantheist Tradition*, 1969). The first shot was fired by De Quincey in *Tait's Magazine* (1834, 1835). J. F. Ferrier followed with a volley, "The Plagiarisms of S. T. Coleridge," in *Blackwood's Magazine* (1840). Both pointed to Coleridge's borrowings from Schelling. In this century, A. A. Helmholtz indicated *The Indebtedness of S. T. Coleridge to A. W. Schlegel* (1907), seconded by G. N. G. Orsini, "Coleridge and Schlegel Reconsidered" (*CL*, 1964); and René Wellek has relentlessly belittled Coleridge, first as a philosophical thinker, in *Immanuel Kant in England* (1933), then as critical theorist, in *History of Modern Criticism* (vol. 2, 1955). Brushing aside the moral issue as irrelevant he has concentrated on the shaky house of philosophy and aesthetics—"here a story from Kant, there a room from Schelling"—that Coleridge tried to build out of materials taken from others. In his chapter "Coleridge's Philosophy and Criticism" in *ERP3*, Wellek has ranged against Coleridge virtually a Panzer division of German philosophers, poets, and critics who served as influences: besides Schelling, Kant, and A. W. Schlegel, also Fichte, Jacobi, Mendelssohn, Tennemann, Maass, Schiller, Herder, Lessing, Jean Paul Richter, Solger, Oken, Schubert, Ritter, and Steffens.

Among the ranks of Coleridge's defenders heroic stands have been made by J. C. Hare, who answered De Quincey in "Samuel Taylor Coleridge and the English Opium Eater" (*British Magazine*, 1835); by Sara Coleridge, who responded to Ferrier in her 1847 edition of *Biographia Literaria;* indirectly by J. H. Muirhead, who spirited Coleridge into the camp of the neo-idealists as a founder of the voluntaristic form of idealistic philosophy, in *Coleridge as Philosopher* (1930); and by R. H. Fogle, in *The Idea of Coleridge's Criticism* (1962), who incautiously relies on an unpublished dissertation to dismiss the nebulous question of Coleridge's substantial indebtedness as one purely of historical sources (see also his chapter "The Romantic Movement" in *Contemporary Literary Scholarship*, ed. Lewis Leary, 1958), thereby justifying his critical feint to concentrate on the exposition of a brilliant mind "at once consistent and capable of growth, with fixed principles but limitless boundaries," the key to which are the principles of organic unity and the reconciliation of opposites. Although Orsini in *Coleridge and German Idealism* (1969) lays out clearly and fairly the evidence of Coleridge's plundering of Kant, Fichte, and Schelling, as quotation, paraphrase, and assimilation, and resolutely refutes the notion that Coleridge prefigures the German idealist philosophers by way of Greek thinkers and seventeenth-century divines, he waffles on the issue of Coleridge's importance as a philosopher, postponing final judgment until complete publication of all the manuscripts. McFarland in *Coleridge and the Pantheist Tradition* (1969) extends the discussion to include not only the German philosophical idealists but also Platonists, Neoplatonists, Cambridge Platonists, Bruno, Boehme, Spinoza, and Leibniz. Forthrightly acknowledging Coleridge's indebtedness to past philosophers, McFarland turns this fact to tactical advantage in an attractive hypothesis about Coleridge's mind. Borrowings "so honeycomb his work as to form virtually a mode of composition" by mosaic organization, which arrives at an architectonic whole by way of a harmonious reticulation of bits and pieces of ideas and data. This ingenious apologetic has prompted Wellek to invoke the Geneva Convention of rules on "syncretistic thought" (*CL,* 1970, and *ERP3*).

So hung the issue—in a sort of World War I stalemate, with sorties back and forth across a no-man's-land lit up by occasional rockets—when Fruman's *Damaged Archangel* marshaled a massive offensive against the arguments that Coleridge had quoted from memory or from old notes and had, from a precocious age, anticipated in good English terms much of what was subsequently developed and systematized as German idealist philosophy. Fruman contends that Coleridge's extensive and artfully concealed plagiarisms derive from an insecure personality caused by a childhood deprived of love and family security, leading him to maintain his image as a many-sided genius, a wunderkind, by whatever dishonest means he could. Despite the unfair legalistic form in which his brief against Coleridge is couched and despite the unattractive moralistic tone—or perhaps, in part, because of it—Fruman captivated the unwary non-Coleridgean and hostile non-Romanticist, as indicated by reviews of the book and by the occasional neo-Fruman article like E. H. King's "Beattie and Coleridge: New Light on the Damaged Archangel" (*WC,* 1976), which intemperately demotes Coleridge "without the inspiration of Wordsworth's presence or the abundant resources of the great German writers" to "a minor transitional figure like Beattie."

Critics who have deplored Fruman's unfair rhetorical strategies and corrected his misrepresentations of evidence include Barfield (*Nation,* 12 June 1972), Beer (*RES,* 1973), and Foakes (*EIC,* 1974). The latter concentrates on Coleridge's differences from A. W. Schlegel. McFarland (excursus note 1 in *Coleridge and the Pantheist Tradition,* 1969) reviews the Coleridge-Schlegel relationship and their mutual indebtedness for the concept of organic form to "what had become a Romantic commonplace."

The most exhaustive answer to Fruman's charges is McFarland's in "Coleridge's Plagiarisms Once More: A Review Essay" (*YR,* 1974). He accuses

Fruman of distorting and omitting evidence and of failing to distinguish between the greater part of Coleridge's writing, where plagiarism is no issue, and the unpublished lectures, journalism, and hastily written publications (presumably *Biographia Literaria* and such a poem as "Hymn before Sunrise"), where it is the issue. Less directly but no less effectively, the editions of *Biographia Literaria* (*CC* 7), *Marginalia* (*CC* 12), and *Notebooks* (3), with their detailed and precise identification of Coleridge's reading, quoting, paraphrasing, annotating, contesting, elaborating, extending, and combining, will eventually work to mute the controversy.

The salutary effect of Fruman's attack on Coleridge's veracity and on his erudition has been to force Coleridgeans to try to clarify a débat beclouded as much by the obfuscations of Coleridge as by the feints of critics bent on treating his philosophical indebtedness and his verbal borrowings as the same thing, a description of the second automatically defining the first. No one any longer denies Coleridge's eclecticism. What exercises the imagination of his defenders is whether "plagiarism" properly describes his often inexplicable and unnecessary resort to another's words and whether these acts diminish his importance as a thinker. There has been much reexamining of Coleridge's derivativeness and of the quality and play of his mind.

Recognizing that McFarland's theory of Coleridge's "reticulating habit of mind" fails to explain "particularly flagrant borrowings in the *Biographia Literaria*," where composition by mosaic organization of materials breaks down, Jerome C. Christensen in a rhetorical analysis, "Coleridge's Marginal Method in the *Biographia Literaria*" (*PMLA,* 1977; rpt. in *Coleridge's Blessed Machine of Language,* 1981), analyzes chapters 5, 6, and 7 to establish marginal discourse as a characteristic of Coleridge's dialectic. Christensen reconstructs the occasion of Coleridge's writing chapter 5, showing how Coleridge used Mackintosh as a primary text against which to play a role of "conservative revisionist and reluctant controversialist." Coleridge needed neither to contest Mackintosh nor to plagiarize Maass in overthrowing Hartleian associationism. He does not *use* them to make an argument so much as he annexes their body of thought—Mackintosh's lectures, Maass's text—into his statement to supply a sustaining text that he can surround with marginalia. Thus, Coleridge's discourse is an equivocal combination of marginal comment (which allows him to employ the rhetorician's nonsyllogistic aims of persuasion) accompanied by borrowed text (which relieves him of responsibility for systematic discourse). Approaching Coleridge's presumed plagiarism from a learned historical overview of the contextual relationships in the European philosophical community, McFarland in "A Complex Dialogue: Coleridge's Doctrine of Polarity and Its European Contexts" (*Reading Coleridge,* ed. Crawford, 1979; rpt. in *Romanticism and the Forms of Ruin,* 1981) places the centrality of Coleridge's concern with polarity and the pervasiveness of its aperçu in his thought within the cultural and intellectual perception of his contemporaries as heirs to a philosophical tradition stretching back through Boehme and Bruno to the predecessor of them all, Heraclitus. Intended, in part, as a rebuke of Barfield's and Appleyard's synchronic approach to Coleridge, McFarland insists that the communal dimension of Coleridge's thought is necessary to appreciate the centrality of his place in the intellectual climate of his time. (Although he does not deal with Coleridge, McFarland further explores this issue in "The Originality Paradox" [*NLH,* 1974] in terms of the dichotomies of the individual and society and the individual and tradition, in the Romantic period.) Coleridge's endemic incompleteness, fragmentation, and ruin become for McFarland, in a moving tribute to Coleridge's intellectual honesty, a testament to his awareness of the crisis of doubt afflicting the Western mind, as contrasted to the systems of Hegel and Schelling, whose completed wholes are now seen, from our perspective, as exercises in the mechanism of denial rather than as living witnesses to the age.

Support for McFarland's view that philosophy is a shared communal endeavor ("There are no Robinson Crusoes of the intellect. . . . Texts are possible only in context") appears massively and substantively in James Engell's *The Creative Imagination: Enlightenment to Romanticism* (1981), which concludes with a chapter on Coleridge as "at once a culminating and an original figure" in the century's effort to establish a common vocabulary and accepted definition as regards the imagination. Ideas on the imagination worked out by British empirical and associationist psychology went to Germany by way of Tetens and Kant reading Alexander Gerard, followed by Schelling reading Tetens and Kant, and then returned as German idealist philosophy to England by way of Coleridge reading Tetens, Kant, and Schelling. Engell emancipates Coleridge from the slavish copying of the German idealists that recent pan-Teutonic critics have insisted is the whole story and remodels him as a polymath creatively fusing ideas of the imagination from two primary philosophical systems, Aristotelian and Platonic, the It-is and the I-am, into a dynamic critical-philosophical instrument granting constitutive powers to the reason and uniting the individual (mind, being) with the natural world.

Other witnesses to the originality of Coleridge's mind are Laurence S. Lockridge, Kathleen Coburn, D. M. MacKinnon, and Rosemary D. Ashton. Lockridge, "Explaining Coleridge's Explanation: Toward a Practical Methodology for Coleridge Studies" (*Reading Coleridge,* ed. Crawford, 1979), pleads for a genetic approach that tracks Coleridge in those passages in which he "has left concrete traces of himself in the act of thinking," glorying in perplexity and wonder—contrary to Keats's influential observation (in a letter of 21–27 Dec. 1817), based on Coleridge's formal, public, and published writings, that Coleridge's mind "would let go by a fine isolated verisimilitude caught from the Penetralium of mystery, from being incapable of remaining content with half-knowledge." In the notebooks one finds a Coleridge "creatively engaged" in acts of cognitive exploration that transcend the mechanical objectives of plagiarism and lead us to the "core" of his mental life. Coburn notes with the wisdom accumulated in a lifetime of observation of Coleridge's mind that Coleridge borrows only when his own thinking has reached almost the same point as his creditor's, allowing him fully to enter into the other's thought, to see its further implications and applications, and to load it with his own accumulated knowledge (introduction to her edition of *The Philosophical Lectures of Samuel Taylor Coleridge,* 1949). If Harold Bloom laments repeatedly (see "Coleridge: The Anxiety of Influence," *Diacritics,* 1972; *New Perspectives on Coleridge and Wordsworth,* ed. Hartman, 1972; introduction to *Selected Poetry [by] Samuel Taylor Coleridge,* 1972; and *Figures of Capable Imagination,* 1976) that Coleridge's poetic ambitions were never realized because he "refused the full exercise of a strong poet's misprisions" in his "revisionary" impulses toward Milton and Wordsworth, MacKinnon contrariwise praises him in "Coleridge and Kant" (*Coleridge's Variety: Bicentenary Studies,* ed. Beer, 1974) as a "strong philosopher" misreading Kant's *Inaugural Dissertation* to emancipate himself from Schelling's *Naturphilosophie* and to formulate an unfettered intellectual ascent to the ultimate. Furthermore, according to this professional philosopher, the diversity of Coleridge's references to Kant, along with his "obstinate insistence" on assimilating the transcendental philosophy not to repeat Kant's ideas but to advance beyond their "formulation by novel application," renders superficial the charges of plagiarism. And Ashton in *The German Idea: Four English Writers and the Reception of German Thought 1800–1860* (1980) reveals that an answer to the vexed questions of Coleridge's place in the history of the English reception of German literature—why he was ambivalent in his response to Goethe and *Faust* (an early statement of this appears in *RES,* 1977), why he avoided directly acknowledging Kant in his letters of 1801–03 and in his publications, why he disguised Schelling as "a continental philosopher," and why he obscured his German reading, in general—may lie in part in the fanatical distaste felt by the English for things German from around 1800 to the 1820s. Desirous of acceptance in the literary world and fearful of being tarred with the prejudice against German obscurity and mysticism, Coleridge during these decades hid his partisanship for the new ideas coming out of Germany. Concise and succinct on Coleridge's departures from Kant, Ashton contends, like MacKinnon, that Coleridge absorbed Kant's critical methodology and ideas more thoroughly than did any other person of his generation, and where he dissents from Kant it is out of dislike, not misunderstanding.

The defense of Coleridge acquires an unexpected postulate from D. M. Fogel's "Compositional History of the *Biographia Literaria*" (*SB,* 1977). Having established that Coleridge started in late July–early August 1815 to expand ten or twelve pages of metaphysics ("probably not much more than the present" ch. 5) into what became chapters 6–13, Fogel hypothesizes that because Coleridge was "under fierce pressure from Gutch and Morgan to send the *Biographia* to press" in September he was forced, as he sped to complete chapters 12 and 13, to plunder Schelling's *Abhandlungen* for chapter 12 and that the anxiety about falling so far behind in delivery of the manuscript may have prompted the evasive letter to "C" in chapter 13. The indications are that he wrote chapters 12 and 13 at white heat, since in a footnote to chapter 12 he refers to "this morning (16th September 1815)" and the manuscript was mailed 19 September.

The record of the last dozen years suggests that Coleridge has emerged from the baptism of fire occasioned by Fruman's angry fusillade with his reputation as a brilliant thinker intact and his standing as a seminal figure in nineteenth- and twentieth-century thought as secure and high as it has ever been.

As a further attempt to get at the essential person and to resolve the apparent contradictions of utterances and actions, McFarland plumbs "Coleridge's Anxiety" (*Coleridge's Variety: Bicentenary Studies,* ed. Beer, 1974; rpt. in *Romanticism and the Forms of Ruin,* 1981) in Freudian and Heideggerian terms, until Coleridge becomes prototypical of Western man of the past two hundred years facing courageously the undefined burden of being. And Coburn pays tribute in "Coleridge and Restraint" (*UTQ,* 1969) to his lifelong flight from the "intolerableness of one constraining situation after another" and his attendant allegiance to the free life finding its appropriate form.

For loved ones who figure significantly in Coleridge's life the following books have not yet been superseded: Griggs's biographies of the children Hartley (1929) and Sara (*Coleridge Fille,* 1940); Stephen Potter's edition of Mrs. Coleridge's letters to Tom Poole (*Minnow among Tritons,* 1934), which will be supplemented by Lefebure's biography and edition of further letters (c. 150), mostly to family, deposited in the Humanities Research Center, University of Texas at Austin; and Whalley's *Coleridge and Sara Hutchinson, and the Asra Poems* (1955). Nor should H. W. Howe's modest little book describing *Greta Hall: Home of Coleridge and Southey* (1943; rev. 1977, with additional revisions by Robert S. Woof) be overlooked. It recreates a sense of the sounds, scenes, and life that filled the house during Coleridge's and Southey's tenancies, and provides a history plus a legible floor plan of the three-storied structure, with the uses and family occupancies of the rooms identified.

Historical and Literary Criticism of the Poetry

GENERAL EVALUATIONS

I noted a dozen years ago, in *ERP3,* that a major reevaluation of Coleridge was under way. Whereas living memory of the man and the vitality of his theology kept him alive to the early Victorians and a "handful of golden poems" (E. K. Chambers, *Samuel Taylor Coleridge,* 1938) fascinated the late Victorians and the early generations of this century, the prose writings, with their tireless display of mental industry, astound the self-reflexive "postmoderns" at the nether end of the twentieth century. This is not to say that the poetry is currently neglected but to say that it now shares honors equally with the prose, much as a star athlete does when a younger brother who has outgrown him in size challenges him in prowess as well. Two recent books, otherwise unexceptional and of slight value only as elementary introductions, reflecting the emergent Coleridge are Katharine Cooke's *Coleridge* (1979) and Richard Holmes's *Coleridge* (1982). The former, for example, gives equal importance in separate chapters to Coleridge the poet, the playwright, the literary critic, the political journalist, the political theorist, the theologian, and the philosopher. Only in the relative neglect of the poetry written after "Dejection" does it fail to signify the whole Coleridge.

One sign of the new Coleridge is acceptance of him as poet-philosopher. The prevailing view from Carlyle through Pater to Chambers was that Coleridge ceased to be a poet because he fell into "the high seas of theosophic philosophy, the hazy infinitude of Kantean transcendentalisms, with its 'sum-m-mjects' and 'om-m-mjects' " (Carlyle; rpt. in *Coleridge the Talker,* ed. R. W. Armour and R. F. Howes, 1940). That coin no longer has currency among Coleridgeans, who perceive Coleridge's philosophizing as an intrinsic and necessary trait of his mind, as essential to the poet as to the metaphysician. As Lockridge says, "There is a theoretical continuity between the poet who writes *The Ancient Mariner* and the moralist who speaks of the postulates of humanity" (*Coleridge the Moralist,* 1977). Poet and philosopher uniquely and naturally inhabit the one person; and recent analysts of Coleridge's writings extrapolate unapologetically and without prejudice equally from the poems and the prose. This is the position of Haven in *Patterns of Consciousness* (1969), who assumes that Coleridge's is a unified sensibility. The psychic configurations Coleridge discovered introspectively to be patterns of his consciousness—symbolized in the figures of the Mariner and Wedding-Guest—supply him with the fundamental principles of his philosophical speculations no less than with the subjects of his poetry. E. S. Shaffer similarly reveals in *"Kubla Khan" and* The Fall of Jerusalem: *The Mythological School in Biblical Criticism and Secular Literature 1770–1880* (1975) the syncretic tendencies of Coleridge's poetic and religious mythmaking. How normative to Coleridge and his compeers was the union of poetry and philosophy McFarland demonstrates in a dazzling, wide-ranging survey of European Romantic thinkers, poets, and philosophers, and of the diasparactive underside—incompleteness, fragmentation, and ruin—of their *Sehnsucht* for order and wholeness in their lives, in their literature, and in their perception of the world ("Fragmented Modalities and the Criteria of Romanticism," in *Romanticism and the Forms of Ruin,* 1981). Central to Coburn's Alexander Lectures, *Experience into Thought: Perspectives in the Coleridge Notebooks* (1979), is her sensitive realization of a poet whose lonely imagination allies him with other great rebellious and curious, original and courageous, thinkers in history: Boehme, Giordano Bruno, Paracelsus. Coleridge as one of the great magician poet-philosophers of history, self-allegorized as the Ancient Mariner, is also Elizabeth Sewell's version of the man in " 'As I Was Sometime Milan': Prospects for a Search for Giordano Bruno, through Prospero, Coleridge, and the Figure of Exile" (*Mosaic,* 1975). And Leslie Brisman never doubts, in a discussion of "Coleridge and the Supernatural" (*SIR,* 1982), the propriety of linking the sensory perception of Coleridge's poems with the spiritual intuition of his definition of the reason.

Of older books dealing with Coleridge's poetry, Humphry House's *Coleridge* (1953), with its sensitive descriptive analyses especially of "The Ancient Mariner," "Kubla Khan," "Dejection," and "Frost at Midnight," remains the seminal starting point for much criticism. John Livingston Lowes's *The Road to Xanadu* (1927), by contrast, while still honored for reversing the patronizing dismissal of Coleridge as one who had not lived up to his potential, which prevailed at the start of this century, and for initiating a reassessment of Coleridge's achievement, has slipped into the category of an exciting "read" that now occasions embarrassment and even, among some, outright contempt for its faulty psychology and deficient criticism. Two of the earliest surveys of the poems are Max F. Schulz's *The Poetic Voices of Coleridge* (1963), which emphasizes their innovative forms, and George

Watson's *Coleridge the Poet* (1966), which locates their stylistic variety in traditional genres wherever possible.

The scholar-critic who has striven most thoroughly the past two decades to meet Coleridge the poet on the grounds of his lifelong ideational pursuits is John Beer. His *Coleridge the Visionary* (1959) is still the best scrutiny of Coleridge's reading in occult and mythological literatures and of how that learning contributes to the symbolic structuring of the poems of the annus mirabilis, particularly "The Ancient Mariner" and "Kubla Khan." Beer's brief is that the poems are expressions of an imagination that seized for a brief time on a limited myth of the Fall and of redemption linking society and the physical universe in an ultimate spiritual order. In follow-up articles and books Beer has continued to probe Coleridge's reading and thinking about the preternatural in the years prior to the Malta trip. In "Coleridge and Poetry: I. Poems of the Supernatural" (*S. T. Coleridge,* ed. Brett, 1971) he gives a chronologically ordered analysis of Coleridge's attempts to write poetic romances that might as exercises in the supernatural yield transcendent knowledge. In "Ice and Spring: Coleridge's Imaginative Education" and "A Stream by Glimpses: Coleridge's Later Imagination" (*Coleridge's Variety,* ed. Beer, 1974, and *Coleridge's Poetic Intelligence*, 1977), Beer explores the cognitive-poetic patterns of Coleridge's speculations based on his readings of the Neoplatonists, Boehme, English empiricists, and manifold other now obscure writers—together making up the "facts of mind" and facts of science, the phantasmagoric powers and beliefs of the ancients and the scientific experiments and theories of the late eighteenth century that provide the context for Coleridge's poetry of a divinely ordered universe of self-renewing energy. Beer admits that his construct of Coleridge's world picture is suppositious; yet he does not always curb his learned enthusiasm to connect Coleridge's thought with the scientific knowledge of the day, esoteric, occult, avant-garde, experimental, and empirical alike, on the assumption that Coleridge's "extremely delicate and perceptive intelligence" had mastered it all. Beer should be read with caution, yet read, for his is a thoughtful summary of a fascinating range of parascientific theories and cogitations in the air at the end of the eighteenth century sufficient to satisfy even Coleridge's appetite for ideas. The system-making value Beer assigns to the mythological and occult reading of Coleridge is indirectly corroborated by Anya Taylor's *Magic and English Romanticism* (1979) and her "Intimations of Immortality: Coleridge's World of Spirits" (*Cithara,* 1982) and by Warren Stevenson's two studies "Divine Analogy: A Study of the Creation Motif in Blake and Coleridge" (*Romantic Reassessments* 25, ed. James Hogg, 1972) and "The Myth of the Golden Age in English Romantic Poetry" (*Salzburg Studies in English Literature* 109, ed. Hogg, 1981).

No less positive or speculative is the tack taken by M. H. Abrams, *Natural Supernaturalism: Tradition and Revolution in Romantic Literature* (1971), that Coleridge, along with other major English and German Romantic poets, reformulates inherited theological beliefs in secular philosophical terms. For Abrams the "root-principle throughout Coleridge's thought . . . is a generative conflict-in-attraction of polar forces, which part to be reunited on a higher level of being." Abrams follows the parabola of this "all living process" as it "moves along a circular and ascending course" powered by the "spiritual journey" of "The Ancient Mariner" and the "imagination impaired" of "Dejection: An Ode." In both poems, so Abrams' argument runs, Coleridge reaches upward for realization of "a shared life between the elementary polarity of mind and nature."

Not all the appraisals of Coleridge's achievement are ready to credit his poetic-philosophical play of mind as working always positively on his behalf. Misdirected religious expectations and uncontrollable psychological fears are diagnosed as at the root of Coleridge's shaky hold on his creative imagination. Marshall Suther in *The Dark Night of Samuel Taylor Coleridge* (1960) has Coleridge abandoning poetry making when it failed to usher him into the "complete presence and union in full knowledge" of the absolute. Geoffrey Yarlott in *Coleridge and the Abyssinian Maid* (1967) blames the slow withering of Coleridge's poetic imagination on guilty entrapment by his lifelong emotionally immature dependence on stalwart masculine and affectionate female figures. E. E. Bostetter in *The Romantic Ventriloquists* (1963; rpt. 1975) attributes Coleridge's floundering poetically after 1800 to his inability to resolve the moral ambivalence seemingly intrinsic in a universe he wished to believe was purposeful.

Bostetter is among the first, and possibly the most influential, of many critics to locate Coleridge's poetic inhibitions in his distrust of the "terrifying activity of the unconscious" and in his increasing reliance on the "conscious will." Others are Patricia Adair, *The Waking Dream: A Study of Coleridge's Poetry* (1967); L. D. Berkoben, *Coleridge's Decline as a Poet* (1975); and Anne K. Mellor, "Guilt and Samuel Taylor Coleridge" (in *English Romantic Irony,* 1980). Berkoben analyzes sun, moon, weed, and mold imagery in the poetry for indication of Coleridge's imaginative exploration of a natural world that appears to be less than benign and of a God more punitive than redemptive. Philosophically and theologically Coleridge professed a universe of cosmic harmony, with poetry functioning as a conveyor of this order; but the writing of poetry tended to release his latent yet deeply felt fears that he inhabited a moral world gone awry, with freedom of the will thwarted and distinctions between good and evil blurred. Rather than risk loss of faith in a Christian God, he suppressed his poetic urge—but not quite, for Coleridge never stopped writing poetry, and Berkoben concedes that the late poems yield up a purposeless universe in which the individual is alienated from beatitude by the puzzle of evil. Beth Lau perceives in the imagery of "Coleridge's Reflective Moonlight" (*SEL,* 1983) similar dramatic tensions at work in Coleridge's poetry. Mellor is the most recent critic to approach Coleridge as neurotically divided at the source of his genius. Using as her frame of reference the two world visions of Romantic irony (an ontological reality of dynamic, unconscious, amoral, and creative force) and of Christian theology (a moral order of coherent and psychological necessity), Mellor tabulates Coleridge's guilt-ridden ambivalence and the resultant dichotomy afflicting the major poems. She finds them wavering irresolutely between conflicting allegiances to the "Free Life" or the "Confining Form," the unconscious imagination's chaotic abundance or the understanding's limiting systems. Like Empson-Pirie (*Coleridge's Verse: A Selection,* 1973) she sees Coleridge instinctively distancing himself from an unpredictable, active universe in favor of the comforting orthodoxy of a Christian explanation. The result in a poem like "The Ancient Mariner" is a "painful tension" between the 1798 narration of the "Mariner's inexplicable, agonizing, joyful experience of a chaotic universe" and the 1817 glossist's Christian vision of a "sensible, rational, moral . . . ordered and just universe." Empson so deplores Coleridge's substitutions in "The Ancient Mariner" of "angels" for "spirits of the air" that with quirky directness, in one of the more eccentric reclamations of Coleridge's original intentions, he prints early versions and removes later layers of Christian piety in a bid to protect Coleridge from his own deceit.

Coleridge sought to realize through his poetry a unified self but was thwarted—so much criticism avers—by unresolved gaps of one sort or another in his psyche, vision, and expression. For David Morse, *Romanticism: A Structural Analysis* (1982), Coleridge is an instance of the Romantic artist as hero who grapples with the impossible task of recovering completely and perfectly in the poem the original vision. For Paul A. Magnuson, *Coleridge's Nightmare Poetry* (1974), Coleridge fails to construct an integrated individuality grounded in the external reality of nature and other persons. Starting with the "one Life" concept Coleridge "progresses" from a literature of joy and visionary delight (the Conversation poems) to one dwelling on isolation and loss ("The Ancient Mariner," "Christabel," "Dejection," and *Remorse*) with "Kubla Khan" transitional. Magnuson's fresh readings of the Conversation poems show Coleridge trying through the mediation of other minds—the Wordsworths, Lamb, Hartley Coleridge—to experience the oneness of existence closed to his perception. Thus, Magnuson transforms Coleridge poignantly into an observer of another's participation in the "one Life," a participant himself only ab extra through sympathetic identification with a loved one. For Kelvin Everest, in *Coleridge's Secret Ministry: The Context of the Conversation Poems 1795–1798* (1979), the "ministry" is to find an audience. The problem of audience and the ideal of the perfect reader as envisioned by the Romantic poets and by Coleridge are also examined by Morris Eaves, "Romantic Expressive Theory and Blake's Idea of the Audience" (*PMLA,* 1980); by Robert DeMaria, Jr., "The Ideal Reader: A Critical Fiction" (*PMLA,* 1978); and, in more formally restricted fashion, by James H. Averill, "The Shape of *Lyrical Ballads* (1798)" (*PQ,* 1981). Like Magnuson, Everest sees an insecure Coleridge turning away in the Conversation poems from a public voice to a private idiom that addresses an intimate circle of friends and celebrates the value of retirement. Everest is insightful as regards the context of the poems, especially the millenarian ideal in the 1790s of a select group of individuals sharing property and love in natural rustic surroundings and the links of this ideal of familial equality with Hartleian and Godwinian ideas, with the French Revolution, and with the radical Christian community. In the conflicting climate of radical political activity and counter conservative nationalism, Coleridge felt increasingly isolated by his class from the common people and by his principles from his social and intellectual fellows. Only in the private and informal voice of the Conversation poems does he achieve a modicum of success. Faulty tone and language in the public portions of these poems betray the failure of relationship between

Coleridge and a wide audience and confirm the dependence of his conversational idiom on a secure sense of audience. The polarities of solitary sublime experience versus social and ethical interaction are the focus of Fred V. Randel's analysis of "Reflections," "Fears in Solitude," and "Lines . . . Elbingerode" in "The Mountaintops of English Romanticism" (*TSLL*, 1981). Slighter estimates of Coleridge's losing battle against the demons of doubt concerning his powers of creativity and against his excessive self-conscious impulse are offered somewhat categorically by Fred Kaplan in *Miracles of Rare Device: The Poet's Sense of Self in Nineteenth-Century Poetry* (1972) and by Philip Hobsbaum in "Coleridge the Ice-Skater" (*Listener*, 1972).

The wide-screen absorption of Coleridge's mind insistently filtering its cogitations through multipoetic forms has left critics sorting through a disparate spectrum of ideas and responses in the hope of getting at the essential poet, and of isolating key attitudes informing his poetry. For Whalley, "Coleridge's Poetic Sensibility" (*Coleridge's Variety*, ed. Beer, 1974), it is Coleridge's skill with words more than his quicksilver sensitivity to experience that is the electrometer of his shaping coadunating imagination; for Patricia M. Ball, *The Science of Aspects: The Changing Role of Fact in the Work of Coleridge, Ruskin and Hopkins* (1971), his intense act of observation; for McFarland, "Problems of Style in the Poetry of Wordsworth and Coleridge" (*Romanticism and the Forms of Ruin*, 1981), his aspiration to imitate the Miltonic sublime, complicated in part by his belief that the proper poetic voice mingles poetry and philosophy, prompting his "false sublime" or "hysterical sublime," and in part by a cultural shift away from the limiting tradition of genre toward an appetitive poetry absorbing new subject matters and new forms of treatment; for Frederick L. Beaty, *Light from Heaven: Love in British Romantic Literature* (1975), his effort to idealize love into a spiritual possession of absolute goodness, for the therapeutic relief it brought his unrequited passion for Sara Hutchinson, without denying altogether the rightness and feasibility of earthly love; for Schulz, "Coleridge and the Enchantments of Earthly Paradise" (*Reading Coleridge*, ed. Crawford, 1979), his disquietude when he tries to partake poetically of "Eden's bowers" extended temporally, terrestrially, and cosmically by the end of the eighteenth century to comprise the whole earth and the endless reaches of space; for Angus Fletcher, " 'Positive Negation': Threshold, Sequence, and Personification in Coleridge" (*New Perspectives on Coleridge and Wordsworth*, ed. Hartman, 1972), his liminal mentality; for Michael G. Cooke, "The Manipulation of Space in Coleridge's Poetry" (*New Perspectives on Coleridge and Wordsworth*, 1972), his anxious sense of jeopardy and exposure before the random intimidation of unprotected space, which lends special resonance to his eagerness for a sacred retreat; and for Jerome J. McGann, *The Romantic Ideology: A Critical Investigation* (1983), his sense of spiritual aridity, disclosed poetically in the dominant theme of loss.

The kaleidoscopic Coleridge presented here perhaps finally resists the capability of any valence, unless it be the tension generated between irreconcilables pulling Coleridge first in one direction and then in the other. That is the implication of both Fletcher's and Cooke's subtle analyses of Coleridge's desperate poetics. As Cooke observes, Coleridge tries to ameliorate his feelings of dread either by duplicating through his powers as poet the spontaneous power of nature or by proposing a continuity between secure dell and unrelieved plain through radiation of love outward from bower to wide world of heaven and sea.

The vacillation of Coleridge literally and symbolically between a secure place of retirement and the threatening world at large is recurrently pointed to by critics, for example, D. G. James, *The Romantic Comedy* (1948), and Schulz (*JEGP*, 1962). Leonard Orr, "Coleridge's Dell by the River: Tension between the Enclosed and the Open" (*RS*, 1979), further traces from somewhat peccable logic and commonplace point of view, in poems up to and including "Kubla Khan," Coleridge's oscillating espousal first of the safety and domestic joy symbolized in the bower enclosure and then of the visionary freedom of the imagination symbolized in the river coursing through the Edenic dell. More reassuringly precise and historical is Patricia Parker's "The Progress of Phaedria's Bower: Spenser to Coleridge" (*ELH*, 1973), which attributes Coleridge's ambivalence toward the bower to the bower's complex literary associations. A topos of rejuvenating imaginative repose, it is also, at a human level, not without its suspiciously Circe-like lure of indolence and consequent threat to the vocation of poetry.

Coleridge used to be irresistible to psychoanalytical critics, Freudian (Beverly Fields, *Reality's Dark Dream*, 1967) and Jungian (Maud Bodkin, *Archetypal Patterns in Poetry*, 1934) alike; now he is a lure to those whose methodologies derive from current discourse theories and so-called postmodernist philosophies. Coleridge's self-conscious deployment of language, his sensitivity to the dialectics of communication and the need to insinuate meaning, and his complex psyche, with its habitual reach for truth and counterinstinct for duplicity, make his writings seem designed for the heuristics of critics who foray into what Jerome C. Christensen (*ELH*, 1978) calls "the terrain of subfictions" that comprises the landscape of Coleridge's thought. Thus, in a provocative adaptation of Julian Jayne's hypothesis in *The Origin of Consciousness in the Breakdown of the Bicameral Mind* (1977), Edward Proffitt, "Romanticism, Bicamerality, and the Evolution of the Brain" (*WC*, 1978), explains Coleridge's "two vastly different kinds of poem: the incantatory versus the conversational" as products of right-brain and left-brain orientations. Meena Alexander, *The Poetic Self: Towards a Phenomenology of Romanticism* (1980), selects "The Eolian Harp," "This Lime-tree Bower," and "Frost at Midnight" as instances of the isolated inward self's quest for an external ordered selfhood. And Richard A. Rand, "Geraldine" (*Glyph*, 1978), generalizes in the language of Derrida that Coleridge's poetry ("Christabel," "Frost at Midnight," and "A Tombless Epitaph") encrypts, or covers up, in the body of its text the meaning of its signature, carrying the meaning "as an invisible or unacknowledged but powerful force, material, individual, and persisting." Since many of these meta- or postmodernist critics have tackled the prose or concentrate on a single poem, principally "The Ancient Mariner," they are reviewed in those respective sections and subdivisions.

Some other theorists who cast wider nets, however, can be dealt with here. David Simpson, *Irony and Authority in Romantic Poetry* (1979), cites "The Ancient Mariner," "Kubla Khan," and "The Eolian Harp" for employing as part of the speaking voice a metacommentary that heuristically apes the reader-speaker relationship. Because this relationship is ironic, it leaves between poem and reader an empty space, an indeterminacy brought about by the author's abdication of his habitual closural role. Pointing to "definite methodological principles" justifying Coleridge's "notoriously 'fragmentary' output," Simpson suggests that Coleridge left his discourse "deliberately incomplete" to bring his readers into the discourse, enticing them to engage in the same mental and imaginative exploration as the author. In this context the poem becomes a heuristic model for growth in consciousness. Kathleen M. Wheeler, *The Creative Mind in Coleridge's Poetry* (1981), even more arbitrarily reorders the priorities, relationships, and meanings of "Kubla Khan," "The Ancient Mariner," "The Eolian Harp," "Frost at Midnight," and "This Lime-tree Bower," treating them as self-reflexive commentaries on the act of participatory reading and on the poem as an aesthetic representation, or self-mirroring model, of Coleridge's presumed philosophy of art. Wheeler on occasion so blithely disregards poetic context and intentionality one is moved to disbelief that Coleridge could have had in mind, or wished to foster, quite such a "strong" reading when in the *Friend* he demanded of the reader thought and attention. Jean-Pierre Mileur, *Vision and Revision: Coleridge's Art of Immanence* (1982), best formulates the contingency of Coleridge's relationship to his poems and the process by which Coleridge the poet-creator evolved into Coleridge the critic-reader. In his poetry—from "The Eolian Harp" to "Dejection"—Coleridge confronts an inner self as a mysterious other threatening to evade the emotional equilibrium and control sought by way of the poetic statement. The poems become, in their manifested intentionality, fragmentary documents of his imperfectly realized poetic intentions. He accordingly moved to complete his poems through the context of revision—the preface to "Kubla Khan," the gloss to "The Ancient Mariner," the conclusion to part 2 of "Christabel"—and to redefine his intellectual development from poet to critic in keeping with his perception that literature needs a critic-reader to complete its meaning. Tilottama Rajan, *Dark Interpreter: The Discourse of Romanticism* (1980), shifts perspective to look at what the unclosed space in the poem tells us about the Romantic poet. She perceives Coleridge deploying his poetry less as an heuristic design on the reader than as an instrument to carry on an uneasy dialogue with self-projected ideals almost impossible of attainment. Although semiaware of the gap between his perceptions and his imagination and of the tenuous mediation that words provide between thought and thing—and hence of the uncertain authority of poetic vision—Coleridge persists in logocentric belief in the transcendent truth of his poetic self-projections. This too is an intriguing Coleridge, although one not so consciously methodological and resourceful as Simpson's, Wheeler's, and Mileur's, a Coleridge who structures his Conversation poems in terms of negations and reversals rather than of affirmations and developments, claiming epiphanies by vicarious creation of surrogates and narcissistically fielding an imagination whose vision is persistently self-echoing and persistently separated from fact. In the late poems his imagination has lost faith in its own illusions and grinds out a rhetoric unconvincing even to itself. Edward Kessler, *Coleridge's Metaphors of Being* (1979), defines the late Coleridge as suspended between thoughts and things, bent on reconciling the created and creating parts of nature into representation of ideal being. Drawing on the Heideggerian discrimination of being, as opposed to a completed life, Kessler sees Coleridge reaching after this balance of opposing forces by means of poetry. Hence the deliberate unfinished form of the late poems: to be fully formed is to be inert, since a completed life is an arrested life—phantoms (objects of earth) lacking in spiritual growth. Modulating yet full statements, abstract yet symbolic, these poems reflect Coleridge's effort to transcend material forms without spinning off into the empyrean. Despite an open-ended critical-philosophical methodology, Kessler has written the best treatment yet of the post-1802 poetry. (For further comment see in this section "'Dejection: An Ode,' Late Poetry, and Drama.") Arden Reed, *Romantic Weather: The Climates of Coleridge and Baudelaire* (1983), fixates on meteorology—particularly the operative climate of mist and sunlight—as a system of signs and as topos to map Coleridge's poetics backwards from "Reason" to "Religious Musings," with full readings of "Constancy to an Ideal Object," "Frost at Midnight," "The Ancient Mariner," essay 15 of the *Friend,* and chapter 13 of *Biographia Literaria.* The weather lowers not insignificantly in a poetry describing a world still responsive to the fallout of Newtonian physics, but Reed's treatment is more keyed to the thunder and lightning of Michel Serres, Jacques Derrida, Ferdinand de Saussure, and Paul de Man. Under this scrutiny Coleridge's poetry circles about the dualities of truth and obscurity, illumination and mystification, unable to resolve the duplicitous relationship of the imagination to nature and to the written word, which leads as problematically to damnation as to salvation. The critical aperçus of these books elicit profoundly interesting perceptions of Coleridge and his poetry, but the occasional barbarity of language does violence to ear and mind, a fault common to much of postmodernist criticism as it seeks to verbalize what is left unvoiced in the poetic discourse, what has been for the poet almost beyond the linguistic range of conscious perceptions but which lies encoded, and encrypted, in the tropes of the text.

Other studies of a general nature touching on one facet or another of Coleridge as poet are: I. A. Richards, "Coleridge: The Vulnerable Poet" (*YR,* 1959); Francis Scarfe, "Coleridge's Nightscapes" (*EA,* 1965); Lura Nancy and Duilio T. Pedrini, *Serpent Imagery and Symbolism: A Study of the Major English Romantic Poets* (1966); Alice Chandler, *A Dream of Order: The Medieval Ideal in Nineteenth-Century Literature* (1970); R. A. Durr, *Poetic Vision and the Psychedelic Experience* (1970); Lionel Stevenson, "The Mystique of Romantic Narrative Poetry," *Romantic and Victorian: Studies in Memory of William H. Marshall,* edited by W. Paul Elledge and Richard L. Hoffman (1971); Harold Bloom, *The Ringers in the Tower: Studies in Romantic Tradition* (1971); Allan Grant, *A Preface to Coleridge* (1972); Oswald Doughty, "Coleridge and the 'Gothic Novel' or 'Tales of Terror'" (*EM,* 1972); George H. Gilpin, "The Strategy of Joy: An Essay on the Poetry of Samuel Taylor Coleridge" (*Romantic Reassessments* 3, ed. Hogg, 1972); Jeanne Halpern, "Coleridge's Aviary: A Field Guide to Bird Imagery in His Poems" (*Rackham Literary Studies,* 1974); N. F. Blake, "Coleridge's Poetic Language," *Literature of the Romantic Period 1750–1850,* edited by R. T. Davies and B. G. Beatty (1976); and J. R. de J. Jackson, *Poetry of the Romantic Period* (1980).

POETIC ORIGINS; LITERARY INFLUENCES;
SOCIOPOLITICAL, HISTORICAL, AND CULTURAL
INDEBTEDNESS

The industry of searching out the genesis of poems has abated spectacularly, concurrent with the decline in authority of *The Road to Xanadu* and with the upsurge in critical methodologies leaning toward linguistics, the social sciences,
and phenomenological philosophies. Not that there is any lack of ongoing efforts
to explain Coleridge's poetry by way of his presumed reading of this or that piece
of literature, as the excursus at the end of this section indicates; and "The Ancient
Mariner" and "Kubla Khan" still garner the greatest number of debts to other letters and literatures. It is just that the faiths of an older generation in this mode of
literary criticism no longer enlist many passionate adherents. Indeed, Leslie
Brisman, "Coleridge and the Ancestral Voices" (*GaR*, 1975; rpt. in *Romantic Origins*, 1978), ironically apotheosizes "Kubla Khan" as itself in search of cultural and
mythic origins. The effect of this assault on the literary continuity of a poem is to
empty it of further lexical congruence—and inconsequentially to put the source
hunters out of countenance. No matter, perhaps, for the source-bearing vein of
Coleridge's poems seems mined, temporarily at least, of its richest ore. A sign of
the played-out Coleridgean lode, if not of the changing critical temper as well, is
the laborious distinction between "influence" and "inspiration" developed by
Robert F. Fleissner, "Shakespeare Again in Xanadu" (*RS*, 1975). Fleissner invokes
the concept of inspiration, untied to specific echoes or analogies, to get from
Alph to Xanadu faster than any critic writing today—although not at times without a touch of jeu d'esprit (as in "*Hwaet! Wē Gar Dēna:* 'Kubla Khan' and Those
Anglo-Saxon Words," *WC*, 1974).

Another sign of the exhausted inventory of influences on Coleridge, which
may equally be signaling the rise in his reputation as a thinker influencing others, is that the past yields its attraction to the future. From looking backward the
industry of searching out parallels has turned to looking forward. If Coleridge
drew his raw materials for poems from the primary resources of others, he in
turn supplied literary heirs with materials and products for their writings. Thus,
the critical search and discovery for indebtedness avidly goes on, but with
Coleridge the creditor rather than the debtor (see excursus at the end of this
section).

Relatively silent also are the noisy debates of several decades ago over the
dating of "Kubla Khan," the authorship of "The Mad Monk" (although Parrish has
tried to keep the issue alive, by reiterating in *The Art of the* Lyrical Ballads [1973]
his brief for Wordsworth's claim to the poem), and the reciprocal poetic lend-
lease that went on between Coleridge and Wordsworth. David B. Eakin's survey
"Coleridge's Early Poetry: Toward an Articulation in 'The Eolian Harp' " (*CP*, 1978)
is, contrariwise, self-effacing, careful not to make larger claims than the poems of
1790–93 can sustain. In brief, Eakin would have it that these poems reveal
Coleridge groping toward the introspective perceptions of a poetic sensibility in

rapport with nature that he realizes for the first time in "The Eolian Harp."

What attempts there are to place this or that of Coleridge's poems within a historical context are of sterner scholarly stuff than the run-of-the-mill parallel mongering. Prickett in *Coleridge and Wordsworth: The Poetry of Growth* (1970) draws on Newtonian optics, Lockian psychology, and technical developments in science to explicate Coleridge's deployment of the Brockenspecter, corona or "glory" (as in "Constancy to an Ideal Object"), as an image of the imagination's mediation between real and ideal worlds. The highly original study "Vaughan, Wordsworth, Coleridge and the *Encomium Asini*" (*ELH*, 1975) by Leah Sinanoglou Marcus resuscitates "To a Young Ass" by deftly situating it in a long tradition of rebellious counterstands against the existent social order. Good as are Marcus' historical perceptions, vastly more rigorous antiquarian powers have gone into E. S. Shaffer's reconstruction (*"Kubla Khan" and* The Fall of Jerusalem: *The Mythological School in Biblical Criticism and Secular Literature 1770–1880,* 1975) of the Higher Criticism that flourished in England in the 1790s in the Beddoes and Priestley circles and that contributed to Coleridge's ambitions to write a religious epic poem that would reflect the biblical mythography of his age.

Coleridge maintained lifelong both theoretical and practical concerns for the body politic, and its exercise of civil and social authority. His early activities in Bristol were highly politicized, and his twenty-year association with the *Morning Post* and *Courier* dealt as often as not with governmental policies. Yet this preoccupation with political and social matters as background to his poetry is only occasionally touched on. Carl R. Woodring's *Politics in the Poetry of Coleridge* (1961) and *Politics in English Romantic Poetry* (1970) after twenty and ten years respectively continue as standard studies of the subject. Several recent articles, however, add shading to Woodring's chiaroscuro. Besides Everest's glance (*Coleridge's Secret Ministry,* 1979) at the impact of a revolutionized ethos on Coleridge's private and public poetic voices, Karl Kroeber, "Coleridge's 'Fears': Problems in Patriotic Poetry" (*Clio,* 1978), and David Aers, Jonathan Cook, and David Punter, *Romanticism and Ideology: Studies in English Writing, 1765–1830* (1981), explore how the sociopolitical reverberations of Coleridge's thought impinge on his poems. In "Fears in Solitude," according to Kroeber, Coleridge could still converse with his compatriots while speaking in solitude to himself. By 1809–10 he cannot assume that this poetically personal form of address automatically includes society at large. All well and good up to here, but then Kroeber makes this limited poetic instance muster an answer to the big question of why Coleridge to all intents and purposes ceased to consider himself a poet. Intellectually isolated, a private poet dependent on a self he never trusted, Coleridge was bound to lose faith in himself, Kroeber believes, when he could no longer define himself against his society as a true patriotic poet. Aers, Cook, and Punter in acute analyses of the rhetorical ploys of the early poetry, pre-1795 and post-1795, suggest that Coleridge never squarely faced the real social issues of his day but regularly withdrew into solipsistic reverie, providential pattern, and idealistic Christian generalities and apologetics.

Whereas Beer (*Coleridge the Visionary,* 1959) emphasizes the priestly and artistic pretensions of Kubla Khan in his discussion of the man of genius and the man of action, looking askance for the most part at their possible political implications, and Woodring ("Coleridge and the Khan," *EIC,* 1959) cautiously identifies the Khan as an Asiatic despot bent on appropriating for his pleasure the unencompassable sacred, Norman Rudich, "Coleridge's 'Kubla Khan': His Anti-Political Vision" (*Weapons of Criticism: Marxism in American and Literary Tradition,* ed. N. Rudich, 1976), baldly reads the poem against the backdrops of Coleridge's political recantation in "France: An Ode" and of his morally fervent patriotism in "Fears in Solitude" as a statement of basically reactionary political prophecy. In this context "Kubla Khan" marks the climax of Coleridge's complex ideological transformation from advocacy of political activism to cultivation of the sacred poetic mission of defending aesthetic and moral values against incompatible state power. Beer and Woodring are wise to signify the political undertones of the poem tentatively and on its own terms, for Rudich with unsubtle Marxist reductivism makes Napoleon "the occasion and the model for Coleridge's anti-political vision," although stopping short of actually equating the French emperor with the Oriental satrap. It may be an act of wisdom on the part of Coleridgeans to have generally skirted the topic of politics in Coleridge's major poems as being too sublimated for even the finest critical scapel. Such is one conclusion to be drawn from Brisman's Freudian-Derridean unmasking (in *Romantic Origins,* 1978) of the man from Porlock who acts out for the beleaguered imagination of Coleridge the role of the censoring conscience come fortuitously to interrupt his visionary recreation of a sociopolitical-religious paradise. As an interesting sidelight to the whole question, none of this deters Beer from discussing "poems of political prophecy" in the introduction to his Everyman's edition of *Coleridge's Poems* (1975).

Nevertheless, Stuart Peterfreund, "Coleridge and the Politics of Critical Vision" (*SEL,* 1981), and Robert Sternbach, "Coleridge, Joan of Arc, and the Idea of Progress" (*ELH,* 1979), have tried to define Coleridge's "failed political vision of European history," respectively, by extrapolating from Coleridge's writings, "The Destiny of Nations," "Kubla Khan," and *Biographia Literaria,* a Coleridgean solution to the historical disjunctions between the realities of political vision and the ideals of critical vision, and by juxtaposing successive portions of "The Destiny of Nations," the early 1794 lines Coleridge contributed to Southey's *Joan of Arc,* and the later 1795–96 section that Coleridge published in 1797 as "The Visions of the Maid of Orleans. A Fragment." Theirs is a sad story of Coleridge's loss of confidence in the moral and rational progress of history, which intractably refuses reformation. As Sternbach puts it, one of the deep and recurrent tensions in the poetry of Coleridge derives from his "desire for the rational perfectibility of man" while beset with "an inward imaginative acknowledgment of the ambiguousness of human nature." That Coleridge never quite stopped dreaming in poetic terms about an ideal moral state is succinctly demonstrated by J. D. Coates, who documents "Coleridge's Debt to Harrington: A Discussion of *Zapolya*" (*JHI,* 1977). Like Harrington, Coleridge locates the stability of his ideal state in a country gentry whose traditional values rest on the religious cultivation of inner and moral truth rather than on the empirical pursuit of mechanistic and materialistic ends. In the evolution of Coleridge's lifelong effort to define the body politic, *Zapolya* in a sense occupies the midpoint between his short-lived early antiproperty phase of pantisocracy and his mature triadic organization of society into landowners and yeomen, commercial-manufacturing and professional orders, and clerisy of *On the Constitution of the Church and State* (1829).

A small start has been made toward determining Coleridge's appreciation of the other arts, his use of their modes of perception and renderings of reality in his poetry, and his role in relating them theoretically to literature; but much more remains to be done. According to Coleridge he had no ear for music, but not unsurprisingly he took "the intensest delight" in it. He studied the violin while at Cambridge, numbered as friend the violinist and musical instrument inventor Charles Clagget, and was an avid concert goer. His susceptibility to opera is indirectly adumbrated in Edgar C. Knowlton's "A Coleridge Allusion to Angelica Catalani (1780–1849)" (*N&Q,* 1978), which discusses a leading soprano in London in 1812–13. Erland Anderson, "Harmonious Madness: A Study of Music Metaphors in the Poetry of Coleridge, Shelley and Keats" (*Romantic Reassessments* 12, ed. Hogg, 1975), and Sue E. Coffman, "Music of Finer Tone: Musical Imagery of the Major Romantic Poets" (*Romantic Reassessments* 89, ed. Hogg, 1979), document Coleridge's use of musical imagery as idea and as metaphor, showing musical tropes to be remarkably pervasive in Coleridge's poetry and central to his imaginative apprehension of a harmonious world of nature. Startling, nevertheless, is Anderson's claim, undocumented except for references to Shelley and Keats, that links between contemporary musical taste and Coleridge's theory of imagination proved seminal for the nineteenth century. As for art, Woodring tabulates "What Coleridge Thought of Pictures" (*Images of Romanticism,* ed. Karl Kroeber and William Walling, 1978). Two other articles in the same collection—James A. W. Heffernan, "The English Romantic Perception of Color," and Ronald Paulson, "Turner's Graffiti: The Sun and Its Glosses"—comment on Coleridge's richly chromatic sense of nature, from white to red, in "The Ancient Mariner," and on the analogies between the "bloody" sun in that poem and in Turner's paintings, especially *Slavers Throwing Overboard the Dead and Dying* (exhibited 1840). In "Reflections on Reflections in English Romantic Poetry and Painting" (*BuR,* 1978), Heffernan pursues with cross-disciplinary critical sensitivity the typologies of Coleridge and Turner, and the receptivity of both men, as Romantics, to the idealizing power of the natural world. James B. Twitchell, *Romantic Horizons: Aspects of the Sublime in English Poetry and Painting, 1770–1850* (1983), devotes a chapter to the same connections between "The Ancient Mariner" and Turner's *Slavers.*

To seek a useful listing of source studies, even though they have abated in recent years in *furor parturitus,* is a Sisyphean task. Included here are ones of the immediate past I thought either representative, relevant, provocative, critically useful, intellectually bizarre (but not wholly foolish), or intriguing. The order of presentation follows in (1) and (3) the chronology of Coleridge's poems and in

(2) first English, then American writers chronologically to the present. On major poems the citations proceed from early, particular, and individual to late, general, and multiple.

(1) *Influences on Coleridge:* (early poems) A. Harris Fairbanks, " 'Dear Native Brook': Coleridge, Bowles, and Thomas Warton, the Younger" (*WC,* 1975), on "To the River Otter"; Arthur Johnston, "The Source of Coleridge's 'Imitated from the Welsh' " (*YES,* 1976); Daniel Stempel, "Revelation on Mount Snowdon: Wordsworth, Coleridge and the Fichtean Imagination" (*JAAC,* 1971); ("Kubla Khan") H. W. Piper, "Mount Abora" (*N&Q,* 1973), and "Two Paradises in *Kubla Khan*" (*RES,* 1976); R. F. Fleissner, " 'Kubla Khan' as an Integrationist Poem" (*Negro Amer. Lit. Forum,* 1974); Eugene L. Stelzig, "The Landscape of 'Kubla Khan' and the *Valley of Rocks*" (*WC,* 1975); (Conversation poems) James H. Averill, "Coleridge's 'The Eolian Harp' and James Thomson's 'An Ode on Aeolus Harp' " (*ELN,* 1979); John Barnard, "An Echo of Keats in 'The Eolian Harp' " (*RES,* 1977); Barbara Leah Harman, "Herbert, Coleridge, and the Vexed Work of Narration" (*MLN,* 1978), on Conversation poems; John Gutteridge, "Scenery and Ecstasy: Three of Coleridge's Blank Verse Poems" (*New Approaches to Coleridge,* ed. Sultana, 1981), on "The Eolian Harp," "This Lime-tree Bower," and "Reflections"; Ann Matheson, "The Influence of Cowper's *The Task* on Coleridge's Conversation Poems" (*New Approaches to Coleridge,* ed. Sultana, 1981); ("Dejection: An Ode") Elizabeth Bieman, "Devils' Yule and Mountain-Birth: Miltonic Echoes in Coleridge's 'Dejection Ode' " (*Milton and Romantics,* 1976); Julia DiSteffano Pappageorge, "Coleridge's 'Mad Lutanist': A Romantic Response to Ann Radcliffe" (*BRH,* 1979), on "Dejection: An Ode"; (post-"Dejection" poems) W. L. Braekman, "An Imitation by Samuel Taylor Coleridge of a Medieval German Love Song" (*Neophil,* 1972), on "The Blossoming of the Solitary Date-tree"; and George M. Ridenour, "Justification by Faith in Two Romantic Poems" (*WC,* 1979), on "Limbo." For a sampling of the bewildering variety of sources that have been put forward for "Kubla Khan"—"the majority of [which] cease to be interesting because they illuminate nothing"—see Fruman, *Coleridge, the Damaged Archangel* (1971), which also cites a wealth of borrowings in other of Coleridge's poems.

(2) *Coleridge's Influence on Other Writers:* (Romantics) On the Shelley-Byron circle (Charles E. Robinson, *ELN,* 1971; C. Darrel Sheraw, *KSMB,* 1972), on Peacock (H. M. Robinson, *N&Q,* 1979), on Keats (Jack Stillinger, *WC,* 1971; Rosemarie Maier, *JEGP,* 1971; Frank W. Pearce, *KSJ,* 1975), (Victorians) on Tennyson (Robert F. Fleissner, *RS,* 1971; Philip Pittman, *VIJ,* 1973; June Steffensen Hagen, *AN&Q,* 1975), on Hopkins (William A. Dumbleton, *ArielE,* 1972), on J. S. Mill (Glenn K. S. Man, *Revue de l'Univ. d'Ottowa,* 1975), on Newman (J. Beer, *The English Mind,* ed. Hugh Sykes Davies and George Watson, 1964; David J. DeLaura, *Hebrew and Hellene in Victorian England: Newman, Arnold, and Pater,* 1969), on Arnold (DeLaura, *PLL,* 1972; DeLaura, *Nineteenth-Century Literary Perspectives: Essays in Honor of Lionel Stevenson,* ed. Clyde de L. Ryals, 1974), on Lewes (William Baker, *Library,* 1976), on Rossetti (Virginia Surtees, *The Paintings and Drawings of Dante Gabriel Rossetti (1828–1882): A Catalogue Raisonné,* 1971), on Wilde (Burton R. Pollin, *RLV,* 1974), (moderns) on Forster (Fleissner, *Indian Literature,* New Delhi, 1971), on Yeats (Beryl Rowland, *OL,* 1971; George Bornstein, *Roman-*

tic and Modern: Revaluations of Literary Tradition, 1977), on Pound (Beer, *TLS,* 1973), on Auden (James McClellan, *NDQ,* 1979), on Tolkien (Jan Wojcik, *Renascence,* 1968), (nineteenth-century Americans) on Emerson (Kenneth Walter Cameron, *ESQ,* 1971; Barry Wood, *PMLA,* 1976; rpt. *Emerson's Nature: Origin, Growth, Meaning,* ed. M. M. Sealts, Jr., and A. E. Ferguson, 1979), on Thoreau (Richard A. Hocks, *CentR,* 1973), on the American transcendentalists and on Poe (Alexander Kern, *New Approaches to Coleridge,* ed. Sultana, 1981), on Hawthorne (R. H. Fogle, *Criticism,* 1971, rpt. *The Permanent Pleasure: Essays on Classics of Romanticism,* 1974; Mario L. D'Avanzo, *SSF,* 1973; Harry J. Cargas, *New Laurel R,* 1975; John E. Holsberry, *TSLL,* 1979), on Poe (Michael Black, *NLH,* 1975), (twentieth-century Americans) on O'Neill (Frank R. Cunningham, *Eugene O'Neill N,* 1979), on Frost (Ronald A. Sharp, *PLL,* 1979), on Stevens (Robert DeMaria, Jr., *Genre,* 1979; Herbert J. Stern, *SoR,* 1979), on Wolfe (Rainer Lengeler, *N&Q,* 1973); on Borges (W. P. Fitzpatrick, *Studies in Humanities,* 1977), on Carson McCullers (Mary Dell Fletcher, *SCB,* 1975), and on Le Guin (Peter S. Alterman, *Ursula K. Le Guin,* ed. J. D. Olander and M. H. Greenberg, 1979).

Then there are those writers and thinkers who derive less an identifiable idea or fact from this or that piece of Coleridge's writings than a mode of cognition, a way of analyzing and organizing human experience, historical-religious perceptions, and sociopolitical concerns. On the pervasive impact of Coleridge in nineteenth- and twentieth-century England, and in twentieth-century America, see Graham Hough, "Coleridge and the Victorians," *The English Mind* (ed. Davies and Watson, 1964); David Newsome, *Two Classes of Men* (1974), the Birkbeck Lectures of 1972, which consider the rival religious traditions at Victorian Oxford and Cambridge; John Mander, *Our German Cousins* (1974), who examines the transmission of Kantian philosophy to the English and the religio-social basis of Broad Church Christian socialism; Albert Rothenberg and Carl R. Housman, editors, *The Creativity Question* (1976), who survey and explore the tradition starting in the nineteenth century that holds individual originality in high esteem; R. J. Reilly, *Romantic Religion: A Study of Barfield, Lewis, Williams, and Tolkien* (1971), who pursues the aesthetic and religious ideas that vitalized these men's minds; Eileen Mackinlay, *The Shared Experience* (1969), who recounts her successes and failures with West Country College students in a writing class pervaded by the "presence" of Coleridge and his perception of the processes of his imagination; Newton P. Stallknecht, "Poetry and the Lure of the Real: Some Reflections on S. T. Coleridge, Wallace Stevens and Marianne Moore" (*Texte und Kontexte: Studien zur deutschen und vergleichenden Literaturwissenschaft,* ed. Manfred Durzak, Eberhard Reichmann, and Ulrich Weisstein, 1973), who uses Coleridge's remarks on the imagination and the poetic consciousness to gloss Stevens' poetic objectives; and Robert Lewis Sayon, *Open to Criticism* (1971), a radio-television reviewer and producer who draws on Coleridge to formulate a criticism comprehending popular arts that focuses broadly on the humanistic and philosophical, not "merely the esthetic."

(3) *Heterodox and Unclassifiable Relationships:* D. H. Reiman, "Christobell; or, The Case of the Sequel Preemptive" (*WC,* 1975), identifies Anna Jane Vardill as the author of the "presumptuous" rhymed couplet attempt to complete

"Christabel" in 1815; R. Haven, "Anna Vardill Niven's 'Christobell': An Addendum" (*WC,* 1976), counts the number of times "Christobell" has been "found" and wonders despairingly how such "finds" can be averted by better bibliographies; A. Harris Fairbanks, "Coleridge's Opinion of 'France: An Ode' " (*RES,* 1975), deplores Coleridge's put-down of "that dull ode"; and Marshall Brown, "Towards an Archeology of English Romanticism: Coleridge and Sarbiewski" (*CL,* 1978), mounts a Foucault-oriented comparative study.

"THE ANCIENT MARINER," "KUBLA KHAN," "CHRISTABEL"

The interpretative history of "The Ancient Mariner" has become so extensive and so complex that critiques of the poem have begun to read like biblical exegeses, each critical point prefaced by a précis of received opinions on the issue. There are two taxonomic attempts at digesting this vast disparate body of writings. Schulz (" 'The Ancient Mariner,' " *ERP3*) arranges the material historically according to interpretation (moral, religious, philosophical) and according to critical methodology (sources, symbolist, mythicist, psychoanalytic, formalist). Mary L. T. Milton ("Introduction: Major Issues in Coleridge Criticism," *The Poetry of Samuel Taylor Coleridge: An Annotated Bibliography of Criticism, 1935 –1970,* 1981) follows loosely the establishment of the main themes and the chronology of events in the poem, her discussion keyed in at all points to her annotated bibliography.

The chief critical positions have been staked out now for about twenty years, handily recapitulated by Sarah Dyck (*SEL,* 1973) and Raimonda Modiano (*MLQ,* 1977). These view the poem as a sacramental vision of crime, punishment, and redemption and, at a secondary thematic level, as an exposition of the creative imagination's apprehension of the "one Life" (Robert Penn Warren, "A Poem of Pure Imagination," *KR,* 1946; rpt. and exp. with an edition of the poem, 1946; rpt. with additional notes, *Selected Essays,* 1958), as a nightmarish tale of senseless suffering (E. E. Bostetter, "The Nightmare World of *The Ancient Mariner,*" *SIR,* 1962; reiterated in *The Romantic Ventriloquists,* 1963, 1975), as a prophetic allegory of Coleridge's personal life (Whalley, "The Mariner and the Albatross," *UTQ,* 1947), as a poetic structuring of Coleridge's speculative readings in occult and mythological literatures linking humanity and the physical universe with an ultimate eternal and divine order (Beer, *Coleridge the Visionary,* 1959), as a subtle psychodrama of the human mind organizing its conscious experience of a world that lies beyond its material and factual measurement (Beer, *Coleridge's Poetic Intelligence,* 1977), and as a poetic workshop for Coleridge's later metaphysics (Irene H. Chayes, "A Coleridgean Reading of 'The Ancient Mariner,' " *SIR,* 1965).

The overarching critical division has been between the Warrenists, who would read the poem as confirmation of a supernatural benevolent universe, and the Bostetterites, who are skeptical of the intelligibility of that universe. The aim in much recent criticism has been to chip away at the inconsistencies and contradictions inherent in these standard positions, in the hope of clarifying, if not resolving, the basic conflicts. The other tactic adopted is to place the contrary worlds of the poem in irresolvable tension to one another. Applying with the rigor of a textbook exercise the test of logic to the problematics of the poem's moral, the Mariner's freedom of will, and the supernatural world's benevolence or malevolence, George Bellis, "The Fixed Crime of 'The Ancient Mariner'" (*EIC*, 1974), concludes that none of the critics who have hazarded answers—Lowes, Babbitt, Gingerich, Clarke, Bostetter, Beer—are absolutely right. Through a series of tortuous hypotheses Bellis establishes that all events in the poem are supernaturally influenced, including sinful ones, which precede and confirm the agency of salvation. James B. Twitchell, "The World above the Ancient Mariner" (*TSLL*, 1975), justifies the sacramental vision of oneness in terms of the Neoplatonic apparatus of tutelary spirits and natal demons who supply a psychodramatic dimension to the thematic and architectonic structure of the poem (and here Twitchell gets suppositious) by mirroring the Mariner's psychological "progression" in knowledge of the unified material and spiritual worlds. For Prickett, *Romanticism and Religion* (1976), the poem is both a psychological drama and a religious experience, sorting out into two "incompatible yet interdependent worlds" of psychological fact and mysterious Christian truths, with neither alone satisfactory and neither together wholly adequate, between which is enacted the drama of the Mariner's fall and redemption through grace. Less charitably inclined towards the universe of "The Ancient Mariner" is Abe Delson, "The Symbolism of the Sun and Moon in 'The Rime of the Ancient Mariner'" (*TSLL*, 1974). Delson goes to great lengths to show that past commentators have been wrong in insisting that the moon and sun are symbolically either favorable or unfavorable, when in fact both have "alternatingly benevolent and malevolent" associations, with their beneficent power "always transitory and their final association . . . malevolent." All but the die-hard Warrenists committed to a symbolic frame in their reading of the poem have suspected this for a long time. Delson, in a less sound effort to discredit the physical world (and to salvage Coleridge's positive position on God), is also at pains to separate the religious-Christian references in the poem from the nature references. Much subtler, and wittily persuasive, is Reed's discussion of "The Ancient Mariner" (in *Romantic Weather*, 1983), which resolves the Warren-Bostetter circle of yes-no by contending the futility of arguing either side of the case, since the poem is irredeemably duplicitous. Singling out its commitment to doubling, its making and unmaking of congruence implicit in the pun on rime (rhyme), Reed identifies the text with the Mariner, the story of his riming (i.e., the freezing of his blood in spiritual death) with the rhymer. The poem, its language forever fixed in the embodiment of both-and—sacramental blessing and senseless cursing—ensures that the Mariner can never be redeemed, because the rhyming of his riming would cease to exist should he be unrimed.

A sign of the centrality of "The Ancient Mariner" in twentieth-century poetics, as well as of the weakening authority of Warren's interpretation, is that two new-mode critical theorists have chosen to set forth the "excessive limitings" of New Criticism as adumbrated in Warren's reading of "The Ancient Mariner." Homer Obed Brown, "The Art of Theology and the Theology of Art: Robert Penn Warren's Reading of Coleridge's *The Rime of the Ancient Mariner*" (*Boundary 2*,

1979), establishes the restrictive intellectual assumptions behind Warren's creative critical act vis-à-vis the poem. His division of the poem into primary and secondary themes (which are actually parts of *one* fused theme) is dictated by his desire to reconcile the two traditional conflicting approaches: the moralist's and the artistic purist's, the Babbitts' and the Loweses'. Warren's closed system, however, proliferates new divisions—literal-metaphoric references, good-bad metaphors—and excludes from consideration those events whose explanation falls outside the symbolic order Warren has framed: the Mariner's continued alienation, the exorbitant supernatural machinery, the chance occurrences. Jonathan Arac, "Repetition and Exclusion: Coleridge and New Criticism Reconsidered" (*Boundary 2*, 1979), adds to this critique of New Criticism's exclusionary reading Warren's arbitrary opposition of the imagination (and poetry) to the understanding (and science) when it should have been in Coleridgean terms the reason to the understanding. The latter dichotomy, however, introduces the question of whether religion eventually displaced Coleridge's poetic activity, which Warren wished to avoid. Nor does Coleridge's reason-understanding equation allow for the opposition of poetry to science, which he does wish to preserve. Warren accordingly remains within the context of the poem, thereby keeping a distance between it and its Coleridgean origins, while maintaining the fiction of poem and its origins being continuous. Both Brown and Arac also repudiate Warren's reliance on the symbol to unite his divided reading and are thus in accord with Paul de Man's powerful indictment of the Romantic symbol for pretending identity where allegory more honestly acknowledges in the repetition of differences that identity can never be reached (see "Intentional Structure of the Romantic Image," 1960; rpt. in *Romanticism and Consciousness: Essays in Criticism,* ed. Bloom, 1970; and "The Rhetoric of Temporality: Allegory and Symbol, Irony," *Interpretation: Theory and Practice,* ed. Charles S. Singleton, 1969). All in all Brown and Arac have done a critically suave hatchet job on Warren. One could charge Arac with not playing scrupulously fair, however, since Warren can show that there are Coleridgeans who contend that the imagination as defined in the *Biographia Literaria* is performing the function Coleridge later assigned to the reason.

Implicit in much of the criticism so far discussed is an undeclared question of how fully the poem works out its statement. L. J. Swingle, "On Reading Romantic Poetry" (*PMLA*, 1971), includes "The Ancient Mariner" among poems that ask, not answer, questions; Cooke, *The Romantic Will* (1976), characterizes it as a narrative founded on the willed ontological adventure of discovering the "spontaneous self" moment by moment in a finite world, while looking wistfully beyond the self to an "ideal world" that the form of the poem does not make room for the self to partake of; and Brisman, *Romantic Origins* (1978), offers its successive versions as a post-Bloomian confirmation of the originative power of imagination, ever reborn, to recreate its cultural past. Disdainful of the Mrs. Barbaulds who yearn for closure, more and more critics find antic cognitive and verbal resonance in what they perceive to be the refusal of "The Ancient Mariner" (and "Kubla Khan") to resolve the discourse. Almost forty years ago Huntington Brown called attention to the persona of the glossist (*MLQ*, 1945).

Deconstructionists, phenomenologists, and critical skeptics of varying hues are seizing on the interplay between poetic narrator and prose glossist as an ironic model of the rhetorical experience that is the reader's. Simpson, *Irony and Authority in Romantic Poetry* (1979), neatly formulates the grounds of the exchange. The reader, like the glossist and his observations, poses a constant reductive threat to the discourse of the poetic narrator. The poem thus incorporates parodically its own metacommentary in the tension between two ways of construing the Mariner's tale: between experiencing it and interpreting it. This uncertainty factor fascinates such diverse critics as L. M. Grow, "The Search for Truth: [the Glossist's] Book Learning versus [the Mariner's] Personal Experience in *The Rime of the Ancient Mariner*" (*Coranto,* 1977), and Lawrence Lipking, "The Marginal Gloss: Notes and Asides on Poe, Valéry, 'The Ancient Mariner,' the Ordeal of the Margin, *Storiella as She Is Syung,* Versions of Leonardo, and the Plight of Modern Criticism" (*CritI,* 1977). According to Lipking only when the gloss was added did "The Ancient Mariner" become a legitimate poem as propounded by the *Biographia Literaria.* With the superbly knowing civilized mind of the glossist casting a secondary imagination over the events of the narrative to make sense of its parabolic events, the poem reproduces rhetorically the eye of the reader snaking back and forth between text and margin, interrupting and interpenetrating one script with another. Thus does the poem create "out of two different phases of seeing" a simultaneous ordering of multiple worlds of perception.

No less subtle or provocative on the dialectic of gloss and text are Sarah Dyck's "Perspective in *The Rime of the Ancient Mariner*" (*SEL,* 1973), with its contention that in the dramatic exchange between the gloss-editor who introduces, articulates, and stresses the moral theme, the Mariner who has a vital experience he can neither understand nor communicate, and the Wedding-Guest whose response is stunned silence, Coleridge was looking for answers to a mystery that "will not be systematized"; Raimonda Modiano's "Words and 'Languageless' Meanings: Limits of Expression in *The Rime of the Ancient Mariner*" (*MLQ,* 1977), with its elaboration of the discrepancy between the Mariner's unorthodox experiences and the orthodox verbal strategies he adopts to communicate them to the Wedding-Guest; Frances Ferguson's "Coleridge and the Deluded Reader: *The Rime of the Ancient Mariner*" (*GaR,* 1977), with its Mrs. Barbauldian uncertainty about the moral conclusion and, more problematically, about the gap between the moralistic gloss and the main text, which never reaches such an assured value judgment; and Wheeler's *Sources, Processes and Methods in Coleridge's* Biographia Literaria (1980), with its ironic view of the gloss as a parody of the passive reader imposing conventional terminology, superstitious signs, and moralistic blame, guilt, and remorse on a poetic narrative whose cosmic import demands a higher imaginative level of self-conscious participation (a reading reiterated and further developed as an instance of Coleridge's presumed philosophy of art in her *The Creative Mind in Coleridge's Poetry,* 1981).

However bright and challenging these explorations of the poem's form, they do not move our perception of "The Ancient Mariner" far off the critical center of the 1940s and 1950s ethical consensus. A brilliant synthesis by Jerome J.

McGann of Coleridge's own exegetical practices and of current critical ideas, "The Meaning of *The Ancient Mariner*" (*CritI*, 1981), provides a theoretical model for reopening the poem to critical analysis—which Brown and Arac for all their analytical subtlety neglect to do. Interpreting as a hermeneutic model the series of variant forms through which the poem evolved in Coleridge's hands, McGann postulates that the poem's indeterminate meaning at any moment is the ongoing history of its relationship with its readers. McGann's argument is too wide-ranging and subtle to do justice to here. Briefly, he invokes Coleridge's religious writings and their practice of Higher Criticism, which treats the text exegetically as the product of communal accretion and of ever more sophisticated layers of interpolated meaning. "The Ancient Mariner" is such a text, with originally four layers of development: the original Mariner's tale, the ballad narrative of that story, the editorial gloss, and Coleridge's own view of his invented materials— which provide the ground for revisionist treatment of the poem. As a mediated text it is for us the praxis of a living social and historical resource. Although it invites diverse readings, its hermeneutics restrict these to a theistic and Christian English natural text. Thus, McGann opens "The Ancient Mariner" to interpretative innovation while avoiding disruption of tradition.

Instead of treating the poem as a revisionist text, the other original departure from the received opinions of the past few decades clears away the sacramental accretions of poet and readers. As long ago as 1964 in the *Critical Quarterly* William Empson had dismissed the Christian plan of atonement-by-suffering as an excrescence. In one of the more eccentric editions, in collaboration with David Pirie, of *Coleridge's Verse: A Selection* (1973), Empson gives textual imprimatur to his persuasion, printing the 1798–1800 version of "The Ancient Mariner," which rescues it from Coleridge's own later thoughts and redeems its references to the economic and social circumstances of its time. The poem becomes again what it was originally according to Empson, a study in neurotic guilt that is accidentally also a masterpiece about the maritime expansion. J. R. Ebbatson, "Coleridge's Mariner and the Rights of Man" (*SIR,* 1972), seizes on Empson's hints. Declaring against the standard views of the poem as a Christian epic or a Freudian confession or a Jungian archetype or an existential paradigm, Ebbatson asserts its politico-economic attack on the slave trade specifically and on colonial expansion generally.

The issue as enjoined by Empson-Pirie and McGann raises a serious critical question. What is the true text of "The Ancient Mariner"? That both Empson-Pirie and McGann ground their contrary answers on Coleridge's practice points up the difficulty of determining the poem before determining its meaning. Indeed, the shadow of the hermeneutical circle casts further suspicion on whatever text is chosen. "The Ancient Mariner" is as if made for the deconstructionists.

In the meantime historians of literature offer multiple conflicting definitions of the poem based on its presumed generic origins. Albert Friedman's *The Ballad Revival* (1961) still presents the best summary of the relationship of "The Ancient Mariner" to the traditional and minstrel ballads. G. Malcolm Laws, *The British Literary Ballad: A Study in Poetic Imitation* (1972), with far fewer details classifies "The Ancient Mariner" as a ballad of the supernatural in the mode of the horror tale, although highly miscellaneous and without direct imitation of any folk or broadside ballad type. Less reticent about sources and intentions, James B. Twitchell boldly advances *"The Rime of the Ancient Mariner* as Vampire Poem" (*College Literature*, 1977; rpt. *The Living Dead: A Study of the Vampire in Romantic Literature*, 1981). In the 1798 version Coleridge, presumably taken with the recent success of German vampire poems, capitalized on the vogue with his own tale of multiple vampire possession: first the blood thirst of the Mariner and fellow seamen and then the Mariner's psychic possession of the Wedding-Guest. Subsequent versions of the poem attempt to cover up this youthful poetic indiscretion with an overlay of Christian explanation. In *The Living Dead*, Twitchell treats the vampire theme more suggestively, as a metaphor for energy transfer and as "an implicit parable of creation that somehow involves precise interaction between artist, audience, artifact, and subject matter." In this context, the reader shares the Wedding-Guest's possession and energy transfer. Richard Payne, " 'The Style and Spirit of the Elder Poets': *The Ancient Mariner* and English Literary Tradition" (*MP*, 1977–78), persuasively demonstrates that the poem's idiom is an authentic rendering of a broad section of the British literary tradition before the eighteenth century. When Coleridge revised for the 1800 "Ancient Mariner" he dropped Northernisms but retained the "lost natural idiom" of the Renaissance and even added new archaisms of a Spenserian and Shakespearean color. Less persuasive is Warren Stevenson's composite "literalist" and symbolist placement of the narrative backward in time to a pre-Magellan circumnavigation of the world (*"The Rime of the Ancient Mariner* as Epic Symbol," *DR*, 1976). Nor does it help to type the poem a "little epic" or epyllion (Northrop Frye's terminology) with medieval diction and a Renaissance narrator, reflective of the displacement of the medieval religious ethic by Renaissance science. Reacting to R. H. Fogle's denial (*TSE*, 1957) that "The Ancient Mariner" belongs to the quest genre, since it has a circular structure, Anca Vlasopolos, *"The Rime of the Ancient Mariner* as Romantic Quest" (*WC*, 1979), contends that the Mariner is a failed quest hero, unable to make sense of his voyage and doomed to repeat it until he understands its meaning. Merton A. Christensen, "Udolpho, Horrid Mysteries, and Coleridge's Machinery of the Imagination" (*WC*, 1971), turns Coleridge's contempt for the Gothic into a justification for believing that Coleridge used Gothic elements in "The Ancient Mariner" to create a superstitious mind imagining the terrible supernatural events he describes. And H. W. Piper, " 'The Ancient Mariner,' Biblical Allegory, Poetic Symbolism and Religious Crisis" (*SoRA*, 1977), derives the poem's symbolist method from allegorical prophecy (especially biblical and eschatological), Gothic symbolism, and natural religion.

Free-wheeling associations of "The Ancient Mariner" with Sanskrit poetic theory are made by Krishna Rayan, *Suggestion and Statement in Poetry* (1972); with the multidimensional sense of movement and the Augustinian problem of the existence and experience of evil in the mind of a man who tends toward pantheism, by John Cornwell, *Coleridge: Poet and Revolutionary* (1973); with totem ritual, by H. S. Visweswariach, "Motive-Finding in 'The Rime of the Ancient Mariner' "

(*Literary Criterion* [Bombay], 1969); with archetypal themes, by Christian LaCassagnère, Introduction to *Samuel Taylor Coleridge, Poèmes* (1975); with any number of national legends, mythologies, and traditions, by the Welsh artist-poet David Jones, *An Introduction to* The Rime of the Ancient Mariner (1972); with the aesthetic theories of Schiller, by Daniel Stempel, "Coleridge's Magical Realism: A Reading of *The Rime of the Ancient Mariner*" (*Mosaic,* 1978); with Hegelian "contrite consciousness," by Raymond Benoit, *Single Nature's Double Name: The Collectedness of the Conflicting in British and American Romanticism* (1973); with Coleridge's own pronouncements generally on poetry, by Charles Richard Sanders, "*The Ancient Mariner* and Coleridge's Theory of Poetic Art" (*Romantic and Victorian: Studies in Memory of William H. Marshall,* ed. W. Paul Elledge and Richard L. Hoffman, 1971; rpt. *Carlyle's Friendships and Other Studies,* 1977); with Coleridge's comments specifically on the "two cardinal points of poetry . . . a faithful adherence to the truth of nature and the power of giving the interest of novelty by the modifying colors of imagination," by Theo Steinmann, "What Ailed the Ancient Mariner?" (*Dutch Quarterly Rev. of Anglo-American Letters,* 1979); with the Eucharist, by Hal Blythe and Charlie Sweet, "Agape and *The Rime of the Ancient Mariner*" (*WC,* 1979); with Poulet's definition of Romantic time and Coleridge's exposition of "Time, Real and Imaginary," by Avery F. Gaskins, "Real and Imaginary Time in 'The Rime of the Ancient Mariner'" (*NDQ,* 1969); and with the geography and spirit of the West Country, Minehead, Watchet, and Bridgewater Bay, by Ursula Codrington, *Coleridge at Nether Stowey* (1972). And for the fun of it—as well as for an instance of how all-purpose is the world Coleridge has constructed in "The Ancient Mariner"—don't miss Charles R. Larson's "Coleridge's Ancient Mariner and the Skinner Box" (*CEA,* 1974), which lampoons the poem for its lack of modern relevance, in terms of the Skinnerian behavioral, stimulus-response environment found on board ship.

Studies attempting a "long-needed explanation" of "the wedding as an ever-present background" have multiplied. Woodring, "The Mariner's Return" (*SIR,* 1972), and Beaty, *Light from Heaven: Love in British Romantic Literature* (1975), remind us respectively that "The Ancient Mariner" ends in the reconciliation of homeland and hospitality and of material and spiritual kingdoms. The latter justifies the wedding as a frame to the narrative. Other studies trying to make sense of the poem, and its conclusion, in terms of love and hate as biblically inspired or existentially endured include Mario L. D'Avanzo, "Coleridge's Wedding-Guest and Marriage-Feast: The Context" (*Univ. of Windsor Review,* 1972); Kenneth Wolman, "The Ancient Mariner's Unethical World" (*English Record,* 1973); Charles E. May, "Objectifying the Nightmare: Cain and the Mariner" (*BSUF,* 1973); Lorne J. Forstner, "Coleridge's 'The Ancient Mariner' and the Case for Justifiable 'Mythocide': An Argument on Psychological, Epistemological and Formal Grounds" (*Criticism,* 1976); and Arnold E. Davidson, "The Concluding Moral in Coleridge's *The Rime of the Ancient Mariner*" (*PQ,* 1981).

Psychoanalytical readings, mostly Freudian or Jungian, have fallen off in numbers since Maud Bodkin, Kenneth Burke, and David Beres pioneered readings of "The Ancient Mariner" as a mythic recreation of death and rebirth (*Archetypal Patterns in Poetry,* 1934), as Coleridge's symbolic solution to his marital difficulties

(*The Philosophy of Literary Form*, 1941; rev. 1957), and as expression of his guilty feelings of love-hate for his mother (*IJP*, 1951). Leon Waldoff in "The Quest for Father and Identity in 'The Rime of the Ancient Mariner'" (*Psychoanalytic Review*, 1971) adds the rebellion of the son (and self) against parental power and the resultant guilt-laden alienation. Bent on reconciling the theoretically formalist interpretations of the poem with psychoanalytical readings of it as dream, Joseph C. Sitterson, Jr., "'The Rime of the Ancient Mariner' and Freudian Dream Theory" (*PLL*, 1982), concentrates on defining the extent to which infantile fantasy figures as an exclusive determiner of meaning. Most of the standard critical positions since Warren are reviewed in the course of the argument. Ross Woodman in "Shaman, Poet, and Failed Initiate: Reflections on Romanticism and Jungian Psychology" (*SIR*, 1980) characterizes the Mariner as a failed shaman. Trapped by an inadequate psychology the Romantic poet is unable to bring back from his sortie into the collective unconscious knowledge to heal the split between human life and nature. Instead, he is a sacrifice to what he finds, believing the myth and repeating the old taboos. That is the symbolic failed journey the Ancient Mariner takes. Returned, he tries to communicate his experience to the Wedding-Guest but can only utter moral platitudes.

As with "The Ancient Mariner" critical assumptions about "Kubla Khan" have reached a considerable degree of stability. The guns that once thundered over the dating of the poem, the role of opium in its creation, the reliability of the preface as a witness to its origins, and the nature and extent of its fragmentariness are silent. On these issues Elisabeth Schneider's *Coleridge, Opium and Kubla Khan* (1953; rpt. 1966), whose reexamination of them caused much of the furor at the time, is the best place to start. Most important, the poem's internal unity and completeness (M. L. T. Milton devotes one third of her survey of "Kubla Khan" criticism 1935–70 to this question) for ordinary interpretive purposes is now taken for granted. More than one critic actually makes a virtue out of the poem's generic, or external, fragmentation, for example, McFarland (*Romanticism and the Forms of Ruin*, 1981), and Timothy Bahti, "Coleridge's 'Kubla Khan' and the Fragment of Romanticism" (*MLN*, 1981). Simpson (*Irony and Authority in Romantic Poetry*, 1979) tags it a prototypical Romantic poem whose "whole" in its "infinite working and re-working of details already lost to immediate perception but regained and intensified through imaginative recollection" is a never-completed inventory of loss and gain. For Simpson "Kubla Khan" in its series of regressing visions or groups of images is a fragment itself fragmented, and therefore a model of "the various limitations imposed by narrative time, memory, and language."

The "standard" interpretations as I summarized them in *ERP3* still determine the boundaries for the general run of critiques. Hence, Marshall Suther's *Visions of Xanadu* (1965) continues to be useful for its dispassionate analysis of where conflicts occur. Beginning with G. Wilson Knight (*The Starlit Dome*, 1941; reiterated in *Neglected Powers*, 1971) the poem has been read as a paradisal vision reconciling within the boundaries of the garden the mysterious cycle of life and the sacred extremes of earth, with Kubla overseeing it all like a God. This "Edenic hypothesis" has its gnostic offshoot, of which Beer (*Coleridge the Visionary*, 1959) is the principal adherent, looking on Xanadu as a false paradise and the

Khan as a failed genius. A poem about divine creativity is easily extended symbolically to include the nature and act of poetic creation, and the conscious workings of the imagination. W. Stevenson, "'Kubla Khan' as Symbol" (*TSLL*, 1972; rpt. in "Divine Analogy: A Study of the Creation Motif in Blake and Coleridge," *Romantic Reassessments* 25, ed. Hogg, 1972), observes that "Kubla Khan" criticism came of age in the sixties. No radical challenge to the holy writ enunciated then has come along in the interim—unless one counts Richard Hoffpauir's iconoclastic put-down "'Kubla Khan' and the Critics" (*ESC*, 1976), which is a reputation study of the poem's reception from 1816 (when the prefatorial account was almost universally accepted and the poem itself considered meaningless) through the rest of the century (from about 1870 on it enjoyed the status of an ideal lyric) to the present. The modern acceptance of the poem's greatness and the attempts at interpretation of it, particularly the symbolist readings, have goaded Hoffpauir to a harsh indictment of the poem's form and content. Not surprisingly, there is little agreement on the genre to which it belongs or on the meaning it expresses. "Never has so much been said by so many about so little." Thus does orthodoxy generate its own heresy! A positive gain from all this clangor is that the article provides what amounts to a checklist of interpretations, helpful so long as one keeps in mind that the analysis and taxonomy reflect Hoffpauir's crotchets.

In fact, there is a preoccupation in much current criticism of the poem with the need to review the central dogmas as prelude to offering a clarification of this or that article of belief. Thus, Stevenson (*TSLL*, 1972) attempts to synthesize the orthodox readings into one grand unified statement that makes Xanadu representative at once symbolically of the unfallen world and literally of the world after the Fall and likens Kubla to the poet narrator, both working to overcome the ravages of the Fall through creating by fiat a portion of God's eternal reality. Like Blake's Los building the city of Golgonooza, the poet of "Kubla Khan" is one of a succession of visionary singers of divine creation who restore imaginatively "at once and ever" a sense of heavenly fulfillment. Less oracular, McFarland, "The Origin and Significance of Coleridge's Theory of Secondary Imagination" (*New Perspectives on Coleridge and Wordsworth*, ed. Hartman, 1972), simply insists that the poem's emphasis is theological, concerned primarily with the creation and loss of Eden. The imagination theme to his way of thinking is a misreading, since the imagination for Coleridge is a tool of limited critical use, its main function being epistemologically to link his poetic and systematic theological and philosophical interests rather than to describe aesthetically how poetry is written. But McFarland's is a minority, almost schismatic voice apropos of "Kubla Khan," and it derives from his perspective of the post-*Biographia* Coleridge of the *Opus Maximum*.

The present rage is to read "Kubla Khan" self-reflexively—in short to elevate the secondary theme to primary importance. Toward this end (in addition to works mentioned earlier in the subsection "General Evaluations") A. B. England, "'Kubla Khan' Again: The Ocean, the Caverns, and the Ancestral Voices" (*ArielE*, 1973), seeks to correct the contradiction inherent in interpreting both the fountain's source and the "lifeless ocean" as emblematic of the unconscious mind from which issues imaginative outbursts of inspiration. In England's reading,

"Kubla Khan" describes the inherent conflict between two kinds of mental activity: the spontaneous energetic overflow of inspiration being deprived of its life by an excess of analytical ratiocination. Anthony John Harding, "Inspiration and Historical Sense in 'Kubla Khan'" (*WC*, 1982), redefines the conflict in terms of two kinds of religious language, with the first section of the poem being an oracular utterance conveying a mythological apprehension of divine reality, while the second section contains the poet's normative historical, or timebound, judgment of the truth of his inspired vision. Charles I. Patterson, Jr., "The Daemonic in *Kubla Khan*: Toward Interpretation" (*PMLA*, 1974), considers "Kubla Khan" a poem "tightly focused on the esthetic alone" and "decidedly not in the mainline of Coleridge's poetry." It concentrates on presenting an extreme aesthetic experience of daemonic amorality, of uninhibited aspiration of mind pressing beyond human limitations to a glimpse of perfect beauty.

Perceptible in all this self-reflexivity is a shift of focus from the first to the last part of the poem and from a poem describing an external earthly scene to one defining its own development, and in the process becoming the kind of poem that it is describing. Coleridge was sensitive to the idealist abyss that threatens self-confirming versions of reality, and Rolf Breuer, "Coleridge's Concept of Imagination—With an Interpretation of 'Kubla Khan'" (*Romanticism, Modernism, Postmodernism*, in *BuR*, 1980), considers "Kubla Khan" to be such a poem. Part 1 presents itself as a poem about the poet's imagination, and therefore about the process of writing poetry. Part 2 stands in relation to part 1 as metatext to text. Part 2 then translates as a poem about a poem about writing poetry. As an instance of self-cognition (like all self-reflexive thought structures) "Kubla Khan" can never end. It is a mirrored image of itself, part 2 reflecting part 1, and in that sense it is self-confirmatory and complete, but in an infinite recension. This incompleteness *sui causa* of the self-contained work of art is the real subject of "Kubla Khan." A. C. Goodson, "Kubla's Construct" (*SIR*, 1979), is concerned with the poem's internal consistency as a system of phonemic signals, apart from its representation of things. Attacking the school of critics who impose on the language of the poem a "'factual-visual consistency' which it does not possess," Goodson describes the first two stanzas as composed of a series of linguistic oppositions, with the third stanza reverting to representational idiom, setting off the miracle of the first two stanzas in relief and designating the self-sustaining flight of its presentation. "Kubla Khan" in these terms reveals the Romantics (or at least Coleridge) on the threshold of discovering language as a domain apart from its referentiality. In the hands of the structuralists and deconstructionists "Kubla Khan" has ironically regressed to the pure construct it was in Lowes's book.

Such critical heuristics are a long way from the traditional stances of E. S. Shaffer, *"Kubla Khan" and* The Fall of Jerusalem: *The Mythological School in Biblical Criticism and Secular Literature 1770–1880* (1975), and of Donald Pearce, "'Kubla Khan' in Context" (*SEL*, 1981). "Kubla Khan" is a hieroglyph of all the mythological texts of a communal past, avers Shaffer, its syncretized geography the sum of oriental epic idylls, of eighteenth-century biblical poems, and of Higher Criticism's desupernaturalized treatments of Revelation. Its contexts,

Pearce insinuates, include the Devonshire countryside fixed in Coleridge's mind by his terrifying all-night vigil by the river as a small boy, by the heroic paradigm of his princely power as a child over his family, and by the drying up of his poetic genius. The latter corresponds to the dependence of the poet on the damsel's inspired song, which effectively transforms the work into a poem about suspended powers. Even here, within the bastion of old-fashioned historical interpretation, rears the deconstructed ghost of the man from Porlock, come as Brisman's metaphoric aspect of the public Coleridge to interrupt the composition of "Kubla Khan."

A few other studies (besides those already cited here and in *ERP3*) address the demonic and the daemonic, the psychoanalytical, and the structural: Nicolas K. Kiessling, "Demonic Dread: The Incubus Figure in British Literature" (*The Gothic Imagination*, ed. G. R. Thompson, 1974); Donald P. Haase, "Coleridge and Henry Boyd's Translation of Dante's *Inferno:* Toward a Demonic Interpretation of 'Kubla Khan' " (*ELN*, 1980); Lawrence Kramer, "That Other Will: The Daemonic in Coleridge and Wordsworth" (*PQ*, 1979); Norman Mackenzie, " 'Kubla Khan': A Poem of Creative Agony and Loss" (*EM*, 1969); Eugene H. Sloane, "Coleridge's *Kubla Khan:* The Living Catacombs of the Mind" (*AI*, 1972); Joseph Sgammato, "A Note on Coleridge's 'Symphony and Song' " (*WC*, 1975); Alicia Martinez, "Coleridge, 'Kubla Khan,' and the Contingent" (*CP*, 1977); Edward Strickland, "The Topography of Initiation of 'Kubla Khan' " (*Ball State Univ. Forum*, 1981); and William Benzon, "Metaphoric and Metonymic Invariance: Two Examples from Coleridge" (*MLN*, 1981). Finally, Norman Fruman, in separate chapters on "Kubla Khan" and "Dreams" (*Coleridge, the Damaged Archangel*, 1971), sloshes together into one matrix "the tension and turbulence of [Coleridge's] chaotic inner life": the "unresolved incestuous conflicts, hatred of women, divided personality, fear of sex, homosexual impulses, female demons issuing threats and punishments, and fiends in the guise of loved ones," to fashion an updated Lowesian deep well of unconscious distortions from whose nether reaches the Coleridgean imagination dipped to produce "The Ancient Mariner," "Kubla Khan," and "Christabel."

The interpretation of "Christabel" still eludes consensus. Although critics are beginning to develop a discernible set of assumptions, they have not reached the measure of agreement that obtains for "The Ancient Mariner" and "Kubla Khan." The concern of early criticism was with the poetic fragment's achieved and projected story (conjectures of how Coleridge planned to complete the poem begin with James Gillman and the poet's son Derwent), its contemporary reception, its prosody (although there has been no significant essay on its versification since Ada Snell's in the *Fred Newton Scott Anniversary Papers*, 1929), and its generic connections with legend, religious allegory, and the Gothic tale. For summaries of the older criticism, see Virginia L. Radley, "*Christabel*: Directions Old and New" (*SEL*, 1964), and my survey in *ERP3*. On the fairy lore, folklore, and supernatural elements in "Christabel," see John Adlard, "The Quantock *Christabel*" (*PQ*, 1971), and Elizabeth M. Liggins, "Folklore and the Supernatural in 'Christabel' " (*Folklore*, 1977).

Sparked by essays of Charles Tomlinson (in *Interpretations: Essays on Twelve English Poems*, ed. John Wain, 1955; rpt. 1972) and of Roy P. Basler (*SR*, 1943; rpt. in *Sex, Symbolism, and Psychology in Literature*, 1948; rpt. 1980), who both, however, still conjectured within the framework of generic literary preoccupations, critical attention has concentrated on the psychosexual in the relationship of good and evil explored by the poem, with emphasis on the role of Geraldine. Concurrent with the psychosexual-moral bias is an effort to get at Coleridge psychologically through the subterfuges and misalliances of the poem. Despite the marked shift of critical focus, the continuing fluidity of "Christabel" interpretation is illustrated by the recent attempt of one critic to synthesize all these ingredients into a unified reading of the poem. Susan M. Luther in *"Christabel* as Dream-Reverie" (*Romantic Reassessment* 61, ed. Hogg, 1976) assembles previous formalistic and psychoexperiential hypotheses, plus Coleridge's own psychological theories, along with his reported remarks about his plans for finishing the poem and about his likening the action of "Christabel" to that of Crashaw's "Hymn to Sainte Teresa." They add up to a dream reverie of Christabel in which she undergoes "self-imposed . . . martyrdom," projecting her guilty feelings of sexuality onto the ghost Geraldine in the subconscious wish to grow into maturity by such self-initiation. In this critical "reconciliation of opposites" Coleridge makes a poor showing. He failed to finish "Christabel" because his aspiration to write an epic led him to extend the modest form of the dream reverie anticlimactically beyond his fully realized "idea" of it in part I. The value of Luther's essay and of Michael D. Patrick's *"Christabel:* A Brief Critical History and Reconsideration" (*Romantic Reassessment* 11, ed. Hogg, 1973) lies in their doggedly anachronistic concentration on the ingredients that make up the nineteenth- and early twentieth-century critical history of the poem. Other articles dealing in old-fashioned ways with the interlocking good and evil of the poem and with the resultant psychological tensions and moral ambiguities are Robert H. Siegel's "The Serpent and the Dove: 'Christabel' and the Problem of Evil" (*Imagination and the Spirit: Essays in Literature and the Christian Faith Presented to Clyde S. Kilby*, ed. Charles A. Huttar, 1971), Roland Bouyssou's *"Christabel* et les Ballades du Sortilège Vert" (*Caliban*, 1976), and H. W. Piper's "The Disunity of *Christabel* and the Fall of Nature" (*EIC*, 1978).

The eddying uncertainties about Coleridge's literary materials and intentions—when contrasted to the convictions of A. H. Nethercot, *The Road to Tryermaine* (1939), about its machinery of the preternatural—are everywhere visible in the post-Nethercot criticism trying to come to grips with these problems. Nethercot's most unapologetic heir, James B. Twitchell, *The Living Dead: A Study of the Vampire in Romantic Literature* (1981; see also *Expl*, 1976), not without ingratiating humor, finesses the lamia motif with the more critically interesting theme of psychic energy transfer, which raises theoretical questions about the artist-audience relationship. Several other critics dare to suggest that the shallow and silly Gothic conventions—bombastic language and banal villainy—are being parodied. So contend Edward Duffy, "The Cunning Spontaneities of Romanticism" (*WC*, 1972), and Edward Dramin, " 'Amid the Jagged Shadows': Christabel and the Gothic Tradition" (*WC,* 1982). Less Gothic-oriented but no less predicated on the assumption that "Christabel" is not what it seems is Gordon K. Thomas' "Rueful Woes, Joyous Hap: The Associate Labor of 'The Idiot Boy' and 'Christabel' " (*WC,* 1983), which hypothesizes that the poem is an exposé of the misuse of language, of the false utterance and the oracular word. As if such indirect undermining of the persistent effort (like Constance Hunting's "Another Look at 'The Conclusion to Part II' of *Christabel,*" *ELN,* 1975) to locate a unity of purpose only doubtfully present in the fragment that is "Christabel" were not enough, that effort is explicitly excoriated by Edwin Thumboo, " 'Christabel': Poem or Fragment" (*Literary Criterion* [India], 1973).

Despite Thumboo's salutary warning, the search goes on to find an underlying psycho-moral coherence in Coleridge's probe of evil originating in good intentions, as Walter H. Evert puts it in "Coadjutors of Oppression: A Romantic and Modern Theory of Evil" (*Romantic and Modern: Revaluations of Literary Tradition,* ed. George Bornstein, 1977). Is "Christabel" a story of evil triumphant (Bostetter, *PQ,* 1957; rpt. *The Romantic Ventriloquists,* 1963, 1975) or potentially ennobling (Terry Otten, *BuR,* 1969; rpt. *After Innocence: Visions of the Fall in Modern Literature,* 1982)? Or is the vision of horror Geraldine brings Christabel balanced against the salutary experience of the world she also introduces into the castle (Gerald Enscoe, *Eros and the Romantics: Sexual Love as a Theme in Coleridge, Shelley and Keats,* 1967)?

The predilection of critics has been to rehabilitate Geraldine. Abe Delson surveys in "The Function of Geraldine in *Christabel:* A Critical Perspective and Interpretation" (*ES,* 1980) the changing interpretations from negative to positive of Geraldine's role in the narrative. As Bate shrewdly hints in his biography of Coleridge (1968), if "Coleridge-as-habitual-usher" is identifiable in Christabel, and Christabel partakes in part of Geraldine, then there must be a part of Coleridge residual also in Geraldine and she cannot be all bad. In two articles, "The Limitations of Langdale: A Reading of *Christabel*" (*EIC,* 1970) and " 'Thoughts so all unlike each other': The Paradoxical in *Christabel*" (*ES,* 1971), Macdonald Emslie and Paul Edwards see the relationship of Christabel and Geraldine as a necessary evil if Christabel is to grow from innocence into the complex state of adult sexual consciousness that is the human condition. R. H. Fogle delicately hints at the same possibility in his sensitively "Coleridgean" climactic chapter to *The Idea of Coleridge's Criticism* (1962). Geraldine is thus a demonic spirit whose evil produces good. In stressing Christabel's growth by way of initiation into evil, Emslie and Edwards link up not only the worlds of life and death, sunlight and cavern darkness, imaged in "Kubla Khan," but also the contrary conjectures of James Gillman (Geraldine is a figure of evil) and Derwent Coleridge (she is an agent of ultimate good). Jonas Spatz, "The Mystery of Eros: Sexual Initiation in Coleridge's 'Christabel' " (*PMLA,* 1975), draws the inevitable conclusion and identifies Geraldine as a projection of the sexual woman whom Christabel at once yearns and fears to become if she is to fulfill her essential role as daughter and wife. Spatz cites Coleridge's sentiments regarding sex, love, and marriage to justify this sexual maturing of Christabel. Michael E. Holstein, "Coleridge's *Christabel* as Psychodrama: Five Perspectives on the Intruder" (*WC,* 1976), then

turns Geraldine into a near-sympathetic phantasm and the real heroine, by transforming her into the dark, chthonic, buried shadow of the self (hence shared half
of Christabel) and the psychological drama into a "morally neutral situation." Holstein accomplishes this feat, however, with suspect critical feints. The quasi-
Jungian reading makes sense psychologically but renders absurd the events of the
poem. And could Coleridge have ever adopted a neutral attitude toward the
moral ambiguity of sexual initiations? Undeterred by such a possible caveat, both
Delson (*ES,* 1980) and Jane A. Nelson, "Entelechy and Structure in *Christabel*"
(*SIR,* 1980), take for granted Christabel's progress from adolescence to womanhood, considering the bedroom scene the arena where Geraldine's unspecified,
but functionally positive, sexuality figures as lover and mother to allow Christabel
to experience roles otherwise denied her. The transformations of Geraldine receive rhetorical apotheosis in the hands of Richard A. Rand (*Glyph 3,* 1978), who
treats her, and the undisclosed "mark" of her sorrow and "seal" of her shame, as
a text—indeed, the major rhetoric of signs, within "the sequence of readings,
known as 'Christabel'"—that Christabel, Sir Leoline, Bard Bracy, and we the readers are unable to decipher because of its noncommunication of its story. The
trouble with attempts to get at the psychic mystery of Geraldine is that sooner or
later they involve psychological explanations of Coleridge's own desolate loneliness and motherlessness (Coburn, *UTQ,* 1955–56), or his lovelessness (Yarlott,
Coleridge and the Abyssinian Maid, 1967), or his fear of godlessness (Bostetter,
The Romantic Ventriloquists, 1963, 1975), or his symbiotic relationship with
Wordsworth (W. Stevenson, *"Christabel:* A Reinterpretation," *Alphabet,* 1962), or
his terror of female power and its threat to a stable world of appearances and
consequences (Sarah McKim Webster, "Circumspection and the Female in the
Early Romantics," *PQ,* 1982). The interpretation of "Christabel" as emblematic of
Coleridge's unconscious sexual ambiguities and self-doubts as a poet continue to
flourish with unabated zeal—and with psychoanalytically predictable results and
some strange conclusions. Among the most sensible and sensitive of these is Barbara Schapiro's "'Christabel': The Problem of Ambivalent Love" (*Literature and
Psychology,* 1980; rpt. *The Romantic Mother: Narcissistic Patterns in Romantic
Poetry,* 1983). For Schapiro, Coleridge's is an oral-fixated personality tormented
by obsessive-compulsive destructive feelings for the mother imago, which poor
Christabel, alternately associated with the ambivalent mother and the guilty child,
acts out with Geraldine. Twitchell, "'Desire with Loathing Strangely Mixed': The
Dream of *Christabel*" (*Psychoanalytic Review,* 1974; rpt. in part in *The Living
Dead,* 1981), contends that the focal point of the poem is the poet himself enacting the sexual desires of the son for his mother but displaced in dream life
across sexual lines in the action of Christabel, who sleeps with Geraldine both as
a "lover" and "like a child," so that she (and Coleridge) have it, in a sense, both
ways. Lacking Twitchell's jeu d'esprit and, with it, his defense against the tasteless,
the humorless, and the improbable, Rosemarie Maier, "The Bitch and the Bloodhound: Generic Similarity in 'Christabel' and 'The Eve of St. Agnes'" (*JEGP,* 1971),
elevates (that is, she contends that Coleridge attempts to elevate) an act of violation of innocence—Geraldine's homosexually disguised rape of Christabel—to an
unrealizable "level of cosmic, metaphysical significance" and thus dooms the

poem to incompletion; while Wendy S. Flory, "Fathers and Daughters: Coleridge and 'Christabel' " (*Women and Literature,* 1975), blames Geraldine's vengeful and denigrated sense of her female identity (her lesbianism) on a homosexual affair postulated between Sir Leoline and Lord Roland when young men, with the whole sorry drama of affairs a tribute to Coleridge's realization that his low esteem for his wife jeopardized his relationship with his children. Yet another reading of the poem as homoerotic psychodrama (how delighted Hazlitt and Tom Moore would have been with these confirmations of their worst surmises; see *ERP3*) is Edward Proffitt's " 'Christabel' and Oedipal Conflict" (*RS,* 1978).

So that this survey of the state of "Christabel" interpretations does not end on too negative a note, I have left to last mention of Edward Strickland's "Metamorphosis of the Muse in Romantic Poesis: *Christabel*" (*ELH,* 1977), which weds Bloom's poetic misprision theory and Jung's archetypal anima to define Geraldine along with other preternatural females who are both destroyer and preserver, "cradling madonna as well as seductress of the imagination," in the "dialectics of visionary poesis, as emblems of vision and metamorphoses of the Muse." In short, "Christabel," like other Romantic narratives, offers us an "image of the subliminal exploration of the imaginative process."

It remains to be seen whether Strickland's move to align the criticism of "Christabel" with current self-reflexive poetics, as has already happened to "The Ancient Mariner" and "Kubla Khan," prefigures a turning away from the critical limitations of the "psychological borderland where matters of religion overlap with matters of sex" (H. House). The signs are modest at best. To read "Christabel" as a satire or a parody is self-delimiting. Strickland's and Susan Luther's contextual studies are still in varying degrees psychoanalytically oriented. Robert Schwartz, "Speaking the Unspeakable: The Meaning of Form in 'Christabel' " (*Language Quarterly,* 1980), appears, at first, to offer in his extreme rhetorical stance an alternative to the psychoanalytical methodologies; but (as with Luther) he appears unresponsive to the yeasty ferment of contemporary aesthetic theorizing and makes his point, in part, by following the time-honored practice of pummeling part 2 and of concentrating on Christabel as martyr and center of the poem. This is not surprising. Of Coleridge's major poems, "Christabel" has been most conservative in its interpretive parameters, least open to a variety of critical approaches.

CONVERSATION POEMS

Ever since House (*Coleridge,* 1953), followed by Albert Gérard (*EC,* 1960; *JEGP,* 1961; *English Romantic Poetry,* 1968), showed how faithfully the Conversation poems enact Coleridge's imaginative experience of nature, the poems have received steady critical attention and praise as a poetic form central to the measure of Coleridge and of the Romantic sensibility. Still, there is merit in Morris Dickstein's admonishment in "Coleridge, Wordsworth, and the 'Conversation Poems' " (*CentR,* 1972), cautioning critics not to sink Coleridge the poet in a zeal to comprehend the whole Coleridge being born in the *Collected Coleridge.* I am not sure, though, that his modest assessment of the Conversation poems will carry them very far into the hearts of contemporary readers. He admires the mode of the Conversation poem, with its dialectic between selfhood and vision, its naturalistic adherence to fact transfigured by a sensory fadeout (the bodily eye tranquilized) leading to spiritual afflatus; but he judges that Coleridge's Conversation poems fail as often as they succeed in realizing this goal. Coleridge uncontrollably alternates between isolated visionary and circumstantial personal moments, the latter conveying a sense of lost opportunities. This compulsion to the untransmuted private reference forces him to become the poet of "The Pains of Sleep" (which Richard Gravil, *ChLB*, 1982, would add to the list of Conversation poems!). There is about Dickstein's assessment of Coleridge the faint aroma of the poet versus philosopher heresy; and one's suspicions are not allayed when he complains that in Bate's biography Coleridge the poet "is almost marginal."

In his anchoring the Conversation poem at one end of its centrifugal-centripetal movement in selfhood, Dickstein speaks in concert with the current preoccupation concerning these poems. Several decades ago critics concentrated on the conceptualization, structural principles, and philosophical sources. The best of such studies include, besides House's and Gérard's, R. H. Fogle's (*TSE*, 1955), R. A. Durr's (*ELH*, 1959), J. D. Boulger's (*JEGP*, 1965), and W. Schrickx's (*REL*, 1966). Now critics are bent on reading the Conversation poems as witness to what Frederick Garber calls Coleridge's "Hedging Consciousness" (*WC*, 1973). The language and critical strategies employed vary but the focus remains remarkably steady. It is on Coleridge's "search for identity" (A. R. Jones's observation in an otherwise unremarkable Housian evaluation, "Coleridge and Poetry: II. The Conversational and Other Poems," in *S. T. Coleridge*, ed. Brett, 1971). A key word is "tension," and the characteristic concept is of a man engaged in a balancing act between extremes. Even conventional surveys of Coleridge's changing perception of the "one Life" in nature—for example, Ronald C. Wendling's "Dramatic Reconciliation in Coleridge's Conversation Poems" (*PLL*, 1973)—elect to define the drama in terms of the contradictory impulses in Coleridge for joyous self-affirmation and for paralytic self-doubt, issuing in a sense of estrangement from life and suspension of imaginative powers. For Garber it reduces to Coleridge's ambivalent relationship to the world surrounding the self: his compulsion to hold the mind aloof at battle with a concomitant need to surrender to and identify with the impressions of sense. Similar slighter analyses of Coleridge's efforts toward self-definition are found in E. San Juan, Jr.'s "Samuel Taylor Coleridge: 'The Eolian Harp'" (*Poetics: The Imitation of Action, Essays in Interpretation*, 1979), on the "tension between the painful solitude of the speaker and his aspirations to destroy the limitations of the ego"; in Michael E. Holstein's "Poet into Priest: A Reading of Coleridge's Conversation Poems" (*UTQ*, 1979), on the tentative, exploratory construction of an ideal poet-priest personality whose emergence structures the poems; in Frederick Kirchhoff's "Reconstructing a Self: Coleridge's 'Frost at Midnight'" (*WC*, 1979), on the recreation (Kirchhoff is applying Heinz Kohut's theories of the exhibitionist self) of an idealized parent image out of a narcissistic personality; and in Richard Eldridge's "On Knowing How to Live: Coleridge's 'Frost at Midnight'" (*Philosophy and Literature*, 1983), on the general subjunctive features of human temporal existence as a guide for making the self intelligible to oneself and as a justification for moral rules of behavior.

Paul A. Magnuson reminds us in "The Dead Calm in the Conversation Poems" (*WC,* 1972; rpt. *Coleridge's Nightmare Poetry,* 1974) that these poems contain other "centers of perception" to whom Coleridge turns when his perceiving "I" is balked in its effort to engage nature. Through his imaginative identification with Sara in "The Eolian Harp," with Lamb and the Wordsworths in "This Lime-tree Bower," and with Hartley in "Frost at Midnight," Coleridge strives to break out of the empty imprisonment of self. Kelvin Everest, *Coleridge's Secret Ministry: The Context of the Conversation Poems 1795 –1798* (1979), has Coleridge, in his search for an idiom, abandoning the effort to communicate with an external public world in favor of the familiar address that prevails among intimate friends and family. Only by such an extreme strategy can he free his voice for poetic utterance. However Garber, Magnuson, and Everest seem to differ in their diagnoses of Coleridge's crisis of identity and in the semiotic forms their analyses take, they present facets of the same Coleridge struggling to define a consciousness that neither lapses into solipsism nor loses itself in identification with the multitudinous world.

The extent and range of Coleridge's achievement in the Conversation poems remain open to measurement and judgment by other means as well. Invoking the religious meditation as analogue, Reeve Parker, *Coleridge's Meditative Art* (1975), reads the poems not as organic entities or as confessional utterances but as the artistic shapings of the materials of distress, with Coleridge employing his analogical imagination, his playfulness of language, and his distress and anxiety, to shape a highly wrought poetic art confirming a Christian resolution of human suffering. Coleridge's posit of a benevolent sacramental world figures as half of a running "debate" with the contrary desolation of Wordsworth's 1796–97 poems ("The Ruined Cottage," "Salisbury Plain," "Guilt and Sorrow," and "The Female Vagrant"). A second richly suggestive analogue, Parker demonstrates, is Wordsworth's image of the self as poet, a limning of the integrated being Coleridge aspired to emulate. Parker's most successful exposition of the Wordsworth (and Milton) analogues is his fine reading of "To William Wordsworth" (originally published as "Wordsworth's Whelming Tide: Coleridge and the Art of Analogy," in *Forms of Lyric,* ed. Reuben A. Brower, 1970; rpt. *Coleridge's Meditative Art;* and *English Romantic Poets: Modern Essays in Criticism,* ed. M. H. Abrams, 1975), a poem whose paean of praise for *The Prelude* becomes also through invocation of "Lycidas" Coleridge's elegy for his own demise as a poet. An unintended minor footnote to Parker's richly suggestive study is Avery F. Gaskins' "Coleridge: Nature, the Conversation Poems and the Structure of Meditation" (*Neophil,* 1975), which sees the structural pattern of the seventeenth-century meditative poem as an analogue of the Conversation poem.

For discernment of overall patterns of imagery, paradigms of form, and contours of meter, see Jill Rubenstein, "Sound and Silence in Coleridge's Conversation Poems" (*English,* 1972); George H. Gilpin, "Coleridge and the Spiral of

Poetic Thought" (*SEL*, 1972); and Janet Ruth Heller, "Enjambment as a Metrical Force in Romantic Conversation Poems" (*Poetics*, 1977).

Of individual poems the only major concern of earlier decades that still worries readers is the unity of "The Eolian Harp." William H. Scheuerle, "A Reexamination of Coleridge's 'The Eolian Harp'" (*SEL*, 1975), questions the assumption that Coleridge added the "one Life" passage in 1817 so he could repudiate it as the "shapings of the unregenerate mind." No less questionable, though, is Scheuerle's alternative thesis that "The Eolian Harp" delineates disparate aesthetico-metaphysical speculations: the "one Life" lines celebrating the imagination's active joyous realization of a harmonious world, while the "organic Harp's" musings to which the retractation lines refer describe the fancy's passive receptivity to outside influences. Douglas B. Wilson, "Two Modes of Apprehending Nature: A Gloss on the Coleridgean Symbol" (*PMLA*, 1972), in a discussion of the poem's presumed and actual pantheism and of the two senses (*natura naturans* and *natura naturata*) in which Coleridge refers to nature, likewise affirms that the original version with the harp passage justifies Coleridge's fears of pantheism and his retractation; but the final version with the addition of the "one Life" lines renders the conclusion irrelevant or out of keeping with what has gone before.

Although not directly concerned with the anticlimactic repudiation of all that has gone before in the poem, M. H. Abrams, "Coleridge's 'A Light in Sound': Science, Metascience, and Poetic Imagination" (*Proceedings of the American Philosophical Society*, 1972), gives the "one Life" lines the richest interpretation they have ever received. The lines are replete with Coleridge's reading in Boehme and other esoteric writers, Schelling, Newton's *Opticks*, and the biblical account of creation. This matrix of metaphysical-scientific ideas is subsumed by Coleridge under the dynamic law of polarity to explain ontologically how the phenomenal world came into being and how science severed the individual's imaginative relation to it. In his explication Abrams demonstrates one of those rare instances when Coleridge is writing with extreme ease philosophical verse of the kind he continually sought but seldom realized.

As for the other Conversation poems, Fred V. Randel, "Coleridge and the Contentiousness of Romantic Nightingales" (*SIR*, 1982), and Wallace Jackson, *The Probable and the Marvelous: Blake, Wordsworth, and the Eighteenth-Century Critical Tradition* (1978), rescue "The Nightingale" from relative neglect. Randel persuasively demonstrates that Coleridge sustains "throughout every portion of ... 'Nightingale' a debate with Milton." This resourceful marshaling of parallels between the two poets challenges Bloom's derogation of Coleridge by showing that Coleridge's endorsement of the organic analogue supports his swerve from Milton instead of crippling his poetic powers. Jackson uses "The Nightingale," in conjunction with "Christabel," to illustrate some of the "peculiar resonances" of Romantic verse in whose celebration of life is often heard a dark inchoate strain of demonic energy. Coleridge's imagination exposes the "fears and compulsions of which the self-consciousness is made" by "allowing to come to the surface an undercurrent of the speaker's emotional life that seizes upon the terms of his prior, more controlled, perceptions" as the instrument of enactment. In this instance, the malign emotions that appear in the father-maiden situation of "Christabel" reappear in disguised form in the nightingale-serpent imagery of the third and fourth stanzas of "The Nightingale." Thus is a poem long dismissed for its commonplace perspective revealed to have a more complicated world embedded in its statement than previous generations of Romantic scholars believed existed. Anne K. Mellor, "Coleridge's 'This Lime-tree Bower My Prison' and the Categories of English Landscape" (*SIR*, 1979), extends the dimensions of that poem's prototypical Romantic affirmation of nature to encompass the eighteenth-century categories of the picturesque, the beautiful, and the sublime. "This Lime-tree Bower" emerges somewhat doctrinarily through comparisons of the scenes in the poem with landscape paintings as a "paradigm of the historical movement in England from an objective to a subjective aesthetics at the end of the eighteenth century."

Since House praised "Frost at Midnight" as one of Coleridge's most successful and revelatory poems it has steadily garnered kudos. Besides the many studies already mentioned, above and in *ERP3*, Fred Kaplan, "Coleridge's Aesthetic Ministry" (in *Miracles of Rare Device: The Poet's Sense of Self in Nineteenth-Century Poetry*, 1972), and Barbara Schapiro (in *The Romantic Mother*, 1983) single it out as "a rare achievement" for Coleridge when the "demons of self-doubt" that "dominated his major years of creativity" were "momentarily conquered." Kaplan makes intelligent observations about the antithetical imagery of the poem, although he forces the language hard to yield up more than abides residually in it or is invested in it by the context. Shapiro, in a fine reading of the poem, extends its reference to include Coleridge's angry and aggressive feelings for the mother, which he separates intact from the self to achieve a true serenity involving an unbroken reciprocal relation with nature. Going against the tide of this approbation, Reed (*Romantic Weather*, 1983) has the perverse distinction of offering a negative view of the poem. It exhibits a Coleridge trapped in his own system of signs, the universally praised synthesis at the end an arbitrary invoking of the supernatural language of nature. Less ad hominem in his rigorous analysis, Rand (*Glyph 3*, 1978) discovers that the poem's tropology "deconstructs the hierarchy of values that it claims to uphold."

"DEJECTION: AN ODE," LATE POETRY, AND DRAMA

Ernest de Selincourt published the newly discovered "Verse Letter to [Asra]" as long ago as 1937 (*ES;* rpt. *Wordsworthian and Other Studies*, 1947). Written 4 April 1802 (so dated by Coleridge) it was the foundry from which Coleridge assembled the metal of "Dejection" (published 4 Oct. 1802). Their relative merits have enlisted advocates in each poem's cause. The "Verse Letter" is admired for its comprehensive statement about Coleridge's domestic and personal situation, its sincere personal tone, and its unity of theme and emotion and of motif and metaphor. "Dejection" is praised for giving successful poetic expression to a lament over the loss of creative imagination, in effect for its realization of a poetic form and statement that effectively questions its theme. At the same time neither poem has got off scot-free; both are charged with being thematically confusing and structurally flawed. That is the position of House (*Coleridge*, 1953). On the relationship of the two poems with Wordsworth's "Resolution and Independence" and "Ode: Intimations of Immortality" as part of an ongoing dialogue between the two poets about the poetic act, still the place to start are the articles of Fred M. Smith (*PMLA*, 1935) and George W. Meyer (*TSE*, 1950), supplemented by Heath, *Wordsworth and Coleridge* (1970). Bloom in *A Visionary Company* (1961; rev. 1971) and Parker in *Coleridge's Meditative Art* (1975) add "To William Wordsworth" to the debate. Milton Teichman in "Wordsworth's Two Replies to Coleridge's 'Dejection: An Ode'" (*PMLA*, 1971) extends the dialogue between the two poets to include Wordsworth's "Stanzas Written in My Pocket-Copy of Thomson's 'Castle of Indolence,'" which Teichman interprets as Wordsworth comforting Coleridge after the admonishment of "Resolution and Independence" (Lucy Newlyn, *WC*, 1981, modifies Teichman's conclusions by contending that Wordsworth inadvertently wrote two self-portraits). And Jonathan Wordsworth, *William Wordsworth: The Borders of Vision* (1982), puts forward "The Barberry-Tree" as having "a far better claim than most poems of the period to be taking a serious view of Coleridge's position" in "Dejection" and offering itself playfully to Coleridge as an antidote to his gloom and anguish.

On the epistemology and metaphysics of the imagination's interaction with the sensible world in "Dejection" there is a succession of discussions: I. A. Richards, *Coleridge on Imagination* (1934; rpt. 1965); Newton P. Stallknecht (*PMLA*, 1934; rpt. *Strange Seas of Thought*, 1945, 1958); A. O. Lovejoy (*ELH*, 1940); and Suther, *The Dark Night of Samuel Taylor Coleridge* (1960).

"Verse Letter" receives a formidable endorsement in the Empson-Pirie selective edition of Coleridge's verse (1972), where it is printed in place of "Dejection." Pirie had prefigured their preference in "A Letter to [Asra]" (*Bicentenary Wordsworth Studies in Memory of John Alban Finch*, ed. Jonathan Wordsworth, 1970), a full-scale study that broaches the topic of perception not as a narrow philosophical issue but as part of a comprehensive personal disability inseparable from other problems Coleridge raises in the poem. Approaching perception from this angle prompts Pirie to conclude, contrary to the assumption of those using "Dejection" as their text, that joy is the result, not the cause, of union with nature. Pirie also finds especially satisfying the way the poem adumbrates the complex interdependent human relationships in the final image affirming Sara as a dove warming, and being warmed by, those she loves.

Pirie's is an all-out assault on the critical position that "Verse Letter" is an early version of a poem on the way to becoming "Dejection." Because "Dejection" shifts from the theme of alienation from people ("Verse Letter") to the theme of alienation from nature, he argues that they are different poems. Neither should be viewed through the lens of the other. Few critics, however, appear to share Pirie's judgment that "Verse Letter" is aesthetically the more interesting poem, since "Dejection" continues to get the lion's share of attention. Certainly, the implicit direction of Gerald Aronow's by now late-in-the-day comparative study "The Metamorphoses of Coleridge's 'Dejection'" (*Hebrew Univ. Studies in*

Literature, 1980) suggests that he has not got Pirie's message. In his survey of what he determines to be the three major stages of change and growth—from "Verse Letter" to 1802 *Morning Post* "Dejection" to 1817 *Sibylline Leaves* "Dejection"—Aronow concentrates on the ambiguous meaning and vague reference of the "natural man" passage (stanza 6) and "Reality's dark dream" lines (stanza 7). Like R. H. Fogle (*ELH,* 1950) and Coburn (*Major English Romantic Poets,* ed. Clarence D. Thorpe et al., 1957), but for a different reason, Aronow concludes that the 1802 "Dejection," because of its deletion of the "natural man" lines (they were put back in 1817), is intended as a sign to Wordsworth of Coleridge's renewal of joy and creativity, thanks to the reactivation of his imagination in the writing of "Verse Letter." Presumably the 1817 version reverts to despair. Susan Hawk Brisman and Leslie Brisman, "Lies against Solitude: Symbolic, Imaginary, and Real" (in *The Literary Freud: Mechanisms of Defense and the Poetic Will,* ed. Joseph H. Smith, *Psychiatry and the Humanities* 4, 1980), provide quite different grounds for claiming that the poem ends on a triumphant note. Theirs is a psychoanalytical confirmation that assimilates the overt turns in addressee as stages of a discourse whose strategy is the recathexis of poetic identity. In a brilliant application of Bloom's Freudian-based theory of the poet resolving his Oedipal relationship with previous literary history and of Lacan's description of three kinds of addressees created by the poet as means of escaping solitude, they show Coleridge shifting in the last two stanzas of "Dejection" from recapitulation of an "original presence" (Milton and Wordsworth in the successive tales of the wind and lute), to creation of an "imaginary other" (the self who establishes poetic space for his own fiction of the eddying soul by rewriting Wordsworth's Lucy poem), to evocation of a "real auditor" (Sara).

The positioning of "Dejection" within the aesthetics and tradition of the odic form has enlisted some stimulating, albeit contrary, critical conjectures. A. Harris Fairbanks, "The Form of Coleridge's Dejection Ode" (*PMLA,* 1975), supplements M. H. Abrams' pioneering discrimination of the greater Romantic lyric (*From Sensibility to Romanticism,* ed. Hilles and Bloom, 1965) by analyzing the ways "Dejection" differs from the Conversation poems, the differences unfortunately emphasized by ignoring or blurring similarities. Wielding Hegelian strategies of dialectical opposition, Cyrus Hamlin, "The Hermeneutics of Form: Reading the Romantic Ode" (*Boundary 2,* 1979), holds up "Dejection" as the model for subsequent Romantic odes. Its ironic form of discourse permits the poet a flexible range of voices for translating Romantic death into reconcilement with the absolute. In "Dejection" the mediating lute voices, for example, mirror the poet's mind as figures of renewal of spirit and affirmation of joy. Not so, opines Paul H. Fry in "The Wedding Guest in 'Dejection'" (*The Poet's Calling in the English Ode,* 1980). The inherently ironic voice of the ode is liminal. As a vehicle of "the hidden wish for apocalypse" it measures, in fact, the counter boundaries of the poetic imagination. Delimitation to the humane is its true mode. Thus, the suppressed theme of "Dejection," supported by the logic of the poem, upholds the poet's dejection, not the joyous wedding of his imagination to nature, as the sole and necessary origin of his creativity. Reed (*Romantic Weather,* 1983), on other grounds, similarly contends that the poem complicates and undermines its movement from dejection to joy. The most inclusive of these studies, George Dekker's *Coleridge and the Literature of Sensibility* (1978), provides illuminating excursuses on the intellectual background of "Dejection": the generic role, usage, and tradition of the aeolian lute, the greater and lesser ode, and the loco-descriptive poem; the epistemological and religio-natural meanings of "joy" as "the great unifying and animating principle of the Universe"; and the diverse philosophical and religious ideas of world harmony. Dekker also tops Pirie's argument for the "Verse Letter" being the original, and hence superior, poem by upsetting the accepted textual chronology with the startling proposal that "Verse Letter" is not the first draft of "Dejection." Rather, several stanzas (1–3 especially) may have been composed well before 4 April 1802, with "Verse Letter" subsequently formed in part by interjections of personal references into those finished lines.

In the context of Dekker's heroic recreation of the intellectual seasons governing the weather of "Dejection," the other critical treatments of the poem's structure and meaning inadvertently mutate to the "stifled, drowsy, unimpassioned" strain that Coleridge laments in the opening lines of the poem. The symbolic action of the lute image and the correlative extent to which the perceiving mind of the bard is either a passive receiver (identified with the lute) or active shaper (like the wind) of experience are the subject of John O. Hayden, "Coleridge's 'Dejection: An Ode'" (*ES*, 1971); W. Paul Elledge, "Fountains Within: Motivation in Coleridge's 'Dejection: An Ode'" (*PLL*, 1971); Donald R. Swanson, "The Growth of a Poem: Coleridge's *Dejection*" (*BSUF*, 1971); Panthea Reid Broughton, "The Modifying Metaphor in 'Dejection: An Ode'" (*WC*, 1973); Barbara F. Lefcowitz, by way of Coleridge's narcissistic overevaluation of his powers, in the "Omnipotence of Thought and the Poetic Imagination: Blake, Coleridge, and Rilke" (*Psychoanalytic Review*, 1972); and Francis Fike, "Correspondent Breeze: The Course of a Romantic Metaphor" (*Renascence*, 1979).

"The Picture," following—allegorically veiled—in the path of "Verse Letter" and published a scant month before "Dejection," has received scant attention. Discounting its bland imaginative alchemy, Michael J. Kelly, "Coleridge's 'Picture, or The Lover's Resolution': Its Relationship to 'Dejection' and Its Sources in the Notebooks" (*Costerus*, 1972), tries laudably to wedge the poem into "a more respectable place in Coleridge's canon." Kelly's is a useful placement of "The Picture" in the context of Coleridge's movements in August 1802, but the poem's central statement remains no less "fuzzy" if somewhat less "obscure" than before.

"Hymn before Sun-rise," which once generated attention because of its plagiarized parallels to the German language poem of Friederike Brun (amply studied by Adrien Bonjour, *Coleridge's "Hymn before Sunrise,"* 1942), is all but totally neglected now except for Fruman's citing of it for the wrong reasons and for Geoffrey Hartman's singling it out, in "Reflections on the Evening Star: Akenside to Coleridge" (*New Perspectives on Coleridge and Wordsworth*, ed. Hartman, 1972), as a prime instance of Coleridge's laboring historically and personally under the burden of originality. Afflicted by the curse of believing himself inherently secondary when measured against past and present poets, Coleridge counterfeits creativity and thereby himself as a poet. For an instant in the "Hymn" he recovers his poetic voice through the willed imitation of a sublime voice.

Thus, Hartman aligns himself with Bloom (*Shelley's Mythmaking,* 1959), who charitably excuses the stridency of "Hymn" as stemming from Coleridge's not inconsiderable effort to revitalize modes of Christian orthodoxy and to challenge the poet of *Job.* Parker devotes a chapter to "Hymn" in *Coleridge's Meditative Art* (1975).

The austere quality of the Highgate poetry has attracted few defenses in this century, other than modest appreciations by Richards (*Coleridge's Minor Poems,* 1960), Schulz (*TSE,* 1960; rpt. *The Poetic Voices of Coleridge,* 1963), and Whalley (*PTRSC,* 1964). Renewed interest in Coleridge the theologian and the rise of phenomenological hermeneutics, however, have directed readers to these poems in larger numbers. James D. Boulger, in particular, has concentrated on them in the final chapter of *Coleridge as Religious Thinker* (1961), in "Coleridge: The Marginalia, Myth-Making, and the Later Poetry" (*SIR,* 1972), and in a long section of *The Calvinist Temper in English Poetry* (1980). At first, Boulger blames the late poems' deficiencies, especially their failure of emotional commitment, on Coleridge's move from an aesthetic to an ethical condition and, in the shift, to an exchange of his youthful religious sense of the oneness of self and nature for the Kantian semidualism in which soul-spirit is separated from nature. Subsequently, Boulger attributes Coleridge's inability in the Highgate years to produce poetry "not necessarily of the highest order" to his retreat from an early relish for occult mythmaking, in favor of restrictive Christian views of divine reality and of the scientific discoveries of his day, neither of which he could shape into a new imaginative cosmos. Most recently, Boulger makes a religiously erudite, nondogmatic case for Coleridge in the late poetry as historically authenticating the continuation of the Calvinist sensibility into the nineteenth century, especially as regards original sin, the origin of evil, and election. Angela G. Dorenkamp, "Hope at Highgate: The Late Poetry of Samuel Taylor Coleridge" (*Barat Review,* 1971), likewise blames the low-keyed spirit of the late poetry on Coleridge's acceptance of the nature-spirit dichotomy, to which is added a resignation in God's will. In a more upbeat overview assuming that "philosophy and theology . . . were correlate to, and not hostile to," the poems 1807 to 1834, John L. Mahoney, " 'The Reptile's Lot': Theme and Image in Coleridge's Later Poetry" (*WC,* 1977), argues that Coleridge wrote "poems of remarkable power" on themes of alienation and loss, world weariness and ennui, and emotional and imaginative paralysis, in a clotted, highly complex, and frequently disconnected language and imagery anticipating the modern style. Unfortunately, Mahoney's interpretation is not as philosophically searching as Boulger's or Dorenkamp's. In a similar, more persuasive act of reclamation, J. Robert Barth, "Coleridge's Constancy to His Ideal Object" (*WC,* 1983), assimilates Boulger's, Prickett's, and Kessler's readings of "Constancy to an Ideal Object" to layer its epistemological concentration on the relation of thought to object with a personal level of lament for lost love. Arden Reed (*Romantic Weather,* 1983) also treats the poem as a central document in the mapping of Coleridge's poetic climates.

The late poems receive the most positive reading from Edward Kessler, *Coleridge's Metaphors of Being* (1979), who is concerned with how, as metaphors, they reveal the mind transfiguring reality to unsettle the understanding and prepare the way for being. Despite an opaque methodology, which one reviewer remarks is an ontology in search of an order, Kessler works to rehabilitate poetry that has always seemed to be abstract and fragmentary. Like McFarland (*Romanticism and the Forms of Ruin*) and D. F. Rauber ("The Fragment as Romantic Form," *MLQ,* 1969), Kessler has conceptualized a theory, this one compounded of Coleridge's religio-metaphysical aspirations and aesthetic principles, to justify poems that resist conclusion. In demonstrating how they mediate between physical and spiritual states, between things and thoughts, Kessler discusses most of the important late poems from "Phantom" and "The Blossoming of the Solitary Date-tree" to "Love's Apparition and Evanishment," including invaluable explications of the key symbols eddy-rose, phantom, and limbo.

Since Bloom's pioneering effort at resuscitation of "Limbo" it has occupied a special status among the late poems; and three articles have subsequently devoted varying amounts of attention to it: Fletcher, " 'Positive Negation': Threshold, Sequence, and Personification in Coleridge"; Cooke, "The Manipulation of Space in Coleridge's Poetry" (both, already noted, in *New Perspectives on Coleridge and Wordsworth,* ed. Hartman, 1972); and Daniel P. Deneau, "Coleridge's 'Limbo': A 'Riddling Tale'?" (*WC,* 1972), which deals with its tangled textual history and vexing resistance to a coherent reading.

Of the major Romantic poets only Coleridge produced a verse drama (*Remorse*) with a successful West End run (in 1813, for 20 days). He also wrote a second verse play, *Zapolya* (1815; published 1817), as well as fragmentary starts of other plays, and made verse translations of Schiller's *The Piccolomini* and *The Death of Wallenstein* (1800). They all contain fine poetry. The latter translations have been compared by Lilian R. Furst, *The Contours of European Romanticism* (1979), to Benjamin Constant's adaptation of Schiller's Wallenstein drama into French in 1809. She analyzes the impact of native literary traditions on the two translations and summarizes their receptions and subsequent histories.

Coleridge's forays into the theater have attracted modest but persistent scholarly attention (see *ERP3*). His dramatic skills and deficiencies are analyzed by Richard M. Fletcher, *English Romantic Drama, 1795 – 1843: A Critical History* (1966); by Pratyush Ranjan Purkayastha, "The Romantics' Third Voice: A Study of the Dramatic Works of the English Romantic Poets" (*Poetic Drama and Poetic Theory* 41, ed. Hogg, 1978); by Om Prakash Mathur, "The Closet Drama of the Romantic Revival" (*Poetic Drama and Poetic Theory* 35, ed. Hogg, 1978); by Brian Morris, "Coleridge and Other People" (*WC,* 1979); by Donald G. Priestman, "Godwin, Schiller and the Polemics of Coleridge's *Osorio*" (*BRH,* 1979); and by Erika Gottlieb, " 'Poison in the Wine': Coleridge's *Remorse*" (in *Lost Angels of a Ruined Paradise: Themes of Cosmic Strife in Romantic Tragedy,* 1981). Fletcher compares *Remorse* to Wordsworth's *The Borderers,* and presents Coleridge's dramatic effectiveness in a sympathetic light. Purkayastha, Mathur, Morris, and Gottlieb deal with Coleridge's shortcomings as a dramatist, his failure to create a hero in *Remorse* as a counterpart to the play's villain, his incapacity for entering into the mind of an imagined character alien to himself, and his Romantic confusion of political, personal, and mythic forms of the hero-villain-rebel, father-son, Cain-Abel, and God-Satan patterns of authority and oppression.

Still others who have critically examined Coleridge's plays are M. J. Vosluisant, "Nature et surnature dans les poèmes dramatiques de Coleridge, *Remorse* et *Zapolya*" (*Proceedings of the Centre du Romantisme Anglais,* 1977 – 79); Jibon Banerji, "*Osorio* and *Remorse*" (*Bulletin of the Department of English,* Univ. of Calcutta, 1978); and John David Moore, "Coleridge and the 'Modern Jacobinical Drama': *Osorio, Remorse,* and the Development of Coleridge's Critique of the Stage, 1797 – 1816" (*BRH,* 1982). Moore argues for Coleridge's use of *Remorse* to criticize the popular theater by identifying Gothicism with Jacobinism.

Prose Writings

GENERAL REFLECTIONS ON SUBSTANCE, STRUCTURE, AND STYLE

Forty-seven years ago R. J. White wrote defensively that "The prose works [of Coleridge] are not a second-best, save as a brother may be second-best to his sister. They are of the same parent, and the same spirit breathes in them" (*The Political Thought of Samuel Taylor Coleridge,* 1938). Yet for most of this century they have been acknowledged, if at all, grudgingly and distantly, with the exception of *Biographia Literaria,* which has occupied a special place of honor in twentieth-century criticism. It was not always so. Owen Barfield reminds us in an appreciative review ("Coleridge Collected," *Encounter,* 1970) of the prose writings to appear so far in *Collected Coleridge* that Coleridge's writings on religion reigned supreme after his death during the years when theology continued to be a matter of general interest and importance. Following that period of influence, though, they and the other prose works sank into relative obscurity, treated through most of this century as a "sprawling corollary" to Coleridge's theory of the imagination. With the *Collected Coleridge* this period of neglect draws to its close, and a third period dawns. The deplorable fact is that of the major Romantic writers Coleridge alone survives with a canon as yet unfixed. On the creation of the Coleridge canon, see McFarland, "A Coleridgean Critique of M. H. Abrams" (*High Romantic Argument: Essays for M. H. Abrams,* ed. Lawrence Lipking, 1981). As volume succeeds volume in the *Collected Coleridge,* however, scholars and critics are rising to the challenge of sifting, evaluating, and shaping the Coleridge canon into a matrix of both poems and prose works.

The concentration on chronology, sources, and plagiarism by scholars from J. L. Haney's *The German Influence on S. T. Coleridge* (1902) to Fruman's *Damaged Archangel* (1971) seems (for the moment) to have spent its force. Wellek summarizes the achievement of this scholarship precisely and at length in "Coleridge's Philosophy and Criticism: I. The Sources" (*ERP3*). The discussion is in two separate sections, so one should not overlook the second section, covering material from 1956.

Most recently focus has shifted from tracing Coleridge's indebtedness to placing him within the larger European intellectual community and assaying his contribution to the never-ending advance and dissemination of philosophical knowledge from generation to generation, an endeavor viewed as historically accumulative more than individually innovative. The most vociferous and eloquent advocate of this perception of the way ideas are transmitted is McFarland. A parallel tactic is for critics now to adopt a perspective more akin to the way Coleridge read and wished his books to be read: that is, to bring the truest philosophy and criticism of the day to bear on a text in a sincere effort not only to grasp its insights but also to assimilate the best of the new and the old in scientific data and human "facts of mind." This empathic approach to the "Selfconscious imagination" of Coleridge, as Coburn christens it in her Riddell Memorial Lectures of 1973, subtitled *A Study of the Coleridge Notebooks in Celebration of the Bi-Centenary of His Birth 21 October 1772* (1974), generally recognizes that the fulcrum of his "exertion and projection of himself into the broad world of human affairs" was psychological. Lest we forget in all the fanfare over his subtle-souled psychology and his vitalist philosophy, Whalley, "The Aristotle-Coleridge Axis" (*UTQ,* 1973), elects to remind us in a minority report of the rational, particularly Aristotelian, quality also of Coleridge's imagination.

Recent assays of the way Coleridge consciously confronts reality have mostly, though, resorted to dialectical patterns appropriate to one who invariably thought in terms of opposites to' be reconciled. Renouncing genetic and biographical approaches for the idea or organizing insight that guides Coleridge's mind, Barfield in "Either: Or" (*Imagination and the Spirit,* ed. Huttar, 1971) looks at the distinction Coleridge drew between the self and the not-self and in *What Coleridge Thought* (1971) sets forth an informed and sympathetic analysis of the philosophy of polarity underlying much of Coleridge's thought from the *Friend* and *Biographia Literaria* to *Church and State.* In a lively and illuminating response to Douglas Wilson's review of *What Coleridge Thought,* Barfield reiterates ("Barfield on Coleridge: An Exchange," *Denver Quarterly,* 1972) his belief that polarity (union as well as distinction) proffers the central assumption of all Coleridge's thought. In overlapping articles, "Coleridge and Kant: Poetic Imagination and Practical Reason" (*BJA,* 1968) and "Coleridge: Philosopher and Theologian as Literary Critic" (*UTQ,* 1969), Roy Park sees Coleridge coping through his middle years with the conflicting attractiveness of an experiential (intuitive) apprehension of reality and a constitutive (theistic) rendering of that reality. McFarland, *Coleridge and the Pantheist Tradition* (1969), locates the basic tension in Coleridge's ambivalent apprehension of the world in pantheistic and trinitarian terms. For J. A. Appleyard, "Coleridge and Criticism: I. Critical Theory" (*S. T. Coleridge,* ed. Brett, 1971), the poles around which Coleridge's mind moves, at least in his critical theory, are "idealist metaphysics and empirical psychology." For E. S. Shaffer, "The 'Postulates in Philosophy' in the *Biographia Literaria*" (*CLS,* 1970), polar tension inheres in Coleridge's persistent effort to incorporate aspects of empiricism into his philosophy, thereby avoiding the split between the rational or sciental and the aesthetic and moral. For Jerome C. Christensen, *Coleridge's Blessed Machine of Language* (1981), the poles are Hartleian associationism, from whose *"streamy* Nature" Coleridge never completely wrenched free, and the willed consciousness of the moral mind.

Less extended attention has been paid to the means—language and prose style—by which Coleridge sought with uncertain success, and justifiable hesitancy, to engage heart and head of his readers and auditors. In "Coleridge's Political Sermons: Discursive Language and the Voice of God" (*MP,* 1973), a searching analysis from the 1795 Lectures to *The Statesman's Manual,* David R. Sanderson isolates the peculiar tendency of the Coleridgean argument abruptly to drop its painstaking multiplication of distinctions and in a leap of faith to enunciate an intuited conclusion. The problem, as Sanderson defines it, is that Coleridge until about 1816–17 uses the discursive language of the understanding (definition, analysis, and generalization) to convey the cognitions of the reason. Frustrated by a constant breakdown in communication because of his resorting to an empirical prose for converting his reader, Coleridge turned in *The Statesman's Manual* toward greater dependence on the higher authority of scriptural language: the revealed Word and the oracular voice of God. Sanderson may be pulling the strings of language too taut by reducing Coleridge's to the empirical and the oracular; but the "radically different states of mind" they reflect coalesce remarkably well with Coleridge's lifelong struggle to unite the philosophy of scientific materialism with metaphysical and poetic modes of apprehending reality, in short, to unite science with theology, philosophy, and poetry.

The finest coupling to date of Coleridge's philosophical principles with his repeated pronouncements on (and exercises of) prose style is Christensen's chapter "The Method of *The Friend"* in *Coleridge's Blessed Machine of Language* (1981). In a densely written essay on the "amicable chiasmus" that figures the concept of method, Christensen links critic (writer) and letters in a "transitive integration of opposites" through its impression on the page. The reverberative chiasmus, which Christensen pursues, not just in the *Friend* but in the *Biographia Literaria* too, combines Coleridge-Wordsworth, critic-poet, original critic of genius – anonymous man of letters, propriety-property, text-illustration, and private conscience – public pronouncement. The product, as well as vehicle, of method is the seventeenth-century English periodic style. Its studied courting of obscurity and deferral of meaning leads to an ultimate imaginative and moral intelligibility that ensures the reflective discourse of reason and the communication of truth. Arraigned against this style is the Anglo-Gallican, whose rapidity of mode leads to an immediate perspicuity that prevents the proper centering of attention. The former is virtuous, difficult, willed; the latter, mendacious, pointed, breathlessly epigrammatic, and uncontrolledly associationist. The one in its self-reflection produces an economy of language that enriches the nation with moral acts made the law; the other impoverishes the nation with its commercial and sophistical debasement of wisdom into political fanaticism. The method of the critic of genius orders thought into a blessed machine of language; the artifice of the anonymous reviewer and the empirical philosopher (modern sophists both) transfigures the mind into an infernal mechanism of the marketplace.

Additional studies of Coleridge's prose style and of his remarks on the subject of prose writing are Paul K. Alkon, "Critical and Logical Concepts of Method from Addison to Coleridge" (*ECS*, 1971), Lynn M. Grow, "The Prose Style of Samuel Taylor Coleridge" (*Romantic Reassessments* 54, ed. J. Hogg, 1976), and John R. Nabholtz, "Romantic Prose and Classical Rhetoric" (*WC*, 1980), which analyzes Coleridge's employment of classical rhetoric in *Conciones ad Populum* (1795) and *The Statesman's Manual* (1816).

On Language

Underlying Coleridge's apprehension of reality is the word: it is "the first Birth of the Idea, and its flexible Organ" (*Friend* 1: 474), the "Alphabet of Physics no less than of Metaphysics, of Physiology no less than of Psychology" (*CL* 4: 688). Accordingly he approached the study of language with all the weighty gravity his mind could muster; and scholars have begun to treat his views with compensatory seriousness. Richards, *Coleridge on Imagination* (1934), tags Coleridge an early semasiologist. George J. Steiner, *After Babel* (1975), praises Coleridge as one of the few writers "who have said anything new and comprehensive" regarding language. Timothy J. Corrigan (*PQ*, 1980) calls him the "foremost neologist of the nineteenth century." And Emerson R. Marks, *Coleridge on the Language of Verse* (1981), pays tribute to Coleridge's "lexical bent of mind," to his pervasively linguistic approach to all knowledge, and to his awe before the miracle of language and the lifelong immersion of every human being in words. More speculatively, Marks also credits Coleridge in his effort to penetrate the mystery of language and the special superior expressiveness of poetic utterance, with uncanny anticipation of twentieth-century structuralism, especially that of Roman Jakobson. Barfield gracefully and appreciatively reviews "Coleridge's Enjoyment of Words" (*Coleridge's Variety*, ed. Beer, 1974): Coleridge's humorous and serious coinings, his feel for classical languages, his sensitivity to the past history of words, his delight in archaisms, his resurrection and desynonymization of words—an awareness of language "as a motion in the depths of his being" that puts him in the company of Sir Thomas Browne, Milton, and Lewis Carroll and reveals itself more in his prose than in his poetry. Finally, Coburn, who is without peer in her near-psychic sensitivity to the movement of Coleridge's mind, applauds "I.A.R. and S.T.C." (in *I. A. Richards: Essays in His Honor*, ed. Reuben Brower, Helen Vendler, and John Hollander, 1973) for their attendance to words as the moral imperatives and cultural subsumptions of society and the means by which chaos is tamed and order found.

The degree to which words represented to Coleridge "living powers"—'substance vivante' (Paul Deschamps, *La Formation de la pensée de Coleridge 1772–1804*, 1964)—or guides to truth, is increasingly appreciated by critics in our linguistically conscious times as they survey the boundaries of Coleridge's forays into the domain of language. Robert DeMaria, Jr., demonstrates in "Coleridgean

Names" (*JEGP*, 1978) how proper names function for Coleridge in an absolute sense. Like the organic analogy with being, they indicate one of a kind. They are "god-terms," as in the language of the natural sciences, untranslatable, tautegorical rather than allegorical, denoting the ideal type divorced from relativism. The development of a system of names by invention, appropriation, or desynonymization or by analogy to science thus becomes identical for Coleridge with the progress and process of knowledge.

Given the central place in Coleridge's criticism of naming, or making language, it is not surprising that desynonymization assumes a large role in his linguistic considerations. In a historically framed evaluation of Coleridge's theory of desynonymy, Paul Hamilton, *Coleridge's Poetics* (1983), puts forward the thesis that in desynonymy Coleridge had a philosophy of language that would have supplied his practical criticism with the theoretical base he had hoped to find in the transcendental philosophy. Unhappily, when his theory of desynonymy "threatened to use the common means of social communication as the model of philosophical discovery," Coleridge repressed the theory out of conservative anxieties for its radical implications for change, his late political, social, and religious thinking intuitively opting for conservation and fixedness. Hamilton places these linguistic concerns of Coleridge within the larger context of the sociophilosophical controversies of the eighteenth century. With similar historical care, James C. McKusick, "Coleridge and Horne Tooke" (*SIR*, 1984), examines Coleridge's response to the noun-verb controversy and Tooke's role in the formation of Coleridge's philosophy of language. Joel W. Weinsheimer, "Coleridge on Synonymity and the Reorientation of Truth" (*PLL*, 1978), and Timothy Corrigan, "Coleridge, the Reader: Language in a Combustible Mind" (*PQ*, 1980), explore the "relativist" conceptualizations of truth that desynonymy forced Coleridge to devise to avoid poetic interpretation becoming mere duplication. According to Weinsheimer, Coleridge conceives of the act of reading as a recurrent questioning of the integrity of the text. The text must be perpetually represented and reappropriated by each reader—which is the function of the poet, and of the critic. Corrigan aligns Coleridge with those whom he calls, after George Steiner (*NLH*, 1972), relativists in nineteenth-century linguistic theorizing (the rival position is universalist). To such relativists "no two languages construe the same world." Accordingly, Coleridge opts for the fields of knowledge in every age having their peculiar languages "which do not just rephrase meaning but in many ways make meaning." Corrigan's article is the lead-off chapter of his *Coleridge, Language, and Criticism* (1982), which carefully attends to four "discursive extra literary languages" that Coleridge naturalizes in his criticism. In the 1790s Coleridge's writing is encoded with such political terms as "benevolence" and "egotism." In the 1800–12 Shakespeare criticism Coleridge's terminology of "passion," "dream," "interest," and "curiosity" actualizes the discourse of contemporary psychology. From 1814 to 1819 (discussion of which appeared initially in *JHI*, 1980) the challenge of modern science causes Coleridge to leaven the theoretical and practical criticism of the *Biographia Literaria* with scientific tropes and to establish a homology between a world of science and a world of poetry. After 1820 language accommodating the literary text to a theological meaning invades Coleridge's commentary, as in his lecture on Aeschylus' *Prometheus* in 1825 to the Royal Society of Literature. Although Corrigan's thesis is modestly argued, it tends to separate Coleridge's critical language into fictional linguistic paradigms (see Modiano's review, *WC,* 1983) that purvey a "minor fiction" that Coleridge's prose comprises discrete multiple styles.

In further formulations of Coleridge's philosophy of language, C. Miles Wallace, "Coleridge's Theory of Language" (*PQ,* 1980), finds Coleridge typically at once empirical and metaphysical, with words for him mediating between mind and object, between human and divine, relating idea to thing, and—by the analogy of law, method, and language with the correlative Logos of God—connecting symbolically human knowledge to divine knowledge. Michael Kent Havens, "Coleridge on the Evolution of Language" (*SIR,* 1981), surveys Coleridge's position on etymology and desynonymization, positing a threefold pattern of linguistic evolution from an original unity ("infinite I Am") to a polar division of verbal and nominal forces, which philosophers and historical accident develop into clear and distinct discourse, while poets are forever restoring the resultant fragmented verbal world to its original integration. In this process language becomes the prime witness to the historical evolution of consciousness, both the product of and the contributor to human intelligence.

Corrigan gives us a Coleridge who appears preoccupied with the consequences of the sign. Wallace devises for us a Coleridge whose linguistic cogitations resonate eclectically with concern for the nature and origin of signs. And Havens has Coleridge in an inclusive straddle, appropriating the issue fore and aft. Is Coleridge with untypical practicality bent on defining the role of language in the creation of knowledge? Or is he, beset by the Hartleian paralysis over the source of words (see Christensen's chapters on this question in *Coleridge's Blessed Machine of Language,* 1981), trying to solve the question of linguistic origin? For all their apparent assertion a curious tentativeness marks these attempts to establish Coleridge as a proto-linguist. Needed now is an esemplastic linguist to reconcile what everyone is talking about. As Wellek is fond of saying, "much remains to be done."

Not everyone treats Coleridge's expressive and theoretical gifts so reverently. At times the waywardness of language betrays even one with his linguistic self-consciousness, and poststructuralist critics delight in disclosing the instances when Coleridge, in their eyes, is duped by words into rhetorical "fictions" rather than truth and into observations that reveal uncomfortable affinities of truth and virtue with their opposites. That is the thrust of Frances Ferguson's "Coleridge on Language and Delusion" (*Genre,* 1978; summarily prefigured in a different context in *Boundary 2,* 1976), as also of Arden Reed's remarks (in *Romantic Weather,* 1983) on chapter 13 of the *Biographia* and essay 14 of the *Friend.* Ferguson suggests with disarming whimsy that Coleridge's "apparently descriptive philosophical statements were continually being invaded by—and reinforced by—prescriptive definitions which were somewhat at odds with the drift of his argument." The example she singles out is the sacrosanct definition of imagination and fancy in chapter 13 of *Biographia Literaria.* Fancy, although disparaged for dealing mechanically with ossified diction, is defined in the finite-infinite language of the preceding discussion of imagination. The disturbing consequence is to make the fancy "an oxymoronic equivalent of the dialectical secondary imagination," a view Reed advances on the grounds of the secondary imagination's capacity to produce difference as much as oneness, thus ever threatening to dissipate its own aesthetics and hence its and fancy's mutual replicating powers to seek the contrary ends of novelty and staleness. Symbol and allegory similarly tend, in spite of Coleridge's desynonymizing efforts, to collapse into one faculty by way of the latter's defined formlessness. Ferguson concludes that on the one hand Coleridge's religious commitment to the divine word validates language as an instrument of God's communication with human beings, but on the other hand his dissatisfaction with the temporally finite condition of words leads at times almost to condemnation of them as such. Thus, Coleridge is forever shuttling between the horns of wishing for words the cognitive power of reference and of fearing that such power may dupe individuals into believing that language does constitute the thing it signifies. The extremity of this critical act of debunking posits Coleridge as a deluded Blakean specter, the victim of a linguistic skepticism that is a far cry from the Logos security he formulates out of transcendental idealism and Christian Trinitarianism. Actually, if Ferguson's verve for pushing textual circumstances to absolutist generalizations is discounted, her deconstruction of text leaves her not too distant from Weinsheimer's evaluation of textual integrity and the role of the reader: " 'Truth' becomes such a vexed issue in Coleridge's accounts of language and literature" that he requires contributory understanding of a reader, "an imaginary friend" who "can fill the gaps in language by continually inputting, and thereby insuring, meaning."

Nor does everyone grant Coleridge near-magical prescience in the history and theory of language. Gerald L. Bruns, *Modern Poetry and the Idea of Language: A Critical and Historical Study* (1974), has Coleridge abortively working toward a linguistical system that assimilates philosophy and poetry as complementary activities of discourse into a dialectic of analysis and synthesis, thought and feeling, reason and imagination. The function of the word is to mediate between the mind and the world (Bruns here anticipates Wallace), by fabricating an immediate relationship between the two. Words can best do this when the historical process of desynonymizing has built up a language of distinctions among words originally equivalent in meaning. Unfortunately, as with so much of his system making, Coleridge left only brilliant gleams of insight into the nature of semantics, gleams that Bruns unkindly tags "The outline of a system that was never brought to birth."

ON EDUCATION

Lamb once observed that, although Coleridge had itinerantly jobbed from one Unitarian pulpit to another for only a brief period in young manhood, he never stopped "preaching" to his contemporaries. Lamb's justly famous observation could with equal validity, except for the loss of playful wit, have taken a pedagogical turn of reference. Coleridge was all his life a self-processing student of truth and learning, his lectures, lay sermons, friendly monologues, autobiographia, and table talk his means outside the classroom of instructing his generation. Surprisingly, despite this Ancient Mariner compulsion to lecture at anyone who would stop and listen, the formal educative intentions of Coleridge have been little investigated. Erdman (*BNYPL,* 1956) reconstructs in a two-part essay Tom Wedgwood's visionary plan to get a skeptical Coleridge and Wordsworth involved in education as the first step in its reform. William Walsh, *The Use of Imagination: Educational Thought and the Literary Mind* (1959), praises Coleridge's developmental conception of learning, whereby the child's knowledge of self and world undergoes transformations into an ever more comprehensive unity. Walsh finds Coleridge in his resistance to "finality and completeness" to be "the first truly modern consciousness." In a general survey, *Coleridge: The Work and the Relevance* (1967), Walsh, while philistinic about Coleridge as philosopher, theologian, and aesthetician, reiterates his appreciation of Coleridge as humane theorist and prefigurer if not direct progenitor of much modern educational philosophy. And Prickett examines the impact of Coleridge's "Idea of the Clerisy" (in *Reading Coleridge,* ed. Crawford, 1979) on nineteenth-century educational theory and practice (see below, the subsection "On Political Economy and Social Theory" for further reference to this article's analysis of the influence *Church and State* exerted on educational goals in Victorian England).

Aside from these tentative placements of Coleridge in the history of education, there is only Philip E. Hager's "The English Romantics and Education" (*AntigR,* 1976), an informative but brief summary of the monitoring procedures for the education of young children by older ones introduced by the Anglican Andrew Bell (1753–1832) and the nonconformist Joseph Lancaster (1778–1838) and an equally brief review of Coleridge's mixed feelings about the monitorial system, his praise of Bell in one of the 1808 lectures, in the 1809–10 *Friend,* and in the 1813 Bristol lecture "The New System of Education," and his subsequent nonpartisan position on the Bell-Lancaster controversy. J. R. de J. Jackson gives us a tantalizing glimpse (see above, "Editions") of Coleridge in the early 1820s trying to establish weekly classes for young gentlemen who find irresistible the blandishments of philosophy and theology and the mellifluous notes of Coleridge's voice. Coleridge's informed concern about education reflects the beat of his pulse over many decades. The modest contribution to our understanding of the subject surveyed here justifies additional study.

ON SCIENCE

Coleridge's involvement in the scientific discoveries and disputes of his day dates from his participation in Humphry Davy's experiments with nitrous oxide at the Pneumatic Institution of Dr. Thomas Beddoes in 1799–1800. Suzanne R. Hoover, "Coleridge, Humphry Davy, and Some Early Experiments with a Consciousness-Altering Drug" (*BRH,* 1978), rehearses the story of these experiments and Coleridge's reticence regarding them as a context to her examination of their relevance to the later drug problem. Coleridge subsequently studied chemistry with more enthusiasm than disciplined method, as much for new poetic images as for new scientific facts. He attended Davy's chemistry lectures in the early 1800s at the Royal Institution and avidly followed Davy's discoveries of chemical elements in the hope they would confirm the existence of a living copula binding the measurable and immeasurable energies of the universe into a divine design of balanced polarities. Coburn, "Coleridge: A Bridge between Science and Poetry" (*Proceedings of the Royal Institution of Great Britain,* 1973; rpt. in *Coleridge's Variety,* ed. Beer, 1974), reviews the friendly rivalry that spurred on both Coleridge and Davy during these years and defends Coleridge's interest in current theories and factual discoveries about the composition of the physical universe. Coleridge culminates this line of scientific speculation with *Theory of Life,* a discourse on the organic individuation of the natural world. It was written probably between 1818 and 1823 on the occasion of the Abernethy-Lawrence vitalist-mechanist controversy over the source of life, which climaxed with Abernethy's 1819 Hunterian oration. The fullest account of its provenance is J. H. Haeger's "Coleridge's 'Bye Blow': The Composition and Date of *Theory of Life*" (*MP,* 1976). An exposition of its organicism is to be found in Fogle's *The Idea of Coleridge's Criticism* (1962). A sympathetic comparison of its speculative evolutionary theory to the received empirical theory, along with a stronger claim for Coleridge's influential presence in the transition from classical to modern physics and chemistry, is set forth in Barfield's chapter "Coleridge and the Cosmology of Science" (in *What Coleridge Thought,* 1971). Barfield treats of the biological aspects and the contemporary controversy over the definition of life in another chapter, simply entitled "Life." George R. Potter's early look (*PMLA,* 1925) at Coleridge's struggle to develop an idea of evolution acceptable to his philosophy of life is still helpful. H. W. Piper, "Coleridge's Views on Evolution in 1795" (*The Active Universe,* appendix A, 1962), a follow-up of Potter, in part, finds Coleridge in *The Destiny of Nations* (lines 283–95) presuming an evolution, not pace Erasmus Darwin as the product of environment, but (*nisus formativus*) as an example of divine power acting providentially and organically through the organizing potency in nature. And A. Taylor, "Continuities and Chasms: Coleridge on Beasts and Men" (*Interspace and the Inward Sphere,* ed. Norman A. Anderson and Margene E. Weiss, 1978), summarizes Coleridge's continued effort to solve the problem of "where human beings begin and animals leave off." So much for the subject of Coleridge and evolution.

Coleridge's "Romantic Vision of the World," as Abrams terms it (*Coleridge's Variety,* ed. Beer, 1974), posits a single system embracing nature, the individual, and mind. A dynamic cosmic ecology constructed out of the elemental powers of light and sound under the "praepotence" of gravitation in combination with the contrary forces of attraction and repulsion, contraction and dilation, it is bent on revealing an ultimate concord between empirical science and mental-spiritual revelation. Positive accounts of this metascience are given by Beer in his books on Coleridge and on Wordsworth (see above, "Criticism of the Poetry"), by way of the poetic forms it takes; by Barfield in *What Coleridge Thought,* by way generally of the dynamic philosophy and Coleridge's speculative bracketing of the natural world with the laws of polarity; and by Abrams in "Coleridge's 'A Light in

Sound': Science, Metascience, and Poetic Imagination" (*PAPS*, 1972), by way of the "one Life" passage in "The Eolian Harp." Abrams acknowledges that Coleridge draws heavily on Schellingian *Naturphilosophie* to shape this post-Newtonian world picture; but because Abrams' final focus is the poem "The Eolian Harp" he remains unconcerned about and uncensorious of the extent to which Coleridge "depended on the daring phantasms of the *Naturphilosophie*" for his concept of nature. The same is true of Craig W. Miller's scientific exposition, "Coleridge's Concept of Nature" (*JHI*, 1964). Both McFarland, excursus note 18 on Coleridge and scientific thought (*Coleridge and the Pantheist Tradition*, 1969), and Wellek (*ERP3*) find dismaying that "Coleridge's most ambitious forays into science were a mixture of slavish dependence on, and rivalry with, the school of Schelling" (this quotation and the previous one are from McFarland) and censure Miller's failure to note this damning fact.

Coleridge's scientific speculations have been judged wanting in experimental method and fanciful in premises and conclusion. Typical is the indictment, narrowly defined by empirical assumptions and laboratory techniques, of Maurice Schofield, "Southey, Coleridge and Company" (*Contemporary Rev.*, 1977), that the Romantic poets were dilettantes in chemistry and that Coleridge's efforts to become "a formidable chemist" dissolved into frivolity under the experiments with laughing gas at the Pneumatic Institution. Another is the charge of S. V. Pradhan, "Kant's *Dissertation*, Coleridge's Imagination and Metascience" (*DR*, 1975), that Coleridge attempted for his own religious peace of mind to humanize science into accommodating his perception of the world. Pradhan deplores the respect accorded a science practiced in the realm of metaphysics, which is heavily derivative and which did nothing to change the science of its day. Evidence justifying Pradhan's condescension is to be found in the fragmentary essay "On the Passions," which reveals the intrinsic conflict in Coleridge between the psychologist and the metaphysician, the scientist and the theologian. Bostetter (*JHI*, 1970) describes the manuscript as "one of the most daring of Coleridge's scientific speculations." In it Coleridge tries to adapt to the evolutionary process the "bad" passions of fear, rage, and lust as necessary appetites of growth rather than deny them as moral forces of evil. Yet, when he realizes his argument is leading him away from Christian dogma toward a kind of scientific humanism Coleridge finds it easier to abandon the essay than to reconcile its premises with his religious postulates.

Some historians of science, however, are discovering Coleridge to be a fascinating thinker and writer, and a useful representative figure in the scientific wars waged in the early nineteenth century. In the vanguard of this inquiring attitude toward Coleridge is Trevor H. Levere, who has been making good use of Coleridge's marginalia in scientific books and of his notebooks of 1816–28 (*CN* 3–4). In four articles—"Coleridge and Romantic Science" (*Science, Technology, and Culture in Historical Perspective*, ed. L. A. Knafla, M. S. Staum, and T. H. E. Travers, 1976), "Coleridge, Chemistry, and the Philosophy of Nature" (*SIR*, 1977), "S. T. Coleridge: A Poet's View of Science" (*Annals of Science*, 1978), and "S. T. Coleridge and the Human Sciences: Anthropology, Phrenology, and Mesmerism" (*Science, Pseudoscience, and Society*, ed. M. P. Hanen, M. J. Osler, and R. G. Weyant,

1980)—Levere puts the case for respectfully treating Coleridge's "extensive and . . . profound" interest in science as a reflection of the dichotomies in scientific theory current at the time. Coleridge was a "fringe member of two scientific communities": the Anglo-French allegiance to analysis, dissection, abstraction, mechanism, and crude empiricism; and the German philosophical tradition that also "cared deeply about exact observation" but valued in addition synthesis, unification, organicism, and rationality. In Coleridge's eyes Anglo-French mechanistic thought of the late eighteenth century, with its atoms and imponderable fluids, was bad science; German dynamic thought, with its idealism and reliance on reason rather than on the unqualified senses, was good science. He regarded poets and scientists as engaged in complementary forms of creative activity, all bent on seeking out the relations in nature that affirm the unity of the universe and of life. Since Coleridge's aim was to provide a· foundation of scientific knowledge supportive of philosophy, and culminating in theology, his science was dynamic, stressing development, interconnectedness, and productive unity. It was in conformity with the law of polarity and opposed to mechanical and corpuscular science. Levere cautions one to handle Coleridge's analogies carefully, for they do not mean equivalent/same so much as they do a field of forces at once similar and different. Coleridge's polar dynamical chemistry may appear obscure and strange to us but it is important to our grasping the mainline of his intellectual development after 1816. It is "not merely the tedious aberration of a brilliant but erratic mind," it is "the strangeness of original thought based on intimate knowledge, and contributing to a brilliant intellectual synthesis."

Levere has capped these studies of Coleridge's effort to unite the two worlds of nature and mind, in a book misleadingly titled *Poetry Realized in Nature: Samuel Taylor Coleridge and Early Nineteenth-Century Science* (1981). It traces the abiding and central importance of chemistry, and secondarily of the earth sciences and of physiology, to Coleridge's teleological view of life. Coleridge had a remarkable grasp of the science of his day ("For a poet, it was unique"); and Levere places him squarely within the scientific experimental and speculative controversies of the early nineteenth century, particularly in the decade after 1816.

The historical importance of Coleridge as a conduit of ideas from philosophers to scientists in the first half of the nineteenth century is also receiving some attention. Leslie Pearce Williams, *Michael Faraday, a Biography* (1965), attributes to Coleridge responsibility for the main transmission of German transcendental idealism to two generations of English scientists. Kant's anti-atomic view of the universe as a plenum filled with forces rather than with matter, resulting in the reduction of all physical phenomena to attraction and repulsion, was a fundamental insight guiding the research of English scientists from Ritter and Davy to Faraday, with Coleridge functioning as intermediary by way of Davy for Faraday's antimaterialist ideas. Thomas L. Hankins, "Triplets and Triads: Sir William Rowan Hamilton and the Metaphysics of Mathematics" (*Isis,* 1977), reveals how Coleridge's urging on Hamilton the study of Kant in 1832–34 led Hamilton, who had read the *Friend* on the law of polarity in 1830, to search unsuccessfully for a concept of mathematical triplets as an analogue to the concept of philosophical triads, on the theoretical assumption that the laws applicable to philosophical idealism also governed the fundamental nature of matter. Abrams recognized thirty years ago in "Mechanical and Organic Theories" (*The Mirror and the Lamp*, 1953; rpt. as "Mechanical and Organic Psychologies of Literary Invention," in *English Literature and British Philosophy*, ed. S. P. Rosenbaum, 1971) Coleridge's role in applying the organism as an aesthetic model to the process and products of literary invention and to the living imagination (on analogy with the living plant) as distinguished from the mechanical fancy, as part of his all-out war against the "Mechanico-corpuscular Philosophy." Now a scientist, Philip C. Ritterbush, "Organic Form: Aesthetics and Objectivity in the Study of Form in the Life Sciences" (*Organic Form: The Life of an Idea*, ed. G. S. Rousseau, 1972), reiterates Abrams' literary-historical perceptions, assigning to Coleridge a leading role in synthesizing the organic form of plants with the organic concept of aesthetics. And W. K. Wimsatt, "Organic Form: Some Questions about a Metaphor" (*Organic Form*, ed. Rousseau, 1972), similarly credits Coleridge with avoiding the implication that a poem, to be organic, must contain vegetable imagery or look in form like a plant, while acknowledging that Coleridge drew from A. W. Schlegel the five properties plants and poems share (analyzed by Abrams at some length also), which "in turn," as Coleridgean analogues, "become archetypal for a moderate English tradition."

Given Coleridge's lifelong preoccupation with his own physical disorders, "There is a need," as Levere observes, "for a major study of STC and the doctors." What little attention has been directed to Coleridge and the therapeutic sciences, however, has been more promising than fulfilling. R. Guest-Gornall, "Samuel Taylor Coleridge and the Doctors" (*Medical History*, 1973), reviews the history of Coleridge's medical treatment, his contact with physicians, and his ailments, real and imagined. Guest-Gornall notes that the school physician at Christ's Hospital when Coleridge was in attendance was William Pitcairn, who "had made a reputation through the use of opium in typhoid fever," and that Coleridge insisted on having all four of his children vaccinated for smallpox. John Harris, "Coleridge's Readings in Medicine" (*WC*, 1972), particularizes the broad interest Coleridge shows in basic physiology, hygiene, pathology, and pharmacopoeia as part of his twofold attempt to diagnose his own illnesses and to understand the phenomenon of psychosomatic disorders. And Modiano, "Coleridge's Views on Touch and Other Senses" (*BRH*, 1978), explores how Coleridge came to believe that the skin is "a Terra Incognita in Medicine" (*CN* 1, no. 1826). Modiano sketches a story of how late eighteenth-century scientific interest in the relationship of the senses to one another led gradually to a more appreciative attitude among Romantic poets toward the lower senses. Consonant with his own experience Coleridge perceived a synonymy between touch and the affective powers, which led him to refine touch into a higher faculty of aesthetic perception. The sense of touch palpably connects the self to the external world and thus provides a mode of consciousness that mediates between subject and object.

One should not forget in the recent respect tendered Coleridge's scientific speculations that he contributed little directly to the mainstream of the experimental disciplines, whose development has been triumphantly empirical and atomistic. Nor has he figured in the advances of psychology. For all his anticipatory grasp of truths about the human psyche and physique that we now take for granted, Coleridge tends—as David S. Miall, "The Meaning of Dreams: Coleridge's Ambivalence" (*SIR*, 1982), indirectly observes—to translate his observations of the mind into matters of the will and of moral significance. Coleridge's concept of science was essentially backward-looking. His attempt to organize the sciences philosophically in support of a theory of divinely initiated cosmic evolution and genetically developed powers was the "last ditch stand" of a conservative mind. So McFarland ("Coleridge's *Magnum Opus*," in *Romanticism and the Forms of Ruin*, 1981) vividly sums up Coleridge's heroic gesture of resistance "at the innermost ramparts of Christianity," against the atheistic flood tide of Spinozistic and Darwinian thought, pantheistic, evolutionary, scientific, and utilitarian, threatening in the nineteenth century to engulf all moral values and all vestiges of God.

ON POLITICAL ECONOMY AND SOCIAL THEORY

The political opinions and activities of Coleridge continue to pique scholars. Still unanswered to the satisfaction of all are questions concerning his historical and intellectual sources, his apparent repudiation in later years of the generous moral and social concerns of his youth, his relationship with the newspapers and journals of his day, his mature views on culture and social reform, and his influence on later generations.

In an effort to discern a recurrent policy of concern in the varied and seeming volte-faces, waverings, and hesitancies checkering Coleridge's political utterances and social temporizings, John Colmer follows up his ground-breaking chronological account in *Coleridge: Critic of Society* (1959) with "Coleridge and Politics" (*S. T. Coleridge*, ed. Brett, 1971), which summarily surveys the whole of them again, stressing the fundamental consistency of their Christian commitment. He refutes the old-fashioned unexamined judgment that Coleridge was "the heir to Burke," affirms Godwin as central to the ideational context of the 1795 lectures, and while recognizing the religious grounds of Coleridge's rejection of Paine and Godwin, contends that "for all his connections with Unitarian radicalism, he had little sympathy for the narrow sectarian aims of English dissent." Colmer also finds in the 1795 lectures the themes that were to preoccupy the "mature political thought" of Coleridge: "the freedom of the press, the communication of truth, the importance of desynonymizing key terms, the function of education in effecting social reform, the creation of an elect (an interesting anticipation of his later idea of the 'clerisy'), the analysis of the forces that cause a loss of national character, the relationship between private and public morality, and above all the importance of relating all political issues to 'fixed and determinate principles of action.'"

The 1971 publication of the *Collected Coleridge* volume of the 1795 lectures on politics and religion, however, stirred up fresh debate about Coleridge's revolutionary activities in Bristol from 1795 to 1797. Mann's estimate in the Introduction (see above, "Editions") of Coleridge's radicalism and its ideological affinities is challenged in a review article, "'Bliss was it in that dawn': The Matter of Coleridge's Revolutionary Youth and How It Came to be Obscured" (*TLS*, 6 Aug. 1971). The anonymous reviewer (E. P. Thompson?) contends that the opinions Coleridge reveals, especially in the fifth and sixth theological lectures, are close to those of William Frend and Gilbert Wakefield and more seditious than later accounts suggest, so much so that if Coleridge had not retired to Nether Stowey he might have eventually talked himself into prison. To the reviewer's way of thinking, Coleridge was more involved with the provincial reform movement than Mann allows. The immediate context of Coleridge's attitudes is less his reaction to Godwin (which Mann stresses) than his espousal of the sentiments of the radical Christian dissenters, especially since Godwin's voice received little hearing in the provinces. Furthermore, the evaporating solidarity of the reform movement in 1796 not only explains much about Coleridge's actions at the time but also suggests extenuating reasons for his bungling indifference to the *Watchman*'s short life. The *TLS* reviewer keeps a firm grip on the contempt he feels for the "often overrated" polymath intellect of Coleridge and for the "distinct apostasy" of Coleridge toward the social ardency of his youth. Less controlled is an exchange between Watson and Beer ("The Revolutionary Youth of Wordsworth and Coleridge," *CritQ*, 1976, 1977). Beer refutes Watson's truculent insistence that Coleridge was a violent revolutionist and political extremist in his undergraduate days, questions Watson's evidence, and insists that there is "surprisingly little inconsistency between [Coleridge's] earlier and his later statements about his youthful opinions." Watson in reply in the same issue refuses to recant but interprets anew Beer's reinterpretation of his interpretation of events. More measured, and useful, explanations of Coleridge's "apostasy" than those rehashed in the Watson-Beer exchange are found in Aers, Cook, and Punter's *Romanticism and Ideology* (1981), in Marilyn Butler's *Romantics, Rebels and Reactionaries* (1981), and in the special collection of essays "Coleridge: The Politics of the Imagination" (*SIR*, 1982), by R. F. Storch, Michael Fischer, Jerome Christensen, and Raimonda Modiano, who argue that Coleridge, whose equivocations are often a sign of his discomfort with direct political action, strove to rise above partisan politics in his persistent search for general principles. These reasonable estimates of Coleridge the political theorist are prefigured by Elizabeth Sewell's "Coleridge on Revolution" (*SIR*, 1972), which demonstrates that his use of the term and the concept both positively and negatively does not bespeak ambivalent attitudes so much as the comprehensive method of the dynamic philosophy and the polar logic. Coleridge never ceased to see himself as a revolutionist, according to Sewell, but over the years the concept undergoes an interesting change: from alluding to political revolution it evolves in middle and later life to mean ideational revolutions of the mind, especially in the fields of philosophy and education. So is regurgitated an issue defined and much discussed previously (see Crane Brinton, *Political Ideas of the English Romanticists*, 1926; Colmer, *Coleridge: Critic of Society*, 1959; and Woodring's two books on political ideas in the poetry of Coleridge and the other Romantics). A footnote to the issue, with a voice out of the past who remembered Coleridge when he was a "down right

zealous leveler," is Burton R. Pollin and Redmond Burke's "John Thelwall's Marginalia in a Copy of Coleridge's *Biographia Literaria*" (*BNYPL*, 1970). An alternative
to Thelwall's view of Coleridge's political divagations is given in Edward Duffy's
Rousseau in England (1979). In an intelligent exposition, Duffy shows how
Coleridge's ambivalent attitude toward Rousseau was complicated by his sharing
with Blake, Wordsworth, and Burke the dismissal of Rousseau as the proto-
Jacobin, the embodiment of the philosophe—an estimate of Rousseau originating
in abstractions of political dogma rather than in attentiveness to specifics.

We know a great deal about the political journalism of Coleridge, thanks to
the labors of Erdman. Besides the copious notes and informed introduction to
his edition of *Essays on His Times* (*CC* 3, 1978), Erdman has added considerable
chiaroscuro to our sketchy picture of Coleridge in the Grub Street world of
London: as editorial writer for the *Morning Post* (in *Power and Consciousness*,
ed. C. C. O'Brien and W. D. Vanech, 1969), as parliamentary reporter (in *Speech
Monographs*, 1960), and as reviewer of his own *Second Lay Sermon* (in *SIR*, 1961).
Most recently, in collaboration with P. M. Zall, Erdman studies "Coleridge and
Jeffrey in Controversy" (*SIR*, 1975). And in "Coleridge and the 'Review Business':
An Account of His Adventures with the *Edinburgh*, the *Quarterly* and *Maga*
[*Blackwood's Magazine*]" (*WC*, 1975), he further traces with tolerant bemusement the sorry story of Coleridge's Gulliverian confrontations with the Brobding-
nagian world of Jeffrey, Lockhart and Company of rascally publishers and booksellers. Erdman makes the most of the tale of genius entangled with human folly:
of Coleridge's courtship of the review editors for work and his temptations—not
always resisted in thought, although his failure to translate intention into deed
usually saved him—to trim his beliefs to fit the politically uncongenial *Edinburgh
Review* and the religiously compatible *Eclectic Review*. Coleridge's protestations
in the *Biographia Literaria* against reviewing to the contrary, his remedy of the
evil was evidently "to out-review the Reviews," if only he could bestir himself to
write them and the periodicals would print them without too many changes—
but alas! he couldn't! and alas! when he did they wouldn't.

Two unfriendly appraisals of *Essays on His Times, The Watchman*, and the
Friend (instigated by *Collected Coleridge* editions of these works) are worth
reading for their minority report on Coleridge the journalist. They are Thomas H.
Landress' "The Politics of Samuel Taylor Coleridge" (*SR*, 1973) and E. P. Thompson's intemperate tonic (for haters of Coleridge) of vituperation against the
Morning Post and *Courier* leaders (*WC*, 1979): a "surfeit of Pharisaism and
cliché . . . in political judgment, disloyal, egocentric, and wholly irresponsible
. . . and unprincipled." Studies of limited value because of their old-fashioned ap-
proach to the subject or their use of now dated sources are Oswald Doughty's
"Coleridge as Statesman" (*EM*, 1969), on *The Statesman's Manual*; R. W. Harris'
"Coleridge and the Philosophy of Conservatism" in *Romanticism and the Social
Order 1780–1830* (1969), which is based on pre–*Collected Coleridge* and
Coleridge Notebooks editions; and Garrett Clarke's "Coleridge's Utopia Revisited"
(*Soundings*, 1972), on the pantisocracy venture.

The mature social and political theories of Coleridge are to be found in the
Friend, the two *Lay Sermons*, and *On the Constitution of the Church and State*.

Critics from J. S. Mill to Raymond Williams have accordingly used them as touchstones for the conservative idea of the individual and society as a moral organism, which Coleridge offers as an alternative to the utilitarian arrangement between individual and institution conceived by positivist minds.

The influence of *Church and State* on the Victorians was heterodox. In *Coleridge to* Catch-22: *Images of Society* (1978) Colmer devotes two chapters to analyzing the impact of its philosophy of society and of its psychology of government on Arnold and Mill. Arnold's division of society into barbarians, philistines, and populace is judged less open than Coleridge's, whose vision of society includes provision for movement from class to class. And Mill unwittingly demonstrates the acuity of his characterization of Coleridge as a seminal thinker, by advancing again and again ideas as his own "that have been unconsciously assimilated from Coleridge." Prickett, "Coleridge and the Idea of the Clerisy" (in *Reading Coleridge,* ed. Crawford, 1979), concentrates on the educational and religious importance of *Church and State* for the Victorians. Whereas some found the essay, in its argument for a "narrowly secular establishment, privileged and conservative in outlook" and supportive of the status quo, two groups of Victorian social and intellectual activists drew on it for inspiration. The secular clerists Mill, Arnold, and Pattison used it to advocate reform of Oxford and Cambridge, while the religious Coleridgeans Maurice, Kingsley, and Hare adapted its Christianizing goals to the educational ideal of working men's colleges. Some of the same ground is covered by John Barrell in the introduction to his edition of *Church and State* (1972), particularly Mill's effort to synthesize Bentham's pragmatic acceptance of the Industrial Revolution with Coleridge's denouncement of it and Arnold's dilution of Coleridge's national cultivation to a state-protected culture. Barrell's bias is that of the political left so ably represented by E. P. Thompson and Raymond Williams. Consequently, his evaluation of *Church and State* as a classic work of conservative thought in English should be supplemented by Colmer's introduction to the work in *Collected Coleridge* (see "Editions"), which concentrates historically on its ecclesiastical and theological backgrounds as much as on its political overtones. Despite his leftist leanings Barrell conveys a keen appreciation at once of the English nature of Coleridge's conservative constitutionalism, which shies away from the cultural relativism of German Romantic conservatism, and of the uncompromising theoretical form of his political thought, which is incompatible with the pragmatism characterizing British conservatism of the past hundred years.

Anthony John Harding, *Coleridge and the Idea of Love: Aspects of Relationship in Coleridge's Thought and Writing* (1974), determines that for Coleridge collective political freedom is inseparable from individual moral freedom. Instead of relying on abstract principles to guarantee this ideal body politic, Coleridge returns always to the solid ground of the individual's inner impulses and moral decisions as the common denominator of the social state. Where political structures are in question, only the individual in the concrete, answerable to God, matters. A community is interdependent, its unity confirmed through human love by the final cause of divine love. Its aim is accordingly the cultivation of those qualities and faculties that characterize our humanity. Hence the corresponding moral imperative of an enlightened government to promote the well-being of all, a communal idea of love that led Coleridge to the advanced sociopolitical position of advocating against the prevalent economic theory of Ricardo, Smith, and Malthus the governmental right, even duty, to interfere on behalf of suffering groups of people. Putting theory into practice Coleridge actively supported the Peel Bill on child labor in 1818. If there is a fault in this enlightened social concern, it is his uncritical reliance on the spiritual motivation of the politician. Indirectly adumbrating this penchant of Coleridge's, Daniel M. McVeigh, "Political Vision in Coleridge's *The Statesman's Manual*" (*WC*, 1983), defends the functional role of Coleridge's religious thought in his political theorizing. To the idea of love as a kind of civic cement, Colmer, "Coleridge and the Life of Hope" (*SIR*, 1972), adds the life-giving and unifying potency of hope as an important ingredient in the development and education of the whole human being and in the positive functioning of government.

A topic that has generated a mild flurry of speculative interest is Coleridge's position on the allied questions of slavery and racial equality, triggered by his shift from ardent advocacy of abolition in the 1790s, through a moderated attitude of paternalism in the first three decades of the nineteenth century, to a theory of race, based on Blumenbach's "scale of dignity," that is more interested in harmonizing science with theology than in confronting and accommodating the emerging biological research on race. The most judicious studies are by J. H. Haeger, "Coleridge's Speculations on Race" (*SIR*, 1974); Barbara T. Paul-Emile, "Samuel Taylor Coleridge as Abolitionist" (*ArielE*, 1974); and Eva Beatrice Dykes, *The Negro in English Romantic Thought* (1942).

Owen Barfield treats "Man in History and in Society" in *What Coleridge Thought* (1971). No less unconventional in viewpoint than Coleridge's own offering of Christian homilies in the guise of political tracts for the times, the operating premise for Barfield is that *Theory of Life* looms as large as *The Statesman's Manual*, the *Friend*, and *Church and State* in these calculations, because for Coleridge "the true idea of society can never be grasped in isolation from the true idea of history." Barfield's method is to polarize the concrete concerns of Coleridge's social thinking into teleological ideas involving the relation of whole to parts, the growth of consciousness into universal and particular oneness, and the process of evolution from totality to unity.

The seminal concept of culture (cultivation is the term Coleridge uses) as a general social condition binding human relations in a vital and active historical process is credited to Coleridge by Raymond Williams in *Culture and Society: 1780–1950* (1958; rpt. 1966) and linked to all the familiar Coleridgean polarities as an act of reconciliation whose goal is a state of spiritual perfection, not an accumulation of social values, by M. Sathya Babu, "Coleridge's Concept of Culture" (*Literary Studies: Homage to Dr. A. Sivaramasubramonia Aiyer*, ed. K. P. Kesava Menon, M. Manuel, and K. Ayyappa Paniker, 1973). Colmer, in *Coleridge to Catch-22* (1978), with his eye in part on the forms the idea of culture took in the later nineteenth and twentieth centuries, distinguishes three concepts of culture traceable to Coleridge: (1) a process of human perfection, (2) a way of life defined by institutions, art, or literature, and (3) the sum of intellectual and artistic works. No one before Coleridge, Colmer concludes, had given learning, science, and the arts—culture—so crucial a role in the state.

This review of Coleridge as political and social thinker should not conclude without mention of several fine older studies by nonliterary scholars already discussed at greater length in *ERP3*. William F. Kennedy, *Humanist versus Economist: The Economic Thought of Samuel Taylor Coleridge* (1958), gives Coleridge high marks for his humane brand of laissez-faire economics that balances affirmation of self-interested individualism with advocacy of state intervention. He judges Coleridge's appraisal in the *Second Lay Sermon* (1817) of the postwar Napoleonic depression and his arguments on government spending, taxation, national debt, and business cycles as superior to Malthus' and Ricardo's recommendations of public policy. He concludes that to Coleridge's emphasis on the value and meaning of life as a legitimate question for economists is owed the anxious desire of Victorian economic theorists from Mill to Keynes to avoid being trapped in empirical and mechanical—antihumanistic—concerns. David P. Calleo, *Coleridge and the Idea of the Modern State* (1966), assesses the relevance of Coleridge's concept of the national state. Finally, Robert Preyer, *Bentham, Coleridge, and the Science of History* (1958), examines the neglected area of Coleridge's historical theorizing, evaluates its influence on the next generation of historians in their rebellion against eighteenth-century Lockian rationalist history, and analyzes the distinctions and similarities of the three major historiographies of the nineteenth century: German absolute idealist, Germano-Coleridgean intellectual idealist, and Benthamite relativist.

BIOGRAPHIA LITERARIA AND THE FRIEND

Annoyance with the *Biographia Literaria* echoes down through the years. It has been labeled "the greatest book of criticism in English and also one of the most exasperating books written in any language" (Arthur Symons) and has been likened to "Coleridge's whole life" in that "it cannot seem to hold a straight course but wanders continually from one subject to another" (Orsini). Coleridge with ingratiating candor calls it an "immethodical miscellany," even as his calculated marshalling of consonants, the alliterating rush of *m*'s and *l*'s, mitigates the harshness of the self-decrying judgment. With equivalent duplicity McFarland tags it as one of Coleridge's "rubble-heap works," while paying tribute to the "diasparactive" epiphanies of Coleridge's mind as honest and heroic analogues of the existential shape of human endeavors (*Romanticism and the Forms of Ruin*, 1981). Its waywardness is like a siren's song to critics, hinting that all was not well in its conception and then providing them with errancies and improprieties to explain symptomatically its failures of heart and mind, especially its quailing before the self-assigned task of constructing a philosophical base for the imagination. Coleridge was confused, they say, frustrated by his emotion toward Wordsworth (Cooke), by his ambivalence toward Schelling (Appleyard and

McFarland), and by his uncertainty about the acts of perception and creativity (Appleyard). Harassment and exhaustion, say others (McFarland and D. M. Fogel), caused him to compromise between his rigorous ideals of composition and the demands of a livelihood (J. R. de J. Jackson), and to cut chapter 13 short (Fogel and Bate). But decorum in the sickroom when Coleridge is the patient is hard to maintain. Such solemn diagnoses are swept aside by the facetious quackery of Eugene L. Stelzig's "Coleridge's Failed Quest: The Anti-climax of Fancy/Imagination in *Biographia Literaria*" (*Univ. of Mississippi Studies in English*, 1980), which summarizes, as if no critical history of the case existed, all the elementary symptoms, pranks, tricks, divagations, and collapses of argument that have been superstitiously charged over the years to the *Biographia*.

Concurrent with all this eager pulse taking is a contrary insistence on the essential health of author and book. In a propaedeutic diagnosis thirty years ago, "The Integrity of the *Biographia Literaria*" (*E&S*, 1952), Whalley determined the bloodline to be Coleridge's need to establish the poetic genius of Wordsworth and, by extension, the nature of the great philosophical poem and the standards by which it should be judged. Bate gives the official imprimatur of the *Collected Coleridge* to this inspired perception, enunciating it in his introduction to the *Biographia Literaria* (*CC* 7), adjusted to include the psychological element of competition dividing the two poets and the need of Coleridge to demonstrate his own genius with a comparable body of work. U. C. Knoepflmacher, "A Nineteenth-Century Touchstone: Chapter XV of *Biographia Literaria*" (*Nineteenth-Century Literary Perspectives: Essays in Honor of Lionel Stevenson*, ed. Clyde de L. Ryals, 1974), seeks to corroborate this view with a bit of special pleading. Chapter 15 defines true poetic genius, ostensibly illustrated by analysis of some Shakespearean verse, but the real target, Knoepflmacher believes, is Wordsworth. The chapter is designed to recall him from the pseudodramatic and pseudonarrative poetry of *The Excursion* back to the distinctly personal meditations of *The Prelude*. In the same vein, Richard Mallette, "Narrative Technique in the 'Biographia Literaria'" (*MLR*, 1975), attends to the modulation of Coleridge's voice into an authoritative apostle of the ideal poet as Wordsworth; while Patrick Parrinder, *Authors and Authority: A Study of English Literary Criticism and Its Relation to Culture, 1750–1900* (1977), reads the *Biographia Literaria* less altruistically, as a series of strategies to outflank the positive, abstract rationalism of Wordsworth's Preface to the *Lyrical Ballads*. If hope for the apotheosis of the poetic imagination seems to be prompted by Wordsworth, much of the *Biographia*, particularly the second half, "is dominated by Coleridge's obsession with contradicting Wordsworth, correcting his views and stating the terms on which he may be accepted as a great writer." All else in the *Biographia* Parrinder downgrades to Shandean facade. More theoretically explicatory of Coleridge's developing belief that poetry culminates not in great poets but in the timeless simultaneity of a Great Tradition and that interpretation or hearing takes priority over, or at least becomes as important as, creation or speaking is Jean-Pierre Mileur's contention (*Vision and Revision: Coleridge's Art of Immanence*, 1982) that in the *Biographia*, especially volume 2, Coleridge corrects his initial mistaken relationship with Wordsworth. From viewing himself as fellow poet, Coleridge redefines himself within the context of his critique of Wordsworth as one whose critical imagination and textualizing consciousness symbiotically brings completion to the poetic voice.

The current discovery of the book's "formulated system" in the "formulating self" of the critic receives its impetus from Cooke's *"Quisque Sui Faber:* Coleridge in the *Biographia Literaria"* (*PQ,* 1971). Although Coleridge never fully defines his "paramount object, the imagination," he succeeds in his secondary goal of self-presentation inferentially via the act of his mind rather than in the facts of an explicit biography and obliquely via his relationships to books, to other writers of the past and present, and above all to Wordsworth. Out of the double awareness of Coleridge's focus on his forming the idea as much as on the idea itself and out of his participation in the discussion as biographical subject as much as in his detachment from it as critic, emerges the being of Coleridge and the entity of the *Biographia.* Cooke's conclusion is that the imagination, although not fully realized philosophically, is revealed at work, in process, diffused throughout the *Biographia Literaria.* This emphasis on the autobiographical leads Cooke subsequently in *The Romantic Will* (1976) to minimize the aesthetic thrust of the imagination in favor of its ontological purposiveness. Through the perception of the primary imagination the individual moves toward self-conscious being, and through the unifying act of the secondary imagination moves toward conception or meaning whereby the unity and value of the world in the eyes of God become a possible part of human knowledge. Like Cooke, Gene M. Bernstein, "Self-Creating Artifices: Coleridgean Imagination and Language" (*MP,* 1979), plays up the imagination as a psychological-ontological instrument reconciling subject and object in such aesthetic acts of self-knowledge as the Conversation poems and *Biographia Literaria,* through which means individuation takes place. C. M. Wallace, "The Function of Autobiography in *Biographia Literaria"* (*WC,* 1981), attributes to this self-reflexive construct of a persona, who illustrates the process of thought and validates the consequent ideas, the readiness of the reader to trust the *Biographia,* however seemingly digressive.

The self-reflexive premise also informs the most ambitious attempt to demonstrate that the *Biographia* is a consciously planned (from at least 1808 onward) and self-consciously conceived "treatise of imagination *on* imagination." This is Wheeler's barbarously titled *Sources, Processes and Methods in Coleridge's* Biographia Literaria (1980). Drawing on the phenomenology of reading theory of Georges Poulet, the reader-response theory of Stanley Fish, the implied-reader process of Wolfgang Iser, and related discourse theories of the German Romantic ironists, especially Karl Solger's definition of irony and Friedrich Schlegel's philosophy of "creative" criticism, Wheeler transforms the *Biographia Literaria* into a self-reflexive exchange between author and reader by way of book and reader, which has as one of its goals the growth in intellectual self-consciousness of the reader. The *Biographia Literaria* offers "a philosophy of the phenomenology of perception, working at the immediate practical level of engaging the reader in a project of self-criticism and knowledge." It is designed not to be read as a discursive statement but as an imaginative work whose form is a mirror of its meaning, with specific metacritiques scattered through its pages indirectly containing descriptions of the method and mode by which the book is intended to interact with the reader. Leaning heavily on the analogical mode, Wheeler transforms the *Biographia Literaria* into an extended piece of metacriticism, making it an early do-it-yourself book on cognitive skills, and every neophyte reader of it a Humpty Dumpty of words. There is much learning assembled here and some sensible perceptions of the *Biographia Literaria* as "a shaping matrix." Given the intense engagement of Coleridge with any text he reads, Wheeler's thesis has a ring of rightness about it. Unfortunately, she forces the metastructure of the book more than she plumbs it. Less critically dissonant is Lawrence Buell's "The Question of Form in Coleridge's *Biographia Literaria*" (*ELH*, 1979), which examines in the symbiosis of *The Prelude* and the *Biographia* the double-edged meaning for Coleridge of discovering the era's greatest poet: his need to proclaim the dependence of his critical identity on Wordsworth and to assert its independence of Wordsworth, which has him at one and the same time constructing and deconstructing a self stylistically and discursively in the disparity of the philosopher-critic's tight and cohesive argument vis-à-vis the journalist's discontinuous and casual format. Through the simultaneous comparison of what he has done with what he promises to accomplish, Coleridge paradoxically labors to dismantle the self being built up in the *Biographia.* Thus is the work a harbinger of the open self-questioning antiform.

The most comprehensive—and I suspect seminal—unraveling of Coleridge's constant act of self-definition through the two-way flow of his mind between the topics of original poetic genius (Wordsworth) and of original critical genius (Coleridge) is Christensen's comparably original "The Genius in the *Biographia Literaria*" (*SIR*, 1978; rpt. as part of an expanded set of referents in *Coleridge's Blessed Machine of Language,* 1981). Christensen neatly assimilates the best of the two theories (as represented by Whalley and Cooke) about the unity of the *Biographia* in a perceptive exposition of how Coleridge in a "habitual textual movement" establishes his own genius while extolling Wordsworth's. The chiasmus by which Coleridge repeats this self-presentation becomes under Christensen's deconstruction, particularly of chapter 4, the pervasive maneuver of *Biographia Literaria* and the key to its unity. Coleridge's strategy is to weave into one texture repetitions of passages quoted from his and others' works, thus deflecting attention, however slightly, from Wordsworth the poet to Coleridge the recollector and critic.

Christensen is not alone in his bold deconstruction of the *Biographia Literaria.* The duplicitous "panoply of errancies, anomalies, and promiscuities" informing a literary work that bears the message of unity and authorial integrity has attracted other like-minded critics now that D. M. Fogel's "Compositional History of the *Biographia Literaria*" (*SB*, 1977) has established a reliable chronology. Focal points for these critics are the verbal and rhetorical evasions of chapters 12 and 13. Grosvenor Powell, "Coleridge's Imagination and the Infinite Regress of Consciousness" (*ELH*, 1972), lucidly sets forth the conditions of the regress in which the union of knowing and being in self-consciousness lands Coleridge. Unable to bridge the gap between mind and matter and unable to break out of the idealist regress without leaving self-consciousness undefined, Coleridge terminates the argument, writes the famous letter from "a friend," and concludes with the even more famous definitions of the primary and secondary imaginations and of the fancy. It is Coleridge's sealing of the gap between subject and object by this imaginative act of imagination that fascinates the doyenne of Derrideans and, in her train, such others as Brisman and Christensen. Gayatri Chakravorty Spivak's target in "The Letter as Cutting Edge" (*YFS*, 1977) is less Coleridge than his heirs the New Critics. Still, her Lacanian psychoanalysis of why he seeks philosophical certainty for what is endemic to the relation of text and subject is suggestive when placed, whether with or without the phallus-castration trope of her critical mechanism, in the context of Christensen's blessed machine of deconstruction. Quoting Derrida that "I is not a being," Spivak calls attention to the maneuver by which Coleridge invents an autonomous self, a letter-writing alter ego who grounds his being—however rhetorically the man of the letter is "merely a man of letters" (*Biographia Literaria*, ch. 11) without existence outside the text—and allows the knowing I to proceed to the desired conclusion, the definition of the imagination.

Less concentrated specifically on the Wordsworth-and-self-reflexive strategies, although appreciative of the role played in the *Biographia*'s critical discourse by the autobiographical format and the richly metaphorical presence of Coleridge's "self," Catherine Miles Wallace's *The Design of 'Biographia Literaria'* (1983) ambitiously attempts a full-scale defense of the rhetorical intricacies of its discourse. Wallace is especially skillful in analysis of sections in the *Biographia* where Coleridge seemingly bungled the transition, and is judicious in discussions of fancy's role in poetry-making, of the relation of language to subject and object, and of the Coleridge-Wordsworth quarrel over the language and meter of poetry. Her relentless attention to the minutiae of each chapter, however, produces a wearying sameness that makes one long for an alleviating shift in tone, play of wit, alteration of viewpoint—if only for the moment. One positive legacy of current critical theory is the recognition that the *Biographia* is the literary artifact of a poet-philosopher with an incomparable gift for the memorable phrase and a modern sensibility for the metatext. His other consciously crafted prose works, like sleeping Snow Whites, await similarly resourceful critics not blinkered by a mythology about the sporadic delirium of Coleridge's creative imagination and the hobby-horsical mania of his metaphysicalizing. A start has been made in this direction by several redoubtable young critics. Christensen in "The Symbol's Errant Allegory" (*ELH*, 1978) analyzes number 19 of the 1809 *Friend* (considered below in the section "On Aesthetics and Literary Criticism") and in "Politerotics: Coleridge's Rhetoric of War in *The Friend*" (*Clio*, 1979) looks at essays 5 and 10 of Section the First of the 1818 *Friend*, characterizing the autoerotic play of Coleridge's eddying rhetoric as always turning back on itself in its moral project of distinguishing true from false, and principle from principal, to meditate on the reliability of its own argument. Arden Reed in "Coleridge, the Sot, and the Prostitute: A Reading of *The Friend*, Essay XIV" (*SIR*, 1980; rpt. *Romantic Weather*, 1983) astutely dissects how the essay "enacts its own hypothesis that obscurity is

more powerful than clarity." And Deirdre Coleman examines why Coleridge included "A Horrid [German] Tale in *The Friend* [No. 13]" (*WC,* 1981).

On Aesthetics and Literary Criticism

René Wellek is right to remark at the outset of his review of recent scholarship
on the subject ("From 1956," *ERP3*) that in Coleridge's thought aesthetics is intimately involved with philosophy, and practical criticism is "at least in ambition"
the offspring of aesthetics and philosophy. In this and the following section I
have separated them even though each sentence brings home to me that I am
caught in the dilemma of the organicist who denies his intentions with every reference to parts.

The previous version of this subchapter summarizes cogently and equitably
(so long as one keeps in perspective Wellek's crotchet that most important
Coleridgean ideas are traceable to the Germans) the older scholarship on the
sources and influences of Coleridge's aesthetical theory and his practical criticism. Wellek himself examines with considerable specificity in *A History of Modern Criticism: 1750–1950* (vol. 2, *The Romantic Age,* 1955) not only the German
works from which Coleridge quoted and paraphrased in his major prose writings
but also the key terms and ideas (art-nature, symbol-allegory, genius-talent,
organic-mechanical, reconciliation of opposites) Coleridge adopted. Wellek
grants Coleridge most originality as a theoretician of poetry, and most importance as a transmitter of German thought to an English-speaking world. Coleridge
combines the English empirical and associationist tradition with the German
metaphysical and dialectical school, causing him (unsuccessfully, Wellek concludes) to ally the principle of pleasure-pain and the emotive poet with the concepts of poetic unity and of the symbol. Wellek notes Coleridge's tendency to psychological criticism but is not inclined to explore its originality or aesthetic
implications. He is content instead to relate it to the English eighteenth-century
tradition of character study.

Wellek's strong opinions have not gone unchallenged. The harshest "correction" has been at the hands of Manfred Wojcik, an East German scholar at pains to
divorce Coleridge from Platonic and Kantian idealism and to link him with Aristotelian mimesis. In three long articles, "The Mimetic Orientation of Coleridge's
Aesthetic Thought," "Coleridge and the Problem of Transcendentalism," and
"Coleridge: Symbolization, Expression, and Artistic Creativity" (*Zeitschrift für
Anglistik und Amerikanistik,* 1969, 1970, 1971), Wojcik relentlessly (and unfairly)
pummels Wellek for historically linking Coleridgean and German Romantic aesthetics to modern symbolist formalism when the line of continuity leads rather to
the modern theory of Marxist realism. Wojcik as philosophical gymnast manages
this by contending that for Coleridge art is not an analogue but an imitation of
nature and the symbol is referentially related to a world outside itself. Furthermore, since artistic creation is essentially a process of perfection and unification
the true work of art in its symbolization of the particular reveals the universal, by
which Wojcik means the general. Thus does Coleridge get from a representation

of nature to an ideal model of life. Marxist aesthetics similarly has preserved the symbol in its materialist reinterpretation of the typical. A minor sidelight to this attack on formalist aesthetics is that Wojcik takes Coleridge seriously as the spokesman of English Romanticism, disclosing no perturbations or reservations about Coleridge's connections with German aesthetics and philosophy. Among the many debits one could charge against Wojcik is his careless citing of early (for example, "Religious Musings") and late (for example, the *Friend*) evidences of Coleridge's thought as if they all were caught in amber at some mythical moment that simultaneously fused and fixed them ever after. More reasonable evaluations that recognize that Wellek is conversant (see "Romanticism Re-examined," *Romanticism Reconsidered,* ed. Northrop Frye, 1963) with the illogicality of New Criticism's concepts deriving from Coleridge's poetics are Ronald S. Crane's "The Bankruptcy of Critical Monism" (*MP,* 1948; rpt. *Critics and Criticism: Ancient and Modern,* 1952) and Frank Lentricchia's "The Place of Cleanth Brooks" (*JAAC,* 1970) and "Coleridge and Emerson: Prophets of Silence, Prophets of Language" (*JAAC,* 1973). The aesthetics of the *Biographia Literaria* is anchored in a Schellingian monistic idealism, which fuses the artistic, cognitive, and ethical into a visionary act of imagination that unites finite and infinite in the oneness of subject and object. Lentricchia observes that such an aesthetics consumes the object and is hence antithetical to the contextualist celebration of a world of things. That Coleridge may, in fact, have approached Schelling gingerly and at arm's length, E. S. Shaffer suggests in "The 'Postulates in Philosophy' in the *Biographia Literaria*" (*CLS,* 1970). Her subtle analysis shows Coleridge trying to play down the excessive idealism of Schelling's constructive method, by omitting from the chapter 12 account a technical justification of intellectual intuition and by heading the chapter with references to intuition as it appears in Plato and Plotinus, in an effort to put Schelling's newfangled and contrived position on traditional philosophical ground. Shaffer sees Coleridge proposing by these feints that the imagination is a mode of cognition, not a "general *noetic.*" McFarland in *Coleridge and the Pantheist Tradition* (1969) dismisses the "wistful imposition" of Schellingian philosophy in chapter 12 as of "brief duration" in the development of a Coleridgean poetics, while Douglas Moffat, "Coleridge's Ten Theses: The Plotinian Alternative" (*WC,* 1982), dispenses with the Schellingian referent altogether in favor of Plotinus, whose "nous" gives a context to the "patchwork of borrowed passages and pious assertions" of the ten theses that renders them a "coherent, theistic development of Coleridge's idea of the 'self-consciousness' " and of the conscious will.

There are many older general discussions of Coleridge's aesthetics still helpful: J. Isaacs, "Coleridge's Critical Terminology" (*E&S,* 1936); C. D. Thorpe, "Coleridge as Aesthetician and Critic" (*JHI,* 1944); W. J. Bate, "Coleridge on Art" (*Perspectives of Criticism,* ed. Harry Levin, 1950); and Abrams, *The Mirror and the Lamp* (1953). Fogle, *The Idea of Coleridge's Criticism* (1962), emphasizes the concepts of organic unity and the reconciliation of opposites, while Emerson R. Marks demonstrates in "Means and Ends in Coleridge's Critical Method" (*ELH,* 1959) that the distinction between means and ends is incompatible with Coleridge's organicist and symbolist views and is a "salutary correction of extreme organicism." Appleyard, *Coleridge's Philosophy of Literature* (1965), follows Coleridge in his swerves and veers from 1791 to 1819 to develop a concept of poetry only to bear witness to its collapse in *Biographia Literaria* from the epistemological overload of Coleridge's attempt to solve the problem of perception. Failing to furnish a theory of knowledge in which the imagination functions at once as a synthesizing and mediating faculty and as the all-knowing "faculty of insight into ultimate philosophical and religious truths," Coleridge abandons interest in a theory of literature and shifts in 1818 for the rest of his life to a religious solution of the epistemological question. Appleyard covers the same ground in "Coleridge and Criticism: I. Critical Theory" (*S. T. Coleridge,* ed. Brett, 1971) in more summary fashion. More quixotically daring is J. R. de J. Jackson's *Method and Imagination in Coleridge's Criticism* (1969), which expands Coleridge's theory of method into an all-purpose cognitive, analytical, critical, and communicative principle. In addition to subsuming Coleridge's turn to theology, Jackson salutarily insists that Coleridge's philosophy must be mastered if his theoretical and practical criticism is to be understood "on his own ground." The book that in many ways began the modern appreciation of Coleridge as a critical theorist— I. A. Richards' *Coleridge on Imagination* (1934; rpt. 1965)—is still regarded with affection and esteem. This is perhaps in part because Richards takes Coleridge seriously even though he transforms the Romantic poet's idealist epistemological interfaces with reality into materialist psychology. Richards appreciates Coleridge for viewing the mind as an "active, self-forming, self-realizing system," which is "plainly an immense improvement" over the sensationalist conception of it as a "mental storehouse"; and Richards in his modern adaptation of Coleridge's thought has much to say suggestively about the wind harp (and the doctrines of being and acting), diction and meter, and the coalescence of subject-object. The influence this book and Richards have enjoyed in the academic community is memorialized in the collection *I. A. Richards: Essays in His Honor* (ed. Reuben Brower, Helen Vendler, and John Hollander, 1973), which contains an interview of Richards, entitled "Beginnings and Transitions," in which he reminisces in part about the writing of *Coleridge on Imagination,* and essays by Coburn and Willey on the kinship of "I.A.R. and S.T.C."

In other works examining specific aspects of aesthetics, Raymond Williams, *The Long Revolution* (1961), assesses Coleridge's seminal role in the transformation of imitative theories of art to creative ones; E. M. Wilkinson and L. A. Willoughby, in an introduction to an edition of Schiller's *On the Aesthetic Education of Man* (1967), compare the intellectual affinities of Schiller and Coleridge; Orsini and Gates, "The Quest for Aesthetic Truth: Croce and Coleridge" (in *Thought, Action and Intuition: A Symposium on the Philosophy of Benedetto Croce,* ed. Palmer and Harris, 1975), cite similar uses of idealist principles by the two critics, Croce to combat nineteenth-century positivism, Coleridge eighteenth-century empiricism; John N. Serio, "Coleridge and the Function of Nature in Romantic Poetry" (*BSUF,* 1978), invokes Susanne Langer's theory of art to corroborate the practicality of drawing on the external world of form to express an internal world of feeling; C. M. Wallace, "Coleridge's *Biographia Literaria* and the Evidence for Christianity" (*Interspace and the Inward Sphere,* ed. N. A. Anderson and M. E. Weiss, 1978), incautiously sketches forth a secondary theme in the *Biographia* of crisis of faith and its resolution by means of the secondary imagination's self-conscious linkup of *scire* and *esse,* the act of knowing an object being equivalent to consciousness of the "absolute in its pure but relative form, [and] of the divine in its human form"; and Marks, *Coleridge on the Language of Verse* (1981), analyzes Coleridge's original contribution to the aesthetics of mimesis and the copy-imitation antithesis. Vinayak Krishna Gokak, *Coleridge's Aesthetics* (1975), which among other things tries to assign taste an esemplastic role equivalent to that of the imagination, is bewilderingly eclectic in his combining of Fogle, Bate, Jackson, and Indian mysticism.

Coleridge's theory of imagination has evoked mixed reaction, from Wordsworth to Wellek. A "source-book" of Coleridge's statements on the imagination, with extensive notes (which tend to ignore indebtedness), has been compiled by John Spencer Hill, *Imagination in Coleridge* (1978). Excerpts, listed chronologically, confirm that Coleridge had little to say about the imagination after 1818. An introduction, descriptive rather than analytical, and incautious at times in its assumptions about Coleridge's early reading of Platonists and German metaphysicians, traces the development of his theory of the imagination. More cautionary expositions of the Coleridgean theory of the imagination are to be found in David Keppel-Jones, "Coleridge's Scheme of Reason" (*Literary Monographs,* 1957), and in McFarland, *Coleridge and the Pantheist Tradition* (1969), excursus 13. Among the main points of contention are the relationships of the primary and secondary imaginations to fancy and of imagination to reason. One school of thought has equated the primary imagination with the reality making of ordinary perception, secondary imagination with the literary and consciously willed creative faculty of the mind, and fancy with the arbitrary arrangement of remembered images according to laws of association. J. Shawcross' introduction to his edition of the *Biographia Literaria* (1907) offered an early formulation of this view, emphasizing the psychological and philosophical links of the fancy and the two imaginations respectively to Kant's reproductive, productive, and aesthetic functions. For many decades influential, Shawcross is now considered inadequate by some and faulty by others in his grasp of the operation of the imagination, particularly in his foggy description of its nexus between the philosophic reason's intuition and the sensible world, as defined in the *Biographia.* James V. Baker, *The Sacred River: Coleridge's Theory of Imagination* (1957), sets forth these distinctions with special emphasis on the balance of conscious and unconscious powers in the imagination and on the passive associations of the fancy. There are those, beginning with Wordsworth, who argue that imagination and fancy describe degrees of the same process rather than faculties performing mental tasks different in kind. Wheeler, *Sources, Processes and Methods in Coleridge's* Biographia Literaria (1980), handily digests the advocacy, pro and con, that has seesawed over this question through the nineteenth and twentieth centuries, although one needs to keep in mind that she is not a disinterested observer. See, also, Barbara Hardy, "Distinction without Difference: Coleridge's Fancy and Imagination" (*EIC,* 1951), and Willey on defense of the distinction in *Coleridge on Imagination and Fancy* (Warton Lecture, *Proceedings of the British*

Academy, 1946). Others would relegate the imagination to an intermediary process of transmuting and funneling ideas of the reason and images of the sense into a single stream of awareness. W. J. Bate (in *Perspectives of Criticism,* ed. H. Levin, 1950) advances this view, along with the proposition that the imagination-fancy dichotomy is not descriptive of "two levels of imaginative 'intensity,' " nor is it an arbitrary division of the creative process into "fusion" and "aggregation," so much as Coleridge's way of defining what the imagination is not by separating it from what in the past had been considered a mere image-making faculty. In recent years a younger group of Coleridgeans has moved the primary imagination into coalescence with reason and the religious sense of the unity of things (discussed below). Finally, in a minority demur from all this psychological and transcendental categorization, Sascha Talmor, "Fancy and Imagination in Coleridge's Poetics" (*Durham Univ. Journal,* 1982), contends that Coleridge, in fact, used the terms in his own critical remarks quite simply as an evaluative yardstick, as "descriptive empirical criteria of poetic excellence."

The history of the confusion of the terms *imaginatio* and *phantasia* from antiquity through the Renaissance, leading to the changing definition, reversal of roles, and desynonymization of the terms in the eighteenth century, and of Coleridge's role and place in this intellectual and cultural transaction is handily available in a variety of studies. Bate and J. Bullitt's pioneering "Distinctions between Fancy and Imagination in Eighteenth-Century Criticism" (*MLN,* 1945) anticipates what has become a mini–critical industry. Brett, *Fancy and Imagination* (1972), gives a concise, reliable introduction to the history of the evolving definition of imagination and fancy in eighteenth-century England, with some emphasis on the Cambridge Neoplatonist tradition and with a full chapter on Coleridge's distinctions between the terms. Wallace Jackson, *Immediacy: The Development of a Critical Concept from Addison to Coleridge* (1973), traces "a century of continuous discourse" from Addison to Alison contributing to a theory of imagination. Originating in an idea of immediacy that starts as an instrument of moral consciousness by which the mind ascends from art to God, the concept graduates to a maxim of practical criticism in the hands of early pragmatists, becomes an essential emotive element of the sublime, then a constitutive part of the equipment of genius, and finally the determining ground or material cause of Romantic imagination. It is at this point in the narrative that Coleridge appears to construct a theory of imagination "partly derived from Schelling." Enlisted under the aegis of the reason, the imagination reconciles poetry and morality, asserts the basis for distinguishing between creative and appreciative and between genius and taste, and closes the schism between human beings and nature. Thus, Coleridge's aesthetic-religious epistemology is grounded, too easily and with too vague and inadequate inclusion of the consequent and concurrent German development of these ideas, in the British aesthetic tradition, with Coleridge as legatee of English empirical thought, despite his reaction to it.

The limitations of Wallace Jackson's overview are amply rectified in James Engell's bountiful *The Creative Imagination: Enlightenment to Romanticism* (1981), which is the most comprehensive treatment to date of the complicated story of the metamorphoses of the imagination in the eighteenth century. Engell touches base seemingly with every English and German thinker on the subject. The story starts with Hobbes and climaxes with Coleridge, who is portrayed as the heir and synthesizer of all that has gone before. By the finale the imagination has evolved into a faculty of multipower. It comprehends both passive and active forces in the mind, unifying disparate experiences and creating the individual's world. As the principle of individuation it reconciles antitheses and polarities, the self with the external, and self-consciousness with the object. It transcends nature to apprehend a universal world. It is the mark of genius, comprehending the productive and reproductive, the inventive and creative. Engell is excellent on the common effort of the British empirical psychologists and the German transcendental philosophers to establish viable definitions and a common vocabulary as regards the function of the imagination, the problem of creativity, and the relationship of the mind to nature. Under this scrutiny the dichotomy between those who contend for the German idealist philosophers as the source of Coleridge's ideas and those who espouse a native British strain is united into one continuous developing tradition that receives its fructifying culmination during the early decades of the nineteenth century in the esemplastic élan of Coleridge's writings.

One should know the worst as well as the best. Mary Warnock, *Imagination* (1976), presents a lucid exposition of two hundred years of philosophical attempt from Hume to Sartre to define the role of the imagination in acts of perception, conception, reproduction, and creation. But it is at the price of an unexamined argument—at least in her chapter on Coleridge and Wordsworth—that is persistently hostile to Coleridge, determined to confirm Fruman's allegations of plagiarism and Wellek's of unsystematic thinking. On the basis of circumstantial and casual parallels, her charges grow sequentially in authoritative certainty: "There can be little doubt that . . . ," "It is virtually certain," "We should not risk . . . therefore claiming any of Coleridge's views as his own original thought," "There seems to be no doubt that Coleridge accepted [Schelling's theory of art in *The System of Transcendental Idealism*] lock, stock, and barrel." She alleges that Coleridge was a reader with neither historical sense nor the ability to distinguish things which are different and, accordingly, was prepared to treat the Kantian reason as genuinely identical to Platonic ideas; that he was uninformed about philosophy, knowing only "what, for the time being, he likes"; and that he was confused about Kant, thought Fichte and Schelling far more original than they were, and misconstrued the comparative stature of Kant and his followers.

An example of Warnock's scholarship is that she assigns the derivation of Coleridge's two-part imagination to Schelling, missing McFarland's reconstruction in "The Origin and Significance of Coleridge's Theory of Secondary Imagination" (*New Perspectives on Coleridge and Wordsworth*, ed. Hartman, 1972) of Coleridge's indebtedness for the threefold division of the imagination "backward beyond Kant to Tetens." The limitations of Warnock's stand are indirectly revealed also in Eike Schmitz's "Coleridge, Maass, and Tetens on Imagination: A Reconsideration" (*Archiv für das Studium der Neueren Sprachen und Literaturen*, 1976). Schmitz refines McFarland's thesis by affirming that Coleridge follows the lead of Tetens when he defines the powers of the secondary imagination but "relies entirely on the theory of association as it is summarized by Maass" for his account of fancy. Furthermore, neither provides Coleridge with an exact model for the imagination. While Tetens conceives of the imagination as fusing elements into unity, he has in mind elements that are similar. The imagination for Tetens does not blend multeity (or dissimilar elements) into unity. Contrariwise, while Maass does not distinguish primary from secondary imagination in their reproductive and productive functions (Kant's terms), he does wish to liberate the associationist system from necessitarianism. To Schmitz both Tetens and Maass stand at the end of a period. Although bent on liberating the mind from the despotism of the mechanical paradigm, they still think with the epistemological concepts of a previous tradition. Coleridge stands at the beginning of a new period that describes the processes and products of the mind in organic terms. Still, Schmitz's argument is that Coleridge, because he draws on Tetens and Maass, does not reject the mechanical theory of associationism entirely but incorporates it into a dualistic theory of poetry with two controlling analogues—the machine and the plant. Substantiating this estimate of the continuing hold on Coleridge's mind of associationism is the analysis of Christensen in the first two chapters of *Coleridge's Blessed Machine of Language* (1981). Christensen concludes that "Coleridge never *overthrows* Hartleian association, but he does continually interrupt it."

Appleyard draws a firm line between the early perceptual-aesthetic and late mediatory-theological roles of the imagination. The latter final development, first adumbrated in an appendix to *The Statesman's Manual* (1816), assigns imagination the task (parallel to that of religious faith) of giving the intuitions of the reason a language by way of its product the symbol. The question, however, of how much the post-*Biographia* swerve from aesthetics to religion is contained, at least implicitly, in the 1815 definition of the imagination continues to nag at critics. Weighing the evidence pro and con, Roy Park (*BJA,* 1968; *UTQ,* 1969) grants that the bias of Coleridge's mind was toward a constitutive rendering of poetic reality, with the function of the imagination analogous to that of the practical reason in Kant's ethical system. Nevertheless, despite Coleridge's wish to use art to bridge the gap between the ideal and the real, thereby escaping the dualistic impasse consequent upon Kant's view that ideas are regulative and art possesses only subjective validity, Park concludes that in the period of Coleridge's greatest activity as a literary critic he never identifies imagination with reason. At most his is an attempt to perceive them as correlative. The resultant ambiguity in Coleridge's theory of poetry, as Wellek notes more than once, derives from the basic disparity "between an organistic, idealistic superstructure and an empiricist psychological groundwork."

Not everyone shares Park's dispassionate turn of mind. Some find irresistible the noumenal substructure visible at times in Coleridge's remarks about the imagination. A key observation for them is an endpaper note of Coleridge's, in Tennemann's *Geschichte der Philosophie,* setting up a complicated hierarchical scale of mental faculties that allows them to stratify the imagination into dual empirical and transcendent roles. On this evidence James Boulger, "Coleridge on Imagination Revisited" (*WC,* 1973), takes issue with his own earlier writings that demoted the imagination from its supreme importance for poetry in the *Biographia* to a significant but "subordinate place in the scheme" of Coleridge's final philosophical and religious position. Now Boulger assigns coordinate status to imagination and reason. By means of the symbol, which subsumes the eternal and the temporal, the imagination functions equally as a philosophical and a poetic activity in mediating ultimate ideas. It is "thus both an organ of perception functioning in a systematic view of reality and an artistic power turning images into symbols which mediate special truths to other minds." J. R. de J. Jackson, *Method and Imagination in Coleridge's Criticism* (1969), even more doctrinally identifies the reason with the primary imagination: unconscious in its eternal repository, and primary in its immediate apprehension, of the divine. Wellek is surely right to find this interpretation "impossible to accept" (*ERP3*). So, also, believes S. V. Pradhan, "Coleridge's 'Philocrisy' and His Theory of Fancy and Imagination" (*SIR*, 1974). Instead of assimilating the *Biographia* theory of the imagination to the Tennemann endnote, as Jackson does, Pradhan discriminates it from the diagrammatic scale, on the ground that the former is a special theory of art and the latter a general theory of human knowledge. Pradhan is, however, overingenious and combative, bent on "correcting" previous critics. He formulates an understanding that squints in two directions, functioning intellectually in mediation with reason (via the imagination) and empirically in mediation with sense perception (via fancy). He similarly divides the mode of operation of the secondary imagination in its mediation between reason and understanding into philosophical (perception) and aesthetic (artistic creation) functions. To turn from Pradhan's supersubtle discriminations to Prickett's alignment of the imagination (in *Coleridge and Wordsworth: The Poetry of Growth*, 1970) synchronically with perception and creativity ("a single and indivisible act") by symbolic means is to return to philosophical civility if not fresh perspicuity. Cooke in *The Romantic Will* (1976) emphasizes that through the conjoinment of imagination and will the sensible world is conceptualized into a value-impregnated whole. By that post-*Biographia* ploy, coupled with "The Ancient Mariner" as chief exhibit, Cooke strives to stake out the no-man's-land between experiential and constitutive grounds. And C. M. Wallace in *The Design of 'Biographia Literaria'* in like strategy, by aligning the will in Coleridge's definition of the imagination with his later triune definition of the reason (will-reason-faith), extends the function of the primary imagination to include knowledge of God.

Engell has assimilated most of these varying explanations of the imagination in his lengthy introduction to *Biographia Literaria* (*CC* 7). He handles historically the distinction between fancy and imagination, carefully separates primary (involuntary) from secondary (willed) imagination, and sets forth the hints of a philosophical imagination embedded in the commentary of the *Biographia*. Engell fleshes out the scanty remarks there by finding implicit in them the later task Coleridge assigns the imagination: in its primary role mediating sense impressions and in its philosophical role mediating ideas. Engell presents the imagination engaged in a reconciliation of self and nature on three different but analogous levels (perceptual, artistic, and philosophical), its goal a grand synthesis of the material and spiritual, Platonic and empirical. Engell makes of the

Coleridgean imagination a "thing of beauty." One may not be ready to accord it, however wondrous and attractive, such formal order. Yet one will have to contend with this "fearful symmetry" when devising an alternative explanation. The literature on Coleridge and the imagination is voluminous. Listed below are some approaching the subject from uncommon perspectives: Georges Poulet, *The Metamorphoses of the Circle* (1966), on the synthesis of self and not-self, center and circle; Herbert Mainusch, *Romantische Aesthetik* (1969), on the vagueness and insubstantiality of Coleridge's concepts of the imagination and fancy; Daniel Stempel, "Revelation on Mount Snowdon: Wordsworth, Coleridge, and the Fichtean Imagination" (*JAAC,* 1971), on the Fichtean, rather than Schellingian, identity of Coleridge's primary and secondary imaginations; Michael Munday, "John Wilson and the Distinction between Fancy and Imagination" (*SIR,* 1974), on Wilson's use of the concepts in his reviews from 1817 to 1830; Patricia Mavis Jenkins, "Coleridge and the Perils of the Unbridled Imagination" (*P&L,* 1977), on Coleridge's misgivings about aspects of the imagination; and Taylor, *Magic and English Romanticism* (1979), on the magical powers of the imagination.

The context of Coleridge's famous definition of the symbol in *The Statesman's Manual* is scriptural, its primary function religious: "the translucence of the eternal through and in the temporal." (See the "Religion and Theology" subsection below.) The symbol is also accorded philosophical and aesthetic configurations. Philip C. Rule, "Samuel Taylor Coleridge: A Christian in Search of an Aesthetic" (*Christianity and Literature,* 1974), attempts a broadly humanistic definition of the symbol as both an aesthetic and a religious nexus between the self and the physical world and God. It is such a "basic spirit-matter relationship," he believes, "that underlies Coleridge's view of reality." In an analysis limited to the notion that philosophical ideas develop in direct transmission from originator to secondhand user, Patricia A. Ward, "Coleridge's Critical Theory of the Symbol" (*TSLL,* 1966), sketches the German background to establish the source of his ideas of the symbol as a synthesis of the universal and the particular (Schiller and Goethe), as a representative of the ultimate reality of the universe in a fusion of the infinite in the finite (Schelling), and as a product of the imagination (Schlegel). Broadly comparative, Margery Sabin, *English Romanticism and the French Tradition* (1976), discriminates Coleridge's ideas and psychological grounding of the symbol particularly as they define Anglo concepts of beauty and taste, and imitation of nature, from later nineteenth-century Gallic theory as revealed in Baudelaire. Similarly comparative, Anca Vlasopolos, *The Symbolic Method of Coleridge, Baudelaire, and Yeats* (1983), lucidly summarizes the standard interpretation of the Coleridgean symbol and applies it to the Conversation poems, "The Ancient Mariner," and "Dejection"—all symbol-making poems of varying success in transforming nature into symbols or in recovering an inner paradise. The traditional view of Coleridge's aesthetics and literary practice is represented in Patricia M. Ball's *The Science of Aspects: The Changing Role of Fact in the Work of Coleridge, Ruskin and Hopkins* (1971). Coleridge's delight in the object serves the larger search for a comprehensive understanding of an organic, divine universe. His text is "body ... striving to become mind," fact transfigured into symbol, phenomena spiritualized in the belief that there is a direct bridge from senses to spiritual insights. Working at the practical level of the confusion attendant on the symbolic interpretations of "The Ancient Mariner," "Kubla Khan," and "Christabel," H. W. Piper, "Coleridge, Symbolism and the Tower of Babel" (*New Approaches to Coleridge,* ed. Sultana, 1981), provides a measured overview of the types of theory (Freudian, Jungian, and those of classical myths and of Cassirer and Mircia Eliade) applied to Coleridge and of the Romantic theories and modes (the idea of God in nature, or natural symbolism, and Gothic, apocalyptic, and literary modes) adopted by Coleridge.

Coleridge's distinction between symbol and allegory has aroused more response than summarized here. See also Mary Rahme, "Coleridge's Concept of Symbolism" (*SEL,* 1969); L. C. Knights, "Idea and Symbol: Some Hints from Coleridge," in *Further Explorations* (1965); and Gay Clifford, *The Transformations of Allegory* (1974).

Contrary antisymbolist poetics, sparked by Paul de Man's spirited resurrection of allegory, in "The Rhetoric of Temporality" (*Interpretation: Theory and Practice,* ed. C. Singleton, 1969), has placed Coleridge's differentiation of symbol from allegory (a "pseudo-dialectic between subject and object") under skeptical reexamination. Jonathan Culler, "Literary History, Allegory, and Semiology" (*NLH,* 1976), in a further effort to rehabilitate allegory, relegates the symbol (and Coleridge, whose preference for it makes him very much of his time) to the historical moment when Romantic concern concentrated on the fundamental problem of the relation between subject and object. Culler's premises, however, are unintentionally subverted by the combination of ambivalence and ambiguity in Coleridge's critical attitude toward allegory. Patricia Ward remarks that Coleridge in his practical criticism fails to use the symbol as a critical tool but employs allegory as a critical principle "much more vigorously," a view seconded by John Gatta, Jr., "Coleridge and Allegory" (*MLQ,* 1977), who stresses the hesitancies residual in Coleridge's denunciation of allegory. He notes that Coleridge tended before 1816 to associate it with imagination, not fancy, and readily to dramatize his ideas with "allegorical fable." Only after 1816 does he begin to define allegory sharply from symbol, but even then its binary mode continued attractive to his complexly divided self and his associationist-Platonic divergencies. Two critics find Coleridge's discursive promotion of the symbol further breached by the obdurate discontinuities of signification. Ferguson, "Reading Heidegger: Paul de Man and Jacques Derrida" (*Boundary 2,* 1976), reviewed in the section "On Language," in testing the de Man effort to redeem the deceptions of literary language by way of its intersection with the presumed truth of philosophy, concludes that the former contextually invade and contaminate the latter in the chapter 13 definition of imagination. Christensen, "The Symbol's Errant Allegory: Coleridge and His Critics" (*ELH,* 1978), in a deft reading of "Christmas Out of Doors" (no. 19 of the 1809 *Friend*) finds symbol modulating into allegory, the consequence of a prose figuration that resonates between signifier and signified. Thus does the practice of writing subvert theory, its impersonations of anonymity masking a will to self-recognition and its claims of authenticity co-opting it into acts of inauthenticity. A desire to mediate the controversy over Coleridge's definitions of symbol-allegory informs John A. Hodgson's "Transcendental Tropes: Coleridge's Rhetoric of Allegory and Symbol" (*Allegory, Myth, and Symbol,* ed. Morton W. Bloomfield, 1981; Harvard English Studies 9). Straddling rhetorical-religious analyses of the two modes of figuration, Hodgson substitutes for the rhetorical opposition of synechdochic and metaphoric tropes, which he believes to be a false issue, the "genuine, significant crux ... of determined versus arbitrary figuration, the true and inescapable issue for any rhetoric that would strive to be transcendental." From this perspective the post–*Statesman's Manual* Coleridge becomes a critic whose efforts to explain rhetorically the "two alternative modes of representing the spiritual mysteries of Christianity" led him "in his last decade ... more than any other finally to understand and reveal the uniquely privileged status" of the allegorical mode, which he had so frequently and successfully worked to depreciate.

As for Coleridge on the sublime, Thorpe in *Wordsworth and Coleridge: Studies in Honor of George McLean Harper* (ed. Griggs, 1939) laboriously assembles Coleridge's pronouncements, with a straightforward Kantian analysis of it in relation to the beautiful; and David B. Morris, *The Religious Sublime: Christian Poetry and Critical Tradition in 18th-Century England* (1972), rehearses the shift in thinking about the religious sublime that transformed it at midcentury onward from a quality inherent in things to an awe resident in the interchange of the mind with external grandeur. Tension between the two modes of the sublime and the beautiful, and Coleridge's fusion of them, has garnered the bulk of critical attention. E. S. Shaffer, in "Coleridge's Theory of Aesthetic Interest" and in "Coleridge's Revolution in the Standard of Taste" (both in *JAAC,* 1969), sets forth his reconciliation of Kant with Burke, and his equation of the beautiful with the sublime, into a single aesthetic. Invoking the Kantian definition of the sublime (*Critique of Judgment*), Thomas Weiskel, *The Romantic Sublime: Studies in the Structure and Psychology of Transcendence* (1976), attributes Coleridge's preference for the beautiful to his attachment to immediate objects of sense. Reluctant to renounce them for the sake of the mind's transcendent aspirations, he is unable to fulfill the conditions of sublimation (recognition of a supersensible faculty beyond the power of the imagination to encompass nature's magnitude) that is the primary psychic source of the sublime. Raimonda Modiano, "Coleridge and the Sublime" (*WC,* 1978), refutes this claim by showing that Coleridge is more in accord with Herder and Richter than with Kant and Schelling on the sublime. Coleridge rejects Kant's sublimation of the imagination to the reason, since for him the sublime resides neither in the mind's rupture from sensible forms nor in the antecedent crisis of imagination's painful laboring to extend itself to heights it cannot reach. Rather the sublime constructs a gradual, not convulsive, passage from sensible to transcendent. It pertains to supersensible ideas but does not require an instantaneous leap over the empirical world or the pain or terror of large gestures. By arguing that the sublime can emerge from beautiful objects, Coleridge empties Kant's formula of much of its weight. There is some justification, however, for Wellek's sweeping into oblivion the distinction as being historically a minor achievement of Coleridge (see *ERP3*).

In the second volume of *Biographia Literaria* (chs. 17 – 22) Coleridge turns to Wordsworth's theories of poetic language and meter and to his poems, correcting Wordsworth's theoretical illogicalities and misconceptions and defining his poetical strengths and weaknesses. While this attempt of Coleridge's simultaneously to put poetry on a firm philosophical footing and to establish the principles of Wordsworth's poetry is praised as one of the best critiques of Wordsworth, it has generated partisan controversy as well. On the credit side are two vigorous defenses of Coleridge, one by Raysor (*PMLA,* 1939) and the other by Engell in the introduction to *Biographia Literaria* (*CC* 7). Raysor is out to counteract the pejorative attitude expressed toward Coleridge by such writers as F. L. Lucas whose voices dominated the pro-Wordsworthian atmosphere of the first half of the twentieth century. Consequently, his assertiveness—the essay on Wordsworth is "the finest critical essay in English literature" and "the richest theoretical discussion of poetic diction in English criticism"—may sound at times shrill to our ears; nevertheless Raysor limns faithfully the main lines of disagreement that characterized the Coleridge-Wordsworth controversy a half century ago. More secure in the current esteem in which Coleridge is held, Engell serenely reviews the *Biographia* chapters on Wordsworth and poetic language as part of Coleridge's fundamental concern with the difference between copy and imitation. One would never guess from Engell's discussion that critical storm clouds still hover over the chapters and militant Wordsworthians still probe the critical ordinances articulated there. A spirit of acrimony animates the attack launched by Don H. Bialostosky in "Coleridge's Interpretation of Wordsworth's Preface to *Lyrical Ballads*" (*PMLA,* 1978). Bialostosky contends that Coleridge was motivated by the desire to refute, not clarify, Wordsworth and that for polemical purposes he persistently and perversely misreads Wordsworth's intentions. Particularly reprehensible in Bialostosky's eyes is that Coleridge defines the arguments over the choice of poetic subject and of language according to what Wordsworth's Preface can be taken to mean instead of what Wordsworth probably meant it to mean. One expects Bialostosky, adopting this tack, to review the Coleridge-Wordsworth disagreements within the context of the poets' collaborative discussions of these matters over several years, as Parrish does (see above, "Biographies"). Instead, to arrive at an accurate sense of what Wordsworth intended, Bialostosky relies (as he accuses Coleridge of doing) on his own semantic-logical analysis of the words Wordsworth wrote.

There is every reason to believe that the issues fundamentally dividing the two poets were rooted as much in sincere misunderstandings and changing ideals, if not always or entirely, as in philosophically conflicting assumptions and aims. To determine the reasons for "the persistent attacks of an otherwise staunch defender," Paul Hamilton, *Coleridge's Poetics* (1983), brings historical common sense and dispassionate fairness to the grounds of the controversy, analyzing the poetical and literalist-symbolic nature of Coleridge's criticism of Wordsworth against the backdrop of the efforts in the eighteenth century to settle the dualities of word-thing, philosophy-poetry, and mind-matter. To explain Coleridge's changing appreciation of Wordsworth's poetry, Roy Park in "Coleridge's Two Voices as a Critic of Wordsworth" (*ELH,* 1969) offers a lucid exposition of Coleridge's shift of allegiance from an experiential characterization of an ideal universe to a Christian constitutive theory of the universal. Park calls our attention to Coleridge's tact in following the early ideal in his public criticism of Wordsworth in *Biographia Literaria* and restricting his constitutive bias to private remarks, particularly about *The Excursion* and late poetry. Park also notes Coleridge's failure to recognize that both he and Wordsworth had altered—"and neither for the better." Christensen in "Wordsworth's Misery, Coleridge's Woe: Reading 'The Thorn'" (*PLL*, 1980) explicates the puzzled effort of Coleridge to account for the "unmeaning repetitions, habitual phrases, and other blank counters" (*BL*, ch. 17) Wordsworth litters throughout "The Thorn." Christensen means his explication as an addendum to Parrish's account of Wordsworth's dramatic method, which in its exculpation of Wordsworth fails to pursue far enough an inquiry into Coleridge's argument about poetic diction and into Coleridge's objection to the dramatic mode.

The intellectual relationship of Coleridge and Wordsworth is extended by B. R. Breyer to include "Wordsworth's Pleasure: An Approach to His Poetic Theory" (*SHR*, 1972) and refined by Pradhan in "Fancy and Imagination: Coleridge versus Wordsworth" (*PQ*, 1975). Hayden, *Polestar of the Ancients: The Aristotelian Tradition in Classical and English Literary Criticism* (1979) and "Wordsworth and Coleridge: Shattered Mirrors, Shining Lamps?" (*WC*, 1981), has Coleridge and Wordsworth straddling mimetic and expressionistic theories, thereby discrediting Abrams' use of them to date the start of Romantic expressionism in 1800. Like Whalley, Hayden insists that Coleridge subscribes to the Aristotelian aperçu of an external world by way of its imaginative imitation. While Coleridge emphasizes a creative theory, this is not the same as expressionist theory, a distinction Abrams fails to make.

As regards the contemporary scene, Hayden, "Coleridge, the Reviewers, and Wordsworth" (*SP*, 1971), and Nathaniel Teich, "Coleridge's *Biographia* and the Contemporary Controversy about Style" (*WC*, 1972), show that Coleridge was not so widely separated from the periodical reviewers of his time in his discussion of Wordsworth's theory of language and his critique of Wordsworth's poems as he may have wished to imply. However much he tried to distance himself from the anonymous reviewers Coleridge could not entirely free himself intellectually from the contemporary controversy in the periodicals, which, in abusing Wordsworth, was part of a historical process of challenge and reassessment taking place in matters of poetic language and style.

Apropos of Coleridge's critical practice in general, R. H. Fogle as a sort of utility man in these matters summarizes handily in "Coleridge and Criticism: II. Critical Practice" (*S. T. Coleridge*, ed. Brett, 1971) its virtues and its consistency with general principles, particularly in the Shakespearean, Miltonic, and Wordsworthian criticism. Fogle also analyzes in separate chapters in *The Idea of Coleridge's Criticism* (1962) how the character studies are part of the study of Shakespeare's dramatic structure and how the poetical defects of Wordsworth are mirror images of the excellences. Equally insistent that Coleridge's metaphysical views and his practical criticism are inseparable is E. S. Shaffer, "Iago's Malignity

Motivated: Coleridge's Unpublished 'Opus Magnum'" (*SQ*, 1968). Arguing the opposite tack is Morris Weitz in *Hamlet and the Philosophy of Literary Criticism* (1964).

Coleridge put an end to the critical hesitation over Shakespeare's breaking of rules and the attendant difficulty of measuring Shakespeare's achievement "by proclaiming loudly and clearly that the works of Shakespeare were the products of the creative imagination, a faculty which makes its own rules as it goes along." That is the conclusion of G. N. G. Orsini and B. T. Gates, "The Quest for Aesthetic Truth: Croce and Coleridge" (in *Thought, Action, and Intuition: A Symposium on the Philosophy of Benedetto Croce*, ed. L. M. Palmer and H. S. Harris, 1975). And they add that Coleridge has had no less impact on posterior Shakespearean criticism: "by this resounding defense, Coleridge was able to pave the way for the twentieth century's more detailed account of the works of Shakespeare, Bradley's for example." So successful was promulgation of the idea that for Coleridge the "[p]sychology of character or of situation" was more important than "the play as a piece of stagecraft" (Wellek, *History of Modern Criticism: 1750–1950*, vol. 2, 1955) that it spawned reactions of differing hues about his contribution to the past one hundred years of Shakespeare criticism.

Apologists for Coleridge's psychological approach include D. Snyder, "A Note on Coleridge's Shakespeare Criticism" (*MLN*, 1923); Roberta Morgan, "The Philosophical Basis of Coleridge's *Hamlet* Criticism" (*ELH*, 1939); Sylvan Barnet, "Coleridge on Shakespeare's Villains" (*SQ*, 1956); and Joseph W. Donohue, Jr., *Dramatic Character in the English Romantic Age* (1970), who insists that Coleridge's interest in penetrating to the inner reality of the dramatic character rested on "fixed canons ... of criticism ... deduced from the nature of man." That Coleridge examines the plays and characters for illumination of "certain central principles" and moral truths at work in human life is also the credo of Peter Hoheisel, "Coleridge on Shakespeare: Method amid the Rhetoric" (*SIR*, 1974).

Chief revisionist of the Bradleian coloring of Coleridge's Shakespeare criticism is M. M. Badawi, whose *Coleridge: Critic of Shakespeare* (1973; see also *EIC*, 1960) methodically takes up one after another the issues central to Shakespeare criticism in the eighteenth and nineteenth centuries and Coleridge's relationship to them: beauties, dramatic illusion, formal structure, character analysis, rhyme, puns, versification, imagery and metaphor, dramatic unities, and Shakespeare's artistry. Badawi believes that Coleridge is a moral, rather than psychological, critic of Shakespeare. Badawi also recognizes that Coleridge in his Shakespeare discourses is primarily bent on illustrating a general theory of poetry and general principles of criticism but that the theory appears at times in conflict with the critical practice because of a Hartleian-Kantian bifurcation, with a pleasure-giving theory at odds with an organicist apprehension of reality. Other revisionists opting for a theatrical-enlightened Coleridge are Barbara Hardy and J. R. de J. Jackson. Hardy in "'I Have a Smack of Hamlet': Coleridge and Shakespeare's Characters" (*EIC*, 1958) contends that Coleridge is the progenitor of E. E. Stoll, L. C. Knights, and G. Wilson Knight as much as of Bradley. Jackson in "Coleridge on Dramatic Illusion and Spectacle in the Performance of Shakespeare's Plays"

(*MP,* 1964) and in "Coleridge on Shakespeare's Preparation" (*REL,* 1966) observes that Coleridge records most of his observations on Shakespeare's mastery of stagecraft in his marginalia and manuscript remains. David Ellis and Howard Mills in "Coleridge's Hamlet: The Notes versus the Lectures" (*EIC,* 1979) compare to the notes and marginalia the lectures reported and the snippets anthologized and commented on by critics like Bradley. They conclude that these secondhand reports too often distort Coleridge into a character critic when his criticism is balanced between attention to outward reality and meditation on inward thoughts. Further demythifying of Coleridge's Shakespeare criticism is the subject of Clifford Davidson's "Organic Unity and Shakespearian Tragedy" (*JAAC,* 1971). Coleridge never applied his pronouncements on organic theory to his Shakespeare criticism in any detailed, satisfactory way, says Davidson. Yet, modern critics have appropriated Coleridge's theories of "unity and multeity" and therefore seek an interdependence of parts and organic whole that has little to do with Shakespeare's casual manner of working up a play: his ready versification of prose materials, his willing assignment of set speeches to whoever is conveniently on stage at the time, and his unconcern for causation.

In 1956 Wellek ended his review of the influence and reputation of Coleridge optimistically: one "can today even speak of a Coleridge revival." Sixteen years later he updated this section with the sadder and wiser observation that "the influence and reputation of Coleridge still has not been studied very fully . . . much needs further exploration and more precision" (see *ERP3*). Wellek was right in both 1956 and 1972, but in two different senses. The truth is that Coleridge's critical ideas and marvelous phrases have to a large extent become coin of the literary realm. They are more often picked up and used—sometimes knowingly, at other times thoughtlessly—than examined, tested, and validated. Another ten years have passed and I can only reiterate that neither Coleridge's miscellaneous critical comments on writers in the English tradition nor his influence on writers and critics in the nineteenth and twentieth centuries has received any kind of systematic treatment. The less than single page devoted to the topic in 1956 more than doubled in 1972, and the modest interest in the impact of Coleridge on nineteenth-century American religious thinkers, transcendentalists, and critics expanded to include the English Victorians, the New Critics, and a handful of modernist poets—but all in a desultory manner. Nor should the misleading title of L. S. Sharma's *Coleridge: His Contribution to English Criticism* (1982) be taken seriously. The book is a stale general summary, dated in scholarship, of Coleridgean critical principles, and its cursory remarks about the New Critics contribute little fresh understanding of Coleridge's impact on the nineteenth and twentieth centuries. Most fully scrutinized has been the transmission of Coleridge's organic aesthetic to the formalist and symbolist critics, with connections rehearsed by Murray Krieger (*The New Apologists for Poetry,* 1956), Frank Kermode (*Romantic Image,* 1957), G. S. Fraser (*Vision and Rhetoric,* 1959), Richard Foster (*The New Romantics,* 1962), Pasquale DiPasquale, Jr. (*JAAC,* 1968), Gunther H. Lenz (*Die Dichtungstheorie S. T. Coleridges,* 1971), and Emerson Marks (*SR,* 1964; *Coleridge on the Language of Verse,* 1981) and irreconcilables dwelled on by Crane (*Critics and Criticism,* 1952), Lentricchia (*The Gaiety of Language,*

1968; *JAAC,* 1973), Abrams ("Coleridge, Baudelaire, and Modernist Poetics," in *Immanente Aesthetik, Aesthetische Reflexion,* ed. Iser, 1966), and Gerald Graff (*Poetic Statement and Critical Dogma,* 1970).

During the past decade even that attention to the presence of Coleridge in our own immediate critical tradition has slackened. I have absorbed most of what there is—Paul de Man and sundry poststructuralist critics who have continued the Neo-Aristotelians' assault on the New Critics through the sapping of Coleridge—into relevant sections, so that there is little additional beyond a few earlier miscellaneous items listed in *ERP3* and more recent ones cited below.

In the chapters "Poetic Diction: Wordsworth and Coleridge" and "Imagination: Wordsworth and Coleridge," now somewhat dated as regards Coleridge, that Wimsatt wrote for *Literary Criticism: A Short History* (1957; Wimsatt contributed chs. 1–24, 32; Cleanth Brooks, chs. 25–31), Wimsatt admonishes readers that Coleridge's theory of poetry is less a general theory than one slanted toward the particular kind of poetry he and Wordsworth wrote; Cleanth Brooks in "Coleridge as a Metaphysical Poet" (in *Romanticism: Vistas, Instances, Continuities,* ed. Thorburn and Hartman, 1973), graciously alludes to this reproof, acknowledging that Coleridgean poetics is too limited to satisfy modern critical needs. Whereas metaphysical poems stress tension in disparity, Romantic poetry is less aware of "disparity in stated likeness" than of "discerning the design and unity latent in a multiform sensuous picture." Despite this concession, Brooks appreciates the capacity of Coleridge in his scattered critical comments on Donne, Herbert, and Crashaw to recognize their analogical powers "to fuse the apparently contradictory and to harmonize the discordant."

Additional facets of Coleridge's practical criticism are examined by Michael Ferber in "Coleridge's 'Anacalyptic' Blake: An Exegesis" (*MP,* 1978–79); Michael Reynard Richards in "The Romantic Critics and John Donne," *Romanticism, Modernism, Postmodernism* (*BuR,* 1980); and Frederick Garber in *The Autonomy of the Self from Richardson to Huysmans* (1982), which looks at Coleridge's 1818 Lecture remarks on Sterne.

ON PHILOSOPHY

There is need for someone to undertake a history of the seesaw reception of Coleridge as a philosopher. The obligatory beginning is John Stuart Mill's influential comparison of Coleridge to Bentham (*Westminster Review,* 1840; rpt. *Dissertations and Discussions,* 1857), as much now for reasons of literary nostalgia and historical theatricality as for philosophical grounding. Still, Mill's mid-nineteenth-century impression of Coleridge is of value for its striking contrast to the condescending dismissal of him by the Oxford Hegelians later in the century (see Graham Hough, "Coleridge and the Victorians," *The English Mind: Studies Presented . . . to Basil Willey,* ed. Hugh Sykes Davies and G. Watson, 1964); and scholars in this century—even those not inclined overly to praise—have persisted in keeping alive the generous and unexpected approbation of Mill, the chief Utilitarian thinker of his day (see *Mill on Bentham and Coleridge,* ed. F. R. Leavis, 1950;

rpt. 1962; and Glenn K. S. Man, "John Stuart Mill on Bentham and Coleridge," *Revue de l'Univ. d'Ottawa*, 1975). Walter Pater also has some acute pages on Coleridge's mind (*Westminster Review*, 1866; rpt. with additions and deletions in *Appreciations*, 1889). How seriously Coleridge is to be taken as a thinker exercised scholars throughout the latter half of the nineteenth century, opinion waxing and waning like a generational tidal wave. Leslie Stephen sums up the cautionary judgment of the age in his *DNB* (1887) article: Coleridge's admirers must abandon "any attempt . . . to extract a philosophical system from his works" and limit themselves to claims for his "having done much to stimulate thought."

The modern affirmation is first voiced, in the teeth of disapprobation, by J. H. Muirhead in *Coleridge as Philosopher* (1930), an admiring compendium of Coleridge's opinions on logic, metaphysics, nature, morals and ethics, politics, fine arts ("disappointingly thin," rightly opines Wellek), and religion. Muirhead, a prominent neo-idealist philosopher, claims for this "body of philosophical thought" greater coherence than most are willing to grant and overemphasizes its originality and contribution to a voluntaristic theory of being. At the same time Wellek, in *Kant in England 1793 – 1838* (1931), thumped for the contrary: there is "a fundamental lack of real philosophical individuality in Coleridge." Nor has Wellek changed his mind. "I have still to be convinced," he concludes in *ERP* (1956), "that Coleridge deserves a place among independent and original speculative philosophers," a judgment he let stand when he updated his review for the 1972 *ERP3*.

With immense erudition and admirable lucidity Wellek documents the presence of Kantian ideas in Coleridge's notes, marginalia, *Friend*, lectures of 1808, the essays "On Taste" and "On the Principles of Genial Criticism concerning the Fine Arts," *Biographia Literaria, Aids to Reflections*, and the manuscript "Logic." His thoroughness and fairness at once censure Coleridge for philosophical puerility and unwittingly absolve him. Here are two judgments issued sentences apart from each other:

> But from the point of view of philosophy one has, I think, to admit a fundamental weakness, incoherence and indistinctness of his thought.

> Historically, of course, Coleridge is immensely important and can scarcely be overrated as a transmitter of ideas.

How Coleridge can be both incoherent and indistinct in his thought and yet a brilliant transmitter of ideas is an essential key to the paradox of Coleridge's vitality and originality that Wellek, his mind set on the fixed origin and identity of a theory, never thinks to explore. One knows, of course, that Wellek is alluding in Coleridge to weakness of *systematic* philosophizing; yet in concentrating undeviatingly on the source of an idea and on the first ordered and coherent authorship of it, he is on target in one narrow sense and woefully off the mark in all those intricate processes of mind ("that whole vast, sprawling, complicated structure . . . christened Samuel Taylor," Owen Barfield) that endear Coleridge to readers. Citing the *Friend*, Wellek concludes: "Still we cannot but feel that a mind very foreign to Kant's has written this book and has given to Kantian ideas an in-. terpretation which is essentially unKantian." Precisely. But the un-Kantian ideas are not for lack of understanding. Many have attested to Coleridge's mastery of Kant, among them, MacKinnon, "Coleridge and Kant" (*Coleridge's Variety,* ed. Beer, 1974), and Pradhan, "Kant's *Dissertation* and Coleridge's Imagination and Metascience" (*DR,* 1975). In his tracing of Kant in Coleridge—the source and ground of Coleridge's criticism of Kant and of Kant's influence on Coleridge—Wellek gives us a truth about Coleridge the philosopher, but it is a truth that Coleridgeans increasingly find relatively uninteresting, unrevealing, and unimportant (see R. H. Fogle's review of the third edition of *ERP,* in *WC,* 1973).

The study of Coleridge calls for a different set of assumptions than Wellek brings to it. Wellek is nevertheless a responsible historian of criticism, however resistant he may be to Coleridge's virtues. In setting forth what he considers Coleridge's intellectual deficiencies he is prompted again and again by the clarity and honesty of his perception to adumbrate alternative ways of evaluating Coleridge. He agrees with Lovejoy, "Coleridge and Kant's Two Worlds" (*ELH,* 1940; rpt. *Essays in the History of Ideas,* 1948), that "Kant opened for [Coleridge] the gate back into the emotionally congenial fields of evangelical faith and piety" but rejects this use of Kant by Coleridge as a falling "back into a sterile dualism of the head and heart, knowledge and faith, intellect and intuition" (*ERP3*). Yet, it is Coleridge's stubbornly independent borrowing of his way through German ideal- ist philosophy that Orsini, *Coleridge and German Idealism* (1969), contrariwise, finds remarkable about Coleridge's mission of reconciling idealism with theism, using as a Christian apologia the reason-understanding distinction specifically to rear a Christian metaphysic on a transcendental foundation. On a different tack in refutation of Wellek, Modiano, *"Naturphilosophie* and Christian Orthodoxy in Coleridge's View of the Trinity" (*Pacific Coast Philology,* 1982), contends that Coleridge does not so much bend and misrepresent philosophy in the service of triune Christianity as he modifies the concept of the Trinity according to princi- ples of the dynamic philosophy to include a fourth, and supreme, element of a God, as prothesis, who is absolute will and absolute subjectivity. Wellek sums up Coleridge's philosophical accomplishment as "merely the heterogeneous combi- nation of different systems," the "poetical flights and the incoherence" of a poet and critic unable "to think consistently and originally." The distinguished Cambridge theologian and philosopher MacKinnon also determines (*Coleridge's Variety*) that Coleridge read Kant as a poet. But he does not arrive at Wellek's pe- jorative conclusion. Probing to get at the intentions of Coleridge, MacKinnon pic- tures a poet preoccupied with the problem of self-knowledge and, bent on emancipating himself from Schelling's *Naturphilosophie,* learning from Kant not to repeat ideas but to assimilate their sense and advance beyond their "formula- tion by novel application." In an illuminating account of Coleridge's lifelong ef- fort to devise a moral faith out of the unity of human will with divine will and an imaginative faith out of the continuity of our creative powers with the uncon- scious processes of nature, Dorothy Emmet, "Coleridge and Philosophy" (*S. T. Coleridge,* ed. Brett, 1971), sensibly insists that Coleridge was an astute observer of the mind's operations and a serious thinker who should not be judged by the standards of systematic philosophy. His metaphysics "was an attempt to hold these two faiths together, not so much by clear abstract argument as by claims to insight in experiences where the inner and outer worlds met in symbolizing vision."

Coleridge's was fundamentally a poetic and religious mind struggling to reconcile with the moral self a world of disparate and not always congenial concepts. His philosophical opinions are the product of his search for solace and salvation. To approach him on these grounds nullifies many of Wellek's objections without reducing our capacity to take Coleridge seriously as a thinker. It is this insight into Coleridge's unsystematic, intuitive, and unchronological approach to ideas as a poet rather than as a systematic philosopher that causes Orsini, in part, to hedge his judgment of the ultimate value of Coleridge's philosophical thought while unhesitatingly praising his grasp of Fichte and the early Schelling and his zealous and brilliant transmission of transcendental idealism to England. This reserve on Orsini's part, however, in no way qualifies an intelligible exposition (*Coleridge and German Idealism*) of the Kantian transcendental analytic and dialectic, unity of apperception, doctrine of categories, ethics, and aesthetics, the Fichtean "I," the Schellingian *Naturphilosophie,* and the Hegelian dialectic—nine chapters in all—and a careful discrimination of what, how much, and where Coleridge took from these philosophies and when and in what he departs from them.

Coleridge "on his own terms" is the goal of Barfield in *What Coleridge Thought* (1971). Deliberately minimizing psychological, biographical, and historical comparative interpretations, this book offers an exegesis of the internal structure and continuities of Coleridge's thought. Barfield conceives "the root of Coleridge's thought" to be the universal law of polarity—or the "Polar Logic"—that Coleridge placed against the increasingly exclusive reliance in his day on the understanding and the senses. Coleridge is thus at the center of the contemporary scientific concern about the evolving polarity between the human being and nature, struggling to oppose to mechanico-corpuscular empiricism a system grounded equally in the material world and in the mind. Coleridge was not out to eliminate quantitative measurement of the natural world. He wished to adjudicate phenomena apprehended by the understanding to their proper limited places in our total experience, for there is another realm governed by polarity whose apprehension is "the basic act of imagination." These two realms—call them what you will (as Barfield unabashedly does)—comprise phenomena-noumena, naturata-naturans, outer-inner, matter-mind, sensuous-supersensuous. With this as his working premise Barfield explicates the function and place in Coleridge's "Constructive Philosophy" of the key mental faculties imagination and fancy, and reason and understanding. Another appreciative digest of key Coleridgean terms as they figure in Coleridge's late philosophy is Keppel-Jones's "Coleridge's Scheme of Reason" (*Literary Monographs,* 1967). Emmet in "Coleridge on Powers in Mind and Nature" (*Coleridge's Variety,* ed. Beer, 1974) dwells on the inner necessity of philosophy for Coleridge, by which means he worked to "master variety," linking the inorganic, mental, and aesthetic into one living system. And Haven in *Patterns of Consciousness* (1969) harnesses Coleridge's philosophy to his psychological need "to find a language, a set of symbols in terms of which he could describe and make intelligible his own experience of himself in the universe."

While *What Coleridge Thought* is admired for a cogent explanation of the doctrine of polarity, the book is criticized for "freezing" this thought according to what Barfield presumes it was "towards the End of [Coleridge's] Life." An underlying consistency in Coleridge's thinking, however, does not warrant the working premise of Barfield "that later views are for the most part implicit in the earlier." Coleridge may have deviated remarkably little in his cognitive goals but the means of reaching them changed repeatedly. Coburn points out (in her introduction to *Coleridge: A Collection of Critical Essays,* 1967) that Muirhead's book fails ultimately, despite his zest and affection for Coleridge, because Muirhead did not take fully into account the phases of Coleridge's thought. McFarland makes a similar charge against Barfield for restricting his discussion of imagination and fancy to their avatar in chapters 12–13 of *Biographia Literaria,* "mostly the thought of Schelling" that Coleridge "worked through and rejected rather than what he finally endorsed." McFarland has been an ardent spokesman for the thesis that philosophical meaning inheres in an intellectual tradition, with the individual thinker nestled within a nurturing history of texts and ideas. To demonstrate the difference between his and Barfield's treatments of "Coleridge's Doctrine of Polarity," McFarland surveys "Its European Contexts" as part of "A Complex Dialogue" (*Reading Coleridge,* ed. Crawford, 1979; rpt. in *Romanticism and the Forms of Ruin,* 1981) in which Coleridge figures as one contributor among many to the forms the idea has taken in Western philosophy from Heraclitus to Nietzsche. He isolates three forms of the doctrine—the logical opposition of subject and object, the physical opposition of attractive and repelling forces, and the phenomenon of magnetic polarity analogized from electrical phenomena—that pervaded Romantic philosophizing and provided part of the intellectual hegemony of the age.

Coleridge's intellectual allegiances to contemporary and past philosophers have been studied extensively. There are innumerable general accounts tracing his odyssey from associationist necessitarianism to transcendental idealism, and from Unitarianism to Trinitarianism. Most suffer from making the trip appear easier and its route better marked than it is. They should be used only as introductions providing an overall perspective, for they lack details about junkets, side trips, divagations, and backtracking. As reliable a guide as any, albeit old-fashioned, is Willey, whose chapter on Coleridge in *Nineteenth-Century Studies: Coleridge to Matthew Arnold* (1949) is a warm-up exercise for the full-scale itinerary in *Samuel Taylor Coleridge* (1972). Both studies, however, like the chapter in *The English Moralists* (1964), treat the odyssey as essentially a religious pilgrimage. Another travelogue, this one intertwined with Wordsworth's and touching on only the high points, is given in Melvin Rader's *Wordsworth: A Philosophical Approach* (1967). Elio Chinol's *Il pensiero di S. T. Coleridge* (1953) is chronologically neat; Radley's *Coleridge* (1966) is responsibly reliant on the scholarship; Emmet's "Coleridge and Philosophy" (*S. T. Coleridge,* ed. Brett, 1971), though brief, is reasonable and measured; and Wendell V. Harris' *The Omnipresent Debate: Empiricism and Transcendentalism in Nineteenth-Century English Prose* (1981) is helpful in reviewing Coleridge's never quite adequate formulation of the interaction of the reason and the understanding and their role in his thinking about government and politics, religion and morality, and aesthetics and poetry.

Haven (*JHI*, 1959) and Appleyard, *Coleridge's Philosophy of Literature* (1965), lead one with a sure sense for landmarks through the labyrinth of Coleridge's love-hate affair with Hartley: the attractiveness of Hartley's "scientific" support for religious feeling and the repulsiveness of the necessitarian chains defacing Hartleian associative psychology. Restricted in thesis but intensely searching in fresh ways is Christensen, *Coleridge's Blessed Machine of Language* (1981). Although Christensen may set too much store by Coleridge's affection for Hartley ("as important as any other intellectual influence in Coleridge's career"), he chronicles with more verbal energy than the subject has summoned up in previous commentators reasons for Coleridge's holding Hartley in high regard. Like Coleridge, Hartley, that "great master of Christian Philosophy" (*CL* 1), "had dedicated himself to the candid demonstration that a single law could harmonize all phenomena." Christensen is especially illuminating on how the divergent editions of *Observations on Man* offered Coleridge conflicting models of a quietist theodicy and a political activism that "enfranchised uncertainty, divergency, vacillation, and even apostasy." True to his Derridean fealties, Christensen focuses, in part, on the inadequacy of Hartley to account for the origin and development of "alphabetical Writing," which becomes for word-conscious Coleridge a problem in the willed control of a language infused with the sacred ambivalence of "God's awful instauration."

As for the early, continuing, and late affinities of Coleridge for Plato and the Neoplatonists, Haven (*JHI*, 1959) persuasively argues that Coleridge was engrossed with them more for their "*records* of experience" than for their "*explanations*"—as confirmation of the parallel development of his own experience—and that Coleridge studied them thoroughly and systematically from 1800 to 1810. In support of Haven's contention that there is little evidence of Coleridge's reading the Neoplatonists in the 1790s, Orsini in *Coleridge and German Idealism* (1969) debunks contemporary claims for Coleridge's precocious knowledge, by testing the record of his reading and finding it largely hypothetical, with Coleridge getting much mileage out of minimal exposure to a few writers, probably in English translation and, in the case of Plato, dated. Bishop C. Hunt, Jr., in "Coleridge and the Endeavor of Philosophy" (*PMLA*, 1976) makes capital out of the association of Coleridge with an outmoded Platonic view of philosophy. He perceives the Neoplatonic tradition providing Coleridge with a model incorporating mind and soul, that is, a gnosis leading to union with the divine. Such a conception of philosophy as being a fundamentally religious endeavor gave support to his lifelong quest for theological consolation and enabled his resistance to the seductive promises of German idealism. Still helpful older studies of Coleridge's youthful interest in the Neoplatonists and in the Cambridge Platonists are Deschamps, *La Formation de la pensée de Coleridge, 1772–1804*

(1964), and Schrickx (*REL*, 1966). On Coleridge's affection for Boehme and occult and scientific writers the best guide is Beer, who explores this area of European intellectual history with indefatigable enthusiasm in all his books (see above, "Biographies" and "Historical and Literary Criticism of the Poetry").

On Coleridge vis-à-vis Kant and the other German transcendental philosophers, Wellek (*ERP3*) should be consulted. A curious relic from the first decade of this century has surfaced and is worth mentioning if only because its author is a distinguished French man of letters. Although it originates in a source-hunting perspective no longer functionally pertinent to present approaches to Coleridge's intellectual growth and proceeds without benefit of the notebooks, Gabriel Marcel's *Coleridge et Schelling* (1971), begun in 1909, is an unprejudiced typological study of a philosophical relationship, with emphasis on the genesis of Coleridge's metaphysical ideas, on his personal traits, and on the philosophy of the mind expressed in *Biographia Literaria,* as they relate to the ideas of Schelling. More illustrative of current efforts to place Coleridge within his philosophical milieu is MacKinnon's analysis (*Coleridge's Variety,* ed. Beer, 1974) of Coleridge's independent use (even abuse) of Kant's *Inaugural Dissertation,* a diagnosis seconded by Pradhan (*DR,* 1975).

The case for Coleridge's initial infatuation with pantheism is put by Piper in "The Pantheistic Sources of Coleridge's Early Poetry" (*JHI,* 1959) and in *The Active Universe: Pantheism and the Concept of Imagination in the English Romantic Poets* (1962). Coleridge's subsequent lifelong dread of pantheism, while unable "either really to accept—or wholeheartedly to reject" it, receives exhaustive documentation in McFarland's erudite *Coleridge and the Pantheist Tradition* (1969). Although McFarland probably "overstates ... the paradigmatic importance of Spinoza and Spinozism for Coleridge" (as one critic has remarked), there is no blinking away the emotional centrality for Coleridge the poet and philosopher of the "I am—it is" dichotomy. The imagination of Coleridge the poet found the "it is" irresistible; the heart and mind of Coleridge the man of God went with the "I am." Eventually, he opted for a Trinitarian solution. McFarland documents this intellectual-affective odyssey of Coleridge as part of the fatal attraction felt for Spinoza by the Romantic European intellectual community at large—the "Spinozistic Crescendo" McFarland terms it. McFarland performs elegant mental gymnastics to explain Coleridge's reliance on Schelling at the time of the *Biographia Literaria,* while all the time downgrading Schelling and upgrading Jacobi in importance to Coleridge. In the final analysis it is Coleridge the gymnast who hopes to reconcile the "I am" and the "it is" by moving "out of the sphere of philosophy into the sphere of religion," where his beloved Spinoza posed no danger. Lore Metzger, in printing an essay Coleridge wrote on Spinoza for the *Encyclopaedia Metropolitana* ("Coleridge's Vindication of Spinoza: An Unpublished Note," *JHI,* 1960), supports the view that Coleridge persisted in his appreciation of Spinoza the man and mind while deploring Spinoza's mistake of starting his system of thought with God as the "Ground of the Universe" instead of as the living God of Revelation.

Coleridge and the Pantheist Tradition comprises three long essays and nineteen marvelous excursus notes on such overlooked and overworked topics and figures as "Toland and the Word Pantheism," "The Connexion between Poetry and Pantheism," "The New Cosmology," "The Personal Influence of Jacobi," "Swedenborg," "Leibniz and Descartes," "The Religious Heterodoxy of Hartley, Priestley, and Godwin," and "Coleridge's Indebtedness to A. W. Schlegel." The first essay deals with the question of what constitutes philosophical originality and what defines Coleridge's plagiarism. This issue is reviewed in the "Biographies" section. The second deals with Spinoza and the dilemmas of pantheism that beset Coleridge. This issue is summarized in the present subsection. The third deals with the Trinitarian resolution Coleridge finally accepted. This issue is considered in the subsection on religion. The diffusion of McFarland's book throughout this review points up a categorizing problem endemic in the study of Coleridge and attendant to this review and may partly explain the disappointing sense conveyed by the "Philosophy" subsection that interest in Coleridge as a philosopher has fallen off from that of earlier decades in this century, when scholars of Muirhead and Wellek's stature were debating his philosophical importance. With this said, the evidence still points to a drop in attention to the relation of Coleridge and formal philosophy. Critical and theoretical interests of the younger literary scholars lead them more readily in aesthetic and linguistic than in philosophical directions. Let Christensen's announced strategy in *Coleridge's Blessed Machine of Language* speak for the best and freshest of the young Coleridgeans. Despite the pervasive presence of Hartley in the philosophical maneuvers of his book, Christensen avers: "I do not seek to reproduce what Coleridge thought; rather, my goal, both more primordial and more attainable, is to produce the way Coleridge writes."

ON RELIGION AND THEOLOGY

There is growing recognition of the centrality of religion to Coleridge, despite the protests of a dwindling number of naysayers—"boring" and "dead" to all outside a narrow professional circle, opines Fruman, *Coleridge, the Damaged Archangel* (1971). The question in the past was not whether it colored the commentary of Coleridge but to what degree it figured in the web of philosophy that Coleridge wove. As John J. Duffy, "Problems in Publishing Coleridge: James Marsh's First American Edition of *Aids to Reflections*" (*NEQ,* 1970), shows, the early New England disciples and antagonists thought Coleridge had fruitfully, or dangerously (depending on one's bias), philosophized religion. For other accounts of the uneasy transfusion of Coleridge's religio-philosophical synthesis into American culture, see Peter C. Carafiol, "James Marsh's American *Aids to Reflection*: Influence through Ambiguity" (*NEQ,* 1976); Anthony John Harding, "James Marsh as Editor of Coleridge" (*Reading Coleridge,* ed. Crawford, 1979); Duffy, *Coleridge's American Disciples: The Selected Correspondence of James Marsh* (1973); and, of course, Marsh's "Preliminary Essay" (1829) to his edition of *Aids,* which Shedd reprinted (along with a lengthy introduction of his own on Coleridge's religious beliefs and metaphysical system) in volume 1 of his 1853 edition of Coleridge's prose writings. Abrams—accenting the positive side of this inclination of Coleridge, which he elaborates in *Natural Supernaturalism* (1971) into a "general enterprise" among German and English Romantic thinkers— observes that Coleridge "carried on a lifetime's struggle to save what seemed to him the irreducible minimum of the Christian creed within an essentially secular metaphysical system." There is corresponding readiness, however, to see Coleridge bending aesthetics and philosophy to the service of faith rather than yielding to the contrary secularizing thrust championed by Abrams. Leslie Brisman, in a wide-ranging exposition, "Coleridge and the Supernatural" (*SIR,* 1982), places Coleridge's thought within an all-encompassing religious frame of reference, which invokes Coleridge's spiritual progress and familiar nature-supernatural, symbol-allegory, miracles-faith, reason-imagination-understanding formulations to link the early poet-aesthetician with the late theologian-transcendentalist. Jean-Pierre Mileur (*Vision and Revision: Coleridge's Art of Immanence,* 1982) brilliantly discusses Coleridge as the "prophetic reader" whose move to a reading of the Bible, because of its central importance to his sense of the human and literary experience of reality, is the logical and inevitable capstone of his life. McFarland puts it well when he calls the *Magnum Opus* Coleridge's heroic stand for faith in God and in Christian values against the intellectual trends toward atheism of Spinozic evolutionism and scientific progressivism in the nineteenth century (*Romanticism and the Forms of Ruin,* 1981).

The detailed and comprehensive survey of Philip C. Rule, "Coleridge's Reputation as a Religious Thinker: 1816–1972" (*HTR,* 1974), is the best overview of the subject. The American reception of Coleridge's religious writings preceded the British, thanks to James Marsh, and Rule provides a working bibliography of books and articles dealing with the impact of Coleridge on the educational theory of the University of Vermont, on Marsh, and on his peers and disciples to John Dewey (from 1829 to the 1870s). Among British thinkers—Newman in *British Critic* (1839), Mill in *Westminster Review* (1840), Maurice in the dedicatory essay to Derwent Coleridge in *Kingdom of God* (1848), F. J. A. Hort in *Cambridge Essays* (1856)—who warmed their minds at the fire of Coleridge's religious teachings, the manner and method of inquiry were as important as the substance and theology. By the 1860s, however, Coleridge was being relegated to a theological back burner as a rationalist, pseudopantheist, and confuser of philosophy and theology. Alfred Benn, *The History of English Rationalism in the Nineteenth Century* (1906), repeats the standard objections. More favorable estimates are John Tulloch's in *Movements of Religious Thought in Britain during the Nineteenth Century* (1885; see also his exchange with Traill in *Fortnightly Review,* 1885); Walter Pater's "Coleridge as a Theologian" (included as part of the 1866 article on Coleridge in *Westminster Review* but deleted from the essay on Coleridge in *Appreciations,* 1889, which is a composite of the remainder of the *Westminster* article and of new matter on Coleridge's poetry; the omitted portions were then reprinted with title in *Sketches and Reviews,* 1919); and the staunch Anglican Vernon F. Storr's *Development of English Theology in the Nineteenth Century 1800–1860* (1913), which praises Coleridge for affirming the spiritual authority of the Bible despite Higher Criticism's disclosures of historical and doctrinal inconsistencies and for advocating the Christian trustworthiness of individual spiritual experience. During the period between world wars little curiosity was shown in Coleridge's religious thought. The exception is Muirhead (*Coleridge as Philosopher,* 1930), and his bias is the nineteenth-century one that Coleridge philosophized religion. A reassessment of Coleridge as theologian began at the end of World War II. Here, Rule's entries multiply, with judicious annotations of articles and books (most of which Wellek also cites in *ERP3*): Willey (*Nineteenth Century Studies,* 1949; rpt. 1966) on the nondemonstrable spiritual truths pervading Coleridge's writings and making him one of the greatest of nineteenth-century "prophets," plus a chapter in *The English Moralists* (1964) on Coleridge as preeminently a religious thinker; Hugh Parry Owen (*Critical Quarterly,* 1962) on Coleridge's theory of revelation and biblical inspiration; Benjamin Sankey (*TSLL,* 1964) on Coleridge's vitalistic approach to nature; and H. Jackson Forstman (*Journal of Religion,* 1964) on Coleridge's approach to the doctrine of election.

In the past two decades, as Rule makes clear, professional theologians and historians of religion are once again taking Coleridge seriously. Ray L. Hart, *Unfinished Man and the Imagination: Toward an Ontology and a Rhetoric of Revelation* (1968), draws repeatedly on Coleridge in his discussion of the imagination and its Augustinian roots, of the inward and outward man, of imaginative synthesis, and of the symbol as an embodiment of communication with God. Jan Henricus Walgrave, *Unfolding Revelation: The Nature of Doctrinal Development* (1972), devotes several pages to Coleridge's proselytizing the dynamic theory of the German philosophical idealists in England. One hears Coleridge compared more and more with continental theologians—particularly Kierkegaard and Schleiermacher. The focus is on his ideas of how the imagination and the symbol figure in religious belief. He is praised for his insights into the psychology of belief, for his defense of transcendent reality and of the integrity of the spirit, and for his pioneering recognition that language and the paradigmatic textuality (immanent and transcendent at once) of the Bible are binding agents in the sacramental symbiosis of the worlds of the social and spiritual, natural and noumenal. Even a study as aesthetically oriented as Mileur's *Vision and Revision* has for its contextual goal Coleridge's conception of the Bible as a self-initiating and self-referential text. In these matters Coleridge speaks again to our age's rediscovery of "God-language" and to our concern with the nature of belief.

Much attention has been directed to the impact on nineteenth-century English thought of such Coleridgean ideas as a national church and the interdependent growth in harmony, not hostility, of social, cultural, and religious institutions. (See, e.g., C. K. Gloyn, *The Church in the Social Order: A Study of Anglican Social Theory from Coleridge to Maurice,* 1942.) Ben Knights, *The Idea of the Clerisy in the Nineteenth Century* (1978), examines, in depth, the idealism inherent in Coleridge's social model and surveys its impact on precepts of order, progress, education, and the status quo in the rest of the century. *Coleridge and the Broad Church Movement: Studies in Samuel Taylor Coleridge, Dr. Arnold of Rugby, J. C. Hare, Thomas Carlyle and F. D. Maurice* (1942) is C. R. Sanders' still standard work on the subject, although it is now unavoidably reduced in effectiveness by its reliance on the Coleridgean printed materials of forty years ago. Access to the notebooks, letters, and manuscript writings of Coleridge should allow a future historian to expatiate on Sanders' synoptic digest of Coleridge's theological opinions. In *Yesterday's Radicals: A Study of the Affinity between Unitarianism and Broad Church Anglicanism in the Nineteenth Century* (1971), Dennis G. Wigmore-Beddoes in a brief discussion locates in Coleridge's early Unitarianism his later opposition to the doctrine of original sin, his open-minded attitude toward the results of science, his concern for freedom of thought in religion, and his tendency to rationalistic interpretation of doctrine. He concludes that "especially pervasive" and of "profound religious influence, particularly in the Anglican Broad Church," were Coleridge's views on the inspiration of the Bible and on the nature of the Church. Bernard M. G. Reardon, *From Coleridge to Gore: A Century of Religious Thought in Britain* (1971), calls Coleridge "a soul *naturaliter christiana*" and interprets nineteenth-century British theology as a history of the influence on it of Coleridge's ideas about the spiritual life of man: his personal approach to religion as a process of life proved in the act, with the incarnation and atonement, the Trinity, sin, and redemption not simply dogmas of faith but regulative and practical norms of experience. Reardon contends that Coleridge "achieved a more intelligent grasp of the nature and implication of the biblical problem than was possessed by any other Englishman of his time."

One of the nineteenth-century religious thinkers whose theological tenets are often compared with Coleridge's is the Roman Catholic convert Cardinal Newman. An early student of the "striking similarity between Coleridge and Newman" is D. G. James, *The Romantic Comedy* (1948). John Coulson, *Newman and the Common Tradition: A Study in the Language of Church and Society* (1970), confirms much of biographical interest ("something of a Coleridgean tradition in Newman's Oratory") underscoring the reported affinities of Coleridge and Newman. Coulson compares Newman's conception of the church with Coleridge's idea of a visible and invisible church, and analyzes the extent to which they and F. D. Maurice were members of a common tradition. It is in Coleridge's fiduciary use of language that Coulson finds a common bond between the Oxford Movement and the Broad Church theology of F. D. Maurice. Religious assertions are linguistically similar to poetic assertions in structure. Each hovers between the literal and the metaphorical (and the actual and the metaphysical), reconciling opposites and qualifying contradictions. Each is a self-verifying language system "partaking of the reality it has rendered intelligible." Prickett, *Romanticism and Religion: The Tradition of Coleridge and Wordsworth in the Victorian Church* (1976), also reveals similarities, more than differences, in the religious thinking of Newman and Maurice. In "The Living Educts of the Imagination: Coleridge on Religious Language" (*WC*, 1973), Prickett had stitched Coleridge's poetic and religious discursiveness into an intertwined intellectual activity, knotted by idea and symbol into a single vision of the mundane and the transcendent. In *Romanticism and Religion* he reiterates this perception, extending its poetic-religious containment of the world to include the polity of the mid-century conservative and liberal religious groups. Along with Newman and Maurice, Keble, Arnold, and Hort were part of a literary as much as of a theological tradition, and thus did not consider it strange to coalesce the two. Consequently, they benefited alike from the new set of conceptual tools and the new climate of thought and feeling given them by Coleridge in their struggle to preserve the English Church. Like Coulson, Prickett finds Coleridge's idea of the church as the Body of Christ and as a community of men of equal vitality to Tractarians and to Christian Socialists. In more general terms, Michael Bright scrutinizes "English Literary Romanticism and the Oxford Movement" (*JHI*, 1979).

A minority report of sorts characterizes David Newsome's Birkbeck Lectures, *Two Classes of Men: Platonism and English Romantic Thought* (1972). Identifying Coleridge's trichotomous logic with a Platonic rationale for the Trinity and Newman's *via media* with an Aristotelian mean supporting the idea of a Christian church, Newsome stresses divergences between Coleridge and Newman. For Newman the sacraments are rooted in history rather than conveyed solely and symbolically in poetic language. They are facts and events as well as signs. Yet Newsome admits that the two men were in tandem on many spiritual assumptions: that faith signals a conviction of the whole person, not just an intellectual acquiescence; that an "idea" describes the inner ethos, or quality, of something; and that knowledge represents the integration of the sciences ministering to the same truth. In a provocative appendix A, Newsome points out that Coleridge is precise when making hierarchical distinctions between, for example, reason and understanding, imagination and fancy, but vague when it comes to lateral relationships such as between the philosophical quality of reason and the poetical attributes of imagination.

Further instance of Coleridge's impact on the generations of Christian apologists who followed him is explored in A. J. Hartley's "Frederick Denison Maurice, Disciple and Interpreter of Coleridge: 'Constancy to an Ideal Object'" (*ArielE*, 1972). Its underlying argument is that nineteenth-century Coleridgeans, despite their knowing the older Coleridge more than the younger, did not dismember him by severing his poetry from his philosophy. Hartley cites "Constancy to an Ideal Object" as a poem expressive to Maurice of Coleridge's Christianity, a poem taking us "straight to the heart of Coleridge's theology." Mid-century theologians widely embraced the idea that Christian truth can and should be taught through symbols. In the instance of Sterling, however, the precept led to unexpected secularizing of the symbol. This is the thesis of Harding's "Development and Symbol in the Thought of S. T. Coleridge, J. C. Hare, and John Sterling" (*SIR*, 1979). Because Coleridge accepted a functional correspondence between the symbol and personal, credal, and vital development, Sterling despairingly concluded that the religious symbol was itself subject to development. Since he could not hold fast to even a select few Christian symbols of the Divine, and be certain of their fixedness, he shifted his attention to the poetic symbol connecting us with our own nature, and that way, with Being itself. More on Coleridge and the Apostles of Cambridge, particularly on Hare, is given in Robert O. Preyer's "The Romantic Tide Reaches Trinity: Notes on the Transmission and Diffusion of New Approaches to Traditional Studies at Cambridge, 1820–1840" (in *Victorian Science and Victorian Values: Literary Perspectives*, ed. James Paradis and Thomas Postlewait, 1981).

General studies of Coleridge's religion abound. To the two essays by Willey already mentioned should be added his "Coleridge and Religion" (*S. T. Coleridge*, ed. Brett, 1971), and his *Samuel Taylor Coleridge* (1972), both chronological surveys following the thread of faith in Coleridge's life leading from Unitarianism to Christian Trinitarianism. Skillful expositions of reason and understanding are to be found in all of them. Although he surveys the lifetime spiritual odyssey of Coleridge, Hoxie N. Fairchild in the third volume of *Religious Trends in English Poetry* (1949) stresses the early years and the evidence of the poems. From the point of view of a doctrinaire Anglican, Fairchild dismisses Coleridge as a "sentimental pragmatist" who platonized Kant and was given to subjective and pantheistic denials of the "it is" and the Outer Light in favor of the "I am" and the Inner Light. Boulger, in both *Coleridge as Religious Thinker* (1961) and *The Calvinist Temper in English Poetry* (1980; reviewed in the section " 'Dejection: An Ode,' Late Poetry, and Drama"), concentrates on the mature theology of the late years. He insists that if the unpublished notebooks and the *Magnum Opus* are included with the published religious works the total represents a near-completed reconsideration of Christian faith in modern times. Boulger's Coleridge sits formidably in the midst of the theological controversies of the day, salvaging historical Christianity from the sterile habits of mind of Lockeans, rationalists, and evidence writers, by accommodating it to post-Kantian modes of thought. As an apologist redivivus for the Christian mysteries, who is at the same time open-minded toward the persuasions of the Higher Criticism, Coleridge invokes in their support metaphysical-psychological-personal levels of witness to explain the submission of the individual will to the Divine Will rather than to the visible church and its sacraments, dogmas, and traditions. Boulger is also excellent in detailing Coleridge's struggle to extricate himself from the absolute monism of Schellingian subjectivity in which God and consciousness are one. The problem for Coleridge was how to accommodate Kantian semidualism with its recognition of an Other outside self without rejecting entirely the harmony of the subject-object reconciliation. Whereas Boulger is analytical, J. Robert Barth, *Coleridge and Christian Doctrine* (1969), is taxonomical, systematizing Coleridge's religious thinking on the one and triune God, sacred scripture (revealed and inspired), sin, redemption, justification, the Church, sacraments, prayer, death and immortality. Barth considers these traditional religious questions with the precision of a theologian picking his way through a dogmatics, informed by the knowledge that he is a Roman Catholic priest dealing with a staunch Protestant of the Church of England whose beliefs are receptive to Augustinian and Lutheran precepts. Like Boulger, Barth addresses what Coleridge meant by speculative and practical reason, will, and conscience as faculties of religious cognition and volition and how he diverges from the Kantian regulative imperative. Barth emphasizes that Coleridge's theology grows out of his personal practical religious needs, which often beset him uneasily with the imperative of moral action haunch to haunch with dependence on God for redemption. David Pym, *The Religious Thought of Samuel Taylor Coleridge* (1978), covers much the same doctrinal ground as Boulger and Barth from the perspective of the Higher Criticism and of the contributions to Coleridge's teaching made by Hort, Hare, and Maurice. Not unexpectedly, Coleridge looms historically important in the transition from eighteenth-century rationalism to nineteenth-century historicism. Pym draws extensively on the unpublished notebooks to reveal Coleridge as superior to all nineteenth-century English religious thinkers except Newman. Minor errors in biographical fact, disregard of up-to-date Coleridge scholarship, and a judgmental writing style detract from the book's virtues and suggest that the book was intended more for the divinity student of nineteenth-century English church history than for the literature student of Coleridge and the Romantics.

It is generally recognized now that Coleridge translates the necessary logic of Kant into articles of faith. He alters Kant's concept of the practical reason in accordance with his own constitutive views of the mind and its apprehension of the ideas of God, freedom, and immortality. Both Boulger and Barth explore these "heretical" fallings away of Coleridge from Kant in considerable detail. Key documents for establishing the informed independence of Coleridge's thinking, as opposed to its being confused misunderstanding, are Kant's *Inaugural Dissertation* of 1770 and Coleridge's *Aids to Reflection* (1825). Both MacKinnon (*Coleridge's Variety*, ed. Beer, 1974), and Ann Loades, "Coleridge as Theologian: Some Comments on His Reading of Kant" (*JTS*, 1978), find Coleridge choosing to draw on the *Dissertation* and its options regarding God (one may write of God as he is in himself, rather than "as if" he exists) even though in the later *Critiques* Kant rejects this position, allowing a limited "knowledge" of God only in predicates *ens realissimus* of this world. Coleridge insists, however, on knowing the nature of divine activity and on assigning it as best one may "*exempli gratia* such detail as our imagination can integrate with it." Shaffer, "Metaphysics of Culture: Kant and Coleridge's *Aids to Reflection*" (*JHI*, 1970), pits Coleridge in argument with Kant's fear of the application of reason to traditional religious faith. Kant believed in the need to protect reason, which is corruptible in the individual while true reason is universal and unchangeable. Coleridge realized that the test of a rational religion is whether it can serve the ends of devotion and at the same time meet the attacks of the Enlightenment. Believing that if it fell short of this test it would go under, Coleridge devises in *Aids* modes of thought that are rational and aesthetic-moral and include the idea of culture. He thus stakes out a middle ground between God and the Devil, expanding the realm of Kant's aid to reflection, by bringing closer together the empirical and transcendental than Kant allowed. Coleridge's departure from Kant explains, for Loades, why Coleridge had little effect in the 1830s and 1840s on the transmission of Kant to the English. While Kant refreshed Coleridge's grasp of his own theological tradition, Coleridge did not depend on Kant for the vitality of his own religious thinking. Nor did Coleridge's contribution to theology—as Newman, Maurice, Hare, and Hort, who held him in esteem, knew—depend on his presenting himself as a Kantian philosopher and theologian.

Expositions of the liberties Coleridge took with the Kantian practical and speculative reasons are given by Willey, Barfield, Boulger, and Barth, among many. There is also a concise exposition in Bate (*Perspectives of Criticism,* ed. H. Levin, 1950). On the relation of imagination-fancy to reason-understanding,

Wheeler (*Sources, Processes and Methods in Coleridge's* Biographia Literaria, 1980) meliorates J. R. de J. Jackson's—and, one could add, Engell's, C. M. Wallace's, and Brisman's—tendency to identify the primary imagination with reason, allowing only that they seem to overlap "at certain points." She spoils this sensible, albeit vague, conclusion with her all-encompassing addendum that their common ground lies in the distinction Coleridge is fond of reverting to between organic and mechanical, active and passive, intuitive and discursive, method and arrangement, symbol and allegory, "and so on." Wheeler hypothesizes that reason-understanding can supersede imagination-fancy without their being "precisely identical" because of the "distinction, though definitely not a division," between philosophy and poetry. This leads her to detect in *Biographia Literaria* and *The Statesman's Manual* stylistic and terminological configurations (poetic formulation and aesthetic concerns) that are at variance with the philosophical and theological patterns of the *Friend* and *Aids to Reflection.* Wheeler appears to be practicing creative reading of the kind Coleridge is presumed (ipso Wheeler) to be advocating and demonstrating in the *Biographia.* There is still margin for further investigation.

How symbol making—and symbol perceiving—is for Coleridge "essentially a religious act" is examined by two members of Roman Catholic orders. In "Symbol as Sacrament in Coleridge's Thought" (*SIR,* 1972), amplified in *The Symbolic Imagination: Coleridge and the Romantic Tradition* (1977), Barth defines the Coleridgean symbol as sacramental in its mediation between a subject and a reality other than the self. Its alignment of the real world with the ideal world allows one to participate in the divine creative act of the infinite I am. For Abrams, Romanticism naturalized the supernatural and humanized the divine. For Barth the other way around comes closer to the truth—at least when the symbol is involved. The natural is supernaturalized and the human divinized. The Romantic symbol thus staples the transcendent world of spiritual reality with the immanent world of time and space in a consubstantial act of imaginative vision that self-reflexively relates internal and external. Through the mediatory power of the symbol Coleridge takes a position midway between a literal and a metaphysical allusion to reality in the hope of reaching fundamentalists and rationalists. The shaky ground here lies in assuming that the simple existence of a symbol is evidence in itself of the truth of a hidden transcendent order.

Among some Catholic theologians the symbol is a suspect concept, undermining biblical authority rather than educing Christian life, and tantamount to anthropomorphism, agnosticism, univocalism, and subjectivism. M. Jadwiga Swiatecka, *The Idea of the Symbol: Some Nineteenth Century Comparisons with Coleridge* (1980), boldly interjects herself into this controversy by way of an analysis of the Coleridgean symbol. In the process of explaining with great clarity how it is intricately constitutive as well as regulative of the knowledge of a triune God, she adduces a lucid definition in terms of the interrelationships of God, idea, nature, man, reason, and imagination. She also shows how a symbol differs in kind from a poetic metaphor. In its presupposing and indicating the whole scheme of things, the symbol is more than a literary device. It is the "visible tip of an ontological iceberg." That Coleridge failed to articulate this full weltanschauung is revealed in his not clarifying the parity of the Bible (the Logos, symbol of God's knowledge and power of creation) and other forms of art and literature. With these preliminary definitions taken care of, Sister Swiatecka then teases out the similarities and differences in Coleridge's, Carlyle's, and Newman's uses of the concept (rebuking Coulson for lack of semantic rigor in his desynonymizing the symbol of Coleridge and Newman) and examines the near neglect of the term by Hazlitt, De Quincey, and other contemporaries.

F. J. A. Hort (*Cambridge Essays,* 1856) observes that moral philosophy need not detain one long, since Coleridge had little to say about it. Laurence S. Lockridge, *Coleridge the Moralist* (1977), revises this nineteenth-century estimate limited to Coleridge's published works by expanding the range of commentary to include the *Magnum Opus* and other manuscript and notebook writings. The guiding assumption of this highly original study is Coleridge's belief that moral awareness defines us as humans. Lockridge considers not only Coleridge's theoretical examination of moral principles but also the degree to which the ironic moral paradox of the daily personal behavior of Coleridge the sinner mediates and liberalizes Coleridge the moral theorist. As Coleridge perceived it the complex moral task for everyone is at once to disarm the abysmal will below the reach of consciousness, synonymous with evil and the absence of moral control, and to discover and articulate the conscious powers of a free will that promotes human feeling and imagination, and free participation in nature and in the human community. To realize this moral freedom Coleridge oscillates from advocacy of duty governing action to promotion of the developing conscious self, from "preoccupation with what the self ought to do to a consideration of what the self may become." Lockridge does not flinch from Coleridge's moral theory, which reflects his personal needs, as does so much of his thought, and hence which introduces a psychological approach to questions of morality. Coleridge's is a sensibility that prefigures the existential recognition that one inhabits an ironic universe but that yet refuses to protect itself by playing the ironist.

On a corollary track Harding, *Coleridge and the Idea of Love: Aspects of Relationship in Coleridge's Thought and Writing* (1974), follows Coleridge's developing experience of love and his evolving elaboration and redefinement of its spiritual significance through separate phases of his lifetime into a moral system: from recreation to completion of self through love of another (1795–1803), to perfection of self through love of God (1804–13), to the connection of human with divine (1814–34). Harding invokes Willey's three-stage historical progress of modern humanism—the theocratic humanism of Hooker, Milton, and Locke; the intermediate de-Christianized "man-centred humanism" of Hume and the idealist Romantic poets and philosophers; and the positivist humanism of Comte, Mill, and Marx—to pinpoint Coleridge's "man-centred humanism," at once complex and individualistic, combining elements of the first two stages into a personal form, which gives due recognition to the empirical "I" while not excluding the noumenal and ultimately heavenward-prone "I." One note of caution about this solid study. Its references are to the photo-facsimiles of the notebooks in the Library of Jesus College, Cambridge, which are bound in groupings of two to five and foliated in toto, not according to each notebook pagination, and which count only photographic pages. Thus foliation does not correspond to the *Collected Notebooks* numeration, which follows the British Museum foliation of numbering each notebook as a separate unit and of counting missing pages as if in place.

The Coleridge honored in today's criticism is appreciated for his delicately perceptive yet powerfully ratiocinative intellect. Regardless of the shape his thought takes—whether poetic or critical or theological—his antennaelike sensibility displays an almost preternatural receptivity to the refluxes of the world around him. Leslie Stephen wrote presciently in the 1880s that "Coleridge alone among English writers is in the front rank at once as poet, as critic, and as philosopher." Coburn reminds us in the narration of her *Pursuit of Coleridge* (1977) of how fragile is the reputation of thinkers, the evenhanded tribute of Stephen having yielded in the early decades of this century to grudging acknowledgment of Coleridge as the failed author of one masterpiece and two brilliant fragments. Thanks in large measure to Coburn's labors the fortunes of Coleridge have had a dramatic renewal since those years of nadir. Barth summarizes this rebirth in a review (*WC,* 1976) of *Coleridge's Variety* (ed. Beer, 1974). He observes that the collection of essays ushers us into the third age of Coleridge studies in this century: there was "first the poet," "then came the age of Coleridge the critic and literary theorist," and now begins "the age of Coleridge the thinker." Without losing sight of the other Coleridges, *Coleridge's Variety* dwells relatively little on his poetry and literary criticism, but a great deal on his philosophy, theology, psychology, and scientific knowledge. Thus does the spell of the "sibylline shadow" cast by the "polymath and genius of Highgate ... over much of nineteenth-century English thought" (Dickstein, *CentR,* 1972) stretch its myriad-minded aura across the waning decades of the twentieth century also.

GEORGE GORDON, LORD BYRON

John Clubbe

Contents

Introduction

This essay builds on the earlier versions by Samuel C. Chew (1950, 1956) and the 1972 revision of Chew's work by Ernest J. Lovell, Jr. Though I have drawn on Chew's and Lovell's essays in preparing my own, particularly in discussions of older work, I have recast, restructured, and rewritten what I have taken. A major difference between this essay and the Chew-Lovell version is far more frequent mention of articles, although nothing approaching complete coverage was possible. Nor do I mention unpublished dissertations. Since the earlier versions omitted much that I regard as important, I have thought it best to give space to significant scholarship that appeared before the last revision of this guide.

I have included two new sections, "Prose" and "Ideas and Beliefs" (a catchall term), and vastly expanded the "Reputation and Influence" section. In the longer sections I have attempted to bring together essays on related subjects, for scholars often seem distressingly unaware of previous work on their subjects. The extraordinary proliferation of critical studies has necessitated my dividing the earlier section on criticism into one on general studies and another on individual works. Biographical research on Byron has also proceeded apace, though not to the same extent. Still, commentary on biographical studies does not preponderate in this essay, as it did in the earlier versions. I have, however, divided the discussion of biography into the nineteenth century and the twentieth century. I have not indicated reprints, since virtually all studies in English of Byron, biographical and critical, written before 1965 were reprinted in the late 1960s and the 1970s. Books substantially revised I indicate by a second date.

I have attempted to cover the ground through 1983. I also consider whatever books and articles of subsequent years have come my way.

For useful suggestions on earlier drafts of this essay, I am deeply grateful to John Spalding Gatton, Peter W. Graham, Peter J. Manning, Leslie A. Marchand, Michael Rees, and William St. Clair. My collaborators on this volume, Stuart Curran and Jack Stillinger, have read and helpfully commented on the completed essay, as have Frank Jordan, Donald H. Reiman, and the volume's official readers. For looking over sections on which they possess special competence, I wish to thank Hubert F. Babinski, Cynthia Bathurst-Rodgers, Alice Levine, and my Kentucky colleagues Jerome Meckier and Donald A. Ringe. Several members of the American Byron Society kindly took the trouble to write to me about their work and that of others, and to them I am also indebted. Without the courteous and efficient aid of the University of Kentucky's interlibrary loan department, particularly Vivien MacQuown and Barbara Hale, my progress would have been slower than it was. Lastly, I wish to express my deepest appreciation to J. A. Bryant, Jr., former chairman of the English department, for his generosity in arranging the semester's leave from teaching duties that made possible the writing of the first draft of this essay.

Bibliographies

Oscar José Santucho, *George Gordon, Lord Byron: A Comprehensive Bibliography of Secondary Materials in English, 1807 – 1974* (1977), is the first volume to which the prospective student of Byron should turn. Filling a long-perceived gap in research on the poet, it begins with reviews of Byron's initial volume of poetry in 1807 and ends in 1974. Santucho maps out nineteenth- and twentieth-century commentary on Byron as never before. He lists entries chronologically, a policy that avoids overlapping but may cause annoyance to a researcher interested in studying, say, the reception of *Childe Harold* over the past century. Since the index lists only authors, such a researcher would have to wade patiently, entry by entry, through most of the volume. The editor's decision to restrict himself to English-language materials is at first glance regrettable, for European scholars have done more work on Byron than on any other Romantic. But doing so keeps his volume within manageable compass and is justifiable in view of Erwin A. Stürzl's planned bibliography of foreign language materials. Less fortunate, perhaps, is Santucho's decision to omit all newspaper accounts of Byron. Granted that any attempt at comprehensiveness here would have been doomed to failure, still the editor would have increased the volume's usefulness by noting newspaper accounts as he came across them. Six appendixes, on such subjects as "Places Associated with Byron" and "Byron in Drama, Fiction, and Poetry," enhance its value. Santucho annotates entries that are ambiguously titled and omits few items. The standard of accuracy is high. Prefacing Santucho's bibliography is Clement Tyson Goode, Jr.'s, comprehensive 160-page critical overview of research on Byron, which introduces and nicely complements the chronological listing of entries. As does Santucho, Goode divides the response to Byron into ten stages, beginning with Byron's lifetime and concluding with the resurgence of critical activity in 1957 – 74, which receives one fourth of his commentary. Occasionally, one finds a misstatement—for example, that "all of the pivotal resource material on Byron is gradually being accumulated into publication." Would it were so, but a mass of manuscripts, especially letters and diaries of Byron's contemporaries, has not seen publication. Goode has familiarized himself with a great quantity of material and has established a useful perspective on it. As with the bibliography, errors are few and unimportant.

Volume 3 of *The New Cambridge Bibliography of English Literature,* edited by George Watson (1969), contains H. G. Pollard's section on Byron. Like the original work, the *New CBEL* follows a basically chronological arrangement of entries; consequently, for quick reference one should know the date of the book or article sought for. Furthermore, the publications of a single scholar or critic are grouped together at that point determined by the date of his or her earliest publication listed. Thus the arrangement is neither strictly chronological nor alphabetical. The effective terminal date for Byron entries may be set at 1962, although Pollard includes a few later publications. Selective rather than exhaustive, the section has major omissions, and students using it (or any other comprehensive bibliography) should check elsewhere for studies omitted. Pollard's *New CBEL* entry supersedes his section in the original *CBEL* (1941) and that by Anne Elliott in the *Supplement* (1957), which, however, contains entries not to be found in the *New CBEL.*

The list of editions, translations, biographies, critical works, and miscellaneous Byroniana in volumes 49 and 50 of the new *British Library General Cata-*

logue of Printed Books to 1975 (1980) is of course limited to the library's very extensive holdings. This catalog incorporates not only the earlier *British Museum General Catalogue of Printed Books* (1959–66), effective to 1955, but also the *Ten-Year Supplement* (1968), listing acquisitions between 1956 and 1965, and the *Five-Year Supplement* (1971). The student may also wish to consult various British Museum publications listing its manuscript holdings.

Volume 7 of E. H. Coleridge's edition of Byron's *Poetry* has an admirable bibliography of editions of the collected poetical works, of individual poems and groups of poems, and of translations. Collations, though not so meticulously detailed as the collector of rare books may wish, are sufficient for the student who needs to identify a particular edition. Coleridge's lists are not quite complete for the period before 1904, and they require supplementing for the period since that date. More particularly designed for the collector is Thomas James Wise's *Bibliography of the Writings in Verse and Prose of George Gordon Noel, Baron Byron* (2 vols., 1932–33). Fortunately Byron did not come within the compass of Wise's notorious activities as a fabricator of "rarities"; consequently this bibliography, apart from omissions, is fairly reliable if occasionally inexact insofar as it covers the poet's own works. A major limitation of Wise's bibliography is that he based it on the books he happened to own. When he had the first issue of a poem, he listed it as such. But he had the second issue of *Childe Harold,* cantos 1 and 2, so he listed it as "the first edition." He is especially inadequate on *Don Juan's* numerous issues, editions, and piracies. The catalog of Byroniana in volume 2 is also very incomplete, for notwithstanding Wise's arrogant assertion that it contains everything of importance, many works are omitted. Covering much the same ground as Wise's *Bibliography* but in briefer form is the Byron section in his catalog of the *Ashley Library* (11 vols., 1922–36), a collection now in the British Museum. Important additional bibliographical information is recorded by John Carter in *TLS* (27 Apr. and 4 May 1933), Davidson Cook on "Fare Thee Well" in the same journal (18 Sept. 1937), and Graham Pollard and John Carter on pirated collections of Byron (16 Oct. 1937). Supplementing the above is Francis Lewis Randolph's *Studies for a Byron Bibliography* (1979). Left incomplete at its author's death, this work often usefully amplifies and corrects Wise. In three parts, it lists first and later editions, volumes in which works by Byron were first published, and privately printed and suppressed Byron editions. Greatly needed is a complete, carefully prepared descriptive bibliography of Byron's own works. Given the often complex publishing history of his many publications—for example, *English Bards and Scotch Reviewers*—such a venture would present the bibliographer with a formidable challenge.

A major collection devoted wholly to Byron is that formerly in the possession of Herbert C. Roe of Nottingham, England, and now appropriately housed in the poet's ancestral home, Newstead Abbey, outside Nottingham. The Corporation of Nottingham issued an elaborate catalog, with commentary, entitled *The Roe-Byron Collection, Newstead Abbey* (1937), which covers not only Byron's works in first and later editions and many autograph manuscripts but also a large collection of Byroniana and many mementos and other objects associated with the poet. The Library of the University of Texas also contains a rich collection of

Byron rarities, for which see R. H. Griffith and H. M. Jones, *A Descriptive Catalogue of an Exhibition of Manuscripts and First Editions of Lord Byron Held in the Library of the University of Texas* (1924), and Willis W. Pratt's compilations, *Lord Byron and His Circle: A Calendar of Manuscripts in the University of Texas Library* (1947) and "Lord Byron and His Circle: Recent Manuscript Acquisitions" (*LCUT*, 1956). T. G. Steffan, "The Byron Poetry Manuscripts in the Library of the University of Texas" (*MLQ*, 1947), provides useful supplementary information. The 150th anniversary of the poet's birth was celebrated at the Henry E. Huntington Library with an exhibition recorded by Ricardo Quintana in *Byron: 1788–1938* (1938). See also H. C. Schulz, "English Literary Manuscripts in the Huntington Library" (*HLQ*, 1968) and *Guide to Literary Manuscripts in the Huntington Library* (1979). Thomas M. Simkins, Jr., discusses Duke University's fine collection of early editions of Byron in "The Byron Collection in the Rare Book Room of Duke University Library" (*Library Notes* [Duke Univ.], 1951). Other major institutions with notable Byron holdings include Yale, Harvard, and the Morgan Library. George K. Boyce in "Modern Literary Manuscripts in the Morgan Library" (*PMLA*, 1952) notes the library's holdings of Byron manuscripts, which include *Beppo, The Corsair, Manfred, Marino Faliero, Mazeppa*, cantos 1–4 of *Don Juan, The Prophecy of Dante*, and *Werner.* An inkling of the extraordinarily rich hoard of Byron manuscripts in the archives of John Murray, Byron's publisher, is contained in the *Bibliographical Catalogue of First Editions Proof Copies & Manuscripts of Books by Lord Byron* (1925). In 1969 appeared the *Catalog of Books and Manuscripts at the Keats-Shelley Memorial House in Rome.* Students should also consult the Byron holdings listed in the *Index of English Literary Manuscripts,* volume 4: 1800–1900, part 1, A–G, compiled by Barbara Rosenbaum and Pamela White (1982). This volume notes the location of Byron's poems, prose, diaries, notebooks, as well as his marginalia in printed books and manuscripts. It has particular use for poems not yet included in the ongoing McGann edition. Those seeking the location of Byron's other writings will find it invaluable.

The sesquicentennial of Byron's death in 1974 led a number of institutions to publish catalogs of the exhibits held on their premises. By far the most sumptuous of these catalogs was put out by the Victoria and Albert Museum, *Byron,* by Anthony Burton and John Murdoch (1974), which lists books, manuscripts, and memorabilia drawn from major British collections. *Lord Byron in Greece* (1974) catalogs an exhibition arranged by the British Council and the Benaki Museum. "Byron in the Gennadius Library" (*Griffon,* 1975) commemorates that library's exhibit in Athens. *Lord Byron: A Sesquicentennial Exhibition Catalogue* (rpt. in *TSLL,* 1975), compiled by Sally Leach, lists holdings at the Humanities Research Center at the University of Texas. The Carl H. Pforzheimer Library and the New York Public Library put out *Byron on the Continent* (1974), which lists the items on exhibit, with perceptive commentary by Donald H. Reiman and Doucet Devin Fischer on Byron's relationship to his age. The Pforzheimer Library now has the first draft of "Fare Thee Well" and *Beppo,* nearly a hundred letters by Byron and many more to him, and other rarities. *Byron* (1974) commemorates the University of Pennsylvania's holdings, which William H. Marshall had previously described in "The Byron Collection in Memory of Meyer Davis, Jr." (*Library Chronicle* [Univ. of Pennsylvania], 1967).

Still the largest list of English Byroniana, with "a representative selection from the Byroniana of other countries," is in Samuel C. Chew's *Byron in England: His Fame and After-Fame* (1924). This list could be much amplified, for though little of any consequence is omitted of English authorship, the foreign items, which were restricted in number for reasons of space, stand in need of considerable expansion. Students should note that Chew in his text discusses a number of items not listed in his bibliography. A valuable supplement to more formal bibliographical aids, recording moreover a few exceedingly rare items omitted from one or another of the compilations already mentioned, is *Byron and Byroniana: A Catalogue of Books* (1930) issued by the scholarly London bookseller Elkin Mathews. Many rare books are also among the 429 items in *Lord Byron* (1980), a catalog put out by C. C. Kohler. This collection is now at Johns Hopkins.

Older surveys of Byron research include Ernest Bernbaum's article "Keats, Shelley, Byron, and Hunt: A Critical Sketch of Important Books and Articles Concerning Them Published in 1940–1950" (*KSJ*, 1952), which gives four pages to Byron, and Leslie A. Marchand's "Recent Byron Scholarship" (*EM*, 1952), which discusses books published since 1921. An expanded and updated version (through 1957) of Marchand's essay appeared in *Essays in Literary History Presented to J. Milton French*, edited by Rudolph Kirk and C. F. Main (1960). Willis W. Pratt's "A Decade of Byron Scholarship: 1946–1956, A Selective Survey" (*KSJ*, 1958) is also valuable and tries to avoid retreading the ground covered by Bernbaum and by Marchand in his earlier article. In the bibliography to his *English Literature 1815–1832* (1963) Ian Jack comments selectively on first editions of Byron as well as on modern studies. Richard Harter Fogle's Goldentree Bibliography, *Romantic Poets and Prose Writers* (1967), intended for undergraduates, has an excellent section on Byron that lists critical discussions under individual poems. Even better (and more up-to-date) is the Byron chapter in Donald H. Reiman, *English Romantic Poetry, 1800–1835: A Guide to Information Resources* (1979). *Byron Criticism since 1952: A Bibliography*, edited by Ronald B. Hearn and others (1980), may also be noted, though it is seriously incomplete and full of errors.

Of the annual bibliographies, the student should probably begin with "The Romantic Movement: A Selective and Critical Bibliography," published in *ELH* (1937–49), *PQ* (1950–64), *ELN* (1965–79), and by Garland Press (1980–   ). Often reviewers have annotated the articles and books, and reviews of books are also listed. This bibliography contains useful cross-listings to treatments of Byron in general studies, a particularly valuable feature since many studies not specifically on Byron discuss him. A. C. Elkins, Jr., and L. J. Forstner have collected the first thirty-five bibliographies: *The Romantic Movement Bibliography, 1936–1970* (7 vols., 1973). The last volume is a comprehensive index. Since 1952 the annual bibliography in *KSJ* has provided the fullest coverage of work done on Byron. It encompasses more categories than other bibliographies—for example, translations and doctoral dissertations, and sometimes it briefly annotates entries. D. B. Green and E. G. Wilson collected in volume form the first twelve bibliographies (July 1950–June 1962) in 1964, and Robert A. Hartley the next twelve (July 1962–December 1974) in 1978. Both volumes have single cumulative indexes. Other important annual bibliographies, both published in England, are in *YWES* (since 1921) and in the Modern Humanities Research Association's *ABELL* (also since 1921). American scholars are more familiar with the annual bibliography put out by the Modern Language Association of America (since 1922 and, since 1956, international in coverage). Until 1969 it appeared in the September, formerly the June, issue of *PMLA,* and since 1970 it has continued as the *MLA International Bibliography.*

Selected or specialized bibliographies appear in many of the larger volumes or works discussed subsequently. Particularly recommended are those by Ernest J. Lovell, Jr., *His Very Self and Voice: Collected Conversations of Lord Byron* (1954); Leslie A. Marchand, *Byron: A Biography* (3 vols., 1957); Peter L. Thorslev, *The Byronic Hero: Types and Prototypes* (1962); M. K. Joseph, *Byron the Poet* (1964); Leslie A. Marchand, *Byron's Poetry: A Critical Introduction* (1965); and Truman Guy Steffan's edition of *Cain* (1968). The second edition of Steffan's and Willis W. Pratt's variorum *Don Juan* (4 vols., 1971) contains a bibliographical "Appendix: *Don Juan* in the Sixties" at the end of volume 4, as well as the earlier "Survey of Commentary on *Don Juan,*" both by Pratt. See also the bibliography in Edmond Estève's *Byron et le romantisme français* (1907), particularly useful in charting early French interest, and that in Robert Escarpit, *Lord Byron: Un tempérament littéraire* (2 vols., 1955, 1957), annotated and helpfully divided into sections dealing with criticism of individual poems, Byron's influence in various countries, and other matters of importance. To gauge how great the interest in Byron has grown in the United States since Escarpit prepared his bibliography, we may note that only six percent of the items in it derive from this country, against sixteen percent for both France and Germany and a lopsided forty-nine percent for Great Britain.

Beyond the scope of most student explorations is Lawrence F. McNamee's *Dissertations in English and American Literature* (1967; supplement 1, 1969; supplement 2, 1974), which lists dissertations, published and unpublished, in American, British, and German universities.

Editions and Selections: Poetry

Byron scholars have eagerly awaited *Lord Byron: The Complete Poetical Works,* a new edition prepared by Jerome J. McGann for the Oxford English Texts series. Volumes 1 and 2 (of seven) appeared at the end of 1980, volume 3 in 1981. Volume 4 (the 1816 poems through *Marino Faliero*) and volume 5 (*Don Juan*) are in press, and the remaining two will follow subsequently. McGann's edition "has two primary aims: to establish a complete collection of Byron's poetical works, and to reproduce a correct text of those works." Though indebted to the great Murray editions of the past—including John Wright's of 1832–33 and E. H. Coleridge's of 1898–1904, the latter until now standard—McGann has advanced on all fronts our knowledge of Byron's oeuvre: new poems, new texts of familiar poems, and magnificent commentaries that bring new and familiar materials more sharply into focus than before. The major contribution to the study of Byron the poet in recent decades, his edition gives us as close as can humanly be established definitive texts for the Byronic canon.

The edition includes (or will include) a number of poems published in articles during the past decades, among them, T. G. Steffan's thorough presentation of "The Edinburgh Ladies Petition and Reply" (*UTSE*, 1948). Steffan concluded that Byron wrote only the "Reply"; McGann assigns the entire poem to him. Like a number of other earlier publications of Byron's poems, Steffan's retains its value, in this case as a recondite survey of the contemporary scientific knowledge that the poem satirizes. Another earlier publication is Ward Pafford, "Byron's 'To Those Ladies': An Unpublished Poem" (*KSJ*, 1952). McGann deems a de Gibler forgery six stanzas assigned to 1819 (in the *Griffon* of the Gennadius Library, 1970) and apparently will assign to the *Dubia* (poems that may or may not be authentic) the witty mock review of Rosa Matilda's epic on the Prince Regent that David V. Erdman attributed to Byron in *KSJ*, 1970. Interim reports by McGann about his editorial discoveries include "Editing Byron's Poetry" (*ByronJ*, 1973), "The Murray Proofs of 'Don Juan' I–II" (*ByronJ*, 1977), and "The Correct Text of *Don Juan*, I, 190–198" (*TLS*, 30 July 1976).

Given Byron's complex relationships with his publisher, John Murray, and with Murray's literary "Senate," McGann has wisely made his decisions for copy texts on a poem-by-poem basis. For poems published before 1816 he usually favors a later edition; for those after 1816, an earlier, often the first. He has also assiduously sought out manuscripts and proofs of Byron's poems in public and private collections all over the world and has collated countless manuscripts and printed versions in order to ensure that each poem appears (as far as can be established) as Byron intended it to appear. This work has led him "to alter the received text of a large number of poems." Extended reviews by Jack Stillinger (in *JEGP*, 1982—of volume 1 only), Ian Jack (in *Review*, ed. James O. Hoge and James L. W. West, 1982), J. Drummond Bone (in *MLR*, 1983), and by Donald H. Reiman (in *KSMB*, 1983) evaluate the new edition.

The table of contents in volume 1 numbers the poems and presents them in approximate chronological order. The first volume contains the poems through 1811, 173 in all, thirty-five of which are hitherto unpublished or uncollected. These "new" poems McGann conveniently identifies in the table of contents by an asterisk. The eighty-six new poems or poetic fragments derive chiefly from Byron's early years, though McGann has located a few from all periods of the poet's career. Most of these poems are not of first importance, but several are and will quietly alter our perception of the rest of Byron's canon. Often political or sexual in nature, of a frankness that made them unsuitable for contemporary publication, they give us—as do the unexpurgated letters and journals in Leslie A. Marchand's edition—a fuller sense of Byron's genius. At the bottom of each page McGann gives all substantive textual variants and at the back of each volume the poet's notes, followed by McGann's own editorial commentary. He also drops a few poems from the canon. His last volume, when published, will contain the *Dubia* (supplementing those noted in Chew's *Byron in England*) and an updated list of false and spurious poems.

The major works in volume 1 are the pieces that make up *Hours of Idleness,* Byron's first public collection; *English Bards and Scotch Reviewers; Hints from Horace;* and *The Curse of Minerva.* McGann's discussion of *Hours of Idleness* sets out as never before the various metamorphoses of this much-revised volume. McGann gives us not only a new text for *Hints from Horace,* written in 1812 though not published in toto until 1831, but also a full account of that undervalued poem's complicated history. Following E. F. Boyd, he usefully reminds us that Byron's revived interest in having *Hints* published in 1820 coincides with Byron's prose defenses of Pope and his renewed attacks on contemporary poets and critics. Byron's dating of 17 March 1811 for *The Curse of Minerva* is seriously misleading, McGann reveals, for Byron wrote most of the poem in November 1811, *after* he had returned from the Near East.

Volume 2 wisely breaks chronology to include the four cantos of *Childe Harold's Pilgrimage.* Since the text of *Childe Harold* is "one of the most reliable in the Byron canon," McGann offers few emendations for cantos 1 and 2, but for canto 3 he restores Byron's unpublished political notes and for canto 4 he prints for the first time Byron's corrections (in the prose dedication to Hobhouse) to his discussion of classical and Romantic poetry. The abundant new manuscript material for *Childe Harold,* while not significantly altering the received text, has allowed McGann to prepare a more sophisticated commentary to the poem than hitherto available. For example, he sets out more clearly than before the differences among the various manuscripts of canto 3. However, students may find McGann's presentation of his commentary to *Childe Harold* somewhat confusing. Usually his own notes are intermixed with Byron's, but for cantos 1, 2, and 4 he gives first all of Byron's notes, then his own. McGann believes his procedure the best of the several awkward possibilities, but it will cause confusion. (Though it is mentioned in the editorial introduction to volume 1, he does not remind his readers of it at the beginning of volume 2.) McGann also somewhat abridges Byron's appendix of extracts of modern Greek attached to the first two cantos, an improvement over E. H. Coleridge, however, who had jettisoned the entire appendix.

Volume 3, devoted largely to the tales and taking Byron up to his departure from England in April 1816, contains *Waltz, The Giaour, The Corsair, Lara,* "Ode to Napoleon Buonaparte," *Hebrew Melodies, The Siege of Corinth,* and *Parisina.* Among its thirty-two pieces new or previously uncollected are a number of satirical epigrams, including a series of nine squibs entitled "Imitations of Martial." Many of the unpublished poems, like the Martial imitations, come from the Lovelace collection. A poem-by-poem reading of this volume allows us to perceive how Byron grew as a poet during his years in England. McGann has sorted out with exemplary clarity the complex compositional and publication history of *The Giaour,* that "snake of a poem," as Byron called it, which lengthened "its rattles every month." McGann's examination of the manuscripts of the poems often alters our understanding of their chronological relationships to each other. His most considerable feat of redating involves *The Siege of Corinth* and *Parisina*, published together in 1816. The manuscripts "strongly suggest that both *Siege* and *Parisina* developed out of an original MS. tale, begun in 1812 and continued in 1813," and that *The Siege* "was pieced together at various times between 1813 and 1815." Thus two of Byron's latest published tales turn out to be among the earliest in inception.

McGann's commentaries constitute one of the glories of these volumes. They explain complicated matters lucidly. In addition, McGann's long involvement as a critic of Byron's poetry lends authority to his judgments on poems as well as on textual matters. He has attempted to identify all the literary allusions of a poet at once solidly rooted in literary tradition and highly original: a hopeless task but one in which he has succeeded better than anyone before him, for his notes pick up a number of hitherto unnoticed literary echoes and point out, as well, parallel passages in Byron's poetry and letters. The commentary also brings out as never before Byron's intense involvement with contemporary issues and events. The poet, who thought he was "born for opposition," writes with most fire against individuals and measures he detested, particularly, it seems, the Prince Regent, against whom he directed more poems than we have realized. McGann points out (in the commentary to *Parisina*) that Byron "habitually used older historical situations—and especially people and events from the Italian Renaissance—to highlight analogous circumstances in the contemporary English and European political scene." He also settles, one hopes forever, some troublesome minor matters, for example, the identification of the Mrs. Wilmot for whom Byron wrote "She Walks in Beauty." I disagree with his identifying the addressee of "Stanzas for Music" ("There be none of Beauty's Daughters") as Claire Clairmont. Earlier, Leslie Marchand and, more recently, Jean Hagstrum have seen the poem as part of the Thyrza group to John Edleston, but I would argue that Byron addresses it to his half-sister, Augusta.

Students may at first find McGann's edition somewhat difficult to use. I regret that he does not repeat at least the relevant parts of the table of contents and list of abbreviations in succeeding volumes, a convenience that would obviate the virtual necessity of having the first volume at hand when consulting later ones. The contents pages in volume 1 are not paginated; volume 2 has no contents pages; only in volume 3 are we given a contents page with pagination. The running heads, for example, "Poetical Works 1812," are of little help and can be downright misleading, particularly as the above designation covers not only *Childe Harold* 1 and 2, indeed published in that year, but also *Childe Harold* 3, published in 1816, and 4, published in 1818. Omission of the title of a poem at the beginning of his commentary (McGann identifies it by number only) also will cause inconvenience. Each volume has an index of first lines but not one of titles, the lack of which will hamper students in finding poems. On the positive side, the Clarendon Press has provided attractive type and page layout, with lines numbered for easy reference. In short, one cannot but be immensely grateful to McGann for bringing off this long-awaited edition. Byron scholarship will be years in assimilating the wealth of its materials. In his *A Critique of Modern Textual Scholarship* (1983) McGann discusses several of Byron's poems within the context of modern textual practice.

Announced for 1985 publication (and not seen by me) are the first four volumes devoted to Byron in the series entitled *The Manuscripts of the Younger Romantics*. The initial Byron volumes, edited by Jerome J. McGann and Alice Levine, reproduce facsimiles of manuscripts in the Pierpont Morgan Library. The series will contain not only original manuscripts but also fair copies and proofs, as well as related materials, so that one can study the creative process from first conception to final manuscript version. Students interested in Byron as a poet of process will find much to interest them in these drafts, which often reveal major differences from published texts. Publication of subsequent volumes in this series will shed light on poems included in earlier volumes because the original manuscript of a poem, the fair copy, and the proofs are not always (or even often) in one repository. Thus to study the evolution of a poem one may well have to jump around the volumes. Not in every case, however. For example, the editors have wisely reserved the first draft of "The Castled Crag of Drachenfels" (in the Morgan Library) for publication with the rest of the *Childe Harold* manuscripts. Once the rich treasures of the Murray archives appear in facsimile, the student of Byron will have almost a superabundance of material with which to study the workings of the poet's mind as he composed. Although McGann used the Byron manuscripts being reproduced in preparing his edition, a look at the originals—and these facsimiles may be the closest we can conveniently get to them—makes real, as nothing else can, the process of composition. Students will discover that establishing a text involves the making of many choices, some of them controversial. Perusing these volumes makes them, in effect, editors of Byron.

Until the appearance of McGann's Oxford edition, the standard edition of Byron's poetry was that edited by Ernest Hartley Coleridge and published in seven volumes by John Murray (1898–1904). It superseded John Wright's valuable edition (17 vols., 1832–33) and is still very much worth consulting. Coleridge did not enlarge considerably the corpus of Byron's poetry; the only notable item that he published for the first time is the fragmentary beginning of the seventeenth canto of *Don Juan*. But a feature of immense value in Coleridge's work was the recording for the first time of a great number of variant readings existing in the manuscripts (for the most part those in the Murray archive). The most important editorial problem was that of punctuation; and here Coleridge, inexplicably, followed the texts in the edition of 1831 instead of those in the edition of 1832–33, which are undoubtedly better. Coleridge's elaborate annotation is informative and sometimes brilliant but occasionally erratic and disproportionate to the significance of the subject.

Of the numerous one-volume editions of the *Poems* with claims to completeness, the edition edited by E. H. Coleridge and published by John Murray (1905) constitutes a reissue of Coleridge's text from his seven-volume edition. That published in 1905 by Houghton Mifflin (in the "Cambridge Poets") was edited and introduced by Paul Elmer More. Ione Dodson Young keyed her concordance to this edition, thus giving it particular value. In 1975 Houghton Mifflin reprinted the volume, retaining the original pagination, with a new introduction by Robert F. Gleckner. The edition published in 1904 by Oxford University Press, edited by Frederick Page, has been, like the one-volume Coleridge and More editions, many times republished. In 1970 Oxford reissued it in paperback, slightly revised by John Jump. The texts of these three editions differ chiefly in matters of punctuation and capitalization.

Of editions of individual poems, the most important is *Byron's* Don Juan, a variorum edition edited by Truman Guy Steffan and Willis W. Pratt in four volumes (1957, rev. 1971). (I discuss Steffan's introductory volume, *Byron's* Don Juan: *The Making of a Masterpiece*, below under "Criticism: Individual Works.") Using the first edition as the basis of their text, which makes up volumes 2 and 3, the editors have printed immediately below each stanza all the available variants, drawn chiefly from "sixteen first drafts, one for each canto; several first draft fragments; the first draft of the unfinished seventeenth canto; and fair copies of the first eight cantos." Thus it is now possible to examine Byron's thousands of deletions, additions, and revisions. The quantity and range of Pratt's notes, which take up volume 4, reflect the various splendor of the poem itself, as it reaches out into all phases of existence in the early nineteenth century—political, literary, scientific, and artistic—displaying fully a panorama of the life and culture of the time. Interpolated pages at the end of volume 4 of the 1971 edition contain new notes. The second edition also has numerous corrections in the text. Penguin Books has published a modernized version of this text (1973, 1977, 1982), with variants and notes by Steffan and Pratt, now joined by Esther Steffan. The text gains in readability what it has lost in authority. The 1982 edition, with further revised notes, mostly suggested by my review in *KSJ*, 1975, is now the best available one-volume edition of *Don Juan*.

For his edition of *Cain* (1968) Steffan based the text on a manuscript at the University of Texas at Austin and collated it with seven editions. The new text differs from that of earlier editions chiefly in regard to capitalization, punctuation, and italics. Variants are recorded in the notes. I discuss Steffan's elaborate commentary on the poem under "Criticism: Individual Works." In *Byron's Hebrew Melodies* (1972) Thomas L. Ashton offers a meticulously edited text of the poems that constitute *Hebrew Melodies*. His text has been "collated from the extant manuscripts, with the editions of the Hebrew Melodies published in Byron's lifetime, with authoritative later editions, and with other relevant sources." He reproduces all variants and decipherable deletions. Of the four known copies of Byron's suppressed *Fugitive Pieces* (1806), one was edited in facsimile by Marcel Kessel in 1933. Volume 7 of *Shelley and His Circle, 1773–1822* will contain a new text of *Beppo* edited by McGann.

Ione Dodson Young's *Concordance to the Poetry of Byron* (4 vols., 1965), based on More's 1905 Cambridge Edition, filled a long-apparent need. Also valuable is *A Concordance to Byron's* Don Juan, edited by Charles W. Hagelman, Jr., and Robert J. Barnes (1967), which uses the 1957 variorum edition of the poem and includes sixteen rejected stanzas and 634 complete-line variant readings.

More volumes of selections of Byron's poetry exist than can be listed here. Early and mid – nineteenth century selections are still worth consulting as indications of contemporary taste. Two slightly later editions possess a place of their own in the history of English literature: Algernon Charles Swinburne compiled *A Selection from the Works of Lord Byron* (1866) with an eloquent introduction (rpt. in his *Essays and Studies,* 1875), and Matthew Arnold edited *Poetry of Byron* (1881) with an equally celebrated preface (rpt. in Arnold's *Essays in Criticism, Second Series,* 1888). Among anthologies of later date Richard A. Rice's *The Best of Byron* (1933, rev. 1942) is tastefully selected and competently introduced. The Odyssey Press has devoted two volumes to Byron: *Don Juan and Other Satiric Poems,* edited by Louis I. Bredvold (1935), and *Childe Harold's Pilgrimage and Other Romantic Poems,* edited by Samuel C. Chew (1936). Both have good introductions, bibliographies, and extensive notes. Other selections include A. Quiller-Couch and D. Nichol Smith, *Byron: Poetry and Prose* (1940); Peter Quennell, *Byron: Selections from Poetry, Letters and Journals* (1949), very full but leaving out *Manfred*; Edward E. Bostetter, *Byron: Selected Poetry and Letters* (1951, rev. 1972); Leslie A. Marchand, *Selected Poetry* (1951, rev. 1967), a generous selection but without annotation, with the revised edition including parts of *Don Juan;* Marchand's *Don Juan* (1958) in the Riverside series; W. H. Auden, *The Selected Poetry and Prose of Byron* (1966), the edition most often found in bookstores but unfortunately idiosyncratic in its emphases on the satires and prose; William H. Marshall's Riverside *Selected Poems and Letters* (1968), a selection of generous proportions, with introduction, notes, and bibliography, but omitting *Don Juan;* and three volumes of *Byron's Poems* in Everyman's Library, the whole most casually edited by V. de Sola Pinto in 1963. (The *Childe Harold* volume was reissued in 1975 under the nominal editorship of John D. Jump.) The Norton Critical Edition of *Byron's Poetry,* edited by Frank D. McConnell (1978), does not measure up to that series' usually high standards of editorial work. McConnell more or less reprints E. H. Coleridge's turn-of-the-century text; leaves out, as does Coleridge, the indicative subtitle, "A Fable," of *The Prisoner of Chillon*; and introduces new errors, omitting, for example, *Manfred's* subtitle and motto. The choice of texts is also strange: *Childe Harold* represented by cantos 1 and 3, with snippets of 4; *Don Juan* by 1, parts of 2, 5, 9, and 16. McConnell's introductions and notes contain a number of glaringly erroneous statements, for example, that Byron began experimenting in ottava rima only in 1817. He includes a few of Byron's letters, nine modern critical essays, and "Images of Byron," a selection from Francis Jeffrey to the present.

The lack of good teaching texts for Byron is a major pedagogical problem today in courses on Romanticism. McGann's one-volume Oxford Standard Authors Edition, based on his text in the seven-volume edition and drawing on his commentaries there, is scheduled for 1985 publication. It will include most of the poetry and a selection of the prose. It will have new texts for poems not yet published in the seven-volume edition, including *Don Juan,* where we may expect to see major changes.

Editions and Selections: Letters

The appearance of Leslie A. Marchand's now-standard edition, *Byron's Letters and Journals* (12 vols., 1973–82), constituted a literary event of the first importance, for Byron, with Keats and the Carlyles, is one of the great letter writers of the century. Marchand's volumes contain, as the title pages announce, "the complete and unexpurgated text of all the letters available in manuscript and the full printed version of all others." About 2,900 letters are now known, largely as a result of his indefatigable researches over the past several decades, nearly 1,700 more than available in Rowland E. Prothero's turn-of-the-century edition. We now have other letters in their entirety that before we had only in part. While many of the best of Byron's letters have long been available, readers of Marchand's edition will find a number they have not seen before. Others already familiar will be read in substantially new texts, for Marchand publishes more than eighty-five percent of the letters from manuscripts or from facsimiles of manuscripts. Although the new edition does not radically change our picture of Byron, it fleshes it out, not merely through greater detail but by bringing diverse materials together in chronological order and in one place. Volume 11, in addition to the letters from Greece written in 1823–24, contains over fifty letters found too late for inclusion in chronological order in earlier volumes, as well as fourteen important letters to Scrope Davies that turned up in late 1976 at a Barclays Bank in London in a trunk untouched since 1820. This volume also has a section of additions and corrections to the first ten volumes. Ian Jack in *Review*, edited by Hoge and West (1982), adds to Marchand's list of corrections. A few letters not in Marchand are listed in the Rosenbaum and White *Index to English Literary Manuscripts.* Byron wrote a number of other letters, and several of these turn up each year. Nor does Marchand's edition contain Byron's formal, critical "letters," for example, those in defense of Pope to William Lisle Bowles (for which see "Prose"). The indexes to individual volumes are limited to proper names, but volume 12 has, along with an anthology of Byron's bons mots, a comprehensive index.

We read the letters as Byron wrote them, spelling and punctuation unmodernized. Marchand, by giving Byron's stylistic vagaries and erratic punctuation, allows the reader to capture the special flavor of the poet's mental processes as he moves quickly from one subject to another. Scholars may regret that Marchand does not indicate whether a letter has seen print before, nor will they find annotation as full as desirable. For more detailed information Marchand often refers readers to Prothero's edition (discussed below), where the notes are of such quality and amplitude that they will always be useful for students of Byron. Indeed, it would be highly desirable to have a volume of supplementary annotation and commentary to the Marchand edition comparable to the splendid concluding volume that James Corson has recently provided for the Grierson edition of Scott's letters. Also, Marchand's decision in volumes 7 to 11 to divide some of Byron's longer letters into paragraphs, "where a pause or change of subject is indicated," goes directly against modern editing practice. Besides paragraphing,

Marchand's text is open to question on other matters of editorial procedure (see, for example, Lovell's review in *KSJ*, 1975, and Drummond Bone's in *ByronJ*, 1979), but on the whole it seems reliable. Marchand sums up his experiences as editor in "The Manuscripts of Byron's Letters" (*Literary Research Newsletter*, 1979).

Marchand's edition contains few references to letters addressed *to* Byron by, among others, Murray, Kinnaird, and Leigh Hunt. Obviously it is necessary to read both sides of a correspondence in order to understand better the meaning of a relationship. A number of these correspondences have survived, chiefly in the Murray archive. *"To Lord Byron": Feminine Profiles Based upon Unpublished Letters 1807–1824*, edited by George Paston (Emily M. Symonds) and Peter Quennell (1939), is an interesting selection of letters from this archive—with accompanying commentary—addressed to the poet by thirteen women associated with him. Supplementing the tales of the lovelorn in this volume is Iris Origo's charming narrative "The Innocent Miss Francis and the Truly Noble Lord Byron" (*KSJ*, 1952). Other correspondences (or journals) are being edited or reedited—including those by Teresa Guiccioli, Shelley, Mary Shelley, Thomas Moore, and Hobhouse. But several major correspondences need to find their editors. Editing them not only would supplement our knowledge of Byron but would also augment valuably our understanding of Regency England.

The Victorians experienced Byron's letters largely through Thomas Moore's *Letters and Journals of Lord Byron, with Notices of His Life* (1830). Moore's two volumes had a liberating effect, still largely unexplored, on nineteenth-century prose, of which the most penetrating discussions remain Ruskin's in *Fiction, Fair and Foul* and *Praeterita. Letters and Journals*, edited by Rowland E. Prothero (later Lord Ernle) in six volumes (1898–1901), superseded Moore's collection and even today retains its usefulness for the quality of the editor's annotation. Prothero's texts of the letters are not always reliable, however, for he took many from printed sources. A large number of documents supplementary to the correspondence and diaries may be found in his appendixes: the texts of Byron's parliamentary speeches, the texts in the controversy with William Lisle Bowles on the merits of Pope's poetry, the texts on both sides of the quarrel with Robert Southey, and much other valuable material.

In the interval between Prothero and Marchand, Byron letters were published in the Earl of Lovelace's *Astarte* (1905); in the revised edition (1921), by the Countess of Lovelace, of that work; in *Lord Byron's Correspondence*, edited by John Murray (2 vols., 1922), which includes in bowdlerized form some of Byron's most interesting letters to Lady Melbourne, John Cam Hobhouse, and Douglas Kinnaird; in Iris Origo's *Byron: The Last Attachment* (1949), which contains the text of 156 letters and notes written by Byron to Teresa Guiccioli, as well as much other new material from the Gamba papers, other Italian sources, the Murray archives, and elsewhere; and in *Byron: A Self-Portrait*, edited by Peter Quennell (2 vols., 1950), which has slightly fewer than the fifty-six new letters the editor claims he has included. Not noted here are a number of articles since 1950 that publish new letters, since included in the Marchand edition. Now and then these articles retain value because of the background or context supplied, for example,

D. B. Green's in *KSJ,* 1956. Occasionally letters held by one institution have had separate publication, for example, T. G. Steffan's edition of forty-one letters, *From Cambridge to Missolonghi: Byron Letters at the University of Texas* (1971).

One-volume selections of Byron's letters abound. The best for comprehensiveness and the quality of its text is *Lord Byron: Selected Letters and Journals,* prepared by Marchand (1982). From his twelve-volume edition he has culled 134 complete letters, memorable passages from a number of others, the whole of the Alpine Journal of 1816 and the journal written in Cephalonia (Byron's last), as well as a self-contained selection from the poet's other journals. Older collections include *Lord Byron in His Letters,* edited by V. H. Collins (1927); *Letters of Lord Byron,* edited by R. G. Howarth (1933, rev. 1962) and introduced by André Maurois; *Byron: A Self-Portrait,* edited by Quennell (2 vols., 1950), a comprehensive selection with a complete text of the journals and "Detached Thoughts"; Quennell's *Byronic Thoughts: Maxims, Reflections, Portraits from the Prose and Verse of Lord Byron* (1961); *The Selected Letters of Lord Byron,* edited by Jacques Barzun (1953) with a stimulating introduction (rpt. in *The Energies of Art,* 1956); and *Byron: Selected Prose,* edited by Peter Gunn (1972), which gives a graphic impression of Byron's epistolary genius over the course of his career.

Biography: Nineteenth Century

To separate the study of Byron's work from that of his character and career is difficult, probably impossible. It has, in fact, often been remarked that moral judgments of the man and criticism of the poetry have been persistently fused and confused. Most biographies contain a certain amount of literary criticism, and few works of literary criticism before 1950 (other than studies of special topics) wholly separate from consideration the man behind the work. Of Byron we may say what Walter Jackson Bate has said of Samuel Johnson, that he was one of the "great experiencing natures." The human richness of his life fascinated the nineteenth century. It continues to fascinate in the twentieth. To the extent that a biography is a work of literary art created by a writer of human sympathy and psychological acumen, it can be supplemented but never superseded. More than any of the other Romantic poets, Byron attracted biographical attention in the nineteenth century as those who had known him hastened to put down their impressions.

No biography of Byron was ever authorized by his surviving relatives. The nearest approach to an official life was the commentary that Thomas Moore interwove in his *Letters and Journals of Lord Byron, with Notices of His Life* (2 vols., 1830), for which Moore garnered a number of valuable firsthand accounts of Byron from his friends and relatives. Those from whom he obtained information include Sir Walter Scott, who contributed his recollections of Byron, and Mary Shelley, whose written account (since lost) of the Swiss summer of 1816 stands behind Moore's narrative of that period. On Mary's contribution, see Paula R. Feldman, "Mary Shelley and the Genesis of Moore's *Life* of Byron" (*SEL,* 1980). Moore's own friendship with Byron began in November 1811 and ended with

Byron's death, although after 1816 he saw Byron only once for a few days on the Continent. John Murray soon issued a one-volume edition of Moore's *Life*, profusely annotated by Scott, Jeffrey, and others, and in this form it remained the standard biography into the twentieth century. Moore's personal knowledge of Byron, his often acute psychological analysis of the poet's character, and the primary documents he included or subsumed in his narrative make his biography still well worth consulting. For somewhat unfairly hostile discussion of it within the context of other period biographies, see Joseph W. Reed, Jr., *English Biography in the Nineteenth Century 1801–1839* (1966). See also Moore's "Notes for Life of Lord Byron" in his *Prose and Verse*, edited by Richard Herne Shepherd (1878). Biographies of Moore by Howard Mumford Jones (1937), Terence de Vere White (1977), and, especially, Hoover H. Jordan (2 vols., 1975) have much of value on Byron, as do Moore's own letters and journal. W. S. Dowden has edited the *Letters* (2 vols., 1964), for which see also the corrections noted in *PBSA*, 1969. Dowden is now reediting the journal from the original manuscript. His forthcoming six-volume edition will replace Lord John Russell's notoriously incomplete and inaccurate version (8 vols., 1853–56). Volume 1 appeared in 1983 and contains a number of references to Byron not included in the Russell edition. Dowden's "'Let Erin Remember': A Re-examination of the Journal of Thomas Moore" (*RUS*, 1975) discusses the significant differences between the manuscript and Russell's edition by focusing on passages dealing with Byron (and Sheridan). Hoover H. Jordan, "Byron and Moore" (*MLQ*, 1948), corrects the view that perceives Byron as the giant, Moore as the dwarf. Byron looked up to Moore for most of his life, though Moore's influence, poetic and personal, was strongest up to 1816, after which Byron's exile kept them largely apart. Jordan adduces interesting parallels between *Poems of Thomas Little* and *Hours of Idleness*. Thérèse Tessier, whose two books on Moore have interest for students of Byron, is at work on a study of the Byron-Moore relationship.

After Byron's death a number of writers thought to capitalize on their acquaintance with him by publishing books. It is often difficult to distinguish sharply between books that include original material and those that are hastily assembled compilations to catch a market. Several of these early biographies contain information not available in more recent accounts; others are useful chiefly in indicating how contemporaries viewed Byron. Although students should evaluate these books with caution and even with skepticism, many will yield unexpected insights into Byron. A multitude of them (including a number not mentioned in these pages) are evaluated in Samuel C. Chew's *Byron in England* (1924). Among the first in the field was Robert C. Dallas' *Recollections of the Life of Lord Byron, from the Year 1808 to the End of 1814* (1824). It is somewhat misleadingly entitled, for the intimacy between the two men reached its peak in 1812, and Dallas did not see Byron during Byron's Eastern tour of 1809–11. French and American editions (1825) contain material that John Cam Hobhouse, Byron's literary executor, managed to suppress in England. Dallas was immediately followed by Thomas Medwin, who knew Byron between November 1821 and March 1822 and who published his *Conversations of Lord Byron* also in 1824. This volume has been authoritatively edited by Ernest J. Lovell, Jr. (1966), with extensive contemporary commentary. Medwin's authenticity is more generally accepted today than it was several decades ago. The *Conversations* should be supplemented by Medwin's *Angler in Wales* (2 vols., 1834), in which he more openly passes judgment on Byron. On Medwin, see Lovell's excellent *Captain Medwin: Friend of Byron and Shelley* (1962).

It is regrettable that John Cam Hobhouse, who knew Byron better than any of his other friends did, never wrote a full-scale study. Hobhouse's journal, edited by his daughter, Lady Dorchester, as *Recollections of a Long Life* (6 vols., 1909 – 11), records impressions of Byron during his first tour, his life following in London, and his travels in Switzerland and Italy. Hobhouse gives an especially full account of Byron at the time of his marriage and separation, for which see also Hobhouse's "Byroniana" at the end of the second volume. Lady Dorchester published only a fraction of the total journal, perhaps one fifth of what Hobhouse wrote, and even by Victorian standards her editing of the manuscript is lax. (Almost all the journal is now in the British Library; the volumes for 3 Jan. to 1 July 1814 and for 29 Mar. 1815 to 5 Apr. 1816 are in the Berg Collection of the New York Public Library.) Scholars have infrequently consulted the original volumes of the journal, which shed light on numerous aspects of Byron's life, for example, his stay in Milan in 1816, where he met Stendhal and several Italian literary notabilities. Bits of Hobhouse's journal have recently been published by John Clubbe (see under *Manfred*) and by George M. Rosa (see under "Reputation and Influence: Europe. France"). Hobhouse's *A Journal through Albania* . . . (1 vol. and 2 vols., 1813), which chronicles his year with Byron in the Mediterranean (1809 – 10), was subsequently revised as *Travels in Albania* . . . (2 vols., 1855). The earlier editions have details on Byron not available in the later one, which, however, has information (with documents) about the controversies that swirled around Byron after his death. See also Hobhouse's *Substance of Some Letters, Written . . . during the Last Reign of the Emperor Napoleon* (1816, rev. 1817), in which most of the letters are to Byron, as the title page of the second edition openly declares, and *Historical Illustrations of the Fourth Canto of Childe Harold* . . . (1818, rev. 1818). Michael Joyce in *My Friend H: John Cam Hobhouse* (1948) makes use of Hobhouse's letters to Byron and also of unpublished portions of his diary. See also Robert E. Zegger, *John Cam Hobhouse: A Political Life, 1819 – 1852* (1973). Peter W. Graham has greatly advanced our understanding of the Hobhouse-Byron relationship through his edition, *Byron's Bulldog: The Letters of John Cam Hobhouse to Lord Byron* (1984).

An important early account is John Galt's *Life of Byron* (1830), which incorporates the author's firsthand impressions of Byron, chiefly in 1809 – 12, the period of the poet's first tour and the early months of his return to England. Doris Langley Moore, whose *The Late Lord Byron* (1961) contains acute commentary on nineteenth-century accounts of Byron, has validly criticized Galt's pretentiousness and vindictiveness. To be used even more cautiously than Galt are [John Watkins], *Memoirs of the Life and Writings of . . . Lord Byron* (1822), a work interesting mainly as showing one side of Byron's contemporary reputation, for it treats Byron as a "chartered Libertine" and fears his influence in morals, poetry, and politics; the pseudonymous (by "George Clinton," actually Sir James Bacon, P. C.) *Memoirs of the Life and Writings of Byron* (1824), a huge, boring compilation; Sir Egerton Brydges, *Letters on the Character and Poetical Genius of Lord Byron* (1824), a shrewd critical evaluation; Sir Cosmo Gordon (possibly a pen name), *The Life and Genius of Lord Byron* (1824); [Alexander Kilgour's] *Anecdotes of Lord Byron* (1825), an interesting compilation; and [Matthew Iley's] *Life, Writings, Opinions, and Times of . . . Lord Byron* (3 vols., 1825), a compilation full of spurious material, interesting mainly as a manifestation of popular interest. In French, we have *Lord Byron* (1824) by Louise Swanton Belloc, the most important early French biographer (one who corresponded with Stendhal about Byron), and the Marquis Carlo de Salvo, *Lord Byron en Italie et en Grèce* (1825), which contains material used by few biographers since. The most interesting contribution by an American is perhaps Andrews Norton's long critique in the *North American Review,* reprinted in London as *A Review of the Character and Writings of Lord Byron* (1826).

Leigh Hunt knew Byron in London, and he and his family lived in Byron's house in Pisa for some months in 1822. Six years later he published the most hostile book on Byron ever written by one who knew him: *Lord Byron and Some of His Contemporaries* (2 vols., 1828). In his *Autobiography* (1850, rev. 1860), reedited by J. E. Morpurgo in 1949, Hunt tempers his attacks on Byron. Isaac Nathan, Byron's collaborator on the *Hebrew Melodies,* put down his impressions of Byron in 1815–16 in *Fugitive Pieces and Reminiscences of Lord Byron . . .* (1829). During the poet's last days in Italy he often met one of the most beautiful hypocrites of the age, Lady Blessington, and in 1834 she published her *Conversations of Lord Byron.* Ernest J. Lovell, Jr.'s edition (1969) utilizes substantial material not previously published, and his introduction fully explores the relations between Byron and Lady Blessington. The *Conversations* should be supplemented by her *Idler in Italy* (2 vols., 1839).

James Hamilton Browne described Byron on his voyage to Greece in two articles in *Blackwood's Edinburgh Magazine* (1834). On the island of Cephalonia Byron met an impressionable Scottish army doctor and Methodist divine, James Kennedy, who wrote *Conversations on Religion with Lord Byron and Others* (1830). Although carelessly edited by his widow, who was almost certainly unaware that Byron was quizzing her husband, it is one of the most reliable of the book-length accounts of the poet's conversation. This period was also recorded by the young Pietro Gamba, brother of Teresa Guiccioli, in *A Narrative of Lord Byron's Last Journey to Greece* (1825). Other major witnesses of Byron's final months in Greece include Leicester F. C. Stanhope, *Greece in 1823 and 1824, to Which Are Added Reminiscences of Lord Byron* (1824; 2nd ed. 1825), also containing recollections by George Finlay, later the historian of Greece (Stanhope's first edition does not contain Finlay); Edward Blaquiere, *A Narrative of a Second Visit to Greece, including Facts Connected with the Last Days of Lord Byron* (1825); Julius Millingen, *Memoirs of the Affairs of Greece, with Various Anecdotes of Lord Byron* (1831), a rather drab account by a physician who attended Byron during his last illness; and William Parry, *The Last Days of Lord Byron* (1825).

Parry is the best, being blunt, humorous, and sympathetically understanding of his subject. A note by William St. Clair in *KSJ,* 1970, reveals that Parry was greatly helped in writing the book by a ghostwriter, Thomas Hodgskin. G. Wilson Knight in *Byron and Shakespeare* (1966) has interesting observations on Byron's relationship with Parry at Missolonghi.

Estimates of the reliability of all these informants, and many others, appear in Lovell's *His Very Self and Voice: Collected Conversations of Lord Byron* (1954) and Doris Langley Moore's *The Late Lord Byron* (1961). On Byron's apparently irrepressible need to mislead and mystify would-be Boswells, see the discerning analysis by St. Clair, "Bamming and Humming" (*ByronJ,* 1979). The student should be forewarned that a number of older accounts are not merely inaccurate but totally fictitious, for example, *Extract of a Letter, Containing an Account of Lord Byron's Residence in the Island of Mitylene,* published with *The Vampyre* (1819); *Narrative of Lord Byron's Voyage to Corsica and Sardinia . . .* (1824); and two articles in the *New Monthly Magazine* of 1835, the second signed "A.D." Mention should also be made here of the rather scurrilous *Don Leon* poems that purport to describe Byron's behavior to Lady Byron during their marriage. G. Wilson Knight surmised them to be by George Colman the Younger. Doris Langley Moore (in a 1976 editorial note to a reissue of her *Late Lord Byron*) more convincingly attributes *Don Leon* to Richard Paternoster ("Byronicus") and *Leon to Annabella* to another, and later, hand. On these poems, see the work of G. Wilson Knight and Louis Crompton, discussed under "Biography: Twentieth Century."

The second half of the nineteenth century featured several of the more spectacular biographical studies of Byron. Edward John Trelawny, who met Byron in January 1822 and sailed to Greece with him, published in 1858 his *Recollections of the Last Days of Shelley and Byron,* most recently edited by J. E. Morpurgo (1952). This and Trelawny's *Records of Shelley, Byron, and the Author* (1878), an elaboration and revision of the above, should be read in the light of Anne Hill's article "Trelawny's Family Background and Naval Career" (*KSJ,* 1956) and William St. Clair's revisionist biography, *Trelawny: The Incurable Romancer* (1977), both of which demonstrate Trelawny's remarkable talent for making fiction out of (occasional) fact. David Wright prepared a useful edition of Trelawny's *Records* for the Penguin English Library in 1973. H. Buxton Forman's edition of his *Letters* (1910) has many inaccuracies and includes only a fraction of the known surviving letters. St. Clair and Paula R. Feldman are now preparing a complete scholarly edition.

Teresa Guiccioli, who met Byron in April 1819 and remained his mistress until he left Italy in July 1823, assembled late in life *My Recollections of Lord Byron* (1 vol. in French, 1868; English trans., 2 vols., 1869). Although in accordance with the conventions of her day she could not be expected to tell the truth about her relation with Byron, the book deserves a careful reading by anyone interested in Byron's biography. It can be supplemented by Willis W. Pratt, "Twenty Letters of the Countess Guiccioli, Chiefly Relating to Lord Byron" (*UTSE,* 1951). Henri Guillemin in "Lamartine, Byron et Mme Guiccioli" (*RLC,* 1939) prints a number of letters from her to Lamartine about Byron. Forthcoming volumes of *Shelley and*

His Circle will include a great mass of new material on La Guiccioli. Her 1,700-page "Vie de Lord Byron en Italie," the manuscript of which is in the Biblioteca Classense in Ravenna, also contains much of value. Erwin A. Stürzl has published in the Salzburg Studies in English Literature a facsimile of the manuscript in French (9 vols., 1983). No transcription or translation is provided. The text is difficult to read, in part because the ink has faded badly, but much of it can be read with an effort. A tenth volume—containing an introduction by Stürzl— is promised. One may hope that the Salzburg edition will not preclude the eventual publication of a scholarly, annotated edition of this important source for Byron's life.

In addition to the biographical studies by Trelawny and Teresa Guiccioli, there appeared *Medora Leigh: A History and an Autobiography,* edited by Charles MacKay (1869), who includes original material on Byron and who supposes that Medora was Byron's daughter. In the next year Harriet Beecher Stowe's *Lady Byron Vindicated,* bitterly hostile toward Byron for his treatment of his wife, came out in volume form. [John Fox], *Vindication of Lady Byron* (1871), continued the attack on Byron for his behavior. The controversy over Byron fanned by these books (it also raged unchecked in contemporary periodicals) strongly colored the later Victorian view of Byron. It is reflected, for example, in Arnold's preface to his *Poetry of Byron* (1881) and, most brilliantly, in Trollope's indictment in *The Eustace Diamonds* (1873) of Lizzie Eustace's values through her fascination with Byron's "Corsair" image. Also denigrating to Byron, though possessing insight into the poet, is John Cordy Jeaffreson, *The Real Lord Byron* (2 vols., 1883). Rectifying the imbalance were John Morley's trenchant essay of 1870, the English translation (1872) of Karl Elze's solid and thoughtful full-length *Life of Lord Byron* (1870), and John Nichol's penetrating, brief *Byron* (1880). *Memoir of the Rev. Francis Hodgson,* edited by James T. Hodgson (2 vols., 1878), also presents a favorable portrait by one of Byron's Cambridge friends. Leslie A. Marchand has recently surveyed this relationship in " 'Childe Harold's Monitor': The Strange Friendship of Byron and Francis Hodgson" in *The Evidence of the Imagination,* edited by Donald H. Reiman et al. (1978).

Biography: Twentieth Century

GENERAL STUDIES

Modern biographers take their start from Lord Lovelace's *Astarte, a Fragment of Truth concerning... Lord Byron* (1905). In his famous but so nearly unreadable book—unreadable because the "fragment of truth" is so thickly swathed in inappropriate erudition, unnecessary digression, and angry prejudice—the poet's grandson revived the charge of incest that Harriet Beecher Stowe had made against Byron and Augusta Leigh in her *Lady Byron Vindicated* (1870) and buttressed it with fresh documentary evidence. The new edition of *Astarte,* which his widow, Lady Lovelace, issued in 1921, is an improvement on the original. Passages not germane to the subject were omitted and thirty-four unpublished letters of Byron (thirty-one to his sister, three to his wife) were added. R. E. Prothero expressed his conviction that the Lovelaces had established their case in "The End of the Byron Mystery" (*The Nineteenth Century and After,* 1921).

The biographies published during the nineteenth century were all incomplete and some of them badly distorted. Thus the way was open for a new full-length narrative of the poet's entire life. In 1912 Ethel C. Mayne published her two-volume *Byron,* an ample biography and the work of a serious, conscientious, and judicious writer. Mayne was the first biographer to accept the evidence in *Astarte* as proving the charge of incest. Throughout her long book she displays a fine and discriminating insight into her subject's character, in its strength as well as in its weakness. In 1924 she abridged her original two volumes into one and revised the work in the light of new evidence in *Lord Byron's Correspondence* (1922). Use was also made of fresh material in the Countess of Airlie's *In Whig Society, 1775–1818* (1921), a collection of unpublished letters by members of the Lamb family, including Lady Melbourne, whom Byron knew well and admired greatly. Mayne's revised edition is still on the whole a satisfactory life of Byron. It must be said, however, that her documentation is inadequate and her chronology loose and vague. Students may be repelled by her gushing style and sentimental tone. She takes up the cudgels for Lady Byron in *The Life and Letters of Anne Isabella, Lady Noel Byron* (1929), which uses the Lovelace papers and quotes extensively from them.

A biography called forth by the centennial of Byron's death is J. D. Symon's *Byron in Perspective* (1924)—in distorted perspective, one is constrained to remark, for Symon puts disproportionate emphasis on the poet's childhood in Aberdeen and on the influence of this early Scottish environment on his imagination and poetry. The Scottish influence is proclaimed as a new discovery, argued for, and exaggerated in T. S. Eliot's essay on Byron in *From Anne to Victoria,* edited by Bonamy Dobrée (1937), and reprinted in Eliot's *On Poetry and Poets* (1957) and in *English Romantic Poetry: Modern Essays in Criticism,* edited by M. H. Abrams (1960, rev. 1975).

Sir John C. Fox in *The Byron Mystery* (1924) reviewed the evidence for Byron's incest with his half-sister, Augusta, and handed down the verdict of guilty. His book, a rather dry legalistic treatise written from the point of view of one trained in law, should have settled the question once and for all but did not. In regard to this relationship, we may note that Augusta was Byron's *half*-sister, that she and Byron had grown up almost entirely apart, and that they came to know each other only in maturity. Another centennial biography, Roger Boutet de Monvel's *Vie de Lord Byron* (1924), focuses on Byron's life after he left England in April 1816.

John Drinkwater's *The Pilgrim of Eternity: Byron—A Conflict* (1925) contains admirable characterizations of Hobhouse, Shelley, Dallas, Moore, Hunt, Lady Blessington, Galt, Trelawny, and the companions of Byron in Greece who after his death rendered accounts of their experiences. Drinkwater firmly integrates Byron's character and career with his achievement as a poet. Critical judgments of the poems are incidental to his narrative purpose, but (with exceptions) they are felicitous and sensitive, the pronouncements of one who was himself a poet and who wrote with dignity and understanding. Drinkwater sets a high value on the historical tragedies, *Marino Faliero, The Two Foscari,* and *Sardanapalus,* as we would expect from a writer who had himself won conspicuous success in this department of drama.

Albert Brecknock's *Byron: A Study... in the Light of New Discoveries* (1926) is by a resident of Nottingham who writes informatively on the topography of the Byron country but superficially on other matters. He had long since issued a smaller work, *The Pilgrim Poet: Lord Byron of Newstead* (1911), which has still some small value for its excellent illustrations.

Helene Richter's *Lord Byron: Persönlichkeit und Werk* (1929) is one of the most reliable and authoritative of all books on Byron. It superseded such earlier biographies as Karl Elze's and rivaled the best that had been produced in England. Richter makes much of the conflicting elements of classicism and romanticism in Byron's character, tastes, and writing, a dichotomy she had already studied in an article, "Byron, Klassizismus und Romantik" (*Anglia,* 1924). In the skillful weaving together of a narrative of the poet's life, an analysis of his character, and an estimate of his work lies the value of this fine study.

By an odd coincidence no fewer than three, very dissimilar French writers—Charles Du Bos, André Maurois, and Maurice Castelain—were about this time engaged in the study of Byron. Du Bos's *Byron et le besoin de la fatalité* (1929, rev. 1957) may be classified among biographies rather than critical studies devoted primarily to the poetry, but actually Du Bos, in his preface, disclaims any intention to write either. His object, he says, is "exclusivement psychologique." His concern is to probe the secret workings of the conscience and to extract the ultimate drop of significance from every situation. His sinuous, undulating style avoids simplification in favor of involution and abstruseness. The result is a difficult, subtle, sometimes profound, and never altogether convincing study of Byron as *l'homme fatal.* Much is made of the delineations of the "Byronic hero," most notably in the portrait—which Du Bos holds to be a self-portrait—of Lara. Disregarding the rationalistic, critical, and satiric side of Byron's nature, Du Bos emphasizes the element of predestinarianism inherited from the Calvinism that Byron tried to reject but could not wholly rid himself of. Students may prefer to acquaint themselves with this book in Ethel Mayne's competent English version, *Byron and the Need of Fatality* (1932), in itself a revision of the 1929 edition. André Maurois published his *Byron* in 1930, and an English translation by Hamish Miles appeared in the same year. It is on an ampler scale and is a more serious piece of work than the same author's better-known *Ariel ou la vie de Shelley.* Unlike that work, it is not fictionalized biography; but though it is documented and makes use of a small amount of unpublished information it must be approached with caution. For the sake of dramatic effect Maurois occasionally takes liberties with chronology. He passes over subjects of importance, for example, Byron's quarrel with Southey or *The Vision of Judgment,* with the easiest unconcern, for no better reason, it would seem, than that their introduction would interrupt the lucid flow of the narrative. Maurois's psychology is clever, but he seldom sees beneath the surface of character. Into a revised version (1952) of the French text, but not of the English, Maurois inserted some entertaining matter from Iris Origo's *The Last Attachment* and from Peter Quennell's *Byron: A Self-Portrait.* Supplementary to this biography is Maurois's *Byron et les femmes* (1934). On a smaller scale, not so rich in the detail of personalities and not so amusing but more critical and trustworthy, is Maurice Castelain's *Byron* (1931), one of the best brief biographies. It has not been translated into English.

Peter C. Quennell's *Byron: The Years of Fame* (1935) was followed by *Byron in Italy* (1941). The first installment takes its title from Byron's life in London during the four years between the appearance of *Childe Harold* in March 1812 and his final departure from England in April 1816. It is somewhat misnamed, for these years were the years of notoriety rather than of the substantial and lasting fame that grew to European proportions during Byron's remaining eight years on the Continent. The setting is vivid, the narrative sparkling, and the psychology clear-cut though not original or profound. But Quennell evinces little critical insight into the poetry. In the second volume he attains a somewhat better adjustment of values but, even so, often loses sight of the poetry in elaborating on the picturesqueness of Byron's personality. In 1974 Quennell republished both volumes together, lightly revised, as *Byron.* Supplementary to this work is a short biography, *Byron* (1934). Quennell recounts his long involvement with Byron in a chapter of *The Sign of the Fish* (1960).

Until recently, Allegra, Byron's daughter by Claire Clairmont, attracted more attention than Ada, his daughter by Lady Byron. Armistead C. Gordon's *Allegra: The Story of Byron and Miss Clairmont* (1926) was soon superseded by Iris Origo's *Allegra* (1935), a revised edition of which appeared as part of *A Measure of Love* (1957). In *Claire Clairmont, Mother of Byron's Allegra* (1939), R. Glynn Grylls (Lady Mander) made use of unpublished passages in Claire's journal and of other fresh material. In manner, though not in substance, the narrative is, unfortunately, fictionalized. The episode of the unhappy affair with Byron is the high point in the story; but this is a biography of Claire, and it contains much not immediately pertinent to the study of Byron. Grylls also wrote biographies of Mary Shelley (1938) and of Trelawny (1950), both of which deal significantly with Byron.

Austin K. Gray's *Teresa, or Her Demon Lover* (1948), a narrative of Byron's relationship with Teresa Guiccioli and of her life after his death, is based on careful research but is somewhat fictionalized in a fashion indicated by the flashy title. In the English edition (1948) the title is changed to *Teresa: The Story of Byron's Last Mistress.* On the basis of unpublished documents, including the Gamba papers, Iris Origo in *The Last Attachment* (1949) told more fully than before the story of Byron and La Guiccioli. She weaves translations of the letters and other documents into her narrative (in English) and in an appendix gives the complete Italian text of Byron's many letters to his "last attachment." This work enriches greatly our knowledge of Byron's life in Italian society and of his relations with conspiratorial patriots, the *Carbonari.* Its publication was an event of major importance in the history of Byron studies.

Mention may be made here of four other books: T. G. Barber, *Byron —and Where He Is Buried* (1939); Duncan Gray's brief sketch *Life and Work of Lord*

Byron (1945); C. E. Vulliamy's chatty, unreliable *Byron* (1948); and Theodore G. Ehrsam, *Major Byron: The Incredible Career of a Literary Forger* (1951), which details what little is known about the forgeries by the "Major" (who sometimes assumed the nom de plume "de Gibler") of manuscripts by Byron, Shelley, and Keats.

G. Wilson Knight's *Lord Byron: Christian Virtues* (1952) lurks on the periphery of biographies. No other book has ever praised Byron so extravagantly. Beginning with the assertion that Byron is "our greatest poet in the widest sense of the term since Shakespeare," Knight has, before the close, hinted more than once at an analogy between Byron and his companions in Greece and Christ and the disciples. He assembles evidence of the poet's love of animals, his courage, benevolence, asceticism, self-discipline, humility, endurance, energy, courtesy, tact, forgiveness of wrongs, gratitude, unselfishness, tenderness, sweetness of disposition, hatred of tyranny and oppression, opposition to war save in the cause of freedom, and his qualities of statesmanship and leadership. Byron is a "superman," a Socrates, a Paul, a Zarathustra, a Gandhi, a Messiah; he is "Shakespearean drama personified"; he is "poetry incarnate." Knight does not tamper with the evidence quoted and rarely resorts to special pleading. Yet obviously something is wrong. The altogether admirable Byron who emerges bears only occasional resemblance to the flawed, striving human that we discover in other studies. Although Knight's conclusions cannot be trusted, his marshaling of evidence and the breadth of his knowledge remain impressive. He possesses an exceptional command of Byron's poetry and life. His claims for Byron's greatness as poet and man may seem less startling today, after Byron has undergone a major revaluation, than when he first made them. Students may, however, safely disregard his *Lord Byron's Marriage: The Evidence of Asterisks* (1957) unless they are interested in an account with generous quotations of the two rare *Don Leon* poems, here attributed to George Colman the Younger and treated—implausibly—as major evidence of the cause of Byron's separation from his wife. Knight concludes that the poet had "only one failing: homosexuality, together with its extension into the marriage-relationship," and that the cause of the separation was Byron's unnatural or unconventional sexual relations with Lady Byron, which were carried on, presumably, for the year that they lived together, before she realized what was happening to her. Knight, in order to prove Byron's homosexuality, suggests that his affairs with Caroline Lamb and even Teresa Guiccioli were only platonic—which is nonsense. The book is drawn wholly from published sources.

Not a biography but very useful to the student of Byron's life, character, and opinions is *His Very Self and Voice: Collected Conversations of Lord Byron* (1954), in which Ernest J. Lovell, Jr., assembled in chronological order the recollections and impressions of some 150 men and women who had the privilege of listening to Byron as he talked on all manner of subjects, from grave to frivolous. Lovell left aside the two principal records of Byron's conversations, those set down by Thomas Medwin and Lady Blessington, for subsequent publication (in 1966 and 1969). He does not include Byron's own records of, and comments on, his talk on the ground that they are easily accessible in editions of the letters and journals. Not all the accounts Lovell included were by friends or admirers of the poet.

Leigh Hunt is here with his bitter memories, as are Byron's wife and her parti-
sans. Against these we may set the recollections of such men as Hobhouse,
Shelley, and Thomas Moore.

Since its appearance, Leslie A. Marchand's *Byron: A Biography* (3 vols., 1957)
has been the standard life. The immensity of Marchand's task is suggested by the
fact that Byron's existence was already one of the most fully documented in literary history. In addition to the many volumes of the poet's letters and journals, a
remarkable number of major informants who knew Byron published memoirs or
biographies. In the twentieth century, at least ten full-length biographical studies
dealing with selected periods of Byron's life had appeared. With such a mass of
biographical matter already published, it is especially noteworthy that Marchand
looked at Byron with a fresh, unbiased eye, for the poet lives again in these
pages, which draw on an immense quantity of unpublished material, brought
alive by Marchand's own pilgrimage in the footsteps of Byron. (That pilgrimage is
vividly evoked in Richard D. Altick's *The Scholar Adventurers*, 1950.) The abundance of new materials effectively removed any temptation to give undue importance to a document or letter merely because it had not before been published.
The result is a sane, scholarly, and balanced view of the poet's life. Not least
among the virtues of this book is its scrupulous accuracy throughout. Although
Marchand, who did not have access to the Lovelace papers, does not solve finally
the question of Medora Leigh, he does provide answers to all the other major
questions (short of a full-scale psychological analysis), and his is now the first biography that students interested in a detailed presentation of the facts of Byron's
life should consult. His focus is almost entirely on the day-to-day existence of
the man. He does not pay much attention to the works or to the interaction between man and poet, nor does he set Byron in much detail against the age. (For
fuller discussion of the biography's achievements and limitations, see Ernest J.
Lovell, Jr., "Byron and the Problems of Literary Biography," *SAQ*, 1958.) In view of
Marchand's culminating work, I need mention here only a few essays of specialized biographical importance that have appeared since 1950. These include James
A. Notopoulos, "New Sources on Lord Byron at Missolonghi" (*KSJ*, 1955); Willis W.
Pratt, "Byron's 'Fantastic' Will of 1811" (*LCUT*, 1951); and William H. Marshall, "A
Byron Will of 1809" (*LC*, 1967).

Marchand's one-volume *Byron: A Portrait* (1970) is based on his three-volume study. Not merely an abridgment, it incorporates important research done in
the 1960s, particularly on Lady Byron and Augusta Leigh. Students seeking an introduction to Byron's life or wishing to gain an overall sense of his career should
begin with this book.

Even on Byron's already well-documented existence new perspectives based
on new material keep turning up. The 1960s and 1970s witnessed a flurry of significant biographical activity, most notably by Doris Langley Moore, who has made
several major contributions to our knowledge of Byron's life. *The Late Lord
Byron: Posthumous Dramas* (1961) is the first book-length study of the intricate
twistings and windings, "the dramas, tensions, feuds, frauds, and blunders," that
characterized the lives of Byron's friends, relatives, and acquaintances, as they

tried to deal with, or themselves caused, events that followed the poet's death. But Moore also reveals much about Byron as he lived on in the minds of those who knew him. She draws on the Lovelace papers (now on deposit at the Bodleian), the Hobhouse diaries, the great archives of John Murray, the Abinger collection (most of which is also on deposit at the Bodleian), and other manuscript sources. (In a pamphlet, *The Great Byron Adventure,* 1959, she tells the story of how she gained access to the Lovelace papers, until the early 1970s the most restricted of access of the major Byron collections.) Moore's first chapter contains a superb account of the burning after Byron's death of his memoirs, a subject she dealt with teasingly in the shrewdest of all novels on Byron, *My Caravaggio Style* (1959). Her chapter on Thomas Medwin, which passes severe moral judgments, offers a much less sympathetic view of its subject than does Lovell in his *Captain Medwin: Friend of Byron and Shelley* (1962). In her analyses of the personalities involved she is never afraid to take sides, yet her views carry conviction. No one can ever again write about Byron the man without consulting this book.

Moore's *Lord Byron: Accounts Rendered* (1974) views Byron through the history of his finances, an approach that until recent decades no biographer would have thought to take. What might seem forbidding if not hostile terrain becomes under her expert guidance an utterly fascinating narrative of Byron from a genuinely new perspective. Her reconstruction of the Italian years makes extensive use of the papers of Lega Zambelli, Byron's Italian secretary, in the British Library. They lay bare "Byron's domestic economy so minutely . . . that there can scarcely be anything comparable in the annals of famous men." But since the Zambelli papers deal only with the period in Italy, she returns to the incomparable Murray archives to fill in the picture for the earlier years, beginning with the poet's irresponsible father and his much underestimated mother. Her book becomes more than an account of Byron's finances: using the "vast pecuniary documentation as the connecting thread," she weaves in effect a coherent account of Byron's life, often stopping to consider neglected or little-known incidents if her new material warrants it or if it sheds light on Byron's character or behavior. Her title *Accounts Rendered* indicates this larger purpose, her study being as much an interpretation of Byron's increasing sense of responsibility as an analysis of his finances. No one is more knowledgeable than Moore in the byways of Byron biography, and she puts her knowledge to good use in a number of appendixes that take up related matters that did not fit into her narrative. For example, her appendix 2, "Byron's Sexual Ambivalence," evinces her particular combination of massive common sense, psychological acuity, and exceptional command of sources, published and unpublished.

Moore's *Ada Countess of Lovelace: Byron's Legitimate Daughter* (1977) is the first full biography of Ada. Famous from her birth, "Ada, daughter of my heart" (as Byron, who had last seen her at the age of one month, apostrophized her in *Childe Harold* 3), emerges as an intriguing figure in her own right and, in personality, a fascinating, ultimately disastrous mixture of her parents' qualities. Ada married William King (later the first Earl of Lovelace) at a young age, had several children in rapid succession, demonstrated an impressive mathematical gift, and strove valiantly throughout her life to achieve a career of her own. Her gambling debts and her desperate efforts to conceal them form one of Moore's most vivid chapters. Equally gripping is her account of Ada's prolonged, excruciating dying from cancer of the uterus, a narrative comparable to the grimmest death scenes in Victorian fiction. The inflexible Lady Byron tried to dominate her daughter and her son-in-law, indeed everyone with whom she had dealings, and in significant ways she dominates this book. Using the abundant primary materials in the Lovelace collection (then under Lady Wentworth's iron hand), the Bodleian, and other depositories, Moore gives not only a considered account of Ada but also, through her, graphic glimpses into the realities of woman's life during the first half of the nineteenth century. Supplementary to Moore's biography is Dorothy K. Stein, "Lady Lovelace's Notes: Technical Text and Cultural Context" (*VS,* 1984), which analyzes her work describing Charles Babbage's "Analytical Engine."

Malcolm Elwin has also made several impressive contributions to Byron biography. *Lord Byron's Wife* (1962) is now the definitive account of its announced subject and of the poet's relations with Annabella. After presenting in depth her early life, the book closes with a detailed narrative, copiously documented, of the first four months of 1816. It draws heavily on the rich hoard of the Lovelace papers and corrects the bias and inaccuracies evident in Mayne's *Life and Letters of . . . Lady Byron.* Elwin clearly demonstrates the increasing unreliability of Annabella's deliberately composed accounts of Byron's words and actions, establishing their dates of origin and contrasting with telling effect her earlier and later reports of the same episode or conversation with Byron. He quotes with great generosity from his original sources, which comprise perhaps one half of his book. *Lord Byron's Wife* dispels finally the "mystery" behind the separation of Byron from his lady. The separation seems to have come about not because of homosexuality, or unusual sexual practices, or incest with Augusta but because of total incompatibility between the pair, "unhappy differences" as the never-used draft bill to compel execution of the deed of separation put it.

Two other books by Elwin illuminate the context of Byron's biography. *The Noels and the Milbankes: Their Letters for Twenty-Five Years 1767–1792* (1967) documents with commentary the earlier history of Lady Byron's family. Elwin's posthumous *Lord Byron's Family: Annabella, Ada, and Augusta 1816–1824,* edited by Peter Thomson (1975), describes the interactions during Byron's lifetime of the three persons mentioned in the title. Elwin elucidates as never before the "limited friendship" between Annabella and Augusta (of which Byron knew nothing). It came into being after his departure for the Continent when Annabella hypocritically tried to "reclaim" Augusta by insisting on regularly reading Byron's letters to her. Elwin's presentation of the situation in England illumines Byron's baffled response in Italy. Again drawing on the Lovelace papers, Elwin weaves a narrative composed in almost equal parts of biographical commentary, social history, and generous quotations from original documents. Elwin's three books, it should be noted, by no means exhaust the research potential of the Lovelace collection. In fact, with a few notable exceptions, students of Byron have yet to make use of the wealth of archival material in it and in other manuscript collections.

Peter Gunn and Catherine Turney consider, respectively, Byron's half-sister, Augusta, and her daughter, considered by some to be also *his* daughter, Medora Leigh. In *My Dearest Augusta* (1968) Gunn largely dispels the myth of Augusta as the scatterbrained "Goose" of earlier biographies by convincingly presenting her not only as warmhearted and humorous but also as able and intelligent. If not possessing (like Astarte in *Manfred*) "a mind to comprehend the universe," Augusta emerges with a mind that comprehended Byron and as very much a person in her own right. Gunn makes Byron's attraction for her much more understandable. Based only on published sources, his nicely synthesized and vividly written account devotes two thirds of its space to the years through 1816, when Byron left England, and only the final third to the period afterward (Augusta died in 1851). Gunn is not convinced that Medora Leigh is Byron's child. Nor is Leslie A. Marchand, who writes in his 1970 *Byron* that "no positive proof survives on either side of the question." One who is convinced is Catherine Turney, who in *Byron's Daughter: A Biography of Elizabeth Medora Leigh* (1972) claims Byron as "father of the child." Her book presents the fullest available history of Elizabeth Medora, or "Libby," but contains an unsettling number of factual errors and, though drawing on some archival work, relies largely on published sources. In *Ada,* Doris Langley Moore provides a more realistic assessment of Medora as well as considerable fresh material on which to form an estimate. For her, Medora is *not* Byron's daughter.

Bernard Grebanier's *The Uninhibited Byron: An Account of His Sexual Confusion* (1970) adds to rather than clarifies the confusion. His book is full of unfounded speculation and dubious methodology, for example, his use of Disraeli's novel *Venetia* to simulate Byron's relationship with his mother. Grebanier also takes the *Don Leon* poems, which so intrigued G. Wilson Knight in *Lord Byron's Marriage,* to interpret Byron's relationship with Annabella. Although these poems are perhaps not to be discounted entirely, they afford more grounds for fueling speculation than for ascertaining truth. Limited to published sources, Grebanier's study also retells without adding anything new the stories of Byron's involvement with Caroline Lamb and with Augusta.

John S. Chapman in *Byron and the Honourable Augusta Leigh* (1975) attempts by tortuous and inaccurate use of evidence to reopen the case against incest. His argument fails to prove that it did not occur. On the whole, the final word may be left with Marchand: "The extant evidence that Byron had sexual relations with Augusta does not amount to *legal* proof. All that can be said is that the circumstantial evidence in Byron's letters to Lady Melbourne cannot be ignored, and that certain aspects of his life and correspondence cannot be explained sensibly in any other terms." In 1975 Margot Strickland in *The Byron Women* devoted chapters to eight of the females whose correspondence with Byron had been quoted by Paston and Quennell in *"To Lord Byron"* (1939).

A number of illustrated biographies have appeared in recent years. Derek Parker's *Byron and His World* (1968) is virtually an iconography of Byron, with 128 pages of pictures of the poet, his family, friends, enemies, and the places where he lived or with which he was otherwise associated. The biographical commentary, although seldom concerned with the illustrations, is gracefully written. The pictures are of unequal quality and reliability. In 1969 Mondadori put out Italian and French editions of *George Byron,* a lavishly illustrated picture book that includes reproductions of a number of rarely seen paintings inspired by Byron's poems. Peter Brent's *Lord Byron* (1974) has fine illustrations, including a number of color plates, and an innocuous text. Another picture book is Vera Cacciatore's *Shelley and Byron in Pisa* (1961). Also well illustrated is Frederick Raphael's *Byron* (1982), a clever book by a clever man. Raphael's "The Byronic Myth" (*ByronJ,* 1984) probes the elusive mythic dimensions of Byron's continuing appeal. Gilbert Martineau's pleasant *Lord Byron: La Malédiction du génie* (1984) does not seem overly concerned with accuracy and adds nothing to what is known about Byron. Altogether the most readable of recent popular biographies is Elizabeth Longford's vivid *Life of Byron* (1976).

More an interpretation than a biography, Gabriel Matzneff's *La Diététique de Lord Byron* (1984) disclaims being a work of scholarship. The book radiates for its subject the enthusiasm of the dedicated admirer. Matzneff believes that professional and nonprofessional approaches can complement and illumine each other, and in this case they most certainly do. By "diététique" Matzneff means not merely the diets that obsessed Byron since adolescence but, even more, "his philosophy of existence and his *art de vivre:* the manner in which this cheerful pessimist, this generous egoist, this austere epicure, this impassioned skeptic . . . loved, wrote, and reacted to society and to God." Written with wit and elegance, Matzneff's personal statement of admiration ponders the Byronic character from multiple angles and often comes up with fresher insights than do the sober academic studies from which it professes to distance itself. A man of letters himself, Matzneff knows his Byron and has thought about life. Every page in this book reflects his understanding of both.

A number of biographical studies have appeared in briefer form. Ernest Bernbaum provided a concise sketch of Byron's life and character in his *Guide through the Romantic Movement* (1930, rev. 1949). Worth mentioning also is Sir Herbert Read's psychological interpretation, *Byron* (1951), in the Writers and Their Work series put out by the British Council. Arguably the best succinct life of Byron is David Erdman's forty-page essay in volume 3 of *Shelley and His Circle,* edited by Kenneth Neill Cameron (1970). Erdman's strongly political interpretation of Byron is considered below under "Ideas and Beliefs." Specialized studies include Howard O. Brogan, "Byron So Full of Fun, Frolic, Wit, and Whim" (*HLQ,* 1974), a well-documented defense of Byron's genial personal qualities, and his "Lady Byron: 'The Moral Clytemnestra of Her Lord' " (*DUJ,* 1974), a summary of the new materials in Elwin's and Moore's interpretations of Lady Byron's character. Myra Stark, "The Princess of Parallelograms, or the Case of Lady Byron" (*KSJ,* 1982), argues that, however unpleasant she may have been personally, Lady Byron has not been given credit by her and Byron's biographers for her serious intellectual interests and for her support of midcentury feminist agitation. A. P. Hudson, "The 'Superstitious' Lord Byron" (*SP,* 1966), focuses particularly on whether or not Byron believed in ghosts. On this subject, see also Wolfgang Franke's essay under "Mature Satires" and, a related study, Elizabeth Longford's somewhat speculative "Byron and Satanism" (*Illustrated London News,* 1977). Thérèse Tessier's

"Aux racines de l'Eros byronien: Les révélations de la correspondance" (in *Romantisme anglais et Eros,* with preface by Christian La Cassagnère, 1982) considers Byron's emotional life as revealed in the first three volumes of Marchand's edition of the *Letters and Journals.*

On the fringes of Byron biography is Peter Shankland's *Byron of the Wager* (1975), on Byron's grandfather, and A. L. Rowse's *The Byrons and the Trevanions* (1977), which argues for the importance of the conjunction of the Byron and Trevanion strains in making the poet the man he was. Rowse has little to say directly on Byron but claims that Byron's Cornish inheritance helped determine his temperament, "for he was the most autobiographical and egotistic of writers." Rowse also has an article on this subject in *Byron: A Symposium,* edited by John Jump (1975). Violet W. Walker and Margaret J. Howell have completed an as yet unpublished book, "The House of Byron: A History of the Family from the Norman Conquest."

Byron has a way of taking over those around him. What happened to Shelley in his lifetime seems to be happening to the successive volumes of *Shelley and His Circle* in ours. Students of Byron's biography should not miss volumes 3 and 4, edited by K. N. Cameron (1970). In volume 3, as noted earlier, David V. Erdman surveys Byron's "Life and Works"; in 4, his " 'Fare Thee Well'—Byron's Last Days in England" adds greatly to our knowledge of the complex political motivation behind the newspaper attacks on Byron in 1816. Shorter essays, including one by Gavin de Beer on Byron and Shelley's tour around Lake Geneva in 1816, provide necessary background for the letters and poems published. Volumes 5 and 6, edited by Donald H. Reiman (1973), contain a number of Shelley's letters to Byron, with enlightening commentary. Volume 6 also has an appendix of Byron manuscripts. The forthcoming volumes 7 and 8, also edited by Reiman, contain documents from 1816 to 1820 and center on Byron. Volume 7 includes a new text of *Beppo* and an essay on it by Jerome J. McGann, many letters to Byron, letters from Byron and Fanny Silvestrini to Teresa Guiccioli, as well as other Byroniana of late 1819. Doucet Devin Fischer contributes essays on Byron's Venetian mistresses and on "Countess Guiccioli's Byron." Volume 8, covering part of 1820, has in addition to more Byron letters over 120 notes and letters from Teresa Guiccioli to Byron. Other essays and commentaries on Shelley material refer to Byron. Later volumes will also have a strong Byron interest. With the publication of volumes 7 and 8, the completion of Marchand's *Byron's Letters and Journals,* and the gradual completion of McGann's *Lord Byron: The Complete Poetical Works,* with its valuable commentaries, the grounds are being prepared for a possible new surge of biographical activity.

One manifestation of this new surge is Louis Crompton's essay "*Don Leon,* Byron, and Homosexual Law Reform" (in *Literary Visions of Homosexuality,* ed. Stuart Kellogg, 1983). Crompton's essay appears, reworked, as part of the epilogue to his *Byron and Greek Love: Homophobia in 19th-Century England* (1985). In this book title and subtitle share equal billing. Three of the nine chapters focus on homophobia in Regency England. Even in the Byron chapters, Crompton often interrupts his narrative to discuss English attitudes regarding homosexuality, attitudes that in the early nineteenth century often changed from year to year. Despite having two chief foci, Crompton neatly meshes foreground (Byron) with background (homophobia). He agrees with Doris Langley Moore that Byron was "a bisexual in whom the heterosexual element predominated," and one may read his study as an elaborate footnote to her appendix "Byron's Sexual Ambivalence" in *Lord Byron: Accounts Rendered*. Crompton believes, however, "that the heterosexual-homosexual balance in Byron's makeup shifted from time to time." He tries "to analyze and—to the extent that such mysteries can be accounted for—give some suggestions as to why the homosexual side of [Byron's] nature came to the fore at certain moments of his life." This he does with considerable success. He could not have written his study without the new biographical material made available in recent decades, notably in Marchand's edition of Byron's letters but also in the work of Elwin, Moore, and Marchand himself. On the basis of this material, Crompton argues "that Byron's bisexuality was far more central to his experience and personality than his biographers have so far been willing to grant." He finds, for example, that Byron's "most urgent reason for traveling to the East" was his need to satisfy his homosexual urges. No one will deny that Byron viewed the East as a land where freer sexual mores prevailed, but one may still believe, even after Crompton, that Byron wished to leave England to experience freedoms other than sexual. However, by isolating the bisexual strand in Byron's emotional makeup, Crompton makes clear its relation to the larger picture. As much a study of Byron's sexuality as of his bisexuality, this book helps to explain the behavior and creativity of a man for whom the sexual drive was of tremendous urgency.

Although less concerned with Byron's poetry than with his biography, Crompton illuminates passages in a number of poems, chiefly lyrics written early and late, those to "Thyrza," John Edleston (inexplicably "Edlestone" throughout), and to Lukas Chalandrutsanos. References in *Childe Harold* and *Don Juan*, in stanzas published and unpublished, come into focus—for example, those to William Beckford. Crompton also finds Byron's bisexuality a factor in the psychology of the Byronic hero, a subject one wishes he had explored more than he does. But he has opened up Byron—and by extension other nineteenth-century writers—in ways that should stimulate discussion. This study is informed by Crompton's impressive knowledge of literature treating homosexuality in England and in Europe and of laws affecting homosexuals; by excursions back into antiquity, forward into the present, and into non-Western as well as Western cultures; and by detailed exposition, whenever relevant, of the Regency background. By casting his net widely, Crompton throws light both on Byron and on the emotional currents of Byron's age. He makes good use of unpublished materials, including key letters to Byron from Charles Skinner Matthews, the poet's close friend at Cambridge. He has interesting things to say about Hobhouse but, surprisingly, does not appear to have looked at Hobhouse's journal. We need not agree with every interpretation Crompton advances—indeed, he often advances alternative ones himself or agrees with those proposed by others—but this book convinces largely because its author knows his material, on Byron no less than on homosexuality, and presents it without stridency or polemics.

PARTIAL BIOGRAPHIES

Southwell (1806–07). Several monographs illuminate one or another period or episode in Byron's life. In *Byron at Southwell: The Making of a Poet* (1948), Willis W. Pratt worked, so far as regards fresh material, within the limitations of the manuscripts at the University of Texas, but though his study largely repeats familiar facts regarding Byron's holidays from Harrow and Cambridge, Pratt includes some unpublished verse and a number of new letters.

The Mediterranean (1809–11). Gordon Kent Thomas, *Lord Byron's Iberian Pilgrimage* (1983), gracefully narrates Byron's 1809 visit to Portugal and Spain. Thomas corrects earlier accounts in detail, glosses the Iberian stanzas of *Childe Harold* 1, and points out the lasting significance of Byron's sojourn for his life and writings. A useful map and numerous illustrations complement the text. William A. Borst's *Lord Byron's First Pilgrimage* (1948) enlarges our understanding of the first two cantos of *Childe Harold* by placing the poem in the context of records of contemporary travel in the Iberian Peninsula, the Mediterranean, and the Near East. Borst traces in detail the beginnings of Byron's cosmopolitanism, his reaction against British insularity, and his sympathy with Greek aspirations for independence. Supplementary to Borst is C. G. Brouzas' monograph *Byron's Maid of Athens: Her Family and Surroundings* (*WVUPP*, 1949). Hugh Tregaskis, *Beyond the Grand Tour: The Levant Lunatics* (1979), has a chapter on Byron and Hobhouse. William St. Clair, *Lord Elgin and the Marbles* (1967), provides valuable background for Byron's first visit to Greece. Stanton Garner's "Lord Byron and Midshipman Chamier in Turkey" (*KSJ*, 1981) contains a firsthand description from an 1832 novel of Byron aboard the *Salsette* in 1810 on his way to Constantinople. Terence Spencer's *Fair Greece, Sad Relic: Literary Philhellenism from Shakespeare to Byron* (1954) is essential reading for anyone wishing to understand Byron's view of Greece.

Switzerland (1816). Claire-Eliane Engel's *Byron et Shelley en Suisse et en Savoie: Mai-octobre 1816* (1930), though inaccurate in details, retains some value for the Swiss period. Heinrich Straumann's Nottingham lecture, *Byron and Switzerland* (1948–49), traces the poet's movements and emotions during the summer of 1816. It has a useful little map of his travels in the Alps. H. W. Häusermann's *The Genevese Background* (1952) adds detail on Byron's sojourn of 1816, as does Gavin de Beer's "Meshes of the Byronic Net in Switzerland" (*ES*, 1962; rev. and in French in *Etudes de Lettres*, 1970). In 1911 W. M. Rossetti edited the diary of John William Polidori, Byron's traveling physician in 1816. The letters of Percy and Mary Shelley, and Mary's introduction to the 1831 edition of *Frankenstein*, supplement Polidori's account of this period. Marion Kingston Stocking edited in 1968 *The Journals of Claire Clairmont, 1814–1827.* With David Stocking, she is preparing an edition of the letters of Charles and Claire Clairmont and of Fanny Godwin. Claire, Byron's mistress in 1816, was the mother of Allegra, born in January 1817. Few accept as genuine today the reminiscences attributed to Claire in William Graham's *Last Links with Byron, Shelley, and Keats* (1898). Elma Dangerfield, *Byron and the Romantics in Switzerland* (1978), has interesting illustrations. A full-length study of the Swiss period, setting Byron against his contemporaries and his times, may eventually be expected from John Clubbe.

Pisa (1821–22). Without altering in essentials a familiar story, C. L. Cliné in *Byron, Shelley, and Their Pisan Circle* (1952) has filled in gaps in our knowledge and has placed this new information against the background of Byron's life in Tuscany in 1821–22. Cline's book, based on archival research in Italy and careful in its scholarship, valuably supplements other biographies. For further details of the Pisan sojourn, one may turn to the journal of Edward E. Williams, edited with other materials by Frederick L. Jones in 1951. William H. Marshall's *Byron, Shelley, Hunt, and the* Liberal (1960) opens with a survey of the relations between the three writers prior to Hunt's arrival in Pisa in 1822 and of the speculations in England concerning the forthcoming *Liberal.* Subsequent sections deal with each of the journal's four numbers and the public reaction to them, followed by a discussion of the "Aftermath: 1823–1828." Marshall's book, the standard work on its subject, traces an important chapter not only in the lives of those concerned but also in the history of publishing. If while abroad Byron usually avoided the English, he welcomed Americans—the subject of Paul R. Baker's "Lord Byron and the Americans in Italy" (*KSJ,* 1964).

Greece (1823–24). Byron's curiosity about Greece and his two visits to that country have always aroused interest. I have already mentioned William A. Borst on his first sojourn. Harold Nicolson's *Byron: The Last Journey: 1823–1824* (1924), obviously written under the influence of Lytton Strachey, belongs to the "depedestalizing" school of biography, the mode of the 1920s. It largely supersedes Richard Edgecumbe's *Byron: The Last Phase* (1909), covering the same period though looking back to Byron's arrival in Pisa in November 1821. Nicolson's literary affiliation is apparent not only in the cold brilliance of the style but also in a detached objectivity distrustful of all sentiment. Yet the narrative, which in its initial stages resembles a cynical comedy of society, gradually changes in tone as Byron's bearing and conduct during the last journey win the sympathy and even the admiration of this cautious, clever skeptic. Even today this book remains one of the most intelligent, the most humanizing, the most touching of the biographical works on Byron. To the 1940 edition Nicolson added a valuable supplementary chapter summarizing Hobhouse's marginalia in his copy of Moore's *Byron.*

The records of the Greek Committee, which was organized in England to promote philhellenism and possible intervention in the Greek War of Independence and to which Byron was attached, have been examined and published by Esmond S. de Beer and W. Seton in "Byroniana: The Archives of the London Greek Committee" (*The Nineteenth Century and After,* 1926). *Les Philhellènes et la Guerre de l'Indépendance,* edited by Eugène Dalleggio (1949), prints letters from the Greek deputies to Byron. Among recent studies, Elizabeth Longford's *Byron's Greece* (1975) focuses both on the first visit and on the return. Throughout, the text comes alive in Jorge Lewinski's stunning photographs. Every study of the Greek War of Independence, in which Byron played a small but memorable part, considers his involvement. The authoritative account is Douglas Dakin, *The Greek Struggle for Independence 1821–1833* (1973), which sets Byron's role in perspective within the larger conflict. Equally comprehensive is William St. Clair, *That Greece Might Still Be Free: The Philhellenes in the War of Independence* (1972), which considers in detail the extensive foreign participation. Joseph Braddock, *The Greek Phoenix* (1972), chronicles the familiar story of Byron's involvement, as does C. M. Woodhouse in *The Philhellenes* (1969). A popular account is David Howarth, *The Greek Adventure: Lord Byron and Other Eccentrics in the War of Independence* (1976). For many related studies see below "Reputation and Influence: Europe. Greece."

BYRON AND HIS LITERARY CONTEMPORARIES

The Major Romantics. Studies of Byron often neglect the poet's interactions with other figures and with the social context. As Augustine Birrell long ago observed, "it is only by reading the lives and letters of his astonished contemporaries that you are able to form some estimate of the power of Byron." Notable lacunae in this regard are up-to-date accounts of his relationships, poetic and personal, with a number of his major contemporaries. The student might begin with Chew's chapter "The Opinions of Great Contemporaries" in *Byron in England.* A useful overview, taking in critics such as Lamb as well as the poets, is Nina Diakonova, "Byron and the English Romantics" (*ZAA,* 1970). The forum "On Byron" (*SIR,* 1977) often relates Byron to his major contemporaries. John Clubbe and Ernest J. Lovell, Jr., in *English Romanticism: The Grounds of Belief* (1983), passim, consider Byron's relationship to the older, as well as to the younger, generation of Romantics. (For Byron's awareness of earlier writers, see the section below, "Byron and Literary Tradition.")

Shelley. Only Byron's relationship with Shelley has been thoroughly explored. "The friendship between Byron and Shelley was the most important relationship in the experience of either," declares John Buxton, without excessive exaggeration, in *Byron and Shelley: The History of a Friendship* (1968). The two poets saw each other on intimate terms, in Switzerland and Italy, for a total of about twelve months. Buxton's account supersedes Manfred Eimer's in *Die persönlichen Beziehungen zwischen Byron und den Shelleys* (1911) and Isabel C. Clarke's in her popularized *Shelley and Byron: A Tragic Friendship* (1934). Although Buxton states that he has dealt only briefly with the effect of the friendship on each's poetry, the pages on this subject are among his best. Unfortunately, he makes little use of unpublished material, and the scarcity of notes makes it difficult to determine sources for his statements. Frederick L. Jones's edition of Shelley's *Letters* (2 vols., 1964) contains much matter of significance to the student of Byron. Students should also consult the massive biographies of Shelley by N. I. White (2 vols., 1940; rev. 1947) and Richard Holmes (1975), the latter, however, often inaccurate in detail. Charles E. Robinson's *Shelley and Byron: The Snake and Eagle Wreathed in Fight* (1976), discussed subsequently in "Criticism: General," takes up the poetic interaction between Byron and Shelley, but Robinson also outlines the biographical context. Nathaniel Brown, *Sexuality and Feminism in Shelley* (1979), has an intriguing discussion of Byron's sexuality in contrast to Shelley's. Also worth consulting are D. G. James's Nottingham lecture, *Byron and Shelley* (1951), which argues (wrongly, in my view) that "Shelley was not what Byron needed" when in 1816 there was "a chance that he might escape from the poison of Romanticism," and E. A. Stürzl's overview, "Byron & Shelley: A Study in Literary Inter-relations" (*ByronJ*, 1979). Donald H. Reiman scatters astute observations on the relationship between the two poets in volumes 5 and 6 of *Shelley and His Circle*, as does J. Drummond Bone, "On 'Influence,' and on Byron and Shelley's Use of Terza Rima in 1819" (*KSMB*, 1981).

Wordsworth. The recently published love letters between Wordsworth and his wife indicate that Byron and Wordsworth met early in May 1812. Since Byron offered to frank Wordsworth's letters home, the two men must have begun on terms of some cordiality. But the relationship did not remain unclouded for long. It became arguably the bitterest of Romantic rivalries, and one of enormous (and fruitful) consequence for Byron. In awaiting a comprehensive study of the Byron-Wordsworth relationship, we may savor Hazlitt's various pithy comparisons (most easily traced through the index to the P. P. Howe edition of his *Complete Works*) and A. C. Swinburne's "Wordsworth and Byron" (1884; rpt. in *Miscellanies,* 1886), hostile to Byron. See also Ernest J. Lovell, Jr., on their respective attitudes toward nature, in *Byron: The Record of a Quest* (1949), and Michael G. Cooke, "Byron and Wordsworth: The Complementarity of a Rock and the Sea" (*WC,* 1980), which, covering much ground in brief compass, nicely juxtaposes related themes, for example, each's attitude toward the sea. Cooke's essay has been republished in *Lord Byron and His Contemporaries: Essays from the Sixth International Byron Seminar,* edited by Charles E. Robinson (1982). See also studies by Gordon K. Thomas and Peter J. Manning in *Byron: Poetry and Politics,* edited by Erwin A. Stürzl and James Hogg (1981). Thomas' "Strange Political Bedfellows: Inkel and Wordsworth in Iberia" reveals more affinities between Wordsworth's and Byron's political positions, particularly in regard to Spain and Portugal, than one might have supposed. Thomas returns to the Byron-Wordsworth relationship in two important articles, "Wordsworth, Byron, and 'Our Friend, the Storyteller' " (*Dutch Quarterly Review of Anglo-American Letters,* 1983) and "Allies and Guerillas: The Peninsula Campaigns of Wordsworth and Byron" (*WC,* 1983). I mention Manning's study ("Tales and Politics: *The Corsair, Lara,* and *The White Doe of Rylstone*") under "Criticism: Individual Works." Marilyn Butler acutely discusses Byron's later attitude toward Wordsworth in her review of McGann's Don Juan *in Context* (*EIC,* 1978). M. L. Peacock's edition of *The Critical Opinions of William Wordsworth* (1950) reprints the poet's comments on Byron.

Coleridge and Blake. Byron-Coleridge remains another major lacuna. E. L. Griggs, who earlier published Coleridge's five letters to Byron in "Coleridge and

Byron" (*PMLA*, 1930), offers a brief sketch of their acquaintance in 1815–16 in the introduction to volume 3 of the *Collected Letters of Samuel Taylor Coleridge* (1959). Byron also comes under discussion in George Whalley's "Coleridge and John Murray" (*QR*, 1951). *Coleridge's Miscellaneous Criticism*, edited by T. M. Raysor (1936), reprints a number of hostile comments on Byron's poetry and views. Jerome McGann speculates on Byron's response to the *Biographia* in *Don Juan in Context*. Like most of his contemporaries, Byron never heard of Blake, but Blake knew of Byron and responded particularly to Byron's *Cain*. See Leslie Tannenbaum, "Byron's *Cain* and Blake's *The Ghost of Abel*" (*MP*, 1975); Irene Tayler, "Blake Meets Byron on April Fool's" (*ELN*, 1978); and Martin Bidney, "*Cain* and *The Ghost of Abel*: Contexts for Understanding Blake's Response to Byron" (*BS*, 1979). Bernard Blackstone's writings on Byron often set the younger poet against Blake.

Southey and Landor. Byron's important, complex relationship to Robert Southey awaits authoritative discussion. *New Letters of Robert Southey*, edited by Kenneth Curry (2 vols., 1965), contains references to Byron. The first part of Fannie E. Ratchford's "Notes on Byron" (*TxSE*, 1924) is on the Byron-Southey quarrel. See also C. L. Cline, "Byron and Southey: A Suppressed Rejoinder" (*KSJ*, 1954); E. L. de Montluzin, "Southey's 'Satanic School' Remarks: An Old Charge for a New Offender" (*KSJ*, 1972–73); W. R. Runyan, "Bob Southey's Diabolical Doggerel: Its Influence on Shelley and Byron" (*WC*, 1975); and the commentary in McGann's Oxford edition. A study of this relationship, making use of unpublished materials in the Murray archive, in the Huntington Library, and in other depositories, would form an illuminating chapter in the literary history of the age. Southey and Byron's quarrel also plays a part in R. H. Super, "Landor and the 'Satanic School'" (*SP*, 1945), which chronicles Landor's irascibility toward Byron and his poetry.

Scott, Hazlitt, Jeffrey. John Clubbe has studied the personal relationship between the two most popular writers of the age in "Byron and Scott" (*TSLL*, 1973) and "After Missolonghi: Scott on Byron, 1824–1832" (*LC*, 1974). Byron's example in his "Detached Thoughts" inspired Scott to keep a journal, most recently edited by W. E. K. Anderson (1972), in which Byron is often mentioned. James A. Houck, "Byron and William Hazlitt" (in Robinson's *Lord Byron and His Contemporaries*), is a nice beginning, although it focuses more on Hazlitt than on Byron and views Byron too exclusively from Hazlitt's point of view. See also Patrick L. Story, "Byron's Death and Hazlitt's *Spirit of the Age*" (*ELN*, 1969), and, for suggestive insights into the ways they affected each other, John Kinnaird, *William Hazlitt: Critic of Power* (1978), and David Bromwich, *Hazlitt: The Mind of a Critic* (1983). The huge number of references to Byron in the Howe edition of Hazlitt's *Complete Works* suggests the need for further work. James A. Greig, *Francis Jeffrey of the* Edinburgh Review (1948), surveys Jeffrey's puzzled, admonitory, but usually supportive reviews of Byron's successive volumes. J. Thomas Dwyer has prepared a handy "Checklist of Primary Sources of the Byron-Jeffrey Relationship" (*N&Q*, 1960). A chapter in Keith Walker's *Byron's Readers...* (1979) discusses this relationship. See also Muriel J. Mellown's "Francis Jeffrey, Lord Byron, and *English Bards, and Scotch Reviewers*" (*SSL,* 1981).

Mary Shelley. Two older studies by Ernest J. Lovell, Jr., retain their value: "Byron and the Byronic Hero in the Novels of Mary Shelley" (*UTSE,* 1951), which reveals Byron to be the prototype of major figures in several of her novels, and "Byron and Mary Shelley" (*KSJ,* 1952), which traces her absorbed interest in Byron the man. Betty T. Bennett's projected three-volume *Letters of Mary Wollstonecraft Shelley* (2 vols. to date, 1980–) will supersede Frederick L. Jones's edition (2 vols., 1944). Mary Shelley's journal, incompletely edited by Jones in 1947, has now been reedited in toto as *The Shelley Journals* by Paula R. Feldman and Diana Pugh (2 vols., forthcoming). In addition, Byron often figures in the numerous discussions of *Frankenstein.* See, among others, William Walling, *Mary Shelley* (1972), and Christopher Small, *Mary Shelley's* Frankenstein: *Tracing the Myth* (1973).

Keats, Lamb, Peacock, Clare. George Cheatham, "Byron's Dislike of Keats's Poetry" (*KSJ,* 1983), succinctly analyzes Byron's chief comments on Keats (omitting, however, the comment of 1821 where Byron finds Keats "sublime as Aeschylus"). The most convincing reassessment is Wolf Hirst's "Lord Byron Cuts a Figure: The Keatsian View" (*ByronJ,* 1985), which shrewdly reevaluates Keats's statements about Byron. For Byron's influence on Keats, see C. L. Finney, *The Evolution of Keats's Poetry* (2 vols., 1936), passim. Keats is paired with Byron in rather special ways in Anya Taylor, *Magic and English Romanticism* (1979), and also in the central chapter of Christopher Ricks, *Keats and Embarrassment* (1974), which argues that Byron asks "a continuing consideration in relation to Keats." John I. Ades discusses "Charles Lamb's Judgment on Byron and Shelley" (*PLL,* 1965). It was decidedly negative. *The Letters of Charles and Mary Anne Lamb,* edited by Edwin W. Marrs, Jr. (3 vols. to date, 1975–), has scattered references to Byron. Howard Mills in *Peacock: His Circle and His Age* (1968) suggests parallels—to Byron's detriment—between *Don Juan's* English cantos and the world of Peacock's novels. Marilyn Butler, *Peacock Displayed: A Satirist in His Context* (1979), reevaluates Mr. Cypress of *Nightmare Abbey,* Peacock's critique of Byronic misanthropy. Nicholas A. Joukovsky, "Peacock's Sir Oran Haut-ton: Byron's Bear or Shelley's Ape?" (*KSJ,* 1980), considers whether Sir Oran-Haut-ton in *Melincourt* owes a debt to the bear Byron kept at Cambridge. *Thomas Love Peacock: Memoirs of Shelley and Other Essays and Reviews,* edited by Mills (1970), reprints Peacock's long review essay on volume 1 of Moore's *Byron.* In the 1840s John Clare in his delusion assumed a Byronic identity and wrote "Child [sic] Harold" and "Don Juan," "continuations" of Byron's poems, as well as "Hebrew Melodies." Mark Minor discusses Byron's impact in "Clare, Byron, and the Bible: Additional Evidence from the Asylum Manuscripts" (*BRH,* 1982).

Madame de Staël and Beckford. Frederick S. Frank has explored well Byron's interesting relationship with Madame de Staël in "The Demon and the Thunderstorm: Byron and Madame de Staël" (*RLC,* 1969), which neglects, however,

Byron's own reminiscences of her, first published in *Murray's Magazine* in 1887. George Ridenour in an appendix to *The Style of* Don Juan (1960) intriguingly suggests that the *mobilité* of Corinne, the titular heroine of Madame de Staël's most famous novel, and her talent as *improvvisatrice* influenced Byron's masterpiece. See also Ernest Giddey's "Byron and Madame de Staël" in Robinson's *Lord Byron and His Contemporaries*. On Byron and Beckford, see André Parreaux's two articles (*EA*, 1955) and Giddey's "Byron and Beckford" (*ByronJ*, 1978).

BYRON AND THE REGENCY

Byron's relationship to the larger life of Regency England remains underinvestigated. A vast quantity of materials on the Regency has become available in public collections in recent years. These include the Hobhouse, Holland, and Melbourne (Lamb family) papers (the last open to scholars only since 1980) in the British Library, as well as the Abinger and Lovelace collections, both now on deposit in the Bodleian. For background, see Marjorie Villiers, *The Grand Whiggery* (1939), rather too chatty. Better are Arthur Bryant, *The Age of Elegance 1812–1822* (1950); Ellen Moers, *The Dandy: Brummell to Beerbohm* (1960); Donald A. Low, *That Sunny Dome: A Portrait of Regency England* (1977), in which Byron occupies most of two of the book's eight chapters; and E. Tangye Lean, *The Napoleonists* (1970), discussed below under "Ideas and Beliefs. Politics." In *Portrait of the Prince Regent* (1953; rpt. in *EDH,* 1955) Dorothy Margaret Stuart scrutinizes Byron's attacks.

Holland House. From 1812 to 1816 Byron was part of the group of Whig luminaries who gathered at Holland House, for which see Lloyd Sanders, *The Holland House Circle* (1908); the Earl of Ilchester's *The Home of the Hollands 1605–1820* (1937); Derek Hudson's briefer *Holland House in Kensington* (1967), which takes the story down to the house's bombing during the 1940 blitz; and Leslie Mitchell's *Holland House* (1980). The Holland (Fox family) papers in the British Library have more on Byron's relationship with Holland House to 1816 than one would divine from Henry Richard Vassall Fox, third Lord Holland, *Further Memoirs of the Whig Party 1807–1821* (1905), which remains essential for context. In *The Sovereign Lady: A Life of Elizabeth Vassall, Third Lady Holland, with Her Family* (1974) Sonia Keppel allots a chapter to Byron's relationship with the Hollands.

Other members of the Holland House circle include Richard Brinsley Sheridan, Sir Humphry Davy, Samuel Rogers, Thomas Moore, and John Cam Hobhouse. On Sheridan, see Jack C. Wills, "Lord Byron and 'Poor Dear Sherry,' Richard Brinsley Sheridan," in Robinson's *Lord Byron and His Contemporaries.* Sheridan's impact on Byron, overwhelming in Byron's young maturity but difficult to pinpoint, needs further investigation. Wills points out Sheridan's role as model on Byron's life and prose and broaches the influence his comedy had on *Don Juan.* Anne Treneer, *The Mercurial Chemist: A Life of Sir Humphry Davy* (1963), discusses Byron's relations with Sir Humphry both in London and in Italy. Samuel Rogers' poem *Italy* contains a tribute to Byron's genius. His other writings, and the records of his conversation, often mention Byron. The student should begin with Ernest Giddey, "Byron and Samuel Rogers" (*ByronJ,* 1979), concise and illuminating, but may also wish to consult R. Ellis Roberts, *Samuel Rogers and His Circle* (1910). For Byron's relationships with Moore and Hobhouse, see the paragraphs above under "Biography: Nineteenth Century."

A tangential member of this circle was Caroline Lamb, with whom Byron was soon launched on a tempestuous affair that is coolly narrated in Lord David Cecil, *The Young Melbourne* (1939; republished in 1954 as part of *Melbourne*), and also in Philip Ziegler, *Melbourne* (1976). In 1816 Caroline published *Glenarvon,* a sensational treatment of Byron, discussed by Clarke Olney (*UKCR,* 1956), John Clubbe (*WC,* 1979), and Malcolm Kelsall (*ByronJ,* 1981; rpt. in *Byron: Poetry and Politics,* ed. Stürzl and Hogg). Dorothy Margaret Stuart, *Dearest Bess: The Life and Times of Lady Elizabeth Foster, Afterwards Duchess of Devonshire* (1955), notes several points of contact with Byron. On Byron and Lady Melbourne, we begin with Mabell, Countess of Airlie, *In Whig Society 1775 – 1818* (1921), and continue with Clubbe, "Byron's Lady Melbourne" (*ByronJ,* 1984).

Davies and Kinnaird. In 1976, Byron's letters to Scrope Berdmore Davies were found in a long-forgotten trunk in a Barclays Bank. Already the bibliography attached to this extraordinary discovery looms large. On the Byron and Shelley manuscripts in the trunk, see Judith Chernaik and Timothy Burnett, "The Byron and Shelley Notebooks in the Scrope Davies Find" (*RES,* 1978). On Davies, see John Clubbe's revisionist "Scrope Davies Reconsidered" (*ByronJ,* 1978) and Burnett's *The Rise and Fall of a Regency Dandy: The Life and Times of Scrope Berdmore Davies* (1981), a popular account that makes good use of the materials in the trunk. In *Lord Byron: Accounts Rendered* Doris Langley Moore has clarified Byron's important relationship with "my trusting and trustworthy trustee and banker and Crown and Sheet Anchor Douglas Kinnaird the Honourable." An edition of Kinnaird's letters to Byron is in order.

Others. A number of studies touch on or discuss Byron's dealings with other persons more or less significant in his life. Caroline M. Duncan-Jones, *Miss Mitford and Mr. Harness: Records of a Friendship* (1955), includes material on Byron and a friend of his youth, as does Robert Mortenson's "Byron and William Harness: Early Recollections of Lord Byron" (*PBSA,* 1971). A. L. Rowse contributes "Byron's Friend, Bankes: A Portrait" (*Encounter,* 1975). Byron finds his place in Warren Derry's biography of the poet's old Cambridge professor, *Dr. Parr: A Portrait of the Whig Dr. Johnson* (1966). Harold Nicolson's "Mr. William Fletcher" in *Small Talk* (1937) renders an ironic sketch of Byron's valet. Richard Findlater, *Joe Grimaldi: His Life and Theatre* (1955, rev. 1978), discusses Byron's relations early in life with the famous comedian. Appendix 6 of Werner W. Beyer's *The Enchanted Forest* (1963) chronicles Byron's acquaintance with William Sotheby ("bustling Botherby" in *Beppo* and a main target of Byron's satire in *The Blues*), the translator of Wieland's *Oberon*. This translation influenced several episodes of *Don Juan,* as E. F. Boyd had earlier pointed out in her *Byron's* Don Juan (1945). Louis F. Peck, *A Life of Matthew G. Lewis* (1961), frequently mentions Byron. Sheila Birkenhead in *Peace in Piccadilly: The Story of Albany* (1958) vividly chronicles Byron's residency in 1814. Stendhal's *Correspondence* (vol. 1 [1800–21], ed. Henri Martineau and V. del Litto, 1962) has references to Byron in Milan in October 1816. They are more authentic than Stendhal's discussion in *Rome, Naples, and Florence, in 1817* (1818). See also the items on Stendhal noted under "Reputation and Influence: Europe. France." Iris Origo in *A Measure of Love* (1957) includes a sketch of Byron's Italian friend the Countess Marina Benzoni. The Countess Albrizzi's "Character of Byron," originally published in 1826, is partially translated in Moore's life; Prothero prints the complete Italian text in volume 4 of his edition of the *Letters and Journals.* Leslie A. Marchand expertly chronicles another personal association in "Lord Byron and Count Alborghetti" (*PMLA,* 1949). Michael Sadleir narrates *The Strange Life of Lady Blessington* (1933, rev. 1947), while Willard Connely, *Count D'Orsay: The Dandy of Dandies* (1952), deals with the life of her companion, whom Byron knew at Genoa. Connely's earlier *The Reign of Beau Brummell* (1940) briefly discusses Byron's admiration of Brummell. The voluminous diary of Henry Crabb Robinson has much on Byron. See *Henry Crabb Robinson on Books and Their Writers,* edited by Edith J. Morley (3 vols., 1938), as well as the earlier compilation *Diary, Reminiscences, and Correspondence,* edited by Thomas Sadler (3 vols., 1869). Patrick O'Leary, *Regency Editor: A Life of John Scott* (1983), comments on Byron's involvement with the gifted, temperamental editor. On Byron and Francis Hodgson, see the final paragraph under "Biography: Nineteenth Century."

Byron and his publishers.   The important subject of Byron and his publishers demands a full-scale modern treatment comparable to those recently accorded Keats, Tennyson, and Dickens. Publishing history has come into its own in recent years, yet, having to make do with the inadequate Wise and the incomplete Randolph bibliographies, we know less than we might about the publication history of Byron's works. A comprehensive study should make full use of the abundant archival material and perhaps publish John Murray II's extensive correspondence with his most famous author. Samuel Smiles's *A Publisher and His Friends: Memoir and Correspondence of the Late John Murray* (2 vols., 1891) is still a mine of information, with many documents from the Murray archives, on this important relationship. See also the discussion in volume 1 of Escarpit's *Lord Byron: Un tempérament littéraire.* Mary Luytens provides a distillation of Murray's career in "The Impresario of Albemarle Street" (*TLS,* 24 Nov. 1979). The firm's fortunes in Victorian times are recounted with verve by "George Paston" in *At John Murray's* (1932). On Murray's chief literary adviser, see R. B. Clark, *William Gifford: Tory Satirist, Critic, and Editor* (1930), and John D. Jump, "Lord Byron and William Gifford" (*BJRL,* 1975), largely based on Clark. On another member of the Murray "Senate," Isaac D'Israeli, see C. L. Cline's "Unpublished Notes on the Romantic Poets by Isaac D'Israeli" (*UTSE,* 1941) and James Ogden,

Isaac D'Israeli (1969), which devotes several pages to Byron and D'Israeli, whose compilations Byron once affirmed he had "read oftener than perhaps those of any English author whatever." Further insight into the publishing practices of the times is afforded in Ben Harris McClary, *Washington Irving and the House of Murray* (1969). On Byron's later relations with Murray and the beginning of his relationship with John Hunt, see Hugh J. Luke, "The Publishing of Byron's *Don Juan*" (*PMLA*, 1965), and William H. Marshall, *Byron, Shelley, Hunt, and the* Liberal (1960). An excellent study is Leslie A. Marchand's "John Hunt as Byron's Publisher" (*KSJ*, 1959). See also Thilo von Bremen, *Lord Byron als Erfolgsautor: Leser und Literaturmarkt im frühen 19. Jahrhundert* (1977), discussed below under "Reputation and Influence: Great Britain."

The Byron Society.   The Byron Society was founded in London in 1876 but lapsed in 1939. In 1971 it was revived and in late 1973 it began publication of the *Byron Journal,* which, appearing each year on the poet's birthday (22 Jan.), includes articles on Byron, book reviews, and notices of Byron-related activities. International in its organization, the society has committees or corresponding members in over two dozen countries. It sponsors programs and lectures and offers annually a tour of a country of Byron interest. The host country usually sponsors a seminar at which scholarly papers are given. Several national committees have their own newsletters, for example, the American *Byron Society Newsletter* (1973 –). Through its publications, its meetings, its tours, its seminars, and the interaction of its members that all these activities provide, the Byron Society fosters the study and appreciation of Byron.

   In 1912 funds for an annual "Byron Foundation Lecture" were raised by public subscription at University College, Nottingham. The first lecture was given in 1919, the most recent that I am aware of in 1969. Many of the published lectures are noticed in due course.

Criticism: General

To 1960

During the first half of the twentieth century, interest in Byron's life, as distinct from his poetry, was very great. Critical attention to what he wrote lagged far behind. Today, the pendulum has swung in the other direction, at least in the United States. True, major advances continue to be made in our knowledge of Byron's life. But in the early 1960s a critical reevaluation of his poetry began, one that underwent an extraordinary efflorescence in the late sixties and one that has maintained its momentum throughout the seventies and into the eighties. During the past two decades, it seems safe to say, the poetic achievement of no other Romantic poet has been so thoroughly reconsidered as has Byron's. M. H. Abrams once spoke of "the apparent difficulty of saying unobvious things about [Byron's] poetry." That statement could not be made today, not even by a hostile critic, as the poems have met with and continue to meet with an increasingly sophisticated critical response.

In the nineteenth and early twentieth centuries biographical criticism often crudely simplified the relationship between Byron's life and his poetry. Then for thirty years the New Critics and their disciples inveighed against the "Intentional Fallacy." Unlike Shelley, whom they often attacked, and Keats, whom they often admired, Byron was largely ignored by the New Critics. Why bother, after all, with a poet of whom T. S. Eliot said that if he "had distilled his verse, there would have been nothing whatever left"? The critical methodologies that supplanted the New Criticism—structuralist, poststructuralist, and deconstructionist—have left Byron largely unscathed. The poetry of a man who in life fiercely resisted systems of any kind, who rooted himself firmly in time and space, itself resists systemization. Nor can the historical dimension be scanted. In recent years, a number of critics have again reexamined Byron's poems within the spectrum of his life. One of the oldest approaches to Byron—one recognized, with varying degrees of sophistication, by many nineteenth-century writers, by W. W. Robson in 1957, and by Northrop Frye in 1963—turns out to hold renewed promise in the writings of, for example, Bernard Blackstone, Jerome J. McGann, and Peter J. Manning, who analyze with skill the ways in which Byron's life affected what he wrote. Recently, McGann has argued that to elucidate the poetry the critic has to be aware of biographical detail. Criticism has neglected Byron's personal poetry, he says, "because our modern critical habits have made it virtually impossible for us to approach these poems in the proper way." For Byron at least, "fine details of biographical history are necessary to the literary critic." In short, the poems are separable from the life only at the risk of critical distortion and loss of richness in critical understanding.

For those who may believe that the great critical issues concerning Byron's poetry approached solution only during the last half-century or less, with the advent of "modern" criticism, *Byron: The Critical Heritage* (1970), edited by Andrew Rutherford, offers a salutary corrective. This volume reprints critical comments ranging from Brougham's attack on *Hours of Idleness* in the *Edinburgh Review* of 1808 to Arthur Symons' chapter on Byron in *The Romantic Movement in English Poetry* of 1909. In between, constituting the first half of the book, are examples of criticism written by Byron's contemporaries, almost all of it during Byron's lifetime. Here we find, among others, Coleridge, Scott, Wordsworth, Jeffrey, Gifford, Lockhart, Jane Austen, Keats, Leigh Hunt, Croker, Hazlitt, John Wilson, and Shelley. These critiques are helpfully grouped in terms of Byron's individual poems or of genres such as the Oriental tales and the dramas. The second half of the volume reprints often substantial portions of major documents of Victorian criticism by Carlyle, Macaulay, Newman, Thackeray, George Eliot, Swinburne, John Morley, Ruskin, Arnold, Saintsbury, and Paul Elmer More. Although this collection is limited almost wholly to English critics, there are selections from Continental writers, among them Goethe and Mazzini. Here we have Hazlitt's trenchant observations on Byron's poetry in *The Spirit of the Age* (1825), as well as Macaulay's essay, originally a review of Moore's biography but in fact a reconsideration of Byron in the widely ranging nineteenth-century manner. Rutherford's introduction is excellent. Brief headnotes preface the selections.

Five volumes of Donald H. Reiman's *The Romantics Reviewed* (9 vols., 1972)—Part B: Byron and Regency Society Poets—reproduce in facsimile most of the reviews that Byron received in his lifetime. These volumes are a boon for students who do not have access to the original periodicals. The contemporary response is not only interesting as an indication of earlier critical taste but also of considerable intrinsic importance, for Byron during much of his career was extremely susceptible to what others thought of his poetry and often wrote (or rewrote) in response to criticism. If, as Hazlitt observed, "the arts are not progressive," neither, we should remember, is criticism. An essay written in 1980 is not necessarily superior to one written in 1820, particularly when we realize that Byron's poetry attracted the attention of the best minds of his generation—among them, Jeffrey, Scott, Lockhart, and Hazlitt himself. The poetry probably received as much excellent criticism during the fifteen years from 1809 to 1824 as it has in the fifteen years since the late 1960s. Reiman's invaluable volumes allow us to read this body of earlier criticism in virtually its entirety.

To gain an overview of the extent of the critical response to Byron's writings in his lifetime, the student should turn to William S. Ward's listing, *Literary Reviews in British Periodicals, 1798–1820* (2 vols., 1972), which has more entries for Byron than for any other poet. Ward has subsequently published a volume on the years 1821–26 (1977). John O. Hayden, *The Romantic Reviewers 1802–1824* (1968), devotes a well-informed chapter to Byron's varying reception in the reviews. Hayden's appendix 2 is a handy checklist of reviews of the Romantic writers, beginning with Byron. *Romantic Bards and British Reviewers,* edited by Hayden (1971), reprints a number of them. Theodore Redpath, *The Young Romantics and Critical Opinion 1807–1824: Poetry of Byron, Shelley, and Keats as Seen by Their Contemporary Critics* (1973), includes a 120-page chapter of extracts, preceded by a commentary, illustrating Byron's reception. *British Literary Magazines. II: The Romantic Age, 1789–1836,* edited by Alvin Sullivan (1983), contains useful background information on journals that reviewed Byron. For other discussions of the nineteenth-century response, see under "Reputation and Influence." Students should also be aware that many still-useful studies of Byron appeared, particularly in Germany, in the four or five decades after 1870—too soon to be picked up in the MLA and other bibliographies and, like the early biographies of him, often forgotten even by Byron scholars.

In reaction to the often crude biographical criticism of the past, one older study, William J. Calvert's *Byron: Romantic Paradox* (1935), stands out conspicuously as an attempt to study the poet in his work, not in his personal career. Calvert's title suggests that Byron's poetry has value apart from the autobiographical, self-revelatory significance that may or may not lie implicit in much of it. A book that sets forth the historical significance of Byron's "place" in English poetry without the record of his personal life was well worth writing in the 1930s, and Calvert produced his with good sense, enthusiasm, and wit. The "paradox" that he sets before the reader is in several of its manifestations a familiar one, recognized to some extent by Byron himself. Fundamental is the vacillation between loyalty to eighteenth-century classicism and adherence to the new Romantic fashions in thought, emotion, and poetry. Byron cannot be understood unless set against the background of the classical and reasonable tradition of the preceding age of which, paradoxically, he was the direct heir and the convinced champion, for if on one side of his nature he had his share in Werther's sorrows, on the other he was an intellectual descendant of Voltaire. Spontaneous and emotional in temperament, he remained intellectually sophisticated and obedient to tradition. This essential dichotomy Calvert studies and displays. G. R. Elliott's "Byron and the Comic Spirit" (*PMLA*, 1924; rpt. in *The Cycle of Modern Poetry*, 1929) complements Calvert's discussion by arguing that Byron in his last years was moving toward "a Stoic acceptance of life" and was close to attaining "the balance and poetic comeliness of the true comic spirit."

Useful studies in the twentieth century before Calvert, a number of them resulting from the centennial of Byron's death, include Oliver Elton's "The Present Value of Byron" (*RES*, 1925; rpt. in *Essays and Addresses*, 1939), which discriminates among Byron's lyrics and praises his power in narrative verse. Elton had earlier written an excellent chapter on Byron for his *Survey of English Literature, 1780–1830* (1912). Also worth noting among the centennial tributes are essays by C. H. Herford (*Holborn Review*, 1924); W. P. Ker (*Criterion*, 1925; rpt. in Ker's *Collected Essays*, 1925), with remarks on Byron's prosody and literary affiliations; a number of the pieces in *Byron, the Poet* (1924), edited by W. A. Briscoe; H. W. Garrod's lecture *Byron: 1824–1924* (1924; rpt. in *The Profession of Poetry*, 1929); H. Hensley Henson's *Byron* (1924); Lord Ernle (R. E. Prothero), "The Poetry of Byron" (*Quarterly Review*, 1924); C. E. Lawrence, "The Personality of Byron" (*Edinburgh Review*, 1924); Prince D. S. Mirsky, "Byron" (*London Mercury*, 1924); and, in the United States, Howard Mumford Jones, "The Byron Centenary" (*YR*, 1924), this last a tonic reaffirmation of the breadth of Byron's vision. Ernest de Selincourt's "Byron" in *Wordsworthian and Other Studies* (1947, but this essay written in 1933) has interest now chiefly as representative of the older, patronizing attitude to Byron.

Recent decades have witnessed a remarkable resurgence of critical interest in the poetry of Byron, so great as to signal a thorough reversal of earlier, often negative, assessments. W. W. Robson, in his lecture *Byron as Poet* (1957; rpt. in *Critical Essays*, 1966), understood that no clear line need be drawn between the man and his works. "Byron's personality is as much the subject for a critical essay on Byron, as it is for a biography." In the Dying Gladiator passage in *Childe Harold* 4, Byron speaks "in the accents of a great European tradition of the public style." Excellence without obscurity in the colloquial mode had been a virtue recognized in Byron since the 1930s. After a sensitive discussion of "Lines on Hearing That Lady Byron Was Ill" and "Epistle to Augusta," Robson concludes that the style is not Regency but "dateless."

It is difficult to do justice to the subtlety and complexity of Robert Escarpit's *Lord Byron: Un tempérament littéraire* (2 vols., 1955, 1957). Escarpit effectively rejects the simplistic notion that Byron wrote only to relieve himself of feelings of guilt, a motive that fails to explain why he also published what he wrote. He argues that Byron found his true vocation at last as a man of action in Greece, and thus he views Byron's voluntary exile in 1816 as "en réalité un retour": an odyssey of some years leading him finally back again to Greece "pour y 'engager' son existence," in an effort to achieve "l'affranchissement de sa personne." Escarpit recognizes the resemblances between Childe Burun and Don Juan and the way in which the resultant poems are a "mélange des genres." He also recognizes the attention that Byron, although periodically renouncing authorship, paid to the opinion of his public and to the advice of Murray. In short, Byron looked on the publication of each poem as an experiment with his popularity, an adventure or experience in which he risked a reputation. Rejecting the oversimplified concept of Byron as satirist and Byron as Romantic, Escarpit discerns three Byronic modes, frequently overlapping in the same poems—lyrical, rhetorical, and narrative—and devotes the final three quarters of his book to them. Thus he can discuss the lyrical element not only in Byron's short poems but also in almost all his other works. Escarpit concludes, however, that for Byron the man of action the narrative form—both dramatic and nondramatic—was the superior form and that, no matter which modes he seems to adopt, his poetic output is a form of action. The second volume opens with a survey of Byron's prose, "surtout une prose d'idées," introductory to a discussion of his "rhétorique en vers": the "classical" satires, *Childe Harold,* and the great satires in ottava rima. Escarpit argues that Byron in *Childe Harold* achieves the illusion of a confrontation between external reality and certain intellectual "données." Everything in cantos 3 and 4 is seen through the lens (or lenses) of Byron's reading, which has become part of him. In effect, all Byron's art tends toward a dualistic equilibrium or balance, a double affirmation of the world and himself, though in the last two cantos, unlike the first two, a portion of Byron's private life has become a public thing, and it is the world, now, which "se rattache au moi." The pages dealing with *Beppo* and *Don Juan* are disappointing, being too often heavily descriptive, and the new sources suggested for *Juan* are merely asserted, not demonstrated. The portrait of the Byronic literary temperament that emerges finally, by no means a familiar one, demands consideration. Escarpit's Byron engages in the act of writing as a refuge against chaos, including that within himself, and so organizes or creates both self and his world by an act of combative will almost military in its disciplined thrust. Thus even when Byron wrote, he was a man of action, finding his equilibrium in the gesture of writing rather than in the thing written or in any indestructible image of his agonies. Earlier, Escarpit had published *De quoi vivait Byron?* (1952), on the poet's finances, and in 1965 he prefaced a selection of French translations, *Byron,* with a long interpretative essay.

In the degree of hostility expressed toward Byron's poetry, Paul West's *Byron and the Spoiler's Art* (1960) stood, until recently, unique among modern critical studies. Although West scorns the biographical approach to Byron and those who employ biography as an aid to critical analysis, he repeatedly makes biographical assertions himself, many of them related only indirectly to the poetry. He believes all Byron's writing is what he calls "release writing," a "spontaneous overflow." "His style does not develop, does not improve between *English Bards* (1809) and *Don Juan*"—an extraordinary (mis)statement. Not untypically, as here, his criticism takes the form of assertion rather than of reasoned argument. For West, *Don Juan* is merely "a rag-bag of interesting exhibits." We are also told that Byron "was not a literary critic." He "only rarely made up his own mind about problems of form." West's flashy and superficial book has occasional insights, even of some brilliance, but overall it is a disappointment.

Byron: A Collection of Critical Essays, edited by West (1963), demonstrated that the critical revolt against Byron and his poetry, fueled by the New Criticism of the 1930s and 1940s, had run its course. Of the fourteen essays selected by West, only one is undisguisedly hostile (West's own essay on the plays) and one perhaps is of mixed tone (Mario Praz's chapter from his *Romantic Agony,* 1933, which seems dated and unconvincing today). Helen Gardner is excellent on *Don Juan* in a review article (1958) of the variorum edition of Steffan and Pratt, as she recognizes Byron's "intellectual vitality and vivacity," his "toughness and temperamental resilience." Gilbert Highet in "The Poet and His Vulture" (1954) contemplates Byron's "unrelenting pessimism," which "sounds like the considered verdict of an educated, experienced, reflective man," one whose mind helped mold those of Heine, Lamartine, Musset, Leopardi, Pushkin, and Berlioz. "Probably he is the last of the great satiric poets writing in English." Bertrand Russell and John Wain also call attention to Byron's immense influence on the Continent. In this collection one may find a startling variety of Byrons: Byron the schizophrenic and the paranoiac; Byron the Shakespearean; Byron the symbolist, Satanist, and surrealist; Byron the Augustan; Byron the careless craftsman as well as the diligent reviser; Byron the mythical force; and several other Byrons. As one might expect from such a varied collection, no coherent image of the poet emerges.

The 1960s

Andrew Rutherford's *Byron: A Critical Study* (1961) is always clear, usually convincing, free of arcane critical jargon and of vague abstractions far removed from the poem's concrete world of universal particulars, and respectful of the poem's evidence. Rutherford roots his criticism in the reality of Byron's life and personality but uses these only to throw light on the poems, which he normally reads with sensitivity. He divides his attention about equally between the Romantic and satiric poems, excludes the plays, and orders his chapters chronologically. He does not disguise his preference for Byron's later satires. This leads him to undervalue Byron's Romantic poetry; in fact, his book is far more convincing on the later than on the earlier Byron. Its wide availability as a paperback during the past two decades has even made it a barrier in getting the whole of Byron to be taken seriously. Rutherford finds that the "central weakness" of the first two cantos of *Childe Harold* "lies in his [Byron's] failure to establish any significant relationship" between the title character and the narrator. Of the heroes of the six verse tales that Byron wrote before leaving England in 1816, Rutherford concludes, "it is impossible to take them seriously, either as symbolic figures or as representations of human nature." The protagonist of *Childe Harold* 3 "shows a marked advance," for narrator and hero have here become essentially one. The poem has an admirable unity despite flaws of tone and consistency in the character of the protagonist, whom Rutherford finds "unsatisfactory." This canto he describes as "extremely good bad poetry." On the next page he asserts, surprisingly, that *The Prisoner of Chillon* is "indeed the best" of Byron's nonsatiric work. One of Rutherford's virtues is that he stimulates readers repeatedly to reexamine their own judgments of these poems. *Manfred,* though important, he deems a "failure." The variety of moods and styles in *Childe Harold* 4 permit Byron "to express [more] adequately his own complex nature" and point to the achievement of the mature satires. Rutherford recognizes *Beppo*'s uniqueness. To *Don Juan* he gives five of his thirteen chapters, and in them he discusses the poem's composition, resurveying ground covered by Steffan and agreeing with Steffan that the English cantos possess certain weaknesses and that the unifying theme of the entire poem is in some way illusion or appearance versus reality. *Don Juan*'s "strengths and weaknesses are both related to the poem's inclusiveness." A final chapter, reflecting even more than elsewhere the book's Leavisite bias, argues that *The Vision of Judgment* is Byron's "masterpiece, aesthetically perfect, intellectually consistent, highly entertaining, and morally profound."

William H. Marshall's *The Structure of Byron's Major Poems* (1962) is concerned, as its title suggests, with the larger organization of a selected number of the poems, many of which Marshall reads as increasingly successful dramatic monologues. He analyzes plot structure, characterization, motivation both conscious and less than conscious, and, most centrally, dramatic irony. Marshall's perspective also includes some theological or philosophical criticism, as well as psychological. After dealing in two early chapters with Byron's work before 1816, he considers the productions of Byron's "Middle Phase," 1816–18, and finds that in these (and later) poems Byron "demonstrated his growing acceptance of imperfection in man's capacities and of disorder in human affairs as the basis for sublimational order in art." *Manfred* is "essentially a sustained soliloquy," in which the title character, like Childe Harold of canto 3, fails in his attempts to remake his vision of the world and thus ceases "to struggle toward resolution." The structure of *Childe Harold* 3 reveals "a nonmechanical symmetry of which the Rhine Journey is obviously the center and the opening and closing addresses by the speaker to his daughter are the bounds. The second half of the poem mirrors the first half, and the total poem possesses organic wholeness rather than merely an accidental sequence of personal passages." Perhaps the most valuable of Marshall's discussions appears in chapter 6, which deals with *The Lament of Tasso, Mazeppa,* and *The Prophecy of Dante,* poems that have suffered from relative critical neglect. *Beppo* and *Don Juan* Marshall deals with briefly in a final chapter, *The Vision of Judgment* not at all.

M. K. Joseph's *Byron the Poet* (1964) regularly comes up with insights both original and convincing, expressed with clarity, grace, and precision. Its comprehensiveness, high level of insight, and careful exposition make it the first book that students beginning their study of Byron's poetry should read. Surveying the whole canon of Byron's poetry, Joseph emphasizes the inventiveness and variety of the early *Childe Harold,* its combination of sentiment and satire or burlesque, and the clear separation of hero and narrator, the former intended as "a negative moral example." Joseph has a gift for quoting the best of the early Byron (for example, *Childe Harold* 2.5–6 on the ruined temple of the skull) and providing a fresh and imaginative analysis of it. He also considers the nature of the description in that poem and its relation to the eighteenth-century topographical poem. Interesting short discussions take up the heroes of the tales and Byron's search after form and variety of meter. His essay on *The Island* does not deal with the problem of the comic Ben Bunting. Chapter 3, "The Later *Childe Harold,*" opens with the brief section "Byron as Tourist" and moves on to consider "The Author and the Pilgrim," "Nature and Man," "Art and Man," and other subjects. The sensitive criticism is not thesis-ridden or forced into any preconceived structure, nor is it limited to purely verbal or other textual concerns. The chapter on the dramas emphasizes Byron's originality in contrast to the melodramatic rant and complexity of most of the plays of his day. Aware of the prevailing views of Byron's poetry, Joseph reflects them reliably and accurately but also provides important critical insights of his own. I discuss his excellent treatment of *Don Juan* under "Criticism: Individual Works."

In the preface to *Byron's Poetry: A Critical Introduction* (1965), Leslie A. Marchand says that his "purpose has been to write an introduction to Byron's poetry for twentieth century students and readers in the light of what is now known of the life, character, and psychology of the poet, and of the intellectual and literary milieu in which he wrote." In doing so he has tried "neither to overemphasize nor to neglect the biographical interpretation." The eighteen chapters of the book show him judiciously and carefully analyzing all of Byron's longer poems and many of the shorter. The well-organized chapters succinctly cover a great mass of material, present the poems by genre (under such headings as "Popean Satires" and "Historical Dramas") and, within the genre, in chronological order. About one third of the book he devotes to *Don Juan*; his opening and closing chapters consider Byron's meaning and value for our time. Unlike so many others who have written on Byron, Marchand advocates no central thesis and reveals no marked critical bias, though he does stress (sensibly, in my opinion) "mobility of mind" as Byron's "greatest strength." And Marchand's own commonsense "mobility" permits him to do justice to the diversity of Byron's oeuvre. This study gains immeasurably from Marchand's unequaled knowledge of Byron's life.

It is difficult to decide whether to discuss G. Wilson Knight's *Byron and Shakespeare* (1966) under the heading of biography or of criticism. Although similarities or correspondences between the two great poets often throw unexpected light on Byron, Knight is guilty of frequent intellectual excesses. He sweeps up evidence uncritically from every possible source, often without considering chronology or making allowance for circumstances or the recipient of a letter or the reliability of the reporter of a conversation. But the repeated juxtaposition of passages from both poets reveals how well Byron stands up beside the master. The great flaw of the book lies in its extravagant and often unconvincing argument. The thesis is that Byron *lived* Shakespeare's plays; biographical parallels are drawn with the plays; and because Knight feels the man and his poetry cannot be separated, he demonstrates that Byron also *wrote* like Shakespeare. What is certain is that Byron spent many hours reading Shakespeare, remembered much of this reading, and quoted repeatedly from the plays, as the indexes to the Coleridge-Prothero edition of Byron's *Works* long ago demonstrated.

Much thought and reading have gone into Robert F. Gleckner's *Byron and the Ruins of Paradise* (1967), which focuses chiefly on the Romantic poems written before Byron left England in 1816, the poems written in Switzerland, and the fourth canto of *Childe Harold,* written in Italy the next year. Gleckner makes a convincing case for the quality of these poems in arguing with great persistence that Byron contemplated, consistently and from the first, "a frighteningly dark and coherent vision . . . of the human condition," which "develops gradually into the myth of man's eternal fall and damnation in the hell of human existence, the myth of what I choose to call the ruins of paradise and the consequent human condition." Michael G. Cooke has observed—with considerable justice—that Gleckner's study constitutes "a sort of amplified monograph, a topology of perennial gloom in Byron's work," for Gleckner relentlessly depicts Byron as a peculiarly modern poet-prophet of doom. To support his thesis, he devotes most of his book to the nonsatiric poems and plays, leaving insufficient space for *Beppo* and *Don Juan* and giving only passing mention to *The Vision of Judgment.* (Nor is Gleckner much interested in the Byronic comedy of love.) His use of quotation, especially from the letters and journals, is uncritical and highly selective, designed to support his thesis. He frequently fails to consider the self-dramatizing qualities of Byron's mind. The discussion of the poetic "I" (Byron the poet), the narrator, and the title character of *Childe Harold* is unconvincing. Gleckner's greatest strength lies in his calling us back repeatedly to Byron's nonsatiric poetry, especially that of the earlier years; his greatest flaw, in his attempts to claim for Byron both too much and too little. He reads Byron through a glass darkly, filtering out much of the light and denying the balance of Byron's vision. This is an incomplete view, one that Gleckner partially rectifies in a subsequent study of Byron's satires (*SIR,* 1979). It is too much to claim that the poet of *Childe Harold* 3 is "Everyman" or that Manfred "is the human condition" or that in *Childe Harold* 4 "the particulars of his [Byron's? the narrator's?] little span on earth become human history and *la condition humaine.*"

W. Paul Elledge in *Byron and the Dynamics of Metaphor* (1968) has excluded the satires and limited his analysis to six romantic poems and three plays, but he has defined his topic broadly. The term "metaphor" he almost always uses interchangeably with the terms "image," "figure," and "configuration" "to suggest the general principle of comparison in Byron's poetry." His study was an effective counter, for the 1960s, to the New Critical dismissal of Byron. In the poems and plays that he considers Elledge discovers four dominant "metaphorical vehicles for illuminating the paradoxical composition of human nature": fire and clay, light and darkness, "organic growth and mechanical stasis," and "the image of the counterpart (or the *Doppelgänger* motif)." His three central chapters deal with *The Corsair, Lara,* and *Parisina* (1813–15); *The Prisoner of Chillon, Childe*

Harold 3, and *Manfred* (1816 – 17); and *Marino Faliero, Sardanapalus,* and *Cain* (1820 – 21). The discussion of *The Prisoner of Chillon* distorts the position of the poem's narrator unfairly; that of *Childe Harold* 3, though often illuminating, suffers occasionally from imprecision. For example, Elledge uses interchangeably the terms "Harold," "narrator," and "speaker." Nor does he wholly convince in his effort to refute the "erroneous notion that the narrator is a static figure," arguing that he is "partially successful" in his "search for spiritual equilibrium." But Elledge is also aware that Harold, in "protest[ing] too much," is capable of an "exercise in self-deception." One might wish that he had explored further this dramatic irony. Elledge comes off best in his treatment of Cain, whose fire and clay he analyzes most impressively in terms of Cain's impassioned pursuit of knowledge (balanced against his murderous temper) and of his loving care of the earth (balanced against his contempt for the claylike bonds of merely human limitations), with the devil serving as doppelgänger throughout.

Jerome J. McGann's *Fiery Dust: Byron's Poetic Development* (1968) is one of the most important books about Byron to appear in the twentieth century. Using a number of approaches or methods (critical, textual, biographical), neglecting neither the intellectual nor the psychological elements in Byron's artistic development, McGann addresses himself directly to the problem of the poet's expression of self in his works, a "poetry of sincerity" (however different from Wordsworth's). Admittedly unbalanced in its coverage of Byron's oeuvre, *Fiery Dust* concerns itself centrally with *Childe Harold's Pilgrimage,* in all its cantos, dealing with it in a way not then customary, as a single poem, to reveal the clear development of the narrator from the first through the fourth canto and to establish this poem as the normative foundation for the argument following, which points out the basic continuity of a developing self in all Byron's poetry, through his last great masterpieces. McGann deals seriously with the problem of biography in art, as Byron, through his writing, explores and creates his own personality. As the narrating poet is the true hero of *Childe Harold,* so also is Byron the narrator of *Beppo,* the norm of the civilized man, citizen of the world, in that poem. Similarly, we should not interpret the narrator of *Don Juan* as a "persona" in any usual sense of the word, but as a "person," the historical Byron, with the result that to appreciate either poem "not only fully, but properly, we must be familiar with Byron's life." This is still a bold argument today for many critics, if no longer so among Byronists, but *Fiery Dust* is a bold book and its argument persuasive. McGann is the first scholar to publish a reasonably complete account of the manuscript versions of the great threefold or fourfold poem that is *Childe Harold's Pilgrimage* and of the way in which it grew in length and artistry. He succeeds in making the first two cantos much more interesting than many other readers have found them to be. His pages should draw readers back even to a reperusal of *Hours of Idleness.* Besides it and *Childe Harold,* McGann discusses four tales and five plays: *The Giaour, The Prisoner of Chillon, Mazeppa,* and *The Island;* and *Marino Faliero, The Two Foscari, Sardanapalus, Cain,* and *Heaven and Earth.* Solid and illuminating as are these analyses, McGann's study is somewhat random in its consideration of Byron's other poems. His neglect of Byron's major satire he makes good in Don Juan *in Context* (1976), discussed subsequently. McGann's later reservations about positions taken in *Fiery Dust* (in his *The Romantic Ideology: A Critical Investigation,* 1983) do not negate the value of the earlier book.

Paul G. Trueblood describes his *Lord Byron* (1969, rev. 1977) as a "modest book" addressed to "the student and general reader." More a work of synthesis than of critical and biographical originality, it provides a useful, eclectic, noncontroversial summary of a number of dominant critical views and gives "considerable attention to Byron's life" on the assumption that an understanding of Byron the man "is prerequisite to a critical assessment" of Byron the poet. For his biographical account, Trueblood relies chiefly on Marchand's life of Byron, and for his discussion of *Don Juan* on E. F. Boyd's and his own studies of the poem. The revised edition includes citations from critics whose work has appeared since the first edition.

Michael G. Cooke's *The Blind Man Traces the Circle: On the Patterns and Philosophy of Byron's Poetry* (1969) has remained since its publication a central study of Byron's mind and poetry. Cooke discovers common stylistic and philosophic features in poems and genres remarkably diverse, early and late. Chapter 1 examines a handful of Byron's lyrics and gives them (in Earl R. Wasserman's words) an "intensive metaphysical reading." Chapter 2 argues that "agnosticism is what *Childe Harold* [3] asserts." The poem contradicts itself repeatedly in its assertions about a transcendental spirit of nature and reveals "the central disarray of Byron's experience." The main character of canto 3 is "reconnoitering avenues to emotional and moral security when he knows he contains in himself the insuperable barrier to success," but Cooke does not discuss the irony of this situation. Chapter 3 deals, not always convincingly, with *Manfred, Cain,* and "Ode to Napoleon Buonaparte." Chapter 4 argues that "the question of knowledge ... occup[ies] a central position in Byron's work." Cooke examines "the imagery of contradiction" in *Don Juan, Mazeppa,* and *Childe Harold* 3 – 4. He studies the ambivalence in Byron's poetry, its "readiness to face up to duality," its "extraordinary accuracy in rendering the simultaneity of plural states." Chapter 5, Cooke's best, is on *Don Juan.* It opens with a survey of recent criticism of the poem, moves on to a particularly interesting discussion of the influence of Restoration comedy on it, and argues that *Don Juan* is "a multiform statement of obligatory irresolution," aiming toward "a state of disequilibrium" in "reader and society," to create "a universe of the unpredictable" and the "recognition of disorder where it has been blinked or denied." Cooke finds, in short, that "the primary bent" of Byron's philosophy "must be termed skeptical." His book deals only briefly with *Beppo* and *The Vision of Judgment.* The last chapter asks "whether we can find in Byron's verse some affirmative philosophic position." It ringingly and convincingly asserts that there is a "viable option in Byron's thought, the peculiar form of humanism and stoicism that may be called counter-heroic." Cooke's tightly argued study has the virtue of frequently forcing one to pause and reexamine one's own positions. Throughout, the author remains nicely aware of and charitable toward other opinions while presenting his own distinct and well-argued point of view.

A number of shorter studies, most of them published in the 1960s, may be brought together here. The Byron chapter in Harold Bloom's *The Visionary Company* (1961, rev. 1971) offers a reading of a number of Byron's poems, excluding the biographical context, that combines apt quotation with intelligent summary in a less arcane style than that of the author's subsequent books. Ian Jack's excellent chapter on Byron in his volume of the Oxford History of English Literature, *English Literature, 1815 – 1832* (1963), sets the poet convincingly against his age. Jack gives the Romantic poems short shrift while praising the satires. Northrop Frye's somewhat disappointing essay in *Fables of Identity* (1963) finds Byron "a tremendous cultural force that was life and literature at once." Divided into three parts (an introduction to Byron's life, a discussion of the lyrics, tales, dramas, and satires, and another on Byron's afterfame), it restates Byron's obvious strengths and weaknesses, making along the way a number of dubious judgments. The chapter on Byron in Allan Rodway, *The Romantic Conflict* (1963), attempts too much and succeeds best when discussing less-read works such as *The Prophecy of Dante* and *The Age of Bronze,* the latter termed "magnificent rhetorical satire." Patricia M. Ball's chapter in *The Central Self* (1968) intelligently reveals the continuity of Byron's imaginative thrust over much of his canon. In *The Heart's Events* (1976) Ball nicely sets Byron's poems of the separation against Wordsworth's Lucy lyrics. An older essay still of value is S. de Ullmann, "Romanticism and Synaesthesia: A Comparative Study of Sense Transfer in Keats and Byron" (*PMLA,* 1945). Two general assessments are Francis M. Doherty's *Byron* (1968) and A. Craig Bell's slight *Byron: His Achievement and Significance* (1976). Articles that contribute to our understanding of Byron the poet include John Lauber's "Byron's Concept of Poetry" (*DR,* 1967 – 68); Roland Bartel's "Byron's Respect for Language" (*PLL,* 1965); and Anne Barton's Nottingham lecture, *Byron and the Mythology of Fact* (1968), a stimulating analysis of the effect that Byron's reverence for fact had on his literary creations. Obscurantist in style (and content) is Frank D. McConnell's "Byron's Reductions: 'Much Too Poetical'" (*ELH,* 1970; rpt. in his edition of *Byron's Poetry,* 1978).

THE 1970S AND AFTER

The achievements of Byron criticism in the 1970s, although not so spectacular as those of the late 1960s, are still considerable in their own right. Until the major books of 1967 – 69, critical work on Byron lagged far behind that on the other Romantic poets. This situation has now changed appreciably. The studies by Gleckner, McGann, and Cooke were conceived and worked out independently and, since they appeared within a year-and-a-half period, hardly influenced one another. The scholarship of the 1970s has built on the insights in these (and earlier) books and has taken up the questions they posed. The Romantic poems that Gleckner, McGann, and Cooke often focused on so brilliantly continue to attract first-rate work. The many facets of *Don Juan,* to which a great deal of the Byron criticism of the 1970s was devoted, now appear even more in evidence, although we still lack a major study that encompasses the poem's diversity within a

full examination of its literary, social, and political context. A similar situation
holds true for the plays: much work, most of it uneven, but few comprehensive
studies that combine penetrating criticism with proper attention to the dramatic
traditions within which Byron worked. McGann's new edition of the poems, with
its commentary, and the fuller context of Byron's life provided by Marchand's *Letters and Journals* will undoubtedly give as much impetus to critical as to biographical studies.

John D. Jump's *Byron* (1972), published as a Routledge Author Guide, is a
cautious, straightforward, somewhat dull book that will not lead beginning students of Byron astray or perhaps excite them much either. After an informative
introductory chapter, "An Age of Revolutions," Jump provides solid studies focusing on major works. He includes a chapter on Byron's prose and chapters on
the later satirical poems (the longest on *Don Juan*). *Childe Harold* he considers
briefly and the Oriental tales even more briefly. The rest is silence. In 1975 Jump
edited *Byron: A Symposium,* most of whose nine essays (noted separately) derive
in one way or another from the previous year's sesquicentennial celebrations.
Jane Kirchner's *The Function of the Persona in the Poetry of Byron* (1973), in the
Salzburg series, competently discusses its announced subject.

Bernard Blackstone's *Byron: A Survey* (1975) offers a virtuoso reading, stylistically and critically, of nearly all Byron's major poems. Blackstone has emerged as
the inheritor of the unfulfilled renown of G. Wilson Knight, with whom by temperament and iconoclastic bent he seems to have much in common. Now the
reigning *savant terrible* of the Byronic world, he combines an impressive grasp
of the poet's canon with an abundance of original and often startling insights, the
whole imbedded in much hocus-pocus and in much that is downright silly. His
style is often irritating, his organization erratic, his use of other poets for comparison elliptical or unnecessary. With his distinctive vocabulary, his outrageous
analogies, his disorganized presentation, Blackstone may put off the student at
first but usually, as here, he yields his rewards. Despite (or perhaps because of)
its author's idiosyncrasies, the book has many strengths. One is what Blackstone
calls "topocriticism." He possesses acute sensitivity to the Eastern landscapes that
Byron knew well and often longed for in imagination. His Byron emerges as very
much a poet of sight, one who prided himself on the accuracy of his descriptions.
Blackstone is often penetrating in exploring these dimensions of Byron's poetry,
for, like Byron, his familiarity with the European scene, particularly Greece and
the Near East, affords him a European rather than an English perspective. Though
Blackstone affects to scorn previous scholarship (and scholars), he has read
widely in secondary work on Byron. He has the virtue, like Wilson Knight before
him, of stimulating one to argue, to disagree, to formulate or reformulate one's
own opinions. Blackstone often reads Byron through a Blakean (and Eliotic) lens,
which can distort his vision as much as Knight's Shakespearean perspective distorted his. But Blackstone emerges as a careful reader of Byron's poetry who has
much to say of value in relating the poetry to the life. As might be expected, he is
strongest on the Eastern poems, but he is also consistently interesting on the lyrics, on *Childe Harold,* and on *Don Juan,* to which he devotes sixty pages.
Blackstone has also replaced Herbert Read's 1951 *Byron* in the Writers and Their

Work series with not one but three studies: *Lyric and Romance*; *Literary Satire, Humour and Reflection*; and *Social Satire, Drama and Epic* (1970, 1971). An earlier piece, "Guilt and Retribution in Byron's Sea Poems" (*RES*, 1961; rpt. in *The Lost Travellers*, 1962), takes up Byron's "relations" with the sea, beginning with *Hours of Idleness*, pausing over *The Island*, and culminating in the Haidée episode in *Don Juan*. On the same topic is Monique Brosse's essay "Byron et la mer" in *Romantisme*, 1974.

Charles E. Robinson's *Shelley and Byron: The Snake and Eagle Wreathed in Fight* (1976) is a detailed, documented study of the literary interactions between the two poets. Robinson has carefully read each poet's works, heeded the biographical background, and come up with numerous connections unperceived by earlier scholars. He demonstrates that Shelley experienced his major intellectual relationship not with Keats, with whom he is traditionally associated, but with Byron, and that their friendship ranks in its importance for literature with that of Wordsworth and Coleridge. Shelley was the only man of letters Byron knew well during his years in Italy, and for both poets the relationship established was of incalculable importance. Whereas Byron the poet awed Shelley, Byron the man left him alternately amazed, despondent, and, finally, bitterly resentful. Byron, for his part, liked Shelley instantly and, though often bewildered by his poetry, never failed to admire Shelley's personal qualities. Robinson has a stronger case arguing for Byron's literary influence on Shelley than for Shelley's on Byron. In regard to the latter, since Byron's comments on Shelley's poems are few and usually noncommittal, Robinson often has to formulate his argument from internal evidence. In this he indulges in frequent overreadings of poems as he relentlessly pursues and insists on a reciprocal response to each other's works to the exclusion of more likely (and often explicitly stated) literary sources. His unremitting focus on Byron and Shelley ultimately distorts their relationship. It is extremely unlikely, for example, that *Alastor* significantly influenced *Manfred* (as Robinson argues in his second chapter). Nor can the poem "All hail, Mont Blanc," which he attributes to Byron, chiefly to serve as a pendant to Shelley's "Mont Blanc," be convincingly assigned to him. More satisfying is Robinson's analysis of *Prometheus Unbound*'s debt to *Manfred*, which here receives its first detailed investigation. A number of Robinson's other comparative readings of Byron's poems in the light of Shelley's "influence" fascinate in their own right, even though the case often fails to convince. His book is, as it should be, more on Shelley than on Byron, and his readings of Shelley's poems are more successful than his readings of Byron's. Though often awkwardly written and presented, Robinson's study is one that no student of Byron's most important literary relationship can fail to benefit from. It is also one to be used with caution, for it is much more speculative than it admits regarding their reciprocal influence.

The announced purpose of Peter J. Manning's *Byron and His Fictions* (1978) is to apply the insights of psychoanalysis to Byron's life in order to elucidate his poetry—a purpose it fulfills with distinction. Manning divides the book into three parts: the first on the early poems, the Oriental tales, *Childe Harold*, and *Manfred*; the second on the historical and speculative dramas; the third on *Don Juan*. His penetrating, undoctrinaire, and virtually jargon-free study brings out as

never before the complexities of Byron's psychological makeup, how his relationships with his mother and with the father he hardly knew, later with his half-
sister and his wife, influenced the situations and interactions among characters in
his poems. On *Don Juan,* for example, Manning categorically affirms that "a
reader who excludes on principle Byron's tantalizing play with the demarcations
between biographical revelation and fiction sacrifices the essential quality of the
poem." Although cantos 1–4 of *Don Juan* "cannot be taken as literal autobiography, . . . they offer a revealing picture not of Byron's outer, but of his inner life."
That inner life lies everywhere subsumed in Byron's poetry, but not until *Don
Juan* was Byron able to sustain an extended ironic focus on it in a literary work.
"Manfred and the later cantos of *Childe Harold* suffer because the personal material is undigested," Manning argues, not quite fairly. "Awkwardly digested" yes,
"undigested" no. His chapters "History and Allusion," "The Fictions of Reality,"
and "Heroes and Heroines, Artists and Readers" subtly explore the autobiographical configurations that lie concealed in *Don Juan*'s rich texture. Those unconvinced of the validity of psychoanalysis as a tool able to clarify the underlying biographical structure of literary works would do well to read Manning's exemplary
study, which covers virtually the entire corpus of Byron's poetry. It demonstrates
that psychoanalytical criticism of Byron, after several false starts and embarrassing performances, has come of age.

Philip W. Martin's *Byron: A Poet before His Public* (1982) is the most hostile
book on Byron's poetry published in this century. It is also among the silliest. Asserting with some justice that Byron's literary contexts "have remained largely
unexplored," Martin purports to analyze Byron's relationship with his audience.
But what could have been a contribution to the study of Byron's intellectual context quickly deteriorates into a hit-or-miss study of Byron's sources. Poems stand
or (more usually) fall on their use of sources. Byron had nothing better to do in
writing, it appears, than decide which sources might best be used to dupe his
public. Martin offers one source-hunting excursus after another, all but a few of
dubious value, for he generally chooses only those that show Byron to least advantage. To seek out the poet at his worst and then to adopt the least favorable
interpretation of what he is doing—that is Martin's notion of the critic's task. Occasionally Martin even expresses surprise that Byron does not fit the procrustean
bed of his own narrow sympathies. "The history of Byron's poetry is a history of
self-deceit," he concludes. Alas, poor Byron! Martin makes many firm statements
about Byron's methods of composition, but not once does he trouble himself to
cast even a casual glance at a manuscript. Rarely do his discussions bear on the
poems themselves. Some chapters—like the one on *Cain,* for example—never
even get to the work ostensibly under discussion. How this parody of scholarly
methodology, at once shoddy and pretentious, managed to get by a doctoral
committee, much less by readers for a university press, must remain a minor
mystery. Somewhat in the same opinionated, humorless vein as Martin's book,
the Byron chapter in A. D. Harvey's *English Poetry in a Changing Society* (1980)
presents Byron's poems within the context of other, chiefly minor poets of the
period. *Byron: Wrath and Rhyme,* edited by Alan Bold (1983), includes nine es-

says of varying merit, several of which I discuss more appropriately elsewhere. Forthcoming is J. Drummond Bone's *Byron*, an introductory study for students.

Important articles on Byron of the 1970s and after include Brian Wilkie's "Byron: Artistry and Style" (in *Romantic and Victorian*, ed. W. Paul Elledge and Richard L. Hoffman, 1971), an eloquent defense of both artistry and style that examines how Byron's rhetorical art emerged out of the oratorical tradition; George Watson's "The Accuracy of Lord Byron" (*CritQ*, 1975), a wide-ranging examination of Byron's apparently conflicting claims of factual accuracy and careless composition; Gilbert Phelps's "The Byronic Byron" (in Jump's *Byron: A Symposium*), a fine interpretive essay on the Romantic poems; Bernard Beatty's "Lord Byron: Poetry and Precedent" (in *Literature of the Romantic Period 1750–1850*, ed. R. T. Davies and Beatty, 1976), a penetrating study of Byron's theory of poetry as it informed his poetic practice. I discuss Mark Storey's chapter on Byron in *Poetry and Humour from Cowper to Clough* (1979) under "Ideas and Beliefs: Comedy." In *Poetry of the Romantic Period* (1980) J. R. de J. Jackson focuses particularly (and somewhat pedestrianly) on *Childe Harold, Manfred, Cain, The Vision of Judgment*, and *Don Juan*. Difficult to classify because of its range of reference is Kurt Heinzelman's "Byron's Poetry of Politics: The Economic Basis of the 'Poetical Character'" (*TSLL*, 1981). The Byron chapter in Warren Stevenson, *The Myth of the Golden Age in English Romantic Poetry* (1981), briefly covers the terrain. Jürgen Klein, "Byron's Ideas of Democracy: An Investigation into the Relationship between Literature and Politics" (in *Byron: Poetry and Politics*, ed. Stürzl and Hogg, 1981), focuses, despite its title, less on politics than on the concept of "immediacy" in Byron. Philip Drew pursues the elusive theme of freedom, chiefly in *Manfred* and *Don Juan*, in a section of his *The Meaning of Freedom* (1982). More theoretically based is J. Drummond Bone's "The Rhetoric of Freedom" (in *Byron: Wrath and Rhyme*, ed. Bold), a succinct and enlightening discussion of the theme, with particular relation to *Childe Harold 3, Manfred*, and *Beppo*. Geoffrey Carnall, "Byron as Unacknowledged Legislator" (also in the Bold volume), offers a shrewd assessment of Byron's character, chiefly as it manifests itself within the political scene. Jennie Calder, "The Hero as Lover: Byron and Women" (also in Bold), deals intelligently with a (surprisingly) neglected subject. The Byron chapter in Ian Jack, *The Poet and His Audience* (1984), expertly surveys Byron's ever-changing relationship with his readers. The focus, however, is on Byron, not on who made up his readership—a subject meriting further investigation.

Donald H. Reiman's chapter "Byron and the 'Other,'" in his forthcoming *Romantic Inquiry*, is an intelligent, often searching study of Byron's psychology and poetry, both set against the context in which Byron thought and wrote. The poet's skepticism made him keep his distance from the "Other." "Byron's greatness as a poet lies in his comprehensive vision and in his ability to touch so many chords in the depths of human life." For Reiman, *"Don Juan . . . transforms Byron into the greatest of the British Romantics."* Another solid general interpretation of Byron is Drummond Bone's chapter on the poet in his forthcoming *On Romanticism*.

BYRON AND LITERARY TRADITION

Scholars have often investigated Byron's relationships with, and indebtedness to, earlier writers. Yet wide gaps remain in our knowledge of his awareness of literary tradition, in part because Byron's apparent insouciance often deludes us into misjudging the range of his knowledge and reading. We know less than we might about how he used literary allusions, how he read, even what he read.

Classical literature.   Byron received an excellent classical education. Though in later years he often made light of the drudgery involved, his classical studies left their imprint on everything he wrote. His touchstones for literary excellence remain Homer and Aeschylus. The pervasive influence of classical literature and history on his poetry has not been adequately explored, though there are signs that this situation is changing. Gilbert Highet provides a brief introduction to the subject in *The Classical Tradition: Greek and Roman Influences on Western Literature* (1949), as does John Buxton in "Greece in the Imagination of Byron and Shelley" (*ByronJ,* 1976). General studies that discuss Byron, written by master hands, are Harry Levin, *The Broken Column* (1931), and Douglas Bush, *Mythology and the Romantic Tradition in English Poetry* (1937). No comprehensive investigation exists of Byron's interest in Greek tragedy, particularly Aeschylus, whom he thought "sublime," though John Clubbe takes up Byron's lifelong interest in Prometheus, with special focus on the Aeschylean dimensions of *Manfred,* in "'The New Prometheus of New Men': Byron's 1816 Poems and *Manfred*" (in *Nineteenth-Century Literary Perspectives,* ed. Clyde de L. Ryals, Clubbe, and B. F. Fisher IV, 1974). Elizabeth Atkins long ago discussed (and overstated) "Points of Contact between Byron and Socrates" (*PMLA,* 1926), more a study of their respective ways of viewing phenomena than of influence. Bernard Blackstone's elaborate speculations in "Byron and the *Republic:* The Platonic Background to Byron's Political Ideas" (in *Byron: Poetry and Politics,* ed. Stürzl and Hogg, 1981) cloud rather than clarify the subject. That "external verification" for Byron's knowledge of Plato is difficult to come by does not in the least deter Blackstone. Jerome J. McGann thoughtfully discusses Byron's ambivalent response to Horace, whom he "hated so" (however "not for thy faults, but mine"), and Horace's influence on the poet's major satire in Don Juan *in Context* (1976); E. Kegel Brinkgreve in "Byron and Horace" (*ES,* 1976) also surveys Byron's familiarity with the Roman poet. Both supersede the discussion in Mary Rebecca Thayer, *The Influence of Horace on the Chief English Poets of the Nineteenth Century* (1916). Frederick L. Beaty in "Byron's Imitations of Juvenal and Persius" (*SIR,* 1976) details in exemplary fashion the ways in which these writers served as models. To my knowledge, no one has explored the influence on Byron of Lucretius, to whom he often refers. See also the studies noted for individual poems, for example, Clearman's on *English Bards,* Ogle's on *The Bride of Abydos,* which looks at the poem's debt to Ovid's *Metamorphoses,* and Emrys Jones on *The Vision of Judgment*; the discussions of Byron's interest in epic (Homer particularly) noted in the section on *Don Juan*; and Arthur D. Kahn's two studies, one on pastoral in

The Island, the other on Seneca's influence on *Sardanapalus.* Under "Reputation and Influence: Europe. Greece" I mention a number of related studies.

The Bible. Byron had the Bible constantly by him and knew it, particularly the Old Testament, very well—so well, in fact, that Goethe conceived Byron's mission to be to dramatize the Old Testament. The Bible's influence can be followed poem by poem in Travis Looper's *Byron and the Bible: A Compendium of Biblical Usage in the Poetry of Lord Byron* (1978). It notes allusions from each poem, listed alphabetically, first under the heading of Old Testament, then of the New. Biblical allusions turn out to be more numerous than generally suspected, for, consciously and unconsciously, Byron made the Bible part of the texture of his poetry. Looper's introduction usefully surveys previous discussions of Byron's interest in religion and traces his lifelong interest in the Bible. Studies of *Cain* often discuss biblical influence. The few pages on Byron in Murray Roston's *Prophet and Poet: The Bible and the Growth of Romanticism* (1965) also focus on *Cain*.

English literature. A. P. Hudson in "Byron and the Ballad" (*SP,* 1945) has investigated Byron's love of, and intimate acquaintance with, the ballads of the Border country, which he constantly quoted, often echoed, and occasionally imitated. Byron knew his Shakespeare intimately. As his letters and journals indicate, he often looked to him in moments of crisis. G. Wilson Knight, from his chapter in *The Burning Oracle* (1939) through *Byron and Shakespeare* (1966), has championed Shakespearean models for Byron's conduct and Shakespearean analogues for his poetry (and life). Students should approach Knight's writings—here brilliantly suggestive analyses, there parodies of scholarly investigation—with caution. A sober recent study is A. A. Jelistratowa, "Byrons Verhältnis zu Shakespeare" (*Shakespeare-Jahrbuch,* 1971). The brief discussion of Shakespearean allusions in Byron's journals in Robert A. Fothergill's *Private Chronicles* (1974) is excellent. E. A. Stürzl has authoritatively traced "Byron's Literary Pilgrimage among Elizabethan and Jacobean Authors" (*ByronJ,* 1978). Jerome J. McGann points out in "Milton and Byron" (*KSMB,* 1974) that Byron's interest, which emerged as early as 1812, came to the fore with the poet's identification with Milton in the poems of 1816–17. McGann also takes up briefly *Cain* and *Don Juan.* Joseph Anthony Wittreich's *The Romantics on Milton* (1970) conveniently collects Byron's references. Michael G. Cooke in "The Restoration Ethos of Byron's Classical Plays" (*PMLA,* 1964) discusses a late phase of Dryden's influence. Pope inspired Byron's chief extended pieces of literary criticism, his replies to the Rev. W. L. Bowles's strictures on Pope's poetry. This subject led to J. J. Van Rennes's monograph *Bowles, Byron, and the Pope-Controversy* (1927), but Prothero had already assembled in the fifth volume of his edition of the *Letters and Journals* all the essential documents. Upali Amarasinghe, *Dryden and Pope in the Early Nineteenth Century* (1962), is useful on the Pope controversy as well as on the larger subject of its title. G. Wilson Knight's *Laureate of Peace: The Poetry of Pope* (1955) includes lengthy consideration of "Byron's adulation of Pope," whereas Michael G. Cooke

acutely distinguishes between Pope's classicism and Byron's in the first chapter of
The Blind Man Traces the Circle. James L. Tyne, "Terrestrial and Transcendental
Man as Viewed by Swift and Byron" (*Enlightenment Essays,* 1977), contrasts
each's satiric vision. Howard O. Brogan in "Byron and Dr. Johnson, 'That
Profoundest of Critics' " (*BNYPL,* 1976) details Byron's allusions to Johnson, whose
influence helped buoy Byron's poetic principles. In "Byron and Johnson: The Dialectics of Temerity" (*JES,* 1980) Bernard Blackstone, taking "temerity" (from *Ram-
bler* 129) as his theme, suggestively draws parallels, biographical and literary, with
a focus on each writer's travelogues. On Byron and Sterne, see the discussion in
E. F. Boyd's and András Horn's books on *Don Juan* (1945, 1962), Earl R. Wasserman's note in *MLN* (1955), and J. Drummond Bone's in *ByronJ* (1981); on Byron
and Fielding, see Boyd, Horn, and Itsuyo Higashinaka's note in *ByronJ* (1984).
Though Horn and A. B. England in their studies of *Don Juan* present a number of
interesting analogies that indicate Byron's wide acquaintance with eighteenth-
century poetry, prose, and drama, the subject has yet to receive comprehensive
treatment. Byron soaked himself in Gibbon, but I have found no good study of
this subject, or of his reading in the Enlightenment philosophers, Hume especially. Heinrich Hartmann in *Lord Byrons Stellung zu den Klassizisten seiner Zeit*
(1932) studies Byron's opinions of, and relations with, poets such as Rogers in
whose verse the earlier mode survived. William A. Covino, "Blair, Byron, and the
Psychology of Reading" (*Rhetoric Society Quarterly,* 1981), reveals Byron in *Don
Juan* flouting eighteenth-century models of coherence and unity advocated by
Blair. Philip Hobsbaum, "Byron and the English Tradition" (in *Byron: Wrath and
Rhyme,* ed. Bold), relates Byron to contemporary litterateurs, including John
Herman Merivale and William Stewart Rose.

The Scottish influence on Byron is affirmed in Symon's biography (1924),
proclaimed as a new discovery in T. S. Eliot's essay on Byron (1937), developed in
W. W. Robson's lecture *Byron the Poet* (1957), specified in Roderick S. Speer's
"Byron and the Scottish Literary Tradition" (*SSL,* 1979), but strongly denied in An-
drew Rutherford's "Byron, Scott, and Scotland" in Robinson's *Lord Byron and His
Contemporaries.* Tom Scott's preposterous essay "Byron as a Scottish Poet" (in
Byron: Wrath and Rhyme, ed. Bold) will leave unconvinced all but the most per-
fervid of the Scots who wish to claim Byron as part of their literary patrimony.
Not preposterous but too single-minded in intent, Everard H. King's "Beattie and
Byron: A Study in Augustan Satire and Romantic Vision" (*Aberdeen University Re-
view,* 1980) overstates Byron's admitted debt in *Childe Harold* to Beattie's
Minstrel. J. Minto Robertson, "Byron and Burns—A Comparison" (*Burns Chroni-
cle,* 1946), is a popular introduction by a Burns enthusiast.

European literature.   Giovanna Foà in *Lord Byron. Poeta e Carbonaro* (1935)
offers a readable survey of Byron's rapport with Italian literature from Dante to
Alfieri, then examines the poet's relationships with contemporary Italian literary
figures and with the *Carbonari,* the Italian fighters for freedom. The survey by
W. P. Friederich of Byron's interest in Dante in *Dante's Fame Abroad* (1950) subsumes previous scholarship. See also Oswald Doughty, "Dante and the English

Romantic Poets" (*EM,* 1951); Frederick L. Beaty, "Byron and the Story of Francesca da Rimini" (*PMLA,* 1960); the chapter (in Spanish) in Pujals, *Lord Byron en España* (1982); and that in Charles Dédéyan, *Dante dans le romantisme anglais* (1983), which finds that Byron's works "reflète une grande admiration et une influence certaine du poète florentin." The most recent examination, Steve Ellis' *Dante and English Poetry: Shelley to T. S. Eliot* (1983), has a well-informed if maundering chapter entitled "Dante as the Byronic Hero." See also DeSua and de Palacio under "Romantic (and Other) Poems: Translations."

That Byron knew well the works of Giambattista Casti is beyond dispute, but P. G. Vassallo in "Casti's *Animali Parlanti,* the Italian Epic and *Don Juan:* The Poetry of Politics" (in Stürzl and Hogg's *Byron: Poetry and Politics*) does not convince me in all his large claims for Casti's influence on *Don Juan.* Vassallo republished this essay in *Byron: The Italian Literary Influence* (1984), an often path-breaking reconsideration of Byron's reading in Italian literature. The first two of the seven chapters examine "Byron's Early Italian Interest" and "Byron, Dante and Italy." Chapters 3 – 6, the most original part of the study, take up Casti's influence on Byron. Full consideration of Byron's reading in Casti has long been overdue and Vassallo makes an impressive case for the Italian's influence on Byron's poetry. The concluding chapter—on Byron's debt to Pulci—may be Vassallo's best. Vassallo is especially helpful on Byron's translation of Pulci's *Morgante Maggiore,* less convincing on *The Vision of Judgment,* whose tone and spirit he claims Pulci affected. Vassallo's study yields a number of valuable insights, yet it often falls into the trap of source studies, that is, of seeing the works it contemplates within a predetermined focus. Though a milestone in charting Byron's Italian reading, the book remains finally somewhat unconvincing. Italian influence appears nearly everywhere in Byron's poetry. Granted, it may often be found, more than has hitherto been recognized, but in my view it does not exist to the extent that Vassallo claims it does. Analogues and parallels do not necessarily denote influence. Vassallo ignores or downplays scholarship that does not accord with his interpretations and unerringly finds what he wants to find. He makes little use of most items listed in the bibliography. There are a few rash statements (e.g., p. 22, in regard to the literary derivation of *Childe Harold*) and a few outright errors (e.g., p. 49, where the author conflates *Childe Harold* 3 and 4). On the positive side, Vassallo does chart Italian influence on Byron more thoroughly than anyone has before. And he does usefully remind us how much Byron was a *literary* poet: "It was Byron's reading rather than the physical actuality of being in a foreign country [Italy] which was the primary source of his inspiration."

On other aspects of the reciprocal relationship between Byron and Italian literature, see Martha King, "Early Italian Romanticism and *The Giaour*" (*ByronJ,* 1976), and Robert B. Ogle, "A Byron Contradiction: Some Light on His Italian Study" (*SIR,* 1973), on Byron's reading of literary histories by Sismondi and Ginguené. Aurelio Zanco's "L'Alfierismo' del Byron" in his *Shakespeare in Russia e altri saggi* (1945) rejects Foà's large claims for Alfieri's influence. A still useful survey is Anna Pudbres, "Lord Byron, the Admirer and Imitator of Alfieri" (*Englische Studien,* 1904).

The Variorum *Don Juan* revealed that Byron knew Montaigne, but it remained for Richard I. Kirkland in "Byron's Reading of Montaigne: A Leigh Hunt Letter" (*KSJ,* 1981) to establish that Byron had Cotton's translation by him daily for several months in 1822. Kirkland briefly suggests the dimensions of this important influence, as does Hermione de Almeida in her study of Byron and Joyce, discussed in the section on *Don Juan.* De Almeida also makes a number of interesting analogies between Byron and Rabelais, indicating the desirability of a comparative study. Anthony Close in *The Romantic Approach to* Don Quixote (1978) sets in perspective Byron's remarks on Cervantes in *Don Juan.* On Molière, we have Abraham Avni, "Molière and the Writers of the English Romantic Era, especially Byron," in *Molière and the Commonwealth of Letters,* edited by Roger Johnson et al. (1975). Jacques Voisine includes a chapter on Byron in his magisterial *J.-J. Rousseau en Angleterre à l'époque romantique* (1956), and Edward Duffy, though focusing on Shelley, has perceptive observations on Byron in *Rousseau in England: The Context for Shelley's Critique of the Enlightenment* (1979). Elizabeth Brody Tenenbaum, *The Problematic Self: Approaches to Identity in Stendhal, D. H. Lawrence and Malraux* (1977), opens with a comparison between Byron and Rousseau, each embodying "diametrically opposite poles of Romantic thought." Harold Orel's "Lord Byron's Debt to the Enlightenment" (in *Studies on Voltaire and the Eighteenth Century,* ed. Theodore Besterman, 1963; rpt. in Orel's *English Romantic Poets and the Enlightenment: Nine Essays on a Literary Relationship,* in *Studies on Voltaire and the Eighteenth Century,* vol. 103, ed. Besterman, 1973) is chiefly on Rousseau, Voltaire, and, too briefly, Gibbon. Byron knew eighteenth-century French literature even more thoroughly than we realize. In Italy Byron read the French classics by preference, and a study of their influence comparable to Vassallo's of the Italian is much to be desired. Other of Byron's literary relationships I discuss under "Reputation and Influence."

Byron's reading.   The books Byron read are an important index to his thought and writing. His library was auctioned in 1816 to raise money for his European sojourn; a second auction—of books accumulated since 1816—took place in 1827, after his death. The 1827 sale included, in effect, only the remnants of Byron's library, for many books were withheld and Byron certainly read (and owned) books other than those listed in the catalog. The catalogs for both sales are conveniently available in volume 1 of *Sales Catalogues of Libraries of Eminent Persons,* edited by A. N. L. Munby (8 vols., 1971), who reprints the British Museum copies (which indicate prices paid). Earlier, Gilbert H. Doane had edited the *Catalogue of the Library of the Late Lord Byron, Sold in 1827* (1929), and William H. Marshall "The [1816] Catalogue for the Sale of Byron's Books" (*LC,* 1968). Anyone doing specialized research involving Byron's reading, or possible reading, or the influence of what he read on what he wrote, should consult these lists to determine whether Byron had read the work in question and, if he had, in what edition. No one should assume, however, that because a particular work does not appear in one of these (or under "Books Read" in Prothero's index to the *Letters and Journals*) that Byron had not read it. He is one of the most allusive (as well as elusive) of authors, and his writings—prose as well as poetry—are still incompletely annotated. The Rosenbaum and White *Index to English Literary Manuscripts,* volume 4 (1982), notes the location of a few of the books in which Byron scribbled marginalia. E. F. Boyd's chapter, "Byron's Library and His Reading" (in *Byron's Don Juan,* 1945), is judicious and well-informed. Ludwig Fuhrmann's *Die Belesenheit des jungen Byrons* (1903) documents the enormous range of Byron's reading to 1816. Roy E. Aycock has investigated "Lord Byron and Bayle's Dictionary" in *YES,* 1975. In "Byron and Bayle" (*Newsletter of the Austrian Byron Society,* 1979) Paulino Lim, Jr., takes up Byron's interest in Bayle in regard to *Don Juan's* skepticism. Other connections deserving further study include Byron's extensive knowledge of Isaac D'Israeli's compilations and his reading in the Restoration and eighteenth-century dramatists, Pope, Fielding, and Scott, even in the Bard of Avon himself.

Criticism: Individual Works

The review of scholarship on Byron's poems that follows is divided into three sections and within each section is roughly chronological. The first section covers the poetry that Byron wrote in the years before his exile, in Switzerland, and in his first year in Italy. At the end of this section I discuss *The Island* (1823) and Byron's translations. The second section deals with the later satires (*Beppo, The Vision of Judgment,* and *Don Juan*). The third considers Byron's dramas, with the exception of *Manfred,* which I take up with the other poems written in Switzerland.

Many of the major critical readings of Byron's poems occur not in articles but in the book-length studies discussed in the preceding sections. By and large I do not refer to them here. Nor do I usually notice articles subsequently published as parts of books. When an article contains significant discussion of several works, I usually refer to it under the first work and, whenever possible, mention it again if considerable space separates it from the earlier reference. Aside from *Don Juan,* Byron's major poems have not yet received the critically sophisticated book-length studies that the major poems of other Romantic poets have often received. A number of these poems merit such in-depth discussion, others need to find their champions, while with still others—for instance, *Hints from Horace, The Lament of Tasso, The Age of Bronze*—almost everything remains to be done. Such investigations should be among the future tasks for Byron scholarship.

ROMANTIC (AND OTHER) POEMS

By now no one will doubt the inadequacy of "Romantic" as an inclusive term for the poets in this volume. No more successfully does it encompass the poems included in this section. Students may find discussions of terminology confusing, but they should realize that the issue goes beyond taxonomy. It goes to the heart of the enormously complex interrelationships among Byron's poems. Strictly speaking, few of the poems fall wholly into a single category, whether "romantic," "satiric," "lyric," or any other. Viewed from an organizational perspective different from the one I have adopted here, Byron's satires and dramas might well be considered, in their very different ways, "Romantic" poems. But other designations for Byron's early poems—for example, Blackstone's "Lyric and Romance"—I find misleading and no less confusing. "Romantic" has the virtue, at least, of long tradition behind it. At this point one risks less confusion using it than using any other term.

Lyrics. Byron wrote lyrics all his life but until the late 1960s discussions of them were few. Leonard C. Martin's Nottingham lecture, *Byron's Lyrics* (1948), asserts that the poet's best lyrics transcend mere personality and, because of their noble style, deriving from the Greek or Roman classics and from the Bible, "can be called classical." The books by Gleckner, McGann, and Cooke offer analyses of individual poems in *Hours of Idleness* and *Hebrew Melodies.* The early lyrics are valued in themselves and as significant anticipations of major emphases in poems to come. William S. Ward discusses sixteen reviews of Byron's first public volume in "Byron's *Hours of Idleness* and Other than Scotch Reviewers" (*MLN,* 1944). On the relationship of background to text, specifically on "Go—triumph securely" and "When We Two Parted," see Jerome J. McGann, "The Significance of Biographical Context: Two Poems by Lord Byron," in *The Author in His Work,* edited by Louis L. Martz and Aubrey Williams (1978). In an analysis of "So we'll go no more a-roving" (in *Versdichtung der englischen Romantik,* ed. T. A. Riese and Dieter Riesner, 1968) Hans-Jürgen Diller makes a cogent case for Byron as a lyric poet Diller's "Wie Byrons Lyrik gemacht ist" (in *Byron-Symposium Mannheim 1982,* ed. Werner Huber and Rainer Schöwerling, 1983) finds that because the lyrics are the expressions of a famous-infamous man readers can identify with them. Via Russian formalist criticism, he argues for the successful realization of Byron's lyrics as rhetoric. Jean H. Hagstrum's "Byron's Songs of Innocence: The Poems to 'Thyrza'" (in *Evidence in Literary Scholarship,* ed. René Wellek and Alveiro Ribeiro, 1979) is a balanced essay, sensitive to Byron's lyric genius and undoctrinaire in its conclusions. Ronald A. Schroeder, "The Rejection and Redefinition of Romance in Byron's Early Poetry" (*Univ. of Mississippi Studies in English,* 1981), is excellent on Byron's early attitude toward "romance." One might wish for studies of Byron's elegiac lyrics. See also under *"Hebrew Melodies"* and *"Poems of 1816"* in this section.

Early satires. The early satires include *English Bards and Scotch Reviewers, Hints from Horace, The Curse of Minerva,* and *Waltz: An Apostrophic Hymn. English Bards* is an important if not fully achieved poem, and it deserves more critical commentary than it has had. Mary Clearman, "A Blueprint for *English Bards and Scotch Reviewers*: The First Satire of Juvenal" (*KSJ,* 1970), argues convincingly for the first satire as the controlling model. Peter J. Manning, "Byron's *English Bards and Scotch Reviewers*: The Art of Allusion" (*KSMB,* 1970), considers in particular Charles Churchill's important (if unnamed) presence in the poem.

Thomas Lockwood's *Post-Augustan Satire: Charles Churchill and Satirical Poetry, 1750 – 1800* (1979) valuably presents the background, in particular Churchill's works, out of which Byron's satires emerged. Michael E. Bassett, "Pope, Byron and Satiric Technique" (*Satire Newsletter*, 1968), points out analogies. Muriel J. Mellown, "Francis Jeffrey, Lord Byron, and *English Bards, and Scotch Reviewers*" (*SSL*, 1981), notes that Byron's critical opinions often closely follow Jeffrey's (and the *Edinburgh's*).

Critics of Byron usually avoid taking up *Hints from Horace,* yet the poem would repay analysis in regard not only to its ostensible model, the *Ars Poetica,* but also to Pope's *Imitations of Horace.* Byron enters William St. Clair's *Lord Elgin and the Marbles* (1967) chiefly through his savage attack on Elgin in *The Curse of Minerva.* In *Waltz* the poet denounced the recent introduction of the dance from Germany into England, where it rapidly became a fashionable craze among the bon ton. In "Byron's *Waltz*: The Germans and Their Georges" (*KSJ,* 1969), William Childers expertly sets Byron's poem within this contemporary context. David V. Erdman in *KSJ,* 1970, supplements Childers. Robert D. Hume, "The Non-Augustan Nature of Byron's Early Satires" (*RLV,* 1968), focuses particularly on *Waltz.*

Childe Harold's Pilgrimage.   The critical turnabout on *Childe Harold's Pilgrimage,* Byron's major Romantic poem, finds reflection in Francis Berry, "The Poet of *Childe Harold*" (in Jump's *Byron: A Symposium*). A poet himself, Berry came to maturity believing T. S. Eliot's influential dictum of 1937 that Byron "would seem the most nearly remote from the sympathies of every living poet." Forty years later, Berry, like many others, responds to the Romantic Byron "with enormous pleasure and admiration," finding in him a poet who had a sure sense of his audience and who used language with distinction. Childe Harold's Pilgrimage *and* Don Juan: A Casebook, edited by Jump (1973), anthologizes representative published criticism on the two poems that illustrates this shift in sensibility. Comments by Byron and his contemporaries compose the first part, Victorian assessments the second. Ten longer pieces follow, about equally divided between the two poems and most of them taken from more recent criticism, including the studies by Calvert, West, Karl Kroeber, Rutherford, Joseph, and Marchand (1965). Among discussions in critical books, that in McGann's *Fiery Dust* remains indispensable. In Georg Roppen and Richard Sommer, *Strangers and Pilgrims: An Essay on the Metaphor of Journey* (1964), Roppen offers a sustained reading of *Childe Harold,* with particular focus on the latter two cantos. Other studies worth noting include Sir Harold Nicolson's lecture entitled *The Poetry of Byron* (1943), chiefly on *Childe Harold*; Carl Woodring, "Nature, Art, Reason and Imagination in *Childe Harold*" (in *Romantic and Victorian,* ed. Elledge and Hoffman, 1971), a terse evaluation of *Childe Harold* as a unified poem; Bernard Blackstone, " 'The Loops of Time': Spatio-Temporal Patterns in 'Childe Harold' " (*ArielE,* 1971), an expansion of his discussion from the second of his Writers and Their Work pamphlets on Byron; and Malcolm Kelsall, "The Childe and the Don" (*ByronJ,* 1976), a timely reminder that from the beginning the Romantic and the satiric existed side by side in Byron and cannot easily be separated. Bernard A. Hirsch's

"The Erosion of the Narrator's World View in *Childe Harold's Pilgrimage,* I – II" (*MLQ,* 1981) works best as an intelligent running commentary on the poem's contents with illuminating remarks on the shifting narrative voices. In an important article, Michael Vicario, "The Implications of Form in *Childe Harold's Pilgrimage*" (*KSJ,* 1984), investigates the subtitle "A Romaunt," explores the tradition of eighteenth-century Spenserian imitation (Thomson, Beattie), and finds that "although Byron subjects the conventions with which he works to severe scrutiny and constant redefinition, he nevertheless does achieve a qualified affirmation of romance in the face of contemporary history and amidst the ruins he contemplates." The argument is more convincing for cantos 1 and 2 than for 3 and 4. Ronald A. Schroeder, "Ellis, Sainte-Palaye, and Byron's 'Addition' to the 'Preface' of *Childe Harold's Pilgrimage* I – II" (*KSJ,* 1983), demonstrates the value of carefully reading Byron's prose preface. Specifically on canto 2 is Blackstone's "Byron's Greek Canto: The Anatomy of Freedom" (*YES,* 1974), idiosyncratic as ever, though with occasional moments of illumination. On the reasons for *Childe Harold's* popularity, see Andrew Rutherford's Nottingham lecture, *Byron the Best-seller* (1964). See also the separate discussions for cantos 3 and 4.

Tales.   The tales include *The Giaour, The Bride of Abydos, The Corsair, Lara, The Siege of Corinth,* and *Parisina. The Prisoner of Chillon, Mazeppa,* and *The Island,* also among Byron's tales, I take up in appropriate chronological order later in this section. Hermann Fischer, *Die romantische Verserzählung in England: Versuch einer Gattungsgeschichte* (1964), has an interesting chapter on Byron's experiments in narrative that led to *Childe Harold* and the tales. Fischer's "Metre and Narrative Rhetoric in Byron" (*ByronJ,* 1982) nicely introduces this complex subject, again focusing on the tales and *Childe Harold.* A still useful survey of the background is Harold Wiener's solidly researched "Byron and the East: Literary Sources of the Turkish Tales" in *Nineteenth-Century Studies,* edited by Herbert Davis, William C. DeVane, and R. C. Bald (1940). The many references to Byron in Colette Le Yaouanc's *L'Orient dans la poésie anglaise de l'époque romantique (1798 – 1824)* (1975) stress the reality behind his Oriental settings. On the tales, the student should consult particularly McGann's detailed commentary in volume 3 of the *Complete Poetical Works,* where the twists and turns of Byron's poetic career from 1812 to 1816, when he left England, are mapped out as never before.

The Giaour.   *The Giaour* has in recent years attracted the most attention. Several critical studies, for instance, Gleckner's *Byron and the Ruins of Paradise* and McGann's *Fiery Dust,* analyze it in depth. For some works— *Childe Harold, Hebrew Melodies, Cain,* and *Don Juan*—scholars have studied in detail Byron's extensive revisions; other works—*English Bards, The Corsair, Sardanapalus*—have suffered relative neglect. William H. Marshall in "The Accretive Structure of Byron's 'The Giaour'" (*MLN,* 1961) argued that in expanding *The Giaour* from 407 to 1,334 lines, from the first to the seventh editions, Byron made "this snake of a poem" incoherent. Several studies since have argued the opposite view. In "The Development of *The Giaour*" (*SEL,* 1969) Michael G. Sundell finds that Byron's accretions prove him capable of "purposeful and careful revision." Frederick Garber in "Byron's 'Giaour' and the Mark of Cain" (*EA*, 1975) agrees with Gleckner and McGann that the many-times-enlarged *Giaour* has "an impressive, occasionally awkward inner coherence." He points out how Byron's accretions subtly alter characterization and situation. Daniel P. Watkins, "Idealism in Byron's 'The Giaour'" (*USF Language Quarterly*, 1981), sensibly steers between Marshall and McGann-Gleckner on the poem's fragmentary nature—and worth. Peter B. Wilson in "'Galvanism upon Mutton,' Byron's Conjuring Trick in *The Giaour*" (*KSJ*, 1975) views the poem as fundamentally unsatisfactory but does not succeed in explaining why. Frederick W. Shilstone, "Byron's *The Giaour*: Narrative Tradition and Romantic Cognitive Theory" (*RS*, 1980), interestingly examines Byron's poem, within the framework of modern theories of perception, as "an aesthetic experiment in human perception." One of the works considered in Daniel P. Deneau's *Byron's Narrative Poems of 1813: Two Essays* (1975) is *The Giaour*, which Deneau analyzes carefully and with frequent reference to, and participation in, the scholarly debate.

Other tales.   Deneau's other chapter (in the work just cited) finds *The Bride of Abydos* a less accomplished poem than does Gleckner in *Byron and the Ruins of Paradise*. Robert B. Ogle in "The Metamorphosis of Selim: Ovidian Myth in *The Bride of Abydos*" (*SIR*, 1981) points out Byron's debt to Ovid in five allusive adaptations of the *Metamorphoses* in canto 2 of Byron's poem. A solid study. Gloria T. Hull's "The Byronic Heroine and Byron's *The Corsair*" (*ArielE*, 1978) argues for the importance of the neglected heroines, with particular focus on Medora and Gulnare. William H. McCarthy, Jr., examines "The First Edition of Byron's 'Corsair'" in the *Colophon*, 1936. Peter J. Manning's "Tales and Politics: *The Corsair, Lara*, and *The White Doe of Rylstone*" (in *Byron: Poetry and Politics*, ed. Stürzl and Hogg, 1981) is a subtle piece of detective work into Byron's politics—his public image even more than his personal beliefs—as they manifest themselves in several of his tales. William H. Marshall's intriguing study "Byron's *Parisina* and the Function of Psychoanalytic Criticism" (*Personalist*, 1961) forms part of his *Structure of Byron's Major Poems* (1962). Still of use on *The Siege of Corinth* is Eugen Kölbing's critical edition (1896).

Hebrew Melodies.   Thomas L. Ashton in *Byron's Hebrew Melodies* (1972) establishes for the first time the definitive canon of these poems. His monograph-length introduction subsumes most previous scholarship. He untangles with fine skill the complex negotiations between Byron and Isaac Nathan, the Jewish music master who by dint of long siege and clever strategy persuaded the poet to write poems on biblical themes to accompany his "ancient" Hebrew melodies. Particularly valuable is Ashton's placing of the poems within the dramatic awakening of nationalistic sentiment that occurred in the aftermath of the French Revolution. One may not wish to go all the way with him when he claims in his preface that "if Byron is to be Byron the poet, his lyric talent needs to be valued equally with his satiric genius." Yet he convinces us, in the end, that "the Hebrew melodies occupy a significant place in the evolution of romantic lyricism." Valuable earlier work includes Karl Adolf Beutler, *Über Lord Byrons "Hebrew Melodies"* (1912), a meticulous poem-by-poem analysis, and Joseph Slater, "Byron's *Hebrew Melodies*" (*SP,* 1952), which shows that in these poems Byron did not concern himself with religious problems but voiced a sympathy with Jewish nationalistic aspirations that foreshadowed his devotion to the cause of liberty in Italy and Greece. Nahum Sokolow in chapter 18 of his *History of Zionism* (1919) had discussed Byron's influence on the movement. Edward Sarmiento, "A Parallel between Lord Byron and Fray Luis de Léon" (*RES,* 1953), points out similarities between Byron's Hebrew melody, "When coldness wraps this suffering clay," and several of Léon's poems. Edmund Miller in "Byron's Moonshine: Alternative Readings in the Ironic Mode" (*ByronJ,* 1985) illumines the irony in "She Walks in Beauty." Frederick W. Shilstone in "The Lyric Collection as Genre: Byron's *Hebrew Melodies*" (*CP,* 1979) argues well the case for Byron as a lyric poet. A facsimile edition of Isaac Nathan's settings of *Hebrew Melodies,* prepared by Frederick Burwick and Paul Douglass, will be forthcoming.

Poems of 1816.   The poems of 1816 include *The Prisoner of Chillon; Childe Harold* 3; a number of Byron's shorter pieces, among them "Darkness," "The Dream," "Prometheus," and "Epistle to Augusta"; and his dramatic poem, *Manfred.* Since these works have a familial relationship, studies of one work often discuss others. John Clubbe provides a perspective on the biographical background out of which they emerged in " 'The New Prometheus of New Men': Byron's 1816 Poems and *Manfred*" (in *Nineteenth-Century Literary Perspectives,* ed. Ryals, Clubbe, and Fisher, 1974). Douglas Grant, "Byron: The Pilgrim and Don Juan" (in *The Morality of Art,* ed. D. W. Jefferson, 1969), recreates the way contemporaries read the 1816 poems. Another general study, focusing on the influence of Wordsworth and especially Coleridge, is Edwin M. Everett, "Lord Byron's Lakist Interlude" (*SP,* 1958). See also the relevant pages of Paul H. Fry, "The Absent Dead: Wordsworth, Byron, and the Epitaph" (*SIR,* 1978).

On *The Prisoner of Chillon,* see Gerald C. Wood, "Nature and Narrative in Byron's 'The Prisoner of Chillon' " (*KSJ,* 1975). Everett's "Lakist Interlude" examines the parallels between this poem and *The Rime of the Ancient Mariner.*

A splendid essay, suggesting interrelationships among the poems of 1816 and evidencing Byron's insistence on the mind's power to create its own world, is Ward Pafford's "Byron and the Mind of Man: *Childe Harold* III – IV and *Manfred*" (*SIR,* 1962). Patricia M. Ball has written an introduction for students, Childe Harold's Pilgrimage *Cantos III and IV and* The Vision of Judgment (1968). Kenneth A. Bruffee in "The Synthetic Hero and the Narrative Structure of *Childe Harold* III" (*SEL,* 1966) builds on Marshall's controversial argument regarding the poem's design in *The Structure of Byron's Major Poems* (1962). John A. Hodgson, "The Structures of *Childe Harold* III" (*SIR,* 1979), elaborates, from a structuralist perspective, on Marshall's discussion. Michael V. DePorte, "Byron's Strange Perversity of Thought" (*MLQ,* 1972), provides a penetrating treatment of the theme of madness in Byron and of the third canto's possible indebtedness to Swift's "Digression on Madness." On Byron's perception of the natural world, see Ronald Tetreault, "Shelley and Byron Encounter the Sublime: Switzerland, 1816"

(*RLV,* 1975), and the chapter in J. R. Watson's *Picturesque Landscape and English Romantic Poetry* (1970). Martin Brunkhorst's illustrated essay "Byrons Rheinreise: Vorläufer und Nachfolger" (in *Byron-Symposium Mannheim 1982,* ed. Huber and Schöwerling) explains how patterns of artistic response to a landscape develop. Byron's experience of the Rhine was in part shaped by his precursors (Beckford, Ann Radcliffe, Sir John Carr); in turn, it influenced those who came after (Mary Shelley, Turner, Bulwer). In "The 'Castled Crag of Drachenfels': Funktionswechsel eines Landschaftsbildes" (*Arcadia,* 1982) Brunkhorst discusses this context more fully. Fred V. Randel, "The Mountaintops of English Romanticism" (*TSLL,* 1981), compares Byron's treatment of mountains—in *Childe Harold* 3, "Prometheus," and *Manfred,* with even a glance at Shooter's Hill in *Don Juan*—with that of the other major Romantics. Hans-Jürgen Diller, "Form und Funktion der Apostrophen in Byrons *Childe Harold's Pilgrimage*" (*Anglia,* 1964), analyzes the rhetorical art of a poet who often apostrophized people, places, and abstract qualities. Robert Lance Snyder's "Byron's Ontology of the Creating Self in *Childe Harold* 3" (*BuR,* 1980) relies too heavily on a gaggle of modern pundits to advance our understanding of Byron's poem. Ronald F. Lunsford, "Byron's Spatial Metaphor: A Psycholinguistic Approach" (in *Linguistic Perspectives on Literature,* ed. Marvin K. L. Ching, Michael C. Haley, and Lunsford, 1980), demonstrates what can be done to a Byron poem, in this case *Childe Harold* 3, using the tools of linguistic analysis, complete with graphs and other aids. Sheila Emerson in "Byron's 'One Word': The Language of Self-Expression" (*SIR,* 1981) studies Byron's reflexive language in developing the context of the "*one* word" passage of stanza 97.

George M. Ridenour's excellent "Byron in 1816: Four Poems from Diodati" (in *From Sensibility to Romanticism,* ed. Frederick W. Hilles and Harold Bloom, 1965) discusses "Epistle to Augusta," "Darkness," "The Dream," and "A Fragment." Specifically on "Epistle to Augusta" is Robert R. Harson's "Byron's 'Tintern Abbey'" (*KSJ,* 1971). On this poem and "Lines on Hearing that Lady Byron was Ill" see W. W. Robson's *Byron the Poet* (1957). Michael G. Cooke's essay in Robinson's *Lord Byron and His Contemporaries* includes an intriguing discussion of "The Dream." Nancy M. Goslee, "Pure Stream from a Troubled Source: Byron, Schlegel and Prometheus" (*ByronJ,* 1982), argues that "Prometheus" is indebted to the interpretation of Aeschylus advanced in A. W. Schlegel's *Lectures.* On "Prometheus," see also the pages in M. Byron Raizis, *From Caucasus to Pittsburgh: The Prometheus Theme in British and American Poetry* (1982). John Clubbe examines "Byron's 'Monody on Sheridan': The Poem in Its Context" (*Papers on Language and Literature,* ed. Sven Bäckman and Göran Kjellner, 1985). For the biographical and political context surrounding "Fare Thee Well" and other poems written before Byron left for Switzerland, see David V. Erdman's essay in volume 4 of *Shelley and His Circle* (1973).

A superb essay on the dramatic poem *Manfred* (Byron never called it a "play") is Stuart M. Sperry, "Byron and the Meaning of 'Manfred'" (*Criticism,* 1974), which claims, convincingly, that Manfred's climactic confrontation with the fiend "is really an aspect of Byron's confrontation with himself." Other recent interpretations include K. McCormick Luke, "Lord Byron's *Manfred:* A Study of Alienation from Within" (*UTQ,* 1970), which examines Manfred as a character "bound only by the unconscious confines of his own mind," and James Twitchell, "The Supernatural Structure of Byron's *Manfred*" (*SEL,* 1975), which, by way of showing that the poem's spirit world not only has unexpected importance in itself but also reflects psychological changes in the protagonist, explains several difficult passages more convincingly than before. In *The Living Dead* (1981) Twitchell discusses *Manfred* within the vampire tradition (see below under "Prose"), and in *Romantic Horizons* (1983) he considers the poem within the context of John Martin's watercolors (see below under "Art"). Maria Hogan Butler provides "An Examination of Byron's Revisions of *Manfred,* Act III" (*SP,* 1963). Unconvincing in its analysis of Byron's "comic world" but with excellent readings of key passages is David Eggenschwiler, "The Tragic and Comic Rhythms of *Manfred*" (*SIR,* 1974). Adolf Büchi, *Byrons* Manfred *und die historischen Dramen* (1972), relates the poem to the history plays. Erika Gottlieb's chapter on *Manfred* in *Lost Angels of a Ruined Paradise: Themes of Cosmic Strife in Romantic Tragedy* (1981) convinces me that the mystery of the Creation and Fall help to explain the play. James D. Boulger in *The Calvinist Temper in English Poetry* (1980) explores "Manfred as magus in relation to eastern tales, and the play itself as a type of the saint's play." Daniel M. McVeigh in "Manfred's Curse" (*SEL,* 1982) offers the best available discussion of "The Incantation," written before *Manfred* and published separately by Byron as well as in the poem. Gerhard Stilz, "Byrons *Manfred* und die romantische Subjekt-Objekt Problematik" (in *Byron-Symposium Mannheim 1982,* ed. Huber and Schöwerling), argues that the Romantic dichotomy of subject versus object fundamentally shapes *Manfred.* Armin Geraths' "Byron: *Manfred*" (in *Das Englische Drama: Vom Mittelalter bis zur Gegenwart,* ed. Dieter Mehl, vol. 2, 1970) covers the main cruces of this problematic poem, as does the chapter in Rolf Eichler's *Poetic Drama: Die Entdeckung des Dialogs bei Byron, Shelley, Swinburne und Tennyson* (1977).

In regard to the literary tradition from which *Manfred* emerged, Bertrand Evans, "Manfred's Remorse and Dramatic Tradition" (*PMLA,* 1947), develops in patient and convincing detail an idea suggested long since by Chew, that the literary forerunners of *Manfred* are to be discovered not so much in the Gothic novel as in Gothic drama. (For a different view, see Ernest J. Lovell, Jr., "The Literary Tradition: Sources and Parallels of the Zeluco Theme" in *Byron: The Record of a Quest.*) Evans indicates an impressive number of parallels in characters and situations and makes it evident that Byron, who in his earlier years was a devotee of the theater, was steeped in memories of Gothic plays. Edward Engelberg in *The Unknown Distance* (1972) focuses on the differences between *Faust* and *Manfred.* John Clubbe's 1974 essay on the Prometheus theme in Byron argues that Aeschylus' *Prometheus Bound,* not *Faust* or the Gothic tradition, provided the major literary inspiration for *Manfred.* Byron's sojourn in the Bernese Oberland in September 1816 provided the spectacular visual stimulation. In "Byron in the Alps: The Journal of John Cam Hobhouse, 17–29 September 1816" (in Clubbe and Giddey, *Byron et la Suisse: Deux Etudes,* 1982), Clubbe uses Hobhouse's largely unpublished journal of this trip to recreate the circumstances that led Byron to take up *Manfred* again. Charles E. Robinson in *Shelley and Byron* (1976) claims, without warrant in external evidence, that Byron's reading of *Alastor* strongly influenced *Manfred.* Valuable on the background is Maurice J. Quinlan, "Byron's *Manfred* and Zoroastrianism" (*JEGP,* 1958). Peter L. Thorslev in "Incest as Romantic Symbol" (*CLS,* 1965) provides a European perspective for the poem's incest theme. Jürgen Klein, *Byrons romantischer Nihilismus* (1980), contains an extended discussion of nihilism in *Manfred.* Sherwyn T. Carr in "Bunn, Byron and *Manfred*" (*NCTR,* 1973) documents *Manfred*'s first appearance on the stage, the Covent Garden production of 1834.

***Childe Harold's Pilgrimage,* Canto 4.** Milton Wilson in "Traveller's Venice: Some Images for Byron and Shelley" (*UTQ,* 1974) discusses several images used by both poets within an English literary tradition stretching back to the Renaissance. Byron's friend John Cam Hobhouse wrote extensive notes for *Childe Harold,* but in "The Influence of Hobhouse on *Childe Harold's Pilgrimage,* Canto IV" (*RES,* 1961) Andrew Rutherford finds exaggerated Hobhouse's claim that he directly influenced Byron in this canto. See also Ball's introductory guide to cantos 3 and 4, noted earlier in this section.

Mazeppa. The student should begin with the comprehensive analysis in chapter 2 of Hubert F. Babinski's *The Mazeppa Legend in European Romanticism* (1974), which supersedes a number of earlier studies. Other chapters consider Byron's sources and the enormous impetus that Byron's poem gave to the Mazeppa legend in subsequent European Romanticism. Babinski's valuable study reminds us that Byron's poetry exerted European force and that others of his poems gain in significance when viewed within a European context. Three articles by Irène Sadowska-Guillon, "Mazeppa, héros romantique: Le thème dans les littératures anglaises, françaises, polonaises, et russes" (*Les Lettres Romanes,* 1982), have more to say about the larger subject than about Byron's poem.

The Prophecy of Dante. See Beverly Taylor's "Byron's Use of Dante in *The Prophecy of Dante*" (*KSJ,* 1979) and Chester H. Mills's brief study (*ByronJ,* 1980). For Byron's interest in Dante, see "Byron and Literary Tradition."

The Island. Important discussions before the 1970s are Escarpit's in *Lord Byron: Un tempérament littéraire* and McGann's in *Fiery Dust.* More recent studies include Robert D. Hume, "*The Island* and the Evolution of Byron's 'Tales'" (in *Romantic and Victorian,* ed. Elledge and Hoffman, 1971); Arthur D. Kahn, "The Pastoral Byron: Arcadia in *The Island*" (*Arcadia,* 1973), which investigates the poem's echoes of the classical tradition of pastoral; and P. D. Fleck, "Romance in Byron's *The Island*" (*ByronJ,* 1975; rpt. in Jump's *Byron: A Symposium*).

Translations. Byron was interested in translation all his life and was an exacting translator himself. He decried the injustices done his poems in translation: *traduttore, traditore!* His first volume, *Hours of Idleness,* is virtually an anthology of translations and adaptations. These and subsequent translations—from classical Greek (Aeschylus, Euripides, Anacreon), Latin (Vergil, Horace, Catullus), Italian (the first canto of Pulci's *Morgante Maggiore* and bits of Dante and possibly

Casti), Spanish, Portuguese, modern Greek, Turkish, and Armenian—have never received the comprehensive attention that Shelley's have. Often lovely and invariably neglected in studies of Byron's poetry, the translations remain the Cinderellas of his canon. Still useful as an introduction is F. Maychrzak's "Lord Byron als Übersetzer" (*Englische Studien*, 1895). Virtually alone on its subject is Panos Morphopoulos, "Byron's Translation and Use of Modern Greek Writings" (*MLN*, 1939), which investigates Byron's knowledge of modern Greek and his translations of three modern Greek songs, 1809–11. William J. DeSua in *Dante into English* (1964) rates favorably Byron's translations from Dante. One who finds the affinities between Byron and Dante "assez superficielles" is Jean de Palacio in "Byron traducteur et les influences italiennes" (*RLMC*, 1958), an important study of Byron's translations, particularly of canto 1 of Pulci's *Morgante Maggiore* and its influence on *Don Juan*. D. B. Gregor has succinctly described "Byron's Knowledge of Armenian" (*N&Q*, 1951). Byron learned the Armenian he knew at the Armenian Monastery of San Lazzaro, an island in the Venetian lagoon. Arpena Mesrobian brings together the known facts of Byron's stay in *Armenian Review*, 1974.

MATURE SATIRES

Still useful as an introduction is Claude M. Fuess's *Lord Byron as a Satirist in Verse* (1912). Fuess recognizes Byron's satiric power but maintains, surprisingly and mistakenly, that his "philosophic satire" is "shallow and cynical" and that "he took no positive attitude towards any of the great problems of existence." Fuess discusses Byron's satire in both its general aspects: the place it had in the tradition of formal English satire descended from the Augustan Age, immediately from Gifford and ultimately from Pope, and the Italianate satire in the mock-heroic tradition that derives from Pulci, Berni, and Casti, and was immediately suggested by John Hookham Frere's English imitation of the Italian masters. For well-balanced accounts of English imitations of Italian comic epics, consult R. D. Waller's lengthy introduction to his edition of Frere's *The Monks and the Giants* (1926) and an older study by Albert Eichler, *John Hookham Frere, sein Leben und seine Werke, sein Einfluss auf Lord Byron* (1905).

More recent studies of Byron's satiric art include Robert F. Gleckner in "From Selfish Spleen to Equanimity: Byron's Satires" (*SIR*, 1979), which, after surveying the debate over the satires, considers *English Bards, The Curse of Minerva, The Giaour*, and *Parisina*, before offering extended scrutiny of *Don Juan*. W. Ruddick in "Don Juan in Search of Freedom: Byron's Emergence as a Satirist" (in Jump's *Byron: A Symposium*) views the later satires as a gradual liberation from earlier encumbering forms. In the same volume P. M. Yarker's "Byron and the Satiric Temper" traces the growth of Byron's satiric thrust by informatively discussing the romances as well as the satires. Yarker does not deal directly with *Don Juan*. Erwin A. Stürzl's "Stylistic Media of Byron's Satires" in *Studies in the Romantics,* a volume of the Salzburg Romantic Reassessment series (81.3; 1982), discusses the figures of speech that Byron used.

Beppo. In "The Devil a Bit of Our *Beppo*" (*PQ,* 1953) Truman Guy Steffan examines the original draft of Byron's first ottava rima tale, and, in so doing, not only establishes the chronology of its composition but reveals Byron's artistic principles. Two articles by Attilio Brilli (in Italian) in *Paragone* (1971, 1972) focus, respectively, on Byron's use of myth, chiefly in *Don Juan* but also in *Beppo,* and on *Beppo*'s rhetorical art. R. B. Sangiorgi in "Giambattista Casti's 'Novelle Galanti' and Lord Byron's 'Beppo'" (*Italica,* 1951) argues for Casti's influence. Forthcoming on the poem (in vol. 7 of *Shelley and His Circle*) is Jerome J. McGann's "'Mixed Company': Byron's *Beppo* and the Italian Medley."

The Vision of Judgment. Although acknowledged by almost everyone to be among Byron's undeniable masterpieces, *The Vision of Judgment* has received little critical attention except in books. Mention should again be made of Patricia M. Ball's Childe Harold's Pilgrimage *Cantos III and IV and* The Vision of Judgment (1968), useful for general orientation. William Walling's "Tradition and Revolution: Byron's *Vision of Judgment*" (*WC,* 1972) is particularly good on relating the dramatic qualities of *The Vision* to Byron's historical plays. Emrys Jones, "Byron's Visions of Judgment" (*MLR,* 1981), argues from internal evidence for the poem's debt to Seneca's "Apotheosis of Claudius" and to Erasmus' *Julius Exclusus,* both of which—according to Jones—served as models for Byron's satire. Building on Carl Woodring's discussion in *Politics in English Romantic Poetry,* Stuart Peterfreund in "The Politics of 'Neutral Space' in Byron's *Vision of Judgment*" (*MLQ,* 1979) gives the detailed consideration to social and political background that many other Byron poems still await. Peterfreund identifies the individuals on whom Byron based his characters and the setting as the House of Lords. "The recovery of the historical dimension of Byron's poem should go a long way toward making the poem comprehensible," he writes, and I agree. Two works for which such recovery has not yet been undertaken are *The Blues* and Byron's last satire, *The Age of Bronze.*

Don Juan. If the nineteenth century valued the Byron of *Childe Harold,* the twentieth does not disguise its preference for the late satires, in particular *Don Juan.* Virginia Woolf, in her diary in 1918, concluded, "It is the most readable poem of its length ever written," its "method . . . a discovery by itself. It[']s what one has looked for in vain—a[n] elastic shape which will hold whatever you choose to put into it." For Auden, *Don Juan* is "the most original poem in English." More has been written on it, particularly in this century, than on any other poem by Byron. In the pages that follow I begin by discussing book-length or otherwise substantial studies of *Don Juan* in roughly chronological order. The sixties and seventies witnessed an explosion of articles on *Don Juan.* The divergent viewpoints and approaches in these studies indicate that no critical consensus on the poem has yet been reached. In order to aid students in picking their way through this maze of scholarship, I have tried to group essays loosely; inevitably, essays on one subject will have application to others.

Alan Lang Strout in his 1947 reprint of one of the best pieces of criticism that Byron received in his lifetime, *John Bull's Letter to Lord Byron* (1821), produces documentary proof that the author was John Gibson Lockhart. Strout annotates the text voluminously, and his introduction discusses the interest that the great contemporary periodicals displayed in Byron. In a long appendix he brings together all the Byron references in *Blackwood's Magazine,* 1817–25.

P. G. Trueblood's *The Flowering of Byron's Genius: Studies in* Don Juan (1945) focuses on three aspects of the poem. The first is its inception and growth. Here Trueblood emphasizes (in fact, overemphasizes) two points: the influence of the Countess Guiccioli and the example of Henry Fielding. Trueblood then surveys contemporary reviews and notices in English periodicals and newspapers, confining himself to these because, as he explains, Chew covered the pamphlet criticism in *Byron in England.* The generally unfavorable reception of the early installments of the poem influenced Byron to reorient his plans. This change Trueblood considers in the third part of his book, which studies the significance of the satire and traces its development as Byron's interest shifted from light social satire and the "mannerly obscene" to the cosmopolitan criticism of the latter part, surveying the European world in general and England in particular. The general tenor of Trueblood's argument and his conclusion are that, contrary to the frequent charges of hostile reviewers in Byron's day, Byron's satiric genius did not find expression in mere negation but that on the contrary his fiercely witty attacks on hypocrisy and cant form the obverse to the idealism that is always implicit and sometimes explicit in *Don Juan.*

One of the most valuable portions of Elizabeth French Boyd's monograph *Byron's* Don Juan: *A Critical Study* (1945) is her survey of Byron's *Belesenheit* and of *Don Juan's* literary background. She covers not only the Italian poets from Pulci to Casti and their English imitators, Frere and Rose, but also parallels and analogues (not always necessarily direct "sources") ranging from ancient and medieval tales of romance and adventure to contemporary fiction of such contrasting kinds as the Gothic romance and the discussion novels of Thomas Love Peacock. The resemblances that Boyd indicates between *Don Juan* and Wieland's *Oberon* (which Byron knew in William Sotheby's translation) are particularly interesting in view of W. W. Beyer's demonstration of the same poem's influence on Keats's imagination. Boyd also discusses possible indebtedness to Thomas Hope's novel *Anastasius,* a question earlier handled by Anton Pfeiffer in *Thomas Hopes* Anastasius *und Lord Byrons* Don Juan (1913). She suggests that for the Russian episode Byron may have owed something to Casti's *Poema Tartaro.* No direct evidence exists that Byron read this work, but he did know and admire Casti's *Animali Parlanti* and *Novelle Galanti.* The parallels Boyd adduces, though not numerous, are striking. Other portions of her book have to do with Byron's concept of "epic satire," with the essential characteristics of "Don Juanism," and with the wide horizons of the poet's experience, observation, and comment, embracing not only "Love—Tempest—Travel—War" but also a great variety of topics touched on in the characteristic digressions.

In "Byron and the Colloquial Tradition in English Poetry" (*Criterion,* 1939; rpt. in *The English Romantic Poets,* ed. M. H. Abrams, 1960), Ronald Bottrall argued that Byron took only the externals of his manner from the Italian poets and that he stands in a well-established line of succession from older English writers. This tradition Byron revitalized by introducing into his verse the colloquial force of his prose. Beside Bottrall's opinion that *Don Juan* is "the greatest long poem in English since *The Dunciad,*" we may put the more cautious but more surprising praise in T. S. Eliot's 1937 essay, in which Eliot deplores what he considers to be Byron's stylistic ineptitudes but recognizes in *Don Juan* an emotional sincerity, a hatred of hypocrisy, and a "reckless, raffish honesty." More guarded is Mark Van Doren, who holds in *The Noble Voice* (1946) that though Byron "flounders brilliantly" in *Don Juan* he misses the heart of comedy. Marius Bewley in "The Colloquial Mode of Byron" (*Scrutiny,* 1949; rpt. as "The Colloquial Byron" in *Masks and Mirrors,* 1970) shows that in this mode Byron follows a tradition traceable back to the Caroline poets of the early seventeenth century. In "The Romantic Imagination and the Unromantic Byron" (also in *Masks and Mirrors*) Bewley insists that Byron's satiric bent puts him closer to Swift's world than to his own and thus leaves him essentially incompatible with the other Romantics. C. M. Bowra's chapter on *Don Juan* in *The Romantic Imagination* (1949) retains its value after more than thirty years.

Truman Guy Steffan incorporated several of his essays (*MP,* 1947; *SP,* 1949; *UTSE,* 1952) into the introductory volume to the Variorum *Don Juan,* entitled *The Making of a Masterpiece* (1957, rev. 1971). This volume is divided into three main parts and five appendixes. Part 1, "Chronicle," places the poem in its biographical setting, tracing the circumstances and times of its composition and quoting generously from Byron's letters. Part 2, "The Anvil of Composition," analyzes "Byron's writing as it progressed through his nine hundred manuscript pages." It "speculates about the artistic and psychological motivations for the accretive stanzas, summarizes the facts about the quantity of manuscript correction, sketches the interests and purposes that emerge from the various foci of revision, and . . . defines and illustrates abundantly the major principles that account for Byron's many verbal changes." The most interesting and valuable of the three parts, part 2 is essential to any study of the poem. Somewhat less satisfactory is part 3, "An Epic Carnival," a canto-by-canto "holiday tour" intended to introduce *Don Juan* "to less special readers and to quicken their admiration." Confessedly and deliberately repetitious, this long discussion contains much paraphrase, summary, and forthright character analysis until finally the massed detail becomes almost overwhelming. It is also often difficult to accept Steffan's reading of Byron's characters, for example, Julia and Lambro. Unlike a number of later critics, who find him writing at the top of his form in the English cantos (11 – 16), Steffan rates the earlier cantos more highly. Among the appendixes are a useful and detailed "Chronology" of composition and publication and "A Reference List of Accretive Stanzas," canto by canto. "Stanzas Showing the Full Process of Manuscript Composition" prints twenty-four stanzas just as Byron wrote and revised them line by line, with interesting editorial and critical comment.

With great originality George M. Ridenour's *The Style of* Don Juan (1960) explores the poem in terms of "two organizing themes, the Christian myth of the Fall and the classical rhetorical theory of the styles." Ridenour also finds "a third, non-thematic mode of organization, the continuing presence of the speaker or *persona*," which "in its relations with the protagonist, makes it possible for the poem to move," that is, gives to it "a developing dramatic action," from a state of innocence to experience. Chapter 1 provides a sensitive, subtle, and enlightening examination of the "Dedication" of *Don Juan* within the perspective of Augustan satiric theory and practice (and their classical predecessors). It distinguishes between Byron's use of the plain, middle, and high styles and demonstrates his debts and triumphs of tone. Ridenour reveals the "Dedication" to be "an elaborately traditional satire in the Augustan manner," in which Byron speaks "from behind the traditional satiric mask." Chapter 2 introduces "the Christian doctrine of the Fall [as] a *metaphor* which Byron uses to express his own personal vision," asserted to be "elaborately coherent." Thus, if his view of human nature "is not remarkably optimistic, neither is it broodingly grim." No one who has read Ridenour can ever again read either the "Dedication" or the Haidée episode in the old simple way. Chapter 3 associates "first and passionate love" with Adam's fall, describes it as an "ambrosial sin" but still a sin, and identifies it with Promethean fire. Chapter 4 defines the action of *Don Juan* as a "process of gradually narrowing the gap between speaker and protagonist." Chapter 5 is concerned with "the specifically rhetorical aspects of the art of *Don Juan*." Elsewhere, Ridenour demonstrates Byron's mastery of such traditional elements as alliteration, assonance, consonance, internal rhyme, puns, zeugma, metaphor, conceit, and tone, the latter of "special importance." He has two appendixes, one on the relation between *Childe Harold* and *Don Juan,* the other on Madame de Staël's influence on *Don Juan*'s narrative technique.

András Horn's *Byron's* Don Juan *and the Eighteenth Century English Novel* (1962), concerned with Fielding, Sterne, and Smollett, demonstrates first that Fielding's influence on Byron's poem is clear but that its extent is not overwhelming. Horn does not press his thesis excessively or generalize beyond his evidence, recognizing that the three novelists whose influence on Byron he explores represent only a small part of the poet's total experience. Sterne's influence he sees in the form of an intrusive first-person narrator, whose presence repeatedly creates the appearance that he is destroying the artistic illusion, and in the relative formlessness of both *Tristram Shandy* and *Don Juan.* Smollett's influence exerts itself in the tradition of the picaresque novel, which tends to create a "conglomerate," achieving great variety of reality, an illusion of totality, but with little interest in unity of plot.

Edward E. Bostetter edited, with an excellent introduction, *Twentieth Century Interpretations of* Don Juan: *A Collection of Critical Essays* (1969). Nine of the sixteen essays were originally published in the 1960s. The volume includes selections from the works of Eliot, Boyd, Steffan, West, Ridenour, Rutherford, Joseph, and Gleckner. In addition, it has excerpts from the comments of Virginia Woolf, William Butler Yeats, Ernest J. Lovell, Jr., W. H. Auden, Karl Kroeber, Brian Wilkie, Alvin B. Kernan, and E. D. Hirsch, Jr. Bostetter's introduction traces the changing circumstances in Byron's life that influenced the composition of *Don Juan* and thus its form and style, surveys the shifting critical reception of the poem in our time, and explores the reasons for its continuing and increasing popularity. Ernest J. Lovell, Jr., in "Irony and Image in *Don Juan*" (originally published in *The Major English Romantic Poets*, ed. Thorpe, Baker, and Weaver, 1957) finds the unifying principle of the poem in "the basically ironic theme of appearance versus reality" and explores "the consistently organic relation between episode and theme" as a prelude to a discussion of style. W. H. Auden, reviewing Marchand's *Byron: A Biography* in 1958, observes that in description of "the motion of life, the *passage* of events and thoughts," Byron is "a great master." Alvin B. Kernan in the excellent climactic chapter of his *The Plot of Satire* (1965) argues persuasively that Byron's "sense of life as endless movement and change" determined the "central rhythm," the "controlling concept of the poem, its basic action," a pattern that "comprehends and is made up of the movements of all the component parts, characters, events, metaphors, settings, stanza form, rhythms, and rhymes." This being true, it then follows that "in every case, what he holds up to ridicule is some attempt to restrain life, to bind and force it into some narrow, permanent form." Finally, E. D. Hirsch, Jr., in "Byron and the Terrestrial Paradise," an essay in *From Sensibility to Romanticism*, edited by Frederick W. Hilles and Harold Bloom (1965), extends and revises Ridenour's views on the metaphorical centrality in *Don Juan* of a Fall from Eden. Other essays in Bostetter's volume are treated elsewhere. See also the discussions reprinted in John Jump's "casebook" *Childe Harold* and *Don Juan* (1973), noted above.

Bostetter's chapter on Byron in *The Romantic Ventriloquists: Wordsworth, Coleridge, Keats, Shelley, Byron* (1963) offers a reasonable and readable account of *Don Juan*, its background and origins. He discusses such topics as Byron's ideas concerning man's relation to the deity and the universe, man's physical nature, Byron's motives for writing, the development of his heroes, existential elements in his view of human life, man's insignificance in the universe, the remarkable similarity of *Cain* and *The Vision of Judgment*—and the ways in which all these elements or developments influenced the writing of *Don Juan*. Byron is here viewed intriguingly as the only one of the Romantic poets to come to terms successfully with the complexities of the early nineteenth century and to refuse to retreat into an illusioned world view.

M. K. Joseph's discussion of *Don Juan* occupies about half of his *Byron the Poet* (1964). It summarizes briefly the composition of the poem, surveys Byron's use of his sources (including nonliterary sources), and considers his models in the Italian comic epic, the picaresque novel, improvisation, and conversation. Joseph offers a subtle, enlightening, and always interesting consideration of the poem's narrator and related problems, as well as one of the best analyses in print of the imagery and diction of the poem. He follows this with an account of the themes of the poem—love, war, nature, "the poem itself and its moral intention"—and of the function and kinds of scene or setting and characters. Another chapter discusses the morality of *Don Juan*, chiefly in terms of Byron's treatment of love and war. "The Age of Cant" considers the implications of the terms "enthusiasm," "system," and "cant," in the political, poetical, religious, and moral realms. This chapter, however, is centrifugal and often moves away from the poem. A concluding chapter deals with the irony of *Don Juan,* and an appendix provides a table showing the proportion of narrative to comment and digression in each canto.

Several book-length studies of *Don Juan* appeared in the 1970s. A. B. England's *Byron's* Don Juan *and Eighteenth-Century Literature: A Study of Some Rhetorical Continuities and Discontinuities* (1975) sets the poem within the inherited Augustan tradition, making not only expected analogies with Pope's poetry but also unexpected ones with Swift's. *Don Juan*'s rhetoric, England argues, "is more characteristically continuous with the poetry of Swift, especially insofar as that poetry manifests the use of the 'burlesque style.'" He explores this subject in his second chapter, "Byron, Swift, Butler, and Burlesque," the heart of his book, where he finds "genuine continuities" between Swift and Byron. But England's argument unfairly delimits Byron's masterpiece, whose antecedents are as much Italian as English, and one wonders how differently Byron would have written *Don Juan* if he had never known Swift or Butler. England's first chapter, "Byron, Pope, and Moral Satire," and his third, *"Don Juan, Tom Jones,* and Comic Narrative," relate Byron to more orthodox eighteenth-century traditions and ones to which Byron frequently proclaimed his allegiance. By his cultivation of "various kinds of rhetorical discontinuity and disorder . . . Byron expresses his alienation from Pope's and Fielding's world view." Maybe so, but England's discussion of Byron's response to Pope lacks the critical discrimination of Cooke's in the first chapter of *The Blind Man Traces the Circle.* The author seems more at home with eighteenth-century works than with *Don Juan.* He is right not to insist too heavily on the analogies he draws, which compel our interest more as patterns of thought than as evidence of direct influence, though the latter may exist. Even for a short book England's is repetitious, verbose, and, despite a number of insights, somewhat vaguely focused. It is also more a book of the midsixties than of the midseventies, for the bibliography makes no mention of pivotal Byron studies that appeared in the late sixties. Excerpts from it appeared as "The Style of *Don Juan* and Augustan Poetry" in Jump's *Byron: A Symposium.*

The great merit of Jerome J. McGann's Don Juan *in Context* (1976) is that it asks hard questions and answers some of them more thoughtfully than any critic has before. McGann brings an impressive critical gift to bear on the poem, both on a theoretical level and in discussions of individual passages, discussions that we leave with a keener awareness of multiple meanings and of the larger context surrounding Byron. By "context" McGann means the melding of influences that affected Byron not only during the years he worked on *Don Juan* but throughout his maturity. These include, among other matters, the events of his life; his evolving response to Milton, man as well as poet; his surprisingly informed awareness of classical literary tradition, almost malgré lui, particularly the works of Juvenal, Cicero, and Horace; his important and not completely explored involvement with Italian literature; and his reaction to the poetry and literary theorizing of the other Romantics. On all these subjects, McGann breaks new ground. Four introductory chapters chart Byron's gradual movement to become the poet of *Don Juan*; the last hundred pages focus on the poem itself. The early chapters consider the modes of thinking of the pre-Italy Byron, usually with *Don Juan* discernible on the horizon, but also ask why the poet wrote as he did before 1817. McGann has astute points to make about Byron's chameleonic being and understands as well as anyone the ways in which the poetry reflected the life at a particular time. Chapters on *Don Juan*'s style, form, and content direct our gaze to the poem proper. The first builds on Ridenour's *The Style of* Don Juan but goes further in unraveling the various traditions of classical rhetoric that went into the poem. Byron's awareness of writing in a defined tradition enabled him in *Don Juan* to surmount the problems that, in McGann's view, Wordsworth faced less successfully in *The Prelude*. The chapter on form develops this argument by focusing on Byron's response to his fellow Romantics, showing that the poet, who knew he was "born for opposition," developed major components of his poetics in resistance to the theories of his Romantic contemporaries. Thus Byron began *Don Juan* in part at least to refute their notions of poetry. Only the last chapter—on *Don Juan*'s content—disappoints slightly, for McGann succeeds better in illuminating the context than in coming to grips with the poem's themes and imagery, its ironic and satiric techniques, its characters, its intricate juggling of narrative stance and digressive mode, its vital (and still incompletely understood) relation to the contemporary political scene and to the disillusioned postwar world in which Byron wrote his poem. For example, how were *Don Juan*'s course and content affected by the uncomprehending response of Byron's friends in England? Why did these friends, themselves men of the world and hitherto thoroughly sympathetic to Byron's poetry, react to *Don Juan* "with wonder and apprehension and even loathing"? These are questions deserving further investigation. Marilyn Butler, reviewing this book in *EIC*, 1978, brilliantly extends the dimensions of McGann's "context" by arguing that in *Don Juan* Byron flings down the gauntlet to the Wordsworth of *The Excursion*, "challenging him to the contest as the great poet of the age, and Milton's heir." *Don Juan* is Byron's "counter-*Excursion*: comic where Wordsworth is solemn, skeptical where Wordsworth is Christian, liberal where Wordsworth is conservative, extrovert and panoramic where Wordsworth locates a succession of personal histories in one retired spot." Also arising from McGann's book was "On Byron" (*SIR*, 1977), in which three critics of note—Ridenour, McGann himself, and Donald H. Reiman—participated in a stimulating forum on *Don Juan*. Ridenour begins by noting his disagreements with McGann's Don Juan *in Context*; McGann's reply, focusing on Byron's relation to Romanticism, prompts a further rejoinder from Ridenour and a valuable statement by Reiman on *Don Juan*'s epic qualities.

Beyond the linguistic range of most is a fine book by Attilio Brilli, *Il Gioco del Don Juan: Byron e la Satira* (1971). Its three sections examine "Choice and Function of a Myth," "Metaphor and Symbol," and "Language, Rhetoric, and Style." Charles J. Clancy, *Lava, Hock and Soda-Water: Byron's* Don Juan (1974), in the Salzburg series, gives a canto-by-canto tour of the poem.

The most recent book-length study, Hermione de Almeida's *Byron and Joyce through Homer:* Don Juan *and* Ulysses (1981), provides further evidence that *Don Juan* still speaks to us directly in the twentieth century. (On Joyce's lifelong interest in Byron, see under "Reputation and Influence. Great Britain.") De Almeida regards *Ulysses* and *Don Juan* as "epic equivalents, each functioning for the post-Kantian era in much the same way as Homer's epics did for early Greek civilization." She has densely written chapters on their relationship to the *Odyssey*, myth and tradition, the hero, society, and styles. A final chapter reiterates her argument that the two modern works belong "conclusively in one literary era." Perhaps so, though Byron and Joyce are not the first writers of their respective centuries that one would pair together. Most observers, de Almeida concedes, regard them as "typically antithetical." Yet even the skeptical will find enlightening her juxtaposition of Byron with Joyce. Every chapter, at once a close argument with critics and firmly independent in judgment, succeeds in the juxtaposition of its two primary texts. And like that of Byron and Joyce, de Almeida's own style, aphoristic and self-aware, even gives forth an occasional exotic bloom. She maps out *Don Juan*'s relationships to the mainstream of European literature, Homer before all, but also to the Renaissance masters, Ariosto, Rabelais, Montaigne, and Cervantes. She handles this long historical perspective with ease and, refreshingly, views Byron as a European as much as an English poet, a recognition more often accorded on the Continent than in English-speaking countries. Drawing on Friedrich Schlegel, she offers a finely perceptive discussion of *Don Juan*'s romantic irony, which she calls, after Schlegel, "transcendental buffoonery." Equally valuable is her analysis of Byron's language. "Where other writers approach things and concepts first, and then invoke words to describe these, words come first for Byron and Joyce: through them they approach the world and its contents." As Byron himself insisted, "*true* words are *things*." Neither writer had much use for theory. Byron, we remember, detested systems. At times, however, de Almeida may place too heavy an intellectual burden on Byron's poem. She also tends to blur the historical dimension and the (very great) differences in outlook between the early nineteenth and the early twentieth century. *Don Juan* and *Ulysses*, almost exactly a hundred years apart, may both be post-Kantean, but they are also much more. Still, her juxtaposition succeeds brilliantly in its primary aim. No one can look at either writer in quite the same way again.

An authoritative account of the origins and different versions of the great story to which Byron's masterpiece is loosely attached is still Georges Gendarme de Bévotte's *La Légende de Don Juan* (1906). See also Armand E. Singer, *The Don Juan Theme, Versions and Criticism: A Bibliography* (1965; 3rd supplement, 1973; 4th, 1975; 5th, 1979; all 3 in *WVUPP*). Neither Leo Weinstein, *The Metamorphoses of Don Juan* (1959), nor Oscar Mandel, *The Theater of Don Juan: A Collection of Plays and Views, 1630–1963* (1963), has much to say on Byron's poem, though the latter volume usefully brings together, with commentary, treatments of the legend from the seventeenth through the twentieth centuries, from Tirso de Molina and Molière to Montherlant and Frisch. Nor do any of the essays in *Don Juan: Darstellung und Deutung*, edited by Brigitte Wittman (1976), deal specifically with Byron's poem, but they do suggest its European context. The parallels Roger B. Saloman draws between the Cervantean and the Byronic vision in "Mock-Heroes and Mock-Heroic Narrative: *Don Juan* in the Context of Cervantes" (*SLitI,* 1976), though interesting and suggestive, are not finally convincing.

Byron referred to *Don Juan* as "an epic as much in the spirit of our day as the Iliad was in Homer's." He understood epic tradition so well that he knew exactly where it could be parodied. Many commentators on the poem take up its relation to the epic, from Boyd, who finds the epic qualities "subordinate architectural ornaments"; to Steffan, who dismisses them; to Ridenour, whose analysis of them was often groundbreaking; to de Almeida, whose examination of the poem's affinities to Homer's *Odyssey* is fundamental. The most influential discussion remains Wilkie's chapter in *Romantic Poets and Epic Tradition* (1965), which, viewing epics not as a genre but as works within a tradition, finds *Don Juan* an "epic of negation" but nonetheless an epic. Assuming that Byron "wanted to show life itself as ultimately without meaning," Wilkie deals convincingly with the "bewildering variety" of epic elements in *Don Juan.* John Lauber in *"Don Juan* as Anti-Epic" (*SEL,* 1968) offers an almost convincing point-by-point argument against the poem being (what Byron called) a "real Epic," which, judged by conventional standards, it is not. But during the nineteenth century the idea of what constitutes an epic underwent extensive modification. Even before, a number of major works—*The Divine Comedy, Don Quixote, The Faerie Queene*—had in fact altered, as Byron was well aware, the classical tradition of epic. With the term stretched to include a number of works not formally epics, most recent commentators place *Don Juan* somewhere within this larger epic tradition. Arthur D. Kahn, "Byron's *Single Difference* with Homer and Virgil: The Redefinition of the Epic in *Don Juan*" (*Arcadia,* 1970), discusses Byron's use of Homer and Vergil as foils in reinterpreting classical epic. Lloyd N. Jeffrey, "Homeric Echoes in Byron's *Don Juan*" (*SCB,* 1971), points out the poem's many Homeric allusions. Donald H. Reiman in *"Don Juan* in Epic Context" (*SIR,* 1977) argues that C. S. Lewis' discussion of "Primary Epic" clarifies Byron's intent in writing an epic whose modernity we can only now appreciate. George de Forest Lord's chapter in *Trials of the Self: Heroic Ordeals in the Epic Tradition* (1983) claims that Byron revoked rather than revised epic tradition.

E. D. H. Johnson in *"Don Juan* in England" (*ELH,* 1944) finds that Byron's strictures on the English moral and social code and his indictments of English hypocrisy originated in a misunderstanding of contemporary ethical standards that was in turn due to his limited experience of English society. The attacks on a hypocrisy that comprehended moral degradation were valid for the entourage of the Prince Regent at Carlton House and for certain other circles of the Whigs but not for English society as a whole. The unfavorable reception of the poem was in part owing to an indignant repudiation of these satiric accusations; and this reception merely served in turn to confirm Byron in his convictions. Johnson argues his case well but underestimates both the breadth of Byron's observations and the extent of British cant. He usefully reminds us that by the time Byron wrote *Don Juan* his personal experiences of English society were dated by several years: the poem reflects conditions prevalent in 1812–16 rather than those characteristic of 1819–23, by which time a more conservative moral code was creeping across England. Without denying Johnson's argument, we may also remember that Byron kept up with the English scene through correspondence, the periodicals Murray sent him, visits from, among others, Hobhouse and Moore, and, in 1823, the company of the Blessingtons. In "Aristocratic Individualism in Byron's *Don Juan*" (*SEL,* 1977) J. Michael Robertson finds that Byron uses the "aristocratic tradition to show his individuality" and that the poet's attitude toward aristocratic values—among them, individuality, inconsistency, a casual attitude toward poetry, a colloquial tone of conversation, skepticism, and cynicism—imbues the poem. In "The Byron of *Don Juan* as Whig Aristocrat" (*TSLL,* 1976) Robertson reveals that, "in a number of indirect and sometimes amusing ways, parts of *Don Juan* parallel the conduct and attitude of the Whig aristocracy." Robertson's valuable exercises in social history remind us that to comprehend Byron and his poetry we must keep in mind the important Whig context.

Surprisingly, critics have not often considered Byron's romantic irony in depth. A number of recent studies on romantic irony, discussed in Frank Jordan's introductory chapter, have value for Byron. Noteworthy among earlier discussions is Helene Richter's chapter in *Lord Byron: Persönlichkeit und Werk.* In *English Romantic Irony* (1980) Anne K. Mellor presents an alternate version of English Romanticism, one that M. H. Abrams chose to ignore in *Natural Supernaturalism.* For Mellor, "Byron's mature works are probably the most masterful artistic example of romantic irony in English," and, like de Almeida in *Byron and Joyce through Homer* but in more detail, she draws on the theoretical writings of Friedrich Schlegel to outline various kinds of romantic irony. Mellor devotes the bulk of the long Byron chapter to irony in *Don Juan,* illuminating as she proceeds a number of the poem's other facets: women, Juan, the narrator, their interactions, prosody, "transcendental buffoonery" (which Schlegel considered the essence of romantic irony), nature, military glory, poetry, rhyme. Although she notes that gloom-ridden interpretations of the poem hold the field, she aligns herself (rightly, in my view) with those who believe that "such pessimistic readings of *Don Juan* seem . . . to seriously underestimate the open-endedness of Byron's imagery and vision." Like de Almeida, too, she views Byron not exclusively as an English poet but as one cognizant of and working within a European tradition. Consult also in this regard the useful chapter on *Don Juan* in Lilian R. Furst's *Fictions of Romantic Irony* (1984).

Two important essays of the 1960s relate Byron's satire to his dramas: D. M. Hassler III, "*Marino Faliero,* the Byronic Hero, and *Don Juan*" (*KSJ,* 1965), and James R. Thompson, "Byron's Plays and *Don Juan*: Genre and Myth" (*BuR,* 1967; rpt. in *Byron's Poetry,* ed. McConnell).

An informative chapter in Karl Kroeber's *Romantic Narrative Art* (1960) views the poem "as a precursor of a new kind of novel writing," anticipating "later novels rather than rework[ing] earlier models." In the long final section of *Poetry towards Novel* (1971) John Speirs examines *Beppo, The Vision of Judgment,* and *Don Juan* in relation to nineteenth-century poetry and the novel. The kinship Speirs establishes reflects the development from poetry into the novel.

Byron once said that "almost all Don Juan is *real* life—either my own—or from people I knew." T. G. Steffan, in "The Token-web, the Sea-Sodom, and Canto I of *Don Juan*" (*UTSE,* 1947), is concerned not with literary sources but with the contribution that Byron's own experiences in Venice made to the beginning of the poem. Steffan has incorporated others of his essays into the introductory volume of the Variorum *Don Juan.* After Steffan, no one has explored the autobiographical vein of the poem more perceptively than Frederick L. Beaty. In "Byron and the Story of Francesca da Rimini" (*PMLA,* 1960) Beaty suggests an identification in canto 1 of Augusta Leigh with Julia and of Byron with Juan; in "Byron's Conception of Ideal Love" (*KSJ,* 1963) he takes up the Haidée episode and *The Island*; in "Harlequin Don Juan" (*JEGP,* 1968) he investigates Byron's possible English and Italian sources, finding that one of the theatrical depictions of the contemporary London stage, "a Harlequin Don Juan, was probably the immediate progenitor of Byron's character"; and in "Byron on Malthus and the Population' Problem" (*KSJ,* 1969) he skilfully analyzes Byron's long involvement with Malthusian ideas, particularly in *Don Juan.* Beaty incorporated reworkings of several of his essays into a book, *Light from Heaven: Love in British Romantic Literature* (1971). In a piece subsequent to it, "Byron's Longbow and Strongbow" (*SEL,* 1972), he argues against the traditional associations of these figures in *Don Juan* and also examines Byron's response to the classic-Romantic debate, which at first the poet reacted violently against but which by 1823 he had grown to accept. Andrew Gurr, "Don Byron and the Moral North" (*ArielE,* 1972), rather crudely tries to show how the first canto of this "intimately biographical poem" emerged out of Byron's personal disaster in England and subsequent exile. Michael Goldberg, "Passion through Reason's Glass: Byron in the Toils of Middle Age" (in *Generous Converse,* ed. Brian Green, 1980), intriguingly argues that "middle age is, if not the main subject, at least an informing principle of" *Don Juan.* Goldberg's tantalizingly brief study chronicles Byron's many-faceted struggle against middle age.

By far the most perceptive psychological discussion occurs in Manning's *Byron and His Fictions.* Mabel P. Worthington, "Byron's *Don Juan*: Certain Psychological Aspects" (*L&P,* 1956), is one of the few earlier psychoanalytic studies still worth consulting, as is her *"Don Juan* as Myth" (*L&P,* 1962). W. Paul Elledge in "Byron's Hungry Sinner: The Quest Motif in *Don Juan*" (*JEGP,* 1970) subtly analyzes the dominant pattern of eating and drinking in the poem, viewing it, ultimately, as a "bare quest of the child for a mother-substitute." Candace Tate, "Byron's *Don Juan*: Myth as Psychodrama" (*KSJ,* 1980), scrutinizes the sexual implications in canto 1, showing how Byron reshaped the Don Juan myth to confront his own past.

In "The Mode of Byron's *Don Juan*" (*PMLA,* 1964) Ridenour answers Marshall's argument about narration in *The Structure of Byron's Major Poems.* He demonstrates the existence of a single narrating voice capable of speaking in a variety of tones to express a variety of coherent attitudes, clarifies the various values or ideals that this voice admires and champions, and thus denies that the ironies of the poem ever "collapse into absurdity." He asserts convincingly that the poem "is in fact a satire in the real sense. . . . It is important to resist the notion that all skepticisms are alike, all ironies equally corrosive." Ridenour's second appendix to *The Style of* Don Juan, "Mobility and Improvisation," also contains valuable insights into the poem's narrative method. In "The 'Desultory Rhyme' of *Don Juan*: Byron, Pulci, and the Improvisatory Style" (*ELH*, 1978), Lindsay Waters traces Byron's style in *Don Juan* to its roots in the Italian improvisatory tradition that began in the early eighteenth century. His sketch of earlier improvised poetry provides the context for Byron's choice of Pulci as model. But Giorgio Melchiori in his Nottingham lecture, *Byron and Italy* (1958), finds the major influence on the ottava rima satires to be, not Boiardo, Pulci, or Berni, but Ariosto, "who remained all the time his first model, as he had originally been a formative influence" on *Childe Harold* 1 – 2. David Parker goes over familiar ground in "The Narrator of *Don Juan*" (*ArielE*, 1974), arguing that Byron's failure to establish his true identity was not a handicap but a key to his success. More authoritative is Leslie A. Marchand's "Narrator and Narration in *Don Juan*" (*KSJ*, 1976). Günther Blaicher, "Der immanente Leser in Byrons *Don Juan*" (*Poetica* 1976), discusses how Byron's addresses to the "reader" varied with the public reaction to his poem. Blaicher develops the subject in regard to the English cantos in a pamphlet, *Vorurteil und literarische Stil: Zur Interaktion von Autor und zeitgenössischem Leserpublikum in Byrons* Don Juan (1979). Helmut Castrop, "Byron's Methods of Engaging His Audience's Response in *Don Juan*" (in *Byron-Symposium Mannheim 1982,* ed. Huber and Schöwerling), focuses on Byron's interaction with his readers in the first two cantos, not neglecting the poem's neglected preface, unpublished until 1901. Gordon K. Thomas in "Wordsworth, Byron, and 'Our Friend, the Storyteller'" (*Dutch Quarterly Review of Anglo-American Letters,* 1983) argues intriguingly that *Don Juan*'s preface foreshadows the narrator's importance in the poem. Eleanor Wikborg, "The Narrator and the Control of Tone in Cantos I – IV of Byron's *Don Juan*" (*ES*, 1979), sometimes belabors the obvious in describing Byron's irony and deliberate ambiguity. Martin Maner, "Pope, Byron, and the Satiric Persona" (*SEL*, 1980), points out how Byron uses the narrative masks of the "literary naif" and the "naive moralist" to make his ironic thrusts. Noteworthy among earlier analyses of the narrator's digressive mode is Joseph's chapter in *Byron the Poet.*

On religion, see C. N. Stavrou's overwritten but helpful "Religion in *Don Juan*" (*SEL*, 1963); Charles R. McCabe, "A Secret Prepossession: Skepticism in Byron's *Don Juan*" (*Renascence,* 1975), which thoughtfully follows up Cooke's claim that Byron's skepticism is "counter-heroic humanism"; and David J. Leigh, *"Infelix Culpa:* Poetry and the Skeptic's Faith in *Don Juan*" (*KSJ*, 1979), which charts the critical debate before concluding that "Byron's poetic creed against all creeds remains a masterpiece of skeptical theodicy." Travis Looper's compendium, *Byron and the Bible,* detailing the many biblical echoes in *Don Juan,* should stimulate further studies. Byron's own religious views I consider under "Ideas and Beliefs."

Only yesterday, it seems, T. S. Eliot was inveighing against Byron for his sloppy language. Today the situation has virtually reversed itself, though studies of Byron's language lag behind those of the other major Romantic poets. Mark Storey in *Poetry and Humour from Cowper to Clough* has positive remarks on Byron's handling of the written word, as does de Almeida, who in *Byron and Joyce through Homer* puts Byron in the same league with the twentieth-century word master. Long before, Byron's contemporary reviewers could see that, even in the first *Childe Harold,* Byron had effected something new with language. Jeffrey, for one, praised his diction, which, "though unequal and frequently faulty, has on the whole a freedom, copiousness and vigour, which we are not sure that we could match in any contemporary poet." The title of Peter J. Manning's excellent *"Don Juan* and Byron's Imperceptiveness to the English Word" (*SIR,* 1979) picks up on Eliot's charge—only to refute it—that Byron did not discriminate in his use of language. Peter Porter, "Byron and the Moral North: The Englishness of *Don Juan"* (*Encounter,* 1974), offers a lively defense of Byron's Englishness of style and manner as opposed to the artifice of Shelley's "special poetic diction" and Wordsworth's nonexistent "language of men." "Byron restored the social role to English poetry" through *Don Juan,* "the skewer of Byron's kebab." R. M. Brownstein, "Byron's *Don Juan:* Some Reason for the Rhymes" (*MLQ,* 1967), examines the multifarious purposes for which Byron created his rhymes. Thomas Bourke, *Stilbruch als Stilmittel: Studien zur Literatur der Spät- und Nachromantik* (1980), contains a long section on Byron as a late Romantic, as well as on Hoffmann and Heine. His wide-ranging if overly derivative discussion of *Don Juan* examines Byron's shifting levels of style to achieve the different effects that he wished. Ina Schabert, "Zur Ideologie der poetischen Sprachstrukturierung: George Herbert und Byron" (*Anglia,* 1978), more on Herbert than on Byron, includes interesting comments on poetic language in *Don Juan.* Ernest Giddey, "Borrowings from Foreign Languages in Byron's Poetry with Special Reference to *Don Juan"* (in *Studies in the Romantics,* a volume of the Salzburg Romantic Reassessment series [81.3], 1982), discusses Byron's borrowings from half a dozen languages. Frederick Garber in "Self and the Language of Satire in *Don Juan"* (*Thalia,* 1982) illuminates Byron's expert use of language and the relationship of language to cant and to character. Garber is particularly acute on those who misuse language (Castlereagh, Brougham, Donna Julia).

The section on *Don Juan* in Robert M. Torrance's *The Comic Hero* (1978) illustrates the difficulties in speaking fruitfully about Byron's comedy. John Cunningham's elegantly written and discerning study *The Poetics of Byron's Comedy in* Don Juan (1982) throws more light on the subject, as does Edward Proffitt's "Byron's Laughter: *Don Juan* and the Hegelian Dialectic" (*ByronJ,* 1983). Some of the useful distinctions made by Heinrich Neudeck in *Byron als Dichter des Komischen* (1911) have never been followed up. See also under "Ideas and Beliefs: Comedy."

A few articles deal specifically with the poem's individual episodes. Frederick W. Shilstone, "A Grandfather, a Raft, a Tradition: The Shipwreck Scene in Byron's *Don Juan*" (*TSL*, 1980), argues for the importance of the *Narrative* of Captain John Byron, "my grand-dad," and of the infamous *Medusa* shipwreck (inspiration for Gericault's celebrated canvas). Andrew M. Cooper, "Shipwreck and Skepticism: *Don Juan* Canto II" (*KSJ*, 1983), after observing affinities between *Mazeppa* and the shipwreck episode, moves on to analyze selected stanzas of the latter. Nina Diakonova defends "The Russian Episode in Byron's *Don Juan*" (*ArielE*, 1972), and Katherine Kernberger in "Power and Sex" (*ByronJ*, 1980) analyzes the role reversals experienced by the protagonists. We need further investigations into the background of these and other episodes (several the length of Byron's earlier narratives). The English cantos, in particular, cry out for detailed treatment.

General essays include Austin Wright's "The Byron of *Don Juan*" in *Six Satirists* (1965), Leonard W. Deen's "Liberty and License in Byron's *Don Juan*" (*TSLL*, 1966), and Edwin Morgan's "Voice, Tone, and Transition in *Don Juan*" (in *Byron: Wrath and Rhyme*, ed. Bold). Hugh J. Luke's "The Publishing of Byron's *Don Juan*" (*PMLA*, 1965) is thorough. Terence L. Lisbeth, "The Motif of Imagination in Byron's Bluestocking Allusions" (*MSE*, 1974–75), focuses on *Don Juan*. Michael G. Cooke, "Byron's *Don Juan*: The Obsession and Self-Discipline of Spontaneity" (*SIR*, 1975; rpt. in *Acts of Inclusion*, 1979), begins with an enlightening discussion of the "fragment" in European Romanticism—*Don Juan* is one—before going on to treat the poem as a set of variations on the Juan-Julia episode. Cooke draws interesting parallels between *Don Juan* and *The Prelude*. Thomas L. Ashton in "Naming Byron's Aurora Raby" (*ELN*, 1969) ingeniously presents the reasons for Byron's creation of this name. Charles J. Clancy, "Aurora Raby in *Don Juan*: A Byronic Heroine" (*KSJ*, 1979), finds Aurora's "character in many respects that of the typical Byronic hero transmuted into feminine form." More traditional in its analysis is Claude Bergerolle, "Révolte sexuelle et liberté individuelle dans le 'Don Juan'" (*Romantisme*, 1974). One may also mention Jean Perrin's "Le Mythe du héros dans le *Don Juan* de Byron ou l'héroïsme de l'antihéros" (in *Le Mythe du héros*, ed. N. J. Rigaud, 1982), too dependent on the theories of others but perceptive when the author looks at the poem with his own eyes. Gerald C. Wood in "The Metaphor of the Climates and *Don Juan*" (*ByronJ*, 1978) explores Byron's fascination with climate and the role climate plays in determining temperament (a notion earlier advanced by Madame de Staël). Wolfgang Franke in "*Don Juan* and the Black Friar: A Byronic Variant of the Ghost Story" (in the *Constance Byron Symposium*, 1977) perceptively discusses Byron's attitude toward ghosts. In the same volume Hans-Jürgen Diller studies "The Function of Verse in Byron's *Don Juan*," and Helmut Viebrock reconsiders "The Fall from Perfection: A Major Motif in Byron's *Don Juan*." Paul Fleck in "Romance in *Don Juan*" (*UTQ*, 1976) scrutinizes the elements and devices of romance in the poem.

On *Don Juan*'s afterfame, see Jay A. Ward, *The Critical Reputation of Byron's* Don Juan *in Britain* (1979, originally completed in 1966), and Charles J. Clancy, *Review of* Don Juan *Criticism 1900 to 1973* (1974). James and Horace Smith's *Re-*

jected Addresses (1812) inaugurated a vast number of imitations, parodies, and continuations of Byron's poems, particularly of *Childe Harold* and *Don Juan*. To my knowledge, the subject has never been dealt with in detail, although Hans Raab, *Über die Fortsetzungen von Lord Byrons* Don Juan (1913), competently considers some thirteen (by no means all) of the continuations, and Chew's *Byron in England* discusses in passing a number of these and other works, many of them difficult to find even in large libraries. Michèle Paris, "Les Avatars du Héros: A propos d'une parodie du *Don Juan* de Byron" (in *Le Mythe du héros*, ed. N. J. Rigaud, 1982), takes up the first continuation of cantos 1 and 2, William Hone's lively *Don Juan* (1819). Not exactly a "continuation" but an account of a modern-day Juan's adventures (in the United States!) is Eric Linklater's novel *Juan in America* (1931).

Dramas

Even today little consensus exists regarding the position of Byron's plays within Romantic literature, within the tradition of English drama, or even within Byron's own canon. Not only Byronists but others can rate the plays very highly indeed, for example, George Steiner, who claims in *The Death of Tragedy* (1961) that "they are of the first interest to anyone concerned with the idea of tragedy in modern literature." Yet with the exception of *Manfred* and possibly *Cain,* the plays are among Byron's least-read works. Despite a recent surge of scholarly activity, a number of hard questions remain about their antecedents, their language, Byron's intentions in bypassing Shakespeare, his claims to return to Greek models, to Seneca, and to modern writers who adapted the classical tradition, Alfieri among them. More than any other part of Byron's literary achievement (except the prose), the dramas cry out for understanding and critical attention. Why did Byron write plays, after all? Perhaps, as Bernard Beatty has suggested, to oppose "Romantic neo-Shakespearean tragedy"—against which Byron wrote what Beatty refers to as, "arguably, the most carefully pondered body of drama in English after that of Ben Jonson." Nor, with the notable exception of *Marino Faliero,* have scholars adequately charted the social and political context in Italy as well as in England out of which the plays emerged. Although I largely restrict the following paragraphs to articles and to specialized studies, the student will find important discussions of individual plays in a number of books, for example, those by McGann, Elledge, and Manning, discussed in "Criticism: General."

General studies. Greatly needed is a fresh survey of Byron's work as a dramatist that will fully supersede Samuel Chew's monograph *The Dramas of Lord Byron: A Critical Study* (1915), which has long held the field and which continues to have use as a point of departure. Chapters entitled "The Drama of the Romantic Period" and "Byron and the Contemporary Drama" precede discussions of individual plays. Chew adds three useful appendixes, "Byron and the Dramatic Unities," "*Manfred* and *Faust*," and "Shakespearean Echoes in *Marino Faliero*." Still a valuable study is David V. Erdman's "Byron's Stage Fright: The History of His Ambition and Fear of Writing for the Stage" (*ELH*, 1939). Siegfried Korninger's "Die geistige Welt Lord Byrons" (*RLMC*, 1952) offers a thoughtful analysis of Byron's own "geistige Natur" chiefly as it finds expression in the dramas, with particular focus on *Manfred*. Bonamy Dobrée's Nottingham lecture, *Byron's Dramas* (1962; rpt. in his *Milton to Ouida*, 1970), although far from uncritical, provided in its day a calm and sensible antidote to Paul West's somewhat hysterical discussion of the plays in *Byron and the Spoiler's Art* (1960). Dobrée finds that Byron's verse is "eminently sayable" and "admirable stage speech"; his plays, if properly pruned, can be most effectively staged. Yet in the past two decades one can count stage productions on the fingers of one hand. The chapter in G. Wilson Knight's *The Golden Labyrinth: A Study of British Drama* (1962) introduces the student to Knight's thinking on Byron's dramas and on Byron the dramatist within the larger subject indicated by the subtitle. John W. Ehrstine, "Byron and the Metaphysics of Self-Destruction" (in *The Gothic Imagination: Essays in Dark Romanticism*, ed. G. R. Thompson, 1974), focuses on the Prometheus myth as it appears not only in the "axial" poems of 1816–17 but also in a number of Byron's works not usually associated with the myth. This essay, in revised form, constitutes Ehrstine's introductory chapter to *The Metaphysics of Byron: A Reading of the Plays* (1976), a useful study that complements but does not exactly supersede Chew's. Ehrstine takes up each play sequentially (appendixes deal in less detailed fashion with *Werner* and *The Deformed Transformed*) and, eschewing biographical background, focuses squarely on the text.

The nineteenth-century stage. In contemplating work on Byron's dramas, the student should understand the conditions of the Romantic stage and the traditions of acting that prevailed at the time. Two studies by Joseph W. Donohue, Jr., present this contemporary context: *Dramatic Character in the English Romantic Age* (1970) and *Theatre in the Age of Kean* (1975). Students of Byron will benefit from the model study of an individual play, not by Byron but by Shelley, that is Stuart Curran's *Shelley's Cenci* (1970). In "Edmund Kean and Byron's Plays" (*KSJ*, 1972–73) Peter J. Manning traces Byron's fascination with the famous actor and argues that Kean's acting influenced several of the plays, *Sardanapalus* particularly. In *Byron Tonight: A Poet's Plays on the Nineteenth Century Stage* (1982) Margaret J. Howell focuses on how Victorian actor-managers adapted Byron's "closet dramas to the melodramatic and spectacular requirements of the contemporary theatre." She pays close attention to the differences between the often drastically shortened and rewritten acting versions that have survived and the published versions. Her book is thus more a chapter in the history of the nineteenth-century stage than a contribution to our knowledge of the plays as literature. Her five chapters take up in turn *Marino Faliero, Sardanapalus, Manfred, The Two Foscari,* and *Werner.* She includes a useful list of biographical sketches of the men who had a share in establishing Byron's posthumous fame as a Victorian dramatist. One of her two appendixes deals valuably with recent Byron productions, the other with "Byron's Alleged Stage Fright"—a somewhat unconvincing refutation of Erdman's 1939 essay. Howell believes that Byron was indeed sincere when he said that he did not write for the stage. The question remains open, depending on how one reads Byron's own statements, with a strong possibility that Byron both did and did not wish his plays staged.

The Salzburg Studies in English Literature devotes a number of volumes in its Romantic Reassessment series to Byron. Though the Salzburgers on the dramas are of varying quality, the specialist will seek them out. The most useful is Boleslaw Taborski, *Byron and the Theatre* (1972; all but the last chapter written in 1952), which focuses on Byron's association with the Drury Lane management committee and on contemporary reviews of staged Byron plays. Like the Howell volume, which it complements, it is more a study of the stage history than a critical examination of Byron's dramas. Taborski takes up more thoroughly most of the matters that Howell does. The chapter in Joan Mandell Baum, *The Theatrical Compositions of the Major English Romantic Poets* (1980, but written at least ten years earlier), nicely restates basic information about the plays' performances. Other titles in the Salzburg series are self-descriptive: Paulino M. Lim, *The Style of Lord Byron's Plays* (1973); Allen Perry Whitmore, *The Major Characters of Lord Byron's Dramas* (1974); and B. G. Tandon, *The Imagery of Lord Byron's Plays* (1976). Tandon's "Dialogue in Byron's Dramas" appears in *New Light on Byron* (1978). Om Prakash Mathur devotes the longest chapter of *The Closet Drama of the Romantic Revival* (1978, but written in 1963) to Byron. P. R. Purkayastha, *The Romantics' Third Voice: A Study of the Dramatic Works of the English Romantic Poets* (1978), builds on Taborski's study. M. S. Kushwaha, *Byron and the Dramatic Form* (1980), learned and thorough, scrutinizes Byron's eight plays with close attention to relevant scholarship. Overelaborate in its rehearsal of earlier scholarship, Zamiruddin's *Byron and the Drama of Ideas* (1982) concerns itself with the "thought content" of the plays. Kavita A. Sharma, *Byron's Plays: A Reassessment* (1982), is a competent survey. E. A. Stürzl has written (in German) a useful, wide-ranging survey of Byron's views on dramatic theory in a volume he edited, *Essays in Honour of Professor Cyrus Hillway* (1977).

The history plays.   In this section I consider *Marino Faliero, The Two Foscari,* and *Sardanapalus. Werner*—more a psychological than a historical drama—I treat at the end. Michael G. Cooke, "The Restoration Ethos of Byron's Classical Plays" (*PMLA,* 1964; rpt. in part in *The Blind Man Traces the Circle*), posits interesting analogies between Byron's thoughts on poetry and Dryden's, with particular focus on *Sardanapalus'* affinities with *All for Love* and, to a lesser degree, *Marino Faliero's* with Otway's *Venice Preserved.* William Ruddick, "Lord Byron's Historical Tragedies" (in *Nineteenth Century British Theatre,* ed. Kenneth Richards and Peter Thomson, 1971), considers *Marino Faliero* and *Sardanapalus* as "plays addressed to the ear and to the inward eye." Valuable also on these plays and on *The Two Foscari* is Anne Barton's " 'A Light to Future Ages': Byron's Political Plays" (in Jump's *Byron: A Symposium*). Though he does not mention Byron's plays, Robert Finley in "The Venetian Republic as Gerontocracy: Age and Politics in the Renaissance" (*JMRS,* 1978) indirectly illumines the background of *Marino Faliero* and *The Two Foscari.* John P. Farrell in *Revolution as Tragedy: The Dilemma of the Moderate from Scott to Arnold* (1980) finds Byron's political moderation "not a deliverance but a ceaseless struggle." "The models of classical tragedy served [Byron] by providing a discipline of form in which [he] could explore with some detachment a tragic action distinctive" of his time. Noteworthy are Farrell's discussions of the political implications of *Marino Faliero, Sardanapalus,* and *Cain.* D. M. De Silva, "Byron's Politics and the History Plays" (in *Byron: Poetry and Politics,* ed. Stürzl and Hogg, 1981), presents the somewhat revisionist argument that Byron displayed "a lack of enthusiasm for the egalitarian aspects of democracy, and an ingrained respect for a traditional social hierarchy." Taking a broader view of the histories than most, Daniel P. Watkins, "Violence, Class Consciousness, and Ideology in Byron's History Plays" (*ELH,* 1981), illustrates and illuminates the plays' social concerns.

Though modern taste seems to agree with Byron that *Sardanapalus* is "his best tragedy," more has been written on *Marino Faliero* than on any other. Lucille King established, after Chew, "The Influence of Shakespeare on Byron's *Marino Faliero*" (*UTSE,* 1931). In "A Political Interpretation of Byron's *Marino Faliero*" (*MLQ,* 1942), E. D. H. Johnson studies the play in the light of contemporary affairs in Italy as well as in England, arguing that in the person of the Doge, who is party to a conspiracy against the social class to which he himself belongs, Byron reflects his own position as an aristocrat in sympathy with movements of revolt. Two articles by Thomas L. Ashton further sharpen our understanding of the political context: "The Censorship of Byron's *Marino Faliero*" (*HLQ,* 1972) and "*Marino Faliero*: Byron's 'Poetry of Politics' " (*SIR,* 1974). In "The Moral Ambiguity of 'Marino Faliero' " (*AUMLA,* 1974) G. W. Spence argues against the view that Byron's sympathies lie with the Doge. Useful also is John D. Jump, "A Comparison of 'Marino Faliero' with Otway's 'Venice Preserved' " (*ByronJ,* 1977). I did not find convincing Philip J. Skerry's overschematized argument in "Concentric Structures in *Marino Faliero*" (*KSJ,* 1983) that underlying the play's structure are four concentric circles: personal, political, historical, and eternal. His observations on imagery are helpful, however.

In default of articles on *The Two Foscari,* students should turn to the chapters in McGann, *Fiery Dust*; in Cooke; and in Manning. For Verdi's interest in the play, see under "Music."

Sardanapalus has attracted excellent work in recent years. In addition to the chapters in McGann, Elledge, and Manning, we have Cooke's 1964 *PMLA* piece; Horst Oppel's solid, carefully presented introductory study (in German) in *Das englische Drama im 18. und 19. Jahrhundert,* edited by Heinz Kosok (1970); and Richard R. Pemberton, "Ironie et tragédie: Le 'Sardanaple' de Byron" (*Romantisme,* 1974). Frederick W. Shilstone, "Byron's 'Mental Theatre' and German Classical Precedent" (*Comparative Drama,* 1976), discusses Byron's interest in German drama, finds *Manfred* and *Sardanapalus* examples of "mental theatre," and argues for the influence of Grillparzer's *Sappho* on *Sardanapalus.* Arthur D. Kahn in "Seneca and *Sardanapalus*: Byron, the Don Quixote of Neo-Classicism" (*SP,* 1969) makes a convincing case for Seneca's influence on "every page of *Sardanapalus*." Hermann Fischer's "*Sardanapalus*: Selbstdramatisierung und Distanz" (in *Byron-Symposium Mannheim 1982,* ed. Huber and Schö-werling) relates the play's idiosyncrasies and paradoxes to Byron's biography. Charles J. Clancy takes on the large subject "Death and Love in Byron's *Sardanapalus*" (*ByronJ*, 1982), whereas Gordon Spence in "Moral and Sexual Ambivalence in *Sardanapalus*" (*ByronJ*, 1984) charts a course between McGann in *Fiery Dust* and Allen Perry Whitmore in *The Major Characters of Lord Byron's Dramas* (1974). Martin K. Nurmi has examined "The Prompt Copy of Charles Kean's 1838 Production of Byron's *Sardanapalus*" (*Serif,* 1968) and Margaret J. Howell has described the younger Kean's spectacular 1853 production of the play (*ByronJ*, 1974). Inge Krengel-Strudthoff, "Archäologie auf der Bühme—das wiederstandene Ninive: Charles Keans Ausstattung zu *Sardanapalus* von Lord Byron" (*Kleine Schriften der Gesellschaft für Theatergeschichte,* 1981), demon-strates more thoroughly than before how much Layard's recently published *Nineveh and Its Remains* influenced Kean's sets.

Although *Werner* is set in a historical time and contains references to histor-ical figures, the play—unlike *Faliero, Foscari,* and (to a lesser extent) *Sardana-palus*—dramatizes no demonstrably historical events. For this reason, "psycho-logical drama" might be a more apt term for it than "history." Karl Stöhsel, *Lord Byrons Trauerspiel* Werner *und Seine Quelle* (1891), should still be cited in default of modern treatments. T. H. V. Motter's "Byron's *Werner* Re-estimated" (in *Essays in Dramatic Literature,* ed. Hardin Craig, 1935), puts a higher value on that play, principally on the score of its fitness for presentation on the stage, than does Chew. Helen Damico, "The Stage History of *Werner*" (*NCTR,* 1975), chroni-cles the play's vigorous theatrical life on two continents. Marvin Spevack edited, with an introduction, *Werner, a Tragedy: A Facsimile of the Acting Version of William Charles Macready* (1970). Terry Otten's *The Deserted Stage* (1972) has a chapter entitled "Byron's *Cain* and *Werner*."

Speculative dramas. The speculative dramas include *Manfred* (considered earlier), *Cain, Heaven and Earth,* and *The Deformed Transformed.* The last two are unfinished. Byron defined a "mystery" as a "tragedy on a sacred subject," meaning a biblical play like those of the Middle Ages. Because he subtitled *Cain* and *Heaven and Earth* "A Mystery," critics have occasionally borrowed the term to refer to these four plays. More accurate would be "speculative dramas," a term (which I adopt) used by several critics. Charles Dédéyan's *Le Thème de Faust dans la littérature européenne* (vol. 2, 1955) has particular reference to *Manfred, Cain,* and *The Deformed Transformed.* W. P. Fitzpatrick's "Byron's Mys-teries: The Paradoxical Drive Toward Eden" (*SEL,* 1975) interprets *Cain* and *Heaven and Earth* as reworkings of the basic human paradox present in "Prome-theus." Anya Taylor in *Magic and English Romanticism* (1979) discusses magical elements in the four plays, which she considers a "tetralogy, however unfinished, on the problems of human limitations and the will to escape from them."

More work has been done on *Cain* than on any other of Byron's speculative dramas. Since 1968 students have benefited from Truman Guy Steffan's *Lord*

Byron's Cain: *Twelve Essays and a Text with Variants and Annotations,* which includes brief accounts of the play's composition and publication, followed by "Byron's Views of the Play," *"Cain"* in Chancery," and a discussion of Byron's dramatic theory. All this is useful to have in one place but does not greatly add to what was already known. "The God of This World" considers thirteen numbered ideas that appear in the play, and "The Orthodox Family" describes the conformist characters. An analysis of Cain, Lucifer, and Adah follows. Somewhat more interesting are the accounts of Byron's "Re-creation of Genesis," the imagery of the play, the medley of language (not always successfully blended), and the metrics (remarkably free). A description of the manuscript, owned by the University of Texas at Austin, precedes the text and variants. Following the notes, seven eighths of them concerned with analogues, there is a lengthy "Survey of *Cain* Criticism," extending from the opinions of members of Byron's circle to the comments of twentieth-century critics. Earlier work on *Cain* includes Régis Messac, "Cain et le problème du Mal dans Voltaire, Byron et Leconte de Lisle" (*RLC,* 1924), which discusses the play's affinities with Voltaire, particularly his tales; and R. W. Babcock, "The Inception and Reception of Byron's *Cain"* (*SAQ,* 1927), which supplements the chapter in Chew's *Dramas of Lord Byron* and "The Reception of *Cain"* in *Byron in England.* See also Constantine N. Stavrou, "Milton, Byron, and the Devil" (*Univ. of Kansas City Review,* 1955). Edward E. Bostetter in "Byron and the Politics of Paradise" (*PMLA,* 1960; largely rpt. in *The Romantic Ventriloquists,* 1963) argues that "Byron deliberately exploits the clash" between old and new values. "He uses the Biblical cosmos as the setting for the first act, superimposes upon it in the second act the cosmos of nineteenth-century scientific speculation, and in the third act returns to the Biblical cosmos." In a related study, Stephen L. Goldstein, "Byron's *Cain* and the Painites" (*SIR,* 1975), reveals *Cain's* affinities to radical thinking by setting it against the geological controversies of the day as they found reflection in the radical press. Leonard Michaels in "Byron's *Cain"* (*PMLA,* 1969) argues, against Bostetter, that Byron does not, in fact, exploit "the clash between old and new cosmologies, but rather that he has no real belief— however much he chooses to exploit it—in the value of abstract speculation on the great matters of theology and metaphysics." His conclusion that *Cain* "has strong affinities with contemporary theatre of the absurd" does not convince. David Eggenschwiler in "Byron's *Cain* and the Antimythological Myth" (*MLQ,* 1976) concludes that "in its use of traditional myth" the play "is an extraordinary dramatic experiment and a forerunner of much modern drama." Jerome J. McGann in "Staging Byron's *Cain"* (*KSMB,* 1968) describes *Cain's* first complete production in English—at the University of Chicago. Taborski's essay on the Russian Stanislavsky's 1920 production and the Pole Grotowski's 1960 production (in *Byron: Poetry and Politics,* ed. Stürzl and Hogg, 1981) covers in part the same ground as the last chapter of his *Byron and the Theatre.* Robert Mortensen, "The Copyright of Byron's *Cain"* (*PBSA,* 1969), after carefully studying the evidence, finds that Murray did not ask for a jury trial to uphold his copyright—thus leaving the play uncopyrighted. Wolf Z. Hirst in "Byron's Lapse into Orthodoxy: An Unorthodox Reading of *Cain"* (*KSJ,* 1980) argues provokingly but (in my view) unconvincingly that the play is "not antireligious, that it accepts rather than reverses the Scriptural position, and that the hero's attacks upon God are dramatically invalidated." Hirst follows this essay with another on *Cain* in *Byron: Poetry and Politics.* Ruth Mellinkoff in *The Mark of Cain* (1981) briefly relates Byron's drama to the long literary and iconographical tradition surrounding this figure. Murray Roston, "The Bible Romanticized: Byron's *Cain* and *Heaven and Earth*" (in his *Biblical Drama in England: From the Middle Ages to the Present Day,* 1968), views both plays as "a disguised reinterpretation of the theme of the Fall." Leslie Brisman's chapter "Byron: Troubled Stream from a Pure Source" (in *Romantic Origins,* 1978) presents an unrewarding structuralist reading of *Cain* (and of *Lara*). Not for the unwary. Terry Otten in *After Innocence: Versions of the Fall in Modern Literature* (1982) offers an existential reading colored by Blake. Daniel M. McVeigh, " 'In Caines Cynne': Byron and the Mark of Cain" (*MLQ,* 1982), has written well on *Cain*—and on Byron. Paul A. Cantor, "Byron's *Cain:* A Romantic Version of the Fall" (*KR,* 1980; rpt. in *Creature and Creator: Mythmaking in English Romanticism,* 1984), reads the play as an expression of Byron's (asserted) gnosticism. His essay is innocent of virtually all the scholarship mentioned in this paragraph.

Daniel P. Watkins, "Politics and Religion in Byron's *Heaven and Earth*" (*ByronJ,* 1983), offers a solid discussion of its announced subjects. On *The Deformed Transformed,* see Charles E. Robinson's important essay "The Devil as Doppelgänger in *The Deformed Transformed:* The Sources and Meaning of Byron's Unfinished Drama" (*BNYPL,* 1970) and Watkins' splendid analysis of conflicting currents of thought, "The Ideological Dimensions of Byron's *The Deformed Transformed*" (*Criticism,* 1983).

Prose

Byron's prose scintillates from earliest manhood. Already at Harrow and Cambridge Byron handled the language with singular grace and ease. His youthful poems, though revaluated in recent years, interest chiefly as harbingers of achievement to come. But the letters Byron wrote in his early twenties, among them the brilliant sequence to Lady Melbourne describing his entanglement with Lady Frances Wedderburn Webster, dazzle in their accomplished artistry. At this time, the autumn of 1813, Byron was between *The Giaour* and *The Bride of Abydos.* Yet if his career as a poet was firmly established, his career as a parliamentary orator and writer of prose never got off the ground. With the publication of *Childe Harold,* "nobody," Byron later recalled, "ever thought about my *prose* afterwards, nor indeed did I—it became to me a secondary and neglected object." And neglected by critics it has largely remained. Yet Byron seems to have preferred prose to poetry. Lady Byron's "preference for *prose,*" he notes in a late letter, "(strange as it may now seem) *was* and indeed *is* mine." W. H. Auden, deciding how best to introduce Byron to students, would have them "read *all* of the prose" before tackling the poetry. "It does not matter where one opens the prose," he observes; "from the earliest years till the end, the tone of voice rings true and utterly unlike anybody else's." In effect, Byron's prose, as G. Wilson Knight wrote in 1953, "in historical and literary comment, oratory, letters and journals is in range, variety, and power, among the great achievements of English literature." With the completion of the Marchand edition of the letters and journals, we are in a better position to appreciate the prescience of Knight's observation.

Byron's prose falls under at least five headings: his letters and journals (which constitute the bulk of it); his prefaces and the often extensive notes to the poems; his three parliamentary speeches; his formal critical writings, which include several early reviews, "Reply to Blackwood's *Edinburgh Magazine*," two letters to the Rev. William Lisle Bowles, and the jeu d'esprit "Letter to the Editor of 'My Grandmother's Review'"; and a number of short or incomplete narratives, not all published. If Byron's memoirs had survived, they would be valued not only as a lively autobiography but also, perhaps, as the capstone of his achievement in prose. By and large, Romantic prose has not been examined for its literary artistry in the way that Victorian prose has been during the past several decades. Although Byron's prose bulks larger in size than his poetry, critics have accorded it only an infinitesimal fraction of the attention they accord the poetry. The prose does not have the poetry's long tradition of critical discourse behind it, nor have the prose and the poetry often been considered together. Nina Diakonova, "Byron's Prose and Byron's Poetry" (*SEL*, 1976), stands almost alone in attempting to move beyond hackneyed restatements that the ironic mode of *Don Juan* emerged equally from prose and poetry. By juxtaposing passages from both media, she points out similarities and dissimilarities and studies the style of the letters alongside that of the poems. Byron's "parallel experiments in prose and verse," she concludes, "paved the way to the realistic mid-nineteenth century European novel."

Letters and journals.   Although the letters of writers from the eighteenth century through the twentieth century have often been admired, the idea that the personal letter can be literature in its own right has not yet gained widespread acceptance. Nor has the study of it emerged from its infancy. Byron's letters reveal, as Ruskin and Wilson Knight have demonstrated, a Shakespearean range of character and situation. Equally subtle are modulations in tone and mood. The protean nature of Byron's being exhibits itself best in his correspondence, for nowhere else can he present a slightly different conception of himself to each recipient. Many of his finest letters he wrote with a particular audience in mind, one often larger than the actual addressee; for example, he knew others would read those he directed to John Murray from Italy. His letters were admired as virtuoso performances by their recipients, and they were admired by reviewers, Lockhart notably, when a substantial number appeared in print for the first time in Moore's *Life* of Byron. But only recently have they begun to gain the recognition they deserve both for their intrinsic merit and for the influence they have exerted on subsequent prose style. Thanks to Leslie A. Marchand's edition, we may now read them, not as successive Victorian editors bowdlerized them, but as Byron wrote them, in all their spontaneity and onrushing flow. They are central both to Byron's literary achievement and to the development of his afterfame.

Ruskin remains the most acute critic of Byron's prose. His major observations occur in *Fiction, Fair and Foul* (1880) and *Praeterita* (1885–89) (the passages are conveniently reprinted in *The Literary Criticism of John Ruskin*, ed. Harold Bloom, 1965). G. Wilson Knight's *Byron's Dramatic Prose* (1953; rpt. in *Poets of Action*, 1967) considers, with well-selected excerpts, qualities of the prose. Charles Keith earlier surveyed "Byron's Letters" (*QQ*, 1946), as did Robert Escarpit in volume 2 of *Lord Byron: Un tempérament littéraire*. More recently, John D. Jump has provided an informative chapter on the prose in his *Byron* (1972), returning to the subject in *Byron: A Symposium*. L. M. Findlay offers a learned, critically sophisticated view in "'Perpetual Activity' in Byron's Prose" (*ByronJ*, 1984). Robert A. Fothergill, *Private Chronicles: A Study of English Diaries* (1974), considering the diary as a literary genre, focuses intelligently on Byron's 1813–14 journal and sets the poet as a diarist against Scott and Haydon. In *The Art of Autobiography in 19th and 20th Century England* (1984) A. O. J. Cockshut includes brief discussion of Byron's letters and journals, especially of "Detached Thoughts." Intelligent exploration of the autobiographical impulse in Byron, of the relation between life and literature, remains a largely uncharted sea. In "Byron as a Romantic Poet" (in *English Romanticism: The Grounds of Belief*), John Clubbe and Ernest J. Lovell, Jr., ponder the implications for Byron's art of a passage from the 1816 Journal to Augusta. Marchand's introduction to volume 1 of *Byron's Letters and Journals* sensitively evaluates many facets of the poet's epistolary genius. Marchand covers some of the same ground in his introduction to the one-volume selection. Most editors of selections (noted in "Editions and Selections: Letters") discuss the literary qualities of the letters. In addition, Elizabeth Drew considers the artistry of the letters in *The Literature of Gossip: Nine English Letterwriters* (1964), as does John Clubbe in "Byron in His Letters" (*SAQ*, 1975), "Byron's Letters: The Poet as Prosaist" (*SAQ*, 1978), and "Byron as Autobiographer" (*SAQ*, 1983), on which these paragraphs draw.

Prefaces and notes. Few have discussed Byron's prefaces and notes to his poems, the latter often quite extensive. The notes often have an interest—biographical, historical, stylistic—well beyond their immediate purpose, namely, to elucidate the work or passage in question. Sometimes a note will even contradict the meaning of the text. *Childe Harold* 2 exhorts the Greeks to gain their freedom, whereas one of its notes denies that they will ever "be sovereign as heretofore, and God forbid they ever should." In addition to their value as commentary, the notes often have considerable distinction in their own right as prose. Unfortunately, most volumes of selections from the poetry usually omit or, at best, severely abridge Byron's notes, which often changed from edition to edition, as he dropped some, added others, revised still others. The student seeking out the poet's own commentary to his poems should consult both the original editions and McGann's Oxford edition. Several studies noted under *"Childe Harold"* and *"Don Juan"* take up the prefaces to those poems. See particularly, for *Childe Harold*, Ronald A. Schroeder's essay, and, for *Don Juan*, essays by

Gordon K. Thomas and Frederick Garber. In an intriguing study, John F. Schell, "Prose Prefaces and Romantic Poets: Insinuation and Ethos" (*JNT,* 1983), discusses Byron's prefaces to *Childe Harold* and *The Vision of Judgment* within a tradition of authorial presentation that goes back to the classical *insinuatio*.

Parliamentary speeches. Byron's parliamentary speeches, first published in 1824, are models of rhetoric but have usually been viewed either as biographical documents or as expressions of liberal sentiment in early nineteenth-century England. Byron's rhetorical art in them, as in his other prose, deserves thorough and detailed investigation. A beginning is made in the Byron chapter of Roger Sales's *English Literature and History 1780 – 1830: Pastoral and Politics* (1983).

Criticism. Byron the critic gets a scant page in the third volume of René Wellek's *History of Modern Criticism* (1955). If not a major critic, he is a far more interesting one than many suppose. On this subject almost all remains to be done. In part, the problem is that Byron wrote little formal criticism and scattered obiter dicta everywhere; in part, it is that he doubted the value of poetry and seems at times to adopt a cavalier attitude toward writing. "What the devil had I to do with scribbling?" he interrogates his journal on 17 March 1814. He admits that he would "think better" of himself if he had the "sense to stop now." But he never did for long, and moods of irritation caused by this need to write continually surged over him. In 1823, inquiring about his daughter Ada, he exclaims, "I hope the Gods have made her anything save *poetical*—it is enough to have one such fool in a family." How much of this discontent is affectation, how much sincere? An intriguing question, one in Byron's case easily susceptible to misinterpretation, and one that needs to be answered in different ways, with different emphases, for various periods of his life.

Any study of Byron's critical opinions, formal and informal, in verse as well as prose, must emphasize the "Augustan" elements in his disposition, taste, and practice. Older surveys drawing together his pronouncements in letters, journals, poems, and prefaces to poems are Clement T. Goode's *Byron as Critic* (1923) and Margot Eisser's *Lord Byron als Kritiker* (1932). Nathan A. E. Carb, Jr., "Byron as Critic: Not a Neo-Classicist" (*WVUPP,* 1958), argues briefly for the essentially autobiographical and subjective character of Byron's literary criticism. Bruce Wallis in *Byron: The Critical Voice* (2 vols., 1972) has provided a useful compendium of Byron's opinions. Volume 1 gives alphabetically by topics Byron's recorded comments, many embedded in the letters and journals, on numerous subjects, for example, "art vs. nature" and "epic poetry." Volume 2 gives his opinions on his own work and on that of others. Wallis' introduction points out the problems facing those interested in Byron's criticism and urges "the need for a serious reestimation of his critical stature." The studies by Heinrich Hartmann on Byron's relationship to his neoclassical contemporaries or near comtemporaries and by J. J. Van Rennes on the Pope-Bowles-Byron controversy I have mentioned under "Criticism: General." As noted there, Prothero reprints Byron's two important letters to Bowles as an appendix to volume 5 of his *Letters and Journals;* in an appendix to volume 4 he includes the playful "Letter to the Editor of 'My Grandmother's Review'" as well as the important "Reply to Blackwood's *Edinburgh Magazine.*" W. S. Ward in "Lord Byron and 'My Grandmother's Review'" (*MLN,* 1949) supplies the background for Byron's attack, and Philip B. Daghlian discusses the manuscript, proofs, and publication of the observations on *Blackwood's Magazine* (*RES,* 1947). Since Marchand was not able to include Byron's critical writings in his edition, there is plainly a need for a scholarly edition of them, properly introduced and annotated. The Clarendon Press has commissioned Andrew Nicholson to prepare such an edition. It might reveal that Byron's own practice as a poet, which sometimes seems inconsistent and sometimes even bizarre, is in fact a carefully reasoned affirmation of his values as critic. Such is the intriguing argument advanced by Bernard Beatty ("Lord Byron: Poetry and Precedent," in *Literature of the Romantic Period 1750–1850,* ed. R. T. Davies and Beatty, 1976), who claims that after 1816 Byron wrote poem after poem in order to assert his critical position. J. Drummond Bone's "Byron's Ravenna Diary Entry: What Is Poetry?" (*ByronJ,* 1978) examines one of his 1821 observations, "What is Poetry?—The feeling of a former world and Future."

Narratives. Byron read novels avidly all his life, and this reading stimulated him to begin several prose fictions of his own. Though he recognized early that his talent was for poetry, contemporaries regretted that he had not written more in the category of imaginative prose. His first prose piece, "The Death of Calmar and Orla," an avowed imitation of Ossian, appeared in *Hours of Idleness.* In November 1813, after beginning a novel, he "burnt it because the scene ran into *reality.* . . . In rhyme, I can keep more away from facts." Such hesitancy may explain why "A Fragment," untitled when set down in 1816 but so designated when published in 1819, remains Byron's best-known but most puzzling exercise in narrative. Apparently about a vampire, it indirectly caused enormous reverberations, for it was this tale that John William Polidori read in manuscript in 1816, heard Byron continue orally, and used for his own version, *The Vampyre* (1819), which inaugurated the vampire vogue in England and particularly in France. On this subject see Richard Switzer, "Lord Ruthven and the Vampires" (*FR,* 1955), and Kenneth A. Bruffee, "Elegiac Romance" (*CE,* 1971; rev. in *Elegiac Romance,* 1983); the latter has a perceptive discussion of both Byron's and Polidori's tales. One who argues (unconvincingly) that Byron's tale is not about a vampire is James B. Twitchell in *The Living Dead: A Study of the Vampire in Romantic Literature* (1981). Twitchell considers it (and *Manfred*) within the larger context of the Romantic interest in vampires. During Byron's years in Italy Murray frequently urged him to make a new departure in prose, but Byron never seriously responded to Murray's exhortations, unless we take the mature satires to be his response. He did make several attempts to write in prose, all, however, quickly abandoned. "Italy, or *Not* Corinna: A Travelling Romance by an Ecrivain en Poste," dated 19 August 1820, begins as a skit on Sotheby's *Farewell to Italy.* Prothero reprints it as an appendix to volume 4 of the *Letters and Journals.* R. M. Wardle in "The Motive for Byron's 'George Russell of A'" (*MLN,* 1950) corrects E. H. Coleridge (who includes the piece in his vol. 5) by pointing out that Byron's target was not John Scott but *Blackwood's Magazine.* A short narrative begun on 6 February 1823 Prothero entitles "An Italian Carnival" and publishes as an appendix to his volume 6.

The survival of a copy of Byron's memoirs—the manuscript was burned in John Murray's chambers a few months after the poet's death—would undoubtedly give further impetus to the study and appreciation of the prose. Several copies were made and perhaps twenty contemporaries read them, but no copy has yet come to light, though the recent discovery of important Byron manuscripts and letters in the Scrope Davies trunk has raised hopes that eventually one will. Wilfred S. Dowden discusses this (admittedly very slight) possibility in "Byron's Letters and 'Journals': A Note" (in Robinson's *Lord Byron and His Contemporaries*).

Ideas and Beliefs

Man, says Shakespeare's Benedick, "is a giddy thing." Byron would have agreed. His thoughts on a number of subjects are often challenging, often inconsistent, rarely dull. He valued what the Renaissance called *sprezzatura*—the quality of doing everything, even difficult tasks, with ease and nonchalance. Although Shaw once deemed Byron "as little of a philosopher as Peter the Great," we should not take the poet's well-known detestation of philosophic systems ("When a man talks of his system, it is like a woman's talking of her *virtue.* I let them talk on") as evidence of lack of interest in ideas or in abstract speculation. All his life his mind churned, his pen raced across the page. His handwriting, he once said, "is that of one who thinks much, rapidly—perhaps deeply—but rarely with pleasure." "Words," for him, were "things." And despite the dazzling stanzas praising inconstancy in *Don Juan* 2, Byron's own seeming inconsistencies sometimes even resolve themselves into underlying consistency. Long ago, Howard Mumford Jones lamented that criticism of Byron was "not enough concerned with his thought. Since Macaulay's famous essay writers have dealt with the Byronic hero too exclusively and too little with Byronic ideas" (*Texas Review,* 1924). Jones's own pages still provide a wide-ranging and suggestive introduction to Byron's thought within the intellectual context of 1750–1850. In the sixty years since Jones wrote his essay, with the honorable exception of politics and, to a lesser degree, of religion, scholarship on Byron's ideas and beliefs has hardly moved out of the Stone Age. In this section I consider Byron's thoughts on only a few subjects. Exigencies of space do not permit giving cross-references to many discussions in studies that deal primarily with other matters.

Religion.   Byron's religious position has elicited much controversy. The poet as usual put the matter most compactly: "I deny nothing, but doubt everything." E. W. Marjarum in *Byron as Skeptic and Believer* (1938) has studied the religious aspect of the Byronic paradox. His four chapters—on doctrinal Christianity, skepticism, naturalism, and Catholicism—succinctly examine Byron's shifting positions, with all-too-brief mention of such important influences as Lucretius and Spinoza. Baffling contradictions remain, for this intellectual child of the age of Bayle and Hume and Voltaire was also the heir of a darkly Calvinistic tradition and was yet receptive to currents of religious and metaphysical thought and emotion in his own age. Although Byron temporarily succumbed to Wordsworthian metaphysics (which Shelley "dosed" him with in the summer of 1816), his more usual position was closer to that of the eighteenth-century deists, with attendant doubts as to the immortality of the soul. Even so, Byron's emotional instability separates him from the cool rationalism of Voltaire. The attraction that the Roman Catholic Church exerted on him was chiefly due to his curiosity and sense of the picturesque; he never seriously considered accepting its dogmas.

When we have made allowances for fundamental differences in point of view, we may learn much from the chapter on Byron's religious opinions in Hoxie N. Fairchild's *Religious Trends in English Poetry* (vol. 3, 1949). Fairchild's treatment of the problem is unavoidably unsympathetic (he is a convinced Anglo-Catholic) but nonetheless valuable as serving to correct other estimates. He remarks that Byron's sense of the limitations of and evil in human nature combined with his superstitiousness to prevent him "from denying that Christianity, which he was unable to accept." In an earlier, briefer consideration of the same problem, in *The Romantic Quest* (1931), Fairchild had characterized Byron's mind as "too idealistic to refrain from blowing bubbles, and too realistic to refrain from pricking them." He had a "certain desperate integrity" of intellect that rendered him unable to "dupe himself" when faced with the "toughness of facts." A brief recent account is C. M. Woodhouse, "The Religion of an Agnostic" (*ByronJ*, 1978). The introduction to Travis Looper's compendium *Byron and the Bible* (1978) reviews other studies. The last chapter of James D. Boulger's *The Calvinist Temper in English Poetry* (1980) focuses on the Calvinist element in Byron's poetry, notably in the Romantic poems, particularly *Childe Harold, Manfred,* and several of the 1816 poems. Boulger concludes that "no other poet was so deeply affected by the dark and negative side of Calvinist thought and tradition."

Byron's interest in Islam is the subject of Bernard Blackstone's long essay "Byron and Islam: The Triple Eros" (*JES,* 1974). Blackstone, who understands Islam to be as much a civilization as a religion, considers Byron's involvement with the East as evidenced in his youthful reading in Oriental poetry and travel books, his tour of 1809–11, and the tales he wrote on Eastern subjects through 1816. Blackstone has read widely in Eastern history and literature, its customs and lore. Much of what he claims regarding Eastern influence on Byron is speculative, he candidly admits, and as speculation not altogether or often convincing. The latter part of his essay takes up Eastern influence on Byron's tales (supplementing Harold Wiener's discussion, noted under "Criticism: Individual Works"). Blackstone's arguments are full of intellectual fireworks and contain numerous startling claims, but when the smoke has cleared Byron emerges pretty much as before. Like his *Byron: A Survey,* "Byron and Islam" succeeds best as a passionate plea to respond to Byron within a total context, one that includes the places in which he lived and wrote, the sights he saw and described, the books he read and commented on. Worth noting again in this connection is Maurice J. Quinlan, "Byron's *Manfred* and Zoroastrianism" (*JEGP*, 1958).

Science. Scholars have not adequately investigated Byron's understanding of the scientific thought of his day. He read widely in, among others, Buffon, Cuvier, and Sir Humphry Davy. The essay by Jones cited earlier (*Texas Review*, 1924) suggests directions to explore. Jones finds Byron "preeminently a cosmological poet," with interests "in metaphysics, in the philosophy of history, in theology." His "dilating imagination" made him an "emotional pioneer" in exploring the "grandiosity of Romantic metaphysics." Still the most comprehensive study of this aspect of Byron's thought is Manfred Eimer's *Byron und der Kosmos* (1912). Several subjects that Eimer takes up—Byron's interest in astronomy, cosmogony, and paleontology—have rarely been discussed since by students of the poet. Recently, however, Edward E. Bostetter in "Masses and Solids: Byron's View of the External World" (*MLQ*, 1974) has sensitively illumined Byron's varied, empirical perception of the natural world. Heide N. Rohloff's lengthy essay "The Disturbing Challenge of Fact: Lord Byron and Romanticism" (in *The Hannover Byron Symposium, 1979*, ed. James Hogg, 1981) discusses Byron's understanding of the universe and of scientific and philosophical tradition (including Locke). *Cain*, as we might expect, comes in for extensive consideration. On this work see also Goldstein's essay (*SIR*, 1975), cited earlier, and, concerning science in the early Byron, Steffan's essay "The Edinburgh Ladies Petition and Reply" (*UTSE*, 1948).

Nature. In *Byron: The Record of a Quest* (1949) Ernest J. Lovell, Jr., thoughtfully surveys the poet's concept and treatment of nature. His study supersedes Ernst Wilmink, *Lord Byrons Naturgefühl* (1913). Lovell considers the tradition of the picturesque and Byron's handling of it; the conflict between the urban and the rural; the theme of the beauties of nature lost on a mind temperamentally disinclined to absorb them; the "rejection of feigned emotion" as a fundamental element in Byron's temperament; and the persistence, with many fluctuations, of deistic thought in his poems and prose writings. Blackstone's "Byron and the Levels of Landscape" (*ArielE*, 1974) also discusses the poet's view of nature, ranging widely over the Byronic corpus, though with particular focus on *Childe Harold*, and relating Byron to other poets. What still has not been adequately studied are the sensory, emotional, historical, and spiritual associations that Byron derived from the spirit of place in many lands—an elusive subject but an important one.

Symbolism. The studies by Marjarum, Eimer, Fairchild, Blackstone, and Lovell penetrate to the profounder levels of the poet's thought that often lie hidden beneath the glittering surface. From another angle of approach, G. Wilson Knight's "The Two Eternities: An Essay on Byron" (in *The Burning Oracle*, 1939; rpt. as "Byron: The Poetry" in *Poets of Action*, 1967) attempts to reach these levels. Knight's well-known technique is warmly applauded by some scholars, firmly rejected by others. His claim to recognize metaphysically significant themes beneath the surface of symbols has never been more disconcertingly illustrated than in his interpretation of Byron, the least symbolic of our major poets. Knight discovers the meaning of Byron's imagery more richly (as one would expect) in the Romantic than in the satiric work.

The Byronic hero (and heroine).   On the Romantic, Byronic *Heldentypus* there are discussions in E. M. Sickels' *The Gloomy Egoist* (1932); in Mario Praz's *The Romantic Agony* (1933), especially chapter 2 (on the descent of the Byronic hero from the Miltonic Satan to the diabolical de Sade, concluding— preposterously—that "the distance does not seem so great between the Divine Marquis and the Satanic Lord"); and in Eino Railo's *The Haunted Castle* (1927), especially chapters 6 and 7. See also Carl Lefevre's article "Lord Byron's Fiery Convert of Revenge" (*SP*, 1952), a study of the renegade aristocrat as a type of the Byronic hero, with particular focus on the tales and *Marino Faliero.*

The standard study is now Peter L. Thorslev's *The Byronic Hero: Types and Prototypes* (1962), which finds that the Byronic hero was "the figure with the most far-reaching consequences for nineteenth-century Western literature." The subject, as Thorslev's bibliographical notes reveal, is a much-studied one. In his view, "all the elements of the Byronic Hero existed before him in the literature of the age." Thorslev "seeks out the origins of the Byronic Hero, not in Byron's personality, but in the cultural and especially the literary milieu of the age in which he lived." He defines and traces the Byronic hero's development in *Childe Harold,* the first four romances, *Manfred,* and *Cain.* Finally, he places "the Byronic Hero in the Romantic Tradition." Thorslev refers to the satires incidentally or not at all. His chapter titles indicate the main prototypes: "The Child of Nature," "The Hero of Sensibility: Man of Feeling or Gloomy Egoist," "The Gothic Villain," "The Noble Outlaw," "Faust," "Cain and Ahasuerus," "Satan and Prometheus." The author, then, is concerned with large areas and broad generalizations. Only the last seventy-two pages focus directly on Byron's heroes. Elsewhere, references to the poetry are few. The central chapters (2–8), valuable as wide-ranging commentary, often emphasize the relationships between types. Chapter 9, on *Childe Harold,* does not convince in its discussion of the main characters in cantos 1 and 2, but Thorslev clearly demonstrates that the early Harold is kin to a number of the prototypes mentioned above. Chapter 11 regards Manfred as "representative of almost every one of the hero-types of the Romantic movement." The book closes by discussing "The Byronic Hero and Heroic Tradition."

In "The Byronic Heroine: Incest and the Creative Process" (*SEL*, 1981) Joanna E. Rapf views Byron's heroines within the context of feminist writing and of Jung. She discusses the women in *Don Juan,* then goes back to earlier females in the tales, *Childe Harold,* and *Manfred.* In Rapf's view, Byron was "unable to accept the female side of the creative process" and thus "turned to humor." She concludes "that Byron's relationship with his feminine ideal, his creative unconscious, was incestuous" and that "in Byron's fallen world, self-love is the only enduring love possible without guilt." Also touching on the Byronic heroine are the essays by Gloria T. Hull (cited under *The Corsair*) and Charles J. Clancy (under *Don Juan*).

Christian Kreutz, *Das Prometheussymbol in der Dichtung der englischen Romantik* (1963), has a long, solidly documented chapter on Byron's weltanschauung, his image of Prometheus, and his Promethean heroes.

Politics.   Byron proclaimed freedom and detestation of cant to be his two abiding concerns. "I wish men to be free," he writes in *Don Juan.* "As much from mobs as kings—from you as me." For Swinburne, Byron was "never earnest save in politics." Goethe once called Byron's poems "repressed parliamentary speeches." Their political dimensions are all-important. Carl Woodring in *Politics in English Romantic Poetry* (1970) deals learnedly and authoritatively with Byron's faith in the possibilities of life as it reveals itself in political terms in his poetry. He analyzes political elements in all Byron's major poems and in many of the lesser ones. Although the specialized studies noted in subsequent paragraphs must still be consulted, Woodring's superb chapter on Byron largely subsumes much earlier work, including Herbert Grierson's "Byron and English Society" (1922; rpt. in *The Background of English Literature,* 1925), which takes in religious as well as political background; Dora Neill Raymond, *The Political Career of Lord Byron* (1924), which gathers the material together but does not subject it to thorough examination; Crane Brinton's chapter in *Political Ideas of the English Romanticists* (1926); and V. de Sola Pinto's Nottingham lecture, *Byron and Liberty* (1944). Robert Escarpit provides an overview, "Byron, figure politique" (*Romantisme,* 1974), revised in English as "Byron and France: Byron as a Political Figure" in *Byron's Political and Cultural Influence in Nineteenth-Century Europe: A Symposium,* edited by Paul Graham Trueblood (1981). Other essays in this volume—many discussed elsewhere—are also of value on Byron's politics. John P. Farrell's chapter, "Byron: Rebellion and Revolution," in *Revolution as Tragedy: The Dilemma of the Moderate from Scott to Arnold* (1980), argues that more than anything else Byron was a moderate. "The major characteristic, as well as the major significance, of Byron's political temper is precisely his sustained ambivalence and caution, particularly when revolution becomes the chief issue." Actually, Byron's political commitment waxed and waned as circumstances dictated: he had more radical moments than Farrell realizes. *Byron: Poetry and Politics,* edited by Erwin A. Stürzl and James Hogg (1981), contains seventeen essays of varying merit on the relationship between Byron's poems and his politics, among them, Peter J. Manning's astute piecing together of overlooked bits of evidence, "Tales and Politics: *The Corsair, Lara,* and *The White Doe of Rylstone.*" Other essays in this volume I note more appropriately elsewhere. The most recent study I have seen, Roger Sales's chapter in *English Literature and History 1780–1830: Pastoral and Politics* (1983), offers a lively run-through of Byron's political ideas, with interesting observations about style in oratory. With all the work done on Byron's politics during the past fifteen years, the subject would seem to be well worked over. Actually, it is not. As I read through Jerome McGann's new edition of the poems in the light of the editor's excellent commentary, I sense that we are just beginning to perceive the extraordinary pervasiveness of the political dimension of Byron's poetry. Malcolm Kelsall's forthcoming study of Byron's politics should help fill the gap.

Several studies by David V. Erdman focus sharply on Byron's attitude toward the political scene. During his years in London the poet moved in the antigovernmental milieu whose center was Holland House. In "Lord Byron and the Genteel Reformers" (*PMLA*, 1941) Erdman demonstrates that Byron's attitude toward reform is that assumed in these Whig circles. In "Lord Byron as Rinaldo" (*PMLA*, 1942) he shows that the political views of Lady Oxford had an appreciable influence on Byron's activities in Parliament. In "Byron and Revolt in England" (*Science & Society*, 1947) he estimates Byron's influence on the social and economic disturbances in England following the defeat of Napoleon and the poet's attitude toward these manifestations of a revolutionary spirit. In "Byron and 'The New Force of the People' " (*KSJ*, 1962) he documents Byron's ambivalent response to the spirit of the new democratic age. Erdman's " 'Fare Thee Well'—Byron's Last Days in England" (in vol. 4 of *Shelley and His Circle*) adds greatly to our knowledge of the newspaper attacks on Byron in 1816 and their complex political motivation. His "Life and Works" of Byron in volume 3 emphasizes the poet's political interests. *Romantic Rebels*, edited by K. N. Cameron (1973), reprints both essays.

The obvious truth that Byron, whatever his self-contradictions along other lines, never wavered or faltered in his hatred of oppression is developed by Wilfred S. Dowden in "The Consistency of Byron's Social Criticism" (*Rice Inst. Papers*, 1950). Two further studies by Dowden discuss the unease Byron caused Austrian authorities (who controlled northern Italy, where Byron lived during 1816–22): "Byron and the Austrian Censorship" (*KSJ*, 1955) and "Byron through Austrian Eyes" in *Anglo-German and American-German Crosscurrents*, edited by P. A. Shelley and Arthur O. Lewis, Jr. (1962).

Byron's attitude toward revolution, as reflected in his poetry, forms the subject of Bertrand Russell's "Byron and the Modern World" (*JHI*, 1940), in which Byron, "the aristocratic rebel," is contrasted with the "proletarian rebel" of our own day. The poet's essential function, Russell argues, is to liberate the human personality from social convention and social morality. This essay, somewhat condensed, reappears in his *History of Western Philosophy* (1945). Ronald Paulson's *Representations of Revolution (1789–1820)* (1983) examines a number of painters and writers, including (briefly) Byron, who have tried to come to grips with the phenomenon of revolution.

Byron and Napoleon. Napoleon never ceased to fascinate Byron. Examination of the many allusions to the French emperor in the poems, letters, and journals leads to the conclusion that Byron was of two minds, admiring the hero and individualist while denouncing the conqueror; in sympathy with the supreme antidynastic offspring of the French Revolution while satirizing the low ambition that sought to establish his own dynasty; and after Waterloo keenly aware that the fall of the emperor was not the triumph of liberalism but the restoration of reactionary despotism. The related larger problem of the influence of French revolutionary thought on Byron has not been the subject of detailed, separate investigation since Edward Dowden's and A. E. Hancock's now somewhat outmoded studies of that influence on the English poets. Gerhart Eggert's *Lord Byron und Napoleon* (1933) supplemented and largely superseded P. Holzhausen's *Bonaparte, Byron, und die Briten* (1904). More recently, a brilliant, erratic, but compelling study by E. Tangye Lean, *The Napoleonists: A Study in Political Disaffection 1760–1960* (1970), has greatly furthered our comprehension of English attitudes toward Napoleon. Readers of this book cannot fail to increase their understanding of the thralldom that Napoleon exerted over certain contemporaries. Lean, who spent over twenty years researching the Napoleonist syndrome in English political life, examines the careers of a number of the emperor's conspicuous supporters in England—all Whigs, Byron among them, but including also John Cam Hobhouse, Samuel Whitbread, Lord and Lady Holland, Thomas Moore, Elizabeth Inchbald, Hazlitt, and Capel Lofft—to trace the common strands in their diverse backgrounds that led them to become such unabashed admirers. Lean's account of the Whigs' empathetic involvement with Napoleon's fortunes, in conjunction with the European image of him as a dynamic, self-made man of destiny, helps put into perspective Byron's own self-identification. James Hogg's "Byron's Vacillating Attitude towards Napoleon" (in *Byron: Poetry and Politics,* ed. Stürzl and Hogg) is more a review of previous scholarship with generous quotations from Byron than an original synthesis. On the Napoleon poems of the other Romantic poets as well as Byron's, see Bernhard Reitz, " 'To Die as Honor Dies': Politics of the Day and Romantic Understanding of History in Southey's, Shelley's, and Byron's Poems on Napoleon" (in *The Hannover Byron Symposium, 1979,* ed. Hogg). Andrew Nicholson in "Form and Content in Byron's Poetry and Prose" (*ByronJ,* 1985) differentiates shrewdly between Byron's prose and poetic responses to Napoleon. John Clubbe is working on a reassessment of Byron's shifting attitudes toward Napoleon.

History. Byron once remarked that "The moment I could read—my grand passion was *history.*" We may better understand much of his poetry with some knowledge of contemporary events and personages. The more we know of the historical characters mentioned in the poems, the more his lines impress with the ring of truth. His pen portraits—among them, Napoleon, Rousseau, Souvarov—are masterfully drawn psychological studies. J. Philip Eggers, "Byron and the Devil's Scripture: The Poet as Historian" (*Clio,* 1975), intelligently discusses the manifestations of Byron's passion for history in all major and most minor works. Clifford M. Byrne's disappointing "Byron's Cyclical Interpretation of History" (*McNeese Review,* 1967) presents, with little analysis, passages from the poetry that illustrate Byron's sense of history as a blind, immoral pattern of cycles of destruction. One may speculate whether Byron was familiar with the Goethean concept that epochs of creativity alternate with epochs of destruction. An intriguing study by a philosopher is Roger Hausheer's "Byron and the Philosophical Foundations of the European Romantic Revolt" (in *The Hannover Byron Symposium, 1979,* ed. Hogg), which studies Byron against the background of European intellectual history.

Time. Byron was obsessed by time. He had an acute sense of himself as a being living in time, and time is one of the great themes in his poetry. He begins one letter *"Sunday—Monday morning—3 o'clock in my doublet & hose— swearing,"* wonders what effect the publication of his letters in the twentieth century will have, and, playing with Petrarch, precisely dates the beginning of Julia's seduction of Juan to 6 June, "about the hour / Of half-past six—perhaps still nearer seven." No wonder that W. H. Auden has remarked about Byron's un-Byronic "obsession with a clock routine. If his hours were bohemian—rising at two in the afternoon and retiring at three in the morning—their regularity was bourgeois, as, indeed, is essential to any writer who hopes to leave a substantial body of work." Michael Goldberg's essay on Byron's fascination with middle age (under *Don Juan*) is pertinent here. See also Itsuyo Higashinaka, "Byron's Sense of Ageing" (*ByronJ*, 1979), which treats Byron's preoccupation with his own age and with the aging process from 1816 to the end; and Koichi Yakushigawa, " 'Time Is, Time Was, Time's Past': Byron's Struggle with Time" (in *Studies in the Romantics*, 1978), which brings together, without much analysis, a number of Byron's references to time. More searching is Ronald A. Schroeder, "Byron's Sense of Time and Age before 1810" (*ByronJ*, 1983). The subject of time in Byron needs more discussion than it has received.

Comedy. "The days of Comedy are gone, alas," laments Byron in *Don Juan*. In regard to critical appreciation of his own comedy, human and poetic, the days have never quite arrived. Goethe, reviewing *Don Juan*, thought "English poetry ... already in possession of something we Germans totally lack: a cultured comic language." Auden considers Byron more a "comedian" than a satirist and "by far the greatest of English comic writers." Mark Storey's chapter on Byron in *Poetry and Humour from Cowper to Clough* (1979) provides the beginnings of an investigation. Although Storey is perceptive on Byron's poetry, *Childe Harold* and *Don Juan* in particular, and on Byron's language, the Byronic comedy remains as elusive as ever. Academic critics will have to learn to understand why they smile in reading Byron. On romantic irony and comedy in *Don Juan*, see the relevant paragraphs under that poem.

Human nature. Rolf P. Lessenich's *Lord Byron and the Nature of Man* (1978), in reaching the conclusion that Byron lived a life of utter despair, owes a considerable (and acknowledged) debt to Gleckner's *Byron and the Ruins of Paradise*. Though often irritatingly opinionated, Lessenich's is more often a trenchant, thoughtful study that contains much subtle psychological probing of Byron the thinker. One should read Lessenich expecting to disagree but also expecting to learn from his firm grasp of Byron's elusive nature and from his mastery of scholarship. In separate chapters he discusses "Hypocrisy and Irony," "The Stagnation of Progress," and "The Worthlessness of Life," but the core of his study is the central section analyzing human passion in Byron and in his writings. By the close, we agree, if we had doubted before, that "the prejudiced concept of the non-designing and non-thinking romantic nobleman can no longer be maintained." Byron's thinking is never presented so convincingly as here. Lessenich firmly and rightly repudiates Morse Peckham's interpretation of Byron as embodying "negative Romanticism" (in "Toward a Theory of Romanticism," *PMLA,* 1951; rpt. in *The Triumph of Romanticism,* 1970). For Lessenich, "neither psychologically nor historically can Byron simply be put away as an unaccomplished romantic." His impact on subsequent Romanticism, particularly in Europe, was vast.

Reputation and Influence

"Ah me, what perils do environ / The man who meddles with Lord Byron," once lamented an unhappy contemporary (Charles Armitage Brown). Byron, let us admit, has often exerted an alarmingly strong hold on others. It can be personal or poetic or, more likely, both. The hold was strong in England and America, stronger on the Continent, strongest of all in Eastern Europe, where it was often as much political as literary. Those who "meddled" with Byron might regret having done so, or the influence itself might be negative, but in the nineteenth century few souls, as Arnold said of his own response, did not feel "him like the thunder's roll." With Scott he represents English Romanticism abroad and, with Shakespeare, English poetry. His influence, overwhelmingly potent in the nineteenth century, continues vital in the twentieth.

This survey confines itself to Great Britain, the United States, and Europe. I have with regret left out studies that take up Byron's influence in South America, in the British Commonwealth, in Asia, and in other parts of the world. In fact, my coverage gets more selective the farther east I go. Even for Greece, Russia, and Eastern Europe, I have cited only a few of the available studies. For these countries and for countries not covered, as well as for many shorter studies of influence in Britain, America, and Europe, students should begin by consulting the annual bibliographies in *KSJ,* where they will find references to vast numbers of translations and editions of Byron's works in many of the world's languages. Fernand Baldensperger's and Werner P. Friederich's *Bibliography of Comparative Literature* (1950) also includes a number of entries attesting to Byron's European fame.

GREAT BRITAIN

"It is to be deplored that scarcely any moral good is derivable from the splendid poetry of Lord Byron," wrote T. H. Lister in the eighth (1854) edition of the *Encyclopaedia Britannica.* "The tendency of his works is to shake our confidence in virtue, and to diminish our abhorrence of vice;—to palliate crime, and to unsettle our notions of right and wrong." Ah me . . . Samuel C. Chew's *Byron in England: His Fame and After-Fame* (1924) records the history of the vicissitudes and fluctuations of the poet's reputation in his own country. Although Steffan's work has superseded Chew's chapters on the reception of *Don Juan* and *Cain,* the chapters "The Pamphlets of the Separation" and "Miscellaneous Byroniana: 1816–1824" remain virtually the only available discussions. Supplementing Chew in some particulars, and containing interesting illustrations, is Mario Praz's *La Fortuna di Byron in Inghilterra* (1925). Richard A. Rice's *Lord Byron's British Reputation* (Smith Coll. Studies, 1924) is still an excellent brief survey. The above volumes carry the discussion up to the centennial of Byron's death. Clement Tyson Goode, Jr.'s substantial overview of English-language research on Byron to 1974, which prefaces O. J. Santucho's 1977 bibliography, complements all the above for this period but proves more valuable for the years since.

Andrew Rutherford in his Nottingham lecture, *Byron the Best-Seller* (1964), explores the reasons for the poet's popular success in his own day. Harold, "the pilgrim without a faith," and the heroes of the early verse tales, "rebels without a cause," function like "projections, symbols, 'objective correlatives' of the deep frustration and disillusion of a generation" growing up amid the problems deriving from the French Revolution. Harold-Byron, the traveler without a destination, is also engaged in an interior journey, exploring the self. Thus the Byronic theme of the isolation of the artist spoke to every sensitive individual's growing sense of alienation from society. The discussion of *Don Juan,* with brief remarks also on *Beppo* and *The Vision of Judgment,* is both enlightening and amusing. Available in the Salzburg series are Herman M. Ward's *Byron and the Magazines, 1806–1824* (1973, originally 1940) and Keith Walker's *Byron's Readers: A Study of Attitudes towards Byron 1812–1832* (1979, originally 1966), which seeks to illuminate how the ordinary reader of the time responded to Byron. Walker has cogent chapters on the contemporary reception of *Childe Harold,* on the evangelical readers of the *Christian Observer,* on dissenting readers of the *Eclectic Review* and the *Monthly Repository,* on radical and working-class readers, on Jeffrey's response to Byron, on Byron biography 1819–28, and on Moore's *Life.* William Ruddick, "Byron in England: The Persistence of Byron's Political Ideas" (in Trueblood's *Symposium* volume), intelligently surveys Byron's impact on liberal thought, literary as well as political, taking the story down to Orwell and Auden. In *Lord Byron als Erfolgsautor: Leser und Literaturmarkt im frühen 19. Jahrhundert* (1977), Thilo von Bremen examines in detail, with specific reference to Byron, the important subject of the artist's relation to his public. In this connection see also the paragraph on Byron's relationship with his publishers in "Biography: Twentieth Century." Useful are the following articles: W. S. Dowden, "A Jacobin Journalist's View of Lord Byron" (*SP,* 1951), on Richard Phillips and the *Monthly Magazine*; R. W. Duncan, "Byron and the London *Literary Gazette*" (*Boston Univ. Studies in English,* 1956); Elmer L. Brookes, "Byron and the *London Magazine*" (*KSJ,* 1956); and Kenneth W. Davis, "Byroniana in the *Literary Guardian:* Vindications" (*PLL,* 1983). Josephine Bauer's 1953 study of the *London Magazine* also discusses Byron's reception in its pages.

The full dimensions of Byron's impact on nineteenth-century English literature remain to be charted. Byron exists, first of all, as a subject in novels virtually in his own person. But except for Caroline Lamb's *Glenarvon* and Mary Shelley's novels, "Byron in Fiction" remains a relatively unexplored subject since Chew's chapter of that title in *Byron in England*. During the past 150 years innumerable novels and plays have been written about Byron, virtually none of which I mention in these pages. Study of these works might prove enlightening as indicators of the different facets of Byron's personality that have elicited attention at different times. Mario Praz, *The Hero in Eclipse in Victorian Fiction* (1956), and, particularly, Donald D. Stone, *The Romantic Impulse in Victorian Fiction* (1980), informatively discuss Byron's (and the Byronic hero's) influence on Victorian novelists. The latter study, though insufficiently aware of the dips in Byron's reputation in the mid-nineteenth century, contains excellent discussions of Byron in Trollope, Disraeli, Charlotte Brontë, Mrs. Gaskell, George Eliot, Dickens, and Meredith. It is the first place that students interested in the Romantics' influence on the Victorian novelists should turn. David R. Eastwood, "Trollope and Romanticism" (*VN,* 1977), correctly observes that Byron is Trollope's prime Romantic target but barely scratches the surface of a huge subject. Robert M. Polhemus, "Being in Love in *Phineas Finn/Phineas Redux:* Desire, Devotion, Consolation" (*NCF,* 1982), finds *Don Juan* a source for Trollope's treatment of love in these novels. Something of a curiosity is N. John Hall's *Salmagundi: Byron, Allegra, and the Trollope Family* (1973), which contains various manuscripts relating to Byron by Frances Trollope and son Anthony. On Disraeli, see S. B. Liljegren, *Essence and Attitude in English Romanticism* (1945), which has a chapter "Disraeli, *Don Juan* and Byron" (and also one entitled "The Psychology of the Byronic Hero and His Heart"). Peter Graham points out (in an essay forthcoming in *VN*) that the first editions of Disraeli's novels are much more Byronic in essence and in language than are the revised versions we usually read today. William R. Harvey takes up "Charles Dickens and the Byronic Hero" (*NCF,* 1969), discussing, among others, Steerforth in *David Copperfield,* Sydney Carton in *A Tale of Two Cities,* and Eugene Wrayburn in *Our Mutual Friend.* Several studies examine the response of the Brontë sisters to Byron: Helen Brown, "The Influence of Byron on Emily Brontë " (*MLR,* 1939), chiefly on her poetry; Ann L. Livermore, "Byron and Emily Brontë " (*QR,* 1962), unconvincing on parallels between Byron's domestic upset of 1816 and "The Dream" as they affected *Wuthering Heights*; and two identically titled essays by Winifred Gérin, "Byron's Influence on the Brontës" (*KSMB,* 1966; *EDH,* 1972), on the impact that Byron's poems and Finden's illustrations to them had on all the Brontës. Covering much the same ground, the latter essay is a revision of the former and is currently the best introduction to the subject. See also Gérin's biographies of Charlotte (1967) and of Emily (1971). K. M. Newton focuses on the Byronic Don Silva in "Byronic Egoism and George Eliot's *The Spanish Gypsy*" (*Neophil,* 1973). After an excellent review of scholarship on Byron's Victorian influence, Uwe Böker in "Lord Byron, Flaubert, and Mrs. Braddon" (in *Byron-Symposium Mannheim 1982,* ed. Huber and Schöwerling) investigates the effect of Byron and the Byronic hero on Mary Elizabeth Braddon's life and writings, particularly *The Doctor's Wife* (1864), a novel that bears some resemblance to *Madame Bovary.* Studies of W. H. White ("Mark Rutherford") often mention Byron's important influence on White's novels and autobiographical works.

Outside of the novel less has been done. On Arnold, see Leon Gottfried's excellent discussion in *Matthew Arnold and the Romantics* (1963). On the divergent approaches to Byron of Arnold and Swinburne, see Andrew Lang's witty poem "To Lord Byron" in *Letters to Dead Authors* (1886) and H. J. C. Grierson's wide-ranging essay "Lord Byron: Arnold and Swinburne" (1920; rpt. in *The Background of English Literature*, 1925). On Carlyle, we have Charles Richard Sanders, "The Byron Closed in *Sartor Resartus*" (*SIR*, 1963; rev. as "The Carlyles and Byron" in *Carlyle's Friendships and Other Studies*, 1977), perceptive and thorough. On Ruskin, see R. W. Chambers, *Ruskin (and Others) on Byron* (1925; rpt. in *Man's Unconquerable Mind*, 1939), and Robert F. Gleckner, "Ruskin and Byron" (*ELN*, 1965), which considers Ruskin's comments on the opening lines of *The Island*. Lloyd N. Jeffrey in *Thomas Hood* (1972) expertly hunts down Byronic echoes in Hood's comic poetry. Byron's influence on Tennyson, Browning, Swinburne, Macaulay, Froude, and other Victorians is occasionally mentioned in studies on these figures but awaits detailed scholarly investigation. Tennyson admired Byron enormously in youth, held strong reservations in middle life, but eventually came to find him "great." B. J. Leggett in "Dante, Byron and Tennyson's 'Ulysses' " (*TSL*, 1970) argues that the indebtedness to *Childe Harold* 3 may exceed that to Dante. W. Whitla briefly examines Byron's influence on Browning's early poems in "Sources for Browning in Byron, Blake and Poe" in *Studies in Browning and His Circle* (1974). Lionel Stevenson in " 'My Last Duchess' and *Parisina*" (*MLN*, 1959) argues for a debt to Byron's poem. William A. Coles details an extensive involvement in "Thomas Noon Talfourd on Byron and the Imagination" (*KSJ*, 1960). Philip Collins' Nottingham lecture, *Thomas Cooper, the Chartist: Byron and the 'Poets of the Poor'* (1969), informatively details, by examining Cooper's career and those of others, the enthusiasm that many working-class poets and thinkers felt for Byron. Elizabeth Longford's *A Pilgrimage of Passion: The Life of Wilfred Scawen Blunt* (1979) traces Blunt's vein of Byronic self-identification. Kenneth A. Bruffee in *Elegiac Romance* touches briefly on significant Byronic echoes in *Lord Jim* and "Youth." At the end of the century Oscar Wilde saw himself, like Byron, as "a man who stood in symbolic relation to the art and culture of [his] age." Rolf Eichler in "Dandytum und Narzissmus: Selbstfindung in Leben und Werk Byrons und Wildes" (in *Byron-Symposium Mannheim 1982*, ed. Huber and Schöwerling) contrasts the personalities of both figures, concluding that each found ways and means of establishing his identity through dandyism and narcissism.

"Before me now lies Byron and behind," wrote Lawrence Durrell (echoing *Don Juan* 14.9) in his poem "Byron." Major writers of this century have often thought of Byron, particularly of *Don Juan* and the prose, as they shaped their own creative visions. Yeats, writing to H. J. C. Grierson in 1926, found in *Don Juan* examples of "common personal speech," an ideal that Yeats achieved increasingly in his own poetry. Byron was "the one great English poet—who sought it constantly." Yeats, who earlier had admired Byron's poetic energy, puts him in Phase Nineteen of *A Vision* (1922), exemplary of those for whom "unity of Being is no longer possible, for the being is compelled to live in a fragment of itself and to dramatise that fragment. . . ." Virginia Woolf in her essay "Byron and Mr. Briggs" (first published in *YR*, 1979) affirms that "prose was his medium; satire his genius." Yet she would find it difficult "to forget hours spent racing before the wind through Byron's Cantos" in *Don Juan.* Although James Joyce wrote no extended comment on him, Byron was one of Joyce's favorite poets. His lifelong enthusiasm extends from Stephen-Joyce's defense of Byron in *A Portrait* to his attempt in 1930–31 to write an opera libretto based on *Cain,* whose titular hero he admired greatly. Clarice Short has pointed out parallels between *The Prisoner of Chillon* and "A Little Cloud" of *Dubliners (MLN,* 1957). Leopold Bloom in *Ulysses* gives Molly a copy of Byron's works during their courtship. And Byron lives on in *Finnegans Wake,* for which see Robert F. Gleckner's essay in *Twelve and a Tilly,* edited by J. P. Dalton and Clive Hart (1966). Hermione de Almeida, *Byron and Joyce through Homer:* Don Juan *and* Ulysses (1981), though not specifically concerned with literary parallels, makes wide-ranging analogies between the two writers. See also her "Byron, Joyce, and the Modern Epic" (*SAQ,* 1983). Graham Hough's Nottingham lecture, *Two Exiles: Lord Byron and D. H. Lawrence* (1956; rpt. in *Image and Experience,* 1960), points out similarities and differences between the two as international figures. Lawrence in *John Thomas and Lady Jane,* the second version of *Lady Chatterley's Lover,* which was not published in England until 1972, sets with insistent echoes the final rendezvous of the lovers in the countryside near Hucknall, "the old, old countryside where Byron walked so often, and Mary Chaworth." Byron inspired the young Auden's "Letter to Lord Byron" (part of *Letters from Iceland,* 1937). Over the next thirty years Byron, particularly the Byron of the ottava rima satires and the prose, remained an important model for Auden in his poetry and in his justification of light verse. In 1938 he said that Byron "fashioned a style of poetry which for speed, wit, and moral seriousness combined with a lack of pulpit pomposity is unique, and a lesson to all young would-be writers." Victor Luftig in "Auden and Byron" (*BJ,* 1984) provides an excellent overview of this relationship. He terms the "Letter to Lord Byron" "perhaps the most remarkable tribute to, and example of, Byronic writing in the twentieth century." Edward Mendelson in *Early Auden* (1981) also notes the Byronic influence. Auden, who once described himself as "particularly interested" in Byron, wrote an illuminating essay on Marchand's biography for the *New Yorker* (26 Apr. 1958) and discussed *Don Juan* in *The Dyer's Hand and Other Essays* (1962)—the title itself comes from Byron's poem—and more recently in the *New York Review of Books* (18 Aug. 1966; rpt. in *The American Literary Anthology,* ed. John Hawkes, John Ashbery, and William Alfred, 1968). Ina Schabert, "Liberales Denken und repressive ästhetische Gestaltung: Zur Poetic von Byron und Auden" (in *Byron-Symposium Mannheim 1982,* ed. Huber and Schöwerling), outlines the close affinities between the two in matters of poetic theory, particularly the discrepancy between aesthetic form and the adequate representation of external reality. See also Carlos Baker, *The Echoing Green: Romanticism, Modernism, and the Phenomenon of Transference in Poetry* (1984). A number of references in George Orwell's *Collected Essays* indicate familiarity with Byron.

UNITED STATES

W. E. Leonard's monograph *Byron and Byronism in America* (1905) has long been outdated. Subsequent scholarship has moved to fill in the gaps. Chew in "Byron in America" (*American Mercury,* 1924) summarizes and to a slight degree supplements Leonard's monograph. Charles E. Robinson describes "The Influence of Byron's Death on America" (*ByronJ,* 1977). Also of value here is Marios Byron Raizis and Alexander Papas, *American Poets and the Greek Revolution, 1821–1828: A Study in Byronic Philhellenism* (1971). Byron was long interested in the United States and other countries of the Western Hemisphere and persistently toyed with the idea of emigrating to South America. See B. R. McElderry, "Byron's Interest in the Americas" (*Research Studies of the State College of Washington,* 1937); J. J. Jones, "Lord Byron on America" (*UTSE,* 1941); and John Clubbe, *Byron's Natural Man: Daniel Boone & Kentucky* (1980), which has a particular focus on the Daniel Boone stanzas in *Don Juan.*

Most American literary figures of the nineteenth century knew Byron's works quite well. Though Washington Irving and Byron never met, they shared the same publisher and were fascinated by each other, as Byron's letters and Irving's journals attest. Irving wrote up his impressions of a sojourn in Byron's ancestral home in a volume, *Miscellanies (Abbotsford, and Newstead Abbey),* of 1835. Elliot W. Hoffman in the *Byron Society Newsletter* (1978–79) briefly chronicles Irving's interest in Byron. Benjamin Lease in *That Wild Fellow John Neal and the American Literary Revolution* (1972) comments on Neal's overwhelming Byronic affinities. Lease's *Anglo-American Encounters: England and the Rise of American Literature* (1982) has concise discussions of Byron and Thoreau and Byron and Harriet Beecher Stowe. George H. Soule, Jr., "Byronism in Poe's *Metzengerstein* and *William Wilson*" (*ESQ,* 1978), valuably surveys earlier work on Byron's influence on Poe, which includes Roy Basler, "Byronism in Poe's 'To One in Paradise'" (*AL,* 1937), and Richard P. Benton, "Is Poe's 'The Assignation' a Hoax?" (*NCF,* 1963). Dennis Pahl, "Recovering Byron: Poe's 'Assignation'" (*Criticism,* 1984), does not find Poe's tale a hoax. Katrina E. Bachinger, "Poe's Vote for Byron: The Problem of Its Duration" (in *Byron: Poetry and Politics,* ed. Stürzl and Hogg), argues convincingly that, whatever public renunciation of Byron Poe made, he remained "loyal and committed to him." Examining "Poe's enduring Byronism" in life and art, Bachinger concludes that "Poe's tales form . . . the most elaborate, perceptive, and varied fictional depiction of Byron and the Byronic situation that has ever been or is ever likely to be written." Bachinger's "An Autumn at Newstead: A Source for Poe's 'The Fall of the House of Usher'" (*ByronJ,* 1985) ties Poe's tale to his reading of Washington Irving's evocative description in *Newstead Abbey.* Thomas Philbrick has a brief discussion of Byronic influence on *The Red River* in *James Fenimore Cooper and the Development of American Sea Fiction* (1961). H. N. Kleinfield in "Infidel on Parnassus: Lord Byron and the *North American Review*" (*NEQ,* 1960) finds that that journal's hostility to Byron the man was tempered by occasional praise of the poetry. Richard Harter Fogle explores

Hawthorne's debt in "Byron and Nathaniel Hawthorne" in *Romantic and Victorian*, edited by Elledge and Hoffman. Ely Stock in "The Biblical Context of *Ethan Brand*" (*AL*, 1965) finds Byron's *Cain* an important source for Satan (and for Ethan's character). Janet Harris in "Reflections on the Byronic Hero in Hawthorne's Fiction" (*Nathaniel Hawthorne Journal*, 1977) offers a number of partially convincing thematic parallels. Michael G. Cooke, "Hawthorne and Byron" (*ByronJ*, 1985), nicely illumines the novelist's debt in *The Marble Faun* to *Childe Harold* 4. The major American historians—among them, Bancroft, Prescott, Motley, Parkman—all read and admired Byron, but to my knowledge the subject remains unexplored. For example, investigation of the Byronic epigraphs and allusions in the first edition of Francis Parkman's *The Oregon Trail* (1849) might result in an intriguing essay. Edward Fiess in "Melville as a Reader and Student of Byron" (*AL*, 1952) discusses Melville's annotations to a sixteen-volume edition of Byron; Fiess has a later note on Melville's borrowings from the "Ocean" stanzas in *Childe Harold* 4 (*ELN*, 1966). See also Joseph J. Mogan, Jr., "*Pierre* and *Manfred*: Melville's Study of the Byronic Hero" (*PLL*, 1965). In *The Novels of Harriet Beecher Stowe* (1969) Alice C. Crozier, after discussing Stowe's defense of Lady Byron in her *Lady Byron Vindicated* (1870), finds that the abhorred Byron turns out to have been "the single greatest literary and imaginative influence" on Stowe's novels. James O. Hoge details "Byron's Influence on the Poetry of William Gilmore Simms" (*ELWIU*, 1975). One of Henry James's best-known short novels, *The Aspern Papers* (1888), came into existence after James heard of Captain Silsbee's attempt to lay siege to the aging Claire Clairmont for the Byron and Shelley manuscripts she allegedly possessed. (On the background to this attempt, see Marion K. Stocking's essay in *The Evidence of the Imagination*, ed. Reiman et al., 1978.) Byron was a lifelong fascination for James as Adeline R. Tintner reveals in her survey, "Henry James and Byron: A Victorian Romantic Relationship" (*ByronJ*, 1981). In "Frederick Winterbourne, James's Prisoner of Chillon" (*Studies in the Novel*, 1977) Carl Wood draws interesting analogies between Byron's poem and *Daisy Miller.* Byron's influence at times overwhelms the Western poet Joaquin Miller.

For an estimate by Paul Elmer More, a turn-of-the-century New Humanist, see K. B. Newell, "Paul Elmer More on Byron" (*KSJ*, 1963). John Lauber, "Truthtelling as Politics: Byron and Pound" (in *Byron: Poetry and Politics,* ed. Stürzl and Hogg), compares the *Cantos* to *Don Juan,* to Byron's advantage, as poems expressing postwar disillusionment. Alice Levine's valuable "T. S. Eliot and Byron" (*ELH*, 1978) points out parallels between *Childe Harold* and *The Waste Land,* in the process giving a sensitive reading of Eliot's influential essay on Byron. Hers "is not a study of direct influence, but of the unconscious, sub-surface relationship between two poets." Also on Eliot's essay, but taking on larger issues as well, is Helmut Viebrock, "Eliot and Byron: Wechselseitige Enthüllung" in *Zur Aktualität T. S. Eliots,* edited by A. P. Frank and Viebrock (1975). For Fitzgerald, one might begin with Kenneth A. Bruffee's observation in *Elegiac Romance* that "Gatsby's fabricated autobiographical tale is patently Byronic." Carlos Baker's edition of Hemingway's *Selected Letters 1917–1961* (1981) indicates that Byron was one of the novelist's role models. "We ought," wrote Hemingway to Charles

Scribner in 1949, "to keep copies of our letters like Mr Lord Byron and Murray." And so they did. Nabokov knew his Byron well: he quotes tellingly from *Childe Harold* 3 in *Lolita* and from "The Dream" in *The Real Life of Sebastian Knight* and frequently refers to Byron in his commentary to Pushkin's *Eugene Onegin*. Several critics have argued for analogues between *Don Juan* and John Berryman's *Dream Songs*.

EUROPE

"Outside Great Britain Lord Byron continues to be the central figure of English Romanticism," Jorge Luis Borges has written in this century. Borges but echoes Adam Mickiewicz, who in 1835 claimed, with pardonable exaggeration, that "Byron's influence on all contemporary literature is everywhere manifest; for all works subsequent to this great poet bear the stamp and the seal of his genius." During the nineteenth century innumerable translations and editions of Byron's works appeared in every European country, and abroad he probably still remains the most written about of the English Romantics. The nations of Europe (now joined by India and Japan) continue to contribute substantially to Byron scholarship. American and British bibliographies do not always pick up these contributions, thus leaving English-language scholars unaware of the quality and extent of European and other scholarship. Escarpit's bibliography in *Lord Byron: Un tempérament littéraire* usefully documents the European influence.

On the Continent the early nineteenth century in England was long known as the "Age of Byron." Europeans valued the dark, alienated, "Romantic" Byron, with *Manfred* probably looming as the most significant work in the nineteenth-century consciousness. The self-exiled Byron spoke to them as a fellow citizen of the world. For reasons why, see H. A. Taine's *History of English Literature* (1863, trans. 1871), which devotes a massive chapter to Byron, "the last the greatest and most English" of the Romantic poets, and Georg Brandes' deceptively titled *Naturalism in Nineteenth Century English Literature* (1875, trans. 1905), actually a history of the English Romantic movement, which allots seven of its twenty-four chapters to Byron.

Byron's Political and Cultural Influence in Nineteenth-Century Europe: A Symposium, edited by P. G. Trueblood (1981), provides a modern overview of Byron's towering position in the nineteenth-century world. Twelve chapters assess Byron's significance, country by country, with the poet emerging as a major disseminator of progressive liberal thought. Douglas Dakin contributes a solid prefatory chapter on the historical background, Trueblood a conclusion, "Byron and Europe." Although this well-organized book contains little new material, it does bring between two covers considerable information about Byron's afterfame in Europe.

Gerhart Hoffmeister's *Byron und der europäische Byronismus* (1983) traverses much ground rapidly. The student new to the subject will find in it helpful overviews of Byron's European influence, examined country by country; the mature scholar will find particularly useful the bibliographies appended to each chapter. Hoffmeister includes (as I do not) dissertations. An introductory chapter on Byron, the Byronic hero, and Byron's influence in England is followed by a much longer one, entitled "Byrons europäische Wirkung," in which Hoffmeister examines the poet's reception in Italy, Spain, France, the Slavic countries, and Germany. The third chapter, on Byron as exponent of "weltanschaulicher Strömungen," takes up philhellenism, pessimism, weltschmerz, titanism, and satanism. The final chapter redefines as *"Byronismus"* Byron's effect on music, on art, and on subsequent life-styles (e.g., dandyism). " *'Byronismus'* arises from an attitude at once pessimistic and aristocratic toward bourgeois life, the world, and even God." Throughout, Hoffmeister understandably focuses more on the nineteenth century than on the twentieth. Wide-ranging rather than deep, his discussions often introduce names and works only to drop them. There are errors of fact and incomplete and inaccurate bibliographical citations, but these are perhaps inevitable for someone covering in brief compass so large a subject. Any student interested in Byron's afterfame will profit from the excellent overview that this book offers.

On the European Byron, see also Desmond Powell, "Byron's Foreign Critics" (*Colorado-Wyoming Journal of Letters,* 1939), a still useful survey of French, German, and American criticism of Byron; H. G. Schenk's chapter in *The Mind of the European Romantics* (1966), which claims that "no other Romantic, with the exception of Chateaubriand, embodied so many aspects of Romanticism"; and Ernest Giddey, "Les Trahisons de Byronisme" (*Etudes de Lettres,* 1970), which suggestively traces the impact on the European imagination of the various strands of Byronism after Byron's death. This influence launched dozens of Byronic epigones but also had effect on the greatest of the century and after, among them, as Northrop Frye points out in his essay on Byron in *Fables of Identity* (1963), Delacroix, Berlioz, Pushkin, Nietzsche, Balzac, Stendhal, Dostoevsky, Melville, Conrad, Hemingway, A. E. Housman, Thomas Wolfe, D. H. Lawrence, and Auden. Modern no less than nineteenth-century fiction would be a diminished thing without the Byronic hero. Bertrand Russell and John Wain, in their studies reprinted in *Byron: A Collection of Critical Essays,* edited by Paul West, also call attention to Byron's immense influence on the Continent, as do the cogent pages in Morse Peckham's *Beyond the Tragic Vision* (1962).

France.   Josef Danhauser's painting "Liszt at the Piano" (1840) includes, among other figures, George Sand, Hugo, Dumas, Paganini, and Rossini. Behind them all is a framed portrait of Byron. Without Byron, the French Romantics would not have composed, painted, or written as they did. Edmond Estève's *Byron et le romantisme français: Essai sur la fortune et l'influence de l'oeuvre de Byron en France de 1812 à 1850* (1907) has maintained its authority as a thorough piece of investigation. The initial discussion of what may be called "pre-Byronic Byronism," especially in the writings of Chateaubriand, has much interest and value. Estève's bibliography charts Byron's early influence in France and early French editions of his works. Georges Roth's *La Couronne poétique de Byron*

(1924) is a handy anthology of French tributes, mostly poetic, inspired by Byron from 1816 to 1836. Estève's own exemplary "Byron en France après le romantisme: Le Byronisme de Leconte de Lisle" (*RLC,* 1925) carefully follows that writer's early fascination with Byron. The story, not precisely of Byron's influence but of his "fortune," is carried far beyond Estève's temporal limits in an article by E. P. Dargan on "Byron's Fame in France" (*VQR,* 1926) and in a short monograph by W. J. Phillips, *France on Byron* (1941). See also René Canat, *L'Hellénisme des romantiques* (vol. 1, 1951), which traces the impact of Byron's Hellenism on nineteenth-century French literature. Under "Byron and His Literary Contemporaries" I have discussed Byron's relationship with Madame de Staël. Robert Escarpit's "Misunderstanding in France" (*ByronJ,* 1975) surveys Byron's French after-fame, with particular focus on Amédée Pichot's deceptive, inaccurate, and widely disseminated translations of Byron and how they (mis)formed the French and European image of Byron, French being the leading European language at this time. Michèle Maréchal-Trudel, *Chateaubriand, Byron et Venise: Un mythe contesté* (1978), argues that Chateaubriand's image of Venice in his *Mémoires d'Outre-Tombe* owes much to Byron. Book 7 of the *Mémoires* evidences that Chateaubriand resented Byron's fame yet was irresistibly drawn to him and to the image of Venice in his work: "Byron et Venise deviennent sous sa plume deux thèmes entrelacés n'existant presque que l'un par l'autre." John Greene glances over Byron's influence on Barbey d'Aurevilly in *RLM,* 1970. The poet figures more significantly in Geneviève Delattre's *Les Opinions littéraires de Balzac* (1961). See also S. R. B. Smith, *Balzac et l'Angleterre* (1953). Pierre Nordon has examined "Alfred de Musset et l'Angleterre" (*Les Lettres Romanes,* 1968), a multipart article, of which the installment in the February number takes up "le Byronisme." J. R. Hewitt in "Musset apprenti de Byron: Une nouvelle conception du Moi poétique" (*RHL,* 1976) believes that Musset's ability to refine his narrative method came in part through study of *Don Juan.* James S. Patty surveys Nerval's knowledge of Byron in "Byron and Nerval: Two Sons of Fire" in *Studies in Honor of Alfred G. Engstrom* (1972). The introduction to volume 1 of the forthcoming Pléiade *Vigny,* edited by André Jarry and François Germain, will discuss Byron and Vigny. Geoffrey Strickland, "Stendhal, Byron et John Cam Hobhouse" (*SC,* 1965), builds on Doris Langley Moore's chapter in *The Late Lord Byron.* George M. Rosa, "Stendhal Raconteur: A Partly Unpublished Record of Reminiscences and Anecdotes" (*Studi Francesi,* 1978), publishes from manuscript the passages from Hobhouse's journal relating to Stendhal in Milan in 1816—when he was often in Byron's company. Still to be discussed adequately is Byron's presence in Stendhal's novels, though Rosa has made a start. In "Byronism and 'Babilanisme' in *Armance*" (*MLR,* 1982) he demonstrates that Stendhal in his first novel largely casts Octave in the mold of the Byronic hero, particularly as drawn in *Childe Harold* and the tales. In "The Tempest and the Rock: An Intertextual Study of Two Images in Stendhal's *De l'Amour*" (*RomN,* 1983) Rosa adduces a further instance of Stendhal's reading in Byron, this time of a passage in *Don Juan.* C. W. Thompson, "Les clefs *d'Armance* et l'ambivalence du génie romantique du Nord" (*SC,* 1982–83), finds Byron a possible model for Octave and argues that not impotence but sexual ambivalence constitutes Octave's "secret." E. Barineau, "*Les feuilles d'automne* et les *Mémoires de Lord Byron*" *(MP,* 1958), studies the impact of Moore's *Life* on Hugo's volume of poems. E. Souffrun considers "Le Byronisme de Théodore de Banville" *(RLC,* 1963). M. H. Matheny in "Baudelaire's Knowledge of English Literature" *(RLC,* 1970) includes Byron among others, but for a study of most of the references to Byron the student should turn to Philip F. Clark's "Baudelaire and Byron: A Premise for Comparison" *(ByronJ,* 1981), which reappears, in extended form, as "Charles Baudelaire: Facets of Byron's French Legacy" in *Byron: Poetry and Politics,* edited by Stürzl and Hogg. André Vandegans, "Anatole France et Byron avant 1873" *(RLC,* 1949), concentrates on *Heaven and Earth's* influence on France's youthful drama *La Fille de Cain.* Two articles in the special Byron issue of *Romantisme* (1974) explore the interest the poet aroused in Lautréamont and Delécluze.

Recent French interest in Byron's poetry is indicated by Aurélien Digeon's translation of *Don Juan* (2 vols., 1954, 1955), by Paul Bensimon's and Roger Martin's translations of *The Prisoner of Chillon* and canto 3 of *Childe Harold* (1971), with excellent introduction and notes by Bensimon, and by Martin's rendering of the complete *Childe Harold* (1974).

Switzerland. Ernest Giddey's careful, detailed study of "La renommée de Byron à Genève et dans le canton de Vaud (1816–1824)" appears as part of Clubbe and Giddey's *Byron et la Suisse* (1982). See also Giddey's "Byron and Switzerland: Byron's Political Dimension" (in Trueblood's *Symposium* volume), chiefly on the Swiss Philhellenes, a study that builds on an earlier contribution by Giddey to *ByronJ* (1977).

Italy. Byron resided in Italy for nearly seven years, a longer time than he lived in any other country during his maturity. Anna B. McMahan compiled from the poems and prose *With Byron in Italy* (1906), an old but fairly good anthology; its abundant illustrations follow Byron's footsteps through Italia. A stimulating survey is Giorgio Melchiori's Nottingham lecture, *Byron and Italy* (1958). Melchiori's subsequent "Byron and Italy: Catalyst of the *Risorgimento*" (in Trueblood's *Symposium* volume), chiefly on Mazzini and Cavour, is in part a reworking of the Nottingham lecture and of a piece in *ByronJ,* 1977, on the influence of Byron's death in Italy. Byron occupies a prominent place in C. P. Brand's important *Italy and the English Romantics* (1957); specifically on Byron is Brand's "Byron and the Italians" *(ByronJ,* 1973). The chapter in Kenneth Churchill's *Italy and English Literature 1764–1930* (1980) nicely chronicles the "immense significance" of Italy for Byron. In Italian are the studies by V. G. Muoni, *La fama del Byron e il Byronismo in Italia* (1903); Arturo Farinelli, *Byron e il byronismo* (1924); A. Porta, *Byronismo italiano* (1928); and, particularly helpful, U. Bosco's article "Byronismo italiano" *(La Cultura,* 1924). Max Simhart discusses *Lord Byrons Einfluss auf die italienische Literatur* (1909).

Byron numbered Ugo Foscolo among the "great names" of living Italians. They never met, but Foscolo assisted Hobhouse in a history of Italian literature that Hobhouse appended to his *Historical Illustrations of the Fourth Canto of*

Childe Harold. Hobhouse quarreled with Foscolo, and Byron was drawn in reluctantly. E. R. Vincent told the full story, based on materials in the Murray archive, in *Byron, Hobhouse, and Foscolo: New Documents in the History of a Collaboration* (1949). See also Vincent's biography *Ugo Foscolo: An Italian in Regency England* (1953) and Carlo Maria Franzero, *A Life in Exile: Ugo Foscolo in London, 1816–1827* (1977). Mario Praz draws general parallels in "Byron and Foscolo," *Renaissance and Modern Essays,* edited by G. R. Hibbard (1966). On Leopardi, see Attilio Brilli, "Byron e Leopardi: il riso dei morti" (*SUSFL,* 1971). J. H. Whitfield's biography *Giacomo Leopardi* (1954) also considers this last relationship. Herbert W. Smith, "Byron and Silvio Pellico" (*ByronJ,* 1979), outlines the two men's awareness of each other. Beatrice Corrigan, "The Byron-Hobhouse Translations of Pellico's 'Francesca'" (*Italica,* 1958), seems to prove, by printing the relevant correspondence, that though Byron and Hobhouse began a translation of Pellico's drama *Francesca da Rimini,* the published fragments that remain are Hobhouse's. Angeline Lograsso, "Byron traduttore del Pellico" (*Lettere Italiane,* 1959), argues, rather less convincingly, for Byron's partial share in the translation. As seems too often to be the case with the studies discussed in this section, Smith, Corrigan, and Lograsso do not appear aware of each other's work.

Among twentieth-century Italian studies of Byron's poetry, outstanding is Guido Ferrando's introduction to his edition of *Manfred* (1926), as is Aldo Ricci's to *Childe Harold* 3 and the 1816 lyrics (1924). Ricci has also edited *Parisina, The Prisoner of Chillon,* and cantos 1–2 and 4 of *Childe Harold*; and Ferdinando Milone, *Cain.* All are in the excellent Biblioteca Sansoniana Straniera series. See also "Music," below.

Spain and Portugal. E. Allison Peers's *History of the Romantic Movement in Spain* (2 vols., 1940) frequently mentions Byron. Esteban Pujals, *Espronceda y Lord Byron* (in Spanish; 1951, rev. 1972, 1982), is standard. Pujals' *Lord Byron en España y otros temas byronianos* (1982) usefully brings together several pieces published earlier. The chapter on "visión poética" appeared in Trueblood's *Symposium* volume as "Byron and Spain: Byron's Poetic Vision of Spain." It focuses chiefly on the first cantos of *Childe Harold* and *Don Juan,* with a glance at the neglected *Age of Bronze.* Pujals takes up "major themes" in Byron's poetry: love, the romantic interpretation of nature, life and death. Traversing all Byron's poetry, these chapters will have less to offer English-speaking readers than those specifically on Byron in Spain and his response to the Spanish milieu. The chapter on Byron and Espronceda dates from 1948 and is superseded by the author's own subsequent research. The last chapter considers Gaspar Núñez de Arce's 1879 poem the *Última Lamentación de Lord Byron,* by way of Lamartine's *Le Dernier chant du pèlerinage d'Harold* and Auden's "Letter to Lord Byron."

Other studies include Philip H. Churchman, "Byron and Espronceda" and "The Beginnings of Byronism in Spain," in the *Revue Hispanique,* 1909 and 1910. Peers's "Sidelights on Byronism in Spain" (*Revue Hispanique,* 1920) supplements and corrects Churchman's 1910 survey by examining the response to Byron in *El Europeo,* 1823–24. Geoffrey N. Ribbons, "Bécquer, Byron y Dacarrete" (*Revista de Literatura*, 1953), touches on Byron's influence. Jorge A. Marbán has studied "Unamuno y Lord Byron" (*SAB*, 1976). D. G. Samuels considers the revitalization of Byron's influence after 1870 in "Some Byronic Influences in Spanish Poetry" (*HR*, 1949) and "Critical Appreciations of Byron in Spain (1900–1929)" (*HR*, 1950). See also Sarmiento under "*Hebrew Melodies*." For a sense of what Byron meant to a nineteenth-century Spaniard see Emilio Castelar's *Life* (English trans., 1875).

The title of F. de Mello Moser's "Byron and Portugal: The Progress of an Offending Pilgrim" (in Trueblood's *Symposium* volume) indicates the Portuguese attitude toward Byron, whose comments in *Childe Harold* Moser terms "surprisingly harsh, unmitigated, and even stressed by explicit contrast with the landscape."

Germany. The problem of Byron's relations with Germany is solely one of reciprocal literary influence, for the poet was in that country but once and for a short time only (when he made the journey up the Rhine in 1816) and seems to have taken no interest in German public affairs. F. W. Stokoe examines the debt Byron's imagination owed to Germany in chapter 7 of *German Influence in the English Romantic Period, 1788–1818* (1926). More limited in scope but more reliable in treatment is M. Roxana Klapper, *The German Literary Influence on Byron* (1974), which specifically deals with the German sources of Byron's works: chapter 1, on Byron's relationship to German literature, Germany, and Germans; 2, a lengthy discussion of *Faust*'s influence on *Manfred;* 3, a comparison of Goethe's *Werther* with *Childe Harold.*

Byron knew little German, Goethe read but spoke no English, and the two men never met. Drawing on J. G. Robertson's 1925 *Goethe and Byron,* itself a fine study, E. M. Butler in *Byron and Goethe: Analysis of a Passion* (1956) uses unpublished material connected with Goethe and also unpublished letters from Kinnaird and Murray to Byron in the Murray archive to make a genuine contribution to Byron studies. Butler has much of interest to say on Byron's opinion of the Germans and on the work of Goethe, on Goethe's confusions concerning Byron (deriving from Caroline Lamb's *Glenarvon* and from a misreading of *Manfred* as autobiography), and on the story of Byron's several attempted dedications to Goethe, the imbroglio ending finally with the dedication of *Werner* and the second edition of *Sardanapalus* to the German poet. Part 2 discusses Thomas Medwin's role in securing Goethe's tribute to Byron, published in Medwin's *Conversations of Byron,* and Goethe's reaction to Medwin's book and to William Parry's *Last Days of Byron.* Part 3 suggestively analyzes Byron as Euphorion in *Faust* 2, arguably the most splendid poetic monument erected to one poet by another in recent times, and the continuing influence of Byron on Goethe and through him on the later history of the world. Briefer but also illuminating is Butler's Nottingham lecture, *Goethe and Byron* (1949–50). See also the excellent pages on Byron in Fritz Strich, *Goethe and World Literature* (English trans., 1949), which amply convince us that "no other contemporary occupied Goethe's thoughts so continuously and so deeply."

Byron's influence on nineteenth-century German literature was great. See the chapter "Byron and *Weltschmerz*" in L. M. Price, *English Literature in Germany* (1953, superseding earlier versions of 1919, 1932), and Cedric Hentschel, *The Byronic Teuton* (1939), disappointing because chiefly concerned with an aspect of the German temperament. Hentschel's "Byron and Germany: The Shadow of Euphorion" (in Trueblood's *Symposium* volume) covers the ground from Goethe to modern times, by way of Bismarck, Pückler-Muskau, Grabbe, Heine, Nietzsche, even Ludwig II, with a glance at Austria. See also Rainer Schöwerling, "Lord Byron and German Literary Criticism: Some Remarks on the Reception and Influence of Byron and his *Don Juan*" (in the *Constance Byron Symposium*, 1977), and Horst Oppel's brief overview in *Englische-deutsche Literaturbeziehungen* (vol. 2, 1971). Hans-Werner Nieschmidt in *Christian Dietrich Grabbe: Zwei Studien* (1951) explores Byron's influence. More centrally on the subject is Ulrich Wesche, *Byron und Grabbe: Ein geistesgeschichtlicher Vergleich* (1978). On Heine's debt to Byron's poetry, one turns first to Thomas Bourke's chapter "Heines Stimmungsbrechung" in his *Stilbruch als Stilmittel* (noted above under "*Don Juan*"). Two older studies still of use are F. Melchior, *Heines Verhältnis zu Lord Byron* (1903), and Wilhelm Ochsenbein, *Die Aufnahme Lord Byrons in Deutschland und sein Einfluss auf dem jungen Heine* (1905). David S. Thatcher has carefully examined "Nietzsche and Byron" (*NietzscheS*, 1974).

Austria. Erwin A. Stürzl's "Byron and Grillparzer" (in Robinson's *Lord Byron and His Contemporaries*) surveys Byron's knowledge of the Austrian dramatist before taking up Grillparzer's complex relation to Byron. See also Frederick W. Shilstone's article noted above in discussion of *Sardanapalus* and Stürzl's "Byron and the Poets of the Austrian Vormärz" (*ByronJ*, 1981; also in *Byron: Poetry and Politics*, ed. Stürzl and Hogg), well-documented and thorough for the years between Waterloo and the 1848 revolutions. Siegfried Korninger, "Lord Byron und Nikolaus Lenau" (*EM*, 1952), argues at length for Byron's considerable influence on the Austrian poet and epic dramatist.

Holland. Beyond the linguistic range of most of us are two large monographs in which the influence in Holland is demonstrated: T. Popma, *Byron en het Byronisme in de Nederlandsche Letterkunde* (1928), and U. Schults, *Het Byronianisme in Nederland* (1929). Unscholarly in presentation but with numerous references to Byron, James Anderson Russell's *Dutch Romantic Poetry: The English Influence* (1961) reveals Byron's impact to be second only to Scott's. J. H. A. Lokin's brief "Byron's Influence on Dutch Literature" (*ByronJ*, 1983) argues that the influence was most strongly felt during 1830–40.

Scandinavia. On Byron in Norwegian literature, see Sigmund Skard, "Byron i norsk litteratur i det nittande hundreåret" (*Edda*, 1939). B. J. Tysdahl, "Byron, Norway, and Ibsen's *Peer Gynt*" (*ES*, 1975), briefly discusses Byron's reputation in nineteenth-century Norway and the influence of the Byronic hero. Peter Simonson takes up (in Norwegian) Byron's influence on Ibsen's *Hedda Gabler*

(*Edda*, 1962). Erik Frykman introduces "Byron and Swedish Literature" (*ByronJ*, 1978); in Swedish is Frykman's similarly titled but expanded study (*Samlaren*, 1977). Stig Sjöholm, "Fröding och Byron" (*Edda*, 1939), considers Byron's influence on the Swedish poet. On Byron and Icelandic literature, the solitary reaper has been Richard Beck, who in "Grimur Thomsen—A Pioneer Byron Student" (*JEGP*, 1928) calls attention to this Icelandic poet, important in introducing readers to Byron in Denmark and Iceland. Beck continued with "Gísli Brynjúlfsson: An Icelandic Imitator of *Childe Harold's Pilgrimage*" (*JEGP*, 1929).

Russia. Byron exerted a tremendous hold on nineteenth-century Russian literature, a hold that lingers today. If one thinks that the Russian Byron is only the gloomy egotist of *Childe Harold,* then one should peruse Isaiah Berlin's recollections (in *Personal Impressions,* 1980) of an interview he had with Anna Akhmatova shortly after World War II. Before reading from her poetry, she told Berlin "she wished to recite two cantos from Byron's *Don Juan* to me. . . . She closed her eyes and spoke the lines from memory, with intense emotion." Nina Diakonova and Vadim Vacuro provide an overview, "Byron and Russia: Byron and Nineteenth-Century Russian Literature" (in Trueblood's *Symposium* volume). Most Russians knew Byron's poems only through wretched French translations. G. R. V. Barratt in *Ivan Kozlov: A Study and a Setting* (1972) and in *I. I. Kozlov: The Translations from Byron* (1972) discusses Kozlov's role as Byron's chief Russian translator. "Thanks to his translations, Byron, virtually unknown in 1819, was by 1825 'a mighty hero among Russians.'" Barratt's "Somov, Kozlov, and Byron's Russian Triumph" (*CRCL,* 1974) reveals Byron's impact on liberal Russians. Kenneth H. Ober and Warren U. Ober, "Žukovskij's Translation of *The Prisoner of Chillon*" (*SEER*, 1973), discuss the creative changes in this version of Byron's poem, generally considered the best translation it has received into Russian. An important older study of Byron's influence is V. I. Maslov, *The Major Period of Byronism in Russia* (in Russian; 1915).

Much has been written on Pushkin as Byron's Russian heir. The seminal book (in Russian) remains V. Zhirmunskii, *Byron and Pushkin* (1924). See also Ernest J. Simmons, *English Literature and Culture in Russia (1553–1840)* (1935); his "La Littérature anglaise et Pouchkin" (*RLC,* 1937); Walter N. Vickery, "Byron's *Don Juan* and Pushkin's *Evgenij Onegin:* The Question of Parallelism" (*Indiana Slavic Studies,* 1967); John Bayley's *Pushkin: A Comparative Commentary* (1971), which frequently mentions Byron; the chapter "Ryleev, Pushkin, and Mazeppa" in Babinski's *The Mazeppa Legend in European Romanticism;* and Sona Stephan Hoisington, *"Eugene Onegin:* An Inverted Byronic Poem" (*CL,* 1975). Pushkin's *Letters,* translated by J. Thomas Shaw (3 vols., 1963), contains numerous references to Byron, as does Nabokov's commentary to his edition of *Eugene Onegin.* Byron was equally influential on Lermontov, whose work was a culminating point of Russian Byronism. See W. J. Entwhistle, "The Byronism of Lermontov's *A Hero of Our Time*" (*CL,* 1949); three essays by Joseph T. Shaw, "Byron, the Byronic Tradition of the Romantic Verse Tale in Russian, and Lermontov's *Mtsyri*" (*Indiana Slavic Studies,* 1956), "Lermontov's *Demon* and the Byronic Oriental Verse Tale"

(*Indiana Slavic Studies,* 1958), and "Byron, Chênedollé, and Lermontov's 'Dying Gladiator' " (in *Studies in Honor of John C. Hodges and Alwin Thaler,* ed. R. B. Davis and J. L. Lievsay, 1961), which scrutinizes Pushkin's poem based on the passage in *Childe Harold* 4; and Nina Diakonova, "Byron and Lermontov: Notes on Pechorin's 'Journal' " (in Robinson's *Lord Byron and His Contemporaries*), which argues that Byron's prose style influenced Lermontov's in *A Hero of Our Time.* Arnold B. McMillin, "Byron and Venevitinov" (*SEER,* 1975), finds Byron's presence in the imagery of the lyrics of the Russian Keats, despite Venevitinov's lack of reference to Byron. I have come across no studies of Byron and Dostoevsky, yet do we not have in Raskolnikov's pathetic craving in *Crime and Punishment* to become another Napoleon an epigone of the Byronic hero? David Matual in "Chekhov's 'Black Monk' and Byron's 'Black Friar' " (*International Fiction Review,* 1978) reveals the debt of Chekhov's tale to *Don Juan.* According to Matual, Byron's influence outlived Romanticism into "an age of realistic prose." Pavlo Bylypovych, "Shevchenko and Romanticism" (in *Shevchenko and the Critics 1861–1980,* ed. George S. N. Luckyj, 1980), traces lines of affinity between Byron and the Ukrainian poet. A well-received study of Byron from a Russian perspective (and in Russian) is Diakonova's *Byron in the Years of His Exile* (1974).

Eastern Europe.   Marian Zdziechowski, *Byron and His Century* (in Polish, 2 vols., 1892, 1906), is a major comparative study, obviously influenced by Taine and Brandes, that contains a wealth of material not found in Western languages. Volume 1 deals with France, Germany, and Italy; volume 2, with Czechoslovakia, Russia, and Poland. For Poland, the student might begin with Juliusz Zuławski's "Byron's Influence in Poland" (*ByronJ,* 1974; rev. in Trueblood's *Symposium* volume). An important earlier study is Stanisław Windakiewicz, *Walter Scott and Lord Byron with Reference to Polish Romantic Poetry* (in Polish; 1914). See also Stefan Treugutt, "Byron and Napoleon in Polish Romantic Myth" in Robinson's *Lord Byron and His Contemporaries.* Babinski's *The Mazeppa Legend* takes up Byron's influence on Słowacki, as does Jean Fabre in *RSH,* 1961. George Gömöri traces "The Myth of Byron in Norwid's Life and Work" (*SEER,* 1973). Essays by Jean Fabre and Giovanni Maver in *Adam Mickiewicz 1789 – 1855: In Commemoration of the Centenary of His Death* (1955) consider Byron's influence on the Polish poet. For Czechoslovakia, see René Wellek, "Mácha and Byron" (*SR,* 1937; rpt. in his *Essays on Czech Literature,* ed. Peter Demetz, 1964), and Henri Granjard, "Le Byronisme de Mácha" (*RLC,* 1954). In "A Byronic Hero in Slovak Literature" (*SEER,* 1956) Gudrum Apel explores Byron's impact on the poetry of Janko Král'. For Romania, see Ileana Verzea, *Byron and Byronism in Romanian Literature* (in Romanian; 1977), and her briefer "Comments on Byronism in Romanian Literature" (*CREL,* 1978). The appended French summary of László Imre's study of *Don Juan* and the Hungarian "verse novel" (*Studia Litteraria,* 1980) implies that Byron's poem strongly influenced the form's development. We should keep in mind that Byron's impact in Eastern Europe has often been as much personal—and political—as literary. In *The Byronic Hero* Peter Thorslev recalls that when he mentioned Byron's name to a Hungarian freedom fighter, he was immediately interrupted—"There was one who would have been with us."

Greece. Most biographies treat extensively Byron's two sojourns in Greece, for which see the paragraphs under "Partial Biographies." Harold Spender's *Byron and Greece* (1924) contains a short introduction but is in the main a convenient and well-arranged anthology of verse, letters, and journals. The final chapter of Terence Spencer's *Fair Greece, Sad Relic: Literary Philhellenism from Shakespeare to Byron* (1954) surveys "Byron's Poetical Inheritance of Philhellenism," that is, the poets who had written of Greece in the three quarters of a century before Byron. Spencer's Nottingham lecture, *Byron and the Greek Tradition* (1959), serves as an excellent introduction to the subject. See also Karl Brunner's "Griechenland in Byrons Dichtung" (*Anglia,* 1937) and Leslie A. Marchand's "Byron's Hellenic Muse" (*ByronJ,* 1975). On the relation of Byron's tales to the contemporary vogue of Oriental travel books, see, in addition to the studies by Wiener (discussed above with the tales) and Blackstone (under "Ideas and Beliefs"), Wallace Cable Brown, "Byron and the English Interest in the Near East" (*SP,* 1937). Brown also published two other articles dealing with this vogue in *PQ* (1936, 1937) that do not bear directly on Byron. Byron has a place in James M. Osborne's survey "Travel Literature and the Rise of Neo-Hellenism in England" (*BNYPL,* 1963). More than the usual picture book, Fani-Maria Tsigakou's *The Rediscovery of Greece: Travellers and Painters of the Romantic Era* (1981) has a solid text as well as stunning illustrations. Anahid Melikian's *Byron and the East* (1977) covers the ground systematically but lacks critical sophistication. Discussions of poems consist largely of paraphrase and plot summary. Her first chapter, "The English Romantics and the East," oddly focuses on *Vathek* and *Lalla Rookh.* Successive chapters take up Byron's youthful pilgrimage, the Oriental tales, *Beppo,* and *Don Juan,* with the last on Byron's activities at the Armenian monastery on San Lazzaro in 1816–17 and his interest in the Greek revolution. Kiriakoula Solomou surveys the influence of Greek poetry, classical and modern, on Byron's work (*ByronJ,* 1982). Robin Fletcher considers "Byron in Nineteenth Century Greek Literature" in *The Struggle for Greek Independence,* edited by Richard Clogg (1973). M. Byron Raizis in "The Greek Poets Praise 'The Britannic Muse'" (*Balkan Studies,* 1979) chronicles the response to Byron's personality, philhellenism, and poetry by successive generations of Greek poets. See also Raizis and Alexander Papas, *American Poets and the Greek Revolution, 1821–1828: A Study in Byronic Philhellenism* (1971), and their anthology *The Greek Revolution and the American Muse: A Collection of Philhellenic Poetry, 1821–1828* (1973). Many will find William St. Clair's "Literature and Politics: The Case of Byron and Greece" (*EDH,* 1980) enlightening on the ways Byron and his poetry have affected perceptions of modern Greece, both in England and in Greece itself.

We should remember that the "Greece" Byron visited was then part of the Ottoman Empire and that, during his first trip at least, he thought of himself as being in Turkey, as the title of Hobhouse's journal indicates, *A Journey through*

Albania and Other Provinces of Turkey. . . . Byron's use of Turkish as opposed to Greek themes and materials deserves more study than it has received.

ART

No one has had much to say about Byron's interest (or lack of interest) in art. Statements by Byron that he disliked painting "unless it reminds me of something I have seen, or think it possible to see" have deterred investigations. Yet, as canto 4 of *Childe Harold* would indicate, the subject has possibilities. Against Byron's rude dismissal of Rubens ("a very great dauber") and of the Flemish school (he "utterly detested despised & abhorred" it), we may set Stendhal's observations after taking Byron through Milan's Brera Gallery: "I admired the depth of sentiment with which the great poet comprehended the most opposite painters: Raphael, Guercino, Luini, Titian, etc. *Hagar Dismissed by Abraham* electrified him; from that moment admiration made us quite speechless; he improvised for an hour, and better, in my opinion, than Madame de Staël." There is more here than the early nineteenth-century's low estimate of Rubens (compare Blake's response!) and Byron's unswerving devotion to prevailing neoclassical canons of taste, exemplified by Reynolds' *Discourses* and the high contemporary evaluation given to the Italian sculptor Canova. On Byron's response to art as well as more particularly to sculpture, Stephen A. Larrabee's chapter in *English Bards and Grecian Marbles: The Relationship between Sculpture and Poetry Especially in the Romantic period* (1943) retains its value. Larrabee finds that although Byron "affected" to possess "no feeling for art," he yet revealed "an unmistakable sensitivity to works of art," sculpture in particular. Clearly he protested his ignorance too much. On this subject, see also Watkins' discussion (in his essay on *The Deformed Transformed*) of Byron's use of Cellini.

The portraits of Byron bear out his characterization of *mobilité* "as an excessive susceptibility of immediate impressions." No portrait by one painter much resembles portraits by other painters. Unfortunately, no detailed iconography of Byron exists such as is available for Keats or for Wordsworth. Useful as an introductory survey is Suzanne Hyman, "Contemporary Portraits of Byron" in Robinson's *Lord Byron and His Contemporaries.* More sophisticated in presentation is the chapter in David Piper's *The Image of the Poet: British Poets and their Portraits* (1982). Further detail is supplied by F. G. Kitton (*Magazine of Art,* 1894); W. A. Shaw's two-part study (*Connoisseur,* 1911), to be used with caution; and R. R. Tatlock (*Burlington Magazine,* 1924). Extremely valuable as a running commentary to the portraits is Doris Langley Moore's "Byronic Dress" (*Costume,* 1971). John Clubbe has discussed "The West Portrait of Byron" (*ByronJ,* 1980). In "William Edward West's Portrait of Teresa Guiccioli" (*ByronJ,* 1979) he draws attention to this artist's rendering of Teresa, the best early representation but long presumed lost. Edmund Blunden's "On a Portrait by Mrs. Hunt" (*KSMB,* 1955) gives the background to her 1823 silhouette of Byron in riding dress. John Kenworthy-Browne in "Byron Portrayed" (*Antique Collector,* 1974) considers the sculptured likenesses. Students of caricature should not miss either William

Hone's "The Lord of the Faithless" in *The Men in the Moon; or, The "Devil to Pay"* (1820) or Max Beerbohm's "Lord Byron Shaking the Dusk of England from His Shoes" in *The Poets' Corner* (1904) or his "But for Missolonghi," a marvelous rendering of an imaginary later Byron—looking like Karl Marx (*Zuleika Dobson,* ed. N. John Hall, 1985). The National Portrait Gallery in London has announced for 1985 publication a major catalog entitled *Regency Portraits.* Covering the period 1790–1830, it studies the more than 800 portraits owned by the gallery. It also brings together much of what is known about other portraits of the Romantic poets. Richard Walker wrote the catalog, and Doris Langley Moore served as consultant for the Byron section. *Byron,* the catalog prepared by Anthony Burton and John Murdoch in 1974 for the sesquicentennial exhibit at the Victoria and Albert Museum, also contains much miscellaneous information about the likenesses of Byron.

Illustrated editions of Byron's poems abounded during the nineteenth century and continue into the twentieth. Several collected editions published in Byron's lifetime contained illustrations (a number are reproduced in McGann's Oxford edition), as did numerous editions after his death. These early published illustrations—by Stothard, Westall, Heath, Colin, the Findens—were extremely influential in promoting the Byronic image and the Byronic myth. The subject remains almost untouched by scholarly investigation. Many of the engravings by William and Edward Finden in *Illustrations of the Life and Works of Lord Byron* (3 vols., 1833–34) are based on original sketches by distinguished artists, including Turner; other sketches were in turn redrawn by distinguished artists, again including Turner. The accompanying descriptions of the illustrations are by William Brockeden. Finden's *Illustrations* introduced many to the Byronic world, including the Brontës. In addition to the illustrated individual and collected editions, there were frequent separate publications of illustrations. Among the best known of these were *The Byron Gallery* (1832, rev. 1847); the forty-odd illustrations that George Cruikshank contributed to "George Clinton's" (Sir James Bacon's) *Memoirs of the Life and Writings of Lord Byron* (1824; the illustrations were also published separately in 1825); and *Finden's Byron Beauties; or, The Principal Female Characters in Lord Byron's Poems* (1836), in which a prose commentary, with appropriate snippets from Byron's poems, accompanies the plates. This last volume was republished many times, often under somewhat different titles. Owners of volumes of Byron illustrations could, if they wished, break up their volumes to use as interleaves to make their own illustrated Byron. Needed is a history of Byron-inspired illustrations on the lines of Robert Halsband's study of the illustrations for *The Rape of the Lock.* Cynthia Bathurst-Rodgers is currently studying the illustrations and how they relate to Byron's poetry.

In England and even more in France, Byron's poetry had considerable influence on nineteenth-century art. John Dixon Hunt, "Wondrous Dark and Deep: Turner and the Sublime" (*GaR,* 1976), considers the impact of the Romantic poets, Byron in particular, on Turner. Turner viewed Switzerland through Byron's eyes, as we learn in *Turner in Switzerland* (1976), introduced by John Russell. Leonée Ormond's lecture "Turner and Byron in Switzerland" is synopsized in

ByronJ, 1978. Kenneth Churchill in *Italy and English Literature 1764–1930* (1980) briefly discusses Turner's developing response to Byron's Italy, of which the most conspicuous manifestation is Turner's painting *Childe Harold's Pilgrimage—Italy.* Also valuable is Martin Meisel, "The Material Sublime: John Martin, Byron, Turner, and the Theater" in *Images of Romanticism,* edited by Karl Kroeber and William Walling (1978) and reprinted in Meisel's *Realizations* (1983). A chapter of James Twitchell's *Romantic Horizons: Aspects of the Sublime in English Poetry and Painting, 1770–1850* (1983) compares *Manfred* with Martin's watercolor *Manfred and the Witch of the Alps.* See also Ranjan Kumar Ravel, "Vortex as the Vehicular Form in Byron and Turner" (*Literary Criterion,* 1982). In addition to Turner and Martin, Byron and Byron's poetry influenced Ford Madox Brown, John Everett Millais, and the American Thomas Cole, all three of whom have paintings on Byron subjects, as do a host of now largely forgotten artists whose works have disappeared or lie in museum basements. Richard D. Altick has completed a large-scale study of the relation between literature and art in the nineteenth century, in which Byron will have his place. Babinski in *The Mazeppa Legend* has an appendix that includes works of art inspired by *Mazeppa,* several of which (and other Byron-inspired paintings) are conveniently reproduced in *George Byron,* a volume put out by Mondadori in 1969, and in Peter Quennell, *Romantic England: Writing and Painting, 1717–1851* (1970). Robert Copeland's "Ceramic View of Byron Country" (*Country Life,* 1976) tells of a porcelain service with scenes from Finden's *Illustrations* that enjoyed considerable popularity for several decades in the mid–nineteenth century.

Byronic subjects appear in the work of numerous French painters, Delacroix conspicuously. He is Byron's greatest interpreter in painting. Byron inspired as many of his major paintings—over a dozen—as did Shakespeare. In addition, close parallels exist between the two men, as the many references to Byron in Delacroix's *Journal* testify. See the pioneering study by G. H. Hamilton, "Eugène Delacroix and Lord Byron" (*Gazette des Beaux-Arts,* 1943), followed by subsequent articles in the same journal (1944, 1949); his "Delacroix's Memorial to Byron" (*Burlington Magazine,* 1952); and an essay in *Studies in Art and Literature for Belle da Costa Greene,* edited by Dorothy Miner (1954). Others who have written on this subject include C. R. Parsons, "Eugène Delacroix and Literary Inspiration" (*UTQ,* 1964); Lee Johnson, "Delacroix and *The Bride of Abydos*" (*Burlington Magazine,* 1972), a scholarly treatment of Delacroix's four versions of *Selim and Zuleika,* 1849–57; Jack J. Spector, *Delacroix: The Death of Sardanapalus* (1974), in which Byron is frequently mentioned; Hazel Pierce, "Lord Byron Illuminated: Eugène Delacroix" (*Platte Valley Review,* 1979), on Delacroix's paintings inspired by *The Giaour, Sardanapalus, Marino Faliero,* and *The Two Foscari; F. W. J.* Hemmings, "A Focal Figure in the Romantic *Fraternité des Arts:* Sardanapalus" (in *Literature and Society . . . ,* ed. C. A. Burns, 1980), excellent on the affinities of Delacroix's *Sardanapalus* (and also *Liberty Leading the People*) to Byron's play; and John Spalding Gatton's equally excellent "Portraits of a Doge: Delacroix's Reading of Byron's *Marino Faliero*" (*ByronJ,* 1981). See also two essays by Frederick Garber—"Conceiving Energy: Byron and

Delacroix" (*Comparatist,* 1980), on Byron's *Giaour* and Delacroix's paintings of 1827 and 1835, and "Beckford, Delacroix and Byronic Orientalism" (*CLS,* 1981), which, in seeking to define "Orientalism," illumines all three figures. Three notes in the *Burlington Magazine* (1983) take up (and add to) Delacroix's Byronic subjects. In addition, most books on Delacroix say something about Byron's influence. Neal MacGregor, "Girodet's Poem *Le Peintre*" (*Oxford Art Journal,* 1981), discusses Girodet's borrowings from *Childe Harold.*

MUSIC

Music, for Byron, was "a strange thing." It affected him deeply. Alice Levine has written that his "influence on European music is, after Shakespeare's, greater than that of any other English or American poet." Her "Byron and the Romantic Composer" in Robinson's *Lord Byron and His Contemporaries* nicely introduces the subject, with particular focus on Berlioz and Schumann. Levine is also preparing a much-needed catalog of the hundreds of songs set to Byron's words. John P. Anderson provided the first extensive listing of music composed for Byron's poems as part of the bibliography unobtrusively attached to Roden Noel's *Life of Lord Byron* (1890). Volume 1 of Bryan N. S. Gooch and David S. Thatcher, *Musical Settings of British Romantic Literature: A Catalog* (2 vols., 1982), contains the most complete listing of songs set to, and other musical forms based on, Byron's works. The *New Grove Dictionary of Music and Musicians* (1980) points out that among the composers who set Byron's poems as songs were Loewe, Mendelssohn, Schumann, Wolf, Musorgsky, Balakirev, Rimsky-Korsakov, Gounod, and Busoni. For further information, students should consult not only studies of composers but the various histories of English and European music (e.g., for England, *The Romantic Age,* ed. Nicholas Temperley, 1981).

Two succinct general introductions are Danièle Pistone's "Byron et les musiciens" (*Romantisme,* 1974) and F. W. Brownlow's "Byron and the Musicians of His Time" (*ByronJ,* 1978). Both suggest the range of Byron's impact on English and European music, as does, in a wider context, Paul Chancellor's "British Bards and Continental Composers" (*Musical Quarterly,* 1960). Ronald Stevenson's "Byron as Lyricist: The Poet among the Musicians" (in *Byron: Wrath and Rhyme,* ed. Bold) makes several interesting points in a scattershot way. Edward E. Bostetter has apt remarks on Byron and Berlioz in *MLQ,* 1974. Glyn Court in "Berlioz and Byron and *Harold in Italy*" (*Music Review,* 1956) denies that Byron influenced Berlioz' work and life in major ways. But Stuart M. Sperry, Jr., "The *Harolds* of Berlioz and Byron" (*Your Musical Cue* [Indiana Univ.], 1968), argues convincingly for Byron's influence on *Harold in Italy,* "the finest evocation of the Byronic sensibility in musical literature." Fritz Strich, "Byrons Manfred in Schumanns Vertonung" (in *Festgabe Samuel Singer,* ed. Harry Maync, 1930), has more on Byron than on Schumann but argues suggestively that the latter's "milder, more harmonious art" completes Byron's poem. See also Ardelle Striker, "*Manfred* in Concert: An American Premiere" (*BRH,* 1982). The premiere is

Edwin Booth's 1869 New York performance of Byron's poem with Schumann's music, the first of a number of performances.

Over forty operas are based on works by Byron. In "Byron and Rossini" (*Opera News*, 19 Mar. 1966) Leslie A. Marchand has carefully brought together the known facts regarding Byron's interest in Rossini's music. Giacomo Antonini briefly considers Byron's "Impact on Italian Opera" (*ByronJ*, 1973). Two of Verdi's operas—*I Due Foscari* and *Il Corsaro*—are based on Byron. On the former, see Scott Stringham, *"I Due Foscari:* From Byron's Play to Verdi's Opera" (*WVUPP*, 1970)—which discusses Verdi's transformation, with his librettist Piave, of Byron's drama—and, especially, the chapter in Vincent Godefroy, *The Dramatic Genius of Giuseppe Verdi* (vol. 1, 1975), an expert handling of Byronic influences. On *Il Corsaro,* see the pages in Julian Budden, *The Operas of Verdi* (vol. 1, 1973), and David Lawton, "The Corsair Reaches Port" (*Opera News*, June 1982). Antonini's "Donizetti and Byron" (*Donizetti Society Journal,* 1974) examines Donizetti's "three operas directly inspired by Byron, and a fourth to which one of Byron's poems greatly contributed to the spirit of the work." Antonini suggests as well the breadth of Byron's influence on other Donizetti operas. Gary Schmidgall, *Literature as Opera* (1977), considers Byron in relation to Tchaikovsky's *Eugene Onegin,* itself based on an ironic reading of Pushkin's poem. The above studies of Verdi, Donizetti, and Tchaikovsky indicate the need for a book on Byron's influence on opera comparable in scale to Jerome Mitchell's study of the Scott operas. There are also operas about Byron himself, including Virgil Thomson's *Lord Byron*.

In the twentieth century we have, amid much else, songs by Hindemith, Thomson's opera, an impressive musical setting of "Ode to Napoleon Buonaparte" (1944) for orchestra and *Sprechgesang* solo by Arnold Schoenberg, Raffaello de Banfield's one-act opera *Lord Byron's Love Letter* (1960), with libretto by Tennessee Williams, the English composer Alan Bush's *Byron Symphony* (1961), and, by the young German composer Aribert Reimann, a powerful 1979 piece for baritone and string quartet, "Unrevealed," based on the Byron-Augusta relationship.

BYRON TODAY

What value does Byron have for the present? Willis W. Pratt in "Byron and Some Current Patterns of Thought" (*The Major English Romantic Poets,* ed. Clarence D. Thorpe et al., 1957) finds Byron's "mind playing with facility and grace upon a great many subjects, forming them into a contrapuntal pattern that has much of the modern temper about it." For Leslie A. Marchand, in "Byron and the Modern Spirit" (in the same volume), the poet's "recognition of the disparity between the mind's conception of perfection and what we actually believe is achievable in our personal lives or the life of man brings him closer to the twentieth century than any of his contemporaries." Erwin A. Stürzl in "Byron—unser Zeitgenosse" (*New Light on Byron,* 1978) also finds Byron's attitudes and ideas of remarkable cogency for our time. Still noteworthy in its evaluation of Byron's modernity is the final chapter of Lovell's *Byron: The Record of a Quest* (1949). Its enumeration of the various components of Byron's personality and achievement recalls for us the extraordinary breadth of his activities—and of his appeal. "He was, briefly, one of the last of the English poets to try to make himself a complete man—poet, scholar, lover, sportsman, world traveller, statesman, soldier, and administrator. It is the Greek idea of wholeness, modified of course by the European Renaissance. Byron's ideal, expressed by word and deed from first to last, was to make of himself a man equally at ease on horseback, swimming in the sea, admiring a picturesque view, writing at his desk, or directing the affairs of a nation fighting for its freedom. He hated specialists, and none more than the mere speculator about this existence, these dreamers, as he called them. Action before philosophy every time." Or, to give Byron the last word, "I have lived, and am content."

PERCY BYSSHE SHELLEY

Stuart Curran

Contents

Since the emphasis of this bibliography is on contemporary tools for research on Shelley, the older foundations on which modern scholarship have rested must of necessity be slighted. The student or scholar interested in earlier developments in Shelley studies is particularly urged to consult the third edition of this bibliography, written by Donald H. Reiman, himself building on the labors of Bennett Weaver before him. The sections on individual works are richly detailed, fairly balanced, yet judicious, a model of guidance through the intricacies of interpretation. Those on the development of the text and the vagaries of Shelley's biography are simply unparalleled. Since we lack anything approaching definitive versions of the text and the life, such a lucid presentation of the problems involved is itself of essential help. The authority of these sections underlies Reiman's own numerous and significant endeavors to rectify major textual and biographical omissions or errors, a continuing scholarly labor to which all current work on Shelley is indebted. The same high standards everywhere inform his contributions to the 1972 edition of *The English Romantic Poets.*

Bibliographies

Students of Shelley are fortunate in at last having an authoritative enumerative bibliography. Clement Dunbar's *A Bibliography of Shelley Studies: 1823 – 1950* (1976) endeavors to list all writing on the poet between his death and the point at which modern Shelley studies began to compile systematic bibliographical records. Dunbar's bibliography numbers over 3,300 items, five times the number previously recorded, and it can safely be said to supersede all compendia for the period he covers. The organization is chronological, with parenthetical symbols loosely indicating the orientation of the particular listing. As rich as this trove is, its chronological plan, coupled with an index limited solely to author and periodical and cross-referencing that is too simple to reveal complexity of detail, poses considerable difficulty for anyone trying to trace the critical history of a particular work or subject. On balance, it might be said that no bibliographical index can substitute for careful perusal of the contents. Still, the value of a work that subsumes all previous enumerations and then adds richly to them far outweighs occasional frustrations of access. It should be noted that the Anglo-American bias of the bibliography is virtually absolute: translations and criticism not written in English are excluded.

Dunbar's bibliography is designed to lock exactly into the annual bibliographies prepared since its inception for the *Keats-Shelley Journal,* "Keats, Shelley, Byron, Hunt, and Their Circle." The first twenty-five of these, beginning in 1950, where Dunbar's record leaves off, have been collected in two separate volumes. The first (1964, 1966), collected by David Bonnell Green and Edwin Graves Wilson, covers the period from 1 July 1950 to 30 June 1962; the second (1978), collected by Robert A. Hartley, covers 1 July 1962 to 31 December 1974. (Later bibliographies are published with the annual volume of the *Journal.*) The organization of these collected bibliographies preserves the original yearly format, but the index points to any substantial discussion of a particular work, allowing the student swift and accurate bibliographical access. In addition, many of the items are briefly described. A listing of relevant doctoral dissertations, most writing in languages other than English, and a virtually complete record of book reviews are notable features of these bibliographies. Clement Dunbar continues his valuable service to the scholarly community as current editor of the *Keats-Shelley Journal* bibliography. More copiously annotated entries regularly appear in the pages of *The Romantic Movement: A Selective and Critical Bibliography*, for many years under the general editorship of David V. Erdman. Once a periodical supplement (*ELH*, 1937–49; *PQ*, 1950–64; *ELN*, 1965–79), *The Romantic Movement* is now produced in an annual volume by Garland Publishing. The *MLA Bibliography*, meanwhile, balances its lack of annotation with a global network of contributors and a relatively quick listing to produce the most current compilation of writing relating to Shelley.

The few bibliographical treatments of Shelley studies not in English are now well out-of-date but still of service. Among these are Henri Peyre's *Shelley et la France* (1935) and, less centrally, Hélène Lemaitre's *Shelley, poète des éléments* (1962); note also Solomon Liptzin's *Shelley in Germany* (1924). Lucas Verkoren's review of Shelley studies in the Netherlands (*Levende Talen*, 1950) is written in Dutch, but Boris Gilenson's similar survey for the Soviet Union (*Soviet Literature*, 1963) is in English. Barring an attempt to resurrect a European bibliography for Shelley, one looks to the *Catalog of Books and Manuscripts at the Keats-Shelley Memorial House in Rome* (1969), compiled by Joan S. Ring, as at least including within the necessary limitations of an author catalog much of the varied Continental literature concerned with Shelley.

For notices of the author during his lifetime the standard reference for many years was Newman Ivey White's compilation *The Unextinguished Hearth* (1938), which profited from his vast knowledge of the poet's life and milieu. This book has been slightly updated by James E. Barcus' edition of *Shelley: The Critical Heritage* (1975); but the major modern compendium of reviews and critical notices appears in facsimile in Donald H. Reiman's *The Romantics Reviewed: Contemporary Reviews of British Romantic Writers* (1972). The chapter on Shelley in Reiman's *English Romantic Poetry, 1800–1835: A Guide to Information Sources* (1979) provides a useful overview of the major scholarship and criticism, updating the more detailed perspective offered in the third edition of this bibliography.

For the descriptive bibliography of Shelley first and early editions, the standard works of references are H. Buxton Forman's *The Shelley Library*, published for the Shelley Society in 1886; Ruth S. Granniss' *A Descriptive Catalogue of the First Editions in Book Form of the Writings of Percy Bysshe Shelley* (1923), which accompanied the Grolier Club centennial observance; and the sumptuously produced *A Shelley Library* (1924) by Thomas J. Wise. His major collection, also described in his *Catalog of the Ashley Library* (1922–36), is still basically intact in the British Library. The chief treatment of Shelley publications from the *Posthumous Poems* of 1824 through various pirated editions to Mary Shelley's four-volume *Poetical Works of Percy Bysshe Shelley* in 1839 is the authoritative work of Charles H. Taylor in *The Early Collected Editions of Shelley's Poems* (1958). There is probably room for further work of a descriptive kind, inasmuch as modern methods of systematic collation have not been brought to bear on either the first or the early editions.

A description of manuscript holdings, of course, cannot substitute for their actual consultation but can at least indicate what is to be found where. Forman and Wise record their holdings within their respective collections listed above. Forman also described at length and with perhaps excessive running linkage the three Shelley notebooks in the collections of the Henry E. Huntington Library: *Note Books of Percy Bysshe Shelley... in the Library of W. K. Bixby* (1911). If one finds his commentary drawing toward the fictional at times, one acknowledges that none of the other Shelley notebooks, principally held in the Bodleian Library, Oxford, has been so carefully described. Among other American holdings, another Huntington Library manuscript, Edward Williams' transcript of *Hellas* corrected by Shelley, is described by Bennett Weaver in volume 8 of the University of Michigan's Publications in Language and Literature (1932). Other manuscripts in this collection are detailed by H. C. Schulz in "English Literary Manuscripts in the Huntington Library" (*HLQ,* 1968). A short sketch of the holdings of the Pierpont Morgan Library done by George K. Boyce appears in *PMLA,* 1952. The fair-copy notebook of Shelley's poems at Harvard is reproduced in facsimile and with notes by George Edward Woodberry as the *Harvard Shelley Notebook* (1929). (The Silsbee notebook at Harvard, whose purchase from Claire Clairmont prompted Henry James's *The Aspern Papers,* has never been described in full.) In the previous edition of this bibliography Donald H. Reiman noted that Woodberry had confused the hands of Shelley and Mary Shelley in the *Harvard Shelley Notebook*; errors of transcription qualify as well the discussion by Frederick L. Jones of the notebook now in the Library of Congress (*SP,* 1948). The Shelley manuscripts at the University of Texas have had three successive enumerations: *An Account of an Exhibition of Books and Manuscripts of Percy Bysshe Shelley* (1935), Willis W. Pratt's *Lord Byron and His Circle: A Catalogue of Manuscripts in the University of Texas Library* (1948), and Pratt's "Lord Byron and His Circle: Recent Manuscript Acquisitions" (*LCUT,* 1956). Shelley manuscripts in the collection of Texas Christian University have been transcribed by Lyle H. Kendall, Jr., in *A Descriptive Catalogue of the W. L. Lewis Collection. Part One: Manuscripts* (1970). There are a few Shelley manuscripts indexed in the *Catalog of Books and Manuscripts at the Keats-Shelley Memorial House in Rome* (1969), already referred to.

The bulk of manuscripts for Shelley and the Shelley circle is contained in three great collections, those of the Bodleian Library, Oxford, of Lord Abinger (on deposit at the Bodleian), and of the Carl H. Pforzheimer Library in New York. Much of the Bodleian collection came through the bequest of Lady Jane Shelley, widow of the poet's son Sir Percy Florence Shelley, in 1893. Portions of this bequest are described in three publications: C. D. Locock, *An Examination of the Shelley Manuscripts in the Bodleian Library* (1903), which concentrates on the poetic texts; A. H. Koszul, *Shelley's Prose in the Bodleian Manuscripts* (1910); and R. H. Hill, *The Shelley Correspondence in the Bodleian Library* (1926). Two additional bequests from the family collection were made to the Bodleian Library in 1948 and 1962 by Sir John Shelley-Rolls and by his widow. The first of these was described by Neville Rogers in *TLS*, 27 July, 3 August, and 10 August 1951, and subsequently in the lengthy examination of his *Shelley at Work* (1956; 2nd ed. 1967). The Bodleian collections have been microfilmed for Duke University, the University of Wisconsin, Milwaukee, and various scholars but are otherwise not available in facsimile. The collection of James Scarlett, eighth Baron Abinger, has likewise been microfilmed for various libraries, including the Bodleian, Duke University, and the University of Texas. Portions of the microfilms are described by Lewis Patton in *Library Notes* (Duke Univ., 1953). The Lord Abinger collection centers on the manuscripts of William Godwin, Mary Wollstonecraft, Mary Wollstonecraft Shelley, and various of her and her husband's friends: a large portion was transcribed in the lax manner of the day by Sir Percy Florence and Lady Jane Shelley for *Shelley and Mary* (1882), a privately printed edition of 1,243 pages. Twelve copies were supposedly printed, but there appear to be at least twice that number in existence. A substantial amount of this material remains otherwise unpublished a hundred years later, most of that, however, being only peripherally concerned with Shelley. That there are treasures in the Lord Abinger collection that have escaped microfilming is testified to by the recent discovery of a transcript for an important Shelley letter by David M. Stocking and Marion Kingston Stocking (*KSMB*, 1980). Plans afoot for producing a series of facsimiles of major Romantics manuscripts, under the general direction of Donald H. Reiman, would have as one priority making generally available to scholars at least the Shelley notebooks housed in the Bodleian. This would allow for a systematic understanding of their contents that has eluded all but a handful of scholars who have worked independently with them. But such facsimiles can never substitute for their actual physical examination. The brief report on the watermarks of two of the notebooks by Carlene A. Adamson (*KSMB*, 1982) freshly demonstrates this truth.

The third major repository of Shelley manuscripts is the Carl H. Pforzheimer Library, which has been systematically publishing its major holdings in the monumental edition of *Shelley and His Circle, 1773–1822*. Projected for twelve weighty volumes, this undertaking establishes a diplomatic text and exhaustive bibliographical description of each manuscript, surrounding them with invaluable commentary, discursive essays, illustrations, maps, and facsimiles of manuscripts. Many scholars have contributed to this venture, the first four volumes of which were under the general editorship of Kenneth Neill Cameron (vols. 1–2, 1961; vols. 3–4, 1970) and subsequent volumes (of which vols. 5–6 were published in 1973, vols. 7–8 projected for 1985) under the general editorship of Donald H. Reiman. The six volumes in print cover Shelley's life through the end of 1819. *Shelley and His Circle, 1773–1822* is a landmark of scholarship that has established numerous definitive texts and resolved many questions concerning Shelley's life, the lives and works of a number of acquaintances, and the contexts of their writings.

Several other valuable bibliographical tools should be mentioned. *A Bibliography of Shelley's Letters* (1927) by Seymour de Ricci attempts to trace the complete provenance of all the correspondence then known and is still of value for its detection of forgeries. Irving Massey, in *Posthumous Poems of Shelley* (1969), edited one of the copybooks in which Mary Shelley prepared texts for her editions of Shelley, collating them with Shelley drafts in the Bodleian and Huntington Libraries. Shelley students must still rely on F. S. Ellis' *Lexical Concordance to the Poetical Works of Percy Bysshe Shelley* (1892), which is dependable, but its value is diminished by its age, its being keyed to the titles of H. Buxton Forman's two-volume edition (1882), and thus by its exclusion of a full century of subsequent editorial work. Since such editorial labors, to which we now turn, are far from complete, a new concordance is not to be anticipated in the foreseeable future.

Editions

Neither Shelley's poetry nor his prose is completely available in a reliable version, and even the letters, edited by Frederick L. Jones in 1964, have prompted suggestions for so many additions and corrections that a new edition would be desirable. Although it is sardonically amusing that so much critical writing unwittingly fleets over such textual thin ice, it is also fair to observe that none of the other English Romantic poets, not even Byron, presents so many formidable obstacles to an editor. Most of Shelley's mature poetry was written after he left England, and very little of it could be said to have been supervised through press by him. In addition, the mature Shelley published relatively few of the lyrics he wrote; the rest were resurrected from such notebooks as survived his death and Mary's relocation to England. Add to this lost poems, lost manuscripts, the simple ravages of time—not to mention an all but indecipherable hand in some of the draft manuscripts—then add to these the customary nineteenth-century sense of decorum that protected reputations by selective editing and suppression, and one has a veritable Gordian knot that has not been unthreaded in a century and a half. As mentioned before, an estimable survey of the development of the texts has been provided by Donald H. Reiman in the third edition of this bibliography. For our purposes there are five editions of the poetry that command a contemporary student's attention: those by Thomas Hutchinson, Roger Ingpen and Walter E. Peck, Neville Rogers, Judith Chernaik, and Donald H. Reiman and Sharon B. Powers.

The primary edition of the poems for much of this century was that done by Thomas Hutchinson for the Oxford University Press in 1904, which was disseminated beginning in 1905 in the Oxford Standard Authors series. It was reset in 1934 and again in 1969, the latter with negligible corrections provided by G. M. Matthews. Long available in a paperback edition, the Hutchinson edition does not incorporate poems or textual authorities that have come to light since 1904, and, though in many respects a more conservative edition than the important Victorian texts, it is chiefly valuable to the contemporary student where no reliable text has superseded its contents. Its own Victorian bias is observable in its attempt to hide *Queen Mab* amid the selection of juvenilia at the back of the book. The Julian edition of the *Complete Works of Shelley* in ten volumes (1926–30), edited by Ingpen and Peck, has limitations similar to those of Hutchinson, to which are added quixotic emendations and choices for copy text. The textual notes, however, are far more substantial than those of Hutchinson. It is generally cited for reference simply because everything is in one place, but then the volumes containing the letters are wholly outdated and the text for the poetry is less reliable than Hutchinson's.

The Clarendon Press of Oxford University has published two of the projected four volumes of Shelley's complete poetry (vol. 1, 1972; vol. 2, 1975) edited by Neville Rogers. There are recognizable improvements to be honored here: a number of poems never before included in a complete edition, principally those of Shelley's youth, are printed in their proper sequence, and the textual apparatus is more complex and sophisticated than in the earlier editions. And yet, paradoxically, the increased access to manuscript and textual sources makes this edition one to be used only with great caution and with more independent knowledge of the history of Shelley texts than is possessed by any but a few devoted scholars. Rogers, operating on a principle that editors—even the succession of editors—have an obligation to improve a text wherever there is reason to believe it faulty, gives himself extreme latitude in determining what is printed, and the textual notes often do not provide an accurate account of variant alternatives. Rogers has defended his approach against what he calls textual fundamentalists in "The Editing of Shelley's Manuscripts" (*KSMB*, 1972), but he has made few converts to flying in the face of scholarly advancement. The procedures now generally in acceptance among modern authorities are applied to the special problems of Shelley by Donald H. Reiman in "Editing Shelley," his contribution to *Editing Texts of the Romantic Period*, a symposium edited by John D. Baird (1972). In addition to idiosyncratic textual principles, Rogers pursues in his editorial notes a relentless thesis that Shelley was a latter-day Platonist, a view that is no longer critically central. Again, it requires considerable prior knowledge to separate those notes that are genuinely new and valuable scholarly contributions from those with a restrictive interpretive bias. One authoritative critic, surveying the first two volumes of the Clarendon edition, was moved to call it "a disservice to a great English poet and a scandal to British scholarship." Yet so prestigious is the press and so costly is such an undertaking that one does not easily foresee another press soon projecting a definitive edition of Shelley's poetry.

In the meantime, the student and scholar rely on two highly accurate and valuable sources for a limited number of Shelley texts. Judith Chernaik's *The Lyrics of Shelley* (1972) offers scrupulously reconstructed texts (with all variants then available) for two dozen of Shelley's lyrics. The only limitations here are those of number and kind: within her constraints Chernaik has performed an admirable service, completely renovating, for instance, two important poems: "To Constantia," where her detective work uncovered an ephemeral printing that solved the problem of the order of its stanzas, and "The Indian Girl's Song," which in its earlier form, "The Indian Serenade," suffered first from Mary Shelley's mistaken tinkering and then from the consequent derision of inimical critics. *The Lyrics of Shelley,* one should observe, incorporates the textual discoveries Chernaik recorded in *TLS* (6 Feb. 1969) and in *KSJ* (1970). By far the most praised and invaluable edition of Shelley in recent years has been that prepared for the series of Norton Critical Editions by Donald H. Reiman and Sharon B. Powers, *Shelley's Poetry and Prose* (1977). This volume has become the standard student text and, for want of a more complete and scholarly edition, the standard textual reference for critical writing on Shelley as well. Although the format does not allow for textual apparatus, the edition was prepared in full knowledge of possible variants and within the consistent and conservative editorial boundaries outlined by Reiman in "Editing Shelley." Along with the major poems are the essays "On Life" and "On Love," as well as *A Defence of Poetry,* each included in a form that supersedes previous texts. One naturally wishes that the format of the series did not sacrifice printing even more of Shelley's writing for critical judgments on it. Selections from standard critics are undoubtedly useful for students, and the pages here represent some of the best thinking on Shelley for its time: as the years move on, however, some of it has become rather dated in viewpoint or approach. There are a handful of typographical errors to be rectified in a future edition: for the time being, these are conveniently enumerated by Reiman in *KSJ,* 1981. All in all, this is an accurate, reliable, economically annotated edition, one that prints a larger, better rounded selection of Shelley's writings (including all the poetry of *Queen Mab,* for instance) than any comparable student edition. Indeed, there simply is no comparable student edition. For the first time in the more than a century and a half since the poet's death, the Reiman-Powers edition offers what anyone might have thought would have taken less time to produce, a reliable text for most of Shelley's major poems. There is nothing in sight that will substitute for it.

The only possible competition is provided by the *Selected Poems* (1977) edited by Timothy Webb for the Everyman series. Webb too has checked his authorities firsthand. The weakness here is one of length, which allows Webb little opportunity to print the longer poems, necessitating, for instance, an abridged version of *Prometheus Unbound.* Webb's annotations are intelligent and well-balanced, however, and the introduction, concentrating on Shelley's sense of craft and of tradition, is one of the sanest overall perspectives on Shelley, claiming comparison with the splendid introductory essay Harold Bloom wrote for his New American edition—"The Unpastured Sea: An Introduction to Shelley"—easily available in the collection *The Ringers in the Tower* (1971). The other student editions are more or less out-of-date in texts and notes. These include the Modern Library edition (1951), edited (without notes) by Carlos Baker; the Rinehart edition (1951), organized topically by Kenneth Neill Cameron; Neville Rogers' *Selected Poetry,* originally published for Riverside (1968) and assimilated by Oxford when that went out of print, an edition with all the defects of the Clarendon edition and far less poetry; and the Cambridge edition of 1901, originally edited by George Woodberry and reissued with a new introduction by Newell Ford in 1975, a volume whose very existence in print testifies to the general unconcern of trade publishers with assuming responsibility for classic authors or for their readers.

More specialized textual studies of Shelley testify to the same problems encountered in attempting to establish a definitive text. The *Esdaile Notebook*, containing fifty-seven poems from Shelley's youth, was bought by the Carl H. Pforzheimer Library in 1962. Edited first by Kenneth Neill Cameron (1964), the notebook was reedited two years later by Neville Rogers. The seemingly needless duplication was actually fruitful, since a number of issues arose between the editors and among their reviewers. These are resolved by Cameron in what constitutes a definitive edition, with all known variants, printed as appendix 2 (containing 150 pages) to *Shelley and His Circle*, volume 4.

A similar duplication of effort with *Prometheus Unbound* is less clearly resolved. Lawrence John Zillman used the first edition of the poem, complete with obvious misprints, as copy text for *Shelley's* Prometheus Unbound: *A Variorum Edition* (1959), with his textual notes confusedly divided between the major surviving manuscript, the first and subsequent editions on the one hand and a melange of draft materials on the other, these last being printed as an appendix. Reacting to the numerous questions raised by this procedure, Zillman returned to the problem of the text, relieved of the complex apparatus necessary for a variorum, and attempted a more rigorous reconstruction of the text in *Shelley's* Prometheus Unbound: *The Text and the Drafts* (1968). Here, however, he veered to the opposite extreme, giving authority to notebook drafts over what were clearly Shelley's second thoughts. And the omissions, minor though they undoubtedly are, certainly qualify the fulfillment of the aim enunciated in Zillman's subtitle: "Toward a Modern Definitive Edition." The most serious problem faced by any editor of this work is that Shelley's errata list, which was apparently incorporated with other emendations in early editions of the poem, is lost and with it an objective means of determining his final intentions. A new edition, which will attempt to resolve lingering issues, is being prepared by Neil Fraistat, whose efforts will also include the nine poems Shelley published with his lyrical drama. In the meantime, aided by Zillman's valuable introductory textual history, one can discern from his apparatus the essential points of contention.

The vexed textual history of another major poem has come to a sounder ending, again through the cooperative efforts of two authorities. "The Triumph of Life," left incomplete and thus a temptation for the ingenuity of editors from Mary Shelley on, has in the last two decades been restored to as close as scholarship can determine it was when Shelley's death interrupted its composition. In three crucial articles G. M. Matthews gave new readings of "The Triumph of Life" and other late lyrics: "The 'Triumph of Life' Apocrypha" (*TLS*, 5 Aug. 1960), " 'The Triumph of Life': A New Text" (*SN*, 1960), and "Shelley and Jane Williams" (*RES*, 1961). Donald H. Reiman raised a challenge to the latter article in "Shelley's 'The Triumph of Life': The Biographical Problem" (*PMLA*, 1963) and, using Matthews' work, attempted a full-scale presentation of the text, its content, and meaning in *Shelley's "The Triumph of Life": A Critical Study* (1965). Matthews' review in *JEGP* (1967) stipulated as yet unresolved questions, and the minor changes that result are incorporated in the Reiman-Powers edition, which is at this juncture the most reliable text of the poem.

Facsimile editions for most of the volumes published by the mature Shelley were prepared by the Shelley Society during its brief but highly active life in the 1880s and 1890s. These volumes have been generally reprinted, and they can be quite useful to the scholar. The poetic volumes include *Alastor, Rosalind and Helen, The Cenci, The Masque of Anarchy, Epipsychidion, Adonais,* and *Hellas.* The latter three were so closely copied after the original editions as to reproduce the colored wrappers as well as the type: Thomas J. Wise so obviously loved rare books as to extend his interest to forging them as well.

Outside of formal editing projects, the number of insights derived by modern Shelley scholars from a meticulous scrutiny of his drafts and notebooks would require a litany of virtually all the prominent active interpreters of Shelley. Suffice it to say that nearly every major study of Shelley in recent years contains incidental renderings of manuscript material nowhere else available in print. There are, beyond these, important fresh readings of poetic texts that supplement the editions noted above, and they are here cited in the chronological sequence of the poems concerned: Charles E. Robinson, " 'Roots' to 'Rocks' in Shelley's 'Alastor' " (*AN&Q,* 1979); Stuart Curran, "Shelley's Emendations to the *Hymn to Intellectual Beauty*" (*ELN,* 1970); notes on the textual crux "But for such faith" in "Mont Blanc" by Joan Rees (*RES,* 1964) and John Kinnaird (*N&Q,* 1968); E. B. Murray, "Mont Blanc's Unfurled Veil" (*KSJ,* 1969); on the text of these companion poems, discovered in the Scrope Davies notebook in 1976, consult (though the transcripts do not agree in all particulars) Neville Rogers (*KSMB,* 1977) and the more authoritative account of Judith Chernaik and Timothy Burnett (*RES,* 1978); G. M. Matthews on the solitary identity of the separated pieces "To Fanny Godwin" and "To William Shelley"—"Whose Little Footsteps? Three Shelley Pieces Re-Addressed"—in the festschrift for Cameron, *The Evidence of the Imagination,* edited by Reiman et al. (1978); G. M. Matthews, "A New Text of Shelley's Scene for *Tasso*" (*KSMB,* 1960); G. M. Matthews, "*Julian and Maddalo*: The Draft and the Meaning" (*SN,* 1963); E. B. Murray, "Gnashing and Wailing in *Prometheus Unbound*" ([on *PU* 1.345–46] *KSJ,* 1975); Stuart Curran, "Shelley's Satiric Fragment on a Heavenly Feast: A Corrected Text" (*N&Q,* 1970); Joseph A. Raben, "Shelley's 'Invocation to Misery': An Expanded Text" (*JEGP,* 1966); Joseph A. Raben, "Shelley's 'The Boat on the Serchio': The Evidence of the Manuscript" (*PQ,* 1967); R. B. Woodings, "Shelley's Widow Bird" (*RES,* 1968). Finally, it should be noted that in 1970 Scolar Press published a facsimile of *Epipsychidion, Together with Shelley's Manuscript Draft* and that Anthony D. Knerr's *Shelley's* Adonais: *A Critical Edition* (1984) transcribes relevant drafts from the Bodleian notebooks.

The state of Shelley's numerous and highly accomplished translations is considerably better settled since the publication of Timothy Webb's *The Violet in the Crucible: Shelley and Translation* (1976). Although Webb does not have room to publish a definitive text, he freshly transcribes all Shelley's translations (which will appear in the Oxford *Prose* described in the next paragraph) and in the course of his critical examination continually revises the texts printed in the

Hutchinson edition. In a separate article Webb has also established a new text for Shelley's translation of the Homeric "Hymn to Venus" (*RES,* 1970). Earlier work on the Italian translations was contributed by Jean de Palacio—in "Shelley and Dante: An Essay in Textual Criticism" (*RLC,* 1961) and "Shelley Traducteur de Dante: Le Chant XXVIII du Purgatoire" (*RLC,* 1963)—and, dealing with Shelley's own writing in Italian, by Parks C. Hunter, "Textual Differences in the Drafts of Shelley's 'Una Favola'" (*SIR,* 1966) and Jean de Palacio, "Shelley traducteur de soi-même" (*RSH,* 1975). Complementing Webb on the *Faust* translations are Robert C. Casto's "Shelley as Translator of *Faust:* The 'Prologue'" (*RES,* 1975) and Roxana Klapper's monograph in the series of Salzburg Studies, *The German Literary Influence on Shelley* (1975), which reprints the over one thousand lines of Shelley's literal prose translations from *Faust.* Shelley's extensive translations from Plato have been well edited by James A. Notopoulos in *The Platonism of Shelley* (1949), with an addendum—"New Texts of Shelley's Plato"—published in *KSJ,* 1966.

The state of Shelley's prose is even less secure than that of the poetry. With much of it unpublished during his lifetime and with minor pieces and fragments still in the process of identification and dissemination, the prose has until comparatively recently never been accorded the status it deserves in regard to rhetorical style, subtlety of thought, and range of speculation. As handmaiden to the poetry, marked by endemic textual problems, even fundamental disputes over dates of composition, the prose has suffered from editorial whim only less serious because fewer have taken their turn with it. For all these reasons the new and systematic edition of the complete writings of Shelley in prose, whose volumes will shortly begin to appear from the Clarendon Press, Oxford, is eagerly awaited. The editors—E. B. Murray for Shelley's original writings and Timothy Webb for the translations—not only recreate the earlier Anglo-American editorial collaboration embodied in Ingpen and Peck but also bring to their labors well-earned reputations for broad learning, critical taste, and scrupulous scholarship. Just as important, both Murray and Webb have already demonstrated themselves authorities in textual editing. The result should be a landmark in Shelley studies.

And yet, until the appearance of this edition, Shelley's prose simply rests in limbo. The common student text, David Lee Clark's *Shelley's Prose; or, The Trumpet of a Prophecy* (1954), has at last gone out of print, and no one can really be sorry to see it go. The editor's zany eccentricities and hobbyhorses, though amusing to the independently proficient, were continually transformed into distortion of fact by students and novice scholars. Clark's datings are frequently years wide of the mark, as his texts are freely rendered with little concern for authority. The two remaining student texts are tailored to special concerns and represent no textual advance: they are *Shelley's Critical Prose,* edited by Bruce R. McElderry, Jr. (1967), and *Political Writings including "A Defence of Poetry,"* edited by Roland Duerksen (1970). For want of alternatives and because it is both reasonably complete and accurate, the standard text of Shelley's prose remains that of volumes 5–7 of the Ingpen and Peck edition, except where it can be updated.

The updating can begin with dating itself. The efforts of James A. Notopoulos—"The Dating of Shelley's Prose" (*PMLA*, 1943)—are today more useful for demonstrating the problems confronting scholars than for dependably resolving them. Stuart Curran and Joseph Wittreich marshall arguments for recasting one traditional date in "The Dating of Shelley's 'On the Devil, and Devils' " (*KSJ*, 1972–73). A crucial revision of date, along with a definitive text, is given the fragment "On Love" by Donald H. Reiman in *Shelley and His Circle*, volume 6. P. M. S. Dawson incorporates such modern revisions, along with his own independent corrections, in an appendix to *The Unacknowledged Legislator: Shelley and Politics* (1980). This table, though substantiating evidence is omitted, is accepted as the most authoritative chronology available and should be consulted by anyone adducing conclusions from Shelley's prose.

In briefly noting prose pieces discovered since the Ingpen and Peck and the Clark editions, we might begin with the longest, Shelley's review of a performance by the Improvvisatore Sgricci, printed in the original Italian with English translation by P. M. S. Dawson (*KSMB*, 1981). Claude Brew has provided "A New Shelley Text: Essay on Miracles and Christian Doctrine" (*KSMB*, 1977), for which Emily Sunstein has supplied a companion piece by Mary Shelley (*KSMB*, 1981). Along the same lines, a fragmentary "Definition of the Term 'Atheist' " is printed by Timothy Webb in *Shelley: A Voice Not Understood* (1977). More difficult of access is the extensive examination of the manuscript "Speculations on Metaphysics and Morals" conducted by Tatsuo Tokoo in "Bodleian Shelley MSS Re-examined: A Re-edited Text of Some of Shelley's Prose Works in the Bodleian MSS. (1)" and printed in *Humanities: Bulletin of the Faculty of Letters, Kyoto Prefectural University* (1981). Even more removed from common attention—it has never been reprinted—is the five-page draft of an essay proposing a homeland for the Jewish people published in *The Shelley Memorial Volume by Members of the English Club, Imperial University of Tokyo* (1922), edited by Takeshi Saito. Two years earlier there had finally appeared one of Shelley's major political documents, *A Philosophical View of Reform*, edited by T. W. Rolleston. How extensively edited it was has appeared from the scrupulous transcription from the manuscript conducted by Donald H. Reiman in *Shelley and His Circle*, volume 6. This transcription largely invalidates the commonly accepted text without providing a reading text in its stead. For that one again must await the Murray edition. In the meantime, as a further and imperative stopgap, E. B. Murray has recorded over 80 corrections to standard readings of the prose in "Annotated Manuscript Corrections of Shelley's Prose Essays" (*KSJ*, 1977). Murray has also examined the textual authority of the "Notes on Sculptures" (*KSJ*, 1983). Finally, although the Reiman-Powers edition provides the most advanced text of *A Defence of Poetry*, a major addition to our knowledge of this work is provided by Fanny Delisle's *A Study of Shelley's* A Defence of Poetry: *A Textual and Critical Evaluation* (Salzburg Studies, 2 vols., 1974), which prints major variants from the manuscripts as well as a helpful summary of editorial and critical contexts.

For Shelley's letters the standard edition is that edited by Frederick L. Jones (2 vols., 1964), but besides numerous minor points of dating and transcription raised by subsequent scholars, two of the letters (nos. 413 and 545) are not authentic and many, principally those in the Pforzheimer collection, are not included. The Jones edition should thus be supplemented by letters published in *Shelley and His Circle* and in Lyle Kendall's *Descriptive Catalogue of the W. L. Lewis Collection of Texas Christian University,* by the corrections suggested by John Buxton (*BL,* 1972), and by such additions as the adolescent verse epistle transcribed by Neville Rogers (*KSMB,* 1973), the two letters on the Greek revolution sent to liberal periodicals that Charles E. Robinson has unearthed (*KSMB,* 1980, 1981), and the important letter to the Gisbornes previously mentioned, edited by David M. Stocking and Marion Kingston Stocking (*KSMB,* 1980). Jones should be greatly credited for having included in his edition at least some of the missives of Shelley's correspondents, but there is more even in *Shelley and Mary* (1882) than he transcribes, as well as in such volumes as R. Brimley Johnson's *Shelley–Leigh Hunt: How Friendship Made History* (1928) or W. S. Scott's edition of Hogg's correspondence in *New Shelley Letters* (1948), which subsumes the earlier limited editions of *The Athenians, Harriet and Mary,* and *Shelley at Oxford.* When a new edition of the Shelley letters is contemplated—and that will surely happen after *Shelley and His Circle* has been completed—one would hope that economic necessities would make practical a better representation of the complete correspondence. This need may be lessened with publication of the Peacock letters, being undertaken by Nicholas A. Joukovsky for the Oxford Press, and a projected edition of the letters of Hunt. In the meantime, the most essential secondary trove of letters, Mary Shelley's, is being reedited on modern principles and with numerous additions by Betty T. Bennett for the Johns Hopkins University Press: the first volume, running to 1827, appeared in 1980, the second in 1983. The new edition of the journal kept by the Shelleys, being prepared by Paula Feldman and Diana Pugh, has been long awaited, since the Jones edition of 1947 omitted much that was vital. Other relevant records of the Shelley circle are in the journals and letters of Maria Gisborne and Edward Williams, edited by Jones in 1951, and in *The Journals of Claire Clairmont, 1814–1827,* expertly rendered by Marion Kingston Stocking with the assistance of David Mackenzie Stocking (1968). The Stockings are currently preparing an edition of the letters of Charles and Claire Clairmont and of Fanny Godwin, which will presumably subsume the relevant parts of *Shelley and Mary,* otherwise unavailable elsewhere until now. (The Godwin letters in this collection have never been independently edited.)

The previous edition of this bibliography began and ended the commentary on texts by emphasizing that they were in a state of flux. The most sanguine view that one can express more than a decade later would celebrate an edition of the complete prose by Murray and Webb that is not yet published; an edition of the poetry, the Reiman-Powers, that is necessarily incomplete and lacking textual apparatus; and two further volumes of *Shelley and His Circle* in print that make one only impatient for the other half of the series still to come. And then there is the new Oxford edition of the poetry, also half in print, whose virtues are so heavily offset by major shortcomings that one looks to future volumes with trepidation. In short, all is still flux. And the best advice one can offer anyone working on Shelley is that there is no way of reading what he wrote or of interpreting it responsibly without mastering the complexities of the present state of the text and compensating as shrewdly as possible for its inadequacies. *Caveat lector—caveat scriptor.*

Biography

From the perspective of history the early biographies of Shelley by his friends are almost more informative by their incompatibility than by their recital of indisputable fact or the insights of propinquity. Taken together with the fragmenting of his Italian circle after his death and the almost incestuous attempt to recreate it (the prime example being the startling marriage of Jane Williams and Thomas Jefferson Hogg), the early lives reveal a magnetic personality less forceful perhaps than Byron's but just as indomitable and ultimately as unfathomable. Shelley's power over his associates in death, one is tempted to say, was even more dynamic than in life.

Donald H. Reiman in the previous edition of this bibliography ably discriminated among the early biographies, citing relevant commentary on them by contemporaries and later scholars. To his chronological list of Mary Shelley (1824, 1839), Thomas Medwin (1833, 1847), Thomas Jefferson Hogg (1858), Lady Jane Shelley (1859), Edward John Trelawny (1858; rewritten in 2 vols, 1878), and Thomas Love Peacock (1858–62), one should perhaps add the first account by a close friend, the extended tribute by Leigh Hunt in *Lord Byron and Some of His Contemporaries* (1828), and the one least tainted by literary controversy, Horace Smith's "A Graybeard's Gossip about His Literary Acquaintances," published in the *New Monthly Magazine* (Oct. and Nov. 1847). All but the last of these are partial, more or less self-aggrandizing, and devoted to a particular aspect of the "Shelley legend"; even Smith shares with the others a limited period of true intimacy with his subject. Mary Shelley, constrained by Sir Timothy's control over her annuity, added circumspection to her hagiographic remembrances. Hunt used his brother radical's humanity and selflessness as a stick with which simultaneously to pummel reactionaries at home and Lord Byron in the grave. Medwin, who grew up with Shelley in Sussex but had virtually nothing to do with the adult Shelley before reappearing less than two years before his death, proclaimed him a Platonist, his meager stone being responsible for a subsequent avalanche. Hogg, Shelley's bosom associate for the few months at Oxford, whom the mature Shelley distanced with increasing caution, was by the time of his biography a stuffy, conservative barrister, whose self-congratulatory common sense demanded a caricatured "poet" as foil. The *Shelley Memorials* of Lady Jane Shelley constitute a Victorian family record, written against Hogg and rigorously protective, as if the baronetcy had descended directly from the poet rather than from Sir Timothy. The macho Trelawny, that wonderful fictionalist of Shelley's life and others', knew Shelley for the poet's last nine months and bought the gravesite next to his as if to protect him for eternity: that, at least, is the sensibility of the recollections. Only Peacock, outraged like the family over Hogg's caricature, attempts to "see

Shelley plain"; and his well-rounded portrait would seem to overcome the limitation of Shelley's necessary distancing in Italy, did not Hogg set the agenda and Peacock's partiality to the memory of Harriet, Shelley's first wife, continually intrude. Among the numerous biographies of later Victorians, well characterized by Reiman, the great monument is clearly Edward Dowden's *Life* (2 vols., 1886). Dowden was a scholar by profession and a writer of gifts, who was still able to document the life from associates of Shelley. Moreover, the family gave him access to its archives so that he could produce a standard, objective life of the poet. Such a standard life in Victorian England almost naturally demanded the suppression of evidence.

This brief survey, even omitting significant portions of the nineteenth century and the whole of twentieth-century biographical accounts (including what remains the standard measure, Newman Ivey White's massive two-volume *Shelley* of 1940, rev. 1947), goes far to explain the single recent biography, *Shelley; the Pursuit* by Richard Holmes (1974). Undoubtedly, there is a stunning incongruity between Shelley's unconventional and even tumultuous life and the attempts to render it saintly or bookishly dignified. Holmes's major effort is to limn a recognizably human portrait, and in large part he succeeds admirably. At the same time, paradoxically, the steadfast refusal to suppress evidence and a continual urge to debunk encrusted myths can themselves lead to gross distortion, as Holmes accentuates every unpaid bill, every flare of passion, every indication of obsessive behavior. Some highly respected scholars (e.g., Cameron in his detailed critique in *KSJ,* 1976) have taken strong exception to the tendentiousness of the argument and the journalistic profile that it often serves. Lifelike it is, but it is rather the life of soap operas—and is it Shelley? There are two unresolved enigmas in Shelley's life to which Holmes pays very close attention: the alleged assassination attempt in Wales and the "Neapolitan charge." Holmes is willing to credit the basic truth of the Welsh adventure, buttressing his argument by measuring the rooms of Tan-yr-allt (seemingly the only evidence of original research in the book). The result is impressive, though it has not been universally convincing. But the argument that in December 1818 both Elise Foggi, the Shelleys' servant, and Claire Clairmont gave birth to children, the latter stillborn, fathered by Shelley is ingenious to the point of being preposterous. In indulging such urges toward the sensational, Holmes loses the authority one must demand of a biographer, as he also does in all his literary judgments. This is truly unfortunate, since Holmes had the opportunity, as he also possessed the talent, to write a biography that would define Shelley for this generation of his readers. Instead, any balanced perspective must return us to Newman Ivey White's somewhat ponderous, but richly detailed, judicious, and unslanted account of Shelley. If White at times seems far more the reserved scholar than one himself possessed of a Shelleyan temperament, he is trustworthy in regard to fact, as far as it was known nearly a half century ago.

Perhaps the closest we have to a later authoritative biography is represented in the first hundred pages of Kenneth Neill Cameron's *Shelley: The Golden Years* (1974), which picks up where *The Young Shelley: Genesis of a Radical* (1950)—itself crucial for the period of Shelley's childhood and adolescence—left off.

Cameron is especially attuned to Shelley the political thinker, and his strong sense of the public person usefully counterbalances Holmes's more internalized portrayal. Cameron's more particularized biographical studies are scattered throughout the first four volumes of *Shelley and His Circle*. Some of these, including his accounts of associates like Godwin and Hunt, are gathered with contributions by other authors—Eleanor Nicholes on Mary Wollstonecraft and Peacock, Sylva Norman on Mary Shelley, and David Erdman on Byron are most noteworthy—under the title *Romantic Rebels* (1973). By no means does this exhaust the biographical value of *Shelley and His Circle*—Cameron's account, in volume 3, of the carriage Harriet wanted skillfully weaves from ephemeral documents an incisive depiction of a foredoomed marriage—but for those who cannot afford the complete series for their personal libraries, *Romantic Rebels* is a valuable anthology. The same tradition continues in the later volumes of this series, as is evident from Donald H. Reiman's impressive essay on the relations of Shelley and Keats in volume 5. One might also note here that *Shelley and His Circle* is turning out to contain a greater wealth about minor literary figures of the time than, perhaps, any publication since the *DNB*.

In recent years there have been several additions to the biographical record not yet assimilated into general writing on the poet and his circle. Sally Hand has traced Shelley's incongruous American roots to the extent that early records allow in "Timothy Shelley, 'Merchant of Newark': The Search for Shelley's American Ancestor" (*KSJ*, 1980). The Irish political milieu into which Shelley intruded himself in 1812 has been greatly illuminated by P. M. S. Dawson in "Shelley and the Irish Catholics in 1812" (*KSMB*, 1978; subsumed within *The Unacknowledged Legislator*, 1980) and by E. B. Murray in "The Trial of Mr. Perry, Lord Eldon, and Shelley's *Address to the Irish*" (*SIR*, 1978). Phillips G. Davies has called attention to a local murder as part of the background to the episode at Tan-yr-allt (*KSMB*, 1972). Emily Sunstein's shrewd detective work has led to identification of "Louise Duvillard of Geneva, the Shelleys' Nursemaid" (*KSJ*, 1980), with implications detracting from Holmes's supposition—following Ursula Orange, "Elise, Nursemaid to the Shelleys" (*KSMB*, 1955)—that Shelley fathered a child by her. John Buxton has followed his genial *Byron and Shelley* (1968) with an essay, "Greece in the Imagination of Byron and Shelley" (*ByronJ*, 1976), that forms part of his *The Grecian Taste: Literature in the Age of Neo-Classicism, 1740–1820* (1978). On Shelley's relations with Byron both C. L. Cline's *Byron, Shelley, and Their Pisan Circle* (1952) and William H. Marshall's *Byron, Shelley, Hunt, and the "Liberal"* (1960) retain value. Charles E. Robinson's acute sense of detail in *Shelley and Byron: The Snake and Eagle Wreathed in Fight* (1976), more concerned with subtleties of literary interaction, creates by far the best chronicle of their association. At times, especially in his speculations on the anxiety Byron caused Shelley in his last months, the study is provocative rather than definitive, but the scholarship is meticulous and the attempt to read the nuances of the poets' interior lives is continually probing. Erwin Anton Stürzl reviews all such accounts of the two poets (*ByronJ*, 1979), then undertakes a brisk tour of the subject himself. The authoritative writing on the Shelleys' Swiss sojourn has been contributed by Gavin de Beer, especially in volumes 3 and 4 of *Shelley and His Circle*. Ronald Tetreault compares the reactions of the two poets in "Shelley and Byron Encounter the Sublime: Switzerland, 1816" (*RLV,* 1975). P. M. S. Dawson argues that Shelley's view of Keats was influenced by Byron in "Byron, Shelley, and the 'New School,'" published among the proceedings of the first two international Shelley conferences (1978 and 1980) at Gregynog, Wales, *Shelley Revalued* (ed. Kelvin Everest, 1983).

Shelley's relations with Mary have received considerable attention in the upsurge of interest in her writing, much of it, though, through a risible distortion of the record. One might single out as an example Christopher Small's *Mary Shelley's* Frankenstein: *Tracing the Myth* (1973; published in England as *Ariel like a Harpy: Shelley, Mary, and* Frankenstein, 1972, where Mary does not even get top billing). Small identifies Victor Frankenstein with "the Shelleyan ideal" and then barges through the life and rummages the works to present Shelley as an untrustworthy neurotic unable to cope with reality. The portrait is more extreme even than Hogg's but otherwise is written to the same formulaic script, with Mary cast as the sensible contrast, her feet on the ground, able unlike her husband to confront the ambiguities of life. It is amazing how often such willful misrepresentations of Shelley figure in writing on Mary; but it should be observed as well that Mary's husband has always had a distorting effect on her biography. With the completion of Betty T. Bennett's edition of Mary's letters it will be possible to assess her entire life afresh. That is the admirable motive behind at least one major biography (by Emily Sunstein) currently under way. In the meantime, to the books on Mary by R. Glynn Grylls (1938), Elizabeth Nitchie (1953), and Jean de Palacio (1970) should be added Noel Gerson's *Daughter of Air and Water* (1973) and Jane Dunn's *Moon in Eclipse* (1978), both written for the general reader and adding nothing to the record, and William Walling's *Mary Shelley* (1972), a biocritical study of economical excellence. *Mary Shelley: An Annotated Bibliography* compiled by W. H. Lyles (1975) is a welcome reference tool, and its minor weaknesses in regard to the shorter fiction are repaired by the bibliography assembled by Charles E. Robinson in *Mary Shelley: Collected Tales and Stories* (1976).

Except for the Stockings' edition of the *Journals,* nothing has been added to the essential record on Claire Clairmont, daughter of Godwin's second wife, compiled by R. Glynn Grylls (1939) and Iris Origo (*A Measure of Love,* 1957). G. M. Matthews has sensitively illuminated the effect of the suicide of Mary's sister, Fanny Godwin, on Shelley in "Whose Little Footsteps? Three Shelley Pieces Re-Addressed" in the Cameron festschrift, *Evidence of the Imagination,* edited by Reiman et al., a model for the application of biographical knowledge to literary texts. Don Locke's *A Fantasy of Reason: The Life and Thought of William Godwin* (1980) adds little to our understanding of Shelley's relationship with Godwin, but it is interesting to have the relationship rehearsed from Godwin's perspective. Similarly, Shelley looms large in Marilyn Butler's brilliant *Peacock Displayed: A Satirist in His Context* (1979), which more than the studies by Howard Mills and Carl Dawson, both good books, emphasizes the intellectual and ideological grounds for the rich friendship of Shelley and Peacock: its many virtues are replicated in her "Myth and Mythmaking in the Shelley Circle" (*ELH,* 1982), which explores what Shelley learned from Peacock. Sylva Norman has added greatly to our knowledge of Peacock after Shelley left his circle, in "Peacock in Leadenhall Street," published in volume 6 of *Shelley and His Circle*. In volume 5 of this collection there is a similarly distinguished estimate of the life and career of Edward John Trelawny by R. Glynn Grylls, somewhat updating her full-length biography of 1950. The most recent account of this fascinating man, *Trelawny: The Incurable Romancer* by William St. Clair (1977), has more documents to rely on than any previous life, yet must fill the still large and, it would appear, deliberate lacunae with sometimes ingenious research into such matters as the life of midshipmen during the Regency. Another of the curious figures in Shelley's life about which much too little has been known is the publisher for most of his mature writing, Charles Ollier, about whom Charles E. Robinson generously educates us. His documentation of Ollier's extensive association with Blackwood's—published in *Shelley Revalued* (1983)—helps explain the favorable reviews Shelley received from that archly conservative journal. Other associates of the poet's in Italy have been portrayed in now standard books: Elizabeth Nitchie, *The Reverend Colonel Finch* (1940); Edward C. McAleer, *The Sensitive Plant: A Life of Lady Mount Cashell* (1958), and Ernest J. Lovell, *Captain Medwin* (1962). The endearing intelligence and charm of Lady Mount Cashell (Mrs. Mason) are embodied in the witty verses she wrote on Shelley's aversion to the pious Reverend Dr. Nott, who preached to the English in Pisa in 1822: Paula Feldman presents these in "Shelley, Mrs. Mason and the Devil Incarnate: An Unpublished Poem" (*LCUT,* 1979). There are two additions to our knowledge of Shelley's last weeks. Diana Pugh suggests professional reputation as the reason for aspersions of foul play traceable to the builder of his boat in "Captain Roberts and the Sinking of the *Don Juan*" (*KSMB,* 1975). Stuart Curran transcribes and comments on three letters of Horace Smith, relating, among other news, accounts of the Shelleys and then the poet's death to an English friend. These merely confirm our knowledge but reaffirm as well how much Shelley was of interest to liberal-minded English contemporaries. See "The View from Versailles: Horace Smith on the Literary Scene of 1822" (*HLQ,* 1977).

Criticism

THE CRITICAL FOUNDATION

The past fifteen years have been for the study of Shelley's works and thought, as for all of English Romanticism, a period of rapid development and healthy invigoration. So intense has it been that the emerging discourse sometimes seems to have little in common with the consolidated picture of Shelley the historically minded critic draws from the burst of activity that followed World War II. Yet, even as this new generation of scholars and interpreters rejects many of the conclusions (and not a few of the premises) of its predecessors, in other respects it is indebted to the pioneering work that sought a consistent, intellectually valid definition of Shelleyan thought to replace the vague, flighty, and morally irresponsible figure inherited from Babbitt, Eliot, Leavis, and their followers. Timothy

Webb's opening chapter in *Shelley: A Voice Not Understood* (1977) provides the most recent account of ideological and critical distortions visited on Shelley by the New Humanists and New Critics. Webb was preceded by sharp rejoinders issued in C. S. Lewis' "Shelley, Dryden, and Mr. Eliot" (*Rehabilitations*, 1939), Frederick Pottle's "The Case of Shelley" (*PMLA*, 1952), and G. M. Matthews' "Shelley's Lyrics," included among the essays celebrating G. Wilson Knight, *The Morality of Art*, edited by D. W. Jefferson (1969). While such devastating counterarguments revealed the inadequacy in critical penetration and judgment of those who attacked Shelley, other critics set to work to represent a poet rather more secure from attack.

For a full account of the critical perspective from the 1940s to the mid-1960s, the reader should consult Kenneth Neill Cameron's "Shelley Scholarship, 1940–1953" (*KSJ*, 1954) and the lucid presentation of Donald H. Reiman in the third edition of this bibliography. From a later vantage point one can see the consolidation of Shelley studies in this period as frequently incorporating a defensive posture in formulations as distorted in their way as those of Eliot and Leavis. Confronted by such conservative moral earnestness, Shelley's own moral earnestness was firmly, if speciously, grounded in Plato. Nothing could be more conservative than to juxtapose Shelley's deep knowledge of Greek against the Horatian pretensions of his detractors or to enforce a systematic Platonism as having priority over Eliot's Anglo-Catholicism. The line of thought initiated by Thomas Medwin in the first full-scale biography was promoted by Carl Grabo, a truly singular scholar, whose *The Magic Plant* (1936) was the defining study for more than a decade, then fully consolidated in Joseph Barrell's setting of the Greek revival against the French philosophes in *Shelley and the Thought of His Time* (1947), in Carlos Baker's attempt to set Shelley within traditional modes of thought and literature in *Shelley's Major Poetry: The Fabric of a Vision* (1948), and in James A. Notopoulos' *The Platonism of Shelley* (1949). Each of these works retains its value: Barrell for his recognition of the philosophical complexities converging on Shelley; Baker for his source studies and his application of Renaissance literary values to Shelley's writing; Notopoulos for bringing together Shelley's translations of Plato. But each also uses a vague conception of Platonic essences as a means of begging major questions; and the appearance of such influential studies within three years established patterns of thought that became endemic to Shelley criticism within the next decade. Platonism is an assumed premise in Neville Rogers' *Shelley at Work: A Critical Inquiry* (1956; rev. 1967) as in all Rogers' later writing on Shelley, in Milton Wilson's *Shelley's Later Poetry* (1959), in David Perkins' *The Quest for Permanence: The Symbolism of Wordsworth, Shelley, and Keats* (1959), and, converted to the more slippery mysticism of Orphic thought, in Ross Woodman's *The Apocalyptic Vision in the Poetry of Shelley* (1964). These are all valuable books, contributing enduring ideas for the understanding of Shelley's art and its contexts; yet one recognizes that the combined effect was to render Shelley an angel, effectual only in aesthetic terms, committed to universal ideals rather than minute particulars, to eternity rather than mortal time—a Novalis without Christianity.

Two contrary movements in Shelley studies existed simultaneously with, and frequently without relation to, this placing of Shelley "far in the Unapparent." The one has, until very recently, been the domain of one master scholar, Kenneth Neill Cameron, who in two books and in a remarkably varied flood of major articles has repeatedly called attention to the political radical's commitment to the renovation of his society in every aspect. *The Young Shelley: Genesis of a Radical* (1950) retains all its early freshness and enthusiasm and is still perhaps the finest analysis of the development of the revolutionary ideas that coalesced in *Queen Mab*. Reverting to the dichotomy of influences defined by Barrell, one realizes that for Cameron Shelley's principal education was in the French tradition to which his adherence never faltered. This Shelley is a proto-Marxist, a materialist and a necessitarian, England's greatest propagandist for the ideals of the French Revolution and an artist and thinker best understood within the political and philosophical agitation of his time. In *The Young Shelley* and *Shelley: The Golden Years* (1974), which absorbs many of the relevant intermediate essays, Cameron pursues this aspect of Shelley relentlessly, coming down hard on one side of much-disputed issues (e.g., necessitarianism) and with minutely documented knowledge of the intellectual and political ferment of the time. Looking back a generation from the present vantage point, one thinks of Cameron wading through a sea of Platonists in the style of his great precursor as a proselyte for the socialist Shelley, G. B. Shaw, who in "Shaming the Devil about Shelley" (1892; printed years later in *Pen Portraits and Reviews,* 1932) recounts attending the dignified, even rarefied, official celebration of Shelley's centenary in the afternoon and a boisterous workingman's tribute from old Chartists and new Marxists in the evening.

Perhaps it was the recognition that the debate between socialists and Platonists had a decidedly Victorian ring to it—these were more or less the factions of the short-lived Shelley Society in London during the 1880s and 1890s—that prompted more particular attention to the intricacies of and interconnections between Shelley's artistic means and his philosophical thinking. Or perhaps there was an implicit understanding that not everyone is either an Aristotelian or a Platonist. In 1954 appeared two very different but ultimately complementary studies of seminal importance for modern Shelley criticism: Peter Butter's *Shelley's Idols of the Cave* and C. E. Pulos' *The Deep Truth: A Study of Shelley's Scepticism.* Butter's concern, somewhat in the line of Richard Harter Fogle's *The Imagery of Keats and Shelley* (1949), was with recurring symbolic and mythic patterns in Shelley's poetry, which he traced, independent of extra-artistic grounding, as pure exercises of the imagination. The aesthetic adventurer through these "countries of the mind," as one of Butter's chapter titles puts it, has curious affinities with the philosophical thinker depicted by Pulos, balanced between empirical and idealist traditions and profoundly influenced by his reading of Sir William Drummond's calm explosion of all philosophical dogmas in *Academical Questions* (1805). Pulos' short monograph, establishing Shelley as intellectual explorer of possibilities, as alive to all traditions but committed to no single dogma, and as a consistent and sophisticated philosophical thinker, is the keystone of virtually all subsequent Shelley scholarship, bearing an anomalous weight on its slight but eminently solid balance. The bulk of modern Shelley criticism has been engendered by the joining of the perspectives of Butter and Pulos, fusing the free artist and free intellectual. The immediate effect of such a juncture, almost of necessity, was two books in the same year (1959) that simply altered the terms of discourse, Harold Bloom's *Shelley's Mythmaking* and Earl R. Wasserman's *The Subtler Language: Critical Readings of Neo-Classic and Romantic Poems*. So much has in the intervening years been added to Bloom's early exploration of the mythopoeic impulses of Shelley's art that his explanation of the process in terms of dissolving distinctions between self and other, insistently invoking Martin Buber on the differences between I-It and I-Thou, seems somewhat mechanical and reductive. (The new Bloom, who sees all of Shelley in terms of an alleged anxiety over Wordsworth, is perhaps open to the same charge.) *Shelley's Mythmaking*, however, both in its sensitivity to literary values and its charting of a dialectical pattern in which the poet drives toward and retreats from his mythopoeic ideal, was a liberating force for further scholarship. So, it goes without saying, was Wasserman's *Subtler Language*. The essays on "Mont Blanc," "The Sensitive Plant," and *Adonais*, set alongside others on Denham, Dryden, and Pope, at once established a new standard for the reading of Shelley. Though essentially a historian of ideas, Wasserman set out as if he were the last of the New Critics to explore and colonize the worlds of these poems, establishing a methodology so penetrating and perspicacious that, with this single publication, the New Critical attack on Shelley was silenced—indeed, put to shame. Wasserman here manifested his peculiar greatness as Shelley critic, reading with such analytical penetration that, whether his ingenious imagination overwhelmed his text with complexity or his thesis was actively resisted by it, as often happened, it scarcely mattered. With his rigorous philosophical precision, extensive learning, and critical acumen a new measure was set for Shelley criticism. Later commentators could take exception to stretched interpretations—for instance, an alleged contradiction between the first two stanzas of "Mont Blanc"—or to a methodological narrowness that excluded biographical and political concerns, but Shelley had been proved more than a match for Wasserman's intellectual sophistication. This element above others established the firm foundation for modern Shelley criticism.

MAJOR STUDIES

This section, somewhat arbitrarily, will limit its scope to books of the past two decades whose aim has been to make a large critical statement about Shelley's art and thought. Those of more limited pretensions, many of them excellent, and all essays, again some of them of considerable influence, are reserved for later sections. This arrangement, then, is no indication of comparative value but is simply a means to chart with relative ease the course of recent developments in Shelley studies.

James Rieger's *The Mutiny Within: The Heresies of Percy Bysshe Shelley* (1967) is not the simplest work with which to begin, though chronology insists on it. Writing stylishly about the most esoteric matters, Rieger is alternatingly brilliant and mystifying. Although he sees Shelley as beginning and ending with the Socratic maxim that one knows only that one knows nothing, Rieger means "heresy" seriously. His Shelley is less an adherent of Platonism than of the Neoplatonic and Gnostic heresies of the early church, deeply questioning the efficacy of life in this world or the value of art, driven finally to suicide. This is a refined version of Benjamin Kurtz's comparatively silly *The Pursuit of Death: A Study of Shelley's Poetry* (1933), but it cannot free itself of the tendentious demands of its thesis. Rieger's study shines with certain poems where the context is relevant and Shelley's knowledge of the esoteric can be substantiated—especially with *The Cenci* and the "Ode to the West Wind"—but he credits Shelley with a contemporary rather than early nineteenth-century access to knowledge of the heretical, and his portrayal of a self-contradictory poet willfully engaging in obscurantism is inherently unattractive to the modern impulse to demonstrate Shelley's breadth and intellectual consistency. Rieger's argument for suicide has been meticulously rebutted by other scholars.

Donald H. Reiman's study of "The Triumph of Life" is discussed in a subsequent section; his *Percy Bysshe Shelley* (1969) sets the paradigm for what can be accomplished within the strict limitations of the Twayne English Authors Series. Constrained by brevity and a chronological assimilation of biography and literary criticism so that there is neither leisure to pause nor room to expatiate, Reiman's study is the best general introduction to Shelley within such limits. The approach is centrist, honoring the social activist, the philosophical speculator, and the artist equally and offering economical interpretive readings with ample citation of requisite scholarship. Historically speaking, this study actually demonstrated for the first time the value of the skeptical thesis of Pulos for viewing Shelley whole (and, one might add, healthy). It is by its very nature an effort of consolidation: the kinds of disturbing questions raised by Rieger, whatever Reiman might think of them, really can have no place in such a treatment.

Judith Chernaik's *The Lyrics of Shelley* (1972) shares this sense of humane balance. Although its subject excludes much of Shelley's major poetry, Chernaik shrewdly compensates by conceiving of the lyrics as a distillation of the full range of Shelley's distinctive concerns. Sensitive reading abounds, but what gives Chernaik's study an importance beyond her unfailingly intelligent criticism is her recognition of how self-conscious of his role as poet Shelley was and how, in exploring its possibilities, he found imaginative freedom and fulfillment. The second half of *The Lyrics of Shelley* is devoted to the textual analyses recommended earlier. The critical section, straightforwardly honoring the breadth of Shelley's claims as lyricist, forms a compact, unified, and undogmatic statement about his mind and art.

Earl R. Wasserman's *Shelley: A Critical Reading* (1971) could not be more opposite in its approach. A great sprawl of a book, incorporating virtually everything the author had written previously on Shelley, Wasserman's summa raises far more questions than it can resolve, actually contradicts itself on the crucial issue of Shelley's belief in a transcendental reality, continually threatens to swamp its readers in metaphysical complexities, and even ignores Shelley's last major poem. Still, it is a work of continuous intellectual excitement with seminal power over the subsequent development of Shelley criticism. One might note, for the record, that Wasserman, apparently convinced by his critics, here suppresses his argument for discrepancies in the opening lines of "Mont Blanc"; less happily, he also suppresses from his treatment of "The Sensitive Plant" in *The Subtler Language* the stimulating discussion of Spenser's influence on Shelley. The section on *Adonais* is virtually the same and stands even today, thirty years after its first version (*ELH,* 1954), as the richest and deepest statement on that poem ever written. From his important essay "Shelley's Last Poetics" (published in *From Sensibility to Romanticism,* ed. Harold Bloom and Frederick Hilles, 1965) Wasserman adapts the discussion of *A Defence of Poetry* but deletes his account of the supposed dialogue between Byron and Shelley on *Hamlet.* Everything substantial in Wasserman's study of *Shelley's* Prometheus Unbound (1965), however, is included and added to in *Shelley: A Critical Reading.*

Though individual interpretations are incorporated in a subsequent section, a general perspective on Wasserman's influential study can indicate its main lines of development and the values it upholds. Continually distinguishing Shelley's dual (and increasingly troubling) commitments to an objective world in need of reform and the mind's vulnerable creative energies, Wasserman emphasizes a wide-ranging skepticism that represents a continual struggle to find a point of rest between dynamic contradictions. The first of four sections is devoted to this restless skepticism, in which Wasserman draws together such works as the early "Refutation of Deism," "Alastor," "Julian and Maddalo," and *The Cenci* as metaphysical dialogues exploring conflicting impulses with a compassionate awareness of human imperatives. The second broad section, "Speculations on Metaphysics," involves a painstaking—some would say intellectually painful—analysis of Shelley's "intellectual philosophy," whose metaphysical abstractions based on the prose just manage not to overwhelm the poems included. Part 3, "The Poetry of Idealism: Utopia," assimilates the earlier reading of *Prometheus Unbound* with the most extensive commentary on *Hellas* yet written. The last section, "The Poetry of Idealism: Immortality," uses *Epipsychidion* and *Adonais* to argue for the force of Shelley's longing for a transcendental absolute in the late poems. That weight, however, tends to ignore Shelley's continuing social preoccupations and to obviate the earlier arguments for skepticism. One might conclude that Wasserman wants it both ways, which itself might suggest the extent to which Shelley did. The all-but-contradiction arising from such equal stress on utopian and immortal longings is potentially confusing to readers who wish less ambiguous conclusions than Wasserman finally allows, but it cannot detract from the accumulated intricacy of Wasserman's readings or the massive learning by which they are buttressed. Disagreements abound among his successors, but Wasserman's *Shelley: A Critical Reading* has established many of the grounds over which the primary disputes of contemporary Shelley studies are waged.

Kenneth Neill Cameron's *Shelley: The Golden Years* (1974) has already been mentioned in several contexts. Of even greater length than Wasserman's, this study of Shelley after *Queen Mab* represents a powerful counterweight to Wasserman's idealist and interiorized vision of Shelley. The first hundred pages, as noted, constitute a sane and unsensational biographical account, and details from the biography, and with it the contemporary social picture, continually reinforce Cameron's criticism. Cameron is unable to conceive of Shelley outside of a grounded historical context, and where that position coincides with Shelley's own artistic imperatives, Cameron is an impressive commentator, lucidly bringing together the necessary contexts to enliven his subject historically. With some poems—for example, *Prometheus Unbound* as an allegory of the French Revolution—the interpretive stance seems unnecessarily narrow; with others, mainly lyrics, the approach offers Cameron little opportunity for more than paraphrase. Cameron is a true master of modern Shelley criticism: his nearly hundred pages of finely printed footnotes are a compendium of what has been thought on Shelley and a goldmine of relevant historical documentation. Cameron, aiming to unify his important research from the past, probably breaks less new ground than Wasserman does; but where Wasserman is unnecessarily intricate or introverted or simply speculative, Cameron (perhaps in tacit defiance) returns us to a solid, historically valid base.

Stuart Curran's *Shelley's Annus Mirabilis: The Maturing of an Epic Vision* (1975), by contrast, is dedicated to Wasserman's memory (he died in 1973) and is intended in part as a friendly correction of Wasserman's approach to Shelley's canon. Although concentrating on the great outpouring of writing from the autumn of 1818 through early 1820, this study is actually concerned with Shelley up through *Prometheus Unbound.* Instead of seeing Shelley increasingly split between contradictory allegiances, Curran observes him overcoming the inner contradictions that plagued his early efforts to forge a coherent epic vision, *Queen Mab* and *The Revolt of Islam,* and doing so by aspiring to create an undogmatic and humanist equivalent to the epic range of Dante and Milton. His "Hell is a city much like London," as he puts it in "Peter Bell the Third"; and in that poem, "Julian and Maddalo," and *The Cenci* Curran sees Shelley anatomizing a culture whose structures enclose and necessarily corrupt its denizens. Curran suggests that the numerous similarities between *The Cenci* and *Prometheus Unbound* are a means of contrasting this self-defeating inferno with a realizable paradise, both being products of human will. The purgatorial struggle of the poet to convert the one to the other is represented as the central focus of the odes of this period—"Ode to the West Wind," "Ode to Liberty," "Ode to Naples"—and of such political writings as "The Mask of Anarchy" and the "Philosophical View of Reform" later recast into *A Defence of Poetry.* Curran thus asserts a unified and temperamentally dialectical vision able to subsume contraries (including Shelley's own dual impulses to artistic creativity and social reform) and a vision that constitutes itself through a deliberate assimilation of the crucial structures of Western art, philosophy, science, and religion. The emphasis here on the informing power of syncretic mythology—classical, Christian, Indian, and especially Zoroastrian—in *Prometheus Unbound, The Cenci,* and "Ode to the West Wind" is massively documented.

Charles E. Robinson's *Shelley and Byron: The Snake and Eagle Wreathed in Fight* (1976) takes its subtitle from the first canto of *The Revolt of Islam,* thus signaling its primary concern with Shelley. By means of his intimate documentary knowledge and a delicate sensitivity to verbal echoes and structural parallels,

Robinson is able for the first time to suggest the remarkable extent to which these two poets played off against each other's writings. At first, Robinson argues, Shelley continually invokes an idealist's perspective against Byron's fatalism; but in the late years, the balance tends to reverse, with Byron turning to the comic epic and romance as Shelley increasingly stressed human and imaginative limitations. The underlying thesis is just and the scholarship impeccable, but Robinson does tend to chart the relationship as more an antagonism than the facts warrant and sees the literary dialogue in rather strong moralistic terms. The portrait of Shelley in his last year as being overwhelmed by Byron's presence in a classic anxiety of influence is the most provocative aspect of the study, one to which some critics have taken strong exception. But there is bound to be room for disagreement where such a previously unexplored and rich area for criticism as this literary relationship exists. It is very much to Robinson's credit that one can draw different conclusions on the strength of his meticulously presented and continually illuminating evidence, which unquestionably establishes this relationship as one very much like that of Wordsworth and Coleridge, at once fruitful and psychologically troubling.

With *Shelley: A Voice Not Understood* (1977) Timothy Webb ended the anomalous twenty-year hiatus of major British studies of Shelley. Like Reiman's, though it is organized around subject rather than chronology, this is an exemplary introduction to Shelley. Its polemical opening chapter may represent the last time that Eliot, Leavis, and their company need to be taken head-on; but the very silence of Britain on Shelley is perhaps the strongest indication of why Webb felt the necessity for such an assault on various misunderstandings of Shelley's aims and achievements. Webb's perspective coalesces around Shelley as a farsighted cultural thinker, whose visionary ideas are solidly based in traditional knowledge, whether he means to subvert it or, as is more often true, to invoke it in order to confront and educate his present culture. This is an admirably and comfortably learned book, but for all its understanding of and respect for Shelley's own learning, its most salutary aspect may be its insistence on Shelley's practicality and on the pervasive importance of a political stance in all his writing. The study includes an especially salient discussion of Shelley's balanced critique and celebration of Christian and Greek thought.

Webb's Shelley is a strong optimist, a public spokesman for a counterculture with numerous and vital roots. The poet delineated in Lloyd Abbey's *Destroyer and Preserver: Shelley's Poetic Skepticism* (1979) is virtually the opposite, one whose "career is a demonstrative exercise in self-destruction or, at least, self-repudiation," who is so tormented by the skepticism he is bound to embrace that it at last renders his social vision and his imaginative celebration alike hollow. This is an extreme view to be drawn from a reading of only eight poems. The thesis is really centered on "The Triumph of Life" as a profoundly pessimistic culmination of Shelley's life, and the clarity of Abbey's approach allows him to provide an exceptionally fine articulation of the complexities of imagery and structure in Shelley's last major poem. So driven a thesis, however, forces what many readers will see as a distortion of the last two acts of *Prometheus Unbound* as an ironic, static dream. More troubling perhaps is the very conceptual structure of the book, which, ostensibly tracing the impact of skeptical thinking in Shelley, differentiates between an "empirical skepticism" about the grounds of knowledge and a "Platonic skepticism" in which one might recognize what Abbey calls "eternal Forms" but be unable to represent them adequately. "Platonic skepticism" is by its nature a contradiction in terms, and frequently Abbey confuses issues by a facile use of the phrase. His book is valuable for its recognition of pervasive patterns of mirroring in image and structure throughout the poetry, but an analysis so ostensibly philosophical needs greater precision than Abbey employs. It hardly need be said that an undifferentiated "skepticism" can be as reductive as the vague Platonism that now bears the onus of critical disrespect.

P. M. S. Dawson's *The Unacknowledged Legislator: Shelley and Politics* (1980) is the most recent of the several substantial attempts to ground Shelley's political thinking in the contexts of his time. Except for a valuable elucidation of the social vision underlying *Prometheus Unbound* and "The Triumph of Life," Dawson's concern is generally with Shelley's political prose. Since the bulk of that dates from Shelley's English years, there is something of a built-in imbalance to Dawson's undertaking that cannot really be rectified by the quick reading of late poems with which his study ends. It is at its best with the very early Shelley, demonstrating his allegiances to the specific program of the aristocratic Whigs (though Dawson sees him pointedly taking issue with their logical conclusions precisely where this liberal faction hedged), balancing with remarkable lucidity the rival claims of Thomas Paine and William Godwin on Shelley's attention, and deepening our knowledge of the complicated political matrix of Ireland into which Shelley inserted himself in 1812. Like Cameron and Gerald McNiece (*Shelley and the Revolutionary Idea,* 1969) before him, Dawson proves how much enlightenment for Shelley's writing is to be gained through a grounding in specific historical detail.

Michael Scrivener (*Radical Shelley: The Philosophical Anarchism and Utopian Thought of Percy Bysshe Shelley,* 1982) is wont to pay less attention to Shelley's place in mainstream liberal politics and much more to how he fits into the radical subculture of English Jacobinism. His book is a survey of Shelley's career from beginning to end, whose virtue is a completeness Dawson cannot match, but the corresponding flaw is a tendency to stretch into paraphrase of the writings that are peripheral to his focus. Scrivener is most enlightening where he extends his discussion into new territory, for instance, on Shelley as pamphleteer, and he pays more attention to the political prose than any previous full-length treatment has. The result is an often fruitful comparison with the major radical journalists of the Regency, from Leight Hunt to Cobbett and Hone.

With Richard Cronin's *Shelley's Poetic Thoughts* (1981) we have the first modern, full-length distillation of a subject in Shelley studies whose significance has increased markedly in recent years. Though the title might suggest a general interpretation, its terms are meant to convey Cronin's accentuation of linguistic and stylistic elements in Shelley's poetry. His introductory treatment of the philosophy of language in the century after Locke is especially valuable for being constantly pointed toward Shelley's practice. Cronin's interests range from minute examination of language and image patterns to an exploration of generic contexts of the poems. Though his large aim is to determine where and how Shelley successfully marries form and content, he is often most revealing in showing the linguistic strategies by which Shelley resists a closure of either language or form. As is the general practice of British criticism, there is a tendency here to sort out good and bad. Such a judgmental bias, the plague of Shelley criticism a generation ago, can be refined as it is here; but it still is open to question on the basis of the critic's operating assumptions and methodological slant, not to mention the mix of artistic and ideological contexts in which Shelley's poems were written, the audiences they were intended to reach, and like considerations.

Cronin's interests are duplicated and expanded by William Keach's *Shelley's Style* (1984), which is the latest of the major Shelley studies of this survey and among the very best. Keach knows Enlightenment linguistic theory thoroughly, and he sets Shelley in subtle ambivalence against it, beginning with a close examination of the near contradictions of the *Defence of Poetry,* then gradually subsuming the entire canon, and ending with a complex and moving account of the late lyrics. Keach's eyes and ears are uncommonly keen, and there is scarcely a page of his book that does not produce original insight. Though the title indicates the minute attention Keach devotes to matters of style, it does not suggest the largeness of his conceptual inquiry, which is as much philosophical as linguistic. Keach's ease with poststructuralist criticism portends a new phase of Shelley studies, where the relevance of such theoretical postulates can be taken for granted, even as they are themselves put to rigorous intellectual testing. And in revealing how significant is Shelley's attention to meter and rhyme, as well as figurative trope, Keach represents a unitary critical posture that is also a healthy portent of the future. So originally perceptive a book is bound to stimulate further exploration by other critics. To end with *Shelley's Style* is, in other words, to begin anew, implicitly acknowledging how far from exhausted are the energies of the new wave in Shelley criticism.

If one attempts to summarize so diverse a group of general studies, one recognizes that all share a healthy respect for Shelley's open-minded growth, his refusal to dogmatize, and the artistry he sought to accommodate to an imaginative and intellectual freedom. Cameron, Dawson, and Scrivener honor the principles underlying Shelley's political thought, but each emphasizes his latitude as to strategy and his sensible acknowledgment of short-term aims. Cronin and Keach, rather interestingly, apply a similar approach in dealing with the interior organization of the poetry. Reiman, Chernaik, and Webb portray an essentially healthy mind whose analytic powers serve a practical humanism. Curran, laying greater stress on Shelley's preoccupation with evil and its purgatorial cost, nonetheless celebrates Shelley's dialectical openness to experience. If a darker portrait emerges from the career as seen by Rieger and Abbey and in the latter part of Wasserman's book, still the constant is a skeptical attitude toward dogmatic fixities, the dimensions of which Shelley, in this view, found increasingly comprehensive and thus increasingly problematic. None of these approaches, however they may conflict in their particular emphases, reverts to the old pattern of recording

Shelley's beliefs or reducing him to a systematic scheme. That Shelley's breadth of concerns—aesthetic, philosophical, psychological, political, and of course personal—is difficult to focus within a single unified perspective is indubitable; but the general studies of the recent past seem united in their willingness, like the figure they portray, to explore without blinkered constraints.

SHELLEY'S THOUGHT

Recent full-length treatments of Shelley have had the effect of enlarging our sense of the complexities of his thought and art by liberating him and the discourse about him from the common reductive biases of the past. Yet, there remains an obvious problem. If earlier generations of readers were wont to derive schematic systems of belief from Shelley, they did not exactly create them—or at least all of them—out of thin air. How does one reconcile his broad skepticism with the ideas promulgated through his writings? And, furthermore, is there a continuity between the early Shelley, who wrote a socialist manifesto in the notes to *Queen Mab,* and the Shelley of "The Triumph of Life," whom critics increasingly see as displaying the insubstantiality of all codified systems? These and their corollaries are still vexed questions, and the lack of easy solution suggests both the value of a grain of salt in discussions of what Shelley thought and the need for greater sophistication.

That Shelley thought uncommonly well and often is now undisputed. His fluency in seven languages, his accumulation of learning, and his range of interests, all suggestive of a latter-day Renaissance man, are daunting to his interpreters. Equally daunting are seeming inconsistencies—between rival philosophical systems, between the continual assertion of progress and the veneration for classical Greece (or between the very notion of progress and his diatribes against the inadequacies of English and European society), between his optimistic vision of human liberation and his clear obsession with evil (or between the very urge toward perfection and its complementary accentuation of human inadequacy). Such a list could be extended much further. What it simply implies is the interpreter's need for critical sensitivity to the restless play of Shelley's mind, to his continual intellectual growth, to his abiding self-questioning, and to his Socratic respect for cerebration for its own sake.

Or is this last characteristic Platonic? The extent to which Shelley still appears in general criticism with this label pinned to his shirt suggests how long exploded conceptions can persist and how tempting it is for humanists to resolve the flux of things by categories and niches. The simple philosophical grounds on which this rubric is inappropriate have been supplied, to refer only to studies already named, in Reiman, Curran, Webb, the fifth chapter of Pulos' *Deep Truth,* and, combining succinctness and analytical sophistication, in Wasserman. If the only answer to such honest and concentrated animadversions is that to be found in the combination of vitriol, vagueness, and sanctimoniousness characterizing William J. McTaggart's "Some New Inquiries into Shelley's Platonism" (*KSMB,* 1970), the inquiry should simply be at rest. That is not to say that Shelley did not read Plato with admiration—the text he owned in Italy has been recently identified by Ronald Tetreault in "Shelley's Folio Plato" (*KSJ*, 1981)—but he read him (as one supposes we read him today) not for a revelation of immutable truth but for the brilliance, subtlety, and humane insight of his discourse. Shelley's skepticism, the exact opposite of deduction from Platonic ideas and thus a mirror resemblance, is in perfect accord with Socrates' maxim that one's only knowledge is that one cannot finally know. With that caveat, which simply removes belief and proselytizing from the picture, one can profit greatly from the knowledge of Shelley's reading, annotation, and translation of Plato supplied by Notopoulos in *The Platonism of Shelley* (1949) and by Rogers in *Shelley at Work* (1956, rev. 1967)—which is to say, a knowledge composed of psychological and linguistic insight, images, mythic fragments, or, to put it simply, literary and human rather than divine truths.

A skeptical idealism like Shelley's, however, is anything but simple, and it is scarcely ever abstract, even when it is concerned with conceptual structures. The fullest elaboration of Shelley's "intellectual philosophy"—contained in the second and third parts of Wasserman's *Shelley: A Critical Reading*—runs well over a hundred pages. But then, the native British empirical tradition, stemming from Locke and including such diverse minds as Berkeley, Hume, Hartley, Godwin, and Drummond, constitutes a rich school of philosophy with which Shelley was well familiar. Although Pulos' examination of the power of Drummond's influence had been generally preceded by G. S. Brett in "Shelley's Relation to Berkeley and Drummond" (*Studies in English [University College, Toronto]*, 1931), by the doctoral thesis of Hans Liedtke, *Shelley—durch Berkeley und Drummond beinflusst?* (Griefswald, 1933), and by John Laird, *Philosophical Incursions into English Literature* (1946), Pulos brought a hitherto lacking philosophical and historical sophistication to his analysis. *The Deep Truth* is thus an essential tool of Shelley studies. So, one might add, is Drummond's *Academical Questions*, at long last returned to print, through the offices of Terence Hoagwood and Scholars' Facsimiles (1985).

The principal treatments of Shelley's relationship with the British empirical tradition are, besides that of Pulos, in Cameron's *The Young Shelley* and Wasserman's *Shelley: A Critical Reading*. Thomas Reisner uses the familiar Lockean trope as the basis for his "Tabula Rasa: Shelley's Metaphor of the Mind" (*ArielE*, 1973), but the discussion is less philosophically precise than the title would suggest. Harry White's title—"Shelley's Defence of Science" (*SIR*, 1977)—is also misleading, for this is a splendid examination of Hume's influence on Shelley's conception of the imagination as rudimentary, underlying even scientific discovery and analysis. The parallel, but in many respects conflicting, line of French thinking associated with the philosophes and their revolutionary heirs (including Godwin and Priestley in England) has drawn a number of Shelley students, beginning with Joseph Barrell in *Shelley and the Thought of His Time*. Barrell's basic dichotomy between rationalism and emotionalism is simpleminded, but his tracing of the main developments in French thought still commands respect. Cameron's *Young Shelley* is also valuable in this respect, as are relevant passages in *Shelley: The Golden Years*, but his earlier essays allow for fuller elucidation: in particular, the considerable impact of the Count Volney traced in "A Major Source of *The Revolt of Islam*" (*PMLA*, 1941). The fullest exposition of this line of thinking, accentuating its political ramifications, is in Gerald McNiece's *Shelley and the Revolutionary Idea* (1969). The relevance of other intellectual currents of French radicalism, primarily in anthropology, is examined by Curran in *Shelley's Annus Mirabilis*. For the importance of Rousseau to Shelley, Barrell's simplistic account is superseded by the much more discerning and complex picture offered by Donald H. Reiman in *Shelley's "Triumph of Life": A Critical Study* (1965) and, most recently, by the historically knowledgeable work of Edward Duffy—*Rousseau in England: The Context for Shelley's Critique of the Enlightenment* (1979)—which also offers a large backdrop in the response of other English Romantic writers. The main extension of the French Enlightenment tradition in England was pursued by William Godwin, particularly in the seminal manifesto of intellectual anarchism, *An Enquiry Concerning Political Justice*. Shelley's philosophical interest in Godwin was greatly complicated by their strained personal relations, and the two aspects are sometimes difficult to discriminate. The finest recent accounts of where Shelley and Godwin agree and disagree are in Dawson's *Unacknowledged Legislator* and Scrivener's *Radical Shelley*. An interesting supplement, suggesting how Shelley would characteristically revise what he adopted from Godwin, is offered by Michael Hyde in "Notes on Shelley's Reading of Godwin's *Enquirer*" (*KSJ*, 1982). Earlier treatments of this major influence can be found in Cameron's *Young Shelley* (also his general essay on Godwin for *Shelley and His Circle*, vol. 1, which is reprinted in *Romantic Rebels*) and in Rieger's *Mutiny Within*. The most debated principle deriving from Godwin and the French materialists is that of necessitarianism. Among earlier examinations those by S. F. Gingerich ("Shelley's Doctrine of Necessity *versus* Christianity," *PMLA*, 1918), Frank B. Evans ("Shelley, Godwin, Hume, and the Doctrine of Necessity," *SP*, 1940), and Carlos Baker (*Shelley's Major Poetry*) are still worth consulting. The foremost modern exponent for the doctrine of necessity as a constant premise in Shelley is Cameron, but he has been frequently countered, most recently in the libertarian arguments put forward by Wasserman and Curran. That the issue is not easily resolved is evident in the thoughtful questions raised by Stuart Sperry in "Necessity and the Role of the Hero in *Prometheus Unbound*" (*PMLA*, 1981). This fine essay is likely to prompt further examinations of the problem, which is, in a real sense, the abiding philosophical problem of modern Shelley studies.

The notion of a historical necessity is, of course, crucial to Marxist politics and to its roots in the European Enlightenment. Thus it is virtually impossible, even if Wasserman by and large attempted it, to separate Shelley's strictly philosophical speculations from their political ramifications. The major expositions of Shelley's politics have already been mentioned. To Cameron's two books should be added articles from which they draw but which retain independent value: "The Social Philosophy of Shelley" (*SR*, 1942), "Shelley, Cobbett, and the National Debt" (*JEGP*, 1943), "Shelley and the Reformers" (*ELH*, 1945), the aforementioned "A Major Source of *The Revolt of Islam*," as well as "The Political Symbolism of *Prometheus Unbound*" (*PMLA*, 1941, 1943). Gerald McNiece's *Shelley and the Revolutionary Idea* (1969) is especially strong for marking thematic continuities in

European radical literature, Scrivener's *Radical Shelley* (1982) and Dawson's *Unacknowledged Legislator* (1981) for lucidly setting Shelley within the context of Regency political agitation. (Dawson's essays "Shelley and the Irish Catholics in 1812" and " 'King over Himself': Shelley's Philosophical Anarchism" [*KSMB*, 1978, 1979] are assimilated within that study.) J. P. Guinn in *Shelley's Political Thought* (1969) and Art Young in *Shelley and Nonviolence* (1975) offer general overviews and emphasize Shelley as a forerunner of Gandhi, a view questioned by Harry White in assessing "Relative Means and Ends in Shelley's Socio-Political Thought" (*SEL*, 1982).

Donald H. Reiman has recently offered valuable insights on the extent to which Shelley's rural upbringing and aristocratic connections coincide to determine his political emphases in "Shelley as Agrarian Reactionary" (*KSMB*, 1979). Roland Bartel's "Shelley and Burke's Swinish Multitude" (*KSJ*, 1969) suggests how richly resonant are political metaphors for a work like *Swellfoot the Tyrant*. More generalized ideological considerations are involved in the essays by Renée Winegarten, "The Anarchist Response: Shelley" (*Writers and Revolution: The Fatal Lure of Action*, 1974), Rolf P. Lessenich, "Godwin and Shelley: Rhetoric versus Revolution" (*SN*, 1975), and Kenneth Neill Cameron, "Shelley and Marx" (*WC*, 1979). Similar to the latter in placing Shelley's thought within the efforts of nineteenth-century socialism is Siddig Kalim's "Robert Owen and Shelley" (*Explorations*, 1969). Shelley sets the context, though a very general one, for John C. Garrett's *Utopias in Literature since the Romantic Period* (1968). As one might expect, critics of a Marxist persuasion have produced a sizable body of work on Shelley. The best overall statement from this perspective remains Manfred Wojcik's "In Defence of Shelley" (*ZAA*, 1963; excerpted in *Shelley*, ed. R. B. Woodings, 1968). The most extensive Marxist treatment is by Rüdiger Hillgärtner, *Bürgerlicher Individualismus und revolutionäre Moral: Percy Bysshe Shelley* (1974), which, concerned with social and personal contradictions Shelley inherited from Godwin, is both abstruse and donnishly limited to the period of Shelley's late adolescence. Thomas Metscher's "Shelley und Hölderlin: Zur Kritik bürgerlicher Literaturwissenschaft" (*Gulliver: German/English Yearbook*, 1976) mounts an exemplary Marxist critique of writing on the "Ode to the West Wind." The same volume contains Heinrich Schwinning's "Der Maskenzug der Anarchie." Such Teutonic methodological scrupulosity could scarcely be farther removed from the tone and approach of Paul Foot's *Red Shelley* (1980), which is by intention not academically responsible but is unfailing in the enthusiasm and energy with which it smites infidels.

The major elucidation of the impact of political themes on Shelley's art is the final chapter, of monograph length, of Carl Woodring's *Politics in English Romantic Poetry* (1970), though it might be said as well that his third chapter, entitled "Varieties of Romantic Experience," is virtually a starting point for any serious examination of the political contexts of Romantic literature. The best part of the Shelley chapter is the lengthy analysis of *Prometheus Unbound*, which is inspired criticism. A similar matching of political themes, historical contexts, and critical profundity centered on the same work is a now classic essay of Shelley scholarship, G. M. Matthews' "A Volcano's Voice in Shelley" (*ELH*, 1957). Two fine recent essays interpret Shelley's more explicitly political poetry within the contexts of radical vernacular verse and suggest both its successes and failings: Richard Hendrix concentrates on "The Mask of Anarchy" in "The Necessity of Response: How Shelley's Radical Poetry Works" (*KSJ*, 1978), whereas Stephen C. Behrendt surveys Shelley's career as an author of polemical verse in "The Exoteric Species: The Popular Idiom in Shelley's Poetry" (*Genre*, 1981).

The extent to which Shelley uses historical allusion for political purposes is glanced at, though the focus must be elsewhere, in Betty T. Bennett's "The Political Philosophy of Mary Shelley's Historical Novels: *Valperga* and *Perkin Warbeck*" (in *The Evidence of the Imagination*, ed. Reiman et al.). The notion (or notions) of history in Shelley would profit from greater attention. William Royce Campbell's survey of the canon from this standpoint in "Shelley's Philosophy of History: A Reconsideration" (*KSJ*, 1972 – 73) posits an ongoing struggle between good and evil as ultimate historical forces and sees Shelley's early meliorism hardening into a cyclical view of culture. Wasserman's attempt to reconcile these conflicting notions in his analysis of *Hellas* (*Shelley: A Critical Reading*) suggests how complicated and subtle the problems are. Campbell's "Shelley's Concept of Conscience" (*KSJ*, 1970) traces a similar darkening of Shelley's vision. Against that view one might consult Norman Thurston's humane essay "Shelley and the Duty of Hope" (*KSJ*, 1977), with its insistent reminder that Shelley often deliberately adopted a negative posture to elicit a distinct response from his readers. The notion of hope as a duty came to Shelley through Coleridge: Charles E. Robinson has examined the transmission in "The Shelley Circle and Coleridge's *The Friend*" (*ELN*, 1971).

Richard Holmes's anthology *Shelley on Love* (1982) is a British coffee-table (or is it bedstand?) book suggestive of how central and extensive are Shelley's thoughts on the subject. What *Shelley: The Pursuit* might have taught Holmes is how ambivalent they are as well. The principal expositions of the concept of love in Shelley tend to neglect the darker sentiments for the personal and social values Shelley celebrated. Early treatments, generally placing Shelley within Enlightenment traditions, include Floyd Stovall's "Shelley's Doctrine of Love" (*PMLA*, 1930), Roy R. Male's "Shelley and the Doctrine of Sympathy" (*TxSE*, 1950), Daniel Stempel's "Shelley and the Ladder of Love" (*KSJ*, 1966), and Seraphia Leyda's " 'Love's Rare Universe': Eros in Shelley's Poetry" (in *Explorations of Literature*, ed. Rima Drell Reck, 1966). Gerald Enscoe's chapter "The Physical Basis of Love in Shelley's *Alastor* and *Epipsychidion*" in *Eros and the Romantics* (1967) was obviously intended to correct a perceived imbalance, but the chapter title says it all. Frederick L. Beaty explores both personal love and social benevolence as parallel but progressive concepts in the relevant sections of his *Light from Heaven: Love in British Romantic Literature* (1971). James O. Allsup, in *The Magic Circle: A Study of Shelley's Concept of Love* (1976), tends to platonize his treatment of nine Shelley poems. There is a closer attention to minute particulars of the imagery here than in the historically defined studies, but conceptual particularities are elided by continual reduction to the language of eros and agape. This kind of reductiveness is an enduring problem in writing on a notion so conducive to being made amorphous: one may question whether Roland Duerksen's "Shelley's

'Deep Truth' Reconsidered" (*ELN,* 1975) as love gives that phrase or *Prometheus Unbound* much in the way of new dimensions. Love as a complementary union of the soul with its epipsyche (a term, of course, never used by Shelley) has been much written about. James C. Evans sees a dangerous circularity in "Masks of the Poet: A Study of Self-Confrontation in Shelley's Poetry" (*KSJ,* 1975), and Masao Miyoshi similarly emphasizes the sense of fragmentation involved (*The Divided Self,* 1969). A more optimistic tack is taken by E. B. Murray in his " 'Elective Affinity' in *The Revolt of Islam*" (*JEGP,* 1968), by Jean Hagstrum in "Eros and Psyche: Some Versions of Romantic Love and Delicacy" (*CritI,* 1977), as well as in the relevant pages of Marilyn Butler's *Romantics, Rebels, and Reactionaries* (1981).

One may hope that the publication of Nathaniel Brown's *Sexuality and Feminism in Shelley* (1979) will mark a watershed in writing about Shelley's ideas of love. So often confined to the musty corridors of intellectual history or inflated to an enormous presence that is lacking interior substance, it is neither in Brown's exposition. On the one hand, Brown goes much further than previous commentators in revealing the ubiquity of erotic imagery in Shelley; and on the other, he analyzes Shelley's views on marriage, friendship, equality of the sexes, and gender identity with a modern psychological sophistication as well as historical accuracy. This is an openly celebratory book, yet the thinking is so clear and so insightful that Brown's sense that Shelley charted paths to sexual liberation and social community far in advance of his age (and ours) is likely to persuade. Shelley's darker recognitions about the destructive capacities of love unfortunately do not figure in Brown's perspective; and, indeed, there is no comprehensive treatment of them, perhaps for understandable reasons. Shelley's conception of rape as a psychological and metaphysical violation has been broached in Curran's *Shelley's* Cenci (1970), and a number of studies of "Alastor" and "The Triumph of Life," in particular, focus on a much less benign view of the fixations of love and the compulsions of sexuality. The second term of Brown's title, however, is represented through a cogent, wide-ranging account of both the cultural situation of women at the beginning of the nineteenth century and the way Shelley's thought fit in with contemporary calls for its amelioration. We are long accustomed to discussions of Godwin's influence on Shelley, but this is the first serious exploration of Wollstonecraft's.

Studies of Shelley's "religious" thought are now so dated that almost none can serve as a dependable base for further study. Ellsworth Barnard's *Shelley's Religion* (1937) is the best of them, the kind of book that no one ever writes anymore, filled with passion, rich in anathemas, its anticlericalism lending a quaint nostalgia to the whole. It goes without saying that it is undependable, but it is one of the most enjoyable books ever written on Shelley. The pervasive underlying religious impulses in Shelley figure in Curran, Rieger, Wasserman, and Ross Woodman (*The Apocalyptic Vision in the Poetry of Shelley,* 1964). David Robertson's reading of the "Hymn to Intellectual Beauty" against Psalm 90 suggests the value of more specific approaches (*The Old Testament and the Literary Critic,* 1977). I. A. Richards has written on *Prometheus Unbound* as a sacred book in the epilogue to his *Beyond* (1974), and Joanna Rapf sees parallels in the drama with Teilhard de Chardin (*KSMB,* 1979); while Webb's "Shelley and the Religion of

Joy" (*SIR,* 1976) is filled in in *Shelley: A Voice Not Understood.* Both Edward Duffy's "Shelley, the Trinity, and the Enlightenment" (*ELN,* 1981) and Leslie Brisman's "Mysterious Tongues: Shelley and the Language of Christianity" (*TSLL,* 1981) testify to Shelley's awareness of Christian traditions. The call should once again go out for a treatment of this subject by a critic versed in modern theological conceptions, to which, paradoxically, Shelley as thinker is much attuned.

Similarly, Shelley's considerable knowledge and use of—even at times his intuitive advances over—the science of his day could profit from the examination of a trained historian of science. This discipline has so far contributed only modestly to the possibilities for literature in this period: for instance, in D. M. Knight's survey "The Physical Sciences and the Romantic Movement" (*History of Science,* 1970). These scientific aspects of Shelley's thought and work have long fascinated his literary critics, and in Britain even professional scientists have been drawn into Shelley's camp. One thinks immediately of Desmond King-Hele, the astronomer, whose *Shelley: His Thought and Work* (1960), although not always sure of its sympathies, invariably comes to life when the vital spark of scientific interest is ignited. He has returned to this interest in "Shelley and Erasmus Darwin" (*Shelley Revalued,* 1983). One of the most remarkable critical exegeses of recent years was furnished by a professional meteorologist, F. H. Ludlam, whose "The Meteorology of Shelley's Ode" (*TLS,* 1 Sept. 1972) testifies to the minute accuracy of Shelley's depiction of the west wind: the replies of Desmond King-Hele and Peter Bradshaw of 22 September, with Ludlam's response of 29 September, extend the discussion. Interest in this subject was whetted by A. N. Whitehead's conception of Shelley as potentially "a Newton among chemists" in *Science and the Modern World* (1925), which offered Carl Grabo the title for the first major effort to show the depth of scientific learning underlying *Prometheus Unbound. A Newton among Poets* (1930), however much its discoveries have been amplified by later critics, remains richly suggestive. Peter Butter extends our awareness of how the formulations of contemporaries like Erasmus Darwin and Humphry Davy touch all Shelley's writing in a valuable chapter of *Shelley's Idols of the Cave.* Laura E. Crouch's "Davy's *A Discourse Introductory to a Course of Lectures on Chemistry:* A Possible Scientific Source of *Frankenstein*" (*KSJ,* 1978) is just as applicable to Shelley. The main recent writing on Shelley and science has concentrated on *Prometheus Unbound.* Thomas Reisner describes and analyzes "Some Scientific Models for Shelley's Multitudinous Orb" (*KSJ,* 1974). The third chapter of Curran's *Shelley's Annus Mirabilis* investigates the relativistic "Physics of Paradise." Lloyd Jeffrey is suggestive, if far too brief, in treating "Cuvierian Catastrophism in Shelley's *Prometheus Unbound* and *Mont Blanc*" (*SAB,* 1978). Jeffrey published four articles on reptiles, birds, mammals, and insects in *KSJ* between 1958 and 1976: these are incorporated, with corrections and additions (and a new section on plants), in *Shelley's Knowledge and Use of Natural History* (Salzburg Studies, 1976). Shelley's knowledge of optics and light was considerable. Aside from the general critical literature, especially as it treats *Adonais* and "The Triumph of Life," the interested reader might consult Robert A. Hartley, "Phosphorescence in Canto I of 'The Revolt of Islam'" (*N&Q,* 1973), and Martha

Banta, "Adonais and the Angel: Light, Color, and the Occult Sublime" (*WC*, 1977), comparing light values in Shelley and Turner. Still and all, given Shelley's penetrating knowledge of contemporary science, such a paragraph should be longer. That this kind of secure knowledge is not often found in literary scholars is true enough, but a substantial scholarly base is already present. There is much more to be done.

On the number of interests that might be grouped under the rubric of Shelley's aesthetics, there is little in the way of consensus. Perspective, as one might anticipate, organizes the argument. Historically oriented analyses have attempted to place Shelley's aesthetics within the bounds of Enlightenment thought. The largest and most influential perspectives are offered in Wasserman's important essay "Shelley's Last Poetics" (*From Sensibility to Romanticism*, 1965, incorporated with some deletions in *Shelley: A Critical Reading*) and in Earl J. Schulze's *Shelley's Theory of Poetry: A Reappraisal* (1966). John E. Jordan valuably locates Shelley's *Defence of Poetry* within the context of Peacock's "Four Ages of Poetry" in the introduction of his joint edition of the two works (1965). Fanny Delisle's two-volume *Study of Shelley's A Defence of Poetry* (1974) has already been mentioned for its textual contributions, but its variorum commentary is also exceedingly helpful for picking through past critical debates. John S. Flagg's "Shelley and Aristotle: Elements of the *Poetics* in Shelley's Theory of Poetry" (*SIR*, 1970) rides its thesis harder than an objective view might warrant, but the essay was endeavoring to right a balance at that point tipped heavily toward Platonic conceptions. Other interpreters have tried to remove Shelley from that dichotomy altogether. Jan Cohn juxtaposes Shelley with I. A. Richards (*KSJ*, 1972–73) on the social and moral utility of poetry, whereas Horace G. Posey, Jr., in "Shelley and Modern Aesthetics" (*BuR*, 1971) would see Shelley as generally pointing the way toward a Crocean expressionism, a position open to many objections from which the author looks the other way. John Wright's monograph *Shelley's Myth of Metaphor* (1970) is densely argued, provocative, and intellectually acute, drawing inspiration from modern theorists like Morse Peckham and Colin Turbayne and suggesting that Shelley recognized, far in advance of his time, the extent to which all formulations are essentially metaphorical. Recently, deconstructive criticism has begun to find a friendly voice in Shelley. The volume of criticism from Yale, *Deconstruction and Criticism* (1980), to which I return in discussing criticism of "The Triumph of Life," does not quite recognize how far Shelley's own language supports a full-scale Derridean argument. One critic who does recognize it is Jerrold E. Hogle, whose "Shelley's Poetics: The Power as Metaphor" (*KSJ*, 1982) is a remarkable attempt to ground (if one can use such a term where its very validity is in question) Shelley's aesthetic in an absolute skepticism akin to that of contemporary aesthetic theory. Arguing even more intensely than Wright that all Shelley's thought is based on his conception of metaphor and that metaphor is a succession of traces without absolute origin or end, Hogle has produced as constructive a deconstructive reading as may exist, worth contemplation alike for its fine intellection, its conceptual breadth, and its mastery of Shelley. One expects such an essay to exert a strong force on subsequent Shelley criticism.

There are numerous ancillary interests in the general area of aesthetics—
Shelley's use of imagery, stylistics, versification—that I consider in a later section.
Several important writings that concern themselves with large issues of his poetics, however, might be more appropriately noted here. Northrop Frye's essay
"Mythos and Logos" (*YCGL,* 1969) compares the theoretical conceptions of Sidney
and Shelley, and his "The Critical Path: An Essay on the Social Context of Literary
Criticism" (*Daedalus,* 1970; expanded in his book by this title, 1971) uses Shelley's *Defence* as a point of reference. So does John Robert Leo, who finds centered in it a "Criticism of Consciousness" (*PLL,* 1978). Lloyd Abbey's "Shelley's Repudiation of Conscious Artistry" (*ESC,* 1975) suffers from one's realization that,
whatever Shelley may appear to say to create such an impression, his practice
wholly belies it. W. Paul Elledge's "Good, Evil, and the Function of Art" (*TSL,*
1969) is far too short to satisfy the needs of the argument that Shelley's pervasive
dualism betrays his sense of public role. John Ross Baker's questioning of
whether there is a unity underlying the various ways in which poetry is
conceptualized by Shelley ("Poetry and Language in Shelley's *Defence of Poetry,*"
JAAC, 1981) is provocative, but insufficiently informed by the relevant treatments
of the subject. Stuart Sperry in a thoughtful study of modes of Romantic irony
places Shelley midway between Keats, in whom the mode is inherent, and Byron,
who self-consciously exploits it (in *Romantic and Modern: Revaluations of Literary Tradition,* ed. George Bornstein, 1977). Finally, Michael Murrin in the postscript to his important study *The Veil of Allegory* (1969) has a brief but telling exposition of metaphorical values in Shelley that he sees as the logical conclusion
of his overall account.

SOURCES AND LITERARY CONTEXTS

Shelley's magisterial command of European cultural traditions is almost inseparable from his thinking and artistic achievement, and most important studies of his
thought and art attempt to honor this deep engagement with the past. With the
sophistication in literary methodology experienced over the last decades, the
earlier search for merely transferable sources and echoes has been supplanted by
the recognition of his purposeful allusion, an almost temperamental inclination
to invoke and play against contexts, even to emphasize them so as to alter or subvert that very foregrounding. Thus, though earlier scholars have often discerned
important contexts for Shelley's writing, the extent of scholarly rethinking has invalidated many of their conclusions.

The starting point for this consideration are the reading lists kept by Shelley
and Mary, supplemented by references in their letters, which can be found in the
index to White's *Shelley* and appendix 8 of Jones's edition of the *Letters.* In addition, Walter E. Peck's *Shelley: His Thought and Work* (2 vols., 1927) and *Shelley
and His Circle* contain information about and transcriptions of Shelley's annotation in his library. Still, such basic tools must be further supplemented by works
cited by Shelley in his other writings, by those mentioned in the reminiscences
of his friends, and even by works that figure so prominently in the writings of his

close literary associates—primarily Mary Shelley, but also Byron, Hunt, and Peacock as well—that Shelley's awareness of them is virtually certain: F. B. Curtis
exemplifies this process in "Shelley and the Hookham Circulating Library in Old
Bond Street" (*KSMB*, 1982). By the same token, one can presume Shelley's secondhand familiarity with works through a variety of channels, for instance, the
lengthy encapsulating reviews of contemporary periodicals. To keep up with
Shelley's reading is a daunting scholarly (and educational) experience, but without question there have been major advances made in our knowledge through
recognition of the multiple contexts of his thought and writing.

The most reliable guide to Shelley's knowledge and use of classical authors
has been provided by Timothy Webb in his two books, *Shelley: A Voice Not Understood* (1977, esp. ch. 7) and *The Violet in the Crucible: Shelley and Translation*
(1976). The latter work, indeed, may constitute the definitive statement to date on
how Shelley read and assimilated not only the major Greek authors but also
Dante and other medieval Italians, Calderón, and Goethe. Webb's command of
these languages and literatures is so minute as to allow him to register when
Shelley mistranslates and usually to explain how the slip could have occurred.
Webb has separately considered the impact of Euripides in "Shelley and the Cy-
clops" (*KSMB*, 1972). Other valuable treatments of Shelley's debt to Greek writing
include the particular emphasis on Plato in Notopoulos' *Platonism of Shelley* and
Rogers' *Shelley at Work*, where, once one smelts away the dross of the thesis,
there remains abundant ore of knowledge and sensitivity; and also in E. M. W.
Tillyard's "Shelley's *Prometheus Unbound* and Plato's *Statesman* (*TLS*, 1932).
Stephen J. Rogers, Jr., in *Classical Greece in the Poetry of Chénier, Shelley, and
Leopardi* (1970), tends to be reductively abstract in discussing Shelley, but he is
unquestionably learned in classical writings. Shelley's neo-Hellenism has been
discussed by P. Carter, "Shelley and the Greek Spirit" (*Art and Artists*, 1977), and
by John Buxton, whose "Greece in the Imagination of Byron and Shelley"
(*ByronJ*, 1976), juxtaposing the two as respectively drawn to modern and ancient
Greece, is incorporated in *The Grecian Taste: Literature in the Age of Neo-
Classicism, 1740–1820* (1978). Roy R. Male, "Young Shelley and the Ancient Moralists" (*KSJ*, 1956), and Male and Notopoulos, "Shelley's Copy of Diogenes
Laertius" (*MLR*, 1959), investigate specific minor influences. Other specific Greek
contexts for individual works are noted in the later survey of criticism. It might
be said in conclusion that the modern critics most concerned with Shelley's
nondogmatic use of Greek thought and literature are Wasserman, Curran, and
Webb.

Much less has been done with Latin influences, though Shelley was fluent
and broadly educated in the language: he is said, for instance, to have translated
half of Pliny's *Natural History* while at Eton. One Latin writer in particular,
Lucretius, had a marked influence: Paul Turner's "Shelley and Lucretius" (*RES*,
1959) is a starting point for this consideration, which has been pursued in references to "Mont Blanc" by Jane Phillips (*CML*, 1982). Mary Rebecca Thayer's *The Influence of Horace on the Chief English Poets of the Nineteenth Century* (1916)
touches on Shelley, and occasionally Horace is discerned behind the tone of
Shelley's more meditative poems of the Italian years; but the subject is deserving

of a more intense scrutiny. Too intense a scrutiny characterizes Richard Acker-man's *Lucans* Pharsalia *in den Dichtungen Shelleys* (1896).

Although Shelley spoke and wrote Italian with ease, his associations in Italy, unlike Byron's, were mainly with his own countrymen. Virtually no influence from contemporary Italian letters has been remarked by scholars, but that of me-dieval Italian has been explored sufficiently to suggest that there is much yet to do. Corrado Zaccheti's *Shelley e Dante* (1922), Werner P. Friederich's *Dante's Fame Abroad* (1950), and Oswald Doughty's "Dante and the English Romantic Poets" (*EM*, 1951) are fairly general in their claims. In range and specificity the most valuable treatment occurs in the final two chapters of Webb's *Violet in the Crucible*. Dante's particular impact on *Epipsychidion* has been argued by Rogers in *Shelley at Work*, by Reiman and Wasserman, by Richard E. Brown (*CL*, 1978), and by Earl Schulze (*SIR*, 1982), but the subject is by no means exhausted. Fred L. Milne, "Shelley's *The Cenci:* The Ice Motif and the Ninth Circle of Dante's Hell" (*TSL*, 1977), cites a specific application of Dante's imagery, whereas Richard Harter Fogle's concern in "Dante and Shelley's *Adonais*" (*BuR*, 1967; rpt. in *The Permanent Pleasure*, 1974) is the contrast between Dante's hierarchical and Shelley's dialectical modes of thought. Herbert G. Wright, *Boccaccio in England from Chaucer to Tennyson* (1957), glances at Shelley; more to the point is the es-say by Marchesa Enrica Viviani Della Robbia, "Shelley e il Boccaccio" in *Rivista Americana Italica* (1959). These and later Italian writers figure in C. P. Brand's *Italy and the English Romantics* (1957). Although Shelley read both Ariosto and Tasso and drafted fragments toward a play on Tasso, the former's name scarcely intrudes on criticism and the latter enters almost exclusively in terms of his sup-posed correspondences with the Maniac in "Julian and Maddalo." As with medie-val Italian writing, the authoritative statement on Shelley's curious affinity for Calderón is provided by Webb. Earlier accounts include those of Rogers in *Shelley at Work*, Eunice Joiner Gates, "Shelley and Calderón" (*PQ*, 1937), and Salvador de Madariaga, *Shelley and Calderón and Other Essays* (1920).

The understanding of Shelley's sources in German writing has been en-larged by M. Roxana Klapper's *The German Literary Influence on Shelley* (Salzburg Studies, 1975), which includes a survey of Shelley's acquaintance with sixteen German writers, then concentrates on his response to two works, Schubart's "Der ewige Jude" and Goethe's *Faust*. This study largely supersedes the chapter on Shelley in Frank W. Stokoe's *German Influence in the English Ro-mantic Period, 1788–1818* (1926). Webb's *Violet in the Crucible* has an excellent chapter on *Faust* and Shelley, and other accounts include Francis G. Steiner, "Shelley and Goethe's *Faust*" (*RLMC*, 1951), Robert C. Casto, "Shelley as Translator of *Faust*" (*RES*, 1975), and Leland Phelps, "Goethe's *Faust* and the Young Shelley," in *Wege der Worte: Festschrift für Wolfgang Fleischhauer*, edited by Donald Riechel (1978). The influence of two earlier German writers on Shelley has been underrated. One is Spinoza, where the significant statements—Sophie Bernthsen, *Der Spinozimus in Shelleys Weltanschauung* (1900), and Carl Grabo, "Spinoza and Shelley" (*Chicago Jewish Forum*, 1942)—need updating. The other is Winckelmann, whose presence in Shelley's aesthetic conceptions has only recently been acknowledged, mainly in relation to Shelley's writings on art (see below).

The French influence on Shelley is largely political, and the major studies previously noted should be quickly repeated in this context. Gerald McNiece sets the somewhat turbulent intellectual world of eighteenth-century France in admirable balance in *Shelley and the Revolutionary Idea* (1969). Earlier studies dealing with aspects of this philosophical and political tradition include Walter E. Peck, "Shelley and the Abbé Barruel" (*PMLA*, 1921), considerations of the influence of Volney's *Ruins of Empire* on *Queen Mab* by L. Kellner (*Englische Studien*, 1896) and on *The Revolt of Islam* by Cameron (*PMLA*, 1941), and Israel J. Kapstein, "Shelley and Cabanis" (*PMLA*, 1937). Amiyakumar Sen includes a chapter entitled "Shelley and the French Revolution" in *Studies in Shelley* (1936). The complex position occupied by Rousseau in Shelley's intellectual life has been most recently investigated by Edward Duffy in *Rousseau in England: The Context for Shelley's Critique of the Enlightenment* (1979), which combines its account of Rousseau's contemporary English reception with critical sensitivity. There was an earlier German monograph on the general influence of Rousseau: Hans Meyer's *Shelley und Rousseau* (1934). Donald L. Maddox casts Rousseau as the prototype of the Poet in "Alastor": "Shelley's *Alastor* and the Legacy of Rousseau" (*SIR*, 1970)—and, of course, virtually any significant treatment of "The Triumph of Life" must touch on the portrait of Rousseau there. Duffy's final chapter focuses directly on this issue: there are also substantial accounts in Abbey's *Destroyer and Preserver* and in Reiman's *Shelley's "The Triumph of Life": A Critical Edition*.

The only other non-English influence on Shelley is that exercised by Eastern cultures and traditions. There is a chapter surveying Shelley's canon descriptively in Colette Le Yaouanc, *L'Orient dans la poésie anglaise de l'époque romantique (1798–1824)* (1975). A more scholarly attempt to lay the ground for Shelley's knowledge and use of Eastern traditions, mainly Persian and Indian, is provided in Curran's *Shelley's Annus Mirabilis*. Several essays on "The Indian Girl's Song" (see below) have noted specific links with Persian and Indian writings. Shelley knew more about the Orient than any of the major Romantics except Byron; that there has not been more scholarly and critical interest in this subject probably reflects our difficulties in recreating the historical knowledge.

Shelley's knowledge of the literature of Renaissance England was not only extensive but also continually dynamic for his writing. The early essays on Shelley and Shakespeare by David Lee Clark (*PMLA*, 1939), Sara R. Watson (*PMLA*, 1940), Frederick L. Jones (*PMLA*, 1944), and Beach Langston (*HLQ*, 1949) contented themselves largely with cataloging supposed echoes. Later critics have emphasized complementary or contending conceptual structures in the two writers. Thus, Martin V. Svaglic in "Shelley and *King Lear*" (in *Nineteenth-Century Literary Perspectives*, ed. Clyde de L. Ryals, 1974) maintains that Shelley found the tragedy so compelling because Lear's progress approximates an archetypal Shelleyan pattern, whereas Paul A. Cantor argues in "'A Distorting Mirror': Shelley's *The Cenci* and Shakespearean Tragedy" (*HES*, 1976) that Shakespeare and Shelley embody radically different notions of tragic conflict, the one between self and world and the other wholly within the self. (In both cases that formulation would seem excessively simple.) Most questions of Shakespearean influence have focused on *The Cenci*: for a survey of the grounds and general bibliographical information, see chapter 2 of Curran's *Shelley's* Cenci (1970). D. M. Harrington-Lueker argues the primary context of *Macbeth* in "Imagination versus Introspection: *The Cenci* and *Macbeth*" (*KSL*, 1983). William Hildebrand notes a Shakespearean context for *Prometheus Unbound* 3.1 in "Jupiter, Demogorgon, and Lear" (*Serif*, 1971). Two other essays on Shakespeare and Shelley move further afield: Earl R. Wasserman takes a broad view in "Shakespeare and the English Romantic Movement" (in *The Persistence of Shakespeare Idolatry*, ed. Herbert M. Schueller, 1964) and Barry Weller relates the late lyrics to *The Tempest* in "Shakespeare, Shelley, and the Unbinding of the Lyric" (*MLN*, 1978). Little impact from non-Shakespearean drama has been suggested. Else von Schaubart's *Shelleys Tragödie* The Cenci *und Marlowes Doppeldrama Tamburlaine* (Paderborn, 1965) strikes one as pure invention.

Carlos Baker, who wrote his doctoral dissertation on the subject, is especially alive to the influence of Spenser in *PMLA*, 1941, and in *Shelley's Major Poetry*; among earlier Shelley scholars, see also Jones in *PMLA*, 1942. Harold Bloom finds many Spenserian traces in *Shelley's Mythmaking*, and Wasserman pursues a valuable digression on the relationship in *The Subtler Language*. Edwin R. Silverman rightly suggests the importance of Spenser's *Astrophel* to *Adonais* in *Poetic Synthesis in Shelley's Adonais* (1972), but then synthesis turns out to mean that Spenser wrote Shelley's poem. For an overview of the main lines of Spenserian influence one might consult the Shelley entry in *The Spenser Encyclopedia* (1985–) contributed by Stuart Curran. As noted, Northrop Frye has used Shelley and Sidney as poles for his discussion in "Mythos and Logos" (*YCGL*, 1969). The richest of all Renaissance contexts for Shelley is that provided by Milton, and it is rich indeed. Earlier echo hunting has in recent work given way to an increasingly sophisticated understanding of the dynamics of influence. Raymond Dexter Havens' standard *The Influence of Milton on English Poetry* (1922) devotes surprisingly little space to Shelley. As with Spenser, Baker touched on the Miltonic element in Shelley separately (*MLN*, 1940) before treating it where appropriate throughout *Shelley's Major Poetry*. Frederick L. Jones formulated a catalog of echoes in "Shelley and Milton" (*SP*, 1952), and Ronald Pelletier has pursued a number of parallels in his series of notes (*N&Q*, Mar. and July 1960, Jan. and Dec. 1961; *KSJ*, 1962, 1965). Bloom, Wasserman, and Curran in their books continually demonstrate the force exercised by Shelley's temperamental affinity with Milton, especially on *Prometheus Unbound*. That work is also the Shelleyan focus in Curran's "The Mental Pinnacle: *Paradise Regained* and the Romantic Four-Book Epic" in *Calm of Mind*, edited by Joseph Wittreich (1971). Ants Oras sees the chariot of the Son in *Paradise Lost* 6 as the prototype for the chariot of the Earth in *Prometheus Unbound* 4: "The Multitudinous Orb: Some Miltonic Elements in Shelley's Poetry" (*MLQ*, 1955). Leslie Brisman raises his perspective to a large conceptual plane, viewing Shelley's various efforts to arrest time as aspects of a Miltonic legacy (*Milton's Poetry of Choice and Its Romantic Heirs*, 1973). From the opposite perspective Joseph Raben has written several essays on Miltonic elements in Shelley's style as demonstration of literary uses of computers: see *Literary Data Processing Conference Proceedings* (*MLA*, 9–11 Sept. 1964) and *Analyses of Communications Contents* (ed. George Gerbner et al., 1969). Raben has also documented "Milton's Influence on Shelley's Translation of Dante's Matilda Gathering Flowers" (*RES*, 1963). The extent to which one can construct a subsuming context from loose verbal parallels is brought to a test by Luther L. Scales, Jr., as he asserts an intense preoccupation with Milton in "Alastor" (*KSJ*, 1972–73). Philip Wade has found Shelley responsible for the Miltonic element in *Frankenstein* (*Milton and the Romantics*, 1976), and Ross Woodman has argued for a subversion of the Miltonic context posed for *Adonais* in "Shelley's Urania" (*SIR*, 1978) and "Milton's Urania and the Romantic Descendants" (*UTQ*, 1979). Joseph Wittreich's questioning of the customary reading of Shelley's remarks on Satan ("The Satanism of Blake and Shelley Reconsidered," *SP*, 1968) is verified and expanded in Stuart Curran's "The Siege of Hateful Contraries: Shelley, Mary Shelley, Byron and *Paradise Lost*" in *Milton and the Line of Vision* (ed. Wittreich, 1975). Curran also contributed the Shelley entry in the *Milton Encyclopedia* (1979). Wittreich's earlier collection *The Romantics on Milton* (1970) draws together the various remarks on Milton of Shelley and other English Romantic writers, and in its introductory chapter offers a large view of why Milton's impact on this period was so immense.

Shelley's high estimate of Sir Francis Bacon has elicited two essays in the older tradition: David Lee Clark's "Shelley and Bacon" (*PMLA*, 1933) and William O. Scott's "Shelley's Admiration for Bacon" (*PMLA*, 1958). A number of books and essays detailing the influence of British empirical philosophy on Shelley were noted in relation to studies of his thought in the previous section. Outside of the work of philosophers, English influence on Shelley between Milton and the Romantics has largely been ignored. An exception is E. H. King's "Beattie and Shelley: The Making of the Poet" (*ES*, 1980), whose claims for parallels are far too broad. Shelley's early and continuing love for the Gothic colors many of his writings: the only general interpretation of this is John V. Murphy's *The Dark Angel: Gothic Elements in Shelley's Works* (1975), which has neither theoretical nor critical insight to recommend it. The earlier cataloging of Gothic attributes and surveying of its historical development in various literary forms—such as one finds in Montague Summers' *The Gothic Quest* (1938) and Bertrand Evans' *Gothic Drama from Walpole to Shelley* (1947)—have their value but in recent years have given way to an understanding much more grounded in psychology and anthropology. Little of that has yet impinged on our understanding of the Gothic element in Shelley.

The profound effect on Shelley of his contemporaries deserves far more detailed treatment than it has received. The range of Shelley's reactions to Wordsworth has been charted by J. C. Echeruo in "Shelley on Wordsworth" (*ESA*, 1966). Harold Bloom began as early as *The Visionary Company* (1963) to read

Shelley's major works as a response to Wordsworth. By the time of *The Anxiety of Influence* (1973) Bloom could speak of Shelley as being "terrorized" by Wordsworth's Intimations Ode. The fourth chapter of *Poetry and Repression* (1976), "Shelley and His Precursors," deals with both Milton and Wordsworth. Wasserman's reading of "Alastor" in *Shelley: A Critical Reading* turns on the references to Wordsworth in that poem; and that view is extended by Yvonne M. Carothers, who sees the narrator as a Wordsworth who comes to recognize his own failings (*MLQ*, 1981). William Keach, in "Obstinate Questionings: The *Immortality Ode* and *Alastor*" (*WC*, 1981) focuses even more directly on Shelley's quotation of Wordsworth in the poem and argues that Shelley shows himself to be an astute reader of the ode. The other poem in which Wordsworth figures prominently is "Peter Bell the Third." F. W. Bateson has resurrected some gossip-laden suppressed verses (*EC*, 1967), and Jack Benoit Gohn has sifted the evidence finely enough that he feels he can answer affirmatively the question "Did Shelley Know Wordsworth's *Peter Bell?*" (*KSJ*, 1979). The most extensive recent commentary on the treatment of Wordsworth in that poem is in Curran's *Shelley's Annus Mirabilis*. Donald Reiman brings the later course of poetry in English to bear on his distinction between Wordsworth's pastoralism and Shelley's Gothic sensibility in "Wordsworth, Shelley, and the Romantic Inheritance" (*RP&P*, 1981). A. C. Bradley includes an essay "Coleridge—Echoes in Shelley's Poems" in *A Miscellany* (1929), and Joseph Raben offers "Coleridge as the Prototype of the Poet in Shelley's *Alastor*" (*RES*, 1966), but here again is an area of a complicated ambivalence that needs further thought. Hector Munro's "Shelley and Coleridge" (*KSMB*, 1970) tries to establish evidence for Coleridge's later attitude toward Shelley but leaves Coleridge's impact on him mainly unexplored. Charles E. Robinson helpfully identifies acquaintance with a distillation of the *Friend* in "The Shelley Circle and Coleridge's *The Friend*" (*ELN*, 1971).

Recent years have brought us much more detailed accounts of Shelley's interactions with his contemporaries among the younger Romantics. The principal literary relation is clearly that between Shelley and Mary. Much criticism of her writings, especially on *Frankenstein*, avoids a historical base or an attempt to establish a context within her husband's writings; and frequently when such a context is invoked, as noted earlier, the effect is one of gross distortion. Still, Mary continually sounds themes, sometimes making them more accessible, of importance in Shelley's writing; and without doubt the intellectual and literary interaction was of such mutual vitality that each illuminates the other's writing. The caricature of Shelley pursued by Christopher Small in *Mary Shelley's* Frankenstein: *Tracing the Myth* (1973) has been mentioned. Much subtler is Peter Dale Scott's argument that both Victor and Clerval have components of Shelley (and Shelley largely as a representative figure in his time): "Vital Artifice: Mary, Percy, and the Psychopolitical Integrity of *Frankenstein*," included in *The Endurance of* Frankenstein (ed. George Levine and U. C. Knoepflmacher, 1979). Scott makes pointed comparison with *The Revolt of Islam*, whereas the latter part of Paul Sherwin's exploration of the limits to psychoanalytic interpretations of the novel—*"Frankenstein*: Creation as Catastrophe" (*PMLA*, 1981)—focuses suggestively on "Alastor." Curran extends the discussion to *The Cenci* and *Prometheus Un-*

bound in "The Siege of Hateful Contraries" (*Milton and the Line of Vision,* ed. Wittreich, 1975). James Rieger's commentary in his important edition of the novel, which adopts the first edition with the revisions Mary had intended for a second (and also prints all variants from the customary edition of 1831), argues that Shelley had so decided a part in the writing of *Frankenstein* that he should be viewed as a collaborator. This text, originally published by Bobbs-Merrill and then inexplicably allowed to go out of print, was reissued in 1982 by the University of Chicago Press. E. B. Murray has independently gone back through the manuscript evidence indicating Shelley's role, the most significant matter being that the last thirteen pages of the fair copy are in Shelley's hand, and concludes that beyond those final pages, and even perhaps there, his role was actually minimal ("Shelley's Contributions to Mary's *Frankenstein,*" *KSMB,* 1978). On that issue the essay cited above by Philip Wade, suggesting that Shelley urged the Miltonic context of the novel on Mary, should be recalled (*Milton and the Romantics,* 1976). Rieger's "Shelley's Paterin Beatrice" (*SIR,* 1965; included in *The Mutiny Within*) discovers in Mary's second published novel, *Valperga,* important backgrounds for *The Cenci.*

The most useful general account of the somewhat strained friendship with Keats is provided by Donald H. Reiman—"Keats and Shelley: Personal and Literary Relations"—in *Shelley and His Circle,* volume 5. Stuart Curran argues that Keats's writings, particularly those of the 1820 volume, impinge directly on the language and meaning of *Adonais* in "*Adonais* in Context" (*Shelley Revalued,* ed. Kelvin Everest, 1983). A more critical attitude toward his fellow poet informs a notebook fragment concerning him, according to Fred L. Milne in "Shelley on Keats: A Notebook Dialogue" (*ELN,* 1976). The interaction of Shelley with Peacock and with the circle surrounding him is best illuminated by Marilyn Butler in *Peacock Displayed* (1979). Cameron's ideas about the impact of Peacock's abortive epic *Ahrimanes* on *The Revolt of Islam* (*MLQ,* 1942) have been sifted and adjusted in *Shelley and His Circle,* volume 3. With John Buxton's and Charles Robinson's books on Shelley and Byron, discussed above, we now possess a much richer awareness of the dynamics of this relationship. Robinson's extensive documentation, on top of his scholarly presentation, makes his the book to begin with for interpretive purposes. The impact of some of Shelley's less familiar contemporaries on his thought and art has been repeatedly acknowledged by the more historically minded of his critics and biographers. Cameron's writings are exemplary in this respect. The importance of a now-forgotten piece of utopian fiction is stressed by Walter Graham in "Shelley and *The Empire of the Nairs*" (*PMLA,* 1925). G. F. McFarland has traced the background of praise for Shelley from an unexpected quarter in "Shelley and Julius Hare: A Review and a Response" (*BJRL,* 1975). Lewis Schwartz in two notes helped to identify sympathetic reviewers of the early poetry: of *Queen Mab* in *KSJ,* 1970, and *The Revolt of Islam* in *N&Q,* 1971. Given the dearth of multiple analyses of any single contemporary influence on Shelley, the attention paid to Charles Brockden Brown is slightly amusing. A general picture was drawn by Melvin T. Solve in "Shelley and the Novels of Brown" (*Fred Newton Scott Anniversary Papers,* 1929) and by Eleanor Sickels in "Shelley and Charles Brockden Brown" (*PMLA,* 1930). A more specific influence has been suggested by Rosemary R. Davies in "Charles Brockden Brown's *Ormond*: A Possible Influence upon Shelley's Conduct" (*PQ,* 1964).

Shelley's sources in the visual arts have received increasing attention. For years the standard reference was Ilse Köhling O'Sullivan's *Shelley und die bildende Kunst* (1927), which by language and scarcity was able to exert little influence. The chapter on Shelley in Stephen A. Larrabee's *English Bards and Grecian Marbles: The Relationship between Sculpture and Poetry, Especially in the Romantic Period* (1943) was self-evidently limited but at least a start. The sharpening recognition of how strongly neoclassical is Shelley's temperament is reflected in John Buxton's "Shelley's Neo-Classical Taste" (*Apollo,* 1972). Frederic S. Colwell has moved the discussion to a new plane in his careful examination of Shelley's art criticism and of the ways the Italian art he saw (or might have seen) in 1818–19 impinged on his poetry: "Shelley on Sculpture: The Uffizi Notes" and "Shelley and Italian Painting" (*KSJ,* 1979, 1980). It is here and in the investigation of Nancy Goslee, particularly in "Shelley's 'Notes on Sculpture': Romantic Classicism in *Prometheus Unbound*" (*Comparatist,* 1980), that the strongest argument for the impact of Winckelmann has been made. In addition to these learned and provocative essays Colwell has argued specifically against seeing Botticelli's *Birth of Venus* as an influence on *Prometheus Unbound* 2: "Shelley's Asia and Botticelli's Venus: An Infectious Shelley Myth" (*KSMB,* 1979). Yet another famous painting has long been linked to Shelley's *The Cenci.* Its historical backgrounds and contemporary significance are extensively documented by Barbara Groseclose in "A Portrait Not by Guido Reni of a Girl Who Is Not Beatrice Cenci" (*SECC,* 1982). A surprising number of essays have focused on the union of contraries Shelley described in his poem celebrating the head of the Medusa attributed to Leonardo da Vinci: Neville Rogers, "Shelley and the Visual Arts" (*KSMB,* 1961); Daniel J. Hughes, "Shelley, Leonardo, and the Monsters of Thought" (*Criticism,* 1970); and Jerome J. McGann, "The Beauty of the Medusa: A Study in Romantic Literary Iconology" (*SIR,* 1972). There is likewise a series of essays establishing Shelley's temperamental and affective links with Turner: Karl Kroeber, "Experience as History: Shelley's Venice, Turner's Carthage" (*ELH,* 1974); John Dixon Hunt, "Wondrous Deep and Dark: Turner and the Sublime" (*GaR,* 1976); Martha Banta, "Adonais and the Angel: Light, Color, and the Occult Sublime" (*WC,* 1977); R. F. Storch, "Abstract Idealism in English Romantic Poetry and Painting," in *Images of Romanticism: Verbal and Visual Affinities,* edited by Karl Kroeber and William Walling (1978). The only substantial treatment of Shelley's links with contemporary political caricatures is offered by Michael Scrivener in *Radical Shelley.*

As with Shelley's relations to the visual arts, his musical backgrounds and influence have begun to attract critical attention. Early surveys of this aspect were conducted by Neville Rogers in "Music at Marlow" (*KSMB,* 1953) and Jean de Palacio in "Music and Musical Themes in Shelley's Poetry" (*MLR,* 1964). Chernaik touches on this subject continually in *The Lyrics of Shelley,* and it forms the central concern of Erland Anderson's *Harmonious Madness: A Study of Musical Metaphors in the Poetry of Coleridge, Shelley, and Keats* (1975). The brief discussion in Curran's *Shelley's* Cenci on how Shelley's interest in opera is manifested in his dramatic writing is much expanded and its concerns enlarged to include ballet in Ronald Tetreault's "Shelley at the Opera" (*ELH*, 1981), the most sophisticated essay thus far on how Shelley's poetry is permeated by his knowledge of music. The other side of the picture has been admirably represented in the bibliography of Burton Pollin, *Music for Shelley's Poetry* (1974), supplemented in *KSJ*, 1982. That bibliography provides an indispensable basis for much future thinking about Shelley's influence.

Another source for Shelley's thought is obvious but surprisingly little pursued: that of his extensive travels. An example of how indelibly specific scenes could permeate his imaginative conceptions is provided by Donald H. Reiman in "Roman Scenes in *Prometheus Unbound*, III.iv" (*PQ*, 1967). Milton Wilson has followed up his chapter on Italian settings in *Shelley's Later Poetry* with a fascinating account, "Traveller's Venice: Some Images for Byron and Shelley" (*UTQ*, 1974), which is, however, of greater application to Byron than to Shelley.

SHELLEY'S ART

Unquestionably, the sources for Shelley's thought are not markedly different from those impinging on his artistic practices: the two cannot easily be separated. That Shelley was, with Blake, a profoundly mythopoeic writer can be seen from the perspective of how that impulse continually animates and harmonizes his poetic universe (Harold Bloom's approach in *Shelley's Mythmaking*) or from the recognition of the ideological as well as artistic consequences of his deep learning in comparative religions and anthropology, the area illuminated by Wasserman and Curran. The second chapter of Curran's *Shelley's Annus Mirabilis* goes further than previous scholarship—Edward Hungerford's jejune *Shores of Darkness* (1940) and Albert J. Kuhn's "English Deism and the Development of Romantic Mythological Syncretism" (*PMLA*, 1956)—in identifying the mythography on which Shelley extensively relied, particularly in *Prometheus Unbound*; the annotations here are copious. On syncretic mythology itself the broadest background is to be found in Paul Korshin's *Typologies in England, 1650–1820* (1982). Frederic S. Colwell brings a similar kind of learning to bear on another such work in "Shelley's 'Witch of Atlas' and the Mythic Geography of the Nile" (*ELH*, 1978). The plethora of daemonic mediators in Shelley was once used to support allegations of Platonic belief: John J. Lavelle in "Shelley's Pythagorean Daemons" (*Evidence of the Imagination*, ed. Reiman et al.), as his title indicates, shifts to firmer ground in his recognition of the mythic character of this species but cannot escape the suspicion that Shelley could have managed his demons without schooling from a mad and dogmatic French mystic (Fabre d'Olivet).

Particular extrapolations from classical Greek myth have been noted by a number of scholars. A general view is offered by John Ower, "The Epic Mythologies of Shelley and Keats" (*WascanaR*, 1969). The section on Shelley in Patricia Merivale's *Pan the Goat-God* (1969) is brief but is supported by citations of many interesting versions of the musical contest held between Apollo and Pan: those from the Renaissance and eighteenth century serve as context for Shelley.

Jean Perrin analyzes "The Actaeon Myth in Shelley's Poetry" (*E&S,* 1975), and Joseph Raben discusses "Shelley the Dionysian" (*Shelley Revalued,* 1983). In the same volume will be found Marilyn Butler's overview of the subject, "Myth and Mythmaking in the Shelley Circle." One recurrent symbol, the tail-eating serpent, has drawn repeated scholarly attention. Aside from connotations for the figure suggested in the books by Notopoulos, Rogers, Wasserman, and Curran, there are three separate essays. H. B. de Groot surveys the symbol in Blake, Coleridge, and Shelley in "The Ouroboros and the Romantic Poets" (*ES,* 1969), and Daniel J. Hughes has undertaken a more systematic and penetrating comparison in "Blake and Shelley: Beyond the Ouroboros" (*William Blake: Essays for S. Foster Damon,* ed. Alvin Rosenfeld, 1969). Robert Hartley goes over the same ground with much greater knowledge: his "The Ouroboros in Shelley's Poetry" (*JEGP,* 1974) emphasizes the serpent as a revolutionary political emblem. A like extension of symbolic connotations into a political realm is accomplished by G. M. Matthews in his classic essay "A Volcano's Voice in Shelley" (*ELH,* 1957).

It is impossible to note every author who has attempted to elaborate on, let alone simply to explain or unravel, the symbols of Shelley's poetry. The early essay of William Butler Yeats "The Philosophy of Shelley's Poetry" (1900) contained an influential examination of Shelley's leading symbols, confirmed in the brief essay on *Prometheus Unbound* of 1932. Carl Grabo's monographs on individual poems, *Prometheus Unbound* and *The Witch of Atlas* (both 1935), are focused especially on symbolic patternings. So also is G. Wilson Knight's *The Starlit Dome* (1941), Butter's *Idols of the Cave,* and Rogers' *Shelley at Work.* The subtitle of David Perkins' *Quest for Permanence* (1959) is "The Symbolism of Wordsworth, Shelley, and Keats." And if Richard Harter Fogle in *The Imagery of Keats and Shelley* seems more interested in comparing kinds of images, in that book (and in his later essays gathered into *The Permanent Pleasure*) he is ultimately concerned with the symbolic in Shelley. Particular symbols have been isolated for exploration: Carlos Baker, "The Traditional Background of Shelley's Ivy-Symbol" (*MLQ,* 1943); Newell F. Ford, "The Symbolism of Shelley's Nightingales" (*MLR,* 1960) and "The Symbolism of Shelley's Swans" (*SIR,* 1962); the three essays on Shelley's symbolic fluidity by Daniel J. Hughes, "Coherence and Collapse in Shelley, with Particular Reference to *Epipsychidion*" (*ELH,* 1961), "Potentiality in *Prometheus Unbound*" (*SIR,* 1963), and "Kindling and Dwindling: The Poetic Process in Shelley" (*KSJ,* 1964); Peter L. Thorslev, "Incest as Romantic Symbol" (*CLS,* 1965); and Curt R. Zimansky, "Cause and Effect: A Symbolism for Shelley's Poetry" (*JEGP,* 1979). In recent years the study of Shelleyan symbolism has become a preoccupation of French structuralist and phenomenological critics. Hélène Lemaitre's *Shelley: Poète des éléments* (1962) began the movement that flowered—perhaps "effulged" is the better term for a book over eight hundred pages long—in Jean Perrin's *Les Structures de l'imaginaire Shelleyan* (1973). Perrin's Shelley is a rhapsodic worshiper of nature and also a Platonist: as the first seems distinctly inappropriate and the two in conjunction are contradictory, so Perrin's interpretations also often seem to stretch Shelley's poetry beyond the recognizable. And yet, his magnified concentration on various symbols makes one constantly see afresh, even if one must adjust for distortions. Perrin has continued this line of investigation in "La Chaîne dans la poésie de Shelley," in *La Raison et l'imagi-naire*, papers from a 1970 conference at Rennes (1973), and in "La symbolique de la transcendance dans la poésie de Shelley," published in *Cahiers du Centre du Romanticisme Anglaise* (Univ. de Clérmont, 1978).

Two good books devoted to the distinctive qualities of Shelley's imagery take rather opposite tacks. Glenn O'Malley, in *Shelley and Synaesthesia* (1964), explores analogies among the senses from "Alastor" to *Adonais* as a means toward a complex aesthetic harmony, a wholeness that subsumes contraries. Jean Hall, in *The Transforming Image: A Study of Shelley's Major Poetry* (1981), like Daniel J. Hughes and other recent critics, emphasizes potentiality rather than completeness as a Shelleyan virtue. His art is one of endless transformation, in the mind as on the page: the poet is thus a maker of images who is himself continually created by his symbols. The artist and his art are in this sense mirrorlike, both constantly in motion. The thesis has much in common with John Wright's *Shelley's Myth of Metaphor,* and in its brevity *The Transforming Image* shares that book's tendency to suggest more than it can define.

Many of the treatments of Shelley's symbolism are as much analyses of his style as of his image patterns. The problem in stylistics until quite recently was to find an approach suitable to Shelley's distinctive and complex practices. Joseph Raben's computer investigations of the 1960s—already mentioned in terms of Miltonic influence on Shelley—never were sufficiently developed to frame a dependable methodology for others to use. And the strong linguistic orientation of Timothy Austin's "Constraints on Syntactic Rules and the Style of Shelley's 'Adonais': An Exercise in Stylistic Criticism" (*PLT,* 1979) has yielded little true insight on the poem. The more particularized linguistic investigation of Roger Murray's "A Case for the Study of Period Styles" (*CE,* 1971), concerned with the use of interrogatives in Byron and Shelley, is more successful. The study of how Shelley's syntax and imagery are keyed to ideas has made extraordinary advances of late, each one seeming to spark fresh thinking among its successors. Richard Cronin's *Shelley's Poetic Thoughts* has most to offer when, finished with what appear obligatory plot summaries, Cronin can focus intensely on the propriety and complex interplay of Shelley's syntax. Perhaps the best introduction to the importance of this subject for Shelley is in Stuart Peterfreund's "Shelley, Monboddo, Vico, and the Language of Poetry" (*Style,* 1981); Peterfreund extends his inquiry into the interrelations of the formal and the referential in "The Two Languages and the Ineffable in Shelley's Major Poetry" (in *The Ineffable from Dante to Beckett,* ed. Peter S. Hawkins and Anne Howland Schotter, 1984). Susan Hawk Brisman's " 'Unsaying His High Language': The Problem of Voice in *Prometheus Unbound*" (*SIR,* 1977) is richly suggestive in exploring the relation of speech to words and words to things in the lyrical drama. Likewise attending to its singular depth of nuance, V. A. De Luca—in "The Style of Millennial Announcement in *Prometheus Unbound*" (*KSJ,* 1979)—reveals the stylistic strategies by which Shelley maintains the openness of a social vision that one would expect to be closed. Frederick Burwick similarly shows the extent to which syntactic ambivalence, minutely observed, fits Shelley's overall design in "The Language of Causality in *Prometheus Unbound,*" (*KSJ,* 1982). Rather in the same line is Timothy Webb's contribution to the collection *Shelley Revalued* (1983), a subtle exploration of how negatives function to effect in the drama. William Keach has concentrated on a broad array of technical means and their intellectual ramifications in *Shelley's Style* (1984), incorporating his earlier essays, "Reflexive Imagery in Shelley" (*KSJ*, 1975) and "Shelley, Rhyme, and the Arbitrariness of Language" (*RP&P*, 1982). All the essays mentioned here, though shifting emphases and sometimes disagreeing on the terms of analysis, are in basic sympathy with the writings of Daniel J. Hughes and Jean Hall, noted above, and with the aesthetics of process so carefully laid down and radically insisted on in Jerrold Hogle's "Shelley's Poetics: The Power as Metaphor" (*KSJ*, 1982). Indeed, one sees in the area of stylistics a growing consensus that Shelley's linguistic and rhetorical strategies reflect his largest intellectual ends. With such a concentrated and illuminating burst of attention on Shelley as linguistic philosopher and artist, there is a distinct sense in which *Deconstruction and Criticism* — with "The Triumph of Life" more or less serving as a point of reference to Bloom, de Man, Derrida, Hartman, and J. Hillis Miller — just made it under the wire.

The increased interest in the correlation of stylistic devices and natural characteristics with Shelley's ideas has not yet led to a revival of interest in matters of versification and prosody, perhaps because that aspect of the discipline of letters is so technical and itself so little touched by the major advances in linguistic and stylistic analysis of recent years. The two general treatments of Shelley's versification are generations out of date: Armin Kroder's German monograph *Shelleys Verskunst* (1903) and Louise Propst's *An Analytical Study of Shelley's Versification* (1933). Two pieces by French critics narrow the focus but likewise bring it closer to our own ken. Charles Marie Garnier's "A Metrical Study of the Lyrical Parts in Shelley's 'Prometheus Unbound' " (*Langues Vivantes*, 1937) provides the basis for the use of that poem as the exemplary text in Georges Faure's *Les Eléments du rythme poétique en anglais moderne* (1970).

STUDIES OF INDIVIDUAL WORKS

The survey undertaken here must by its nature be out of proportion, with minor works emphasized to the same extent as major and with the setting of commentaries whose brevity may embody a condensed brilliance alongside those that may say relatively little at considerable length. Furthermore, such a survey must emphasize specifically pointed essays and notes at the expense of interpretations that occur as incidental discussions in full-length books. That much of value must be passed over in these circumstances is inevitable, and thus the studies singled out here should be viewed as the starting point for research not the inclusive perimeters.

The standard treatments of the juvenilia of Shelley are those encountered in Cameron's *The Young Shelley* and Hughes's *Nascent Mind of Shelley*, to which should be added the commentary for the Esdaile Notebook in *Shelley and His Circle*, volume 4, and that offered by Cameron and Rogers in their editions of this

collection. Marjorie Levinson offers a stimulating account of the program discernible in the "Posthumous Fragments of Margaret Nicholson," in *The Romantic Fragment Poem: A Critique of a Form* (1986). Bertram Dobell's account of "The Wandering Jew" in the Shelley Society Publications (1887) has been brought up to
modern knowledge by Neville Rogers in the notes to the first volume of the Clarendon edition and by S. G. Andrews' essay "Shelley, Medwin, and *The Wandering
Jew*" (*KSJ*, 1971). Shelley's sources are pinpointed by Roxana Klapper in *The German Literary Influence on Shelley;* a broader traditional context is in George K.
Anderson, *The Legend of the Wandering Jew* (1965). The more playfully demonic
early ballad "The Devil's Walk" is placed within its contemporary setting by C.
Darrel Sheraw in "Coleridge, Shelley, Byron, and the Devil" (*KSMB*, 1972).
Shelley's adolescent forays into Gothic fiction continue to fascinate critics, in part
because they are so excruciatingly bad. It is perhaps fitting that they have provoked what is arguably the worst modern study of Shelley, *Shelley and Zastrozzi:
Self-Revelation of a Neurotic* (1965) by the British psychologist Eustace Chesser,
who attributes to quirks of Shelley's personality what are clichés of the Gothic
tradition and who bases his argument on Shelley's letters to Hogg that are corrupted by Hogg's artful changing of pronouns. Standard writings on the Gothic
fiction are A. M. D. Hughes, "Shelley's *Zastrozzi* and *St. Irvyne*" (*MLR*, 1912);
Frederick L. Jones, "*Alastor* Foreshadowed in *St. Irvyne*" (*PMLA*, 1934); and David G.
Halliburton, "Shelley's Gothic Novels" (*KSJ*, 1967). There is surprisingly little
added to the account in John V. Murphy's *The Dark Angel: Gothic Elements in
Shelley's Works* (1975). A new sophistication enters the discussion with Andy
Antippas, "The Structure of Shelley's *St. Irvyne*: Parallelism and the Gothic Mode
of Evil" (*TSE*, 1970). The finest study of these works, encompassing all Shelley's
attempts at prose narrative, in which linear and atemporal structures are continually seen at odds, is that by Jerrold E. Hogle, "Shelley's Fiction: 'The Stream of
Fate'" (*KSJ*, 1981). The two Gothic novels have been reprinted in the Arno Press
series with an introduction by Frederick Frank (1977).

There is little separate commentary on the early polemical and philosophical
prose. Harold Orel's "Another Look at 'The Necessity of Atheism'" (*Mosaic,* 1969;
slightly rev., *Studies in Voltaire and the Eighteenth Century,* 1973) paradoxically
argues deistic roots; see also Bice Chiapelli's *Il pensiero religioso di Shelley*
(1956). Pulos in *The Deep Truth* is helpful in setting "A Refutation of Deism"
within eighteenth-century controversies, and Wasserman interprets its carefully
manipulated dialogue as a characteristic Shelleyan strategy. Shelley's intellectual
development is charted by John Freeman in "Shelley's Early Letters" (*Shelley
Revalued,* 1983). The Irish political tracts have recently been historically
grounded by P. M. S. Dawson in *The Unacknowledged Legislator* (1980) and by
E. B. Murray (*SIR*, 1978). A lengthy treatment of the early prose, centering it on
the unified vision of *Queen Mab*, is offered by Michael Scrivener in *Radical
Shelley,* and Cameron's large and persuasive view of the ideological importance of
that poem is also worth recall. Curran in *Shelley's Annus Mirabilis* stresses contradictions within the thought of *Queen Mab* but argues for a unified metaphorical structure. The complications of the two attempts to recast the poem as "The
Daemon of the World" and "The Queen of the Universe" are set forth by

Cameron in *Shelley and His Circle,* volume 4. William Hildebrand develops a generic link among these early poems and "Alastor" in "Shelley's Early Vision Poems" (*SIR,* 1969), a notion extended across Shelley's canon in Leslie Brisman's *Romantic Origins* (1978).

"Alastor," in the twenty-five years since Milton Wilson declared it the *Hamlet* of Shelley studies, has amply fulfilled his description. There seems no end in sight in the effort to resolve its confusions or to fathom its archetypal power. One can, however, observe distinct lines of thought within the multitude of interpretations. Early source studies—for example, L. H. Allen, "Plagiarism, Sources, and Influences in Shelley's *Alastor*" (*MLR,* 1923); Kenneth Neill Cameron, "*Rasselas* and *Alastor*" (*SP,* 1943); Jerome W. Archer, "*Kubla Khan, Queen Mab,* II.4 – 79; VIII.70 – 103, and *Alastor,* 81 – 94, 163 – 172" (*SP,* 1944)—established generic and thematic links. Another such line has been the fruitless but curiously illuminating attempt to identify Shelley's obsessive Poet with a particular contemporary. The naive assumption that this is a self-portrait, which usually ignores the poem's complicated double stance, appears again and again in earlier, and especially in hostile, criticism (as if the poem were objective documentary evidence rather than a created artifact). No more tenable is the attempt to identify the Poet's desires and experiences as those of the actual Wordsworth—Paul Mueschke and Earl L. Griggs, "Wordsworth as the Prototype of the Poet in Shelley's *Alastor*" (*PMLA,* 1934), whose arguments were countered by Marcel Kessel, "The Poet in Shelley's *Alastor:* A Criticism and a Reply" (*PMLA,* 1936), but have recently been renewed by Yvonne M. Carothers, "*Alastor*: Shelley Corrects Wordsworth" (*MLQ,* 1981)—or of Coleridge—Joseph Raben, "Coleridge as the Prototype of the Poet in Shelley's *Alastor*" (*RES,* 1966), predictably refuted by Timothy Webb, "Coleridge and Shelley's *Alastor:* A Reply" (*RES,* 1967)—or of Rousseau—Donald L. Maddox, "Shelley's *Alastor* and the Legacy of Rousseau" (*SIR,* 1970). Wrongheaded as such specific identifications were, they nonetheless emphasized the extent to which Shelley's Poet embodied a recognizably Romantic drive. There was also an extended debate over the poem's consistency, which began with Raymond Dexter Havens (*PMLA,* 1930, 1931), who was answered by M. C. Weir (*PMLA,* 1931), and which was then resumed by Harold Leroy Hoffman in his monograph Alastor: *An Odyssey of the Soul* (1933) and by Frederick L. Jones (*ELH,* 1946; *SP,* 1947). The most lucid early claim for the overall unity of the poem and preface was asserted by Evan K. Gibson in "*Alastor*: A Reinterpretation" (*PMLA,* 1947). Yet another critical line has been to trace the relationship between "Alastor" and Keats's *Endymion*: this was initiated by an essentially foolish essay, Leonard Brown's "The Genesis, Growth, and Meaning of *Endymion*" (*SP,* 1933), then more seriously examined in J. D. Wigod's "The Meaning of *Endymion*" (*PMLA,* 1953) and, most recently, in Miriam Allott's "Keats's *Endymion* and Shelley's *Alastor,*" printed in *Literature of the Romantic Period, 1750 – 1850,* edited by R. T. Davies and B. G. Beatty (1976). As these critics seem intent on covering Keats's embarrassments by their disdain for Shelley's poem, one might wish a reconsideration of this interesting subject from a less bardolatrous perspective. A recent and suggestive critical line, relating the poem to its immediate context, was begun by William J. McTaggart's rapid survey

"The Design and Unity of Shelley's *Alastor* Volume" (*KSMB*, 1972) and renewed in a probing essay by Neil Fraistat in *KSJ* (1984).

In surveys such as this, earlier essays of limited aims and sound common sense tend to get lost next to those with grand, if implausible, claims: one such is Arthur E. DuBois' "Alastor: Spirit of Solitude" (*JEGP*, 1936), which set the general lines of inquiry for William H. Hildebrand's monograph *A Study of Alastor* (Kent State Research Series, 1954). Albert S. Gérard's *'Alastor, or the Spirit of Solipsism"* (*PQ*, 1954) is reprinted as a chapter entitled "The Hopeless Quest" in his *English Romantic Poetry: Ethos, Structure, and Symbol in Coleridge, Wordsworth, Shelley, and Keats* (1968). Gérard's view of the poem as a dialectical exploration has been a shared assumption in more recent commentary. Bryan Cooper—"Shelley's *Alastor*: The Quest for a Vision" (*KSJ*, 1970)—sees death as the driving force and the final love-death reflected in symbols with dual associations: fire, the wild, waste. John C. Bean traces an allegory of the quest for spiritual knowledge with greater specificity than other critics (and perhaps the poem) have allowed in "The Poet Borne Darkly: The Dream-Voyage Allegory in Shelley's *Alastor*" (*KSJ*, 1974). James C. Evans' "Masks of the Poet: A Study of Self-Confrontation in Shelley's Poetry" (*KSJ*, 1975) begins by interpreting "Alastor" as an allegory of the Poet's pursuing his perfected self through art, then wanders off across the canon in search of doubles. The suggestion by T. J. Spencer—in "Shelley's 'Alastor' and Romantic Drama" (*Transactions of the Wisconsin Academy*, 1959)—that the Hippolytus myth stands behind the poem has been more specifically proposed in reference to Euripides' tragedy by Henning Krabbe (*N&Q*, 1980). Luther Scales has surrounded the poem by the scaffolding of *Paradise Lost* in "The Poet as Miltonic Adam in Shelley's *Alastor*" (*KSJ*, 1972–73), though many readers might wonder whether a movement from Satanic struggle to Adamic insight accurately characterizes the poem.

By far the most influential reading of the poem in recent criticism is that in Wasserman's *Shelley: A Critical Reading*, an interpretation so elaborately argued that almost no essay directly concerned with the poem since has tried to establish an independent perspective. Wasserman sees the narrator's role not as simply celebratory of the Poet but as almost, if unconsciously, adversarial; and, though later readers have generally found his structuring of the relationship of the two unnecessarily complicated, the sense of the poem as enacting an implicit dialogue has dominated criticism for the past decade. Norman Thurston, in "Author, Narrator, and Hero in Shelley's *Alastor*" (*SIR*, 1975), complicates the framework even further by introducing Shelley as a third consciousness in preface and poem. Ronald Tetreault, in "Quest and Caution: Psychomachy in Shelley's *Alastor*" (*ESC*, 1977), sees Shelley's skeptical attitude as undermining both figures in the poem; and Lisa M. Steinman, in "Shelley's Skepticism: Allegory in *Alastor*" (*ELH*, 1978), likewise recognizes an extreme skepticism underlying the narrative. The most recent criticism has backed away from the overly ingenious schematization fostered by Wasserman and those in his wake, preferring to see Shelley testing his own tendencies in the career of his Poet: sophisticated psychoanalytic models are employed in Frederick Kirchhoff's "Shelley's *Alastor*: The Poet Who Refuses to Write Language" (*KSJ*, 1983) and in Edward Strickland's concentration on narcissistic patterns in the poem (*KSJ*, 1984). Barbara Schapiro, in *The Romantic Mother* (1983), crudely suggests an adolescent oedipal fixation in Shelley.

Modern interpretation of "Mont Blanc" rests on the foundations established by two early essays: Israel Kapstein's "The Meaning of Shelley's *Mont Blanc*" (*PMLA*, 1947) and Charles H. Vivian's "The One 'Mont Blanc'" (*KSJ*, 1955), as well as Wasserman's probing explication in *The Subtler Language* (somewhat recast for *Shelley: A Critical Reading*). The most significant readings of the poem since have been Judith Chernaik's (in *The Lyrics of Shelley*), Spencer Hall's elucidation of its wholly skeptical nature (*SP*, 1973), and Gerald McNiece's "The Poet as Ironist in 'Mont Blanc' and 'Hymn to Intellectual Beauty'" (*SIR*, 1975), which accentuates Shelley's rhetorical strategies. The function of rhyme has also been suggestively explored in William Keach's *Shelley's Style* (1984). As in McNiece's essay, many critics treat "Mont Blanc" and the "Hymn to Intellectual Beauty" together or in the light of each other. Chernaik, for instance, is also excellent in writing about the "Hymn." Its most meticulous critical interpretation is that offered by Spencer Hall, "Power and the Poet: Religious Mythmaking in Shelley's 'Hymn to Intellectual Beauty'" (*KSJ*, 1983). Coleridge's "Hymn before Sunrise" is increasingly regarded as a further context for "Mont Blanc": see, for instance, John Rieder's "Shelley's Mont Blanc: Landscape and the Ideology of the Sacred Text" (*ELH*, 1981). A further consideration of Shelley's view of the sacred in his "Hymn" is undertaken by David Robertson in *The Old Testament and the Literary Critic* (1977). The recurring textual crux of "Mont Blanc"—"But for such faith"—has been well treated by Joan Rees (*RES*, 1964) and John Kinnaird (*N&Q*, 1968); E. B. Murray takes on another such problem in "Mont Blanc's Unfurled Veil" (*KSJ*, 1969). Shelley's corrections to the "Hymn" are enumerated by Stuart Curran (*ELN*, 1970). But the texts of these two poems seem destined to be a continuing center of controversy, for new variants surfaced with the discovery of the fair copies in the Scrope Davies notebook: see the accounts by Neville Rogers (*KSMB*, 1977), Judith Chernaik and Timothy Burnett (*RES*, 1978), and Dewey Faulkner (*YR*, 1979). Roland Duerksen ingeniously reads the two sonnets discovered in this notebook as elaborations of these major poems (*BRH*, 1980). Erland Anderson briefly examines the first of the sonnets in *ELN*, 1979.

If "Alastor" is the *Hamlet* among Shelley texts, *The Revolt of Islam* qualifies as *The Excursion*, more honored in the breach than in the observance and generally read as a matter of principle. Though the number of separate interpretations is not great, several are of high quality. Shelley's forced revisions have dominated textual commentary. Neville Rogers, in basically reverting to the initial text (in the Clarendon edition, vol. 2), offers ample annotations. These are buttressed by the nearly fifty pages of Donald H. Reiman's account in *Shelley and His Circle*, volume 5, which includes shrewd surmises about the structure based on an examination of the manuscripts, a succinct representation of those manuscripts, and a summary of the publication problems. Claude C. Brew, in a monograph published by the Keats-Shelley Memorial Association in 1971—*Shelley and Mary in 1817: The Dedication to* The Revolt of Islam—charts the process of composition in this much revised passage. The epic claims of the poem are analyzed in Brian

Wilkie's valuable *Romantic Poets and Epic Tradition* (1965) and by Curran in *Shelley's Annus Mirabilis.* The symmetries of the structure are Richard H. Haswell's major concern in "Shelley's *The Revolt of Islam:* 'The Connexion of Its Parts'" (*KSJ,* 1976). The symmetries of character are as purposeful, argues E. B. Murray in "'Elective Affinity' in *The Revolt of Islam*" (*JEGP,* 1968), a viewpoint somewhat modified in the interests of growth and experience by Stuart Sperry in "The Sexual Theme in Shelley's *The Revolt of Islam*" (*JEGP,* 1983). Other recent essays include Anthony Arthur's "The Poet as Revolutionary in *The Revolt of Islam*" (*XUS,* 1971) and Harold Orel's "Shelley's *Revolt of Islam*: The Last Great Poem of the English Enlightenment?" twice published in *Studies in Voltaire and the Eighteenth Century* (1972, 1973). Earlier writings to which critics habitually return are Kenneth Neill Cameron's "A Major Source for *The Revolt of Islam*" (*PMLA,* 1943), Wilfred S. Dowden's monograph *Shelley's Use of Metempsychosis in "The Revolt of Islam"* (*Rice Inst. Pamphlets,* 1951), and Frederick L. Jones's "Canto I of *The Revolt of Islam*" (*KSJ,* 1960). The avowedly propagandistic nature of this poem makes it a central document for considerations of Shelley's religious and political views before his Italian exile distanced him from an immediate focus on English society. The prose works that accompany his thinking along these lines have, until recently, never received the attention they deserve. Ernest J. Lovell, Jr., and John Clubbe, in "Shelley's Prose: The Growth of a Moral Vision" (*PSt,* 1980), place these works within a developing but unified perspective. They have been most extensively considered by Michael Scrivener in *Radical Shelley.*

It is hard to imagine a major work by another poet of Shelley's stature as neglected as has been "Rosalind and Helen": one must revert many years to find more than a cursory treatment, and the older essays demand running mental adjustment to a modern critical framework. These are Raymond Dexter Havens' interpretation (*JEGP,* 1931) and that of Bennett Weaver in "Pre-Promethean Thought in Three Longer Poems of Shelley" (*PQ,* 1950). The minor masterpiece "Lines Written among the Euganean Hills" has been less neglected, but there is only one essay whose attention is fixed squarely on that poem: fortunately, Donald H. Reiman's analysis "Structure, Symbol, and Theme" (*PMLA,* 1962) is an exemplary critical reading. Karl Kroeber has suggestively extrapolated from the poem a statement about history in "Experience as History: Shelley's Venice, Turner's Carthage" (*ELH,* 1974). It might be noted that with this poem one enters the period when Shelley's interaction with Byron reached a peak of creative intensity, so that Robinson provides valuable background on and insight into these writings. "Ozymandias," written much earlier but published with these poems, has been paradoxically much more celebrated: typical discussions of the sources of the sonnet are contributed by Johnstone Parr and H. M. Richmond (*KSJ,* 1957, 1962); and Horace Smith's sonnet written in competition with Shelley's is printed and discussed by M. K. Bequette in *KSJ,* 1977.

It is a nonevent worth celebrating that no new candidates for the identity of the Maniac in "Julian and Maddalo" have been proposed since the last edition of this guide, which is to say that criticism has shifted entirely from such peripheral issues to analysis of the imagery, characters, and structure of the poem. Again, the major impulse to this critical orientation is Wasserman's probing study in *Shelley:*

A Critical Reading. His basic thesis—that the poem inconclusively represents contradictory philosophies as a means of engaging the reader's active
compassion—is disarmingly simple; but Wasserman consolidated the undogmatic
approaches of James L. Hill ("Thematic Structure in Shelley's *Julian and
Maddalo*," *ELH*, 1968) and of Reiman. That the skeptical premise of these critics is
not universally accepted is evidenced by Charles Robinson's lengthy exposition of
the Maniac as a Byronic hero (and the poem as thus a sharp attack on Byron) or
by Bernard A. Hirsch in "'A Want of That True Theory': *Julian and Maddalo* as
Dramatic Monologue" (*SIR*, 1978), which takes Julian to task for his moral
insensitivity and other failings. A counterargument for Julian's moral sophistication and basic decency has been made by Curran in *Shelley's Annus Mirabilis*.
Richard E. Brown in "Self-Resolution in Shelley's *Julian and Maddalo*" (*Rocky
Mountain Review*, 1975) argues against Wasserman that the irresolution at the
end testifies not to paralysis but to a balanced integration of views. In recent writing the poem's ideological and political ramifications have been subtly probed:
see Kelvin Everest's "Shelley's Doubles: An Approach to *Julian and Maddalo*"
(*Shelley Revalued*, 1983) and Marjorie Levinson's powerful analysis of alienation
in *The Romantic Fragment Poem: A Critique of a Form* (1986). Among earlier
studies perhaps the most significant is that of G. M. Matthews, "'Julian and
Maddalo': The Draft and the Meaning" (*SN*, 1963).

"Julian and Maddalo" and *The Cenci* have often been linked because of their
dramatic nature, their ambiguities, and their unblinking representation of what
Shelley in the dedication of his tragedy called "sad reality." The standard treatment of *The Cenci* is Stuart Curran's *Shelley's* Cenci: *Scorpions Ringed with Fire*
(1970). Divided into sections covering the work as poem and as stage vehicle, the
commentary focuses on the versification, patterns of imagery, the representation
of characters, and the large psychological and metaphysical questions Shelley
raises, then turns to an examination of contemporary drama and stage usage as
contexts, demonstrates the work's viability as a stage vehicle and the variety of
approaches it has elicited through its stage history, and concludes with an exploration of Shelley's dramaturgy from the perspective of the modern stage. The one
area of controversy in the book, in which Curran argues for a radical critical
rethinking, is his view that Beatrice is not corrupted into behaving like her father
but, in terms of her culture and her predicament, is faced with no alternative but
her father's death. This has not drawn many adherents in print. The contrary perspective, which sees the tragedy as concerned with Beatrice's moral degenera-
tion, is ably represented by Robert F. Whitman in "Beatrice's 'Pernicious Mistake'
in *The Cenci*" (*PMLA*, 1959) and more recently by Walter H. Evert in "Coadjutors
of Oppression: A Romantic and Modern Theory of Evil" (included in the volume
Romantic and Modern: Revaluations of Literary Tradition, ed. George Bornstein,
1977). Both perspectives can reduce to single vision, the one defending Beatrice
in terms of sentimentalized abstractions like innocence (see Erika Gottlieb, "Cosmic Allegory in *The Cenci*," *AJES*, 1978; rpt. in *Lost Angels of a Ruined Paradise*,
1981), the other attacking her with a shrill moralism inappropriate to art, especially to tragedy. Among studies in full-length books Rieger's identification of the

Shelleys' knowledge of the Gnostic sect of Paterini—originally published as "Shelley's Paterin Beatrice" (*SIR*, 1965)—firmly establishes the metaphysical and theological issues of the tragedy; Joseph W. Donohue, Jr., devotes chapter 7 of *Dramatic Character in the English Romantic Age* (1970), still the best study of the aesthetics of Romantic drama, to an analysis of *The Cenci* as "The Drama of Radical Innocence" (originally published in *KSJ*, 1968), forcing a double vision on its audience; a similar ambivalence is traced by Wasserman to the double view of the entire age concerning the French Revolution (this being virtually his only descent into the political dynamics of Shelley's culture); Curran returns to the tragedy in *Shelley's Annus Mirabilis,* tracing links to the victimization of Io in Aeschylus' *Prometheus Bound* and accentuating the importance of the play's anti-Christian perspective. The best of a generally weak mix, *Essays on Shelley,* edited by Miriam Allott (1982), is Michael Worton's "Speech and Silence in *The Cenci.*"

Among other useful studies of sources and analogues, one might consult Truman Guy Steffan's "Seven Accounts of the Cenci and Shelley's Drama" (*SEL*, 1969); Fred L. Milne's tracing the association of evil and coldness to Dante in "Shelley's *The Cenci:* The Ice Motif and the Ninth Circle of Dante's Hell" (*TSL*, 1977); Paul Cantor's distinction between Shelleyan and Shakespearean tragedy (*HES*, 1976); and D. M. Harrington-Lueker on the organic rationale for Shelley's allusions to *Macbeth* (*KSJ*, 1983), the most recent among the essays on Shelley and Shakespeare already cited. Note also Richard A. Davison's sense of an echo from John Webster (*AN&Q*, 1967) and William D. Sims-Gunzenhauser's "Conflict of the Inner Self in Goethe's *Iphigenie* and Shelley's *Cenci*" (*Neophil*, 1979). Among other historically centered arguments Fred L. Milne has suggested the feast of the Holy Innocents as ironic context for the death of Beatrice's brothers (*Expl*, 1976); James B. Twitchell in "Shelley's Use of Vampirism in *The Cenci*" (*TSL*, 1979; rpt. in *The Living Dead: A Study of the Vampire in Romantic Literature*, 1981) easily establishes the symbolic link but rather contradicts the legendary exigencies by condemning Beatrice for killing her vampirelike father; and Barbara Groseclose concentrates on the famous portrait of Beatrice and other artistic renderings in "A Portrait Not by Guido Reni of a Girl Who Is Not Beatrice Cenci" (*SECC*, 1982). Other recent critical essays on the drama are of lesser interest: Ronald L. Lemoncelli's "Cenci as Corrupt Dramatic Poet" (*ELN*, 1978) interprets Beatrice as text, which is rather like executing her in French; Harry White questions whether Shelley is not justifying violent revolution in "Beatrice Cenci and Shelley's Avenger" (*ELWIU*, 1978), and James D. Wilson in "Beatrice Cenci and Shelley's Vision of Moral Responsibility" (*ArielE*, 1978) seems to be suggesting that an immortal realm is implicitly affirmed by so corrupt a mortal realm, a logical fallacy that Shelley would have been quick to catch. Adding nothing new are Sara Nasi Miller, "Irony in Shelley's *The Cenci*" (*MSE*, 1969), Arlene R. Thorn, "Shelley's *The Cenci* as Tragedy" (*Costerus*, 1973), P. Jay Delmar, "Evil and Character in Shelley's *The Cenci*" (*MSE*, 1978), and Eugene R. Hammond, "Beatrice's Three Fathers: Successive Betrayal in Shelley's *The Cenci*" (*ELWIU*, 1981). Several of the earlier essays on the tragedy are still worth consulting: Joan Rees's "Shelley's Orsino: Evil in

The Cenci" (*KSMB*, 1961), Paul Smith's "Restless Casuistry: Shelley's Composition of *The Cenci"* (*KSJ*, 1964), and Charles L. Adams' defense of the drama's structure, "The Structure of *The Cenci"* (*Drama Survey*, 1965).

On the dramatic propriety of *The Cenci* for a Regency theater, on its validity as stage vehicle, and on the history of productions Curran's study (1970) subsumes the prior critical literature. Other theatrically oriented commentary includes that of Richard M. Fletcher's valuable *English Romantic Drama, 1795–1843* (1966); Donohue's *Dramatic Character in the English Romantic Age* (1970), already cited; and Terry Otten's *The Deserted Stage: The Search for Dramatic Form in Nineteenth-Century England* (1972). An astute dramatic and imagistic analysis is offered by Richard Hornby on the basis of his directing a University of Calgary production in *Script into Performance: A Structuralist View of Play Production* (1977). This production clearly portrayed Beatrice as corrupted by her father and degenerating through the play; the opposite approach was taken by the 1976–77 New York production briefly described by Stuart Curran in *KSJ*, 1978. Although tangential, Antonin Artaud's adaptation of *The Cenci* has attained something of a cult status (though all comparisons give the dramatic and literary nod to Shelley: e.g., Albert E. Rickert in *BSUF*, 1973). Artaud's text and his various pronouncements concerning the play can be found in volumes 4 and 5 of his *Oeuvres complètes* (1964). The English translation, by Simon Watson Taylor, was published in 1969; and Artaud's commentaries are translated, along with additional matter, in the lengthy "Antonin Artaud's *Les Cenci:* Performance, Blocking, Diagrams, Reviews" (*TDR*, 1972). See also M. Labelle, "Artaud's Use of Shelley's *The Cenci:* The Experiment in the Théâtre de la Cruauté" (*RLC*, 1972). Finally, Shaw's brilliant review of the 1886 Shelley Society production has been reprinted in the *Shaw Review* (1972).

Critics (e.g., Rieger, Reiman) have noted in passing the curious links of image and structure between *The Cenci* and *Prometheus Unbound*. Wasserman analyzes these extensively; even more so does Curran in *Shelley's Annus Mirabilis*. Between them the remarkable degree to which the two dramas play off against each other is greatly illuminated. Their conclusions about what it all signifies are rather different.

Prometheus Unbound has itself elicited the largest amount of, and frequently the best, criticism on Shelley, especially in the last quarter century. It is virtually impossible to be fair to the range, specificity, or larger integrations of the more sophisticated writing on Shelley's lyrical drama, particularly during this period. What that means in effect—and it is difficult here not to sound condescending about herculean labors—is that the six hundred or so pages of commentary in Lawrence Zillman's variorum edition (1959) represent the codification of scholarship before this rapid, sustained, and learned critical elaboration, bringing together a massive bulk of either what is simply wrong in the face of modern principles of criticism or what the reader does not need to know—or both. Of course, it requires considerable knowledge to recognize what one need not know. A fundamental problem with *Prometheus Unbound,* which the variorum ignores, is its mode. Critics who try to read it literally find themselves enmeshed in what appear contradictions: much early criticism suffers from this, but it persists among modern interpreters as well, as is exemplified by the view of Holmes and Abbey that the retirement of Prometheus and Asia to their cave resolves the work in a detached quietism ill-suited to its political aspirations. Generally more successful are those critics who interpret the drama as symbolic and psychological in mode, a perspective that now appears to have drawn a critical consensus behind it. Again, Wasserman's analysis, though his definition of Prometheus as the "One Mind" has prompted much questioning, has been widely influential. Since none of Shelley's works was more painstakingly crafted, it goes without saying that a basic knowledge of and respect for the accumulated critical understanding of the poem should protect student and critic alike from making inappropriate demands of it.

The longest and most valuable early interpretations include Grabo's Prometheus Unbound: *An Interpretation* (1935), Bennett Weaver's *Prometheus Unbound* (1957), and the accounts in Carlos Baker's *Shelley's Major Poetry* and Milton Wilson's *Shelley's Later Poetry.* Wasserman's Prometheus Unbound: *A Critical Reading* (1965) is expanded in *Shelley: A Critical Reading*; critically astute, the discussion is sometimes densely philosophical in orientation. Another work devoted entirely to the drama, William H. Hildebrand's monograph in the Salzburg Studies series—*Shelley's Polar Paradise: A Reading of* Prometheus Unbound (1974)—is a running explication, but what it loses in overall perspective and contexts is made up for in its attention to particulars of Shelley's language and imagery. Among other book-length studies of recent years, Curran's two sizable chapters in *Shelley's Annus Mirabilis* represent the furthest scholarly advance thus far in relating Shelley's use of geography (superseding Joseph Raben's "Shelley's *Prometheus Unbound:* Why the Indian Caucasus?" *KSJ,* 1963) and syncretic mythology to his aims and also explore correspondences between the microcosm of the psyche and the macrocosm of a scientific universe. With a more generalized perspective Northrop Frye reveals Shelley's mythic universe in the long chapter devoted to this poem in *A Study of English Romanticism* (1968). Charles Robinson (*Shelley and Byron*) documents the extent to which *Prometheus Unbound* engages in a dialogue with Byron's *Manfred* and *Childe Harold's Pilgrimage.* Jean Hall (*The Transforming Image,* 1980) concentrates on the significance of the lyrical, while Richard Cronin (*Shelley's Poetic Thoughts,* 1981) examines the evolving dramatic structure. The value of Shelley's conception of lyrical drama is noted in many commentaries; Jerome Christensen explores how this generic alloy develops in Romantic literature in *WC,* 1981.

The major interpretations of the political contexts and reverberations of *Prometheus Unbound* are in Cameron's *PMLA* essay of 1943 (assimilated within *Shelley: The Golden Years*), Woodring's *Politics in English Romantic Poetry* (1970), and Dawson's *Unacknowledged Legislator* (1980). All significant interpretations of the poem are concerned with its rich patterns of imagery, but among those concentrating specifically on this aspect are Richard Harter Fogle in "Image and Imageless: A Limited Reading of *Prometheus Unbound*" (*KSJ,* 1952), included in *The Permanent Pleasure* (1974), and Sarah Dyck's monograph "The Presence of That Shape: Shelley's *Prometheus Unbound*" (*Costerus,* 1972). Frederic S. Colwell's two essays (*KSJ,* 1979, 1980) on Shelley's interest in art in Italy focus strongly on its effects on this poem, as does Nancy Goslee's essay in *Comparatist* (1980). Georges Faure's *Les Eléments du rhythme poétique en anglais moderne* (1970) uses the poem as its exemplary text: its aim is to advance Charles Marie Garnier's "A Metrical Study of the Lyrical Parts in Shelley's *Prometheus Unbound*" (*Langues Vivantes,* 1937): these are really investigations of scansion in both the blank verse and complexly patterned lyrics. To the important essays on the language in the work by Susan Hawk Brisman (*SIR,* 1977), V. A. De Luca (*KSJ,* 1979), Frederick Burwick (*KSJ,* 1982), and Timothy Webb (*Shelley Revalued,* 1983), one can add Leonard N. Neufeldt's "Poetry as Subversion: The Unbinding of Shelley's Prometheus" (*Anglia,* 1977), whose own rhapsodic style rather subverts analysis; Anya Taylor's "Shelley's Occult Drama," printed in *Literature and the Occult,* edited by Luanne Frank (1977), and as chapter 6 of Taylor's *Magic and English Romanticism* (1979), an essay whose premises are palatable only with grains of salt; and Norman Thurston's "The Second Language of *Prometheus Unbound*" (*PQ,* 1976).

On the complexities of Shelley's recasting of Aeschylus the main writings are Bennett Weaver's "*Prometheus Bound* and *Prometheus Unbound*" (*PMLA,* 1949), James C. Hurt's "*Prometheus Unbound* and Aeschylean Dramaturgy" (*KSJ,* 1966), and Wasserman's. On the relation of Shelley's work to other versions of the myth, besides Wasserman, Curran, and Robinson, one should consult Christian Kreutz, *Das Prometheussymbol in der Dichtung der englischen Romantik* (1963), Raymond Trousson, *Le Thème de Prométhée dans la littérature européenne* (Geneva, 1964), and James A. Harvie, "The Promethean Syndrome" (*CLS,* 1976), which compares Shelley and Lermontov. The psychological validity of Shelley's representation of Prometheus is intelligently underscored by Leon Waldoff in "The Father-Son Conflict in *Prometheus Unbound*: The Psychology of Vision" (*Psychoanalytic Review,* 1975). Psychological issues combine with arcane traditions in Ross Woodman's "The Androgyne in *Prometheus Unbound*" (*SIR,* 1981). Stuart Sperry probes the extent to which free will is exhibited and tempered in "Necessity and the Role of the Hero in *Prometheus Unbound*" (*PMLA,* 1981). Other general treatments include the influential essay of Daniel J. Hughes, "Potentiality in *Prometheus Unbound*" (*SIR,* 1963); I. A. Richards' view of the poem as a sacred text in "The Mystical Element in Shelley's Poetry" (*The Aryan Path,* 1959) and in the epilogue to *Beyond* (1973); William Ernest Ray, "The Education of Prometheus" (*Interpretations,* 1973); William H. Hildebrand, "On Three Prometheuses: Shelley's Two and Mary's One" (*Serif,* 1974); Roland Duerksen, "Shelley's 'Deep Truth' Reconsidered" (*ELN,* 1975), on love, and "Shelley's Prometheus: Destroyer and Preserver" (*SEL,* 1978), on the paradoxes of self-annihilation; and John Ower, "The Aesthetic Hero: His Innocence, Fall, and Redemption" (*BuR,* 1977). Of the several French interpretations of this work the most substantial is *La Mystique du* Prometheus Unbound *de Shelley: Essai d'interpretation* (1970) by C. da Cassagnère. J.-G. Ritz includes an essay, "Le Dynamisme prophétique de Shelley dans *Prometheus Unbound,*" in the collection "Le Romantisme anglo-américain" in *EA,* 1971.

A number of essays focus on particular characters or scenes. Frederick A. Pottle's "The Role of Asia in the Dramatic Action of Shelley's *Prometheus Unbound*" has become a justified classic since its publication in *Shelley: A Collection of Critical Essays* (ed. George M. Ridenour, 1965). It is joined in penetration and eloquence by William H. Hildebrand's "Naming-Day in Asia's Vale" (*KSJ*, 1983). Duncan Williams, in "Shelley's Demogorgon" (*WVUPP*, 1970), rather neatly undermines most definitions of this enigmatic presence, but he could have subjected his own ("Eternity") to a comparable critique. On this figure, see also G. M. Matthews' "A Volcano's Voice in Shelley" (*ELH*, 1957), Richard Cronin's complementary "A Tidal Murmur in Shelley" (*N&Q*, 1977), Pierre Vitoux's "Jupiter's Fatal Child in *Prometheus Unbound*" (*Criticism*, 1968), and the analyses of Wasserman and Curran. Mildred S. McGill undertakes to explain "The Role of Earth in Shelley's *Prometheus Unbound*" (*SIR*, 1968). On the dynamics of the first act of the drama, see James R. Bennett, "*Prometheus Unbound*, Act I, 'The play's the thing' " (*KSJ*, 1974), and Daniel J. Hughes, "Prometheus Made Capable Poet in Act One of *Prometheus Unbound*" (*SIR*, 1978). E. B. Murray's "Gnashing and Wailing in *Prometheus Unbound*" (*KSJ*, 1975) probes the language of the Furies, and William H. Hildebrand analyzes at considerable length the third and fourth spirit songs (*KSJ*, 1971). Hildebrand's essay on Asia cited above (*KSJ*, 1983) concentrates on the first scene of the second act; Priscilla St. George attends to its very end in "Another Look at Two Famous Lyrics in *Prometheus Unbound*" (*JEGP*, 1968). Donald H. Reiman suggests how much Shelley's setting influenced his writing in "Roman Scenes in *Prometheus Unbound*, III.iv" (*PQ*, 1967). Michael Hyde glances at what was "The Lockean Ending of Shelley's Original Conclusion to *Prometheus Unbound*," that is to say, the third act (*N&Q*, 1980). On the fourth act specifically, one could consult James B. Twitchell, "Shelley's Metapsychological System in Act IV of *Prometheus Unbound*" (*KSJ*, 1975), Joanna E. Rapf, "A Spirit in Search of Itself: Non-Narrative Structure in Act IV of Shelley's *Prometheus Unbound*" (*KSMB*, 1979), and Daniel M. McVeigh's "Aeschylus' *Adamantinoi Desmoi* and a Line from Act IV of Shelley's *Prometheus Unbound*" (*ELN*, 1980).

The poems Shelley published with *Prometheus Unbound* are among his most famous: almost all of them figure in the perceptive analyses of Chernaik's *Lyrics of Shelley*; the one study linking them as a whole with the lyrical drama is the richly suggestive chapter in Neil Fraistat's *The Poem and the Book: Interpreting Collections of Romantic Poetry* (1985). Individual poems in the volume have accumulated a sizable body of commentary. On "The Sensitive Plant," aside from its treatment in the major studies, one can consult Priscilla St. George's "The Styles of Good and Evil in 'The Sensitive Plant' " (*JEGP*, 1952), Donald Davie's influential celebration of Shelley's urbane style in *Purity of Diction in English Verse* (1952; rpt. 1966, 1972), Wasserman's lengthy explication in *The Subtler Language* (rpt. with some deletions in *Shelley: A Critical Reading*), Robert M. Maniquis' "The Puzzling Mimosa: Sensitivity and Plant Symbols in Romanticism" (*SIR*, 1969), and the interesting psychoanalytic interpretation in Richard S. Caldwell's " 'The Sensitive Plant' as Original Fantasy" (*SIR*, 1976). The fragment of "A Vision of the Sea" has received little attention: Carl H. Ketcham offers an explication (*SIR*, 1978), and Elsie F. Mayer has sifted the evidence of the draft for bio-graphical elements in "Notes on the Composition of 'A Vision of the Sea'" (*KSJ*, 1979). By contrast, "The Cloud" and "To a Skylark" have attracted a substantial body of criticism, yet much of it is very dated, prompted by and reflecting New Critical biases in interpretation. "The Cloud" has perhaps best been handled in large studies of Shelley, where the dynamic processes embodied in the poem can be related to larger themes. Several brief notices—by James E. Cronin (*N&Q*, 1950), Mignonette E. Harrison (*Expl*, 1953), and Allan H. MacLaine (*KSJ*, 1959)— deal with individual images, while Stella P. Revard has discovered affinities with Aristophanes' *Clouds* (*ELN*, 1978). Donald Pearce's "The Riddle of Shelley's Cloud" (*YR*, 1972) is genial, though not rigorous, criticism; more systematic are Horst Meller's treatment (in English) in *Versdichtung des englischen Romantik*, edited by Teut Riese and Dieter Riesner (1968) and Helmut Klinger's "Shelley und die Idee der Wolke" (*Sprachkunst*, 1977). Beverly Taylor surveys the general ground in "Shelley's Philosophical Perspective and Thematic Concerns in 'The Cloud'" (*Interpretations*, 1980). Parks C. Hunter is very persuasive in arguing for "Undercurrents of Anacreontics in Shelley's 'To a Skylark' and 'The Cloud'" (*SP*, 1968). "To a Skylark" is treated by E. M. W. Tillyard in *Poetry: Direct and Oblique* (1934), E. Wayne Marjarum, "The Symbolism of Shelley's 'To a Skylark'" (*PMLA*, 1937), Stewart C. Wilcox in "The Scientific Bird" (*CE*, 1949) and "The Sources, Symbolism, and Unity of Shelley's 'Skylark'" (*SP*, 1949), Newell F. Ford in "Shelley's 'To a Skylark'" (*KSMB*, 1960), and Jean H. Hagstrum in "Romantic Sky-larks" (*Newberry Library Bulletin*, 1959). Donald Sutherland, in his eccentric but often penetrating *On, Romanticism* (1971), devotes a quite extraordinary portion of his third chapter to an explication of the poem. James Allsup in *The Magic Circle* (1976) sees the skylark as a mediating figure between the earthly and divine.

Early studies of the "Ode to the West Wind" that retain their value include Israel J. Kapstein's "The Symbolism of the Wind and the Leaves in Shelley's 'Ode to the West Wind'" (*PMLA*, 1936), Richard Harter Fogle's "The Imaginal Design of Shelley's 'Ode to the West Wind'" (*ELH*, 1948; rpt. in *The Permanent Pleasure*, 1974), and Stewart C. Wilcox's "The Prosodic Structure of 'Ode to the West Wind'" (*N&Q*, 1950) and "Imagery, Ideas, and Design in Shelley's 'Ode to the West Wind'" (*SP*, 1950). F. R. Leavis made one of his classic misstatements about this poem: the critical controversy he unleashed is rehearsed by Colin Redford in "Critical Argu-ments" (*SoR*, 1976). The definitive rejoinder is supplied by the scientific analysis of the imagery in F. H. Ludlam's "The Meteorology of Shelley's Ode" (*TLS*, 1 Sept. 1972; with replies on 22 and 29 Sept. 1972). On this aspect of the imagery one should also consult C. C. Clarke's "Shelley's Tangled Boughs" (*DUJ*, 1961); another aspect is raised by Eban Bass's "The Fourth Element in 'Ode to the West Wind'" (*PLL*, 1967). On the rhetorical mode of the poem, a valuable overview is supplied by Irene H. Chayes in "Rhetoric as Drama: An Approach to the Romantic Ode" (*PMLA*, 1964); see also Francis Berry (*Poet's Grammar*, 1958) and Coleman O. Parson's "Shelley's Prayer to the West Wind" (*KSJ*, 1962). On the same subject but less dependable are William H. Pixton's "Shelley's Commands to the West Wind" (*SAB*, 1972) and S. Viswanathan's "Antiphonal Patterns in Shelley's 'Ode to the West Wind'" (*PLL*, 1972). The general political aims of the poem are illuminated in J. J. Oversteegen's view, "A Case of Whig History" (in *Comparative Poetics*, ed. D. W. Fokkema et al., 1975), and by the German essays by Horst Meller (*Archiv*, 1976) and Thomas Metscher ("Shelley und Hölderlin," *Gulliver*, 1976). Helen E. Haworth's brief analysis of the marriage of sonnet and terza rima (*KSJ*, 1971) is original and perceptive, and the subject is learnedly pursued through both English and Italian poetry by François Yost in "Anatomy of an Ode: Shelley and the Sonnet Tradition" (*CL*, 1982). Inventive might be the appropriate term for Paul Fry's chapter on the poem in *The Poet's Calling in the English Ode* (1980), which is heavily indebted to Bloom's notion that Shelley is forever in Wordsworth's shadow: Fry finds deep significance in the poem's sonic values, while Richard Cronin (*Shelley's Poetic Thoughts*) is persuasive in his account of syntactical values. The most detailed readings of the poem in recent full-length studies include Rieger's demonstration of its Pythagorean underpinnings in *The Mutiny Within* and Curran's reading of it as a purgatorial song of secular Christian triumph in *Shelley's Annus Mirabilis*. Curran sees similar generic patterns also implicated in the "Ode to Liberty" and "Ode to Naples." Judith Chernaik's excellent account of the "Ode to Liberty" should also be consulted for that underregarded poem; too brief, though right in its suppositions, is John Buxton's "Shelley and the Tradition of the 'Progress Piece' " (*KSMB*, 1972).

Little has been published on "Peter Bell the Third." Curran reads it as supplying a contemporary notion of the dynamics of hell; while Jack Benoit Gohn has helpfully brought together the evidence on whether Shelley actually had read Wordsworth's *Peter Bell* (*KSJ*, 1979). For Shelley's other major satirical work the standard essay still is Newman Ivey White's "Shelley's *Swellfoot the Tyrant* in Relation to Contemporary Political Satire" (*PMLA*, 1921), though it is somewhat updated by Roger Sales in *English Literature in History, 1780–1830: Pastoral and Politics* (1983). The underlying metaphor has been traced through political writing by Roland Bartel in "Shelley and Burke's Swinish Multitude" (*KSJ*, 1969). Ann Thompson analyzes how unconventional is Shelley's use of this mode in "Shelley and 'Satire's Scourge' " (*Literature of the Romantic Period*, ed. R. T. Davies and B. G. Beatty, 1976). One might wish to consult as well Allan Rodway's view of Shelley in *English Comedy: Its Role and Nature from Chaucer to the Present Day* (1975). There is much more written on "The Mask of Anarchy," though, as with Leavis' sense of its solitary worth in the canon or Holmes's raising it to the pinnacle of Shelley's achievement, the tinge of political sympathies constantly affects readings of the poem. This is true whether, as in Thomas Edwards' discussion in *Imagination and Power: A Study of Poetry on Public Themes* (1971), one thinks Shelley should have been more a man of the people, or, as in Richard Hendrix' "The Necessity of Response: How Shelley's Radical Poetry Works" (*KSJ*, 1978), the critic sees a perfect match among idea, mode, and audience. The best treatment of the poem's historical bases is Kenneth Neill Cameron's in *Shelley: The Golden Years*. The poem has long appealed to Marxist critics: the most recent such interpretation is Heinrich Schwinning's substantial "Der Maskenzug der Anarchie" (*Gulliver*, 1976). Earlier (1938) Bertolt Brecht translated (or adapted) the first twenty-five stanzas: these are printed in his brief essay on the breadth and variety of the realistic mode in *Brecht Versuche* (1956) and are interpreted by

S. S. Prawer (*Comparative Literature Studies: An Introduction*, 1973) and by Richard Cronin in *Shelley's Poetic Thoughts*. Cronin supplies the best commentary on Shelley's relation to the ballad tradition; Curran, on the backgrounds supplied by the masque tradition.

The revision in title and text accomplished by Judith Chernaik in *The Lyrics of Shelley* forever transforms the sing-song prettiness of "The Indian Serenade" to the hesitant sonorities of "The Indian Girl's Song." Her discussion is invaluable: see also the attempt to ground the dramatic nature of the poem in Chauncey B. Tinker, "Shelley's 'Indian Serenade' " (*YULG*, 1950), B. A. Park's "The Indian Elements of the 'Indian Serenade' " (*KSJ*, 1961), and Richard Levin's "Shelley's 'Indian Serenade': A Re-Revaluation" (*CE*, 1963). The Anglo-Asiatic milieu of the poem also forms the subject of Satya Pahori's "Shelley's 'Indian Serenade': Hafiz and Sir William Jones" (*OJES*, 1974 – 75).

"The Witch of Atlas" is a poem that, like "Julian and Maddalo," has experienced a wholesale shift in critical approach in recent years. The early source hunting that surfaces in Carl Grabo's Neoplatonic reading, *The Meaning of "The Witch of Atlas"* (1935), and Kathrine Koller's *MLN* essay (1937) certainly has value. That line of investigation continues in Frederic S. Colwell's "Shelley's 'Witch of Atlas' and the Mythic Geography of the Nile" (*ELH*, 1978). The red herring of Keats's influence proposed by John Livingston Lowes ("*The Witch of Atlas* and *Endymion*," *PMLA*, 1940) was netted the next year by David Lee Clark—"What Was Shelley's Indebtedness to Keats?"—and by Carlos Baker—"Spenser and *The Witch of Atlas*" (both *PMLA*, 1941). John E. Jordan's "Wordsworth and 'The Witch of Atlas' " (*ELH*, 1942) sensibly establishes a contemporary context for the poem. Beginning with Bloom's *Shelley's Mythmaking*, the search for sources and echoes gave way to concern with the autonomy of the poem in tone and mythic creation. David Rubin's "A Study of Antinomies in Shelley's *The Witch of Atlas*" (*SIR*, 1969) is a perceptive exposition of the polarized image patterns of the poem. Although Jean Watson Rosenbaum's dubious notion that Shelley is trying to symbolize an ecstatic state of mind ("Shelley's Witch: The Naked Conception," *CP*, 1977) posits a unified intention, Richard Cronin (*KSJ*, 1977; rev. *Shelley's Poetic Thoughts*) carefully measures language and event to support a continual dialectic between imaginative and moralist poetics. Andelys Wood, observing the same ironies with detailed attention to patterns of imagery, suggests that "Shelley's Ironic Vision: *The Witch of Atlas*" (*KSJ*, 1980) is evidence of a weakening poetic faith. On the contrary, asserts Jerrold E. Hogle in the longest, most impressive, but also most provocative of modern readings—"Metaphor and Metamorphosis in Shelley's 'The Witch of Atlas' " (*SIR*, 1980)—the Witch is Shelley's most extreme celebration of imaginative play (*jeu*), and the poem's "irony" is simply a hardheaded recognition of what it is like to live amid never-ending transformations. The remarkable, if unintentional, dialogue of these last three fine essays reveals the extent to which the critical energies aroused by this poem in recent years are best embodied in articles rather than books.

The critical history of *Epipsychidion* has also shifted its ground in the last decade or so. Earlier readings tended to concentrate on the poem as biographical allegory: the classic statement of this view can be found in Kenneth Neill Cameron's "The Planet-Tempest Passage in *Epipsychidion*" (*PMLA*, 1948), which is subsumed in *Shelley: The Golden Years*. Whether Shelley's feelings for Emilia Viviani were "Platonic"—elaborately demonstrated by Carlos Baker in *Shelley's Major Poetry*—or were physical—as argued disparagingly by Edward E. Bostetter in "Shelley and the Mutinous Flesh" (*TSLL*, 1959; rpt. in *The Romantic Ventriloquists*, 1963) and enthusiastically by Gerald Enscoe (*Eros and the Romantics*, 1967)—may seem a critically naive inquiry to later readers. Increasingly, they have come to see the poem as an attempt to modernize the romance ideal of Dante's *La vita nuova*: Reiman's brief argument in *Percy Bysshe Shelley* (1969) was taken up by Wasserman and is pressed in both of Timothy Webb's books. It is also central to the overviews supplied by Richard E. Brown, "The Role of Dante in *Epipsychidion*" (*CL*, 1978), and in greater detail by Earl Schulze, "The Dantean Quest of *Epipsychidion*" (*SIR*, 1982). As established as this context is by now, the critical literature suggests that it is also richer and more complex than any one account has thus far revealed. It needs as well to be linked to the other major stream of criticism of *Epipsychidion*, which sees the poem as continuously self-reflexive, concerned with its own making. Jean Hall's celebration of the poem's wish-fulfillment composes one of the best sections of *The Transforming Image* (1980). Hall is preceded by Frank D. McConnell in "Shelleyan 'Allegory': *Epipsychidion*" (*KSJ*, 1971) and, with emphasis on dialectical pressures, by Daniel J. Hughes's important "Coherence and Collapse in Shelley, with Particular Reference to *Epipsychidion*" (*ELH*, 1961) and by John F. Slater's "Self-Concealment and Self-Revelation in Shelley's *Epipsychidion*" (*PLL*, 1975). Michael H. Bright has suggested analogues for "The Pleasure-House in Shelley's 'Epipsychidion'" (*AN&Q*, 1978). Earlier, the context of Chaucer's Knight's Tale was proposed by Enrica Viviani della Robbia, "Shelley e il Boccaccio" (*Italica*, 1959); and Neville Rogers undertakes to explain links (in idea as well as in manuscript) with Shelley's Italianate fragments "Fiordispina" and "Ginevra" in *Shelley at Work* (1956, 1967).

The major critical disagreement over Shelley's late poetry, starting with "The Witch of Atlas" and *Epipsychidion* and culminating in readings of "The Triumph of Life," is whether it testifies to world-weariness or to a combined celebration of and healthy skepticism about the imagination. Criticism of *Adonais* seems increasingly to split over this issue, as is documented almost to the point of contradictions in the historical synthesis of Anthony D. Knerr's *Shelley's Adonais: A Critical Edition* (1984). Almost all modern criticism of the poem is indebted to (and rather overwhelmed by) the truly brilliant and penetrating reading of Earl Wasserman, which began as an *ELH* essay of 1954 and was progressively incorporated in *The Subtler Language* and *Shelley: A Critical Reading*. So commanding is this essay that it has implicitly reinforced the notion of the poem as enacting an ecstasy of despair, especially when taken with such other strong readings as those of Milton Wilson (*Shelley's Later Poetry*) and Ross Woodman, whose view of Shelley's "psychic suicide" in *The Apocalyptic Vision of Shelley's Poetry* (1964) continues to underpin his more recent essays, "Shelley's Urania" (*SIR*, 1978) and "Milton's Urania and the Romantic Descendants" (*UTQ*, 1979). In addition, all of the Platonic school of Shelley studies uses *Adonais* as an ultimate justification, with basically the same line of interpretation. The alternative approach to the poem includes a broad spectrum of critical opinion. Kenneth Neill Cameron, beginning with his explication of the stanzas on the venal critic, "Shelley vs. Southey: New Light on an Old Quarrel" (*PMLA*, 1942), expands his view of the poem's ideological base into a surprisingly comprehensive argument in *Shelley: The Golden Years*. A similar orientation, stressing the sardonic diatribe of Shelley's preface, distinguishes Timothy Webb's account in *Shelley: A Voice Not Understood*. John Wright's important monograph *The Myth of Metaphor* relies on *Adonais* as its central text, reading the poem as self-reflective of its own creativity. Angela Leighton, in "*Adonais:* The Voice and the Text" (*KSMB*, 1980), is concerned with the same process, though from a deconstructive vantage point. That an "aesthetic" approach to the poem need not be wholly turned in on itself is demonstrated in the good sense of Reiman's view of the poem as a created and dramatic artifact rather than a rhapsodic confession (*Percy Bysshe Shelley*). The self-dramatizing mode of the poem also figures in Ronald E. Becht's "Shelley's *Adonais:* Formal Design and the Lyric Speaker's Crisis of Imagination" (*SP,* 1981). Such an approach revivifies and sophisticates an older line of criticism that saw the poem in the light of its forebears. The earliest of these is perhaps William Michael Rossetti's introduction and notes to his edition of the poem (1891). The Spenserian background is examined in T. P. Harrison's "Spenser and Shelley's *Adonais*" (*TxSE*, 1933) and becomes the driven thesis of Edwin Silverman's *Poetic Synthesis in Shelley's* Adonais (1972). The relevance of Dante is emphasized by Richard Harter Fogle in his transcription of the notes on the poem by Shelley's friend and Dante scholar John Taaffe ("John Taaffe's Annotated Copy of *Adonais,*" *KSJ,* 1968), though Fogle sees the two poets as having opposite temperaments in "Dante and Shelley's *Adonais*" (*BuR*, 1967; rpt. in *The Permanent Pleasure*, 1974). Michael Cooke compares Shelley's poetic strategies with those of Milton's *Lycidas* in *Acts of Inclusion* (1979). Ostensibly following the same line, Eric Smith's *By Mourning Tongues: Studies in English Elegy* (1977) misses its opportunity with a conventional reading of the poem that makes little of its context. Stuart Curran, mounting his argument on the conventions of the pastoral elegy and on the numerous echoes of Keats in the poem, attempts a synoptic reading bridging Shelley's aesthetic and political concerns in "*Adonais* in Context" (in *Shelley Revalued,* 1983).

Hellas has begun to receive increased attention in recent years, partly because it had been so unjustly neglected, partly because the first concerted modern attempt to offer a coherent reading of the poem, Wasserman's in *Shelley: A Critical Reading,* suggested the complexity of the issues involved in the work. Nonetheless, his lengthy exposition on the contexts provided, in classical literature, by Aeschylus' *Persians,* and, in modern Italian culture, by literary improvisation, were noteworthy additions to our understanding. The fullest account of the political dimensions of this second lyrical drama is provided by Carl Woodring in *Politics in English Romantic Poetry.* Scrivener (*Radical Shelley*) is also useful here, as is Timothy Webb (*Shelley: A Voice Not Understood*) for Shelley's Hellenic allegiances. On all such subjects the pioneering essay by Newman Ivey White,

"The Historical and Personal Backgrounds of Shelley's *Hellas*" (*SAQ*, 1921), still retains a remarkable vigor. Jerome J. McGann's view—in "The Secrets of an Elder Day: Shelley after *Hellas*" (*KSJ*, 1966)—that the poem is divided against itself is implicitly contradicted in Wasserman's subtle reading and has been directly challenged in Constance Walker's "The Urn of Bitter Prophecy: Antithetical Patterns in *Hellas*" (*KSMB*, 1983), which breaks ground in its careful examination of the work's dramaturgy.

If *Hellas* has provoked increasing attention of late, the fragment of a drama "Charles the First" has almost dropped from critical sight. Of major studies in the last dozen years only Scrivener's *Radical Shelley* gives it serious consideration. He draws well on the earlier studies in literary and historical sources conducted by Newman Ivey White (*JEGP*, 1922) and Kenneth Neill Cameron (*MLQ*, 1945) and the two important essays by R. B. Woodings, "Shelley's Sources for *Charles the First*" (*MLR*, 1969), the most authoritative of these examinations, and " 'A Devil of a Nut to Crack': Shelley's *Charles the First*" (*SN*, 1968), which is more critical in scope. On the late lyrics, McGann's "Secrets of an Elder Day" (*KSJ*, 1966) is sensitive to tone and verbal patterning, arguing for an increasing humanism in the poems to Jane Williams; James Allsup, whose *Magic Circle* draws its title from one of them, conversely sees a straining for the immutable; Barry Weller is perhaps less successful in claiming the relevance of *The Tempest* to these poems than in understanding their intrinsic values ("Shakespeare, Shelley, and the Binding of the Lyric," *MLN*, 1978). For all the late lyrics Judith Chernaik's *Lyrics of Shelley* is dependable for its continual perceptiveness. More searching in aim, the last chapter of Keach's *Shelley's Style* suggests a pervasive ambivalence of motive and value in these poems. The unconfessional nature of many of Shelley's lyrics has been convincingly demonstrated in G. M. Matthews' essay on the subject in *The Morality of Art*, edited by D. W. Jefferson (1969). These recent studies all take Shelley's command of his lyric craft as a given, unlike his detractors of a generation and more ago, who poured much ink on the pages of poems like "When the lamp is shattered" and claimed that the resultant obscurity was Shelley's fault. The noncritical controversy that resulted is so far behind us that it needs no rehearsal here.

Real controversy continues to grow around "The Triumph of Life," especially since its text has been stabilized (see above) and critics have at least that certainty in confronting this enigmatic fragment. The point of departure for modern conceptions of the poem is Donald H. Reiman's *Shelley's "The Triumph of Life": A Critical Study, Based on a Text Newly Edited from the Bodleian Manuscript* (1965), the terms of whose title offer dually justified claims. The minor adjustments to the text later made by Matthews and Reiman do not diminish the importance of this textual recovery, nor can the involved apparatus obscure the lengthy and judicious analysis of the poem, its milieu, and its sources that precedes it. So much has been written on the poem since that one might do best simply referring students of its earlier critical history to Reiman's bibliography and his synthesis of earlier commentary. Reiman reads the poem as exemplifying a seasoned and mature optimism, a view that is tested and more or less confirmed (with disagreements over local details abounding) by David Quint, in his fine "Representation and Ideology in *The Triumph of Life*" (*SEL,* 1978); by Linda E. Marshall, "The 'Shape All Light' in Shelley's *Triumph of Life*" (*ESC,* 1979), which perhaps too easily resolves the ambiguities of that figure; and by Fred L. Milne, "The Eclipsed Imagination in Shelley's 'The Triumph of Life'" (*SEL,* 1981). Other commentators have seen a much darker poem, ranging from a vision of despair to a virtual suicide note, the argument attempted by James Rieger. These include McGann's "Secrets of an Elder Day," already cited; John Hodgson's "The World's Mysterious Doom: Shelley's *The Triumph of Life*" (*ELH,* 1975); Merle R. Rubin's "Shelley's Skepticism: A Detachment Beyond Despair" (*PQ,* 1980); and, most forcefully, Lloyd Abbey's reading in *Destroyer and Preserver* (1979). Perhaps in this camp should be placed the authors of *Deconstruction and Criticism* (ed. Harold Bloom et al., 1979), though the congenitally word-weary critics of Yale seem themselves to favor the worldweary excessively. In Paul de Man's "Shelley Disfigured" one finds combined an out-of-date critical context and idiosyncratic readings with real subtlety of thought. But the abyss does tend to yawn. J. Hillis Miller, "The Critic as Host," emphasizes the irreconcilability of the "logocentric metaphysics and nihilism" featured in the poem. Jacques Derrida bows in the direction of Shelley's poem only once and then to note ambiguities in the title as translated into French that do not exist in English. Reacting to this volume, in particular the nihilistic overtones of de Man's essay, Lisa M. Steinman, "From 'Alastor' to 'The Triumph of Life': Shelley on the Nature and Source of Linguistic Pleasures" (*RP&P,* 1983), stresses the depth and continuity of Shelley's skepticism throughout his career. Although wont, like de Man, to see Shelley as coming to sudden awareness in 1822, Tilottama Rajan contributes the most persuasive and commanding poststructuralist reading of "The Triumph of Life" (in *Dark Interpreter: The Discourse of Romanticism,* 1980), viewing it as a deliberately conceived and labyrinthine puzzle without solution. Her incidental but lengthy comparison with Keats's "Fall of Hyperion" is an inspired revitalization of an old academic exercise. Likewise William Keach suggestively shows how stylistic elements deliberately enforce the poem's ambiguities in *Shelley's Style.* The debate over the means and ends of Shelley's last poem is unlikely ever to be resolved, but it has in the past two decades illuminated the subtle complexities of the poem to a remarkable degree, and one expects that process to continue even as there is likely never to be a firm consensus as to its meaning. In the meantime, an even firmer sense of the poem's dating has been contributed by Betty T. Bennett and Alice Fredman (*KSJ,* 1982).

REPUTATION AND INFLUENCE

Shelley's impact on the nineteenth century was enormous, and it is enormously problematical. The breadth of his interests made him a natural repository for proselytizing, and the caricatures of the early biographies resonated through the ensuing decades. It is safe to say that almost no Victorian was able, in Browning's famous phrase, "to see Shelley plain." And if Shelley criticism in the second half of the twentieth century is wont to congratulate itself collectively on at last establishing secure bases for interpretation of his life and works, the implicit corollary is that such a foundation could not be relied on earlier in our own century. Paradoxically, now that Shelley's name no longer sounds a battle cry or provokes stereotypical responses, he has lost much of his influence on the course of letters and politics. Our Shelley is no longer the Shelley of legend, and mental adjustments are constantly needed—and frequently are not made—in our assessments of his influence.

Much knowledge has been gained about Shelley and much more documentary evidence for his influence has been accumulated since Newman Ivey White's researches; and yet both *The Unextinguished Hearth,* the study of contemporary reviews, and the two-volume *Shelley* remain standard and reliable reference guides to the subject. James E. Barcus' *Shelley: The Critical Heritage* (1975) adds surprisingly little to what was already known. More is to be gained by perusing Francis Mason's *A Study of Shelley Criticism...from 1818 to 1860* (1937). For a fluent account of Shelley's influence in the Victorian period, Sylva Norman's *Flight of the Skylark: The Development of Shelley's Reputation* (1954) is unsurpassed; it has, however, been supplemented by Carl Woodring—"Dip of the Skylark" (*KSJ,* 1960) and by Norman herself in "Twentieth-Century Theories on Shelley" (*TSLL,* 1967). Also useful is Nancy Fogarty's monograph in the Salzburg Studies series on the development of Shelley criticism in England and America between 1916 and 1971, *Shelley in the Twentieth Century* (1976). Julia Power's *Shelley in America in the Nineteenth Century* (1940) is, again, standard. New sources of information suggest the need for an updating of this subject; less necessary, perhaps, but still of value would be a modernization of our knowledge of Shelley's impact on the continent, for which we rely on the older studies of Henri Peyre, Solomon Liptzin, and Boris Gilenson noted in the first section. Further knowledge along these lines is to be found in Konrad Gorski's "The Reception of Shelley in Polish Literature," which appears in a festschrift for E. M. Hill, edited by R. Auty et al., *Gorski Vijenic* (1970); B. M. Baxter's study of the Dutch transmission, *Albert Vernay's Translations from Shelley's Poetical Works* (1963); and M. Abdel-Hai's "Shelley and the Arabs: An Essay in Comparative Literature" (*JArabL,* 1972).

The afterlife of Shelley's political ideas has been comparatively well charted, though the continuity of discovery suggests that the survey is far from complete. Newman Ivey White's "Shelley and the Active Radicals of the Early Nineteenth Century" (*SAQ,* 1930) has been advanced by Kenneth Muir's essay "Shelley's Heirs" (*Penguin New Writing,* ed. John Lehmann, 1945), by Siddig Kalim's study "Robert Owen and Shelley" (*Explorations,* 1969), by O. Madden's "Consideration of Shelley's Reputation in the Eighteen-Thirties" (*Essays in English Romanticism,* 1981), and by Bouthaina Shaaban's account "Shelley in the Chartist Press" (*KSMB,* 1983). More specialized, yet still of moment for the history of political thought in the nineteenth century, are the studies of Shelley's fortunes with the censors: see A. W. Bagley, "*Queen Mab* and the Pirates" (*New Zealand Monthly Review,* 1977), and the two essays by Donald Thomas "Press Prosecutions of the Eighteenth and Nineteenth Centuries" and "The Prosecution of Moxon's Shelley" (*Library,* 1977, 1978). Shelley's political impact later in the century has usually centered on Shaw:

Harold F. Brooks's "Shavian Sources in the Notes to *Queen Mab*" (*ShawR*, 1977) is a direct exposition of this sort. The January 1972 issue of the *Shaw Review* is entirely devoted to Shelley's influence, though the focus tends to be more literary than political. A balanced overview is provided by Roland Duerksen (*PMLA*, 1963), which is incorporated within his ranging study of *Shelleyan Ideas in Victorian Literature* (1966). The influence is seen from the alternate perspective in Julian B. Kaye's *Bernard Shaw and the Nineteenth-Century Tradition* (1958). Duerksen has been especially helpful in suggesting ways in which George Eliot and George Henry Lewes responded to Shelley. For the latter figure one should also consult Donald H. Reiman's "Shelley in the Encyclopedias" (*KSJ*, 1963) and Alice R. Kaminsky's *George Henry Lewes as Literary Critic* (1968).

A minor industry has grown up around Shelley's impact on Browning, who testified to it most pertinently in his *Essay on Shelley*. Much of the writing on this subject ignores the remarkable distortion masked in Browning's celebration of his precursor. One critic who does not is Harold Bloom, who, confronting a paradigm of misprision, is quick to remove Shelley from Wordsworth's shadow and place Browning within Shelley's. *A Map of Misreading* (1975) extends the shadow among other major Victorians as well. Frederick A. Pottle's *Shelley and Browning: A Myth and Some Facts* (1923) inaugurated both this subject and Pottle's long critical devotion to Shelley studies. The most extensive reading of Browning's works in relation to Shelley has been conducted by Paul A. Cundiff in *Robert Browning: A Shelleyan Promethean* (privately printed, 1977). More restrained in claims is Herbert Tucker's study of the early Browning, *Browning's Beginnings: The Art of Disclosure* (1980). Tucker returns to the subject in "Memorabilia: Mnemonic Imagination in Shelley and Browning" (*SIR*, 1980). Other general treatments of this subject include Richard C. Keenan's "Browning and Shelley" (*BIS*, 1973), Loy D. Martin's "Browning: The Activation of Influence" (*VN*, 1978), and the running discussion in John Maynard's *Browning's Youth* (1977). More specialized still are Lawrence Poston's "Browning's Career to 1841" (*BIS*, 1975) and "Shelley the Almost-Christian: An Early Victorian Commonplace" (*SBHC*, 1981), as well as the readings of Shelleyan influence in *Pauline* by Thomas J. Collins (*VP*, 1965) and Clyde de L. Ryals (*Genre*, 1976) and in *Sordello* by Michael G. Yetman (*VP*, 1975). Harold Bloom's well-known study "Browning's *Childe Roland*: All Things Deformed and Broken" (*Ringers in the Tower*, 1971) has elicited responses on the Shelleyan context by Philip Raisor (*TSL*, 1972) and Mario L. D'Avanzo (*SEL*, 1977). Raisor has also suggested a Shelleyan focus for "Love among the Ruins" (*VP*, 1976). Shelley also enters the lists in Paul F. Mattheisen's lengthy treatment of *The Ring and the Book* (*Literary Monographs*, 1970). Browning's aesthetics are differentiated from what he thought Shelley's to be in Thomas J. Collins' "Browning's *Essay on Shelley*: In Context" (*VP*, 1964) and in A. R. Jones's study of Browning's dramatic monologues (*CQ*, 1967). The context is conceived from another perspective in James McNally's "Browning's Political Thought" (*QQ*, 1970).

No such elaborate literature exists for Shelley's influence on other Victorian writers. Tennyson's interest in *Adonais* is reflected in Ian A. Kennedy's "*In Memoriam* and the Tradition of the Pastoral Elegy" (*VP*, 1977). Edward Chetham has assessed "Emily Brontë and Shelley" (*BST*, 1978), and Mark A. Weinstein suggests Shelley's influence on notions of spontaneous creativity in *William Edmondstoune Aytoun and the Spasmodic Controversy* (1968). The significance of Shelley for the Pre-Raphaelite group has begun to receive greater attention. Robert M. Cooper makes note of it in *Lost on Both Sides: D. G. Rossetti, Critic and Poet* (1970), and David Riede undertakes a more particularized examination in "Shelleyan Reflections in the Imagery of D. G. Rossetti" (*VP*, 1981). Harris Chewning describes his brother's important role in "William Michael Rossetti and the Shelley Renaissance" (*KSJ*, 1955), while George Landow explains the distance maintained by William Holman Hunt (*PRR*, 1979). Terry L. Myers has devoted three essays to the examination of Shelley's impact on Swinburne's poetry and poetics (*VP*, 1976; *PLL*, 1978; *PRR*, 1980). Arnold's problems with Shelley are placed in perspective in Leon Gottfried's *Matthew Arnold and the Romantics* (1963). The more salutary response of Hardy is noted by Phyllis Bartlett ("Hardy's Shelley," *KSJ*, 1955, and "Seraph of Heaven: A Shelleyan Dream in Hardy's Fiction," *PMLA*, 1955). A broad survey by George Stavros, "Oscar Wilde on the Romantics" (*ELT*, 1977), is brought down to some interesting particulars of literary influence in Philip K. Cohen's *The Moral Vision of Oscar Wilde* (1978).

Shelley's influence on American writers of the nineteenth century has also drawn increased speculation. Two essays, by Kent Ljundquist and Lou Ann Kriegisch, have suggested the impact of *Adonais* on Poe's "Eleonora" (*PoeS*, 1977, 1978). The importance of *The Cenci* to Hawthorne's fiction has been noted by Roland Duerksen, "The Double Image of Beatrice Cenci in *The Marble Faun*" (*MichA*, 1969), and by Robert L. White, " 'Rappaccini's Daughter,' *The Cenci*, and the Cenci Legend" (*SA*, 1968). Mario L. D'Avanzo has seen the impact of *Prometheus Unbound* on "The Dynamics of Myth in *Moby-Dick*" (*BBr*, 1971), while Mary K. Saunders has traced it in *Leaves of Grass* (*WWR*, 1968). A psychoanalytic comparison of "Alastor" and "Out of the Cradle Endlessly Rocking" has also been attempted by Barbara Schapiro (*AI*, 1979).

Of modernists, the most directly indebted to Shelley—but to a Shelley almost unrecognizable to contemporary students—is Yeats, who saw the earlier poet in something of a mirror. Harold Bloom's *Yeats* (1970), where he first developed his anxiety theory to explain poetic influence, places Shelley within a continuum of poets, ranging from Milton to Yeats, who both suffer and create anxiety. Narrower in focus but less tendentious in thesis is George Bornstein's *Yeats and Shelley* (1970). His lengthy account is justified both by the particulars of the influence and by Yeats's complicated reaction to it. Bornstein has also described "Yeats's Copy of Shelley at the Pforzheimer Library" (*BRH*, 1979). A much less detailed treatment of this relationship is H. C. Merritt's "Shelley's Influence on Yeats" (*YES*, 1971). Another modernist with complicated and eccentric views of Shelley is Lawrence. Michael Steig concentrates on the fiction in "Fantasy and Mimesis in Literary Character: Shelley, Hardy, and Lawrence" (*ESC*, 1975), while Merle R. Rubin turns to the influence on Lawrence's poetry (*TSLL*, 1981). How Shelley influenced Virginia Woolf's conceptions of androgyny is Nathaniel Brown's concern in *KSJ*, 1984. Finally, reaching toward a contemporary application is Robert Bertholf's "Shelley, Stevens, and Robert Duncan: The Poetry of Approximations" (in *Artful Thunder: Versions of the Romantic Tradition in American Literature,* ed. Robert J. DeMott and Sanford E. Marovitz, 1975). And more finally still might be considered Timothy R. Lucas' "The Old Shelley Game: Prometheus and Predestination in Burgess' Works" (*MFS,* 1981), which offers some hope that, old game or not, Shelley's works are still in the field.

Though it is presumptuous on such an occasion and even pernicious, as restricting the possible range of inquiry, to formulate a list of scholarly and critical desiderata, there is also a danger of losing obvious implications amid a deluge of bibliographical minutiae. To begin then with the end: however much individual literary critics may wish to modify or oppose the Freudian determinism of Bloom's model of literary influence, Bloom is surely right to demand a more sophisticated theoretical understanding of intellectual transmission than was allowed for by the echo and source hunting of the past. As study of Victorian literature and culture has taken immeasurable strides in the last several decades, so it should now be possible to understand Shelley's place in the ongoing dynamics of that culture from a perspective at once unconstrained by the limited biases of the past and subtler in its calibrations. Naturally, the same is true with Shelley's own multiple inheritances, not only from such literary giants as Dante, Spenser, and Milton but from his contemporaries and from the currents of anthropology, philosophy, theology, and science. The general loss of the classical education Shelley possessed in abundance makes that all the more difficult, but Shelley's learning must then stand as a continual challenge to our own and at the very least should encourage a healthy self-doubt about easy scholarly answers to complicated cultural problems. Although the journals bloat and the book shelves fill up to provide the bases for a bibliographical survey such as this, any impartial assessment would suggest that the revolution in Shelley studies in the past generation is far from played out and that, as the critical consensus becomes elaborated, some earlier scholarship is simply invalidated and much more scholarship demands careful adjustment to a new perspective.

To put the matter in starker terms, where there is no text either for the poetry, the prose, or the letters that is sufficiently reliable, where the biography on which scholarship rests is nearly a half century old, and where the popular notion of Shelley is so sharply at odds with the most advanced critical estimations, there are obvious scholarly imperatives for the intrepid. The recent spurt of studies from a political perspective has refined our comprehension of this aspect of Shelley more than might have been expected, but it now needs consolidation and some testing. No greater test could be imagined than that which is currently arising from within the study of Shelley's philosophical and aesthetic speculations. If Shelley is beginning to emerge as a forerunner of deconstruction, the theorists and the historical critics need to open a spirited dialogue. As the limits of Shelley's skepticism become expanded, it is in the interests of everyone—and that is to say, all contemporary intellectuals—to acknowledge that Shelley saw the liberty of mind, society, and art as aspects of a single process and to ascertain how such manifold and disparate ends as were unified within his encyclopedic consciousness could remain consistent for him and for us. That simply demands from Shelley's critics both the meticulous historical grounding and the bold imaginative vision they have always demanded of him.

JOHN KEATS

Jack Stillinger

Contents

Bibliographical Materials

If we set aside general knowledge and life experience, the student of Keats mainly needs to know the editions, the biographies, and the bibliographical guides to the scholarship and criticism. Since the bibliographical guides will themselves give information about editions and biographies, they have fair claim to be the most primary of all the research tools available. It is an unhappy fact that, increasingly, students (and, I must add, a great many of their teachers) do not know how to use the bibliographical guides to research and consequently cannot "do their homework" (which is library work) in finding out the previous scholarship on a topic and relating their own new contributions to what is already in print. As evidenced in manuscripts submitted to *KSJ* and other periodicals with a special interest in English Romantic literature, amateurism is growing at an alarming rate, and it shows up most frequently and most immediately in the writers' seeming lack of awareness of the current state of knowledge on whatever they are writing about. I invite particular attention to this brief opening section.

The only comprehensive Keats bibliography in book form is J. R. MacGillivray's *Keats: A Bibliography and Reference Guide with an Essay on Keats' Reputation* (1949), a listing of both primary and secondary works from 1816 through 1946. This is intricately organized, much too selective, and very poorly indexed, but nevertheless constantly useful. As a guide to the scholarship and criticism of the later nineteenth century and the early decades of the twentieth, before the annual bibliographies in *PMLA* and *ELH* were begun (see just below), it is indispensable.

Sister Pio Maria Rice's "John Keats: A Classified Bibliography of Critical Writings ... in Periodicals ... 1947–1961" (in 2 issues of *BB*, 1965) attempts to cover the next fifteen years after MacGillivray leaves off. In addition to the Keats chapters (earlier versions of the present essay) by Clarence D. Thorpe and David Perkins in the three previous editions of *The English Romantic Poets: A Review of Research,* there are selected bibliographical lists in Ian Jack's *English Literature, 1815–1832* (1963), Richard Harter Fogle's *Romantic Poets and Prose Writers* (1967), volume 3 of the *New CBEL* (ed. George Watson, 1969), and Donald H. Reiman's *English Romantic Poetry, 1800–1835: A Guide to Information Sources* (1979). But the really essential tools are the annual bibliographies of research, of which the three most serviceable (and most up-to-date) are (1) that begun in *PMLA* (1922–69) and continued in the *MLA International Bibliography* (1970–   ); (2) that begun in *ELH* (1937–49), continued in *PQ* (1950–64) and *ELN* (1965–79), and now issued by Garland Publishing (*The Romantic Movement: A Selective and Critical Bibliography,* ed. David V. Erdman, 1980–   ); and (3) that in *KSJ* (1952–   ). The second and third of these are selectively annotated (the former sometimes with page-long descriptions and evaluations), and both include notice of reviews. Two British publications, *YWES* (1921–   ) and the Modern Humanities Research Association's *Annual Bibliography of English Language and Literature* (also 1921–   ), are somewhat less helpful, the former because it is overly selective, the latter because it is running several years behind schedule; but they nevertheless invariably contain items overlooked or otherwise omitted in the three American lists just mentioned.

The first thirty-five bibliographies of the *ELH-PQ-ELN* series are reprinted with an index volume in *The Romantic Movement Bibliography, 1936–1970: A Master Cumulation,* edited by A. C. Elkins, Jr., and L. J. Forstner (7 vols., 1973); those of the first twenty-five volumes of *KSJ* are reprinted with indexes in two volumes entitled *Keats, Shelley, Byron, Hunt, and Their Circles: A Bibliography,* edited by David Bonnell Green and Edwin Graves Wilson (1964) and Robert A. Hartley (1978). These last works, because of the comprehensiveness of the *KSJ* listings and the excellence of the indexing, are the most useful of all for the quarter century that is covered. In consulting them, and the annuals for the more recent years, it is usually best to proceed in reverse chronological order (starting with the latest and then working backward); the cumulative accretion of references to earlier scholarship is thus available from the beginning of the investigation.

Two annual publications are centrally concerned with Keats—*KSJ* (issued by the Keats-Shelley Association of America) and *KSMB* (issued by the Keats-Shelley Memorial Association in Britain), both of which have review sections, *KSJ* from its beginning and *KSMB* since 1979. Besides these, the main periodicals publishing work on Keats are, in order of frequency, *SIR, PMLA, ELH, SEL,* and *EIC,* and the most important of the many reviewing journals are *MLR, RES, N&Q, JEGP, WC* (the Summer issue of each year), and *SEL* (the "Recent Studies" survey each autumn).

Editions, Concordance, Manuscripts, Other Textual Materials

Keats's three original volumes—*Poems* (1817), *Endymion* (1818), and *Lamia, Isabella, The Eve of St. Agnes, and Other Poems* (1820)—are bibliographically described by T. J. Wise (in "A Bibliography of the Writings of John Keats," *The John Keats Memorial Volume,* 1921, and again in vol. 3 of *The Ashley Library,* 1923) and, with slightly superior accuracy, by MacGillivray in the first section of his *Keats: A Bibliography and Reference Guide.* Photographic facsimiles have been published of two of the three volumes (*Poems* and *Lamia* in the Noel Douglas replicas, both 1927, and a different copy of *Lamia* in the Scolar Press facsimiles, 1970), and the original *Endymion* has been reproduced in a type facsimile, edited by H. Clement Notcutt (1927); this last has more than a score of errors that reappear in later texts (e.g., H. W. Garrod's) purportedly based on the original printing of 1818.

The three original volumes contain forty-five poems, five of which had already been published earlier in magazines. Nine additional poems first appeared in periodicals and a gift annual during Keats's lifetime, and the rest—close to two thirds of the 150 titles currently in the canon—were first published after his death, the most recent in 1939. The specific details of all these publications, as well as a systematic account of their sources of text and the various relationships among the known manuscripts behind them, are set forth in Jack Stillinger's *The Texts of Keats's Poems* (1974).

The first posthumous collection of the poems, reprinting the contents of the three volumes plus four short pieces from other printed sources, was the Keats section of *The Poetical Works of Coleridge, Shelley, and Keats,* published by A. and W. Galignani in Paris in 1829, a work that largely determined the canon and the texts in both England and the United States for the next several decades, even after more and better texts became available. The most significant enlargements of the canon in the nineteenth century were those made by Richard Monckton Milnes (later Lord Houghton), who published forty new poems from a variety of manuscript sources in *Life, Letters, and Literary Remains, of John Keats* (2 vols., 1848) and then *The Fall of Hyperion* separately in 1857 and a handful of additional short pieces in the Aldine edition that initially appeared in 1876 and served as the most popular edition of Keats until the Oxford Standard Authors edition took over.

The serious scholarly editing of the poems dates from 1883, when Harry Buxton Forman produced the first of his numerous collected editions. Ernest de Selincourt published a valuable critically annotated *Poems* in 1905, and Sidney Colvin issued a chronologically arranged two-volume edition in 1915, but for more than five decades—almost until World War II—the standard texts were Forman's, even though Forman himself died in 1917. Subsequent editors, including H. W. Garrod in the Oxford English Texts *Poetical Works* (1939; 2nd ed., 1958) and—partly by way of Garrod—Miriam Allott in *The Poems* (1970), have drawn heavily on his work. Forman especially exerted influence through his Oxford Standard Authors edition of 1906 and later years; even Garrod's revised O.S.A. edition of 1956, which is still frequently (but mistakenly) used for scholarly citation, is but a selectively patched-up version of the earlier O.S.A. texts.

At present the most elaborate textual edition, based on still further investigation and checking of the manuscripts and early printings following publication of *The Texts of Keats's Poems,* is Stillinger's *The Poems of John Keats* (1978). This includes a record of all substantive variants having any claim to be considered authoritative, lengthy notes detailing transmission and first publication of the texts, and several appendixes, among them a forty-two-page list of the editor's emendations of the copy texts. Miriam Allott's *The Poems* (1970; 3rd impression, with corrections, 1975) is the most fully annotated of the critical editions, with modernized texts and a great deal of information about historical context, sources, and analogues. The four other most usefully annotated complete editions of the poetry are *The Poems,* edited by E. de Selincourt (1905; 5th ed., 1926); *Complete Poems and Selected Letters,* edited by Clarence DeWitt Thorpe (1935); *The Complete Poems,* edited by John Barnard (1973; 2nd ed., 1976); and *Complete Poems,* edited by Jack Stillinger (1982), a "reading" edition using the texts established in 1978. The best of the numerous selected editions (which, by ignoring *Otho the Great, The Jealousies,* and some other esoterica, has room for all of Keats's most famous letters) is Douglas Bush's *Selected Poems and Letters* (1959).

The new *Concordance to the Poems of John Keats* by Michael G. Becker, Robert J. Dilligan, and Todd K. Bender (1981), citing Stillinger's 1978 edition as the standard for reference and quotation, is the more valuable for covering not only the texts themselves but substantive variants (including cancellations) in Stillinger's apparatus. This replaces the concordance by Dane Lewis Baldwin et al. (1917), which was keyed to H. B. Forman's O.S.A. texts.

R. M. Milnes published all or parts of about eighty of Keats's letters in his *Life, Letters, and Literary Remains* of 1848. By the time of H. B. Forman's first collected edition, *The Poetical Works and Other Writings* (4 vols., 1883), the number of known letters had grown to nearly two hundred. Forman's son, Maurice Buxton Forman, expanded the canon from 231 to 244 in four successive Oxford editions (1931, 1935, 1947, 1952), and the number today stands at 251. The definitive edition for the last twenty-five years has been *The Letters of John Keats, 1814 – 1821,* edited by Hyder Edward Rollins (2 vols., 1958), clearly superior to all predecessors in texts, datings, annotation, and indexing. Among several selected editions, Robert Gittings' *Letters . . . A New Selection* (1970) deserves special notice; Gittings to an extent did his work independently of Rollins, and a three-page appendix defends several differences from Rollins in text, dating, and some other specifics. Rollins was the most painstaking of twentieth-century scholars, but even his work is not wholly free from error, and more authoritative sources of text show up from time to time. (W. H. Bond reports on the holograph of Rollins' transcript-based no. 77, to Reynolds, now dated 17 Apr. 1818, in *KSJ,* 1971; and the holograph of no. 21, to George and Tom Keats, 15 Apr. 1817, was sold at Sotheby's on 27 June 1972.) But the most serious reediting of the letters at present would produce only minor (mostly cosmetic) improvements; Rollins' work will continue as standard in the foreseeable future.

For both poems and letters, the preeminent collection of manuscripts, both holographs and transcripts, is that at Harvard, formed on the basis of Amy Lowell's collection for her biography of 1925 and Arthur A. Houghton, Jr.'s acquisitions and gifts in more recent decades. Other important collections are at the Pierpont Morgan Library, the British Library, and the Keats House, Hampstead; but small groups and single manuscripts are scattered throughout Great Britain and the United States, and there are scraps of holograph in Rome and Geneva. For locations of the poetry manuscripts the best sources of information are section 2 of Stillinger's *The Texts of Keats's Poems* and the textual notes and appendix 5 in his 1978 edition (the details will appear again, more compactly, in the forthcoming vol. 4 of *Index of English Literary Manuscripts,* the Keats section compiled by Barbara Rosenbaum). The individual "histories" in section 4 of *The Texts of Keats's Poems* include references to published facsimiles of the manuscripts, of which there are a great many; the handsomest among them are those in *"Hyperion": A Facsimile of Keats's Autograph Manuscript,* with introductions and notes by Ernest de Selincourt (1905); *The Keats Letters, Papers, and Other Relics Forming the Dilke Bequest in the Hampstead Public Library,* edited by George C. Williamson (1914); and *The Odes of Keats and Their Earliest Known Manuscripts,* introduced with notes by Robert Gittings (1970). Stuart M. Sperry's "Richard Woodhouse's Interleaved and Annotated Copy of Keats's *Poems* (1817)" (Univ. of

Wisconsin *Literary Monographs,* 1967) is an especially valuable record of Wood-house's commentary and transcripts in the interleaved volume now in the Huntington Library. For manuscripts of the letters, the most up-to-date information is that given in the first footnote to each letter in Rollins' edition.

The collected editions of H. B. Forman, of which the latest is the Hampstead edition, *The Poetical Works and Other Writings,* revised by M. B. Forman (8 vols., 1938–39), remain useful for Keats's magazine reviews, marginalia, and some other miscellanea. To these may be added Caroline F. E. Spurgeon's *Keats's Shakespeare: A Descriptive Study* (1928), an account, with transcriptions (much more copious than Forman's), of Keats's underscorings and comments in two editions of Shakespeare's plays now at Keats House and Harvard; *The Romantics on Milton,* edited by Joseph Anthony Wittreich, Jr. (1970), containing the most accurate transcripts of Keats's markings in two copies of *Paradise Lost* at Keats House; Helen E. Haworth, "Keats's Copy of Lamb's *Specimens of English Dramatic Poets*" (*BNYPL,* 1970), describing Keats's marked copy in the Berg Collection; and *John Keats's Anatomical and Physiological Note Book,* edited by Maurice Buxton Forman (1934), a transcription of holograph lecture notes, now at Keats House, that Keats made at Guy's Hospital in 1815–16. Amy Lowell's account of Keats's markings and annotations in six books now at Harvard, including canto 1 of *The Faerie Queene* and Mateo Alemán's *Guzman de Alfarache,* in appendix C of her *John Keats* (1925), only partly overlaps with material in Forman; some of her transcriptions of the marginalia have been corrected by Norman A. Anderson (*KSJ,* 1974), and her description of one of the books is supplemented by Charles I. Patterson, "The Keats-Hazlitt-Hunt Copy of *Palmerin of England* in Relation to Keats's Poetry" (*JEGP,* 1961). Robert Gittings includes as appendix A in *The Mask of Keats* (1956) a full record of Keats's markings in volume 1 of Cary's Dante, now at Yale. The provenances and some other details concerning these and a handful of other books, twenty-five in all, that were once in Keats's possession are given in Frank N. Owings, Jr., *The Keats Library* (*A Descriptive Catalogue*) (n.d. [1978]).

Modern editions of letters and other papers by members of Keats's circle are listed near the end of the next section.

Biographies and Biographical Materials

The many intentions and attempts to produce a biography of Keats, beginning with the publisher John Taylor's announcement of a proposed memoir in the *New Times* for 29 March 1821, five weeks after the poet's death, are well documented in Rollins' *The Keats Circle* (see below). Several friends besides Taylor, including Charles Cowden Clarke, John Hamilton Reynolds, and Charles Brown, also had thoughts of writing Keats's life, and discord quickly arose among them over the possession and use of papers, information, and unpublished poems. Leigh Hunt's portrayal of the poet in *Lord Byron and Some of His Contemporaries* (2 vols., 1828) constitutes the first significant piece of Keats biography in print, and there was occasional notice of him in biographical and literary encyclo-pedias in the 1830s and 1840s. Charles Brown finally wrote out a "Life of John Keats" for a lecture at the Plymouth Institution in 1836. But the earliest full-length biography—based on Brown's lecture, his transcripts of the poems, and a vast collection of manuscripts, facts, and reminiscences from others who knew Keats—was Milnes's two-volume *Life, Letters, and Literary Remains* of 1848. Other biographies followed as Keats came to take his self-predicted place "among the English Poets"—Sidney Colvin's *Keats* in the English Men of Letters series (1887) and William Michael Rossetti's *Life of John Keats* in the Great Writers series (also 1887) were the most notable of those later in the century—but still Milnes's work, in a new edition of 1867 (minus the "literary remains") and then in cheap reprints of this version in the New Universal Library, Everyman's Library, and the Oxford World's Classics, remained the standard life of the poet until the 1920s.

While we have most, we do not have all of the material that Milnes brought together, and his work of 1848 even today is our best or only source for a handful of Keats's poems and continues to be of historical interest for its role in the estab-lishment of Keats's reputation. Other nineteenth-century works that remain valua-ble as firsthand sources, even though they have been repeatedly and heavily drawn on in subsequent biographies, are Hunt's *Lord Byron* (1828) and his *Auto-biography* (1850; rev. ed. 1860; ed. J. E. Morpurgo, 1948); Brown's "Life of John Keats" (first published, ed. Dorothy Hyde Bodurtha and Willard Bissell Pope, in 1937; subsequently included in vol. 2 of *The Keats Circle*); Benjamin Robert Haydon's *Autobiography* (first published, ed. Tom Taylor, in 3 vols., 1853; ed. Malcolm Elwin, 1950—see below for Haydon's *Diary*); C. C. Clarke's "Recollec-tions of Keats" (*Atlantic Monthly*, 1861; rev. in Charles and Mary Cowden Clarke's *Recollections of Writers*, 1878); *The Papers of a Critic. Selected from the Writings of the Late Charles Wentworth Dilke. With a Biographical Sketch by His Grand-son, Sir Charles Wentworth Dilke* (2 vols., 1875); and William Sharp's *The Life and Letters of Joseph Severn* (1892).

Of the score or more biographies of Keats written in the present century, six are conspicuously better than the rest. Three of these—by Colvin, Lowell, and Hewlett—were produced before microfilm and other copying devices (not to mention research grants and jet air travel) made British and American resources more or less equally accessible to scholars on both sides of the Atlantic, but they nevertheless continue to prove useful and in the main dependable. Sidney Colvin's *John Keats: His Life and Poetry, His Friends, Critics, and After-Fame* (1917; 3rd ed. 1920), a work two and a half times as long as his English Men of Letters *Keats* of 1887, is usually considered the most levelheaded and factually re-liable of the biographies before 1963, and it contains information—for example, from a Woodhouse notebook destroyed by fire in 1883—not elsewhere available. Amy Lowell's *John Keats* (2 vols., 1925), twice as long as Colvin's, is another major work of research and interpretation. This has what was in its time an abundance of new materials (including three new poems by Keats and two others, "The Poet" and "Gripus," that have since been removed from the canon or classified as questionable). It also has an unhurried expansiveness of a sort no longer affordable; Lowell's chapter on *Endymion* is 144 pages long, and even her index (52 double-column pages) bristles with forthright critical opinions, as in this small sampling of entries under *Otho the Great:* "dreary and stupid, II, 294; failure, I, 227; II, 277, 293, 294; finished, II, 293; forced product, II, 281; hack work, II, 294; hybrid, II, 293; nothing brought in by, II, 410; potboiler, II, 282." Dorothy Hewlett's *Adonais: A Life of John Keats* (1937; 3rd rev. ed., *A Life of John Keats,* 1970) is shorter and more readable than the two preceding works and is specially concerned to present Keats "in period" and to detail the contemporary reception of his three volumes. Fourteen brief appendixes in the 1970 version correct, and enlarge on, certain details in the light of more recent scholarship.

The other three major biographies are all works of the 1960s, two of them appearing within five weeks of each other in 1963. Aileen Ward's *John Keats: The Making of a Poet* was the first out, on 6 September 1963, and was advertised as "the first new full-scale biography of [Keats] in more than twenty-five years." Walter Jackson Bate's *John Keats* was officially published on 14 October, but review copies of both works were made available in August, and reviewers seemed almost pathologically obsessed to take sides, elevating one (whichever it happened to be) at the expense of the other. Ward's book won the 1964 National Book Award for arts and letters, as well as some other prizes; Bate's won the 1964 Pulitzer Prize for biography and, again, some other prizes. At this remove, two decades later, we can more reasonably congratulate ourselves on having both works.

Ward's biography (here and there emended in the Compass Books paperback of 1967) is well researched, well documented, and at the same time quite readable. Ward is especially good on the political and other public events of Keats's time, sound in her presentation of most of the people in Keats's circle, and generous with a great many specific suggestions concerning dates, sources, identifications, and also some acute observations on Keats's imagery—for example, the series of images of medicine and disease running through *Isabella.* She is less good on Keats himself; the attempt at psychoanalytic portrayal (influenced by Otto Rank, among others) is amateurish, and there is some novelistic embroidering on sources. But the net result is certainly on the positive side; the work, repeatedly cited, obviously maintains its usefulness.

Bate's biography (slightly corrected in the Galaxy paperback of 1966, and in the most recent issue subtitled *The Growth of a Genius*) is of another order of magnitude and has claims to be considered one of the best critical biographies ever written of any poet. Bate's versatility is amazing; he is equally adept at explaining a poem, describing a style, evaluating an influence, characterizing a friend of Keats, assessing Keats's modernity, and digging out the details of the Keats family inheritance. His interweaving of facts with poems, poems with letters, early letters with later poems, later poems with significant biographical developments of a year or two earlier is masterly, and the book is written throughout with a large, commonsense understanding of both human nature and the problems of literary art. It is not always easy to use as a reference work; one may have to read or skim several pages to find a specific fact, and Rollins' thirty-three-page list of "Events in the Life of Keats" near the front of his edition of the *Letters* is always handier for simple chronology. But for comprehensiveness and all-around intelligence, Bate's work would seem to be about as "definitive" as we are likely to get in the biographical department.

One might suppose that these works of 1963 would have rendered further biographies superfluous, at least for a long time to come, but Robert Gittings' *John Keats* (1968), the culmination of a series of significant publications that began with *John Keats: The Living Year* (1954) and continued with *The Mask of Keats: A Study of Problems* (1956) and *The Keats Inheritance* (1964), successfully holds its own among the competition. It does not change our view of Keats in any really important respect, and it makes no attempt at sustained interpretation of the poems. But it does contribute substantially to our knowledge of Keats's origins and early life, to our understanding of the influences operating on his mind and art, and to the texture of factual details that help recreate his day-to-day existence. Even while occasionally outreaching himself in his quest for precision in datings and other matters, Gittings is the most factually dependable of all the modern biographers, and he is excellent on Keats's sources and especially (as in *John Keats: The Living Year*) on the importance of nonliterary influences—places that Keats visited, things that he saw. In sum, the array of good biographies is remarkable. One might prefer Bate for overall presentation and interpretation of Keats's life and then consult Gittings and Ward on specific details, but any serious student of the poet should know and have at hand all three.

Among shorter critical biographies (which, as a category, tend to merge with the introductory general studies mentioned below under "Criticism"), the best by a considerable margin is Douglas Bush's *John Keats: His Life and Writings* (1966). Bush had already written masterfully and comprehensively on Keats in, among other works, *Mythology and the Romantic Tradition in English Poetry* (1937), "Keats and His Ideas" (in *The Major English Romantic Poets: A Symposium in Reappraisal*, ed. C. D. Thorpe et al., 1957), and his introduction and notes for the Riverside *Selected Poems and Letters* (1959). The concise biography of 1966 is full of wise observations about Keats's life and letters and seasoned interpretations of the poems, a distillation of several decades' learning and reflection.

There have been a great many specialized biographical studies over the years, of which only a few can be singled out here. Keats's early schooling is treated in a popular but intelligent work by Morris Marples, *Romantics at School* (1967), and is further illuminated by some new discoveries in Stuart M. Sperry, "Isabella Jane Towers, John Towers, and Keats" (*KSJ*, 1979), and Joan Coldwell, "Charles Cowden Clarke's Commonplace Book and Its Relationship to Keats" (*KSJ*, 1980). For Keats's medical training we have, among other works, Sir William Hale-White, *Keats as Doctor and Patient* (1938); Walter A. Wells, *A Doctor's Life of John Keats* (1959); and Donald C. Goellnicht, *The Poet-Physician: Keats and Medical Science* (1984), this last an extensive and well-documented tracing of the great many "scientific resonances" in Keats's poems and letters. C. D. Thorpe has contributed "Wordsworth and Keats—A Study in Personal and Critical Impression" (*PMLA*, 1927) and "Keats and Hazlitt: A Record of Personal Relationship and Critical Estimate" (*PMLA*, 1947) and Donald H. Reiman "Keats and Shelley: Personal and Literary Relations" (in *Shelley and His Circle*, vol. 5, 1973). Nelson S.

Bushnell's *A Walk after John Keats* (1936) is a day-by-day account of Keats's Scottish tour in the summer of 1818. For Keats's finances we have, in addition to the standard biographies and a host of articles too numerous to list here, Gittings' *The Keats Inheritance* (1964). Guy Murchie, *The Spirit of Place in Keats* (1955), identifies and describes a number of places that Keats visited or lived in, and Timothy Hilton, *Keats and His World* (1971), gives us pictures of most of them. Donald Parson, *Portraits of Keats* (1954), with ninety-four plates, is the best source of information about the many sketches, paintings, silhouettes, and busts of the poet.

After Keats's letters themselves, the richest single source of biographical information is *The Keats Circle: Letters and Papers, 1816–1878,* edited by H. E. Rollins (2 vols., 1948). This work, supplemented by Rollins' *More Letters and Poems of the Keats Circle* (1955; 2nd ed. of *KC* and *More Letters* together, 1965), makes available the texts of nearly four hundred letters and other documents at Harvard and the Morgan Library written by friends, relatives, and, later in the century, students and scholars of the poet. They include Brown's "Life" of Keats and much of the rest of the material collected by Milnes for his *Life* of 1848, papers collected by Amy Lowell for her biography of 1925, and letters and memoranda from Woodhouse's scrapbook in the Morgan. These form a substantial (and very readable) body of evidence concerning the development of Keats's reputation in the nineteenth century. There is also much of more immediate biographical and critical interest—for example, Brown's list of Keats's books (80 items), an illuminating correspondence between Woodhouse and Keats's publisher Taylor, and Woodhouse's description of "K's mode of writing Poetry" in some remarks on "When I have fears."

Other primary documents concerning the Keats circle (in addition to the nineteenth-century works mentioned earlier in this section) include *The Letters of John Hamilton Reynolds,* edited by Leonidas M. Jones (1973); *The Letters of Charles Armitage Brown,* edited by Jack Stillinger (1966); *Letters of Fanny Brawne to Fanny Keats, 1820–1824,* edited by Fred Edgcumbe (1937); and *The Diary of Benjamin Robert Haydon,* edited by W. B. Pope (5 vols., 1960–63). Thirty-nine additional Reynolds letters have been published in *Letters from Lambeth: The Correspondence of the Reynolds Family with John Freeman Milward Dovaston, 1808–1815,* edited by Joanna Richardson (1981), and twenty-five others in articles by Donald Lange (*N&Q* and *MLR,* both 1977), John Clubbe (*KSJ,* 1981), Anne Kaier (*KSJ,* 1981), and Joanna Richardson (*KSMB,* 1982), and appendix A of L. M. Jones's *The Life of John Hamilton Reynolds* (1984); an additional Brown letter has been published by Jones (*KSMB,* 1979—there is another, unpublished, to Mrs. Leigh Hunt, 19 Nov. 1840, in the Berg Collection). Twentieth-century editions of Reynolds' *Poetry and Prose,* edited by George L. Marsh (1928), and *Selected Prose,* edited by L. M. Jones (1966), are valuable, especially the latter, which contains a lengthy list of Reynolds' published and unpublished writings, several hundred items in all. A half dozen of Brown's magazine articles are included in *Some Letters & Miscellanea of Charles Brown,* edited by M. B. Forman (1937). For Hunt's writings we have, among others, *Poetical Works,* edited by H. S. Milford (1923), Edmund Blunden's *Leigh Hunt's "Examiner" Examined* (1928), re-

printing thirteen of Hunt's pieces (plus a half dozen articles by other hands), and
Lawrence Huston Houtchens and Carolyn Washburn Houtchens' editions of
Hunt's *Dramatic Criticism* (1949), *Literary Criticism* (1956), and *Political and
Occasional Essays* (1962); there is a comprehensive bibliographical essay on Hunt
in the Houtchenses' *The English Romantic Poets & Essayists: A Review of Research
and Criticism* (rev. ed. 1966).

For the lives of members of the Keats circle it is usually best to start with
Rollins' biographical sketches at the front of *The Keats Circle* and his edition of
Keats's *Letters*—two dozen in the former, twenty in the latter—which give not
only the principal facts but also references to the most important sources of information. The lives of two of Keats's siblings are chronicled by Naomi Joy Kirk,
"Memoir of George Keats" (in vol. 1 of H. B. Forman's Hampstead edition, 1938),
and Marie Adami, *Fanny Keats* (1938). Clayton E. Hudnall and Paul Kaufman have
written interestingly (and independently of each other) on an early group of
Keats's acquaintances in "John Hamilton Reynolds, James Rice, and Benjamin Bailey in the Leigh Browne–Lockyer Collection" (*KSJ*, 1970) and "A Keats Circle by the
Sea" (*EM*, 1971). Then there are a number of useful biographies of Keats's other
close friends—Richard D. Altick's *The Cowden Clarkes* (1948); Eric George's *The
Life and Death of Benjamin Robert Haydon* (1948) and Clarke Olney's *Benjamin
Robert Haydon, Historical Painter* (1952); Edmund Blunden's *Leigh Hunt: A Biog-
raphy* (1930) and Louis Landré's *Leigh Hunt (1784–1859): Contribution à
l'histoire du Romantisme anglais* (2 vols., 1935–36); Leonidas M. Jones's *The Life
of John Hamilton Reynolds* (1984); Blunden's *Keats's Publisher: A Memoir of John
Taylor* (1936) and Tim Chilcott's *A Publisher and His Circle: The Life and Work of
John Taylor* (1972); Sheila Birkenhead's *Against Oblivion: The Life of Joseph
Severn* (1943) and her larger and more thoroughly documented *Illustrious
Friends: The Story of Joseph Severn and His Son Arthur* (1965); William Garrett's
Charles Wentworth Dilke (1982), a volume in the Twayne English Authors series,
containing an extensive list of Dilke's published writings; and Joanna Richardson's
Fanny Brawne: A Biography (1952) and *The Everlasting Spell: A Study of Keats
and His Friends* (1963), the latter centering on Dilke and Charles Brown.
Richardson has also recently published *Keats and His Circle: An Album of Portraits* (1980), a collection of 163 portraits of Keats, his family, his friends and their
families and friends, and, the prize of them all, a hitherto unknown photograph
of Fanny Brawne, in her fifties, looking every bit as beautiful and elegant as we
always knew she would be.

Criticism

The critical works on Keats and his poems (like those, I should suppose, on any
other major literary artist) are nearly impossible to organize and classify in a way
that makes good sense. Books that profess to be about Keats's art turn out really
to be about his ideas (and of course sometimes vice versa); titles tend to be noncommittal ("On the Poetry of Keats," "Keats and His Poetry," "Keats the Poet") or
else simply incomprehensible ("The Finer Tone," "The Hoodwinking of

Madeline"); much of the best commentary on individual poems is in fact contained in the "general studies" and also in some of the biographies mentioned in the preceding section (particularly Bate's and Bush's), and then some of the specialized studies and interpretations of individual poems have comprehensive results that would qualify for inclusion in a more general category. The best source-and-influence studies end up as critical interpretations, and so do a great many of the works produced by the various other specialized research and critical methodologies.

Consider just a couple of random examples. Gittings' *John Keats: The Living Year* (1954) is a biography of Keats's life and career during a single year (21 Sept. 1818 – 21 Sept. 1819), an important and controversial study of Keats's sources, and a collection of interpretive commentary on his major poems. Christopher Ricks's *Keats and Embarrassment* (1974) is more than anything else a sustained meditation on selected passages of Keats's letters and poems but also qualifies (and fortunately, since we have no category called "sustained meditation") as a psychoanalytic investigation of Keats's personality and his art, a discourse on Keats's imagination, a study of his poetic style and characteristic imagery, and a more general contribution to aesthetics (what Keats's art *is* and what it *does*). Obviously these books could be mentioned and, if there were room, described under several different headings, and the same is true of many other works at hand. The prudent user of this essay will see the virtual necessity of keeping everything in mind all at once—and not just the whole of this section but the preceding and following sections as well!

The present section on criticism is subdivided into three parts. "General Studies" treats, in order, the most enduring of the comprehensive works produced before 1960, the most useful book-length critical studies of the 1960s and 1970s, a half dozen book-length "introductions" to Keats, a selection of shorter works (mainly book chapters and introductory essays), and finally a brief list of collections of essays on Keats. "Specialized Studies," the most heterogeneous part of the entire essay, begins with studies of Keats's ideas and "philosophy" per se, branches out into ideas as themes, "preoccupations," and controlling myths in the poems, then takes up work on Keats's style, narrative technique, and other aspects of his art, and finally considers investigations of his sources and influences and his relation to literary tradition. The third part, "Studies of Individual Works," is mainly an elaborate listing of the best recent interpretations, beginning with those on the *Poems* of 1817 and proceeding chronologically (according to composition of the poems) through *Endymion, Isabella, The Eve of St. Agnes,* and so on to the end.

GENERAL STUDIES

Works before 1960. There are a great many valuable critical comments by Keats's contemporaries, especially Woodhouse, Clarke, and Bailey, scattered through *The Keats Circle* and other works mentioned in the preceding section and elsewhere (e.g., Woodhouse's note originally inscribed near the front of the larger of his two books of poetry transcripts at Harvard, beginning "There is a great degree of reality about all that Keats writes," is worth more than many modern essays, and his well-known comment to Taylor that Keats's revisions of *The Eve of St. Agnes* rendered the poem "unfit for ladies, & indeed scarcely to be mentioned to them among the 'things that are'" is of first importance concerning both Keats's and his publishers' ideas of their contemporary audience). One pays homage to F. M. Owen's *John Keats: A Study* (1880), the first book-length critical study (still occasionally cited for its allegorical interpretation of *Endymion*). Matthew Arnold's essay on Keats (originally an introduction to the Keats selections in T. H. Ward's *The English Poets,* vol. 4, 1880; rpt. in Arnold's *Essays in Criticism: Second Series,* 1888) is still frequently quoted, especially the fervent ending of the penultimate paragraph: "No one else in English poetry, save Shakespeare, has in expression quite the fascinating felicity of Keats, his perfection of loveliness. 'I think,' he said humbly, 'I shall be among the English Poets after my death.' He is; he is with Shakespeare." And Robert Bridges' essay (privately printed 1895, then published as an introduction to Keats's *Poems,* 1896; rpt. in Bridges' *Collected Essays, Papers, &c.,* 1929) is also mentioned from time to time. Apart from these, however, the principal older critics whose works continue to be cited are all twentieth-century writers: Murry, Garrod, Ridley, Finney, Caldwell, Ford, Wasserman, Gittings (in his books of the 1950s), Pettet, Slote, and Blackstone. If one adds the names of two of the earlier biographers—Colvin and Lowell—and those of Clarence Thorpe (for his *The Mind of John Keats,* discussed below among specialized studies) and Douglas Bush (for his treatment of Keats in *Mythology and the Romantic Tradition* and his introduction and commentary in the Riverside edition) the list of the most important Keats critics before 1960 is pretty nearly complete.

John Middleton Murry is the author of two very influential books, *Keats and Shakespeare: A Study of Keats' Poetic Life from 1816 to 1820* (1925—reissued by the original publisher at least eight times between 1926 and the late 1960s) and *Studies in Keats* (1930), a work that was three times "enlarged and drastically revised" as, successively, *Studies in Keats: New and Old* (1939), *The Mystery of Keats* (1949), and *Keats* (1955). The initial work of 1925, an attempt to tell "the story of [Keats's] inward life," grew out of Murry's interest in such things as "the history of the human soul since the Renaissance," "the adventure of the individual mind exploring the universe for truth," and "the rediscovery of the essential reality of religion" and his "astonishing" (and belated) discovery not only that his two greatest spiritual heroes, Shakespeare and Keats, had so much in common but that "Keats himself was far more conscious than I had ever been of the strange relation between himself and Shakespeare!" As might be gathered from these quotations (from the preface and the introductory chapter), Murry's study is highly personal and, by today's standards, somewhat muddleheaded; Murry is a precursor of some more recent metaphysical critics here and abroad. But there are numerous insightful comments, and the book is not to be rejected out of hand. The second, companion work—*Studies in Keats* through *Keats*—is in its various forms a collection of individual essays on the principal women in Keats's life (Fanny

Brawne, Fanny Keats, Isabella Jones), his relationships with some other writers (Milton, Wordsworth, Blake), some separate poems and passages (e.g., the Chapman's Homer sonnet, the Cave of Quietude passage in *Endymion* 4), and miscellaneous topics like "Keats and Friendship" and "Keats and Claret" (this last the subject, with a different emphasis, of 14 letters in the London *Times,* 17 Feb. – 11 Mar. 1977). Most of these retain something of their original value and interest, and in any case they are what subsequent critics read and reacted to over a period of several decades.

H. W. Garrod's *Keats* (1926; 2nd ed., 1939), part of which was originally delivered as the Oxford Poetry lectures for 1925, is notable chiefly for the author's sustained attack on Amy Lowell's biography (the first of a series of sporadic hostilities between British and American Keatsians that continued into the 1950s), for some outrageous statements that are now quoted mainly to be refuted (e.g., "upon whatever page of Keats' poetry there falls the shadow of a living woman, it falls calamitously like an eclipse" and "I think [Keats] the great poet he is only when the senses capture him, when he finds truth in beauty, that is to say, when he does not trouble to find truth at all"), and finally for some quite sound discussion of Keats's odes, focusing on the development of the ode stanza out of experiments with the sonnet and on some problems of coherence in "Ode on a Grecian Urn."

A much more substantial work is M. R. Ridley's *Keats' Craftsmanship: A Study in Poetic Development* (1933). Based on careful examination of manuscripts and transcripts now mainly at Harvard, the Morgan Library, and the British Library and taking off from Woodhouse's account of "K's mode of writing Poetry," this is the first detailed investigation into the processes of composition as revealed by Keats's cancellations and revisions in his drafts. Some of the facts of textual history and readings of the manuscripts would now be corrected in the light of more recent work in *The Texts of Keats's Poems* and the apparatus and notes to the 1978 *Poems,* but Ridley's descriptions of Keats's verbal craftsmanship continue to be sound and illuminating. In the realm of interpretation there are naturally some blindnesses (for instance, the notion that in *Lamia* 1.191 – 96 Keats wrote "six lines which have a specious appearance of reflective profundity, and in fact mean as nearly as may be exactly nothing"), but there are some very smart interpretive suggestions as well—for example, that "if in most places where Keats uses the word 'truth' (with its connotation of 'correspondence') we substitute the word 'reality', we are likely to come nearer to his meaning." Ridley also offers a great many facts and suggestions concerning Keats's sources.

Claude Lee Finney's *The Evolution of Keats's Poetry* (2 vols., 1936), originating as a Harvard dissertation under John Livingston Lowes and completed some fourteen years later when Finney was on the faculty of the University of Illinois (which still enjoys the benefit of the 18 volumes of photostats of Keats manuscripts that he collected), is an impressive compilation, more than eight hundred pages long, of basic information concerning chronology, sources, influences, biographical facts, and interpretation. It treats virtually every poem that Keats wrote and concludes with a lengthy bibliographical account, "Manuscript Material for the Study of Keats's Life and Poetry," particularly valuable at the time for its detailed descriptions of the Woodhouse notebooks at Harvard and the Morgan Library and its information about the many manuscripts that were then in private collections. Nowadays, nearly five decades later, it is still a standard work, one of the half dozen or so most useful for the general study of Keats's poems.

James Ralston Caldwell's *John Keats' Fancy: The Effect on Keats of the Psychology of His Day* (1945) and Newell F. Ford's *The Prefigurative Imagination of John Keats: A Study of the Beauty-Truth Identification and Its Implications* (1951), although more specialized than Finney's work, still qualify as general studies. Caldwell investigates the Hartleian associationalism that was the standard psychology of Keats's time and discovers a great many Hartleian elements in the poems. As a study of Keats's aesthetics, whether in theory or in practice, it is severely limited, but its analysis of the mental processes and "trains" of imagery in poems and passages, especially the poems of Keats's first volume and *Endymion,* is quite valuable. Ford's work, as its subtitle suggests, focuses on the beauty-truth identification at the end of "Ode on a Grecian Urn," but the subject has implications for *Endymion* and the rest of the major poems of 1818 and 1819 as well. Ford employs (and advertises) a lexicographical method of assessing meanings of key terms ("truth," "ethereal," "empyreal," "sensations," "spiritual," etc.) by collecting and scrutinizing all the separate uses in their contexts. The most fundamental text for this work, Keats's letter to Bailey of 22 November 1817, is subjected to sentence-by-sentence analysis, and its most important idea, the prefigurative (prophetic) character of the imagination, becomes the focal point of the study. Ford finds elements of the prefigurative imagination throughout Keats's career. Directly and indirectly the work has had considerable influence on subsequent Keats criticism.

Earl R. Wasserman, whether or not he knew of Ford's work, produced a brilliant and illogical extension of *The Prefigurative Imagination* two years later in his *The Finer Tone: Keats' Major Poems* (1953). Wasserman's principal texts are two passages of book 1 of *Endymion*—the Hymn to Pan, with its reference to "the very bourne of heaven," and the lines about "fellowship with essence" beginning at 777—and again Keats's letter to Bailey of 22 November 1817, which supplies Wasserman's title ("we shall enjoy ourselves here after by having what we called happiness on Earth repeated in a finer tone and so repeated"). On the basis of these, and with a little help from Kenneth Burke and the notion of "mystic oxymoron," Wasserman arrives at "the three cardinal principles of Keats' mind: his aspiration is to ascend to a condition of beauty-truth which is to be found in heaven's bourne; the pleasure thermometer is the means; and self-annihilation is the condition." In five central chapters this scheme is rigorously and minutely applied to "Ode on a Grecian Urn," "La Belle Dame," *The Eve of St. Agnes, Lamia,* and "Ode to a Nightingale," with results that are at once dazzling and lopsided. To an extent Wasserman reads 1819 poems as if they had been written in 1817, and it has seemed to some subsequent critics that Keats himself outgrew his early metaphysical speculations before his interpreter did. At times Wasserman writes as if Keats's characters (e.g., Madeline and Porphyro, Lycius and Lamia) had read not only Keats's letters and *Endymion* but *The Finer Tone* as well. But the study is conducted with energy and audacity; it commanded (and still commands) attention and stimulated some of the best Keats criticism of the decade following its publication.

Wasserman's work is typical of the general studies produced in the last thirty years in being both flawed and quite useful at the same time. No single book gives a completely satisfactory account of Keats overall (Keats is much too complex and many-sided to be encompassed in book length), but almost without exception each has something to offer in the way of new information and suggestions for interpretation, new critical uses of the facts of Keats's life and letters, and fresh connections among Keats's writings and between his and other writers' works. This is certainly true of Robert Gittings' *John Keats: The Living Year* (1954), which caused more than a little agitation among Keatsians by elevating Isabella Jones, a friend of Keats's publisher Taylor and other members of the circle, to an importance in Keats's life nearly equal to that of Fanny Brawne. (This book and Gittings' *The Mask of Keats,* 1956, are treated below among works on Keats's sources.) It is also true of E. C. Pettet's *On the Poetry of Keats* (1957), a lengthy and somewhat disorganized study, down-to-earth and anti-Wasserman in tendency, concluding that "even when Keats is writing at his most rhapsodic . . . he never loses sight of actuality." Pettet sometimes sounds as if he had more important business elsewhere ("in several instances," he says of his work, "the interests and writing of one [chapter] led directly to another. There are even moments when I fancy that the book may have some degree of shape"), and his interpretive positions are now and then overly simple and exclusionary: *Endymion* is "a tale of 'pure deliciousness' "; "there can be no other way of reading [*The Eve of St. Agnes*] than as a great affirmation of love"; "we must surely regard *To Psyche* as Keats's epithalamion to Fanny Brawne"; "the urn's message is perhaps not really difficult to understand." But then, along with (indeed, almost in spite of) statements like these, there are serious and clever interpretations of many parts of Keats's best poems. Pettet is capable both of calling attention to the "vague and obscure" character of the opening lines of "Ode on a Grecian Urn"—"if we choose to dwell on their meaning"!—and then, a page or so later, of offering a very sharp explanation of what they mean. One can learn much from the work without fully agreeing on any specific point.

Bernice Slote's *Keats and the Dramatic Principle* (1958) is a highly original critical study based on solid biographical and historical research. The ostensible subject is Keats's interest in, and connections with, the drama and theater of his time and the influence of these on his poetry. But the treatment is broad and comprehensive, and it captures some of the basic qualities of Keats's greatest work. The first section begins with Keats's famous letter to Woodhouse on the poetical character ("it has no self . . . no Identity") and establishes the essentially dramatic stance of his own artistic sensibility; the second section surveys his activities as playgoer, theatrical reviewer, and frustrated playwright; the third investigates his increasing use of character, scene, and dramatic voice in his shorter poems and the dramatic and playlike qualities of *Lamia.* The final chapter is the best discussion in print of the complexity of the autobiographical relationships between Keats's life and the characters and happenings in his poems. The chapter is entitled "The Submerged Continent," and the main point is that what we know about the biography and sources of a poet, even one so well documented as Keats, represents a mere island or two when compared to the submerged continent of matters—the subsurface "incalculable complexities of the creative life"—that we really can learn nothing about: we are quite rightly advised to be skeptical of "single, surface measurements."

Bernard Blackstone's *The Consecrated Urn: An Interpretation of Keats in Terms of Growth and Form* (1959) is also a highly original work but in a different sense. My Byron colleague in the present volume speaks of Blackstone as a "*savant terrible*" combining "an impressive grasp of [Byron's] canon with an abundance of original and often startling insights, the whole imbedded in much hocus-pocus and in much that is downright silly." This would be an apt description of *The Consecrated Urn* as well, a work that approaches Keats on a "botanico-physiologico-cosmogonical [not to mention tragical-comical-historical-pastoral] slant." Blackstone is a self-confessed "inveterate Platonist" who is convinced that Keats read Blake and the hermetic philosophers and that these are the key to unlock his poems. One of Blackstone's primary texts is a sonnet called "The Poet," then in the Keats canon, which has images of an excursion "into the charmed air," a "talisman to call up spirits rare," "secret essence," "premature and mystic communings," "unearthly intercourses"—all of which would be of sensational interest these days if Keats had in fact written the poem (but it is now attributed to John Taylor and dated after Keats's death). Blackstone uses the sonnet as a means of access to *Endymion,* the poem that he treats at greatest length. "*Endymion,* which by any standards is Keats's major work...contains in germ or in flower every single aspect of Keats's thinking and feeling and knowing.... In all that follows (with the partial exception of *Hyperion*) Keats simply detaches and writes variations upon the themes of his master-work." The book is full of such half-truths; negatively capable readers will know how to value them.

General studies of the 1960s and 1970s. The most frequently cited general critics of more recent years are Evert, Patterson, Dickstein, Stillinger, Sperry, and Ricks. Walter Evert's *Aesthetic and Myth in the Poetry of Keats* (1965) is a detailed investigation of Keats's use of the myths associated with Apollo in his various roles as god of the sun, poetry, astronomy, and medicine and a great many images connected with these myths—gold, nightingales, wine, the lyre, sunshine, wind, water, and so on. Beginning with the very early "Ode to Apollo" (1815), Evert finds enough recurrences of these elements to argue that "the late-Greek conception of the god Apollo" is central to the themes and structures of much of Keats's work, in a positive way in the earlier pieces and *Endymion* and then in an inverse, negative way as Keats detaches himself from that conception in the great poems of 1819. As with any attempt to explain Keats in terms of a single myth, idea, symbol, or structure, the successful outcome depends to an extent on the critic's ingenuity and the reader's willingness to look the other way when he or she comes to a recalcitrant poem or passage. But Evert's close readings of the poems—*Endymion* in particular (in an 89-page chapter), as well as the verse epistle to Reynolds, "La Belle Dame," *Lamia,* and the Hyperion fragments, among other notables—are excellent. One continually returns to these to have one's thinking straightened out; the interpretations remain sharp and up-to-date even while the central myth fades on the horizon.

John Jones's *John Keats's Dream of Truth* (1969) is more elusive, owing in part no doubt to the unhelpfulness of the five section headings—"The Feel I Have," "The Abstract Idea," "Snailhorn Perception," "Havens of Intenseness," "The Labyrinthian Path" (all from Keats's letter to Haydon of 8 Apr. 1818, where in context they make some sense)—and a prose style that the *TLS* reviewer described as "frequently either glutinous or lumpish." More than one serious scholar of my acquaintance has read all the other books on Keats but failed in the attempt to get through this one. It is, like Christopher Ricks's much more readable *Keats and Embarrassment,* a work heavily influenced by John Bayley's "Keats and Reality" (*Proceedings of the British Academy,* 1962; rev. and exp. in Bayley's *The Uses of Division: Unity and Disharmony in Literature,* 1976) and therefore is specially interested in Keats's orientation in the world of "feel," sensation, and sensuality. It is not now much cited (except by Bayley, Ricks, and, most recently, Helen Vendler in her new book on the odes) but probably deserves to be consulted nevertheless for the occasional detail that everyone else has missed. Unfortunately the index is not much more helpful than the section headings. Jones may have had a higher audience in mind.

Charles I. Patterson, Jr.'s *The Daemonic in the Poetry of John Keats* (1970) is an ambitious attempt to explain Keats not in the commoner terms of actual versus ideal but in terms of actual versus "the daemonic," a concept that is variously a metaphor ("for a particular area or activity of the human consciousness influenced by much that wells up from the unconscious"), a psychological state ("a sharply focused trance in which a person still perceives specific objects and situations vividly and concretely, but with a daemonic intensity and fixation upon only those qualities and aspects of these objects that are desirable to him"), an experience related to actuality (where the "specific objects and situations" usually are), and a realm located somewhere else ("experience out of this world, beyond the actual and its limitations, beyond the moral and immoral into joy and ecstasy"). Obviously the concept is not well defined—perhaps there are too many definitions, with a damaging degree of conflict and contradiction among them—and its place in Keats's poems is accordingly somewhat murky, as is the account of Keats's development first toward and then away from the concept, ending with "the triumph of the anti-daemonic" in "To Autumn." Patterson has, however, provoked some critics out of their complacency with the simpler received schemes for understanding Keats's poetry, and in any case he provides intelligent discussions of the major poems—*Endymion,* "La Belle Dame," and *Lamia* in particular—that must be taken seriously in any survey of interpretations.

Morris Dickstein's *Keats and His Poetry: A Study in Development* (1971), another ambitious work of loose definitions, offers "a reading of Keats' development in terms of his changing attitudes toward 'consciousness,' what Keats calls 'the thinking principle,' by which he means not pure intellection so much as self-awareness and awareness of the world that surrounds, nurtures, and conditions the self." The focus is important, because Keats's concern with thinking, consciousness, and problems of the self had at that time received very little critical attention. In the overall scheme, Dickstein charts a progress from early escape poetry to attempts to transcend (rather than lose) the self, and finally to an acceptance of self, consciousness, and a tragic vision of life and the world. For some critics the scheme lacks coherence (mainly because the terms, and especially the values attached to them, seem to change around rather arbitrarily). What stands out, however, is the poem-by-poem exploration of these matters. There are lengthy discussions of *Endymion* and most of the great odes, but Dickstein concentrates especially on a sizable number of poems that are usually slighted or ignored—for example, "In drear nighted December," "Sonnet to Sleep," and the poems of the Scottish walking tour of 1818. The anonymous *TLS* reviewer faulted Dickstein for seeming to be unacquainted with the work of John Bayley and John Jones; all the other reviewers praised the book highly, especially for its readability.

Jack Stillinger's *The Hoodwinking of Madeline and Other Essays on Keats's Poems* (1971), while in part a collection of pieces already separately published in journals, is included here among general studies because all the essays proceed from the same view of what Keats's poems are principally about, namely that they

> center on a single basic problem, the mutability inherent in nature and human life, and openly or in disguise they debate the pros and cons of a single hypothetical solution, transcendence of earthly limitations by means of the visionary imagination. . . . Keats came to learn that this kind of imagination was a false lure, inadequate to the needs of the problem, and in the end he traded it for the naturalized imagination, embracing experience and process as his own and man's chief good.

The initial chapter sorts out the main concerns of the poems in Keats's first volume, and the last chapter attempts to relate Keats to Wordsworth in a redefinition of Romanticism; those in between treat the major works from *Endymion* through the odes, with special emphasis on dreaming, visionary imagination, and antiromantic skepticism. The shortest review of the book, referring to the chapter on *The Eve of St. Agnes* (rpt. half a dozen times since its original appearance as an essay in 1961), was a couplet by R. H. Fogle in the Phi Beta Kappa *Key Reporter*: "Alack for Madeline, poor hoodwink'd maid— / By Porphyro then, now Stillinger betrayed." It might be noted that Stillinger, having started out as a Keats critic some twenty-five years ago by censuring Bush's description of *St. Agnes* as "no more than a romantic tapestry of unique richness of color," is nowadays assigning seminar reports on the color imagery of the poem and showing photographic slides of tapestries and stained glass.

Bhabatosh Chatterjee's *John Keats: His Mind and Work* (1971), written and published in India, is a three-part study of "Keats's spiritual quest as revealed in his letters and poems." The first part "examines the nature of Keats's quest and his uncertainties before several ideals"; the second more specifically treats "the comic in Keats"; the third (constituting three fifths of the book) is a detailed commentary on the poems in chronological order. It is a large work of compilation—twenty-four chapters, 487 pages, 830 notes at the back, most of which cite Keats scholars and critics from Milnes through writers of the later 1960s—and might be used (via the index) as a guide to some of the available opinions on various matters. Chatterjee himself adds little to those opinions, but for an audience unfamiliar with them the work could provide a great deal in the way of facts, interpretations, and references.

Stuart M. Sperry's *Keats the Poet* (1973) is currently the most widely and frequently cited of all recent books on Keats, and deservedly, for it contains some of the most intelligent critical analyses in print. The opening chapter establishes the importance of "sensation" in both Keats's early critical thinking and his practice as a poet and surveys the philosophical and aesthetic theories underlying the concept as Keats uses it. The second introductory chapter, entitled "The Chemistry of the Poetic Process," is a brilliant investigation of the relationship of critical and philosophical terms in Keats's poems and letters—for example, "abstract," "spirit," "essence," "intense," "distill," "empyreal," "ethereal," "sublime"—to their literal meanings in the chemistry of Keats's day. The rest of the book is an examination of specific poems in the usual chronological order, from a selection of 1816 – 17 pieces to *The Fall of Hyperion* and "To Autumn." At the outset the work is intended "to trace the intellectual and poetic development of John Keats from the beginning to the end of his career," but the continuing argument that is supposed to hold the analyses together—that Keats was principally concerned with problems of the poetic process—becomes less and less prominent until, in the last third of the book, it virtually disappears. I thought this a fault when I reviewed the work in 1974; I'd now consider it a virtue: rather than force a thesis on his materials, Sperry has written an excellent book of commentary and made a considerable contribution in the form of new and valuable insights into specific poems and passages.

The most original of modern studies of Keats, however—even more so than Blackstone's, where the originality is frequently merely a kind of perverse eccentricity—is Christopher Ricks's *Keats and Embarrassment* (1974), a book that received more numerous and more searching reviews than any other work on Keats since the major biographies of a decade earlier. Ricks begins with three propositions: "First, that embarrassment is very important in life. Second, that one of the things for which we value art is that it helps us to deal with embarrassment, not by abolishing or ignoring it, but by recognizing, refining, and putting it to good human purposes. . . . Third, that Keats as a man and a poet was especially sensitive to, and morally intelligent about, embarrassment." This is not the way books about Keats usually begin. The reader is instantly attracted by the freshness of the approach, and, as one of the reviewers remarked, it is a difficult book to stop reading. Like Bayley and John Jones before him, but much more interestingly and usefully, Ricks is concerned with Keats's sensuousness, especially in the extreme indulgences of that sensuousness that produced such phrasings as "Those lips, O slippery blisses," "O he had swoon'd / Drunken from pleasure's nipple," and "his erewhile timid lips . . . poesied with hers in dewy rhyme," phrasings some of Keats's critics have wished that Taylor or Woodhouse had edited out of existence. Considered as a general study of Keats's poetry, the work has severe limitations: it focuses mainly on the early poems and *Endymion,* slighting the work of 1819 (most notably the odes and the Hyperion fragments), and it largely ignores the poems as individual works of art and says nothing about their subjects, themes, plots, characters, structures, and the like routine matters. As a study, with general implications, of some undeniably characteristic elements of Keats's style and imagery—"the hotly disconcerting, the potentially ludicrous, distasteful, or blush-inducing"—and why Keats was interested in them, and how we respond to them, it is of first importance. Ricks also gives a great deal of attention to Keats's letters and quotes them at considerable length; passages are somehow made to seem brand-new even to someone who has been reading them for decades.

Ronald A. Sharp's *Keats, Skepticism, and the Religion of Beauty* (1979) seeks to recast conflicting impulses in Keats's poetry and letters into a more compatible relationship of problem and solution. The problem: "How can a religious and metaphysical skeptic find a source of endurance and affirmation in a world of unavoidable suffering?" The solution: "Keats develops a fully humanized religion of beauty, paradoxically rooted in skepticism and offered as an alternative not to the inescapably painful world but to the Christian response to that world." One does not usually number Keats, especially Keats the poet, among the theologians of the world, but Sharp makes an interesting case in this study, mustering large parts of major works to support his thesis. Disapproving critics have pointed to lapses in his knowledge of religious history and serious flaws of logic in his argument (see in particular the review by Robert M. Ryan, *JEGP,* 1981), and even those who admire the work object to the depiction of Keats as a man who never wavered once he had made up his mind ("In Keats," says Sharp, "we have an extraordinary example of a poet whose essential ideas about life and poetry were almost fully conceived from the beginning of his poetic career"). Still it is a well-written study, solidly grounded in knowledge of the considerable body of earlier Keats criticism, and, like a number of the other works surveyed here, valuable for individual insights even when it falters on the main point.

The most recently published of the general studies (as of this writing, in the summer of 1983) was actually drafted in nearly complete form two decades ago—Dorothy Van Ghent's posthumous *Keats: The Myth of the Hero,* revised and edited by Jeffrey C. Robinson (1983). Van Ghent's work seeks to establish "a single synoptic action or master plot" recurring in (and serving to unify and interrelate) major and minor poems from *Endymion* through *The Fall of Hyperion*: a gifted young man, full of aspirations and confusion, desires to become his "anti-self," a type of Adonis or Apollo; three female characters (maiden, witch, and goddess) help or hinder his progress; gods and *numina* inhabit the natural and supernatural settings; and so forth. Not surprisingly, the various elements can be found in at least most of the texts minutely examined (*Endymion,* the major narratives of 1818–19, the poems and letters to Fanny Brawne, the great odes, the Hyperion fragments). The study is indebted to Joseph Campbell, Robert Graves, Jessie Weston, and other mythographers who played an important part in criticism during the 1950s and 1960s but are now generally considered out of date.

What saves it from being merely a period piece is Van Ghent's surpassing critical intelligence. The work is full of fresh observations about the poems, especially concerning their stories, characters, and actions, and there are excellent discussions of such topics as the women in *Endymion,* the "ravished brides" of the later narratives, the framing stanzas of "La Belle Dame," the parodic tone of *Lamia,* the essential differences between Keats and Spenser, the mythological-literary backgrounds of his relationship with Fanny Brawne, and the symbolism of the Grecian urn.

As I said earlier, none of these general studies gives a completely satisfactory explanation of Keats overall, and there is none that I would recommend to the exclusion of all the others. The interesting thing is that each of them has an authentic basis in Keats's work. Hartleian psychology, the prefigurative imagination, the mystic oxymoron of paradise in heaven's bourne, the strong penchant toward the dramatic, the Apollo myth, the daemonic, the acute awareness of self and consciousness, the interest in dreaming and visionary imagination, the antiromantic skepticism, the prolonged concern with the poetic process, embarrassment, the worship of beauty, the myth of the hero—all of these (and more) are present, frequently at the same time and in the same passages and contexts. Keats is greater than the sum of his critics. It is probably this multitudinous complexity that explains why he seems so inexhaustible—and why his critics can read and teach him with enthusiasm year after year and still find something more in his works on every new occasion.

"Introductions" to Keats. Douglas Bush's *John Keats: His Life and Writings* (1966), mentioned earlier as the best of the shorter critical biographies, would be an ideal introduction to the poet. But there is another category of publication, somewhat shorter than Bush's volume—say, in the 60- to 190-page range—and more openly aimed at beginning students and interested readers outside the academy: the general introduction that rehearses the biographical facts, discusses the best-known poems, and sometimes surveys the criticism. Works in this category do not usually have a thesis, and they make no great claims for originality of interpretations; nevertheless they are, or can be, very useful for the audience addressed. Three of the half dozen examples at hand were published at about the same time as Bush's book: Fred Inglis' *Keats* (1966), an engaging and intelligent series of chapters on "The Intellectual Background," "The Life," "The Letters," and then the major poems, ending with "Conclusion: Why Read Keats?"; Robin Mayhead's *John Keats* (1967), a businesslike tour of Keats's earliest poems, *Endymion,* some of the other narratives, the odes (to which more than a third of the book is given), and the Hyperion fragments; and Norman Talbot's *The Major Poems of John Keats* (1968), which is much narrower in scope (treating only 3 of the odes and *The Fall of Hyperion,* 4 poems in all) and, most unfortunately in a work of this sort, rather tedious. Inglis' would appear to be the most substantial and recommendable of the three. Miriam Allott's *John Keats* (1976), a sixty-page pamphlet in the British Council's Writers and Their Work series, consists of a pleasant, readable essay and an impressive annotated bibliography that covers some 125 items.

The two most recent works in this category are William Walsh's *Introduction to Keats* (1981) and Wolf Z. Hirst's *John Keats* (also 1981), the latter in the Twayne English Authors series. Walsh's book begins well, with a fine description of Keats's character and sensibility and intelligent discussion of the early poems and *Endymion*, then declines into a disproportionately lengthy survey of the letters (really not much more than a stringing together of quotations), and ends up with little to say of the poems of 1819 (the final chapter consists of 2 pages on *The Eve of St. Agnes*, 2 on *Lamia*, and 15 on the odes). There are many errors in datings and other facts; the whole is rather shoddy and amateurish. Hirst's book, by contrast, while written for a similar audience and organized on a roughly similar scheme—introductory account of the life and career, summary of the main ideas in the letters, followed by description and interpretation of the poems—is a readable and scholarly work of very high quality throughout. Hirst has a firm grasp of both the standard and the latest Keats scholarship and does an excellent job of synthesizing others' research and opinions with his own. The book is well documented, and the eight-page annotated bibliography is particularly good. Teachers as well as students can learn from this one.

Shorter works (chapters and essays).   Keats usually gets a chapter to himself in the literary histories and surveys of the period. Samuel C. Chew's treatment in *A Literary History of England* (ed. Albert C. Baugh, 1948; 2nd ed. 1967) is representative but of course long out of date. The Keats chapter in Ian Jack's *English Literature, 1815–1832* (1963), another standard work, is more satisfactory. But the seventy-five pages on Keats in Harold Bloom's *The Visionary Company: A Reading of English Romantic Poetry* (1961; rev. ed. 1971), a book originally intended, like Ernest Bernbaum's *Guide through the Romantic Movement* of thirty years earlier, as a companion volume to an anthology of the poetry, constitute a brilliant series of close readings and interpretations, from "Sleep and Poetry" and *Endymion* through the narratives and odes to a final section ("Tragic Humanism") on *The Fall of Hyperion*, "To Autumn," and the "Bright star" sonnet. Parts of the work, especially the discussions of the odes, have been several times reprinted in collections of criticism; indeed, Bloom has a considerable (and deserved) reputation as a Keats critic primarily on the basis of this single long chapter. (His later theorizing about Keats's sources is separately treated below.)

A somewhat related form is the introductory essay prefixed to a selection of poems or letters. Lionel Trilling's "The Poet as Hero: Keats in His Letters" (in *The Opposing Self,* 1955), which is repeatedly cited for some important statements about Keats's character and ideas and his relation to Romanticism, was originally the introduction to an edition of *Selected Letters* (1951). Paul de Man's introduction to a *Selected Poetry* (1966), also frequently cited, is full of brilliant suggestions not always clearly connected with one another—they have to do with Keats's place among the Romantics and his general standing in our own century, the prospective pattern of his work, his mythologizing tendency throughout and the particular myth of poetry as thawing agent, his treatment of love, the significance of his final poems, the simultaneity of generality and individuality in his work. Stanley Kunitz' "The Modernity of Keats" (in *A Kind of Order, a Kind of Folly: Essays and Conversations,* 1975), an excellent general essay, is in part based on Kunitz' introduction to an edition of Keats's *Poems* (1964). Alfred Kazin's "Rome: A Meditation on Keats" (*ASch,* 1976–77; rpt. in *Contemporaries: From the 19th Century to the Present,* rev. ed. 1982), a well-informed and beautifully written general appreciation of the poet, was never used as an introductory essay but should have been. The two most recent essays in this category are Ernest J. Lovell, Jr., and John Clubbe's "Keats the Humanist" (*Kentucky Review,* 1982; rpt. in Clubbe and Lovell's *English Romanticism: The Grounds of Belief,* 1983) and Jack Stillinger's introduction to the *Complete Poems* (1982).

There are four other works that I include here among general studies, although each could claim a prominent place among the specialized studies as well. David Perkins' *The Quest for Permanence: The Symbolism of Wordsworth, Shelley, and Keats* (1959) is a study of the three Romantics' different ways of coping with problems of time and mortality, and it is a thoroughgoing exploration of their use of symbolism and their characteristic ways of structuring poems, especially their lyrics; but it is even more a series of major essays in interpretation and revaluation. The three substantial chapters on Keats, who is the hero of the book, contain excellent discussion of the poet's (and the poems') attitudes toward process, permanence, and the visionary imagination. Perkins emphasizes Keats's skepticism; his suggestion that "the over-all course of [Keats's] development might be partly described as a periodic, though gradually cumulative, loss of confidence in the merely visionary imagination" is frequently quoted. The last chapter is entitled "The Affirmation of Process," and the conclusion, after a series of fine explications of the poems, is that "the varied speculations which underlie Keats's poetry from 'La Belle Dame' to the ode 'To Autumn' may potentially include a rejection of the romantic quest for permanence."

Albert S. Gérard's *English Romantic Poetry: Ethos, Structure, and Symbol in Coleridge, Wordsworth, Shelley, and Keats* (1968), a refinement and development of work begun in his *L'Idée romantique de la poésie en Angleterre* (1955), is another important study that has symbolism in the title (and the names of several Romantic poets) but conclusions about Keats and his contemporaries of a larger, more general character. In Gérard's view the central impulse of Romantic inspiration is "the *Sehnsucht,* the yearning toward the absolute, the aspiration to oneness and wholeness and organic unity, the dream of perfection," and the crucial problem is to square this impulse with objective perception of the harsh realities of life. Gérard traces a series of movements in the various poets from perplexity to anguish to some sort of reconciliation. His two chapters on Keats focus mainly on the Cave of Quietude episode in *Endymion* 4 (puzzlement), the verse epistle to Reynolds (a transitional piece), and "Ode on a Grecian Urn" (reconciliation). The concluding emphasis on "ontological skepticism" is in harmony with that of Perkins' work a decade earlier.

Patricia A. Parker's *Inescapable Romance: Studies in the Poetics of a Mode* (1979), consisting mainly of four large chapters on Ariosto, Spenser, Milton, and

Keats, presents Keats as "most explicitly the poet of romance among the Romantics" and the one "most clearly [Spenser's] descendant." But romance (here defined as "a form which simultaneously projects the end it seeks and defers or wanders from a goal which would mean ... the end of the quest itself") has undergone a sea change since the days of Spenser; in Keats's poems and letters it is surrounded by ambivalence, inseparable from anxiety, and full of ambiguity and complexity. Parker gives most attention to "Ode to a Nightingale," *Endymion,* and *The Fall of Hyperion* but also offers acute and illuminating comment on a great many other poems in the course of displaying these basic tendencies. Her work is a most intelligent piece of criticism and a welcome correction to the more simplified dichotomizings of the preceding generation of Keatsians. Independently of Parker, Robert Kern's "Keats and the Problem of Romance" (*PQ,* 1979) treats the same subject in somewhat the same way, focusing primarily on *The Eve of St. Agnes* and describing "an inclusive poetry of dream that forestalls barrenness by maintaining a critical perspective on itself, acknowledging its status as dream and in this way directing the reader to issues beyond those of romantic plot alone." Kern's account of Keats's "development from a victim of romance to a serious romancer to a poet, finally, of tragic knowledge" is engagingly written and persuasive, another good antidote to oversimplification.

Collections of essays. The individual pieces, if they have retained their value, are mentioned in the appropriate place above or below in the present survey. This section is simply a brief listing, for convenience, of the most useful collections. *The Major English Romantic Poets: A Symposium in Reappraisal,* edited by Clarence D. Thorpe et al. (1957), contains four original contributions on Keats, by W. J. Bate ("Keats's Style: Evolution toward Qualities of Permanent Value"), Douglas Bush ("Keats and His Ideas"), Cleanth Brooks ("The Artistry of Keats: A Modern Tribute"), and J. M. Murry ("Keats's Thought: A Discovery of Truth"). *John Keats: A Reassessment,* edited by Kenneth Muir (1958), a volume of mostly new essays by members of the English faculty at Liverpool, includes studies of Keats's narratives by Clarisse Godfrey, Miriam Allott, and Muir; analyses of the odes by Kenneth Allott, Arnold Davenport, and Muir; and pieces on Keats's sources, ideas, and style by Joan Grundy, R. T. Davies, David I. Masson, and, again, Muir. *English Romantic Poets: Modern Essays in Criticism,* edited by M. H. Abrams (1960), reprints Bush's and Bate's essays from the 1957 *Reappraisal* volume just mentioned and pieces by Brooks, Wasserman, and Fogle on, respectively, "Ode on a Grecian Urn," "La Belle Dame," and "Ode to a Nightingale"; in the second edition of this work (1975), Abrams drops Bush and Wasserman and adds pieces by Davenport, Stillinger, and Sperry on "To Autumn," *The Eve of St. Agnes,* and *The Fall of Hyperion. Keats: A Collection of Critical Essays,* edited by W. J. Bate (1964), reprints T. S. Eliot's remarks on Keats in *The Use of Poetry and the Use of Criticism,* Bush's Keats chapter in *Mythology and the Romantic Tradition in English Poetry,* part of R. H. Fogle's chapter on synaesthetic imagery in *The Imagery of Keats and Shelley,* Bate's own discussion of negative capability in his 1963 biography, and then critical analyses of particular poems by Stillinger (*St. Agnes*), Bloom ("Psyche," "Melancholy"), Perkins ("Nightingale," *Lamia*), Wasserman ("Grecian Urn"), Bate ("Autumn"), and D. G. James (the Hyperion fragments). *British Romantic Poets: Recent Revaluations,* edited by Shiv K. Kumar (1966), contains reprinted essays by Sperry (on *Endymion*) and Brooks (on "Grecian Urn") and two new pieces by Blackstone (on Keats's ideas) and Kumar (on *Hyperion*). *Critics on Keats,* edited by Judith O'Neill (1967), presents excerpts from sixteen critics, ranging from Lockhart and Croker, writing in 1818, to Aileen Ward in 1963; the selections are quite short, however, sometimes less than two pages, and for the most part are drastic abridgments of the originals. *Keats: The Narrative Poems,* a "casebook" edited by John Spencer Hill (1983), contains eighteen extracts from Keats's letters, a brief section of nineteenth-century commentary (two dozen excerpts in 28 pages), and then more substantial selections from twentieth-century critics, including Sperry (on *Endymion*), Louise Smith (*Isabella*), Wasserman and Stillinger (*St. Agnes*), Walter Houghton ("St. Mark"), Perkins (*Lamia*), Mario D'Avanzo ("La Belle Dame"), Muir (*Hyperion*), and Paul Sheats (*The Fall of Hyperion*). Collections of essays specifically focusing on *The Eve of St. Agnes* and the odes are listed below with the studies of individual works.

SPECIALIZED STUDIES

Ideas, themes, controlling myths.   It ought to go without saying that all the biographies and general critical studies, whether purposely or inadvertently, treat Keats's ideas. Discussions of his subject matter, the main themes of his work, the recurrent myths, plots, characters, attitudes, structures (and so on and on) always have to do with ideas. In a purely narrative analysis of *Lamia,* for example, identifying Lycius as a dreamer necessarily leads to a consideration of such things as the consequences of dreaming, the roles of Lamia and Apollonius in the working out of these consequences, and the attitudes of the narrator toward the principal characters as the consequences become increasingly clear; it is impossible to write even a short paragraph about the events in *Lamia* without at least implying something about the poem's and, at some level, Keats's ideas. The same is true of discussions of Keats's style and other aspects of his artistry: a pleasure-pain oxymoron is a figure of speech and at the same time is obviously the reflection of an idea about human life; the characteristic particularity, concreteness, and textural density of Keats's lines—among the most prominent qualities of his poetic style—embody a complex of attitudes toward (and therefore ideas about) things in the real world. The present section, however, at least in the beginning paragraphs, surveys the scholarship that more openly considers ideas as entities separable from their contexts—Keats's ideas *as* ideas.

The earliest formal work on Keats's ideas—in studies by F. M. Owen, Matthew Arnold, Robert Bridges, Sidney Colvin, Ernest de Selincourt, A. C. Bradley, and Hugh I'A. Fausset, among others—is conveniently reviewed in the first chapter ("Keats, Thinker") of Clarence D. Thorpe's *The Mind of John Keats* (1926), a book that has had a profound effect on subsequent scholars (even on many who never read it but whose views of Keats's mind and art were influenced by those who did). Thorpe's study, though it is nearly sixty years old, remains timely and useful; the chapter titles—"The Dream World and the Actual—An Antithesis," "Gradus ad Parnassum," " 'Sensation' versus Knowledge and Philosophy—Partial Reconciliation," "The 'Mystery,' " "Detachment and Philosophy—Further Reconciliation," "The Imagination," "What Is Beauty?" "Principles and Practice," "What Is Poetry? Conclusion"—point to what Thorpe considered the most important topics, and they do not seem out of date. Thorpe's work is itself negatively capable; he finds (as he himself described it in an earlier version of the present bibliographical essay) not a consistent pattern of thought but tentative conclusions wrested from a set of conflicts—for example, between an impulse toward dream and the claims of the actual, between a leaning toward the merely sensuous in art and life and a craving for knowledge and understanding. Reconciliation of opposing claims was an increasingly conscious aim as Keats saw more clearly the demands of his art and its relationship to the actualities of existence. Thorpe's emphasis on the tentativeness of Keats's gropings is especially worth keeping in mind; more recent scholars have sometimes discovered a greater consistency than the material seems to justify.

Of three general essays on Keats's thinking—Douglas Bush's "Keats and His Ideas" and J. M. Murry's "Keats's Thought: A Discovery of Truth" (both in *The Major English Romantic Poets: A Symposium in Reappraisal,* ed. C. D. Thorpe et al., 1957) and Bernard Blackstone's "The Mind of Keats in His Art" (in *British Romantic Poets: Recent Revaluations,* ed. Shiv K. Kumar, 1966)—both Murry's and Blackstone's are too personal and idiosyncratic to be of much use. Bush's essay, however, is an excellent brief survey of the most important passages in the letters and poems. Following Thorpe, Bush observes that "even in his ripest maturity Keats had not achieved a settled and unified creed but was continually divided against himself." One of the divisions that Bush specially emphasizes is that between negative capability and the famous description (in late April 1819) of the world as a "vale of Soul-making"; the latter idea, says Bush, "seems to be the very opposite of negative capability, since the chameleon poet has no identity, no ethical character, whereas men are not souls 'till they acquire identities, till each one is personally itself.' "

The recent study by Yuichi Midzunoe, *Sapience: The Philosophy of John Keats,* further subtitled *An Epistemological and Mythological Speculation on His "Agonies, the Strife of Human Hearts"* (1978), is, I believe, the first book-length discussion of Keats in English published in Japan (Takeshi Saito's *Keats' View of Poetry,* 1929, was issued in London). A fairly comprehensive work based on wide reading in Keats's letters and poems, English poetry more generally, and the standard Keats scholarship through the middle 1970s, it is rather strangely organized—the "Life of Sensations" letter, negative capability, and the Vale of Soul-making are treated together in the opening chapter—and there are some staggering generalizations (e.g., "The Romantics regard the universe not as static or mechanical but as dynamic and organic. This view of the universe provides the necessary metaphysics in romantic theory"). Still, the various bases are duly touched, and the work serves as another useful reminder, like Thorpe's book and Bush's essay, of what and where the principal ideas are.

Keats's religious views (to begin narrowing the scope somewhat) have until recently been an oddly neglected topic. The earliest separate treatment, Hoxie Neale Fairchild's chapter on Keats in *Religious Trends in English Poetry,* volume 3 (1949), is unsatisfactory for several reasons. More useful are Roger Lloyd, "Keats and the Limitations of Pantheism" (*QR,* 1952); Edward E. Bostetter, "The Eagle and the Truth: Keats and the Problem of Belief" (*JAAC,* 1958); and especially Stuart M. Sperry, "Keats's Skepticism and Voltaire" (*KSJ,* 1963), and Richard E. Brantley, "Keats's Method" (*SIR,* 1983), the last focusing specifically on the Wesleyan Methodist elements in Keats's poems. Lloyd N. Jeffrey, "Keats and the Bible" (*KSJ,* 1961), provides a long list of biblical echoes and allusions in both the poetry and the letters. George Yost, "Keats's Early Religious Phraseology" (*SP,* 1962), and Newell F. Ford, "Holy Living and Holy Dying in Keats's Poetry" (*KSJ,* 1971), examine the religious and ceremonial phrasings, imagery, and tone in the poems. James Benziger's chapter on Keats in *Images of Eternity: Studies in the Poetry of Religious Vision from Wordsworth to T. S. Eliot* (1962) is partly focused, while working through Keats's poems, on the religious ideas behind them. There was, however, no separate book-length study of Keats's religious ideas until the appearance of Robert M. Ryan's *Keats: The Religious Sense* (1976).

Ryan's work, which because of the previous neglect of the topic can be considered one of the most immediately useful of recent books on Keats, is a painstakingly researched investigation of the poet's "religious milieu"—the state (or states) of religion in England at the beginning of the nineteenth century—and the many influences that affected his religious thinking: his early education at Clarke's school at Enfield, the ideas and attitudes that prevailed at Guy's Hospital, his reading in Burnet, Voltaire, and numerous others, his friendships with Hunt, Haydon, Bailey, and, again, numerous others. According to Ryan,

> Keats was neither an evangelist nor an agnostic. He was an earnest seeker after truth who believed in the existence of a Supreme Being and who felt a need to investigate the consequences and ramifications of that belief. He was not an especially original or creative thinker in theology; most of his ideas were borrowed from friends or from books. But he was determined to find his own way in religion, and the system of faith he constructed for himself clearly reflects his own personality.

Ryan focuses most closely on Keats's own writings—the letters thoroughly, the poems hardly at all—and offers interesting new interpretations of some of the best-known passages (such as those on the authenticity of the imagination and on negative capability, in both of which he finds primarily theological rather than aesthetic or literary significance). The book is strong in its grasp of historical context and acute in its analysis of the letters. It has been faulted for neglect of the poetry and for some other omissions and possible distortions of emphasis, but these do not seem serious enough to negate its value as a considerable clarification of Keats's religious thinking.

A handful of fringe items (fringe because they are generally not by Romantics scholars and because they view the poet from, as it were, the outside) may be mentioned as a brief illustration of Keats's genial adaptability to other interests in philosophy and religion: Frederic Will, "A Confrontation of Kierkegaard and Keats" (*Personalist,* 1962); Lucio P. Ruotolo, "Keats and Kierkegaard: The Tragedy of Two Worlds" (*Renascence,* 1964); Edward Carben, "John Keats: Pioneer of Modern Existentialist Thought" (*Trace,* 1964); Pravas Jivan Chaudhury, "Keats and the Indian Ideal of Life and Poetry" (*Personalist,* 1962); Richard P. Benton, "Keats and Zen" (*Philosophy East and West,* 1966); and Stephen H. Ruppenthal, "Keats and Zen Enlightenment" (*Studia Mystica,* 1978). Nathan A. Scott, Jr.'s *Negative Capability: Studies in the New Literature and the Religious Situation* (1969) takes Keats's phrase for its title and quotes the appropriate letter in the preface but does not otherwise have anything to do with our poet.

Keats's political and social ideas have attracted relatively little attention, perhaps with good reason. The best general treatments outside the biographies are a half-century old—Clarence D. Thorpe's "Keats's Interest in Politics and World Affairs" (*PMLA,* 1931) and Herbert G. Wright's "Keats and Politics" (*E&S,* 1933). Allan Rodway discusses Keats and his social concerns in "Radical Romantic Poets" (*The Romantic Conflict,* 1963). Carl Woodring, *Politics in English Romantic Poetry* (1970), holding that "politics has an integral place in Keats's canon," gives seven pages to the poet (roughly a tenth of the space allotted to Byron and a twelfth of that occupied by Shelley). The most detailed examinations of political themes and allusions in specific texts are Aileen Ward's "Keats's Sonnet, 'Nebuchadnezzar's Dream'" (*PQ,* 1955), on the sonnet "Before he went to live with owls and bats," and June Q. Koch's "Politics in Keats's Poetry" (*JEGP,* 1972), on book 3 of *Endymion.*

Keats's aesthetic and literary ideas, by contrast, have been of perennial interest, especially the passages in the letters on Adam's dream and the authenticity of the imagination (to Bailey, 22 Nov. 1817), negative capability in philosophy and literature (to his brothers, late Dec. 1817), egotism in modern poetry (to Reynolds, 3 Feb. 1818), "Axioms" in poetry (to Taylor, 27 Feb. 1818), and the "poetical Character" (to Woodhouse, 27 Oct. 1818). These appear prominently in the biographies and in early studies like Thorpe's *The Mind of John Keats* (see above) and Takeshi Saito's *Keats' View of Poetry* (1929), and they have been in the back, and frequently in the front, of critics' minds as they explore other aspects of Keats's ideas and art. General works having a bearing on some element of aesthetic theory include M. A. Goldberg's *The Poetics of Romanticism: Toward a Reading of John Keats* (1969), which specially emphasizes Keats's relation to "the classicism of ancient Greece as it developed through the eighteenth century"; the Keats section in Michael G. Cooke's *The Romantic Will* (1976), on the poet's "will to art," his conscious desire to be an artist; and Aileen Ward's "'That Last Infirmity of Noble Mind': Keats and the Idea of Fame" (in *The Evidence of the Imagination,* ed. Donald H. Reiman et al., 1978), on his ideas of poetry, genius, and poetic fame. Among the book-length general critical studies described in the preceding section, Sperry's *Keats the Poet,* which keeps an eye on Keats's early and continuing interest in the poetic process, is the most relevant to the topic at hand.

Keats's letter to Bailey on the imagination is discussed in the previously mentioned critical studies by Caldwell, Ford, and Stillinger, among others (*John*

Keats' Fancy, The Prefigurative Imagination of John Keats, and *The Hoodwinking of Madeline,* respectively), and in articles by Earl R. Wasserman, "Keats and Benjamin Bailey on the Imagination" (*MLN,* 1953); Robert M. Ryan, "Keats and the Truth of Imagination" (*WC,* 1973; rpt. as part of ch. 3 in Ryan's *Keats: The Religious Sense*); and W. P. Albrecht, "Keats's 'Truth' and 'A Truth' " (*PQ,* 1978). Keats's ideas of imagination more generally are given brief treatment in Patricia M. Ball's *The Central Self: A Study in Romantic and Victorian Imagination* (1968) and of course more extended treatment in the numerous studies that make much of Keats's "prefigurative imagination," "visionary imagination," "sympathetic imagination," and, as in Dickstein's *Keats and His Poetry,* his interest in consciousness and self-awareness. Leon Waldoff has sorted out the various interpretations in the preface to his own forthcoming comprehensive work on the subject, *Keats and the Silent Work of Imagination.*

The critical idea most often associated with Keats is negative capability, which is the subject of three or four sentences in a letter of late December 1817 but is usually (though not invariably) also connected with Keats's remarks to Woodhouse ten months later on "the poetical Character" ("A Poet is the most unpoetical of any thing in existence; because he has no Identity—he is continually ... filling some other Body"). The leading expounder of this idea for several decades has been W. J. Bate in, among other places, *Negative Capability: The Intuitive Approach in Keats* (1939), which was Bate's undergraduate honors thesis at Harvard, and chapter 10 ("Negative Capability") of his 1963 biography of the poet. Other discussions include Claude Lee Finney, "Keats's Philosophy of Negative Capability in Its Philosophical Backgrounds" (*Vanderbilt Studies in the Humanities,* 1951); Jacob D. Wigod, "Negative Capability and Wise Passiveness" (*PMLA,* 1952); R. T. Davies, "Was 'Negative Capability' Enough for Keats? A Re-Assessment of the Evidence in the Letters" (*SP,* 1958); Nathan Comfort Starr, "Negative Capability in Keats's Diction" (*KSJ,* 1966); Leon M. Guilhamet, "Keats's 'Negative Capability' and 'Disinterestedness': A Confusion of Ideals" (*UTQ,* 1970); Stanley A. Leavy, "John Keats's Psychology of Creative Imagination" (*Psychoanalytic Quarterly,* 1970); John D. Margolis, "Keats's 'Men of Genius' and 'Men of Power' " (*TSLL,* 1970); Margaret Ann Fitzpatrick, "The Problem of 'Identity' in Keats's 'Negative Capability' " (*DR,* 1981); and Shimon Sandbank, "Keats, Altered by the Present" (*CL,* 1983), this last on affinities between Keats's ways of perceiving and those more recently of Pound, Rilke, and Ashbery.

In addition to these, there is a growing list of works, some of them quite sizable, on other, even more elusive critical concepts and terms in Keats's writings—most recurringly "ethereal" and "sublime." Both are among the six words studied lexicographically by R. T. Davies, "Some Ideas and Usages" (in *John Keats: A Reassessment,* ed. Muir, 1958), and we have, further, George Bornstein, "Keats's Concept of the Ethereal" (*KSJ,* 1969); Stuart M. Sperry, "Keats and the Chemistry of Poetic Creation" (*PMLA,* 1970; rev. in Sperry's *Keats the Poet*), on the chemical origins of "sublime," "ethereal," and several other important words; the Keats chapter in W. P. Albrecht's *The Sublime Pleasures of Tragedy: A Study of Critical Theory from Dennis to Keats* (1975); Stuart A. Ende's *Keats and the Sublime* (1976); the scattered references to Keats in Thomas Weiskel's *The Romantic Sub-*

lime: Studies in the Structure and Psychology of Transcendence (1976); and, with some lengthy comments on Ende and Weiskel, Albrecht's "The Tragic Sublime of Hazlitt and Keats" (*SIR,* 1981).

A great many books and essays on Keats, including most of those described above in the section on general critical studies, focus on some recurring idea—sometimes *as* idea but more often in the subsidiary form of theme, motif, myth, metaphor, or structure—as a device for relating poems, passages, and situations in the poems to explain what Keats's work as a whole is "about." Here are some random examples among critical studies not yet mentioned. Mario L. D'Avanzo's *Keats's Metaphors for the Poetic Imagination* (1967), based on the notion that "Keats makes repeated use of certain organizing metaphors and images to describe poetic inspiration, the poetry-making process, and the structure of poetry itself," is a useful compilation of such metaphors and images. Chapter 2, for example, examines "woman as poetry," "the moon and sexuality," and "enthrallment"; chapter 3 is on "sleep and dreams," "flight and wings," "the elf," "the steeds," "the boat," "swimming." The index entry for "Metaphors, individual" is two-and-a-half pages long and includes multiple references to nearly fifty items. Helen E. Haworth, "Keats and the Metaphor of Vision" (*JEGP,* 1968), singles out the vision or visionary experience—representing the functioning of poetic imagination—as a basic metaphor in the poems. James Land Jones's *Adam's Dream: Mythic Consciousness in Keats and Yeats* (1975) is a structuralist attempt to identify in Keats (and Yeats too, who is always hovering in the background) a recurring myth of consciousness in which the Self apprehends, contacts, and finally merges with the Other. Barry Gradman, *Metamorphosis in Keats* (1980), takes "metamorphosis" as "both a principle of form and a bearer of meaning in most of Keats's major poems"—metamorphosis not so much, however, in the Ovidian sense of radical physical change (e.g., the transformations suffered by Circe's lovers in *Endymion* 3) as in the more encompassing but less serviceable sense of "curative, renovating change," most often from illness to health. Tilottama Rajan, *Dark Interpreter: The Discourse of Romanticism* (1980), of which more than a third is devoted to Keats's late romances and the Hyperion fragments, applies deconstructionist methodology to illuminate the "self-negating" aspects of theme and "semiotic anxiety" in the major narratives. Anne K. Mellor's chapter on Keats in *English Romantic Irony* (1980) takes the struggle for "Soul-making" as central to the poems.

Several works treat the themes of love and sex: Miriam Allott, " 'The Feast and the Lady': A Recurrent Pattern in Keats's Poetry" (*N&Q,* 1954); Gerald Enscoe, *Eros and the Romantics: Sexual Love as a Theme in Coleridge, Shelley, and Keats* (1967), which has chapters entitled "Keats and the Triumph of Eros" and "Keats and the Failure of Eros"; Stanley C. Russell, " 'Self-Destroying' Love in Keats" (*KSJ,* 1967); Frederick L. Beaty's partial chapter on Keats in *Light from Heaven: Love in British Romantic Literature* (1971); Anya Taylor's partial chapter on Keats in *Magic and English Romanticism* (1979), again on "self-destroying enthrallments"; and Helen B. Ellis, "Food, Sex, Death, and the Feminine Principle in Keats's Poetry" (*ESC,* 1980).

Style, narrative technique, and other aspects of Keats's artistry. There does not seem, in recent criticism, to be as much interest in Keats's artistry as there used to be. His poetic style was comprehensively considered in the 1930s and 1940s (by Bate and Fogle in particular) but has been slighted in later decades as critics have become increasingly aware of both theoretical and methodological difficulties in the stylistic analysis of literary texts. Narrative technique and structure are of course rigorously pursued these days, but almost exclusively in the novel and other forms of prose fiction. The relative neglect of Keats's art (as opposed, here, to his thought) ought to be something of a scandal, since it was, after all, his art that put him "among the English Poets."

The older critics and biographers had no trouble discussing Keats's style; Ridley, for example, in his study of manuscript alterations in *Keats' Craftsmanship* has his eye constantly on stylistic revisions, and Finney also is primarily interested in style when he describes the various important influences on Keats in *The Evolution of Keats's Poetry.* The most useful study of the subject, though it is now close to forty years old, came in the next decade after Ridley and Finney—W. J. Bate's *The Stylistic Development of Keats* (1945). This is a thoroughgoing work on all aspects of Keats's style in the conventional sense: syntax, diction, imagery, sound patterns, rhythm, meter. It traces Keats's development and his relation to earlier English poetry in these matters, provides full statistical information (for the most part unobtrusively), and incidentally offers sharp critical commentary on the major poems (e.g., "Throughout *Endymion,* it is emphasized that the concrete must be accepted and cherished as the only means of knowing the ideal"). There are seven appendixes, on Keats's verse forms, sonnet structure, metrical variation in the couplets, "caesural distribution," and the like. Possibly the best feature consists in the many quoted examples with scansion marks and/or lines drawn to illustrate the repetitions of vowel sounds; the book is a continuous lesson in how to *read* Keats's poetry.

Bate has also written the best short treatment of the subject, "Keats's Style: Evolution toward Qualities of Permanent Value" (in *The Major English Romantic Poets: A Symposium in Reappraisal,* ed. Thorpe et al., 1957), and he of course pays a great deal of attention to it in his 1963 biography (in which the index entry for "Style, poetic" has 14 subentries and references to more than 80 pages of the book). Other shorter works on style include Cleanth Brooks, "The Artistry of Keats: A Modern Tribute" (in the *Reappraisal* volume just cited), a slight piece in comparison with Bate's in the same collection; Martin Halpern, "Keats and the 'Spirit that Laughest'" (*KSJ,* 1966), on the comic as an aspect of Keats's serious style; Paul D. Sheats, "Stylistic Discipline in *The Fall of Hyperion*" (*KSJ,* 1968); Garrett Stewart, "*Lamia* and the Language of Metamorphosis" (*SIR,* 1976), like the preceding an example of interpretation via style study; G. J. Finch, "Wordsworth, Keats, and 'the Language of the Sense'" (*ArielE,* 1980); and George Yost, "Keats's Poignancy and the Fine Excess" (*SAB,* 1980). Karl Kroeber's *The Artifice of Reality: Poetic Style in Wordsworth, Foscolo, Keats, and Leopardi* (1964) has, in spite of its title, almost nothing to do with "poetic style" but instead is a large tracing of the course of European literature in the early nineteenth century. Three British works already mentioned under general critical studies—Bayley's "Keats and Reality," John Jones's *John Keats's Dream of Truth*, and Ricks's *Keats and Embarrassment*—have, in spite of *their* titles, a great deal to do with Keats's style, especially the more "vulgar," sensuous, and otherwise blush-inducing elements of the earlier poems and *Endymion.*.

Bate (in *Stylistic Development*) is particularly good on the repetition and interplay of vowel and consonant patterns in the poetry. Further work on sound patterns has been done by E. C. Pettet in chapter 3 ("Melody in Keats's 'Poesy'") of *On the Poetry of Keats* (1957); David I. Masson, "The Keatsian Incantation: A Study of Phonetic Patterning" (in *John Keats: A Reassessment*, ed. Muir, 1958), drawing material from the odes and *The Eve of St. Agnes;* and Ann Lozano, "Phonemic Patterning in Keats's 'Ode on Melancholy'" (*KSJ*, 1968), on both "Melancholy" and "To Autumn." D. Ross, "Structural Elements in Keats's Sonnets and Odes" (*Cahiers de Lexicologie*, 1977), is a computer-based study of grammatical and rhetorical structures. Donald C. Freeman, "Keats's 'To Autumn': Poetry as Process and Pattern" (*Language and Style*, 1978), is a still more recent linguistic approach to "syntactic strategy."

Special studies of Keats's diction include George Yost, "Keats's Early Religious Phraseology" (*SP*, 1962), and Nathan C. Starr, "Negative Capability in Keats's Diction" (*KSJ*, 1966), both already mentioned in the preceding section. G. Wilson Knight's "The Priest-like Task: An Essay on Keats" (in Knight's *The Starlit Dome: Studies in the Poetry of Vision*, 1941) is a brilliant piece focusing especially on Keats's language and imagery. For the latter topic the standard book-length treatment is Richard H. Fogle's *The Imagery of Keats and Shelley* (1949), which—in between an introductory chapter defining poetic imagery and a conclusion defending Shelley against the attacks of Eliot, Leavis, Ransom, Tate, and other New Critics—has four substantial chapters on "Imagery of Sensation," "Synaesthetic Imagery," "Empathic Imagery," and "Concrete and Abstract Imagery." Among more recent works on imagery and symbolism are Perkins' *The Quest for Permanence* (described earlier among general critical studies); James D. Boulger's "Keats' Symbolism" (*ELH*, 1961), which views Keats's symbols as a means of uniting the actual and the ideal; Theodor Wolpers' "Zur Struktur der Bildlichkeit bei Keats" (*Anglia*, 1962), an especially discerning and comprehensive survey; D'Avanzo's *Keats's Metaphors for the Poetic Imagination* (see the preceding section); Arthur H. Bell's "'The Depth of Things': Keats and Human Space" (*KSJ*, 1974), a phenomenological study of Keats's spatial imagery; François Matthey's *The Evolution of Keats's Structural Imagery* (1974), which, though rather murky in its principal concept ("structural imagery" refers sometimes to structure, sometimes to imagery), has some interesting diagrams; George Yost's "Keats's Halfway Zone" (*PQ*, 1981), on the halfway zones and states taken to represent Keats's interest in "incomplete revelation"; and John Barnard's "Keats's Tactile Vision: 'Ode to Psyche' and the Early Poetry" (*KSMB*, 1982), on Keats's pictorialism.

Much of the critical commentary on Keats's narrative technique—in such novelistic matters as plot devices, characterization, setting, point of view, author-narrator-audience relationships—is contained in the studies of individual works, especially, of course, the major narratives, listed in a separate section below. A book and a handful of essays of a more general character may be mentioned here. Judy Little's *Keats as a Narrative Poet: A Test of Invention* (1975), the first and only book on its subject, focuses on imagery as the key to structure. In a summarizing passage Little writes that, with *Isabella,* Keats

> learns to "lyricize" the narrative; that is, he shapes and contours the action by means of imagery. During a climactic event in a poem, he crowds a line, or a stanza, with vivid adjectives or metaphors; during the less excited moments of the narration, the description of characters and events is less vivid, and the metaphors tend to be brief or conventional. The imagery "rises" and "sets" in a way that emphasizes the narrative elements of suspense, climax, and resolution.

One may admire this approach and still feel that more comprehensive study and explanation are needed (Karl Kroeber, reviewing the work in *MP,* 1979, posed the interesting question of whether Keats was "lyricizing" the narrative or "narratizing" lyricism); the book in any case calls attention to an important topic for further consideration. Nancy M. Goslee, " 'Under a Cloud in Prospect': Keats, Milton, and Stationing" (*PQ,* 1974), discusses Keats's use of a technique of description ("stationing") taken over from the cult of picturesque landscape. Jacqueline Zeff, "Strategies of Time in Keats's Narratives" (*SEL,* 1977), proposes levels of time as a structuring device in *Endymion* and *Lamia.* William C. Stephenson's "The Performing Narrator in Keats's Poetry" (*KSJ,* 1977) is an intelligent piece on the presence and effect of narrators in Keats's poems, a topic also treated in some detail by Tilottama Rajan in the first of her two chapters on Keats in *Dark Interpreter: The Discourse of Romanticism* (1980). Probably, because of the current outpouring of practical and theoretical work on technique in the novel, we shall soon see considerably more attention paid to the narrative art of Keats's longer poems.

Sources, influences, and Keats's relation to literary tradition.   Everybody for one reason or another, beginning with Keats himself, has been interested in Keats's sources. In literary study generally in the early decades of this century, source hunting was by far the busiest activity, and annotated editions of the poets contained, along with the usual paraphrases and other kinds of critical conversion, an endless parade of what were then called "echoes and borrowings." Keats has received more than the usual share of such attention, and, although the value of the activity as a type of scholarship has more recently been called into question (because so much of the work appears not to have been of any use to anyone), still the sources of his ideas, stories, characters, language, and imagery continue to be a main focus in the scholarly and critical writings. Keats's critics invoke sources on practically every occasion, sometimes without being aware of doing so, as in commenting on a phrase (e.g., relating "tongueless nightingale" in *The Eve of St. Agnes* to the myth of Philomel), or a character (relating Angela to

Juliet's Nurse), or a motivation (comparing that of Isabella's brothers in Keats's poem with that in the English translation of Boccaccio that Keats read), or a style (Huntian in "Calidore," Miltonic in *Hyperion,* "Drydenian heroic" in *Lamia*). Keats criticism carried on without reference to sources is almost unthinkable, and the activity has in fact accelerated rather than slowed down as a result of Robert Gittings' controversial books of the 1950s.

A few cautionary observations may be in order. (1) Some, perhaps much, of the source work on Keats has mistaken an analogue (simply a likeness or another instance of the same thing) for a source. The early scholars were especially prone to this sort of error—Earle V. Weller, for example, in *Keats and Mary Tighe: The Poems of Mary Tighe with Parallel Passages from the Work of John Keats* (1928), in which a great many of the "parallel passages" consisted of ordinary single words ("beauties," "tranced," "flowery," and the like), or Werner W. Beyer, *Keats and the Daemon King* (1947), who traced half of Keats's lines to a single source, William Sotheby's translation of Wieland's *Oberon.* But the tendency shows up in more recent scholarship as well. Allott, for instance, in her edition of *Poems,* says that "waking dream" in the penultimate line of "Ode to a Nightingale" "was probably suggested by Hazlitt's 1818 lecture, 'On Chaucer and Spenser,' " but the phrase also occurs in Cowper, Wordsworth, and Coleridge (among others) and was sufficiently established to merit definition and illustration in the *Oxford English Dictionary.* She and other editors gloss "the joy of grief" in "Fill for me a brimming bowl" as a quotation from Campbell's *The Pleasures of Hope,* but this too occurs in other works and was a commonplace expression in the eighteenth century. Many of the words and phrases once proposed as "echoes" or "borrowings" from specific sources are now better viewed as the common property of all the poets of a certain time writing in English.

(2) Nearly all the sources discovered for Keats's poems are literary sources—words, phrases, characters, and situations in other people's books, articles, and lectures. As Kenneth Muir and F. W. Bateson observe in an important statement on the relative usefulness of different kinds of source work ("Editorial Commentary," *EIC,* 1954), there is also an immense complexity of nonliterary sources underlying Keats's work, most of which we know (and can know) nothing about—a point also made by Bernice Slote in the final chapter of *Keats and the Dramatic Principle.* Even a full account of literary sources, if such were possible, would leave a great deal of source material out of consideration.

(3) A special oddity in the matter of literary sources arises because Keats's early models included some now relatively obscure writers (the eighteenth-century Spenserians and contemporaries and near-contemporaries like James Beattie, Mary Tighe, Tom Moore, George Felton Mathew, Leigh Hunt) while his later models are these days considerably better known (e.g., Shakespeare, Milton, Wordsworth, Dante). The consequence (especially since scholars have much more often concerned themselves with Keats's later work than with the earlier) is that mature poems like *The Eve of St. Agnes,* "La Belle Dame," and the odes are thickly glossed with references to sources while the early poems go relatively untouched, and thus Keats is represented as developing away from originality, and

toward greater derivativeness, as he matures. Knowledgeable Keatsians will not be misled, but the more innocent users of the annotated editions might well be confused by this seeming anomaly.

Notable source studies from the earlier decades of this century include B. Ifor Evans, "Keats's Approach to the Chapman Sonnet" (*E&S*, 1931), an attempt in the manner of John Livingston Lowes, just four years after the appearance of Lowes's *The Road to Xanadu,* to separate out the materials that went into Keats's best-known early sonnet; Douglas Bush, "Notes on Keats's Reading" (*PMLA,* 1935), proposing a wide range of sources; and J. L. Lowes, "Moneta's Temple" (*PMLA,* 1936), a Lowes-like piece on the complex sources of a short passage of description in *The Fall of Hyperion.* There was of course considerable attention given to sources in the early biographies—Colvin's and Lowell's in particular—and in the general critical studies, most enduringly Finney's *The Evolution of Keats's Poetry.* The most interesting source work of the 1950s was by Robert Gittings, in *John Keats: The Living Year* (1954) and *The Mask of Keats: A Study of Problems* (1956), which made much of Keats's reading of Burton, Dante (in H. F. Cary's translation), Chaucer, and Chatterton, among others. Gittings' wild assertions of certainty in questionable matters, like his portrayal of Keats as a poet who could hardly write three consecutive lines without borrowing someone else's phrase or image, provoked considerable comment, much of it negative. But it also stimulated fresh interest in the question of Keats's sources, and Gittings (who retreated from some of these extremes in his biography of 1968) is undoubtedly responsible for the large amount of space given to sources in the latest annotated editions.

The most useful recent work on Keats's sources has been done by W. J. Bate and Harold Bloom—Bate in his 1963 biography and then in the 1969 Alexander Lectures, published as *The Burden of the Past and the English Poet* (1970); Bloom in a series of works beginning with "Keats and the Embarrassments of Poetic Tradition" (in *From Sensibility to Romanticism,* ed. F. W. Hilles and H. Bloom, 1965; rpt. without the notes in Bloom's *The Ringers in the Tower: Studies in Romantic Tradition,* 1971) and continuing in *The Anxiety of Influence: A Theory of Poetry* (1973), *A Map of Misreading* (1975), and *Poetry and Repression: Revisionism from Blake to Stevens* (1976), some of which hardly mention Keats but are nevertheless relevant to the interpretation of Keats in relation to his literary predecessors. Both Bate and Bloom are concerned specifically with the writer's problem—always increasing, as the predecessors' achievements mount up—of how to differ from, and most crucially how to excel, the great literary accomplishments of the past. Source work at its best, as in Bate and Bloom, is the study of writers in the process of coping with this problem. Keats, it turns out, coped remarkably well.

As a matter of practical procedure, the first works that one should consult for Keats's sources, in large elements and minute particulars alike, are the annotated editions—especially those of de Selincourt, Bush, Allott, and Barnard (see "Editions," above)—and then the most comprehensive general studies (like Finney's), the studies of individual works (see the next section), and the standard bibliographies of research (see "Bibliographical Materials," above). There are

many hundreds of source-and-influence studies to be found out (usually their ti-
tles are fairly specific as to scope and connection); the following are a handful of
representative examples. Keats's knowledge and use of the classics is treated by
Herbert Warren, "Keats as a Classical Scholar" (*Nineteenth Century,* 1923); B. Ifor
Evans, "Keats and the Golden Ass" (*Nineteenth Century,* 1926); John Henry
Wagenblass, "Keats and Lucretius" (*MLR,* 1937); and most fully by Douglas Bush,
Mythology and the Romantic Tradition in English Poetry (1937). A recent article
by Leon Burnett, "Heirs of Eternity: An Essay on the Poetry of Keats and Mandel'shtam" (*MLR,* 1981), assesses Keats's and Mandel'shtam's "respective appropriations" of the culture of ancient Greece. Harold E. Toliver, *Pastoral Forms and Attitudes* (1971), considers Keats's relation to pastoral tradition. The influence of
Dante is treated by Gittings in *The Mask of Keats* and by John Saly, "Keats's Answer to Dante: *The Fall of Hyperion"* (*KSJ,* 1965), the latter proposing that Keats
read some of Dante in the original Italian. On Boccaccio's influence the most authoritative work is Herbert G. Wright, *Boccaccio in England from Chaucer to
Tennyson* (1957).

Among the numerous influences of earlier English writers, Chaucer's is stud-
ied by F. E. L. Priestley, "Keats and Chaucer" (*MLQ,* 1944), Gittings in *The Mask of
Keats,* and Ronald Primeau, "Chaucer's *Troilus and Criseyde* and the Rhythm of
Experience in Keats's 'What can I do to drive away' " (*KSJ,* 1974). Assessments of
Shakespeare's influence include works as disparate as Murry's *Keats and
Shakespeare* (1925); Caroline F. E. Spurgeon's *Keats's Shakespeare* (1928); Douglas
Bush's "Keats and Shakespeare" (in *Shakespeare: Aspects of Influence,* ed. G. B.
Evans, 1976); R. S. White's "Shakespearean Music in Keats's 'Ode to a Nightingale' "
(*English,* 1981); and Willard Spiegelman's "Keats's 'Coming Muskrose' and
Shakespeare's 'Profound Verdure' " (*ELH,* 1983). Other Renaissance writers are
the focus in R. S. White's "Sidney's *Arcadia* as a Possible Source for 'The Eve of St.
Agnes' " (*KSJ,* 1979) and Joan Grundy's "Keats and William Browne" (*RES,* 1955)
and "Keats and the Elizabethans" (in *John Keats: A Reassessment,* ed. Muir, 1958).
Burton's influence is treated by Floyd Dell, "Keats's Debt to Robert Burton"
(*Bookman* [New York], 1928); Gittings in *John Keats: The Living Year;* Aileen
Ward, "Keats and Burton: A Reappraisal" (*PQ,* 1961); and Jane Chambers, " 'For
Love's Sake': *Lamia* and Burton's Love Melancholy" (*SEL,* 1982). The influence of
Milton is discussed in, among others, John D. Rosenberg, "Keats and Milton: The
Paradox of Rejection" (*KSJ,* 1957); Victor J. Lams, Jr., "Ruth, Milton, and Keats's
'Ode to a Nightingale' " (*MLQ,* 1973); a series of works by Leslie Brisman that in-
cludes *Milton's Poetry of Choice and Its Romantic Heirs* (1973), "Keats, Milton,
and What One May 'Very Naturally Suppose' " (*Milton and the Romantics,* 1975),
and *Romantic Origins* (1978); Paul Sherwin, "Dying into Life: Keats's Struggle
with Milton in *Hyperion"* (*PMLA,* 1978); Douglas Bush, "The Milton of Keats and
Arnold" (*Milton Studies,* 1978); Meg Harris Williams, *Inspiration in Milton and
Keats* (1982); and of course most of the separate works on *Hyperion* and/or *The
Fall of Hyperion.* Studies of eighteenth-century sources and influences include
H. E. Briggs, "Swift and Keats" (*PMLA,* 1946); Harry M. Solomon, "Shaftesbury's
Characteristics and the Conclusion of 'Ode on a Grecian Urn' " (*KSJ,* 1975); Rob-

ert M. Ryan, "Keats's 'Hymn to Pan': A Debt to Shaftesbury?" (*KSJ*, 1977); Robert Gittings, "Keats and Chatterton" (*KSJ*, 1955; rpt. in *The Mask of Keats*); Nai-tung Ting, "The Influence of Chatterton on Keats" and "Chatterton and Keats: A Reexamination" (*KSJ*, 1956 and 1981); and E. H. King, "Beattie and Keats: The Progress of the Romantic Minstrel" (*ESC*, 1977). A number of eighteenth-century philosophers and aestheticians who are possible sources for Keats's thinking about dreams are discussed in John E. Holsberry, "Hawthorne's 'The Haunted Mind,' the Psychology of Dreams, Coleridge, and Keats" (*TSLL*, 1979).

The influence of writers contemporary with Keats is examined in Thora Balslev, *Keats and Wordsworth: A Comparative Study* (1962); Miriam Allott, "Keats and Wordsworth" (*KSMB*, 1971); Mario L. D'Avanzo, " 'Ode on a Grecian Urn' and *The Excursion*" (*KSJ*, 1974); Kenneth Muir, "Keats and Hazlitt" (*Proceedings of the Leeds Philosophical and Literary Society*, 1951; rpt. in *John Keats: A Reassessment*, ed. Muir, 1958); R. T. Davies, "Keats and Hazlitt" (*KSMB*, 1957); Herschel M. Sikes, "The Poetic Theory and Practice of Keats: The Record of a Debt to Hazlitt" (*PQ*, 1959); Stuart Peterfreund, "Keats's Debt to Maturin" (*WC*, 1982); and the various essays that consider Shelley in relation to *Endymion*—for example, Miriam Allott, "Keats's *Endymion* and Shelley's 'Alastor' " (in *Literature of the Romantic Period*, ed. R. T. Davies and B. G. Beatty, 1976). There are some fifteen articles and notes connecting Keats with Coleridge but no comprehensive study of Coleridge's effect on the younger poet's thinking and writing.

Keats's reading in William Robertson's *History of America* is discussed by Joseph Warren Beach, "Keats's Realms of Gold" (*PMLA*, 1934), and H. E. Briggs, "Keats, Robertson, and *That Most Hateful Land*" (*PMLA*, 1944), and his interest in history more generally by J. Philip Eggers, "Memory in Mankind: Keats's Historical Imagination" (*PMLA*, 1971). Some scientific influences are treated in Charles W. Hagelman, Jr., "Keats's Medical Training and the Last Stanza of the 'Ode to Psyche' " (*KSJ*, 1962); Stuart M. Sperry, "Keats and the Chemistry of Poetic Creation" (*PMLA*, 1970; rev. in Sperry's *Keats the Poet*); and John Barnard, "Sun-Spots in Keats's Epistle 'To My Brother George' " (*KSMB*, 1980), this last on a book frequently mentioned among Keats's sources, John Bonnycastle's *Introduction to Astronomy*. On Keats's interest in Egyptian art and culture see Helen Darbishire, "Keats and Egypt" (*RES*, 1927), and Barbara Garlitz, "Egypt and *Hyperion*" (*PQ*, 1955). Various other influences among the visual arts, including sculpture, are pointed out by Edmund Blunden, "Romantic Poetry and the Fine Arts" (*Proceedings of the British Academy*, 1942); Stephen A. Larrabee, *English Bards and Grecian Marbles: The Relationship between Sculpture and Poetry Especially in the Romantic Period* (1943); D. S. Bland, "Painting and the Poetry of Keats: Some Further Identifications" (*MLR*, 1955); Dwight E. Robinson, "Ode on a 'New Etrurian' Urn: A Reflection of Wedgwood Ware in the Poetic Imagery of John Keats" and "A Question of the Imprint of Wedgwood in the Longer Poems of Keats" (*KSJ*, 1963 and 1967); Ian Jack, *Keats and the Mirror of Art* (1967), which is the one essential work on Keats's acquaintance with the visual arts; and James Dickie, "The Grecian Urn: An Archaeological Approach" (*BJRL*, 1969). Oddly, there does not seem to be any comparable investigation into Keats's knowledge of music. The influence of picturesque landscape is treated in chapter 8 ("Keats and the Pursuit of the Sublime") of J. R. Watson's *Picturesque Landscape and English Romantic Poetry* (1970), and that of contemporary ballet in Carol K. Walker's "*Lamia* as Theater Art" (*KSJ*, 1982). These studies represent just a sampling of the published scholarship. It might not be a bad project to compile a bibliographical list, arranged alphabetically according to author and title, of all the works (however unlikely) that have been proposed as Keats's sources.

STUDIES OF INDIVIDUAL WORKS

Much of the best critical interpretation and commentary on the individual poems is contained in the general studies described in the first part of the "Criticism" section—particularly those by Wasserman, Evert, Patterson, Dickstein, and Sperry. The present section occasionally refers to these but mainly lists, with little additional comment, the more interesting and useful discussions published in the past two or three decades. Some of these are more valuable than others, but, just as with the general critical studies earlier, no one book or article on a major poem can be recommended to the exclusion of all others, and I make no attempt in the next several pages to convey the thesis or argument of each item in a phrase or two (such reductions are frequently misleading and almost always unfair to the authors). It is the cumulative effect that is important, the complexity of response that builds up as one reads more and more of the criticism on a single work. The student or scholar who lacks the time to go through the whole array of interpretive work on a major poem is advised to read (or even skim) the three or four most recent pieces; these will usually refer back to, and characterize, what the critic considers the most useful earlier writings on the poem.

For Keats's initial volume, one might begin with the interpretive commentary written while Keats was still alive by his friend Woodhouse, as transcribed and further commented on by Stuart M. Sperry, "Richard Woodhouse's Interleaved and Annotated Copy of Keats's *Poems* (1817)" (Univ. of Wisconsin *Literary Monographs*, 1967). Other studies of the volume as a whole include Jack Stillinger's "The Order of Poems in Keats's First Volume" (*PQ*, 1969; rpt. in *The Hoodwinking of Madeline*), Wanda Krajewska's "Keats's Romantic Manifesto" (*Kwartalnik Neofilologiczny*, 1980), and Michael E. Holstein's "His Soul's Decree: *Poems* (1817) and Keats's Poetic Autobiography" (*ES*, 1981). Among essays on single poems in the volume, Sperry, "Keats's First Published Poem" (*HLQ*, 1966), provides biographical and critical comment on the sonnet "O Solitude"; J. Burke Severs, "Keats's Fairy Sonnet" (*KSJ*, 1957), argues that the speaker in the sonnet "Had I a man's fair form" is a fairy addressing a loved one who is human; Robert F. Gleckner, "Keats's 'How Many Bards' and Poetic Tradition" (*KSJ*, 1978), examines the sources of Keats's sonnet about his sources. The Chapman's Homer sonnet is discussed by J. M. Murry, "The Birth of a Great Poem" (*Hibbert Journal*, 1928; rpt. several times, most recently as ch. 4 of Murry's *Keats*, 1955); B. Ifor Evans, "Keats's Approach to the Chapman Sonnet" (*E&S*, 1931); Carl Woodring, "On Looking into Keats's Voyagers" (*KSJ*, 1965); Paul McNally, "Keats and the Rhetoric of Association: On Looking into the Chapman's Homer Sonnet" (*JEGP*, 1980); and Lawrence Lipking, *The Life of the Poet: Beginning and Ending Poetic Careers* (1981). The opening poem in the volume is studied phenomenologically by Marjorie Norris, "Phenomenology and Process: Perception in Keats's 'I Stood Tip-toe' " (*KSJ*, 1976). On the closing poem see J. Burke Severs, "Keats's 'Mansion of Many Apartments,' *Sleep and Poetry*, and *Tintern Abbey*" (*MLQ*, 1959). Two relatively early poems not in the first volume are the subjects of Aileen Ward's "Keats's Sonnet, 'Nebuchadnezzar's Dream' " (*PQ*, 1955), on "Before he went to live with owls and bats," and E. B. Murray's "Ambivalent Mortality in the Elgin Marbles Sonnet" (*KSJ*, 1971). Gerald B. Kauvar's *The Other Poetry of Keats* (1969) has more or less random comments—discoverable via the index and an analytic table of contents—on these and most of Keats's other minor pieces.

Endymion has received serious attention in practically all the biographies and book-length studies. F. M. Owen published the first allegorical interpretation in *John Keats: A Study* (1880), and there have been more than a hundred analyses since then, some thirty of them of major proportions. Studies published in the last three decades include Jacob D. Wigod, "The Meaning of *Endymion*" (*PMLA*, 1953); Glen O. Allen, "The Fall of Endymion: A Study in Keats's Intellectual Growth" (*KSJ*, 1957); Carroll Arnett, "Thematic Structure in Keats's *Endymion*" (*TxSE*, 1957); Clarisse Godfrey, " 'Endymion' " (in *John Keats: A Reassessment*, ed. Muir, 1958); Albert Gérard, "Keats and the Romantic *Sehnsucht*" (*UTQ*, 1959; rev. in Gérard's *English Romantic Poetry*, 1968); Robert Harrison, "Symbolism of the Cyclical Myth in *Endymion*" (*TSLL*, 1960); Stuart M. Sperry, "The Allegory of *Endymion*" (*SIR*, 1962; rev. in Sperry's *Keats the Poet*); Walter H. Evert's long second chapter in *Aesthetic and Myth in the Poetry of Keats* (1965); Bruce E. Miller, "On the Meaning of Keats's *Endymion*" (*KSJ*, 1965); Mario L. D'Avanzo, "Keats's and Vergil's Underworlds: Source and Meaning in Book II of *Endymion*" (*KSJ*, 1967); Helen E. Haworth, "The Redemption of Cynthia" (*HAB*, 1967); Northrop Frye, "*Endymion*: The Romantic Epiphanic" (in Frye's *A Study of English Romanticism*, 1968); Morris Dickstein's long third chapter in *Keats and His Poetry* (1971); Stuart Curran, "The Mental Pinnacle: *Paradise Regained* and the Romantic Four-Book Epic" (in *Calm of Mind: Tercentenary Essays*, ed. J. A. Wittreich, Jr., 1971); Leon Waldoff, "From Abandonment to Scepticism in Keats" (*EIC*, 1971); Jack Stillinger, "On the Interpretation of *Endymion*: The Comedian as the Letter E" (in *Romantic and Victorian*, ed. W. P. Elledge and R. L. Hoffman, 1971; rpt. in *The Hoodwinking of Madeline*); Miriam Allott, "Keats's *Endymion* and Shelley's 'Alastor' " (in *Literature of the Romantic Period*, ed. R. T. Davies and B. G. Beatty, 1976); William Garrett, "The Glaucus Episode: An Interpretation of Book III of *Endymion*" (*KSJ*, 1978); Masoodul Hasan, "The Symbolic Mode in *Endymion*" (*AJES*, 1979); Charles I. Patterson, Jr., "The Monomyth in the Structure of Keats's *Endymion*" (*KSJ*, 1982); and Barbara A. Schapiro's Keats chapter in *The Romantic Mother: Narcissistic Patterns in Romantic Poetry* (1983). For surveys of the most influential earlier interpretations—by Bridges, de Selincourt, Colvin, Lowell, Thorpe, Murry, Bush, Finney, and Ford, among others—see in particular the essays by Wigod, Sperry, and Miller.

For poems written in 1818 we have, first of all, two explications of the sonnet "When I have fears"—M. A. Goldberg, "The 'Fears' of John Keats" (*MLQ*, 1957), and Nathaniel Elliott, "Keats's When I Have Fears" (*ArielE*, 1979)—and several studies of the verse epistle to Reynolds: Albert Gérard, "Romance and Reality: Continuity and Growth in Keats's View of Art" (*KSJ*, 1962; rev. in Gérard's *English Romantic Poetry*), which also discusses "Ode on a Grecian Urn"; Mary Visick, " 'Tease us out of thought': Keats's *Epistle to Reynolds* and the Odes" (*KSJ*, 1966); Stuart M. Sperry, "Keats's *Epistle to John Hamilton Reynolds*" (*ELH*, 1969; rev. in *Keats the Poet*); and David Luke, "Keats's Notes from Underground 'To J. H. Reynolds' " (*SEL*, 1979). Commentaries on *Isabella* include Miriam Allott, " 'Isabella', 'The Eve of St. Agnes' and 'Lamia' " (in *John Keats: A Reassessment*, ed. Muir, 1958); Jack Stillinger, "Keats and Romance" (*SEL*, 1968; rpt. in *The Hoodwinking of Madeline*); Billy T. Boyar, "Keats's 'Isabella': Shakespeare's *Venus and Adonis* and the Venus-Adonis Myth" (*KSJ*, 1972–73); and Louise Z. Smith, "The Material Sublime: Keats and *Isabella*" (*SIR*, 1974). There are two articles on the sonnet "On Visiting the Tomb of Burns"—J. C. Maxwell, "Keats's Sonnet on the Tomb of Burns" (*KSJ*, 1955), and George Yost, "A Source and Interpretation of Keats's Minos" (*JEGP*, 1958)—and one on "Old Meg she was a gipsey": Joan Coldwell, " 'Meg Merrilies': Scott's Gipsy Tamed" (*KSMB*, 1981). For discussion of other poems written on the walking tour of the summer of 1818 see the biographies, Dickstein's *Keats and His Poetry*, and Sperry's *Keats the Poet*.

Modern interpretation of *The Eve of St. Agnes* begins with Earl R. Wasserman's chapter on the poem in *The Finer Tone* (1953) and continues with Jack Stillinger, "The Hoodwinking of Madeline: Scepticism in 'The Eve of St. Agnes' " (*SP*, 1961; rev. in *The Hoodwinking of Madeline*); C. F. Burgess, " 'The Eve of St. Agnes': One Way to the Poem" (*EJ*, 1965); Marian H. Cusac, "Keats as Enchanter: An Organizing Principle of *The Eve of St. Agnes*" (*KSJ*, 1968); Rosemarie Maier, "The Bitch and the Bloodhound: Generic Similarity in 'Christabel' and 'The Eve of St. Agnes' " (*JEGP*, 1971); Stuart M. Sperry, "Romance as Wish-Fulfillment: Keats's *The Eve of St. Agnes*" (*SIR*, 1971; rev. in *Keats the Poet*); Brother Baldwin Peter, " 'The Eve of St. Agnes' and the Sleeping-Beauty Motif" (*KSMB*, 1971); G. Douglas Atkins, "*The Eve of St. Agnes* Reconsidered" (*TSL*, 1973); Michael Ragussis, "Narrative Structure and the Problem of the Divided Reader in *The Eve of St. Agnes*" (*ELH*, 1975; rev. in Ragussis' *The Subterfuge of Art*, 1978); Gail M. Gibson, "Ave Madeline: Ironic Annunciation in Keats's 'The Eve of St. Agnes' " (*KSJ*, 1977); Leon Waldoff, "Porphyro's Imagination and Keats's Romanticism" (*JEGP*, 1977); Constance Rooke, "Romance and Reality in *The Eve of St. Agnes*" (*ESC*, 1978); James B. Twitchell, "Porphyro as 'Famish'd Pilgrim': The Hoodwinking of Madeline Continued" (*BSUF*, 1978; rev. as part of ch. 3 in Twitchell's *The Living Dead: A Study of the Vampire in Romantic Literature*, 1981); Robert Kern, "Keats and the Problem of Romance" (*PQ*, 1979); David Wiener, "The Secularization of the Fortunate Fall in Keats's 'The Eve of St. Agnes' " (*KSJ*, 1980); Martin Aske, "Magical Spaces in 'The Eve of St. Agnes' " (*EIC*, 1981); and Jeffrey Baker, "Aphrodite and the Virgin: A Note on Keats's 'Eve of St. Agnes' " (*AntigR*, 1981). *Twentieth Century Interpretations of 'The Eve of St. Agnes'* (ed. Allan Danzig, 1971) reprints the interpretations of Wasserman and Stillinger (above) along with other essays and excerpts, by Herbert G. Wright, Bernard Blackstone, W. J. Bate, and Robert Gittings, and contains a new essay by Clifford Adelman, "The Dangers of Enthrallment."

Virtually every major Keats scholar has written on *Hyperion*. The discussions by Bate (in his 1963 biography) and Evert (in *Aesthetic and Myth*) are especially recommended among works already mentioned in this essay. Specialized studies include Kenneth Muir, "The Meaning of *Hyperion*" (*EIC*, 1952; rpt. in *John Keats: A Reassessment*, ed. Muir, 1958); Edward E. Bostetter's chapter on Keats in *The Romantic Ventriloquists* (1963); Brian Wilkie's chapter on Keats in *Romantic Poets and Epic Tradition* (1965); Shiv K. Kumar, "The Meaning of *Hyperion*: A Reassessment" (in *British Romantic Poets*, ed. Kumar, 1966); Helen E. Haworth, "The Titans, Apollo, and the Fortunate Fall in Keats's Poetry" (*SEL*, 1970); Geoffrey H. Hartman, "Spectral Symbolism and the Authorial Self: An Approach to Keats's *Hyperion*" (*EIC*, 1974; rpt. in Hartman's *The Fate of Reading*, 1975); Nancy M. Goslee, "'Under a Cloud in Prospect': Keats, Milton, and Stationing" (*PQ*, 1974) and "Plastic to Picturesque: Schlegel's Analogy and Keats's *Hyperion* Poems" (*KSJ*, 1981); Pierre Vitoux, "Keats's Epic Design in *Hyperion*" (*SIR*, 1975); Michael Ragussis' chapter 3 ("The Language of Gods and Men: The Fragmented World of the Hyperion Poems") in *The Subterfuge of Art: Language and the Romantic Tradition* (1978); Paul Sherwin, "Dying into Life: Keats's Struggle with Milton in *Hyperion*" (*PMLA*, 1978); Anya Taylor, "Superhuman Silence: Language in *Hyperion*" (*SEL*, 1979); Tilottama Rajan's chapter 4 ("Keats's Hyperion Poems: The Dialogue of Apollo and Dionysos") in *Dark Interpreter: The Discourse of Romanticism* (1980); and Stephen Gurney, "Between Two Worlds: Keats's 'Hyperion' and Browning's 'Saul'" (*SBHC*, 1980).

The most substantial interpretive discussions of "La Belle Dame sans Merci" are those in Wasserman's *The Finer Tone*, Patterson's *The Daemonic in the Poetry of John Keats*, and Sperry's *Keats the Poet*. A great many of the separate works on the poem are mainly concerned with Keats's sources, on which see the "Editorial Commentary" by Muir and Bateson (*EIC*, 1954) already referred to above in the section on sources and influences; the completest array of "echoes and borrowings" in one place is that in the commentary in Stillinger's edition of *Complete Poems* (1982). Separate studies transcending this interest in sources include Francis Lee Utley, "The Infernos of Lucretius and of Keats's *La Belle Dame sans Merci*" (*ELH*, 1958); Bernice Slote, "The Climate of Keats's 'La Belle Dame sans Merci'" (*MLQ*, 1960) and "La Belle Dame as Naiad" (*JEGP*, 1961); Jane Rabb Cohen, "Keats's Humor in 'La Belle Dame sans Merci'" (*KSJ*, 1968); David Simpson, "Keats's Lady, Metaphor, and the Rhetoric of Neurosis" (*SIR*, 1976; see also Simpson's discussion in *Irony and Authority in Romantic Poetry*, 1979); and Judith Weissman, "'Language Strange': 'La Belle Dame sans Merci' and the Language of Nature" (*CLQ*, 1980).

Of the dozen "odes" in the Keats canon—poems that have been so designated by Keats, his transcribers, or his editors—seven are decidedly less famous than the other five. The earliest is the 1815 "Ode to Apollo," beginning "In thy western halls of gold." Then come "God of the golden bow" (headed "Ode to Apollo" in five transcripts and the first published text), "Lines on Seeing a Lock of Milton's Hair" (subtitled "Ode" in the letter copy that Keats made for Bailey), "Mother of Hermes" (referred to as an "ode" in Keats's letter to Reynolds containing the lines, and headed "Ode to May—Fragment" in Woodhouse's transcript and "Fragment of an Ode to Maia" in Forman's edition of 1883), and "Bards of passion and of mirth" ("Ode" in two transcripts and the first published text). Two later items in this category are "Ode on Indolence" and "To Fanny" (titled "Ode to Fanny" in Forman's edition of 1883). But it is of course the five "great odes" that are meant when one speaks of Keats's odes—in their conventional order, "Ode to Psyche," "Ode to a Nightingale," "Ode on a Grecian Urn," "Ode on Melancholy," and "To Autumn." Two of these ("Nightingale" and "Grecian Urn") were first published six months apart in a periodical, *Annals of the Fine Arts;* all five were included in Keats's 1820 volume but not as a distinct group: "Nightingale," "Grecian Urn," and "Psyche" follow the three long narrative poems with which the volume begins, and "Autumn" and "Melancholy" are together (in that order) in a later position, just before the final piece, *Hyperion.* The order in which Keats wrote them is to an extent unsettled. "Psyche" is probably the earliest (around the end of Apr. 1819), "Autumn" is probably the latest (19 Sept. 1819), "Nightingale" comes in between (it is dated May 1819 in several sources deriving from a lost transcript by Charles Brown), but "Grecian Urn" and "Melancholy" are dated only 1819 in reliable sources and could have been written at any time during the year, even before "Psyche" or after "Autumn." These facts have some bearing on several nonfactual matters that continue to challenge critics—the poems' status as a group, their generic characteristics, their thematic relationships, and the progress, development, and structures that can be seen when they are considered (in whatever order) as a sequence.

The great odes have attracted an immense amount of critical attention and provoked many hundreds of interpretations. (Jack Wright Rhodes's *Keats's Major Odes: An Annotated Bibliography of the Criticism,* 1984, the newest bibliographical work on Keats, lists and describes some 875 items—books, articles, reviews, dissertations—from 1820 through 1980.) Practically all the general critical studies of Keats examine them at length. Among more specialized works on the poems as a group we have David Perkins, "Keats's Odes and Letters: Recurrent Diction and Imagery" (*KSJ,* 1953), on the significance of parallel phrasings between the poems and passages in Keats's letters; Robert Gittings' presentation of facsimiles of Keats's extant drafts in *The Odes of Keats and Their Earliest Known Manuscripts* (1970); and the following studies specially focusing on the thematic or structural unity of the group and on problems of interpretation: H. M. McLuhan, "Aesthetic Pattern in Keats's Odes" (*UTQ,* 1943); John Holloway, "The Odes of Keats" (*Cambridge Journal,* 1952; rpt. in Holloway's *The Charted Mirror,* 1960); Robert M. Adams, "*Trompe-l'oeil* in Shakespeare and Keats" (*SR,* 1953; rpt. in Adams' *Strains of Discord,* 1958); Kenneth Muir, "The Meaning of the Odes" (in *John Keats: A Reassessment,* ed. Muir, 1958); D. G. James, *Three Odes of Keats* (W. D. Thomas Memorial Lecture, Univ. of Wales, 1959); Karl Kroeber, "The New Humanism of Keats's Odes" (*Proceedings of the American Philosophical Society,* 1963; rpt. as part of ch. 4 in Kroeber's *The Artifice of Reality,* 1964); Irene H. Chayes, "Rhetoric as Drama: An Approach to the Romantic Ode" (*PMLA,* 1964); Robert F. Gleckner, "Keats's Odes: The Problems of the Limited Canon" (*SEL,* 1965); Gillian Beer, "Aesthetic Debate in Keats's Odes" (*MLR,* 1969); E. Pereira, "John Keats: The Major Odes of 1819" and "John Keats: Three 1819 Odes" (*Unisa English Studies,* 1969 and 1971); Helen Vendler, "The Experiential Beginnings of

Keats's Odes" (*SIR,* 1973); Paul H. Fry's two chapters on Keats in *The Poet's Calling in the English Ode* (1980); Nancy M. Goslee, "Phidian Lore: Sculpture and Personification in Keats's Odes" (*SIR,* 1982); and Helen Vendler's long awaited study, *The Odes of John Keats* (1983). This last, while playing fast and loose with chronology and some other elements of scholarship, has long appreciative essays on the subject, structure, and "constitutive trope" of each of the major odes (plus chapters on "Indolence" and parts of *The Fall of Hyperion*). *Twentieth Century Interpretations of Keats's Odes* (ed. Jack Stillinger, 1968) reprints essays and excerpts, most of which treat the poems individually (and many of which are therefore listed below), by Kenneth Allott, R. H. Fogle, Cleanth Brooks, R. P. Warren, C. I. Patterson, Jacob Wigod, Albert Gérard, W. J. Bate, David Perkins, Harold Bloom, L. M. Jones, Anthony Hecht, F. W. Bateson, Douglas Bush, M. H. Abrams, and Leonard Unger. The editor's introduction, "Imagination and Reality in the Odes of Keats," is reprinted in *The Hoodwinking of Madeline.*

Studies of "Ode to Psyche" include Kenneth Allott, "Keats's 'Ode to Psyche' " (*EIC,* 1956; rpt. in *John Keats: A Reassessment,* ed. Muir, 1958); Leonidas M. Jones, "The 'Ode to Psyche': An Allegorical Introduction to Keats's Great Odes" (*KSMB,* 1958); Max F. Schulz, "Keats's Timeless Order of Things: A Modern Reading of 'Ode to Psyche' " (*Criticism,* 1960); Robert D. Wagner, "Keats: 'Ode to Psyche' and the Second 'Hyperion' " (*KSJ,* 1964); Lloyd N. Jeffrey, "A Freudian Reading of Keats's *Ode to Psyche*" (*Psychoanalytic Review,* 1968); James H. Bunn, "Keats's *Ode to Psyche* and the Transformation of Mental Landscape" (*ELH,* 1970); Homer Brown, "Creations and Destroyings: Keats's Protestant Hymn, the 'Ode to Psyche' " (*Diacritics,* 1976); Leon Waldoff, "The Theme of Mutability in the 'Ode to Psyche' " (*PMLA,* 1977); and John Barnard, "Keats's Tactile Vision: 'Ode to Psyche' and the Early Poetry" (*KSMB,* 1982).

On "Ode to a Nightingale" much of the best interpretive work has again been done in the general critical studies, especially those by Wasserman, Perkins (*The Quest for Permanence*), Evert, and Dickstein. Separate discussions include Allen Tate, "A Reading of Keats" (*ASch,* 1945–46; rpt. in Tate's *On the Limits of Poetry,* 1948); Richard H. Fogle, "A Note on Keats's *Ode to a Nightingale*" (*MLQ,* 1947) and "Keats's *Ode to a Nightingale*" (*PMLA,* 1953; rpt. in Fogle's *The Permanent Pleasure,* 1974); Janet Spens, "A Study of Keats's 'Ode to a Nightingale' " (*RES,* 1952); Katharine M. Wilson, *The Nightingale and the Hawk: A Psychological Study of Keats' Ode* (1964); Marghanita Laski, "The Language of the Nightingale Ode" (*E&S,* 1966); F. Matthey, "Interplay of Structure and Meaning in the *Ode to a Nightingale*" (*ES,* 1968); William N. Dodd, "Keats's 'Ode to a Nightingale' and 'Ode on a Grecian Urn': Two Principles of Organization" (*Lingua e Stile,* 1971); Andrew J. Kappel, "The Immortality of the Natural: Keats' 'Ode to a Nightingale' " (*ELH,* 1978); Allan Chavkin, "Keats's Open Endings" (*RS,* 1979); Christian La Cassagnère, "The 'Ode to a Nightingale' and Keats's Tragic Myth" (*DUJ,* 1980); and Beth Lau, "Keats, Associationism, and 'Ode to a Nightingale' " (*KSJ,* 1983).

On "Ode on a Grecian Urn," Harvey T. Lyon's *Keats' Well-Read Urn: An Introduction to Literary Method* (1958) is a convenient guide to the first 125 years of criticism. The most useful among the earlier essays are Kenneth Burke, "Symbolic Action in a Poem by Keats" (*Accent,* 1943; rpt. in Burke's *A Grammar of Motives,* 1945); Cleanth Brooks, "History without Footnotes: An Account of Keats' Urn" (*SR,* 1944; rpt. in Brooks's *The Well Wrought Urn,* 1947); C. M. Bowra's chapter 6 in *The Romantic Imagination* (1949); Charles I. Patterson, "Passion and Permanence in Keats's *Ode on a Grecian Urn*" (*ELH,* 1954); Leo Spitzer, "The 'Ode on a Grecian Urn,' or Content vs. Metagrammar" (*CL,* 1955); and Jacob D. Wigod, "Keats's Ideal in the *Ode on a Grecian Urn*" (*PMLA,* 1957). More recent studies include Philip Hobsbaum, "The 'Philosophy' of the Grecian Urn: A Consensus of Readings" (*KSMB,* 1964); James Dickie, "The Grecian Urn: An Archaeological Approach" (*BJRL,* 1969); Archibald A. Hill, "Some Points in the Analysis of Keats' *Grecian Urn*" (in *Studies in Language, Literature, and Culture of the Middle Ages and Later,* ed. E. B. Atwood and A. A. Hill, 1969; rpt. in Hill's *Constituent and Pattern in Poetry,* 1976); Marco Mincoff, "Beauty Is Truth—Once More" (*MLR,* 1970); Bruce E. Miller, "Form and Substance in 'Grecian Urn'" (*KSJ,* 1971); Jean-Claude Sallé, "The Pious Frauds of Art: A Reading of the 'Ode on a Grecian Urn'" (*SIR,* 1972); James Shokoff, "Soul-Making in 'Ode on a Grecian Urn'" (*KSJ,* 1975); Pratap Biswas, "Keats's Cold Pastoral" (*UTQ,* 1977–78); John J. Teunissen and Evelyn J. Hinz, "*Ode on a Grecian Urn:* Keats's 'Laocoön'" (*ESC,* 1980); and William F. Zak, "To Try That Long Preserved Virginity: Psyche's Bliss and the Teasing Limits of the Grecian Urn" (*KSJ,* 1982). For commentary specifically on the concluding lines of the poem, which seem not to have mystified Keats's contemporaries but have posed a serious critical problem throughout the present century, see James A. Notopoulos, "'Truth-Beauty' in the 'Ode on a Grecian Urn' and the Elgin Marbles" (*MLR,* 1966); the surveys of previous interpretations in Miriam Allott's edition of *Poems* (1970) and Stillinger's appendix 3 ("Who Says What to Whom at the End of *Ode on a Grecian Urn?*") in *The Hoodwinking of Madeline*; and Harry M. Solomon, "Shaftesbury's *Characteristics* and the Conclusion of 'Ode on a Grecian Urn'" (*KSJ,* 1975).

Much less has been written about "Ode on Melancholy." The most substantial recent discussions are Barbara H. Smith, "'Sorrow's Mysteries': Keats's '*Ode on Melancholy*'" (*SEL,* 1966), and Horace G. Posey, Jr., "Keats's 'Ode on Melancholy': Analogue of the Imagination" (*CP,* 1975). "To Autumn," by contrast, has been, especially in the most recent work, a sort of proving ground for various theories of how best to read and interpret a poem. The methodologies range from "slow reading," as in Reuben A. Brower's handful of pages on the poem in *The Fields of Light: An Experiment in Critical Reading* (1951), to approaches by "genesis," genre, ideology, phenomenology, and linguistic analysis. See, among others, Ernest J. Lovell, Jr., "The Genesis of Keats's Ode 'To Autumn'" (*TxSE,* 1950); Leonard Unger, "Keats and the Music of Autumn" (*Western Review,* 1950; rpt. in Unger's *The Man in the Name,* 1956); Arnold Davenport, "A Note on 'To Autumn'" (in *John Keats: A Reassessment,* ed. Muir, 1958); B. C. Southam, "The Ode 'To Autumn'" (*KSJ,* 1960); James Lott, "Keats's *To Autumn*: The Poetic Consciousness and the Awareness of Process" (*SIR,* 1970); Herbert Lindenberger, "Keats's 'To Autumn' and Our Knowledge of a Poem" (*CE,* 1970); Geoffrey H. Hartman, "Poem and Ideology: A Study of Keats's 'To Autumn'" (in *Literary Theory and Structure,* ed. Frank Brady et al., 1973; rpt. in Hartman's *The Fate of Reading,* 1975); Donald Pearce, "Thoughts on the Autumn Ode of Keats" (*ArielE,* 1975); Thomas Pison, "A Phenomenological Approach to Keats's 'To Autumn'" (in *Phenomenology, Structuralism, Semiology,* ed. Harry R. Garvin, 1976); Donald C. Freeman, "Keats's 'To Autumn': Poetry as Process and Pattern" (*Language and Style,* 1978); Virgil Nemoianu, "The Dialectics of Movement in Keats's 'To Autumn'" (*PMLA,* 1978); Annabel M. Patterson, "'How to load and...bend': Syntax and Interpretation in Keats's *To Autumn*" (*PMLA,* 1979); and Helen Vendler's sixty-two-page chapter on the poem (prefaced with 22 epigraphs) in *The Odes of John Keats.*

For *Lamia,* the most substantial discussions among the general critical studies are those by Wasserman, Slote, Perkins, C. I. Patterson (who begins his chapter with a helpful summary of earlier work on the poem), and Sperry. Separate studies include Georgia S. Dunbar, "The Significance of the Humor in 'Lamia'" (*KSJ,* 1959); Donald H. Reiman, "Keats and the Humanistic Paradox: Mythological History in *Lamia*" (*SEL,* 1971); Richard Benvenuto, "'The Ballance of Good and Evil' in Keats's Letters and 'Lamia'" (*JEGP,* 1972); Warren Stevenson, "*Lamia:* A Stab at the Gordian Knot" (*SIR,* 1972); William C. Stephenson, "The Fall from Innocence in Keats's 'Lamia'" (*PLL,* 1974); R. H. Fogle, "Keats's *Lamia* as Dramatic Illusion" (in *Nineteenth-Century Literary Perspectives,* ed. Clyde de L. Ryals et al., 1974); Barbara Fass's partial chapter on Keats in *La Belle Dame sans Merci and the Aesthetics of Romanticism* (1974); Garrett Stewart, "*Lamia* and the Language of Metamorphosis" (*SIR,* 1976); Coleman O. Parsons, "The Refining of Lamia" (*WC,* 1977); Gene M. Bernstein, "Keats' 'Lamia': The Sense of a Non-Ending" (*PLL,* 1979); Donald Pearce, "Casting the Self: Keats and *Lamia*" (*YR,* 1980); Carol K. Walker, "*Lamia* as Theater Art" (*KSJ,* 1982); Jane Chambers, "'For Love's Sake': *Lamia* and Burton's Love Melancholy" (*SEL,* 1982); and Joseph C. Sitterson, Jr., "Narrator and Reader in *Lamia*" (*SP,* 1982) and "'Platonic Shades' in Keats's *Lamia*" (*JEGP,* 1984).

The Fall of Hyperion is sometimes treated with the earlier *Hyperion* in joint or comparative evaluations; see in particular, among works listed above for *Hyperion,* the items by Muir, Bostetter, Wilkie, Ragussis, Rajan, and Goslee (specifically the essay of 1981). The most useful studies concentrating on *The Fall* are Brian Wicker, "The Disputed Lines in *The Fall of Hyperion*" (*EIC,* 1957); William R. Manierre, "Versification and Imagery in *The Fall of Hyperion*" (*TSLL,* 1961); Stuart M. Sperry, "Keats, Milton, and *The Fall of Hyperion*" (*PMLA,* 1962; rev. in *Keats the Poet*); John Saly, "Keats's Answer to Dante: *The Fall of Hyperion*" (*KSJ,* 1965); Irene H. Chayes, "Dreamer, Poet, and Poem in *The Fall of Hyperion*" (*PQ,* 1967); Paul D. Sheats, "Stylistic Discipline in *The Fall of Hyperion*" (*KSJ,* 1968); Thomas A. Vogler's chapter on Keats in *Preludes to Vision: The Epic Venture in Blake, Wordsworth, Keats, and Hart Crane* (1971); Anne K. Mellor, "Keats's Face of Moneta: Source and Meaning" (*KSJ,* 1976); K. K. Ruthven, "Keats and *Dea Moneta*" (*SIR,* 1976); Warren U. Ober and W. K. Thomas, "Keats and the Solitary Pan" (*KSJ,* 1980); and Benjamin Taylor, "Refusing to Refuse Perplexity: Keats and the Tragic" (*New England Review,* 1980). Yuichi Midzunoe's monograph, *Keats' Poetic Space: "The Fall of Hyperion"* (1981), contains a forty-page analysis (with 22 charts and diagrams), facing texts of *Hyperion* and *The Fall,* and facsimiles of Milnes's first printed version of *The Fall* (1857) and the late transcript by Woodhouse's clerks.

Discussions of lesser poems that Keats wrote in 1819 include Walter E. Houghton, "The Meaning of Keats's *Eve of St. Mark*" (*ELH,* 1946); Jack Stillinger, "The Meaning of 'Poor Cheated Soul' in Keats's 'The Eve of Saint Mark' " (*ELN,* 1968; rpt. in *The Hoodwinking of Madeline*); David Luke, "*The Eve of Saint Mark:* Keats's 'ghostly Queen of Spades' and the Textual Superstition" (*SIR,* 1970); Martin Kallich, "John Keats's Dispassionate Star: A Contextual Analysis" (*BSUF,* 1964); David Ormerod, "Nature's Eremite: Keats and the Liturgy of Passion" (*KSJ,* 1967)—like the preceding, an analysis of the "Bright star" sonnet; Mario L. D'Avanzo, "Keats' 'If by Dull Rhymes' " (*RS,* 1970); Jack Stillinger, "The Context of Keats's 'Fairy's Song' " (*KSJ,* 1961), on "Shed no tear," written for inclusion in a fairy-tale romance by Charles Brown; and three studies of "Ode on Indolence" (the first two interpreting a text that has the stanzas in the wrong order): Margaret Y. Robertson, "The Consistency of Keats's 'Ode on Indolence' " (*Style,* 1970); Howard H. Hinkel, "Growth without Toil: Generative Indolence in Keats" (*TSL,* 1975); and William F. Zak, "The Confirmation of Keats's Belief in Negative Capability: The 'Ode on Indolence' " (*KSJ,* 1976). A late poem to Fanny Brawne, "What can I do to drive away," is analyzed by Paul de Man in his introduction to the Signet Classic edition of Keats's *Selected Poetry* (1966) and by Ronald Primeau, "Chaucer's *Troilus and Criseyde* and the Rhythm of Experience in Keats's 'What can I do to drive away' " (*KSJ,* 1974). The most substantial commentaries on *The Jealousies* (until recently usually referred to as "The Cap and Bells") are those by Gittings in *The Mask of Keats;* Martin Halpern, "Keats and the 'Spirit that Laughest' " (*KSJ,* 1966); and Howard O. Brogan, " '*The Cap and Bells,* or . . . *The Jealousies*'?" (*BNYPL,* 1974). The literary and aesthetic qualities of Keats's letters are explored by David Luke, "Keats's Letters: Fragments of an Aesthetic of Fragments" (*Genre,* 1978), and Susan J. Wolfson, "Keats the Letter-Writer: Epistolary Poetics" (*RP&P,* 1982).

Reputation and Influence

Keats's contemporary and subsequent reputation and his influence on contemporary and later writers (and also artists and musical composers) are more difficult and diffuse concerns than most of the topics surveyed earlier in this essay. In studying reputation there is always the question, reputation with whom? One conventionally goes to the contemporary reviews and other comments in periodicals as the main source of information, but these leave too many things out of the picture—Byron's "gentle reader! and / Still gentler purchaser" as well as other classes of audience, including readers not yet born at the time the writer is writing. A poet's popularity may be a detraction from his or her reputation; and as Wordsworth especially was well aware (see the advertisement at the beginning of the 1798 *Lyrical Ballads*), originality and popular appeal may both be at odds with "our own pre-established codes of decision," the prevailing critical standards. Frequently the poets themselves were of a divided mind concerning whom they were addressing and, at a very basic level of motivation, why; the two commonest spurs, money and immortal fame, have almost never gone hand in hand. Influence is not so complicated—it is merely source study in the reverse direction—but it is nevertheless difficult to bring into focus. In the investigation of Keats's sources, all roads lead to a central terminus in Keats's creativity; in the investigation of his influence on others, the lines of relationship spread out in all directions. Reputation study is primarily an element in the biography of a writer, but it can of course have practical critical significance whenever a writer does (or doesn't do) something out of consideration for his or her reputation; contemporary reviews are sometimes of great interest for their possible effect on the writer's work subsequently, for help in interpretation (as evidence of how the writer's contemporaries read the works), and for indications of extraliterary causes of the writer's reputation. Influence study is theoretically harder to justify; it is really a matter of some later writer's sources, and is of practical usefulness mainly when the scholarly focus is on the later writer.

Keats's contemporary and developing reputation was naturally of interest to his early biographers, especially Colvin, who includes Keats's "Critics and After-Fame" as the last two items of his subtitle and has a forty-page final chapter ("Epilogue") on Keats's fame during the posthumous century between Shelley's *Adonais* and World War I. George L. Marsh and Newman I. White, "Keats and the Periodicals of His Time" (*MP*, 1934), list and describe nearly ninety items consisting of reviews, comments on Keats, and publications by him in periodicals between May 1816 and the end of 1821. James R. MacGillivray, *Keats: A Bibliography and Reference Guide* (1949), includes these (plus others for the same years discovered in the interim) and then continues with a fairly generous record of periodical and other notices from 1822 to the publication of Milnes's biography in 1848 and a more selected list for the years after 1848. There are shorter lists in William S. Ward's bibliographies of *Literary Reviews in British Periodicals* during the Romantic period; Keats appears both in the second volume of the set covering 1798–1820 (2 vols., 1972) and in the volume for 1821–26 (1977). The most elaborate list, presented with introduction, headnotes, texts, and at the end a convenient "Summary of English Publications in Which Keats Is Mentioned, 1816–1821," is Lewis M. Schwartz's *Keats Reviewed by His Contemporaries: A Collection of Notices for the Years 1816–1821* (1973). There are many errors of text and detail in this work (an 8-page errata list of more than 160 items is available from the publisher, Scarecrow Press), along with some claims to novelty that were justifiable when the compilation was first finished in 1968 but not when it was published five years later; still it is the fullest work now in print for the period that it covers. Some of the materials appear again separately in Schwartz's "Keats's Critical Reception in Newspapers of His Day" (*KSJ*, 1972–73), on letters, short reviews, and a sonnet in the *Anti-Gallican Monitor*, the *Sun*, the *St. James's Chronicle*, and the *Kaleidoscope*.

Texts of the contemporary reviews began being reprinted as early as Forman's edition of 1883. Extracts from five reviews of Keats are included in *Contemporary Reviews of Romantic Poetry*, edited by John Wain (1953), and a great many more in *Blake to Browning* (1962), volume 2 of *The Poets and Their Critics*, edited by H. S. Davies. The real burgeoning, however, came in the early

1970s. In the United States appeared *Romantic Bards and British Reviewers: A Selected Edition of the Contemporary Reviews,* edited by John O. Hayden (1971), containing fifteen reviews of Keats from 1817 to 1820, and in England *Keats: The Critical Heritage,* edited by G. M. Matthews (1971), containing about two dozen reviews and notices plus nearly fifty other extracts from letters, journals, reminiscences, early biographical notices, lectures, encyclopedia entries, and the like from 1816 to 1863. The materials in this latter collection are somewhat obscured from view by vague and incomprehensible headings supplied by the editor for about half the items ("A Wanderer in the Fields of Fancy," "A Very Facetious Rhymer," "A Great Original Work," "A Monstrously Droll Poem," etc.); it is nevertheless an immensely useful work and is probably, because it draws on such a variety of other sources besides reviews, the best single compilation of materials on Keats's reputation. *The Romantics Reviewed: Contemporary Reviews of British Romantic Writers,* edited by Donald H. Reiman (9 vols., 1972), was published in the following year; the two volumes of part C, *Shelley, Keats, and London Radical Writers,* contain photographically reproduced texts of twenty-nine Keats items that are especially valuable because, being facsimiles, they of course include the reviewers' lengthy quotations from Keats's poems, for which Hayden, Matthews, Schwartz, and the others simply substitute bracketed line references. (The fact is that Keats's and many other poets' works were frequently known first, and for some readers only, through these long quotations in the reviews.) Theodore Redpath's *The Young Romantics and Critical Opinion, 1807 –1824* (1973) has twenty-two extracts in the Keats section, a fuller compilation than those by Wain and Davies but rather meager and mechanical in comparison with Hayden's and especially Matthews'.

While nothing can take the place of firsthand acquaintance with the reviews themselves, several surveys and summary discussions are readily available. For a long time the most substantial of these was MacGillivray's seventy-page introductory essay, "On the Development of Keats' Reputation," in *Keats: A Bibliography and Reference Guide.* More recently we have John O. Hayden's *The Romantic Reviewers, 1802 –1824* (1968); Matthews' introduction, "Keats's Reputation: The Pattern of Change," in *Keats: The Critical Heritage* (1971); and Schwartz's introductory chapter in *Keats Reviewed by His Contemporaries* (1973). Hayden's work is a study of the critical reception of a dozen Romantic writers, not just Keats; and while his partial chapter on Keats is shorter than the introductions by MacGillivray, Matthews, and Schwartz, he includes a lengthy opening section treating "The Historical Background of the Reviewing Periodicals" and a final section on the reviewers' "Attitudes, Policies, and Practices," thus providing a broader context in which to consider the contemporary reviews specifically concerned with Keats. John U. Peters, "Jeffrey's Keats Criticism" (*SSL,* 1973), analyzes the "intrinsic issues" in Jeffrey's August 1820 review (in the *Edinburgh Review*) of *Endymion* and the *Lamia* volume.

For Keats's reputation and influence in the Victorian period the premier scholarly work is George H. Ford's *Keats and the Victorians: A Study of His Influence and Rise to Fame, 1821 –1895* (1944), which has large sections on

Tennyson, Arnold, and D. G. Rossetti, shorter discussions of Morris, Swinburne, and a handful of lesser writers, and a lengthy bibliography of work done on the subject up to around 1940. Further information based on periodical notices and early editions of the poems is given in Hyder E. Rollins, "Notes on the Vogue of Keats 1821–1848" (in *Elizabethan Studies and Other Essays in Honor of George F. Reynolds*, 1945), and Helen E. Haworth, " 'A Thing of Beauty Is a Joy Forever'? Early Illustrated Editions of Keats's Poetry" (*HLB*, 1973). Keats's influence first appears in the 1820s in the writings of contemporaries and near-contemporaries like B. W. Procter ("Barry Cornwall"), Thomas Hood, and C. J. Wells, and then, beginning in the 1830s and accelerating with the publication of Milnes's biography in 1848, shows up in many more famous nineteenth-century writers—among others, Tennyson, Browning, Arnold, Emily Brontë, Meredith, D. G. and Christina Rossetti, Morris, Swinburne, Hardy, Hopkins, Wilde, and Francis Thompson. The considerable scholarship connecting Keats with these and later English writers, as well as with writers in other countries, English-speaking and otherwise, can be located most easily by means of the indexes in the two collections (ed. Green and Wilson, 1964, and Hartley, 1978) of reprinted *KSJ* bibliographies mentioned in the first section of this essay. Among the more interesting and substantial studies of Keats's influence on nineteenth-century English authors are Edmund Blunden, "Barry Cornwall and Keats" (*KSMB*, 1963); Alvin Whitley, "Keats and Hood" (*KSJ*, 1956); Blunden, "The Poet Hood" (*REL*, 1960); Priscilla Johnston, "Charles Jeremiah Wells: An Early Keatsian Poet" (KSJ, 1977); Clyde de L. Ryals, "The 'Fatal Woman' Symbol in Tennyson" (*PMLA*, 1959); the Keats chapters in William A. Jamison's *Arnold and the Romantics* (1958) and Leon Gottfried's *Matthew Arnold and the Romantics* (1963); Helen E. Haworth, "Arnold's Keats" (*Revue de l'Université d'Ottawa*, 1971); Ann Marie Ross, "Matthew Arnold's Elegiac Essays: The Death and Fame of the Poet of Nature" (*SIR*, 1979); Jeffrey R. Prince, "D. G. Rossetti and the Pre-Raphaelite Conception of the Special Moment" (*MLQ*, 1976); Barbara Fass, "Christina Rossetti and St. Agnes' Eve" (*VP*, 1976); Elizabeth Strode, "The Crisis of *The Earthly Paradise:* Morris and Keats" (*VP*, 1975); and Jerome Bump, "Hopkins and Keats" (*VP*, 1974).

The early awareness of Keats in the United States is documented in Hyder E. Rollins' *Keats' Reputation in America to 1848* (1946), and scholars have seen his influence on the writing and thinking of, among others, Emerson, Hawthorne, Poe, Holmes, Thoreau, Melville, Dickinson, and Henry James. Much of the "detecting" has been published in short articles and notes too numerous to list here. Longer separate studies include Helen E. Haworth, "Emerson's Keats" (*HLB*, 1971); Julian Smith, "Keats and Hawthorne: A Romantic Bloom in Rappaccini's Garden" (*ESQ*, 1966); Norman A. Anderson, " 'Rappaccini's Daughter': A Keatsian Analogue?" (*PMLA*, 1968); Kathleen Gallagher, "The Art of Snake Handling: *Lamia, Elsie Venner,* and 'Rappaccini's Daughter' " (*Studies in American Fiction*, 1975); Marvin B. Perry, Jr., "Keats and Poe" (in *English Studies in Honor of James Southall Wilson*, 1951); and Adeline R. Tintner, "Keats and James and *The Princess Casamassima*" (*NCF*, 1973).

In the twentieth century Keats has attained a seemingly permanent place among the most highly regarded poets in English, and his influence shows up everywhere. Among modern British writers he has been linked with Yeats, Walter de la Mare, Edward Thomas, Forster, Wodehouse, Woolf, Sassoon, Brooke, Owen, Waugh, Auden, Lowry, and Burgess. Longer studies include Donald Pearce, "Yeats and the Romantics" (*Shenandoah,* 1957); John Burrow, "Keats and Edward Thomas" (*EIC,* 1957); Hugh Underhill, "The 'Poetical Character' of Edward Thomas" (*EIC,* 1973); Jon Stallworthy's references to Keats's influence in *Wilfred Owen* (1974); and Rodney Delasanta and Mario L. D'Avanzo, "Truth and Beauty in *Brideshead Revisited*" (*MFS,* 1965). Keats has also influenced Australian poets like Christopher Brennan, Shaw Neilson, and W. J. Turner, and Canadian poets in both English and French.

Keats's heaviest influence, to judge by the frequency of allusion and the amount of space given to it in the journals, has been on twentieth-century American literature. Edwin Arlington Robinson thought Keats's sonnets "the greatest in the English language." Ellen Glasgow called Keats "my poet among poets." Wallace Stevens was constantly in touch with Keats, and his most famous early poem, "Sunday Morning," is full of echoes of the odes ("And shall the earth / Seem all of paradise that we shall know?" can be read as the question that Keats was attempting to answer at the end of "Grecian Urn"). For William Carlos Williams, like Keats a poet trained in medicine, "Keats, during the years at medical school, was my God. *Endymion* really woke me up. I copied Keats's style religiously, starting my magnum opus of those days on the pattern of *Endymion*"; Keats supplies one of the two epigraphs (and Shakespeare the other) on the title page of Williams' first book of poems. Scott Fitzgerald told his daughter that he had read the "unbearably beautiful" "Grecian Urn" a hundred times, adding: "For awhile after you quit Keats all other poetry seems to be only whistling or humming." These quotations are a tiny sampling of the comments that occur in writers' letters, autobiographies, and recorded conversations. Scholars have discerned Keatsian influence on, among others in addition to those just mentioned, Frost, T. S. Eliot, Aiken, MacLeish, Faulkner, Thomas Wolfe, Countee Cullen, John Berryman, Stanley Kunitz, and Denise Levertov, with a special concentration in the works of Fitzgerald and Faulkner. See, for example, Helen Vendler, "Stevens and Keats' 'To Autumn' " (in *Wallace Stevens: A Celebration,* ed. Frank Doggett and Robert Buttel, 1980); Stuart Peterfreund, "Keats's Influence on William Carlos Williams" (*William Carlos Williams Newsletter,* 1977); Richard L. Schoenwald, "F. Scott Fitzgerald as John Keats" (*Boston University Studies in English,* 1957); Tristram P. Coffin, "Gatsby's Fairy Lover" (*Midwest Folklore,* 1960); John Grube, "*Tender Is the Night*: Keats and Scott Fitzgerald" (*DR,* 1964–65); Dan McCall, " 'The Self-Same Song that Found a Path': Keats and *The Great Gatsby*" (*AL,* 1971); Joseph B. Wagner, "*Gatsby* and John Keats: Another Version" (*Fitzgerald-Hemingway Annual,* 1979); Blanche H. Gelfant, "Faulkner and Keats: The Ideality of Art in 'The Bear' " (*Southern Literary Journal,* 1969); J. F. Kobler, "Lena Grove: Faulkner's 'Still Unravish'd Bride of Quietness' " (*Arizona Quarterly,* 1972); Joan S. Korenman, "Faulkner's Grecian Urn" (*Southern Literary Journal,* 1974); Larry M. Sams, "Isaac McCaslin and Keats's 'Ode on a Grecian Urn' " (*SoR,* 1976); and

Ronald Primeau, "Countee Cullen and Keats's 'Vale of Soul-Making' " (*PLL,* 1976).

Keats's poems and letters have of course been translated into most of the written languages of the world, and repeatedly into the dozen or fifteen most common. (Translations are regularly listed at the beginning of the Keats section in the annual *KSJ* bibliography.) French writers known to have read Keats with effect include Baudelaire, Mallarmé, Anatole France, André Gide, and Charles Du Bos. See in particular Jean-François Delesalle, "Baudelaire et Keats" (*Etudes Baudelairiennes,* 1971), and Robert G. Cohn, "Keats and Mallarmé" (*CLS,* 1970). Hofmannsthal and Rilke are among the Germans responding to Keats. See Hanna B. Lewis, "Hofmannsthal, Shelley, and Keats" (*German Life and Letters,* 1974); Heinz J. Dill, "Hofmannsthal and Keats" (*Germanic Review,* 1980); and Frank Wood, "Rilke's 'Keats-Bild' " (*Germanic Review,* 1950). Keats figures prominently in both Gerrit Dekker's *Die Invloed van Keats en Shelley in Nederland gedurende die Negentiende Eeu* (1926) and James A. Russell's *Dutch Romantic Poetry: The English Influence* (1961); Herman Gorter's *Mei* is one of the masterpieces of Dutch poetry influenced by Keats—see Henry Klomp, "*Alastor, Endymion,* and Gorter's *Mei*" (*Kentucky Foreign Language Quarterly,* 1959). Recent Spanish interest in Keats is discussed by José Luis Cano in two essays, "Keats en España" (*Papeles de Son Armadans,* 1956) and "Keats y España" (in Cano's *El escritor y su aventura,* 1966). For recent Japanese interest see Tohru Matsuura, "John Keats and His Influence on Modern Japanese Poetry" (*KSMB,* 1978). I would emphasize that the works cited in these last few paragraphs represent just a small selection of the scholarship on the relationship of Keats to later writers and other literatures.

This essay has mentioned and in some cases described 595 books and articles, and at this point the question might justifiably be raised whether there is anything still to be done on Keats. The short answer is that there is still plenty to be done. In the first place, our bibliographical resources are scattered and patchy. It is probably in the nature of the material that this should be so, but still it would be a considerable help to scholars if someone (or some committee) would redo, enlarge, and extend MacGillivray's bibliography so that we could have, in a single large work, a complete list of publications both of and about Keats's writings.

Then there are several editorial and textual projects that come to mind, even though the texts of the poems have been recently both studied in detail and freshly edited. It would be useful to have in print many more photographic reproductions of Keats's manuscripts. At present, as I mentioned in the section on editions, a relative handful are available in de Selincourt's 1905 facsimile of the *Hyperion* manuscript, Williamson's 1914 publication of manuscripts in the Dilke bequest to the Hampstead Library, and Gittings' 1970 work on the odes; and *The Texts of Keats's Poems* includes references to many others, frequently of poor quality, here and there in books, magazines, and sale catalogs. What is wanted is a more systematic publication, after the manner of the Cornell Wordsworth, of all the extant holographs and a selection of the most authoritative transcripts. It would be valuable, either in connection with photographic reproductions or else independently, to have a descriptive catalog of the Harvard Keats Collection, by far the richest in the world. And much more could be done toward our understanding of how Keats's nonposthumous poems got into print. From the plentiful documentary evidence in letters, poetry manuscripts, transcripts, and proofs one gets an impression of Keats, Taylor, Woodhouse, and other friends all pulling together to make the poems presentable to the public; it is a topic worth investigating at book length.

Finally (in the textual department), it might be a considerable help, especially to students and general readers, to have available a cleaned-up text of Keats's letters. Both Rollins (in the standard edition) and Gittings (in the "new selection") are scrupulous in preserving Keats's oddities of punctuation and capitalization, misspellings and other slips of the pen, and at least some of the cancellations recoverable in the letter manuscripts; Rollins uses several different kinds of bracket, and Gittings in addition prints words that are lined through. These practices are commendable, but they can be something of an obstacle to readers unaccustomed to them. Keats's letters deserve to be presented more accessibly; a principled job of punctuating and respelling for a general audience would, I think, be a good idea. The same might be done with a selection of Keats Circle documents. Consider, as an extreme example, these sentences from Rollins' text of some comments by Woodhouse on Keats's "mode of writing Poetry": "He [Keats] has <not often> said, that he has often not been aware of the beauty of some <of his writings> thought or expr^n until after he has composed & written it down— It has then struck <it> him with <wonder & he has sca> astonishm^t—& seemed <like> rather the prod^n of another person than his own." In Amy Lowell's version, the first in print, the same sentences read: "He has said that he has often not been aware of the beauty of some thought or expression until after he had composed and written it down—It has then struck him with astonishment and seemed rather the production of another person than his own." Rollins' is the more accurate text but, alas, it is very nearly unreadable. Woodhouse's comments are too valuable to be buried in this way.

In the biographical line it may be difficult to think of new projects to undertake. Nevertheless there are practically no specialized studies focusing on Keats's early education, his reading at Clarke's school, his medical training (though Donald Goellnicht's *The Poet-Physician,* received at the last minute, appears to contribute substantially toward answering this need), and specific periods of his adult life such as the walking tour of the summer of 1818. As to criticism, there are many topics still to consider—for example, Keats's and his publishers' views of his audience and how these affected his writing and their publishing; Keats's ideas about and depiction of women (who figure prominently, sometimes as the principal characters, in practically all the narratives and many of the shorter poems); and his relationship to music and some of the other arts (Ian Jack has initiated the study of Keats and the visual arts, but there is much more to be done). If we set aside a handful of unrevised Ph.D. dissertations and Katharine M. Wilson's *The Nightingale and the Hawk* (1964)—the latter actually devoting fewer than twenty pages to its purported subject, the Nightingale ode—no book-length critical treatment of *any* Keats poem has ever been published (a circumstance that makes Keats unique among the major Romantics). *Endymion,* several later narratives, and the great odes as a group are, I should think, obvious candidates for more detailed and comprehensive study than they have so far received. More could be done on Keats's sources; at the end of the section on specialized studies I suggest the desirability of a bibliographical compilation that would bring together in some manageable form the numerous bits and pieces of source work already in print. And of course much more work is needed on the art of Keats's poetry—the style and narrative techniques in particular. Probably we have run out of things to say about most of Keats's ideas, but there seems no end in sight to the investigation of what happens when a reader slowly reads Keats's lines. When we no longer have readers—then Keats scholars and critics will genuinely have something to worry about. In the meantime it's business as usual.

Index

Topical headings appear in boldface. Persons or topics referred to on consecutive pages are indicated by inclusive numbers (e.g., 330–31) without regard to whether the discussion is continuous. References to pages in the chapter "The Romantic Movement in England" appear in the index for each of the poets whenever they are mentioned by name, but the general discussions throughout the chapter should be consulted for their relevance to each of the poets.